The SAGE Encyclopedia of
SOCIAL SCIENCE RESEARCH METHODS

The SAGE Encyclopedia of
SOCIAL SCIENCE
RESEARCH METHODS

VOLUME 2

MICHAEL S. LEWIS-BECK
Department of Political Science, University of Iowa

ALAN BRYMAN
Department of Social Sciences, Loughborough University

TIM FUTING LIAO
Department of Sociology, University of Essex and University of Illinois, Urbana-Champaign

EDITORS

A SAGE Reference Publication

SAGE Publications
International Educational and Professional Publisher
Thousand Oaks ▪ London ▪ New Delhi

For information:

 SAGE Publications, Inc.
2455, Teller Road
Thousand Oaks, California 91320
E-mail: order@sagepub.com

SAGE Publications Ltd.
6, Bonhill Street
London EC2A 4PU
United Kingdom

SAGE Publications India Pvt. Ltd.
B-42, Panchsheel Enclave
Post Box 4109
New Delhi 110 017 India

Printed in the United States of America

Library of Congress Cataloging-in-Publication Data

Lewis-Beck, Michael S.
The SAGE encyclopedia of social science research methods/Michael S.
Lewis-Beck, Alan Bryman, Tim Futing Liao.
    p. cm.
Includes bibliographical references and index.
ISBN 0–7619–2363–2 (cloth)
    1. Social sciences—Research—Encyclopedias. 2. Social sciences—Methodology—Encyclopedias.
I. Bryman, Alan. II. Liao, Tim Futing. III. Title.
H62.L456 2004
300.!72—dc22

                            2003015882

03 04 05 06 10 9 8 7 6 5 4 3 2 1

Acquisitions Editor:	Chris Rojek
Publisher:	Rolf A. Janke
Developmental Editor:	Eileen Haddox
Editorial Assistant:	Sara Tauber
Production Editor:	Melanie Birdsall
Copy Editors:	Gillian Dickens, Liann Lech, A. J. Sobczak
Typesetter:	C&M Digitals (P) Ltd.
Proofreader:	Mattson Publishing Services, LLC
Indexer:	Sheila Bodell
Cover Designer:	Ravi Balasuriya

List of Entries

The Appendix, Bibliography, appears at the end of this volume as well as in Volume 3.

Reader's Guide

Effects Coefficient
Endogenous Variable
Exogenous Variable
Independent Variable
Path Analysis
Structural Equation Modeling

DISCOURSE/CONVERSATION ANALYSIS

Accounts
Conversation Analysis
Critical Discourse Analysis
Deviant Case Analysis
Discourse Analysis
Foucauldian Discourse Analysis
Interpretative Repertoire
Proof Procedure

ECONOMETRICS

ARIMA
Cointegration
Durbin-Watson Statistic
Econometrics
Fixed Effects Model
Mixed-Effects Model
Panel
Panel Data Analysis
Random-Effects Model
Selection Bias
Serial Correlation (Regression)
Time-Series Cross-Section (TSCS) Models
Time-Series Data (Analysis/Design)
Tobit Analysis

EPISTEMOLOGY

Constructionism, Social
Epistemology
Idealism
Interpretivism
Laws in Social Science
Logical Positivism
Methodological Holism
Naturalism
Objectivism
Positivism

ETHNOGRAPHY

Autoethnography
Case Study
Creative Analytical Practice (CAP) Ethnography

Critical Ethnography
Ethnographic Content Analysis
Ethnographic Realism
Ethnographic Tales
Ethnography
Participant Observation

EVALUATION

Applied Qualitative Research
Applied Research
Evaluation Research
Experiment
Heuristic Inquiry
Impact Assessment
Qualitative Evaluation
Randomized Control Trial

EVENT HISTORY ANALYSIS

Censoring and Truncation
Event History Analysis
Hazard Rate
Survival Analysis
Transition Rate

EXPERIMENTAL DESIGN

Experiment
Experimenter Expectancy Effect
External Validity
Field Experimentation
Hawthorne Effect
Internal Validity
Laboratory Experiment
Milgram Experiments
Quasi-Experiment

FACTOR ANALYSIS AND RELATED TECHNIQUES

Cluster Analysis
Commonality Analysis
Confirmatory Factor Analysis
Correspondence Analysis
Eigenvalue
Exploratory Factor Analysis
Factor Analysis
Oblique Rotation
Principal Components Analysis
Rotated Factor

Rotations
Varimax Rotation

FEMINIST METHODOLOGY

Feminist Ethnography
Feminist Research
Gender Issues
Standpoint Epistemology

GENERALIZED LINEAR MODELS

General Linear Models
Generalized Linear Models
Link Function
Logistic Regression
Logit
Logit Model
Poisson Regression
Probit Analysis

HISTORICAL/COMPARATIVE

Comparative Method
Comparative Research
Documents, Types of
Emic/Etic Distinction
Historical Methods
Oral History

INTERVIEWING IN QUALITATIVE RESEARCH

Biographic Narrative Interpretive
    Method (BNIM)
Dependent Interviewing
Informant Interviewing
Interviewing in Qualitative Research
Narrative Interviewing
Semistructured Interview
Unstructured Interview

LATENT VARIABLE MODEL

Confirmatory Factor Analysis
Item Response Theory
Factor Analysis
Latent Budget Analysis
Latent Class Analysis
Latent Markov Model
Latent Profile Model

Latent Trait Models
Latent Variable
Local Independence
Nonparametric Random-Effects Model
Structural Equation Modeling

LIFE HISTORY/BIOGRAPHY

Autobiography
Biographic Narrative Interpretive
    Method (BNIM)
Interpretive Biography
Life History Method
Life Story Interview
Narrative Analysis
Psychoanalytic Methods

LOG-LINEAR MODELS (CATEGORICAL DEPENDENT VARIABLES)

Association Model
Categorical Data Analysis
Contingency Table
Expected Frequency
Goodness-of-Fit Measures
Log-Linear Model
Marginal Model
Marginals
Mobility Table
Odds Ratio
Saturated Model
Sparse Table

LONGITUDINAL ANALYSIS

Cohort Analysis
Longitudinal Research
Panel
Period Effects
Time-Series Data (Analysis/Design)

MATHEMATICS AND FORMAL MODELS

Algorithm
Assumptions
Basic Research
Catastrophe Theory
Chaos Theory
Distribution
Fuzzy Set Theory
Game Theory

MEASUREMENT LEVEL

Attribute
Binary
Categorical
Continuous Variable
Dichotomous Variables
Discrete
Interval
Level of Measurement
Metric Variable
Nominal Variable
Ordinal Measure

MEASUREMENT TESTING AND CLASSIFICATION

Conceptualization, Operationalization, and Measurement
Generalizability Theory
Item Response Theory
Likert Scale
Multiple-Indicator Measures
Summated Rating Scale

MULTILEVEL ANALYSIS

Contextual Effects
Dependent Observations
Fixed Effects Model
Mixed-Effects Model
Multilevel Analysis
Nonparametric Random-Effects Model
Random-Coefficient Model
Random-Effects Model

MULTIPLE REGRESSION

Adjusted R-Squared
Best Linear Unbiased Estimator
Beta
Generalized Least Squares
Heteroskedasticity
Interaction Effect
Misspecification
Multicollinearity
Multiple Regression Analysis
Nonadditive
R-Squared
Regression
Regression Diagnostics

Specification
Standard Error of the Estimate

QUALITATIVE DATA ANALYSIS

Analytic Induction
CAQDAS
Constant Comparison
Grounded Theory
In Vivo Coding
Memos, Memoing
Negative Case
Qualitative Content Analysis

SAMPLING IN QUALITATIVE RESEARCH

Purposive Sampling
Sampling in Qualitative Research
Snowball Sampling
Theoretical Sampling

SAMPLING IN SURVEYS

Multistage Sampling
Quota Sampling
Random Sampling
Representative Sample
Sampling
Sampling Error
Stratified Sampling
Systematic Sampling

SCALING

Attitude Measurement
Bipolar Scale
Dimension
Dual Scaling
Guttman Scaling
Index
Likert Scale
Multidimensional Scaling (MDS)
Optimal Scaling
Scale
Scaling
Semantic Differential Scale
Thurstone Scaling

SIGNIFICANCE TESTING

Alpha, Significance Level of a Test
Confidence Interval

G

GAME THEORY

Game theory extends classical decision theory by focusing on situations in which an actor's result depends not only on his or her own decisions but also on one or more persons' behavior. In this sense, it is a theory of social interaction with a special interest in goal-directed ("rational") behavior.

"Born" by John von Neumann and Oskar Morgenstern (1944), applications of game theory spread from economics to political science, psychology, sociology, and even biology. Key elements of game-theoretic studies are games, players, strategies, payoffs, and maximization. A "game" describes a given situation of social interaction between at least two actors ("players") with all the rules of the game, as well as its possibilities and restrictions. The situation offers the players various alternatives to decide and act ("strategies"). The players' strategies lead to different outcomes along with different utility values ("payoffs"). Based on these key elements, game-theoretic analysis can show which strategy a player will choose when he or she maximizes his or her payoff. Therefore, game theory is more a mathematical discipline than a psychological theory.

Although goal-directed behavior is a presumption of game theory, theoretical results and empirical evidence sometimes can be bizarre. A famous example is the PRISONER'S DILEMMA (PD). The PD is a simple model of a situation of strategic interdependence with aspects of cooperation and conflict. Table 1 shows the PD that Robert Axelrod (1984) used in his computer tournament. Individually seen, defection always leads

Table 1 Prisoner's Dilemma

		Player 2	
		Cooperation	*Defection*
Player 1	Cooperation	3,3	0,5
	Defection	5,0	1,1

to a better payoff than cooperation (and is therefore a "dominant strategy"). The dilemma is that although mutual defection causes a worse result than mutual cooperation, a player has no interest in a one-sided change of his or her strategy. With this characterization, the PD can be a fruitful model of various social situations such as employment relations, an arms race, or free trade. It also illustrates that game-theoretical analysis is most interesting in situations with mixed motives of cooperation and conflict incentives.

Looking at classical methods of data collection, most empirical game-theoretical studies use EXPERIMENTS, COMPUTER SIMULATIONS, and—in a broader sense—CONTENT ANALYSIS. In a content analysis, given documents such as statistics or historical data are analyzed to build a game-theoretic model (e.g., an explanation of political strategic moves at the beginning of World War I). Computer simulations can match a variety of different strategies to simulate the effect of repeated games (iterations), changed parameters, or evolution aspects. Experiments are the best way of testing (game) theoretical findings. The study by Anatol Rapoport and Albert Chammah (1965) about the PD exemplifies the connection of theoretical, experimental, and simulation aspects. For a general introduction, see Gintis (2000).

—Bernhard Prosch

REFERENCES

Axelrod, R. (1984). *The evolution of cooperation.* New York: Basic Books.

Gintis, H. (2000). *Game theory evolving.* Princeton, NJ: Princeton University Press.

Rapoport, A., & Chammah, A. (1965). *Prisoner's dilemma.* Ann Arbor: Michigan University Press.

von Neumann, J., & Morgenstern, O. (1944). *Theory of games and economic behaviour.* Princeton, NJ: Princeton University Press.

GAMMA

Similar to Kendall's tau coefficient (and its variations such as Kendall's τ_b coefficient or Stuart's τ_c coefficient), described in SYMMETRIC MEASURES, Goodman and Kruskal's gamma coefficient is one of the NONPARAMETRIC STATISTICS that describes the relationship between two ordered or rank-order variables X and Y. When there are no tied ranks, all the above coefficients yield the same results. When many tied ranks occur in either variable, the gamma coefficient is more useful and appropriate than tau correlations and will always be greater than Kendall's coefficients.

Given two rank-order variables, X and Y, in a population, the parameter gamma (γ) is defined as the difference between the probability that agreement exists in the order for a pair (X_i, Y_j) and the probability that disagreement exists for a pair (X_i, Y_j) in their ordering, given that there are no ties in the data (Siegel & Castellan, 1988). In other words,

$$\gamma = \frac{\begin{aligned}&p(\text{agreement between } X_i \text{ and } Y_i)\\&\quad - p(\text{disagreement between } X_i \text{ and } Y_i)\end{aligned}}{1 - p(X_i \text{ and } Y_i \text{ are tied})}$$

$$= \frac{\begin{aligned}&p(\text{agreement between } X_i \text{ and } Y_i)\\&\quad - p(\text{disagreement between } X_i \text{ and } Y_i)\end{aligned}}{\begin{aligned}&p(\text{agreement between } X_i \text{ and } Y_i)\\&\quad + p(\text{disagreement between } X_i \text{ and } Y_i)\end{aligned}}.$$

The gamma coefficient of a population can be estimated by a sample using $\hat{\gamma} = \frac{P-Q}{P+Q}$, where P is the number of concordance or agreement, and Q is the number of discordance or disagreement in the sample. The numbers of concordance and discordance are operationalized as follows. In any pair of observations—(X_i, Y_i) for case i and (X_j, Y_j) for case j—concordance occurs when $(X_i - X_j)(Y_i - Y_j) > 0$, which suggests either $Y_i < Y_j$ when $X_i < X_j$ or

Table 1   Ranks of 10 Students on Creative Writing by Two Judges

	Judge X	Judge Y	P	Q
Mr. Lubinsky	1	5	4	5
Ms. Firth	2	4	4	4
Ms. Aron	3	3	4	3
Mr. Millar	4	2	4	2
Ms. Savident	5	1	3	0
Mr. DeLuca	5	1	3	0
Ms. Pavarotti	5	6	3	0
Ms. Lin	6	7	1	0
Mr. Stewart	6	7	1	0
Ms. Barton	7	8	0	0
Σ			27	14

NOTE: $P =$ the number of concordance or agreement; $Q =$ the number of discordance or disagreement.

$Y_i > Y_j$ when $X_i > X_j$. Likewise, discordance exists if $(X_i - X_j)(Y_i - Y_j) < 0$, which suggests either $Y_i < Y_j$ when $X_i > X_j$ or $Y_i > Y_j$ when $X_i < X_j$. The gamma coefficient can range from -1 when $P = 0$ to 1 when $Q = 0$.

An example of the use of this statistic is provided by a situation in which two judges (X and Y) rank 10 students according to their creative writing, with 1 as the lowest rank and 10 as the highest rank. To calculate the gamma coefficient, we first arrange Judge X's rankings in ascending order, as shown in the second column of Table 1. The corresponding rankings from Judge Y are listed in the third column of Table 1. Next, we determine the number of concordance and discordance for each student, starting with the first. Mr. Lubinsky is compared to 9 other students (i.e., Lubinsky vs. Firth, Lubinsky vs. Aron, . . . , and Lubinsky vs. Barton). The number of concordance (i.e., the number of students ranked above 5 by Judge Y) is four, and the number of discordance (i.e., the number of students ranked below 5 by Judge Y) is five. The second student, Ms. Firth, is then compared to the 8 remaining students (i.e., Firth vs. Aron, Firth vs. Millar, . . . , and Firth vs. Barton). The number of concordance (i.e., the number of the remaining students ranked above 4 by Judge Y) is four, and the number of discordance (i.e., the number of the remaining students ranked below 4 by Judge Y) is four.

When there are tied ranks assigned by Judge X, no comparison is made among those cases. For instance, the fifth student, Ms. Savident, is only compared to the remaining students, excluding Mr. DeLuca and Ms. Pavarotti (i.e., Savident vs. Lin, Savident vs.

Stewart, and Savident vs. Barton). The number of concordance (i.e., the number of the remaining students ranked above 1 by Judge Y) is three, and the number of discordance (i.e., the number of the remaining students ranked below 1 by Judge Y) is 0. Following the same procedure, both P and Q for the remaining students can be obtained.

The null hypothesis test for Goodman-Kruskal's gamma can be examined by

$$z = \frac{\hat{\gamma}}{\sqrt{\frac{n(1-\hat{\gamma}^2)}{P+Q}}}$$

when the sample size is large. Note that the upper limit of the standard error is

$$\sqrt{\frac{n(1-\hat{\gamma}^2)}{P+Q}}.$$

Therefore, the z-statistic obtained from the above formula is a conservative estimate.

—Peter Y. Chen and Autumn D. Krauss

REFERENCE

Siegel, S., & Castellan, N. J. (1988). *Nonparametric statistics for the behavioral sciences* (2nd ed.). New York: McGraw-Hill.

GAUSS-MARKOV THEOREM. *See* BLUE; OLS

GEISTESWISSENSCHAFTEN

This is a term that came into common use in the 19th century, referring to the humanities and social sciences. In the context of methodology, it also implies a particular approach to work in these fields, one that emphasizes the role of VERSTEHEN.

There were isolated uses of *Geisteswissenschaften*, or its variants, before 1849, but widespread employment of the term seems to have stemmed from Schiel's translation into German of John Stuart Mill's *System of Logic* (Mill, 1974), in which the term *Geisteswissenschaften* was used to stand for Mill's "moral sciences." Mill regarded psychology as the key moral science, and its method was to be modeled on the natural sciences (*Naturwissenschaften*). However, most of the German historians and philosophers who adopted the term *Geisteswissenschaften* took a very different view. Some earlier German writers, notably Goethe and Hegel, had sought to develop a notion of scientific understanding that encompassed not just natural science but also the humanities and philosophy, thereby opposing empiricist and materialist views of scientific method and their extension to the study of human social life. However, by the middle of the 19th century, attempts at such a single, comprehensive view of scholarship had been largely discredited in many quarters. Instead, influential philosophers argued that the human social world had to be studied in a quite *different* way from the manner in which natural scientists investigate the physical world, although one that had equal empirical rigor. As a result, it is common to find *Geisteswissenschaften* translated back into English as "the human studies" or "the human sciences," signaling distance from the positivist view of social research marked by labels such as *behavioral science*.

One of the most influential accounts of the distinctiveness of the *Geisteswissenschaften* is found in the work of Wilhelm Dilthey (see Ermarth, 1978). He argued that whereas the natural sciences properly approach the study of phenomena from the outside, by studying their external characteristics and behavior, we are able to understand human beings and their products—whether artifacts, beliefs, ways of life, or whatever—from the inside because we share a common human nature with those we study. Another influential 19th-century account of the distinctiveness of the human sciences was put forward by the neo-Kantians Windelband and Rickert. For them, the distinction between the natural and social sciences was not primarily about subject matter; indeed, the neo-Kantians were keen to emphasize that there is only one reality (see Hammersley, 1989, pp. 28–33). Rather, the main difference was between a generalizing and an individualizing form of science. Max Weber drew on both the Diltheyan and neo-Kantian traditions in developing his *verstehende* sociology, in which explanation (*Erklären*) and understanding (*Verstehen*) go together, so that any sociological account is required to be adequate at the level of both cause and meaning (Turner & Factor, 1981).

—Martyn Hammersley

REFERENCES

Ermarth, M. (1978). *Wilhelm Dilthey: The critique of historical reason*. Chicago: University of Chicago Press.

Hammersley, M. (1989). *The dilemma of qualitative method: Herbert Blumer and the Chicago school of sociology*. London: Routledge.

Mill, J. S. (1974). *Collected works of John Stuart Mill: Vol. 8. A system of logic* (Books 4–6). Toronto: University of Toronto Press.

Turner, S. P., & Factor, R. A. (1981). Objective possibility and adequate causality in Weber's methodological writings. *Sociological Review, 29*(1), 5–28.

GENDER ISSUES

Issues relating to gender in social research arose, in the 1970s, out of concerns about the relative invisibility of women and a perceived lack of attention to their lives. Feminists argued that there had been insufficient recognition of how differences in the experiences of women and men, together with changes in the relationships between them, could have significant implications for the ways in which social phenomena are conceptualized and investigated. Areas researched tended to focus on the public spheres of life, those existing outside the private sphere of the home, such as the workplace and school. It was assumed either that the experiences of women could simply be inferred from those of men or that men had the normal or customary kinds of lives, with those of women being treated as unusual or deviant.

GENDER AND RESEARCH

One way of dealing with the gender issue is to treat women and men as separate and to measure the extent of any differences between them, for example, in health and illness or educational attainment. Such an approach, although useful, has been criticized as inadequate on its own because it fails to acknowledge differences in the quality and nature of experiences. Another approach, characteristic of the early stages of gender awareness, was to add studies of women onto those of men. However, although valuable work was produced in areas such as employment and the media, for instance, this was similarly criticized for insufficiently challenging the basic assumptions and concepts that informed such research. It was argued that these were still based on male perceptions and interests, with women being tagged on rather as an afterthought. This led to three developments. First, it was necessary to research additional issues that were particularly pertinent to women. New themes were introduced, ranging from housework, motherhood, and childbirth to sexuality, pornography, and male violence. Second, some of the perspectives and concepts at the very heart of the social science agenda had to be revised or modified. This gave rise to important debates, such as the relative meaning and significance of social class for women and men and whether the accepted distinction between work and leisure was based on gendered assumptions. The third development involved issues to do with the actual methods and procedures of social research. There was heated discussion among feminists, with some suggesting that qualitative, rather than quantitative, research styles were more attuned to rendering the previously hidden aspects of women's lives visible. There has also been much debate as to whether it is either desirable or possible to have a distinct feminist methodology (Ramazanoglu, 2002).

DEFINING AND OPERATIONALIZING GENDER

The most usual definition of gender distinguishes it from biological sex. Whereas sex is taken to denote the anatomical and physiological differences that define biological femaleness and maleness, gender refers to the social construction of femininity and masculinity (Connell, 2002). It is not regarded as a direct product of biological sex but is seen as being differently created and interpreted by particular cultures and in particular periods of historical time. However, a number of issues arise from this usage. To begin with, initial studies of gender relations focused mainly on women and girls to compensate for their previous exclusion. It is only recently that the gendered nature of men, of masculinities, has become the focus of attention. Furthermore, the commonsense usage of the term *gender* has been contested. It has been suggested that there are not, in practice, two mutually exclusive gender categories, as attempts to classify international athletes have demonstrated (Ramazanoglu, 2002). Intersexuality and transexuality disrupt rigid gender boundaries, indicating that body differences may be important after all. Definitions based on dichotomy also overlook patterns of difference among both women and men—for instance, between violent and nonviolent masculinities. Another concern is with the need to relate gender to other forms of difference—for instance, those of ethnicity, sexual orientation, disability, class, and age. Such categories and signifiers mean that gender is always mediated in terms of experience.

There is also the postmodern argument that gender has no pregiven and essential existence. It only exists to the extent that it continues to be performed. Gender is rendered diverse, fluctuating, and volatile rather than a stable and homogeneous identity. Such a stance, however, sweeps away the grounds for focusing on gender issues in the first place. Despite all the above problems, the researcher on gender has to have a more specific place to start. This has led some commentators to talk about research on "gendered lives" (Ramazanoglu, 2002, p. 5) and the need to focus on gender "relations" (Connell, 2002, p. 9) rather than accept gender as a given. This makes the understanding of what constitutes gender a part of any particular empirical investigation. It also makes it a form of patterning of social relations within which individuals and groups act. The central argument is that gender cannot be known in general or in advance of research.

EFFECTS ON THE RESEARCH PROCESS

It has also been claimed that gender can influence the research process, whatever the topic being studied and whether this is from a feminist or nonfeminist perspective. For example, differing gendered perceptions of the social world may influence why a particular project is chosen, the ways in which it is framed, and the questions that are then asked. The gender of the researcher, together with other characteristics, such as age and ethnicity, can affect the nature of the interaction with research participants and the quality of the information obtained. Gender may also be of significance in the analysis and interpretation of data, with men and women "reading" material in differing ways, based on their differing experiences and worldview. There is debate in the literature as to how far these gender effects may be minimized. Views range from those who see them to be inconsequential for research to those who regard them as possible sources of bias. For the latter, it is necessary to be reflexive about the way gender might intrude into research practice and also to make commentary on it available so that this can be part of any critical evaluation process.

—Mary Maynard

REFERENCES

Connell, R. W. (2002). *Gender*. Cambridge, UK: Polity.
Ramazanoglu, C. (with Holland, J.). (2002). *Feminist methodology*. London: Sage.

GENERAL LINEAR MODELS

The general linear model provides a basic framework that underlies many of the statistical analyses that social scientists encounter. It is the foundation for many univariate, multivariate, and repeated-measures procedures, including the T-TEST, (MULTIVARIATE) ANALYSIS OF VARIANCE, (MUTIVARIATE) ANALYSIS OF COVARIANCE, MULTIPLE REGRESSION ANALYSIS, FACTOR ANALYSIS, CANONICAL CORRELATION ANALYSIS, CLUSTER ANALYSIS, DISCRIMINANT ANALYSIS, MULTIDIMENSIONAL SCALING, REPEATED-MEASURES DESIGN, and other analyses. It can be succinctly expressed in a regression-type formula, for example, in terms of the expected value of the random dependent variable Y, such as income as a function of a number of independent variables X_k (for $k = 1$ to K), such as age, education, and social class:

$$E(Y) = f(X_1, \ldots, X_K)$$
$$= \beta_0 + \beta_1 X_1 + \cdots + \beta_K X_K. \qquad (1)$$

All members of the general linear model can be given in the form of (1). For example, a typical analysis of variance model is formed when all the explanatory variables are categorical factors and hence can be coded as DUMMY VARIABLES in X_k. Parameters in the general linear model can be appropriately obtained by ORDINARY LEAST SQUARES estimation. According to the Gauss-Markov theorem, when all the ASSUMPTIONS of the general linear model are satisfied, such estimation is optimal in that the least squares ESTIMATORS are BEST LINEAR UNBIASED ESTIMATORS of the population parameters of β_k.

A basic distinction between the general linear model and the GENERALIZED LINEAR MODEL lies in the response variable of the model. The former requires a continuous variable, whereas the latter does not. Another distinction is the distribution of the response variable, which is expected to be normal in the general linear model, but it can be one of several nonnormal (e.g., BINOMIAL, MULTINOMIAL, and POISSON DISTRIBUTION) distributions. Yet another distinction is how the response variable is related to the explanatory variables. In the generalized linear model, the relation between the dependent and the independent variables is specified by the LINK FUNCTION, an example of which is the identity link of (1), which is the only link used in the general linear model. On the other hand, the link function of the generalized linear model, which is formally expressed by the inverse function in (1) or $f^1[E(Y)]$, can take on nonlinear links such as the probit, the logit, and the log, among others:

$$E(Y) = f(X_1, \ldots, X_K)$$
$$= f(\beta_0 + \beta_1 X_1 + \cdots + \beta_K X_K). \quad (2)$$

Here the identity link is just one of the many possibilities, and the general linear model (1) can be viewed as a special case of the generalized linear model of (2).

Another extension of the general linear model is the GENERALIZED ADDITIVE MODEL, which also extends the generalized linear model by allowing for nonparametric functions. The generalized additive model can be expressed similarly in terms of the expected value of Y:

$$E(Y) = f(X_1, \ldots, X_K)$$
$$= f[s_0 + s_1(X_1) + \cdots + s_K(X_K)], \quad (3)$$

where $s_K(X_K)$ are smoothing functions that are estimated nonparametrically. In (3), not only the $f^1[E(Y)]$ link function can take on various nonlinear forms, but each of the X_K variables is fitted using a smoother such as the B-spline.

Another type of generalization that can be applied to the models of (1) and (2) captures the spirit of the HIERARCHICAL LINEAR MODEL or the models in MULTI-LEVEL ANALYSIS. So far, we have ignored the subscript i representing individual cases. If the subscript i is used for the first-level units and j for the second-level, or higher, units, then the Y_{ij} and X_{ij} variables represent observations from two levels; moreover, the coefficients β_{jk} now are random and can be distinguishable among the second-level units.

Some popular statistical software packages such as SAS and SPSS implement the general linear model in a flexible procedure for data analysis. Both SAS and STATA have procedures for fitting generalized linear and generalized additive models as well as some form of hierarchical (non)linear models.

—Tim Futing Liao

GENERALIZABILITY. *See* EXTERNAL VALIDITY

GENERALIZABILITY THEORY

Generalizability theory provides an extensive conceptual framework and set of statistical machinery for quantifying and explaining the consistencies and inconsistencies in observed scores for objects of measurement. To an extent, the theory can be viewed as an extension of classical test theory through the application of certain ANALYSIS OF VARIANCE (ANOVA) procedures. Classical theory postulates that an observed score can be decomposed into a TRUE SCORE and a single undifferentiated RANDOM ERROR term. By contrast, generalizability theory substitutes the notion of *universe score* for true score and liberalizes classical theory by employing ANOVA methods that allow an investigator to untangle the multiple sources of error that contribute to the undifferentiated error in classical theory.

Perhaps the most important and unique feature of generalizability theory is its conceptual framework, which focuses on certain types of studies and universes. A *generalizability* (G) study involves the collection of a sample of data from a *universe of admissible observations* that consists of *facets* defined by an investigator. Typically, the principal result of a G study is a set of estimated random-effects variance components for the universe of admissible observations. A D (*decision*) study provides estimates of universe score variance, error variances, certain indexes that are like RELIABILITY COEFFICIENTS, and other statistics for a measurement procedure associated with an investigator-specified *universe of generalization*.

In univariate generalizability theory, there is only one universe (of generalization) score for each object of measurement. In multivariate generalizability theory, each object of measurement has multiple universe scores. Univariate generalizability theory typically employs random-effects models, whereas MIXED-EFFECTS MODELS are more closely associated with multivariate generalizability theory.

HISTORICAL DEVELOPMENT

The defining treatment of generalizability theory is the 1972 book by Lee J. Cronbach, Goldine C. Gleser, Harinder Nanda, and Nageswari Rajaratnam titled *The Dependability of Behavioral Measurements*. A recent extended treatment of the theory is the 2001 book by Robert L. Brennan titled *Generalizability Theory*. The essential features of univariate generalizability theory were largely completed with technical reports in 1960–1961 that were revised into three journal articles, each with a different first author (Cronbach, Gleser, and Rajaratnam). Multivariate generalizability theory was developed during the ensuing decade. Research between 1920 and 1955 by Ronald A. Fisher, Cyril Burt, Cyril J. Hoyt, Robert L. Ebel, and E. F. Lindquist, among others, influenced the development of generalizability theory.

EXAMPLE

Suppose an investigator, Smith, wants to construct a measurement procedure for evaluating writing proficiency. First, Smith might identify or characterize essay prompts of interest, as well as potential raters. Doing so specifies the facets in the universe of admissible observations. Assume these facets are viewed as infinite and that, in theory, any person p (i.e., object of measurement) might respond to any essay prompt t, which in turn might be evaluated by any rater r. If so, a likely data collection design might be $p \times t \times r$, where "$\times$" is read as "crossed with." The associated linear model is

$$X_{ptr} = \mu + \nu_p + \nu_t + \nu_r + \nu_{pt} + \nu_{pr} + \nu_{tr} + \nu_{ptr},$$

where the ν are uncorrelated score effects. This model leads to

$$\sigma^2(X_{ptr}) = \sigma^2(p) + \sigma^2(t) + \sigma^2(r) + \sigma^2(pt)$$
$$+ \sigma^2(pr) + \sigma^2(tr) + \sigma^2(ptr), \quad (1)$$

which is a decomposition of the total observed score variance into seven *variance components* that are usually estimated using the expected MEAN SQUARES in a random-effects ANOVA.

Suppose the following estimated variance components are obtained from Smith's G study based on n_t essay prompts and n_r raters:

$$\hat{\sigma}^2(p) = 0.25, \quad \hat{\sigma}^2(t) = 0.06, \quad \hat{\sigma}^2(r) = 0.02,$$
$$\hat{\sigma}^2(pt) = 0.15, \quad \hat{\sigma}^2(pr) = 0.04, \quad \hat{\sigma}^2(tr) = 0.00,$$
$$\text{and } \hat{\sigma}^2(ptr) = 0.12.$$

Suppose also that Smith wants to generalize persons' observed mean scores based on n'_t essay prompts and n'_r raters to these persons' scores for a universe of generalization that involves an infinite number of prompts and raters. This is a verbal description of a D study with a $p \times T \times R$ random-effects design. It is much like the $p \times t \times r$ design for Smith's G study, but the sample sizes for the D study need not be the same as the sample sizes for the G study, and the $p \times T \times R$ design focuses on *mean* scores for persons. The expected score for a person over the facets in the universe of generalization is called the person's universe score.

If $n'_t = 3$ and $n'_r = 2$ for Smith's measurement procedure, then the estimated random-effects variance components for the D study are

$$\hat{\sigma}^2(p) = 0.25, \qquad \hat{\sigma}^2(T) = \frac{\hat{\sigma}^2(t)}{n'_t} = 0.02,$$

$$\hat{\sigma}^2(R) = \frac{\hat{\sigma}^2(r)}{n'_r} = 0.01, \quad \hat{\sigma}^2(pT) = \frac{\hat{\sigma}^2(pt)}{n'_t} = 0.05,$$

$$\hat{\sigma}^2(pR) = \frac{\hat{\sigma}^2(pr)}{n'_r} = 0.02, \quad \hat{\sigma}^2(TR) = \frac{\hat{\sigma}^2(tr)}{n'_t n'_r} = 0.00,$$

$$\text{and } \hat{\sigma}^2(pTR) = \frac{\hat{\sigma}^2(ptr)}{n'_t n'_r} = 0.02,$$

with $\hat{\sigma}^2(p) = .25$ as the estimated universe score variance. The other variance components contribute to different types of error variance.

Absolute error, Δ_p, is simply the difference between a person's observed mean score and the person's universe score. For Smith's design and universe, the variance of these errors is

$$\sigma^2(\Delta) = \sigma^2(T) + \sigma^2(R) + \sigma^2(pT) + \sigma^2(pR)$$
$$+ \sigma^2(TR) + \sigma^2(pTR),$$

which gives $\hat{\sigma}^2(\Delta) = 0.02 + 0.01 + 0.05 + 0.02 + 0.00 + 0.02 = 0.12$. Its square root is $\hat{\sigma}(\Delta) = 0.35$, which is interpretable as an estimate of the "absolute" standard error of measurement for a randomly selected person.

Relative error, δ_p, is defined as the difference between a person's observed deviation score and his or her universe deviation score. For Smith's design and universe,

$$\sigma^2(\delta) = \sigma^2(pT) + \sigma^2(pR) + \sigma^2(pTR),$$

which gives $\hat{\sigma}^2(\delta) = 0.05 + 0.02 + 0.02 = 0.09$. Its square root is $\hat{\sigma}(\delta) = 0.30$, which is interpretable as an estimate of the "relative" standard error of measurement for a randomly selected person.

Two types of reliability-like coefficients are widely used in generalizability theory. One coefficient is called a *generalizability coefficient*, which is defined as

$$E\rho^2 = \frac{\sigma^2(p)}{\sigma^2(p) + \sigma^2(\delta)}.$$

It is the analog of a reliability coefficient in classical theory. The other coefficient is called an *index of dependability*, which is defined as

$$\Phi = \frac{\sigma^2(p)}{\sigma^2(p) + \sigma^2(\Delta)}.$$

Because $\sigma^2(\delta) < \sigma^2(\Delta)$, it necessarily follows that $E\rho^2 > \Phi$. For example, using Smith's data, $E\hat{\rho}^2 = 0.25/(0.25 + 0.09) = 0.74$, and $\hat{\Phi} = 0.25/(0.25 + 0.12) = 0.68$.

—Robert L. Brennan

REFERENCES

Brennan, R. L. (2001). *Generalizability theory*. New York: Springer-Verlag.

Cronbach, L. J., Gleser, G. C., Nanda, H., & Rajaratnam, N. (1972). *The dependability of behavioral measurements: Theory of generalizability for scores and profiles*. New York: John Wiley.

Shavelson, R. J., & Webb, N. M. (1991). *Generalizability theory: A primer*. Newbury Park, CA: Sage.

GENERALIZATION/ GENERALIZABILITY IN QUALITATIVE RESEARCH

The issue of whether one should or can generalize from the findings of qualitative (interpretive/ethnographic) research lies at the heart of the approach, although it is discussed less than one would expect. Its relative absence from the methodological literature is likely attributable to it being seen by many qualitative researchers as a preoccupation of those who take a NOMOTHETIC, specifically quantitative, approach to research. For many qualitative researchers, it is a nonissue because the role of qualitative research is to interpret the meanings of agents within particular social contexts, rather than measuring, explaining, or predicting.

Those who deny the possibility of generalization argue that individual consciousnesses are free to attach different meanings to the same actions or circumstances. Conversely, different actions can arise out of similarly expressed meanings. An "inherent indeterminateness in the lifeworld" (Denzin, 1983, p. 133) is said to follow, which leads to too much variability to allow the possibility of generalization from a specific situation to others. However, a major problem in holding this line is that it is actually very hard not to generalize, in that reports of a particular social setting, events, or behavior will usually claim some typicality (or, conversely, that the reports are in some way untypical of some prior observed regularity).

Those who deny the possibility or desirability of generalization would be correct in their assertions if it was claimed that qualitative research could produce total generalizations, where situation S^{1-n} is identical to S in every detail, or even statistical generalizations, where the probability of situation S occurring more widely can be estimated from instances of s. The first kind of generalization is rarely possible outside of physics or chemistry, and the second (in social science) is the province of survey research. However, it seems reasonable to claim that qualitative research might produce *moderatum* generalizations in which aspects of S can be seen to be instances of a broader recognizable set of features (Williams, 2000). These depend on levels of cultural consistency in the social environment, those things that are the basis of inductive reasoning in everyday life, such as rules, customs, and shared social constructions of the physical environment.

Moderatum generalizations can arise from CASE STUDY research. Case studies can take many different forms—for example, the identification of the existence of a general social principle, the analysis of a social situation, or the extended case study in which people or events are studied over time (Mitchell, 1983, pp. 193–194). Case studies do not depend on statistical generalization from sample to population, as in survey research, but on logical inference from prior theorizing. Theoretical generalization therefore does not aim to say anything about populations but instead makes claims about the existence of phenomena proposed by a theory. This reasoning is common in anthropology, and theoretical corroboration is said to be increased by further instances of a phenomenon in repeated case studies.

Some minimal generalization seems necessary if qualitative research is to have any value in the policy process. If all qualitative research can give us are many interpretations, each with the same epistemological status, then how can we evaluate, for example, social programs or economic policy? Nevertheless, one should be cautious when making even moderatum generalizations from qualitative data (as analogously as one should in claims of meaning in survey data). Even if findings confirm a prior theoretical proposition, it cannot be known how typical they are with any certainty.

—Malcolm Williams

REFERENCES

Denzin, N. (1983). Interpretive interactionism. In G. Morgan (Ed.), *Beyond method: Strategies for social research* (pp. 128–142). Beverly Hills, CA: Sage.

Mitchell, J. (1983). Case and situation analysis. *Sociological Review, 31*(2), 186–211.

Williams, M. (2000). Interpretivism and generalisation. *Sociology, 34*(2), 209–224.

GENERALIZED ADDITIVE MODELS

Additive models recast the LINEAR REGRESSION model $y_i = \alpha + \sum_{j=1}^{k} X_{ij}\beta_j + \varepsilon_i$ by modeling y as an additive combination of nonparametric functions of X: $y_i = \alpha + \sum_{j=1}^{k} m_j(X_{ij}) + \varepsilon_i$, where the ε_i are zero mean, independent, and identically distributed stochastic disturbances. *Generalized* additive models (GAMs) extend additive models in precisely the same way the generalized linear models (GLMs) extend linear models so as to accommodate qualitative dependent variables (e.g., binary outcomes, count data, etc.). The additive model for a continuous outcome is a special case of a GAM, just as ORDINARY LEAST SQUARES regression with normal disturbances is a special type of GLM.

GAMs are especially useful in exploratory work or when analysts have weak priors as to the functional form relating predictors X to an outcome y. In these cases, assuming that the conditional mean function for y, $E(y|X)$ is linear in X is somewhat arbitrary: Although linearity is simple, easy to interpret, and parsimonious, linear functional forms risk smoothing over what might be substantively interesting nonlinearities in $E(y|X)$. GAMs are also useful when prediction motivates the data analysis. By fitting possibly quite nonlinear $m(\ )$ functions, the resulting model will respond to localized features of the data, resulting in smaller prediction errors than those from a linear model.

GAMs can be distinguished from other nonparametric modeling strategies (for a recent comparison, see Hastie, Tibshirani, & Friedman, 2001). With additive GLMs at one extreme and NEURAL NETWORKS at the other, GAMs lie closer to the former than the latter, generally retaining the additivity (and hence separability) of linear regression. GAMs are also generally closer to linear regression models than other techniques such as projection pursuit, alternating conditional expectations, or tree-based methods. GAMs can also be distinguished from parametric approaches to handling nonlinearities, such as simply logging variables, modeling with polynomials of the predictors, or the Box-Cox transformation; the $m(\ )$ functions that GAMs estimate are nonparametric functions that are generally more flexible than parametric approaches. Note also that linear models nest as a special case of a GAM, meaning that the null hypothesis of a linear fit can be tested against a nonparametric, nonlinear alternative; that is, the null hypothesis is that $m(X) = X\beta$, or, in other words, a 1 degree-of-freedom $m(\ )$ versus a higher degree-of-freedom alternative. In practice, a mixture of parametric and nonparametric $m(\ )$ functions may be fit, say, when researchers have strong beliefs that a particular predictor has a linear effect on y but wish to fit a flexible $m(\ )$ function tapping the effect of some other predictor.

GAMs use *linear smoothers* as their $m(\ )$ functions, predictor by predictor. It is possible to fit an $m(\ )$ function over more than a single predictor, but to simplify the discussion, I consider the case of fitting nonparametric functions predictor by predictor: Given n observations on a dependent variable $\mathbf{y} = (y_1, \ldots, y_n)'$ and a predictor $\mathbf{x} = (x_1, \ldots, x_n)'$, a linear smoother estimates $\hat{y}$ at target point x_0 as a weighted average (i.e., a linear function) of the y observations accompanying the x observations in some neighborhood of the target point x_0. That is, $\hat{y} = \hat{m}(x_0) = \sum_{i=1}^{n} S(x_0, x_i; \lambda)y_i$, where $S(\ )$ is a weighting function, parameterized by a SMOOTHING parameter λ, that effectively governs the width of the neighborhood around the target point. The neighborhood width or *bandwidth* governs how much weight observations $i = 1, \ldots, n$ contribute to forming $\hat{y}$ at target point x_0: As the name implies, local fitting assigns zero weight to data points not in the specified neighborhood of the target point x_0, and it is the smoothing parameter λ that determines "how local" is "local."

To motivate these ideas, one should consider LOESS, a popular linear smoother by Cleveland (1979). Given a target point x_0, loess yields $\hat{y}|x_0 = \hat{m}(x_0)$ by fitting a *locally weighted* regression, using the following procedure:

1. Identify the q *nearest neighbors* of x_0 (i.e., the q value of x closest to x_0). This set is denoted $N(x_0)$. The parameter q is the equivalent of the smoothing parameter λ, defined above, and is usually preset by the analyst.

2. Calculate $\Delta(x_0) = \max N(x_0)|x_0 - x_i|$, the distance of the nearest neighbor most distant from x_0.

3. Calculate weights w_i for each point in $N(x_0)$ using the following tri-cube weight function:

$$W\left[\frac{|x_0 - x_i|}{\Delta(x_0)}\right],$$

where

$$W(z) = \begin{cases} (1 - z^3)^3 & \text{for } 0 \leq z < 1; \\ 0 & \text{otherwise.} \end{cases}$$

Note that $W(x_0) = 1$ and that the weights decline smoothly to zero over the chosen set of nearest neighbors, such that $W(x_i) = 0 \ \forall x_i \notin N(x_0)$. The use of the tri-cube weight function is somewhat arbitrary; any weight function that has smooth contact with 0 on the boundary of $N(x_0)$ will produce a smooth fitted function.

4. Regress y on x and an intercept (for local linear fitting) using WEIGHTED LEAST SQUARES, with weights W defined in the previous step. Quadratic or higher order polynomial local regression can be implemented (Fan & Gijbels, 1996, chap. 5) or even mixtures of low-order polynomials. Local constant fitting produces a simple moving average.

5. The predicted value from the local weighted regression is the smoothed value $\hat{y}|x_0 = \hat{m}(x_0)$.

Loess is just one of a number of nonparametric smoothers but demonstrates the key idea; run a regression of y and x in the neighborhood around a target point x_0 (smoothers differ as to how to weight observations in the neighborhood of x_0—that is, the choice of the *kernel* of the nonparametric regression—and in the degree of the local regression), and then report the fitted value of the local regression at x_0 as the estimate of the nonparametric function. Other popular smoothers for nonparametric regression include SPLINE functions, loess, and various other smoothing functions. The spline and the loess, among a variety of smoothers (including the kernel), are typically available software implementing GAMs.

Implementing the linear smoother over a grid of target points traces out a function, the smoothed fit of y against x. In particular, letting the linear smoother produce $\hat{y}_i$ for each observation (i.e., letting $x_0 = x_i, i = 1, \ldots, n$) produces $\hat{\mathbf{y}} = \mathbf{S}\mathbf{y}$, where $\mathbf{S}$ is an n-by-n smoother matrix, formed by stacking n vectors of weights $S(x_i, x_i; \lambda)$, each of length n. Linear smoothers are thus linear in precisely the same way that the predicted values from a least squares regression are a linear function of $\mathbf{y}$: that is, $\hat{\mathbf{y}} = \mathbf{X}\hat{\beta} = \mathbf{H}\mathbf{y}$, where $\mathbf{H} = \mathbf{X}(\mathbf{X}'\mathbf{X})^{-1}\mathbf{X}'$ is the well-known "hat matrix." The smoother matrix $\mathbf{S}$ has many of the same properties as $\mathbf{H}$. In fact, $\mathbf{H}$ is a special case of a linear smoother, and least squares linear regression is the equivalent of an infinitely smooth smoother (formally, "smoothness" is measured by the inverse of the second derivative of the fitted values with respect to the predictors; for a linear model, this second derivative is zero). At the other extreme is a smoother that simply interpolates the data (the equivalent of running a regression with a dummy variable for every observation), and $\mathbf{S} = \mathbf{I}_n$ (an n-by-n identity matrix), with all off-diagonal elements zero (i.e., extreme local fitting). As the bandwidth increases, an increasing number of the off-diagonal elements of $\mathbf{S}$ are nonzero, as data points further away from any target point x_i have greater influence in forming $\hat{y}_i = \hat{m}(x_i)$.

The inverse relationship between the amount of smoothing and the extent to which $\mathbf{S}$ is diagonal means that the degrees of freedom consumed by a linear smoother are well approximated by the trace (sum of the diagonal elements) of $\mathbf{S}$ (Hastie & Tibshirani, 1990, Appendix 2). Because all smoothers fit an intercept term, $\text{tr}(\mathbf{S}) - 1$ is an estimate of the *equivalent degrees of freedom* consumed by the nonparametric component of the linear smoother. This approximation provides a critical ingredient in inference, letting the smoother's residual error variance σ^2 be estimated as

$$\hat{\sigma}^2 = \frac{\sum_{i=1}^{n} \left[y_i - \hat{m}(x_i) \right]^2}{n - \text{tr}(\mathbf{S})},$$

and, in turn, the variance-covariance matrix of the smoothed values is estimated with $\text{var}[\hat{\mathbf{y}}] = \mathbf{SS}'\hat{\sigma}^2$, with pointwise standard errors for the fitted smooth obtained by taking the square root of the diagonal of this matrix. In short, the more local the fitting, the less smoothing and the more degrees of freedom are consumed, with less bias in the $\hat{y}$ but with the price of higher variances.

GAMs extend linear smoothers to multiple predictors via an iterative fitting ALGORITHM known as backfitting, described in detail in Hastie and Tibshirani (1990). The basic idea is to cycle over the predictors in the model, $j = 1, \ldots, k$, smoothing the residual quantity y minus the intercept and the partial effects of the $k - 1$ other predictors against x_j until convergence. The extension to GLM-type models with qualitative dependent variables is also reasonably straightforward; backfitting nests neatly inside the iteratively reweighted least squares algorithm for GLMs developed by Nelder and Wedderburn (1972).

A key question when working with GAMs is whether a simpler, more parsimonious fit will suffice relative to the fitted model. This is critical in helping to guard against overfitting (fitting a more flamboyant function than the data support) and in finding an appropriate setting for the respective smoothing parameters. Simpler, "less local" models (including a linear fit) will nest inside an alternative, "more local" fit, suggesting that likelihood ratio tests can be used to test the null hypothesis that the restrictions embodied in the simpler model are correct. These tests apply only approximately in the nonparametric setting implied by GAMs (for one thing, the degrees of freedom consumed by the GAM are only an estimate) but, in large samples, appear to work well. There are a number of proposals for automatic selection of smoothing parameters in the statistical literature (e.g., Hastie & Tibshirani, 1990, pp. 50–52), and this is an active area of research.

As a practical matter, social scientists should be aware that implementing GAMs entails forgoing a simple single-parameter assessment of the marginal effect of x on y produced by a linear regression or a GLM. In adopting a nonparametric approach, the best way (and perhaps only way) to appreciate the marginal effect of x on y is via a graph of the fitted smooth

of y against x. Beck and Jackman (1998) provide numerous examples from political science, supplementing traditional tables of regression estimates with graphs of nonparametric/nonlinear marginal effects and confidence intervals around the fitted values.

GAMs are the subject of a book by Hastie and Tibshirani (1990), although the literature on nonparametric smoothing (at the heart of any GAM) is immense. Loader (1999) provides an excellent review of local fitting methods; Wahba (1990) reviews the use of splines in nonparametric regression. GAMs are implemented in S-PLUS (for a detailed review, see Hastie, 1992). Wood (2001) provides an implementation in R with automatic selection of the smoothing parameters via generalized cross-validation and smoothing via spline functions.

—Simon Jackman

REFERENCES

Beck, N., & Jackman, S. (1998). Beyond linearity by default: Generalized additive models. *American Journal of Political Science, 42*, 596–627.

Cleveland, W. S. (1979). Robust locally-weighted regression and smoothing scatterplots. *Journal of the American Statistical Association, 74*, 829–836.

Fan, J., & Gijbels, I. (1996). *Local polynomial modelling and its applications*. London: Chapman & Hall.

Hastie, T. J. (1992). Generalized additive models. In J. M. Chambers & T. J. Hastie (Eds.), *Statistical models in S* (pp. 249–307). Pacific Grove, CA: Wadsworth Brooks/ Cole.

Hastie, T. J., & Tibshirani, R. J. (1990). *Generalized additive models*. New York: Chapman & Hall.

Hastie, T. J., Tibshirani, R., & Friedman, J. (2001). *The elements of statistical learning*. New York: Springer.

Loader, C. (1999). *Local regression and likelihood*. New York: Springer.

Nelder, J. A., & Wedderburn, R. W. M. (1972). Generalized linear models. *Journal of the Royal Statistical Society, Series A, 135*, 370–384.

Wahba, G. (1990). *Spline models for observational data*. Philadelphia: SIAM.

Wood, S. (2001). mgcv: GAMs and generalized ridge regression for R. *R News, 1*, 20–25.

GENERALIZED ESTIMATING EQUATIONS

The method of generalized estimating equations (GEE) is an extension of GENERALIZED LINEAR MODELS to repeated-measures (or, in fact, any correlated) data. In the social sciences, this class of MODELS is most valuable for PANEL and TIME-SERIES CROSS-SECTION MODEL data, although it can be used to model spatial data as well.

Consider a generalized linear model for repeated-measures data, where $i = (1, \ldots, N)$ indexes units and $t = (1, \ldots, T)$ indexes time points, such that $E(Y_{it}) \equiv \mu_{it} = f(\mathbf{X}_{it}\beta)$ and $\mathrm{Var}(Y_{it}) = g(\mu_{it})/\varphi$, where $\mathbf{X}$ is an $(NT \times k)$ vector of covariates, $f(\cdot)$ is the inverse of the LINK FUNCTION, and φ is a scale parameter. The GEE estimate of β is the solution to the set of k differential "score" equations:

$$\mathbf{U}_k(\beta) = \sum_{i=1}^{N} \mathbf{D}_i' \mathbf{V}_i^{-1} (\mathbf{Y}_i - \mu_i) = \mathbf{0}, \qquad (1)$$

where

$$\mathbf{V}_i = \frac{\mathbf{A}_i^{1/2} \mathbf{R}_i(\alpha) \mathbf{A}_i^{1/2}}{\varphi}.$$

$\mathbf{A}_i$ is a $t \times t$ diagonal matrix with $g(\mu_{it})$ as its tth diagonal element, and $\mathbf{R}_i(\alpha)$ is a $t \times t$ "working" correlation matrix of the conditional within-subject correlation among the values of Y_{it}. The form of the working correlation matrix is determined by the researcher; however, Liang and Zeger (1986) show that GEE estimates of β and its robust variance-covariance matrix are consistent even in the presence of MISSPECIFICATION of $\mathbf{R}_i(\alpha)$. In practice, researchers typically specify $\mathbf{R}_i(\alpha)$ according to their substantive beliefs about the nature of the within-subject correlations.

GEEs are a robust and attractive alternative to other models for panel and time-series cross-sectional data. In particular, GEE methods offer the possibility of estimating models in which the intrasubject CORRELATION is itself of substantive interest. Such "GEE2" methods (e.g., Prentice & Zhao, 1991) incorporate a second, separate set of estimating equations for the pairwise intrasubject correlations. In addition, GEEs offer the ability to model continuous, dichotomous, ordinal, and event-count data using a wide range of distributions. Finally, GEEs are estimable using a wide range of commonly used software packages, including SAS, S-PLUS, and STATA.

—Christopher Zorn

REFERENCES

Hardin, J. W., & Hilbe, J. M. (2003). *Generalized estimating equations*. London: Chapman & Hall.

Liang, K.-Y., & Zeger, S. L. (1986). Longitudinal data analysis using generalized linear models. *Biometrika, 73*, 13–22.

Prentice, R. L., & Zhao, L. P. (1991). Estimating equations for parameters in mean and covariances of multivariate discrete and continuous responses. *Biometrics, 47*, 825–839.

Zorn, C. J. W. (2001). Generalized estimating equation models for correlated data: A review with applications. *American Journal of Political Science, 45*, 470–490.

GENERALIZED LEAST SQUARES

Consider the LINEAR REGRESSION model $\mathbf{y} = \mathbf{X}\beta + \mathbf{u}$, where $\mathbf{y}$ is a n-by-1 vector of observations on a dependent variable, $\mathbf{X}$ is a n-by-k matrix of independent variables of full column rank, β is a k-by-1 vector of parameters to be estimated, and $\mathbf{u}$ is a n-by-1 vector of disturbances. Via the GAUSS-MARKOV theorem, if

Assumption 1 (A1): $E(\mathbf{u}|\mathbf{X}) = \mathbf{0}$ (i.e., the disturbances have conditional mean zero), and

Assumption 2 (A2): $E(\mathbf{uu}'|\mathbf{X}) = \sigma^2 \mathbf{\Omega}$, where $\mathbf{\Omega} = \mathbf{I}_n$, an n-by-n identity matrix (i.e., conditional on the $\mathbf{X}$, the disturbances are independent and identically distributed or "iid" with conditional variance σ^2),

then the ORDINARY LEAST SQUARES (OLS) estimator $\hat{\beta}_{\mathrm{OLS}} = (\mathbf{X}'\mathbf{X})^{-1}\mathbf{X}'\mathbf{y}$ with variance-covariance matrix $V(\hat{\beta}_{\mathrm{OLS}})\sigma^2(\mathbf{X}'\mathbf{X})^{-1}$ is (a) the BEST LINEAR UNBIASED ESTIMATOR (BLUE) of β, in the sense of having smallest sampling variability in the class of linear unbiased estimators, and (b) a consistent estimator of β (i.e., as $n \to \infty$, $\Pr[|\hat{\beta}_{\mathrm{OLS}} - \beta| < \varepsilon] = 1$, for any $\varepsilon > 0$, or plim $\hat{\beta}_{\mathrm{OLS}} = \beta$).

If A2 fails to hold (i.e., $\mathbf{\Omega}$ is a positive definite matrix but not equal to $\mathbf{I}_n$), then $\hat{\beta}_{\mathrm{OLS}}$ remains unbiased, but no longer "best," and remains consistent. Relying on $\hat{\beta}_{\mathrm{OLS}}$ when A2 does not hold risks faulty inferences; without A2, $\hat{\sigma}^2(\mathbf{X}'\mathbf{X})^{-1}$ is a biased and inconsistent estimator of $V(\hat{\beta}_{\mathrm{OLS}})$, meaning that the estimated STANDARD ERRORS for $\hat{\beta}_{\mathrm{OLS}}$ are wrong, risking invalid inferences and hypothesis tests. A2 often fails to hold in practice; for example, (a) pooling across disparate units often generates disturbances with different conditional variances (HETEROSKEDASTICITY), and (b) analysis of TIME-SERIES data often generates disturbances that are not conditionally independent (serially correlated disturbances).

When A2 does not hold, it may be possible to implement a *generalized least squares* (GLS) estimator that is BLUE (at least asymptotically). For instance, if the researcher knows the exact form of the departure from A2 (i.e., the researcher knows $\mathbf{\Omega}$), then the GLS estimator $\hat{\beta}_{GLS} = (\mathbf{X'\Omega^{-1}X})^{-1}\mathbf{X'\Omega^{-1}y}$ is BLUE, with variance-covariance matrix $\sigma^2(\mathbf{X'\Omega^{-1}X})^{-1}$. Note that when A2 holds, $\mathbf{\Omega} = \mathbf{I}_n$, and $\hat{\beta}_{GLS} = \hat{\beta}_{OLS}$ (i.e., OLS is a special case of the more general estimator).

Typically, researchers do not possess exact knowledge of $\mathbf{\Omega}$, meaning that $\hat{\beta}_{GLS}$ is nonoperational, and an *estimated or feasible* generalized least squares (FGLS) estimator is used. FGLS estimators are often implemented in multiple steps: (a) an OLS analysis to yield estimated residuals $\hat{\mathbf{u}}$; (b) an analysis of the $\hat{\mathbf{u}}$ to form an estimate of $\mathbf{\Omega}$, denoted $\hat{\mathbf{\Omega}}$; and (c) computation of the FGLS estimator $\hat{\beta}_{FGLS} = (\mathbf{X'\hat{\Omega}^{-1}X})^{-1}\mathbf{X'\hat{\Omega}^{-1}y}$. The third step is often performed by noting that $\hat{\mathbf{\Omega}}$ can be decomposed as $\hat{\mathbf{\Omega}} = \mathbf{P}^{-1}(\mathbf{P'})^{-1}$, and $\hat{\beta}_{FGLS}$ is obtained by running the WEIGHTED LEAST SQUARES (WLS) regression of $\mathbf{y^*} = \mathbf{Py}$ on $\mathbf{X^*} = \mathbf{PX}$; that is, $\hat{\beta}_{FGLS} = (\mathbf{X^{*'}X^*})^{-1}\mathbf{X^{*'}y^*}$.

The properties of FGLS estimators vary depending on the form of $\mathbf{\Omega}$ (i.e., the nature of the departure from the conditional iid assumption in A2) and the quality of $\hat{\mathbf{\Omega}}$, and so they cannot be neatly summarized. Finite sample properties of the FGLS estimator are often derived case by case via MONTE CARLO experiments; in fact, it is possible to find cases in which $\hat{\beta}_{OLS}$ is more efficient than $\hat{\beta}_{FGLS}$, say, when the violation of A2 is mild (e.g., Chipman, 1979; Rao & Griliches, 1969). ASYMPTOTIC results are more plentiful and usually rely on showing that $\hat{\beta}_{FGLS}$ and $\hat{\beta}_{GLS}$ are asymptotically equivalent, so that $\hat{\beta}_{FGLS}$ is a consistent and asymptotically efficient estimator of β (e.g., Amemiya, 1985, pp. 186–222; Judge, Griffiths, Hill, & Lee, 1980, pp. 117–118).

In social science settings, FGLS is most commonly encountered in dealing with simple forms of residual autocorrelation and heteroskedasticity. For instance, the popular Cochrane-Orcutt (Cochrane & Orcutt, 1949) and Prais-Winsten (Prais & Winsten, 1954) procedures for AR(1) disturbances yield FGLS estimators. The use of FGLS to deal with heteroskedasticity appears in many econometrics texts: Judge et al. (1980, pp. 128–145) and Amemiya (1985, pp. 198–207) provide rigorous treatments of FGLS estimators of β for commonly encountered forms of heteroskedasticity. Groupwise heteroskedasticity arises from pooling across disparate units, yielding disturbances that are conditionally iid *within* groups of observations; this model is actually a special case of Zellner's (1962) SEEMINGLY UNRELATED REGRESSION (SUR) model. FGLS applied to Zellner's SUR model results in a cross-equation weighting scheme that is also used as the third stage of three-stage least squares estimators (Zellner & Theil, 1962).

FGLS is also used to estimate models for PANEL data with unit- and/or period-specific HETEROGENEITY not captured by the independent variables—for example, $y_{it} = \mathbf{x}'_{it}\beta + v_i + \eta_t + \varepsilon_{it}$, where v_i and η_t are error components (or random effects) specific to units i and time periods t, respectively. The composite error term $u_{it} = v_i + \eta_t + \varepsilon_{it}$ is generally not iid, but its variance-covariance matrix $\mathbf{\Omega}$ can be estimated with the sum of the estimated variances of the error components; provided that $E(u_{it}|\mathbf{x}_{it}) = 0$ and $E(\mathbf{X'\Omega^{-1}X})$ is of full rank, then FGLS provides a consistent estimator of β (see Wooldridge, 2002, chap. 10).

Finally, FGLS estimators can often be obtained as MAXIMUM LIKELIHOOD ESTIMATES (MLEs), generating consistent estimates of β in "one shot." Although the iid assumption (A2) often greatly simplifies deriving and computing MLEs, the more common (and hence more simple) departures from A2 are often tapped via a small number of auxiliary parameters that determine the content and structure of $\mathbf{\Omega}$ (e.g., consider the relatively simple form of $\mathbf{\Omega}$ implied by first-order residual autocorrelation, groupwise heteroskedasticity, or simple error components structures). Thus, the parameters of substantive interest (β) and parameters tapping the assumed error process can be estimated simultaneously via MLE, yielding estimates that are asymptotically equivalent to FGLS estimates.

—Simon Jackman

REFERENCES

Amemiya, T. (1985). *Advanced econometrics*. Cambridge, MA: Harvard University Press.

Chipman, J. S. (1979). Efficiency of least squares estimation of linear trend when residuals are autocorrelated. *Econometrica, 47*, 115–128.

Cochrane, D., & Orcutt, G. H. (1949). Application of least squares relationships containing autocorrelated error terms. *Journal of the American Statistical Association, 44,* 32–61.

Judge, G. G., Griffiths, W. E., Hill, R. C., & Lee, T.-C. (1980). *The theory and practice of econometrics.* Wiley Series in Probability and Mathematical Statistics. New York: John Wiley.

Prais, S. J., & Winsten, C. B. (1954). *Trend estimators and serial correlation.* Chicago: Cowles Commission.

Rao, P., & Griliches, Z. (1969). Small-sample properties of several two-stage regression methods in the context of auto-correlated errors. *Journal of the American Statistical Association, 64,* 253–272.

Wooldridge, J. M. (2002). *Econometric analysis of cross-section and panel data.* Cambridge: MIT Press.

Zellner, A. (1962). An efficient method of estimating seemingly unrelated regressions and tests for aggregation bias. *Journal of the American Statistical Association, 57,* 348–368.

Zellner, A., & Theil, H. (1962). Three-stage least squares: Simultaneous estimation of simultaneous equations. *Econometrica, 30,* 54–78.

GENERALIZED LINEAR MODELS

Generalized linear models (GLMs) expand the basic structure of the well-known linear model to accommodate nonnormal and noninterval measured outcome variables in a single unified theoretical form. It is common in the social sciences to encounter outcome variables that do not fit the standard assumptions of the linear model, and as a result, many distinct forms of regression have been developed: POISSON REGRESSION for counts as outcomes, LOGIT and PROBIT ANALYSIS for dichotomous explanations, exponential models for DURATIONS, gamma models for TRUNCATED data, and more. Although these forms are commonly used and well understood, it is not widely known among practitioners that nearly all of these particularistic regression techniques are special forms of the *generalized linear model.*

With the generalized linear model, explanatory variables are treated in exactly the usual fashion by creating a linear systematic component, $\eta = \mathbf{X\beta}$, which defines the right-hand side of the statistical model. Because the expectation of the outcome variable, $\mu = -\mathbf{y}$, is no longer from an interval-measured form, standard central limit and asymptotic theory no longer apply in the same way, and a "LINK" FUNCTION is required to define the relationship between the linear systematic component of the data and the mean of the outcome

variable, $\mu = g(\mathbf{X\beta})$. If the specified link function is simply the identity function, $g(\mathbf{X\beta}) = \mathbf{X\beta}$, then the generalized linear model reduces to the linear model, hence its name.

The generalized linear model is based on well-developed theory, starting with Nelder and Wedderburn (1972) and McCullagh and Nelder (1989), which states that any parametric form for the outcome variable that can be recharacterized (algebraically) into the *exponential family form* leads to a link function that connects the mean function of this parametric form to the linear systematic component. This exponential family form is simply a standardized means of expressing various probability mass functions (PMFs, for discrete forms) and PROBABILITY DENSITY FUNCTIONS (PDFs, for continuous forms).

The value of the GLM approach is that a seemingly disparate set of nonlinear regression models can be integrated into a single framework in which the processes of specification searching, numerical estimation, residuals analysis, goodness-of-fit analysis, and reporting are all unified. Thus, researchers and practitioners can learn a singularly general procedure that fits a wide class of data types and can also be developed to include even broader classes of assumptions than those described here.

THE EXPONENTIAL FAMILY FORM

The key to understanding the generalized linear model is knowing how common probability density functions for continuous data forms and probability mass functions for discrete data forms can be expressed in exponential family form—a form that readily produces link functions and moment statistics. The exponential family form originates with Fisher (1934, pp. 288–296), but it was not shown until later that members of the exponential family have fixed dimension-sufficient statistics and produce unique MAXIMUM LIKELIHOOD ESTIMATES with strong consistency and asymptotic normality (Gill, 2000, p. 22).

Consider the one-parameter conditional PDF or PMF for the random variable Z of the form $f(z|\zeta)$. It is classified as being an exponential family form if it can be expressed as

$$f(z|\zeta) = \exp[\underbrace{t(z)u(\zeta)}_{\substack{\text{interaction} \\ \text{component}}} + \underbrace{\log(r(z)) + (\log s(\zeta))}_{\text{additive component}}],$$

(1)

given that r and t are real-valued functions of z that do not depend on ζ, and s and u are real-valued functions of ζ that do not depend on z, with $r(z) > 0$, $s(\zeta) > 0$ $\forall z, \zeta$. The key feature is the distinctiveness of the subfunctions within the exponent. The piece labeled *interaction component* must have $t(z)$, strictly a function of z, multiplying $u(\zeta)$, strictly a function of ζ. Furthermore, the *additive component* must have similarly distinct, but now summed, subfunctions with regard to z and ζ.

The canonical form of the exponential family expression is a simplification of (1) that reveals greater structure and gives a more concise summary of the data. This one-to-one transformation works as follows. Make the transformations $y = t(z)$ and $\theta = u(\zeta)$, if necessary (i.e., they are not already in canonical form), and now express (1) as

$$f(y|\theta) = \exp[y\theta - b(\theta) + c(y)]. \qquad (2)$$

The subfunctions in (2) have specific identifiers: y is the canonical form for the data (and typically a sufficient statistic as well), θ is the natural canonical form for the unknown parameter, and $b(\theta)$ is often called the "cumulant function" or "normalizing constant." The function $c(y)$ is usually not important in the estimation process. However, $b(\theta)$ plays a key role in both determining the mean and variance functions as well as the link function. It should also be noted that the canonical form is invariant to random sampling, meaning that it retains its functionality for iid (independent, identically distributed) data:

$$f(y|\theta) = \exp\left[\sum_{i=1}^{n} y_i\theta - nb(\theta) + \sum_{i=1}^{n} c(y_i)\right],$$

and under the extension to multiple parameters through a k-length parameters vector $\boldsymbol{\theta}$:

$$f(y|\boldsymbol{\theta}) = \exp\left[\sum_{j=1}^{k} (y\theta_j - b(\theta_j)) + c(y)\right].$$

As an example of this theory, we can rewrite the familiar binomial PMF,

$$f(y|n, p) = \binom{n}{y} p^y (1-p)^{n-y},$$

in exponential family form:

$$f(y|n, p) = \exp\left[\underbrace{y \log\left(\frac{p}{1-p}\right)}_{y\theta} - \underbrace{(-n \log(1-p))}_{b(\theta)} + \underbrace{\log\binom{n}{y}}_{c(y)}\right]$$

Here the subfunctions are labeled to correspond to the canonical form previously identified.

THE EXPONENTIAL FAMILY FORM AND MAXIMUM LIKELIHOOD

To obtain estimates of the unknown k-dimensional $\boldsymbol{\theta}$ vector, given an observed matrix of data values $f(\boldsymbol{\theta}|\mathbf{X})$, we can employ the standard technique of maximizing the likelihood function with regard to coefficient values to find the "most likely" values of the $\boldsymbol{\theta}$ vector (Fisher, 1925, pp. 707–709). Asymptotic theory assures us that for sufficiently large samples, the likelihood surface is unimodal in dimensions for exponential family forms, so the maximum likelihood estimate (MLE) process is equivalent to finding the k-dimensional mode.

Regarding $f(\mathbf{X}|\boldsymbol{\theta})$ as a function of $\boldsymbol{\theta}$ for given observed (now fixed) data $\mathbf{X}$, then $L(\boldsymbol{\theta}|\mathbf{X}) = f(\mathbf{X}|\boldsymbol{\theta})$ is called a likelihood function. The MLE, $\hat{\boldsymbol{\theta}}$, has the characteristic that $L(\hat{\boldsymbol{\theta}}|\mathbf{X}) \geq L(\boldsymbol{\theta}|\mathbf{X})$ $\forall \boldsymbol{\theta} \in \boldsymbol{\Theta}$, where $\boldsymbol{\Theta}$ is the admissible range of $\boldsymbol{\theta}$ given by the parametric form assumptions.

It is more convenient to work with the natural log of the likelihood function, and this does not change any of the resulting parameter estimates because the likelihood function and the log-likelihood function have identical modal points. Using (2) with a scale parameter added, the likelihood function in canonical exponential family notation is

$$\ell(\theta, \psi | \mathbf{y}) = \log(f(\mathbf{y}|\theta, \psi))$$
$$= \log\left(\exp\left[\frac{\mathbf{y}\theta - b(\theta)}{a(\psi)} + c(\mathbf{y}, \psi)\right]\right)$$
$$= \frac{\mathbf{y}\theta - b(\theta)}{a(\psi)} + c(\mathbf{y}, \psi). \qquad (3)$$

Because all of the terms are expressed in the exponent of the exponential family form, removing this exponent through the log of the likelihood gives a very compact form. The score function is the first derivative of the log-likelihood function with respect to the parameters of interest. For the time being, the scale parameter ψ is treated as a *nuisance parameter* (not of primary interest), and we estimate a scalar. The resulting score function, denoted as $\dot{\ell}(\theta|\psi, \mathbf{y})$, is

$$
\begin{aligned}
\dot{\ell}(\theta, \psi|\mathbf{y}) &= \frac{\partial}{\partial\theta}\ell(\theta|\psi, \mathbf{y}) \\
&= \frac{\partial}{\partial\theta}\left[\frac{\mathbf{y}\theta - b(\theta)}{a(\psi)} + \mathbf{c}(\mathbf{y}, \psi)\right] \\
&= \frac{\mathbf{y} - \frac{\partial}{\partial\theta}b(\theta)}{a(\psi)}.
\end{aligned} \tag{4}
$$

The mechanics of the maximum likelihood process involve setting $\dot{\ell}(\theta|\psi, \mathbf{y})$ equal to zero and then solving for the parameter of interest, giving the MLE: $\hat{\theta}$. Furthermore, the *likelihood principle* states that once the data are observed, all of the available evidence from the data for estimating $\hat{\theta}$ is contained in the calculated likelihood function, $\ell(\theta|\psi, \mathbf{y})$.

The value of identifying $b(\theta)$ the function lies in its direct link to the mean and variance functions. The expected value calculation of (2) with respect to the data (Y) in the notation of (3) is

$$
E_Y\left[\frac{y - \frac{\partial}{\partial\theta}b(\theta)}{a(\psi)}\right] = 0,
$$

$$
\int_Y yf(y)\,dy - \int_Y \frac{\partial b(\theta)}{\partial\theta}f(y)\,dy = 0,
$$

$$
\underbrace{\int_Y yf(y)\,dy}_{E(Y)} - \frac{\partial b(\theta)}{\partial\theta}\underbrace{\int_Y f(y)\,dy}_{1} = 0,
$$

$$
\Rightarrow E[Y] = \frac{\partial}{\partial\theta}b(\theta),
$$

where the second to last step requires general regularity conditions with regard to the bounds of integration, and all exponential family distributions meet this requirement (Gill, 2000, p. 23). This means that (2) gives the mean of the associated exponential family of distributions: $\mu = b'(\theta)$. It can also be shown (Gill, 2000, p. 26) that the second derivative of $b(\theta)$ is the variance function. Then, multiplying this by the scale

parameter (if appropriate) and substituting back in for the canonical parameter produces the standard variance calculation. These calculations are summarized for the binomial PMF:

Table 1   Binomial Mean and Variance Functions

$b(\theta)$	$n\log(1 = \exp(\theta))$
$E[Y] = \frac{\partial}{\partial\theta}b(\theta)\big|_{\theta=u(\zeta)}$	np
$\frac{\partial^2}{\partial\theta^2}b(\theta)$	$n\exp(\theta)(1 + \exp(\theta))^{-2}$
$\mathrm{Var}[Y] = a(\psi)\frac{\partial^2}{\partial\theta^2}b(\theta)\big|_{\theta=u(\zeta)}$	$np(1 - p)$

THE GENERALIZED LINEAR MODEL THEORY

Start with the standard linear model meeting the following Gauss-Markov conditions:

$$
\underset{(n\times 1)}{\mathbf{V}} = \underset{(n\times p)(p\times 1)}{\mathbf{X}\boldsymbol{\beta}} + \underset{(n\times 1)}{\boldsymbol{\varepsilon}},
$$
$$
\underset{(n\times 1)}{E(\mathbf{V})} = \underset{(n\times 1)}{\boldsymbol{\theta}} = \underset{(n\times p)(p\times 1)}{\mathbf{X}\boldsymbol{\beta}}. \tag{5}
$$

The right-hand sides of the two equations in (5) contain the following: $\mathbf{X}$, the matrix of observed data values; $\mathbf{X}\boldsymbol{\beta}$, the "linear structure vector"; and $\boldsymbol{\varepsilon}$, the error terms. The left-hand side contains $E(\mathbf{V}) = \boldsymbol{\theta}$, the vector of means (i.e., the systematic component). The variable, $\mathbf{V}$, is distributed iid normal with mean θ and constant variance σ^2. Now suppose we generalize this with a new "linear predictor" based on the mean of the outcome variable, which is no longer required to be normally distributed or even continuous:

$$
\underset{(n\times 1)}{g(\boldsymbol{\mu})} = \underset{(n\times 1)}{\boldsymbol{\eta}} = \underset{(n\times p)(p\times 1)}{\mathbf{X}\boldsymbol{\beta}}.
$$

It is important here that $g(\ )$ be an invertible, *smooth* function of the mean vector $\boldsymbol{\mu}$.

The effect of the explanatory variables is now expressed in the model only through the link from the linear structure, $\mathbf{X}\boldsymbol{\beta}$, to the linear predictor, $\boldsymbol{\eta} = g(\boldsymbol{\mu})$, controlled by the form of the link function, $g(\ )$. This link function connects the linear predictor to the *mean* of the outcome variable and not directly to the expression of the outcome variable itself, so the outcome variable can now take on a variety of nonnormal forms. The link function connects the stochastic component, which describes some response variable from a wide variety of forms to all of the standard normal theory supporting the linear systematic component through the mean function:

$$g(\mu) = \eta = \mathbf{X}\boldsymbol{\beta}$$

$$g^{-1}(g(\mu)) = g^{-1}\eta = g^{-1}(\mathbf{X}\boldsymbol{\beta}) = \mu = E(\mathbf{Y}).$$

Furthermore, this linkage is provided by the form of the mean function from the exponential family subfunction: $b(\theta)$.

For example, with the binomial PMF, we saw that $b(\theta) = n \log(1 + \exp(\theta))$, and $\theta = \log(\frac{p}{1-p})$. Reexpressing this in link function notation is just $\eta = g(\mu) = \log(\frac{\mu}{1-\mu})$, or we could give the inverse link, $\mu = g^{-1}(\eta) = \frac{\exp(\theta)}{1+\exp(\theta)}$.

The generalization of the linear model as described now has the following components:

1. *Stochastic component:* $\mathbf{Y}$ is the random or stochastic component that remains distributed iid according to a specific exponential family distribution with mean μ.

2. *Systematic component:* $\eta = \mathbf{X}\boldsymbol{\beta}$ is the systematic component with an associated Gauss-Markov normal basis.

3. *Link function:* The stochastic component and the systematic component are linked by a function of η, which is taken from the inverse of the canonical link, $b(\theta)$.

4. *Residuals:* Although the residuals can be expressed in the same manner as in the standard linear model—observed outcome variable value minus predicted outcome variable value—a more useful quantity is the deviance residual described as follows.

ESTIMATING GENERALIZED LINEAR MODELS

Unlike the standard linear model, estimating generalized linear models is not done with a closed-form analytical expression [i.e., $\hat{\beta} = (\mathbf{X}'\mathbf{X})^{-1}\mathbf{X}\mathbf{y}$]. Instead, the maximum likelihood estimate of the unknown parameter is found with a weighted numerical process that repeatedly increases the likelihood with improved weights on each cycle: *iterative weighted least squares* (IWLS). This process, first proposed by Nelder and Wedderburn (1972, pp. 372–374) and first implemented in the GLIM software package, works for any GLM based on an exponential family form (and for some others).

Currently, all professional-level statistic computing implementations now employ IWLS to numerically find maximum likelihood estimates for generalized linear models.

The overall strategy is to apply Newton-Raphson with Fisher scoring to the normal equations, which is equivalent to iteratively applied, weighted *least squares* (and hence easy). Define the current (or starting) point of the linear predictor by

$$\underset{(n \times 1)}{\hat{\eta}_0} = \underset{(n \times p)(p \times 1)}{\mathbf{X}'\boldsymbol{\beta}_0}$$

with fitted value $\hat{\mu}_0$ from $g^{-1}(\hat{\eta}_0)$. Form the "adjusted dependent variable" according to

$$\underset{(n \times 1)}{\mathbf{z}_0} = \underset{(n \times 1)}{\hat{\eta}_0} + \underset{\text{diag}(n \times n)}{\left(\frac{\partial \eta}{\partial \mu}\Big|_{\hat{\mu}_0}\right)} \underset{(n \times 1)}{(\mathbf{y} - \hat{\mu}_0)},$$

which is a linearized form of the link function applied to the data. As an example of this derivative function, the binomial form looks like

$$\eta = \log\left(\frac{\mu}{1-\mu}\right) \Rightarrow \frac{\partial \eta}{\partial \mu} = (\mu)^{-1}(1-\mu)^{-1}.$$

Now form the *quadratic weight matrix*, which is the variance of $\mathbf{z}$:

$$\underset{\text{diag}(n \times n)}{\omega_0^{-1}} = \underset{\text{diag}(n \times n)}{\left(\frac{\partial \eta}{\partial \mu}\Big|_{\hat{\mu}_0}\right)^2} \underset{\text{diag}(n \times n)}{v(\mu)|_{\hat{\mu}_0}},$$

where $v(\mu)$ is the following variance function: $\frac{\partial}{\partial \theta}b'(\theta) = b''(\theta)$. Also, note that this process is necessarily iterative because both $\mathbf{z}$ and ω depend on the current fitted value, μ_0. The general scheme can now be summarized in the three steps:

1. Construct $\mathbf{z}$, ω. Regress $\mathbf{z}$ on the covariates with weights to get a new interim estimate:

$$\underset{(p \times 1)}{\hat{\beta}_1} = \left(\underset{(p \times n)}{\mathbf{X}'}\underset{(n \times n)}{\omega_0}\underset{(p \times p)}{\mathbf{X}}\right)^{-1}\underset{(p \times n)}{\mathbf{X}'}\underset{(n \times n)}{\omega_0}\underset{(n \times 1)}{\mathbf{z}_0}.$$

2. Use the coefficient vector estimate to update the linear predictor:

$$\hat{\eta}_1 = \mathbf{X}'\hat{\beta}_1.$$

3. Iterate the following:

$$\mathbf{z}_1 \boldsymbol{\omega}_1 \Rightarrow \hat{\boldsymbol{\beta}}_2, \hat{\boldsymbol{\eta}}_2$$

$$\mathbf{z}_2 \boldsymbol{\omega}_2 \Rightarrow \hat{\boldsymbol{\beta}}_3, \hat{\boldsymbol{\eta}}_3$$

$$\mathbf{z}_3 \boldsymbol{\omega}_3 \Rightarrow \hat{\boldsymbol{\beta}}_4, \hat{\boldsymbol{\eta}}_4$$

$$\vdots$$

Under very general conditions, satisfied by the exponential family of distributions, the iterative weighted least squares procedure finds the mode of the likelihood function, thus producing the maximum likelihood estimate of the unknown coefficient vector, $\hat{\beta}$. Furthermore, the matrix produced by $\hat{\sigma}^2 (\mathbf{X}' \boldsymbol{\Omega} \mathbf{X})^{-1}$ converges in probability to the variance matrix of $\hat{\beta}$ as desired.

RESIDUALS AND DEVIANCES

One significant advantage of the generalized linear model is the freedom it provides from the standard Gauss-Markov assumption that the residuals have mean zero and constant variance. Unfortunately, this freedom comes with the price of interpreting more complex stochastic structures. The *response* residual vector, $\mathbf{R}_{\text{response}} = \mathbf{Y} - \mathbf{X}\boldsymbol{\beta}$, calculated for linear models can be updated to include the GLM link function, $\mathbf{R}_{\text{response}} = Y - g^{-1}(\mathbf{X}\boldsymbol{\beta})$, but this does not then provide the nice distribution theory we get from the standard linear model.

A more useful but related idea for generalized linear models is the *deviance function*. This is built in a similar fashion to the likelihood ratio statistic, comparing the log likelihood from a proposed model specification to the maximum log likelihood possible through the saturated model (n data points and n specified parameters, using the same data and link function). The resulting difference is multiplied by 2 and called the summed deviance (Nelder & Wedderburn, 1972, pp. 374–376). The goodness-of-fit intuition is derived from the idea that this sum constitutes the summed contrast of individual likelihood contributions with the native data contributions to the saturated model. The point here is to compare the log likelihood for the proposed model,

$$\ell(\hat{\boldsymbol{\theta}}, \psi | \mathbf{y}) = \sum_{i=1}^{n} \frac{y_i \hat{\boldsymbol{\theta}} - b(\hat{\boldsymbol{\theta}})}{a(\psi)} + c(\mathbf{y}, \psi),$$

to the same log-likelihood function with identical data and the same link function, except that it is now with n coefficients for the n data points (i.e., the saturated model log-likelihood function):

$$\ell(\tilde{\boldsymbol{\theta}}, \psi | \mathbf{y}) = \sum_{i=1}^{n} \frac{y_i \tilde{\boldsymbol{\theta}} - b(\tilde{\boldsymbol{\theta}})}{a(\psi)} + c(\mathbf{y}, \psi).$$

The latter is the highest possible value for the log-likelihood function achievable with the given data. The deviance function is then given by

$$D(\boldsymbol{\theta}, \mathbf{y}) = 2 \sum_{i=1}^{n} [\ell(\tilde{\boldsymbol{\theta}}, \psi | \mathbf{y}) - \ell(\hat{\boldsymbol{\theta}}, \psi | \mathbf{y})]$$

$$= 2 \sum_{i=1}^{n} [y_i (\tilde{\boldsymbol{\theta}} - \hat{\boldsymbol{\theta}}) - b(\tilde{\boldsymbol{\theta}}) - b, \psi(\hat{\boldsymbol{\theta}})] \, a(\psi)^{-1}.$$

This statistic is asymptotically chi-square with $n - k$ degrees of freedom (although high levels of discrete granularity in the outcome variable can make this a poor distributional assumption for data sets that are not so large). Fortunately, these deviance functions are commonly tabulated for many exponential family forms and therefore do not require analytical calculation. In the binomial case, the deviance function is

$$D(m, p) = 2 \sum \left[y_i \log \left(\frac{y_i}{\mu_i} \right) + (n_i - y_i) \log \left(\frac{n_i - y_i}{n_i - \mu_i} \right) \right],$$

where the saturated log likelihood achieves the highest possible value for fitting $p_i = y_i / n_i$.

We can also look at the individual deviance contributions in an analogous way to linear model residuals. The single-point deviance function is just the deviance function for the y_ith point:

$$d(\boldsymbol{\theta}, y_i) = -2[y_i (\tilde{\boldsymbol{\theta}} - \hat{\boldsymbol{\theta}}) - (b(\tilde{\boldsymbol{\theta}}) - b(\hat{\boldsymbol{\theta}}))] \, a(\psi)^{-1}.$$

A deviance residual at the point is built on this by

$$\mathbf{R}_{\text{deviance}} = \frac{(y_i - \mu_i)}{|y_i - \mu_i|} \sqrt{|d(\boldsymbol{\theta}, y_i)|},$$

where $\frac{(y_i - \mu_i)}{|y_i - \mu_i|}$ is just a sign-preserving function.

Table 2 Happiness and Schooling by Sex, 1977 General Social Survey

| | Self-Reported Status | Years of Schooling | | | |
		< 12	12	13–16	17 +
Male	Not happy	40	21	14	3
	Pretty happy	131	116	112	27
	Very happy	82	61	55	27
Female	Not happy	62	26	12	3
	Pretty happy	155	156	95	15
	Very happy	87	127	76	15

EXAMPLE: MULTINOMIAL RESPONSE MODELS

Consider a slight generalization of the running binomial example in which, instead of two possible events defining the outcome variable, there are now k vents. The outcome for an individual i is given as a $k - 1$ length vector of all zeros—except for a single one identifying the positive response, $\mathbf{y}_i = [y_{i1}, y_{i2}, \ldots, y_{i(k-1)}]$—or all zeros for an individual selecting the left-out reference category. It should be clear that this reduces to a binomial outcome for $k = 2$.

The objective is now to estimate the $k - 1$ length of categorical probabilities for a sample size of n, $\boldsymbol{\mu} = g^{-1}(\boldsymbol{\eta}) = \boldsymbol{\pi} = [\pi_1, \pi_2, \ldots, \pi_{k-1}]$, from the data set consisting of the $n \times (k - 1)$ outcome matrix $\mathbf{y}$ and the $n \times p$ matrix of covariates $\mathbf{X}$, including a leading column of 1s. The PMF for this setup is now multinomial, where the estimates are provided with a logit (but sometimes a probit) link function, giving for each of $k - 1$ categories the probability that the ith individual picks category r:

$$P(\mathbf{y}_i = r | \mathbf{X}) = \frac{\exp(\mathbf{X}_i \boldsymbol{\beta}_r)}{1 + \sum_{s=1}^{k-1} \exp(\mathbf{X}\boldsymbol{\beta}_s)},$$

where β_r is the coefficient vector for the rth category.

The data used are from the 1977 General Social Survey and are a specific three-category multinomial example analyzed by a number of authors. These are summarized in Table 2. Because there are only three categories in this application, the multinomial PMF for the ith individual is given by

$$f(\mathbf{y}_i | n_i, \boldsymbol{\pi}_i) = \frac{n_i}{y_{i1}! y_{i2}! (n - y_{i1} - y_{i2})!}$$
$$\pi_{i1}^{y_{i1}} \pi_{i2}^{y_{i2}} (1 - \pi_{i1} - \pi_{i2})^{n - y_{i1} - y_{i2}},$$

and the likelihood is formed by the product across the sample. Is this an exponential family form such that

we can treat this as a GLM problem? This PMF can be reexpressed as

$$f(\mathbf{y}_i | n_i, \boldsymbol{\pi}_i) = \exp\left[\underbrace{\left(\frac{y_{i1}}{n_i}, \frac{y_{i2}}{n_i}\right)}_{\mathbf{y}_1'} \right.$$
$$\underbrace{\left(\log\left(\frac{\pi_{i1}}{1 - \pi_{i1} - \pi_{i2}}\right), \log\left(\frac{\pi_{i2}}{1 - \pi_{i1} - \pi_{i2}}\right)\right)'}_{\theta_1}$$
$$- \underbrace{(-\log(1 - \pi_{i1} - \pi_{i2}))}_{b(\theta_2)} n_i$$
$$\left. + \log\underbrace{\left(\frac{n_i}{y_{i1}! y_{i2}! (n - y_{i1} - y_{i2})!}\right)}_{c(y)} \right],$$

where n_i is a weighting for the ith case. This is clearly an exponential form, albeit now with a two-dimensional structure for $\mathbf{y}_i'$ and $\boldsymbol{\theta}_i$. The two-dimensional link function that results from this form is simply

$$\boldsymbol{\theta}_i = g(\pi_{i1}, \pi_{i2})$$
$$= \left(\log\left(\frac{\pi_{i1}}{1 - \pi_{i1} - \pi_{i2}}\right), \log\left(\frac{\pi_{i2}}{1 - \pi_{i1} - \pi_{i2}}\right)\right).$$

We can therefore interpret the results in the following way for a single respondent:

$$\log\left[\frac{P(\text{event 1})}{P(\text{reference category})}\right] = \log\left[\frac{\pi_{i1}}{1 - \pi_{i1} - \pi_{i2}}\right]$$
$$= \mathbf{X}_i \boldsymbol{\beta}_1,$$

$$\log\left[\frac{P(\text{event 2})}{P(\text{reference category})}\right] = \log\left[\frac{\pi_{i2}}{1 - \pi_{i1} - \pi_{i2}}\right]$$
$$= \mathbf{X}_i \boldsymbol{\beta}_2.$$

The estimated results for this model are contained in Table 3. What we observe from these results is that there is no evidence of gender effect (counter to other studies), and there is strong evidence of increased happiness for the three categories relative to the reference category of < 12 years of school. Interesting, the *very happy* to *not happy* distinction increases with

Table 3   Three-Category Multinomial Model Results

| | Intercept | Years of Schooling | | | |
		Female	12	13–16	17 +
Pretty happy	1.129	−0.181	0.736	1.036	0.882
	(0.148)	(0.168)	(0.196)	(0.238)	(0.453)
Very happy	0.474	0.055	0.878	1.114	1.451
	(0.161)	(0.177)	(0.206)	(0.249)	(0.455)

education, but the *pretty happy* to *not happy* distinction does not. The deviance residual is 8.68, indicating a good fit for 6 degrees of freedom (not in the tail of a chi-square distribution), and therefore an improvement over the saturated model.

—Jeff Gill

REFERENCES

Fisher, R. A. (1925). Theory of statistical estimation. *Proceedings of the Cambridge Philosophical Society, 22,* 700–725.

Fisher, R. A. (1934). Two new properties of mathematical likelihood. *Proceedings of the Royal Society of London, Series A, 144,* 285–307.

Gill, J. (2000). *Generalized linear models: A unified approach.* Thousand Oaks, CA: Sage.

McCullagh, P., & Nelder, J. A. (1989). *Generalized linear models* (2nd ed.). New York: Chapman & Hall.

Nelder, J. A., & Wedderburn, R. W. M. (1972). Generalized linear models. *Journal of the Royal Statistical Society, Series A, 135,* 370–385.

GEOMETRIC DISTRIBUTION

A geometric distribution is used to model the number of failures $(n - 1)$ of a binomial distribution before the first success (r). It is a special case of the NEGATIVE BINOMIAL DISTRIBUTION, or PASCAL DISTRIBUTION, when $r = 1$. The geometric distribution is a series of binomial trials. Due to the independence of binomial trials, the desired trial results are multiplied together to determine the overall PROBABILITY of the occurrence of the first success. For example, the geometric distribution would be used to model the number of tosses of a coin necessary to obtain the first "tails."

A discrete RANDOM VARIABLE X is said to have a geometric distribution if it has a probability mass function in the form of

$$P(X = x) = p(1 - p)^{(x-1)}, \qquad (1)$$

where

$$x = 1, 2, 3, \dots \qquad (2)$$

and $p = $ probability of success,

$$0 < p < 1. \qquad (3)$$

For X to have a geometric distribution, each trial must have only two possible outcomes, success and failure. The outcomes of each trial must be statistically independent, and all trials must have the same probability of success over an infinite number of trials.

If X is a random variable from the geometric distribution, it has expectation

$$E(x) = \frac{1}{p} \qquad (4)$$

and variance

$$\text{Var}(x) = \frac{(1 - p)}{p^2}. \qquad (5)$$

The geometric distribution has a special property. It is "memoryless." That means that the probability of observing a certain number of failures in a row does not depend on how many trials have gone before. So, the chance that the next five trials will all be failures after already seeing 100 failures is the same as if you had only seen 10 failures. The distribution "forgets" how many failures have already occurred.

The geometric distribution is analogous to the exponential distribution. The geometric distribution is "discrete" because you can only have an integer number of coin flips (i.e., you cannot flip a coin 1.34 times). The exponential distribution is continuous. Instead of the number of trials to success, it waits for the amount of time for the first success.

—Ryan Bakker

See also DISTRIBUTION

REFERENCES

Johnson, N. L., & Kotz, S. (1969). *Discrete distributions.* Boston: Houghton Mifflin.

King, G. (1998). *Unifying political methodology: The likelihood theory of statistical inference.* Ann Arbor: University of Michigan Press.

GIBBS SAMPLING

Gibbs sampling is an iterative Monte Carlo procedure that has proved to be a powerful statistical tool for approximating complex probability distributions that could not otherwise be constructed. The technique is a special case of a general set of procedures referred to as MARKOV CHAIN MONTE CARLO (MCMC) METHODS. One of the most important applications of Gibbs sampling has been to Bayesian inference problems that are complicated by the occurrence of missing data. Other useful applications in the social sciences have been the analysis of hierarchical linear models and the analysis of item response models. For the reader interested in some of the theory underlying MCMC methods, good overviews can be found in Gelman, Carlin, Stern, and Rubin (1995) and Schafer (1997).

A very simple example is useful in explaining the Gibbs sampler. Suppose one had knowledge of the statistical form of the joint probability distribution of two variables, say, x_1 and x_2. Further suppose that one was primarily interested in the marginal distribution of each variable separately and/or the probability distribution of some function of the two variables (e.g., $x_1 - x_2$). In cases in which the mathematical form of the joint distribution is not complex (e.g., the two variables have a bivariate normal distribution), one can analytically construct the desired probability distributions. However, suppose that the joint distribution is quite nonstandard and analytic procedures are not possible. How does one proceed in this case? If one could draw a Monte Carlo—simulated sample of size N from the joint distribution, empirical relative frequency distributions could be constructed to estimate the distributions of interest. However, suppose it is very difficult to even sample from the joint distribution due to its complexity. Gibbs sampling to the rescue! In many problems, even when one cannot sample from a joint distribution, one can readily construct Monte Carlo methods for sampling from the full conditional distributions, for example, $P(x_1|x_2)$ and $P(x_2|x_1)$. The following iterative scheme is used in Gibbs sampling. Given a starting value for x_1, sample a value for x_2 from $P(x_2|x_1)$. Given the generated x_2, sample a new value for x_1 from $P(x_1|x_2)$. If we continue this iterative scheme for a "sufficiently" long burn-in period, all generated (x_1, x_2) pairs beyond this point can be treated as samples from the desired bivariate distribution. By constructing relative frequency distributions separately for x_1, x_2, and $x_1 - x_2$, one can approximate the desired distributions.

In Bayesian analyses of incomplete data sets, the problem is to construct the posterior distribution of the unknown parameters (UP) using only the observed (O) data. When missing data (M) have occurred, the form of this posterior distribution can be very complex. However, if we let $x_1 = $ UP, $x_2 = $ M, and condition on O, one can readily approximate the desired posterior distribution and various marginal distributions using the Gibbs sampling scheme.

Unresolved issues in using Gibbs sampling are how to determine how long the burn-in period must be to ensure convergence and how to construct the sample given the proper burn-in period.

The BUGS software package (available for free from www.mrc-bsu.cam.ac.uk/bugs/winbugs/contents. shtml) provides a powerful and relatively user-friendly program (and references) for performing a wide range of statistical analyses using Gibbs sampling.

—Alan L. Gross

REFERENCES

Gelman, A., Carlin, J. B., Stern, H. S., & Rubin, D. B. (1995). *Bayesian data analysis.* London: Chapman & Hall.
Schafer, J. L. (1997). *Analysis of incomplete multivariate data.* London: Chapman & Hall.

GINI COEFFICIENT

The Gini coefficient is a measure of inequality of wealth or income within a population between 0 and 1. The coefficient is a measure of the graph that results from the Lorenz distribution of income or wealth across the full population (see INEQUALITY MEASUREMENT). The graph plots "percentage of ownership" against "percentile of population." Perfect equality of distribution would be a straight line at 45 degrees. Common distributions have the shape represented in Figure 1. The Gini coefficient is the ratio of the area bounded by the curve and the 45-degree line divided by the area of the surface bounded by the 45-degree line and the x-axis.

—Daniel Little

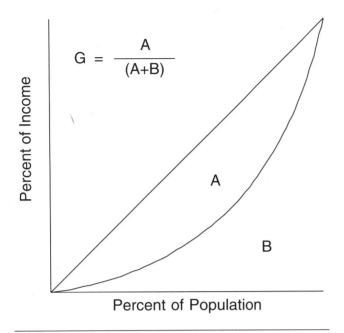

$$G = \frac{A}{(A+B)}$$

Percent of Income

Percent of Population

Figure 1　　Lorenz Distribution of Income

GLIM

GLIM is a statistical software package for the estimation of GENERALIZED LINEAR MODELS. It is flexible in handling user-defined macros. For further information, see the Web site of the software at www.nag.co.uk/stats/GDGE_soft.asp.

—Tim Futing Liao

GOING NATIVE

At the more qualitative end of the research methods spectrum, the phrase "going native" encapsulates the development of a sense of "overrapport" between the researcher and those "under study," to the extent that the researcher essentially "becomes" one of those under study. Seemingly imbued with negative connotations concerning the overembracing of aspects of "native" culture and ways of life by imperial and colonial ruling elites, its origins have often been attributed to Malinowski and his call for anthropologists to participate in the cultures they were observing to enhance their understanding of those cultures and peoples (Kanuha, 2000). Such calls for participation stood in stark contrast to more dominant expectations for any

(social) researcher to be the epitome of OBJECTIVITY. To be "committed," to be *inside* the group, to work *with* the group would result in the wholesale adoption of an uncritical, unquestioning position of approval in relation to that group and their actions; the "standard" of the research would be questioned, its VALIDITY threatened (Stanley & Wise, 1993). The inclusion of the "researcher as person" within the research would be associated with an apparent inability for that researcher to "suitably" distance himself or herself from the events in which he or she was participating, ultimately undermining the "authority" of the voice of the "researcher as academic." However, as Kanuha (2000) notes, such a perspective has been increasingly challenged as

the exclusive domain of academia once relegated only to white, male, heterosexual researchers has been integrated by scholars who are people of color, people from the barrio, and those whose ancestors were perhaps the native objects of their mentors and now colleagues. (p. 440)

Writing from "marginal" perspectives, the role of the researcher—the relationship between "us" and "them" and between the researcher and "researched-community"—has increasingly been deconstructed and problematized in recent years, leading ultimately to increased awareness of the need for critical, reflexive thought regarding the implications of any researcher's positionality and situatedness. A key notion here is that "the personal is the political" (Stanley & Wise, 1993) and vice versa (Fuller, 1999), epitomizing how, for many researchers, personal, political, academic, and often activist identities are one and the same—many researchers are always or already natives in the research they are conducting. As such, they occupy a space in which the situatedness of their knowledges and their positionalities are constantly renegotiated and critically engaged with, a space that necessarily involves the removal of artificial boundaries between categories such as researcher, activist, teacher, and person and proposes instead movement between these various identities to facilitate engagement between and within them (Routledge, 1996). Here there is a continual questioning of researchers' social location (in terms of class, gender, ethnicity, etc.), in addition to the physical location of their research, their disciplinary location, and their political position and personality (Robinson, 1994). In addition, such questioning is included and made transparent within any commentary on the work conducted, highlighted as an integral (and unavoidable) part of the research process, thereby successfully avoiding any false and misleading presentation of the researcher (and research itself) as inert, detached, and neutral.

—Duncan Fuller

REFERENCES

Fuller, D. (1999). Part of the action, or "going native"? Learning to cope with the politics of integration. *Area, 31*(3), 221–227.

Kanuha, V. K. (2000). "Being" native versus "going native": Conducting social work research as an insider. *Social Work, 45*(5), 439–447.

Robinson, J. (1994). White women researching/representing "others": From anti-apartheid to postcolonialism. In A. Blunt & G. Rose (Eds.), *Writing, women and space* (pp. 97–226). New York: Guilford.

Routledge, P. (1996). The third space as critical engagement. *Antipode, 28*(4), 399–419.

Stanley, L., & Wise, S. (1993). *Breaking out again: Feminist ontology and epistemology.* London: Routledge.

GOODNESS-OF-FIT MEASURES

Goodness-of-fit measures are STATISTICS calculated from a SAMPLE of data, and they measure the extent to which the sample data are consistent with the MODEL being considered. Of the goodness-of-fit measures, *R*-SQUARED, also denoted R^2, is perhaps the most well known, and it serves here as an initial example. In a LINEAR REGRESSION analysis, the VARIABLE *Y* is approximated by a model, set equal to $\hat{Y}$, which is a linear combination of a set of *k* EXPLANATORY VARIABLES, $\hat{Y} = +\hat{\beta}_0 + \hat{\beta}_1 X_1 + \hat{\beta}_2 X_2 + \cdots + \hat{\beta}_k X_k$. The COEFFICIENTS in the model, $\hat{\beta}_0, \hat{\beta}_1, \hat{\beta}_2, \ldots, \hat{\beta}_k$, are estimated from the data so that the sum of the squared differences between *Y* and $\hat{Y}$ is as small as possible, also called the SUM OF SQUARED ERRORS (SSE), $SSE = \Sigma(Y - \hat{Y})^2$. R^2 gauges the goodness of fit between the observed variable *Y* and the regression model $\hat{Y}$ and is defined as $R^2 = 1 - \dfrac{SSE}{SST}$, where $SST = \Sigma(Y - \bar{Y})^2$, which is the sum of the squared deviations around the sample mean $\bar{Y}$. It ranges in value from 0, indicating extreme lack of fit, to 1, indicating perfect fit. It has universal appeal because it can be interpreted as the square of the CORRELATION between *Y* and $\hat{Y}$ or as the proportion of the total variance in *Y* that is accounted for by the model.

ADDITIONAL EXAMPLES

Goodness-of-fit measures are not limited to regression models but may apply to any hypothetical statement about the study POPULATION. The following are three examples of models and corresponding goodness-of-fit measures.

The HYPOTHESIS that a variable *X* has a NORMAL DISTRIBUTION in the population is an example of a model. With a sample of observations on *X*, the goodness-of-fit statistic *D* can be calculated as a measure of how well the sample data conform to a normal distribution. In addition, the *D* statistic can be used in the KOLMOGOROV-SMIRNOV TEST to formally test the hypothesis that *X* is normally distributed in the population.

Another example of a model is the hypothesis that the mean, denoted μ, of the distribution of *X* is equal to 100, or $\mu_X = 100$. The *T*-STATISTIC can be calculated from a sample of data to measure the goodness of fit between the sample mean $\bar{X}$ and the hypothesized population mean μ_X. The *t*-statistic can then be used in a *T*-TEST to decide if the hypothesis $\mu_X = 100$ should be rejected based on the sample data.

One more example is the INDEPENDENCE model, which states that two categorical variables are unrelated in the population. The numbers expected in each category of a CONTINGENCY TABLE of the sample data, if the independence model is true, are called the "EXPECTED FREQUENCIES," and the numbers actually observed in the sample are called the "OBSERVED FREQUENCIES." The goodness of fit between the hypothesized independence model and the sample data is measured with the χ^2 (chi-square) statistic, which can then be used with the χ^2 test (CHI-SQUARE TEST) to decide if the independence model should be rejected.

HYPOTHESIS TESTS

The examples above illustrate two distinct classes of goodness-of-fit measures that serve different purposes. Each summarizes the consistency between sample data and a model, but R^2 is a descriptive statistic with a clear intuitive interpretation, whereas D, t, and χ^2

are INFERENTIAL STATISTICS that are less meaningful intrinsically. The inferential measures are valuable for conducting HYPOTHESIS TESTS about goodness of fit, principally because each has a known SAMPLING DISTRIBUTION that often has the same name as the statistic (e.g., t and χ^2). Even if a model accurately represents the population under study, a goodness-of-fit statistic calculated from a sample of data will rarely indicate a perfect fit with the model, and the extent of departure from perfect fit will vary from one sample to another. This variation is captured in the sampling distribution of a goodness-of-fit measure, which is known for D, t, and χ^2. These statistics become interpretable as measures of fit when compared to their sampling distribution, so that if the sample statistic lies sufficiently far out in the tail of its sampling distribution, it suggests that the sample data are improbable if the model is true (i.e., a poor fit between data and model). Depending on the rejection criteria for the test and the SIGNIFICANCE LEVEL chosen, the sample statistic may warrant rejection of the proposed model.

REGRESSION MODELS

A goodness-of-fit statistic is generally applicable to a specific type of model. However, within a class of models, such as linear regression models, it is common to evaluate goodness of fit with several different measures. Following are examples of goodness-of-fit measures used in regression analysis. These fall into two categories: (a) scalar measures that summarize the overall fit of a model and (b) model comparison measures that compare the goodness of fit between two alternative models. Some of the measures described are applicable only to linear regression models; others apply to the broader class of regression models estimated with MAXIMUM LIKELIHOOD ESTIMATION (MLE). The latter includes linear and LOGISTIC REGRESSION models as well as other models with categorical or limited dependent variables.

Scalar Measures

Scalar measures summarize the overall fit of the model, with a single number. R^2 is the best example of this. However, R^2 does have limitations, and there are a number of alternative measures designed to overcome these. One shortcoming is that R^2 applies to linear models only. There is no exact counterpart in nonlinear models or models with categorical outcomes,

although there are several "PSEUDO-R^2" measures that are designed to simulate the properties of R^2 in these situations. A popular pseudo-R^2 measure is the maximum likelihood R^2, denoted $R^2_{\mathrm{ML}} \times R^2_{\mathrm{ML}}$ would reproduce R^2 if applied to a linear regression model, but it can be applied more generally to all models that are estimated with MLE. For the model being evaluated, M_k, with k explanatory variables, there is an associated statistic L_{M_k}, which is the likelihood of observing the sample data given the PARAMETERS of model M_k, and another statistic L_{M_0}, which is the likelihood of observing the sample data given the null model with no explanatory variables, M_0. R^2_{ML} is calculated using the ratio of these two likelihoods, $R^2_{\mathrm{ML}} = 1 - [\frac{L_{M_0}}{L_{M_k}}]^{\frac{2}{n}}$. For categorical outcomes, a more intuitive alternative is the count R^2, R^2_{count}, which is the proportion of the sample observations that was correctly classified by the model. See Long (1997, pp. 102–108) and Menard (1995, pp. 22–37) for more discussion of alternative measures.

A second limitation of R^2 is that it cannot become smaller as more variables are added to a model. This gives the false impression that a model with more variables is a better fitting model. ADJUSTED R^2, denoted R^2_{adj}, is a preferred alternative that does not necessarily increase as more variables are added. It is calculated in such a way that it devalues R^2 when too many variables are included relative to the number of observations, $R^2_{\mathrm{adj}} = 1 - \frac{n-1}{n-p}(1 - R^2)$, with p parameters and n observations.

Akaike's Information Criterion (AIC) is another popular scalar measure of fit. Like R^2_{adj}, it takes into account the number of observations in the sample and the number of variables in the model and places a premium on models with a small number of parameters per observation. For a linear model with n observations and p parameters, AIC is defined as $\mathrm{AIC} = n \ln \left[\frac{\mathrm{SSE}}{n} \right] + 2p$. A more general formulation applies to models estimated with MLE. If L is the likelihood of the sample data given the proposed model, then $\mathrm{AIC} = \frac{2 \ln L + 2p}{n}$. AIC is interpreted as the "per observation contribution" to the model, so smaller values are preferred, and it is useful for comparing different models from the same sample as well as the same model across different samples.

Model Comparison Measures

In addition to providing a summary measure of fit, scalar measures, as described above, can be valuable for evaluating the overall fit of one model relative to another. Increments in R^2, R^2_{adj}, and some pseudo-R^2 measures are included in a general class of model comparison measures that have a PROPORTIONATE REDUCTION OF ERROR (PRE) interpretation. When the fit of a multivariate linear model with k explanatory variables, M_k, is compared to the fit of the null model with no explanatory variables, M_0, the inferential F-statistic, also called the F-RATIO, is directly related to R^2 and is reported automatically in most statistical software packages. The F-statistic has advantages over R^2 in that it serves as the basis for formally testing, with the F-test, the null hypothesis that the fit of a MULTIVARIATE model M_k is not a significant improvement over the null model M_0. This is equivalent to testing the hypothesis that all of the slope coefficients in the model are equal to zero, that is, $\beta_1 = \beta_2 = \cdots = \beta_k = 0$.

Analogous to the F-statistic for linear models is the model χ^2 statistic that applies to the larger class of models estimated with MLE. As the F-statistic is related to R^2, the model χ^2 is related to R^2_{ML}, and as the F-statistic is the basis of the F-test, the model χ^2 is the basis of the LIKELIHOOD RATIO test of the null hypothesis that the fit of a multivariate MLE model, M_k, is not a significant improvement over the null model M_0 or, equivalently, $\beta_1 = \beta_2 = \ldots = \beta_k = 0$. The model χ^2 is a function of the ratio of the two likelihoods described above, L_{M_k} and L_{M_0}, and is calculated as $\chi^2 = -2 \ln[\frac{L_{M_0}}{L_{M_k}}]$.

The F-test and the likelihood ratio test are more broadly applicable than the examples suggest. They can be used to test for improved goodness of fit between any two models, one having a subset of the variables contained in the other. They can test for improvement provided by sets of variables or by a single variable. For MLE models, alternatives to the likelihood ratio test are the Wald test and the Lagrange multiplier test. When testing for a significant contribution to goodness of fit from a single variable, t-tests can be used in linear models and MLE models.

Despite the reliance on hypothesis tests to compare the goodness of fit between two models, these tests need to be used cautiously. Because the probability of rejecting the null hypothesis increases with sample size, overconfidence in these methods when samples are large can lead to conclusions that variables make a significant contribution to fit when the effects may actually be small and unimportant. The Bayesian Information Criterion (BIC) is an alternative that is not affected by sample size. BIC can be applied to a variety of statistics that gauge model improvement, and it offers a method for assessing the degree of improvement provided by one model relative to another. For example, when applied to the model χ^2, which implicitly compares M_k to M_0, $\text{BIC}_{M_k} - \text{BIC}_{M_0} = -\chi^2 + k \ln n$. In general, when comparing any two MLE models, M_1 and M_2, with one not necessarily a subset of the other, $\text{BIC}_{M_1} - \text{BIC}_{M_2} \approx 2 \ln \left[\frac{L_{M_2}}{L_{M_1}} \right]$. Because the model with the more negative BIC is preferred, if $\text{BIC}_{M_1} - \text{BIC}_{M_2} < 0$, then the first model is preferred. If $\text{BIC}_{M_1} - \text{BIC}_{M_2} > 0$, then the second model is preferred. Raftery (1996) suggests guidelines, presented in Table 1, for evaluating model improvement based on the absolute value of the difference between two BICs. See Raftery (1996, pp. 133–139) and Long (1997, pp. 110–112) for more discussion of the BIC.

—Jani S. Little

Table 1   Strength of Evidence for Improved Goodness of Fit

Absolute Value of Difference, $\lvert \text{BIC}_{M_1} - \text{BIC}_{M_2} \rvert$	Strength of Evidence
$0 - 2$	Weak
$2 - 6$	Positive
$6 - 10$	Strong
> 10	Very strong

REFERENCES

Greene, W. H. (2000). *Econometric analysis* (4th ed.). Upper Saddle River, NJ: Prentice Hall.

Long, J. S. (1997). *Regression models for categorical and limited dependent variables.* Thousand Oaks, CA: Sage.

Menard, S. (1995). *Applied logistic regression analysis.* Thousand Oaks, CA: Sage.

Pampel, F. C. (2000). *Logistic regression: A primer.* Thousand Oaks, CA: Sage.

Raftery, A. E. (1996). Bayesian model selection in social research. In P. V. Marsden (Ed.), *Sociological methodology* (Vol. 25, pp. 111–163). Oxford, UK: Basil Blackwell.

GRADE OF MEMBERSHIP MODELS

Grade of Membership (GoM) models produce a classification of a set of objects in the form of fuzzy partitions where persons may have partial membership in more than one group. The advantage of GoM compared to discrete partition classification methods (e.g., CLUSTER ANALYSIS; LATENT CLASS ANALYSIS [LCA]) is that it generally produces fewer classes whose parametric relations to measured variables are easier to interpret. Indeed, LCA may be viewed as a special case of GoM in which classes are "crisp," and persons belong only in one group (i.e., there is no within-class heterogeneity). In factor analysis, the model is constructed to use only second-order (i.e., covariance or correlation matrix) moments so it cannot describe nonnormal multivariate distributions that might arise if there are multiple distinct groups (subpopulations) comprising the total set of cases analyzed.

DESCRIPTION

GoM deals with a family of random variables, $\{Y_{ij}\}_{ij}$, representing measurements. Here i ranges over a set of objects $\mathcal{I}$ (in demography, objects are usually individuals), j ranges over measurements $\mathcal{J}$, and Y_{ij} takes values in a finite set $\mathcal{L}_j$, which, without loss of generality, may be considered as a set of natural numbers $\{1, \ldots, L_j\}$. Every individual i is associated with a vector of random variables $(Y_{ij})_j$, with this vector containing all available information on the individual. The idea is to construct a convex space or "basis," $\{(Y_{kj}^0)_j\}_k, k = 1, \ldots, K$, in the space of random vectors $(Y_{ij})_j$ and, for every individual, coefficients of position on this "basis," $(g_{ik})_k$, such that the equations $\Pr(Y_{ij} = l) = \Sigma_{k=1}^K g_{ik} \Pr(Y_{kj}^0 = l)$, together with constraints $g_{ik} \geq 0, \Sigma_k g_{ik} = 1$, hold. One might treat these as K fuzzy sets, or "pure profiles," with a representative member ($g_{ik} = 1$ for some k) of the kth profile described by $(Y_{kj}^0)_j$. The interpretation of profiles is derived from a posteriori analysis of the coefficients $\lambda_{kjl} = \Pr(Y_{kj}^0 = 1)$ produced by GoM.

The GoM ALGORITHM searches for g_{ik} and λ_{kjl} that maximize the likelihood $\Pi_{i \in I} \Pi_{j \in J} \Pi_{l \in L_j}$ $(\Sigma_{k=1}^K g_{ik} \lambda_{kjl})^{y_{ijl}}$, with constraints $g_{ik} \geq 0, \Sigma_k g_{ik} = 1, \lambda_{kjl} \geq 0$, and $\Sigma_l \lambda_{kjl} = 1$, where y_{ijl} is 1 if the jth measurement on an ith individual gives outcome l and 0 otherwise. If no response is given, then all $y_{ijl} = 0$, and the variable is missing and drops from the likelihood. The λ_{kjl} determine the distribution of Y_{kj}^0—that is, $\Pr(Y_{kj}^0 = l)$—and the g_{ik} are estimates of the grades of membership. Likelihood estimates of g_{ik} are consistent (i.e., as both number of individuals and number of measurements tend to infinity, g_{ik} estimates converge

to true values). As in standard statistical models, the λ_{kjl}, averaged over i, are also statistically consistent.

EXAMPLE

In an analysis of the National Long-Term Care Survey (Manton & XiLiang, 2003), 27 different measures of function coded on binary (2) or quaternary (4) variables were selected. A GoM analysis was performed identifying six profiles ($K = 6$), whose position is defined in terms of the 27 observed variables by six vectors, λ_{kjl}. In this analysis, the first profile has no disability, and the sixth has a high likelihood of almost all functional disability measures. The other four types divide into two pairs of vectors, with one pair describing a graduation of impairment on instrumental activities of daily living and a second pair describing a graduation of activities of daily living impairments. Because there is significant variation in the g_{ik}, no six classes of LCA could describe as much variability as GoM. Because the distribution of the g_{ik}s was not normal, no factor analysis (FA) could have fully described the data (including higher order moments) in as few as six dimensions.

HISTORY AND BIBLIOGRAPHY

The GoM model was first described in 1974 (Woodbury & Clive, 1974). Books (Manton & Stallard, 1988; Manton, Woodbury, & Tolley, 1994) provide a detailed description of the method and give examples of applications. Papers (Tolley & Manton, 1992) also contain proofs of the important statistical properties (e.g., sufficiency and consistency) of the g_{ik} and λ_{kjl} parameter estimates.

—Kenneth Manton and Mikhail Kovtun

REFERENCES

Manton, K. G., & Stallard, E. (1988). *Chronic disease modelling: Vol. 2. Mathematics in medicine.* New York: Oxford University Press.

Manton, K. G., & XiLiang, G. (2003). *Variation in disability decline and Medicare expenditures.* Working Monograph, Center for Demographic Studies.

Manton, K. G., Woodbury, M. A., & Tolley, H. D. (1994). *Statistical applications using fuzzy sets.* Wiley Series in Probability and Mathematical Statistics. New York: John Wiley.

Tolley, H. D., Kovtun, M., Manton, K. G., & Akushevich, I. (2003). Statistical properties of grade of membership models for categorical data. Manuscript to be submitted to *Proceedings of National Academy of Sciences*, 2003.

Tolley, H. D., & Manton, K. G. (1992). Large sample properties of estimates of discrete grade of membership model. *Annals of the Institute of Statistical Mathematics, 41*, 85–95.

Woodbury, M. A., & Clive, J. (1974). Clinical pure types as a fuzzy partition. *Journal of Cybernetics, 4*(3), 111–121.

GRANGER CAUSALITY

Econometrician Clive Granger (1969) has developed a widely used definition of CAUSALITY. A key aspect of the concept of *Granger causality* is that there is no instantaneous causation (i.e., all causal processes involve time lags). X_t "Granger causes" Y_t if information regarding the history of X_t can improve the ability to predict Y_t beyond a prediction made using the history of Y_t alone. Granger causality is not unidirectional; that is, Y_t Granger causes X_t if information about the history of Y_t can improve the ability to predict X_t beyond a prediction made using only the history of X_t.

Granger causality tests may be performed using a bivariate vector autoregression (VAR) model. A VAR for X and Y specifies that each variable is a function of k lags of itself plus k lags of the other variable; that is,

$$Y_t = \beta_0 + \beta_1 Y_{t-1} + \cdots + \beta_k Y_{t-k} + \lambda_1 X_{t-1}$$
$$+ \cdots + \lambda_k X_{t-k} + \varepsilon_t, \qquad (1)$$
$$X_t = \alpha_0 + \alpha_1 X_{t-1} + \cdots + \alpha_k K_{t-k} + \gamma_1 Y_{t-1}$$
$$+ \cdots + \gamma_k Y_{t-k} + \zeta_t. \qquad (2)$$

An F-test or a Lagrange multiplier (LM) test can be used to determine if X Granger causes Y or Y Granger causes X. For example, the LM test to see if X Granger causes Y involves estimating (1) under the assumption that the λs are jointly zero. Residuals from this regression then are regressed on all variables in (1). The R^2 from this second regression $\times T$ (number of observations) is the test statistic (distributed as χ^2, df $= 2k + 1$). Rejection of the null hypothesis implies X Granger causes Y. An alternative VAR representation of the above test has been developed by Sims (1972). The impact of nonstationarity on the validity of these tests is controversial. Granger causality tests also may be implemented in the ARIMA modeling framework (see Freeman, 1983).

The concept of Granger causality has been incorporated into the definitions of exogeneity offered by Hendry and associates (e.g., Charemza & Deadman, 1997, chap. 7). Recognize that one need not establish that X Granger causes Y to warrant inference concerning the effects of X in a single-equation model of Y. It is sufficient to establish that X is *weakly exogenous* to Y (i.e., parameters in the model for Y can be efficiently estimated without any information in a model for X). However, if one wishes to forecast Y, then it is necessary to investigate if X is *strongly exogenous* to Y. Strong exogeneity equals weak exogeneity plus Granger "noncausality" (i.e., Y_t does not affect X at time t or at any time $t + k$). If Y is not strongly exogenous to X, then feedback from Y to X must be taken into account should that feedback occur within the forecast horizon of interest.

—Harold D. Clarke

REFERENCES

Charemza, W. W., & Deadman, D. F. (1997). *New directions in econometric practice* (2nd ed.). Cheltenham, UK: Edward Elgar.

Freeman, J. F. (1983). Granger causality and the time series analysis of political relationships. *American Journal of Political Science, 27*, 325–355.

Granger, C. W. J. (1969). Investigating causal relations by econometric models and cross-spectral methods. *Econometrica, 37*, 24–36.

Sims, C. A. (1972). Money income and causality. *American Economic Review, 62*, 540–552.

GRAPHICAL MODELING

A graphical model is a parametric statistical model for a set of random variables. Under this model, associations between the variables can be displayed using a mathematical graph. Graphical modeling is the process of choosing which graph best represents the data.

The use of mathematical graphs in statistics dates back to the PATH DIAGRAMS of Sewall Wright in the 1920s and 1930s. However, it was not until the seminal paper of John N. Darroch, Steffen L. Lauritzen, and Terry P. Speed, published in 1980, that a way of constructing a graph that has a well-defined PROBABILISTIC interpretation was proposed. This graph has since been called the *conditional independence graph* or *independence graph*, for short.

The (conditional) independence structure between variables X_1 to X_p can be displayed using a

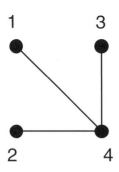

Figure 1   An Independence Graph

mathematical graph with p vertices (dots) corresponding to the p variables in which an edge (line) between vertices i and j is missing if, and only if, X_i and X_j are conditionally independent given the remaining $p - 2$ variables. For example, if X_1 to X_4 satisfy the following conditional independencies—X_1 independent of X_2 given X_3 and X_4, X_1 independent of X_3 given X_2 and X_4, and X_2 independent of X_3 given X_1 and X_4—then their independence graph, displayed in Figure 1, has four vertices and edges missing between the following pairs of vertices: $(1, 2)$, $(1, 3)$, and $(2, 3)$.

Although any set of jointly distributed random variables has an independence graph, the analyst requires, to construct the graph for some given data, a family of models in which conditional independence can easily be parameterized. For CONTINUOUS VARIABLES, multivariate normal distributions are used; for DISCRETE variables, LOG-LINEAR MODELS are used; and for a mixture of discrete and continuous variables, conditional Gaussian distributions are used. When there is a mixture, it is usual to indicate discrete variables by dots and continuous variables by circles in the graph.

When searching for a well-fitting graphical model, it is usual to first calculate the edge exclusion deviances: the LIKELIHOOD RATIO STATISTICS for the tests that each edge, in turn, is missing from the graph. The deviances are then compared with a preselected critical level to obtain a list of significant edges, which must be retained in the graph. The nonsignificant edges are then considered as edges, which could possibly be omitted from the graph, and model selection continues using procedures similar to those used in regression for selecting the best subset of the regressors. Once a well-fitting graph has been selected, information about the associations between the variables can be obtained from the graph using theoretical results, called the Markov properties.

Latent variable models can be represented by including vertices for the unobserved variables. So can Bayesian models by including vertices for the parameters. Directed graphs with arrows, rather than lines, between the vertices or chain graphs with a mixture of lines and arrows can be used to represent (potentially) causal relationships between variables or to distinguish between responses and explanatory variables.

—Peter W. F. Smith

REFERENCES

Darroch, J. N., Lauritzen, S. L., & Speed, T. P. (1980). Markov fields and log-linear models. *Annals of Mathematical Statistics, 43,* 1470–1480.

Edwards, D. (2000). *Introduction to graphical modelling* (2nd ed.). New York: Springer-Verlag.

Whittaker, J. (1990). *Graphical models in applied multivariate statistics.* Chichester, UK: Wiley.

GROUNDED THEORY

Grounded theory refers to a set of systematic inductive methods for conducting QUALITATIVE RESEARCH aimed toward theory development. The term *grounded theory* denotes dual referents: (a) a *method* consisting of flexible methodological strategies and (b) the *products* of this type of inquiry. Increasingly, researchers use the term to mean the methods of inquiry for collecting and, in particular, analyzing data. The methodological strategies of grounded theory are aimed to construct middle-level theories directly from data analysis. The inductive theoretical thrust of these methods is central to their logic. The resulting analyses build their power on strong empirical foundations. These analyses provide focused, abstract, conceptual theories that explain the studied empirical phenomena.

Grounded theory has considerable significance because it (a) provides explicit, sequential guidelines for conducting qualitative research; (b) offers specific strategies for handling the analytic phases of inquiry; (c) streamlines and integrates data collection and analysis; (d) advances conceptual analysis of qualitative data; and (e) legitimizes qualitative research as scientific inquiry. Grounded theory methods have earned their place as a standard social research method and have influenced researchers from varied disciplines and professions.

Yet grounded theory continues to be a misunderstood method, although many researchers purport to use it. Qualitative researchers often claim to conduct grounded theory studies without fully understanding or adopting its distinctive guidelines. They may employ one or two of the strategies or mistake qualitative analysis for grounded theory. Conversely, other researchers employ grounded theory methods in reductionist, mechanistic ways. Neither approach embodies the flexible yet systematic mode of inquiry, directed but open-ended analysis, and imaginative theorizing from empirical data that grounded theory methods can foster. Subsequently, the potential of grounded theory methods for generating middle-range theory has not been fully realized.

DEVELOPMENT OF THE GROUNDED THEORY METHOD

The originators of grounded theory, Barney G. Glaser and Anselm L. Strauss (1967), sought to develop a systematic set of procedures to analyze qualitative data. They intended to construct theoretical analyses of social processes that offered abstract understandings of them. Their first statement of the method, *The Discovery of Grounded Theory* (1967), provided a powerful argument that legitimized qualitative research as a credible methodological approach, rather than simply as a precursor for developing quantitative instruments. At that time, reliance on quantification with its roots in a narrow POSITIVISM dominated and diminished the significance of qualitative research. Glaser and Strauss proposed that systematic qualitative analysis had its own logic and could generate theory. Their work contributed to revitalizing qualitative research and maintaining the ethnographic traditions of Chicago school sociology. They intended to move qualitative inquiry beyond descriptive studies into the realm of explanatory theoretical frameworks, thereby providing abstract, conceptual understanding of the studied phenomena. For them, this abstract understanding contrasted with armchair and logico-deductive theorizing because a grounded theory contained the following characteristics: a close fit with the data, usefulness, density, durability, modifiability, and explanatory power (Glaser, 1978, 1992; Glaser & Strauss, 1967).

Grounded theory combined Strauss's Chicago school intellectual roots in pragmatism and symbolic interactionism with Glaser's rigorous quantitative methodological training at Columbia University with Paul Lazarsfeld. Strauss brought notions of agency, emergence, meaning, and the pragmatist study of action to grounded theory. Glaser employed his analytic skills to codify qualitative analysis. They shared a keen interest in studying social processes. They developed a means of generating substantive theory by invoking methodological strategies to explicate fundamental social or social psychological processes within a social setting or a particular experience such as having a chronic illness. The subsequent grounded theory aimed to understand the studied process, demonstrate the causes and conditions under which it emerged and varied, and explain its consequences. Glaser and Strauss's logic led them to formal theorizing as they studied generic processes across substantive areas and refined their emerging theories through seeking relevant data in varied settings.

Although the *Discovery of Grounded Theory* transformed methodological debates and inspired generations of qualitative researchers, Glaser's book, *Theoretical Sensitivity* (1978), provided the most definitive early statement of the method. Since then, Glaser and Strauss have taken grounded theory in somewhat separate directions (Charmaz, 2000). Glaser has remained consistent with his earlier exegesis of the method, which relied on direct and, often, narrow EMPIRICISM. Strauss has moved the method toward verification, and his coauthored works with Juliet M. Corbin (Strauss & Corbin, 1990, 1998) furthered this direction.

Strauss and Corbin's (1990, 1998) version of grounded theory also favors their new techniques rather than emphasizing the comparative methods that distinguished earlier grounded theory strategies. As before, Glaser studies basic social processes, uses comparative methods, and constructs abstract relationships between theoretical categories. Glaser's position assumes an external reality independent of the observer, a neutral observer, and the discovery of data. Both approaches have strong elements of objectivist inquiry founded in positivism. However, Glaser (1992) contends that Strauss and Corbin's procedures force data and analysis into preconceived categories and thus contradict fundamental tenets of grounded theory. Glaser also states that study participants will tell researchers what is most significant in their setting, but participants often take fundamental processes for granted. Showing how grounded theory can advance constructionist, interpretative inquiry minimizes its positivist cast.

Grounded theory has gained reknown because its systematic strategies aid in managing and analyzing qualitative data. Its REALIST cast, rigor, and positivistic assumptions have made it acceptable to quantitative researchers. Its flexibility and legitimacy appeal to qualitative researchers with varied theoretical and substantive interests.

APPLYING GROUNDED THEORY METHODS

Grounded theory methods provide guidelines for grappling with data that stimulate ways of thinking about them. These methods are fundamentally comparative. By comparing data with data, data with theoretical categories, and category with category, the researcher gains new ideas (Glaser, 1992). Discoveries in grounded theory emerge from the depth of researchers' empirical knowledge and their analytic interaction with the data; discoveries do not inhere in the data. Although researchers' disciplinary perspectives sensitize them to conceptual issues, grounded theory methods prompt researchers to start but not end with these perspectives.

These methods involve researchers in early data analysis from the beginning of data collection. Early analytic work then directs grounded theory researchers' subsequent data collection. Grounded theory strategies keep researchers actively engaged in analytic steps. These strategies also contain checks to ensure that the researcher's emerging theory is grounded in the data that it attempts to explain. Which data researchers collect and what they *do* with them shapes how and what they think about them. In turn, what they think about their data, including the questions they ask about them, guide their next methodological step. Moreover, grounded theory methods shape the content of the data as well as the form of analysis.

Grounded theory directs researchers to take a progressively analytic, methodical stance toward their work. They increasingly focus data collection to answer specific analytic questions and to fill gaps in the emerging analysis. As a result, they seek data that permit them to gain a full view of the studied phenomena. Grounded theory strategies foster gathering rich data about specific processes rather than the general structure of one social setting. These strategies also foster making the analysis progressively more focused and abstract. Subsequently, a grounded theory analysis may provide a telling explanation of the studied phenomena from which other researchers may

deduce hypotheses. Because grounded theory methods aim to generate theory, the emerging analyses consist of abstract concepts and their interrelationships. The following grounded theory strategies remain central to its logic as they cut across all variants of the method.

CODING DATA

The analytic process begins with two phases of coding: open, or initial, and selective, or focused. In open coding, researchers treat data analytically and discover what they see in them. They scrutinize the data through analyzing and coding each line of text (see Table 1, for example).

This line-by-line coding keeps researchers open to fresh ideas and thus reduces their inclinations to force the data into preconceived categories. Such active analytic involvement fosters developing theoretical sensitivity because researchers begin to ask analytic questions of the data. Grounded theorists ask a fundamental question: What is happening here? But rather than merely describing action, they seek to identify its phases, preconditions, properties, and purposes. Glaser and Strauss' early statements specify analyzing the basic social or social psychological process in the setting. Studying the fundamental process makes for a compelling analysis. However, multiple significant processes may be occurring; the researcher may study several of them simultaneously and demonstrate their interconnections. In a larger sense, grounded theory methods foster studying any topic as a process.

This initial coding forces researchers to think about small bits of data and to interpret them—immediately. As depicted in Table 1, grounded theory codes should be active, specific, and short.

Through coding, researchers take a new perspective on the data and view them from varied angles. Line-by-line coding loosens whatever taken-for-granted assumptions that researchers may have shared with study participants and prompts taking their meanings, actions, and words as problematic objects of study. This close scrutiny of data prepares researchers to compare pieces of data. Thus, they compare statements or actions from one individual, different incidents, experiences of varied participants, and similar events at different points in time. Note, for example, that the interview participant in Table 1 mentions that her friend and her husband provide different kinds of support. The researcher can follow the leads in her statements

Table 1   Example of Initial Coding

Line-by-Line Coding	Interview Statement of a 68-Year-Old Woman With Chronic Illness
Reciprocal supporting Having bad days Disallowing self-pity Issuing reciprocal orders Comparing supportive others Defining support role Taking other into account Interpreting the unstated Invoking measures of health/illness Averting despair Transforming suffering Acknowledging other's utmost significance	We're [a friend who has multiple sclerosis] kind of like mutual supporters for each other. And when she has her bad days or when we particularly feel "poor me," you know, "Get off your butt!" You know, we can be really pushy to each other and understand it. But with Fred [husband who has diabetes and heart disease] here to support me no matter what I wanted to do. . . . And he's the reason why I try not to think of myself a lot . . . because he worries. If he doesn't see me in a normal pattern, I get these side glances, you know, like "Is she all right?" And so he'll snap me out of things and we're good for each other because we both bolster, we need each other. And I can't fathom life without him. I know I can survive, you know, but I'd rather not.

to make a comparative analysis of support and the conditions under which it is helpful.

When doing line-by-line coding, researchers study their data, make connections between seemingly disparate data, and gain a handle on basic processes. Then they direct subsequent data collection to explore the most salient processes. Line-by-line coding works particularly well with transcriptions of interviews and meetings. Depending on the level and quality of field note descriptions, it may not work as well with ethnographic material. Hence, researchers may code larger units such as paragraphs or descriptions of anecdotes and events.

Initial coding guides focused or selective coding. After examining the initial codes, researchers look for both the most frequent codes and those that provide the most incisive conceptual handles on the data. They adopt these codes for focused coding. Focused codes provide analytic tools for handling large amounts of data; reevaluating earlier data for implicit meanings, statements, and actions; and, subsequently, generating categories in the emerging theory. Increasingly, researchers use computer-assisted programs for coding and managing data efficiently. Whether such programs foster reductionist, mechanistic analyses remains a question.

MEMO WRITING

Memo writing is the pivotal intermediate stage between coding and writing the first draft of the report.

Through writing memos, researchers develop their analyses in narrative form and move descriptive material into analytic statements. In the early stages of research, memo writing consists of examining initial codes, defining them, taking them apart, and looking for assumptions, meanings, and actions imbedded in them as well as relationships between codes. Early memos are useful to discuss hunches, note ambiguities, raise questions, clarify ideas, and compare data with data.

These memos also advance the analysis because they prompt researchers to explicate which comparisons between data are the most telling and how and why they are. Such comparisons help researchers to define fundamental aspects of participants' worlds and actions and to view them as processes. Subsequently, they can decide which processes are most significant to study and then explore and explicate them in memos. Writing memos becomes a way of studying data. Researchers can then pursue the most interesting leads in their data through further data collection and analysis.

Memo writing enables researchers to define and delineate their emerging theoretical categories. Then they write later memos to develop these categories and to ascertain how they fit together. They compare data with the relevant category, as well as category to category. Writing progressively more theoretical memos during their studies increases researchers' analytic competence in interpreting the data as well as their confidence in the interpretations.

By making memos increasingly more analytic with full coverage of each category, researchers gain a handle on how they fit into the studied process. Then they minimize what can pose a major obstacle: how to integrate the analysis into a coherent framework.

THEORETICAL SAMPLING

As researchers write memos explicating their codes and categories, they discern gaps that require further data collection. Subsequently, they engage in theoretical sampling, which means gathering further, more specific data to illuminate, extend, or refine theoretical categories and make them more precise. Thus, the researcher's emerging theory directs this sampling, not the proportional representation of population traits. With skillful use of this sampling, researchers can fill gaps in their emerging theoretical categories, answer unresolved questions, clarify conditions under which the category holds, and explicate consequences of the category.

Theoretical sampling may be conducted either within or beyond the same field setting. For example, researchers may return to the field and seek new data by posing deeper or different research questions, or they may seek new participants or settings with similar characteristics to gain a fresh view. However, as researchers' emerging theories address generic processes, they may move across substantive fields to study their concepts and develop a formal theory of the generic process. Through theoretical sampling, researchers make their categories more incisive, their memos more useful, and their study more firmly grounded in the data.

CONSTRUCTING AND LINKING THEORETICAL CATEGORIES

Coding, memo writing, and theoretical sampling progressively lead researchers to construct theoretical categories that explain the studied process or phenomena. Some categories arise directly from open coding, such as research participants' telling statements. Researchers successively infer other categories as their analyses become more abstract and subsume a greater range of codes.

Grounded theorists invoke the saturation of core categories as the criterion for ending data collection. But what does that mean? And whose definition of saturation should be adopted? If the categories are concrete and limited, then saturation occurs quickly. Some studies that purport to be grounded theories are neither well grounded nor theoretical; their categories lack explanatory power, and the relationships between them are either unimportant or already established.

For a grounded theory to have explanatory power, its theoretical categories should be abstract, explicit, and integrated with other categories. Thus, grounded theorists complete the following tasks: locating the context(s) in which the category is relevant; defining each category; delineating its fundamental properties; specifying the conditions under which the category exists or changes; designating where, when, and how the category is related to other categories; and identifying the consequences of these relationships. These analytic endeavors produce a fresh theoretical understanding of the studied process.

—Kathy Charmaz

REFERENCES

Charmaz, K. (2000). Grounded theory: Constructivist and objectivist methods. In N. Denzin & Y. Lincoln (Eds.), *Handbook of qualitative research* (2nd ed., pp. 509–535). Thousand Oaks, CA: Sage.

Glaser, B. (1978). *Theoretical sensitivity*. Mill Valley, CA: Sociology Press.

Glaser, B. (1992). *Emergence vs. forcing: Basics of grounded theory analysis*. Mill Valley, CA: Sociology Press.

Glaser, B., & Strauss, A. (1967). *The discovery of grounded theory*. Chicago: Aldine.

Strauss, A., & Corbin, J. (1990). *Basics of qualitative research: Grounded theory procedures and techniques*. Newbury Park, CA: Sage.

Strauss, A., & Corbin, J. (1998). *Basics of qualitative research: Grounded theory procedures and techniques* (2nd ed.). Thousand Oaks, CA: Sage.

GROUP INTERVIEW

Group interviewing is the systematic questioning of several individuals simultaneously in formal or informal settings (Fontana & Frey, 1994). This technique has had a limited use in social science, where the primary emphasis has been on interviewing individuals. The most popular use of the group interview has been in FOCUS GROUPS, but there are additional formats for this technique, particularly in qualitative fieldwork. Depending on the research purpose, the interviewer/researcher can direct group interaction and response in a structured or unstructured manner in formal or naturally occurring settings. Groups can be used in exploratory research to test a research idea, survey question, or a measurement technique. Brainstorming with groups has been used to obtain the best explanation for a certain behavior. Group discussion will also enable researchers to identify key respondents (Frey & Fontana, 1991). This technique can be used in combination with other data-gathering strategies to obtain multiple views of the same research problem. The phenomenological assessment of emergent meanings that go beyond individual interpretation is another dimension of group interviews.

Group interviews can have limited structure (e.g., direction from interviewer) as in the case with brainstorming or exploratory research, or there can be considerable structure as in the case with nominal, Delphi, or most marketing focus groups. Respondents can be brought to a formal setting, such as a laboratory in a research center, or the group can be stimulated in an informal field setting, such as a street corner, recreation center, or neighborhood gathering place. Any group interview, regardless of setting, requires significant ability on the part of the interviewer to recognize an interview opportunity, to ask the questions that stimulate needed response, and to obtain a representative response or one that does not reflect the view of the dominant few and neglect perspectives of otherwise timid participants. The interviewer must be able to draw balance between obtaining responses related to the research purpose and the emergent group responses. Thus, the interviewer can exercise considerable control over the questioning process using a predetermined script of questions, or the interviewer can exercise little or no control over the direction and content of response by simply letting the conversation and response take their own path.

Problems exist when appropriate settings for group interviews cannot be located or when such a setting (e.g., public building, street corner) does not lend itself to an expressive, often conflict-laden, discussion. It is also possible that the researcher will not be accepted by the group as either a member or researcher. The group members may also tend to conformity rather than diversity in their views, thus not capturing the latent variation of responses and making it difficult to approach sensitive topics (Frey & Fontana, 1991). Finally, there is a high rate of irrelevant data; recording and compiling field notes is problematic,

particularly in natural, informal settings; and posturing by respondents is more likely in the group.

Advantages include efficiency, with the opportunity to get several responses at the same time and in the same settings. Group interviews provide another and rich dimension to understanding an event or behavior; respondents can be stimulated by the group to recall events they may have forgotten, and the researcher gains insights into social relationships associated with certain field settings.

—James H. Frey

REFERENCES

Fontana, A., & Frey, J. H. (1994). Interviewing: The art of science. In N. K. Denzin & Y. S. Lincoln (Eds.), *Handbook of qualitative research* (pp. 361–376). Thousand Oaks, CA: Sage.

Fontana, A., & Frey, J. H. (2000). The interview: From structured questions to negotiated text. In N. K. Denzin & Y. S. Lincoln (Eds.), *Handbook of qualitative research* (2nd ed., pp. 645–672). Thousand Oaks, CA: Sage.

Frey, J. H., & Fontana, A. (1991). The group interview in social research. *The Social Science Journal, 28*, 175–187.

GROUPED DATA

Data come from VARIABLES measured on one or more units. In the social sciences, the unit is often an individual. Units used in other sciences could be elements such as a pig, a car, or whatever. It is also possible to have *larger* units, such as a county or a nation. Such units are often made up by aggregating data across individual units. We aggregate the values of a variable across the individual persons and get *grouped data* for the larger unit. Grouped data can consist of data on variables such as average income in a city or number of votes cast in a ward for a candidate.

However, data on aggregates do not always consist of grouped data. If we consider type of government in a country as a variable with values *Democracy, Dictatorship*, and *Other*, then we clearly have data on aggregates of individuals in the countries. But the value for any country is a characteristic of the people who make up the country, and it is not an aggregate of values of any variable across the individuals in that country.

Grouped data exist at various levels of aggregation. There can be grouped data for the individuals who make up a census tract, a country, or a state. The importance of this lies in the fact that aggregation to different levels can produce different results from analyses of the data. Data on different levels may produce different magnitudes of CORRELATIONS depending on whether the data consist of observations aggregated, say, to the level of the county, where we may have data on all 3,000+ counties in the country, or whether the data are aggregated to the level of the state, where we may have data on all 50 states. Thus, analysis results that come from one level of aggregation apply *only* to the level on which the analysis is done. Mostly, they do not apply to units at lower or higher levels of aggregation.

In particular, results obtained from the analysis of aggregate data do in no way necessarily apply to the level of individuals as well. The so-called ECOLOGICAL FALLACY occurs when results obtained from grouped data are thought to apply on the level of the individual as well. In sociology, Robinson (1950) made this very clear in his path-breaking article on this topic. He showed mathematically how an ecological correlation coefficient obtained from grouped data could be very different, both in magnitude and in sign, from the correlation of the same two variables using data on individuals. *Simpson's paradox* is another name used for this phenomenon.

This situation becomes worse when there are group data available, but the individual data have not been observed. In voting, we know the number of votes cast for a candidate as well as other characteristics of precincts, but we do not know how the single individuals voted. Attempts have been made to construct methods to recover underlying individual-level data from group data, but in principle, such recovery will remain impossible without additional information.

In social science data analysis, another common form of grouped data is cross-classified data (i.e., observations cross-classified by the categories of the variables in an analysis). Such cross-classifications are known as CONTINGENCY TABLES and are often analyzed by LOG-LINEAR MODEL.

—Gudmund R. Iversen

See also DATA

REFERENCES

Borgatta, E. F., & Jackson, D. J. (Eds.). (1980). *Aggregate data: Analysis and interpretation.* Beverly Hills, CA: Sage.

Iversen, G. R. (1973). Recovering individual data in the presence of group and individual effects. *American Journal of Sociology, 79,* 420–434.

Robinson, W. S. (1950). Ecological correlations and the behavior of individuals. *American Sociological Review, 15,* 351–357.

GROWTH CURVE MODEL

Growth curve models refer to a class of techniques that analyze trajectories of cases over time. As such, they apply to longitudinal or PANEL data, where the same cases are repeatedly observed. John Wishart (1938) provided an early application of the growth curve model in which he fit polynomial growth curves to analyze the weight gain of individual pigs. Zvi Griliches (1957) looked at the growth of hybrid corn across various regions in the United States and modeled predictors of these growth parameters. Since these early works, growth curve models have increased in their generality and have spread across numerous application areas.

The word *growth* in growth curve models reflects the origin of these procedures in the biological sciences, whereby the organisms studied typically grew over time, and a separate growth trajectory could be fit to each organism. With the spread of these techniques to the social and behavioral sciences, the term *growth* seems less appropriate, and there is some tendency to refer to these models as latent curve models or *latent trajectory models.* We will use the term latent curve models in recognition that the objects of study might grow, decline, or follow other patterns rather than linear growth.

Social and behavioral scientists approach latent curve models from two methodological perspectives. One treats latent curve models as a special case of multilevel (or hierarchical) models, and the other treats them as a special case of STRUCTURAL EQUATION MODELS (SEMs). Although these methodological approaches have differences, the models and estimators derived from multilevel models or SEMs are sometimes identical and often are similar. A basic distinction that holds across these methodological approaches is whether a latent curve model is unconditional or conditional. The next two sections describe these two types of models.

UNCONDITIONAL MODEL

The unconditional latent curve model refers to REPEATED MEASURES for a single outcome and the modeling of this variable's trajectory. We can conceptualize the model as consisting of Level 1 and Level 2 equations. The Level 1 equation is

$$y_{it} = \alpha_i + \beta_i \lambda_t + \varepsilon_{it},$$

where i indexes the case or observation, and t indexes the time or wave of the data. The y_{it} is the outcome or repeated-measure variable for the ith case at the tth time point, α_i is the intercept for the ith case, β_i is the slope for the ith case, and λ_t is a function of the time of observation. The typical assumption is that $\lambda_t = t - 1$. In this case, the model assumes that the outcome variable is adequately captured by a linear trend. Nonlinear trends are available, and we will briefly mention these in our last section on extensions of the model. Finally, ε_{it} is the random DISTURBANCE for the ith case at the tth time period, which has a mean of zero ($E(\varepsilon_{it}) = 0$) and is uncorrelated with α_i, β_i, and λ_t. In essence, the Level 1 equation assumes an individual trajectory for each case in the sample, where the intercept (α_i) and slope (β_i) determine the trajectory and can differ by case. This part of the model differs from many typical social science statistical models in that each individual is permitted to follow a different trajectory.

The Level 2 equations treat the intercepts and slopes as "dependent" variables. In the unconditional model, the Level 2 equations give the group mean intercept and mean slope so that

$$\alpha_i = \mu_\alpha + \zeta_{\alpha i},$$
$$\beta_i = \mu_\beta + \zeta_{\beta i},$$

where μ_α is the mean of the intercepts, μ_β is the mean of the slopes, $\zeta_{\alpha i}$ is the disturbance that is the deviation of the intercept from the mean for the ith case, and $\zeta_{\beta i}$ is a similarly defined disturbance for β_i. The disturbances have means of zero, and they can correlate with each other. Generally, researchers need at least three waves of data to identify all of the model parameters.

The preceding Level 1 and Level 2 equations have the same form in both the multilevel and the SEM approaches to these models. In the SEM tradition of latent curve models, a path diagram is an alternative way to present these models. Figure 1 is a path diagram of the Level 1 and Level 2 equations for an unconditional latent curve model with four waves of data. In

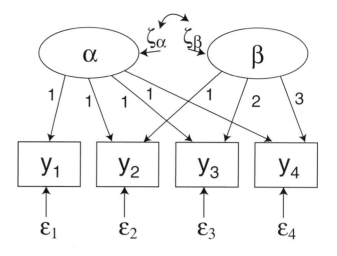

Figure 1   Unconditional Latent Trajectory Model

this path diagram, circles (or ellipses) represent latent variables, observed variables are in squares or rectangles, and disturbances are not enclosed. Single-headed arrows stand for the impact of the variable at the base of the arrow on the variable to which it points, and the two-headed arrows represent an association between the connected variables. One noteworthy feature of the path diagram is that it represents the random intercepts and random slopes as latent variables. They are latent because we do not directly observe the values of α_i and β_i, although we can estimate them. The time trend variable enters as the factor loadings in the SEM approach latent curve models.

When the data are continuous, it is common to assume that the repeated measures derive from a multivariate normal distribution. A maximum likelihood estimator (MLE) is available. In the SEM literature, methodologists have proposed corrections and adjustments to the MLE and significance tests that are asymptotically valid, even when the observed variables are not from a multinormal distribution. If the repeated measures are noncontinuous (e.g., dichotomous or ordinal), then alternative estimators must be used.

To illustrate the unconditional latent curve model, consider bimonthly data on logged total crime indexes in 616 communities in Pennsylvania for the first 8 months of 1995. These data come from the FBI Uniform Crime Reports and allow viewing the trajectory of crime over the course of the year. We estimate a mean value of 5.086 for the latent intercept, indicating that the mean logged crime rate at the first time point (January-February) is 5.086 for these communities.

The mean value of 0.105 for the latent slope indicates that the logged crime rate increases on average 0.105 units every 2 months over this time period. Both of these parameters are highly significant ($p < 0.01$). The significant intercept variance of 0.506 suggests that there is considerable variability in the level of crime in these communities at the beginning of the year, whereas the significant slope variance of 0.007 suggests variability in the change in crime over these 8 months.

CONDITIONAL MODEL

A second major type of latent curve model is the conditional model. Like the unconditional model, we can conceptualize the model as having Level 1 and Level 2 equations. Except in instances with time-varying covariates, the Level 1 equation is identical to that of the unconditional model (i.e., $y_{it} = \alpha_i + \beta_i \lambda_t + \varepsilon_{it}$). The difference occurs in the Level 2 equations. Instead of simply including the means of the intercepts and slopes and the deviations from the means, the Level 2 equations in the conditional latent curve model include variables that help determine the values of the intercepts and slopes. For instance, suppose that we hypothesize that two variables—say, x_{1i} and x_{2i}—affect the over-time trajectories via their impact on a case's intercept and slope. We can write the Level 2 equations as

$$\alpha_i = \mu_\alpha + \gamma_{\alpha x_1} x_{1i} + \gamma_{\alpha x_2} x_{2i} + \zeta_{\alpha i},$$
$$\beta_i = \mu_\beta + \gamma_{\beta x_1} x_{1i} + \gamma_{\beta x_2} x_{2i} + \zeta_{\beta i},$$

where μ_α and μ_β now are the intercepts of their respective equations, and the γs are the regression coefficients that give the expected impact on the random intercept (α_i) or random slope (β_i) of a one-unit change in the x variable, controlling for the other variables in the equation. We still interpret the disturbances of each equation the same way and make the same assumptions with the addition that the disturbances are uncorrelated with the xs. Figure 2 is a path diagram of the conditional Level 1 and Level 2 equations, represented as an SEM.

An advantage of the conditional model is that a researcher can determine which variables influence the intercepts or slopes and hence better understand what affects the individual trajectories. The above Level 2 equations in the conditional model have only two xs, although in practice, researchers can use any number of xs.

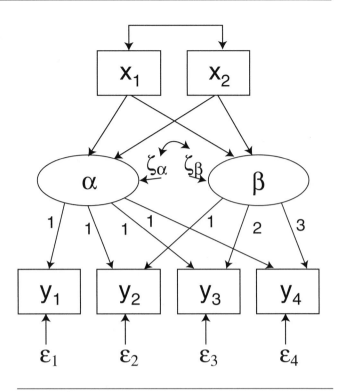

Figure 2   Conditional Latent Trajectory Model

An MLE for the conditional model is available when $\zeta_{\alpha i}$, $\zeta_{\beta i}$, and ε_{it} are distributed multivariate normal and the estimator is conditional on the value of the xs. As in the unconditional model, adjustments to the MLE permit significance testing when this distributional assumption does not hold.

Returning to the violent crime index, we include measures of population density and poverty rates for each community. The estimate of 0.02 ($p < 0.01$) for the effect of the poverty rate on the latent intercept suggests that a 1 percentage point difference in the poverty rate leads to an expected 0.02-unit difference in the level of logged crime at the first time point net of population density. However, the estimate of -0.002 for the effect of poverty on the latent slope indicates that a 1 percentage point increase in the poverty rate has an expected 0.002 decrease in the change in logged crime every 2 months net of population density. Population density has a positive effect on both the latent intercept and latent slope (although the latter narrowly misses significance), indicating that increasing population density increases the level of crime at the first time point and adds marginally to the slope of the trajectory in crime over this time period net of the poverty rate.

EXTENSIONS

There are many extensions to the unconditional and conditional latent curve models. One is to permit nonlinear trajectories in the outcome variable. This can be done by fitting polynomials in time, transforming the data, or, in the case of the SEM approach, freeing some of the factor loadings that correspond to the time trend so that these loadings are estimated rather than fixed to constants. In addition, autoregressive disturbances or autoregressive effects of the repeated measures can be added to the model. Researchers can incorporate time-varying predictors as a second latent curve or as a series of variables that directly affect the repeated measures that are part of a latent curve model. Direct maximum likelihood estimation or multiple imputation can handle missing data. Techniques to incorporate multiple indicators of a repeated latent variable also are available, as are procedures to include noncontinuous (e.g., categorical) outcome variables. In addition, recent work has investigated the detection of latent classes or groups in latent curve models. Furthermore, many measures of model fit are available, especially from the SEM literature. For further discussion of these models within the multilevel context, see Raudenbush and Bryk (2002); see also Bollen and Curran (in press) for a discussion from the SEM perspective. Software packages available to date for estimating latent growth curves include AMOS, EQS, LISREL, and MPLUS for the SEM approach, as well as HLM, MLn, and Proc Mixed in SAS for the hierarchical modeling approach. See the *Encyclopedia of Statistical Sciences* (Kotz & Johnson, 1983, pp. 539–542) and the *Encyclopedia of Biostatistics* (Armitage & Colton, 1998, pp. 3012–3015) for overviews of growth curve modeling in biostatistics and statistics.

—Kenneth A. Bollen, Sharon L. Christ, and John R. Hipp

REFERENCES

Armitage, P., & Colton, T. (Eds.). (1998). *Encyclopedia of biostatistics*. New York: John Wiley.

Bollen, K. A., & Curran, P. J. (in press). *Latent curve models: A structural equation approach*. New York: John Wiley.

Griliches, Z. (1957). Hybrid corn: An exploration in the economics of technological change. *Econometrica, 25,* 501–522.

Kotz, S., & Johnson, N. (Eds.). (1983). *Encyclopedia of statistical sciences*. New York: John Wiley.

Raudenbush, S. W., & Bryk, A. S. (2002). *Hierarchical linear models: Applications and data analysis methods*. Thousand Oaks, CA: Sage.

Wishart, J. (1938). Growth-rate determinations in nutritional studies with the Bacon pig, and their analysis. *Biometrika, 30,* 16–28.

GUTTMAN SCALING

Many phenomena in the social sciences are not directly measurable by a single item or variable. However, the researcher must still develop valid and reliable measures of these theoretical CONSTRUCTS in an attempt to measure the phenomenon under study. SCALING is a process whereby the researcher combines more than one item or variable in an effort to represent the phenomenon of interest. Many scaling MODELS are used in the social sciences.

One of the most prominent is Guttman scaling. Guttman scaling, also known as scalogram analysis and cumulative scaling, focuses on whether a set of items measures a single theoretical construct. It does so by ordering both items and subjects along an underlying cumulative dimension according to intensity. An example will help clarify the distinctive character of Guttman scaling. Assume that 10 appropriations proposals for the Department of Defense are being voted on in Congress—the differences among the proposals only being the amount of money that is being allocated for defense spending from $100,000,000 to $1,000,000,000 at hundred million-dollar increments. These proposals would form a (perfect) Guttman scale if one could predict how each member of Congress voted on each of the 10 proposals by knowing only the total number of proposals that each member of Congress supported. A scale score of 8, for example, would mean that the member supported the proposals from $100,000,000 to $800,000,000 but not the $900,000,000 or $1,000,000,000 proposals. Similarly, a score of 2 would mean that the member only supported the $100,000,000 and $200,000,000 proposals while opposing the other 8 proposals. It is in this sense that Guttman scaling orders both items (in this case, the 10 appropriations proposals) and subjects (in this case, members of Congress) along an underlying cumulative dimension according to intensity (in this case, the amount of money for the Department of Defense).

A perfect Guttman scale is rarely achieved; indeed, Guttman scaling anticipates that the perfect or ideal model will be violated. It then becomes a question of the extent to which the empirical data deviate from the perfect Guttman model. Two principal methods are used to determine the degree of deviation from the perfect model: (a) minimization of error, proposed by Guttman (1944), and (b) deviation from perfect reproducibility, based on work by Edwards (1948). According to the minimization of error criterion, the number of errors is the least number of positive responses that must be changed to negative, or the least number of negative responses that must be changed to positive, for the observed responses to be transformed into an ideal response pattern. The method of deviation from perfect reproducibility begins with a perfect model and counts the number of responses that are inconsistent with that pattern. Error counting based on deviations from perfect reproducibility results in more errors than

the minimization of error technique and is a more accurate description of the data based on scalogram theory. For this reason, it is superior to the minimization of error method.

—Edward G. Carmines and James Woods

REFERENCES

Carmines, E. G., & McIver, J. P. (1981). *Unidimensional scaling* (Sage University Paper Series on Quantitative Applications in the Social Sciences, 07–024). Beverly Hills, CA: Sage.

Edwards, A. (1948). On Guttman's scale analysis. *Educational and Psychological Measurement, 8,* 313–318.

Guttman, L. L. (1944). A basis for scaling qualitative data. *American Sociological Review, 9,* 139–150.

Nunnally, J. C. (1978). *Psychometric theory.* New York: McGraw-Hill.

H

HALO EFFECT

Also known as the *physical attractiveness stereotype* and the *"what is beautiful is good" principle*, halo effect, at the most specific level, refers to the habitual tendency of people to rate attractive individuals more favorably for their personality traits or characteristics than those who are less attractive. Halo effect is also widely used in a more general sense to describe the global impact of a likeable personality, or some specific desirable trait, in creating biased judgments of the target person on any dimension. Thus, feelings generally overcome cognitions when we appraise others.

This principle of judgmental bias caused by a single aspect of a person is grounded in the theory of central traits: Asch (1946) found that a man who had been introduced as a "warm" person was judged more positively on many aspects of his personality than when he had been described as "cold."

Dion, Berscheid, and Walster (1972) asked students to judge the personal qualities of people shown to them in photos. People with good-looking faces, compared to those who were either unattractive or average-looking, were judged to be superior with regard to their personality traits, occupational status, marital competence, and social or professional happiness. This effect was not altered by varying the gender of the perceiver or the target person.

A reverse halo effect can also occur, in which people who possess admired traits are judged to be more attractive. A negative halo effect refers to negative bias produced by a person's unattractive appearance. Halo effect occurs reliably over a wide range of situations, involving various cultures, ages, and types of people. It affects judgments of social and intellectual competence more than ratings of integrity or adjustment (Eagly, Ashmore, Makhijani, & Longo, 1991).

Attempts to evaluate individuals' job performance are often rendered invalid by halo effect: Ratings given by coworkers commonly reflect the attractiveness or likeability of the ratee rather than an objective measure of his or her actual competence. Halo effect also distorts judgments of the guilt of a defendant and the punishment he or she deserves. Raters may be given specific training in an attempt to reduce halo effect, very specific questions may be used, or control items may be included to estimate this bias.

The stereotype that attractive individuals possess better personal qualities is typically false in an experimental situation, where degree of beauty may be manipulated as a true INDEPENDENT VARIABLE and assigned randomly to individuals (e.g., by photos), but in real life, it may be true for certain traits. People who are beautiful, for example, may actually develop more confidence or social skills, creating a self-fulfilling prophecy.

—Lionel G. Standing

REFERENCES

Asch, S. E. (1946). Forming impressions of personality. *Journal of Abnormal and Social Psychology, 41,* 258–290.

Dion, K. K., Berscheid, E., & Walster, E. (1972). What is beautiful is good. *Journal of Personality and Social Psychology, 24,* 285–290.

Eagly, A. H., Ashmore, R. D., Makhijani, M. G., & Longo, L. C. (1991). What is beautiful is good but . . . A meta-analytic review of research on the physical attractiveness stereotype. *Psychological Bulletin, 110,* 109–128.

HAWTHORNE EFFECT

The Hawthorne effect refers to a methodological artifact (see ARTIFACTS IN RESEARCH PROCESS) in behavioral FIELD EXPERIMENTS arising from the awareness of research participants that they are being studied. This awareness leads them to respond to the social conditions of the data collection process rather than to the experimental treatment the researcher intended to study. Somewhat akin to what has been called the "guinea pig effect" in laboratory research, the artifact reduces the INTERNAL VALIDITY of experiments. The term *Hawthorne effect* may also be used in a management context to refer to workers' improved performance that is due to special attention received from their supervisor. Some researchers may confuse these usages, incorrectly interpreting improved performance due to a Hawthorne effect as a desirable outcome for their experiment.

Both effects were observed in a series of studies conducted in the 1920s and 1930s at the Hawthorne Works of the Western Electric Company (Roethlisberger & Dickson, 1939). Investigating the influence of various conditions on work performance, researchers were surprised that each new variable led to heightened levels of productivity, but were even more surprised when increased levels of productivity were still maintained after all improvements to working conditions had been removed. Researchers concluded that this unexpected result had been caused by incidental changes introduced in an attempt to create a controlled experiment.

Although there has been continuing controversy over the exact source of the artifact, and whether there was even evidence for it in the original experiments (Jones, 1992), the Hawthorne studies provided some of the first data suggesting the potential for social artifact to contaminate human research. The Hawthorne effect has been widely considered to be a potential contaminant of field experiments conducted in real-life settings, most notably in education, management, nursing, and social research in other medical settings. Researchers in a wide range of social sciences continue to control for Hawthorne effects, or claim its potential for misinterpretation of their research results.

Rather than procedures preventing its occurrence, the extent of artifact in a study is typically addressed by the inclusion of CONTROL GROUPS to measure the difference in performance on the DEPENDENT VARIABLE between a no-treatment control group and a "Hawthorne" group. The conditions manipulated to create the Hawthorne control group are one of the variables typically thought to generate Hawthorne effects; the others are special attention, a novel (yet meaningless) task, and merely leading participants to feel that they are subjects of an experiment. The EFFECT SIZES associated with each of these Hawthorne control procedures in educational research (Adair, Sharpe, & Huynh, 1989) have been found by meta-analyses (see META-ANALYSIS) to be small and nonsignificant, suggesting that these control groups have been ineffective for assessing artifact.

In spite of this lack of evidence in support of any of its controls and the difficulties in defining the precise nature of the Hawthorne effect, the potential for artifact within field experiments remains. The significance of the Hawthorne studies was to suggest how easily research results could be unwittingly distorted simply by the social conditions within the experiment. In contemporary research, the term *Hawthorne effect* is often used in this broad sense to refer to nonspecific artifactual effects that may arise from participants' reactions to experimentation.

—John G. Adair

REFERENCES

Adair, J. G., Sharpe, D., & Huynh, C. L. (1989). Hawthorne control procedures in educational experiments: A reconsideration of their use and effectiveness. *Review of Educational Research, 59,* 215–228.

Jones, S. R. (1992). Was there a Hawthorne effect? *American Journal of Sociology, 98,* 451–468.

Roethlisberger, F. J., & Dickson, W. J. (1939). *Management and the worker.* Cambridge, MA: Harvard University Press.

HAZARD RATE

A hazard rate, also known as a *hazard function* or *hazard ratio,* is a concept that arises largely in the literatures on SURVIVAL ANALYSIS and EVENT HISTORY

ANALYSIS, and this entry focuses on its usage and estimation in these literatures. However, the estimator of the hazard ratio also plays a key role in the MULTI-VARIATE modeling approach to correcting for sample SELECTION BIAS proposed by Heckman (1979).

The mathematical definition of a hazard rate starts with the assumption that a continuous RANDOM VARI-ABLE T defined over a range $t_{min} \leq T \leq t_{max}$ has a cumulative distribution function (CDF), $F(t)$, and a corresponding PROBABILITY DENSITY FUNCTION, $f(t) \equiv dF(t)/dt$. Frequently, the random variable T is assumed to be some measure of time. The complement of the cumulative probability function, called the survivor function, is defined as $S(t) \equiv 1 - F(t)$. Because it gives the probability that $T \geq t$ (i.e., "survives" from t_{min} to t), it is also known as the survivor probability. The hazard rate (or hazard ratio), $h(t)$, is then defined as

$$h(t) \equiv f(t)/S(t).$$

Speaking roughly and not rigorously, the hazard rate tells the chance or probability that the random variable T falls in an infinitesimally small range, $t \leq T < t + \Delta t$, divided by Δt, given that $T \geq t$, when Δt is allowed to shrink to 0. (Mathematically, one takes the limit as Δt approaches 0.)

Because both the probability density function and the survivor function cannot be negative, the hazard rate cannot be negative. The hazard rate is often regarded as analogous to a probability, and some authors even refer to a "discrete [time] hazard rate" (rather than to a probability) when T is taken to be a discrete random variable. However, for a continuous random variable T, the hazard rate can exceed 1, and, unlike a probability, it is not a unit-free number. Rather, its scale is the inverse of the scale of T. For example, in event history analysis, T might denote the age at which a person experiences some event (marriage, death) or the duration at which someone enters or leaves some status (starts or ends a job). In such instances, the hazard rate might be expressed in units "per year" or "per month."

Because the survivor function equals 1 at t_{min}, the hazard rate equals the probability density function at t_{min}. In addition, because the survivor function is a monotonically nonincreasing function and equals 0 at t_{max} (unless T has a "defective" probability distribution), the hazard rate tends to become an increasingly larger multiple of the probability density function as t increases.

The LIFE TABLE or actuarial ESTIMATOR of the hazard rate in a specified discrete interval $[u, v)$ has a very long history of usage in demography and is still utilized in many practical applications. Its definition is

$$\widehat{h(t)} = \frac{d(u, v)}{(v - u)\{n(u) - \frac{1}{2}[d(u, v) + c(u, v)]\}},$$
$$u \leq t < v$$

where $d(u, v)$ is the number of observations of t falling in the interval $[u, v)$; $n(u)$ is the number of observations that survived until u (i.e., for which $T \geq u$); and $c(u, v)$ is the number of observations censored in the interval $[u, v)$. (See CENSORING AND TRUNCATION for a definition and discussion of censored observations.) One-half appears in the divisor on the right-hand side of the equation because observations within the interval $[u, v)$ are assumed to occur uniformly over the interval.

Another widely used estimator is derived from the Nelson-Aalen estimator of the integrated hazard rate:

$$\widehat{h(t)} = \frac{d(u, v)}{(v - u)n(u)}, u \leq t < v.$$

Cox and Oakes (1984) provide a clear, concise introduction to these and several other common nonparametric estimators of a hazard rate.

Multivariate models of hazard rates can be categorized in various ways. Some are fully parametric models; for example, the hazard rate may be postulated to be a particular function of EXPLANATORY VARIABLES and of the random variable T in a way that reduces to a simple Weibull or Gompertz model in t. Partially parametric models are widely used, in particular, the proportional hazard rate model proposed by Cox (1972). In these models, the hazard rate is assumed to be the product of a nuisance function, $q(t)$, and a parametric function of the explanatory variables, typically $\exp[\beta' x(t)]$.

Fully parametric models include not only proportional hazard rate models, but also nonproportional hazard rate models. For a discussion of these and other types of hazard rate models, along with some social scientific examples, see Tuma and Hannan (1984, Chaps. 3–8). Fully parametric models are usually estimated by MAXIMUM LIKELIHOOD; Cox's proportional model is typically estimated by partial likelihood. In both fully and partially parametric models, the explanatory variables may be time invariant or time varying. The latter type demands either much more complete temporal data on the explanatory variables or fairly restrictive assumptions about how the explanatory variables change when they are incompletely observed over time.

Exploratory analyses of data often suggest that a nonproportional hazard rate model would fit empirical data better than a proportional hazard rate model. Local hazard rate models, proposed by Wu and Tuma (1990), offer a way to model nonproportionality when the sample size is large. The article on the closely related concept of a TRANSITION RATE refers to yet another approach.

—Nancy Brandon Tuma

REFERENCES

Cox, D. R. (1972). Regression models and life-tables (with discussion). *Journal of the Royal Statistical Society, Series B, 34*, 187–220.

Cox, D. R., & Oakes, D. (1984). *Analysis of survival data.* London and New York: Chapman and Hall.

Heckman, J. J. (1979). Sample selection bias as a specification error. *Econometrica, 47*, 153–161.

Tuma, N. B., & Hannan, M. T. (1984). *Social dynamics: Models and methods.* Orlando, FL: Academic Press.

Wu, L. L., & Tuma, N. B. (1990). Local hazard models. In C. C. Clogg (Ed.), *Sociological methodology 1990* (pp. 141–180). Oxford, UK: Basil Blackwell.

HERMENEUTICS

Although hermeneutic literally means "making the obscure plain," it is generally translated as "to interpret" or "to understand." Hermeneutics emerged in 17th-century Germany as a method of biblical interpretation. Later, it was applied to other texts, particularly those that are obscure, alien, or symbolic. The aim is to uncover the meanings and intentions that are hidden in the text, including those of which even the author may not have been aware (known as *philological* hermeneutics). In the context of social research, hermeneutics is concerned with the interpretation of meaningful human action.

ORIGINS OF MODERN HERMENEUTICS

Friedrich Schleiermacher (1768–1834) provided the foundation for modern hermeneutics. Because he saw hermeneutics as a science for understanding any utterance in language, hermeneutics moved from a concern with the analysis of texts from the past to the problem of how a person from one culture or historical period grasps the experiences of a person from another culture or period (known as general hermeneutics).

For Schleiermacher, understanding has two dimensions—grammatical and psychological. Grammatical interpretation corresponds to the understanding of language itself. Psychological interpretation attempts to recreate the act that produced the text and involves placing oneself within the mind of the author in order to know what was known and intended by this person as he or she wrote. Schleiermacher argued that the interpreter, as an outsider, is in a better position than the author to grasp and describe the "totality."

From its background in scriptural and other textual interpretation, hermeneutics came to be seen as the core discipline for understanding all great expressions of human life, cultural and physical. The instigator of this transition, Wilhelm Dilthey (1833–1911), argued that the study of human conduct should be based on the method of understanding (*verstehen*) to grasp the subjective consciousness of the participants, whereas the study of natural phenomena should seek causal explanation (*erklären*). He rejected the methods of the natural sciences as being appropriate for the human sciences and addressed the question of how to achieve OBJECTIVITY in the human sciences. He set out to demonstrate the methods, approaches, and categories—applicable in all the human sciences—that would guarantee objectivity and VALIDITY. Whether he produced a satisfactory answer to the question is a matter of some debate.

In his early work, Dilthey hoped that the foundation of the human sciences would be based on descriptive psychology—an empirical account of consciousness devoid of concerns with causal explanation. He believed that psychology could provide a foundation for the social sciences in the same way that mathematics underlies the natural sciences. All human products, including culture, were seen to be derived from mental life. However, Dilthey came to realize the limits of this position and eventually moved from a focus on the mental life of individuals to understanding based on socially produced systems of meaning. He came to stress the role of social context and what he called "objective mind"—objectifications or externalizations of the human mind, or the "mind-created world," that are sedimented in history, in what social scientists now call culture.

Dilthey now argued that phenomena must be situated in the larger wholes from which they derive their meaning; parts acquire significance from the whole, and the whole is given its meaning by the parts. The dual process of discovering taken-for-granted meanings from their externalized products, and understanding the products in terms of the meanings on which they are based, is known as the *hermeneutic circle*. The interpreter attempts to reconstruct the social and historical circumstances in which a text was produced and then to locate the text within these circumstances. Dilthey continued to assert the view that objective understanding must be the ultimate aim of the human sciences, even if the method is circular.

Dilthey insisted that the foundation for understanding human beings is in life itself, not in rational speculation or metaphysical theories. Life, or human experience, provides us with the concepts and categories we need to produce this understanding. He regarded the most fundamental form of human experience to be *lived experience*—first-hand, primordial, unreflective experience. According to Dilthey, the capacity of another person, or a professional observer, to understand human products is based on a belief that all human beings have something in common. However, he accepted the possibility that human expressions of one group may not be intelligible to members of another group; they may be so foreign that they cannot be understood. On the other hand, they may be so familiar that they do not require interpretation.

Martin Heidegger (1889–1976) was influenced by Dilthey and helped to lay the foundations for one branch of contemporary hermeneutics. Like Dilthey, he also wanted to establish a method that would reveal life in terms of itself. The central idea in Heidegger's work is that understanding is a mode of being rather than a mode of knowledge, an ONTOLOGICAL problem rather than an EPISTEMOLOGICAL one. It is not about how we establish knowledge; it is about how human beings exist in the world. For Heidegger, understanding is embedded in the fabric of social relationships, and interpretation is simply making this understanding explicit in language. Therefore, understanding is an achievement within reach of all human beings.

Heidegger recognized that there is no understanding of history outside of history. To assume that what is really there is self-evident is to fail to recognize the taken-for-granted presuppositions on which such assumed self-evidence rests. All understanding is temporal; it is not possible for any human being to step outside history or his or her social world.

To recapitulate, early hermeneutics arose in order to overcome a lack of understanding of texts; the aim was to discover what the text means. Schleiermacher shifted the emphasis away from texts to an understanding of how members of one culture or historical period grasp the experiences of a member of another culture or historical period. He argued for a method of psychological interpretation, of re-experiencing the mental processes of the author of a text or speaker in a dialogue. This involves the use of the hermeneutic circle, or the process of grasping the unknown whole from the fragmented parts and using this to understand any part. Dilthey then shifted the emphasis to the establishment of a universal methodology for the human sciences, one that would be every bit as rigorous and objective as the methods of the natural sciences. He moved from psychological interpretation to the socially produced systems of meaning, from introspective psychology to sociological reflection, from the reconstruction of mental processes to the interpretation of externalized cultural products. Lived experience provides the concepts and categories for this understanding. For both Schleiermacher and Dilthey, because an interpreter's prejudices would inevitably distort his or her understanding, it is necessary to extricate oneself from entanglement in a sociohistorical context. Heidegger disagreed and regarded understanding as being fundamental to human existence and, therefore, the task of ordinary people. He argued that there is no understanding outside of history; human beings cannot step outside of their social world or the historical context in which they live.

TWO BRANCHES

The views of these early scholars reveal two polarized positions that divide on the claim of whether or not objective interpretation is possible. One, based on the work of Schleiermacher and Dilthey, looked to hermeneutics for general methodological principles of interpretation. It endeavored to establish an objective understanding of history and social life above and outside of human existence. The other, based on the work of Heidegger, regarded hermeneutics as a philosophical exploration of the nature and requirements for all understanding and regarded objectively valid interpretation as being impossible. He claimed that understanding is an integral part of everyday human existence and is therefore the task of ordinary people, not of experts. Although these traditions have persisted, the latter has predominated and has been further developed by Hans-Georg Gadamer.

Gadamer (1989) was not particularly interested in the further development of hermeneutic methods for the social sciences, nor was he specifically concerned with the interpretation of texts. He focused on what is common to all modes of understanding by addressing three questions: How is "understanding" possible? What kinds of knowledge can understanding produce? What is the status of this knowledge?

For Gadamer, the key to understanding is grasping the "historical tradition," or understanding and seeing the world at a particular time and in a particular place within which, for example, a text is written. It involves adopting an attitude that allows a text to speak to us while also recognizing that the tradition in which the text is located may have to be "discovered" from other sources.

When viewed in the context of disciplines such as anthropology and sociology, historical tradition can be translated as "culture" or "worldview," and texts as records of conversations between social participants or with a researcher. Gadamer's position requires us to look beyond what is said to what is being taken for granted while it is being said, to the everyday meaning of both the language used and the situations in which the conversations occur. The aim is to hear beyond the mere words.

Another important feature of Gadamer's approach is the recognition that the process of understanding the products of other traditions or cultures cannot be detached from the culture in which the interpreter is located. He was critical of Dilthey's attempt to produce an "objective" interpretation of human conduct. For Gadamer, a text or historical act must be approached from within the interpreter's horizon of meaning, and this horizon will be broadened as it is fused with that of the act or text. The process of understanding involves a "fusion of horizons" in which the interpreter's own horizon of meaning is altered as a result of the hermeneutical conversation with the old horizon through the dialectic of question and answer. The interpreter engages the text in dialogue, a process that transforms both the text and the interpreter. The interpreter is not trying to discover what the text really means by approaching it with an unprejudiced open mind; he or she is not so much a knower as an experiencer for whom the other tradition opens itself.

For Gadamer, hermeneutics is about bridging the gap between our familiar world and the meaning that resides in an alien world. Collision with another horizon can make the interpreter aware of his or her own deep-seated assumptions and his or her own prejudices or horizon of meaning, of which he or she may have remained unaware; taken-for-granted assumptions can be brought to critical self-consciousness, and genuine understanding can become possible.

Gadamer argued that understanding what other people say is not a matter of "getting inside" their heads and reliving their experiences. Because language is the universal medium of understanding, understanding is about the translation of languages. However, every translation is, at the same time, an interpretation. Every conversation presupposes that the two speakers speak the same language and understand what the other says. But the hermeneutic conversation is usually between different languages, ranging from what we normally regard as "foreign" languages, to differences due to changes in a language over time or to variations in dialect. The hermeneutic task is not the correct mastery of another language but the mediation between different languages. Thus, understanding as the fusion of horizons occurs through language; language allows the mediation, the interpenetration and transformation of past and present. Whether it be a conversation between two people or between an interpreter and a text, a common language must be created. Like Heidegger, Gadamer was interested in ontology, not epistemology, with establishing what all ways of understanding have in common rather than being concerned with problems of method.

Hermeneutics has provided the foundation for some branches of interpretivism, such as the work of Max Weber and Alfred Schütz, and for the logic of abduction.

—Norman Blaikie

REFERENCES

Bauman, Z. (1978). *Hermeneutics and social science.* London: Hutchinson.

Blaikie, N. (1993). *Approaches to social enquiry.* Cambridge, UK: Polity.

Gadamer, H-G. (1989). *Truth and method* (rev. 2nd ed.). New York: Crossroad.

Outhwaite, W. (1975). *Understanding social life: The method called verstehen.* London: Allen & Unwin.

Palmer, R. E. (1969). *Hermeneutics: Interpretation theory of Schleiermacher, Dilthey, Heidegger, and Gadamer.* Evanston, IL: Northwestern University Press.

HETEROGENEITY

Statistics is the study of heterogeneity, so this is a broad topic. Statistical models typically distinguish between observed and unobserved sources of heterogeneity, capturing observed sources in terms of predictors or explanatory variables and relegating unobserved sources to the error term, typically assumed independent of observed covariates. Heterogeneity also arises when individual observations follow different models, leading to a distinction between subject-specific and population-average models. Because these ideas first became popular in demographic applications, we describe them in terms of survival or time-to-event data. The seminal paper here is Vaupel, Manton, and Stallard (1979).

Consider a homogeneous population where the risk that an event such as death will occur at time (or age) t, given that it has not yet occurred, is $\lambda(t)$, both for individuals and for the population as a whole. Consider next a heterogeneous population, and assume that the risk for individual i is $\theta_i \lambda(t)$, where $\theta_i > 0$ is an unobservable representing an individual's frailty, assumed to have a DISTRIBUTION with a mean of 1. It turns out that in such a heterogeneous population, the average HAZARD at age t is not $\lambda(t)$ but $E(\theta_i | T_i > t)\lambda(t)$. The multiplier is the average frailty of survivors to age t, is always less than 1, and declines with t. This implies that even if the risk were CONSTANT for each individual, the average risk in the POPULATION would decline over time as the weaker die first and leave exposed to risk a group increasingly selected for its robustness.

The fact that the risk one observes in a heterogeneous population is not the same as the risk faced by each individual can lead to interesting paradoxes. It has also led to attempts by analysts to control for unobserved heterogeneity by introducing frailty effects in their models, often in addition to observed covariates. ESTIMATION usually proceeds by specifying parametric forms for the hazard and the distribution of frailty. Concerned that the estimates might be heavily dependent on ASSUMPTIONS about the distribution of the unobservable, Heckman and Singer (1984) proposed a nonparametric ESTIMATOR of the distribution of θ_i. But estimates can also be sensitive to the choice of parametric form for the hazard. Unfortunately, one cannot relax both assumptions, because then the model is not identified. Specifically, unobserved heterogeneity is confounded with negative duration dependence in models without covariates, and with the usual assumption of proportionality of hazards in models with covariates; see Rodríguez (1994) for details.

The situation is much better if one has repeated events per individual and frailty is persistent across events, or if one has hierarchical data such as children nested within mothers and frailty is shared by members of a family. In both situations, frailty models are fully identified. For a discussion of multivariate survival, see Hougaard (2000). These models can be viewed as special cases of the models used in MULTILEVEL ANALYSIS. The classical frailty framework corresponds to a random-intercept model, where the mean level of response varies across groups. One can also consider random-slope models, where the effect of a covariate on the outcome, such as a treatment effect, varies across groups. Alternatively, the assumption that frailty is independent of observed covariates can be relaxed by treating θ_i as a fixed rather than a random effect (see FIXED-EFFECTS MODEL).

—Germán Rodríguez

REFERENCES

Heckman, J. J., & Singer, B. (1984). A method for minimizing the impact of distributional assumptions in econometric models for duration data. *Econometrica, 52,* 271–319.

Hougaard, P. (2000). *Analysis of multivariate survival data.* New York: Springer-Verlag.

Rodríguez, G. (1994). Statistical issues in the analysis of reproductive histories using hazard models. In K. L. Campbell & J. W. Wood (Eds.), *Human reproductive ecology: Interaction of environment, fertility and behavior* (pp. 266–279). New York: New York Academy of Sciences.

Vaupel, J. W., Manton, K. G., & Stallard, E. (1979). The impact of heterogeneity in individual frailty on the dynamics of mortality. *Demography, 16,* 439–454.

HETEROSCEDASTICITY. *See* HETEROSKEDASTICITY

HETEROSKEDASTICITY

An assumption necessary to prove that the ORDINARY LEAST SQUARES (OLS) estimator is the BEST LINEAR UNBIASED ESTIMATOR (BLUE) is that the variance of the error is constant for all observations, or HOMOSKEDASTIC. Heteroskedasticity arises when this assumption is violated because the error variance is nonconstant. When this occurs, OLS parameter estimates will be unbiased, but the variances of the estimated parameters will not be efficient. A classic example is the regression of income on savings (Figure 1 provides a hypothetical visual example). We expect

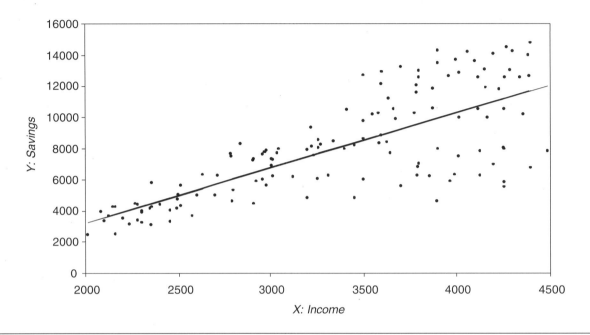

Figure 1   Heteroskedastic Regression

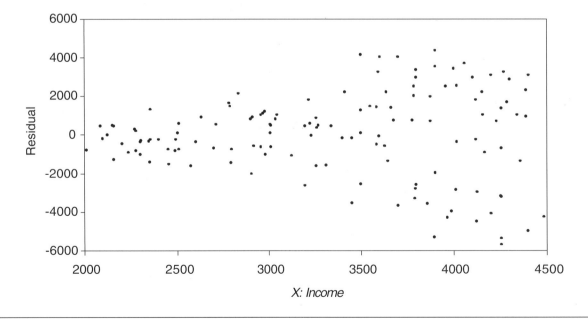

Figure 2   Visualizing Residuals

savings to increase as the level of income rises. This regression is heteroskedastic because individuals with low incomes have little money to save, and thus all have a relatively small amount of savings and small errors (they are all located near the regression line). However, individuals with high incomes have more to save, but some choose to use their surplus income in other ways (for instance, on leisure), so their level of savings varies more and the errors are larger.

A number of methods to detect heteroskedasticity exist. The simplest is a visual inspection of the residuals $\hat{u}_i = (y_i - \hat{y}_i)$ plotted against each independent variable. If the absolute magnitudes of the residuals seem to be constant across values of all independent variables, heteroskedasticity is likely not a problem. If the dispersion of errors around the regression line changes across any independent variable (as Figure 2 shows it does in our hypothetical example), heteroskedasticity may be present. In any event, more formal tests for heteroskedasticity should be performed.

The Goldfeld-Quandt and Breusch-Pagan tests are among the options. In the former, the observations are ordered according to their magnitude on the offending variable, some central observations are omitted, and separate regressions are performed on the two remaining groups of observations. The ratio of their sum of squared residuals is then tested for heteroskedasticity. The latter test is more general, in that it does not require knowledge of the offending variable.

If the tests reveal the presence of heteroskedasticity, a useful first step is to again scrutinize the residuals to see if they suggest any omitted variables. It is possible that all over-predictions have a trait in common that could be controlled for in the model. In the example, a measure of the inherent value individuals place on saving money (or on leisure) could alleviate the problem. The high income-low savings individuals may value saving less (or leisure more) than the average individual. If no such change in model specification is apparent, it may be necessary to transform the variables and conduct a GENERALIZED LEAST SQUARES (GLS) estimation. The GLS procedure to correct for heteroskedasticity weights the observations on the offending independent variable by the inverse of their errors and is often referred to as WEIGHTED LEAST SQUARES (WLS). If the transformation is done, and no other regression assumptions are violated, transformed estimates are BLUE.

—Kevin J. Sweeney

REFERENCES

Berry, W. D. (1993). *Understanding regression assumptions.* Newbury Park, CA: Sage.

Gujarati, D.N. (1995). *Basic econometrics* (3rd ed.). New York: McGraw-Hill.

Kennedy, P. (1992). *A guide to econometrics* (3rd ed.). Cambridge: MIT Press.

HEURISTIC

A tool, device, or rule to facilitate the understanding of a concept or method. For example, to help students learn about SIGNIFICANCE TESTING, they may be offered the following heuristic: In general, a coefficient with a t ratio of 2.0 or more in absolute value will be significant at the .05 level. This heuristic is useful for sorting through t ratios that may have been generated by many REGRESSION runs.

—Michael S. Lewis-Beck

HEURISTIC INQUIRY

Heuristic inquiry is a form of phenomenological inquiry that brings to the fore the personal experience and insights of the researcher. With regard to some phenomenon of interest, the inquirer asks, "What is *my* experience of this phenomenon and the essential experience of others who also experience this phenomenon intensely?" (Patton, 2002).

Humanist psychologist Clark Moustakas (1990) named heuristic inquiry when he was searching for a word that would encompass the processes he believed to be essential in investigating human experience. "Heuristic" comes from the Greek word *heuriskein,* meaning "to discover" or "to find." It connotes a process of internal search through which one discovers the nature and meaning of experience and develops methods and procedures for further investigation and analysis. "The self of the researcher is present throughout the process and, while understanding the phenomenon with increasing depth, the researcher also experiences growing self-awareness and self-knowledge. Heuristic processes incorporate creative self-processes and self-discoveries" (Moustakas, 1990, p. 9).

There are two focusing elements of heuristic inquiry within the larger framework of phenomenology: (a) The researcher *must* have personal experience with and intense interest in the phenomenon under study, and (b) others (coresearchers) who share *an intensity* of experience with the phenomenon participate in the inquiry. Douglass and Moustakas (1985) have emphasized that "heuristics is concerned with meanings, not measurements; with essence, not appearance; with quality, not quantity; with experience, not behavior" (p. 42).

The particular contribution of heuristic inquiry is the extent to which it legitimizes and places at the fore the personal experiences, reflections, and insights of the researcher. The researcher comes to understand the essence of the phenomenon through shared reflection and inquiry with coresearchers as they also intensively experience and reflect on the phenomenon in question. A sense of connectedness develops between researcher and research participants in their mutual efforts to elucidate the nature, meaning, and essence of a significant human experience.

The rigor of heuristic inquiry comes from systematic observation of and dialogues with self and others, as well as depth interviewing of coresearchers.

Heuristic inquiry is derived from but different from PHENOMENOLOGY in four major ways:

1. Heuristics emphasizes connectedness and relationship, whereas phenomenology encourages more detachment in analyzing experience.
2. Heuristics seeks essential meanings through portrayal of personal significance, whereas phenomenology emphasizes definitive descriptions of the structures of experience.
3. Heuristics includes the researcher's intuition and tacit understandings, whereas phenomenology distills the structures of experience.
4. "In heuristics the research participants remain visible.... Phenomenology ends with the essence of experience; heuristics retains the essence of the person in experience" (Douglass & Moustakas, 1985, p. 43).

Systematic steps in the heuristic inquiry process lead to the exposition of experiential essence through immersion, incubation, illumination, explication, and creative synthesis (Moustakas, 1990).

—Michael Quinn Patton

REFERENCES

Douglass, B., & Moustakas, C. (1985). Heuristic inquiry: The internal search to know. *Journal of Humanistic Psychology, 25,* 39–55.

Moustakas, C. (1990). *Heuristic research: Design, methodology, and applications.* Newbury Park, CA: Sage.

Moustakas, C. (1994). *Phenomenological research methods.* Thousand Oaks, CA: Sage.

Patton, M. Q. (2002). *Qualitative research and evaluation methods.* Thousand Oaks, CA: Sage.

HIERARCHICAL (NON)LINEAR MODEL

The hierarchical linear model (HLM) is basic to the main procedures of MULTILEVEL ANALYSIS. It is an extension of the GENERAL LINEAR MODEL to data sets with a hierarchical nesting structure, where each level of this hierarchy is a source of unexplained variation. The general linear model can be formulated as

$$Y_i = b_0 + b_1 X_{1i} + \cdots + b_p X_{pi} + E_i,$$

where i indicates the case; Y is the dependent variable; X_1 to X_p are the independent (or explanatory) variables; E is the unexplained part, usually called the residual or error term; b_0 is called the intercept; and b_1 to b_p are the regression coefficients. Sometimes, the constant term b_0 is omitted from the model. The standard assumption is that the residuals E_i are independent, normally distributed, random variables with expected value 0 and a common variance, and the values X_{hi} are fixed and known quantities.

Examples of nesting structures are pupils nested in classrooms (a two-level structure), pupils nested in classrooms in schools (three levels), pupils nested in classrooms in schools in countries (four levels), and so on. Elements of such nesting structure are called units (e.g., pupils in this example are level-one units, classrooms are level-two units, etc.). For a two-level nesting structure, it is customary to use a double indexation so that, in this example, Y_{ij} indicates the dependent variable for pupil i in classroom j. The hierarchical linear model for two levels of nesting can be expressed as

$$Y_{ij} = b_0 + b_1 X_{1ij} + \cdots + b_p X_{pij} + U_{0j}$$
$$+ U_{1j} Z_{1ij} + \cdots + U_{qj} Z_{qij} + E_{ij}.$$

The first part, $b_0 + b_1 X_{1ij} + \cdots + b_p X_{pij}$, is called the fixed part and has the same structure and interpretation as the first part of the general linear model; the double indexation of the explanatory variables is only a matter of notation. The second part, called the random part, is different. Unexplained variation between the level-two units is expressed by $U_{0j} + U_{1j} Z_{1ij} + \cdots + U_{qj} Z_{qij}$, where Z_1 to Z_q are explanatory variables (usually, but not necessarily, a subset of X_1 to X_p); U_{0j} is called the random intercept; and U_{1j} to U_{qj} are called random slopes (it is allowed that there are no random slopes, i.e., $q = 0$). The variables U_{0j} to U_{qj} are residuals for level two, varying between the level-two units, and E_{ij} is a residual for level one. The standard assumption is that residuals for different levels are independent, residuals for different units at the same level are independent, and all residuals are normally distributed. It is possible to extend the model with random slopes at level one, in addition to the residual E_{ij}; this is a way of formally representing HETEROSKEDASTICITY of the level-one residuals (see Snijders & Bosker, 1999, Chap. 8).

This model can be extended to more than two levels of nesting. For three nesting levels, with units being indicated by i, j, and k, the formula reads

$$Y_{ijk} = b_0 + b_1 X_{1ijk} + \cdots + b_p X_{pijk} + V_{0k}$$
$$+ V_{1k} W_{1ijk} + \cdots + V_{rk} W_{rijk} + U_{0jk}$$
$$+ U_{1jk} Z_{1ijk} + \cdots + U_{qjk} Z_{qijk} + E_{ijk}.$$

The W_{hijk} now are also explanatory variables, with random slopes V_{hk} varying between the level-three units k. The rest of the model is similar to the two-level model. The hierarchical linear model also can be extended to sources of unexplained variation that are not nested but crossed factors (see the entries on MULTILEVEL ANALYSIS and MIXED-EFFECTS MODEL).

HIERARCHICAL NONLINEAR MODEL

The hierarchical nonlinear model, also called hierarchical generalized linear model or generalized linear mixed model, is an analogous extension to the GENERALIZED LINEAR MODEL. It is defined by including random residuals for the higher-level units in the linear predictor of the generalized linear model. Thus, the formulas given above for Y_{ij} and Y_{ijk}, but without the level-one residual E_{ij} or E_{ijk}, take the place of the elements of

the vector defined as the linear predictor $\eta = X\beta$ in the entry on generalized linear models.

—Tom A. B. Snijders

REFERENCES

Goldstein, H. (2003). *Multilevel statistical models* (3rd ed.). London: Hodder Arnold.

Raudenbush, S. W., & Bryk, A. S. (2001). *Hierarchical linear models: Applications and data analysis methods* (2nd ed.). Thousand Oaks, CA: Sage.

Snijders, T. A. B., & Bosker, R. J. (1999). *Multilevel analysis: An introduction to basic and advanced multilevel modeling.* London: Sage.

HIERARCHY OF CREDIBILITY

A term used by Howard Becker (1967) to refer to a differential capacity for the views of groups in society to be regarded as plausible. The term relates to the tendency for many spheres of society to have a clear hierarchy: police/criminal, manager/worker, teacher/student. It has been suggested that when social scientists take the worldviews of those groups that form the subordinate groups in these pairings, they are more likely to be accused of bias. This arises because of the hierarchy of credibility, whereby those in the superordinate positions are perceived by society at large as having the right and the resources for defining the way things are.

—Alan Bryman

REFERENCE

Becker, H. S. (1967). Whose side are we on? *Social Problems, 14,* 239–247.

HIGHER-ORDER. *See* ORDER

HISTOGRAM

Histograms, BAR GRAPHS, and PIE CHARTS are used to display results in a simple, visual way. A bar chart would be used for categorical (nominal) variables, with each bar of the chart displaying the value of some variable. A histogram performs the same function for grouped data with an underlying CONTINUOUS VARIABLE (an ordinal, interval, or ratio distribution). The bars touch to reflect the continuous nature of the underlying distribution. A histogram or bar chart would be used in preference to a pie chart for showing trends across a variable (e.g., over time or by geographical locality). Pie charts are better for showing the percentage composition of a population.

Figure 1 shows the number of moves (changes of householder) recorded against properties where there has been a change of householder in the past year, in the center of a town in northeastern England that has been in decline since the collapse of its major industries but is now undergoing considerable regeneration. The figure shows nearly 150 properties that have had two changes of householder during the year and nontrivial numbers where ownership has been even more volatile. (The data for this figure are taken from Hobson-West & Sapsford, 2001.) As well as being descriptively useful, this kind of graph helps to determine the overall shape of the variable—the extent

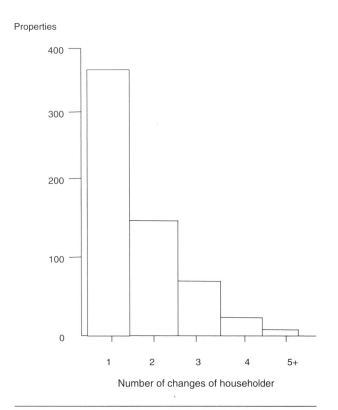

Properties

Figure 1   Number of Changes of Householder in Middlesbrough During 2001

of departure from normality—which in this case is very substantial.

—Roger Sapsford

REFERENCE

Hobson-West, P., & Sapsford, R. (2001). *The Middlesbrough Town Centre Study: Final report.* Middlesbrough, UK: University of Teesside, School of Social Sciences.

HISTORICAL METHODS

Historical methods refers to the use of primary historical data to answer a question. Because the nature of the data depends on the question being asked, data may include demographic records, such as birth and death certificates; newspapers articles; letters and diaries; government records; or even architectural drawings.

The use of historical data poses several broad questions:

1. Are the data appropriate to the theoretical question being posed?
2. How were these data originally collected, or what meanings were embedded in them at the time of collection?
3. How should these data be interpreted, or what meanings do these data hold now?

THEORETICAL QUESTIONS

One way for social scientists to pose questions about contemporary issues is to compare aspects of contemporary society with those of past societies. As C. Wright Mills put it, to understand social life today, one must ask such questions as, "In what kind of society do I live?" and "Where does this society stand in the grand march of human history?" These questions necessarily imply a theory, a set of related propositions that orients the researcher as to where to search for answers. Indeed, to generalize, *any historical question implies a theory,* for without a theory, the social scientist is haphazardly collecting a conglomeration of shapeless facts.

I stress the centrality of an explicit theory to historical method to highlight a key distinction between historical methods used by historians and those used by social scientists. Although historians use theories, their theoretical assumptions are not always explicitly developed. Rather, their theoretical emphases are often contained in the professional classification in which they are placed—say, "military historian," "diplomatic historian," or "social historian"—because these classifications implicitly claim that the activities of a specific group (and hence a particular kind of power or lack of power) is central to the analysis of epochs. Within this profession, as within all academic professions, the centrality of any one category has varied over time. In the late 20th century, the advent of social history (including such specialties as women's history and African American history) *was* an announcement that understanding people who had been historically powerless, even invisible, is vital to grasping the nature of our own time.

APPROPRIATE DATA

Such shifts in categorical emphasis also imply new forms of data. Thus, news reports have less utility to understand the lives of peasants, factory workers, slaves, or maids than they do to write the biography of, say, a military officer—although news stories may tell us how factory workers or slaves were seen by those who had more power than they. Similarly, one can *hope* to understand the differential reaction of European Americans and African Americans to urban riots by comparing mass media and African American media. But unless such reports are placed in a theoretical and comparative context, the researcher can only have *hope*.

Unfortunately, many social scientists embarking on historical inquiries have not been trained in history. In part, this deficiency means that when reading historical accounts, the social scientist may not know either the specific questions those accounts are debating or even the implicit theories that historians are addressing. Without a context, it is difficult to know what to remember, or even what to write on one's ubiquitous note cards or computer files. Similarly, without some appreciation of the lives of people in a specific group living in a specific time and place, one cannot know the meaning or significance of a specific piece of data.

Not having been trained in history also poses another problem: A social scientist may not know the location of archives pertinent to a research problem. Taking a course in historiography, consulting an accomplished historian, checking *Historical Abstracts*, and searching the Internet are all ways to learn what data others have used and thus what types of data may be available.

AN EXAMPLE

Some social scientists work inductively rather than deductively. If a social scientist is proceeding inductively, he or she must know the context. Let me give a seemingly insignificant example—constructing a family tree (an atheoretic enterprise). To delineate a family tree, I recalled my parents', uncles', and aunts' stories abut their childhood. Then, I visited my family's graveyard, pen and paper in hand. I did so because I knew to expect that under each person's English name, I would find his or her name in Hebrew, and that name would follow the expected form "first name middle name, son or daughter of first name middle name," as in "Chava Perl bat [daughter] of Yisroel Avram." By locating the gravestone of Yisroel Avram, I could then learn the name of his father and so on. One stone did not give the name of the deceased father. Rather, in Yiddish (the wrong language), that stone announced "daughter of a good man." An elderly relative had once told me a family secret about the woman whose stone contained Yiddish: She had married her uncle. Examining the placement of graves (whose conventions I knew), I could infer the name of her uncle and also that of her mother. Without having background information, I could not have constructed the family tree. That family tree is simply data waiting for a theoretical frame.

OTHER CONTEXTUAL ISSUES

Contextual questions may be difficult in other ways as well. Reading histories, one wants to know what the historians are debating. (If the historians did not have a point, they would not have bothered to write.) Other nonfictions raise other questions: Reading 19th-century women's diaries requires asking, Was this skill taught in school? Did a teacher read this diary as part of a class assignment? What kind of self-censorship (or external censorship) was involved in the production of any written document? Context—what is said and what is missing—governs meaning in historical data as in ethnographic studies of contemporary life. As is true of any qualitative method, context guides the recognition of theoretically pertinent data, and theory directs the understanding of pertinent contexts.

INTERPRETATION

Theory is particularly pertinent to the interpretation of data, because all theories imply an EPISTEMOLOGICAL stance toward the very existence of data. There are at least two broad ways of viewing interpretative acts. I call them *reproduction* and *representation*. By reproduction, I mean the view that historical accounts accurately capture the essence of a specific time and place. I include here empiricalist epistemologies, such as those that emphasize "the grand march of history." Representation refers to the great variety of POSTMODERNIST views that identify both historical and social scientific writings as "texts," which, as is the case of the data they analyze, are political documents that purposively or inadvertently take sides in struggles for power. However, more discussion about the differences between these broad schools of thought departs from a discussion of historical method.

—Gaye Tuchman

REFERENCES

Himmelfarb, G. (1987). *The new history and the old.* Cambridge, MA: Harvard University Press.

Marcus, G., & Fischer, M. (1986). *Anthropology as cultural critique.* Chicago: University of Chicago Press.

Scott, J. W. (1988). *Gender and the politics of history.* New York: Columbia University Press.

Tuchman, G. (1994). Historical social science: Methodologies, methods, and meanings. In N. K. Denzin & Y. S. Lincoln (Eds.), *Handbook of qualitative research* (pp. 306–323). Thousand Oaks, CA: Sage.

HOLDING CONSTANT. *See* CONTROL

HOMOSCEDASTICITY. *See* HOMOSKEDASTICITY

HOMOSKEDASTICITY

For ORDINARY LEAST SQUARES (OLS) assumptions to be met, the ERRORS must exhibit constant variance. Such uniform variance is called homoskedasticity. If this assumption is not met, that is, if the errors exhibit nonuniform variance, the opposing condition of HETEROSKEDASTICITY obtains, and OLS is no longer the BEST LINEAR UNBIASED ESTIMATOR (BLUE) of model PARAMETERS. Specifically, if the errors are heteroskedastic, the estimated model parameters will remain UNBIASED, but they will not be minimum variance estimates.

To understand the concept of uniform error variance, it is helpful to consider the relationship between two variables, X and Y, and the conditional means and variances of Y with respect to X in a regression. If DEPENDENT VARIABLE Y is related to INDEPENDENT VARIABLE X, then mean values of Y will vary across different values of X. This is the conditional mean of Y given X, written $(Y|X)$. It is known that the regression line of Y on X passes directly through these conditional means. We may then consider the variation in Y at different conditional means. This is known as conditional variation, denoted $\text{var}[Y|X]$. This conditional variation is also referred to as the skedastic function. When homoskedastic, conditional variation will not change across values of X; rather, it will be uniform. This uniform variation is denoted σ^2 (Figure 1 illustrates). The conditional mean of Y given particular values of X $(Y|X)$ increases with X. But the dispersion of errors around those conditional means remains constant throughout.

If the errors are homoskedastic and exhibit no AUTOCORRELATION with each other, they are said to be "spherical." With spherical DISTURBANCE TERMS, the EXPECTED VALUE of the error variance-covariance matrix, $E(\mathbf{UU}')$, reduces to $\sigma^2\mathbf{I}$, and the OLS formulas for model parameters and their STANDARD ERRORS are obtained readily (see SPHERICITY ASSUMPTION). If the disturbances are nonspherical, then OLS becomes problematic and a GENERALIZED LEAST SQUARES (GLS) solution is required.

Because the errors are simply the difference between predicted and observed values of the dependent variable Y, they are themselves expressed in units of Y. Nevertheless, there is no reason to expect

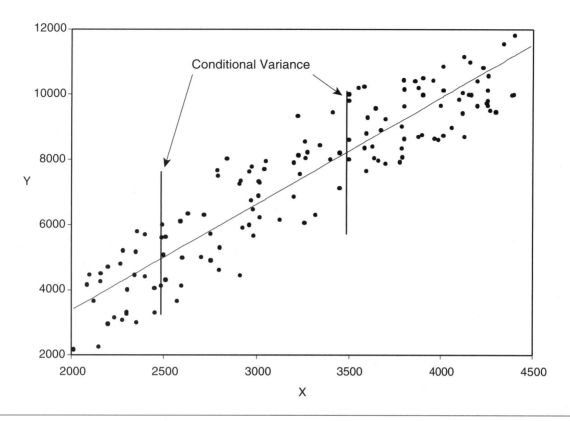

Figure 1   Homoskedastic Errors in Regression

that overall variation in Y, var(Y), will be equal to var($Y|X$), even when that conditional variation is uniform (σ^2). It is expected that our model has explained some of the overall variation in Y, and it is only the conditional variation of the residuals that needs to be uniform (i.e., homoskedastic) for this OLS assumption to be met.

—Brian M. Pollins

REFERENCES

Greene, W. H. (2003). *Econometric analysis* (5th ed.). Upper Saddle River, NJ: Prentice Hall.

Gujarati, D. N. (2003). *Basic econometrics* (4th ed.). Boston: McGraw-Hill.

Kennedy, P. (1998). *A guide to econometrics* (4th ed.). Cambridge: MIT Press.

HUMANISM AND HUMANISTIC RESEARCH

Humanistic research is research that gives prime place to human beings, human meaning, and human actions in research. It usually also works with a strong ethical framework that both respects human beings and seeks to improve the state of humankind in a global context. It allies itself more with the humanities than with science, which it often critiques.

There is, of course, a long history of diverse forms of humanism in world history. The Greek Sophists and Socrates "called philosophy down from heaven to earth" (as Cicero put it). Early humanists of the pre-Renaissance movement, such as Erasmus, did not find their humanism incompatible with religion, but they did sense the abilities of human beings to play an active role in creating and controlling their world. The Italian Renaissance itself was a period in which the study of the works of man—and not simply God—became more and more significant. French philosophers, such as Voltaire, gave humanism a strongly secular base. Alfred McLung Lee (1978), a champion of a humanistic sociology, sees humanism "in a wide range of religious, political and academic movements" (p. 44) and links it to fields as diverse as communism, democracy, egalitarianism, populism, NATURALISM, POSITIVISM, pragmatism, relativism, science, and supernaturalism, including versions of ancient paganisms, Hinduism, Buddhism, Judaism, Roman Catholicism, Protestantism and Mohammedanism (pp. 44–45). It does seems to be one of those words that can mean all things to all people.

In the social sciences, there are clear humanistic strands in psychology (the works of Abraham Maslow, Jerome Bruner, and Robert Coles); anthropology (Gregory Bateson, Margaret Mead, Robert Redfield); and sociology (C. Wright Mills, Peter Berger, the symbolic interactionists). Humanistic psychologists, for example, criticize much of psychology as dehumanizing and trivial, providing elegant experiments but failing to deal with the major ethical crises of our time or the ways in which living, whole human beings deal with them. Within sociology, humanistic research is frequently linked to research that examines the active construction of meanings in people's lives.

As with William James's *Varieties of Religious Experience* or Margaret Mead's *Sex and Temperament in Three Primitive Societies,* humanistic social science usually recognizes the varieties of these meanings. Often employing field research, life stories, and qualitative research—as well as using wider sources such as literature, biographies, photographs, and film—it aims to get a close and intimate familiarity with life as it is lived. Humanistic research tends to shun abstractions and adopt a more pragmatic, down-to-earth approach. Although it usually places great faith in human reason, it also recognizes the role of emotions and feelings, and it puts great emphasis upon the ethical choices people make in creating the good world and the good life.

Humanistic research is attacked from many sides. Scientists have tended to deride its lack of objectivity, determinism, and technical competence. Nihilist philosophers like Nietzsche and Kierkegaard shun its overly romantic view of the human being and dismiss its ethical systems. Many religions are critical because it fails to see humans as worthless and only saved by salvation or divine grace. Most recently, multiculturalists and postmodernists have been concerned that it is often limited to a very specific Western and liberal version of what it is to be human. Criticisms notwithstanding, it acts as a subversive tradition to major scientific tendencies within the social sciences.

—Ken Plummer

See also AUTOBIOGRAPHY, INTERPRETATIVE BIOGRAPHY, LIFE HISTORY INTERVIEW, LIFE HISTORY RESEARCH, ORAL HISTORY, QUALITATIVE RESEARCH, REFLEXIVITY

REFERENCES

Lee, A. M. (1978). *Sociology for whom.* New York: Oxford University Press.
Radest, H. B. (1996). *Humanism with a human face: Intimacy and the enlightenment.* London: Praeger.
Rengger, J. (1996). *Retreat from the modern: Humanism, postmodernism and the flight from modernist culture.* Exeter, UK: Bowerdean.

HUMANISTIC COEFFICIENT

In contrast with a social science that sees the world in terms of "facts" and "things," there is a persistent strand that is concerned with *meaningful, intersubjective social actions and values.* Max Weber's concern with VERSTEHEN is one of the most celebrated of such approaches. The work of Alfred Schutz on PHENOMENOLOGY is another.

During the 1920s and 1930s, another key figure in clarifying this position was Florian Znaniecki (although he is largely neglected today). Both in his methodological note to *The Polish Peasant* (with W. I. Thomas) and in his *The Method of Sociology* (1934), he presents a strong concern with the neo-Kantian distinction between two systems, natural and cultural. Natural systems are given objectively in nature and have an independent existence. They are separate from the experience and activities of people. Cultural systems are intrinsically bound up with the conscious experiences of human agents in interaction with each other.

For Znaniecki (1934), "natural systems are objectively given to the scientist as if they existed absolute independently of the experience and activity of men" (p. 136). They include such things as the geological composition of the earth, the chemical compound, or the magnetic field. They can exist without any participation of human consciousness. "They are," as he says, "bound together by forces which have nothing to do with human activity" (p. 136). In stark contrast, cultural systems deal with the human experiences of conscious and active historical subjects. This cultural system is believed to be real by these historical subjects experiencing it; but it is not real in the same way as the natural system is. The object of study is always linked to somebody's human meanings. Znaniecki (1934) calls this essential character of cultural data the humanistic coefficient, "because such data, as objects of the student's theoretical reflection, already belong to someone else's active experience and are such as this active experience makes them" (p. 136). Thus, if this cultural system was ignored and not seen as a humanistic coefficient, if cultural life was studied like a natural system, then the researcher would simply find "a disjointed mass of natural things and processes, without any similarity to the reality he started to investigate" (p. 137). It becomes central to research into human and cultural life.

Thus, one major tradition of social science has repeatedly stressed the importance of studying this "humanistic coefficient"; of getting at the ways in which participants of historical social life construct and make sense of their particular world—their "definitions of the situation," their "first level constructs." This tradition is exemplified in Thomas and Znaniecki's classic volume *The Polish Peasant in Europe and America,* where a whole array of subjective documents—letters, life stories, case records, and so on—are used to get at the meaning of the experience of migration. This major study anticipated the important development of personal documents, life histories, and participant observation within social science. These are among the core methods that help us get at the humanistic coefficient.

—Ken Plummer

See also VERSTEHEN, SENSITIZING CONCEPTS, LIFE HISTORY METHOD, PARTICIPANT OBSERVATION

REFERENCES

Bryun, T. S. (1966) *The human perspective in sociology: The methodology of participant observation.* Englewoood Cliffs, NJ: Prentice Hall.

Thomas, W. I., & Znaniecki, F. (1918–1920). *The Polish peasant in Europe and America* (Vols. 1 & 2). New York: Dover.

Znaniecki, F. (1934). *The method of sociology.* New York: Farrar and Rinehart.

Znaniecki, F. (1969). *On humanistic sociology: Selected papers* (R. Bierstadt, Ed.). Chicago: University of Chicago Press.

HYPOTHESIS

This is a central feature of scientific method, specifically as the key element in the hypothetico-deductive model of science (Chalmers, 1999). Variations on this model are used throughout the sciences, including social science. Hypotheses are statements derived from an existing body of THEORY that can be tested using the methods of the particular science. In chemistry or psychology, this might be an experiment, and in sociology or political science, the social survey. Hypotheses can be confirmed or falsified, and their status after testing will have an impact on the body of theory, which may be amended accordingly and new hypotheses generated. Consider a simplified example: Classical migration theory states that economic push and pull factors will be the motivation for migration, and agents will have an awareness of these factors. From this, it might be hypothesized that migrants will move from economically depressed areas to buoyant ones. If, upon testing, it is found that some economically depressed areas nevertheless have high levels of inmigration, then the original theory must be amended in terms of either its claims about economic factors, or the agents' knowledge of these, or possibly both.

Rarely, however, is it the case that hypotheses are proven wholly right (confirmed) or wholly wrong (falsified), and even rarer that the parent theory is wholly confirmed or falsified. Through the second half of the 20th century, there was a great deal of debate (which continues) around the degree to which hypotheses and, by implication, theories can be confirmed or falsified. Karl Popper (1959) maintained that, logically, only a falsification approach could settle the matter, for no matter how many confirming instances were recorded, one can never be certain that there will be no future disconfirming instances. Just one disconfirming instance will, however, demonstrate that something is wrong in the specification of the theory and its derived hypothesis. Therefore, in this view, scientists should set out to *disprove* a hypothesis.

Falsification is logically correct, and its implied skepticism may introduce rigor into hypothesis testing, but in social science in particular, hypotheses cannot be universal statements and are often probabilistic. In the example above, no one would suggest that everyone migrates under the particular given circumstances, but that one is more or less likely to migrate. Indeed, in many situations, the decision as to whether one should declare a hypothesis confirmed or falsified may be just a matter of a few percentage points' difference between attitudes or behaviors in survey findings.

Hypotheses can be specified at different levels. Research hypotheses are linguistic statements about the world whose confirmation/falsification likewise can be stated only linguistically as "none," "all," "some," "most," and so on. In qualitative research, a hypothesis might be framed in terms of a social setting having certain features, which, through observation, can be confirmed or falsified. However, in survey or experimental research, hypothesis testing establishes the statistical significance of a finding and, thus, whether that finding arose by chance or is evidence of a real effect. A null hypothesis is stated—for example, that there is no relationship between migration and housing tenure—but if a significant relationship is found, then the null hypothesis is rejected and the alternative hypothesis is confirmed. The alternative hypothesis may be the same as, or a subdivision of, a broader research hypothesis (Newton & Rudestam, 1999, pp. 63–65).

—Malcolm Williams

REFERENCES

Chalmers, A. (1999). *What is this thing called science?* (3rd ed.). Buckingham, UK: Open University Press.

Newton, R., & Rudestam, K. (1999). *Your statistical consultant: Answers to your data analysis questions.* Thousand Oaks, CA: Sage.

Popper, K. (1959). *The logic of scientific discovery.* London: Routledge.

HYPOTHESIS TESTING. *See*
SIGNIFICANCE TESTING

HYPOTHETICO-DEDUCTIVE METHOD

This method is commonly known as the "method of hypothesis." It involves obtaining or developing a THEORY, from which a hypothesis is logically deduced (deduction), to provide a possible answer to a "why" RESEARCH QUESTION associated with a particular research problem. The hypothesis is tested by comparing it with appropriate DATA from the context in which the problem is being investigated.

The foundations of the hypothetico-deductive method were laid by the English mathematician and theologian William Whewell (1847) as a counter to the method of INDUCTION advocated much earlier by Francis Bacon. Whewell debated the notion of induction with his contemporary, John Stuart Mill (1879/1947). He was critical of Mill's view that scientific knowledge consists of forming generalizations from a number of particular observations, and he challenged the view that observations can be made without preconceptions. He rejected the idea that generalizing from observations is the universally appropriate scientific method and argued that hypotheses must be invented at an early stage in scientific research in order to account for what is observed. For him, observations do not make much sense until the researcher has organized them around some conception. In short, he shifted the source of explanations from observations to constructions in the mind of the scientist that will account for observed phenomena.

These conceptions may involve the use of concepts or phrases that have not been applied to these "facts" previously. In Kepler's case, it was *elliptical orbit,* and for Newton, it was *gravitate.* Whewell argued that the process requires "inventive talent"; it is a matter of guessing several conceptions and then selecting the right one. He thought that it was impossible to doubt the truth of a hypothesis if it fits the facts well. In spite of this self-validation, he was prepared to put hypotheses to the test by making predictions and appropriate observations. It is on this latter point that Whewell anticipated Karl Popper's FALSIFICATIONISM.

Popper (1972) was not particularly interested in the notion of hypotheses as organizing ideas. Rather, he was concerned with the view of science in which hypotheses, or conjectures, were produced as tentative answers to a research problem, and were then tested. According to Popper, in spite of the belief that science proceeds from observation to theory, to imagine that we can start with pure observation, as in POSITIVISM, without anything in the nature of a theory is absurd. Observations are always selective and occur within a frame of reference or a "horizon of expectations." Rather than wait for regularities to impose themselves on us from our observations, according to Popper, we must actively impose regularities upon the world. We must jump to conclusions, although these may be discarded later if observations show that they are wrong.

Hence, Popper concluded that it is up to the scientist to invent regularities in the form of theories. However, the attitude must be critical rather than dogmatic. The dogmatic attitude leads scientists to look for confirmation for their theories, whereas the critical attitude involves a willingness to change ideas through the testing and possible refutation of theories. He argued that we can never establish whether theories are, in fact, true; all we can hope to do is to eliminate those that are false. Good theories will survive critical tests.

—Norman Blaikie

REFERENCES

Blaikie, N. (1993). *Approaches to social enquiry.* Cambridge, UK: Polity.

Popper, K. R. (1972). *Conjectures and refutation.* London: Routledge & Kegan Paul.

Mill, J. S. (1947). *A system of logic.* London: Longman, Green. (Originally published in 1879.)

Whewell, W. (1847). *The philosophy of the inductive sciences* (Vols. 1 & 2). London: Parker.

I

IDEAL TYPE

Ideal types are CONSTRUCTS used for data analysis in qualitative social research. The idea that ideal types can be used for systematic comparative analysis of historical data (including life-history data) was originally developed by Max Weber. Weber's methodology of ideal types has been adapted in ideal-type analysis to fulfill the requirements of multi-case study research. Through the use of ideal types, life history data are analyzed systematically on a case-by-case basis, arriving at structural explanations. Ideal-type analysis is a branch of interpretive social research dealing with narrative (textual) data materials that are organized in multiple case trajectories.

HISTORICAL DEVELOPMENT

The idea of ideal type was originally devised by Max Weber to explain sociologically individual cultural phenomena. That is, Weber (1904/1949) constructed ideal types as explanatory schemes when he wished to understand individual case material taken from the "infinite causal web" of social reality (p. 84). Alfred Schütz, another theorist who also used ideal types in his research, realized that not only are ideal types valid constructions for microsociological theory, but the social world itself is organized in ideal-type structures (Schütz, 1932/1967, 1955/1976).

Against this background, Gerhardt (1985, 1994) introduced ideal-type analysis into qualitative research. She applied it in two major studies, demonstrating its systematic scope (Gerhardt, 1986, 1999). The approach has become established in Germany and elsewhere (e.g., Leisering & Leibfried, 1999).

LEVELS OF CASE ANALYSIS

Cases are the focus of ideal-type analysis in three stages of the research act. For one, cases are units of analysis established through data processing; second, cases are selected for their relative capacity of ideal-type representation; and third, case explanation is the ultimate goal of ideal-type analysis. The three levels of case work are the following:

1. *Case reconstruction*, which entails reconstruction of all cases in the data set as a sequence of stages following an analytical scheme. Case reconstruction arranges cases as sequential patterns such that each case can be compared with all other cases in the data set.

2. *Selection of paradigmatic cases*, which is the outcome of comparative analysis of cases (following systematic case reconstruction). When clusters of similar cases emerge, within each cluster, one or more paradigmatic cases can be chosen that epitomize the respective typical pattern.

3. *Case explanation*, which is the eventual objective of the research act, follows structural explanation (see next section). For Weber and also for modern ideal-type analysis, the aim is to explain systematically the developmental dynamics of empirical cases.

ANALYTICAL PROCEDURE

Through analytical procedures on two separate levels, on both of which ideal types are used, descriptions as well as structural explanations are reached. The descriptions serve to construct descriptive types that epitomize the dynamics of the cases. The explanations are geared toward understanding the structural patterns that explain the dynamics of the case material. The use of ideal types to understand patterns of social life on both a descriptive as well as a structural level has two separate stages in the analytical procedure:

1. *Descriptive Ideal Types.* Through comparison between cases as they are reconstructed using the analytical scheme, clusters of similar cases emerge. These may be pictured choosing a paradigmatic case taken as ideal type. The ideal-type case epitomizes the case dynamics in the respective cluster. Through comparison between a paradigmatic case (ideal-type case) and all other cases in the cluster, applying the same procedure to each cluster of cases, a rich picture of case dynamics emerges. This picture shows the pattern in each group as well as that of all groups on a comparative basis. This allows for a variety of comparisons in the empirical material, yielding a tableau of variation of patterns epitomized in ideal-type paradigmatic cases.

2. *Structural Ideal Types.* If the question is asked, "Why do cases develop as they do?" social structures come into the picture. Structural explanation of pattern dynamics is needed. Only through ideal-type-based structural explanation can explanation of individual cases be accomplished. Such explanation determines why a case follows a structural pattern dynamics, which it does more or less closely. To arrive at the selection of ideal-type cases that can be used for structural pattern explanation, a catalogue of case characteristics must be set up that—under the analytical perspective of the research project—defines what would be the features or composition of an optimal case. The ideal-type case chosen on this basis is to be found in the empirical material. The ideal-type case epitomizes the structural pattern, the latter being mirrored in its case characteristics as closely as possible. In-depth analysis of the ideal-type case reveals the structural dynamics of the "pure" type in the structural pattern. Heuristically, to use a Weberian term, the ideal-type case represents the structural pattern for analytical purposes. Analytically, however, not only an optimal case but also a worst-case scenario should be established. Juxtaposing the analytical pictures derived from the best-case as well as the worst-case analytical scenarios yields a prolific tableau of patterns. These patterns define the structural backgrounds of potential case dynamics in the analyzed case material. High- versus low-class status groups and multimarriage versus never-married family background, to name but two, are social structural patterns whose dynamics may be investigated using ideal-type analysis.

Ideal-type cases allow for explanations linking cases with structural patterns. Because social structures are realized to a variable degree in the cases in the data material, their typicality in relation to the ideal-type case(s) helps understand their structural versus individual developmental dynamics. Comparative analysis juxtaposing ideal-type cases with other cases in the data material allows also for analysis of subgroups, and so on, which further enriches the findings achieved through structural pattern explanation.

AN EXAMPLE

Our study of biographies of coronary artery bypass (CABS) patients investigated 60 cases (using 240 interviews). They were selected preoperatively on the basis that each fulfilled four known criteria (social and medical) predicting postoperative return to work. Slightly more than half the cases did eventually return to work postoperatively; the others preferred or were eventually pushed into early retirement. Case reconstruction yielded four patterns, namely successful revascularization/return to work, failure of revascularization/return to work, successful revascularization/early retirement, failure of revascularization/early retirement. These four groups were investigated further using descriptive ideal types (cases paradigmatic for each of the four patterns). In order to explain the case trajectories, all cases were recoded using four criteria of optimum outcome (postoperative absence of symptoms, improvement of income, absence of marital conflict over postoperative decision regarding return to work or retirement, satisfactory doctor-patient relationship). Only two cases fulfilled all four criteria—one a return-to-work case, and the other an early-retirement one. They turned out to differ with respect to a number of explanatory parameters, namely social class, age at the time of CABS, marital status, subjective perception of health status, and—expressed in their narratives—central life interest. Whereas the upper-class, older return-to-work case had a central life interest favoring his job and occupation, the lower-class, younger early-retirement case had a non-work-related central life interest (favoring his leisure and the prospect of old age without work stress). The two ideal-type cases were then used to explain the course of events in all other cases, using cross-case comparative analysis (comparing biographical trajectories against the background of parameters such as, among others, social class). One main result of the study was the following: Return to work or early retirement after CABS depends more on type of central life interest than outcome of revascularization.

IDEAL TYPES AND MEASUREMENT

Max Weber (1904/1949) made it clear that ideal-type analysis aims at measurement. He expressed it as follows: "Such concepts are constructs in terms of which we formulate relationships by the application of the category of objective possibility. By means of this category, the adequacy of our imagination, oriented and disciplined by reality, is *judged*" (p. 93). Following on from Weber, and showing how Weber's ideas of ideal-type methodology can be transformed into a method of modern qualitative research, Gerhardt (1994) writes about case explanation as measurement of the case development in a particular individual biography whose course was pitted against an ideal-type case in the respective data material:

This case explanation may serve as an example of how the individual case often represents chance and unforeseen hazards. These emerge as specific when the case is held against the ideal-type case. Apparently irrational elements, to be sure, explain the case by making understandable its unique dynamics—just as Weber suggested. (p. 117)

—Uta Gerhardt

REFERENCES

Gerhardt, U. (1985). Erzähldaten und Hypothesenkonstruktion. *Kölner Zeitschrift für Soziologie und Sozialpsychologie, 37,* 230–256.

Gerhardt, U. (1986). *Patientenkarrieren: Eine idealtypen-analytische Studie.* Frankfurt: Suhrkamp.

Gerhardt, U. (1994). The use of Weberian ideal-type methodology in qualitative data interpretation: An outline for ideal-type analysis. *BMS Bulletin de Methodologie Sociologique* (International Sociological Association, Research Committee 33), *45,* 76–126.

Gerhardt, U. (1999). *Herz und Handlungsrationalität: Eine idealtypen-analytische Studie.* Frankfurt: Suhrkamp.

Leisering, L., & Leibfried, S. (1999). *Time and poverty in Western welfare states.* New York: Cambridge University Press.

Schütz, A. (1967). *Der sinnhafte Aufbau der sozialen Welt* [Phenomenology of the social world]. Evanston, IL: Northwestern University Press. (Originally published in 1932)

Schütz, A. (1976). Equality and the meaning structure of the social world. In *Collected Papers II* (pp. 226–273). The Hague: Martinus Nijhoff. (Originally published in 1955)

Weber, M. (1949). Die "Objektivität" sozialwissenschaftlicher und sozialpolitischer Erkenntnis ["Objectivity" in social science and social policy]. In *The methodology of the social sciences: Max Weber* (pp. 50–112). New York: Free Press. (Originally published in 1904)

IDEALISM

Idealism is a philosophical position that underpins a great many epistemological stances in social science. All of these share a common view that reality is mind dependent or mind coordinated. Although idealism might be seen as contrary to REALISM, which postulates a mind-independent reality, idealist thought spans a range of positions. These positions do not reject outright the existence of an external reality; rather, they point to the limits of our knowledge of it.

Indeed, one of the most important idealist philosophers, Kant, held that the only way we can conceive of ourselves as mind-endowed beings is in the context of existing in a world of space and time (Körner, 1955, Chap. 4). What is important is that we can know phenomena only through mind-dependent perception of it, we cannot ever know the thing in itself, what he called *noumena*. Kant's *transcendental idealism* has been enormously influential both directly and indirectly, perhaps most importantly in the work of Max Weber. He shifted the issue of knowing away from the thing itself to a refinement of our instruments of knowing, specifically "ideal types." Ideal types are not averages or the most desirable form of social phenomena, but ways in which an individual can reason from a shared rational faculty to a model or pure conceptual type that would exist if all agents acted perfectly rationally. Therefore, Weber's methodology depends crucially on rationality as the product of minds (Albrow, 1990).

Hegel's idealism is very different from Kant's. Kantian philosophy emphasizes the epistemological through a refinement of the instruments of knowing, whereas Hegel emphasizes the ontological through a development of our understanding of mind. Unlike Kant's noumena, Hegel believed mind (and minds as a universal category) could be known through a dialectical process of contradiction and resolution—ironically, a method most famously associated with Marx, a materialist and realist!

Most expressions of idealist social science are not obviously or directly traceable to Kant or Hegel, but simply begin from the premise that the social world consists of ideas, that it exists only because we think it exists, and we reproduce it on that basis. The means of that reproduction is considered to be language, and thus, idealism underpins the "linguistic turn" in social science. An important originator, at least in the Anglophone world, was Peter Winch (1958/1990), who argued that rule-following in social life consisted of linguistic practice and, because language is subject to variation (and shapes culture accordingly), then to know a culture, one must come to know the language of that culture. Winch's philosophy is an important constituent of ETHNOMETHODOLOGY and, less directly, more recent POSTMODERNIST approaches.

—Malcolm Williams

REFERENCES

Albrow, M. (1990). *Max Weber's construction of social theory.* London: Macmillan.

Körner, S. (1955). *Kant.* Harmondsworth, UK: Penguin.

Winch, P. (1990). *The idea of a social science and its relation to philosophy.* London: Routledge. (Originally published in 1958)

IDENTIFICATION PROBLEM

In the social sciences, empirical research involves the consistent ESTIMATION of POPULATION parameters from a prespecified system consisting of data, a parameterized model, and statistical MOMENT conditions. In this context, an identification problem is any situation where the PARAMETERS of the model cannot be consistently estimated. Systems that yield consistent estimates of the model's parameters are *identified*, and those that do not are *not identified*. Sometimes, a system may produce consistent estimates of a subset of its parameters, in which case the identification problem is at the parameter level. Identification problems can be loosely differentiated into two classes: those caused by *insufficient moment conditions*, and those caused by an *overparameterization* of the model. However, there is a substantive degree of overlap in these classifications (an overparameterized model can be thought of

as having too few moment conditions, and vice versa). Simple theoretical and empirical examples of these phenomena are discussed below.

ORDINARY LEAST SQUARES (OLS) regression can be thought of as a solution to an identification problem caused by *insufficient moment conditions*. Consider the simple *deterministic* system

$$y_i = \alpha + x_i\beta + \varepsilon_i, \quad i = 1, \dots, n, \quad (1)$$

where the ε_i are nonrandom slack terms. Equation (1) alone cannot determine the unknown parameters α and β; there are essentially n equations and $n + 2$ unknowns (think of the n slack terms as unknowns, too). Therefore, the system lacks two equations for identification. However, if the slack terms are stochastic errors, then the two OLS moment conditions

$$E(\varepsilon_i) = 0 \text{ (zero-mean condition)}, \quad (2)$$

$$E(x_i\varepsilon_i) = 0 \text{ (exogeneity condition)} \quad (3)$$

provide the two necessary equations to identify consistent estimates of α and β via OLS regression.

The familiar INSTRUMENTAL VARIABLE technique is a leading case of a solution to an identification problem. If the exogeneity condition in equation (3) fails, then the system in equations (1) and (2) lacks one identifying moment condition. If there are suitable instruments z_i for the x_i, then the four additional equations

$$x_i = \gamma + z_i\delta + v_i, \quad i = 1, \dots, n,$$
$$E(v_i) = 0,$$
$$E(z_i v_i) = 0,$$
$$E(z_i \varepsilon_i) = 0,$$

along with equations (1) and (2), identify the parameters: α, β, γ, and δ (effectively, $2n + 4$ equations and $2n + 4$ unknowns, counting the ε_i and v_i as unknowns). Notice that the system defined by equations (1) and (2) is also *identified* (trivially) if $\beta = 0$, so this identification problem could be thought of naively as one of *overparameterization*.

A substantive example of the *overparameterization* class of identification problems is the Simultaneous Equations problem, which is typically solved with parameter restrictions on the system. Simultaneously determined variables in a system containing more than one modeling equation often fail exogeneity conditions like equation (3). For example, if y_i and x_i are simultaneously determined and z_i is EXOGENOUS, then a simultaneous model might be

$$y_i = x_i \beta_1 + z_i \theta_1 + \varepsilon_{1i}, \qquad (4)$$

$$x_i = y_i \beta_2 + z_i \theta_2 + \varepsilon_{2i}, \qquad (5)$$

$i = 1, \ldots, n$, where $\mathrm{E}(\varepsilon_{1i}) = \mathrm{E}(\varepsilon_{2i}) = \mathrm{E}(\varepsilon_{1i}\varepsilon_{2i}) = \mathrm{E}(z_i\varepsilon_{1i}) = \mathrm{E}(z_i\varepsilon_{2i}) = 0$. Neither equation in this system is *identified*. To see this, notice that y_i in equation (4) is correlated with ε_{2i} through x_i in equation (5). Similarly, x_i in equation (5) is correlated with ε_{1i} through y_i in equation (4). Therefore, the entire system fails the OLS exogeneity condition and cannot be consistently estimated. Moreover, some algebra shows that equations (4) and (5) are identical up to parameters, so no solution is forthcoming. If theory suggests the parameter restriction $\theta_1 = 0$, then the equations are not identical, and z_i may be an appropriate instrument for y_i. Then, equation (5) could be consistently estimated using instrumental variable techniques. Equation (4) remains *not identified*, because all of the information contained in the data (x_i, y_i, z_i) has been exhausted. A complete theoretical treatment of identification problems in Simultaneous Equations models can be found in Greene (2003), Kmenta (1997), Schmidt (1976), or Wooldridge (2003).

Manski (1995) presents some empirical examples of the identification problem in applied social science research. For example, Manski's *mixing problem* in social program evaluation is an identification problem. That is, outcomes of controlled social program experiments, administered homogeneously to an experimental treatment sample, may not produce the same results that would exist were the social program to be administered heterogeneously across the population. Therefore, the potential outcomes of a social program across the population may not be identified in the outcomes of a social program experiment. Additionally, the *selection problem* in economic models of wage determination is an identification problem. Market wage data typically exclude wage observations of individuals in the population who choose not to work; therefore, estimates of wage parameters for the general population (working and nonworking), based solely on wage data from those that select into the labor market, may not be identified. In both of these examples, identification is achieved by bringing prior information to bear on the problem; see Manski (1995). Insofar as this prior information can be formulated

as additional moment conditions, the previous mixing and selection problems are identification problems of insufficient moment conditions.

—William C. Horrace

REFERENCES

Greene, W. H. (2003). *Econometric analysis* (5th ed.). Upper Saddle River, NJ: Prentice Hall.

Kmenta, J. (1997). *Elements of econometrics* (2nd ed.). Ann Arbor: University of Michigan Press.

Manski, C. F. (1995). *Identification problems in the social sciences*. Cambridge, MA: Harvard University Press.

Schmidt, P. (1976). *Econometrics*. New York: Marcel Dekker.

Wooldridge, J. M. (2003). *Introductory econometrics* (2nd ed.). Mason, OH: South-Western.

IDIOGRAPHIC/NOMOTHETIC. *See* NOMOTHETIC/IDIOGRAPHIC

IMPACT ASSESSMENT

Impact assessment involves a comprehensive evaluation of the long-term effects of an intervention. With regard to some phenomenon of interest, such as a community development program, the evaluator asks: What impact has this program had on the community, in terms of both intended and unintended effects (Patton, 1997)?

Impact assessment brings a broad and holistic perspective to evaluation. The first level of assessment in evaluation is at the resource or input level: To what extent did the project or program achieve the targeted and needed level of resources for implementation? The second level of assessment is implementation analysis: To what extent was the project or program implemented as planned? The third level of analysis focuses on outputs: To what extent did the project or program produce what was targeted in the original plan or proposal in terms of levels of participation, completion, or products produced? The fourth level of analysis involves evaluating outcomes: To what extent and in what ways were the lives of participants in a project or program improved in accordance with specified goals and objectives? Finally, the ultimate level of evaluation is impact assessment: To what extent, if at all, were outcomes sustained or increased over the long term, and what ripple effects, if any, occurred in the larger context (e.g., community)?

Consider an educational program. The first level of evaluation, inputs assessment, involves looking at the extent to which resources are sufficient—adequate buildings, materials, qualified staff, transportation, and so forth. The second level of evaluation, implementation analysis, involves examining the extent to which the expected curriculum is actually taught and whether it is taught in a high-quality way. The third level of evaluation involves outputs, for example, graduation rates; reduced dropout rates; parent involvement indicators; and satisfaction data (student, parents, and teachers). The fourth level, outcomes evaluation, looks at achievement scores, quality of student work produced, and affective and social measures of student growth. Finally, impact assessment looks at the contribution of the education program to students after graduation, over the long term, and the effects on the broader community where the program takes place, for example, community pride, crime rates, home ownership, or businesses attracted to a community because of high-quality schools or repelled because of poorly performing schools.

In essence, then, there are two dimensions to impact assessment, a *time dimension* and a *scope dimension*. The time dimension is long term: What effects endure or are enhanced beyond immediate and shorter term outcomes? *Outcomes evaluation* assesses the direct instrumental linkage between an intervention and participant changes like increased knowledge, competencies, and skills, or changed attitudes and behaviors. In contrast, *impact assessment* examines the extent to which those outcomes are maintained and sustained over the long term. For example, a school readiness program may aim to prepare young children for their first year of school. The outcome is children's performance during that first year in school. The impact is their performance in subsequent years.

The second dimension of impact assessment is scope. Outcomes evaluation looks at the narrow, specific, and direct linkage between the intervention and the outcome. Impact assessment looks more broadly for ripple effects, unintended consequences, side effects, and contextual effects. Impact assessment includes looking for both positive and negative effects, as well as both expected and unanticipated effects. For example, the desired and measured outcome of a literacy program is that nonliterate adults learn to read. The impacts might include better jobs for those

adults, greater civic participation, and even higher home ownership or lower divorce rates. Therefore, impact assessment looks beyond the direct, immediate causal connection to longer term and broader scope effects.

This broader and longer term perspective creates methodological challenges. Everything and anything is open for investigation because one is seeking unexpected and unanticipated effects as well as planned and foreseen ones. The community is often the unit of analysis for impact assessments (Lichfield, 1996). Comprehensive impact assessment requires multiple methods and measurement approaches, both QUANTITATIVE and QUALITATIVE, and both deductive and inductive reasoning. CAUSAL connections become increasingly diffuse and difficult to follow over time and as one moves into more complex systems beyond the direct and immediate causal linkages between a program INTERVENTION and its immediate outcome. Therefore, impact assessment is also costly.

With greater attention to the importance of systems understandings in social science, impact assessment has become increasingly valued, although challenging to actually conduct.

—Michael Quinn Patton

REFERENCES

Lichfield, N. (1996). *Community impact evaluation*. London: University College Press.

Patton, M. Q. (1997). *Utilization-focused evaluation: The new century text* (3rd ed.). Thousand Oaks, CA: Sage.

IMPLICIT MEASURES

The distinction between *implicit* and *explicit* processes originated from work in cognitive psychology but is now popular in other areas, such as social psychology. Implicit processes involve lack of awareness and are unintentionally activated, whereas explicit processes are conscious, deliberative, and controllable. Measures of implicit processes (i.e., implicit measures) include response latency procedures (e.g., the Implicit Association Test) (Greenwald et al., 2002); memory tasks (e.g., the process-dissociation procedure) (Jacoby, Debner, & Hay, 2001); physiological reactions (e.g., galvanic skin response); and indirect questions (e.g., involving attributional biases).

Implicit measures include such diverse techniques as the tendency to use more abstract versus concrete language when describing group members, preferences for letters that appear in one's own name, and response times to make decisions about pairs of stimuli. In one popular response-time technique for assessing racial biases, the Implicit Association Test (IAT) (Greenwald et al., 2002), participants first perform two categorization tasks (e.g., labeling names as Black or White, classifying words as positive or negative) separately, and then the tasks are combined. Based on the well-substantiated assumption that people respond faster to more associated pairs of stimuli, the speed of decisions to specific combinations of words (e.g., Black names with unpleasant attributes vs. Black names with unpleasant characteristics) represents the implicit measure. In contrast, explicit measures are exemplified by traditional, direct, SELF-REPORT MEASURES.

Perhaps because the various types of implicit measures are designed to address different aspects of responding (e.g., awareness or controllability) and focus on different underlying processes or systems (e.g., conceptual or perceptual), relationships among different implicit measures of the same social concepts or attitudes are only moderate in magnitude and highly variable. In addition, implicit measures have somewhat lower levels of TEST-RETEST RELIABILITY than do explicit measures (Fazio & Olson, 2003).

The relationship between implicit and explicit measures is also modest and variable (Dovidio, Kawakami, & Beach, 2001). One potential reason for the discordance between implicit and explicit measures is that they are differentially susceptible to strategic control. Explicit measures are more transparent and higher in REACTIVITY than are implicit measures. As a consequence, the correspondence between implicit and explicit measures tends to be weaker in more socially sensitive domains. Another explanation for the inconsistent relation between implicit and explicit measures is that people often have dual attitudes about people and objects—one relatively old and habitual, the other newer and conscious. Because implicit measures tap habitual attitudes and explicit measures assess more recently developed attitudes, implicit and explicit measures may be uncorrelated when the two components of the dual attitudes diverge.

In conclusion, implicit measures represent a diverse range of techniques that is fundamentally different from direct, explicit measures in terms of objectives, implementation, assumptions, and interpretation. Moreover, because these are newly emerging techniques, their psychometric properties (RELIABILITY and VALIDITY) tend to be less well substantiated than are those for many established explicit measures (e.g., prejudice scales). Nevertheless, the application of implicit measures has already made substantial contributions for understanding human memory, cognition, and social behavior.

—John F. Dovidio

REFERENCES

Dovidio, J. F., Kawakami, K., & Beach, K. R. (2001). Implicit and explicit attitudes: Examination of the relationship between measures of intergroup bias. In R. Brown & S. L. Gaertner (Eds.), *Blackwell handbook of social psychology: Intergroup processes* (pp. 175–197). Malden, MA: Blackwell.

Fazio, R. H., & Olson, M. A. (2003). Implicit measures in social cognition research: Their meaning and use. *Annual Review of Psychology, 54,* 297–327.

Greenwald, A. G., Banaji, M. R., Rudman, L. A., Farnham, S. D., Nosek, B. A., & Mellott, D. S. (2002). A unified theory of implicit attitudes, stereotypes, self-esteem, and self-concept. *Psychological Review, 109,* 3–25.

Jacoby, L. L., Debner, J. A., & Hay, J. F. (2001). Proactive interference, accessibility bias, and process dissociations: Valid subject reports of memory. *Journal of Experimental Psychology: Memory, Learning, and Cognition, 27,* 686–700.

IMPUTATION

MISSING DATA are common in practice and usually complicate data analyses. Thus, a general-purpose method for handling missing values in a data set is to impute, that is, fill in one or more plausible values for each missing datum so that one or more completed data sets are created. In principle, each of these data sets can be analyzed using standard methods that have been developed for complete data. Typically, it is easier first to impute for the missing values and then use a standard, complete-data method of analysis than to develop special statistical techniques that allow the direct analysis of incomplete data. In social surveys, for example, it is quite typical that the missing values occur on different variables. Income information might be most likely to be withheld, perhaps followed by questions about sexual habits, hygiene, or religion.

Correct analyses of the observed incomplete data can quickly become cumbersome. Therefore, it is often easier to use imputation.

Another great advantage of imputation occurs in the context of producing a public-use data set, because the imputer can use auxiliary confidential and detailed information that would be inappropriate to release to the public. Moreover, imputation by the data producer solves the missing data problem in the same way for all users, which ensures consistent analyses across users.

Imputation also allows the incorporation of observed data that are often omitted from analyses conducted by standard statistical software packages. Such packages often handle incomplete data by LIST-WISE DELETION, that is, by deleting all cases with at least one missing item. This practice is statistically inefficient and often leads to substantially biased inferences. Especially in multivariate analyses, listwise deletion can reduce the available data considerably, so that they are no longer representative of the population of interest. A multivariate analysis based only on the completely observed cases will often lose a large percentage, say 30% or more, of the data, which, minimally, reduces the precision of estimates.

Moreover, basing inferences only on the complete cases implicitly makes the assumption that the missing data are missing completely at random (MCAR), which is not the case in typical settings. In social surveys, special socioeconomic groups or minorities are often disproportionately subject to missing values. If, in such cases, the missingness can be explained by the observed rather than missing variables, the missing data are said to be missing at random (MAR) and can be validly imputed conditionally on the observed variables. Often, it is quite plausible to assume that differences in response behavior are influenced by completely observed variables such as gender, age group, living conditions, social status, and so on.

If the missingness depends on the missing values themselves, then the data are missing not at random (MNAR). (See Little & Rubin, 2002, for formal definitions.) This might be the case for income reporting, where people with higher incomes tend to be less likely to respond, even within cells defined by observed variables (e.g., gender and district of residence). Even in such cases, however, (single or multiple) imputation can help to reduce bias due to nonresponse.

SINGLE IMPUTATION

Typically, imputation is used for item-NONRESPONSE, but it can also be used for unit-nonresponse. Many intuitively appealing approaches have been developed for single imputation, that is, imputing one value for each missing datum. A naïve approach replaces each missing value on a variable with the unconditional sample mean of that variable or the conditional sample mean after the cases are grouped (e.g., according to gender). In regression imputation, a REGRESSION of the variable with missing values on other observed variables is estimated from the complete cases. Then, the resulting prediction equation is used to impute the estimated conditional mean for each missing value. In stochastic regression imputation, a random residual is added to the regression prediction, where the random error has variance equal to the estimated residual variance from the regression.

Another common procedure is hot deck imputation, which replaces the missing values for an incomplete case by the observed values from a so-called donor case. A simple hot deck defines imputation cells based on a cross-classification of some variables that are observed for both complete and incomplete cases (e.g., gender and district of residence). Then, the cases with observed values are matched to each case with missing values to create a donor pool, and the observed values from a randomly chosen donor are transferred (imputed) to replace the missing values.

With nearest neighbor imputation, a distance (metric) on the observed variables is used to define the best donor cases. When the distance is based on the difference between cases on the predicted value of the variable to be imputed, the imputation procedure is termed *predictive mean matching*. In the past decade, considerable progress has been made in developing helpful hot deck and nearest neighbor procedures.

Little (1988) gives a detailed discussion of issues in creating imputations. One major consideration for imputation is that random draws rather than best predictions of the missing values should be used, taking into account all observed values. Replacing missing values by point estimates, such as means, conditional means, or regression predictions, tends to distort estimates of quantities that are not linear in the data, such as VARIANCES, COVARIANCES, and CORRELATIONS. In general, mean imputation can be very harmful to valid estimation and even more harmful to valid inference (such as CONFIDENCE INTERVALS). Stochastic regression imputation and hot deck procedures are acceptable for point estimation, although special corrections are needed for the resulting variance estimates. Methods of variance estimation have been developed for the hot deck and nearest neighbor techniques, but they are limited to specific univariate statistics; for a recent discussion, see Groves, Dillman, Eltinge, and Little (2002).

MULTIPLE IMPUTATION

Imputing a single value for each missing datum and then analyzing the completed data using standard techniques designed for complete data will usually result in standard error estimates that are too small, confidence intervals that undercover, and p values that are too significant; this is true even if the modeling for imputation is carried out absolutely correctly. Multiple imputation (MI), introduced by Rubin in 1978 and discussed in detail in Rubin (1987), is an approach that retains the advantages of imputation while allowing the data analyst to make valid assessments of uncertainty. MI is a MONTE CARLO technique that replaces the missing values by $m > 1$ simulated versions, generated according to a probability distribution indicating how likely the true values are given the observed data. Typically, m is small, such as $m = 5$. Each of the imputed (and thus completed) data sets is first analyzed by standard methods; the results are then combined to produce estimates and confidence intervals that reflect the missing data uncertainty.

The theoretical motivation for multiple imputation is BAYESIAN, although the resulting multiple imputation inference is also usually valid from a frequentist viewpoint. Formally, Bayesian MI requires independent random draws from the posterior predictive distribution of the missing data given the observed data:

$$f(y_{\text{mis}}|y_{\text{obs}}) = \int f(y_{\text{mis}}, \theta|y_{\text{obs}}) \, d\theta$$
$$= \int f(y_{\text{mis}}|y_{\text{obs}}, \theta) f(\theta|y_{\text{obs}}) \, d\theta.$$

(For ease of reading, the colloquial "distribution" is used in place of the formally correct "probability density function.") Because it is often difficult to draw from $f(y_{\text{mis}}|y_{\text{obs}})$ directly, a two-step procedure for each of the m draws is useful:

1. Draw the parameter θ according to its observed-data posterior distribution $f(\theta|y_{\text{obs}})$.

2. Draw the missing data Y_{mis} according to their conditional predictive distribution, $f(y_{\text{mis}}|y_{\text{obs}}, \theta)$, given the observed data and the drawn parameter value from Step 1.

For many models, the conditional predictive distribution $f(y_{\text{mis}}|y_{\text{obs}}, \theta)$ in Step 2 is relatively straightforward due to iid aspects of the complete-data model used. On the contrary, the corresponding observed-data posterior distribution, $f(\theta|y_{\text{obs}}) = f(y_{\text{obs}}|\theta) f(\theta)/f(y_{\text{obs}})$, usually is difficult to derive, especially when the data are multivariate and have a complicated pattern of missingness. Thus, the observed-data posterior distribution is often not a standard distribution from which random draws can be generated easily. However, straightforward iterative imputation procedures have been developed to enable multiple imputation via MARKOV CHAIN MONTE CARLO METHODS; many examples are discussed extensively by Schafer (1997). Such data augmentation procedures (Tanner & Wong, 1987), which include, for example, GIBBS SAMPLING, yield a stochastic sequence $\{(y_{\text{mis}}^{(t)}, \theta^{(t)}), t = 1, 2, \dots \}$ whose stationary distribution is $f(y_{\text{mis}}, \theta|y_{\text{obs}})$. More specifically, an iterative sampling scheme is created, as follows. Given a current guess $\theta^{(t)}$ of the parameter, first draw a value $y_{\text{mis}}^{(t+1)}$ of the missing data from the conditional predictive distribution $f(y_{\text{mis}}|y_{\text{obs}}, \theta^{(t)})$. Then, conditioning on $y_{\text{mis}}^{(t+1)}$, draw a new value $\theta^{(t+1)}$ of θ from its complete-data posterior $f(\theta|y_{\text{obs}}, y_{\text{mis}}^{(t+1)})$. Assuming that t is suitably large, m independent draws from such chains can be used as multiple imputations of Y_{mis} from its posterior predictive distribution $f(y_{\text{mis}}|y_{\text{obs}})$.

Now consider the task of estimating an unknown quantity, say, Q. In the remainder of this section, the quantity Q, to be estimated from the multiply imputed data set, is distinguished from the parameter θ used in the model for imputation. Although Q could be an explicit function of θ, one of the strengths of the multiple imputation approach is that this need not be the case. In fact, Q could even be the parameter of a model chosen by the analyst of the multiply imputed data set, and this analyst's model could be different from the imputer's model. As long as the two models are not overly incompatible or the fraction of missing information is not high, inferences based on the multiply imputed data should still be approximately valid. Rubin (1987) and Schafer (1997, Chapter 4) and their references discuss the distinction between Q and θ more fully.

The MI principle assumes that the complete-data statistic, $\hat{Q}$, and its variance estimate, $\hat{V}(\hat{Q})$, can be regarded as the approximate complete-data posterior mean and variance for Q, that is, $\hat{Q} \approx E(Q|y_{\text{obs}}, y_{\text{mis}})$ and $\hat{V}(\hat{Q}) \approx V(Q|y_{\text{obs}}, y_{\text{mis}})$ based on a suitable complete-data model and prior distribution. Moreover, with complete data, tests and interval estimates based on the large sample normal approximation

$$(\hat{Q} - Q)/\sqrt{\hat{V}(\hat{Q})} \sim N(0, 1)$$

should work well. Notice that the usual MAXIMUM-LIKELIHOOD ESTIMATES and their asymptotic variances derived from the inverted Fisher information matrix typically satisfy these assumptions. Sometimes, it is necessary to transform the estimate $\hat{Q}$ to a scale for which the normal approximation can be applied; for other practical issues, see Rubin (1987), Schafer (1997) and Little and Rubin (2002).

After m imputed data sets have been created, the m complete-data statistics $\hat{Q}^{(i)}$ and their variance estimates $\hat{V}(\hat{Q}^{(i)})$ are easily calculated for $i = 1, \ldots, m$. The final MI point estimate $\hat{Q}_{\text{MI}}$ for the quantity Q is simply the average

$$\hat{Q}_{\text{MI}} = \frac{1}{m} \sum_{i=1}^{m} \hat{Q}^{(i)}.$$

Its estimated total variance T is calculated according to the ANALYSIS OF VARIANCE principle, as follows:

- The "between-imputation" variance

$$B = \frac{1}{m-1} \sum_{i=1}^{m} \left(\hat{Q}^{(i)} - \hat{Q}_{\text{MI}}\right)^2.$$

- The "within-imputation" variance

$$W = \frac{1}{m} \sum_{i=1}^{m} \hat{V}\left(\hat{Q}^{(i)}\right).$$

- The "total variance"

$$T = W + \left(1 + \frac{1}{m}\right) B.$$

The correction $(1 + \frac{1}{m})$ reflects the estimation of Q from a finite number (m) of imputations. Tests and two-sided interval estimates can be based on the approximation $(\hat{Q}_{\text{MI}} - Q)/\sqrt{T} \sim t_\nu$ where t_ν denotes the Student's t-distribution with degrees of freedom

$$\nu = (m-1)\left(1 + \frac{W}{(1 + m^{-1})B}\right)^2.$$

Barnard and Rubin (1999) relax the above assumption of a normal reference distribution for the complete-data interval estimates and tests to allow a t-distribution, and they derive the corresponding degrees of freedom for the MI inference to replace the formula for ν given here. Moreover, additional methods are available for combining vector estimates and covariance matrices, p values, and LIKELIHOOD RATIO STATISTICS (see Little & Rubin, 2002).

The multiple imputation interval estimate is expected to produce a larger but valid interval than an estimate based only on single imputation because the interval is widened to account for the missing data uncertainty and simulation error. Even with a small number of imputations (say, $m = 3$ or 4), the resulting inferences generally have close to their nominal coverages or significance levels. Hot deck procedures or stochastic regression imputation can be used to create multiple imputations, but procedures not derived within the Bayesian framework are often not formally proper in the sense defined by Rubin (1987), because additional uncertainty due to estimating the parameters of the imputation model is not reflected.

Proper MI methods reflect the sampling variability correctly; that is, the resulting multiple imputation inference is valid also from a frequentist viewpoint if the imputation model itself is valid. Stochastic regression imputation can be made proper by following the two-step procedure described previously for drawing Y_{mis} from its posterior predictive distribution, and thus, first drawing the parameters of the regression model (Step 1), and then using the drawn parameter values in the usual imputation procedure (Step 2). Rubin and Schenker (1986) propose the use of BOOTSTRAPPING to make hot deck imputation proper; the resulting procedure is called the approximate Bayesian bootstrap. This two-stage process first draws a bootstrap sample from each donor pool and then draws imputations randomly from the bootstrap sample; it is a nonparametric analogue to the two-step procedure for drawing Y_{mis}. Thus, approximately proper multiple imputations can often be created using standard imputation procedures in a straightforward manner.

COMPUTATIONAL ISSUES

Various single imputation techniques, such as mean imputation, conditional mean imputation, or regression imputation, are available in commercial statistical software packages such as SPSS. With the increasing computational power, more and more multiple imputation techniques are being implemented, making multiple imputation procedures quite easy to implement for both creating multiply imputed data sets and analyzing them.

There are programs and routines available for free, such as the stand-alone Windows program NORM or the S-PLUS libraries NORM, CAT, MIX, PAN, and MICE (also available for R now). NORM uses a normal model for continuous data, and CAT a LOG-LINEAR MODEL for categorical data. MIX relies on a general location model for mixed categorical and continuous data. PAN is designed to address PANEL data. The new missing data library in S-PLUS 6 features these models and simplifies consolidating the results of multiple complete-data analyses after multiple imputation.

Moreover, there are the free SAS-callable application IVEware and the SAS procedures PROC MI and PROC MIANALYZE based on normal asymptotics. PROC MI provides a parametric and a nonparametric regression imputation approach, as well as the multivariate normal model. Both MICE and IVEware are very flexible tools for generating multivariate imputations for all kinds of variables by using chained equations. AMELIA (a free Windows version as well as a Gauss version) was developed especially to fit certain social sciences' needs.

Finally, SOLAS for Missing Data Analysis 3.0 is a commercial Windows program provided by Statistical Solutions Limited. For links and further details, see www.multiple-imputation.com or Horton and Lipsitz (2001).

SUMMARY AND SOME EXTENSIONS

Imputation enables the investigator to apply immediately the full range of techniques that is available to analyze complete data. General considerations and a brief discussion of modeling issues for creating imputations have been given; also discussed has been how multiply imputed data sets can be analyzed to draw valid inferences.

Another advantage of MI for the social sciences may lie in splitting long questionnaires into suitable parts, so that only smaller questionnaires are administered to respondents, promising better response rates, higher data quality, and reduced costs. The missing data are thus created by design to be MCAR or MAR, and can be multiply imputed with good results; for the basic idea, see Raghunathan and Grizzle (1995).

Although Bayesian methods are often criticized because prior distributions have to be chosen, this is also an advantage when IDENTIFICATION PROBLEMS

occur. For example, multiple imputations of missing data under different prior settings allow sensitivity analyses; for an application to statistical matching, see Rubin (1986) or Rässler (2002).

Finally, empirical evidence suggests that multiple imputation under MAR often is quite robust against violations of MAR. Even an erroneous assumption of MAR may have only minor impact on estimates and standard errors computed using multiple imputation strategies. Only when MNAR is a serious concern and the fraction of missing information is substantial does it seem necessary to model jointly the data and the missingness. Moreover, because the missing values cannot be observed, there is no direct evidence in the data to address the MAR assumption. Therefore, it can be more helpful to consider several alternative models and to explore the sensitivity of resulting inferences.

Thus, a multiple imputation procedure seems to be the best alternative at hand to account for missingness and to exploit all valuable available information. In general, it is crucial to use multiple rather than single imputation so that subsequent analyses will be statistically valid.

—Susanne Rässler, Donald B. Rubin, and Nathaniel Schenker

AUTHORS' NOTE: The views expressed in this entry do not necessarily represent the views of the U.S. government, and Dr. Schenker's participation as a coauthor is not meant to serve as an official endorsement of any statement to the extent that such statement may conflict with any official position of the U.S. government.

REFERENCES

Barnard, J., & Rubin, D. B. (1999). Small-sample degrees of freedom with multiple imputation. *Biometrika, 86,* 948–955.

Groves, R. M., Dillman, D. A., Eltinge, J. L., & Little, R. J. A. (2002). *Survey nonresponse.* New York: Wiley.

Horton, N. J., & Lipsitz, S. R. (2001). Multiple imputation in practice: Comparison of software packages for regression models with missing variables. *The American Statistician, 55,* 244–254.

Little, R. J. A. (1988). Missing data adjustments in large surveys. *Journal of Business and Economic Statistics, 6,* 287–301.

Little, R. J. A., & Rubin, D. B. (2002). *Statistical analysis with missing data.* New York: Wiley.

Raghunathan, T. E., & Grizzle, J. E. (1995). A split questionnaire survey design. *Journal of the American Statistical Association, 90,* 54–63.

Rässler, S. (2002). Statistical matching: A frequentist theory, practical applications, and alternative Bayesian approaches. *Lecture Notes in Statistics, 168.* New York: Springer.

Rubin, D. B. (1986). Statistical matching using file concatenation with adjusted weights and multiple imputations. *Journal of Business and Economic Statistics, 4,* 87–95.

Rubin, D. B. (1987). *Multiple imputation for nonresponse in surveys.* New York: Wiley.

Rubin, D. B., & Schenker, N. (1986). Multiple imputation for interval estimation from simple random samples with ignorable nonresponse. *Journal of the American Statistical Association, 81,* 366–374.

Schafer, J. L. (1997). *Analysis of incomplete multivariate data.* London: Chapman and Hall.

Tanner, M. A., & Wong, W. H. (1987). The calculation of posterior distributions by data augmentation (with discussion). *Journal of the American Statistical Association, 82,* 528–550.

INDEPENDENCE

Social scientists are usually interested in empirical questions such as, "Is living in a metropolitan area associated with facing a higher crime rate (Event *B*)?" and "Is making more than $50,000 a year independent of having a college degree?" We answer these kinds of questions with reference to the concept of statistical *independence* and *dependence*. Two "events" are said to be statistically independent of each other if the occurrence of one event in no way affects the PROBABILITY of the other event. This general idea can be extended to any number of independent events that have nothing to do with each other. In contrast, if the occurrence of one event affects the likelihood of the other event, then these two events are said to be associated or statistically dependent.

If two events are independent from each other, the fact that one event has occurred will not affect the probability of the other event. Suppose neither the probability of Event *A* [i.e., $P(A)$] nor the probability of Event *B* [i.e., $P(B)$] is zero. Statistical independence between these two events suggests that the conditional probability of *A* given *B* [i.e., $P(A|B)$] is exactly the same as the marginal (or unconditional) probability of *A* [i.e., $P(A)$]. That is, if *A* and *B* are independent, then $P(A|B) = P(A)$. Likewise, one should expect that the conditional probability of *B* given *A* [i.e., $P(B|A)$] is the same as the probability of Event *B* [i.e., $P(B)$] if these two events are independent of each other. In other words, if *A* and *B* are independent of each other, then $P(B|A) = P(B)$ and $P(A|B) = P(A)$.

The usual definition of statistical independence is that Event *A* and Event *B* are independent if and only if their joint probability [i.e., $P(A \cap B)$] is equal to the product of their respective marginal (or unconditional) probabilities, $P(A) \times P(B)$. Consider two independent Events *A* and *B*. We know $P(A|B) = P(A)$, then because $P(A|B) = \frac{P(A \cap B)}{P(B)}$, we obtain $P(A \cap B) = P(A) \times P(B)$ under the assumption that $P(B) \neq 0$. Likewise, the information $P(B|A) = P(B)$ leads to the same statement $P(B \cap A) = P(A) \times P(B)$ in the same way. This definition of mutual independence can be extended to multiple events. Specifically, Events *A, B, C, . . . , Z*, each having a nonzero probability, are independent if and only if

$$P(A \cap B \cap C \cap \cdots \cap Z)$$
$$= P(A) \times P(B) \times P(C) \times \cdots \times P(Z).$$

Suppose we toss a fair six-sided die twice. Let Event *A* be the occurrence of an odd number and Event *B* be getting an even number. We know that $P(A) = \frac{3}{6} = \frac{1}{2}$ (1 or 3 or 5 occurs) and $P(B) = \frac{3}{6} = \frac{1}{2}$ (2 or 4 or 6 occurs). The probability that the first toss will show an odd number (Event *A*) and the second an even number (Event *B*) is $P(A \cap B) = P(A) \times P(B) = \frac{1}{2} \times \frac{1}{2} = \frac{1}{4}$ because the two tosses are independent from each other. Similarly, the probability of getting three tails from flipping an unbiased coin three times is simply $P(T_1 \cap T_2 \cap T_3) = P(T_1) \times P(T_2) \times P(T_3) = \frac{1}{2} \times \frac{1}{2} \times \frac{1}{2} = \frac{1}{8}$.

Consider an example in which statistical independence does not hold. Table 1 is a CONTINGENCY TABLE showing population cross-classification of a purely hypothetical community. If a resident is randomly selected from this population, what is the probability that this resident will be a white Republican? Let *A* be the event that we get a Republican resident and *B* be the event that we get a white resident. Because there are 860 Republican residents in all, $P(A) = \frac{860}{1480}$ or about .581. Similarly, the probability of getting a white resident is $P(B) = \frac{1100}{1480}$ or about .743. Among the 1,100 white residents, there are 600 people who identified themselves as a Republican. Thus, if we are given the information that a resident is white, the probability of this person's being a Republican is 600/1100 or about .545. Likewise, if we are given the information that a resident is a Republican, the probability of this person's being a white resident is 600/860

Table 1   Population Cross-Classification Showing Statistical Dependence

Ethnic Group	Party Identification			Total
	Democratic	Independent	Republican	
White	400	100	600	1,100
Non-White	100	20	260	380
Total	500	120	860	1,480

or .698. We thus have $P(A) = .581$, $P(B) = .743$, $P(A|B) = .545$, and $P(B|A) = .698$. One can find that $P(A \cap B) \neq P(A) \times P(B)$ in this example because we obtain

$$P(A \cap B) = P(A) \times P(B|A) = .581 \times .698 \cong .406$$
$$\text{or} = P(B) \times P(A|B) = .743 \times .545 \cong .405.$$

Because $P(A) \times P(B) = .581 \times .743 = .432$, we find the joint probability of A and B, that is, $P(A \cap B)$, is not equal to the product of their respective probabilities. Thus, these two events are associated. Statistical methods employed to test independence between variables depend on the nature of the data. More information about the statistical test of independence may be found in Alan Agresti and Barbara Finlay (1997), Agresti (2002), and Richard A. Johnson and Gouri K. Bhattacharyya (2001).

—Cheng-Lung Wang

REFERENCES

Agresti, A. (2002). *Categorical data analysis* (2nd ed.). New York: Wiley Interscience.

Agresti, A., & Finlay, B. (1997). *Statistical methods for the social sciences.* Upper Saddle River, NJ: Prentice Hall.

Johnson, R. A., & Bhattacharyya, G. K. (2001). *Statistics: Principles and methods* (4th ed.). New York: Wiley.

INDEPENDENT VARIABLE

An independent variable is any variable that is held to have a causal impact on another variable, referred to as the DEPENDENT VARIABLE. The notion of what can be taken to be an independent variable varies between experimental and nonexperimental research (see entries on INDEPENDENT VARIABLE (IN EXPERIMENTAL RESEARCH) and INDEPENDENT VARIABLE (IN NONEXPERIMENTAL RESEARCH).

—Alan Bryman

INDEPENDENT VARIABLE (IN EXPERIMENTAL RESEARCH)

A defining characteristic of every true experiment is the independent variable (IV), an adjustable or alterable feature of the experiment controlled by the researcher. Such variables are termed independent because they can be made independent of their natural sources of spatial and temporal covariation. The researcher decides whether or not the IV is administered to a particular participant, or group of participants, and the variable's magnitude or strength. Controlled variations in the IV are termed experimental treatments or manipulations. Variations in the presence or amount of an IV are termed the levels of the treatment. Treatment levels can be quantitative (e.g., 5, 10, 35 mg of a drug) or qualitative (participant assigned to Workgroup A, B, or C). IVs may be combined in FACTORIAL DESIGNS, and their interactive effects assessed. The IV is critical in the LABORATORY EXPERIMENT because it forms the basis for the inference of causation. Participants assigned randomly to different conditions of an experiment are assumed initially equivalent. Posttreatment differences on the DEPENDENT VARIABLE between participants receiving different levels of the IV are causally attributed to the IV.

Crano and Brewer (2002) distinguish three general forms of IVs: social, environmental, and instructional treatments. Social treatments depend on the actions of people in the experiment, usually actors employed by the experimenter, whose behavior is scripted or controlled. In Asch's (1951) classic conformity studies, naïve participants made a series of comparative judgments in concert with others. In fact, these others were not naïve, but were accomplices who erred consistently on prespecified trials. In one condition, one accomplice whose erroneous report was different from that of his peers shattered the (incorrect) unanimity of the accomplice majority. Differences between unanimous and nonunanimous groups were interpreted as having been caused by controlled variations in the uniformity of accomplices' responses.

Environmental treatments involve the systematic manipulation of some feature(s) of the physical setting. In an attitude change experiment, for example, all participants may be exposed to the same persuasive communication, but some may receive the message under highly distracting circumstances, with noise and commotion purposely created for the experiment. Differences in susceptibility to the message between participants exposed under normal versus distracting conditions are interpreted causally, if participants were randomly assigned to the distraction or normal communication contexts, and the experimenter controlled the presence or absence of the distraction.

Instructional manipulations depend on differences in instructions provided to participants. For example, Zanna and Cooper (1974) gave participants a pill and suggested to some that they would feel tense and nervous, whereas others were informed that the pill would help them relax. In fact, the pill contained an inert substance that had no pharmacological effects. Differences in participants' subsequent judgments were attributed to variations in the instructional manipulation, the IV.

For strict experimentalists, factors that differentiate participants (e.g., sex, religion, IQ, personality factors), and other variables not under the control of the researcher (e.g., homicide rates in Los Angeles), are not considered independent and thus are not interpreted causally. However, in some research traditions, variables not under experimental control sometimes are suggested as causes. For example, a strong negative correlation between marriage rates in a society at Time 1, and suicides at Time 2, might be interpreted as marriage causing a negative impact on suicides. Marriage, it might be suggested, causes contentment and thus affects the likelihood of suicide. The opposite conclusion is untenable: Suicide rates at Time 2 could not have affected earlier marriage rates. However, such conclusions are usually (and appropriately) presented tentatively, insofar as a third, unmeasured variable might be the true cause of the apparent relationship. In the present example, economic conditions might be the true causal operator, affecting marriage rates at Time 1, and suicides at Time 2. Owing to the possibility of such third-variable causes, causal inferences based on correlational results are best offered tentatively. In the ideal experimental context, such extraneous influences are controlled, and hence their effects cannot be used to explain differences between groups receiving different levels of the IVs.

—William D. Crano

REFERENCES

Asch, S. E. (1951). Effects of group pressure upon the modification and distortion of judgments. In H. Guetzkow (Ed.), *Groups, leadership, and men* (pp. 177–190). Pittsburgh, PA: Carnegie Press.

Crano, W. D., & Brewer, M. B. (2002). *Principles and methods of social research* (2nd ed.). Mahwah, NJ: Lawrence Erlbaum.

Zanna, M. P., & Cooper, J. (1974). Dissonance and the pill: An attribution approach to studying the arousal properties of dissonance. *Journal of Personality and Social Psychology, 29,* 703–709.

INDEPENDENT VARIABLE (IN NONEXPERIMENTAL RESEARCH)

Also known as EXPLANATORY VARIABLE or input variable, an independent variable—or, more precisely, its effect on a DEPENDENT VARIABLE—is what a researcher analyzes in typical quantitative social science research. Strictly speaking, an independent variable is a variable that the researcher can manipulate, as in EXPERIMENTS. However, in nonexperimental research, variables are not manipulated, so that it is sometimes unclear which among the various variables studied can be regarded as INDEPENDENT VARIABLES. Sometimes, researchers use the term loosely to refer to any variables they include on the right-hand side of a REGRESSION equation, where causal inference is often implied. But it is necessary to discuss what qualifies as an independent variable in different RESEARCH DESIGNS. When data derive from a CROSS-SECTIONAL DESIGN, information on all variables is collected coterminously, and no variables are manipulated. This means that the issue of which variables have causal impacts on other variables may not be immediately obvious. Nonmanipulation of variables in disciplines such as sociology, political science, economics, and geography arises for several reasons: It may not be possible to manipulate certain variables (such as ethnicity or gender); it may be impractical to manipulate certain variables (such as the region in which people live); or it may be ethically and politically unacceptable (such as the causal impact of poverty). Some of these variables (e.g., race, ethnicity, gender, country of origin, etc.) are regarded as "fixed" in the analysis. Contrary to the definition of manipulatibility in experimental research, fixed variables are not at all manipulatible but nevertheless are the ones that can be safely considered and treated as "independent" in nonexperimental research.

With longitudinal designs, such as a PANEL DESIGN, the issue is somewhat more complex, because although variables are still not manipulated, the fact that data can be collected at different points in time allows some empirical leverage on the issue of the temporal and hence causal priority of variables. Strict experimentalists might still argue that the lack of manipulation casts an element of doubt over the issue of causal priority. To deal with this difficulty, analysts of panel data resort to the so-called cross-lagged panel analysis for assessing causal priority among a pair of variables measured at two or more points in time. The line between dependent and independent variables in such analysis in a sense is blurred because the variable considered causally precedent is treated as an independent variable in the first regression equation but as a dependent variable in the second. Conversely, the variable considered causally succedent is treated as dependent in the first equation and as independent in the second. Judging from analyses like this, it appears that the term *independent variable* can be quite arbitrary; what matters is clear thinking and careful analysis in nonexperimental research.

Given that it is well known that it is wrong to infer causality from findings from a single regression run about relationships between variables, which is what are usually gleaned from nonexperimental research, how can we have independent variables in such research? Researchers employing nonexperimental research designs (such as a SURVEY design) must engage in *causal inference* to tease out independent variables. Essentially, this process entails a mixture of commonsense inferences from our understanding about the nature of the social world and from existing theory and research, as well as analytical methods in the area that is the focus of attention. It is this process of causal inference that lies behind such approaches as CAUSAL MODELING and PATH ANALYSIS, to which the cross-lagged panel analysis is related.

To take a simple example: It is well known that age and voting behavior are related. Does that mean that all we can say is that the two variables are correlated? Because the way we vote cannot be regarded in any way as having a causal impact on our ages, it seems reasonable to assume that age is the independent variable. Of course, there may be INTERVENING VARIABLES or MODERATING VARIABLES at work that influence the causal path between age and voting behavior, but the basic point remains that it is still possible and sensible to make causal inferences about such variables.

Making causal inferences becomes more difficult when causal priority is less obvious. For example, if we find as a result of our investigations in a large firm that employees' levels of organizational commitment and their job satisfaction are correlated, it may be difficult to establish direction of causality, although existing findings and theory relating to these variables might provide us with helpful clues. A panel study is often recommended in such circumstances as a means of disentangling cause and effect.

—Alan Bryman and Tim Futing Liao

REFERENCES

Davis, J. A. (1985). *The logic of causal order* (Sage University Paper Series on Quantitative Applications in the Social Sciences, 07–055). Beverly Hills, CA: Sage

Rosenberg, M. (1968). *The logic of survey analysis*. New York: Basic Books.

IN-DEPTH INTERVIEW

In-depth interview is a term that refers to the UNSTRUCTURED INTERVIEW, the SEMISTRUCTURED INTERVIEW, and, sometimes, to other types of INTERVIEW IN QUALITATIVE RESEARCH, such as NARRATIVE INTERVIEWING and LIFE STORY INTERVIEWING.

—Alan Bryman

INDEX

An index is a measure of an abstract theoretical CONSTRUCT in which two or more indicators of the construct are combined to form a single summary score. In this regard, a SCALE is a type of index, and, indeed, the two terms are sometimes used interchangeably. But whereas scales arrange individuals on the basis of patterns of attributes in the data, an index is simply an additive composite of several indicators, called items. Thus, a scale takes advantage of any intensity structure that may exist among the attributes in the data, whereas an index simply assumes that all the items reflect the underlying construct equally, and therefore, the construct can be represented by summing the person's score on the individual items.

Indexes are widely used by government agencies and in the social sciences, much more so than scales. The consumer price index, for example, measures prices in various areas of the economy, such as homes, cars, real estate, consumer goods, and so forth. All of these entities contribute to the average prices that consumers pay for goods and services and therefore are included in the index. This example indicates why an index is generally preferred over a single indicator. Thus, the price of gasoline might spike at a particular time, but the price of other entities may be stable. It would be inaccurate and misleading to base the consumer prices just on the increasing cost of gasoline when the other items remained unchanged.

Furthermore, an index may not be unidimensional. For example, political scientists use a 7-point index to measure party identification. This index is arranged along a continuum as follows: strong Democrat, weak Democrat, independent leaning toward Democrat, independent, independent leaning toward Republican, weak Republican, strong Republican. One can easily see that this index consists of two separate dimensions. The first is a directional dimension, from Democrat through independent to Republican. However, there also exists an intensity dimension, going from strong through weak, independent, weak, and back to strong.

Frequently, governments use indexes of official statistics. For example, the consumer price index is used as a measure of the level of prices that consumers pay, and the FBI's crime index is the sum of the seven so-called index crime rates and is used as an overall indicator of crime in the United States.

—Edward G. Carmines and James Woods

REFERENCES

Carmines, E. G., & McIver, J. P. (1981). *Unidimensional scaling* (Sage University Paper Series on Quantitative Applications in the Social Sciences, 07–024). Beverly Hills, CA: Sage.

Nunnally, J. C. (1978). *Psychometric theory*. New York: McGraw-Hill.

INDICATOR. *See* INDEX

INDUCTION

In logic, induction is a process for moving from particular statements to general statements. This logic is used in the social sciences to produce THEORY from DATA. Many specific instances are used to produce a general conclusion that claims more than the evidence on which it is based. Theory consists of universal GENERALIZATIONS about connections between phenomena. For example, many observed instances of juvenile delinquents who have come from broken homes are used to conclude that "all juvenile delinquents come from broken homes."

This is a popular conception of how scientists go about their work, making meticulous and objective observations and measurements, and then carefully and accurately analyzing data. It is the logic of science associated with POSITIVISM, and it is contrasted with DEDUCTION, the logic associated with FALSIFICATIONISM.

The earliest form of inductive reasoning has been attributed to Aristotle and his disciples, known as *enumerative induction* or *naïve induction*. Later, in the 17th century, induction was advocated by Francis Bacon as *the* scientific method. He wanted a method that involved the "cleansing of the mind of all presuppositions and prejudices and reading the book of nature with fresh eyes" (O'Hear, 1989, p. 16). Bacon was critical of Aristotle's approach and argued that rather than simply accumulating knowledge by generalizing from observations, it is necessary to focus on negative instances. His was an "eliminative" method of induction that required the comparison of instances in which the phenomenon under consideration was both present and absent. Two centuries later, John Stuart Mill elaborated Bacon's ideas in his methods of agreement and difference. In the method of agreement, two instances of a phenomenon need to be different in all but one characteristic, whereas in the method of difference, two situations are required to be similar in all characteristics but one, the phenomenon being present with this characteristic.

Advocates of the logic of induction require that OBJECTIVE methods be used, that data be collected carefully and systematically, without preconceived ideas guiding their selection. Generalizations are then produced logically from the data. Once a generalization is established, further data can be collected to strengthen or verify its claim. Also, new observed instances can be explained in terms of the pattern in the generalization. For example, if the generalization about the relationship between juvenile delinquency and broken homes can be regarded as universal, then further cases of juvenile delinquency can be explained in terms of family background, or predictions can be made about juveniles from such a background. This is known as pattern explanation.

Induction has been severely criticized and rejected by many philosophers of science. The following claims have been contested: that preconceptions can be set aside to produce objective observations; that "relevant" observations can be made without some ideas to guide their selection; that inductive logic has the capacity to mechanically produce generalizations from data; that universal generalizations can be based on a finite number of observations; and that establishing patterns or regularities is all that is necessary to produce explanations (see Blaikie, 1993, Chalmers, 1982, and O'Hear, 1989, for critical reviews). DEDUCTION has been offered as an alternative.

Induction was first advocated as *the* method in the social sciences by Emile Durkheim in *Rules of Sociological Method* (1964) and was put into practice in his study of *Suicide*. In spite of its shortcomings, a modified form of induction is essential in descriptive social research concerned with answering "what" RESEARCH QUESTIONS (see Blaikie, 2000).

—Norman Blaikie

REFERENCES

Blaikie, N. (1993). *Approaches to social enquiry.* Cambridge, UK: Polity.

Blaikie, N. (2000). *Designing social research: The logic of anticipation.* Cambridge, UK: Polity Press.

Chalmers, A. F. (1982). *What is this thing called science?* St. Lucia: University of Queensland Press.

Durkheim, E. (1964). *Rules of sociological method.* Glencoe, IL: Free Press.

O'Hear, A. (1989). *An introduction to the philosophy of science.* Oxford, UK: Clarendon.

INEQUALITY MEASUREMENT

Individuals differ in countless ways. And groups are characterized by different levels of inequality in all the ways in which individuals differ. Several important examples of difference among individuals include income, wealth, power, life expectancy, and mathematical ability. There are inequalities among individuals in each of these dimensions, and different populations have different distributions of various characteristics across individuals. It is often the case that there are also inequalities among subgroups within a given population: men and women, rural and urban, black and white. It is often important to identify and measure various dimensions of inequality within a society. For the purposes of public policy, we are particularly interested in social inequalities that represent or influence differences in individuals' well-being, rights, or life prospects.

How do we measure the degree of inequalities within a POPULATION? There are several important alternative approaches, depending on whether the DISTRIBUTION of the factor is approximately NORMAL across the population. If the factor is distributed approximately normally, then the measurement of inequality is accomplished through analysis of the MEAN and STANDARD DEVIATION of the factor over the population. On this approach, we can focus on the descriptive statistics of the population with respect to the feature (income, life expectancy, weight, test scores): the shape of the distribution of scores, the mean and MEDIAN scores for the population, and the standard deviation of scores around the mean. The standard deviation of the VARIABLE across the population provides an objective measure of the degree of dispersion of the feature across the population. We can use such statistical measures to draw conclusions about inequalities across groups within a single population ("female engineers have a mean salary only 70% of that of male engineers"); conclusions about the extent of inequality in separate populations ("the variance of adult body weight in the United States is 20% of the mean, whereas the variance in France is only 12% of the mean"); and so forth.

A different approach to measurement is required for an important class of inequalities—those having to do with the distribution of resources across a population. The distribution of wealth and income, as well as other important social resources, is typically not statistically normal; instead, it is common to find distributions that are heavily SKEWED to the low end (that is, large numbers of individuals with low allocations). Here, we are explicitly interested in estimating the degree of difference in holdings across the population from bottom to top. Suppose we have a population of size N, and each individual i has wealth W_i, and consider the graph that results from rank ordering the population by wealth. We can now standardize the representation of the distribution by computing the percent of total wealth owned by each percent of population. And we can graph the percent of cumulative wealth against percentiles of population. The resulting graph is the Lorenz distribution of wealth for the population. Different societies will have Lorenz curves with different shapes; in general, greater wealth inequality creates a graph that extends further to the southeast. Several measures of inequalities result from the technique of organizing a population in rank order with respect to ownership of a resource. The GINI COEFFICIENT and the ratio of bottom quintile to top quintile of property ownership are common measures of inequality used in comparative economic development.

—Daniel Little

REFERENCES

Rae, D. W., & Yates, D. (1981). *Equalities*. Cambridge, MA: Harvard University Press.

Sen, A. (1973). *On economic inequality*. New York: Norton.

INEQUALITY PROCESS

The Inequality Process (IP) is a MODEL of the process generating inequality of income and wealth. The IP is derived from the surplus theory of social stratification of economic anthropology. In this theory, success in competition for surplus—wealth net of production cost—concentrates surplus, explaining why evidence of substantial inequality first occurs in the same layer in archeological excavations as the earliest evidence of hunter/gatherers' acquiring agriculture and its surpluses. Gerhard Lenski (1966) extended the surplus theory from the increase in inequality at the dawn of agriculture to the waning of inequality since the Industrial Revolution. Lenski HYPOTHESIZED that more educated people retain more of their surplus.

In words, the IP is as follows:

> People are randomly paired. Each competes for the other's wealth with a 50% chance to win. Each has two traits, wealth and omega, ω, the proportion of wealth lost in a loss. Winners take what losers lose. Repeat process.

Although winners gain, winning streaks are short. Wealth flows to those with smaller ω. Given Lenski's hypothesis, $(1 - \omega_i)$ is the IP's OPERATIONALIZATION of a worker at education level i.

The solution of the equations of IP competition shows that the IP's equilibrium DISTRIBUTION can be approximated by a two-PARAMETER gamma PROBABILITY DENSITY FUNCTION (pdf):

$$f_{it}(x) \equiv \frac{\lambda_{it}^{\alpha_i}}{\Gamma \alpha_i} x^{(\alpha_i - 1)} e^{-(\lambda_{it} x)} \qquad (1)$$

where

$\alpha_i \equiv$ shape parameter of individuals with ω_i,

$$\alpha_i \approx \frac{1 - \omega_i}{\omega_i}$$

$$\omega_i \approx \frac{1}{1 + \alpha_i} \qquad (2)$$

$\lambda_{it} \equiv$ shape parameter of individuals with ω_i,

$$\lambda_{it} \approx (1 - \omega_i) \frac{\left(\frac{w_{1t}}{\omega_1} + \frac{w_{2t}}{\omega_2} + \cdots + \frac{w_{it}}{\omega_i} + \cdots + \frac{w_{It}}{\omega_I}\right)}{\bar{x}_t}, \qquad (3)$$

$x \equiv$ wealth > 0, considered as a random variable,

$\bar{x}_t \equiv$ unconditional mean of wealth at time t,

$w_{it} \equiv$ proportion of population with ω_i at time t.

The IP reproduces (a) the higher mean earnings of the more educated, (b) the lower GINI of their earnings, and (c) the shapes of the distribution of earnings by level of education. The mean of x in $f_{it}(x)$ is

$$\bar{x}_{it} = \frac{\alpha_i}{\lambda_{it}} \approx \frac{\bar{x}_t}{\omega_i \left(\frac{w_{1t}}{\omega_1} + \cdots + \frac{w_{It}}{\omega_I}\right)} \qquad (4)$$

and increases with smaller ω_i, holding the distribution of education, the w_{it}s, constant. The McDonald and Jensen expression for the gamma pdf's Gini is

$$\text{Gini ratio of } f_{it}(x) = \frac{\Gamma(\alpha_i + \frac{1}{2})}{\sqrt{\pi} \, \Gamma(\alpha_i + 1)}. \qquad (5)$$

Given equation (2), Figure 1 shows how the Gini of x in $f_{it}(x)$ rises with greater ω_i. Empirically, the Gini of the earnings of the less educated is higher.

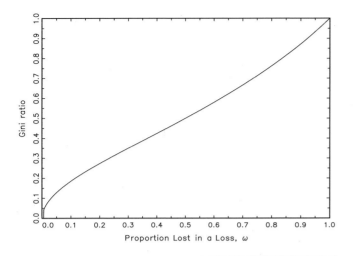

Figure 1   The Graph of the Gini Concentration Ratio of the Gamma PDF Whose Shape Parameter, α, Is Approximately Given by $(1 - \omega)/\omega$, Against ω

Figure 2 shows $f_{it}(x)$ fitting the distribution of wage and salary income of nonmetropolitan workers in the United States in 1987 by level of education. The shape parameter of the gamma pdf fitting distributions in

Figure 2, α_i, increases with education, so ω_i falls with education. The same sequence of shapes reappears throughout the industrial world.

A. B. Z. Salem and Timothy Mount (1974) advocate the two-parameter gamma pdf with no restrictions on its two parameters, the shape and scale parameters, to model income distribution. The parameters of the IP's gamma pdf model, $f_{it}(x)$, are restricted. Both are functions of ω_i. Figure 2 shows one year of the simultaneous fit of the IP's $f_{it}(x)$ to 33 years $\times$ 5 levels of education $=$ 165 distributions. In the example, $f_{it}(x)$ has one parameter taking on five values in the population modeled, five parameter values to estimate. Salem and Mount's method requires estimating (165 $\times$ 2 $=$) 330 parameters. Despite the fewer DEGREES OF FREEDOM, the IP's $f_{it}(x)$ fits nearly as well. Kleiber and Kotz (2003) discuss the IP in their chapter, "Gamma-Type Size Distributions".

—John Angle

REFERENCES

Angle, J. (1986). The Surplus Theory of Social Stratification and the size distribution of personal wealth. *Social Forces, 65,* 293–326.

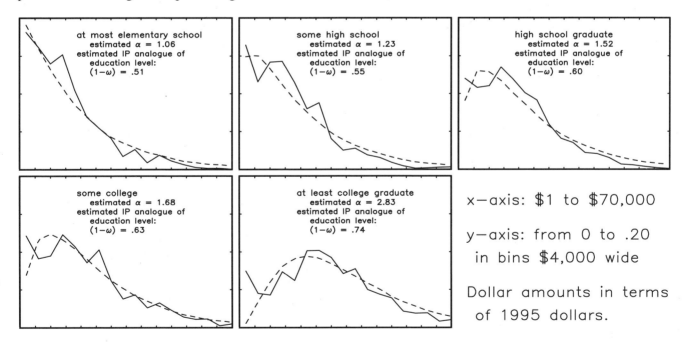

Figure 2   Relative Frequency Distribution of Annual Wage and Salary Income of Workers in 1987 (Residents of Nonmetropolitan Counties of U.S., Solid Curve) and Fitted IP Model (Dotted Curve). Workers Aged 25 to 65. One Year of Simultaneous Fits to Data from 1963 to 1995.

SOURCE: March Current Population Survey.

Angle, J. (2002). The statistical signature of pervasive competition on wage and salary incomes. *Journal of Mathematical Sociology, 26,* 217–270.

Kleiber, C., & Kotz, S. (2003). *Statistical size distributions in economics and actuarial sciences.* Hoboken, NJ: Wiley.

Lenski, G. (1966). *Power and privilege.* New York: McGraw-Hill.

Salem, A., & Mount, T. (1974). A convenient descriptive model of income distribution: The gamma density. *Econometrica, 42,* 1115–1127.

INFERENCE. *See* STATISTICAL INFERENCE

INFERENTIAL STATISTICS

Broadly, statistics may be divided into two categories: descriptive and inferential. Inferential statistics is a set of procedures for drawing conclusions about the relationship between sample statistics and population PARAMETERS. Generally, inferential statistics addresses one of two types of questions. First, what is the likelihood that a given sample is drawn from a population with some known parameter, θ? Second, is it possible to estimate a population parameter, θ, from a sample statistic?

Both operations involve inductive rather than deductive logic; consequently, no closed form proof is available to show that one's inference is correct (see CLASSICAL INFERENCE). By drawing on the CENTRAL LIMIT THEOREM (CLT) and using the appropriate method for selecting our observations, however, making a probabilistic inference with an estimable degree of certainty is possible.

It can be shown empirically, and proven logically through the CLT, that if repeated random samples of a given size, n, are drawn from a population with a mean, μ, the sample means will be essentially normally distributed with the mean of the sample means approximating μ. Furthermore, if the population elements are distributed about the population mean with a VARIANCE of σ^2, the sample means will have a sampling variance of σ^2/n. The standard deviation of the sample means is generally called the STANDARD ERROR to distinguish it from the standard deviation of a single sample.

As the sample size, n, increases, the closer will be the approximation of the distribution of the sample means to the normal distribution. Based on the description of the normal distribution, we know that about 68% of the area (or data points) under the normal curve is found within ± 1 standard deviation from the mean. Because we are dealing with a distribution of sample means, we conclude that 68% of the sample means also will be within ± 1 standard error of the true population mean.

Since the normal distribution is ASYMPTOTIC, it is possible for a given sample mean to be infinitely far away from the population mean. Common sense, however, tells us that although this is possible, it is unlikely. Hence, we have the first application of inferential statistics. A random sample is selected, and a relevant sample statistic such as $\bar{y}$ is calculated. Often, a researcher wants to know whether $\bar{y}$ is equivalent to the known mean, μ, of a population. For example, a sociologist might want to know whether the average income of a random sample of immigrants is equal to that of the overall population. The sociologist starts with the null hypothesis that $\bar{y} - \mu = 0$ against the alternative that $\bar{y} - \mu \neq 0$. The value of $\bar{y}$ is calculated from the sample, and μ and σ^2 are obtained from census values. The quantity

$$z = \frac{\bar{y} - \mu}{\sqrt{\sigma^2/n}}$$

provides an estimate of how many standard deviations the sample mean is from the population parameter. As the difference $\bar{y} - \mu$ increases, the practical likelihood that $\bar{y} = \mu$ decreases, and the more likely it is that the sample is from a population different from the one under consideration. There is only a 5% chance that a sample mean two standard deviations away from the population mean (i.e., a z value larger than 2) would occur by chance alone; the likelihood that it would be three or more standard deviations away drops to less than 0.3%.

The second basic question addressed by inferential statistics uses many of the ideas outlined above but formulates the problem in a different way. For example, a polling company might survey a random sample of voters on election day and ask them how they voted. The pollster's problem is whether estimating the population value, μ, is possible based on the results of the survey. The general approach here is to generate a confidence interval around the sample estimate, $\bar{y}$. Using the sample variance, s^2, as an estimate of the population variance, σ^2, the pollster estimates the standard error for the population as $\sqrt{s^2/n}$.

The pollster decides that being 95% "certain" about the results is necessary. Thus, a 95% confidence interval is drawn about $\bar{y}$ as: $\bar{y} \pm 1.96$ s.e. $(\bar{y})$ or $\bar{y} \pm 1.96\sqrt{s^2/n}$. The pollster now concludes that μ would be within approximately two standard errors of $\bar{y}$ 19 times out of 20, or with a 95% level of confidence.

These two basic approaches can be elaborated to address a variety of problems. For example, we might want to compare two or more sample means to determine whether they are statistically equivalent. This is the same as asking whether all of the samples are members of the same population. We can modify the formulas slightly given the type of information that is available. For example, sometimes the population variance, σ^2, is known, and sometimes it is not. When it is not known, we often estimate it from a sample variance. Similarly, when multiple samples are examined, we might pool their variances, if they are equivalent, to generate a better or more precise overall estimate of the population variance.

Clearly, one element that is central to inferential statistics is the assumption that the sampling distribution of the population is knowable. Using the CLT with nontrivial samples, we find that the sampling distribution approximates the normal distribution when simple random samples are selected. This assumption does not always hold. For example, with small samples, the population variance σ^2 is underestimated by the sample variance, s^2. With small samples, we often use the t-distribution, which is flatter at the peak and thicker in the tails than the normal distribution. The t-distribution is actually a family of distributions. The shape of a specific distribution is determined by the degrees of freedom, which, in turn, is related to the sample size.

In other circumstances, yet other distributions are used. For example, with count data, we often use the chi-square distribution. In comparing variances, we use the F-distribution first defined by Fisher. Occasionally, the functional form of the sampling distribution may not be known. In those circumstances, we will sometimes use what is known as a nonparametric or distribution-free statistic. Social scientists use a variety of these procedures, including such statistics as GAMMA, the KOLMOGOROV-SMIRNOV test, and the various Kendall's tau statistics.

With the advent of inexpensive computing, more scientists are using modeling techniques such as the jackknife and BOOTSTRAPPING to estimate empirical distributions. These procedures are not always ideal but can be used successfully to estimate the sampling distributions for such statistics as the median or the INTERQUARTILE RANGE. Modeling techniques are also useful when complex or nonrandom sampling procedures are used to generate samples.

There are also different frameworks within which the interpretation of results can be embedded. For example, BAYESIAN INFERENCE includes prior knowledge about the parameter based on previous research or the researcher's theoretical judgment as part of the inferential process. The likelihood approach, on the other hand, considers the parameter to have a distribution of possible values as opposed to being immutably fixed. Thus, within this approach, the distribution function of the sample results is judged conditional on the distribution of the possible parameter values.

—Paul S. Maxim

REFERENCES

Agresti, A., & Finlay, B. (1997). *Statistical methods for the social sciences* (3rd ed.). Upper Saddle River, NJ: Prentice Hall.

Hacking, I. (1965). *The logic of statistical inference.* Cambridge, UK: Cambridge University Press.

Maxim, P. S. (1999). *Quantitative research methods in the social sciences.* New York: Oxford University Press.

INFLUENTIAL CASES

One or a few cases may be considered as influential observations in a sample when they have excessive effects on the outcomes of an analysis.

—Kwok-fai Ting

INFLUENTIAL STATISTICS

One or a few cases may be considered as influential observations in a sample when they have excessive effects on the outcomes of an analysis. In other words, the removal of these observations may change some aspects of the statistical findings. Thus, the presence of influential observations threatens the purpose of making generalizations from a wide range of data. For example, a few observations with extremely large or exceptionally small values make the mean a less useful statistic in describing the central tendency of a distribution. Besides parameter estimates, influential observations can also affect the validity of SIGNIFICANCE TESTS and GOODNESS-OF-FIT MEASURES in small and large samples. Because of these potential problems, various influence statistics are formulated to assess the influence of each observation in an analysis.

Influence statistics were first discussed in linear regression analysis and were later extended to LOGISTIC REGRESSION analysis. These statistics attempt to measure two major components: leverage and residuals. Leverage is the power that an observation has in forcing the fitted function to move closer to its observed response. In regression analysis, observations that are further away from the center—that is, the point of the means of all predictors—have greater leverage in their favor. Thus, high-leverage observations are those with outlying attributes that separate themselves from the majority of a sample. A residual is the deviation of an observed response from the fitted value in an analysis. Large residuals are unusual in the sense that they deviate from the expected pattern that is projected by a statistical model. This is a cause of concern because observations with large residuals are often influential in the outcomes of a regression analysis; that is, the exclusion of these observations brings the fitted function closer to the remaining observations.

Graphic plots are useful visual aids for assessing the influence of outlying observations. Figure 1 illustrates three such observations that may have an undue influence on the fitted regression function in a bivariate analysis of hypothetical data. Observation 1 has a high leverage because it lies far away from the center of X, and it will exert a greater influence on the slope of the regression line. Although Observation 2 is near to the center of X, it deviates considerably from the expected value of the fitted regression function. The large residual is likely to affect the goodness-of-fit measure and significant test statistics. Observation 3 combines a high leverage with a large residual, making it more likely to distort the analytical results. For multivariate analyses, partial regression plots are more appropriate for the detection of influential observations because they take into account the multiple predictors in a model.

For quantitative measures, the hat-value is a common index of an observation's leverage in shaping the estimates of an analysis. Residuals are often measured by the studentized residuals—the ratios of residuals to their estimated standard errors. Several widely used influence statistics combine leverage and residuals in their computations. An idea that is common to these measures is the approximation of the consequences of sequentially dropping each observation to

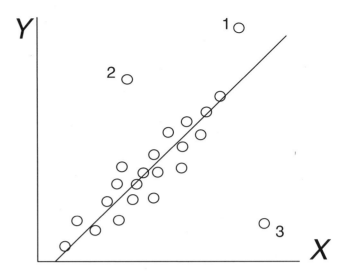

Figure 1   Bivariate Scatterplot With a Regression Line Fitted Without the Outlying Observations

assess its influence in an analysis. DFFITS examines the difference between two fitted response values of the same observation, with and without that observation contributing to the estimation. Cook's distance considers the effects of excluding an observation on all fitted values. DFBETAS evaluates the effects of excluding each observation on regression coefficients.

Influence statistics are heuristic devices that alert analysts of problematic observations in analyses. Although numeric cutoffs have been proposed for these statistics, many of them are suggestive rather than implied by statistical theories, and they should be used with flexibility. Graphic plots of these statistics are useful means of spotting major gaps that separate problematic observations from the rest. In practice, analysts need to replicate the analysis by excluding problematic observations to fully evaluate their actual effects. This does not mean that these observations, even when verified as influential to a given analysis, should be discarded in the final analysis. It is more important to seek the causes of their outlying patterns before looking for remedies. Common causes include coding errors, model misspecifications, and the pure chance of sampling.

—Kwok-fai Ting

REFERENCES

Belsley, D. A., Kuh, E., & Welsch, R. E. (1980). *Regression diagnostics: Identifying influential data and sources of collinearity*. New York: Wiley.

Bollen, K. A., & Jackman, R. W. (1990). Regression diagnostics: An expository treatment of outliers and influential cases. In J. Fox & J. S. Long (Ed.), *Modern methods of data analysis* (pp. 257–291). Newbury Park, CA: Sage.

Collett, D. (1991). *Modelling binary data.* New York: Chapman and Hall.

Cook, R. D., & Weisberg, S. (1982). *Residuals and influence in regression.* New York: Chapman and Hall.

Fox, J. (1991). *Regression diagnostics.* Newbury Park, CA: Sage.

INFORMANT INTERVIEWING

Informant interviews are of a more in-depth, less structured manner (semistructured, unstructured interviews) with a small selected set of informants most often in a field setting. What distinguishes this type of interview from other possible forms (e.g., cognitive tasks, survey interviews) is the depth, breadth, structure, and purpose of the interview format. Informant interviews can be used at various stages of the research enterprise to achieve a variety of different research interview objectives. Johnson and Weller (2002) make the distinction between top-down and bottom-up interviews. Bottom-up informant interviews aid in the clarification of less well-understood topics and knowledge domains and contribute to the construction of more valid STRUCTURED INTERVIEWING formats (e.g., structured questions) used in later stages of the research. Top-down informant interviews aid in the validation and alteration of existing structured questions (e.g., SURVEY questions) leading to the more valid adaptation of existing interviewing forms (e.g., cognitive tasks) to the research context.

An important use of informant interviews concerns the exploration of a less well-understood topic of interest. Informants are selected on the basis of their knowledge, experience, or understanding of a given topical area (Johnson, 1990). In such cases, the interviewer takes on the role of student and directs the interview in such a way as to learn from the informant, who is an expert in the area. Spradley's *The Ethnographic Interview* (1979) provides an excellent discussion of interviewing in this vein in his distinction of "grand tour" and "mini tour" questions in initial stages of interviewing. Grand tours involve asking questions that literally have the informant take the researcher on a tour of a given place, setting, or topical area. Other questions may direct informants, for example, to describe a typical day or a typical interaction. Mini tour questions seek more specific information on any of these more general topics. The objective of these unstructured questions is to learn more about the informant's subjective understanding of social setting, scene, or knowledge domain.

An understanding of local terminology and issues gained in tour type questioning can facilitate the development of more specific questions for informants. There are a variety of more directed and structured informant interview formats that include, for example, taxonomic approaches or free recall elicitation that provide for a more organized and systematic understanding of a given topic on the part of the informants. Furthermore, such interviews can be used to develop more systematic types of questions and scales (i.e., bottom-up) that provide the ability for comparative analysis of beliefs, knowledge, and so on among informants (or respondents). In sum, informant interviews are an essential component of many forms of research, particularly ETHNOGRAPHIC research, in that they provide for the collection of data that contributes significantly to the overall VALIDITY of the research enterprise.

—Jeffrey C. Johnson

REFERENCES

Johnson, J. C. (1990). *Selecting ethnographic informants.* Newbury Park, CA: Sage.

Johnson, J. C., & Weller, S. C. (2002). Elicitation techniques for interviewing. In J. F. Gubrium & J. A. Holstein (Eds.), *The handbook of interview research.* Thousand Oaks, CA: Sage.

Spradley, J. P. (1979). *The ethnographic interview.* New York: Holt, Rinehart and Winston.

INFORMED CONSENT

Voluntary informed consent refers to a communication process in which a potential subject decides whether to participate in the proposed research. *Voluntary* means without threat or undue inducement. *Informed* means that the subject knows what a reasonable person in the same situation would want to know before giving consent. *Consent* means an explicit agreement to participate. Fulfillment of informed consent, thus defined, can be challenging, especially when participants, for situational, intellectual, or cultural reasons, have compromised autonomy, or do not accept the social norms that typically accompany social or behavioral research.

HISTORICAL BACKGROUND

After World War II, it was learned that Nazi scientists had used prisoners in brutal medical experiments. These crimes were investigated at the Nuremberg trials of Nazi war criminals and resulted in development of the Nuremberg Code, which requires that scientists obtain the informed consent of participants. In 1974, the passage of the U.S. National Research Act established the National Commission for the Protection of Human Subjects in Biomedical and Behavioral Research (National Commission), and the use of Institutional Review Boards (IRBs) to oversee federally funded human research. The National Commission conducted hearings on ethical problems in human research, and it learned of biomedical research where concern for informed consent and well-being of subjects was overshadowed by other concerns. In their "Belmont Report," the National Commission formulated three principles to govern human research: respect for the autonomy and well-being of subjects, beneficence, and justice (see Ethical Principles). Informed consent is the main process through which respect is accorded to subjects.

ELEMENTS OF INFORMED CONSENT

The following elements of informed consent were set forth in the U.S. Federal Regulations of Human Research (Federal Regulations):

1. A statement that the study involves research, an explanation of the purposes of the research and expected duration of participation, a description of the procedures to be followed, and identification of any procedures that are experimental
2. A description of any reasonably foreseeable risks or discomforts to the subject
3. A description of any benefits to subjects or others that may reasonably be expected
4. A disclosure of appropriate alternative courses of treatment, if any, that might be advantageous to the subject (relevant primarily to clinical biomedical research)
5. A statement describing the extent, if any, to which confidentiality will be assured

6. For research involving more than minimal risk, a statement of whether any compensation or treatments are available if injury occurs
7. An explanation of whom to contact for answers to pertinent questions about the research, subjects' rights, and whom to contact in the event of a research-related injury
8. A statement that participation is voluntary, refusal to participate will involve no penalty, and the subject may discontinue participation at any time with impunity

Under the Federal Regulations, some or all of these elements of informed consent may be waived by the IRB if the research could not practicably be carried out otherwise. However, in waiving or changing the requirements, the IRB must document that there is no more than minimal risk to subjects; that the waiver will not adversely affect the rights and welfare of the subjects; and, whenever appropriate, that the subjects will be provided additional pertinent information after participation. These elements are often expressed in written form in a fairly standard format and are signed by research participants to indicate that they have read, understood, and agreed to those conditions. The requirement that the information be written or that the consent form be signed may be waived if the research presents no more than minimal risk of harm to subjects and involves no procedures for which written consent is normally required outside of the research context. It may also be waived in order to preserve confidentiality if breach of confidentiality could harm the subject and if the signed consent form is the only record linking the subject and the research.

Misapplication of Informed Consent

Many investigators and IRBs operate as though a signed consent form fulfills ethical requirements of informed consent. Some consent forms are long, complex, inappropriate to the culture of the potential subject, and virtually impossible for most people to comprehend. Confusing informed consent with a signed consent form violates the ethical intent of informed consent, which is to communicate clearly and respectfully, to foster comprehension and good decision making, and to ensure that participation is voluntary.

Why do researchers and IRBs employ poor consent procedures? The Federal Regulations of Human

Research (45 CFR 4) were written to regulate human research sponsored by the Department of Health and Human Services (HHS). Most HHS-sponsored research is biomedical, and not surprisingly, the federal regulations governing human research were written with biomedical research in mind. This biomedical focus has always posed problems for social and behavioral research. These problems became more severe when the Office for Human Research Protection (OHRP) began responding to complaints about biomedical research by suspending the funded research of the entire institution and holding its IRB responsible for causing harm to human subjects. Responsibility was established by inspecting the paperwork of the IRB at the offending institution and noting inadequate paperwork practices. Such highly publicized and costly sanctions against research institutions resulted in an environment of fear in which IRBs learned that it is in their self-interest and that of their institution to employ highly bureaucratic procedures, emphasizing paperwork instead of effective communication. Results of this new regulatory climate include many bureaucratic iterations before a protocol is approved, and requirement of subjects' signatures on long, incomprehensible consent forms.

These problems are further compounded because Subpart A of 45 CFR 46 has been incorporated into the regulatory structure of 17 federal agencies (Housing & Urban Development, Justice, Transportation, Veterans Affairs, Consumer Product Safety, Environmental Protection, International Development, National Aeronautics & Space Administration, National Science Foundation, Agriculture, Commerce, Defense, Education, Energy, Health & Human Services, Social Security, and Central Intelligence Agency). Subpart A, now known as the Common Rule, governs all social and behavioral research at institutions that accept federal funding. Consequently, most IRBs, in their efforts to "go by the book," require a signed consent form even when this would be highly disrespectful (e.g., within cultures where people are illiterate or do not believe in signing documents). Within mainstream Western culture, Singer (1978) and Trice (1987) have found that a significant number of subjects refuse to participate in surveys, studies, or experiments if required to sign a consent form, but would gladly participate otherwise. Among subjects who willingly sign documents, most sign the consent form without reading it.

These problems can be avoided if investigators and IRBs remember to exercise their prerogative to exempt specified categories of research, to conduct expedited review, or to waive written documentation of consent as permitted under 45 CFR 46.117(c), or if they recognize other ways of documenting informed consent (e.g., by having it witnessed, by the researcher's certification that the consent was conducted, or by audio or video recording of the consent procedure). Of most interest is paragraph (2) of 46.117(c) of the Federal Regulations: The IRB may waive the requirement for a signed consent form "if the research presents no more than minimal risk and involves no procedures for which written consent is normally required outside of the research context." Most social and behavioral research presents no more than minimal risk. The statement "no procedures for which written consent is normally required outside of the research context" refers to medical procedures. Consent forms are not used to document the patient's willingness to be interviewed or to complete questionnaires about their medical histories. Therefore, similarly personal questions might be asked of survey research respondents without triggering the requirement of documented informed consent, under the Common Rule. The following recommendations are offered in pursuit of intelligent interpretation of the Common Rule:

Informed consent should take the form of friendly, easily understood communication. When written, it should be brief and simply phrased at such a reading level that even the least literate subject can understand it. Subjects should have a comfortable context in which to think about what they have been told and to ask any questions that occur to them. The consent process may take many forms. For example, if conducting a housing study of elderly people at a retirement community, the interviewers should be mindful of the safety concerns of elders and of possible memory, auditory, and visual impairment. They might begin by holding a meeting at the community's meeting center to explain the purpose of the interviews and to answer any questions. They might arrange with the management to summarize the discussion in the community's newsletter, with photos of the interviewers. In preparation for the interviews, they might make initial contact with individual households by phone. Upon arriving, they might bring along the article so that residents can see that they are admitting bona fide interviewers. The interviewers might give a brief verbal summary of their purpose, confidentiality measures, and other pertinent elements of consent; obtain verbal consent; and provide a written summary of the information for the subjects to keep as appropriate.

If there is some risk of harm or inconvenience to subjects, they should receive enough information to judge whether the risk is at a level they can accept. An adequate informed consent process can sort out those who would gladly participate from those who wish to opt out. There are risks or inconveniences that some will gladly undertake if given a choice, but that they would not want to have imposed upon them unilaterally. Others may decide that the experience would be too stressful, risky, or unpleasant for them.

The researcher should make it clear that the subject is free to ask questions at any time. Subjects do not necessarily develop questions or concerns about their participation until they are well into the research experience. For example, a discussion of confidentiality may not capture their attention until they are asked personal questions.

If subjects can refuse to participate by hanging up the phone or tossing a mailed survey away, the informed consent can be extremely brief. Courtesy and professionalism would require that the identity of the researcher and research institution be mentioned, along with the nature and purpose of the research. However, if there are no risks, benefits, or confidentiality issues involved, these topics and the right to refuse to participate need not be mentioned, when such details would be gratuitous. Detailed recitation of irrelevant information detracts from the communication. Assurances that there are no risks and descriptions of measures taken to ensure confidentiality are irrelevant, irritating, and have been found to reduce response rates. (See PRIVACY AND CONFIDENTIALITY.)

The cultural norms and lifestyle of subjects should dictate how to approach informed consent. It is disrespectful and foolhardy to seek to treat people in ways that are incompatible with their culture and circumstances. For example, a survey of homeless injection drug users should probably be preceded by weeks of "hanging out" and talking with them, using their informal communication "grapevine" to discuss their concerns, answer their questions, and negotiate the conditions under which the survey is conducted. Similar communication processes probably should precede research on runaways and drug-abusing street youngsters of indeterminate age. Such youngsters may be considered emancipated, or alternatively, it is

likely impossible to obtain parental consent because of unavailability of the parent. People who are functionally illiterate, suspicious of people who proffer documents or require signatures, and people from traditional cultures should also be approached in the style that is most comfortable to them. In community-based research, the formal or informal leaders of the community are the gatekeepers. The wise researcher consults with them to learn the concerns and perceptions of prospective subjects, how best to recruit, and how to formulate and conduct the informed consent process. Protocols for research on such populations should show evidence that the researcher is familiar with the culture of the intended research population and has arranged the informed consent and other research procedures accordingly.

Researchers and IRBs should flexibly consider a wide range of media for administering informed consent. Videotapes, brochures, group discussions, Web sites, and so on can be more appropriate ways of communicating with potential subjects than the kinds of legalistic formal consent forms that have often been used.

When written or signed consent places subjects at risk and the signed consent is the only link between the subject and the research, a waiver of informed consent should be considered. One useful procedure is to have a trusted colleague witness the verbal consent. Witnessed consent, signed by the witness, can also be used in the case of illiterate subjects.

In organizational research, both the superior who allows the study and the subordinates who are studied must consent. Both must have veto power. Superiors should not be in a position to coerce participation and should not be privy to information on whether subordinates consented, or to their responses.

Sometimes, people are not in a position to decide whether to consent until after their participation. For example, in brief sidewalk interviews, most respondents do not want to endure a consent procedure until they have participated. After the interview, they can indicate whether they will allow the interview to be used as research data in the study that is then explained to them. A normal consent procedure can ensue.

In summary, informed consent is a respectful communication process, not a consent form. By keeping this definition foremost in mind, the researcher can decide on the appropriate content and format in relation to the context of the research.

Thanks are due Dr. Robert J. Levine for his critical comments of an earlier draft of some of this material.

—Joan E. Sieber

REFERENCES

Fisher, C. B., & Wallace, S. A. (2000). Through the community looking glass: Reevaluating the ethical and policy implications of research on adolescent risk and psychopathology. *Ethics & Behavior, 10*(2), 99–118.

Krueger, R. A. (1994). *Focus groups: A practical guide for applied research* (2nd ed.). Thousand Oaks, CA: Sage.

Levine, E. K. (1982). Old people are not all alike: Social class, ethnicity/race, and sex are bases for important differences. In J. E. Sieber (Ed.), *The ethics of social research: Surveys and experiments* (pp. 127–144). New York: Springer-Verlag.

Marshall, P. A. (1992). Research ethics in applied anthropology. *IRB: A Review of Human Subjects Research, 14*(6), 1–5.

Melton, G. B., Levine, R. J., Koocher, G. P., Rosenthal, R., & Thompson, W. C. (1988). Community consultation in socially sensitive research: Lessons from clinical trials on treatments for AIDS. *American Psychologist, 43,* 573–581.

National Commission for the Protection of Human Subjects of Biomedical and Behavioral Research. (1979). *The Belmont Report*. Washington, DC: U.S. Government Printing Office.

Sieber, J. E. (Ed.). (1991). *Sharing social science data: Advantages and challenges*. Newbury Park, CA: Sage.

Sieber, J. E. (1996). Typically unexamined communication processes in research. In B. H. Stanley, J. E. Sieber, & G. B. Melton (Eds.), *Research ethics: A psychological approach*. Lincoln: University of Nebraska Press.

Singer, E. (1978). Informed consent: Consequences for response rate and response quality in social surveys. *American Sociological Review, 43,* 144–162.

Singer, E., & Frankel, M. R. (1982). Informed consent procedures in telephone interviews. *American Sociological Review, 47,* 416–427.

Stanton, A. L., Burker, E. J., & Kershaw, D. (1991). Effects of researcher follow-up of distressed subjects: Tradeoff between validity and ethical responsibility? *Ethics & Behavior, 1*(2), 105–112.

Trice, A. D. (1987). Informed consent: VII: Biasing of sensitive self-report data by both consent and information. *Journal of Social Behavior and Personality, 2,* 369–374.

U.S. Federal Regulations of Human Research 45 CFR 46. Retrieved from http://ohrp.osophs.dhhs.gov.

INSTRUMENTAL VARIABLE

One of the crucial assumptions in ORDINARY LEAST SQUARES (OLS) estimation is that the disturbance term is not correlated with any of the explanatory variables. The rationale for this assumption is that we assume the explanatory variables and the disturbance have separate effects on the dependent variable. However, this is not the case if they are correlated with one another. Because we cannot separate their respective effects on the dependent variable, estimates are BIASED and inconsistent. Suppose we have a simple linear regression such as $Y = \beta_0 + \beta_1 X + \varepsilon$, where X and ε are positively correlated. As X moves up or down, so does ε, with direction depending on the nature of the correlation. Here, variations in Y associated with variations in X will also be related to those between Y and ε. This implies that we cannot estimate the population coefficients of X and ε precisely. It can be shown that this problem gets worse as we increase the sample size toward infinity.

There are three major cases where correlation between an explanatory variable and the disturbance is likely to occur: (a) The problem can occur when an explanatory variable is measured with error, making it stochastic. This is the so-called errors-in-variables problem. (b) The problem can occur when there is a lagged dependent variable accompanied by auto-correlated disturbances. (c) The problem can occur when there is a simultaneity problem. That is, the dependent variable contemporaneously causes the independent variable, rather than vice versa.

One approach to addressing this problem is to use an instrumental variable in place of the variable that is correlated with the disturbance. An *instrumental variable* is a proxy for the original variable that is not correlated with the disturbance term. In the simple linear regression equation above, an instrumental variable for X is one that is correlated with X (preferably highly) but not with ε. Let's define such a variable, Z, so that $X = Z + v$, where v is a random disturbance with zero mean. If we put this into the original equation above, then we will have $Y = \beta_0 + \beta_1(Z + v) + \varepsilon = \beta_0 + \beta_1 Z + \beta_1 v + \varepsilon = \beta_0 + \beta_1 Z + \varepsilon^*$, where $\varepsilon^* = \beta v + \varepsilon$. Compared to the original equation, in which X and ε are correlated, this is not the case with Z and ε^* in the new equation. This is because ε^* contains βv, which exists independently of Z. As we increase our sample infinitely, the correlation between Z and ε_i^* will approach zero. With such a proxy variable Z in hand, we still may not have an unbiased estimator for the coefficient of X, because a proxy is not equal to the true variable. However, as we increase the sample size, the estimator based upon Z will approach the true population coefficient.

A practical and serious problem with the instrumental variable approach is how to find a satisfactory proxy for an explanatory variable. If we have strong theory, this can guide us. If we don't, however, we have to rely on technical procedures to find it. For example, in TWO-STAGE LEAST SQUARES estimation, we regard as proxies of ENDOGENOUS VARIABLES the predicted values of the endogenous variables in the regressions on all EXOGENOUS VARIABLES. However, there is no guarantee that this kind of atheoretical procedure will provide a good proxy. As a general rule, the proxy variable should be strongly correlated with the original variable. Otherwise, estimates will be very imprecise.

—B. Dan Wood and Sung Ho Park

REFERENCES

Greene, W. H. (2003). *Econometric analysis* (5th ed.). Englewood Cliffs, NJ: Prentice-Hall.

Gujarati, D. N. (1995). *Basic econometrics* (3rd ed.). New York: McGraw-Hill.

Kennedy, P. (1998). *A guide to econometrics* (4th ed.). Cambridge: MIT Press.

INTERACTION. *See* INTERACTION EFFECT; STATISTICAL INTERACTION

INTERACTION EFFECT

Interaction in statistics refers to the interplay among two or more INDEPENDENT VARIABLES as they influence a DEPENDENT VARIABLE. Interactions can be conceptualized in two ways. First is that the effect of each independent variable on an outcome is a conditional effect (i.e., depends on or is *conditional* on the value of another variable or variables). Second is that the *combined effect* of two or more independent variables is different from the sum of their individual effects; the effects are NONADDITIVE. Interactions between variables are termed HIGHER ORDER effects in contrast with the FIRST-ORDER effect of each variable taken separately.

As an example, consider people's intention to protect themselves against the exposure to the sun as a function of the distinct region of the country in which they reside (rainy northwest, desert southwest) and

Table 1   No Interaction Between Region and Risk—Arithmetic Mean Level of Intention to Protect Oneself Against the Sun as a Function of Region of the Country (Northwest, Southwest) and Objective Risk for Skin Cancer

		Region of the Country	
		Northwest	Southwest
Risk of Skin Cancer	Low	6	8
	High	7	9

their high versus low objective risk for skin cancer (see Table 1).

In Table 1, risk and region do not interact. In the northwest, those at low risk have a mean intention of 6; those at high risk have a mean intention of 7, or a 1-point difference in intention produced by risk. In the southwest, high risk again raises intention by 1 point, from 8 to 9. Looked at another way, people residing in the southwest have 2-point higher intention than in the northwest whether they are at low risk (8 vs. 6, respectively) or at high risk (9 vs. 7, respectively). The impact of risk is not conditional on region and vice versa. Finally, risk (low to high) raises intention by 1 point and region (northwest to southwest) raises intention by 2 points; we expect a $1 + 2 = 3$-point increase in intention from low-risk individuals residing in the northwest to high-risk individuals residing in the southwest, and this is what we observe (from 6 to 9, respectively), an *additive* effect of risk and region.

In Table 2, risk and region interact. Low- versus high-risk individuals in the northwest differ by 1 point in intention, as in Table 1 (termed the *simple effect* of risk at one value of region, here northwest). However, in the southwest, the difference due to risk is quadrupled (8 vs. 12 points). Looked at another way, among low-risk individuals, there is only a 2-point difference in intention (6 to 8) as a function of region; for high-risk individuals, there is a 5-point difference (7 to 12). The impact of region is *conditional on* risk and vice versa. Instead of the additive 3-point effect of high risk and southwest region from Table 1, in Table 2, high-risk individuals in the southwest have a 6-point higher intention to sun protect than low-risk individuals in the northwest (12 vs. 6, respectively). The combined effects of region and risk are nonadditive, following the second definition of interaction.

Table 2 illustrates an interaction in terms of means of variables that are either CATEGORICAL (region) or

Table 2 Interaction Between Region and Risk—Arithmetic Mean Level of Intention to Protect Oneself Against the Sun as a Function of Region of the Country (Northwest, Southwest) and Objective Risk for Skin Cancer

		Region of the Country	
		Northwest	Southwest
Risk of Skin Cancer	Low	6	8
	High	7	12

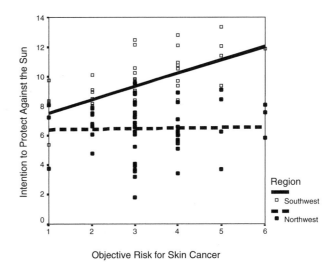

Figure 1 Interaction Between Region of the Country and Objective Risk for Skin Cancer in Prediction of Intention to Protect Against the Sun

NOTE: Region moderates the relationship of risk to intention. In the northwest, there is no effect of objective risk on intention, whereas in the southwest, there is a strong effect of objective risk on intention.

have been artificially broken into categories (risk), as in ANALYSIS OF VARIANCE. TWO CONTINUOUS VARIABLES may interact, or a continuous and a categorical variable may interact, as in MULTIPLE REGRESSION ANALYSIS. Figure 1 shows the interaction between region (categorical) and risk (with people sampled across a 6-point risk scale). Separate regression lines are shown for the northwest and southwest (termed *simple regression lines*). In the southwest (solid line), intention increases dramatically as risk increases. However, in the northwest (dashed line), risk has essentially no impact on intention. Region is a MODERATING VARIABLE or *moderator*, a variable that changes the relationship of another variable (here, risk) to the outcome. Put another way, the impact of risk is conditional on region. The vertical distance between the two lines shows the impact of region on intention. When risk is low (at 1 on the risk scale), the lines are close together; regional difference in intention is small. When risk is high (at 6 on the risk scale), regional difference is large. The impact of region is conditional on risk. Finally, being both at high risk and living in the southwest produces unexpectedly high intention, consistent with our second definition of nonadditive effect.

TYPES OF INTERACTIONS

The interaction between region and risk is *synergistic*: the effects of the variables together are greater than their sum. Being in a region of the country with intense sun (the southwest) and being at high personal risk combine to produce intention higher than the simple sum of their effects, a *synergistic interaction*. Alternatively, an interaction may be *buffering*, in that one variable may weaken the effect of another variable. Stress as an independent variable increases the risk of negative mental health outcomes. Having social support from family and friends weakens (or buffers)

the effect of high stress on mental health outcomes, a *buffering interaction*.

The interaction illustrated in Figure 1 is an ORDINAL INTERACTION; that is, the order of levels of one variable is maintained across the range of the other variable. Here, intention is always higher in the southwest across the range of risk, characteristic of an ordinal interaction. An interaction may be *disordinal* (i.e., exhibit DISORDINALITY). Say that among high-risk individuals, those in the southwest had higher intention than those in the northwest. Among low-risk individuals, however, those in the northwest had higher intention. The interaction would be disordinal. This would be a *cross-over interaction*: Which value of one variable was higher would depend on the value of the other variable.

HISTORICAL DEVELOPMENT

In the 1950s through the 1970s, there was great emphasis on the characterization and interpretation of interactions between categorical variables (factors in the analysis of variance). Cohen (1978) turned attention to interactions between continuous variables in multiple linear regression. A decade later, Jaccard, Turrisi, and Wan (1990) and Aiken and West (1991) extended the methodology for the post hoc probing and interpretation of continuous variable interactions. At present, there is focus on extending the characterization of interactions to other forms of regression analysis (e.g., LOGISTIC REGRESSION) and to interactions among latent variables in STRUCTURAL EQUATION MODELING.

—Leona S. Aiken

REFERENCES

Aiken, L. S., & West, S. G. (1991). *Multiple regression: Testing and interpreting interactions.* Newbury Park, CA: Sage.

Cohen, J. (1978). Partialed products are interactions; partialed powers are curve components. *Psychological Bulletin, 85,* 858–866.

Jaccard, J., Turrisi, R., & Wan, C. K. (1990). *Interaction effects in multiple regression.* Newbury Park, CA: Sage.

Kirk, R. E. (1995). *Experimental design: Procedures for the behavioral sciences* (3rd ed.). Pacific Grove, CA: Brooks/Cole.

INTERCEPT

The intercept is defined as the value of a variable, Y, when a line or curve cuts through the y-axis. In a two-dimensional graph, the intercept is therefore the value of Y when X is zero. The units of the intercept are the same as the units of Y.

There are problems with the interpretation of intercepts in REGRESSION contexts: The zero value of the X variable often lies outside of the range of X observations, so the value of Y when X is zero is therefore not of interest in practical or policy contexts.

However, the intercept is a critical component of regression equations.

$$Y = a + bX$$

or

$$Y_i = \sum_j b_j X_{ij} + \varepsilon_i.$$

The subscript j indicates the different variables, starting with a neutral constant term b_0. The subscript i indicates the cases in the sample data set. The intercept a in the simple bivariate equation corresponds to the constant term b_0 in the multivariate equation. The term b_0 is a multiplicative constant applied to the first variable, X_0, whose values are all set equal to 1. Thus, a variable $X_0 = 1$ is created so that an intercept will be assigned to the whole equation.

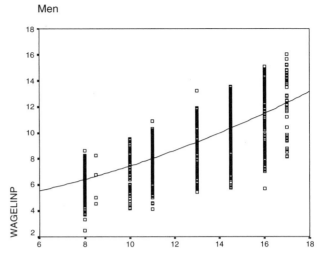

Men

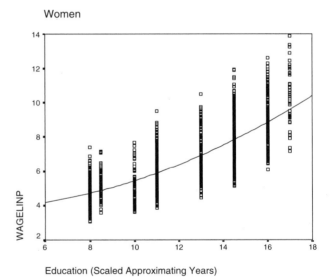

Women

Figure 1   Hourly Wage Predicted by Regression: Education Dummy Variables

SOURCE: British Household Panel Survey, Wave 9, 1999–2000 (ESRC, 2001; Taylor, 2000).

Diagrams can illustrate for both linear and nonlinear equations where the intercept will fall. Some curves have no intersection with the x-axis, and these have no intercept. However, for linear regression, there is always a y-intercept unless the slope is infinite. The y-intercept can be set to zero if desired before producing an estimate.

An example illustrates how the intercept can be of policy interest even while remaining outside the range of reasonable values for the independent variable.

Regression equations for men's and women's wages per hour have been subjected to close scrutiny in view of the gender pay gap that exists in many countries (Monk-Turner & Turner, 2001). Other pay gaps, such as that between a dominant and a minority ethnic group, also get close scrutiny. A wage equation that includes dummy values for the highest level of education shows the response of wages to education among men and women using U.K. 2000 data (Walby & Olsen, 2002). The log of wages is used to represent the skewed wage variable, and linear regression is then used. The predictions shown below are based upon a series of dummy variables for education producing a spline estimate. The predictions are then graphed against years of formal education. The curve shown is that which best fits the spline estimates.

In mathematical terms, the true intercept occurs when $x = 0$, as if 0 years of education were possible. However, the intercept visible in Figure 1 (£5.75 for men and £4.25 for women) forms part of the argument about gender wage gaps: The women's line has a lower intercept than the men's line. Much debate has occurred regarding the intercept difference (Madden, 2000).

In REGRESSION analysis, the constant term in these equations is a factor that depends upon all 32 independent variables in the equation (for details, see Taylor, 2000; Walby & Olsen, 2002). However, the regression constant B_0 is not that which would be seen in this particular $x - y$ graph. B_0 is the constant in the multidimensional space of all the x_is. However, a single graph showing one x_i and the predicted values of y has a visible intercept on the x_i-axis. Assumptions must be made regarding the implicit values of the other x_is; they are usually held at their mean values, and these influence the intercept visible in the diagram of $x - \hat{y}$ (i.e., the predictions of y along the domain of x_i). Two-dimensional diagrams, with their visible intercepts and slopes, bear a complex relation to the mathematics of a complex MULTIPLE REGRESSION.

—Wendy K. Olsen

REFERENCES

Economic and Social Research Council Research Centre on Micro-Social Change. (2001, February 28). *British Household Panel Survey* [computer file] (Study Number 4340). Colchester, UK: The Data Archive [distributor].

Madden, D. (2000). Towards a broader explanation of male-female wage differences. *Applied Economics Letters, 7,* 765–770.

Monk-Turner, E., & Turner, C. G. (2001). Sex differentials in the South Korean labour market. *Feminist Economics, 7*(1), 63–78.

Taylor, M. F., with Brice, J., Buck, N., & Prentice-Lane, E. (Eds.). (2000). *British Household Panel Survey User Manual Volume B9: Codebook.* Colchester, UK: University of Essex.

Walby, S., & Olsen, W. (2002, November). *The impact of women's position in the labour market on pay and implications for UK productivity.* Cabinet Office Women and Equality Unit. Retrieved from www.womenandequalityunit. gov.uk.

INTERNAL RELIABILITY

Most measures employed in the social sciences are constructed based on a small set of items sampled from the large domain of possible items that attempts to measure the same CONSTRUCT. It would be difficult to assess whether the responses to specific items on a measure can be generalized to the population of items for a construct if there is a lack of consistent responses toward the items (or a subset of the items) on the measure. In other words, high internal consistency suggests a high degree of interrelatedness among the responses to the items. Internal reliability provides an estimate of the consistency of the responses toward the items or a subset of the items on the measure.

There are a variety of internal reliability estimates, including CRONBACH'S ALPHA, Kuder Richardson 20 (KR20), SPLIT-HALF RELIABILITY, stratified alpha, maximal reliability, Raju coefficient, Kristof's coefficient, Angoff-Feldt coefficient, Feldt's coefficient, Feldt-Gilmer coefficient, Guttman λ_2, maximized λ_4, and Hoyt's analysis of variance. These estimates can all be computed after a single form of a measure is administered to a group of participants. In the remaining section, we will discuss only KR20, split-half reliability, stratified alpha, and maximal reliability.

When a measure contains dichotomous response options (e.g., yes/no, true/false, etc.), Cronbach's alpha takes on a special form, KR20, which is expressed as

$$\left[\frac{n}{n-1}\right]\left[\frac{\sigma_X^2 - \sum p_i(1-p_i)}{\sigma_X^2}\right],$$

where p_i is the proportion of the population endorsing item i as yes or true, and σ_X^2 is the variance of the observed score for a test with n components.

Split-half reliability, a widely used reliability estimate, is defined as the CORRELATION between two halves of a test (r_{12}), corrected for the full length of the test. According to Spearman-Brown Prophecy formula, split-half reliability can be obtained by $\frac{2r_{12}}{1+r_{12}}$. It can also be calculated by

$$\frac{4r_{12} \times \sigma_1 \times \sigma_2}{\sigma_X^2},$$

which takes VARIANCES into consideration, where σ_1 and σ_2 are the STANDARD DEVIATIONS of the two halves of a test, and σ_X^2 is the variance of the entire test. Cronbach's alpha is the same as the average split-half reliability when split-half reliability is defined by the latter formula. However, if split-half reliability is calculated based on the Spearman-Brown Prophecy formula, Cronbach's alpha is equal to the average split-half reliability *only* when all item variances are the same.

If a test X is not unidimensional and is grouped into i subsets because of heterogeneous contents, stratified alpha and maximal reliability are better choices than Cronbach's alpha and its related estimates. Stratified alpha can be calculated as

$$1 - \sum \frac{\sigma_i^2(1 - \alpha_i)}{\sigma_X^2},$$

where σ_i^2 is the variance of the ith subset and α_i is the Cronbach's alpha of the ith subset. The maximal reliability estimate is appropriate when all items within a subset are parallel, although the items in different subsets may have different reliabilities and variances (Osburn, 2000). Maximal reliability can be derived by

$$R_I = \frac{A}{\frac{I}{[1+(I-1)]\rho} + A},$$

where I = number of subsets, ρ is the common correlation among the subsets

$$A = \frac{n_1\rho_1}{(1 - \rho_1)} + \frac{n_2\rho_2}{(1 - \rho_2)} + \cdots + \frac{n_i\rho_i}{(1 - \rho_i)}, n_i$$

is the number of items in the ith subset, and ρ_i is the reliability of the ith subset.

In general, the alternate-forms reliability is a preferred reliability estimate when compared with internal reliability or TEST-RETEST RELIABILITY. Unfortunately, the required conditions to estimate the alternate-forms reliability are not easily met in practice (see RELIABILITY). Compared to test-retest reliability, internal reliability is flexible and tends not to be affected by problems such as practice, fatigue, memory, and motivation. It is flexible because it requires only a single administration and can be applied to a variety of circumstances, including a test containing multiple items, a test containing multiple subscales, or a score containing multiple raters' judgments. Internal consistency reliability is generally not an appropriate reliability estimate when (a) the test is heterogeneous in content, (b) a battery score is derived from two or more heterogeneous tests, or (c) the test is characterized as a speeded test.

—Peter Y. Chen and Autumn D. Krauss

REFERENCES

Cortina, J. M. (1993). What is coefficient alpha? An examination of theory and applications. *Journal of Applied Psychology, 78,* 98–104.

Feldt, L. S., & Brennan, R. L. (1989). Reliability. In R. L. Linn (Ed.), *Educational measurement* (3rd ed., pp. 105–146). New York: Macmillan.

Osburn, H. G. (2000). Coefficient alpha and related internal consistency reliability coefficients. *Psychological Methods, 5,* 343–355.

INTERNAL VALIDITY

Internal validity refers to the confidence with which researchers can make *causal* inferences from the results of a particular empirical study. In their influential paper on "Experimental and Quasi-Experimental Designs for Research," Campbell and Stanley (1963) characterized internal validity as the sine qua non of experimental research. This is because the very purpose of conducting an experiment is to test causal relationships between an INDEPENDENT VARIABLE and a DEPENDENT VARIABLE. Hence, it is appropriate that the primary criterion for evaluating the results of an experiment is whether valid causal conclusions can be drawn from its results. However, the concept of internal validity can also be applied to findings from correlational research anytime that causal inferences about the relationship between two variables are being drawn.

It is important to clarify that internal validity does not mean that a particular independent variable is the *only* cause of variation in the dependent variable—only that it has some independent causal role. For instance, variations among individuals in their attitudes toward a social program can be caused by many factors, including variations in personal history, self-interest, ideology, and so on. But if the mean attitude of a group of people that has been exposed to a particular persuasive message is more favorable than that of a group of people that did not receive the message, the question of interest is whether the message played a role in causing that difference. We can draw such a conclusion only if no other relevant causal factors were correlated with whether an individual received the message or not. In other words, there are no plausible alternative explanations for the covariation between attitude and receipt of the message. The existence of correlated rival factors is usually referred to as a CONFOUNDING of the experimental treatment because the potential effects of the variable under investigation cannot be separated from the effects of these other potential causal variables.

In this example, the most obvious challenge to causal inference would be any kind of self-selection to message conditions. If participants in the research were free to decide whether or not they would receive the persuasive message, then it is very likely that those who already had more favorable attitudes would end up in the message-receipt group. In that case, the difference in attitudes between the groups after the message was given may have been predetermined and had nothing to do with the message itself. This does not necessarily mean that the message did not have a causal influence, only that we have a reasonable alternative that makes this conclusion uncertain. It is for this reason that RANDOM ASSIGNMENT is a criterial feature of good experimental design. Assigning participants randomly to different levels of the independent variable rules out self-selection as a threat to internal validity.

BASIC THREATS TO INTERNAL VALIDITY

A research study loses internal validity when there is reason to believe that obtained differences in the dependent variable would have occurred even if exposure to the independent variable had not been manipulated. In addition to self-selection as a potential confounding factor, Campbell and Stanley (1963) described several other generic classes of possible threats to internal validity. These are factors that could be responsible for variation in the dependent variable, but they constitute threats to internal validity only if the research is conducted in such a way that variations in these extraneous factors become correlated with variation in the independent variable of interest. The types of potential confounds discussed by Campbell and Stanley (1963) included the following:

History. Differences in outcomes on the dependent variable measured at two different times may result from events other than the experimental variable that have occurred during the passage of time between measures. History is potentially problematic if the dependent variable is measured before and after exposure to the independent variable, where other intervening events could be a source of change.

Maturation. Another class of effects that may occur over the passage of time between measures on the dependent variable involves changes in the internal conditions of the participants in the study, such as growing older, becoming more tired, less interested, and so on. (These are termed *maturation effects* even though some representatives of this class, such as growing tired, are not typically thought of as being related to physical maturation.)

Testing. Participants' scores on a second administration of the dependent variable may be affected by the fact of their having been exposed to the measure previously. Thus, testing itself could be a source of change in the dependent variable. This would also be a problem if some individuals in a study had received prior testing and others had not.

Instrumentation. Changes across time in dependent variable scores may be caused by changes in the nature of the measurement "instrument" (e.g., changes in attitudes of observers, increased sloppiness on the part of test scorers, etc.) rather than by changes in the participants being measured.

Statistical Regression. Unreliability, or error of measurement, will produce changes in scores on different measurement occasions, and these scores are subject to misinterpretation if participants are selected on the basis of extreme scores at their initial measurement session.

Experimental Mortality. If groups are being compared, any selection procedures or treatment differences that result in different proportions of participants dropping out of the experiment may account for any differences obtained between the groups in the final measurement.

Selection-History Interactions. If participants have been differentially selected for inclusion in comparison groups, these specially selected groups may experience differences in history, maturation, testing, and so on, which may produce differences in the final measurement on the dependent variable.

Again, it should be emphasized that the presence of any of these factors in a research study undermines internal validity if and only if it is differentially associated with variations in the independent variable of interest. Events other than the independent variable may occur that influence the outcomes on the dependent variable, but these will not reduce internal validity if they are not systematically correlated with the independent variable.

—Marilynn B. Brewer

REFERENCES

Campbell, D. T., & Stanley, J. C. (1963). Experimental and quasi-experimental designs for research on teaching. In N. L. Gage (Ed.), *Handbook of research on teaching* (pp. 171–246). Chicago: Rand McNally.

Crano, W. D., & Brewer, M. B. (2002). *Principles and methods of social research* (2nd ed.). Mahwah, NJ: Lawrence Erlbaum.

Shadish, W. R., Cook, T. D., & Campbell, D. T. (2001). *Experimental and quasi-experimental designs for generalized causal inference.* Boston: Houghton Mifflin.

INTERNET SURVEYS

The term "Internet survey" refers simply to any SURVEY where the data are collected via the Internet. Internet surveys are having an impact on the survey profession like few other innovations before. In the short time that the Internet (and, more particularly, the World Wide Web) has been widely available, the number of Web survey software products, online panels, and survey research organizations offering Web survey services, either as a sole data collection mode or in combination with traditional methods of survey research, has proliferated. However, the reception within the profession has been mixed, with some hailing online surveys as the replacement for all other forms of survey data collection, and others viewing them as a threat to the future of the survey industry. Although much is still unknown about the value of Internet surveys, research on their utility is proceeding apace.

TYPES OF INTERNET SURVEYS

The Internet can be used for survey data collection in several different ways. A distinction can be made between those surveys that execute on a respondent's machine (client-side) and those that execute on the survey organization's Web server (server-side). Key client-side survey approaches include e-mail surveys

and downloadable executables. In each of these cases, the instrument is transmitted to sample persons, who then answer the survey questions by using the reply function in the e-mail software, entering responses using a word processor, or using software installed on their computers. Once complete, the answers are transmitted back to the survey organization. Server-side systems typically involve the sample person completing the survey while connected to the Internet through a browser, with the answers being transmitted to the server on a flow basis. Interactive features of the automated survey instrument are generated by scripts on the Web server. A key distinction between these two approaches is whether the Internet connection is "on" while the respondent is completing the survey. Web surveys are the prime example of the second type and are by far the dominant form of Internet survey prevalent today.

There are variations of these two basic types. For example, some surveys consist of a single scrollable HTML form, with no interaction with the server until the respondent has completed the survey and pressed the "submit" button to transmit the information. Similarly, client-side interactivity can be embedded in HTML forms using JavaScript, DHTML, or the like. These permit a variety of dynamic interactions to occur without the involvement of the Web server.

The typical Web survey involves one or more survey questions completed by a respondent on a browser connected to the World Wide Web. Sampling of persons may take many forms, ranging from self-selected samples to list-based approaches (see Couper, 2000, for a review). In the latter case, the invitation to participate is often sent via e-mail, with the survey URL embedded in the e-mail message, along with an ID and password to control access. Web surveys are also increasingly used in mixed-mode designs, where mail surveys are sent to respondents, with an option to complete the survey online.

ADVANTAGES OF INTERNET SURVEYS

The primary argument in favor of Internet surveys is cost. Although fixed costs (hardware and software) may be higher than mail, the per-unit cost for data collection is negligible. Mailing and printing costs are eliminated using fully automated methods, as are data keying and associated processing costs. These reduce both the cost of data collection and the time taken to obtain results from the survey.

Another benefit of Web surveys is their speed relative to other modes of data collection. It is often the case that a large proportion of all responses occur within 24 hours of sending the invitation.

Web surveys also offer the advantages associated with self-administration, including the elimination or reduction of interviewer effects, such as socially desirable responding. RESPONDENTS can answer at their own pace and have greater control over the process. At the same time, Web surveys offer all the advantages associated with computerization. These include the use of complex branching or routing, randomization, edit checks, and so on that are common in COMPUTER-ASSISTED INTERVIEWING. Finally, such surveys can exploit the rich, graphical nature of the Web by including color, images, and other multimedia elements into the instruments.

DISADVANTAGES OF INTERNET SURVEYS

The biggest drawbacks of Internet surveys relate to representational issues. Internet access is still far from universal, meaning that large portions of the POPULATION are not accessible via this method. To the extent that those who are covered by the technology differ from those who are not, coverage BIAS may be introduced in survey estimates. Of course, for some populations of interest (students, employees in high-tech industries, visitors to a Website, etc.), this is less of a concern. A related challenge is one of SAMPLE. No list of Internet users exists, and methods akin to RANDOM DIGIT DIALING (RDD) for telephone surveys are unlikely to be developed for the Internet, given the variety of formats of e-mail addresses.

NONRESPONSE is another concern. The response rates obtained in Internet surveys are typically lower than those for equivalent paper-based methods (see Fricker & Schonlau, 2002). In mixed-mode designs, where sample persons are offered a choice of paper or Web, they overwhelmingly choose the former.

Another potential drawback is the anonymity of the Internet. There is often little guarantee that the person to whom the invitation was sent actually completed the survey, and that they took the task seriously. Despite this concern, results from Internet surveys track well with other methods of survey data collection, suggesting that this is not a cause of great concern.

SUMMARY

Despite being a relatively new phenomenon, Internet surveys have spread rapidly, and there are already many different ways to design and implement online surveys. Concerns about representation may limit their utility for studies of the general population, although they may be ideally suited for special population studies (among groups with high Internet penetration) and for those studies where representation is less important (e.g., experimental studies). Given this, Internet surveys are likely to continue their impact on the survey industry as cutting-edge solutions to some of the key challenges are found and as the opportunities offered by the technology are exploited.

—Mick P. Couper

REFERENCES

Couper, M. P. (2000). Web surveys: A review of issues and approaches. *Public Opinion Quarterly, 64*(4), 464–494.

Fricker, R. D., & Schonlau, M. (2002). Advantages and disadvantages of Internet research surveys: Evidence from the literature. *Field Methods, 14*(4), 347–365.

INTERPOLATION

Interpolation means to estimate a value of a FUNCTION or series between two known values. Unlike EXTRAPOLATION, which estimates a value outside a known range from values within a known range, interpolation is concerned with estimating a value inside a known range from values within that same range.

There are, broadly, two approaches to interpolation that have been used in the social sciences. One is mathematical, and the other is statistical. In mathematical interpolation, we estimate an unknown value by assuming a deterministic relationship between two known data points. For example, suppose we are trying to find the 99% critical value for a CHI-SQUARE variable with 11.3 degrees of freedom (e.g., see Greene, 2000, p. 94). Note that chi-square tables are given only for integer values. However, the actual chi-square distribution is also defined for noninteger values. We can interpolate to noninteger values for this example as follows. First, obtain the 99% critical values of the chi-square distribution with 11 and 12 degrees of freedom from the tables. Then, interpolate linearly between the reciprocals of the degrees of freedom. Thus, given that $\chi^2_{11} \leq 0.99 = 24.725$ and $\chi^2_{12} \leq 0.99 = 26.217$, we have

$$\chi^2_{11.3} \leq 0.99 = 26.217 + \frac{\frac{1}{11.3} - \frac{1}{12}}{\frac{1}{11} - \frac{1}{12}}(24.725 - 26.217)$$

$$= 25.209.$$

This example uses linear interpolation. However, there are other problems where interpolation might involve inserting unknown values with nonlinear functions such as a cosine, polynomial, cubic spline, or other functions. The method of mathematical interpolation chosen should be consistent with the desired result.

Statistical interpolation estimates unknown values between known values by relying on information about the dynamics or DISTRIBUTION of the whole data set. Notice here the difference from the mathematical approach. In the previous example, we just draw a linear or smooth line between two data points to get an unknown value, regardless of the specific internal structure of the data set. However, in the statistical method, we are concerned with the specific dynamics and distribution inherent in the data set and project this information to get the unknown value. We can secure this information by either finding a related data set or simply assuming an internal structure of the data. For example, suppose we have a variable X that consists of quarterly TIME-SERIES data, and we want to convert X into a monthly time series. One approach is to find Y, a monthly time series, that is highly correlated with the original X series. We would first eliminate the differences between the quarterly movements of the two data series and then project the monthly series of Y onto X. Different outcomes can be obtained depending on how we eliminate the quarterly differences between X and Y and how we project Y onto the X series. Suppose, however, we are unable to find a data series that is related to X; we can also simply assume an internal dynamic. For example, we might have quarterly data prior to some date, and monthly data after that date (e.g., the University of Michigan's Index of Consumer Sentiment before and after 1978). We could simply assume that the monthly data structure is consistent with the unknown monthly dynamics of the earlier quarterly data. Using this assumption, we could construct an ARIMA model for the X series, in which we specify a combination of AUTOREGRESSIVE, MOVING AVERAGE, and RANDOM WALK movements, and project this specification into the unknown monthly series of X.

There are many technically advanced methods of interpolation that have been derived from the two broad categories discussed above. However, it should be emphasized that none of them can eliminate the uncertainty inherent in interpolation when true values do not exist. This is because it is impossible to find the true value of unknown data. In some cases, interpolation even might end up with a serious distortion of the true data structure. Thus, caution is required when creating and using interpolated data.

—B. Dan Wood and Sung Ho Park

REFERENCES

Friedman, M. (1962). The interpolation of time series by related series. *Journal of the American Statistical Association, 57,* 729–757.

Greene, W. H. (2000). *Econometric analysis* (4th ed.). Englewood Cliffs, NJ: Prentice Hall.

INTERPRETATIVE REPERTOIRE

Social psychological DISCOURSE ANALYSIS aims in part to identify the explanatory resources that speakers use in characterizing events, taking positions, and making arguments. *Interpretative repertoire* is a term used to define those resources with regard to a particular theme or topic. Typically, these themes or topics are sought in interview data on matters of ideological significance, such as race, gender, and power relations. Interpretative repertoires occupy a place in analysis that seeks to link the details of participants' descriptive practices to the broader ideological and historical formations in which those practices are situated.

The essence of interpretative repertoires is that there is always more than one of them available for characterizing any particular state of affairs. Usually, there are two, used in alternation or in opposition, but there may be more. Repertoires are recurrent verbal images, metaphors, figures of speech, and modes of explanation. There is no precise definition or heuristic for identifying them. Rather, the procedure is to collect topic-relevant discourse data and examine them for recurrent interpretative patterns. This resembles the stages of developing GROUNDED THEORY, but it is a feature of interpretative repertoire analysis that it remains closely tied to the details of the discourse data, informed by the procedures of DISCOURSE ANALYSIS, rather than resulting in an abstract set of codes and categories. Interpretative repertoires are best demonstrated by examples.

The first use of the term was by Nigel Gilbert and Michael Mulkay (1984) in a study of scientific discourse, where they discovered two contrasting and functionally different kinds of explanation. There was an *empiricist repertoire*—the impersonal, method-based, data-driven account of findings and theory choice typically provided in experimental reports. There was also a *contingent repertoire*—an appeal to personal motives, insights, and biases; social settings; and commitments—a realm in which speculative guesses and intuitions can operate and where conclusions and theory choice may give rise to, rather than follow from, the empirical work that supports them. Whereas the empiricist repertoire was used in making factual claims and supporting favored theories, the contingent repertoire was used in accounting for how and when things go wrong, particularly in rival laboratories, and with regard to discredited findings.

Margaret Wetherell and Jonathan Potter (1992) conducted interviews with New Zealanders on matters of race and ethnicity. They identified, among others, a *heritage repertoire* in talk about culture and cultural differences. This consisted of descriptions, metaphors, figures of speech, and arguments that coalesced around the importance of preserving traditions, values, and rituals. An alternative *therapy repertoire* defined culture as something that estranged Maoris might need in order to be whole and healthy again. Rather than expressing different attitudes or beliefs across different speakers, each repertoire could be used by the same people, because each had its particular rhetorical uses. The therapy metaphor, for example, was useful in talk about crime and educational failure. Repertoires of this kind, although often contradictory, were typically treated by participants as unquestionable common sense each time they were used. This commonsense status of interpretative repertoires enables links to the study of ideology.

—Derek Edwards

REFERENCES

Gilbert, G. N., & Mulkay, M. (1984). *Opening Pandora's box: A sociological analysis of scientists' discourse.* Cambridge, UK: Cambridge University Press.

Wetherell, M., & Potter, J. (1992). *Mapping the language of racism: Discourse and the legitimation of exploitation.* Brighton, UK: Harvester Wheatsheaf.

INTERPRETIVE BIOGRAPHY

The interpretive biographical method involves the studied use and collection of personal life documents, stories, accounts, and narratives that describe turning-point moments in individuals' lives (see Denzin, 1989, Chap. 2). The subject matter of the biographical method is the life experiences of a person. When written in the first person, it is called an autobiography, life story, or life history. When written by another person, observing the life in question, it is called a biography.

The following assumptions and arguments structure the use of the biographical method. Lives are only known through their representations, which include performances such as stories, personal narratives, or participation in ritual acts. LIVED EXPERIENCE and its representations are the proper subject matter of sociology. Sociologists must learn how to connect and join biographically meaningful experiences to society-at-hand, and to the larger culture- and meaning-making institutions of the past postmodern period. The meanings of these experiences are given in the performances of the people who experience them. A preoccupation with method, with the VALIDITY, RELIABILITY, GENERALIZABILITY, and theoretical relevance of the biographical method, must be set aside in favor of a concern for meaning, performance, and interpretation. Students of the biographical method must learn how to use the strategies and techniques of performance theory, literary interpretation, and criticism. They must bring their use of the method in line with recent STRUCTURALIST and POSTSTRUCTURALIST developments in critical theory concerning the reading and writing of social texts. This will involve a concern with HERMENEUTICS, SEMIOTICS, CRITICAL RACE, FEMINIST, and postcolonial theory, as well as pedagogical cultural studies.

Lives and the biographical methods that construct them are literary productions. Lives are arbitrary constructions, constrained by the cultural writing practices of the time. These cultural practices lead to the inventions and influences of gendered, knowing others who can locate subjects within familied social spaces, where lives have beginnings, turning points, and clearly defined endings. Such texts create "real" people about whom truthful statements are presumably made. In fact, these texts are narrative fictions, cut from the same kinds of cloth as the lives they tell about. When a writer writes a biography, he or she writes himself or herself into the life of the subject written about. When the reader reads a biographical text, that text is read through the life of the reader. Hence, writers and readers conspire to create the lives they write and read about. Along the way, the produced text is cluttered by the traces of the life of the "real" person being written about.

These assumptions, or positions, turn on, and are structured by, the problem of how to locate and interpret the subject in biographical materials. All biographical studies presume a life that has been lived, or a life that can be studied, constructed, reconstructed, and written about. In the present context, a *life* refers to two phenomena: lived experiences, or conscious existence, and person. A person is a self-conscious being, as well as a named, cultural object or cultural creation. The consciousness of the person is simultaneously directed to an inner world of thought and experience and to an outer world of events and experience. These two worlds, the inner and the outer, are opposite sides of the same process, for there can be no firm dividing line between inner and outer experience. The biographical method recognizes this fact about human existence, for its hallmark is the joining and recording of these two structures of experience in a personal document, a performative text.

—Norman K. Denzin

REFERENCE

Denzin, N. K. (1989). *Interpretive biography*. Newbury Park, CA: Sage.

INTERPRETIVE INTERACTIONISM

Interpretive interactionists study personal troubles and turning-point moments in the lives of interacting individuals. Interpretive interactionism implements a critical, existential, interpretive approach to human experience and its representations. This perspective follows the lead of C. Wright Mills, who argued in *The Sociological Imagination* (1959) that scholars should examine how the private troubles of individuals, which occur within the immediate world of experience, are connected to public issues and to public responses to these troubles. Mills' sociological imagination was biographical, interactional, and historical. Interpretive interactionism implements Mills' project.

Interpretive interactionists attempt to make the problematic LIVED EXPERIENCE of ordinary people available to the reader. The interactionist interprets these worlds, their effects, meanings, and representations. The research methods of this approach include performance texts; AUTOETHNOGRAPHY; poetry; fiction; open-ended, creative interviewing; document analysis; SEMIOTICS; LIFE HISTORY; life-story; personal experience and self-story construction; PARTICIPANT OBSERVATION; and THICK DESCRIPTION. The term *interpretive interactionism* signifies an attempt to join traditional SYMBOLIC INTERACTIONIST thought with critical forms of interpretive inquiry, including reflexive participant observation, literary ethnography, POETICS, life stories, and TESTIMONIOS.

Interpretive interactionism is not for everyone. It is based on a research philosophy that is counter to much of the traditional scientific research tradition in the social sciences. Only people drawn to the qualitative, interpretive approach are likely to use its methods and strategies. These strategies favor the use of minimal theory and value tightly edited texts that show, rather than tell.

Interpretive interactionists focus on those life experiences, which radically alter and shape the meanings people give to themselves and their life projects. This existential thrust leads to a focus on the "epiphany." In epiphanies, personal character is manifested and made apparent. By studying these experiences in detail, the researcher is able to illuminate the moments of crisis that occur in a person's life. These moments are often interpreted, both by the person and by others, as turning-point experiences. Having had this experience, the person is never again quite the same. Interpretive interactionists study these experiences, including their representations, effects, performances, and connections to broader historical, cultural, political, and economic forces.

—Norman K. Denzin

REFERENCES

Denzin, N. K. (1989a). *Interpretive biography*. Newbury Park, CA: Sage.

Denzin, N. K. (1989b). *Interpretive interactionism*. Newbury Park, CA: Sage.

Denzin, N. K. (1997). *Interpretive ethnography*. Thousand Oaks, CA: Sage.

Mills, C. W. (1959). *The sociological imagination*. New York: Oxford University Press.

INTERPRETIVISM

Interpretivism is a term used to identify approaches to social science that share particular ONTOLOGICAL and EPISTEMOLOGICAL assumptions. The central tenet is that because there is a fundamental difference between the subject matters of the natural and social sciences, the methods of the natural sciences cannot be used in the social sciences. The study of social phenomena requires an understanding of the social worlds that people inhabit, which they have already interpreted by the meanings they produce and reproduce as a necessary part of their everyday activities together. Whereas the study of natural phenomena requires the scientist to interpret nature through the use of scientific concepts and theories, and to make choices about what is relevant to the problem under investigation, the social scientist studies phenomena that are already interpreted.

ORIGINS

Interpretivism has its roots in the German intellectual traditions of HERMENEUTICS and PHENOMENOLOGY, in particular in the work of Max Weber (1864–1920) and Alfred Schütz (1899–1959). Like Dilthey before them, they sought to establish an objective science of the subjective with the aim of producing verifiable knowledge of the meanings that constitute the social world. Their attention focused on the nature of meaningful social action, its role in understanding patterns in social life, and how this meaning can be assessed.

Rather than trying to establish the actual meaning that a social actor gives to a particular social action, Weber and Schütz considered it necessary to work at a higher level of generality. Social regularities can be understood, perhaps explained, by constructing models of typical meanings used by typical social actors engaged in typical courses of action in typical situations. Such models constitute tentative HYPOTHESES to be tested. Only social action that is rational in character, that is consciously selected as a means to some goal, is regarded as being understandable.

According to Weber (1964, p. 96), subjective meanings may be of three kinds: They may refer to the actual, intended meanings used by a social actor; the average or approximate meanings used by a number of social actors; or the typical meanings attributed to a hypothetical social actor.

Drawing on Dilthey, Weber distinguished between three modes of understanding: two broad types— *rational* understanding, which produces a clear intellectual grasp of social action in its context of meaning, and *empathetic* or appreciative understanding, which

involves grasping the emotional content of the action— and two versions of *rational* understanding, *direct* and *motivational* understanding. *Direct* understanding of a human expression or activity is like grasping the meaning of a sentence, a thought, or a mathematical formula. It is an immediate, unambiguous, matter-of-fact kind of understanding that occurs in everyday situations and that does not require knowledge of a wider context. *Motivational* understanding, on the other hand, is concerned with the choice of a means to achieve some goal.

Weber was primarily concerned with this motivational form of rational action. He regarded human action that lacks this rational character as being unintelligible. The statistical patterns produced by quantitative data, such as the relationship between educational attainment and occupational status, are not understandable on their own. Not only must the relevant actions that link the two components of the relationship be specified, but the meaning that is attached to these actions must also be identified.

Weber acknowledged that motives can be both rational and nonrational, they can be formulated to give action the character of being a means to some end, or they can be associated with emotional (affectual) states. Only in the case of rational motives did he consider that it was possible to formulate social scientific explanations.

Weber regarded meaningful interpretations as plausible hypotheses that need to be tested, and he recommended the use of COMPARATIVE RESEARCH to investigate them. However, if this is not possible, he suggested that the researcher will have to resort to an "imaginary experiment," the thinking away of certain elements of a chain of motivation and working out the course of action that would probably then ensue.

Weber was not primarily concerned with the actor's own subjective meaning but, rather, with the meaning of the situation for a constructed hypothetical actor. Neither was he particularly interested in the specific meanings social actors give to their actions but with approximations and abstractions. He was concerned with the effect on human behavior not simply of meaning but of meaningful social relations. His ultimate concern was with large-scale uniformities. Because he did not wish to confine himself to either contemporary or micro situations, he was forced to deal with the observer's interpretations. Nevertheless, he regarded such interpretations only as hypotheses to be tested.

Weber's desire to link statistical uniformities with VERSTEHEN (interpretive understanding) has led to a variety of interpretations of his version of interpretivism. Positivists who have paid attention to his work have tended to regard the verstehen component as simply a potential source of hypotheses, whereas interpretivists have tended to ignore his concern with statistical uniformities and causal explanation.

Because Weber never pursued methodological issues beyond the requirements of his own substantive work, he operated with many tacit assumptions, and some of his concepts were not well developed. These aspects of Weber's work have been taken up sympathetically by Schütz (1976), for whose work Weber and Husserl provided the foundations. Schütz's main aim was to put Weber's sociology on a firm foundation. In pursuing this task, he offered a methodology of ideal types. Schütz argued that, in assuming that the concept of the meaningful act is the basic and irreducible component of social phenomena, Weber failed, among other things, to distinguish between the meaning the social actor *works with* while action is taking place, the meaning the social actor *attributes to* a completed act or to some future act, and the meaning the sociologist *attributes to* the action. In the first case, the meaning worked with during the act itself, and the context in which it occurs, is usually taken for granted. In the second case, the meaning attributed will be in terms of the social actor's goals. In the third case, the context of meaning will be that of the observer, not the social actor. Weber appeared to assume that the latter is an adequate basis for arriving at the social actor's attributed meaning and that there will be no disputes between actors, or between actors and observers, about the meaning of a completed or future act.

Schütz has provided the foundation for a methodological bridge between the meaning social actors attribute and the meaning the social scientists must attribute in order to produce an adequate theory. He argued that the concepts and meanings used in social theories must be derived from the concepts and meanings used by social actors. In Schütz's version of interpretivism, everyday reality is paramount; he argued that it is the social actor's, not the social investigator's, point of view that is the basis of any accounts of social life. The work of Weber and Schütz has provided the foundations for the major branches of interpretivism.

CRITICISMS

The critics of interpretivism have come from within as well as from without the approach. For example, Giddens (1984) has argued that it is misleading to imply that competent social actors engage in an ongoing monitoring of their conduct and are thus aware of both their intentions and the reasons for their actions. However, it is usually only when actors carry out retrospective inquiries into their own conduct, when others query their actions, or when action is disturbed or breaks down that this reflection occurs. Most of the time, action proceeds without reflective monitoring.

In response to the view of some interpretivists, that the social scientists must just report social actors' accounts of their actions and not interpret or theorize them, Rex (1974) and others have argued that social scientists should be able to give a different and competing account of social actors' actions from what those actors provide. Bhaskar (1979) has referred to this as the *linguistic fallacy,* which is based on a failure to recognize that there is more to reality than is expressed in the language of social actors. Bhaskar (1979) and Outhwaite (1987) have argued that interpretivism also commits the *epistemic fallacy* of assuming that our access to the social world is only through our understanding of interpretive processes—that this is all that exists. Other critics, such as Giddens and Rex, have argued that interpretivism fails to acknowledge the role of institutional structures, particularly divisions of interest and relations of power.

—Norman Blaikie

REFERENCES

Bhaskar, R. (1979). *The possibilities of naturalism: A philosophical critique of the contemporary human sciences.* Brighton, UK: Harvester.

Blaikie, N. (1993). *Approaches to social enquiry.* Cambridge, UK: Polity.

Giddens, A. (1984). *The constitution of society: Outline of the theory of structuration.* Cambridge, UK: Polity.

Outhwaite, W. (1987). *New philosophies of social science: Realism, hermeneutics and critical theory.* London: Macmillan.

Rex, J. (1974). *Sociology and the demystification of the modern world.* London: Routledge & Kegan Paul.

Schütz, A. (1976). *The phenomenology of the social world* (G. Walsh & F. Lehnert, Trans.). London: Heinemann.

Weber, M. (1964). *The theory of social and economic organization* (A. M. Henderson & T. Parsons, Trans.). New York: Free Press.

INTERQUARTILE RANGE

For quantitative data that have been sorted numerically from low to high, the interquartile range is that set of values between the 25th PERCENTILE (or P_{25}) in the set and the 75th percentile (P_{75}) in the set. Because this range contains half of all the values, it is descriptive of the "middle" values in a DISTRIBUTION. The range is referred to as the interquartile range because the 25th percentile is also known as the first QUARTILE and the 75th percentile as the third quartile.

Consider the ordered data set {3, 5, 7, 10, 11, 12, 14, 24}. There are eight values in this set. Eliminating the bottom two (which constitute the bottom 25%) and the top two (which constitute the top 25%) leaves the middle 50%. Their range is 7 to 12, which could be taken to be the interquartile range for the eight observations; however, because P_{25} must be a value below which 25% fall and above which 75% fall, it is conventional to define P_{25} as the value halfway between the boundary values, 5 and 7. This is 6. In like manner, the 75th percentile would be defined as 13, the point halfway between the boundary values 12 and 14. Thus, the interquartile range for the sample dataset is $13 - 6$, or 7.

Reporting interquartile ranges as part of data description enriches the description of central tendency that is provided by point values such as the MEDIAN (or second quartile) and the arithmetic MEAN. The greatest use of the interquartile range, however, is in the creation of BOXPLOTS and in the definition of OUTLIERS or "outside values," which are data values that are quantitatively defined as highly atypical. A widely accepted definition of an outlier is a data value that lies more than 1.5 times the interquartile range above P_{75} or below P_{25} (Tukey, 1977, p. 44ff). In boxplots, these values are given a distinctive marking, typically an asterisk. For the data set above, 24 is an outlier because it is more than $1.5(13 - 6) = 10.5$ units beyond P_{75}.

—Kenneth O. McGraw

REFERENCE

Tukey, J. W. (1977). *Exploratory data analysis*. Reading, MA: Addison-Wesley.

INTERRATER AGREEMENT

Researchers often attempt to evaluate the consensus or agreement of judgments or decisions provided by a group of raters (or judges, observers, experts, diagnostic tools). The nature of the judgments can be nominal (e.g., Republicans/Democrats/Independents, or Yes/No); ordinal (e.g., low, medium, high); interval; or ratio (e.g., Target A is twice as heavy as Target B). Whatever the type of judgments, the common goal of interrater agreement indexes is to assess to what degree raters agree about the precise values of one or more attributes of a target; in other words, how much their ratings are interchangeable. Interrater agreement has been consistently confused with INTERRATER RELIABILITY both in practice and in research (Kozlowski & Hattrup, 1992; Tinsley & Weiss, 1975). These terms represent different concepts and require different measurement indexes. For instance, three reviewers, A, B, and C, rate a manuscript on four dimensions—clarity of writing, comprehensiveness of literature review, methodological adequacy, and contribution to the field—with six response categories ranging from 1 (*unacceptable*) to 6 (*outstanding*). The ratings of reviewers A, B, and C on the four dimensions are (1, 2, 3, 4), (2, 3, 4, 5), and (3, 4, 5, 6), respectively. The data clearly indicate that these reviewers completely disagree with one another (i.e., zero interrater agreement), although their ratings are perfectly consistent (i.e., perfect interrater reliability) across the dimensions.

There are many indexes of interrater agreement developed for different circumstances, such as different types of judgments (nominal, ordinal, etc.) as well as varying numbers of raters or attributes of the target being rated. Examples of these indexes are percentage agreement; STANDARD DEVIATION of the rating; STANDARD ERROR of the mean; Scott's (1955) π; Cohen's (1960) kappa (κ) and Cohen's (1968) weighted kappa (κ_w); Lawlis and Lu's (1972) χ^2 test; Lawshe's (1975) Content Validity Ratio (CVR) and Content Validity Index (CVI); Tinsley and Weiss's (1975) T index; James, Demaree, and Wolf's (1984) $r_{WG(J)}$; and Lindell, Brandt, and Whitney's (1999) $r^*_{WG(J)}$. In the remaining section, we will review Scott's π, Cohen's κ and weighted κ_w, Tinsley and Weiss's T index, Lawshe's CVR and CVI, James et al.'s $r_{WG(J)}$, and Lindell et al.'s $r^*_{WG(J)}$. These indexes have been widely used, and their corresponding NULL HYPOTHESIS tests have been well developed. Scott's π applies to categorical decisions about an attribute for a group of ratees based on two independent raters. It is defined as $\pi = \frac{p_o - p_e}{1 - p_e}$ and practically ranges from 0 to 1 (although negative values can be obtained), where p_o and p_e represent the percentage of observed agreement between two raters and the percentage of expected agreement by chance, respectively. Determined by the number of judgmental categories and the frequencies of categories used by both raters, p_e is defined as the sum of the squared proportions of overall categories,

$$p_e = \sum_{i=1}^{k} p_i^2,$$

where k is the total number of categories and p_i is the proportion of judgments that falls in the ith category.

Cohen's κ, the most widely used index, assesses agreement between two or more independent raters who make categorical decisions regarding an attribute. Similar to Scott's π, Cohen's κ is defined as $\kappa = \frac{p_o - p_e}{1 - p_e}$ and often ranges from 0 to 1. However, p_e in Cohen's κ is operationalized differently, instead as the sum of joint probabilities of the MARGINALS in the CONTINGENCY TABLE across all categories. In contrast to Cohen's κ, Cohen's κ_w takes disagreements into consideration. In some practical situations, such as personnel selection, disagreement between "definitely succeed" and "likely succeed" would be less critical than "definitely succeed" and "definitely fail." Both κ and κ_w tend to overcorrect for the chance of agreement when the number of raters increases.

Tinsley and Weiss's T index, $T = \frac{N_1 - Np_e}{N - Np_e}$, was developed based on Cohen's κ and Lawlis and Lu's χ^2 test of the RANDOMNESS in ratings, where N_1, N, and p_e are the number of agreements across attributes, the total number of attributes rated, and the expected agreement by chance, respectively. Divided by N, the above formula can be rewritten as $T = \frac{p_o - p_e}{1 - p_e}$, where p_o is the proportion of attributes on which the raters agree. The value of p_e is determined by the range of acceptable ratings (r), the number of response categories used to make the judgments about the attributes (A), and the number of raters (K). If an exact agreement is required by researchers (i.e., the range of ratings is zero), $p_e = (\frac{1}{A})^{(K-1)}$. The computation formulas for p_e when $r > 0$ are quite complex; as such, a variety of p_e values can be obtained from Tinsley and Weiss (1975, note 7).

Lawshe's CVR, originally developed to assess experts' agreement about test item importance, is defined as $\text{CVR} = \frac{p_A - .5}{.5} = 2p_A - 1$ and may range from –1 to 1, where p_A is the proportion of raters who agree. If raters judge multiple items, an overall interrater agreement index (CVI) is applied. CVI is defined as $\text{CVI} = 2\bar{p}_A - 1$, where $\bar{p}_A$ is the average of the items' p_A values.

James et al.'s $r_{WG(J)}$ compares the observed variance of a group of ratings to an expected variance from random responding. When one attribute is rated,

$$r_{WG(1)} = 1 - \frac{S_x^2}{S_E^2},$$

where S_x^2 is the observed variance for rating an attribute X and S_E^2 is the variance of random responding. Although there are numerous ways to determine S_E^2, researchers often assume that the distribution of random responding is a discrete uniform distribution (Cohen, Doveh, & Eick, 2001). Given that, S_E^2 can be estimated by $S_{EU}^2 = \frac{A^2 - 1}{12}$, where A^2 is the number of response categories used to make judgments about attribute X. When there are J attributes to be rated,

$$r_{WG(J)} = \frac{J\left(1 - \frac{\bar{S}_x^2}{S_E^2}\right)}{J\left(1 - \frac{\bar{S}_x^2}{S_E^2}\right) + \frac{\bar{S}_x^2}{S_E^2}},$$

where $\bar{S}_x^2$ is the average variance of J attributes. Similarly, S_E^2 can be estimated by S_{EU}^2 if the uniform distribution for random responding is assumed. Similar to the above indexes, the upper bound of $r_{WG(J)}$ is 1. If $r_{WG(J)}$ is negative, James et al. suggest setting it to zero.

Lindell et al.'s $r_{WG(J)}^*$ differs from James et al.'s $r_{WG(J)}$ on two grounds. First, they argued that interrater agreement that is greater than expected by chance is just as legitimate a concept as interrater agreement that is less than expected by chance (Lindell & Brandt, 1999, p. 642). By setting negative values of $r_{WG(J)}$ to zero, Cohen et al. (2001) found a positive bias. Second, James et al.'s $r_{WG(J)}$ is derived from the SPEARMAN-BROWN correction formula, although $r_{WG(J)}$ is an agreement index rather than a reliability index. Lindell et al. questioned the legitimacy of using the Spearman-Brown correction for an agreement index and recommended

$$r_{WG(J)}^* = 1 - \frac{\bar{S}_x^2}{S_E^2}$$

or

$$r^*_{WG(J)} = 1 - \frac{\bar{S}^2_x}{S^2_{EU}}$$

if the uniform distribution is assumed. In general, both $r_{WG(J)}$ and $r^*_{WG(J)}$ are more flexible in a variety of situations than Lawshe's CVR or CVI, as well as Tinsley and Weiss's T index.

—Peter Y. Chen and Autumn D. Krauss

REFERENCES

Cohen, J. (1960/1968). A coefficient of agreement for nominal scales. *Educational and Psychological Measurement, 20,* 37–46.

Cohen, A., Doveh, E., & Eick, U. (2001). Statistical properties of the $r_{WG(J)}$ index of agreement. *Psychological Methods, 6,* 297–310.

James, L. R., Demaree, R. G., & Wolf, G. (1984). Estimating within-group interrater reliability with and without response bias. *Journal of Applied Psychology, 69,* 85–98.

Kozlowski, S. W., & Hattrup, K. (1992). A disagreement about within-group agreement: Disentangling issues of consistency versus consensus. *Journal of Applied Psychology, 77,* 161–167.

Lawlis, G. F., & Lu, E. (1972). Judgment of counseling process: Reliability, agreement, and error. *Psychological Bulletin, 78,* 17–20.

Lawshe, C. H. (1975). A quantitative approach to content validity. *Personnel Psychology, 28,* 563–575.

Lindell, M. K., & Brandt, C. J. (1999). Assessing interrater agreement on the job relevance of a test: A comparison of the CVI, T, $r_{WG(J)}$, and $r^*_{WG(J)}$ indexes. *Journal of Applied Psychology, 84,* 640–647.

Lindell, M. K., Brandt, C. J., & Whitney, D. J. (1999). A revised index of interrater agreement for multi-item ratings of a single target. *Applied Psychological Measurement, 23,* 127–135.

Scott, W. A. (1955). Reliability of content analysis: The case of nominal scale coding. *Public Opinion Quarterly, 19,* 321–325.

Tinsley, H. E., & Weiss, D. J. (1975). Interrater reliability and agreement of subjective judgments. *Journal of Counseling Psychology, 22,* 358–376.

INTERRATER RELIABILITY

Behavioral scientists often need to evaluate the consistency of raters' judgments pertaining to characteristics of interest such as patients' aggressive behaviors in a geriatric unit, quality of submitted manuscripts, artistic expression of figure skaters, or therapists' diagnostic abilities. Inconsistent judgments among raters threaten the validity of any inference extended from the judgment. Interrater reliability measures assess the relative consistency of judgments made by two or more raters.

Ratings made by two raters can be viewed as scores on two alternate forms of a test. Hence, interrater reliability based on two raters can be estimated by a SIMPLE CORRELATION such as PEARSON'S CORRELATION COEFFICIENT or SPEARMAN CORRELATION COEFFICIENT, according to the classical theory presented in RELIABILITY. However, these methods are of little use when there are more than two raters, such as in the case of a navy commander who needs to estimate the consistency of judgments among three officers who evaluate each F-18 pilot's landing performance. The above methods also cannot adequately assess interrater reliability if each pilot is rated by a different group of officers. To assess interrater reliability given the above circumstances, the most appropriate measure would be the INTRACLASS CORRELATION (ICC), which is a special case of the one-facet GENERALIZABILITY study.

Conceptually, the ICC ranges from 0 to 1 in theory (although it is not always the case in reality) and refers to the ratio of the variance associated with ratees over the sum of the variance associated with ratees and error variance. Different ICC formulas are used for different circumstances. We will focus on three basic cases that are frequently encountered in both practice and research. For more complex scenarios, such as the assessment of interrater reliability for four raters across three different times, an application of generalizability theory should be utilized.

The three scenarios, well articulated in the seminal article by Shrout and Fleiss (1979), are as follows: (a) Each ratee in a random sample is independently rated by a *different* group of raters, which is randomly selected from a population; (b) each ratee in a random sample is independently rated by the *sample* group of raters, which is randomly selected from a population; and (c) each ratee in a random sample is independently rated by the sample group of raters, which contains the only raters of interest (i.e., there is little interest in whether the result can be generalized to the population of raters). Each case requires a different statistical analysis, described below, to calculate the correspondent ICC. Specifically, one-way random effects, two-way random effects, and two-way mixed models are appropriate for Case 1, Case 2, and Case 3,

Table 1   Rating Data Used to Demonstrate ICC for Case 1, Case 2, and Case 3

Ratee	Rater 1	Rater 2	Rater 3
A	2	4	7
B	2	4	7
C	3	5	8
D	3	5	8
E	4	6	9
F	4	6	9
G	5	7	10
H	5	7	10
I	6	8	11
J	6	8	11

Table 2   Analysis of Variance Result for Case 1

Sources of Variance	df	MS
Between Ratee	9	6.67
Within Ratee	20	6.33

respectively. Note that all of these ICC indexes are biased but consistent estimators of reliability.

In Case 1, we assume there are 10 ratees, and each ratee is rated by a different group of raters. Specifically, the three raters who rate Ratee C are different from those who rate Ratee E. Based on the data in Table 1 and the ANALYSIS OF VARIANCE result in Table 2, we can calculate the ICC by the formula

$$ICC(1, 1) = \frac{MS_b - MS_w}{[MS_b + (k-1)MS_w]},$$

where MS_b and MS_w are the mean square between ratees and the mean square within ratees, respectively, and k is the number of raters rating each ratee. If there are different numbers of raters rating each ratee, k can be estimated by the average number of raters per ratee. The ICC $(1,1)$, the expected reliability of a single rater's rating, is 0.02, which suggests that only 2% of the variation in the rating is explained by the ratee. If we are interested in the interrater reliability pertaining to the average rating of k raters, we can estimate it by

$$ICC(1, k) = \frac{MS_b - MS_w}{MS_b},$$

which is 0.05.

In the second case, there are 10 ratees who are rated by the same three raters. These raters are a random

Table 3   Analysis of Variance Result for Case 2 and Case 3

Sources of Variance	df	MS
Ratee	9	6.67
Rater	2	63.33
Residual	18	5.403E-15

sample of the rater population. According to Tables 1 and 3, we can calculate the ICC by the formula,

$$ICC(2, 1) = \frac{MS_b - MS_e}{[MS_b + (k-1)MS_e + \frac{k(MS_j - MS_e)}{n}]},$$

where MS_b, MS_j, and MS_e are the mean square between ratees, the mean square between raters, and the mean square error respectively, k is the number of raters, and n is the number of ratees. Based on the sample data, the ICC$(2, 1)$ is 0.35. If we are interested in the interrater reliability pertaining to the average rating of k raters, we can estimate it by

$$ICC(2, k) = \frac{MS_b - MS_e}{MS_b + \frac{MS_j - MS_e}{n}},$$

which is 0.51.

In the final case, there are 10 ratees who are rated by the same three raters. The difference between Case 2 and Case 3 is that we are interested in generalizing the result to the population of raters in Case 2, but we are interested only in the actual raters in Case 3. Similarly, we can use the information in Table 3 and calculate the ICC by the formula

$$ICC(3, 1) = \frac{MS_b - MS_e}{[MS_b + (k-1)MS_e]},$$

and the ICC $(3, 1)$ approximates 1. If we are interested in the interrater reliability pertaining to the average rating of k raters, we can estimate it by

$$ICC(3, k) = \frac{MS_b - MS_e}{MS_b}$$

only if there is no interaction between ratee and rater.

—Peter Y. Chen and Autumn D. Krauss

REFERENCES

Shavelson, R. J., & Webb, N. M. (1991). *Generalizability theory: A primer*. Newbury Park, CA: Sage.

Shrout, P. E., & Fleiss, J. L. (1979). Intraclass correlations: Uses in assessing rater reliability. *Psychological Bulletin, 86*, 420–428.

INTERRUPTED TIME-SERIES DESIGN

The interrupted time-series design provides an estimate of the CAUSAL effect of a discrete intervention. In its simplest form, the design begins from a long series of repeated measurements on a DEPENDENT VARIABLE. The INTERVENTION breaks this TIME SERIES into preintervention and postintervention segments, and a data analysis compares the means of the dependent variable in the two periods. Rejecting the NULL HYPOTHESIS of no difference between the means is taken as evidence that the intervention influenced the series.

Figure 1 illustrates an unusually clear example of the design's logic. The data come from a 1978 study by A. John McSweeny and consist of 180 months of local directory assistance calls in Cincinnati, Ohio. During March 1974, the Cincinnati telephone company began to charge a small fee for answering these calls, which it had previously handled for free. Call volume plummeted, supporting the idea that the fee successfully reduced demands on the service.

In this example, the causal impact of the intervention seems obvious. The number of calls fell immediately and dramatically, and no ready explanation exists for why the drop might otherwise have occurred. More typically, any change in a series will be visually ambiguous, and alternative explanations will be easier to construct. Therefore, applications of the time-series design must address statistical analysis issues, and researchers must entertain rival explanations for an apparent causal effect.

Much of the design's popularity stems from the work of Donald T. Campbell, in collaborations with Julian C. Stanley and Thomas D. Cook. Campbell and his coworkers developed a list of threats to the INTERNAL VALIDITY of causal inferences, where variables besides the one under study might account for the results. Using their list to evaluate common nonexperimental designs, Campbell and coworkers concluded that the interrupted time series had stronger internal validity than did most alternatives.

Its relative strengths notwithstanding, the time-series design is still vulnerable to several important validity threats. One of these is *history,* or the possibility that other events around the time of the intervention were responsible for an observed effect. To make historical threats less plausible, researchers often analyze control series that were not subject to the intervention.

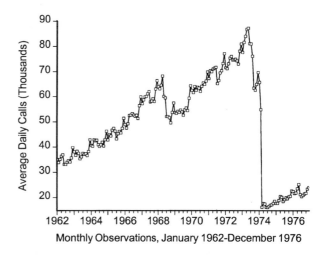

Figure 1   Average Daily Calls (in Thousands) to Cincinnati Local Directory Assistance, January 1962–December 1976

SOURCE: McSweeny (1978).

Lack of change in these series increases confidence that the intervention was the causal agent. In Cincinnati, for example, the telephone company continued to provide free long-distance directory assistance, and this series did not drop after the local assistance fee began.

Statistical analyses of interrupted time-series data often rely on BOX-JENKINS MODELING. Although not absolutely required, Box-Jenkins methods help solve two major analytic problems: nonstationarity and SERIAL CORRELATION. Nonstationarity occurs when a series lacks a constant mean (e.g., when it trends), and serial correlation occurs when later observations are predictable from earlier ones. If not addressed, these features can invalidate tests of the difference between the preintervention and postintervention means.

—David McDowall

REFERENCES

Campbell, D. T., & Stanley, J. C. (1963). *Experimental and quasi-experimental designs for research.* Chicago: Rand McNally.

Cook, T. D., & Campbell, D. T. (1979). *Quasi-experimentation: Design and analysis issues for field settings.* Boston: Houghton-Mifflin.

McDowall, D., McCleary, R., Meidinger, E. E., & Hay, R. A., Jr. (1980). *Interrupted time series analysis.* Beverly Hills, CA: Sage.

McSweeny, A. J. (1978). Effects of response cost on the behavior of a million persons: Charging for directory assistance in Cincinnati. *Journal of Applied Behavior Analysis, 11,* 47–51.

INTERVAL

An interval is a level of measurement whereby the numeric values of the variable are equidistant and have intrinsic meaning. A classic example is income measured in dollars. An income score of $90,000 is immediately understood. Furthermore, the distance between someone with a $90,000 income and someone with a $90,001 income (i.e., one dollar) is equal to the distance between someone with a $56,545 income and someone with a $56,546 income (i.e., one dollar). Interval level of MEASUREMENT allows a high degree of precision and the ready use of MULTIVARIATE statistics. Interval measures are sometimes called QUANTITATIVE, or METRIC, measures. DATA that are interval can be converted to lower levels of measurement, such as ORDINAL or NOMINAL, but information is lost.

—Michael S. Lewis-Beck

INTERVENING VARIABLE. *See* MEDIATING VARIABLE

INTERVENTION ANALYSIS

Interventions in a time series are measures representing disruptions in the course of a series of data extending over a time period. They are often conceptualized for evaluating policy impacts or other discrete introductions in a historical process. In many cases, they are introduced as the experimental treatment in an INTERRUPTED TIME-SERIES DESIGN (McDowall, McCleary, Meidinger, & Hay, 1980). Because estimates of policy interventions or other factors affecting a time series can be BIASED by contaminating factors, such as TREND (nonstationarity), AUTOREGRESSION (sometimes present even when there is no trend, as in cyclical processes), and MOVING AVERAGE components (random shocks that persist over time and then die away), the analytical model is usually specified as the presence or absence of an intervention (0 or 1), plus a noise model from which unspecified time-related effects have been eliminated—a WHITE NOISE process. The equation for this process is usually represented as

$$y_t = \omega I_t + N_t,$$

1. Pulse Function   (I= ....0,0,0,1,0,0,0.....)

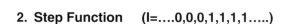

2. Step Function   (I=....0,0,0,1,1,1,1.....)

3. Ramp Function   (I=....0,0,0,1,2,3,4.....)

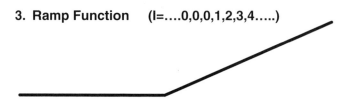

Figure 1   Basic Structures of Interventions

where y_t represents an observation in a time series composed of ωI_t; effects of the intervention; and a *white noise process*, N_t. Effects of the intervention can be evaluated by a *T*-TEST for SIGNIFICANCE of ω. This has the effect of eliminating time-series components extraneous to the impact of the intervention and permits testing of hypotheses regarding impacts of the policy or other intervention.

Although the research takes the form of a QUASI-EXPERIMENTAL design suggested by Campbell and Stanley (see INTERRUPTED TIME-SERIES DESIGN), estimation of the intervention effects may take a variety of specifications. When precise information on the form of the intervention is available, such as yearly reductions in allowable pollution (Box & Tiao, 1975), the intervention should be specified accordingly. Most policy interventions are difficult to specify, however, and require DUMMY VARIABLES representing presence or absence of a policy or program.

1. Rapidly Dampening Pulse Function (I=...0,0,0,1,0,0,0...; δ > 0)

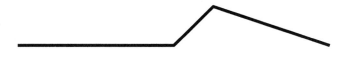

2. Step Function Plus Gradually Increasing Level (I=...0,0,0,1,1,1,1...; δ > 0)

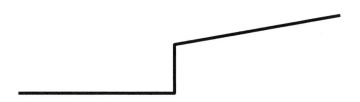

Model 2 can also be modeled as a Step Function plus a Ramp Function by specifying two intervention effects.

3. Step Function Plus Ramp Function (I₁=...0,0,0,1,1,1,1...; I₂=...0,0,0,1,2,3,4...)

Figure 2   Common, Complex Models of Intervention Effects

For these more general effects, there are three basic specification models that account for an intervention (Figure 1).

Tests of these models can be obtained by including a lag of y, y_{t-1}, in the estimating equation,

$$y_t = \delta y_{t-1} + \omega I_t + N_t,$$

and evaluating the parameter, δ, by a t-test. If the analyst has no explicit knowledge as to the form of the intervention, alternative specifications can be tested. Specifically, one may try specification of the intervention in the following manner:

1. If the parameter of a specified *pulse function* (abrupt, temporary effect) is significant and the parameter, δ, is not significant, the intervention effect takes the form of the *pulse function* illustrated in Figure 1.
2. If the parameter of a specified *pulse function* (abrupt, temporary effect), ω, is significant and the parameter, δ, is also significant, the outcome suggests that a *step function* (abrupt, permanent effect) is a better specification.

For example, if the coefficient of the lagged endogenous variable equals 1, the model is identical with a *step function*.

3. If the parameter of a specified *step function*, ω, is significant, but the parameter, δ, is not significant, a *step function* specification is probably correct (Figure 1).
4. If the parameters of both the intervention specified as a *step function* and the lagged time series, y_{t-1}, prove to be significant, alternative model combinations should be investigated.
5. If the parameter of a *pulse function* specification is not significant, but the parameter of y_{t-1} is significant, a *ramp* function (Figure 1) should be investigated.

When ambiguities are detected in the model specifications described above, the model may require more complex, alternative specifications, sometimes as combinations of the basic models (see Figure 2).

These models of interventions represent the most frequently encountered specifications. More complex models, including multiple interventions, are also useful for representing policy and program effects.

Scholars sometimes object that following the Box and Jenkins specification of a white noise process by removing time-related processes is atheoretical. If a researcher believes that specifiable variables may represent alternative rival hypotheses, they may be included as transfer functions. In any case, the process is hardly more atheoretical than so-called ERROR CORRECTION models and has the effect of eliminating contaminating statistical artifacts, such as COLLINEARITY, from the equation.

—Robert B. Albritton

See also INTERRUPTED TIME-SERIES DESIGN

REFERENCES

Box, G. E. P., & Jenkins, G. M. (1976). *Time series analysis: Forecasting and control.* San Francisco: Holden-Day.

Box, G. E. P., & Tiao, G. C. (1975). Intervention analysis with applications to economic and environmental problems. *Journal of the American Statistical Association, 70,* 70–92.

Campbell, D. T., & Stanley, J. C. (1966). *Experimental and quasi-experimental designs for research.* Skokie, IL: Rand McNally.

McDowall, D., McCleary, R., Meidinger, E. E., & Hay, R. A., Jr. (1980). *Interrupted time series analysis.* Beverly Hills, CA: Sage.

INTERVIEW GUIDE

An interview guide, or aide memoire, is a list of topics, themes, or areas to be covered in a SEMISTRUCTURED INTERVIEW. This is normally created in advance of the interview by the researcher and is constructed in such a way as to allow flexibility and fluidity in the topics and areas that are to be covered, the way they are to be approached with each interviewee, and their sequence. The interview guide normally will be linked to the RESEARCH QUESTIONS that guide the study and will cover areas likely to generate data that can address those questions.

An interview guide is a mechanism to help the interviewer conduct an effective semistructured interview. It can take a variety of forms, but the primary consideration is that it enables the interviewer to ask questions relevant to the research focus, in ways relevant to the interviewee, and at appropriate points in the developing social interaction of the interview. An interview guide should help an interviewer to make on-the-spot decisions about the content and sequence of the interview as it happens. This means, for example, deciding whether a topic introduced by the interviewee is worth following up, when to close a topic and open a new one, whether and when to reintroduce something mentioned earlier in the interview, and when and how to probe for more detail. It also usually means deciding on the spot how to word a question in the specific context of a particular interview, rather than reading from a script.

This level of flexibility and specificity cannot be achieved with a standardized list of interview questions, and thus an interview guide should be distinguished from an INTERVIEW SCHEDULE, which contains a formal list of the questions to be asked of each interviewee. Instead, an interview guide might comprise topics headings and key words on cards that can easily be shuffled and reordered. It might include examples of ways of asking about key issues, but it will not list every or even any question in detail. It might include some of the researcher's hunches, or specific issues or events that would be worth probing should they arise. It might include a checklist of areas, or perhaps interviewee characteristics, to ask about at the end of the interview if these have not arisen before.

The quality of an interview guide is dependent upon how effective it is for the researcher and the research in question, rather than upon abstract principles. Therefore, it is vital that interview guides are tested out in a PILOT STUDY and modified accordingly.

—Jennifer Mason

REFERENCES

Kvale, S. (1996). *InterViews: An introduction to qualitative research interviewing.* Thousand Oaks, CA: Sage.

Mason, J. (2002). *Qualitative researching* (2nd ed.). London: Sage.

INTERVIEW SCHEDULE

An interview schedule is the guide an interviewer uses when conducting a STRUCTURED INTERVIEW. It has two components: a set of questions designed to be asked exactly as worded, and instructions to the interviewer about how to proceed through the questions.

The questions appear in the order in which they are to be asked. The questions are designed so they can be administered verbatim, exactly as they are written. The questions need to communicate not only what information is being asked of RESPONDENTS but also the form or the way in which respondents are supposed to answer the question. For example, "Age" does not constitute a question for an interviewer to ask. In a structured interview schedule, the question would supply all the words the interviewer would need: "How old were you on your last birthday?"

Similarly, "When were you born?" does not tell the respondent what kind of answer to provide. "After the Vietnam war," "about 20 years ago," and "in 1971" would all constitute adequate answers to this question, yet they are all different. A good question in an interview schedule would read, "In what year were you born?"

The interview schedule also needs to make clear to interviewers how they are to proceed through the questions. For example:

1. Provide optional wording to fit particular circumstances of the respondent. For example, "Did you (or your husband/wife) buy any stocks in the past 12 months?" The parentheses and the husband/wife wording communicates to interviewers that they have to adapt the question to the respondent's situation. This helps the interviewer word questions properly and ensures that all interviewers adapt question wording in the same, consistent way.

2. Provide instructions for skipping questions. For example, certain questions might be asked only of those who have recently visited a doctor. The interview schedule must identify those people who have and have not been to a doctor's office and provide appropriate instructions to interviewers about which questions to ask and which to skip.

3. Interview schedules also provide instructions to interviewers about where and how to record answers.

Interview schedules can be on paper forms in booklets. Increasingly, interview schedules are computerized for COMPUTER-ASSISTED DATA COLLECTION; the questions to be asked pop up on the computer screen to be read by the interviewer, and answers are recorded by either typing the respondent's words into the computer or by entering a number that corresponds to a particular answer. In either form, the role of the interview

schedule is to provide a PROTOCOL for interviewers to ask and record answers in a consistent way across all respondents and to facilitate the process of getting through the interview smoothly and efficiently.

—Floyd J. Fowler, Jr.

REFERENCES

Converse, J., & Presser, S. (1986). *Survey questions*. Beverly Hills, CA: Sage.

Fowler, F. J., Jr. (1995). *Improving survey questions*. Thousand Oaks, CA: Sage.

Sudman, S., & Bradburn, N. (1982). *Asking questions*. San Francisco: Jossey-Bass.

INTERVIEWER EFFECTS

The increase in VARIANCE of a SAMPLE statistic because of interviewer differences is known as the *interviewer effect*. This increased variance can be modeled as arising from a positive CORRELATION, ρ_{int}, among responses collected by the same interviewer. Under this simple MODEL, it can be shown that variance of the sample mean is increased by a factor of about $1 + (\bar{m} - 1)\rho_{int}$, where $\bar{m}$ is the size of the average interviewer assignment (Kish, 1962).

Studies have shown that ρ_{int} is typically small, often less than 0.02 and nearly always less than 0.10. Even so, it can have a large impact on the STANDARD ERROR of statistics when interviewer assignments are large. For example, the standard error of the sample MEAN of an item having $\rho_{int} = 0.02$ would be nearly doubled in a survey in which the average interviewer assignment size is 150 because its variance would be increased by a factor of $1 + (150 - 1)(0.02) = 3.98$. This suggests that one way to reduce the impact of interviewer differences on survey data is to increase the number of interviewers on staff and reduce their average assignment size.

Interviewer effects are not routinely measured as part of survey operations. To do so, one must interpenetrate interviewer assignments, meaning that the sample units must be RANDOMLY ASSIGNED to them. This is prohibitively expensive in personal visit surveys, but more feasible in telephone survey operations. Even there, though, potential shift effects complicate ESTIMATION. A methodology that allows interviewer and respondent covariates to be accounted for, called MULTILEVEL ANALYSIS, has been adopted for modeling interviewer effects. Software to implement this method is now readily available (e.g., MLwiN) and could help make estimation of interviewer effects in production environments more feasible.

One advantage of measuring interviewer effects is that it allows a more realistic assessment of precision of estimates of means and totals. Another is that it provides a way of assessing and comparing data quality among the survey items. Ideally, this information would help with monitoring and improving interviewer performance. However, it is still not clear how to reduce the magnitude of ρ_{int} for an item, even if it is known to be large. Numerous studies have attempted to find the causes of interviewer effects. Demographic and behavioral characteristics of interviewers, such as race, gender, voice, and demeanor, have been examined. Little evidence has been found to suggest that these characteristics explain the effects. Other research has tried to identify the types of items most affected. Although it seems plausible that sensitive items would be more vulnerable, this has not been clearly shown. There is some evidence that items requiring more interviewer intervention, such as PROBING, have larger interviewer effects, which suggests that more extensive interviewer training in these skills might be useful. However, some studies have suggested that training alone may not be helpful, but the monitoring and feedback possible in a centralized telephone facility may help. Until recently, it was widely accepted that standardized interviewing, which restricts interviewers to a uniform script, was the best approach for controlling interviewer effects. Some research now suggests that a more conversational style, which allows interviewers to paraphrase or clarify responses, may increase the accuracy of responses without increasing ρ_{int} (Schober & Conrad, 1997).

—S. Lynne Stokes

REFERENCES

Biemer, P. P., Groves, R. M., Lyberg, L. E., Mathiowetz, N. A., & Sudman, S. (Eds.). (1991). *Measurement errors in surveys*. New York: Wiley.

Kish, L. (1962). Studies of interviewer variance for attitudinal variables. *Journal of the American Statistical Association, 57*, 92–115.

Schober, M., & Conrad, F. (1997). Does conversational interviewing reduce survey measurement error? *Public Opinion Quarterly, 61*, 576–602.

INTERVIEWER TRAINING

Those who are going to be interviewers on social science research projects almost always benefit from training. The specific mix of skills and techniques they need to learn varies somewhat by whether they are doing STRUCTURED or SEMISTRUCTURED INTERVIEWS.

If interviewers will be doing structured interviews, the basic skills they need to learn include the following:

1. Asking questions exactly as worded
2. Probing incomplete answers in a nondirective way; that is, in a way that does not increase the likelihood of one particular answer over others
3. Recording answers without discretion

When interviewers are doing SEMISTRUCTURED INTERVIEWS, they need to be trained in how to word or ask questions in a way that will elicit the information they need to obtain. The answers to semistructured interviews tend to be in narrative form in the respondents' own words, whereas structured interviews tend to ask respondents to choose one of a specific set of answers. Therefore, semistructured interviewers also have to have more highly developed skills in nondirective probing than is typically the case for a structured interviewer. Specifically, such interviewers need to develop skills at diagnosing the reason why an answer is incomplete and learn an array of nondirective probes that will elicit the information that is needed.

Two skills are common to both kinds of interviewers. First, interviewers usually are responsible for enlisting the cooperation of potential respondents. Thus, they need to learn how to introduce the research project in a way that engages the respondents' interest and makes them willing to accept their role in the interview. Second, interviewers also have to train the respondents in what they are supposed to do during the interview. This is particularly a challenge for structured interviews, in which the behavior of both interviewers and respondents is highly prescribed. For such interviews, it is extremely valuable for interviewers to properly explain to respondents what they are supposed to do and why it is the best way to do it, in order to get them to accept their role and play it well. In contrast, a semistructured interview is less constrained, so training the respondents in their roles is less of a challenge.

There have been several studies that show that the training of structured interviewers has a major effect on how well they conduct interviews and on the quality of data that they collect. Interviewers with minimal training do not perform well. In particular, it has been shown that supervised practice interviewing has a positive effect on interviewing and data quality. For semistructured interviews, we lack systematic studies of the effects of training on the resulting data. However, studies have shown that PROBING answers that are provided in narrative form is among the hardest skills for interviewers to master, and those skills benefit most from training. The same studies suggest that designing appropriate question wording may be even harder and, hence, even more likely to benefit from training.

—Floyd J. Fowler, Jr.

REFERENCES

Fowler, F. J., Jr., & Mangione, T. W. (1990). *Standardized survey interviewing*. Newbury Park, CA: Sage.

Weiss, R. (1995). *Learning from strangers*. New York: Free Press.

INTERVIEWING

In the social sciences, a major method of data gathering is interviewing individuals. Interviews may be formally conducted in social SURVEYS, face-to-face or over the telephone. Or, subjects in a study population, such as members of an indigenous language community in the Andes, can be more or less informally interviewed. At the elite level, interviews may be carried out essentially as conversations, at least ostensibly. The interview method may have to be adapted to the social context in order to achieve the overriding goal of obtaining VALID and useful DATA.

—Michael S. Lewis-Beck

INTERVIEWING IN QUALITATIVE RESEARCH

INTERVIEWING is one of the most frequently used research methods in the social sciences, used in both quantitative SURVEY research and in QUALITATIVE RESEARCH. Qualitative interviewing involves a special kind of conversation, one in which an interviewer (or more than one) asks questions of a respondent or subject (or more than one), on a particular topic or topics, and carefully listens to and records the answers. Some interviews take place over the telephone, and some in person; some are videotaped, whereas most are audiotaped and then transcribed. This discussion of the qualitative interview is based on what is probably the most common form: a single interviewer interviewing a single respondent using an audiotape recorder.

Interviews have been used in the social sciences since the 19th century, when scholars and practitioners began to seek answers to large-scale questions about the human condition. In America, interviews were used as part of the case study method in the social sciences at the University of Chicago during the 1920s and 1930s, together with fieldwork, documentary analysis, and statistical methods (Platt, 2002). After World War II, interviews began to be used extensively in survey research; from that point onward, the quantifiable CLOSED-ENDED QUESTION survey interview became more common than the open-ended qualitative interview.

However, qualitative interviewing remained as a key method in anthropology and is used today in all the social sciences. The purpose of qualitative interviewing in social science research today, as of qualitative research in general, is to understand the meanings of the topic of the interview to the respondent. As Kvale (1996) puts it, the qualitative interview has as its purpose "to obtain descriptions of the life world of the interviewee with respect to interpreting the meaning of the described phenomena" (pp. 5–6). For the sake of simplicity, I illustrate this point mainly with reference to my own qualitative interview-based book on Madwives (Warren, 1987).

In interviews with female psychiatric patients in the late 1950s and early 1960s (Warren, 1987), the eight interviewers wanted to know about the experiences of mental hospitalization from the perspective of the female patients as well as the psychiatrists. They interviewed these women at weekly intervals during and after hospitalization, in some cases for several years. One of the topics they asked about was electroshock or electroconvulsive therapy (ECT). From the point of view of the medical model, ECT is a psychiatric treatment intended to relieve the symptoms of depression, schizophrenia, or other disorders, with side effects that include short-term memory loss. To the women undergoing ECT in the late 1950s and early 1960s, however, the meanings of the treatment were both different (from the medical model) and variable (from one another, and sometimes from one day to another). Some of the women saw it as a form of punishment, whereas others believed that it was a medical treatment, but that its purpose was to erase their troubles from their memories.

Social scientists interview people because they have questions about the life worlds of their respondents. How do mental patients interpret the treatments they are given? What do single women involved in affairs with married men think about their situation (Richardson, 1985)? In order to use the qualitative interview method, these RESEARCH QUESTIONS have to be translated into actual questions for the researcher to ask the respondent. These questions are developed in two contexts: the overall RESEARCH DESIGN, and governmental and institutional guidelines for protection of human subjects.

In social research, qualitative interviewing may be part of a research design that also includes FIELD RESEARCH or other methods, or it may be the only method planned by the researcher. Whatever the overall design, the specific questions asked by the interviewer are related to the topic of interest and to the study designer's research questions. In general, qualitative researchers develop 10 to 15 questions to ask respondents, and they are also prepared to use PROBES to elicit further information. In order to save time, basic demographic information such as gender, age, occupation, and ethnicity can be gathered using a face sheet for each respondent. Then, the rest of the interview time—which may range from 15 minutes to several hours, depending upon the questioner and the talkativeness of the respondent—can be spent on the researcher's topic questions and the respondent's narrative.

In contemporary social science research, qualitative interview studies must concern themselves with federal and institutional human subjects regulations. Although human subjects regulations are discussed elsewhere in this volume, it is important to note the requirements for INFORMED CONSENT and CONFIDENTIALITY in interview research. Generally, the respondents in an interview study are given a letter explaining the purpose of the research (informed consent) and indicating who is sponsoring it—a university department, for example—which they will sign. As with any other social research, the interviewer must promise (and keep that promise!) to make sure that the names and identifying details of all respondents remain confidential.

Once the interviewer has his or her Institutional Review Board (IRB) permissions, has his or her questions formulated, and is ready to go, he or she will have to find people to be interviewed—deciding, first, what types of people to interview (by gender, race, age, and so on), and how many (generally, 20–50). Then, the interviewer must locate specific respondents. The general issue of sampling is discussed elsewhere in this volume; suffice it to say here that the difficulty of finding people to talk to is dependent, in part, on the topic of the interview. If the study is to be on mental patients, for example, the researcher must locate a mental hospital that will give him or her permission to do the research (very difficult in the 2000s), and then gain individual patients' consent—both of which are fraught with difficulty. The study of single women having affairs with married men will probably involve fewer problems, especially if the researcher is a woman around the same age as the respondents she wants to interview. As Richardson (1985) notes, "Finding Other Women to interview was not difficult" (p. x), and getting them to tell their stories was not either, because women in that situation are often eager to talk.

Qualitative interviewing is a special kind of conversation, with the researcher asking the questions and the respondent taking as much time as he or she needs (within some limits!) to tell his or her story; qualitative interviews typically last from a half hour to an hour or more. The types of questions asked include introducing questions ("Can you tell me about . . .?"), probing questions ("Could you tell me more about . . .?"), and specifying questions ("What did you think then . . .?) (Kvale, 1996, pp. 133–134). The interviewer tries not to lead the witness; for example, instead of saying, "Didn't that make you feel awful?" he or she would ask, "How did that make you feel?" The order of questioning proceeds from the most general and unthreatening to, at the end, questions that might cause discomfort to the respondent. The interviewer hopes to gain some rapport with the respondent in the early part of the interview so that more sensitive questions will be acceptable later on.

Audiotaped qualitative interviews are generally TRANSCRIBED, either by the interviewer or by someone else. It is often preferable for the interviewer to transcribe the interviews he or she has done, because he or she is in the best position to be able to interpret ambiguous statements. Paid—or especially unpaid—transcribers lack the firsthand experience with the interview and may lack the incentive to translate the oral into the written word with attention and care. It is important in transcribing and analyzing interviews to remember that an interview is a speech event guided by conversational turn-taking (Mishler, 1986).

Transcripts are used in qualitative interviewing—just as field notes are used in ETHNOGRAPHY—as the textual basis for analysis. Analysis of interview or ethnographic text consists of reading and rereading transcriptions and identifying conceptual patterns. In my study of female mental patients and their husbands in the late 1950s and early 1960s, I noticed two patterns in those interviews that occurred after the women had been released from the mental hospital. Some wives, and some husbands, wanted to forget and deny that the women had been in the mental hospital; the continued weekly presence of the interviewer, however, reminded them of this. So, they either tried to end the interviews, or, when that failed (respondents are sometimes very obedient!), they tried to make the interviews into social events by inviting the interviewer to stay for tea, or by turning the tables and asking questions. Other women were still very troubled and wanted to continue to try to make the interview process into a form of therapy (Warren, 1987). Here are some examples:

> Ann Rand repeated that she would only see the interviewer again if she would have her over to her house. While the interviewer was evasive, Ann said, "then I suppose you still see me as a patient. To me you are either a friend or some kind of authority, now which is it? The way I see it, you either see me as a friend or a patient." (p. 261)

> Mr. Oren asked me if I wanted to join them for dinner, and was rather insistent about this despite my repeated declining. He later invited me to drop over to his place some afternoon, bring along a broad and just let my hair down and enjoy myself.... I was emphasizing the fact that this was my job, probably in the hope of getting him to accept the situation as such and not redefine it. (p. 261)

It is no accident that the first example involves a female interviewer and a female respondent, and the second involves a male interviewer and a male respondent. A housewife in 1960 would not have tried to make a friend out of a male interviewer—indeed, the male

interviewers had difficulty setting up interviews with female respondents—and a husband from the same era would not have invited a female interviewer to "drop over to his place and bring along a broad." The extensive literature on qualitative interviewing documents the significance of gender and other personal characteristics on the interview process—and thus the data that are the subject of analysis. Some feminist qualitative interviewers in the 1970s and 1980s, such as Ann Oakley, noted the particular suitability of interviewing as a method for eliciting the narratives of women (whose everyday lives were often invisible) and for lessening the hierarchical divisions between superordinate researchers and subordinated subjects in social science research (Warren, 2002). Other feminist interviewers in the 1990s and 2000s, such as Donna Luff, note that there are profound differences between women in terms of nationality, race, social class, and political ideology—differences that are not necessarily overcome by the commonalities of gender (Warren, 2002).

Issues of representation and POSTMODERNISM are as relevant to qualitative interviewing in the social sciences as they are to ethnography and other methods. Gubrium and Holstein (2002) have challenged the modernist (and journalistic) notion of interviewees as "vessels of answers" whose responses are just waiting to be drained out of them by interviewers. Gubrium and Holstein's and others' critiques of the interview method (whether these critiques are from postmodernist, feminist, or other stances) focus on the EPISTEMOLOGY of the interview: What kind of knowing is it, and what kinds of knowledge can be derived from it? Various answers to these questions have emerged during the past decade or so, including the framing of interviews as a particular form of talk (Mishler, 1986) with knowledge of linguistic forms to be derived from it—and nothing else. Whether an interview is just a speech event, or can be used as data for understanding respondents' meaning-worlds outside the interview, is an open question at the present time.

Although it is one of the most widely used methods in the social sciences, the qualitative interview is currently subject to considerable epistemological debate. As Gubrium and Holstein (2002) note, we live in an "interview society" in which everyone's point of view is seen as worthy of eliciting, and in which everyone seemingly wants to be interviewed—at least by the media, if not by social scientists. The qualitative interview, like the survey interview in quantitative research, is likely to be used for some time to come to illuminate those aspects of social lives that cannot be understood either quantitatively or ethnographically.

What is it that the qualitative interview can capture that cannot be captured by field research? Although ethnography does, like qualitative interviewing, seek an understanding of members' life-worlds, it does so somewhat differently. Going back to the example of mental hospital research, a field researcher observes staff-patient and patient-patient interaction in the present, coming to conclusions about the patterns and meanings observed in those interactions. An interviewer elicits biographical meanings related to the present but also the past and future; the interview focuses not on interaction (which is best studied observationally) but on accounts or stories about the respondent. Thus, to a field researcher, ECT looks like an easy and inexpensive way for hospitals to subdue unruly patients, whereas to the housewife undergoing ECT, it seems like a punishment for her inability to be what the culture tells her is a good wife and mother.

Interviewing in today's society holds both dangers and promises for the conduct of social science research. Interviewing is an inexpensive and easy way to do research in an interview society where quick results are the bottom line—especially for journalists—producing superficial and cursory results. But it can also be an invaluable tool for understanding the ways in which people live in and construct their everyday lives and social worlds. Without such an understanding, it is impossible to conduct good or useful theoretical, quantitative, or applied research. Whatever the aims of the social scientist—constructing or proving theory, conducting large-scale survey research, or improving social conditions—none of them can be reached without an understanding of the lives of the people who live in the society and the world. Qualitative interviewing, together with ethnography, provides the tools for such an understanding.

—Carol A. B. Warren

REFERENCES

Gubrium, J. F., & Holstein, J. A. (2002). From the individual interview to the interview society. In J. F. Gubrium & J. A. Holstein (Eds.), *Handbook of interview research: Context and method* (pp. 3–32). Thousand Oaks, CA: Sage.

Kvale, S. (1996). *InterViews: An introduction to qualitative research interviewing.* Thousand Oaks, CA: Sage.

Mishler, E. G. (1986). *Research interviewing: Context and narrative.* Cambridge, MA: Harvard University Press.

Platt, J. (2002). The history of the interview. In J. F. Gubrium & J. A. Holstein (Eds.), *Handbook of interview research: Context and method* (pp. 33–54). Thousand Oaks, CA: Sage.

Richardson, L. (1985). *The new other woman: Contemporary single women in affairs with married men.* London: Collier-Macmillan.

Warren, C. A. B. (1987). *Madwives: Schizophrenic women in the 1950s.* New Brunswick, NJ: Rutgers University Press.

Warren, C. A. B. (2002). Qualitative interviewing. In J. F. Gubrium & J. A. Holstein (Eds.), *Handbook of interview research: Context and method* (pp. 83–101). Thousand Oaks, CA: Sage.

INTRACLASS CORRELATION

An intraclass correlation coefficient is a measure of association based on a variance ratio. Formally, it is the ratio of the variance for an object of measurement (σ_{Object}^2) to the object variance plus error variance:

$$(\sigma_{\text{error}}^2)\frac{\sigma_{\text{Object}}^2}{\sigma_{\text{Object}}^2 + \sigma_{\text{error}}^2}.$$

It differs from an analog measure of association known as OMEGA SQUARED (ω^2) only in the statistical model used to develop the sample estimate of σ_{Object}^2. Intraclass correlation estimates are made using the random effects model (i.e., the objects in any one sample are randomly sampled from a population of potential objects) and ω^2 estimates are made using the FIXED EFFECTS MODEL (i.e., the objects in the sample are the only ones of interest and could not be replaced without altering the question being addressed in the research).

Intraclass correlation is best introduced using one of the problems it was developed to solve—what the correlation of siblings is on a biometric trait. If the sample used to obtain the correlation estimate consisted just of sibling pairs (in which sibships are the object of measurement), a Pearson product-moment, interclass correlation could be used, but this procedure would not lead to a unique estimate. The reason is seen with an example. For three sibling pairs $\{1, 2\}$, $\{3, 4\}$, and $\{5, 6\}$, the Pearson r for pairs when listed in this original order $\{1, 2\}\{3, 4\}\{5, 6\}$ is different from the Pearson r for the same pairs if listed as $\{2, 1\}\{3, 4\}\{6, 5\}$, even though the sibling data are exactly the same. The Pearson procedure requires the totally arbitrary assignment of pair members to a set

X and a set Y when, in fact, the only assignment is to sibship. How, then, is one to obtain a measure of correlation within sibship classes without affecting the estimate through arbitrary assignments? An early answer was to double-list each pair and then compute a Pearson r. For the example above, this meant computing the Pearson r for the twice-listed pairs $\{1, 2\}\{2, 1\}\{3, 4\}\{4, 3\}\{5, 6\}\{6, 5\}$.

Double-listing the data for each sibship leads to a convenient solution in the case of sibling pairs, but the method becomes increasingly laborious as sibships are expanded to include 3, 4, or k siblings. A computational advance was introduced by J. A. Harris (1913), and then R. A. Fisher (1925) applied his analysis of variance to the problem. This latter approach revealed that a sibling correlation is an application of the one-way random effects variance model. In this model, each sibling value is conceptualized as the sum of three independent components: a population mean (μ) for the biometric trait in question; an effect for the sibship (α), which is a deviation of the sibship mean from the population mean; and a deviation of the individual sibling from the sibship mean (ε). In its conventional form, the model is written $Y_{ij} = \mu + \alpha_i + \varepsilon_{ij}$. The sibling correlation is then the variance of the alpha effects over the variance of the alpha effects plus epsilon (error) effects:

$$\frac{\sigma_\alpha^2}{\sigma_\alpha^2 + \sigma_\varepsilon^2}.$$

In other words, it is the proportion of total variance in the trait that is due to differences between sibships. For traits that run in families, the correlation would be high; for those that don't, the correlation would be low.

Applying the ANALYSIS OF VARIANCE to the problem of sibling correlation solved the computational inconveniences of the old method, easily accommodated the analysis of data with unequal sibling sizes, and clarified the nature of the correlation as one of the ratio of variances. It also provided a means of computing other forms of intraclass correlation. Sibling correlations represent correlations expressible using a one-way model. There are other correlations of interest that require two- and three-way models. Many of these involve the RELIABILITY of measurements: How reliable are judges' ratings when each of k judges rates each of n performers? How reliably do school students perform across different instructors and subjects? Each of these questions can be addressed by forming variance ratios that are intraclass correlations. In fact, two of the most common reliability measures—CRONBACH'S ALPHA and Cohen's kappa—are expressible as intraclass correlations.

—Kenneth O. McGraw

REFERENCES

Fisher, R. A. (1925). *Statistical methods for research workers* (1st ed.). Edinburgh, UK: Oliver & Boyd.

Harris, J. A. (1913). On the calculation of intraclass and interclass coefficients of correlation from class moments when the number of possible combinations is large. *Biometrika, 9,* 446–472.

McGraw, K. O., & Wong, S. P. (1996). Forming inferences about some intraclass correlation coefficients. *Psychological Methods, 1,* 30–46.

Shrout, P. E., & Fleiss, J. L. (1979). Intraclass correlation: Uses in assessing rater reliability. *Psychological Bulletin, 86,* 420–428.

INTRACODER RELIABILITY

An observer's or coder's judgments about people's behaviors or other phenomena of interest (e.g., violent acts on TV shows or gender stereotypes embedded in children's books) tend to fluctuate across different occasions. Intracoder (intrarater or intraobserver) reliability provides an estimate of the relative consistency of judgments within a coder over time. More specifically, it assesses the amount of inconsistency (i.e., MEASUREMENT ERRORS) resulting from factors such as carefulness, mood, noise, fatigue, and fluctuation of targets' behaviors that occurs during a period of time. Intracoder reliability differs from INTERRATER RELIABILITY in that the latter assesses the relative consistency of judgments made by *two or more* raters (or coders).

The conventional procedure to estimate intracoder reliability is similar to that of TEST-RETEST RELIABILITY, as described below. A coder makes a judgment about targets' behaviors (e.g., number of violent scenes on TV) at two different occasions that are separated by a certain amount of time. The two sets of judgments are then correlated by using various formulas discussed in SYMMETRIC MEASURES. This correlation coefficient represents an estimate of intracoder reliability.

In the remaining section, we will introduce a flexible but less used approach to assess intracoder reliability across multiple occasions based on GENERALIZABILITY THEORY, or G theory (Brennan, 1983; Cronbach,

Table 1   Number of Eye Contacts of 10 Autistic Pupils Observed by One Coder

	Occasions				Pupils	
	Day 1	*Day 2*	*Day 3*	*Day 4*	*Mean*	*SD*
Pupil A	0	2	2	0	1	1.15
Pupil B	2	3	1	1	1.75	0.96
Pupil C	2	0	1	2	1.25	0.96
Pupil D	1	3	0	0	1	1.41
Pupil E	1	0	0	1	0.5	0.58
Pupil F	4	3	2	2	2.75	0.96
Pupil G	1	0	3	0	1	1.41
Pupil H	2	1	0	3	1.5	1.29
Pupil I	3	1	2	0	1.5	1.29
Pupil J	3	1	0	0	1	1.41
Mean	1.9	1.4	1.1	0.9	Overall Mean: 1.33	
SD	1.2	1.26	1.1	1.1	Overall *SD*: 1.19	

Gleser, Nanda, & Rajaratnam, 1972; Shavelson & Webb, 1991). Let's assume a coder has observed the number of eye contacts of 10 autistic pupils 1 hour a day for 4 consecutive days. The observation records are presented in Table 1.

Based on the content in Table 1, we can identify four sources that are responsible for the variation in the coder's observations: (a) differences among autistic pupils (i.e., MAIN EFFECT of pupils), (b) differences within the coder on four occasions (i.e., main effect of occasions), (c) different observations of pupils on different occasions (i.e., INTERACTION EFFECT between pupils and occasions), and (d) unknown errors (e.g., RANDOM ERRORS and unspecified but SYSTEMATIC ERRORS). All sources of variation are assumed random so that we can address the question, "How well does the coder's observation on one occasion generalize to other occasions?" Because the third and the fourth sources cannot be distinguished from the data, both are collectively considered as RESIDUALS. The magnitude of variation resulting from the above sources can be estimated by a VARIANCE COMPONENTS MODEL.

Based on the formulas presented in Table 2, the estimated variance components are derived and reported in Table 3. As seen, the variance component for pupils merely accounts for 4% of the total variance, which suggests that an observation based on *one* occasion can hardly distinguish among pupils' behaviors. A large proportion of variance in residuals further suggests that pupils' eye contacts fluctuate across different occasions.

To assess intracoder reliability, we first identify the appropriate measurement errors of interest, which are determined by the interpretations or decisions made by the researchers. Researchers may desire to interpret the data based on how well a pupil behaves relative to other pupils (i.e., relative decisions), or the absolute number of eye contacts (i.e., absolute decisions). Measurement error for the relative decision (σ_R^2) can be estimated by

$$\hat{\sigma}_R^2 = \frac{\hat{\sigma}_{po,e}^2}{n_o^*},$$

Table 2   Sources of Variance, Correspondent Notations, and Computation Formulas

Source of Variation	Sums of Square	Degrees of Freedom	Mean Squares	Estimated Variance Components
Pupils (p)	SS_p	$df_p = n_p - 1$	$MS_p = SS_p/df_p$	$\hat{\sigma}_p^2 = (MS_p - \hat{\sigma}_{po,e}^2)/n_o$
Occasions (o)	SS_o	$df_0 = n_o - 1$	$MS_o = SS_o/df_p$	$\hat{\sigma}_o^2 = (MS_o - \hat{\sigma}_{po,e}^2)/n_p$
Residuals (po, e)	$SS_{po,e}$	$df_{po,e} = df_p \times df_o$	$MS_p = SS_{po,e}/df_{po,e}$	$\hat{\sigma}_{po,e}^2 = MS_{po,e}$

NOTE: n_p and n_o are number of pupils and number of occasions, respectively.

Table 3   Sources of Variance Based on Data in Table 1

Source of Variation	Sums of Square	Degrees of Freedom	Mean Squares	Estimated Variance Components	Percentage of Total Variance (%)
Pupils (p)	13.53	9	1.50	0.046	4
Occasions (o)	5.68	3	1.89	0.057	4
Residuals (po, e)	35.58	27	1.32	1.318	93

Table 4 Measurement Errors and Intracoder Reliability Estimates Under Different Types of Decisions and Numbers of Occasions

	Relative Decisions		Absolute Decisions	
Occasions	Measurement Error	Intracoder Reliability	Measurement Error	Intracoder Reliability
1 day	1.318	0.033	1.364	0.032
2 days	0.659	0.065	0.682	0.063
3 days	0.439	0.094	0.454	0.091
4 days	0.329	0.122	0.341	0.118
5 days	0.263	0.148	0.272	0.144
10 days	0.131	0.258	0.136	0.252
20 days	0.065	0.411	0.068	0.402
30 days	0.043	0.511	0.045	0.502
40 days	0.032	0.582	0.034	0.574
80 days	0.016	0.736	0.017	0.729
120 days	0.010	0.807	0.011	0.801
160 days	0.008	0.848	0.008	0.843

whereas that for the absolute decision (σ_A^2) can be estimated by

$$\hat{\sigma}_A^2 = \frac{\hat{\sigma}_o^2}{n_o^*} + \frac{\hat{\sigma}_{po,e}^2}{n_o^*},$$

where n_o^* refers to the number of occasions used in the study (e.g., Table 1), or the number of occasions researchers should choose to improve the observation consistency.

For both the relative decision and the absolute decision, intracoder reliability (or termed the generalizability coefficient in G theory) is estimated by

$$G_R = \frac{\hat{\sigma}_p^2}{\hat{\sigma}_p^2 + \hat{\sigma}_R^2}$$

and

$$G_A = \frac{\hat{\sigma}_p^2}{\hat{\sigma}_p^2 + \hat{\sigma}_A^2},$$

respectively. Intracoder reliability estimates under different types of decisions and numbers of occasions are presented in Table 4. As shown, the more occasions a coder observes each pupil, the fewer measurement errors there are. It would require more than 80 days of the coder's observations to reach a satisfactory level of consistency. The data also show poor intracoder reliability when the coder observes the pupils on only four occasions.

—Peter Y. Chen and Autumn D. Krauss

REFERENCES

Brennan, R. L. (1983). *Elements of generalizability.* Iowa City, IA: American College Testing Program.

Cronbach, L. J., Gleser, G. C., Nanda, H., & Rajaratnam, N. (1972). *The dependability of behavioral measurements: Theory of generalizability of scores and profiles.* New York: Wiley.

Shavelson, R. J., & Webb, N. M. (1991). *Generalizability theory: A primer.* Newbury Park, CA: Sage.

INVESTIGATOR EFFECTS

Investigator effects are those sources of artifact or error in scientific inquiry that derive from the investigator. It is useful to think of two major types of effects, usually unintentional, that scientists can have upon the results of their research. The first type operates, so to speak, in the mind, eye, or hand of the scientist. It operates without affecting the actual response of the human participants or animal subjects of the research. It is not interactional. The second type of investigator effect is interactional. It operates by affecting the actual response of the subject of the research.

Noninteractional effects include (a) observer effects, (b) interpreter effects, and (c) intentional effects.

(a) *Observer effects* refer to errors of observation made by scientists in the perception or recording of the events they are investigating. The analysis of a series of 21 studies involving 314 observers who recorded a total of 139,000 observations revealed that about 1% of the observations were in error, and that when errors were made, they occurred two thirds of the time in the direction of the observer's hypothesis.

(b) *Interpreter effects* refer to differences in the theoretical interpretations that different scientists give to the same set of observations. For many years, for example, investigators of the effectiveness of psychotherapy disagreed strongly with one another in the interpretation of the available studies. It was not until systematic, quantitative summaries of the hundreds of studies on the effectiveness of psychotherapy became available that this particular issue of interpreter effects became fairly well resolved.

(c) *Intentional effects* refer to instances of outright dishonesty in science. Perhaps the most common example is simple data fabrication, in which nonoccurring but desired observations are recorded instead of the honest observations of the events purported to be under investigation.

Interactional investigator effects include (a) biosocial, (b) psychosocial, (c) situational, (d) modeling, and (e) expectancy effects.

(a) *Biosocial effects* refer to those differences in participants' responses associated with, for example, the sex, age, or ethnicity of the investigator.

(b) *Psychosocial effects* refer to those differences in participants' responses associated with, for example, the personality or social status of the investigator.

(c) *Situational effects* refer to those differences in participants' responses associated with investigator differences in such situational variables as research experience, prior acquaintance with participants, and the responses obtained from earlier-contacted participants.

(d) *Modeling effects* refer to those differences in participants' responses associated with investigator differences in how they themselves responded to the task they administer to their participants.

(e) *Expectancy effects* refer to those differences in participants' responses associated with the investigator's expectation for the type of response to be obtained from the participant. Expectations or hypotheses held by investigators in the social and behavioral sciences have been shown to affect the behavior of the investigator in such a way as to bring about the response the investigator expects from the participant. This effect, referred to most commonly as the EXPERIMENTER EXPECTANCY EFFECT, is a special case of interpersonal expectancy effects that has been found to occur in many situations beyond the laboratory.

—Robert Rosenthal

See also PYGMALION EFFECT

REFERENCES

Rosenthal, R. (1976). *Experimenter effects in behavioral research: Enlarged edition.* New York: Irvington.

Rosenthal, R., & Jacobson, L. (1968). *Pygmalion in the classroom.* New York: Holt, Rinehart and Winston.

Rosnow, R. L., & Rosenthal, R. (1997). *People studying people: Artifacts and ethics in behavioral research.* New York: W. H. Freeman.

IN VIVO CODING

To understand in vivo coding, one must first understand CODING. A code is a concept, a word that signifies "what is going on in this piece of data." Coding, on the other hand, is the analytic process of examining data line by line or paragraph by paragraph (whatever is your style) for significant events, experiences, feelings, and so on, that are then denoted as concepts (Strauss & Corbin, 1998). Sometimes, the analyst names the concept. Other times, the words of the respondent(s) are so descriptive of what is going on that they become the designated concept. These descriptive words provided by respondents are what have come to be known as in vivo concepts (Glaser & Strauss, 1967).

In vivo concepts are usually snappy words that are very telling and revealing. The interesting thing about in vivo codes is that a researcher knows the minute the idea is expressed by a respondent that this is something to take note of. The term that is used expresses meaning in a way far better than any word that could be provided by the analyst (Strauss, 1987). For example, suppose a researcher were doing a study of what goes on at cocktail parties. One interviewee might say something like,

Many people hate going to cocktail parties, but I love them. When I go, I take the opportunity to *work the scene.* It may seem like idle chatter, but in reality, I am making mental notes about future business contacts, women I'd like to date, possible tennis partners, and even investment opportunities.

Working the scene is a great concept. It doesn't tell us everything that goes on at cocktail parties, but it does convey what this man is doing. And if he does this, then perhaps other people also are *working the scene.* The researcher would want to keep this concept in mind when doing future interviews to see if other people describe actions that could also be labeled as *working the scene.*

In contrast, an analyst-derived code would look something like the following. While observing at another cocktail party, the researcher notices two women talking excitedly about work projects in which they are engaged. In another area, a man and a woman are also talking about their work, and further on, another group of people are doing likewise. The researcher labels this talking about work at a cocktail party as "social/work talk." This term describes what is going on but it's not nearly as snappy or interesting as *working the scene*.

Not every interview or observation yields interesting in vivo codes, but when these do come up in data, the researcher should take advantage of them. It is important that analysts are alert and sensitive to what is in the data, and often, the words used by respondents are the best way of expressing that. Coding can be a laborious and detailed process, especially when analyzing line by line. However, it is the detailed coding that often yields those treasures, the terms that we have come to know as in vivo codes.

—Juliet M. Corbin

REFERENCES

Glaser, B., & Strauss, A. (1967). *The discovery of grounded theory*. Chicago: Aldine.

Strauss, A. (1987). *Qualitative analysis for social scientists*. Cambridge, UK: Cambridge University Press.

Strauss, A., & Corbin, J. (1998). *Basics of qualitative analysis*. Thousand Oaks, CA: Sage.

ISOMORPH

An isomorph is a theory, model, or structure that is similar, equivalent, or even identical to another. Two theories might be conceptually isomorphic, for example, but use different empirical measures and thus be empirically distinct. Or, two theories might appear to be different conceptually or empirically, but be isomorphic in their predictions.

—Michael S. Lewis-Beck

ITEM RESPONSE THEORY

DEFINITION AND APPLICATION AREAS

Tests and questionnaires consist of a number of items, denoted J, that each measure an aspect of the same underlying psychological ability, personality trait, or attitude. Item response theory (IRT) models use the data collected on the J items in a sample of N respondents to construct scales for the measurement of the ability or trait.

The score on an item indexed j ($j = 1, \ldots, J$) is represented by a random variable X that has realizations x_j. Item scores may be

- *Dichotomous*, indicating whether an answer to an item was correct (score $x_j = 1$) or incorrect (score $x_j = 0$)
- *Ordinal polytomous*, indicating the degree to which a respondent agreed with a particular statement (ordered integer scores, $x_j = 0, \ldots, m$)
- *Nominal*, indicating a particular answer category chosen by the respondent, as with multiple-choice items, where one option is correct and several others are incorrect and thus have nominal measurement level
- *Continuous*, as with response times indicating the time it took to solve a problem

Properties of the J items, such as their difficulties, are estimated from the data. They are used for deciding which items to select in a paper-and-pencil test or questionnaire, and more advanced computerized measurement procedures. Item properties thus have a technical role in instrument construction and help to produce high-quality scales for the measurement of individuals.

In an IRT context, abilities, personality traits, and attitudes underlying performance on items are called latent traits. A latent trait is represented by the random variable θ, and each person i ($i = 1, \ldots, N$) who takes the test measuring θ has a scale value θ_i. The main purpose of IRT is to estimate θ for each person from his or her J observed item scores. These estimated measurement values can be used to compare people with one another or with an external behavior criterion. Such comparisons form the basis for decision making about individuals.

IRT originated in the 1950s and 1960s (e.g., Birnbaum, 1968) and came to its full bloom afterwards. Important fields of application are the following:

- *Educational measurement*, where tests are used for grading examinees on school subjects, selection of students for remedial teaching and follow-up education (e.g., the entrance to university), and certification of professional workers with respect to skills and abilities

- *Psychology*, where intelligence measurement is used, for example, to diagnose children's cognitive abilities to explain learning and concentration problems in school, personality inventories to select patients for clinical treatment, and aptitude tests for job selection and placement in industry and with the government
- *Sociology*, where attitudes are measured toward abortion or rearing children in single-parent families, and also latent traits such as alienation, Machiavellianism, and religiosity
- *Political science*, where questionnaires are used to measure the preference of voters for particular politicians and parties, and also political efficacy and opinions about the government's environmental policy
- *Medical research*, where health-related quality of life is measured in patients recovering from accidents that caused enduring physical damage, radical forms of surgery, long-standing treatment using experimental medicine, or other forms of therapy that seriously affect patients' experience of everyday life
- *Marketing research*, where consumers' preferences for products and brands are measured

Each of these applications requires a quantitative scale for measuring people's proficiency, and this is what IRT provides.

This entry first introduces the assumptions common to IRT models. Then, several useful distinctions are made to classify different IRT models. Finally, some useful applications of IRT models are discussed.

COMMON ASSUMPTIONS OF IRT MODELS

Dimensionality of Measurement

The first assumption enumerates the parameters necessary to summarize the performance of a group of individuals that takes the test or questionnaire. For example, if a test is assumed to measure the ability of spatial orientation, as in subtests of some intelligence test batteries, an IRT model that assumes only one person parameter may be used to describe the data. This person parameter represents for each individual his or her level of spatial orientation ability. An IRT model with one person parameter is a strictly unidimensional (UD) model. Alternatively, items in another test may measure a mixture of arithmetic ability and word comprehension, for example, when

arithmetic exercises are embedded in short stories. Here, a two-dimensional IRT model may be needed. Other test performances may be even more complex, necessitating multidimensional IRT models to explain the data structure. For example, in the arithmetic example, some items may also require general knowledge about stores and the products sold there (e.g., when calculating the amount of money returned at the cash desk), and others may require geographical knowledge (e.g., when calculating the distance between cities). Essentially unidimensional models assume all the items in a test to measure one dominant latent trait and a number of nuisance traits that do not disturb measurement of the dominant θ when tests are long. For example, a personality inventory on introversion may also measure anxiety, social intelligence, and verbal comprehension, each measured only weakly by one or two items and dominated by introversion as the driving force of responses.

Relationships Between Items

Most IRT models assume that, given the knowledge of a person's position on the latent trait or traits, the joint distribution of his or her item scores can be reconstructed from the marginal frequency distributions of the J items. Define a vector $\mathbf{X} = (X_1, \ldots, X_J)$ with realization $\mathbf{x} = (x_1, \ldots, x_J)$ and let $\boldsymbol{\theta}$ be the vector with latent traits needed to account for the test performance of the respondents. In IRT, the marginal independence property is known as LOCAL INDEPENDENCE (LI), and defined as

$$P(\mathbf{X} = \mathbf{x}|\boldsymbol{\theta}) = \prod_{j=1}^{J} P(X_j = x_j|\boldsymbol{\theta}). \quad (1)$$

At the behavior level, LI means that during test administration, each item is answered independent of the other items. There is no learning or development due to practice while the respondent tries to solve the items; thus, the measurement procedure does not influence the measurement outcome. However, improving students' ability through practice may be the purpose of a test program, as is typical of dynamic testing. Then, an IRT model may assume that practice produces successively more skills, each represented by a new latent trait. This means that possible dependencies between items during testing not explained by $\boldsymbol{\theta}$ are absorbed by simply adding more θs.

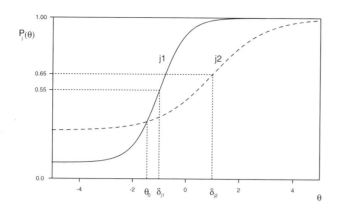

Figure 1 Two IRFs Under the Three-Parameter Logistic Model (Parameter Values: $\gamma_{j1} = 0.10$, $\gamma_{j2} = 0.30$; $\delta_{j1} = -1.00$, $\delta_{j2} = 1.00$; $\alpha_{j1} = 2.00$, $\alpha_{j2} = 1.00$); Intersection Point at $\theta_0 = 1.46$; $P(\theta_0) = 0.36$

Relationships Between Items and the Latent Trait

For unidimensional dichotomous items, the item response function (IRF) describes the relationship between item score X_j and latent trait θ, and is denoted $P_j(\theta) = P(X_j = 1|\theta)$. Figure 1 shows two typical monotone increasing IRFs (assumption M) from the three-parameter logistic model that is introduced shortly. Assumption M formalizes that a higher θ drives the response process such that a correct answer to the item becomes more likely. The two IRFs differ in three respects, however.

First, the IRFs have different slopes. A steeper IRF represents a stronger relationship between the item and the latent trait. IRT models have parameters related to the steepest slope of the IRF. This slope parameter, denoted α_j for item j, may be compared with a REGRESSION COEFFICIENT in a LOGISTIC REGRESSION model. Item j_1 (solid curve) has a steeper slope than Item j_2 (dashed curve); thus, it has a stronger relationship with θ and, consequently, discriminates better between low and high values of θ.

Second, the locations of the IRFs are different. Each IRF is located on the θ scale by means of a parameter, δ_j, that gives the value of θ where the IRF is halfway between the lowest and the highest conditional probability possible. Item j_1 (solid curve) is located more to the left on the θ scale than Item j_2 (dashed curve), as is shown by their location parameters: $\delta_{j1} < \delta_{j2}$. Because the slopes are different, the IRFs intersect. Consequently, for the θs to the left of the intersection

point, θ_0, Item j_1 is less likely to be answered correctly than Item j_2. Thus, for these θs, Item j_1 is more difficult than Item j_2. For the θs to the right of θ_0, the item difficulty ordering is reversed.

Third, the IRFs have different lower asymptotes, denoted γ_j. Item parameter γ_j is the probability of a correct answer by people who have very low θs. In Figure 1, Item j_1 has the lower γ parameter. This parameter is relevant, in particular, for multiple-choice items where low-θ people often guess with nonzero probability for the correct answer. Thus, multiple-choice Item j_2 is more liable to guessing than Item j_1.

Three-Parameter Logistic Model. The IRFs in Figure 1 are defined by the three-parameter logistic model. This model is based on assumptions UD and LI, and defines the IRF by means of a logistic function with the three item parameters discussed:

$$P_j(\theta) = \gamma_j + (1 - \gamma_j)\frac{\exp[\alpha_j(\theta - \delta_j)]}{1 + \exp[\alpha_j(\theta - \delta_j)]}. \quad (2)$$

One-Parameter Logistic Model. Another well-known IRT model is the one-parameter logistic model or Rasch model, also based on UD and LI, that assumes that for all J items in the test, $\gamma = 0$ and $\alpha = 1$ (the value 1 is arbitrary; what counts is that α_j is a constant, a, for all j). Thus, this model (a) is not suited for fitting data from multiple-choice items because that would result in positive γs; (b) assumes equally strong relationships between all item scores and the latent trait ($\alpha_j = a$ for all j); and (c) allows items to differ only in difficulty δ_j, $j = 1, \ldots, J$.

Linear Logistic Multidimensional Model. Figure 2 shows an IRF as a three-dimensional surface in which the response probability depends on two latent traits, $\mathbf{\theta} = (\theta_1, \theta_2)$. The slope of the surface is steeper in the θ_2 direction than in the θ_1 direction. This means that the probability of having the item correct depends more on θ_2 than θ_1. Because θ_2 matters more to a correct answer than θ_1, by using this item for measurement, people are better distinguished on the θ_2 scale than on the θ_1 scale. The two slopes may be different for other items that measure the composite, $\mathbf{\theta}$. The location (not visible in Figure 2) of this item is related (but not identical) to the distance of the origin of the space to the point of steepest slope in the direction from the origin. The γ_j parameter represents the probability of a correct answer when both θs are very low.

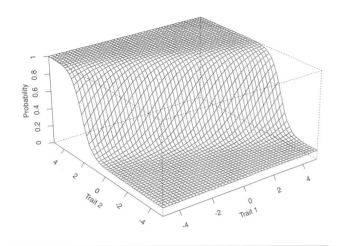

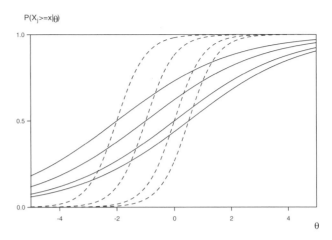

Figure 2   Item Response Surface Under the Linear Logistic Multidimensional Model (Parameter Values: $\gamma_j = 0.10$; $\delta_j = 0.00$; $\alpha_{j1} = 1.00$; $\alpha_{j2} = 2.50$)

Figure 3   ISRFs of Two Items With Five Answer Categories Each, Under the Graded Response Model (No Parameter Values Given)

The item response surface in Figure 2 originated from Reckase's linear logistic multidimensional model (Van der Linden & Hambleton, 1997, pp. 271–286). This IRT model has a multidimensional θ, and slope parameters collected in a vector, α. The item response surface is given by

$$P_j(X_j = 1|\theta) = \gamma_j + (1 - \gamma_j)\frac{\exp(\alpha'_j\theta + \delta_j)}{1 + \exp(\alpha'_j\theta + \delta_j)}.$$

$$(3)$$

Graded Response Model.   Finally, Figure 3 shows the item step response functions (ISRFs) (solid curves) of an item under Samejima's graded response model (Van der Linden & Hambleton, 1997, pp. 85–100) for polytomous item scores. For ordered integer item scores ($x_j = 0, \ldots, m$) and a unidimensional latent trait, each conditional response probability $P(X_j \geq x_j|\theta)$, is modeled separately by logistic functions. These functions have a location parameter that varies between the item's ISRFs and a constant slope parameter. Between items, slope parameters are different. It may be noted that for $x_j = 0$, the ISRF equals 1, and that for a fixed item, the other m ISRFs cannot intersect by definition. ISRFs of different items can intersect, however, due to different slope parameters (see Figure 3). Polytomous IRT models are more complex mathematically than dichotomous IRT models because they involve more response functions and a greater number of item parameters. Many other IRT models exist; see Van der Linden and Hambleton (1997) for an extensive overview.

Nonparametric Models.   The models discussed so far are parametric models because their IRFs or ISRFs are parametric functions of θ. Nonparametric IRT models put only order restrictions on the IRFs but refrain from a more restrictive parametric definition. This is done in an attempt to define measurement models that do not unduly restrict the test data structure, while still imposing enough structure to have ordinal measurement of people on the θ scale. This ordering is estimated by means of the sum of the item scores, which replaces θ as a summary of test performance. Thus, flexibility is gained at the expense of convenient mathematical properties of parametric—in particular, logistic—functions. See Boomsma, Van Duijn, and Snijders (2001) for discussions of parametric and nonparametric IRT models, and Sijtsma and Molenaar (2002) for an introduction to nonparametric IRT models.

APPLICATIONS OF IRT MODELS

Test Construction, Calibration.   IRT models imply the scale of measurement, which is either ordinal or interval. When the IRT model fits the data, the scale is assumed to hold for the particular test. Scales are calibrated and then transformed so as to allow a convenient interpretation. For example, the θ metric can be replaced by the well-known total score or percentile scales. The scale may constitute the basis for individual diagnosis, as in educational and psychological measurement, and for scientific research.

Equating and Item Banks, Adaptive Testing. The θ metric is convenient for the equating of scales based on different tests for the same latent trait, with the purpose of making the measurements of pupils who took these different tests directly comparable. Equating may be used to construct an item bank, consisting of hundreds of items that measure the same latent trait, but with varying difficulty and other item properties. New tests can be assembled from an item bank. Tests for individuals can be assembled by selecting items one by one from the item bank so as to reduce measurement error in the estimated θ as quickly as possible. This is known as adaptive testing. It is convenient in large-scale testing programs in education, job selection, and placement.

Differential Item Functioning. People with different backgrounds are often assessed with the same measurement instruments. An important issue is whether people having the same θ level, but differing on, for example, gender, socioeconomic background, or ethnicity, have the same response probabilities on the items from the test. If not, the test is said to exhibit differential item functioning. This can be investigated with IRT methods. Items functioning differently between groups may be replaced by items that function identically.

Person-Fit Analysis. Respondents may be confused by the item format; they may be afraid of situations, including a test, in which they are evaluated; or they may underestimate the level of the test and miss the depth of several of the questions. Each of these mechanisms, as well as several others, may produce a pattern of J item scores that is unexpected given the predictions from an IRT model. Person-fit methods have been proposed to identify nonfitting item score patterns. They may contribute to the diagnosis of the behavior that caused the unusual pattern.

Cognitive IRT Models. Finally, cognitive modeling has taken measurement beyond assigning scores to people, in that the cognitive process or the solution strategy that produced these scores is part of the IRT model, and measurement is related to a psychological explanation. This approach may lead to the identification of skills that are insufficiently mastered or, at the theoretical level, to a better understanding of the processes underlying test performance.

—Klaas Sijtsma

REFERENCES

Birnbaum, A. L. (1968). Some latent trait models and their use in inferring an examinee's ability. In F. M. Lord & M. R. Novick (Eds.), *Statistical theories of mental test scores*. Reading, MA: Addison-Wesley.

Boomsma, A., Van Duijn, M. A. J., & Snijders, T. A. B. (Eds.). (2001). *Essays on item response theory*. New York: Springer.

Embretson, S. E., & Reise, S. P. (2000). *Item response theory for psychologists*. Mahwah, NJ: Lawrence Erlbaum.

Sijtsma, K., & Molenaar, I. W. (2002). *Introduction to nonparametric item response theory*. Thousand Oaks, CA: Sage.

Van der Linden, W. J., & Hambleton, R. K. (Eds.). (1997). *Handbook of modern item response theory*. New York: Springer.

J

JACKKNIFE METHOD

The jackknife method is a resampling procedure that can be used to generate an empirical SAMPLING DISTRIBUTION. Such distributions can be used to run statistical hypothesis tests, construct CONFIDENCE INTERVALS, and estimate STANDARD ERRORS. The jackknife method is parallel to the BOOTSTRAP and the permutation (or randomization) methods.

Rodgers (1999) presented a TAXONOMY organizing these methods based on size of the resampled samples and whether sampling occurs with or without replacement. The jackknife method involves repeatedly drawing samples without replacement that are smaller than the original sample. Originally, the jackknife was defined as an approach in which one or more data points are randomly deleted, a conceptualization equivalent to randomly sampling without replacement.

The jackknife method was originally developed by Quenouille (1949) and Tukey (1958); Efron (1982), developer of the bootstrap, named it the "Quenouille-Tukey jackknife." The method was summarized by Mosteller and Tukey (1977): "The basic idea is to assess the effect of each of the groups into which the data have been divided... through the effect upon the body of data that results from *omitting* that group" (p. 133). The jackknife has broadened, as implied in Rodgers (1999): "Let the observed data define a population of scores. Randomly sample from this population *without replacement* to fill the groups with *a smaller number of scores than in the original sample*" (p. 46).

In general, an empirical sampling distribution can be generated by deleting one, two, or a whole group of observations; computing a relevant statistic within the new sample; and generating a distribution of these statistics by repeating this process many times.

As an example, consider a research design with RANDOM ASSIGNMENT of 10 participants to a treatment or a control group ($n = 5$ per group). Did the treatment result in a reliable increase? Under the NULL HYPOTHESIS of no group difference, the 10 scores are sorted into one or the other group purely by chance. The usual formal evaluation of the null hypothesis involves computation of a two–independent group t-statistic measuring a standardized mean difference between the two groups, which is then evaluated in relation to the presumed distribution under the null hypothesis, modeled by the theoretical t-distribution. This evaluation rests on a number of parametric statistical assumptions, including normality and independence of errors and homogeneity of variance. Alternatively, the null distribution can be defined as an empirical t-distribution using resampling, a process requiring fewer assumptions.

In the jackknife method, we might decide to delete 1 observation from each group (or, equivalently, to sample without replacement from the original 10 observations until each group has 4 observations). There are 3,150 possible resamples. The t-statistic is computed in each new sample, resulting in a distribution of ts approximating the population t-distribution under the null hypothesis. The original t-statistic is evaluated in relation to this empirical sampling distribution to draw a conclusion about group differences. Furthermore, a standard error of the t-statistic can be estimated from the standard deviation of the resampled t-statistics, and confidence intervals can also be constructed.

—Joseph Lee Rodgers

REFERENCES

Efron, B. (1982). *The jackknife, the bootstrap, and other resampling plans.* Philadelphia: Society for Industrial and Applied Mathematics.

Mosteller, F., & Tukey, J. W. (1977). *Data analysis and regression: A second course in statistics.* Reading, MA: Addison-Wesley.

Quenouille, M. (1949). Approximate tests of correlation in time series. *Journal of the Royal Statistical Society, Series B, 11,* 18–84.

Rodgers, J. L. (1999). The bootstrap, the jackknife, and the randomization test: A sampling taxonomy. *Multivariate Behavioral Research, 34,* 441–456.

Tukey, J. W. (1958). Bias and confidence in not quite large samples [abstract]. *Annals of Mathematical Statistics, 29,* 614.

K

KEY INFORMANT

Also referred to as a key consultant (Werner & Schoepfle, 1987), a key informant is an individual who provides in-depth, expert information on elements of a culture, society, or social scene. Such in-depth information tends to be gathered in repeated sets of SEMI-STRUCTURED and UNSTRUCTURED INTERVIEWS in mostly natural, informal settings (e.g., the key informant's home). Aside from the depth and breadth of information, what sets a key informant apart from other types of interviewees is the duration and intensity of the relationship between the researcher and the informant. Three primary types of interviewees in social research include subjects, respondents, and informants. Subjects are generally individuals interviewed in the course of a social experiment. Respondents are individuals who are interviewed in the course of a social SURVEY. Finally, informants are individuals who are interviewed in a more in-depth, less structured manner (semi-structured, unstructured interviews), most often in a field setting. In any given study, individuals can move from the role of an informant to respondent to subject depending on the interviewing context (e.g., survey, IN-DEPTH INTERVIEW). Key informants are a subtype of informant in which a special relationship exists between interviewer (e.g., ethnographer) and interviewee.

Key informants are selected on the basis of an informant's characteristics, knowledge, and rapport with the researcher. Johnson (1990) describes two primary criteria for selecting informants. The first set of criteria concerns the form and type of expert knowledge and the theoretical representativeness of the informant, where such representativeness refers to the characteristics of the informant with respect to theoretically important factors (e.g., status, position in an organization) or the emergent features of some set of data (e.g., the position of the informant in the distribution of incomes). The second set of criteria concerns the informant's personality, interpersonal skills, and the chemistry between the researcher and the informant. Whereas the first set of criteria places the informant within the framework of the study's goals and objectives, the second set of criteria reflects the important nature of the collaborative relationship between the researcher and key informant. Once the researcher understands the place of an individual within the realm of theoretical criteria, key informant selection can then be based on the potential for rapport, thus limiting potential biases that may arise from selection on the basis of personal characteristics alone.

What further separates key informants from the other main types of interviewees is their potential involvement throughout the various phases of the research enterprise. Key informants and their expert knowledge and advice not only are a source of data but also can be used to develop more valid formal survey instruments (e.g., help in better framing of survey questions), provide running commentaries on cultural events or scenes, aid in the interpretation of study results from more systematically collected data sources (e.g., survey results), and help in determining the VALIDITY and RELIABILITY of data (e.g., genealogies), to mention a few. Key informants are an essential component of any ethnographic enterprise.

—Jeffrey C. Johnson

REFERENCES

Johnson, J. C. (1990). *Selecting ethnographic informants.* Newbury Park, CA: Sage.

Werner, O., & Schoepfle, G. M. (1987). *Systematic fieldwork* (2 vols.). Newbury Park, CA: Sage.

KISH GRID

The Kish grid was developed by Leslie Kish in 1949 and is commonly used by those conducting large-scale sample SURVEYS. It is a technique used in equal-probability SAMPLING for selecting cases at random when more than one case is found to be eligible for inclusion when the interviewer calls at a sampled address or household. For example, a sample of addresses may be drawn from a list of all postal addresses in a given area, and the sample design assumes that each address on that list will contain only one household. When the interviewer calls at the sampled address, he or she may find more than one household at the address and will need to select one at random (or whatever number is specified in the sample design) to include in the sample. Most important, this must be done systematically and in a way that provides a known probability of selection for every household included.

The same problem occurs when selecting an individual within a household. A household may consist of one person only or many persons. Households that contain more than one member of the population become clusters of population elements, so they must be translated from a sample of households to a sample of individuals. If the survey design asks for a specific type of individual to be interviewed (e.g., the person responsible for the accommodation or for all individuals age 16 years or older to be included), the problem of selection does not arise. However, if the survey design asks for one individual to be included from each household, the Kish grid is used to randomly select the individual for inclusion in the sample from each selected household.

The Kish grid is a simple procedure that is easy for interviewers to implement in the field. It provides a clear and consistent procedure for randomly selecting cases for inclusion in the sample with a known probability of selection. The interviewer first needs an objective way to order the members of the household or number of dwellings before they can be selected. To select an individual within a household, the interviewer has a pre-prepared grid that asks him or her to list all the individuals living within the household systematically, usually according to their age and sex, and each person is given a serial number. Who is selected for interview depends on the total number of persons within the household. The grid includes a selection table that tells the interviewer which numbered individual to select. The interviewer simply reads across the table from a column listing the number of persons in the household to the serial number he or she should select for interview. The Kish grid is a standard technique that is widely used and can be adapted to meet the needs of different survey designs.

—Heather Laurie

REFERENCES

Kish, L. (1949). A procedure for objective respondent selection within a household. *Journal of the American Sociological Association, 44,* 380–387.

Kish, L. (1965). *Survey sampling.* New York: John Wiley.

KOLMOGOROV-SMIRNOV TEST

There are two versions, the one-sample GOODNESS-OF-FIT test and the two-sample test.

ONE-SAMPLE TEST

Several alternatives for one-sample tests involving ordinal data are available (Gibbons & Chakraborti, 1992; Siegel & Castellan, 1988) with advantages that vary slightly with the situation. The Kolmogorov-Smirnov one-sample test is purported to be more powerful than the CHI-SQUARE goodness-of-fit test for the same data, particularly when the sample is small. The test is appropriate for ranked data, although it is truly a test for the match of the distribution of sample data to that of the population; consequently, the distributions can include those other than the normal distribution for populations. It also assumes an underlying continuous distribution, even though the data may be in unequal steps (see Gibbons & Chakraborti, 1992), which leads to alternative calculations, as will be seen below.

The test itself compares the *cumulative* distribution of the data with that for the expected population distribution. It assumes an underlying continuous distribution and has a definite advantage over the CHI-SQUARE TEST when the sample size is small, due

Table 1   Data for a Kolmogorov-Smirnov One-Sample Test for Ranked Data Where the Population Distribution Is a Mathematical Function

School Salary	f_o	CF_o School	CF_e County	$CF_{oi} - F_{ei}$ Adjacent Rows	$CF_{o(i-1)} - CF_{ei}$ Offset Rows
9,278	2	0.100	0.131	−0.031	−0.131
10,230	1	0.150	0.168	−0.018	−0.068
11,321	1	0.200	0.218	−0.018	−0.068
13,300	1	0.250	0.326	−0.076	−0.126
14,825	2	0.350	0.422	−0.072	−0.172
16,532	2	0.450	0.535	−0.085	−0.185
18,545	1	0.500	0.664	−0.164	−0.214
21,139	3	0.650	0.804	−0.154	−0.304
22,145	2	0.750	0.847	−0.097	−0.197
24,333	2	0.850	0.918	−0.068	−0.168
28,775	1	0.900	0.983	−0.083	−0.133
30,987	1	0.950	0.994	−0.044	−0.094
32,444	1	1.000	0.997	0.003	−0.047
Total	20				

to the limitation of the minimum expected value. The maximum magnitude of the divergence between the two distributions is the test factor and is determined simply by the largest absolute difference between cumulative *relative* frequencies, the fractions of the whole. This is checked against a table of maximum differences expected to be found for various α.

The difficulty in appropriately applying this test lies in the nature of the intervals for the ranks. There are basically two types of problems illustrated in the literature, each resulting in different applications of the Kolmogorov-Smirnov test. Each of these is presented as *the* way of applying the test by some texts:

- The intervals for the ranks are not well defined, and the underlying distribution is *assumed;* therefore, the test is mathematically determined by a continuous function, for example, a normal or even a flat distribution (see Gibbons & Chakraborti, 1992). Here the sample data are stepped and the population "data" are continuous.

- The intervals are well defined and mutually exclusive, and population data exist for them by interval; thus, the population data are stepped, as well as that for the sample (see Siegel & Castellan, 1988). This makes the test equivalent to the two-sample test in which both samples are stepped.

Some examples will be used to clarify this issue.

Continuous Population Data From a Mathematical Distribution

For example, the following question is asked: Is the distribution of a particular school's salaries typical of those across the county? Here it is assumed that the county distribution of salaries is normal. Table 1 shows the frequency of salaries in the school and the corresponding cumulative relative frequencies for these sample data, in addition to providing a cumulative relative distribution for the population based on a normal distribution. This is shown graphically in Figure 1. It is apparent that there are two possible points of comparison for each data point: the interval above and the interval below. This is shown by the two arrows for one point on the continuous population distribution, which could be considered to be matched with either of the steps below for the sample data.

Therefore, the Kolmogorov-Smirnov test requires the calculation of both differences for all points, the last two columns in Table 1. Then the maximum difference from the complete set is compared to that for the appropriate corresponding α value. The critical $D_{critical}$ can be closely estimated from Table 2.

For this case, if α is chosen to be 0.05, then the maximum allowed is

$$D_{critical} = \frac{1.36}{\sqrt{20 + 1}} = 0.297.$$

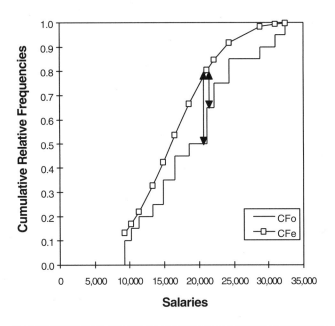

Figure 1   Observed and Expected Cumulative Relative
Frequency Distributions

NOTE: These frequencies refer to a situation in which the
population distribution is assumed and generated from a mathematical function (here a normal distribution).

Table 2   Critical Maximum Differences, $D_{critical}$,
for the Kolmogorov-Smirnov Test

Sample Size	α .10	.05	.01
$25 > n > 10$	$\frac{1.22}{\sqrt{n+1}}$	$\frac{1.36}{\sqrt{n+1}}$	$\frac{1.63}{\sqrt{n+1}}$
$n \geq 25$	$\frac{1.22}{\sqrt{n}}$	$\frac{1.36}{\sqrt{n}}$	$\frac{1.63}{\sqrt{n}}$

Now reexamining Table 1, it can be seen from
the last two columns of the differences that 0.305
exceeds this value, and there is a significant difference
between the school's distribution and that assumed by
the county. A comparison of this test with the CHI-
SQUARE and T-TEST on the same data can be found in
Black (1999). The point to note is that the three tests
for a given set of data not only provide different levels
of *power* but also answer essentially three different
questions.

Stepped Population Data
From a Full Survey

In this situation, the sample data are compared to
actual population data, whereby the frequencies for

each of the ordinal categories for both are known. To
illustrate this, let us use the sample data as before but
compare it to a county register of teachers. The data and
corresponding stepped graphs are shown in Figure 2,
where it becomes obvious that only data within intervals are to be compared. For example, the double-
ended arrow shows the difference between one pair
of intervals. Therefore, the Kolmogorov-Smirnov one-
sample test will only use the adjacent differences in
cumulative relative frequencies (see Table 3), and the
largest difference will be compared with the minimum
for the chosen α. The largest difference is 0.278, which
is less than the 0.297 found above (the sign does not
make any difference here), and therefore there is no
significant difference.

Such a distribution-free comparison will have
advantages in many situations when data do not fit a
predetermined distribution. To carry out the equivalent
test in SPSS, one must use the two-sample function, in
which one of the sets of data is that of the population.

TESTS FOR TWO INDEPENDENT SAMPLES

Not always will designs of studies involving the
comparison of two groups produce interval/ratio data
and lend the resolution of the hypotheses to a t-test. The

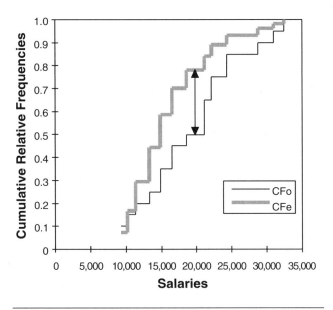

Figure 2   Observed and Expected Cumulative Relative
Frequency Distributions

NOTE: These distributions correspond to the sample and the
population when both sets of data are stepped (i.e., population
data are from a real survey).

Table 3 Data for a Kolmogorov-Smirnov One-Sample Test for Ranked Data Where the Population Distribution Based on Ordinal Population Data

School Salary	f_o School	f_o County	CF_o School	CF_e County	$CF_{oi} - F_{ei}$ Adjacent Rows
9,278	2	260	0.100	0.097	0.003
10,230	1	287	0.150	0.205	−0.055
11,321	1	320	0.200	0.325	−0.125
13,300	1	350	0.250	0.456	−0.206
14,825	2	365	0.350	0.593	−0.243
16,532	2	287	0.450	0.700	−0.250
18,545	1	208	0.500	0.778	−0.278
21,139	3	145	0.650	0.832	−0.182
22,145	2	125	0.750	0.879	−0.129
24,333	2	100	0.850	0.916	−0.066
28,775	1	85	0.900	0.948	−0.048
30,987	1	74	0.950	0.976	−0.026
32,444	1	64	1.000	1.000	0.000
Total	20	2,670			

null hypothesis, H_0, is basically that the nature of the frequency distributions across the categories or levels of the dependent variable is the same for both groups. In other words, does the differentiating characteristic of the two groups (INDEPENDENT VARIABLE) influence the nature of the distribution of the levels or categories of the DEPENDENT VARIABLE?

The Kolmogorov-Smirnov test checks to see if the two samples have been drawn from the same population, again with the assumption of the underlying continuous distribution. The process is the same as above, except in this case, one is comparing adjacent cumulative relative frequencies. This also requires a set of maximums that can be calculated when $n > 25$ and $m > 25$. Then,

$$D(.05) = 1.36\sqrt{\frac{m + n}{mn}}. \qquad (1)$$

For small samples, special tables are needed (see, e.g., Siegel & Castellan, 1988). Alternatively, the probabilities are calculated automatically when using SPSS. Siegel and Castellan (1988) maintain that this test is "slightly more efficient" than the WILCOXON and MANN-WHITNEY U TESTS, but when the samples are large, the reverse tends to be true.

—Thomas R. Black

REFERENCES

Black, T. R. (1999). *Doing quantitative research in the social sciences: An integrated approach to research design, measurement, and statistics*. London: Sage.

Gibbons, J. D., & Chakraborti, S. (1992). *Nonparametric statistical inference* (3rd ed.). New York: Marcel Dekker.

Howell, D. C. (2002). *Statistical methods for psychology* (5th ed.). Pacific Grove, CA: Duxbury.

Siegel, S., & Castellan, N. J. (1988). *Nonparametric statistics for the behavioral sciences*. New York: McGraw-Hill.

KRUSKAL-WALLIS *H* TEST

Also known as the Kruskal-Wallis one-way analysis of variance by ranked data, this test determines whether three or more independent samples belong to the same POPULATION based on MEDIANS. It is analogous to the parametric ONE-WAY ANALYSIS OF VARIANCE (ANOVA). The MANN-WHITNEY U TEST covers the equivalent two-sample situation. The NULL HYPOTHESIS is that the medians are the same as that for the population, with the statistical test checking to see if they are close enough, allowing for natural variation in samples. The data are assumed to be at least ordinal, and there is a single underlying continuous distribution (Siegel & Castellan, 1988).

As with other tests based on rank, this one requires that all the raw data from all the samples be placed in order and assigned a rank, starting with 1 for the smallest, going to N, the number of independent observations for all k samples. The sum of all the ranks for each sample is found and the mean rank for each group is calculated. The assumption is that if the samples are really from the same population with a common mean, then these average ranks should be much the same,

Table 1   Scores for Ratings of Creepies Breakfast Cereal by Three Groups

Men		Women		Children	
Score	*Rank*	*Score*	*Rank*	*Score*	*Rank*
12	8.5	13	6.5	20	1
10	12.5	12	8.5	19	2
7	16.5	11	10.5	18	3.5
7	16.5	10	12.5	18	3.5
6	18.5	9	14.5	16	5
5	20.5	6	18.5	13	6.5
4	23	5	20.5	11	10.5
4	23	4	23	9	14.5
R_I	139		114.5		46.5
n_I	8		8		8
R_i^2/n_i	2415.13		1638.78		270.28
Ri/n_I	17.38		14.31		5.81
			Men-Children	Women-Children	Men-Women
$\alpha/k(k-1)$	0.0083	$\Delta(R/n)$	11.56	8.50	3.06
$z(0.0083)$	2.394	$\Delta(R/n)$ critical	8.46	8.46	8.46

NOTE: Tied ranks are the average of the sequential ranks. $N = 24$; $H = 11.48$; $\alpha = 0.05$; $\chi^2(2) = 5.99$.

allowing for natural variation. This is best seen in the following expression of the Kruskal-Wallis statistic, which reminds one of the calculation of variance:

$$H = \frac{12 \sum_{j=1}^{k} n_j (\bar{R}_j - \bar{R})^2}{N(N+1)}.$$

The statistic is also calculated by a form of the equation that makes it easy to use with raw ranks (Howell, 2002), especially on a spreadsheet (Black, 1999):

$$H = \left[\frac{12}{N(N+1)} \sum_{j=1}^{k} \frac{R_j^2}{n_j} \right] - 3(N+1),$$

where

R_j = sum of ranks in group j, where $j = 1$ to k groups;

$\bar{R}_j$ = average of ranks in group j;

$\bar{R}$ = the grand mean of all ranks;

n_j = number in group j;

N = total subjects in all groups.

When the number of groups is greater than three and the number in each group is greater than four (or even when it is three but the sample is large), then the sampling distribution is close to the CHI-SQUARE DISTRIBUTION. Also, there is a correction that can be applied if there are a large number of ties (more than 25% of the samples), which increases the size of the H statistic (see Siegel & Castellan, 1988). If *all* values of R_i were equal to each other, then H would be 0.

For example, the data in Table 1 show scores on the trial of a new breakfast cereal, Creepies, chocolate-flavored oat cereal shaped like insects. Each person rated the cereal on four 5-point scales: texture, taste, color, and the shapes. Thus, possible scores ranged from 4 to 20. It was suspected that adults would not like them as much as children. The sample was taken so that children and adults did not come from the same families. First, the scores were rank ordered, and then H was calculated as

$$H = \left[\frac{12}{24(24+1)} \sum_{j=1}^{3} \frac{R_j^2}{n_j} \right] - 3(24+1)$$

$$= \left[\frac{12}{600}(4324.2) \right] - 75 = 11.48.$$

When compared to the critical value $\chi^2(df = 2) = 5.99$, it is seen that there is a difference across the three groups.

POST HOC ANALYSIS FOR KRUSKAL-WALLIS

Carrying out pairwise comparisons is simply a matter of testing the differences between pairs of averages of ranks against a standard that has been adjusted to take into account that these are not independent. When the samples are large, their differences are approximately normally distributed (Siegel & Castellan, 1988), and the CRITICAL VALUE is found by

$$\Delta(R_i/n_i)_{\text{crit}}$$

$$= z(\alpha/k(k-1))\sqrt{\frac{N(N+1)}{12}\left(\frac{1}{n_a}+\frac{1}{n_b}\right)}.$$

Assuming that all the sample sizes are the same, this calculation has to be carried out only once. There is an adjustment that can be made if the comparisons are to be done only between each treatment and a control but not between treatments (analogous to Dunnett's post hoc test for ANOVA) (see Siegel & Castellan, 1988). For our example above,

$$\Delta(R_i/n_i)_{\text{crit}}$$

$$= z(.05/3(3-1))\sqrt{\frac{24(24+1)}{12}\left(\frac{1}{8}+\frac{1}{8}\right)}$$

$$= 2.394\sqrt{12.5} = 8.46.$$

From Table 1, it can be seen that the differences between men and children, as well as between women and children, are greater than 8.46, and thus these differences are significant. There is no significant difference between men and women. Therefore, the suspicions were confirmed.

—Thomas R. Black

REFERENCES

Black, T. R. (1999). *Doing quantitative research in the social sciences: An integrated approach to research design, measurement, and statistics.* London: Sage.

Howell, D. C. (2002). *Statistical methods for psychology* (5th ed.). Pacific Grove, CA: Duxbury.

Siegel, S., & Castellan, N. J. (1988). *Nonparametric statistics for the behavioral sciences.* New York: McGraw-Hill.

KURTOSIS

Kurtosis, skewness, and their standard errors are common univariate descriptive statistics that measure the shape of the distribution. Kurtosis is the peakedness of a distribution, measuring the relationship between a distribution's tails and its most numerous values. Kurtosis is commonly used to screen data for NORMAL DISTRIBUTION. Values of skewness, which measures the symmetry of the distribution, and kurtosis, which measures peakedness, are generally interpreted together. By statistical convention, skewness and kurtosis both should fall in the range from +2 to –2 if data are normally distributed. The mathematical formula is as follows:

$$\text{kurtosis} = [\Sigma(X-\mu)^4/(N\sigma^4)] - 3,$$

where

X = individual score in the distribution,

$\bar{X}$ = mean of the sample,

N = number of data points,

σ = square root of variance.

Mathematically, kurtosis is the fourth-ORDER central MOMENT. The kurtosis of a standard normal distribution is 3. By subtracting 3 from kurtosis in the formula, zero kurtosis becomes indicative of a perfect normal distribution.

It is important to obtain an adequate sample size when analyzing kurtosis as the size and even direction of kurtosis may be unstable for small sample sizes. When data are found not to be normally distributed, the researcher may wish to apply some data TRANSFORMATION to produce a normal distribution. Statistical programs typically output histograms, BOXPLOTS, box and whisker plots, stem plots, or STEM-AND-LEAF plots to display a distribution's direction and size of skewness and peakedness. These plots are useful in identifying which transformation technique to use if the data are not normally distributed. As a simple example, a normal curve may be superimposed on a histogram of responses to assess a distribution's shape. Log and square root transformations are the most common procedures for correcting positive skewness and kurtosis, whereas square root transformations correct negative skewness and kurtosis. Cubed root and negative reciprocal root transformations are used to correct extreme negative and positive skew, respectively (Newton & Rudestam, 1999).

Data may be leptokurtic, platykurtic, or mesokurtic depending on the shape of the distribution (Newton & Rudestam, 1999). Large positive values are leptokurtic and illustrate a very peaked distribution, with data clustered around the mean and with thicker or longer tails,

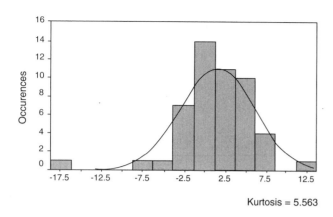

Kurtosis = 5.563

Figure 1   Leptokurtic Data

meaning there are fewer cases in the tails. As shown in Figure 1, which was obtained from hypothetical data, leptokurtic data clustered around the meanand with fewer cases in the tails, in comparison to normally distributed data, resulted in moderate positive kurtosis.

Positive skewness and peakedness indicate that the mean is larger than the median. Large negative values are platykurtic, with histograms indicating a very flat distribution with less clustering around the mean and lighter or shorter tails, meaning there are more cases in the tails than would appear in a normal distribution. Negative skewness and peakedness indicate that the median is larger than the mean. Mesokurtic data approximate a normal distribution, which may be either slightly negative or slightly positive. Low skewness and peakedness reflect relative closeness of the mean and median.

—Amna C. Cameron

REFERENCES

Newton, R. R., & Rudestam, K. E. (1999). *Your statistical consultant: Answers to your data analysis questions.* Thousand Oaks, CA: Sage.

LABORATORY EXPERIMENT

All EXPERIMENTS involve random assignment of participants to the conditions of the study, an INDEPENDENT VARIABLE (IV) and a DEPENDENT VARIABLE (DV). Experiments may be conducted in highly constrained laboratory settings or in field contexts, which generally are characterized by somewhat less control. Both venues offer advantages and disadvantages. In the laboratory, the researcher typically has control over all external forces that might affect the participant—the degree of control over the setting is extreme. In field experiments, this often is not so; hence, conclusions are sometimes more tentative in such contexts, owing to the possibility of the effect of uncontrolled variations.

Random assignment in experimentation means that from a predefined pool, all participants have an equal chance of being assigned to one or another condition of the study. After random assignment, participants assigned to different conditions receive different levels of the IV. In some designs, participants will have been pretested (i.e., assessed on a measure that theoretically is sensitive to variations caused by different levels of the IV). In other designs, only a posttreatment DV is used (see Crano & Brewer, 2002). After the treatment application, they are assessed again, as indicated in Figure 1, which shows two groups, a treated group and a control group (which did not receive the experimental treatment).

In developing an experiment, the theoretical construct that is the central focus of the study, as well as the measures of this CONCEPTUALIZATION, must be defined in terms of observable behaviors or events. This process is termed *operationalization*. Then, participants are assigned randomly to conditions of the experiment, which are defined by different levels of the IV. Sometimes, more than one IV is employed; typically in such cases, each level of one IV is combined with each level of the other(s), resulting in a FACTORIAL DESIGN. Ideally, equal numbers of participants are assigned to each condition formed by the factorial combination. After assignment, participants are exposed to the particular treatment (IV) or combination of treatments (if multiple IVs are used), and the effects of this exposure are observed on the DV.

The laboratory experiment is a highly constrained research technique. Through randomization, participants theoretically are equivalent in all respects, except that some have been exposed to the IV and others have not (or they were systematically exposed

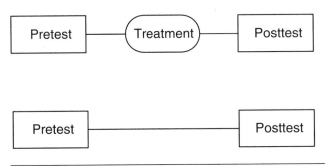

Figure 1   Example of a Pretest/Posttest/Control Group Experimental Design

NOTE: Removing the pretest from treatment and control groups results in a posttest-only/control group design. Random assignment of participants to conditions is assumed in either case.

to different values or levels of the IV). As such, they should not differ on the DV *unless* the IV has had an effect. The high degree of constraint characteristic of laboratory experimental research has caused some to question the generalizability of findings generated in these contexts. Conversely, the randomization and constraint that characterize the laboratory experiment help shield the research from extraneous variables that may affect the DV but that have not been accounted for. The trade-off of generalizability versus control helps define the most appropriate occasion for laboratory experimentation.

The laboratory experiment is the ideal method to determine cause-effect relationships. It is most profitably employed when considerable knowledge of the phenomenon under study already exists. It is not a particularly efficient method to develop hypotheses. However, if the theory surrounding a phenomenon is relatively well developed, and fine-grained hypotheses can be developed on the basis of theory, the laboratory experiment can materially assist understanding the precise nature of the construct in question. It is an ideal method to test alternative explanations of specific predicted causal relationship, facilitating identification of factors that amplify or impede a given outcome.

—William D. Crano

REFERENCE

Crano, W. D., & Brewer, M. B. (2002). *Principles and methods of social research* (2nd ed.). Mahwah, NJ: Lawrence Erlbaum.

LAG STRUCTURE

TIME-SERIES models typically assume that the independent variables affect the dependent variable both instantaneously and over time. This relationship is modeled with a lag structure whose parameters are then estimated by some appropriate method. Focusing on a single independent variable, x, and omitting the error term, the most general lag structure is

$$y_t = \alpha + \beta_0 x_t + \beta_1 x_{t-1} + \beta_2 x_{t-2} + \beta_3 x_{t-3}\ldots.$$

It is impossible to estimate the parameters of such a model because there are an infinite number of them.

A finite distributed lag structure assumes that after some given lag—say, K—x no longer affects y. Here,

the lag structure has only a finite number of parameters, that is, $\beta_{K+1} = \beta_{K+2} = \cdots = 0$. Although this can be estimated in principle, MULTICOLLINEARITY makes estimation of each parameter very difficult unless it is assumed that only one or two lags of x affect current y (and even here multicollinearity may still be a problem). Thus, analysts usually impose some parametric structure on the βs. The most common assumption is that they follow a polynomial structure, such as one that is quadratic in time, as in $\beta_k = \lambda_0 + \lambda_1 k + \lambda_2 k^2$. This restriction means that analysts need only estimate three parameters.

Many analysts prefer to allow for an infinite (or at least unlimited) number of lags of x to affect y, feeling that it is odd to allow for impacts from up to some prespecified lag and then zero impacts thereafter. The most common parameterization for this infinite distributed lag is the geometric lag structure, where the impact of x on y is assumed to decline geometrically, that is, $\beta_k = \beta \rho^k$. This can be algebraically transformed into a model with a lagged dependent variable. The assumption that the impact of x on y declines geometrically with lag length is often plausible. If it is too constraining, analysts can combine the finite and infinite lag structures by allowing the (very) few first lags to be freely estimated, as in the finite lag structure model, with the remaining lags assumed to decline geometrically. This may provide a nice balance between the flexibility of the finite lag model and the simplicity of the infinite geometric lag model without forcing the analyst to estimate too many parameters or falling afoul of multicollinearity problems.

With several independent variables, analysts must choose between the simplicity of forcing them all to follow the same lag structure and the flexibility of allowing for each variable to have its own lag structure. The price of the latter flexibility is that analysts have to estimate many more parameters. Analysts can also use lag structures to model the error process. All the various tools available to time-series analysts, such as correlograms, can be usefully combined with theoretical insight to allow analysts to choose a good lag structure.

—Nathaniel Beck

REFERENCES

Beck, N. (1991). Comparing dynamic specifications: The case of presidential approval. *Political Analysis, 3,* 51–87.

Harvey, A. (1990). *The econometric analysis of time series* (2nd ed.). Cambridge: MIT Press.

Mills, T. C. (1990). *Time series techniques for economists.* Cambridge, UK: Cambridge University Press.

LAMBDA

The lambda coefficient is a measure of strength of relationship between NOMINAL variables. Also known as Guttman's coefficient of predictability, lambda measures the extent to which prediction of a DEPENDENT VARIABLE can be improved by knowledge of the category of a nominal PREDICTOR VARIABLE. It is a proportionate reduction in error measure because it shows how much knowing the value of one variable decreases the prediction error for the other variable. Lambda is an asymmetrical coefficient because its value depends on which of the two variables is the dependent variable because it will generally have a different value when one variable is the dependent variable and the other variable is the independent variable. Reversing the independent and dependent variables changes the value of lambda:

$$\lambda = \left(\sum f_i - M \right)/(N - M),$$

where f_i is the largest cell frequency within category i of the independent variable, M is the largest marginal frequency on the dependent variable, and N is the total number of cases. The denominator is the number of errors in predicting the dependent variable that would be made without knowing the category of the independent variable for that case, whereas the numerator shows how many fewer errors in predicting the dependent variable would be made when knowing the category of the independent variable.

Lambda varies in value between 0 and 1 and does not take on negative values. Whereas most measures of relationship view statistical INDEPENDENCE as their definition of a zero relationship between two variables, lambda instead finds no relationship whenever the modal response on the dependent variable is the same for every category of the independent variable. For example, in analyzing the relationship between the region of the country in which a person lives and the person's favorite color, the lambda value would be 0 if, in every region, more people choose blue as their favorite color than any other color.

Table 1   Favorite Color by Region, No Gain in Prediction

	Northeast	South	West
Blue	60	40	80
Red	20	30	10
Gray	20	30	10

NOTE: $\lambda = 0$ (predicting color from region).

Table 2   Favorite Color by Region, Complete Gain in Prediction

	Northeast	South	West
Blue	100	0	0
Red	0	0	100
Gray	0	100	0

NOTE: $\lambda = 1$ (predicting color from region).

Lambda also has the value of 0 whenever the two variables are statistically independent.

Lambda attains a value of 1 under "conditional unanimity." That is, it interprets a perfect relationship between two variables as the situation in which, for each independent variable category, all cases fall in the same category of the dependent variable. If everyone in the Northeast chooses blue as their favorite color, but everyone in the South chooses gray and everyone in the West chooses red, there would be perfect predictability from knowing a person's region of residence, and therefore lambda would equal 1.

There is also a SYMMETRIC version of lambda, which has the same value regardless of which variable is the dependent variable.

—Herbert F. Weisberg

REFERENCES

Blalock, H. M. (1979). *Social statistics* (Rev. 2nd ed.). New York: McGraw-Hill.

Goodman, L. A., & Kruskal, W. H. (1954). Measures of association for cross classification. *Journal of the American Statistical Association, 49,* 732–764.

Guttman, L. (1941). An outline for the statistical theory of prediction. In P. Horst (with collaboration of P. Wallin & L. Guttman) (Ed.), *The prediction of personal adjustment* (Bulletin 48, Supplementary Study B-1, pp. 253–318). New York: Social Science Research Council.

Weisberg, H. F. (1974). Models of statistical relationship. *American Political Science Review, 68,* 1638–1655.

LATENT BUDGET ANALYSIS

A *budget,* denoted by **p**, is a vector with nonnegative components that add up to a fixed constant c. An example of a budget is the distribution of a day's time over J mutually exclusive and exhaustive activities, such as sleep, work, housekeeping, and so forth. Another example of a budget is the distribution of a $20,000 grant over J cultural projects. Note that components of the time budget add up to 24 hours or 1,440 minutes, and the components of the financial budget add up to 20,000. Without loss of generality, the components of a budget can be divided by the fixed constant c such that they add up to 1. The time budgets of I (groups of) respondents (i.e., $\mathbf{p}_1, \ldots, \mathbf{p}_I$) or the financial budgets of I $20,000 grants can be collected in an $I \times J$ data matrix. Such data are called *compositional data.* The idea of latent budget analysis is to write the I budget as a mixture of a small number, K ($K < I$), of *latent budgets,* denoted by $\beta_1, \ldots, \beta_k$.

Let Y_E be an explanatory variable (e.g., nationality, socioeconomic status, point of time) or an indicator variable with I categories, indexed by i. Let Y_R be a response variable with J categories, indexed by j, and let X be a latent variable with K categories, indexed by K. The budgets can be written as

$$\mathbf{p}_i = [P(Y_R = 1 | Y_E = i), \ldots,$$
$$P(Y_R = j | Y_E = i), \ldots,$$
$$P(Y_R = J | Y_E = i)],$$

for $i = 1, \ldots, I$, and latent budgets can be written as

$$\beta_k = [P(Y_R = 1 | X = k), \ldots,$$
$$P(Y_R = j | X = k), \ldots, P(Y_R = J | X = k)],$$

for $k = 1, \ldots, k$. Let $P(X = k | Y_E = i)$ denote a weight that indicates the proportion of budget $\mathbf{p}_i$ that is determined by latent budget β_k. In latent budget analysis, the budgets $\mathbf{p}_i$ ($i = 1, \ldots, i$) are estimated by *expected budgets* π_i such that

$$\mathbf{p}_i \approx \pi_i = \sum_{k=1}^{K} P(X = k | Y_E = i)\beta_k.$$

The compositional data may be interpreted using latent budgets $\beta_1, \ldots, \beta_K$ in the following procedure:

First, latent budgets $\beta_1, \ldots, \beta_K$ are interpreted and entitled. Comparing the components of the budgets to the components of the independence budget $[P(Y_R = 1), \ldots, P(Y_R = j)]$ can help to characterize the latent budgets. For example, if $P(Y_R = j | X = k) > P(Y_R = j)$, then $\beta_{k,}$ is characterized more than average by component j. Second, the budgets $\pi_1, \ldots, \pi_I$ are interpreted on the basis of the entitled latent budgets by comparing weights $P(X = K | Y_E = i)$ to the average weight

$$P(X = k) = \sum_{i=1}^{I} P(X = k | Y_E = i)P(Y_E = i).$$

For example, if $P(X = k | Y_E = i) > P(X = k)$, then budget π_i is characterized more than average by latent budget β_K.

The idea of latent budget analysis was proposed by Goodman (1974), who called it asymmetric LATENT CLASS ANALYSIS; independently, the idea was also proposed by de Leeuw and van der Heijden (1988), who named it latent budget analysis. Issues with respect to latent budget analysis are discussed in van der Ark and van der Heijden (1998; graphical representation); van der Ark, van der Heijden, and Sikkel (1999; model identification); van der Heijden, Mooijaart, and de Leeuw (1992; constrained latent budget analysis); and van der Heijden, van der Ark, & Mooijaart (2002; applications).

—L. Andries van der Ark

REFERENCES

de Leeuw, J., & van der Heijden, P. G. M. (1988). The analysis of time-budgets with a latent time-budget model. In E. Diday (Ed.), *Data analysis and informatics* (Vol. 5, pp. 159–166). Amsterdam: North-Holland.

Goodman, L. A. (1974). The analysis of systems of qualitative variables when some of the variables are unobservable: I. A modified latent structure approach. *American Journal of Sociology, 79,* 1179–1259.

van der Ark, L. A., & van der Heijden, P. G. M. (1998). Graphical display of latent budget analysis and latent class analysis, with special reference to correspondence analysis. In M. Greenacre & J. Blasius (Eds.), *Visualization of categorical data* (pp. 489–508). San Diego: Academic Press.

van der Ark, L. A., van der Heijden, P. G. M., & Sikkel, D. (1999). On the identifiability of the latent model. *Journal of Classification, 16,* 117–137.

van der Heijden, P. G. M., Mooijaart, A., & de Leeuw, J. (1992). Constrained latent budget analysis. In P. Marsden

(Ed.), *Sociological methodology* (pp. 279–320). Cambridge, UK: Basil Blackwell.

van der Heijden, P. G. M., van der Ark, L. A., & Mooijaart, A. (2002). Some examples of latent budget analysis and its extensions. In J. A. Hagenaars & A. McCutcheon (Eds.), *Applied latent class analysis* (pp. 107–136). Cambridge, UK: Cambridge University Press.

LATENT CLASS ANALYSIS

The basic idea underlying latent class (LC) analysis is a very simple one: Some of the parameters of a postulated statistical model differ across unobserved subgroups. These subgroups form the categories of a categorical latent variable (see LATENT VARIABLE). This basic idea has several seemingly unrelated applications, the most important of which are clustering, scaling, density estimation, and random-effects modeling. Outside social sciences, LC models are often referred to as finite mixture models.

LC analysis was introduced in 1950 by Lazarsfeld, who used the technique as a tool for building typologies (or clustering) based on dichotomous observed variables. More than 20 years later, Goodman (1974) made the model applicable in practice by developing an algorithm for obtaining maximum likelihood estimates of the model parameters. He also proposed extensions for polytomous manifest variables and multiple latent variables and did important work on the issue of model identification. During the same period, Haberman (1979) showed the connection between LC models and log-linear models for frequency tables with missing (unknown) cell counts. Many important extensions of the classical LC model have been proposed since then, such as models containing (continuous) covariates, local dependencies, ordinal variables, several latent variables, and repeated measures. A general framework for categorical data analysis with discrete latent variables was proposed by Hagenaars (1990) and extended by Vermunt (1997).

Although in the social sciences, LC and finite mixture models are conceived primarily as tools for categorical data analysis, they can be useful in several other areas as well. One of these is density estimation, in which one makes use of the fact that a complicated density can be approximated as a finite mixture of simpler densities. LC analysis can also be used as a probabilistic cluster analysis tool for continuous observed variables, an approach that offers many advantages over traditional cluster techniques such as K-means clustering (see LATENT PROFILE MODEL). Another application area is dealing with unobserved heterogeneity, for example, in regression analysis with dependent observations (see NONPARAMETRIC RANDOM-EFFECTS MODEL).

THE CLASSICAL LC MODEL FOR CATEGORICAL INDICATORS

Let X represent the latent variable and Y_ℓ one of the L observed or manifest variables, where $1 \leq \ell \leq L$. Moreover, let C be the number of latent classes and D_ℓ the number of levels of Y_ℓ. A particular LC is enumerated by the index x, $x = 1, 2, \ldots, C$, and a particular value of Y_ℓ by y_ℓ, $y_\ell = 1, 2, \ldots, D_\ell$. The vector notation $\mathbf{Y}$ and $\mathbf{y}$ is used to refer to a complete response pattern.

To make things more concrete, let us consider the following small data set obtained from the 1987 General Social Survey:

Y_1	Y_2	Y_3	Frequency	$P(X = 1|\mathbf{Y} = \mathbf{y})$	$P(X = 2|\mathbf{Y} = \mathbf{y})$
1	1	1	696	.998	.002
1	1	2	68	.929	.071
1	2	1	275	.876	.124
1	2	2	130	.168	.832
2	1	1	34	.848	.152
2	1	2	19	.138	.862
2	2	1	125	.080	.920
2	2	2	366	.002	.998

The three dichotomous indicators Y_1, Y_2, and Y_3 are the responses to the statements "allow anti-religionists to speak" (1 = allowed, 2 = not allowed), "allow anti-religionists to teach" (1 = allowed, 2 = not allowed), and "remove anti-religious books from the library" (1 = do not remove, 2 = remove). By means of LC analysis, it is possible to identify subgroups with different degrees of tolerance toward anti-religionists.

The basic idea underlying any type of LC model is that the probability of obtaining response pattern $\mathbf{y}$, $P(\mathbf{Y} = \mathbf{y})$, is a weighted average of the C class-specific probabilities $P(\mathbf{Y} = \mathbf{y}|X = x)$; that is,

$$P(\mathbf{Y} = \mathbf{y}) = \sum_{x=1}^{C} P(X = x) P(\mathbf{Y} = \mathbf{y}|X = x). \quad (1)$$

Here, $P(X = x)$ denotes the proportion of persons belonging to LC x.

In the classical LC model, this basic idea is combined with the assumption of LOCAL INDEPENDENCE. The L manifest variables are assumed to be mutually independent within each LC, which can be formulated as follows:

$$P(\mathbf{Y} = \mathbf{y}|X = x) = \prod_{\ell=1}^{L} P(Y_\ell = y_\ell|X = x). \quad (2)$$

After estimating the conditional response probabilities $P(Y_\ell = y_\ell|X = x)$, comparing these probabilities between classes shows how the classes differ from each other, which can be used to name the classes. Combining the two basic equations (1) and (2) yields the following model for $P(\mathbf{Y} = \mathbf{y})$:

$$P(\mathbf{Y} = \mathbf{y}) = \sum_{x=1}^{C} P(X = x) \prod_{\ell=1}^{L} P(Y_\ell = y_\ell|X = x).$$

A two-class model estimated with the small example data set yielded the following results:

	$X = 1$ *(Tolerant)*	$X = 2$ *(Intolerant)*
$P(X = x)$	.62	.38
$P(Y_1 = 1|X = x)$	.96	.23
$P(Y_2 = 1|X = x)$	.74	.04
$P(Y_3 = 1|X = x)$	.92	.24

The two classes contain 62% and 38% of the individuals, respectively. The first class can be named "Tolerant" because people belonging to that class have much higher probabilities of selecting the tolerant responses on the indicators than people belonging to the second "Intolerant" class.

Similarly to CLUSTER ANALYSIS, one of the purposes of LC analysis might be to assign individuals to latent classes. The probability of belonging to LC x—often referred to as posterior membership probability—can be obtained by the Bayes rule:

$$P(X = x|\mathbf{Y} = \mathbf{y}) \quad (3)$$
$$= \frac{P(X = x)P(\mathbf{Y} = \mathbf{y}|X = x)}{P(\mathbf{Y} = \mathbf{y})}.$$

The most common classification rule is modal assignment, which amounts to assigning each individual to the LC with the highest $P(X = x|\mathbf{Y} = \mathbf{y})$. The class membership probabilities reported in the first table show that people with at least two tolerant responses are classified into the "Tolerant" class.

LOG-LINEAR FORMULATION OF THE LC MODEL

Haberman (1979) showed that the LC model can also be specified as a LOG-LINEAR MODEL for a table with missing cell entries or, more precisely, as a model for the expanded table, including the latent variable X as an additional dimension. The relevant log-linear model for $P(X = x, \mathbf{Y} = \mathbf{y})$ has the following form:

$$\ln P(X = x, \mathbf{Y} = \mathbf{y}) = \beta + \beta_x^X$$
$$+ \sum_{\ell=1}^{L} \beta_{y_\ell}^{Y_\ell} + \sum_{\ell=1}^{L} \beta_{x,y_\ell}^{X,Y_\ell}.$$

It contains a main effect, the one-variable terms for the latent variable and the indicators, and the two-variable terms involving X and each of the indicators. Note that the terms involving two or more manifest variables are omitted because of the local independence assumption.

The connection between the log-linear parameters and the conditional response probabilities is as follows:

$$P(Y_\ell = y_\ell|X = x) = \frac{\exp(\beta_{y_\ell}^{Y_\ell} + \beta_{x,y_\ell}^{X,Y_\ell})}{\sum_{r=1}^{D_\ell} \exp(\beta_r^{Y_\ell} + \beta_{x,r}^{X,Y_\ell})}.$$

This shows that the log-linear formulation amounts to specifying a logit model for each of the conditional response probabilities.

The type of LC formulation that is used becomes important if one wishes to impose restrictions. Although constraints on probabilities can sometimes be transformed into constraints on log-linear parameters and vice versa, there are many situations in which this is not possible.

MAXIMUM LIKELIHOOD ESTIMATION

Let I denote the total number of cells entries (or possible answer patterns) in the L-way frequency table, so that $I = \prod_{\ell=1}^{L} D_\ell$, and let i denote a particular cell entry, n_i the observed frequency in cell i, and $P(\mathbf{Y} = \mathbf{y}_i)$ the probability of having the response pattern of cell i.

The parameters of LC models are typically estimated by means of MAXIMUM LIKELIHOOD (ML). The kernel of the log-likelihood function that is maximized equals

$$\ln L = \sum_{i=1}^{I} n_i \ln P(\mathbf{Y} = \mathbf{y}_i).$$

Notice that only nonzero observed cell entries contribute to the log-likelihood function, a feature that is exploited by several more efficient LC software packages that have been developed within the past few years.

One of the problems in the estimation of LC models is that model parameters may be nonidentified, even if the number of DEGREES OF FREEDOM is larger or equal to zero. Nonidentification means that different sets of parameter values yield the same maximum of the log-likelihood function or, worded differently, that there is no unique set of parameter estimates. The formal identification check is via the information matrix, which should be positive definite. Another option is to estimate the model of interest with different sets of starting values. Except for local solutions (see below), an identified model gives the same final estimates for each set of the starting values.

Although there are no general rules with respect to the identification of LC models, it is possible to provide certain minimal requirements and point to possible pitfalls. For an unrestricted LC analysis, one needs at least three indicators, but if these are dichotomous, no more than two latent classes can be identified. One has to watch out with four dichotomous variables, in which case the unrestricted three-class model is not identified, even though it has a positive number of degrees of freedom. With five dichotomous indicators, however, even a five-class model is identified. Usually, it is possible to achieve identification by constraining certain model parameters; for example, the restrictions $P(Y_\ell = 1|X = 1) = P(Y_\ell = 2|X = 2)$ can be used to identify a two-class model with two dichotomous indicators.

A second problem associated with the estimation of LC models is the presence of local maxima. The log-likelihood function of a LC model is not always concave, which means that hill-climbing algorithms may converge to a different maximum depending on the starting values. Usually, we are looking for the global maximum. The best way to proceed is, therefore, to estimate the model with different sets of random starting values. Typically, several sets converge to the same highest log-likelihood value, which can then be assumed to be the ML solution. Some software packages have automated the use of several sets of random starting values to reduce the probability of getting a local solution.

Another problem in LC modeling is the occurrence of boundary solutions, which are probabilities equal to 0 (or 1) or log-linear parameters equal to minus (or plus) infinity. These may cause numerical problems in the estimation ALGORITHMS, occurrence of local solutions, and complications in the computation of standard errors and number of degrees of freedom of the goodness-of-fit tests. Boundary solutions can be prevented by imposing constraints or by taking into account other kinds of prior information on the model parameters.

The most popular methods for solving the ML estimation problem are the expectation-maximization (EM) and Newton-Raphson (NR) algorithms. EM is a very stable iterative method for ML estimation with incomplete data. NR is a faster procedure that, however, needs good starting values to converge. The latter method makes use the matrix of second-order derivatives of the log-likelihood function, which is also needed for obtaining standard errors of the model parameters.

MODEL SELECTION ISSUES

The goodness of-fit of an estimated LC model is usually tested by either the Pearson or the likelihood ratio chi-squared statistic (see CATEGORICAL DATA ANALYSIS). The latter is defined as

$$L^2 = 2 \sum_{i=1}^{I} n_i \ln \frac{n_i}{N \cdot P(\mathbf{Y} = \mathbf{y}_i)},$$

where N denotes the total sample size. As in log-linear analysis, the number of degrees of freedom (df) equals the number of cells in the frequency table minus 1, $\prod_{\ell=1}^{L} D_\ell - 1$, minus the number of independent parameters. In an unrestricted LC model,

$$df = \prod_{\ell=1}^{L} D_\ell - C \cdot \left[1 + \sum_{\ell=1}^{L} (D_\ell - 1) \right].$$

Although it is no problem to estimate LC models with 10, 20, or 50 indicators, in such cases, the frequency table may become very sparse and, as a result, asymptotic p values can longer be trusted. An elegant but somewhat time-consuming solution to this problem is to estimate the p values by parametric bootstrapping. Another option is to assess model fit in lower order marginal tables (e.g., in the two-way marginal tables).

It is not valid to compare models with C and $C + 1$ classes by subtracting their L^2 and df values because this conditional test does not have an asymptotic chi-squared distribution. This means that alternative methods are required for comparing models with different numbers of classes. One popular method is the use of information criteria such as the Bayesian Information Criterion (BIC) and the Akaike Information Criterion (AIC). Another more descriptive method is a measure for the proportion of total association accounted for by a C class model, $[L^2(1) - L^2(C)]/L^2(1)$, where the L^2 value of the one-class (independence) model, $L^2(1)$, is used as a measure of total association in the L-way frequency table.

Usually, we are not only interested in goodness of fit but also in the performance of the modal classification rule (see equation (3)). The estimated proportion of classification errors under modal classification equals

$$E = \sum_{i=1}^{I} \frac{n_i}{N} \{1 - \max[P(X = x | \mathbf{Y} = \mathbf{y}_i)]\}.$$

This number can be compared to the proportion of classification errors based on the unconditional probabilities $P(X = x)$, yielding a reduction of errors measure λ:

$$\lambda = 1 - \frac{E}{\max[P(X = x)]}.$$

The closer this nominal R^2-type measure is to 1, the better the classification performance of a model.

EXTENSIONS OF THE LC MODEL FOR CATEGORICAL INDICATORS

Several extensions have been proposed of the basic LC model. One of the most important extensions is the inclusion of covariates or grouping variables that describe (or predict) the latent variable X. This is achieved by specifying a multinomial logit model for the probability of belonging to LC x; that is,

$$P(X = x | \mathbf{Z} = \mathbf{z})$$
$$= \frac{\exp(\gamma_x^X + \sum_{k=1}^{K} \gamma_x^{X, Z_k} \cdot z_k)}{\sum_{r=1}^{C} \exp(\gamma_r^X + \sum_{k=1}^{K} \gamma_r^{X, Z_k} \cdot z_k)},$$

where z_k denotes a value of covariate k.

Another important extension is related to the use of information on the ordering of categories. Within the log-linear LC framework, ordinal constraints can be imposed via ASSOCIATION MODEL structures for the two variable terms $\beta_{x, y_\ell}^{X, Y_\ell}$. For example, if Y_ℓ is an ordinal indicator, we can restrict $\beta_{x, y_\ell}^{X, Y_\ell} = \beta_x^{X, Y_\ell} \cdot y_\ell$. Similar constraints can be used for the latent variable (Heinen, 1996).

In the case that a C class model does not fit the data, the local independence assumption fails to hold for one or more pairs of indicators. The common model-fitting strategy in LC analysis is to increase the number of latent classes until the local independence assumption holds. Two extensions have been developed that make it possible to follow other strategies. Rather than increasing the number of latent classes, one alternative approach is to relax the local independence assumption by including direct effects between certain indicators—a straightforward extension to the log-linear LC model. Another alternative strategy involves increasing the number of latent variables instead of the number of latent classes. This so-called LC factor analysis approach (Magidson & Vermunt, 2001) is especially useful if the indicators measure several dimensions.

Other important extensions involve the analysis of longitudinal data (see LATENT MARKOV MODEL) and partially observed indicators. The most general model that contains all models discussed thus far as special cases is the structural equation model for categorical data proposed by Hagenaars (1990) and Vermunt (1997).

OTHER TYPES OF LC MODELS

Thus far, we have focused on LC models for categorical indicators. However, the basic idea of LC analysis, that parameters of a statistical model differ across unobserved subgroups, can also be applied with variables of other scale types. In particular, three important types of applications of LC or finite mixture models fall outside the categorical data analysis framework: clustering with continuous variables, density estimation, and random-effects modeling.

Over the past 10 years, there has been a renewed interest in LC analysis as a tool for cluster analysis with continuous indicators. The LC model can be seen as a probabilistic or model-based variant of traditional nonhierarchical cluster analysis procedures such as the K-means method. It has been shown that such a LC-based clustering procedure outperforms the more ad hoc traditional methods. The method is known under names such as LATENT PROFILE MODEL, *mixture-model clustering, model-based clustering, latent discriminant analysis,* and *LC clustering.* The basic formula of this model is similar to one given in equation (1); that is,

$$f(\mathbf{Y} = \mathbf{y}) = \sum_{x=1}^{C} P(X = x) f(\mathbf{Y} = \mathbf{y} | X = x).$$

As shown by this slightly more general formulation, the probabilities $P(\ldots)$ are replaced by densities $f(\ldots)$. With continuous variables, the class-specific densities $f(\mathbf{Y} = \mathbf{y} | X = x)$ will usually be assumed to be (restricted) multivariate normal, where each LC has its own mean vector and covariance matrix. Note that this is a special case of the more general principle of density estimation by finite mixtures of simple densities.

Another important application of LC analysis is as a NONPARAMETRIC RANDOM-EFFECTS MODEL. The idea underlying this application is that the parameters of the regression model of interest may differ across unobserved subgroups. For this kind of analysis, often referred to as LC regression analysis, the LC variable serves the role of a moderating variable. The method is very similar to regression models for repeated measures or two-level data sets, with the difference that no assumptions are made about the distribution of the random coefficients.

SOFTWARE

The first LC program, MLLSA, made available by Clifford Clogg in 1977, was limited to a relatively small number of nominal variables. Today's programs can handle many more variables, as well as other scale types. For example, the LEM program (Vermunt, 1997) provides a command language that can be used to specify a large variety of models for categorical data, including LC models. Mplus is a command language–based structural equation modeling package that implements some kinds of LC models but not for nominal indicators. In contrast to these command language programs, Latent GOLD is a program with an SPSS-like user interface that is especially developed for LC analysis. It implements the most important types of LC models, deals with variables of different scale types, and extends the basic model to include covariates, local dependencies, several latent variables, and partially observed indicators.

—Jeroen K. Vermunt and Jay Magidson

REFERENCES

Goodman, L. A. (1974). The analysis of systems of qualitative variables when some of the variables are unobservable: I. A modified latent structure approach. *American Journal of Sociology, 79,* 1179–1259.

Haberman, S. J. (1979). *Analysis of qualitative data: Vol. 2. New developments.* New York: Academic Press.

Hagenaars, J. A. (1990). *Categorical longitudinal data: Loglinear analysis of panel, trend and cohort data.* Newbury Park, CA: Sage.

Hagenaars, J. A., & McCutcheon, A. L. (2002). *Applied latent class analysis.* Cambridge, UK: Cambridge University Press.

Heinen, T. (1996). *Latent class and discrete latent trait models: Similarities and differences.* Thousand Oaks, CA: Sage.

Lazarsfeld, P. F. (1950). The logical and mathematical foundation of latent structure analysis & the interpretation and mathematical foundation of latent structure analysis. In S. A. Stouffer (Ed.), *Measurement and prediction* (pp. 362–472). Princeton, NJ: Princeton University Press.

Magidson, J., & Vermunt, J. K. (2001). Latent class factor and cluster models, bi-plots and related graphical displays. *Sociological Methodology, 31,* 223–264.

Vermunt, J. K. (1997). *Log-linear models for event histories.* Thousand Oaks, CA: Sage.

LATENT MARKOV MODEL

The latent Markov model (LMM) can either be seen as an extension of the LATENT CLASS model for the analysis of longitudinal data or as an extension of the discrete time MARKOV CHAIN model for dealing with measurement error in the observed variable of interest. It was introduced in 1955 by Wiggins and also referred to as latent transition or the hidden Markov model. The LMM can be used to separate true systematic change from spurious change resulting from measurement error and other types of randomness in the behavior of individuals.

Suppose a single categorical variable of interest is measured at T occasions, and Y_t denotes the response at occasion t, $1 \le t \le T$. This could, for example, be a respondent's party preference measured at 6-month intervals. Let D denote the number of levels of each Y_t, and let y_t denote a particular level, $1 \le y_t \le D$. Let X_t denote an occasion-specific latent variable, C a number of categories of X_t, and x_t a particular LC class at occasion t, $1 \le x_t \le C$. The corresponding LMM has the form

$$P(\mathbf{Y} = \mathbf{y}) = \sum_x P(X_1 = x_1)$$

$$\times \prod_{t=2}^{T} P(X_t = x_t | X_{t-1} = x_{t-1})$$

$$\times \prod_{t=1}^{T} P(Y_t = y_t | X_t = x_t).$$

The two basic assumptions of this model are that the transition structure for the latent variables has the form of a first-order Markov chain and that each occasion-specific observed variable depends only on the corresponding latent variable. For identification and simplicity of the results, it is typically assumed that the error component is time homogeneous:

$$P(Y_t = y_t | X_t = x_t) = P(Y_{t-1} = y_t | X_{t-1} = x_t),$$

for $2 \leq t \leq T$. If no further constraints are imposed, one needs at least three time points to identify the LMM. Typical constraints on the latent transition probabilities are time homogeneity and zero restrictions.

The enormous effect of measurement error in the study of change can be illustrated with a hypothetical example with $T = 3$ and $C = D = 2$. To illustrate this, suppose $P(X_1 = 1) = .80$, $P(X_t = 2 | X_{t-1} = 1) = P(X_t = 2 | X_{t-1} = 1) = .10$, and $P(Y_t = 1 | X_t = 1) = P(Y_t = 2 | X_t = 2) = .20$. If we estimate a stationary manifest first-order Markov model for the hypothetical table, we find .68 in the first state at the first time point and transition probabilities of .29 and .48 out of the two states. These are typical biases encountered when not taking measurement error into account: The size of the smaller group is overestimated, the amount of change is overestimated, and there seems to be more change in the small than in the large group.

It is straightforward to extend the above single-indicator LMM to multiple indicators. Another natural extension is the introduction of covariates or grouping variables explaining individual differences in the initial state and the transition probabilities. The independent classification error (ICE) assumption can be relaxed by including direct effects between indicators at different occasions. Furthermore, mixed variants of the LMM have been proposed, such as models with MOVER-STAYER structures. In social sciences, the LMM is conceived as a tool for categorical data analysis. However, as in standard LATENT CLASS ANALYSIS, these models can be extended easily to other scale types.

The PANMARK program can used to estimate the more standard LMMs. The LEM program can also deal with more extended models, such as models containing covariates and direct effects between indicators.

—Jeroen K. Vermunt

REFERENCES

Langeheine, R., & Van de Pol, F. (1994). Discrete-time mixed Markov latent class models. In A. Dale & R. B. Davies (Eds.), *Analyzing social and political change: A casebook of methods* (pp. 171–197). London: Sage.

MacDonald, I. L., & Zucchini, W. (1997). *Hidden Markov models and other types of models for discrete-valued time series*. London: Chapman & Hall.

Vermunt, J. K. (1997). *Log-linear models for event histories*. Thousand Oaks, CA: Sage.

Wiggins, L. M. (1973). *Panel analysis*. Amsterdam: Elsevier.

LATENT PROFILE MODEL

The latent profile model is a LATENT VARIABLE model with a categorical latent variable and continuous manifest indicators. It was introduced in 1968 by Lazarsfeld and Henry. Although under different names, very similar models were proposed in the same period by Day (1969) and Wolfe (1970).

Over the past 10 years, there has been renewed interest in this type of latent variable model, especially as a tool for CLUSTER ANALYSIS. The latent profile model can be seen as a probabilistic or model-based variant of traditional nonhierarchical cluster analysis procedures such as the K-means method. It has been shown that such a model-based clustering procedure outperforms the more ad hoc traditional methods. It should be noted that only a few authors use the term *latent profile model*. More common names are *mixture of normal components*, *mixture model clustering*, *model-based clustering*, *latent discriminant analysis*, and *latent class clustering*.

Possible social science applications of the latent profile model include building typologies and constructing diagnostic instruments. A sociologist might use it to build a typology of countries based on a set of socioeconomic and political indicators. A psychologist may apply the method to combine various test scores into a single diagnostic instrument.

As in LATENT CLASS ANALYSIS, latent profile analysis assumes that the population consists of C unobserved subgroups that can be referred to as latent profiles, latent classes, or mixture components. Because the indicators are continuous variables, it is most natural to assume that their conditional distribution is normal. The most general model is obtained with unrestricted multivariate normal distributions; that is,

$$f(\mathbf{y}) = \sum_{x=1}^{C} P(x) f(\mathbf{y}|\boldsymbol{\mu}_x, \Sigma_x).$$

The equation states that the joint density of the L indicators, $f(\mathbf{y})$, is a mixture of class-specific densities. Each latent class x has its own mean vector $\boldsymbol{\mu}_x$ and covariance matrix $\sum_x$. The proportion of persons in each of the components is denoted by $P(x)$. It should be noted that the model structures resembles quadratic discriminant analysis, with the important difference, of course, that the classes (groups) are unknown.

Several special cases are obtained by restricting the covariance matrix $\sum_x$. Common restrictions are equal covariance matrices across classes, diagonal covariance matrices, and both equal and diagonal covariance matrices. The assumption of equal covariance matrices is similar to the basic assumption of linear discriminant analysis. Specifying the covariance matrices to be diagonal amounts to assuming LOCAL INDEPENDENCE. Such a model can also be formulated as follows:

$$f(\mathbf{y}) = \sum_{x=1}^{C} P(x) \prod_{\ell=1}^{L} f\left(y_\ell | \mu_{\ell x}, \sigma_{\ell x}^2\right).$$

Assuming local independence and equal error variances, $\sigma_{\ell x}^2 = \sigma_\ell^2$, yields a specification similar to K-means clustering. In most applications, however, this local independence specification is much too restrictive.

Recently, various methods have been proposed for structuring the class-specific covariance matrices. A relatively simple one, which is a compromise between a full and a diagonal covariance matrix, is the use of block-diagonal matrices. This amounts to relaxing the local independence assumption for subsets of indicators. More sophisticated methods make use of principal component and factor analysis decompositions of the covariance matrix, as well as structural equation model-type restrictions on the $\sum_x$.

Another recent development is a model for combinations of continuous and categorical indicators. This is actually a combination of the classical LATENT CLASS model with the latent profile model. Another recent extension is the inclusion of covariates to predict class membership.

Software packages that can be used for estimating latent profile models are EMMIX, Mclust, Mplus, and Latent GOLD.

—Jeroen K. Vermunt

REFERENCES

Day, N. E. (1969). Estimating the components of a mixture of two normal distributions. *Biometrika, 56,* 463–474.

Lazarsfeld, P. F., & Henry, N. W. (1968). *Latent structure analysis.* Boston: Houghton Mifflin.

McLachlan, G. J., & Basford, K. E. (1988). *Mixture models: Inference and application to clustering.* New York: Marcel Dekker.

Vermunt, J. K., & Magidson, J. (2002). Latent class cluster analysis. In J. A. Hagenaars & A. L. McCutcheon (Eds.), *Applied latent class analysis* (pp. 89–106). Cambridge, UK: Cambridge University Press.

Wolfe, J. H. (1970). Pattern clustering by multivariate mixtures. *Multivariate Behavioral Research, 5,* 329–350.

LATENT TRAIT MODELS

A latent trait model is a measurement model that describes the relationship between the probability of a particular score on an item (e.g., correct/incorrect, rating on an ordered scale) and the LATENT VARIABLE or the latent trait that explains this score. For an individual responding to a particular item, this probability depends on his or her latent trait value and properties of the item, such as its difficulty and its discrimination power. The term *latent trait model,* a synonym of *item response model,* is not in as much use today.

—Klaas Sijtsma

See also ITEM RESPONSE THEORY

LATENT VARIABLE

Many constructs that are of interest to social scientists cannot be observed directly. Examples are preferences, attitudes, behavioral intentions, and personality traits. Such constructs can only be measured indirectly by means of observable indicators, such as questionnaire items designed to elicit responses related to an attitude or preference. Various types of scaling techniques have been developed for deriving information on unobservable constructs of interest from the indicators. An important family of scaling methods is formed by latent variable models.

A latent variable model is a possibly nonlinear PATH ANALYSIS or graphical model. In addition to the manifest variables, the model includes one or more unobserved or latent variables representing the constructs of interest. Two assumptions define the causal mechanisms underlying the responses. First, it is assumed that the responses on the indicators are the result of an individual's position on the latent variable(s). The second assumption is that the manifest variables have nothing in common after controlling for the latent variable(s), which is often referred to as the axiom of LOCAL INDEPENDENCE.

The two remaining assumptions concern the distributions of the latent and manifest variables. Depending on these assumptions, one obtains different kinds of latent variable models. According to Bartholomew and Knott (1999), the four main kinds are as follows: FACTOR ANALYSIS (FA), latent trait analysis (LTA), latent profile analysis (LPA), and LATENT CLASS ANALYSIS (LCA) (see table).

| | Latent Variables | |
Manifest Variables	Continuous	Categorical
Continuous	Factor analysis	Latent profile analysis
Categorical	Latent trait analysis	Latent class analysis

In FA and LTA, the latent variables are treated as continuous normally distributed variables. In LPA and LCA, on the other hand, the latent variable is discrete and therefore assumed to come from a multinomial distribution. The manifest variables in FA and LPA are continuous. In most cases, their conditional distribution given the latent variables is assumed to be normal. In LTA and LCA, the indicators are dichotomous, ordinal, or nominal categorical variables, and their conditional distributions are assumed to be binomial or multinomial.

The more fundamental distinction in Bartholomew and Knott's (1999) typology is the one between continuous and discrete latent variables. A researcher has to decide whether it is more natural to treat the underlying latent variable(s) as continuous or discrete. However, as shown by Heinen (1996), the distribution of a continuous latent variable model can be approximated by a discrete distribution. This shows that the distinction between continuous and discrete latent variables is less fundamental than one might initially think.

The distinction between models for continuous and discrete indicators turns out not to be fundamental at all. The specification of the conditional distributions of the indicators follows naturally from their scale types. The most recent development in latent variable modeling is to allow for a different distributional form for each indicator. These can, for example, be normal, student, log-normal, gamma, or exponential distributions for continuous variables; binomial for dichotomous variables; multinomial for ordinal and nominal variables; and Poisson, binomial, or negative-binomial for counts. Depending on whether the latent variable is treated as continuous or discrete, one obtains a generalized form of LTA or LCA.

—Jeroen K. Vermunt and Jay Magidson

REFERENCES

Bartholomew, D. J., & Knott, M. (1999). *Latent variable models and factor analysis.* London: Arnold.
Heinen, T. (1996). *Latent class and discrete latent trait models: Similarities and differences.* Thousand Oaks, CA: Sage.

LATIN SQUARE

A Latin square is a square array of letters or ordered symbols in which each letter or symbol appears once and only once in each row and each column. The following are examples of 2×2, 3×3, and 4×4 Latin squares.

A	B		A	B	C		A	B	C	D
B	A		B	C	A		B	A	D	C
			C	A	B		C	D	B	A
							D	C	A	B

The name *Latin square* was given to the squares by the famous Swiss mathematician Leonard Euler (1707–1783), who studied them and used letters of the Latin alphabet.

The three squares in the table above are called *standard squares* because their first row and first column are ordered alphabetically. Two Latin squares are *conjugate* if the rows of one square are identical to the columns of the other. For example, a 5×5 Latin square and its conjugate are as follows:

A	B	C	D	E		A	B	C	D	E
B	A	D	E	C		B	A	E	C	D
C	E	A	B	D		C	D	A	E	B
D	C	E	A	B		D	E	B	A	C
E	D	B	C	A		E	C	D	B	A

A Latin square is *self-conjugate* if the same square is obtained when its rows and columns are interchanged. The 2×2, 3×3, and 4×4 Latin squares above are self-conjugate.

The p different letters in a Latin square can be rearranged to produce $p!(p-1)!$ Latin squares, including the original square. For example, there are $3!(3-1)! = 12$ three-by-three Latin squares. An enumeration of Latin squares of size 2×2 through 7×7 has been made by Fisher and Yates (1934), Norton (1939), and Sade (1951).

Latin squares are interesting mathematical objects and also useful in designing experiments. A *Latin square design* enables a researcher to test the hypothesis that p population means are equal while isolating the effects of two nuisance variables, with each having p levels. Nuisance variables are undesired sources of variation in an experiment. The effects of the two nuisance variables are isolated by assigning one nuisance variable to the rows of a Latin square and the other nuisance variable to the columns of the square. The p levels of the treatment are assigned to the Latin letters of the square. The isolation of two nuisance variables often reduces the MEAN SQUARE ERROR and results in increased power.

Consider the following example. A researcher is interested in comparing the effectiveness of three diets in helping obese teenage boys lose weight. The independent variable is the three kinds of diets; the dependent variable is the amount of weight loss 3 months after going on a diet. Instead of denoting the diets by the letters A, B, and C, we will follow contemporary usage and denote the diets by the lowercase letter a and a number subscript: a_1, a_2, and a_3. The researcher believes that ease in losing weight is affected by the amount that a boy is overweight and his genetic predisposition to be overweight. A rough measure of the latter variable can be obtained by asking a boy's parents if they were overweight as teenagers: c_1 denotes neither parent overweight, c_2 denotes one parent overweight, and c_3 denotes both parents overweight. This nuisance variable can be assigned to the columns of a 3×3 Latin square. The other nuisance variable, the amount that boys are overweight, can be assigned to the rows of the Latin square: b_1 is 20 to 39 pounds, b_2 is 40 to 59 pounds, and b_3 is 60 or more pounds. A diagram of this Latin square design is as follows:

	c_1	c_2	c_3
b_1	a_1	a_2	a_3
b_2	a_2	a_3	a_1
b_3	a_3	a_1	a_2

By isolating the effects of two nuisance variables, the researcher can obtain a more powerful test of the independent variable. An important assumption of Latin square designs is that there are no INTERACTIONS among the nuisance and independent variables. If the assumption is not satisfied, statistical tests will be BIASED.

François Cretté de Palluel (1741–1798), an agronomist, is credited with performing the first experiment in 1788 that was based on a Latin square. His experiment involved four breeds of sheep that were fed four diets and slaughtered on the 20th of 4 consecutive months. The person most responsible for promoting the use of experimental designs based on a Latin square was Ronald A. Fisher (1890–1962), an eminent British statistician who worked at the Rothamsted Experimental Station north of London. Fisher showed that a Latin square or combination of squares could be used to construct a variety of complex experimental designs. For a description of these designs, see Kirk (1995, chaps. 8, 13, and 14).

—Roger E. Kirk

REFERENCES

Fisher, R. A., & Yates, F. (1934). The six by six Latin squares. *Proceedings of the Cambridge Philosophical Society, 30,* 492–507.

Kirk, R. E. (1995). *Experimental design: Procedures for the behavioral sciences* (3rd ed.). Pacific Grove, CA: Brooks/Cole.

Norton, H. W. (1939). The 7 × 7 squares. *Annals of Eugenics, 9,* 269–307.

Sade, A. (1951). An omission in Norton's list of 7 × 7 squares. *Annals of Mathematical Statistics, 22,* 306–307.

LAW OF AVERAGES

RANDOM ERROR decreases proportionally as the number of trials increases. So, by the law of averages, after enough trials, the expected outcome is more likely to be achieved. Take the example of tossing a coin. Out of 100 tosses, one expects 50 heads, but, by chance, it will probably be off that number. Say it was off by 5, by chance. If the number of tosses went up to 1,000, the expectation would again be for half heads. But again, by chance, it would probably be off by some number, say 8. The absolute number of errors has increased, from 5 to 8, but the percentage of tosses in error has decreased, from 5% to eight tenths of 1%. In general, the law of averages says that as the number of tosses increases, the overall percentage of random error decreases. Thus, the distribution of the coin toss gets closer to its expected value of 50% heads.

—Michael S. Lewis-Beck

LAW OF LARGE NUMBERS

One of the most important results in mathematical statistics describing the behavior of observations of a random variable (i.e., observations from surveys based on random SAMPLES) is the law of large numbers. The law of large numbers concerns the difference between the EXPECTED VALUE of a variable and its AVERAGE computed from a large sample. The law states that this difference is unlikely to be large.

The simplest form of the law applies to an event (such as observing that a respondent has a certain characteristic) A, the PROBABILITY of the event (which can be identified with the relative size of the fraction of the population possessing this characteristic) $P(A)$, and its RELATIVE FREQUENCY after n observations, $r(n, A)$. The law of large numbers says that for large enough n, $r(n, A)$ will get arbitrarily close to $P(A)$, with an arbitrarily large probability. More precisely, for arbitrary (small) values a and b, there exists a threshold such that for all sample sizes n greater than this threshold,

$$P(|P(A) - r(n, A)| < a) > 1 - b.$$

The absolute deviation between the probability and the relative frequency of the event is smaller than a with a probability larger than $1 - b$, if the sample size n is large enough. There, however, remains a small probability (less than b) that the deviation is more than a.

This result is important in two aspects. First, the frequentist approach speaks of probability only if the relative frequencies show a kind of stability (i.e., the relative frequencies computed for large sample sizes tend to be close to each other) and postulates that the relative frequencies are manifestations of the directly unobservable probability. The fact that this property is obtained as a result shows that the mathematical theory of probability appropriately incorporates the fundamental assumptions. Second, the law of large numbers

is also a fundamental result of mathematical statistics. In this context, it says that with large enough sample sizes, the estimates (relative frequency of an event) are very likely to be close to the true value (probability of the event).

The previous result does not indicate how large a sample size is needed to get close to the probability with the relative frequency. The following version is more helpful in this aspect. Let $E(X)$ and $D(X)$ be the expected value and the STANDARD DEVIATION of a variable. Then, for arbitrary positive value c,

$$P(|X - E(X)| > cD(X)) < 1/c^2.$$

This result measures the deviation between the observed value (e.g., the relative frequency) and the expected value (e.g., the probability) in units of the standard deviation. The probability that the deviation exceeds c times the standard deviation is less than $1/c^2$. This result applies to any quantity that may be observed in a survey.

For example, a poll is used in a town to estimate the fraction of those who support a certain initiative. If the sample size is, say, 100, the following bound is obtained for the likely behavior of the estimate. From the BINOMIAL distribution, the standard deviation is not more than 5%, and the probability that the result of the poll deviates from the truth by more than 10% (i.e., 2 standard deviations) is less than $1/4 = 0.25$.

—Tamás Rudas

REFERENCE

Feller, W. (1968). *An introduction to probability theory and its applications* (3rd ed.). New York: John Wiley.

LAWS IN SOCIAL SCIENCE

The question of the possibility of social laws has divided social scientists along both disciplinary and epistemological lines. Macroeconomics has traditionally depended on laws, or at least lawlike statements (e.g., the "laws of supply and demand"), whereas most historians would be skeptical of the existence of historical laws. These positions (to which of course there are exceptions) reflect the epistemological foundations of the disciplines.

The epistemological grounds for the rejection of laws can be summarized as the view that there is too much variability deriving from individual consciousness and free will in the social world to permit lawlike regularities. Although the conclusion of this argument may be ultimately correct, it is also often premised on an oversimplified version of what a "law" is. The common notion of a scientific law is one that brooks no exceptions in the predicted behavior of phenomena. Classical laws of physics are often cited, such as gravity, thermodynamics, and so forth. However, most scientific laws have quite different characteristics, and even classical laws will exhibit certain local exceptions and, under certain circumstances (outside of human experience), may break down altogether (Nagel, 1979, chaps. 4, 5).

Laws can express fundamental theoretical principles (such as those in economics), they may be mathematical axioms or experimentally established invariances, or they may express statistical regularities. Although a theory is usually seen to be a more speculative statement about regularities, sometimes the difference between a law and a theory may be no more than a linguistic or social convenience. Thus, although they both enjoy similar degrees of corroboration, one speaks of Newton's laws and Einstein's theories (Williams, 2000, p. 33). If, then, by accepting the possibility of theoretical corroboration, one accepts there can be regularities in the social world, does this entail a commitment to laws that all have the property of claiming the existence of some nonaccidental occurrences? Perhaps regularities in economic and demographic behavior are as predictable, under given circumstances, as those of gases. Statistical laws, at least, would seem to be possible. However, to continue the gas analogy, although certain local conditions (such as temperature or pressure variations) will create statistical fluctuation in the distribution of gases, the characteristics of the exceptions to demographic or economic laws are much more dependent on unique cultural or historical circumstances (Kincaid, 1994). Thus, there will be regularity in the exceptions to physical laws, but demonstrating such regularity in social laws requires reference to other universalist principles such as rationality.

What is perhaps more important than whether there can be social laws is that good evidence suggests that there can be nonaccidental regularities in the social world, even though such regularities may vary in their cultural or historical applicability and extent.

—Malcolm Williams

REFERENCES

Kincaid, H. (1994). Defending laws in the social sciences. In M. Martin & L. McIntyre (Eds.), *Readings in the philosophy of social science* (pp. 111–130). Cambridge: MIT Press.

Nagel, E. (1979). *The structure of science: Problems in the logic of scientific explanation.* Indianapolis, IN: Hackett.

Williams, M. (2000). *Science and social science: An introduction.* London: Routledge Kegan Paul.

LEAST SQUARES

The least squares method—a very popular technique—is used to compute estimations of parameters and to fit data. It is one of the oldest techniques of modern statistics, being first published in 1805 by the French mathematician Legendre in a now-classic memoir. But this method is even older because it turned out that, after the publication of Legendre's memoir, Gauss, the famous German mathematician, published another memoir (in 1809) in which he mentioned that he had previously discovered this method and used it as early as 1795. A somewhat bitter anteriority dispute followed (a bit reminiscent of the Leibniz-Newton controversy about the invention of calculus), which, however, did not diminish the popularity of this technique. Galton used it (in 1886) in his work on the heritability of size, which laid down the foundations of CORRELATION and (also gave the name) REGRESSION analysis. Both Pearson and Fisher, who did so much in the early development of statistics, used and developed it in different contexts (FACTOR ANALYSIS for Pearson and EXPERIMENTAL DESIGN for Fisher).

Nowadays, the least squares method is widely used to find or estimate the numerical values of the parameters to fit a function to a set of data and to characterize the statistical properties of estimates. It exists with several variations: Its simpler version is called ORDINARY LEAST SQUARES (OLS); a more sophisticated version is called WEIGHTED LEAST SQUARES (WLS), which often performs better than OLS because it can modulate the importance of each observation in the final solution. Recent variations of the least squares method are alternating least squares (ALS) and PARTIAL LEAST SQUARES (PLS).

FUNCTIONAL FIT EXAMPLE: REGRESSION

The oldest (and still most frequent) use of OLS was LINEAR REGRESSION, which corresponds to the problem of finding a line (or curve) that best fits a set of data. In the standard formulation, a set of N pairs of observations $\{Y_i, X_i\}$ is used to find a function giving the value of the dependent variable (Y) from the values of an independent variable (X). With one variable and a linear function, the prediction is given by the following equation:

$$\hat{Y} = a + bX. \tag{1}$$

This equation involves two free parameters that specify the intercept (a) and the slope (b) of the regression line. The least squares method defines the estimate of these parameters as the values that minimize the sum of the squares (hence the name *least squares*) between the measurements and the model (i.e., the predicted values). This amounts to minimizing the following expression:

$$\varepsilon = \sum_i (Y_i - \hat{Y}_i)^2 = \sum_i [Y_i - (a + bX_i)]^2, \tag{2}$$

where ε stands for "error," which is the quantity to be minimized. This is achieved using standard techniques from calculus—namely, the property that a quadratic (i.e., with a square) formula reaches its minimum value when its derivatives vanish. Taking the derivative of ε with respect to a and b and setting them to zero gives the following set of equations (called the *normal equations*):

$$\frac{\partial \varepsilon}{\partial a} = 2Na + 2b \sum X_i - 2 \sum Y_i = 0 \tag{3}$$

and

$$\frac{\partial \varepsilon}{\partial b} = 2b \sum X_i^2$$
$$+ 2a \sum X_i - 2 \sum Y_i X_i = 0. \tag{4}$$

Solving these two equations gives the least squares estimates of a and b as

$$a = M_Y - bM_X, \tag{5}$$

with M_Y and M_X denoting the means of X and Y, and

$$b = \frac{\sum (Y_i - M_Y)(X_i - M_X)}{\sum (X_i - M_X)^2}. \tag{6}$$

OLS can be extended to more than one independent variable (using MATRIX ALGEBRA) and to nonlinear functions.

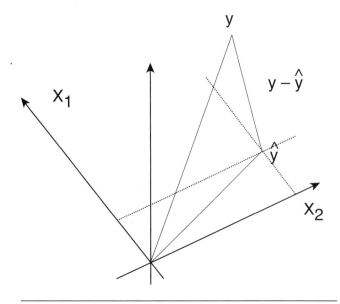

Figure 1   The Least Squares Estimate of the Data Is the Orthogonal Projection of the Data Vector Onto the Independent Variable Subspace

THE GEOMETRY OF LEAST SQUARES

OLS can be interpreted in a geometrical framework as an orthogonal projection of the data vector onto the space defined by the independent variable. The projection is orthogonal because the predicted values and the actual values are uncorrelated. This is illustrated in Figure 1, which depicts the case of two independent variables (vectors $\mathbf{x}_1$ and $\mathbf{x}_2$) and the data vector ($\mathbf{y}$) and shows that the error vector ($\mathbf{y}_1 - \hat{\mathbf{y}}$) is orthogonal to the least squares ($\hat{\mathbf{y}}$) estimate, which lies in the subspace defined by the two independent variables.

OPTIMALITY OF LEAST SQUARES ESTIMATES

OLS estimates have some strong statistical properties. Specifically, when (a) the data obtained constitute a RANDOM SAMPLE from a well-defined POPULATION, (b) the population model is linear, (c) the error has a zero expected value, (d) the independent variables are linearly independent, and (e) the error is normally distributed and uncorrelated with the independent variables (the so-called homoskedasticity assumption), then the OLS estimate is the BEST LINEAR UNBIASED ESTIMATOR, often denoted with the acronym BLUE (the five conditions and the proof are called the Gauss-Markov conditions and theorem). In addition, when the Gauss-Markov conditions hold, OLS estimates are also MAXIMUM LIKELIHOOD estimates.

WEIGHTED LEAST SQUARES

The optimality of OLS relies heavily on the HOMOSKEDASTICITY assumption. When the data come from different subpopulations for which an independent estimate of the error variance is available, a better estimate than OLS can be obtained using weighted least squares (WLS), also called GENERALIZED LEAST SQUARES (GLS). The idea is to assign to each observation a weight that reflects the uncertainty of the measurement. In general, the weight w_i, assigned to the ith observation, will be a function of the variance of this observation, denoted σ_i^2. A straightforward weighting schema is to define $w_i = \sigma_i^{-1}$ (but other, more sophisticated weighted schemes can also be proposed). For the linear regression example, WLS will find the values of a and b minimizing:

$$\varepsilon_w = \sum_i w_i (Y_i - \hat{Y}_i)^2$$
$$= \sum_i w_i [Y_i - (a + bX_i)]^2. \quad (7)$$

ITERATIVE METHODS: GRADIENT DESCENT

When estimating the parameters of a nonlinear function with OLS or WLS, the standard approach using derivatives is not always possible. In this case, iterative methods are very often used. These methods search in a stepwise fashion for the best values of the estimate. Often, they proceed by using at each step a linear approximation of the function and refine this approximation by successive corrections. The techniques involved are known as gradient descent and Gauss-Newton approximations. They correspond to nonlinear least squares approximation in numerical analysis and nonlinear regression in statistics. NEURAL NETWORKS constitute a popular recent application of these techniques.

—Hervé Abdi

REFERENCES

Bates, D. M., & Watts, D. G. (1988). *Nonlinear regression analysis and its applications.* New York: John Wiley.

Greene, W. H. (2002). *Econometric analysis.* New York: Prentice Hall.

Nocedal, J., & Wright, S. (1999). *Numerical optimization.* New York: Springer-Verlag.

Plackett, R. L. (1972). The discovery of the method of least squares. *Biometrika, 59,* 239–251.

Seal, H. L. (1967). The historical development of the Gauss linear model. *Biometrika, 54,* 1–23.

LEAST SQUARES PRINCIPLE.

See REGRESSION

LEAVING THE FIELD

Despite the enormous amount of space devoted to gaining entry in the ethnographic literature, very little attention has been paid to its corollary, *leaving the field.* Also called *disengagement,* leaving the field is the process of exiting from field settings and disengaging from the social relationships cultivated and developed during the research act.

Leaving the field is influenced by the way field-workers gain entry, the intensity of the social relationships they develop in the field, the research bargains they make, and the kinds of persons they become to their informants—or how the researcher and the researched become involved in what Rochford (1992) calls "a politics of experience" (p. 99).

In describing his field experiences with a Buddhist movement in America, Snow (1980) discusses three central issues: (a) information sufficiency, which refers to whether the researcher collected enough data to answer the questions posed by the research; (b) certain extraneous precipitants, which could be institutional, interpersonal, or intrapersonal; and (c) barriers that pressure the ethnographer to remain in the field, such as the feelings of the group concerning the researcher's departure and the overall intensity of field relationships.

In some cases, leaving the field is influenced by the research bargain. This written or unwritten agreement between the researcher and a *gatekeeper* is usually more important at the beginning of the research and is largely forgotten later on. However, the nature of the bargain influences disengagement and helps to shape exit strategies.

Another related issue involves the misrepresentation of the researcher's identity. Although most researchers are overt in their investigations, there are cases when researchers deliberately misrepresent or are unable to be truthful or are unable to maintain their commitment or promises. Informants expect the researchers to live up to their commitments permanently. When the research ends, the level of commitment dissipates, researchers return to their everyday lives, and informants may feel betrayed and manipulated. As researchers prepare to disengage, they need to consider future relationships with their informants, especially if they want to return for further study or clarification.

Gallmeier's (1991) description of conducting FIELD RESEARCH among a group of minor-league hockey players demonstrates the advantages gained by staying in touch with informants. Such revisiting allows the ethnographer to obtain missing data as well as follow the careers of informants who have remained in the setting and thereby observe the changes that have occurred. Revisits also enable the researcher to "take the findings back into the field" (Rochford, 1992, pp. 99–100) to assess the validity of their field reports. Some ethnographers are experimenting with ways to share their findings with informants, actually soliciting their comments on the final analysis and write-up. By giving the respondents the "last word," ethnographers are employing a validity measure referred to as MEMBER VALIDATION. The strength of this approach is that it affords the researched an opportunity to respond to what has been written about them, and it assists the ethnographer in comparing the *etic* with the *emic* perspective.

—Charles P. Gallmeier

REFERENCES

Gallmeier, C. P. (1991). Leaving, revisiting, and staying in touch: Neglected issues in field research. In W. B. Shaffir & R. A. Stebbins (Eds.), *Fieldwork experience: Qualitative approaches to social research* (pp. 224–231). London: Sage.

Rochford, E. B., Jr. (1992). On the politics of member validation: Taking findings back to Hare Krishna. In G. Miller & J. A. Holstein (Eds.), *Perspectives on social problems* (Vol. 3, pp. 99–116). Greenwich, CT: JAI.

Snow, D. (1980). The disengagement process: A neglected problem in participant observation research. *Qualitative Sociology, 3,* 100–122.

LESLIE'S MATRIX

If we know the size and the composition of a population as well as the age-specific fertility and survival (or, alternatively, mortality) rates at the current time, can we project the population size and composition to future times? Leslie's (1945) creative use of MATRIX ALGEBRA is intended for answering this question.

In matrix notation, the population sizes at time $t + 1$, $\mathbf{N}_{t+1}$, is the product of the Leslie matrix, $\mathbf{L}$, and the population sizes at time t, $\mathbf{N}_t$.

$$\mathbf{N}_{t+1} = \mathbf{L}\mathbf{N}_t.$$

This can be written out in vector notation as

$$
\begin{bmatrix} N_{1,t+1} \\ N_{2,t+1} \\ \vdots \\ \vdots \\ N_{J,t+1} \end{bmatrix}
$$
$$
= \begin{bmatrix} F_1 & F_2 & F_3 & \cdots & F_j \\ S_1 & 0 & 0 & \cdots & 0 \\ 0 & S_2 & 0 & \cdots & 0 \\ 0 & 0 & \vdots & \vdots & 0 \\ 0 & \cdots & 0 & S_{j-1} & 0 \end{bmatrix} \begin{bmatrix} N_{1,t} \\ N_{2,t} \\ \vdots \\ \vdots \\ N_{J,t} \end{bmatrix},
$$

where, for $j = 1, \ldots, J$, $N_{j,t}$ is the population size of the jth age group at time t, $N_{j,t+1}$ is the population size of the jth age group at time $t + 1$, S_j is the probability of an individual will survive to the next age group, and F_j is the age-specific fertility of the jth age group.

Let us use a very simple hypothetical example of a population divided into three age classes or groups, each of which has only 10 individuals—hence, $\mathbf{N}_t' = [10, 10, 10]$. Let us further assume that the three age-specific fertility rates are all 0, and the two age-specific survival probabilities are 1 (the survival probability for the last age class is, by definition, 0 as no one lives beyond the upper age limit defined by the last age class). Then, $\mathbf{N}_{t+1}' = [0, 10, 10]$ because everyone survives to the next age class except those in the oldest age class. This population will disappear from the surface of the earth by $t + 3$. Readers familiar with matrix multiplication will quickly see that the result can be obtained from the equation above.

A more realistic situation could have a 30%, 40%, and 30% fertility schedule in the first row of the Leslie matrix, as well as the survival probabilities of 1 again for the first two age groups. In this scenario, we have a constant population size and structure; that is, the three age groups will always contain 10 individuals each, maintaining a *stationary population,* a special case of the useful STABLE POPULATON MODEL. In the real world, however, populations do not follow such beautiful models, but their behaviors can nonetheless be captured by the Leslie matrix.

... ∙∙∙∙lly designed to
∙∙ as the
∙∙ in the
popu-
ap∙ cations
on rate
a study
rs own as
matrix
organi-
r aced by

m ting Liao

population

∙u. n growth to
ly *Mathemati-*

ice of "urban
uctured epi-
ciology, 25,

— ————

A social science ∙∙∙∙y at the MICRO level when individuals are studied, or it can be set at the MACRO level when aggregates of individuals such as cities, counties, provinces, or nations become the UNIT OF ANALYSIS. There is no cut-and-dried definition, and a researcher may choose to analyze a level of analysis between the very micro and the very macro, such as households or neighborhoods.

—Tim Futing Liao

LEVEL OF MEASUREMENT

The level of measurement defines the relation among the values assigned to the ATTRIBUTES of a VARIABLE. Social science researchers conventionally use four such levels: nominal, ordinal, interval, and ratio. For defining these four types of measurement, an increasing number of ASSUMPTIONS are required. For instance, a NOMINAL VARIABLE needs only discrete categories for representing its attributes, an ORDINAL MEASURE has attributes that are ordered, an INTERVAL

measure requires equal distancing among them, and a RATIO SCALE also has a meaningful absolute zero.

—Tim Futing Liao

LEVEL OF SIGNIFICANCE

The level of significance refers to a particular value or level of PROBABILITY a researcher sets in statistical SIGNIFICANCE TESTING of a HYPOTHESIS, commonly known as ALPHA SIGNIFICANCE LEVEL OF A TEST. By social science convention, researchers report the level of significance at the 0.001, 0.01, 0.05, or 0.10 level of making a TYPE I ERROR, although sometimes a lower or higher level of significance is used.

—Tim Futing Liao

LEVENE'S TEST

This test, which was developed by Howard Levene (1960), is a one-way analysis of variance on the absolute deviation of each score from the mean of its group in which the scores of the groups are unrelated. It is an *F* test in which the population estimate of the variance between the groups is compared with the population estimate of the variance within the groups.

$$F = \frac{\text{Between-groups variance estimate}}{\text{Within-groups variance estimate}}.$$

The larger the between-groups variance estimate is in relation to the within-groups variance estimate, the larger the *F* value is and the more likely it is to be statistically significant. A statistically significant *F* value means that the variances of the groups are not equal or homogeneous. These variances may be made to be more equal by transforming the original scores such as taking their square root or logarithm.

Analysis of variance is usually used to determine whether the means of one or more factors and their interactions differ significantly from that expected by chance. One of its assumptions is that the variances of the groups should be equal so that they can be pooled into a single estimate of the variance within the groups. However, if one or more of the groups have a larger variance than the other groups, the larger variance will increase the within-groups variance, making it less likely that an effect will be statistically significant.

Several tests have been developed to determine whether group variances are homogeneous. Some of these tests require the number of cases in each group to be the same or are sensitive to data that are not normally distributed. Levene's test was designed to be used with data that are not normally distributed and where group size is unequal. Milliken and Johnson (1984, p. 22) recommend Levene's test when the data are not normally distributed. Levene's test is the only homogeneity of variance test currently offered in the statistical software of SPSS for Windows.

In factorial analysis of variance, in which there is more than one unrelated factor, Levene's test treats each cell as a group in a one-way analysis of variance. For example, in a factorial analysis of variance consisting of one factor with two groups or levels and another factor with three groups or levels, there will be six ($2 \times 3 = 6$) cells. These six cells will be analyzed as a one-way analysis of variance for unrelated scores. In analysis of covariance, the absolute deviation is that between the original score and the score predicted by the unrelated factor and the covariate.

Rosenthal and Rosnow (1991, p. 340) have recommended that Levene's test can also be used to test the homogeneity of related scores when a single-factor repeated-measures analysis of variance is carried out on the absolute deviation of each score from its group mean.

—Duncan Cramer

REFERENCES

Levene, H. (1960). Robust tests for equality of variances. In I. Olkin (Ed.), *Contributions to probability and statistics* (pp. 278–292). Stanford, CA: Stanford University Press.

Milliken, G. A., & Johnson, D. A. (1984). *Analysis of messy data: Vol. 1. Designed experiments.* New York: Van Nostrand Reinhold.

Rosenthal, R., & Rosnow, R. L. (1991). *Essentials of behavioral research* (2nd ed.). New York: McGraw-Hill.

LIFE COURSE RESEARCH

A key concern of many social scientists is to understand major life events—which can be as simple as completing education, marriage, first birth, and employment—and, in particular, the transition into a particular event as well as the relations between these events throughout one's life span or life course. Life course researchers typically take a dynamic view, as any life course event can be the consequence of past experience and future expectation. Life course research

uses many types of methodology, both qualitative and quantitative, such as the LIFE HISTORY METHOD and EVENT HISTORY ANALYSIS.

—Tim Futing Liao

REFERENCE

Giele, J. Z., & Elder, G. H. (1998). *Methods of life course research: Qualitative and quantitative approaches.* Thousand Oaks, CA: Sage.

LIFE HISTORY INTERVIEW. *See* LIFE STORY INTERVIEW

LIFE HISTORY METHOD

A life story is the story a person tells about the life he or she has lived. For Atkinson (1998), it is "a fairly complete narrating of one's entire experience of life as a whole, highlighting the most important aspects" (p. 8). In social science, life stories exist in many forms: long and short, specific and general, fuzzy and focused, surface and deep, realist and romantic, modernist and postmodernist. And they are denoted by a plethora of terms: *life stories, life histories, life narratives, self stories, mystories, autobiographies, auto/biographies, oral histories, personal testaments,* and *life documents.* All have a slightly different emphasis and meaning, but all focus on the first persona accounting of a life. (For a discussion of this diversity, see Denzin, 1989, pp. 27–49.)

An initial, simple, but helpful contrast can be made between "long" and "short" life stories. *Long life stories* are perhaps seen as the key to the method—the full-length book account of one person's life in his or her own words. They are usually gathered over a long period of time with gentle guidance from the researcher, often backed up with keeping diaries, intensive observation of the subject's life, interviews with friends, and perusals of letters and photographs. The first major sociological use of life histories in this way is generally credited to the publication of Thomas and Znaniecki's five-volume *The Polish Peasant in Europe and America,* which makes the famous claim that life histories "constitute the perfect type of sociological material" (Thomas & Znaniecki, 1918–1920/1958, pp. 1832–1833). One volume of this study provides a 300-page story of a Polish émigré to Chicago, Wladek Wisniewski, written 3 months before the outbreak of World War I. In his story, Wladek describes the early phases of his life in the Polish village of Lubotyn, where he was born the son of a rural blacksmith. He talks of his early schooling, his entry to the baker's trade, his migration to Germany to seek work, and his ultimate arrival in Chicago and his plight there. Twenty years on this "classic" study was honored by the Social Science Research Council "as the finest exhibit of advanced sociological research and theoretical analysis" (see Blumer, 1939/1969, p. vi). Following from this classic work, life histories became an important tool in the work of both Chicago and Polish sociologists. By contrast, *short life stories* take much less time, tend to be more focused, and are usually published as one in a series. They are gathered through in-depth interviews, along with open-ended questionnaires, requiring gentle probes that take somewhere between half an hour and 3 hours. The stories here usually have to be more focused than the long life histories.

COMPREHENSIVE, TOPICAL, AND EDITED

Making another set of distinctions, Allport (1942) suggested three main forms of life history writing: the comprehensive, the topical, and the edited. The *comprehensive life document* aims to grasp the totality of a person's life—the full sweep—from birth to his or her current moment, capturing the development of a unique human being. The *topical life document* does not aim to grasp the fullness of a person's life but confronts a particular issue. The study of Stanley, The Jack Roller, in the late 1920s focuses throughout on the delinquency of his life (Shaw, 1966). The document is used to throw light on a particular topic or issue. The *edited life document* does not leave the story quite so clearly in the subject's voice. Rather, the author speaks and edits the subjects into his or her account—these documents are often used more for illustration. The classic version of this is William James's (1902/1952) *The Varieties of Religious Experience: A Study in Human Nature.* In this book-length study, organized around themes such as "Conversion," "Saintliness," and "Mysticism," James draws from series of case studies of religious experience. No one life dominates—instead, extracts appear in many places.

NATURALISTIC, RESEARCHED, AND REFLEXIVE

A further distinction that is increasingly made lies in what can be called *naturalistic, researched,* and *reflexive* life stories, although there can be overlaps between them. *Naturalistic life stories* are stories that naturally occur, which people just tell as part of their everyday lives, unshaped by the social scientist. Naturalistic life stories are not artificially assembled but just happen in situ. They are omnipresent in those most popular forms of publishing: confessions, personal testaments, and autobiographies. Classically, these may include Rousseau's (1781/1953) *Confessions* or slave narratives such as Harriet A. Jacobs' *Incidents in the Life of a Slave Girl: Written by Herself* (1861). They are first-person accounts unshaped by social scientists.

By contrast, *researched life stories* are specifically gathered by researchers with a wider—usually social science—goal in mind. These do not naturalistically occur in everyday life; rather, they have to be interrogated out of subjects. ORAL HISTORY, sociological LIFE HISTORY, literary biographies, psychological case studies—all these can bring life stories into being that would not otherwise have happened. Both the case studies of Stanley and Wladek cited above would be classic instances of this. The role of researchers is crucial to this activity: Without them, there would be no life story. In their questioning, they shape and generate the stories.

Reflexive and recursive life stories differ from the other two types of life stories by bringing with them a much greater awareness of their own construction and writing. Most earlier life stories would convey a sense that they were telling the story of a life, but these latter kinds of stories become self-conscious and suggest that storytelling is a language game, an act of speech, a mode of writing, a social construction. Whatever else they may say, stories do not simply tell the tale of a life. Here, a life is seen more richly as "composed" or constructed: The writer becomes a part of the writing. In this view, life story research usually involves a storyteller (the narrator of the story) and an interviewer (who acts as a guide in this process), as well as a narrative text that is assembled: producer, teller, and text. The producer and the teller together construct the story in specific social circumstances. Stories can be told in different ways at different times. Stanley (1992) even finds that so many of the most common distinctions that are made—for example, between biography and autobiography—are false: "Telling apart fiction, biography and autobiography is no easy matter" (p. 125). Because of this, she carves out yet another word, *auto/biography*—"a term which refuses any easy distinction between biography and autobiography, instead recognizing their symbiosis"—and applies it to some of her own life (Stanley, 1992, p. 127).

Although life stories have often been criticized for being overly subjective, too idiographic, and nongeneralizable, it is noticeable that in the closing years of the 20th century, such research was becoming more and more popular.

—Ken Plummer

See also Autobiography, Autoethnography, Case Study, Humanism and Humanistic Research, Interpretative Biography, Interviewing in Qualitative Research, Life Course Research, Life History Interview, Narrative Analysis, Narrative Interview, Oral History, Qualitative Research, Reflexivity

REFERENCES

Atkinson, R. (1998). *The life story interview* (Qualitative Research Methods Series, Vol. 44). Thousand Oaks, CA: Sage.

Blumer, H. (1969). *An empirical appraisal of Thomas and Znaniecki (1918–20) The Polish peasant in Europe and America.* New Brunswick, NJ: Transaction Books. (Original work published 1939)

Denzin, N. K. (1989). *Interpretative biography.* London: Sage.

Jacobs, H. A. (1861). *Incidents in the life of a slave girl: Written by herself.* Boston.

James, W. (1952). *The varieties of religious experience: A study in human nature.* London: Longmans, Green & Co. (Original work published 1902)

Plummer, K. (2001). *Documents of life 2: An invitation to a critical humanism.* London: Sage.

Roberts, B. (2002). *Biographical research.* Buckingham, UK: Open University Press.

Rousseau, J.-J. (1953) *The confessions.* Harmondsworth, UK: Penguin. (Original work published 1781.)

Shaw, C. (1966). *The jack roller.* Chicago: University of Chicago Press.

Smith, S., & Watson, J. (2001). *Reading autobiography: A guide for interpreting life narratives.* Minneapolis: University of Minnesota Press.

Stanley, L. (1992). *The auto/biographical I: The theory and practice of feminist auto/biography.* Manchester, UK: Manchester University Press.

Thomas, W. I., & Znaniecki, F. (1918–1920). *The Polish peasant in Europe and America* (5 vols.). New York: Dover.

Thomas, W. I., & Znaniecki, F. (1958). *The Polish peasant in Europe and America* (2 vols.). New York: Dover. (Original five-volume work published in 1918–1920)

LIFE STORY INTERVIEW

A life story is the story a person chooses to tell about the life he or she has lived as completely and honestly as possible, what that person remembers of it, and what he or she wants others to know of it, usually as a result of a guided INTERVIEW by another; it is a fairly complete narrating of one's entire experience of life as a whole, highlighting the most important aspects. A life story is the narrative essence of what has happened to a person. It can cover the time from birth to the present, or before and beyond. It includes the important events, experiences, and feelings of a lifetime.

Life story, LIFE HISTORY, and ORAL HISTORY can be different terms for the same thing. The difference between them is often emphasis and scope. Although a life history or an oral history often focuses on a specific aspect of a person's life, such as work life or a special role played in some part of the life of a community, a life story interview has as its primary and sole focus a person's entire life experience. A life story brings order and meaning to the life being told, for both the teller and the listener. It is a way to better understand the past and the present, as well as a way to leave a personal legacy for the future. A life story gives us the vantage point of seeing how one person experiences and subjectively understands his or her own life over time. It enables us to see and identify the threads that connect one part of one's life to another, from childhood to adulthood.

HISTORICAL AND DISCIPLINARY CONTEXT

Stories, in traditional communities of the past, played a central role in the lives of the people. The stories we tell of our lives today are guided by the same vast catalog of enduring elements, such as archetypes and motifs, that are common to all human beings. These expressions of ageless experiences take a range of forms in different times and settings and come together to create a pattern of life, with many repetitions, that becomes the basis for the plot of the story of a life. Our life stories follow such a pattern or blueprint and represent, each in its own way, a balance between the opposing forces of life. It is within this ageless and universal context that we can best begin to understand the importance and power of the life story interview and how it is fundamental to our very nature. Our life stories, just as myths did in an earlier time, can serve the classic functions of bringing us into accord with ourselves, others, the mystery of life, and the universe around us.

Researchers in many academic disciplines have been interviewing others for their life stories, or for some aspect of their lives, for longer than we recognize. The life story interview has evolved from the oral history, life history, and other ETHNOGRAPHIC and field approaches. As a QUALITATIVE RESEARCH method for looking at life as a whole and as a way of carrying out an in-depth study of individual lives, the life story interview stands alone. It has a range of interdisciplinary applications for understanding single lives in detail and how the individual plays various roles in society.

Social scientists—such as Henry A. Murray, who studied individual lives using life narratives primarily to understand personality development, and Gordon Allport, who used personal documents to study personality development in individuals—began using a life-as-a-whole approach in the 1930s and 1940s. This approach reached its maturation in studies of Luther and Gandhi by Erik Erikson (1975), who used the life history to explore how the historical moment influenced lives.

Today, social scientists reflect a broad interest in narrative as it serves to illuminate the lives of persons in society. The narrative study of lives is a significant interdisciplinary methodological approach (represented by the series edited by Josselson & Lieblich, 1993–1999) that aims to further the theoretical understanding of individual life narratives through in-depth studies, methodological examinations, and theoretical explorations.

As a research tool that is gaining much interest and use in many disciplines today, there are two primary approaches to life stories: CONSTRUCTIONIST and NATURALISTIC. Some narrative researchers conceive of the life story as a circumstantially mediated, constructive collaboration between the interviewer and interviewee. This approach stresses the situated emergence of the life story as opposed to the subjectively faithful, experientially oriented account. In the constructionist perspective, life stories are evaluated not so much for how well they accord with the life experiences in question but more in terms of how accounts of lives are used

by a variety of others, in addition to the subjects whose lives are under consideration, for various descriptive purposes (Holstein & Gubrium, 2000).

The approach used at the University of Southern Maine Center for the Study of Lives is more naturalistic and has evolved from an interdisciplinary context, taking in folklore, counseling psychology, and cross-cultural human development and exploring how cultural values and traditions influence development across the life cycle from the subjective representation of one's life. This approach seeks to understand another's lived experience, as well as his or her relation to others, from that person's own voice. If we want to know the unique perspective of an individual, there is no better way to get this than in his or her voice. This allows that person, as well as others, to see his or her life as a whole, across time—and the parts of it may all fit together as one continuous whole, or some parts may seem discontinuous with others, or both might be possible, as well.

Life stories have gained respect and acceptance in many academic circles. Psychologists see the value of personal narratives in understanding development and personality. Anthropologists use the life history, or individual CASE STUDY, as the preferred unit of study for their measures of cultural similarities and variations. Sociologists use life stories to understand and define relationships as well as group interactions and memberships. In education, life stories have been used as a new way of knowing and teaching. Literary scholars use autobiography as texts through which to explore questions of design, style, content, literary themes, and personal truth. In using the oral history approach, historians find that life story materials are an important source for enhancing local history.

USES OF THE LIFE STORY INTERVIEW

The life story is inherently interdisciplinary; its many research uses can help the teller as well as the scholar understand a very broad range of social science issues better. A life story narrative can be a valuable text for learning about the human endeavor, or how the self evolves over time, and becomes a meaning maker with a place in society, the culture, and history. A life story can be one of the most emphatic ways to answer the question, "Who am I?"

Life stories can help the researcher become more aware of the range of possible roles and standards that exist within a human community. They can define an individual's place in the social order of things and can explain or confirm experience through the moral, ethical, or social context of a given situation. They can provide the researcher with information about a social reality existing outside the story, described by the story.

Life stories can provide clues to what people's greatest struggles and triumphs are, where their deepest values lie, what their quest has been, where they might have been broken, and where they were made whole again. Life stories portray religion, spirituality, worldview, beliefs, and community making as lived experience.

The research applications of the life story interview are limitless. In any field, the life story itself could serve as the centerpiece for published research, or segments could be used as data to illustrate any number of research needs. The life story interview allows for more data than the researcher may actually use, which not only is good practice but also provides a broad foundation of information to draw on. The life story approach can be used within many disciplines, as well as for many substantive issues. To balance out the databases that have been relied on for so long in generating theory, researchers need to record more life stories of women and members of diverse groups. The feminine voice needs to be given more opportunities to be heard and understood. Because how we tell our stories is mediated by our culture, we need to hear the life stories of individuals from underrepresented groups, to help establish a balance in the literature and expand the awareness and knowledge level of us all.

THE METHODOLOGY OF THE LIFE STORY INTERVIEW

Although a fairly uniform research methodology can be applied, and much important data can be gotten from a life story, there is a level of subjectivity, even chance, involved in doing a life story interview. The same researcher may use different questions with different interviewees, based on a number of variables, and still end up with a fairly complete life story of the person being interviewed. Different interviewers may also use different questions, depending on the particular focus of their project. The life story interview is essentially a template that will be applied differently in different situations, circumstances, or settings.

For example, more than 200 questions suggested in *The Life Story Interview* (Atkinson, 1998) can be asked to obtain a life story. These questions are not meant to

be used in their entirety or as a structure that is set in stone. They are suggested questions only, with only the most appropriate few to be used for each person interviewed. There are times when a handful of the questions might actually be used and other times when two or three dozen might be applied; in each case, a different set of questions most likely would be chosen. The best interview is usually the result of carefully chosen OPEN-ENDED QUESTIONS that elicit and encourage detailed, in-depth responses.

The life story interview can be *approached* scientifically, but it is best *carried out* as an art. Although there may be a structure (a set of questions, or parts thereof) that can be used, each interviewer will apply this in his or her own way. The execution of the interview, whether structured or not, will vary from one interviewer to another. The particular interviewee is another important factor. Some life storytellers offer highly personal meanings, memories, and interpretations of their own, adding to the artful contours of their life story, but others may need more help and guidance filling the details.

A life story interview, as carried out at the Center for the Study of Lives, involves the following three steps: (a) *planning* (preinterview)—preparing for the interview, including understanding why a life story can be beneficial; (b) *doing the interview itself* (interviewing)—guiding a person through the telling of his or her life story while recording it on either audiotape or videotape; and (c) *transcribing and interpreting the interview* (postinterview)—leaving out questions and comments by the interviewer, as well as other repetitions (only the words of the person telling his or her story remain, so that it then becomes a flowing, connected narrative in that person's own words). One might then give the transcribed life story to the person to review and check over for any changes he or she might want to make in it. What we will end up with is a flowing life story in the words of the person telling it. The only editing necessary would be to delete repetitions or other completely extraneous information.

The length of a life story interview can vary considerably. Typically, for the kind of life story interviewing being described here, at least two or three interviews with the person are needed, with each one lasting 1 to $1\frac{1}{2}$ hours. This length of interview can usually provide more than enough information to gain a good understanding of the person's life or the research topic.

One characteristic of the life story interview is that it is not a standardized research instrument. Although framed as both an art and a science and requiring much preinterview planning and preparation, the life story interview is a highly contextualized, personalized approach to gathering qualitative information about the human experience. It demands many spontaneous, individual judgments on the part of the interviewer while the interview is in progress. Its direction can be determined in the spur of the moment by unexpected responses to questions or by the way a life is given its particular narrative structure. The quest in a life story interview is to present the unique voice and experience of the storyteller, which may also merge at some points with the universal human experience.

ETHICAL AND INTERPRETATION ISSUES

A number of important conceptual and interpretive issues also need to be considered. Perhaps most important, because we are asking real people to tell us their true stories, and we are attempting to assist and collaborate with them in this process and then take their story to a larger audience, we have to be able to address satisfactorily the important ethical questions about maintaining a consistency between our original intention and the final product. The ethics of doing a life story interview are all about being fair, honest, clear, and straightforward. A relationship develops that is founded on a moral responsibility to ensure that the interests, rights, and sensitivities of the storyteller are protected.

Also important are the interpretive challenges of doing a life story interview. The ultimate aim of the narrative investigation of a human life, using the life stories approach, is the interpretation of experience, a complex matter because both *interpretation* and *experience* are highly relative terms. Subjectivity is thus at the center of the process of life storytelling. Categories of analysis will emerge from a review of each life story text itself, along with a complexity of patterns and meanings, rather than being set from the beginning, as in quantitative studies. A fundamental interpretive guideline is that the storyteller should be considered both the expert and the authority on his or her own life. This demands a standard of RELIABILITY and VALIDITY that is appropriate to the life story interview as a subjective reflection of the experience in question.

There are a multiplicity of perspectives possible, and the narrative arrived at by different interviewers will be representative of a position, just as a portrait painted from the side or from the front is still a faithful portrait. Historical truth may not be the main issue in personal narrative; what matters is if the life story is deemed trustworthy, more than true.

Nevertheless, internal consistency is still important. What is said in one part of the narrative should not contradict what is said in another part. There *are* inconsistencies in life, and people may react to this one way one time and a different way at another time, but their stories of what happened and what they did should be consistent within themselves.

Whether it is for research purposes on a particular topic or question or to learn more about human lives and society from one person's perspective, life stories serve as excellent means for understanding how people see their own experiences, their own lives, and their interactions with others. The approach of the life story interview suggested here may avoid many of the typical research and publication dilemmas if certain primary values are kept in mind. Setting out to help people tell their stories in their own words gives the researcher a very clear intent, as well as final product.

More life stories need to be brought forth that respect and honor the personal meanings the life storytellers give to their stories. Interpretation and analysis of, as well as commentary on, the life story, even though highly individualized and very subjective, can follow the same approach whether this is carried out within the same life story or across many life stories. In most cases and disciplines, the way to best understand a life story is to find the meaning that comes with it, emerges from it, or is waiting to be drawn out from it.

Life storytelling is a process of personal meaning making. Often, the telling of the story can bring about the knowing of it for the first time, and the text of the story can carry its own meaning. Beyond that, each discipline or research project may have its own theoretical or substantive interest being looked for in the story, and this is when the analysis of a life story or a series of life stories can be examined from theoretical or thematic perspectives. The real value of a life story interview is that it allows for and sheds light on the common life themes, values, issues, and struggles that many people might share, as well as on the differences that do exist between people.

—Robert Atkinson

REFERENCES

Atkinson, R. (1998). *The life story interview* (Qualitative Research Methods Series, Vol. 44). Thousand Oaks, CA: Sage.

Erikson, E. H. (1975). *Life history and the historical moment.* New York: Norton.

Holstein, J. A., & Gubrium, J. F. (2000). *The self we live by: Narrative identity in a postmodern world.* New York: Oxford University Press.

Josselson, R., & Lieblich, A. (Eds.). (1993–1999). *The narrative study of lives* (Vols. 1–6). Newbury Park, CA: Sage.

Titon, J. (1980). The life story. *Journal of American Folklore,* 93(369), 276–292.

LIFE TABLE

Life tables are powerful and versatile analytic tools that describe the general parameters of a population's mortality regime such as its age-specific probabilities of survival and mean survival times. Although life tables are most commonly used in the analysis of mortality of human populations, they can be used for any population that is subject to duration-specific probabilities of experiencing one or more "exit events." They have been used, for example, in the study of school enrollment and graduation, labor force participation, migration, marital status, and health and disability. The main attribute of life tables is the ability to compare the parameters of mortality (or some other exit process) across populations without the need to adjust for compositional differences.

Life tables lend themselves to two different types of interpretations: the experiences of a COHORT or the experiences of a stationary population. If the data are period specific, the life table portrays the hypothetical exits of a *synthetic* cohort played out over time. If the data follow the experiences of a *true* (birth) cohort, the life table is called a "generation life table." Generation life tables of human populations are rare because they require the observation of age-specific death rates stretching over the life span of the longest lived individuals in the birth cohort.

If the parameters in a life table are interpreted as representing the mortality experiences of a stationary population, then the numbers of births or entrants into the population are assumed to remain constant with each new cohort experiencing the observed age-specific mortality or exit rates over time. Because the numbers of births, deaths, and age-specific mortality rates remain constant, the total size and the age distribution of the hypothetical stationary population also remain constant.

THE BASIC LIFE TABLE FUNCTIONS

Life tables consist of a series of interconnected columns arrayed by age groups.

- x—exact age x. The values of x range from 0, the youngest possible age, to the oldest possible age, represented by ω. In abridged life tables, the single-year age intervals are aggregated into n-year intervals, x to $x + n$. For human populations, it is common for n to equal 1 for the first age interval, 4 for the second interval, and 5 or 10 for all but the last interval, which is open-ended.

- $_na_x$—the separation fraction. It refers to the fraction of the age interval lived by persons who die between ages x and $x + n$. For all but the youngest and oldest age intervals, the values of $_na_x$ are often set to .50, a value that assumes deaths are spread evenly throughout the interval. Because deaths in the first years of life are concentrated near the beginning of the interval, the separation fractions for the youngest age groups are usually less than .50. There are a variety of suggested values for the separation fractions for the younger ages (see, e.g., Preston, Heuveline, & Guillot, 2001).

- $_nM_x$—the observed age-specific mortality rate for the population aged x to $x + n$. In the formula below, the capital letters M, D, and N refer to the mortality rate, the number of deaths, and the size of the mid-year population between exact ages x and $x + n$, respectively. If the life table describes a national population or subpopulation, the number of deaths is usually derived from vital statistics, and the size of the population is derived from a census:

$$_nM_x = {_nD_x}/{_nN_x}.$$

- $_nq_x$—the proportion of the members of the life table cohort alive at the beginning of the age interval (at exact age x) who die before reaching the end of the age interval. It is the most crucial column in the life table. Except for the youngest and oldest age groups, values of $_nq_x$ are often estimated using the following formula:

$$_nq_x = {_nM_x}/((1/n) + ((1 - {_na_x}) \times {_nM_x})).$$

Because no one survives past the oldest possible age (ω), $_nq_{\omega-n} = 1.0$. Because the

Table 1   Life Table for the U.S. Population, 2000

Age Interval	Death Rate in Population	Separation Fraction	Proportion Dying During Interval	Number Alive at Exact Age x	Number Dying During Interval	Stationary Population Number Alive in Interval	Stationary Population Number Alive Age x and Older	Mean Number of Years of Remaining Life
x to $x+n-1$	$_nM_x$	$_na_x$	$_nq_x$	l_x	$_nd_x$	$_nL_x$	T_x	e_x
0–1	—[a]	0.125	0.0069	100,000	690	99,393	7,684,601	76.8
1–4	0.000328	0.35	0.0013109	99,310	130	396,902	7,585,209	76.4
5–14	0.000186	0.5	0.0018583	99,180	184	990,877	7,188,307	72.5
15–24	0.000815	0.5	0.0081169	98,996	804	985,937	6,197,430	62.6
25–34	0.001080	0.5	0.0107420	98,192	1,055	976,646	5,211,493	53.1
35–44	0.001997	0.5	0.0197726	97,137	1,921	961,769	4,234,847	43.6
45–54	0.004307	0.5	0.0421620	95,217	4,015	932,093	3,273,078	34.4
55–64	0.010054	0.5	0.0957278	91,202	8,731	868,367	2,340,986	25.7
65–74	0.024329	0.5	0.2169046	82,471	17,888	735,272	1,472,618	17.9
75–84	0.056943	0.5	0.4432345	64,583	28,625	502,703	737,346	11.4
85+	0.153244	—[a]	1.0000000	35,958	35,958	234,643	234,643	6.5

a. Value for this cell is not calculated.

under-enumeration of infants is common, $_1q_0$ is often derived from vital statistics data on infant deaths and births (i.e., the infant mortality rate) rather than from the age-specific death rate for infants.

- l_x—the number of persons in the life table cohort alive at exact age x. The value of l_0 is usually set to 100,000. In general, $l_{x+n} = l_x - d_x$.

- $_nd_x$—the number of deaths occurring to people age x to $x+n$.

In general, $_nd_x = l_x \times _nq_x$. Because all persons alive at the beginning of the last interval die by the end of the last interval, $_nd_{\omega-n} = l_{\omega-n}$.

- $_nL_x$—the number of person-years lived by the life table cohort between ages x and $x+n$ or the number of people alive in the stationary population between ages x and $x+n$:

$$_nL_x = (n \cdot l_{x+n}) + (_na_x \cdot _nd_x).$$

Estimating the number of person-years lived in the last age interval (or the number of people alive in the stationary population who are age $\omega - n$ and older) can be problematic. It is customary to use the age-specific mortality rate observed in the population to estimate it:

$$_nL_{\omega-n} = \frac{_nd_{\omega-n}}{_nM_{\omega-n}}.$$

- T_x—the total number of person-years lived by the life table cohort after age x or the total number of people alive in the stationary population ages x and older:

$$T_x = \sum_{x}^{\omega-n} {_nL_x}.$$

- e_x—the average remaining lifetime for people age x:

$$e_x = \frac{\sum_{x}^{\omega-n} {_nL_x}}{l_x} = \frac{T_x}{l_x}.$$

The example provided in Table 1, which is based on data for the total population in the United States in 2000, is a period-specific life table. The life table parameters suggest that the members of a synthetic cohort living out their lives according to the mortality rates observed in the year 2000 will live, on average, 76.8 years, but a bit more than a third of them (35,958/100,000) will experience their 85th birthday. The stationary population generated by the life table, which will experience 100,000 births and 100,000 deaths every year, will have a constant size of 7,684,601 members, of whom 99,393 are between the exact ages of 0 and 1.

GENERAL OBSERVATIONS ABOUT LIFE TABLES

The initial size of the life table cohort is l_0. Because all members of the life table cohort exit the life table through death, the total number of deaths $(\sum_x d_x)$

equals the initial size of the life table cohort (l_0). The total size of the stationary population is T_0. The crude death rate (CDR) and crude birth rate (CBR) of the life table stationary population equal l_0/T_0. The life expectancy at age 0 in the life table population (e_0) is the inverse of the crude death rate (1/CDR). Preston et al. (2001); Shryock, Siegel, and Associates (1973); and Smith (1992), among many others, provide detailed descriptions of life table functions for single-decrement life tables (in which there is only one exit), multiple-decrement life tables (with two or more exits), and increment and decrement life tables (which allow both entrances and exits), as well as their interpretations and uses. They also provide detailed summaries of more complex demographic methods, such as the projection and indirect estimation of populations and the use of stationary and stable population models, which build on the basic life table functions described here.

—Gillian Stevens

REFERENCES

Preston, S. H., Heuveline, P., & Guillot, M. (2001). *Demography: Measuring and modeling population processes.* Oxford, UK: Blackwell.

Shryock, H. S., Siegel, J. S., & Associates. (1973). *The methods and materials of demography.* New York: Academic Press.

Smith, D. P. (1992). *Formal demography.* New York: Plenum.

LIKELIHOOD RATIO TEST

A likelihood ratio test is used to determine whether overall model fit is improved by relaxing one or more restrictions and is usually used to test whether individual coefficients or linear combinations of coefficients are equal to specific values. In general, it can be used to compare any two NESTED models (but not nonnested models). The likelihood ratio test is based on the MAXIMUM LIKELIHOOD principle of the estimates and allows a test for whether differences in the likelihood of the data for two models are systematic or due to SAMPLING ERROR. The likelihood ratio statistic is constructed using the likelihood of the unrestricted model (evaluated at the maximum likelihood parameter estimates), L^*, and the likelihood of the restricted model, LR^*, and is defined as $LR = -2\ln(LR^*/L^*)$. This can be rewritten as $2(\ln L^* - \ln LR^*)$. Because removing model restrictions always increases the likelihood, the likelihood ratio statistic is positive and can be shown to follow a chi-square distribution with m degrees of freedom, where m is the number of restrictions: ($LR \sim X_m^2$). Under the null hypothesis that the restricted model is just as good as the unrestricted model, the expected value of R is 0. Including considerations for sampling error, however, the expected value of LR is the number of restrictions, m. To the extent that there are systematic differences between the models, then the observed value of LR will be greater than m. Using classical hypothesis testing, significance tests can be conducted using the value of LR. ASYMPTOTICALLY, the likelihood ratio test is equivalent to both the Wald test (W) and the Lagrange multiplier test (LM), which is also known as Rao's score test. In small samples, the tests will perform differently, but in the case of linear restrictions, it can be shown that $LM < LR < W$.

—Frederick J. Boehmke

REFERENCES

Kmenta, J. (2000). *Elements of econometrics* (2nd ed.). Ann Arbor: University of Michigan Press.

Maddala, G. G. (1983). *Limited dependent and qualitative variables in econometrics.* Cambridge, UK: Cambridge University Press.

LIKERT SCALE

The Likert (or summated rating) scale is a very popular device for measuring people's attitudes, beliefs, emotions, feelings, perceptions, personality characteristics, and other psychological constructs. It allows people to indicate their position on items along a quantitative continuum. Three features characterize this sort of SCALE. First, there are multiple items that are combined into a total score for each respondent. Second, each item has a stem that is a statement concerning some object (person, place, or thing). This might concern an aspect of the person completing the scale or an aspect of another person or object. Third, the person completing the scale is asked to choose one of several response choices that vary along a continuum. They can be unipolar, ranging from low to high, or bipolar, ranging from extreme negative to extreme positive. These responses are quantified (e.g., from

1 to 6) and summed across items, yielding an interpretable quantitative score.

The development of a Likert scale generally involves five steps (Spector, 1992). First, the construct of interest is carefully defined to clarify its nature and boundaries. Second, format decisions are made and the items are written. Third, the scale is pilot tested on a small SAMPLE to be sure the items are clear and make sense. Fourth, the scale is administered to a sample of 100 to 200 (or more) individuals. An item analysis is conducted to help choose those items that are intercorrelated with one another and form an internally consistent scale. Coefficient alpha is computed as a measure of internal consistency reliability with a target of at least .70 (Nunnally, 1978), although .80 to .90 is more desirable. Finally, research is conducted to provide data on the scale's CONSTRUCT VALIDITY to be sure it is reasonable to interpret it as reflecting the construct defined in Step 1.

The response choices in Likert scales can differ in number of type. The most popular form is the *agree-disagree,* in which respondents indicate the extent to which they agree with each stem. Usually, there are five to seven response choices—for example, *disagree (agree) very much, disagree (agree) somewhat,* and *disagree (agree) slightly.* Other common alternatives are frequency (e.g., *never, seldom, sometimes, often*) and evaluation (e.g., *poor, fair, good, outstanding*).

There has been some debate with bipolar scales about whether there should be an odd number of response choices with a neutral response in the middle (e.g., *neither agree nor disagree*) or an even number without the neutral response. Those advocating an odd number argue that one should not force the ambivalent person to make a choice in one direction or the other. Those advocating an even number point out that the neutral response is often misused by respondents (e.g., to indicate that the item is not applicable) and that it may encourage people to be noncommittal. There is generally little practical difference in results using even or odd numbers of response choices.

—Paul E. Spector

REFERENCES

Nunnally, J. C. (1978). *Psychometric theory* (2nd ed.). New York: McGraw-Hill.

Spector, P. E. (1992). *Summated rating scale construction: An introduction* (Sage University Paper Series on Quantitative Applications in the Social Sciences, Series No. 07–082). Newbury Park, CA: Sage.

LIMDEP

LIMDEP is an integrated computer program for the estimation and analysis of a variety of linear and nonlinear econometric and statistical models for LIMited DEPendent variables and other forms of data, such as survival and sample selection data. For further information, see the Web site of the software: http://www.limdep.com.

—Tim Futing Liao

LINEAR DEPENDENCY

A set of vectors is said to be linearly dependent if any one of the vectors in the set can be written as a linear combination of (some of) the others. More generally, we say that two variables are linearly dependent if

$$\lambda_1 X_1 + \lambda_2 X_2 = 0,$$

where λ_1 and λ_2 are CONSTANTS such that λ_1 or $\lambda_2 \neq 0$. This definition can be expanded to k variables such that a perfect linear relationship is said to exist when

$$\lambda_1 X_1 + \lambda_2 X_2 + \cdots + \lambda_k X_k = 0,$$

where $\lambda_1 \cdots \lambda_k$ are not all zero simultaneously.

To illustrate, consider the following set of data where each of the three (INDEPENDENT) VARIABLES is represented as a vector containing n (the number of observations) values:

$$
\begin{array}{ccc}
X_1 & X_2 & X_3 \\
\end{array}
\begin{bmatrix}
4 & 16 & 12 \\
7 & 30 & 22 \\
12 & 34 & 29 \\
13 & 22 & 24 \\
1 & 50 & 26 \\
\end{bmatrix}.
$$

In this case, X_3 is a perfect linear combination of X_1 and X_2 ($X_{3i} = \frac{1}{2} X_{2i} + X_{1i}$), and therefore, a (perfect) linear dependency exists in this data set.

Linear dependency (among the independent variables) has serious implications for the estimation of regression coefficients. It is a violation of the ASSUMPTION that **X** (the MATRIX of independent variables) is a $n \times k$ matrix with rank k (i.e., the columns of **X** are linearly independent, and there are at least k observations). In addition, it leads to the commonly understood problem of (MULTI) COLLINEARITY.

The implications of linear dependency on the estimation of REGRESSION COEFFICIENTS depend on the degree of the dependency. If there is perfect linear dependency among the independent variables, the regression coefficients cannot be uniquely determined. To see this, consider the following SIMPLE regression model with two independent variables:

$$y_i = \beta_0 + \beta_1 X_{1i} + \beta_2 X_{2i} + u_i.$$

Let $X_{2i} = 2X_{1i}$ (implying a perfect linear dependency between the independent variables). Then, it is the case that

$$y_i = \beta_0 + \beta_1 X_{1i} + \beta_2 2X_{1i} + u_i$$

or

$$y_i = \beta_0 + (\beta_1 + 2\beta_2)X_{1i} + u_i.$$

It should be clear from the last equation that in the presence of a perfect linear dependency, it is not possible to estimate the *independent* effects of X_1 (i.e., β_1) and X_2 (i.e., β_2).

A similar result is obtained in matrix form by noting that if a perfect linear dependency exists in the matrix of independent variables ($\mathbf{X}$), then both ($\mathbf{X}$) and ($\mathbf{X'X}$) are singular, and neither can be inverted. Recalling that the vector of regression coefficients in matrix form is given by $(\mathbf{X'X})^{-1}\mathbf{X'y}$, it is clear that these coefficients cannot be estimated in the presence of perfect linear dependency.

In social science research, it is rarely the case that a perfect linear dependency between independent variables will exist. Rather, it is quite possible that something like "near-perfect" dependency will be present. Near-perfect linear dependency can result in high but not perfect (multi) collinearity.

In the presence of imperfect collinearity, regression coefficients can be estimated, and they are still BLUE (best linear unbiased estimators), as imperfect collinearity violates none of the assumptions of the classical linear regression model (CLRM). However, there remain some nontrivial consequences. Coefficients will have large VARIANCES and COVARIANCES. As a consequence, CONFIDENCE INTERVALS for the coefficients will be wider (and T-STATISTICS will often be insignificant), leading researchers to fail to reject the NULL HYPOTHESIS when it is, in fact, false (i.e., a higher incidence of TYPE II ERRORS). Finally, coefficient estimates and their STANDARD ERRORS can be sensitive to small changes in the data.

—Charles H. Ellis

REFERENCES

Green, W. H. (2000). *Econometric analysis* (4th ed.). Upper Saddle River: Prentice Hall.

Gujarati, D. N. (1995). *Basic econometrics* (3rd ed.). New York: McGraw-Hill.

Kennedy, P. (1998). *A guide to econometrics* (4th ed.). Cambridge: MIT Press.

LINEAR REGRESSION

Linear regression refers to a linear FUNCTION expressing the RELATIONSHIP between the conditional mean of a RANDOM VARIABLE (the DEPENDENT VARIABLE) and the corresponding values of one or more explanatory variables (INDEPENDENT VARIABLES). The dependent variable is a random variable whose realization is composed of the DETERMINISTIC effects of fixed values of the explanatory variables as well as random disturbances. We could express such a relationship as $Y_i = \beta_0 + \beta_1 X_{1i} + \cdots + \beta_k X_{ki} + \varepsilon_i$.

We can speak of either a population regression function or a sample regression function. The sample regression function is typically used to estimate an unknown population regression function. If a linear regression model is well specified, then the expected value of ε_i in the population is zero. Given this expectation, UNBIASED estimates of the population regression function can be calculated from the sample by solving the problem $\hat{Y}_i = \hat{\beta}_0 + \hat{\beta}_1 X_{1i} + \cdots + \hat{\beta}_k X_{ki}$. This equation can also be thought of in terms of estimating a conditional mean as in $E(Y_i|X_i) = \hat{\beta}_0 + \hat{\beta}_1 X_{1i} + \cdots + \hat{\beta}_k X_{ki}$. Both equations give the average values of the STOCHASTIC dependent variable conditional on fixed values of the independent variables. The goal of linear regression analysis is to find the values $\hat{\beta}$ that best characterize $\hat{Y}_i$ or $E(Y_i|X_i)$.

The term *linear regression* implies no particular method of estimation. Rather, a linear regression can be estimated in any of several ways. The most popular approach is to use ORDINARY LEAST SQUARES (OLS). This approach does not explicitly incorporate assumptions about the probability distribution of the disturbances. However, when attempting to relate from the sample to the population regression functions, unbiased and EFFICIENT estimation requires compliance with the Gauss-Markov assumptions. Using OLS, the analyst minimizes the function defined by the sum of squared sample residuals with respect to the regression parameters. Another approach to estimating a linear regression is to use MAXIMUM LIKELIHOOD ESTIMATION. This approach requires the assumption of normally distributed disturbances, in addition to the assumptions of OLS. Using maximum likelihood, the analyst maximizes the function defined by the product of the joint probabilities of all disturbances with respect to the regression parameters. This is called the joint likelihood function. Yet another approach is to use the method of moments. This approach uses the analogy principle whereby moment conditions are used to derive estimates.

With regard to the meaning of linearity, it is useful to clarify that we are not concerned with linearity in the variables but with linearity in the parameters. For a linear regression, we require that predicted values of the dependent variable be a linear function of the estimated parameters. For example, suppose we estimate a sample regression such as $\hat{Y}_i = \hat{\alpha} + \hat{\beta}\sqrt{X_i} + \varepsilon_i$. In this regression, the relation between $\hat{Y}_i$ and X_i is not linear, but the relation between $\hat{Y}_i$ and $\sqrt{X_i}$ is linear. If we think of $\sqrt{X_i}$ instead of X_i as our explanatory variable, then the linearity assumption is met. However, this cannot be applied equally for all estimators. For example, suppose we want to estimate a function such as

$$\hat{Y}_i = \hat{\alpha} + \frac{\sqrt{\hat{\beta}}}{\hat{\alpha}} X_i + \varepsilon_i.$$

This is not a linear regression, but it requires nonlinear regression techniques.

—B. Dan Wood and Sung Ho Park

REFERENCES

Casella, G., & Berger, R. L. (1990). *Statistical inference.* Belmont, CT: Duxbury.

Gujarati, D. N. (1995). *Basic econometrics* (3rd ed.). New York: McGraw-Hill.

LINEAR TRANSFORMATION

A linear transformation is a mathematical function that changes all the values a variable can take into a new set of corresponding values. When the linear transformation is imposed, the units and the shape of the variable's HISTOGRAM change. A wide range of rank-preserving transformations is used in statistics to move from one distribution shape to another. These fall into two groups: linear and nonlinear transformations, as illustrated in Table 1. The nonlinear transformations

give curvature to the relationship, whereas the linear transformations do not.

As a function, such as $X' = 4 + 0.2X$, it is important for all existing values over the range of X to map uniquely onto the new variable X'. Conversions from the Fahrenheit to Celsius temperature scales and in general from imperial to metric units qualify as linear transformations. The logarithmic transformation is a nonlinear transformation.

In general, a linear transformation of a variable X has the form

$$X' = a + bX.$$

The slope of the function with respect to X is constant. In empirical work, it is often necessary to convert earnings to a new currency—for example, $Y_{\text{euro}} = 0.66Y_{\pounds}$ when the exchange rate is 0.66 Euros per Pound sterling, or $Y_{\text{euro}} = RY_{\pounds}$ when the rate in general is denoted R. It is also useful to convert weekly earnings to annual earnings (e.g., $Y_{\text{yrly}} = 52 \cdot Y_{\text{wkly}}$).

More complex linear transformations use more than one source variable. Earnings that include an annual bonus may be summed up by merging the contents of the two variables:

$$Y_{\text{yrly}} = 52 \cdot (H \cdot W) + B,$$

where H = hours per week, W = wage per hour, B = bonus per year, and Y_{yrly} = total annual earnings. Y_{yrly} is a linear transformation of H if and only if W is invariant with respect to H (i.e., no overtime supplement). In general, for a variable X, the transformation function X' is a linear function if

$$\frac{D_X^2}{D_X} = 0.$$

It is possible to see scale construction as a linear transformation process with explicit weights for the different variables comprising the new scale.

In forming linear transformations, a nonzero constant can be used. A multiplicative constant other than 1 changes the VARIANCE, altering the relative dispersion of the variable vis-à-vis its own mean by a proportion. The best-known linear transformation is the standardization of a variable around its mean. To read changes in X in unit-free language (or, equivalently, in terms of standard deviation units), one subtracts X's mean and divides X by its standard deviation

$$X_i' = \frac{(X_i - \bar{X})}{\text{sd}(X)},$$

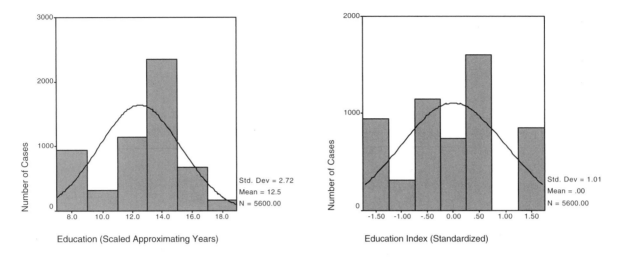

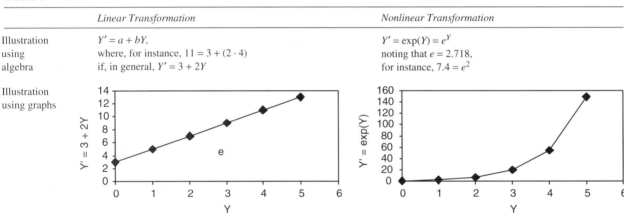

Figure 1 Distribution of a Variable and Its Standardized Variant

SOURCE: British Household Panel Survey, Wave 9, 1999–2000 (Taylor, 2000).

Table 1

	Linear Transformation	*Nonlinear Transformation*
Illustration using algebra	$Y' = a + bY,$ where, for instance, $11 = 3 + (2 \cdot 4)$ if, in general, $Y' = 3 + 2Y$	$Y' = \exp(Y) = e^Y$ noting that $e = 2.718$, for instance, $7.4 = e^2$
Illustration using graphs		

where we define

$$\mathrm{sd}(X) = \sqrt{\frac{\sum_i (X_i - \bar{X})^2}{n - 1}}.$$

The new variable X' is a linear transformation of X because the derivative of X' with respect to X_i is constant over the values of X. The standard deviation is a fixed parameter here. For a normally distributed variable such as levels of education (approximated in years), the standardizing transformation produces the changes illustrated in Figures 1 and 2 in the distribution of X.

The standardizing transformation is sometimes described as producing a Z-distribution if the underlying distribution of X is normal. Z-distributions are standardized normal distributions that have mean zero and a standard deviation of 1. As Figures 1 and 2 show, however, the distribution's shape changes during this procedure.

—Wendy K. Olsen

REFERENCES

Economic and Social Research Council Research Centre on Micro-Social Change. (2001). *British Household Panel*

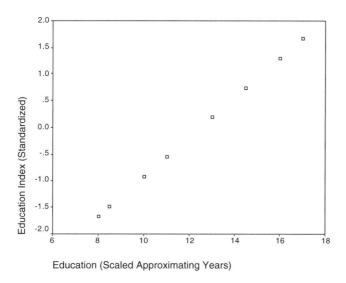

Figure 2

Survey [computer file]. Colchester, UK: The Data Archive [distributor], 28 February. Study Number 4340.

Taylor, M. F. (Ed.) (with Brice, J., Buck, N., & Prentice-Lane, E.). (2000). *British Household Panel Survey User Manual Volume B9: Codebook*. Colchester, UK: University of Essex.

LINK FUNCTION

The link function is what links the random component and the systematic component of GENERALIZED LINEAR MODELS. It is also what connects the possibly nonlinear outcome variable with the linear combination of EXPLANATORY VARIABLES.

—Tim Futing Liao

LISREL

LISREL was the first statistical software package that became widely available to social scientists for performing analysis of LInear Structural RELations models, better known as STRUCTURAL EQUATION MODELS. Today, it can analyze structural equation models of a variety of types of forms, including ordinal and longitudinal data. For further

information, see the Web site of the software: http://www.ssicentral.com/lisrel/mainlis.htm.

—Tim Futing Liao

LISTWISE DELETION

Listwise deletion is a term used in relation to computer software programs such as SPSS in connection with the handling of MISSING DATA. Listwise deletion of missing data means that all cases with missing data involved in an analysis will be ignored in an analysis. Consider the following scenario: We have a sample of 200 cases, we want to produce a set of PEARSON CORRELATIONS for 10 variables, and 50 of the cases have missing data for at least one of the variables. In this instance, the analysis will be performed on the remaining 150 cases. Compare with PAIRWISE deletion.

—Alan Bryman

See also DELETION

LITERATURE REVIEW

A literature review is a summary of what is currently known about some issue or field on the basis of research evidence, and/or of what lines of argument there are in relation to that issue or field. Sometimes reviews are designed to stand alone, perhaps even being substantial book-length pieces of work. More usually, they amount to chapters in monographs or theses; and here their function is to set the scene for the particular study being reported, showing how it fits into the existing literature.

In recent years, some disagreement has emerged about what form literature reviews ought to take. The most common form is what has come to be labeled as *narrative* review, in which the findings and methods of relevant studies are outlined and discussed with a view to presenting an argument about the conclusions that can be drawn from the current state of knowledge in a field. Such reviews can be contrasted with annotated bibliographies and with so-called "systematic" reviews. Recently, there have also been proposals for "interpretive" reviews.

In pure form, an annotated bibliography lists studies, perhaps in alphabetical order, and provides a brief summary of each, with or without an evaluation of their strengths and weaknesses, the validity of their findings, and so forth. There is, however, a spectrum between this and the traditional literature review, in terms of how far the discussion is subordinated to an overall narrative line.

SYSTEMATIC REVIEWING has become quite influential in recent times, notably because it is seen as providing the basis for evidence-informed policymaking and practice (see Cooper, 1998; Light & Pillemer, 1984; Slavin, 1986). Systematic reviews have a number of distinctive features, frequently including the following:

- They employ explicit procedures to determine what studies are relevant.

- They rely on an explicit hierarchy of research designs according to the likely validity of the findings these produce. Studies are included or excluded on the basis of whether they employed a sufficiently strong research design, or in terms of which offer the best evidence available. Generally speaking, RANDOMIZED CONTROLLED TRIALS are at the top of the list.

- They seek to include in the review *all* studies that meet the specified criteria of relevance and validity.

- They aim to synthesize the evidence produced by these studies, rather than simply summarizing the findings of each study and relating these in a narrative or interpretive way. Systematic reviews often focus primarily on quantitative studies and employ statistical META-ANALYSIS for the purpose of synthesis.

In many ways, systematic reviewing is an attempt to apply the canons of QUANTITATIVE methodology to the process of reviewing itself (see Hammersley, 2001).

By contrast, interpretive reviewing involves application of a QUALITATIVE methodological approach. Here, the emphasis is on the interpretative role of the reviewer in making sense of the findings of different studies to construct a holistic picture of the field, a picture that may well reflect the particular interests and sensibilities of the reviewer (see Eisenhart, 1998; Schwandt, 1998). This is a development out of the traditional or narrative review.

In addition, some commentators have proposed what we might refer to as POSTMODERNIST literature reviews (see Lather, 1999; Livingston, 1999; Meacham, 1998). Here, any notion of an authoritative account of current knowledge is rejected on the grounds that the claim to true representation of the world, at the level of particular studies or of a review, can be no more than the imposition of one discursive construction over others; thereby reflecting, for example, the work of power or of resistance to it.

Whatever approach to reviewing is adopted, certain decisions have to be made concerning the following:

- Who is the intended readership?
- How is the review to be structured?
- How are relevant studies to be found, and which studies are to be included?
- How much detail is to be provided about each study discussed; in particular, how much information is to be given about the research methods employed?
- How are the studies and their findings to be evaluated and related to one another?

In many ways, the issue of audience is the primary one because this will shape answers to the other questions, in terms of what background knowledge can be assumed, and what readers will have the greatest interest in. Recently, considerable emphasis has been put on literature reviews designed for "users" of research—in other words, on the literature review as a bridge by which research can be made relevant to policymakers, professional practitioners of one sort or another, and relevant publics. However, literature reviews also play an important function within research communities: in defining and redefining an intellectual field, giving researchers a sense of the collective enterprise in which they are participating, and enabling them to coordinate their work with one another.

—Martyn Hammersley

REFERENCES

Cooper, H. (1998). *Synthesizing research: A guide for literature reviews* (3rd ed.). Thousand Oaks, CA: Sage.

Eisenhart, M. (1998). On the subject of interpretive reviews. *Review of Educational Research, 68*(4), 391–399.

Hammersley, M. (2001). On "systematic" reviews of research literatures: A "narrative" reply to Evans and Benefield. *British Educational Research Journal, 27*(5), 543–554.

Hart, C. (1998). *Doing a literature review.* London: Sage.

Hart, C. (2001). *Doing a literature search.* London: Sage.

Lather, P. (1999). To be of use: The work of reviewing. *Review of Educational Research, 69*(1), 2–7.

Light, R. J., & Pillemer, D. B. (1984). *Summing up: The science of reviewing research.* Cambridge, MA: Harvard University Press.

Livingston, G. (1999). Beyond watching over established ways: A review as recasting the literature, recasting the lived. *Review of Educational Research, 69*(1), 9–19.

Meacham, S. J. (1998). Threads of a new language: A response to Eisenhart's "On the subject of interpretive reviews." *Review of Educational Research, 68*(4), 401–407.

Schwandt, T. A. (1998). The interpretive review of educational matters: Is there any other kind? *Review of Educational Research, 68*(4), 409–412.

Slavin, R. E. (1986). Best-evidence synthesis: An alternative to meta-analytic and traditional reviews. *Educational Researcher, 15*(9), 5–11.

LIVED EXPERIENCE

Human experience is the main epistemological basis for QUALITATIVE RESEARCH, but the concept of "lived experience" (translated from the German *Erlebnis*) possesses special methodological significance. The notion of "lived experience," as used in the works of Dilthey (1985), Husserl (1970), Merleau-Ponty (1962), and their contemporary exponents, announces the intent to explore *directly* the originary or prereflective dimensions of human existence. The etymology of the English term *experience* does not include the meaning of *lived*—it derives from the Latin *experientia,* meaning "trial, proof, experiment, experience." But the German word for experience, *Erlebnis,* already contains the word *Leben,* "life" or "to live." The verb *erleben* literally means "living through something."

Wilhelm Dilthey (1985) offers the first systematic explication of lived experience and its relevance for the human sciences. He describes "lived experience" as a reflexive or self-given awareness that inheres in the temporality of consciousness of life as we live it. "Only in thought does it become objective," says Dilthey (p. 223). He suggests that our language can be seen as an immense linguistic map that names the possibilities of human lived experiences.

Edmund Husserl (1970) uses the concept of *Erlebnis* alongside *Erfahrung,* which expresses the full-fledged acts of consciousness in which meaning is given in intentional experiences. "All knowledge 'begins with experience' but it does not therefore 'arise' from experience," says Husserl (p. 109).

Erfahrungen (as meaningful lived experiences) can have a transformative effect on our being. More generally, experience can be seen in a passive modality as something that befalls us, overwhelms us, or strikes us, and it can be understood more actively as an act of consciousness in appropriating the meaning of some aspect of the world. Thus we can speak of an "experienced" person when referring to his or her mature wisdom, as a result of life's accumulated meaningful and reflective experiences.

In *Truth and Method,* Hans-Georg Gadamer (1975) suggests that there are two dimensions of meaning to lived experience: the immediacy of experience and the content of what is experienced. Both meanings have methodological significance for qualitative inquiry. They refer to "the immediacy with which something is grasped and which precedes all interpretation, reworking, and communication" (p. 61). Thus, lived experience forms the starting point for inquiry, reflection, and interpretation. This thought is also expressed in the well-known line from Merleau-Ponty (1962), "The world is not what I think, but what I live through" (pp. xvi–xvii). If one wants to study the world as lived through, one has to start with a "direct description of our experience as it is" (p. vii).

In contemporary human science, "lived experience" remains a central methodological notion (see van Manen, 1997) that aims to provide concrete insights into the qualitative meanings of phenomena in people's lives. For example, medical science provides for strategies of intervention and action based on diagnostic and prognostic research models, but predictions about the clinical path of an illness do not tell us how (different) people actually experience their illness. PHENOMENOLOGICAL human science investigates lived experience to explore concrete dimensions of meaning of an illness, such as multiple sclerosis (Toombs, 2001) or pain in the context of clinical practice (Madjar, 2001).

Even in the DECONSTRUCTIVE and POSTMODERN work of the more language-oriented scholars such as Jacques Derrida, the idea of lived experience reverberates in phrases such as the "singularity of experience" or "absolute existence." Derrida speaks of this originary experience as "the resistance of existence to the concept or system" and says, "this is something I am always ready to stand up for" (Derrida & Ferraris, 2001, p. 40). In the human sciences, the focus on experience remains so prominent because of its power to crack the constraints of conceptualizations, codifications, and categorical calculations. In addition, the critical questioning of the meaning and ultimate source of lived experience ensures an openness that is a condition for discovering what can be thought and found to lie beyond it.

—Max van Manen

REFERENCES

Derrida, J., & Ferraris, F. (2001). *A taste for the secret.* Cambridge, UK: Polity.

Dilthey, W. (1985). *Poetry and experience: Selected works* (Vol. 5). Princeton, NJ: Princeton University Press.

Gadamer, H.-G. (1975). *Truth and method.* New York: Seabury.

Husserl, E. (1970). *Logical investigations* (Vols. 1–2). London: Routledge & Kegan Paul.

Madjar, I. (2001). The lived experience of pain in the context of clinical practice. In S. K. Toombs (Ed.), *Handbook of phenomenology and medicine* (pp. 263–277). Boston: Kluwer Academic.

Merleau-Ponty, M. (1962). *Phenomenology of perception.* London: Routledge & Kegan Paul.

Toombs, S. K. (2001). Reflections on bodily change: The lived experience of disability. In S. K. Toombs (Ed.), *Handbook of phenomenology and medicine* (pp. 247–261). Boston: Kluwer Academic.

van Manen, M. (1997). *Researching lived experience: Human science for an action sensitive pedagogy.* London, Ontario: Althouse.

LOCAL INDEPENDENCE

Local independence is the basic assumption underlying LATENT VARIABLE models, such as FACTOR ANALYSIS, LATENT TRAIT ANALYSIS, LATENT CLASS ANALYSIS, and LATENT PROFILE ANALYSIS. The axiom of local independence states that the observed items are independent of each other, given an individual's score on the latent variable(s). This definition is a mathematical way of stating that the latent variable explains why the observed items are related to one another.

We will explain the principle of local independence using an example taken from Lazarsfeld and Henry (1968). Suppose that a group of 1,000 persons are asked whether they have read the last issue of magazines *A* and *B*. Their responses are as follows:

Table 1

	Read A	*Did Not Read A*	*Total*
Read B	260	240	500
Did not read B	140	360	500
Total	400	600	1,000

It can easily be verified that the two variables are quite strongly related to one another. Readers of A tend to read B more often (65%) than do nonreaders (40%). The value of phi coefficient, the product-moment correlation coefficient in a 2×2 table, equals 0.245.

Suppose that we have information on the respondents' educational levels, dichotomized as high and low. When the 1,000 people are divided into these two groups, readership is observed in Table 2. Thus, in each of the 2×2 tables in which education is held constant, there is no association between the two magazines: the phi coefficient equals 0 in both tables. That is, reading A and B is independent within educational levels.

The reading behavior is, however, very different in the two subgroups: the high-education group has much higher probabilities of reading for both magazines (0.60 and 0.80) than the low-education group (0.20 and 0.20). The association between *A* and *B* can thus fully be explained from the dependence of *A* and *B* on the third factor, education. Note that the cell entries in the marginal *AB* table, $N(AB)$, can be obtained by the following:

$$N(AB) = N(H) \cdot P(A|H) \cdot P(B|H)$$
$$+ N(L) \cdot P(A|L) \cdot P(B|L),$$

where *H* and *L* denotes high and low education, respectively.

In latent variable models, the observed variables are assumed to be locally independent given the latent variable(s). This means that the latent variables have the same role as education in the example. It should be noted that this assumption not only makes sense from a substantive point of view, but it is also necessary to identify the unobserved factors.

The fact that local independence implies that the latent variables should fully account for the associations between the observed items suggests a simple test of this assumption. The estimated two-way tables according to the model, computed as shown above for

Table 2

	High Education			Low Education		
	Read A	*Did Not Read A*	*Total*	*Read A*	*Did Not Read A*	*Total*
Read *B*	240	60	300	20	80	100
Did not read *B*	160	40	200	80	320	400
Total	400	100	500	100	400	500

$N(AB)$, should be similar to the observed two-way tables. In the case of continuous indicators, we can compare estimated with observed correlations.

Variants of the various types of latent variable models have been developed that make it possible to relax the local independence assumption for certain pairs of variables. Depending on the scale type of the indicators, this is accomplished by inclusion of direct effects or correlated errors in the model.

—Jeroen K. Vermunt and Jay Magidson

REFERENCES

Bartholomew, D. J., & Knott, M. (1999). *Latent variable models and factor analysis.* London: Arnold.

Lazarsfeld, P. F., & Henry, N. W. (1968). *Latent structure analysis.* Boston: Houghton Mifflin.

LOCAL REGRESSION

Local regression is a strategy for fitting smooth curves to BIVARIATE or MULTIVARIATE data. Traditional strategies (such as ordinary least squares [OLS] REGRESSION analysis) are *parametric,* in that they require the analyst to specify the FUNCTIONAL form of Y's dependence on X prior to fitting the curve. In contrast, local regression is NONPARAMETRIC because the ALGORITHM tries to follow the empirical concentration of data points, regardless of the shape of the curve that is required to do so. The smooth curve is fitted without any advance specification of the functional relationship between the variables.

The basic principles underlying local regression have been known since the 19th century. However, it is a computationally intensive analytic strategy, so major developments did not really occur until the late 1970s and early 1980s. Currently, the most popular local regression algorithm is the loess procedure, developed by William S. Cleveland and his associates. The term *loess* (or *lowess,* as it was previously known) is an acronym for *lo*cally weighted regr*ess*ion.

FITTING A LOESS CURVE TO DATA

Assume that the DATA consist of n observations on two variables, X and Y. These data can be displayed in a bivariate SCATTERPLOT, with X values arrayed along the horizontal axis and Y values along the vertical axis. The horizontal axis of the scatterplot also includes a set of m locations, v_j, where j runs from 1 to m. These v_js are equally spaced across the entire range of X values.

Loess uses a "vertical sliding window" that moves across the horizontal scale axis of the scatterplot. The window stops and estimates a separate regression equation (using WEIGHTED LEAST SQUARES) at each of the m different v_js. The width of this window is adjusted so that it always contains a prespecified proportion (often called α) of the total data points. In this sense, each of the m regressions is "local" because it only incorporates the subset of αn observations that falls within the current window. Furthermore, observations included within each local regression are weighted inversely according to their distance from the current v_j; accordingly, observations closer to v_j have more influence on the placement of the local regression line than observations that fall farther away within the current window.

The coefficients from each local regression are used to estimate a predicted value, designated $\hat{g}(v_j)$, for the current window. The m ordered pairs, $(v_j, \hat{g}(v_j))$, are plotted in the scatterplot, superimposed over the n data points. Finally, adjacent fitted points are connected by line segments. The v_js are located relatively close to each other along the horizontal axis, so the series of connected line segments actually appears to be a smooth curve passing through the data points. Visual inspection of the resultant loess curve is used for substantive interpretation of the relationship between X and Y.

The general principles of multivariate loess are identical to the bivariate case. However, the fitting windows, the distances between the v_js and the observations, and the local weights are now calculated within the k-dimensional subspace generated by the k independent variables. The end result of a multivariate loess analysis is a smooth surface that tends to coincide with the center of the data point cloud throughout the entire $(k + 1)$ dimensional space formed by the independent variables and the dependent variable.

LOESS-FITTING PARAMETERS

Loess is a nonparametric fitting procedure. However, there are still some parameters that the analyst must specify prior to the analysis. Selecting the values for these parameters can be a subjective process, but the considerations involved are quite straightforward.

First, there is α, the smoothing parameter. This gives the size of the local fitting window, defined as the proportion of observations included within each local regression. Larger α values produce smoother loess curves. The usual objective is to find the largest α value that still produces a curve that captures the major features within the data (i.e., passes through the most dense regions of the data points).

Second, the analyst must specify whether the local regressions are LINEAR or QUADRATIC in form. This decision is usually based on visual inspection of the data. If the data exhibit a generally MONOTONIC relationship between Y and X, then local linear fitting is sufficient. If there are nonmonotonic patterns, with local minima and/or maxima, then quadratic local regressions provide the flexibility for the fitted surface to conform to the "undulations" in the data.

Third, the analyst must specify whether robustness corrections are to be included in each local regression. Because a relatively small number of data points are included in each local regression, a few discrepant observations can have an adverse impact on the coefficient estimates. The robustness step down-weights the influence of any outlying observations to make sure that the fitted loess curve follows the most heavily populated regions within the data space.

CONCLUSION

The great advantage of local regression methods, such as loess, is that they are very flexible about the exact nature of the relationship between the variables under investigation. Therefore, local regression is an important tool for EXPLORATORY DATA ANALYSIS. In addition, INFERENTIAL procedures have also been developed for the methodology, making it very useful for characterizing NONLINEAR structures that may exist within a data set. The major weakness is that these methods produce graphical, rather than numerical, output—that is, the fitted smooth curve or surface itself. Nonparametric fitting strategies cannot be used to characterize the data in terms of a simple equation. Nevertheless, local regression lets the data "speak for themselves" to a greater extent than traditional parametric methods such as linear regression analysis.

—William G. Jacoby

REFERENCES

Cleveland, W. S., & Devlin, S. J. (1988). Locally weighted regression: An approach to regression analysis by local fitting. *Journal of the American Statistical Association, 83,* 596–610.

Fox, J. (2000a). *Multiple and generalized nonparametric regression.* Thousand Oaks, CA: Sage.

Fox, J. (2000b). *Nonparametric simple regression.* Thousand Oaks, CA: Sage.

Jacoby, W. G. (1997). *Statistical graphics for univariate and bivariate data.* Thousand Oaks, CA: Sage.

Loader, C. (1999). *Local regression and likelihood.* New York: Springer.

LOESS. *See* LOCAL REGRESSION

LOGARITHM

A logarithm is an exponent. It is the power to which a base—usually 10 or e—must be raised to produce a specific number. Thus, in base 10, the logarithm of 1,000 would be 3 because $10^3 = 1,000$. Symbolically, this relationship is also expressed as $\log_{10} 1,000 = 3$. Logarithm FUNCTIONS transform variables from original units into logarithmic units. In the example above, 1,000 is transformed into the base-10 logarithmic unit

Table 1   The Base-10 Logarithm Function and the Relationship Between x and y

x	$y = \log_{10}x$	$10^y = x$	A One-Unit change in $y = a\ 90\%$ Change in x
1	0	$10^0 = 1$	
10	1	$10^1 = 10$	$\{(10 - 1)/1\} \times 100 = 90\%$
100	2	$10^2 = 100$	$\{(100 - 10)/10\} \times 100 = 90\%$
1,000	3	$10^3 = 1,000$	$\{(1,000 - 100)/100\} \times 100 = 90\%$
10,000	4	$10^4 = 10,000$	$\{(10,000 - 1,000)/1,000\} \times 100 = 90\%$
100,000	5	$10^5 = 100,000$	$\{(100,000 - 10,000)/10,000\} \times 100 = 90\%$

of 3. Of the two bases used most frequently (base 10 and base e), the natural logarithm function with the base of e, or approximately 2.7182, is often used for transforming variables to include in REGRESSION MODELS. However, both the common logarithm function (base 10) and the natural logarithm function (base e) are discussed below and demonstrate the properties of logarithms in general.

The common logarithm function transforms x from original units into y, in base-10 logarithmic units. Again, this is denoted $y = \log_{10} x$ or, equivalently, $10^y = x$. The relationship between values of x (in original units) and y (in base-10 logarithmic units) for the base-10 logarithm function is demonstrated in Table 1. Values of x increase by multiples of 10 as values of y increase by 1. So as x gets larger, it requires larger increases to produce a one-unit change in y. For example, as x goes from 10 to 100, y increases by 1, and as x goes from 1,000 to 10,000, y still increases by only 1. This demonstrates a property common to all logarithms, regardless of base; that is, the resulting scale of y shrinks gaps between values of x that are larger than 1. In practice, this "shrinking" effect pulls in large positive values and sometimes prevents having to throw away OUTLIERS that otherwise might complicate regression modeling efforts. Hence, logarithm functions are often used to transform variables with extreme positive values into variables with DISTRIBUTIONS that are more symmetric.

It might seem that including logarithmic TRANSFORMATIONS in regression models would make them difficult to interpret. However, because of the property of logarithms demonstrated in the last column of Table 1, this is not necessarily the case. For a base-10 logarithm, each unit increment in y (logarithmic units) is associated with a constant 90% increase in x (original units). For example, when a base-10 logarithm is used

as an EXPLANATORY VARIABLE in a regression model, the corresponding REGRESSION COEFFICIENT can be interpreted as the expected change in the outcome variable, given a unit change in the explanatory variable (logarithmic units) or a 90% change in the explanatory variable (original units).

The natural logarithm function (using base e) demonstrates other general properties of logarithms. Although logarithmic transformations diminish differences at large positive values of x, they accentuate differences at values of x greater than 0 and less than 1. This property is demonstrated in Figure 1, a graph of the natural logarithm function, denoted either or $y = \ln x$ or $y = \log_e x$. As x takes on smaller fractional values, asymptotically approaching 0, y becomes increasingly negative at an exponential rate. This "stretching" property is why logarithmic functions are used to transform variables, with compression in the region between 0 and 1, into variables that are distributed more like a NORMAL DISTRIBUTION. Figure 1 also demonstrates that the natural logarithm function, like all logarithm functions, is not defined for negative x or for x equal to 0.

—Jani S. Little

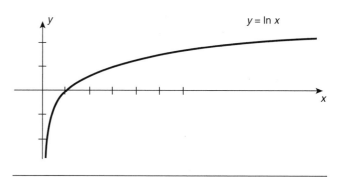

Figure 1   The Natural Logarithm Function

REFERENCES

Hamilton, L. C. (1990). *Modern data analysis: A first course in applied statistics*. Pacific Grove, CA: Brooks/Cole.

Hamilton, L. C. (1992). *Regression with graphics: A second course in applied statistics*. Pacific Grove, CA: Brooks/Cole.

Pampel, F. C. (2000). *Logistic regression: A primer*. Thousand Oaks, CA: Sage.

Swokowski, E. W. (1979). *Calculus with analytic geometry* (2nd ed.). Boston: Prindle, Weber & Schmidt.

LOGIC MODEL

A logic model depicts the theoretical or model ASSUMPTIONS and linkages between program elements and hypothesized intermediate and long-term outcomes. The logic model is often used as a tool by program evaluators during the design phase of the research to conceptualize and guide evaluation strategies by providing a comprehensive framework for data collection and analysis. The model assumptions are often referred to as *program theory* and describe the program components and rationale, the process by which the program is intended to work, and the expected outcomes of the program. The logic model encompasses the key elements of the program THEORY and provides a system-level map, which identifies the interrelationships of the program elements, and the internal and external factors that might influence the hypothesized outcomes.

The key elements of a logic model are depicted in Figure 1 and include the following:

- The program's goals
- The available resources for supporting the program
- The target POPULATIONS or people who are affected by the program
- The program components or key activities that comprise the program
- The program outputs or products that result from the program
- The intermediate and long-term outcomes of the program
- The antecedent variables or factors outside of the program that might affect the outputs of the program
- The intervening or rival events outside of the program that might affect the hypothesized short-term and long-term outcomes of the program

As described by Yin (1998), the strength of a logic model for program evaluators is its depiction of an explicit and comprehensive chain of events or

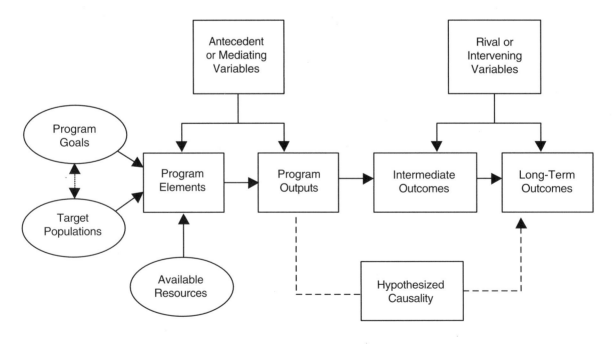

Figure 1   General Program Evaluation Logic Model

interrelationships sufficiently detailed for operational MEASURES to be determined for each step in the chain. The operational measures are used by evaluators as part of the data collection strategy (i.e., which quantitative or qualitative data need to be collected to be able to comprehensively measure the program outputs or outcomes?) and the analysis strategy (i.e., what mediating and rival events might affect program outcomes?).

In a comprehensive logic model, operational measures can include data from multiple sources that can be converged for additional clarity and insight into each stage of the evaluation. For example, an assessment of the intermediate outcomes of the program outputs can vary by target population or stakeholder perspective. Similarly, antecedent or rival variables may affect outputs and outcomes differently for different target populations. Multiple perspectives or inputs rather than a single input into the evaluation strategy better inform the extent to which the desired outcomes of the program have been achieved at each stage of the evaluation.

In addition to program evaluator utility, logic models can also be used by program managers to inform strategies and decisions for program design and implementation, and serve as a framework for reporting program outcomes. Logic models can be used to clarify for stakeholders what critical factors are required to achieve the desired outcomes, what sequence of events are potentially influencing the outcomes, what performance measures are most relevant for different target populations, how program outcomes vary across target populations, what factors beyond the program control influence intermediate and long-term outcomes across program participants or target populations, and what resources are required to achieve the desired outcomes.

—Georgia T. Karuntzos

REFERENCES

Cooksy, L. J., Gill, P., & Kelly, P. A. (2001). The program logic model as an integrative framework for a multimethod evaluation. *Evaluation and Program Planning, 24,* 119–128.

Julian, D. A. (1997). The utilization of the logic model as a system level planning and evaluation device. *Evaluation and Program Planning, 20*(3), 251–257.

Millar, A., Simeone, R. S., & Carnevale, J. T. (2001). Logic models: A system tool for performance management. *Evaluation and Program Planning, 24,* 73–81.

Yin, R. K. (1998). The abridged version of case study research. In L. Bickman & D. J. Rog (Eds.), *Handbook of applied social research methods* (pp. 229–259). Thousand Oaks, CA: Sage.

LOGICAL EMPIRICISM. *See* LOGICAL POSITIVISM

LOGICAL POSITIVISM

Logical positivism, sometimes also called logical empiricism, is an approach to philosophy that developed in the 1920s and remained very influential until the 1950s. It was inspired by rapid and dramatic developments that had taken place in physical science and mathematics. For logical positivists, the main task was to analyze the structure of scientific reasoning and knowledge. This was important because they took science to be the model for intellectual and social progress.

Logical positivism combined EMPIRICISM with the new mathematical logic pioneered by Russell, Frege, and others. Its central doctrine was that all meaningful statements are either empirical or logical in character. This was initially interpreted to mean that they are either open to test by observational evidence or are matters of definition and therefore tautological—a principle that was referred to as the verifiability principle. It ruled out, and was designed to rule out, a great amount of philosophical and theological discussion as literally meaningless. By applying this principle, it was hoped to identify those problems that are genuine ones, as opposed to those that are simply generated by the misuse of language. Not only statements about God or the Absolute but also those about a "real" world beyond experience were often dismissed.

One of the key ideas of logical positivism was a distinction between the context of discovery and the context of justification, between how scientists develop their ideas and what is involved in demonstrating the validity of scientific conclusions. The logical positivists concentrated exclusively on the latter. Moreover, they assumed the unity of science in methodological terms: They denied that there are any fundamental differences between the natural and the social sciences. Indeed, they saw philosophy as itself part of science.

Logical positivist ideas were developed by the Vienna and Berlin Circles, which were small groupings of philosophers, mathematicians, and scientists meeting together in the 1920s and 1930s. The Vienna Circle was the more influential of the two, producing a manifesto and running its own journal. Despite the focus on natural science, several members also had a close interest in social and political issues. Indeed one, Otto Neurath, was a sociologist and became a socialist politician for a short period. The logical positivists regarded their philosophy as capable of playing an important role in undercutting the influence of religion and other sources of irrational ideas. Two other important 20th-century philosophers, Wittgenstein and Popper, had close associations with the Vienna Circle—indeed, Wittgenstein's *Tractatus* was a significant early influence on it—although both were also critics of logical positivism, albeit for different reasons. In the 1930s, key figures in the Vienna Circle began to emigrate to Britain and the United States as a result of the rise of fascism in continental Europe, and this facilitated the spread of logical positivism across the Anglo-American world, as did A. J. Ayer's (1936) best-selling book *Language, Truth and Logic.*

Logical positivism was never a unified body of ideas, and its influence on the development of social science methodology was probably less than is often supposed; although the related doctrine of OPERA-TIONISM certainly did have a strong influence on psychology and, to a lesser extent, on sociology in the first half of the 20th century. In social science, these ideas came into conflict with older views about the nature of science, as well as with the notion that the study of physical and of social reality must necessarily take different forms.

Logical positivists themselves recognized problems with their initial positions and deployed considerable effort and intelligence in trying to deal with these. One problem concerned the epistemic status of the verifiability principle itself: Was it to be interpreted as an empirical statement open to observational test, or was it a tautological matter of definition? Because it did not seem to fit easily into either category, this principle came to be judged as self-refuting by some commentators.

Another problem arose from the logical positivists' empiricism: their assumption that there can be non-inferential empirical givens, such as direct observations, which can provide an indubitable foundation for knowledge. It came to be recognized that any observation, as soon as it is formulated, relies on assumptions, many of which may not have been tested and none of which can be tested without reliance on further assumptions. As a result, the sharp distinction that the positivists wanted to make between theoretical and empirical statements could not be sustained.

The logical positivists also failed to develop a satisfactory solution to the problem of INDUCTION: of how universal theoretical conclusions could be derived from particular empirical data with the same level of logical certainty as deductive argument. Indeed, it became clear that any body of data is open to multiple theoretical interpretations, and this threatened to make scientific theory itself meaningless in terms of the verifiability principle. Given this, the principle came to be formulated in more qualified terms. As a result, it began to provide a more realistic account of science, but the changes endangered any neat demarcation from what the logical positivists had dismissed as meaningless metaphysics.

Logical positivists dominated the philosophy of science until the 1950s, when the problems facing their position became widely viewed as irresolvable. In response, some philosophers (e.g., Quine) retained the spirit of the position while abandoning key elements of it. Others adopted competing accounts of the philosophy of science, such as that of Popper, and sought to build on these—for instance, Lakatos and Feyerabend. There were also some, such as Rorty, who reacted by drawing on pragmatism, on the work of Wittgenstein, and on continental philosophical movements. Radical responses to the collapse of logical positivism sometimes involved reduction of the philosophy of science to its history or sociology, rejection of natural science as a model, and even abandonment of the whole idea that a rational method of inquiry can be identified.

—Martyn Hammersley

REFERENCES

Achinstein, P., & Barker, S. F. (1969). *The legacy of logical positivism.* Baltimore: Johns Hopkins University Press.

Ayer, A. J. (1936). *Language, truth and logic.* London: Victor Gollancz.

Friedman, M. (1991). The re-evaluation of logical positivism. *Journal of Philosophy, 88*(10), 505–519.

Passmore, J. (1967). Logical positivism. In P. Edwards (Ed.), *The encyclopedia of philosophy* (Vol. 5, pp. 52–57). New York: Macmillan.

Reichenbach, H. (1951). *The rise of scientific philosophy.* Berkeley: University of California Press.

LOGISTIC REGRESSION

The situation in which the outcome variable (Y) is limited to two discrete values—an event occurring or not occurring, with a "yes" or "no" response to an attitude question, or a characteristic being present or absent, usually coded as 1 or 0 (or 1 or 2), respectively—is quite typical in many areas of social science research, as in dropping out of high school, getting a job, joining a union, giving birth to a child, voting for a certain candidate, or favoring the death penalty. Logistic regression is a common tool for statistically modeling these types of discrete outcomes.

The overall framing and many of the features of the technique are largely analogous to ordinary least squares (OLS) REGRESSION, especially the linear probability model. Many of the warnings and recommendations, including the diagnostics, made for OLS regression apply as well. It is, however, based on a different, less stringent, set of statistical assumptions to explicitly take into account the limited nature of the outcome variable and the problems resulting from it—because the outcome variable as a function of independent variables can take only two values; the ERROR terms are not continuous, homoskedastic, or normally distributed; and the predicted probabilities are not constrained to behave linearly and not to be greater than 1 and less than 0.

Logistic regression fits a special s-shaped curve by taking a linear combination of the explanatory variables and transforming it by a logistic function (cf. PROBIT ANALYSIS) as follows:

$$\ln[p/(1-p)] = a + BX + e,$$

where p is the probability that the value of the outcome variable is 1, and BX stands for $b_1 x_1 + b_2 x_2 + \cdots + b_n x_n$. The model hence estimates the LOGIT, which is the natural log of the odds of the outcome variable being equal to 1 (i.e., the event occurring, the response being affirmative, or the characteristic being present) or 0 (i.e., the event not occurring, the response being negative, or the characteristic being absent). The probability that the outcome variable is equal to 1 is then the following:

$$p = [\exp(a + BX)]/[1 + \exp(a + BX)]$$
$$\text{or} \quad p = 1/[1 + \exp(-a - BX)].$$

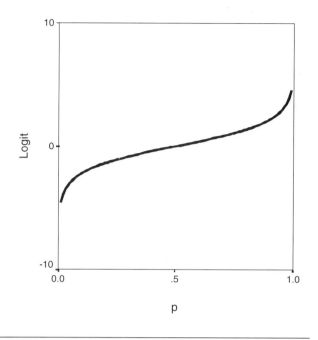

Figure 1   The Relationship Between p and Its Logit

Note that there is a nonlinear relationship between p and its logit, which is illustrated in Figure 1: In the midrange of p there is a (near) linear relationship, but as p approaches the extremes—0 or 1—the relationship becomes nonlinear with increasingly larger changes in logit for the same change in p.

For large samples, the parameters estimated by MAXIMUM LIKELIHOOD ESTIMATION (MLE) are unbiased, efficient, and normally distributed, thus allowing statistical tests of significance. The technique can be extended to situations involving outcome variables with three or more categories (polytomous, or multinomial dependent variables).

EXAMPLE

To illustrate its application and the interpretation of the results, we use the data on the attitude toward capital punishment—"Do you favor or oppose the death penalty for persons convicted of murder?"—from the General Social Survey. Out of 2,599 valid responses in 1998, 1,906 favored (73.3%) and 693 opposed (26.7%) it. The analysis below examines the effects of race (White = 1 and non-White = 0) and education on the DEPENDENT VARIABLE, which is coded as 1 for those who favor it and 0 for those who oppose it, controlling for sex (male = 1 and female = 0) and age.

Table 1   Classification Table

Observed	Predicted		% Correct
	Oppose (0)	Favor (1)	
Oppose (0)	83	605	12.1
Favor (1)	86	1,811	95.5
Overall %			73.3

The standard logistic regression output consists of two parts: one that shows the overall fit of the model and the other that reports the parameter estimates. In the first part, several statistics can be used for comparing alternative models or evaluating the performance of a single model.

1. The model LIKELIHOOD RATIO (LR) STATISTIC, G^2 or L^2, is used to determine if the overall model is statistically significant vis-à-vis the restricted model, which includes only a constant term. It is distributed χ^2 with k degrees of freedom, where k is the number of INDEPENDENT VARIABLES. In the example at hand, we obtain $G^2 = 156.59$, with $df = 4$ and $p < .000$. This model chi-square shows that the prediction model significantly improves on the restricted model.

2. Another method of gauging the performance of the logistic regression model involves the cross-classification of observed and predicted outcomes and summarizes the correspondence between the two with the percentage of correct predictions. For our example, Table 1 shows that the model predicts 73.3% of the cases correctly. In general, the larger the value, the better the model fit. Yet, these results depend a great deal on the initial distribution of the outcome variable.

3. Other statistics—pseudo-R^2s—assessing the overall fit of the model are similar to R^2 in OLS, although they cannot be used for hypothesis testing.

The estimated coefficients are usually provided in the second section of the output in a format similar to that in OLS (see Table 2). The Wald statistic, which is

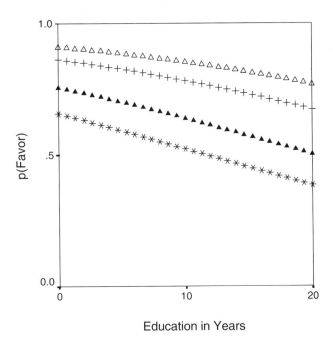

Figure 2   Favoring Death Penalty by Education, Race, and Sex

distributed as χ^2 with 1 degree of freedom, is used to test the hypothesis that the coefficient is significantly different from zero. In our death penalty example, all the independent variables included in the model are significant at the .05 level. The interpretation of the coefficients is fundamentally different, though. The logistic regression coefficients indicate the change in the logit for each unit change in the independent variable, controlling for the other variables in the model. For example, the coefficient for education, −.056, indicates that an additional year of schooling completed reduces the logit by .056. Another, more intuitive, approach is to take the antilog of (i.e., to exponentiate) the coefficient, which gives the statistical effect of the independent variable in terms of odds ratios. It is multiplicative in that it indicates no effect when it has a value of 1, a positive effect when it is greater than 1, and a negative effect when it is less than 1. Each additional year of schooling, for instance, decreases the odds of favoring the death penalty by a factor of .946 when the other variables are controlled for. Still another approach is to calculate predicted probabilities for a set of values of the independent variables. Figure 2 shows the effect of education on the probability of favoring

Table 2   Logistic Regression Coefficient Estimates

Independent Variable	B	SE	Wald Statistic	df	p	Exp
Education	−.056	.016	11.586	1	.001	.946
Age	−.006	.003	4.348	1	.037	.994
Sex (male = 1)	.481	.095	25.843	1	.000	1.617
Race (White = 1)	1.190	.107	124.170	1	.000	3.289
Constant	.922	.271	11.577	1	.001	2.514

the death penalty. Separate lines are generated for non-White female (*), non-White male (▲), White female (+), and White male (△), with age fixed at the sample mean.

—Shin-Kap Han and C. Gray Swicegood

REFERENCES

Liao, T. F. (1994). *Interpreting probability models: Logit, probit, and other generalized linear models.* Thousand Oaks, CA: Sage.

Long, J. S. (1997). *Regression models for categorical and limited dependent variables.* Thousand Oaks, CA: Sage.

Menard, S. (1995). *Applied logistic regression analysis.* Thousand Oaks, CA: Sage.

Pampel, F. C. (2000). *Logistic regression: A primer.* Thousand Oaks, CA: Sage.

LOGIT

The *logit* is the natural logarithm of the *odds* that an event occurs or a state exists. For example, if $P(Y)$ is the probability that someone is a computer user or that someone commits a crime, then $\text{logit}(Y) = \ln[P(Y)/(1 - P(Y))]$. The logit is negative whenever $P(Y)$ is less than .5, and is negative and infinitely large in magnitude when $P(Y) = 0$; it is positive whenever $P(Y)$ is greater than .5, and positive and infinitely large in magnitude when $P(Y) = 1$. If $P(Y) = .5$, because the natural logarithm of 1 is zero, $\text{logit}(Y) = \ln[(.5)/(.5)] = \ln(1) = 0$. The logit of a dichotomous or dichotomized dependent variable is used as the dependent variable in LOGISTIC REGRESSION and LOGIT MODELS.

—Scott Menard

LOGIT MODEL

The logit model was developed as a variant of the LOG-LINEAR MODEL to analyze categorical variables, parallel to the analysis of CONTINUOUS VARIABLES with ORDINARY LEAST SQUARES regression analysis. The basic formulation of the log-linear and logit models begins with the assumption that we are dealing with a CONTINGENCY TABLE of two or more dimensions (represented by two or more variables), each of which has two or more categories, which may be ordered but are usually assumed to be unordered. The analysis of a two-way contingency table for CATEGORICAL variables is a relatively simple problem covered in basic statistics texts. When tables contain three or more categorical variables, however, it quickly becomes cumbersome to consider all the different ways of arranging the multidimensional tables in the two-dimensional space of a page.

Log-linear models are used to summarize three-way and higher-dimensional contingency tables in terms of the effects of each variable in the table on the frequency of observations in each cell of the table; they are also used to show the relationships among the variables in the table. As described by Knoke and Burke (1980, p. 11), the *general log-linear model* makes no distinction between independent and dependent variables but in effect treats all variables as dependent variables and models their mutual associations. The expected cell frequencies based on the model (e.g., F_{ijk} for a three-variable table) are modeled as a function of all the variables in the model. The *logit model* is mathematically equivalent to the log-linear model, but one variable is considered a dependent variable, and instead of modeling the expected cell frequencies, the *odds* of being in one category (instead of any of the other categories) on the dependent variable is modeled as a function of the other (independent) variables instead of the expected frequency being modeled.

THE GENERAL LOG-LINEAR MODEL

Consider as an example a three-way contingency table in which variable A is sex ($0 =$ male, $1 =$ female), variable B is race ($1 =$ White, $2 =$ Black, $3 =$ other), and variable C is computer use, which indicates whether ($0 =$ no, $1 =$ yes) the respondent uses a personal computer. The categories of each variable are indexed by $i = 0, 1$ for A, $j = 1, 2, 3$ for B, and $k = 0, 1$ for C. For a trivariate contingency table, the *saturated model* is the model that includes the effect of each variable, plus the effects of all possible INTERACTIONS among the variables in the model. Using the notation for log-linear models,

$$F_{ijk} = \eta \tau_i^A \tau_j^B \tau_k^C \tau_{ij}^{AB} \tau_{jk}^{BC} \tau_{ijk}^{ABC}, \tag{1}$$

where each term on the right-hand side of the equation is multiplied by the other terms, and

F_{ijk} = frequency of cases in cell (i, j, k), which is expected if the model is correct.

η = geometric mean of the number of cases in each cell in the table, $\eta = (f_{010} f_{020} f_{030}$ $f_{110} f_{120} f_{130} f_{011} f_{021} f_{031} f_{111} f_{121} f_{131})^{1/12}$.

τ_i^A = effect of A on cell frequencies (one effect for each category of A; one category is redundant); similarly, τ_j^B and τ_k^C are the respective effects of B and C.

τ_{ij}^{AB} = effect of the interaction between A and B; effects that occur to the extent that A and B are not independent; similarly, τ_{ik}^{AC} and τ_{jk}^{BC} are the respective interaction effects of A with C and of B with C.

τ_{ijk}^{ABC} = effect of the three-way interaction among A, B, and C.

There is no single standard for log-linear and logit model notation. Goodman (1973) presents two notations, the first of which [the notation used in equation (1)] expresses the row and column variables as exponents to the coefficients and has come to be more frequently used in log-linear analysis. In the second notation, which is used for logit but not general log-linear models and is more similar to the OLS regression format, the row and column variables of the table are expressed as dummy variables $X_1, X_2, \ldots, X_k$. A third notation, often used for log-linear but not logit models, is the fitted marginals notation (Knoke & Burke 1980), involving the use of "curly" brackets to specify effects, for example, representing the saturated model in equation (1) as $\{A\}\{B\}\{C\}\{AB\}\{AC\}\{BC\}\{ABC\}$.

In the multiplicative model of equation (1), any $\tau > 1$ results in more than the geometric mean number of cases in a cell, but $\tau < 1$ results in less than the geometric mean number of cases in the cell. When any $\tau = 1$, the effect in question has no impact on the cell frequencies (it just multiplies them by 1; this is analogous to a coefficient of zero in OLS regression). Because the saturated model includes all possible effects, including all possible interactions, it perfectly reproduces the cell frequencies, but it has no DEGREES OF FREEDOM. As effect parameters (τ) are constrained to equal 1 (in other words, they are left out of the model), we gain degrees of freedom and are able to test how well the model fits the observed data.

Taking the natural LOGARITHM of the saturated model in equation (1) results in the following equation:

$$\ln(F_{ijk}) = \ln(\eta) + \ln(\tau_i^A) + \ln(\tau_j^B) + \ln(\tau_k^C)$$
$$+ \ln(\tau_{ij}^{AB}) + \ln(\tau_{ik}^{AC}) + \ln(\tau_{jk}^{BC}) + \ln(\tau_{ijk}^{ABC}) \tag{2}$$

or

$$V_{ijk} = \theta = \lambda_i^A + \lambda_j^B + \lambda_k^C + \lambda_{ij}^{AB}$$
$$+ \lambda_{ik}^{AC} + \lambda_{jk}^{BC} + \lambda_{ijk}^{ABC}, \tag{3}$$

where $V_{ijk} = \ln(F_{ijk})$, $\theta = \ln(\eta)$, and each $\lambda = \ln(\tau)$ for the corresponding effect. Equations (2) and (3) convert the multiplicative model of equation (1) to an additive model that is more similar to the OLS regression model. In equation (3), the absence of an effect is indicated by $\lambda = 0$ for that effect. For example, if the interaction between A and B has no impact on the cell frequencies, $\lambda_{ij}^{AB} = 0$, corresponding to $\ln(\tau_{ij}^{AB}) = 0$ because $\tau_{ij}^{AB} = 1$ and $\ln(1) = 0$. The additive form of the model has several advantages, as described in Knoke and Burke (1980), including ease of calculating standard errors and thus of determining the statistical significance of the parameters.

THE LOGIT MODEL

In the log-linear model described in equations (1), (2), and (3), all three variables have the same conceptual status. Computer use is treated no differently from sex or race. Substantively, however, we may be interested specifically in the impact of race and sex on computer use. The logit model is a variant of the log-linear model in which we designate one variable as the dependent variable and the other variables as predictors or independent variables. For the dichotomous dependent variable C (computer use) in the saturated model in equation (1), we can express the expected ODDS that a respondent is a computer user, Ω_C, as the ratio between the expected frequency of being a computer user, F_{ij1}, and the expected frequency of not being a computer user, F_{ij0}:

$$
\begin{aligned}
\Omega_C &= (F_{ij1}/F_{ij0}) \\
&= \left(\eta \tau_i^A \tau_j^B \tau_1^C \tau_{ij}^{AB} \tau_{i1}^{AC} \tau_{j1}^{BC} \tau_{ij1}^{ABC}\right) \\
&\quad /\left(\eta = \tau_i^A \tau_j^B \tau_0^C \tau_{ij}^{AB} \tau_{i0}^{AC} \tau_{j0}^{BC} \tau_{ij0}^{ABC}\right) \\
&= \left(\tau_1^C \tau_{i1}^{AC} \tau_{j1}^{BC} \tau_{ij1}^{ABC}\right)/\left(\tau_0^C \tau_{i0}^{AC} \tau_{j0}^{BC} \tau_{ij0}^{ABC}\right), \quad (4)
\end{aligned}
$$

where η, τ_i^A, τ_j^B, and τ_{ij}^{AB} cancel out of the numerator and the denominator of the equation, and all of the remaining terms include the variable C. If we take the natural logarithm of equation (4), the dependent variable becomes the log-odds of computer use, or the *logit* of the probability that the respondent is a computer user: $\ln(\Omega_C) = 2\lambda^C + 2\lambda_i^{AC} + 2\lambda_j^{BC} + 2\lambda_{ij}^{ABC}$ or, reexpressing $\beta = 2\lambda$ and $\text{logit}(C) = \ln(\Omega_C)$,

$$
\begin{aligned}
\text{logit}(C) &= \ln(\Omega_C) \\
&= \beta^C + \beta^{AC} + \beta^{BC} + \beta^{ABC}. \quad (5)
\end{aligned}
$$

In the DUMMY VARIABLE notation mentioned earlier and described or used by, among others, Goodman (1973), Hutcheson and Sofroniou (1999), and Powers and Xie (2000),

$$
\begin{aligned}
\text{logit}(C) &= \beta_0 + \beta_1 X_{A=1} + \beta_2 X_{B=2} + \beta_3 X_{B=3} \\
&\quad + \beta_4 X_{A=1} X_{B=2} + \beta_5 X_{A=1} X_{B=3}. \quad (6)
\end{aligned}
$$

The subscripts on the X variables here indicate which categories are omitted as reference categories; male ($A = 0$) is the reference category for variable A, and White ($B = 1$) is the reference category for variable B. $X_{A=1}$ is the dummy variable for being female; $X_{B=2}$ and $X_{B=3}$ are the dummy variables for

being Black and other, respectively; and the last two terms in the equation represent the interaction between sex and race (A and B). Equations (5) and (6) represent exactly the same model; they are just two different ways of showing which effects are included in the model.

It is also possible to include continuous, interval, or ratio scale predictors in the logit model (DeMaris, 1992). Sometimes, a distinction is made between logistic regression as a method for dealing with continuous predictors, as opposed to logit analysis as a method for dealing with categorical predictors, but this distinction is somewhat artificial. In form, the two models are identical, with both being able to analyze continuous as well as categorical predictors. They differ primarily in the numerical techniques used to estimate the parameters and in how they are usually presented, with the logistic regression model appearing more like the ordinary least squares regression model and the logit model appearing more like the general log-linear model.

LOGIT MODELS FOR POLYTOMOUS VARIABLES

Suppose that instead of computer use as the dependent variable, we have the nominal variable *ice cream preference,* where $1 =$ vanilla, $2 =$ chocolate, $3 =$ strawberry, and $4 =$ other. Among the several possible approaches to analyzing this nominal variable, in which there is no natural ordering to the categories, is the MULTINOMIAL LOGIT model, in which one category (e.g., $4 =$ other) is selected as a reference category, and each of the other categories is separately compared to the reference category. Because the reference category cannot be compared to itself, this results in a series of $k - 1 = 3$ equations, one for each category compared to the reference category, and we add subscripts to the coefficients in equation (6) to indicate which of the other categories we are contrasting with the first category:

$$
\begin{aligned}
\text{logit}(C_1) &= \ln[P(C = 1)/P(C = 4)] \\
&= \ln(F_{ij1}/F_{ij4}) = \beta_1^C + \beta_1^{AC} + \beta_1^{BC} + \beta_1^{ABC}, \\
\text{logit}(C_2) &= \ln[P(C = 2)/P(C = 4)] \\
&= \ln(F_{ij2}/F_{ij4}) = \beta_2^C + \beta_2^{AC} + \beta_2^{BC} + \beta_2^{ABC}, \\
\text{logit}(C_3) &= \ln[P(C = 3)/P(C = 4)] \\
&= \ln(F_{ij3}/F_{ij4}) = \beta_3^C + \beta_3^{AC} + \beta_3^{BC} + \beta_3^{ABC},
\end{aligned}
$$

where $P(C = 1)$ is the probability that C has the value 1, $P(C = 2)$ is the probability that C has the value 2, and so forth, given the values of the predictors, and the equations indicate how well sex and race predict preferences for vanilla [logit(C_1)], chocolate [logit(C_2)], and strawberry [logit(C_3)] as opposed to other flavors of ice cream. The multinomial logit model is more complicated to interpret, with $(k - 1)$ sets of coefficients, but it avoids unnecessary and artificial recoding of the dependent variable into a single dichotomy.

As another alternative, suppose that the dependent variable C represents different levels of academic attainment, with 1 = *less than high school graduation*, 2 = *high school graduation but no college degree*, 3 = *undergraduate college degree but no graduate degree*, and 4 = *graduate (master's or doctoral) degree*. We could construct a multinomial model similar to the one above, but the additional information provided by the natural ordering of the categories, from lower to higher levels of education, may allow us to construct a simpler model. If we again take the fourth category (graduate degree) as the reference category, it is plausible that the impacts of sex and race on the difference between an undergraduate degree and a graduate degree are the same as their impacts on the difference between an undergraduate degree and a high school diploma (i.e., the impacts of sex and race on the transition from one adjacent level to the next are the same regardless of which adjacent levels of education are being compared). If so, we may use the *adjacent categories logit* model, in which $\ln[P(C = k)/P(C = k+1)] = \sum \beta_k^C + \beta^{AC} + \beta^{BC} + \beta^{ABC}$ or, for the four-category dependent variable used here, logit(C) $= \beta_1^C + \beta_2^C + \beta_3^C + \beta^{AC} + \beta^{BC} + \beta^{ABC}$, and only the coefficient for β^C is subscripted to show that we have a different starting point (a *threshold*, much like the intercept in a multinomial logit model) for the logit regression line in each category. Another possibility is the *cumulative logit* model, in which the equation is basically the same, but a different logit is used as the dependent variable: $\ln[P(C \leq k)/P(C > k)] = \sum \beta_k^C + \beta^{AC} + \beta^{BC} + \beta^{ABC}$ or, again, logit(C) $= \beta_1^C + \beta_2^C + \beta_3^C + \beta^{AC} + \beta^{BC} + \beta^{ABC}$ for the four-category dependent variable C = educational attainment. In effect, the adjacent categories and cumulative logit models assume parallel logit regression lines, starting at a different value for each category. Another way to describe this is to say that coefficients for the relationships among the variables are constant, but they have a different starting point for each different level of the dependent variable. Other possible logit models can be constructed to analyze ordered dependent variables, as reviewed, for instance, in Long (1997).

The (dichotomous) logit model or its variant, the LOGISTIC REGRESSION model, is one of two models widely used in the analysis of dichotomous dependent variables and appears to be more widely used than the main alternative, the PROBIT model. The multinomial logit model is probably the model most commonly used by social scientists today to analyze a polytomous nominal dependent variable with two or more predictors. The family of ordered logit models, however, represents only one of several more or less widely used approaches to the analysis of polytomous-ordered categorical dependent variables. Other options in this case, as summarized by Menard (2002), include ordered probit models, treating ordinal dependent variables as though they represented interval or ratio scaled variables, ordinal regression, and the use of structural equation models with polychoric correlations. It is also possible to test whether the slopes are parallel in an ordered logit model; if they are not, a multinomial logit model or some other model may be more appropriate than the ordered logit model, even for ordered categorical data. Broadly speaking, the family of logit models, particularly if we include the special case of logistic regression, is presently the most widely used approach to the analysis of categorical dependent variables in the social sciences.

—Scott Menard

REFERENCES

DeMaris, A. (1992). *Logit modeling*. Newbury Park, CA: Sage.

Goodman, L. A. (1973). Causal analysis of data from panel studies and other kinds of surveys. *American Journal of Sociology, 78*, 1135–1191.

Hutcheson, G., & Sofroniou, N. (1999). *The multivariate social scientist: Introductory statistics using generalized linear models*. London: Sage.

Knoke, D., & Burke, P. J. (1980). *Log-linear models*. Beverly Hills, CA: Sage.

Long, J. S. (1997). *Regression models for categorical and limited dependent variables*. Thousand Oaks, CA: Sage.

Menard, S. (2002). *Applied logistic regression analysis* (2nd ed.). Thousand Oaks, CA: Sage.

Powers, D. A., & Xie, Y. (2000). *Statistical methods for categorical data analysis*. San Diego: Academic Press.

LOG-LINEAR MODEL

Cross-classifications of categorical variables (CONTINGENCY TABLE) are ubiquitous in the social sciences, and log-linear models provide a powerful and flexible framework for their analysis. The log-linear model has direct analogies to the linear model routinely used to perform an ANALYSIS OF VARIANCE. There are, of course, important issues that are particular to contingency tables analysis, and those are the primary focus of this entry.

This entry begins with an exposition of the log-linear model in the context of the 2×2 contingency table, and from the basic concepts and models of this simple setting, extensions or generalizations are made to a illustrate how log-linear models can be applied to applications with more than two categories per variable, more than two variables, or a one-to-one matching between the categories of two variables. The concept and representation of the ODDS RATIO are fundamental to understanding the log-linear model and its applications, and this will be demonstrated throughout.

ASSOCIATION: THE 2×2 CONTINGENCY TABLE, LOG-ODDS RATIO, AND LOG-LINEAR MODEL PARAMETERS

The correlation coefficient is the standard measure for the assessment of (linear) ASSOCIATION between two continuous variables, and the parameters in the classical LINEAR REGRESSION model are readily related to it. The odds ratio is the analogous measure in the log-linear model, as well as numerous generalizations of these models that have been developed for the modeling and analysis of associations between categorical variables. That is, log-linear model parameters have immediate interpretations in terms of log-odds, log-odds ratios, and contrasts between log-odds ratios. The analogy to linear models for analysis of variance is that the parameters in those models have interpretations in terms of means, differences in means, or mean contrasts. In addition, there are immediate connections between log-odds ratios for association and the parameters in regression models for log-odds, just as there are immediate connections between PARTIAL CORRELATIONS and REGRESSION COEFFICIENTS in ordinary linear regression.

The fundamental concepts and parameterization of the log-linear model are readily demonstrated with the consideration of the 2×2 contingency table, as well as sets of 2×2 contingency tables. Let π_{ij} denote the probability associated with the cell in row i and column j of a 2×2 contingency table, and let n_{ij} denote the corresponding observed count. For example, consider the following cross-classification of applicants' gender and admission decisions for all 12,763 applications to the 101 graduate programs at the University of California at Berkeley for 1973 (see, e.g., Agresti, 1984, pp. 71–73):

Table 1   Berkeley Graduate Admissions Data

	Admissions Decision	
Gender	Yes	No
Male	3,738	4,704
Female	1,494	2,827

In this case, $n_{11} = 3,738, n_{12} = 4,704, n_{21} = 1,494$, and $n_{22} = 2,827$. These data were presented in an analysis to examine possible sex bias in graduate admissions, as it is immediately obvious from simple calculations that more than 44% (i.e., $3,738/8,442 > 0.44$) of males were offered admission, whereas less than 35% (i.e., $1,494/4,321 < 0.35$) of females were. Log-linear models can be applied to test the hypothesis that admissions decisions were (statistically) independent of applicants' gender versus the alternative that there was some association/dependence.

A log-linear model representation of the cell probabilities π_{ij} in the 2×2 contingency table is

$$\ln(\pi_{ij}) = \lambda + \lambda_i^R + \lambda_j^C + \lambda_{ij}^{RC},$$

where "ln( )" is used to represent the natural logarithm function and the λ_i^R, λ_j^C, and λ_{ij}^{RC} are row, column, and association parameters, respectively, to be estimated from the data. The model of statistical independence is the reduced model where $\lambda_{ij}^{RC} = 0$ for all pairs (i, j). If the R (row) variable (i.e., applicants' gender) and the C (column) variable (i.e., admissions decision) are not independent of one another, then the association between R and C is represented in terms of the λ_{ij}^{RC}, and a specific contrast of these terms is readily interpreted as the log-odds ratio for assessing the degree of association between R and C; that is,

$$\ln\left(\frac{\pi_{11}\pi_{22}}{\pi_{12}\pi_{21}}\right) = \lambda_{11}^{RC} - \lambda_{12}^{RC} - \lambda_{21}^{RC} + \lambda_{22}^{RC}.$$

Note that, just as with linear models for analysis of variance, restrictions are necessary to identify individual parameters in the log-linear model (e.g., $\lambda_1^R = \lambda_1^C = \lambda_{1j}^{RC} = \lambda_{i1}^{RC} = 0$, for all i and for all j), but the contrast $\lambda_{11}^{RC} - \lambda_{12}^{RC} - \lambda_{21}^{RC} + \lambda_{22}^{RC}$ is identified as the log-odds ratio independent of the identifying restrictions chosen for the individual λ terms.

The method of MAXIMUM LIKELIHOOD is routinely employed to estimate log-linear models and their parameters; in the case of the Berkeley admissions data, the maximum likelihood estimate of the $\ln(\pi_{ij})$ in the model, not assuming that R and C were independent, is $\ln(n_{ij}/N)$, where N is the total sample size. Hence, the maximum likelihood estimate of the log-odds ratio equals $\ln(\frac{3738 \times 2827}{1494 \times 4704}) = 0.41$, and a statistic (see the ODDS RATIO entry for details on the calculation) for testing the NULL HYPOTHESIS that the log-odds ratio equals zero (i.e., statistical independence) equals 10.52— thereby providing strong evidence ($p < .001$) for a departure from independence and hence an association.

A general approach to testing hypotheses within the log-linear model framework is to fit the model under the null hypothesis (independence, in this case) and the ALTERNATIVE HYPOTHESIS (in this case, the unrestricted model that includes the λ_{ij}^{RC} terms). The difference in the LIKELIHOOD RATIO STATISTICS (which we denote here by L^2) for the two models is a test of the null hypothesis against the alternative, and (under certain assumptions) the appropriate reference distribution is a chi-square with DEGREES OF FREEDOM (which we denote here by df) equal to the difference in the (residual) degrees of freedom for the two models. For our example, the null model has $L^2 = 112.40$, and $df = 1$. The unrestricted model in the example, because it is specified with no simplifying assumptions, has residual deviance and residual degrees of freedom both equal to 0. It follows that L^2 for testing the null hypothesis of independence against an unrestricted alternative equals 112.40, and the corresponding p-value is considerably less than .001.

Note that the square root of L^2 (i.e., $\sqrt{112.40} = 10.60$) is numerically close to the value of the test statistic based on the maximum likelihood estimate of the log-odds ratio. Indeed, the similarity between the values of the two test statistics—the first based on

a parameter estimate and its estimated standard error and the second based on the log-likelihood—is not an accident. These two methods to testing hypotheses for log-linear models (and other models estimated by maximum likelihood) are asymptotically equivalent, which intuitively means that they should be numerically very close when the observed sample size is "large."

Log-linear models are in the family of so-called GENERALIZED LINEAR MODELS, and hence software for such models (e.g., the glm function in R or Splus, or proc glm in SAS) can be used to fit and analyze log-linear models.

The standard theory of likelihood-based inference applies to log-linear modeling estimation and testing when the sampling model for the observed cross-classification is either MULTINOMIAL, product-multinomial, or independent POISSON. Inferences are not sensitive to which of these three sampling models was employed, provided that the log-linear model estimated does not violate the sampling assumptions. For example, in the case of product-multinomial sampling, the estimated model must yield estimated cell counts that preserve the relevant multinomial totals. Further discussion of these issues can be found in the general categorical data analysis references for this entry.

MODELS FOR MORE THAN TWO VARIABLES

The development of log-linear models for the setting where there are more than two categorical variables includes both the specification of models in terms of equations and the development of associated concepts of independence. The presentation here focuses on further analysis of 1973 graduate admission data from the University of California, Berkeley. The following data incorporate a third variable (in addition to applicants' gender and admission status): major applied to. Data are presented only for what were the six largest graduate programs at the time, accounting for 4,526 applications and approximately 35% of the total.

The fullest specification of a log-linear model with three variables is

$$\begin{aligned}\ln(\pi_{ijk}) = {} & \lambda + \lambda_i^R + \lambda_j^C + \lambda_k^M + \lambda_{ij}^{RC} + \lambda_{ik}^{RM} \\ & + \lambda_{jk}^{RM} + \lambda_{ijk}^{RCM},\end{aligned}$$

Table 2   Berkeley Admissions Data for Six Majors

| | Admissions Decision | | | |
| | Male | | Female | |
Major	Yes	No	Yes	No
A	512	313	89	19
B	353	207	17	8
C	120	205	202	391
D	138	279	131	244
E	53	138	94	299
F	22	351	24	317

where the additional subscript k indexes the third variable. Adopting the notation from the previous example (i.e., R represents the applicants' gender, and C is used to denote the admissions decision), M is used to denote the major applied to. The log-odds ratio to explore the association between R and C for a specific major is

$$\ln\left(\frac{\pi_{11k}\pi_{22k}}{\pi_{12k}\pi_{21k}}\right) = \ln(\pi_{11k}) - \ln(\pi_{12k})$$
$$- \ln(\pi_{21k}) + \ln(\pi_{22k}),$$

which in turn can be written as

$$\ln\left(\frac{\pi_{11k}\pi_{22k}}{\pi_{12k}\pi_{21k}}\right) = \left(\lambda_{11}^{RC} - \lambda_{12}^{RC} - \lambda_{21}^{RC} + \lambda_{22}^{RC}\right)$$
$$+ \left(\lambda_{11k}^{RCM} - \lambda_{12k}^{RCM} - \lambda_{21k}^{RCM} + \lambda_{22k}^{RCM}\right).$$

It is important to note that in the latter equation, the first contrast of the λ terms does not depend on the level of M, whereas the second contrast does. Let $\theta_k^{RC(M)}$ denote the log-odds ratio for the *conditional association* between gender and admissions decision in the kth major (i.e., $\theta_k^{RC(M)} = \ln(\pi_{11k}\pi_{22k}/\pi_{12k}\pi_{21k})$), and let

$$\delta^{RC} = \lambda_{11}^{RC} - \lambda_{12}^{RC} - \lambda_{21}^{RC} + \lambda_{22}^{RC}$$

and

$$\delta_k^{RCM} = \lambda_{11k}^{RCM} - \lambda_{12k}^{RCM} - \lambda_{21k}^{RCM} + \lambda_{22k}^{RCM}.$$

It then follows that $\theta_k^{RC(M)} = \delta^{RC} + \delta_k^{RCM}$. The obvious implication is that the full model allows for the possibility that any association between R and C could be variable across the levels of M; that is, the δ_k^{RCM} are nonzero, and hence the $\theta_k^{RC(M)}$ are variable

across the majors. On the other hand, a model that excludes the three-factor terms λ_{ijk}^{RCM} (and hence δ_k^{RCM} equals 0) is one in which the association between R and C is assumed to be the same across all majors—this is a model of *homogeneous association,* or *no-three-factor interaction.* Likewise, a model excluding both the λ_{ij}^{RC} terms and the λ_{ijk}^{RCM} terms would yield a log-odds ratio of 0 for the R–C association, given $M = k$, and hence it would be a model assuming that R and C were independent in each of the six majors. This latter model is one of *conditional independence—R and C are independent at each level of $M = k$.

The likelihood ratio test statistic for the homogeneous association model is $L^2 = 20.20$, on five residual df (i.e., six log-odds ratios are constrained to a single value, and hence $df = 6 - 1$). The corresponding p value is approximately equal to .001, indicating some departure from homogeneous association. Fitting the heterogeneous association model (i.e., the full model) to the data yields a perfect fit to the data, and inspection of the estimates $\hat{\delta}_k^{RCM}$ (not presented) shows that association between R and C in major A was markedly different from the other five majors. Indeed, there appears to be little evidence for an association between R and C across the other majors. Therefore, consider fitting the model where δ_k^{RCM} is estimated only when $k = 1$; that is, we constrain $\delta_k^{RCM} = 0$ for all k not equal to 1. The likelihood ratio test statistic is $L^2 = 2.68$ on five residual df (again, we have estimated but one out of six possible log-odds ratios), which indicates an excellent fit to the data.

There is not space here for a more thorough analysis of the Berkeley admissions data, but it is worth noting that the two examples taken in tandem provide for a nice illustration of Simpson's paradox. That is, the association between an applicant's gender and the admissions decision that is evident when we do not consider major suggests bias against female applicants, but when we control for major, we see no overall bias toward one gender. The data do support that females were admitted at a higher rate in the department receiving the largest number of applications, which is in the opposite direction of the bias observed in the two-way table combining all majors. The paradox arises because males and females did not apply to the various majors at the same rates. That is, females were relatively more likely to apply to majors with lower admissions rates, and hence their admissions rate, when combined across majors, is lower.

Table 3   Educational Attainment Data

Respondent's	Oldest Brother's Level (Years)		
Level (Years)	< 12	12	≥ 13
< 12	16	20	16
12	15	65	76
≥ 13	26	69	629

LOG-LINEAR MODELS WITH MORE THAN TWO CATEGORIES: A TWO-WAY EXAMPLE AND REFINING OR MODIFYING THE λ_{ij}^{RC} PARAMETERS

In the general setting of an $I \times J$ cross-classification log-linear model, parameters are still interpreted in terms of log-odds ratios for association; more generally, in a multiway table, they are interpreted in terms of conditional or partial log-odds ratios. For example, in an arbitrary two-way table, contrasts of the association parameters λ_{ij}^{RC} correspond to a log-odds ratio comparing the relative odds of a pair of categories with respect to one variable across two levels of the other; that is,

$$\ln\left(\frac{\pi_{ij}\pi_{i'j'}}{\pi_{ij'}\pi_{i'j}}\right) = \lambda_{ij}^{RC} - \lambda_{ij'}^{RC} - \lambda_{i'j}^{RC} + \lambda_{jj'}^{RC}.$$

Consider the following data from a study of educational attainment. The data are from the 1973 Occupational Changes in a Generation II Survey (Mare, 1994), and here we only consider data for the sons of fathers with 16 or more years of education. The rows correspond to the educational attainment of the survey respondents, and the columns correspond to the educational attainment of the respondents' oldest brothers. The likelihood ratio statistic for testing statistical independence between respondents' educational attainment and oldest brothers' educational attainment is $L^2 = 161.86$. The relevant number of degrees of freedom is four (i.e., $(3-1) \times (3-1) = 4$), the corresponding p value for a chi-square distribution with 4 df is much less than .001, and hence there is strong evidence indicating a departure from independence. We could fit the saturated model to estimate the four identifiable λ_{ij}^{RC}, but instead we use these data to illustrate how more parsimonious models, arrived at by placing restrictions on the λ_{ij}^{RC}, can be developed to explore specific departures from independence.

The first model we consider exploits the fact that the categories for both variables are ordered. Let

$\lambda_{ij}^{RC} = \theta ij$, and then a log-odds ratio comparing any pair of adjacent categories equals θ; that is,

$$\ln\left(\frac{\pi_{ij}\pi_{i+1,j+1}}{\pi_{i,j+1}\pi_{i+1,j}}\right) = \theta.$$

Such a model is referred to as an example of ASSOCIATION MODELS, and in the case of the example, $L^2 = 33.12$ on 3 df for this model. This is a dramatic improvement in fit, but there remains evidence of lack of fit.

Next, consider refining the model further by adding a parameter that enters the model only for observations along the main diagonal—that is, let $\lambda_{ij}^{RC} = \theta ij + \beta I(i = j)$, where $I(i = j) = 1$ if $i = j$; otherwise, it is equal to 0. This model improves the fit further ($L^2 = 6.36$ on 2 df, with a corresponding p value between .025 and .05), and the estimated association parameters are $\hat{\theta} = 0.47$ and $\hat{\beta} = 0.74$. Briefly, $\hat{\theta}$ accounts for a positive association between respondents' education attainment and oldest brothers' educational attainment (i.e., $\theta > 0$), and $\hat{\beta}$ accounts for still greater clustering of the two variables into the identical (i.e., diagonal) categories than under uniform association (i.e., $\beta > 0$).

The two refined models presented here only scratch the surface for illustrating the tools available for modeling association within the log-linear models framework. Indeed, the model of SYMMETRY (i.e., $\pi_{ij} = \pi_{ji}$), which corresponds to the log-linear model where $\lambda_i^R = \lambda_i^C$ and $\lambda_{ij}^{RC} = \lambda_{ji}^{RC}$, fits these data very well (i.e., $L^2 = 3.46$ on 3 df; $p > .25$). The interested reader is referred to the references, as well as the references cited therein, to explore this subject further, including generalizations to nonlinear models for association in two-way tables and in multiway tables.

—Mark P. Becker

REFERENCES

Agresti, A. (1984). *Analysis of ordinal categorical data.* New York: John Wiley.

Agresti, A. (1996). *An introduction to categorical data analysis.* New York: John Wiley.

Agresti, A. (2002). *Categorical data analysis* (2nd ed.). New York: John Wiley.

Mare, R. D. (1994). Discrete-time bivariate hazards with unobserved heterogeneity: A partially observed contingency table approach. In P. V. Marsden (Ed.), *Sociological methodology 1984* (pp. 341–383). Cambridge, MA: Blackwell.

Powers, D. A., & Xie, Y. (2000). *Statistical methods for categorical data analysis.* San Diego: Academic Press.

LONGITUDINAL RESEARCH

Longitudinal research may best be defined by contrasting it with CROSS-SECTIONAL research. Cross-sectional research refers to research in which data are collected for a set of cases (individuals or aggregates such as cities or countries) on a set of variables (e.g., frequency of illegal behavior, attitudes toward globalization) and in which data collection occurs specifically (a) *at* a single time and (b) *for* a single time point or a single interval of time (hereafter, both will be referred to as *periods*). Analysis of purely cross-sectional data can examine *differences between cases* but not *changes within cases.* Different disciplines define *longitudinal research* differently, but a broad definition would include research in which (a) data are collected *for* more than one time period, (b) possibly but not necessarily involving collection of data *at* different time periods, and (c) permitting analysis that, at a minimum, involves the measurement and analysis of change over time within the same cases (individual or aggregate). Longitudinal data have been collected at the national level for more than 300 years, since 1665, and at the individual level since 1759, but longitudinal research in the social sciences has really flourished since the 1970s and 1980s (Menard, 2002).

Although some researchers would consider the collection of data *at* different time periods to be a defining characteristic of longitudinal research, it is also possible in principle to collect *retrospective* data, in which the data are collected *at* a single period but *for* more than one period. For example, a respondent may be asked to report on all of the times he or she has been a victim of crime, or has committed a crime, over a span of years up to and including her or his lifetime. In contrast to retrospective studies, *prospective* longitudinal data collection involves the repeated collection of data with usually short recall periods: crimes committed or victimizations experienced in the past week, month, or year or data on attitudes, beliefs, and sociodemographic characteristics at the instant the data are collected.

Longitudinal research serves two primary purposes: to describe patterns of change and to establish the direction (positive or negative, from Y to X or from X to Y) and magnitude (a relationship of magnitude zero indicating the absence of a relationship) of causal relationships. Change is typically measured with respect to one of two continua: chronological time (for historical change) or age (for developmental change). Sometimes, it is difficult to disentangle the two. If older individuals are less criminal than younger individuals, is this because crime declines with age, or is it possible that older individuals were always less criminal (even when they were younger) and younger individuals will remain more criminal (even as they get older), or some combination of the two? With cross-sectional data, it is not possible to disentangle the effects of history and development. Even with longitudinal data, it may be difficult, but with data on the same individuals both at different ages and different time periods, it at least becomes possible.

There are several different types of longitudinal designs (Menard, 2002), as illustrated in Figure 1. In each part of Figure 1, the columns represent years, and the rows represent subjects, grouped by time of entry into the study. Thus, subjects enter the population or sample ("rows") at different times ("columns"), and subjects who have entered the study at different times may be in the study at the same time (more than one row outlined in the same column), except in the *repeated cross-sectional design,* in which different subjects are studied at each different time (no two rows outlined in the same column).

In a *total population design,* we attempt to collect data on the entire population at different time periods. An example of a total population design would be the Federal Bureau of Investigation's (annual) *Uniform Crime Report* data on arrests and crimes known to the police. Although coverage is not, in fact, 100% complete (the same is true for the decennial census), the intent is to include data on the entire U.S. population. From year to year, individuals enter the population (by birth) and exit the population (by death), so the individuals to whom the data refer overlap substantially but differ somewhat from one period to the next and may differ substantially over a long time span (e.g., from 1950 to the present). FBI data are used to measure aggregate rates of change or trends in arrests and crimes known to the police. The same design structure is present in the *Panel Study of Income Dynamics* (Hill, 1992), which is not a total population design but in which individuals may exit the sample by death or enter the sample by birth or marriage.

Repeated cross-sectional designs collect data on different samples in different periods. Because a new sample is drawn each year, there is in principle no overlap from one year to the next (although it is possible that independent samples will sample a few of

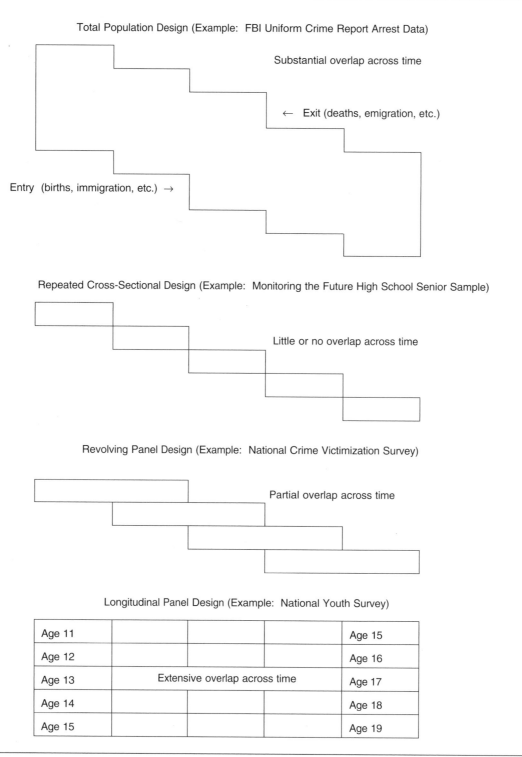

Total Population Design (Example: FBI Uniform Crime Report Arrest Data)

Substantial overlap across time

← Exit (deaths, emigration, etc.)

Entry (births, immigration, etc.) →

Repeated Cross-Sectional Design (Example: Monitoring the Future High School Senior Sample)

Little or no overlap across time

Revolving Panel Design (Example: National Crime Victimization Survey)

Partial overlap across time

Longitudinal Panel Design (Example: National Youth Survey)

Age 11				Age 15
Age 12				Age 16
Age 13	Extensive overlap across time			Age 17
Age 14				Age 18
Age 15				Age 19

Figure 1   Types of Longitudinal Designs

SOURCE: Adapted from Menard (2002).

the same individuals). A good example of a repeated cross-sectional design is the General Social Survey, an annual general population survey conducted by the National Opinion Research Center, which covers a wide range of topics (including marriage and family, sexual behavior and sex roles, labor force participation, education, income, religion, politics, crime and violence, health, and personal happiness) and emphasizes exact REPLICA-TION of questions to permit comparisons across time to measure aggregate-level change (Davis & Smith, 1992).

Revolving panel designs are designs in which a set of respondents is selected, interviewed for more than one time period, then replaced by a new set of respondents. The revolving PANEL design is used in the National Crime Victimization Survey (NCVS; Bureau of Justice Statistics annual). Households are selected and interviewed seven times over a 3-year period: once at the beginning, once at the end, and at 6-month intervals between entry and exit. At the end of the 3-year period, a new household is selected to replace the old household. Replacement is staggered, so every 6 months, approximately one sixth of the households in the NCVS are replaced. It is important to note that the NCVS has historically been a sample of households, not individuals; whenever an individual or a family moved from a household, interviews were conducted not with the original respondents but with the (new) occupants of the original household. Because each household is replaced after 3 years, only short-term longitudinal data are available for individuals. At the national level, however, the NCVS is one of the most widely used sources of data on aggregate changes over time in rates of crime victimization and, by implication, the rate at which those offenses included in the NCVS (limited to offenses with identifiable victims) are committed.

The *longitudinal panel design* is the design most generally recognized in different disciplines as a true longitudinal design. An example of the longitudinal panel design is the National Youth Survey (NYS) (see, e.g., Menard & Elliott, 1990). The NYS first collected data on self-reported illegal behavior, including substance use, *in* 1977 but *for* the preceding year, 1976. It then collected data at 1-year intervals, for 1977 to 1980, and thereafter at 3-year intervals, for 1983 to 1992, and (as this is being written) additional data are being collected on the original respondents and their families in 2003. Unlike all of the types of longitudinal research discussed so far, there is no entry into the sample after the first year. The respondents interviewed in the most recent year were a subset of the respondents interviewed in the first year: Some of the original respondents were not interviewed because of death, refusal to participate, or failure to locate the respondent. In contrast to the General Social Survey, FBI, and NCVS data, the NYS is used less to examine aggregate historical trends in crime than to examine intraindividual developmental trends, and causal relationships to test theories of crime. In this latter context, the NYS has been used to study the time ordering of the onset of different offenses and predictors of offending and to construct cross-time CAUSAL MODELS that can only be tested using longitudinal data (Menard & Elliott, 1990).

POTENTIAL PROBLEMS IN LONGITUDINAL RESEARCH

Longitudinal research potentially has all of the problems of cross-sectional research with respect to internal and external measurement validity; measurement RELI-ABILITY; SAMPLING ERROR; refusal to participate or NONRESPONSE to particular items; the appropriateness of questions to the population being studied; effects of interactions between subjects or respondents and interviewers, experimenters, or observers; relevance of the research; and research costs. Some of these issues are even more problematic for longitudinal research than for cross-sectional research. For example, biases in sampling may be amplified by repetition in repeated cross-sectional designs, and costs are typically higher for a multiple-year longitudinal study than for a single-year cross-sectional study. There are also additional dangers. As already noted, respondent recall failure may result in underreporting of illegal behavior if long recall periods are used. Respondents who are repeatedly interviewed may learn that giving certain answers results in follow-up questions and may deliberately or unconsciously avoid the burden imposed by those questions, a problem known as panel conditioning. Relatedly, the potential problem of interaction between the respondent or subject and an experimenter, interviewer, or observer producing invalid responses may be exacerbated when there is repeated contact between the experimenter, interviewer, or observer and the respondent or subject in a prospective longitudinal design. In later waves of a prospective panel study, respondents may have died or become incapable of participating because of age or illness or may refuse to continue their participation, or researchers may have difficulty locating respondents, resulting in panel attrition. In retrospective research, the corresponding problem is that individuals who should have been included to ensure a more REPRESENTATIVE SAMPLE may have died or otherwise become unavailable before the study begins. Particularly in prospective longitudinal sample SURVEY research, an important question is whether attrition is so systematic or so great that the results of the study can no longer be generalized to the original population on which the sample was based.

Measurement used at the beginning of a longitudinal study may come to be regarded as obsolete later in the study, but changing the measurement instrument means that the data are no longer comparable from one time to the next. An example of this is the change in the way questions were asked in the NCVS in 1992. The new format produced a substantial increase in reported victimizations. A comparison was made between the rates of victimization reported using the old and the new method but only in a single year. Thus, it remains uncertain whether attempts to "adjust" the victimization rates to produce a closer correspondence between the old and the new methods are really successful, especially for examining long-term trends in victimization. In developmental research, a parallel problem is the inclusion of age-appropriate measures for the same concept (e.g., prosocial bonding) across the life course. For example, in adolescence, bonding may occur primarily in the contexts of family of orientation (parents and siblings) and school, but in adulthood, it may occur more in the contexts of family of procreation (spouse and children) and work. One is then faced with the dilemma of asking age-inappropriate questions or of using different measures whose comparability cannot be guaranteed for different stages of the life course.

In cross-sectional research, we may have MISSING DATA because an individual refuses to participate in the research (missing subjects) or because the individual chooses not to provide all of the data requested (missing values). In longitudinal research, we have the additional possibility that an individual may agree to participate in the research and provide the requested data at one or more periods but may refuse or may not be found at one or more other periods (missing occasions). Some techniques for analyzing longitudinal data are highly sensitive to patterns of missing data and cannot handle series of unequal lengths, thus requiring dropping all cases with missing data on even a single variable on just one occasion. Problems of missing data may be addressed in longitudinal research either by imputation of missing data (replacing the missing data by an educated guess, based on other data and the relationships among different variables in the study, sometimes including imputation of missing occasions)

or by using techniques that allow the use of partially missing data in the analysis (Bijleveld & van der Kamp, 1998, pp. 43–44).

LONGITUDINAL DATA ANALYSIS

Longitudinal research permits us to use dynamic models, models in which a change in one variable is explained as a result of change in one or more other variables. Although we often phrase statements about causal relationships as though we were analyzing change, with cross-sectional data, we are really examining how *differences* among individuals in one variable can be explained in terms of *differences* among those same individuals in one or more predictors. It has been relatively commonplace to draw conclusions about *intraindividual change,* or change within an individual respondent, from findings about *interindividual differences,* or differences between different respondents. Under certain conditions, it is possible to estimate dynamic models using cross-sectional data, but those conditions are restrictive and relatively rare in social science research (Schoenberg, 1977). It is generally more appropriate to use longitudinal data and to analyze the data using statistical techniques that take advantage of the longitudinal nature of the data. Longitudinal data analysis techniques, as described in Bijleveld and van der Kamp (1998), Menard (2002), and Taris (2000), include TIME-SERIES analysis for describing and analyzing change when there are a large number of time periods (e.g., changes in imprisonment rates as a function of changes in economic conditions), latent GROWTH CURVE MODELS and HIERARCHICAL LINEAR MODELS for describing and analyzing both short- and long-term change within individual subjects or cases and relationships among changes in different variables (e.g., changes in violent criminal offending as a function of changes in illicit drug use), and EVENT HISTORY ANALYSIS to analyze influences on the timing of qualitative changes (e.g., timing of the onset of illicit drug use as a function of academic performance).

Cross-sectional research cannot disentangle developmental and historical trends, and the description and analysis of historical change require the use of longitudinal data. The description and analysis of developmental trends can be attempted using cross-sectional data, but the results will not necessarily be consistent with results based on longitudinal data. Testing for the time ordering or sequencing of purported causes and effects in developmental data can only be done with longitudinal data. Although there are cross-sectional methods for modeling patterns of mutual causation, more powerful models that allow the researcher to examine such relationships in more detail, including the explicit incorporation of the time ordering of cause and effect, require longitudinal data. Briefly, no analyses can be performed with cross-sectional data that cannot (by analyzing a single cross section) be performed with longitudinal data, but there *are* analyses that can be performed only with longitudinal, not cross-sectional, data. Cross-sectional data remain useful for describing conditions at a particular period, but increasingly in the social sciences, longitudinal data are recognized as best for research on causal relationships and patterns of historical and developmental change.

—Scott Menard

REFERENCES

Bijleveld, C. C. J. H., & van der Kamp, L. J.Th. (with Mooijaart, A., van der Kloot, W. A., van der Leeden, R., & van der Burg, E.). (1998). *Longitudinal data analysis: Designs, models, and methods.* London: Sage.

Davis, J. A., & Smith, T. W. (1992). *The NORC General Social Survey: A user's guide.* Newbury Park, CA: Sage.

Hill, M. S. (1992). *The panel study of income dynamics: A user's guide.* Newbury Park, CA: Sage.

Menard, S. (2002). *Longitudinal research.* Thousand Oaks, CA: Sage.

Menard, S., & Elliott, D. S. (1990). Longitudinal and cross-sectional data collection and analysis in the study of crime and delinquency. *Justice Quarterly, 7,* 11–55.

Schoenberg, R. (1977). Dynamic models and cross-sectional data: The consequences of dynamic misspecification. *Social Science Research, 6,* 133–144.

Taris, T. W. (2000). *A primer in longitudinal data analysis.* London: Sage.

LOWESS. *See* LOCAL REGRESSION

M

MACRO

Aggregate-level analysis is macro; individual-level analysis is micro. Thus, a political scientist may study elections at the macro level (e.g., presidential election outcomes for the nation as a whole) or at the micro level (e.g., presidential vote choice of the individual voter). Furthermore, an economist may study macroeconomic indicators, such as the country's gross domestic product, or the microeconomy of supply and demand for a particular product, say, automobiles. Finally, it should be noted that *macro* is the name applied to a computer program subroutine, as in SAS macros.

—Michael S. Lewis-Beck

MAIL QUESTIONNAIRE

Mailing QUESTIONNAIRES to PROBABILITY SAMPLES can be a cost-effective method to collect information when addresses are available for the POPULATION of interest (e.g., individuals or establishments). Single-mode surveys can be designed that employ mail questionnaires only, or these self-administered questionnaires may be part of a mixed-mode approach that includes other modes of administration (e.g., telephone, Web-based, or in-person INTERVIEWS). A frequently employed dual-mode design is to call sample members who have not returned mailed questionnaires to attempt interviews by telephone. Multimode designs can help reduce NONRESPONSE and often increase the representativeness of the resulting sample.

The SAMPLING FRAME for any RESEARCH DESIGN that includes a mail component can be a set of addresses, such as a list of employees of a firm or members of a professional organization. Note that the lists of addresses in telephone books cannot be relied on for sampling for population studies. The representativeness of samples drawn from telephone listings is compromised by unlisted numbers and households that either have no telephone service or rely solely on cell phones.

To identify members of rare populations for a mail SURVEY, one might use RANDOM-DIGIT DIALING (RDD) techniques. When a household is identified in which a member of the population of interest lives, the interviewer requests the address and a questionnaire can be mailed. Although the advantage of using RDD is that every household with a telephone has a known chance of selection, many people are unwilling to divulge their addresses to strangers who call on the telephone.

Respondent selection can be another challenge with mailed questionnaires (e.g., in situations when addresses, but not names, are known or when parents are required to randomly select one of their children to report on). There are techniques available for designating a respondent or subject (in the case of PROXY REPORTING), but these designs must be carefully planned, and the quality of the resultant sample depends on respondent compliance with sampling instructions.

Researchers have a toolbox of methods to use to develop survey instruments to collect data that can be used to adequately address their research questions. Instrument development often begins with a literature review to identify existing instruments that address the issues at hand. It continues with FOCUS GROUPS conducted in the population(s) of interest to identify salient issues and the terminology that people use to talk about these topics. Candidate survey items are drafted about these domains of interest, and cognitive interviews, intensive one-on-ones with individuals from the target population, are conducted. The goal of these interviews is to identify survey questions and terminology that are not consistently understood. The instrument can then be revised and retested prior to fielding the survey. Instruments also often undergo expert review prior to launching the survey. Here, authorities in the field of interest are asked to propose domains and comment on the suitability of the planned instrument. The last step before fielding a mail questionnaire is a PRETEST. Individuals with characteristics that mirror the target population can be brought together for group pretests. First, participants complete the questionnaire, and then they are debriefed about their experiences with navigating the instrument and any difficulties they may have encountered in answering the questions. Group pretests also allow an estimation of how long it will take respondents to fill out the form.

Characteristics of the target population must be taken into consideration, both when deciding whether to use a mail questionnaire and in the design of mailed instruments. To minimize respondent burden, it is always important to consider the length and reading level of instruments. Instrument length and readability are especially key in mail surveys that include members of more vulnerable populations (e.g., those with poor reading or writing skills, people who are vision impaired, or those who may tire easily because of poor health).

With mailed questionnaires, there is no interviewer present to motivate respondents or to answer their questions. These instruments should be designed to make it easy for people to respond to questions and to successfully navigate skip patterns. CLOSED-ENDED questions that can be answered by simply checking a box or filling in a circle (for data entry using optical scanning techniques) are preferable to open-ended items, for which obtaining adequate answers and standardized CODING of responses can be problematic.

There are certain advantages to the use of mailed questionnaires, including better estimates of sensitive topics. People are more willing to report socially undesirable behaviors (e.g., substance abuse or violence) when there is no interviewer present. Another advantage is the reduced cost of data collection relative to telephone and face-to-face administration. Mailing questionnaires can also be a successful approach to getting survey instruments past gatekeepers and into the hands of sample members, who may find the topic of study salient enough to warrant the investment of time necessary to respond. In addition, because respondents are not required to keep all response choices in memory while formulating their answers, mail administration allows longer lists of response choices than telephone.

The field period for a mail study is generally about eight weeks. Although there are a number of acceptable PROTOCOLS, standard mail survey research often includes three contacts by mail. First, a questionnaire packet is mailed that generally includes a cover letter outlining research goals and sponsors, the survey instrument, and a postage-paid envelope in which to return the completed questionnaire. This mailing is followed in about a week by a postcard reminder/thank you to all sample members. Around 2 to 3 weeks after the initial mailing, a replacement questionnaire packet is sent to all nonrespondents. Response rates are a function of the quality of the contact information available. Imprinting outgoing envelopes with a request for address corrections will yield updated addresses for some sample members who have moved.

The use of systematic quality control measures is key to successful data collection. Sample members should be assigned identification numbers to be affixed to questionnaire booklets to track response. Survey data are then entered, either manually or using optical scanning, to allow statistical analysis.

—Patricia M. Gallagher

REFERENCES

Dillman, D. A. (2000). *Mail and Internet surveys: The tailored design method.* New York: John Wiley.

Fowler, F. J., Jr. (2002). *Survey research methods* (3rd ed.). Thousand Oaks, CA: Sage.

Schwarz, N. A., & Sudman, S. (Eds.). (1996). *Answering questions.* San Francisco: Jossey-Bass.

MAIN EFFECT

The term *main effect* typically is used with reference to FACTORIAL DESIGNS in ANALYSIS OF VARIANCE. Consider a factorial design in which the levels of one factor, A, are crossed with the levels of another factor, B, as follows in Table 1.

Table 1

		Factor B			Marginal Mean
		Level B_1	Level B_2	Level B_3	
Factor A	Level A1	M_{A1B1}	M_{A1B2}	M_{A1B3}	M_{A1}
	Level A2	M_{A2B1}	M_{A2B2}	M_{A2B3}	M_{A2}
	Marginal mean	M_{B1}	M_{B2}	M_{B2}	

The entries in each cell are means and the marginal entries are means for a given level of a factor collapsing across the levels of the other factor. For example, M_{A1} is the mean for Level 1 of Factor A collapsing across the levels of Factor B.

Informally, the term *main effect* refers to properties of the marginal means for a factor. Researchers use the term in different ways. Some will state that "there is a main effect of Factor A," which implies that the marginal means for the factor are not all equal to one another in a POPULATION, a conclusion that is based on the results of a formal statistical test. Others simply refer to the "means comprising the main effect of Factor A," drawing attention to the marginal means but without any implication as to their equality or the results of a statistical test that is applied to them.

There are different methods for calculating marginal means. One method uses unweighted means, whereby the marginal mean is the average of each cell mean that is being collapsed across. For example, M_{A1} is defined as $(M_{A1B1} + M_{A1B2} + M_{A1B3})/3$. A second method is based on weighted means, whereby each of the individual cell means that factor into the computation of the marginal mean is weighted in proportion to the SAMPLE size on which it is based. Means based on larger sample sizes have more weight in determining the marginal mean.

The term *main effect* also is used in LINEAR REGRESSION models. A "main effect" model is one that does not include any INTERACTION terms. For example, a "main effect" MULTIPLE REGRESSION model is

$$Y = a + b_1 X + b_2 Z + e,$$

whereas an "interaction model" is

$$Y = a + b_1 X + b_2 Z + b_3 XZ + e.$$

The presence of the product term in the second equation makes this an interaction model. In regression contexts, a main effect refers to any continuous PREDICTOR in a REGRESSION model that is not part of a product

term or an interaction term. A main effect also refers to any dummy variable or set of DUMMY VARIABLES that is not part of a product term or interaction term. In the following model of all continuous predictors,

$$Y = a + b_1 X + b_2 Z + b_3 XZ + b_4 Q + e.$$

The coefficient for Q might be referred to as representing a "main effect" of Q, but the coefficients for X, Z, and XZ would not be so characterized.

—James J. Jaccard

MANAGEMENT RESEARCH

The academic discipline of management evolved rapidly in the 1960s within the United States and in the 1980s in most other parts of the world and is consequently a relative newcomer to the pantheon of the social sciences. In the early days, it drew very heavily on related disciplines such as economics, sociology, anthropology, statistics, and mathematics. But more recently, there has been a growing appreciation that these related disciplines are inadequate in themselves for handling the complex theoretical and practical problems posed in the management domain.

Three distinctive features of management research imply a need both to adapt traditional social science methods and to identify new ways of conducting research. First, there is a marked difference between the practice of management and the academic theories about management. The former draws eclectically on ideas and methods to tackle specific problems; the latter adopts distinct disciplinary frameworks to examine aspects of management. The adoption of disciplines, ranging from highly quantitative subjects such as finance, economics, and operations research to highly qualitative subjects such as organization behavior and human resource development, makes it hard to achieve consensus on what constitutes high-quality research. It has also led to a sustained debate about the relative merits of adopting monodisciplinary or transdisciplinary perspectives (Kelemen & Bansal, 2002; Tranfield & Starkey, 1998).

The second issue concerns the stakeholders of management research because managers, the presumed objects of study, will normally have the power to control ACCESS and may also be in a position to provide or withdraw financial sponsorship from the researcher.

This means that management research can rarely divorce itself from political and ethical considerations; it also means that specific methods have to be adapted to meet the constraints of managerial agendas (Easterby-Smith, Thorpe, & Lowe, 2002). Thus, for example, it is rarely possible to adopt the emergent or THEORETICAL SAMPLING strategies recommended by the proponents of GROUNDED THEORY because managers may insist on prior negotiation of interview schedules and will severely restrict access due to the opportunity costs of having researchers taking up the time of employees. Hence, the canons of grounded theory have to be adapted in most cases (Locke, 2000).

Third, the practice of management requires both thought and action. Not only do most managers feel that research should lead to practical consequence, but they are also quite capable of taking action themselves in the light of research results. Thus, research methods either need to incorporate with them the potential for taking actions, or they need to take account of the practical consequences that may ensue with or without the guidance of the researcher. At the extreme, this has led to a separation between pure researchers who try to remain detached from their objects of study and ACTION RESEARCHERS or consultants who create change to learn from the experiences. This has also led to the development of a range of methods such as participative inquiry (Reason & Bradbury, 2000) and Mode 2 research (Huff, 2000), which have considerable potential for research into management.

Of course, these three features are widely encountered across the social sciences, but it is their simultaneous combination that is driving the methodological adaptations and creativity encountered in some management research. In some cases, this has resulted in the adaptation and stretching of existing methods; in other cases, it is leading to the evolution of new methods and procedures. Furthermore, these evolving methods are likely to have a greater impact on the social sciences in general due to the sheer scale of the academic community in the field of management and business. At the time of this writing, roughly one third of all social scientists in the United Kingdom work within business schools. No doubt things have progressed even further in the United States.

—Mark Easterby-Smith

REFERENCES

Easterby-Smith, M., Thorpe, R., & Lowe, A. (2002). *Management research: An introduction* (2nd ed.). London: Sage.

Huff, A. S. (2000). Changes in organizational knowledge production. *Academy of Management Review, 25*(2), 288–293.

Keleman, M., & Bansal, P. (2002). The conventions of management research and their relevance to management practice. *British Journal of Management, 13,* 97–108.

Locke, K. D. (2000). *Using grounded theory in management research.* London: Sage.

Reason, P., & Bradbury, H. (2000). *Handbook of action research: Participative inquiry and practice.* London: Sage.

Tranfield, D., & Starkey, K. (1998). The nature, organization and promotion of management research: Towards policy. *British Journal of Management, 9,* 341–353.

MANCOVA. *See* MULTIVARIATE ANALYSIS OF COVARIANCE

MANN-WHITNEY *U* TEST

This is a frequently used test to determine whether two independent groups belong to the same population. It is considered to be one of the most powerful NONPARAMETRIC TESTS available and it is appropriate for data that is at least ordinal. Two groups developed what is essentially the same test, the *Mann-Whitney U-test* and the *Wilcoxon rank-sum test,* thus references in the literature tend to refer to them as one test, the Wilcoxon-Mann-Whitney test. The actual calculations may vary from one reference to another, but the same end is achieved. It is also of use as an alternative to the *T*-TEST when its assumptions of normality and homogeneity of variance cannot be met (Siegel and Castellan, 1988). When the sample sizes are small, it is necessary to have special tables, or depend on a computer-based statistical package to tell what the probability is.

The test is based upon the rank order of the data and is asking whether the two underlying population distributions the same. This is resolved by determining whether the sum of the ranks of one sample is sufficiently different from the overall mean of the ranks of both of the groups to indicate that it is not part of a common POPULATION. The SAMPLING DISTRIBUTION again says that any sample from a population will have a sum of ranks close to the population mean but not necessarily identical. The distribution of the sum of ranks for "large" samples is assumed to be normal with a population MEAN defined as

$$\mu = \frac{1}{2}n_1(n_1 + n_2 + 1)$$

and a standard error of the mean found by

$$SEM = \sqrt{\frac{n_1 n_2 (n_1 + n_2 + 1)}{12}}.$$

Some texts suggest that large can be 10 or more in each group; others will maintain a minimum of 25. In any case, the following approximation is more accurate the larger the sample. It is not difficult to see that the test is based upon the z-TEST,

$$z = \frac{\bar{x} - \mu}{SEM},$$

which, when using the sum of the ranks, W_1, for one of the groups as the sample mean, becomes, using the Wilcoxon approach,

$$z = \frac{W_1 - 1/2 n_1 (n_1 + n_2 + 1)}{\sqrt{\frac{n_1 n_2 (n_1 + n_2 + 1)}{12}}}$$

where

$W_1 =$ the sum of the ranks for one of the two groups,

$n_1 =$ the sample size of one group (≥ 10),

$n_2 =$ the sample size of the other group (≥ 10).

Thus, to carry out the test on sample data, the first task is to arrange all the raw data in rank order and use the order as the data. This will require that when "ties" in scores occur, the subjects having identical scores be assigned equivalent ranks. The z-score is then checked against the appropriate point in the table for the choice of α.

For example, the data in Table 1 shows scores on a Spanish language vocabulary test for two groups after two weeks, each learning the same material by different approaches. The groups were formed by randomly assigning students from a second year class. Group A learned by teacher lead discussions in class with visual aids, and Group B learned by computer based exercises, working on their own. In this case, the score distributions were highly skewed, thus the second column for each set of raw data reflects the ranks for the whole set (both groups combined).

The question is, do they still belong to the same population, allowing for natural variation? The ranks are then added for each group and one of them becomes W_1, as shown. The calculation of z then becomes

$$z = \frac{W_1 - 1/2 n_1 (n_1 + n_2 + 1)}{\sqrt{\frac{n_1 n_2 (n_1 + n_2 + 1)}{12}}}$$

Table 1 Data From a Spanish-Language Test for Two Groups, With Columns Added to List Rank Order

Data A	Rank A	Data B	Rank B
86	2	92	1
78	5	85	3
75	8	80	4
73	10.5	77	6
73	10.5	76	7
72	12	74	9
70	14	71	13
68	16	69	15
64	17.5	64	17.5
60	20	61	19
55	22	57	21
50	25	52	23
46	26	51	24
$W =$	188.5		162.5
$n =$	13		13

NOTE: Tied ranks are the average of the sequential ranks.

$$z = \frac{188.5 - 1/2(13)(13 + 13 + 1)}{\sqrt{\frac{(13)(13)(13+13+1)}{12}}}$$

$$z = \frac{188.5 - 175.5}{\sqrt{380.25}} = \frac{13}{19.5} = 0.67$$

If α were chosen to be 0.05, the minimum value for z would be 1.96 for a significant difference. Therefore, this result indicates that the two groups are not significantly different in their distributions of ranks and would still seem to belong to the same population. In other words, at least for this exercise, there was no difference due to learning approach, assuming all other possible extraneous variables were controlled.

The equivalent Mann-Whitney approach calculates U_1, which is

$$U_1 = n_1 n_2 + \frac{n_1 (n_1 + 1)}{2} - W_1,$$

and then the calculation of z for U_1 (producing the same value as above) becomes

$$z = \frac{U_1 - (n_1 n_2 / 2)}{\sqrt{\frac{n_1 n_2 (n_1 + n_2 + 1)}{12}}}.$$

As Howell (2002) notes, the simple linear relationship results in the two differing only by a constant for any set of samples, making it easy to convert one to the other if the need arises.

—Thomas R. Black

REFERENCES

Black, T. R. (1999). Doing Quantitative Research in the Social Sciences: An Integrated Approach to Research Design, Measurement, and Statistics. London: Sage Publications.

Grimm, L. G. (1993). Statistical Applictions for the Behavioral Sciences. New York: John Wiley & Sons.

Howell, D. C. (2002). *Statistical Methods for Psychology.* (5th ed) Pacific Grove. CA: Duxbury.

Siegel, S., and Castellan, N. J. (1988). *Nonparametric Statistics for the Behavioral Sciences.* New York: McGraw-Hill.

MANOVA. *See* MULTIVARIATE ANALYSIS OF VARIANCE

MARGINAL EFFECTS

In REGRESSION analysis, data analysts are oftentimes interested in interpreting and measuring the effects of INDEPENDENT (or explanatory) VARIABLES on the DEPENDENT (or response) VARIABLE. One way to measure the effects of independent variables is to compute their *marginal effects*. The marginal effect of an independent variable measures the impact of change in an independent variable (e.g., X_i) on the expected change in the dependent variable (e.g., Y) in a regression model, especially when the change in the independent variable is infinitely small or merely marginal.

The marginal effect of an independent variable X on the dependent variable Y can be computed by taking the partial derivative of $E(Y|X)$ with respect to X if the independent variable is *continuous* and thus differentiable. Consider a linear regression model with two independent variables,

$$Y_i = \beta_0 + \beta_1 X_{1i} + \beta_2 X_{2i} + \varepsilon_i,$$

where Y_i is the value of the dependent variable for the ith observation, X_{1i} is the value of the continuous independent variable, X_{2i} is the value of a dichotomous variable that equals either 0 or 1, βs are regression coefficients, and ε_i is the error term, which is assumed to be distributed independently with zero mean and constant variance σ^2. Given the assumption of the classical regression model, the conditional mean of the dependent variable Y is simply $E(Y|X) = \beta_0 + \beta_1 X_{1i} + \beta_2 X_{2i}$. Thus, the marginal effect of X_1 on the expected change in Y in this linear regression model

can be computed by obtaining the partial derivative with respect to X_1, that is,

$$\frac{\partial E(Y|X, \beta)}{\partial X_1} = \frac{\partial(\beta_0 + \beta_1 X_1 + \beta_2 X_2)}{\partial X_1} = \beta_1. \quad (1)$$

The marginal effect of X_2, however, cannot be computed by taking the partial derivative because X_2 is a dichotomous variable and not differentiable. Greene (2002) and Long (1997) suggest using the *discrete change* in $E(Y|X, \beta)$ as the dichotomous variable (in this case, X_2) changes from 0 to 1, holding all other variables constant (usually at their mean) to interpret the marginal effect of a dichotomous independent variable. Symbolically, that is,

$$\frac{\Delta E(Y|X, \beta)}{\Delta X_2} = (\beta_0 + \beta_1 X_1 + \beta_2 \times 1)$$
$$- (\beta_0 + \beta_1 X_1 + \beta_2 \times 0) = \beta_2. \quad (2)$$

From equations (1) and (2), we know that the marginal effect of an independent variable in a linear regression model is simply equal to the parameter β. Thus, interpretation of parameter estimates ($\hat{\beta}_1$ and $\hat{\beta}_2$, in this case) might be described as follows: Holding all other variables constant, a unit increase in X_1 led to, on average, about a $\hat{\beta}$ increase (or decrease, depending on the sign of $\hat{\beta}$) in the dependent variable Y. Note that a unit change for a dichotomous variable is equal to the variable's range because it only takes on value of 0 or 1. Thus, interpretation of regression on DUMMY VARIABLES might be described as follows: Holding all other variables constant, having the attribute of X_1 (as opposed to not having the attribute) led to, on average, an increase (or decrease) of $\hat{\beta}$ in Y.

Interpretation of marginal effects of independent variables in NONLINEAR regression models is far more complicated because the effect of a unit change in an independent variable depends on the values of *all* independent variables and *all* of the model parameters. As a result, in almost no case is the reported coefficient equal to a marginal effect in nonlinear models such as logit, probit, multinomial logit, ordered probit and logit, and event count models.

Consider a binary choice model such as a logit or a probit model,

$$\Pr(Y = 1|\mathbf{X}) = F(\mathbf{X}\boldsymbol{\beta}),$$

in which the link function F is the cumulative distribution for the NORMAL DISTRIBUTION or for the logistic distribution. In either case, the marginal effect of an independent variable is the expected change in the probability due to change in that independent variable. This can also be computed by taking the partial derivative if the data are differentiable. For example, the marginal effect of the kth independent variable (X_k) is given by

$$\frac{\partial \Pr(Y = 1 | \mathbf{X}, \boldsymbol{\beta})}{\partial X_k} = \frac{\partial F(\mathbf{X}\boldsymbol{\beta})}{\partial X_k} = f(\mathbf{XB})\beta_k, \quad (3)$$

where f is either the probability density function for the standard normal distribution or for the logistic distribution, $\mathbf{X}$ is the matrix of values of independent variables for all observations, and $\boldsymbol{\beta}$ is the vector of parameters. Because $f(\mathbf{X}\boldsymbol{\beta})$, which is also known as the scale factor, is nonnegative by definition, equation (3) shows that the direction (or sign) of the marginal effect of X_k is completely determined by β_k. However, the magnitude of its marginal effect is jointly determined by both the values of β_k and $f(\mathbf{X}\boldsymbol{\beta})$. Thus, interpretation of a marginal effect in nonlinear models needs to further consider the nature of the dependent variable (e.g., continuous, dichotomous, ordinal, or nominal), the problem being analyzed, and the probability distribution chosen by a researcher. For more information on the issue regarding marginal effects, one can refer to Long (1997), Greene (2002), and Sobel (1995).

—Cheng-Lung Wang

REFERENCES

Greene, W. H. (2002). *Econometric analysis* (5th ed.). New York: Prentice Hall.

Long, J. S. (1997). *Regression models for categorical and limited dependent variables.* Thousand Oaks, CA: Sage.

Sobel, M. E. (1995). Causal inference in the social and behavioral sciences. In G. Arminger, C. C. Clogg, & M. E. Sobel (Eds.), *Handbook of statistical modeling for the social and behavioral sciences* (pp. 1–38). New York: Plenum.

MARGINAL HOMOGENEITY

Marginal homogeneity is a class of models that equates some of the marginal distributions of a multidimensional contingency table. For a $R \times R$ table, univariate marginal homogeneity is satisfied if the cell probabilities π_{ij} satisfy

$$\sum_j \pi_{ij} = \sum_j \pi_{ji} \quad \text{for all } i.$$

For a $R \times R \times R$ table, bivariate marginal homogeneity is satisfied if the cell probabilities π_{ijk} satisfy

$$\sum_k \pi_{ijk} = \sum_k \pi_{ikj} = \sum_k \pi_{kij} \quad \text{for all pairs } (i, j).$$

—Marcel A. Croon

MARGINAL MODEL

Statistical models that impose constraints on some (or all) marginal distributions of a set of variables as well as, eventually, on their joint distribution are called marginal models. In a multinormal distribution, modeling the marginal distributions does not create special problems because the first- and second-order moments of any marginal distribution are equal to their counterparts in the joint distribution. For CATEGORICAL variables, such a one-to-one correspondence between the parameters of the joint and the marginal distributions does not exist in general, and one has to resort to specially developed procedures for analyzing data by means of marginal models.

Table 1 contains data for a response variable Y that is measured at three time points.

Table 1   Observed Frequency Distribution

	$Y_3 = 1$		$Y_3 = 2$	
	$Y_2 = 1$	$Y_2 = 2$	$Y_2 = 1$	$Y_2 = 2$
$Y_1 = 1$	121	11	41	44
$Y_1 = 2$	4	2	1	12

SOURCE: Data from the National Youth Survey from the Inter-University Consortium for Political and Social Research (ICPS), University of Michigan.

The data reported here were collected on 236 boys and girls who were repeatedly interviewed on their marijuana use. Here we use the data collected in 1976 (Y_1), 1978 (Y_2), and 1980 (Y_3) with responses coded as 1 = never used marijuana before and 2 = used marijuana before.

The corresponding joint probability distribution of Y_1, Y_2, and Y_3 will be represented by $\pi_{123}(y_1, y_2, y_3)$; the bivariate marginal distribution of Y_1 and Y_2 is then given by

$$\pi_{12}(y_1, y_2) = \sum_{y_3} \pi_{123}(y_1, y_2, y_3)$$

and the univariate marginal distribution of Y_1 by

$$\pi_1(y_1) = \sum_{y_2} \sum_{y_3} \pi_{123}(y_1, y_2, y_3).$$

Other marginal distributions can be defined similarly.

The hypothesis that Y_3 and Y_1 are independent given Y_2 imposes constraints on the joint distribution of the three variables, and these can be tested by fitting the LOG-LINEAR MODEL $[Y_1 Y_2, Y_1 Y_3]$ in the original three-dimensional contingency table. If a model only imposes constraints on the joint distribution, it is not a marginal model.

However, instead of formulating hypotheses about the structure of the entire table, one could be interested in hypotheses that state that some features of the marginal distributions of the response variable do not change over time. The hypothesis of univariate marginal homogeneity states that the univariate marginal distribution of Y is the same at the three time points:

$$\pi_1(y) = \pi_2(y) = \pi_3(y) \quad \text{for all } y.$$

In our example, the corresponding observed univariate marginal response distributions are presented in Table 2.

Table 2   Univariate Marginals

	Y_1	Y_2	Y_3
1	217	167	138
2	19	69	98
	236	236	236

For these data, the hypothesis that all three distributions arise from the same probability distribution has to be rejected with $L^2 = 82.0425$ and $df = 2$ ($p < .001$). Hence, in this panel study, there is clear evidence for a significant increase in marijuana use over time. Note that this hypothesis cannot be tested by the conventional CHI-SQUARE TEST for independence because the three distributions are not based on independent samples.

Alternatively, one could be interested in the hypothesis that some of the bivariate marginal distributions are identical, such as

$$\pi_{12}(y_1, y_2) = \pi_{23}(y_1, y_2)$$
$$\text{for all pairs of scores } (y_1, y_2).$$

The corresponding observed bivariate distributions for (Y_1, Y_2) and (Y_2, Y_3) are, respectively, given by Tables 3 and 4.

The hypothesis that both bivariate marginal distributions derive from the same bivariate probability

Table 3   Bivariate Marginal for (Y_1, Y_2)

	$Y_2 = 1$	$Y_2 = 2$
$Y_1 = 1$	162	55
$Y_1 = 2$	5	14

Table 4   Bivariate Marginal for (Y_2, Y_3).

	$Y_3 = 1$	$Y_3 = 2$
$Y_2 = 1$	125	42
$Y_2 = 2$	13	56

distribution is also rejected because $L^2 = 86.0024$ with $df = 4$ ($p < .001$).

A less restrictive hypothesis would equate corresponding association parameters from each bivariate distribution. The assumption of equality of corresponding local ODDS RATIOS in the bivariate marginals π_{12} and π_{23} leads to constraints of the following type:

$$\frac{\pi_{12}(y_1, y_2)\pi_{12}(y_1 + 1, y_2 + 1)}{\pi_{12}(y_1 + 1, y_2)\pi_{12}(y_1, y_2 + 1)}$$
$$= \frac{\pi_{23}(y_1, y_2)\pi_{23}(y_1 + 1, y_2 + 1)}{\pi_{23}(y_1 + 1, y_2)\pi_{23}(y_1, y_2 + 1)}$$
$$\text{for all pairs of scores } (y_1, y_2).$$

In a 2×2 table, there is only one odds ratio to consider. For the present data, it is equal to 8.247 in the marginal (Y_1, Y_2) table and to 12.8205 in the marginal (Y_2, Y_3) table. The hypothesis that both odds ratios are equal cannot be rejected now because $L^2 = 0.4561$ with $df = 1$ ($p = .499$). The estimate of the constant odds ratio in both marginal tables is 11.3463. This result indicates that a strong positive and constant association exists between responses that are contiguous in time. For variables with more than two response categories, alternative marginal models can be formulated that equate corresponding adjacent, cumulative, or global odds ratios.

Finally, one can also impose constraints on conditional distributions defined in terms of the marginals. For example, the hypothesis that the conditional distribution of Y_2 given Y_1 is equal to the conditional distribution of Y_3 given Y_2 leads to the following constraints:

$$\frac{\pi_{12}(y_1, y_2)}{\pi_1(y_1)} = \frac{\pi_{23}(y_1, y_2)}{\pi_2(y_1)}$$
$$\text{for all pairs of scores } (y_1, y_2).$$

For the present data, we have

$$\Pr(Y_2 = 2 | Y_1 = 1) = 0.2535,$$
$$\Pr(Y_2 = 2 | Y_1 = 2) = 0.7368,$$
$$\Pr(Y_3 = 2 | Y_2 = 1) = 0.2515, \text{ and}$$
$$\Pr(Y_3 = 2 | Y_2 = 2) = 0.8116.$$

The hypothesis that corresponding TRANSITION RATES are constant over time could not be rejected with $L^2 = 0.5016$ for $df = 2$ ($p = .778$). The estimates of these constant transition probabilities were the following:

$$\Pr(Y_{t+1} = 2 | Y_t = 1) = 0.2529, \text{ and}$$
$$\Pr(Y_{t+1} = 2 | Y_t = 2) = 0.7959.$$

These results indicate that about 80% of the users at a particular time point continue to do so at the next time point, whereas in the same period, about 25% of the nonusers become users.

Estimating the parameters under a marginal model and testing whether the model provides an acceptable fit to the data both require specifically developed methods. In many cases, the ensuing marginal model can be formulated as a generalized log-linear model for which appropriate estimation and testing procedures have been developed. These procedures perform MAXIMUM LIKELIHOOD ESTIMATION of the probabilities in the joint distribution under the constraints imposed on the joint and the marginal distributions and allow conditional and unconditional tests for the assumed model.

—Marcel A. Croon

REFERENCES

Bergsma, W. (1997). *Marginal models for categorical data.* Tilburg, The Netherlands: Tilburg University Press.

Croon, M. A., Bergsma, W., & Hagenaars, J. A. (2000). Analyzing change in categorical variables by generalized log-linear models. *Sociological Methods & Research, 29,* 195–229.

Vermunt, J. K., Rodrigo, M. F., & Ato-Garcia, M. (2001). Modeling joint and marginal distributions in the analysis of categorical panel data. *Sociological Methods & Research, 30,* 170–196.

MARGINALS

Marginals or marginal distributions are obtained by collapsing a multivariate joint distribution over one or more of its variables. If X, Y, and Z are three discrete random variables with probability distribution $\pi_{XYZ}(x, y, z)$, the marginal distribution of X and Y is given by

$$\pi_{XY}(x, y) = \sum_z \pi_{XYZ}(x, y, z).$$

The marginal distribution of X is given by

$$\pi_X(x) = \sum_y \sum_z \pi_{XYZ}(x, y, z).$$

For continuous variables, summing over a variable is replaced by integrating over it.

—Marcel A. Croon

MARKOV CHAIN

A Markov chain describes one's probability to change state. The focus is on the probability to change state in a discrete period of time, for instance, from political party A to another political preference. It is a process without memory: The probability to be in a state at the present measurement occasion only depends on one's state at the last previous occasion. States at earlier occasions have no additional predictive value. Once we observe a cross-table of two subsequent occasions, we can estimate the transition probability for all combinations in the state space: the probability of A given state A, $\tau_{A|A}$; the probability of other, O, given A, $\tau_{O|A}$; and so on, $\tau_{A|O}$ and $\tau_{O|O}$. Generalization to more states is straightforward.

The Markov chain is due to the Russian mathematician Andrei A. Markov. Interestingly, the Markov chain allows prediction of the distribution over states in the future. With the data example of Table 1, it is easily verified that Party A, starting with 67%, has lost 5% support after 1 year. In the end, this Markov chain will reach an equilibrium, with party A having the preference of 58% of the population, irrespective of the original distribution over states. This can be computed by matrix multiplication of the matrix with transition probabilities, T, with T itself and the result again with T and so on, until all rows of the resulting matrix are the same.

The fit of a Markov chain can be tested if it is applied to PANEL data on three or more occasions. When doing so, the Markov chain predicts too much long-term change in most social science applications. Blumen, Kogan, and McCarthy (1968) therefore postulated a mixture of two sorts of people: Some people change

Table 1   Change of State in Political Preferences

Original State	One Year Later; Frequencies		One Year Later; Transition Probabilities		7-Year Transition Probabilities Assuming a Markov Chain	
	Party A	*Other*	*Party A*	*Other*	*Party A*	*Other*
Party A	750	250	0.75	0.25	0.58	0.42
Other	175	325	0.35	0.65	0.58	0.42

state, and others do not. With a panel observed at three or more occasions, the proportions of "movers" and "stayers" can be estimated.

A pitfall in the analysis of change is that measurement error can blur the outcomes. If independent between occasions, such error will inflate the observed change, unless it is incorporated in a model. The LATENT MARKOV MODEL, also known as the hidden Markov model, allows erroneous responses. Each answer in the state space can occur, but its probability depends on the state one is in. People may have a high probability to answer correctly, and lower probabilities may hold for erroneous responses. This model can be estimated from a panel observed at three or more occasions.

Both approaches can be combined, for instance, assuming that part of the population behaves according to a latent Markov chain and another part consists of stayers. For accurate estimation of such a mixed, partially latent Markov model, it is better to have multiple indicators at each occasion.

A complication arises if people tend to return to states they were previously in, for instance, unemployment in labor market status research. Then previous state membership can be modeled as an exogenous variable, influencing the probability to become unemployed.

Finally, transition probabilities in discrete time are in fact the result of more basic flow parameters in continuous time—TRANSITION RATES or HAZARD RATES—that apply in an infinitesimally small period of time.

—Frank van de Pol and Rolf Langeheine

REFERENCES

Blumen, I., Kogan, M., & McCarthy, P. J. (1968). Probability models for mobility. In P. F. Lazarsfeld & N. W. Henry (Eds.), *Readings in mathematical social science* (pp. 318–334). Cambridge: MIT Press.

Langeheine, R., & van de Pol, F. (1990). A unifying framework for Markov modeling in discrete space and discrete time. *Sociological Methods & Research, 18,* 416–441.

Vermunt, J. K., Rodrigo, M. F., & Ato-Garcia, M. (2001). Modeling joint and marginal distributions in the analysis of categorical panel data. *Sociological Methods & Research, 30,* 170–196.

MARKOV CHAIN MONTE CARLO METHODS

Markov chain Monte Carlo (MCMC) methods are SIMULATION techniques that can be used to obtain a random sample approximately from a probability distribution p by constructing a MARKOV CHAIN whose stationary distribution is p and running the Markov chain for a large number of iterations. One of the most popular application areas of MCMC methods is BAYESIAN INFERENCE. Here MCMC methods make it possible to numerically calculate summaries of Bayesian POSTERIOR DISTRIBUTIONS that would not be possible to calculate analytically.

In many applications, researchers find it useful to be able to sample from an arbitrary probability distribution p. This is particularly the case when one wishes to calculate a numerical approximation to some integral, as is commonly the case in Bayesian inference and, to a lesser extent, likelihood inference. In situations when p is a member of a known family of distributions, it is sometimes possible to use standard pseudo-random number generation techniques to produce an independent stream of pseudo-random deviates directly from p. However, in many practical applications, p is not a member of a known family of distributions and cannot be sampled from directly using standard methods. Nonetheless, MCMC methods can be used in such situations and, in general, are relatively easy to implement.

MCMC methods work not by generating an independent sample directly from p but rather by constructing a sequence of dependent draws from a particular stochastic process whose long-run equilibrium distribution is p. By constructing a long enough sequence of such draws, we can think of the later draws as being approximately from p. More specifically, MCMC methods provide recipes for constructing Markov chains whose equilibrium (or stationary) distribution is the distribution p of interest.

A number of complications arise because the sequence of MCMC draws is not an independent sequence of draws taken directly from p. One complication concerns the number of initial so-called *burn-in* iterations to discard. The idea here is that because the MCMC draws are only approximately from p after running the Markov chain for a long period of time, the initial MCMC draws are not likely to be representative of draws from p and so should be discarded. Another complication involves the determination of how long the Markov chain should be run to obtain a sample that is sufficiently close to a direct sample from p for the application at hand. These issues are discussed at some length in standard reference texts such as Robert and Casella (1999).

Two basic types of MCMC algorithms are commonly used by researchers (although it should be noted that one is actually a special case of the other). The first is what is known as the Metropolis-Hastings algorithm. The second is a type of Metropolis-Hasting algorithm referred to as the GIBBS SAMPLING algorithm.

THE METROPOLIS-HASTINGS ALGORITHM

The Metropolis-Hastings algorithm is a very general MCMC algorithm that can be used to sample from probability distributions that are only known up to a normalizing constant. The Metropolis-Hastings algorithm works by generating candidate values from a candidate-generating density that is easily simulated from and then probabilistically accepts or rejects these candidate values in such a way as to produce a sample approximately from the distribution p of interest.

Suppose we want to draw a random sample from $p(\theta)$ where θ may be multidimensional. The Metropolis-Hastings algorithm is shown in Figure 1.

```
initialize  θ⁽⁰⁾
for (i in 1 to m){
   generate  θ⁽ⁱ⁾_can  from  q(θ|θ⁽ⁱ⁻¹⁾)
   calculate  α ←  f(θ⁽ⁱ⁾_can) q(θ⁽ⁱ⁻¹⁾|θ⁽ⁱ⁾_can)
                   ─────────────────────────
                   f(θ⁽ⁱ⁻¹⁾) q(θ⁽ⁱ⁾_can|θ⁽ⁱ⁻¹⁾)
   set  θ⁽ⁱ⁾ ←  { θ⁽ⁱ⁾_can  with probability min{1,α}
               { θ⁽ⁱ⁻¹⁾  with probability 1 − min{1,α}
   store  θ⁽ⁱ⁾
}
```

Figure 1

where $f(\theta)$ is some function proportional to $p(\theta)$, and $q(\theta|\theta^{(i-1)})$ is the candidate-generating density. Note that the candidate-generating density depends on the current value of $\theta^{(i-1)}$. In situations when the candidate-generating density is symmetric—that is, $q(\theta|\theta^{(i-1)})$ is equal to $q(\theta^{(i-1)}|\theta)$—then these terms cancel in the formula for the acceptance probability α.

THE GIBBS SAMPLING ALGORITHM

The Gibbs sampling algorithm is a special case of the Metropolis-Hastings algorithm in which the acceptance probability is always equal to 1. The Gibbs sampling algorithm generates a sample approximately from some joint distribution p by iteratively sampling from the conditional distributions that make up p.

To see how the Gibbs sampling algorithm works, suppose we have a joint distribution $p(\theta_1, \ldots, \theta_k)$, where it is possible to break the arguments of p into k distinct blocks. Let $p_1(\theta_1|\theta_2, \ldots, \theta_k)$ denote the conditional distribution of θ_1 given the remaining $k-1$ blocks, with similar notation for the other $k-1$ full conditional distributions. The Gibbs sampling algorithm works as shown in Figure 2.

```
initialize  θ⁽⁰⁾₂,...,θ⁽⁰⁾_k
for (i in 1 to m){
   generate  θ⁽ⁱ⁾₁  from  p₁(θ₁|θ⁽ⁱ⁻¹⁾₂,...,θ⁽ⁱ⁻¹⁾_k)
   generate  θ⁽ⁱ⁾₂  from  p₂(θ₂|θ⁽ⁱ⁾₁,θ⁽ⁱ⁻¹⁾₃...,θ⁽ⁱ⁻¹⁾_k)
   .
   .
   .
   generate  θ⁽ⁱ⁾_k  from  p_k(θ_k|θ⁽ⁱ⁾₁,...,θ⁽ⁱ⁾_{k-1})
   store  θ⁽ⁱ⁾₁,...,θ⁽ⁱ⁾_k
}
```

Figure 2

HISTORICAL DEVELOPMENT

MCMC methods have their origins in statistical physics. Metropolis, Rosenbluth, Rosenbluth, Teller, and Teller (1953) proposed what is now known as the Metropolis algorithm to perform the numerical integrations needed to explore certain properties of physical systems. The Metropolis algorithm was generalized by Hastings (1970) to work with nonsymmetric candidate-generating densities. Geman and Geman (1984) introduced what is now referred to as the Gibbs sampling algorithm within the context of image restoration problems. Despite these (and several other) earlier works, statisticians did not fully embrace the potential of MCMC methods until the work of Gelfand and Smith (1990), which showed how MCMC techniques could be used to perform Bayesian inference for models that, up to that point, were regarded as computationally infeasible.

EXAMPLE: SAMPLING FROM A BAYESIAN POSTERIOR DISTRIBUTION

Consider the Bayesian treatment of the simple LOGISTIC REGRESSION MODEL. Suppose we have n observations, and the value of the dependent variable for observation i (y_i) is coded as either a 1 or 0. Assuming one's prior belief about the coefficient vector β is that it follows a normal distribution with mean b_0 and variance-covariance matrix B_0, the posterior density of β is (up to a constant of proportionality) given by

$$p(\beta|y) \propto \prod_{i=1}^{n} \left(\frac{\exp(x_i'\beta)}{1 + \exp(x_i'\beta)} \right)^{y_i}$$
$$\times \left(1 - \frac{\exp(x_i'\beta)}{1 + \exp(x_i'\beta)} \right)^{1-y_i}$$
$$\times \exp\left(-\frac{(\beta - b_0)'B_0^{-1}(\beta - b_0)}{2} \right).$$

To summarize this posterior density, we may want to calculate such quantities as the posterior mean of β and the posterior variance of β. Suppose we want to use the posterior mean of β (defined as $E[\beta|y] = \int \beta p(\beta|y)\, d\beta$) as a Bayesian point estimate. Doing the integration necessary to calculate the posterior mean is a nontrivial matter, even for such a simple model. Another approach to calculating the posterior mean of β is to use an MCMC algorithm to take a large random sample $\beta^{(1)}, \ldots, \beta^{(m)}$ of size m approximately from $p(\beta|y)$ and to estimate the posterior mean of β as

$$\hat{E}[\beta|y] = \frac{1}{m} \sum_{i=1}^{m} \beta^{(i)}.$$

The following Metropolis algorithm in Figure 3 does just that.

```
initialize β⁽⁰⁾
for (i in 1 to m){
   generate β_can⁽ⁱ⁾ ← β⁽ⁱ⁻¹⁾ + z⁽ⁱ⁾
   calculate  α ← f(β_can⁽ⁱ⁾ | y) / f(β⁽ⁱ⁻¹⁾ | y)
   set  β⁽ⁱ⁾ ← { β_can⁽ⁱ⁾ with probability min{1,α}
                 β⁽ⁱ⁻¹⁾ with probability 1 − min{1,α}
   store  β⁽ⁱ⁾
}
calculate  β̄ ← (1/m) Σ_{i=1}^{m} β⁽ⁱ⁾
```

Figure 3

where $z^{(i)}$ is a realization of a zero mean multivariate normal random variable with a fixed variance-covariance matrix drawn at iteration i, and $f(\beta|y)$ is any function that is proportional to $p(\beta|y)$. Note that, in practice, one would discard the first several hundred to several thousand samples of β as burn-in iterations to eliminate sensitivity to the starting value of β.

—Kevin M. Quinn

REFERENCES

Gelfand, A. E., & Smith, A. F. M. (1990). Sampling based approaches to calculating marginal densities. *Journal of the American Statistical Association, 85,* 398–409.

Geman, S., & Geman, D. (1984). Stochastic relaxation, Gibbs distributions, and the Bayesian restoration of images. *IEEE Transactions on Pattern Analysis and Machine Intelligence, 6,* 721–741.

Hastings, W. K. (1970). Monte Carlo sampling methods using Markov chains. *Biometrika, 57,* 97–109.

Metropolis, N., Rosenbluth, A. W., Rosenbluth, M. N., Teller, A. H., & Teller, E. (1953). Equation of state calculation by fast computing machines. *Journal of Chemical Physics, 21,* 1087–1092.

Robert, C. P., & Casella, G. (1999). *Monte Carlo statistical methods.* New York: Springer.

MATCHING

Matching refers to creating sets of TREATMENT and CONTROL units based on their similarity on one or more covariates. In randomized experiments, matching reduces error variance, thus increasing STATISTICAL POWER. In nonrandomized experiments, matching increases similarity of treatment and control groups. Matching in nonrandomized experiments does not equate groups as well as randomization, but it can reduce bias.

Variations of matching include the following. *Matched-pairs* designs match a single control unit to a single treatment unit, yielding equal numbers of units per group. *Matched-sets* designs match one or more treatment units with one or more control units. Groups can be matched on a single variable (*uni-variate* matching) or several variables (MULTIVARIATE matching). *Exact* matching pairs treatment and control units that have the same value on the COVARIATE(S); however, finding an exact match for all units may be difficult. Exact multivariate matching is made easier by collapsing the matching variables into a single variable called a *propensity score*—the predicted probability of treatment or control group membership from a LOGISTIC REGRESSION. *Distance* matching matches pairs or sets of units to minimize the overall difference between control and treatment groups. Variations of exact and distance matching include full matching, optimal matching, and greedy matching (Shadish, Cook, & Campbell, 2002).

Examples of matching include the following: (a) Bergner (1974), who rank ordered 20 couples on pretest scores on a couple communication measure and then randomly assigned one couple from each pair to treatment or control conditions; (b) Cicerelli and Associates (1969), who compared children enrolled in Head Start to eligible but not enrolled children of the same gender, ethnicity, and kindergarten education; and (c) Dehejia and Wahba (1999), who used propensity score matching of those receiving labor training with controls drawn from a national survey. Matching in nonrandomized experiments can cause significant problems if not done carefully (Shadish et al., 2002).

—William R. Shadish and M. H. Clark

REFERENCES

Bergner, R. M. (1974). The development and evaluation of a training videotape for the resolution of marital conflict. *Dissertation Abstracts International, 34,* 3485B. (UMI No. 73-32510)

Campbell, D. T., & Kenny, D. A. (1999). *A primer on regression artifacts.* New York: Guilford.

Cicerelli, V. G., & Associates. (1969). *The impact of Head Start: An evaluation of the effects of Head Start on children's cognitive and affective development* (2 vols.). Athens: Ohio University and Westinghouse Learning Corp.

Dehejia, R. H., & Wahba, S. (1999). Causal effects in nonexperimental studies: Reevaluating the evaluation of training programs. *Journal of the American Statistical Association, 94,* 1053–1062.

Rosenbaum, P. R. (1998). Multivariate matching methods. *Encyclopedia of Statistical Sciences, 2,* 435–438.

Shadish, W. R., Cook, T. D., & Campbell, D. T. (2002). *Experimental and quasi-experimental designs for general causal inference.* Boston: Houghton Mifflin.

MATRIX

A *matrix* can be defined as a rectangular array of real numbers or elements arranged in *rows* and *columns.* The *dimension* or *order* of a matrix is determined by its numbers of rows and columns. For example, **A** is said to be an *m* by *n* (denoted as $m \times n$) matrix because it contains $m \times n$ real numbers or elements arranged in *m* rows and *n* columns, as in

$$
\mathbf{A} = \begin{bmatrix} a_{11} & a_{12} & \cdots & a_{1n} \\ a_{21} & a_{22} & \cdots & a_{2n} \\ \vdots & \vdots & a_{ij} & \vdots \\ a_{m1} & a_{m2} & \cdots & a_{mn} \end{bmatrix},
$$

where a_{ij} ($i = 1, 2, \ldots, m$; $j = 1, 2, \ldots, n$) is an *element* of matrix **A**.

Note that the first subscript for an element of a matrix—that is, a_{ij}—is the index for row and the second subscript for column, counting from the upper left corner. For example, a_{ij} is the value of the element in the *i*th row and the *j*th column. If a matrix **B** is one in which $a_{ij} = a_{ji}$ for all *i* and *j*, then **B** is called a *symmetric matrix.* For example,

$$
\mathbf{B} = \begin{bmatrix} 1 & 4 & 7 \\ 4 & 6 & 5 \\ 7 & 5 & 9 \end{bmatrix}.
$$

An $m \times 1$ matrix is called a *column vector* because it only has one column. Likewise, a $1 \times n$ matrix is called a *row vector* because it only has one row. A 1×1 matrix is simply a number and usually called a *scalar.*

A matrix that has an equal number of rows and columns is called a *square matrix.* For example, the symmetric matrix **B** illustrated above is a 3×3 square matrix. The sum of the diagonal elements of a square matrix is called the *trace* of the square matrix. For example, *trace*(B) = 16. Several particular types of matrices are frequently used in statistical and ECONOMETRIC analysis.

• A *diagonal matrix* is a square matrix such that each element that does not lie in the main (or principal) diagonal (i.e., from the upper left corner to the lower right corner) is equal to zero. That is, $a_{ij} = 0$ if $i \neq j$. For example, **C** is an $m \times m$ diagonal matrix,

$$\mathbf{C} = \begin{bmatrix} a_{11} & 0 & \cdots & 0 \\ 0 & a_{22} & \cdots & 0 \\ \vdots & \vdots & \ddots & 0 \\ 0 & 0 & 0 & a_{mm} \end{bmatrix}.$$

• An *identity matrix* or a *unit matrix* is a special diagonal matrix whose main diagonal elements are all equal to 1. It is usually denoted $\mathbf{I}_m$, where m is the dimension or order of this identity matrix. (Thus, *trace*($\mathbf{I}_m$) = m.) For example, $\mathbf{I}_3$ is an identity matrix,

$$\mathbf{I}_3 = \begin{bmatrix} 1 & 0 & 0 \\ 0 & 1 & 0 \\ 0 & 0 & 1 \end{bmatrix}.$$

• A *triangular matrix* is a particular square matrix that has only zeros either above or below the main diagonal. If the zeros are *above* the diagonal, the matrix is *lower triangular* because nonzero elements are below the diagonal. That is,

$$a_{ij} = \begin{cases} a_{ij}, & \text{for } i \geq j \\ 0, & \text{for } i < j \end{cases}.$$

For example, **D** is a lower triangular matrix,

$$\mathbf{D} = \begin{bmatrix} a_{11} & 0 & \cdots & 0 \\ a_{21} & a_{22} & \cdots & 0 \\ \vdots & \vdots & \ddots & 0 \\ a_{m1} & a_{m2} & \cdots & a_{mm} \end{bmatrix}.$$

In contrast, when the zeros are below the diagonal, the matrix is *upper triangular.*

• A diagonal matrix whose main diagonal elements are all equal is called a *scalar matrix*. For example, the variance-covariance matrix of a LINEAR REGRESSION error variable that follows all the assumptions of classical linear REGRESSION analysis is a scalar matrix given by

$$\mathbf{\Omega} = \begin{bmatrix} \sigma^2 & 0 & \cdots & 0 \\ 0 & \sigma^2 & \cdots & 0 \\ \vdots & \vdots & \ddots & 0 \\ 0 & 0 & \cdots & \sigma^2 \end{bmatrix}.$$

Each of these matrixes has its own properties that are often applied in STATISTICS and econometrics. For example, matrix operations and finding the *transpose* and *inverse* of a matrix are useful tools in statistical and econometric analysis. More information on these topics may be found in Namboodiri (1984) and Chiang (1984) for an elementary discussion and in Golub and Van Loan (1996) for an advanced discussion.

—Cheng-Lung Wang

REFERENCES

Chiang, A. C. (1984). *Fundamental methods of mathematical economics* (3rd ed.). New York: McGraw-Hill.

Golub, G. H., & Van Loan, G. F. (1996). *Matrix computations* (3rd ed.). Baltimore: Johns Hopkins University Press.

Namboodiri, K. (1984). *Matrix algebra: An introduction.* Beverly Hills, CA: Sage.

MATRIX ALGEBRA

Manipulation of matrices can be used to solve complex relationships between several variables over many observations. Although such manipulations are carried out by computer programs for relationships beyond the most simple ones, the three basic MATRIX operations are the same and can be easily demonstrated.

MATRIX ADDITION

The matrices $\mathbf{A} = \lfloor a_{ij} \rfloor$ and $\mathbf{B} = \lfloor b_{ij} \rfloor$ with equal order $m \times n$ may be added together to form the matrix $\mathbf{A} + \mathbf{B}$ of order $m \times n$ such that $\mathbf{A} + \mathbf{B} = \lfloor a_{ij} + b_{ij} \rfloor$. For example, if

$$\mathbf{A} = \begin{bmatrix} a & b \\ c & d \end{bmatrix}$$

and

$$\mathbf{B} = \begin{bmatrix} e & f \\ g & h \end{bmatrix},$$

then

$$\mathbf{A} + \mathbf{B} = \begin{bmatrix} a+e & b+f \\ c+g & d+h \end{bmatrix}.$$

The commutative and associative laws both hold for matrix addition.

MULTIPLICATION BY A NUMBER

If $\mathbf{A} = \lfloor a_{ij} \rfloor$ is a matrix and k is a number, then the matrix $k\mathbf{A} = \lfloor ka_{ij} \rfloor = \mathbf{A}k$. For example, if

$$\mathbf{A} = \begin{bmatrix} a & b \\ c & d \end{bmatrix},$$

then

$$k\mathbf{A} = \begin{bmatrix} ka & kb \\ kc & kd \end{bmatrix}.$$

Note that every element of the matrix is multiplied by the number (unlike multiplying a determinant by a number). Multiplication by a number is commutative.

MATRIX MULTIPLICATION

Two matrices can be multiplied only if they are conformable. To be conformable, the number of columns in the first matrix must equal the number of rows in the second. For the matrices $\mathbf{A} = [a_{ik}]$ with order $m \times p$ and $\mathbf{B} = [b_{kj}]$ with order $p \times n$, the matrix $\mathbf{A} \times \mathbf{B}$ of order $m \times n$ is

$$\mathbf{AB} = \left[\sum_{k=1}^{p} a_{ik}b_{kj} \right].$$

Because the matrices must be conformable, the order of multiplication makes a difference (i.e., matrix multiplication is not commutative). For the resulting matrix $\mathbf{AB}$, we say that $\mathbf{B}$ is premultiplied by $\mathbf{A}$ or that $\mathbf{A}$ is postmultiplied by $\mathbf{B}$. For the case when $m = p = n = 2$, we would have

$$\mathbf{A} = \begin{bmatrix} a_{11} & a_{12} \\ a_{21} & a_{22} \end{bmatrix},$$

$$\mathbf{B} = \begin{bmatrix} b_{11} & b_{12} \\ b_{21} & b_{22} \end{bmatrix},$$

and

$$\mathbf{AB} = \begin{bmatrix} a_{11}b_{11} + a_{12}b_{21} & a_{11}b_{12} + a_{12}b_{22} \\ a_{21}b_{11} + a_{22}b_{21} & a_{21}b_{12} + a_{22}b_{22} \end{bmatrix}.$$

Notice that each element of $\mathbf{AB}$ is the sum of the product of a particular element of $\mathbf{A}$ and a particular element of $\mathbf{B}$. Notice also that the inside number of each product pair is equal (because it is the k value) and that the numbers go from 1 to p (which equals 2 in this case) for each sum. For matrices of unequal size, the product matrices, $\mathbf{AB}$ and $\mathbf{BA}$, may be of a different order than either of the original matrices and may be of different order from each other. It is also possible that one or the other may simply not exist. For example, if $\mathbf{A}_{2 \times 4}$ and $\mathbf{B}_{4 \times 1}$, then $\mathbf{AB}_{2 \times 1}$, but $\mathbf{BA}$ would not exist because the columns in $\mathbf{B}$ do not equal the rows in $\mathbf{A}$. Note that even if $\mathbf{AB}$ and $\mathbf{BA}$ both exist and are of the same size, the two are not necessarily equal.

Following from these three operations, matrix subtraction is accomplished by multiplying the matrix to be subtracted by -1 and then adding the two matrices. Similarly, a form of matrix division requires finding the inverse of the intended divisor matrix and then multiplying that inverse with the second matrix. Calculating the inverse of a matrix involves a series of manipulations, and not all matrices have inverses. In particular, a matrix must be both square and nonsingular (i.e., a nonzero determinant) for it to have an inverse. Thus, if $\mathbf{A}$ is a square and nonsingular matrix, then its inverse, $\mathbf{A}^{-1}$, can be written as

$$\mathbf{A}^{-1} = \left(\frac{1}{|\mathbf{A}|} \right) \text{ adj } \mathbf{A},$$

where $|\mathbf{A}|$ is the determinant of $\mathbf{A}$, and adj $\mathbf{A}$ is the adjoint of $\mathbf{A}$.

An important use of matrix algebra is in the calculation of REGRESSION coefficients. For example, the simple linear regression model may be expressed in matrix terms as $\mathbf{Y} = \mathbf{X}\boldsymbol{\beta}$, where $\mathbf{Y}$ is the column vector of dependent variable values, $\mathbf{X}$ is the matrix of independent variable values, and $\boldsymbol{\beta}$ is the matrix of regression coefficients. Manipulation of the equation using matrix algebra results in the solution, $\boldsymbol{\beta} = \mathbf{X}^{-1}\mathbf{Y}$.

—Timothy M. Hagle

REFERENCES

Cullen, C. G. (1990). *Matrices and linear transformations* (2nd ed.). New York: Dover.

Pettofrezzo, A. J. (1978). *Matrices and transformations.* New York: Dover.

MATURATION EFFECT

The *maturation effect* is any biological or psychological process within an individual that systematically varies with the passage of time, independent of specific external events. Examples of the maturation effect include growing older, stronger, wiser, and more experienced. These examples involve long-lasting changes. The maturation effect also can be transitory as in the case of fatigue, boredom, warming up, and growing hungry.

Campbell and Stanley (1963), in their classic *Experimental and Quasi-Experimental Designs for Research,* identified the maturation effect as one of eight rival hypotheses that could compromise the INTERNAL VALIDITY of an experiment. *Internal validity* is concerned with correctly concluding that an independent variable and not some extraneous variable is responsible for a change in the dependent variable. Internal validity is the sine qua non of experiments.

The simplest EXPERIMENTAL DESIGN that enables a researcher to rule out maturation and some other extraneous variables as rival explanations for a change in the dependent variable is the posttest-only control group design. Following Campbell and Stanley (1963), the design can be diagrammed as follows:

$$
\begin{array}{ccc}
R & X & O \\
R &   & O
\end{array}
$$

The *R*s indicate that participants are randomly assigned to one of two conditions: a treatment condition, denoted by X, and a control condition, denoted by the absence of X. The control condition is administrated to the participants as if it is the treatment of interest. The *O*s denote an observation or measurement of the dependent variable. The order of the events is R followed by X or the control condition and then O. The vertical alignment of the *R*s indicates that the assignment of participants to the two groups occurs at the same time. Similarly, the vertical alignment of the *O*s indicates that the two groups are measured at the same time. RANDOM ASSIGNMENT is an essential feature of the design. It is used to achieve comparability of the participants in the two conditions prior to the administration of the independent variable. If the sample size is large and each participant has an equal chance of being assigned to a particular condition, a researcher can be reasonably confident that known as well as unsuspected extraneous variables are evenly distributed over the conditions. Hence, maturation effects are controlled in the sense that they should be manifested equally in the two groups. The data for this simple design are often analyzed with a t-statistic for independent samples.

The posttest-only control group design can be modified for experiments that have p conditions, where p is greater than 2. The modified design in which $X_1, X_2, \ldots, X_{p-1}$ denote treatment conditions and X_p denotes a control condition is as follows:

$$
\begin{array}{ccc}
R & X_1 & O \\
R & X_2 & O \\
\vdots & \vdots & \vdots \\
R & X_{p-1} & O \\
R & X_p & O
\end{array}
$$

The data for this experiment are usually analyzed using a completely randomized analysis of variance design.

—Roger E. Kirk

REFERENCE

Campbell, D. T., & Stanley, J. C. (1963). *Experimental and quasi-experimental designs for research.* Chicago: Rand McNally.

MAXIMUM LIKELIHOOD ESTIMATION

At the close of the 19th century, Karl Pearson showed that by understanding statistical DISTRIBUTIONS, researchers had a powerful tool for better understanding outcomes from EXPERIMENTS and observational studies. Pearson went one step further, showing that by understanding a small number of CONSTANTS governing statistical distributions—that is, PARAMETERS—we could understand everything about the distributions. So long as we knew the parameters governing some distribution, we did not need to "see" the entire distribution. At the close of the 19th century, the field of parametric statistics was born.

This, of course, was a powerful insight. The problem remained, however, as to precisely how the empirical information from these experiments and observational studies could be harnessed to learn something about those distributional parameters. Pearson's answer to that crucial question was based on collecting as many empirical observations as possible, hopefully from the entire POPULATION, and then calculating characteristics of the empirical distribution—for example, the MEAN, VARIANCE, SKEWNESS, and KURTOSIS. These calculated empirical moments were in turn used to map the empirical distribution on to some known theoretical distribution, typically one of the so-called Pearson-Type distributions (Stuart & Ord, 1987).

At about the same time, a young genius by the name of Ronald Aylmer Fisher—and, by all accounts, Pearson's intellectual superior and to whom Pearson is well known to have been less than accommodating and at times openly hostile (Salsburg, 2001)—proved that Pearson's solutions to the ESTIMATION question were significantly flawed. Fisher showed that Pearson's estimates were oftentimes inconsistent and most always inefficient. By this, Fisher meant that Pearson's estimates for the parameters in a probability distribution were oftentimes not likely to converge in probability to the true population parameter, no matter how much DATA were collected (i.e., they were inconsistent), and that they have more variability from SAMPLE to sample than other ways of obtaining estimates (i.e., they were inefficient).

To replace Pearson's flawed methods with more sound estimation procedures, Fisher centered his attention on the probability of observing the data under different estimates of a distribution's parameters. More precisely, he sought to obtain, under general conditions, the parameter estimate that maximized the probability of observing the data that were collected or, as it is often called, the data likelihood. Not only were these *maximum likelihood estimates* superior in that they in fact maximized the data likelihood, but *maximum likelihood estimators* were also shown to be consistent and efficient and, at a later point, asymptotically unbiased under very general conditions and for a wide range of models and distributions. At the beginning of the 20th century, the method of maximum likelihood was born.

To better understand this method, it is useful to consider some RANDOM VARIABLE on observation i. Denote this random variable as Y_i and the data observed by the researcher as y_i. Suppose we wish to estimate the parameters governing the distribution from which Y_i originates. To do so, we need to know or, as is often the case, assume the form of the distribution of Y_i. To keep things general for the moment, denote the known or assumed distribution of Y_i as $f(Y_i; \theta)$, where θ is either the sole parameter or the vector of parameters governing the distribution of Y_i. In the case where Y_i is

discrete, $f(Y_i; \theta)$ gives the probability that Y_i will take on a specific value y_i and is often called the *probability function*. In the case where Y_i is continuous, $f(Y_i; \theta)$ governs the probability of observing a range of possible values y_i and is often called the PROBABILITY DENSITY FUNCTION.

Let's now assume that N data points $y_1, \ldots, y_N$ are collected in some manner. Precisely how these data are collected (observational, experimental, etc.) is not so important so long as $y_1, \ldots, y_N$ are *independent and identically distributed*, or *iid*. That is, we need to assume, for the data-generating mechanism giving rise to data point y_i and some other data point—say, $y_{i'}$—that for all i and i', (a) observing y_i is independent of observing $y_{i'}$, and (b) the probability (density) functions $f(Y_i; \theta)$ and $f(Y_{i'}; \theta)$ are the same. Of course, there are more or less complex ways to accommodate deviations from these ASSUMPTIONS in maximum likelihood estimation. But for now, let's ignore these additional considerations.

Given the iid assumption, the joint probability (density) function for the data—known as the *data likelihood* or, as Fisher called it, the probability of the sample—is given by the product of the individual probability (density) functions:

$$L(y; \theta) = \prod_{i=1}^{N} f(y_i; \theta). \quad (1)$$

The core of the idea that Fisher hit upon was to find values for θ that maximize equation (1), the likelihood of the data. Because products of runs of numbers present computing difficulties (underflows for small numbers, overflows for large numbers, general loss of precision, etc.), it is common to maximize instead the natural log of the data likelihood, or the log-likelihood,

$$\log\{L(y; \theta)\} = \log\left\{\prod_{i=1}^{N} f(y_i; \theta)\right\}$$
$$= \sum_{i=1}^{N} \log\{f(y_i; \theta)\}, \quad (2)$$

as this gives the same solution as maximizing the FUNCTION in equation (1).

Aside from having the data, we must specify the form of $f(y_i; \theta)$ to find the value of θ that maximizes equations (1) and (2). This value is typically called the *maximum likelihood estimate* and is most often denoted as $\hat{\theta}$. There are many distributions that may be used. Useful continuous distributions include the NORMAL, log-normal, LOGISTIC, beta, exponential, and gamma distributions; useful discrete distributions include the BINOMIAL, MULTINOMIAL, NEGATIVE BINOMIAL, and POISSON. Most introductory probability and statistics textbooks give a sampling of important distributions researchers may wish to consider (see, e.g., Hogg & Tanis, 1988). Eliason (1993) also provides examples in this regard. An important consideration when choosing an appropriate distribution is to consider the form of the observed y_is in relation to the range allowed by a candidate distribution. For example, it may make little sense to choose a distribution where y_i is allowed to traverse the entire range of real numbers (as, for example, with the normal distribution) when the range of the observed data y_i is strictly positive (as, for example, with market wages) or is bounded between 0 and 1 (as, for example, with probabilities).

The normal distribution is by far the most commonly used distribution in the social sciences, either explicitly or, perhaps more often the case, implicitly. Moreover, it is common in didactic pieces such as these to assume a normal distribution and to then show that the maximum likelihood estimator for the mean of the distribution, often denoted μ, is the sample mean

$$\frac{1}{N} \sum_{i=1}^{N} y_i.$$

Although important, this is a well-known result, can be found in many sources, and, worst of all, can give an *incorrect* impression that these techniques must assume normality.

So, to make this more interesting and to show that all that is required is that we assume *some* distribution, let Y_i be distributed as a gamma random variable. The gamma distribution can take on many forms, although it is often considered in its chi-square-like form, that is, right-skewed with the distribution anchored on the left at zero. It is also the parent distribution to the exponential and the CHI-SQUARE. Perhaps more important from a social science perspective, the gamma distribution is interesting in that many reward and related distributions (e.g., wealth, wages, power, etc.) tend to follow a typical gamma distribution.

As considered in Eliason (1993), the two-parameter gamma distribution, with parameters $\mu = E\{Y_i\}$ (i.e., μ gives the expected mean value of Y_i) and

$\nu = E\{Y_i\}^2 / V\{Y_i\}$ (i.e., ν gives the ratio of the squared expected value over the variance of Y_i), is given by

$$f(y_i; \theta = [\mu, \nu]) = \left(\frac{1}{\Gamma\{\nu\}}\right)\left(\frac{\nu}{\mu}\right)^{\nu} y_i^{(\nu-1)} \exp\left\{\frac{-\nu y_i}{\mu}\right\}. \quad (3)$$

To find the maximum likelihood solution for the parameter that governs the central tendency of this distribution, μ, let's first take the natural log of the gamma density in equation (3),

$$\log\{f(y_i; \theta = [\mu, \nu])\} = -\log\Gamma\{\nu\} + \nu\log\{\nu/\mu\} + (\nu - 1)\log\{y_i\} - (\nu y_i/\mu). \quad (4)$$

The log-likelihood for the data is then given by the sum of these natural logs,

$$\log\{L(y_i; \theta = [\mu, \nu])\} = -N\log\Gamma\{\nu\} + \nu N\log\{\nu/\mu\} + (\nu - 1)\sum_{i=1}^{N}\log\{y_i\} - (\nu/\mu)\sum_{i=1}^{N} y_i. \quad (5)$$

The next step involves a working knowledge of first derivatives, as we need to calculate the first derivative of equation (5) with respect to the parameter of interest, μ, to solve for the maximum likelihood solution for μ. Although calculating first derivatives may be difficult, understanding first derivatives need not be. That is, a first derivative simply gives the rate of change of some function relative to something else. In this case, that function is the log-likelihood in equation (5), and the something else is the parameter μ, which is given by

$$\frac{\partial \log\{L(y_i; \theta = [\mu, \nu])\}}{\partial \mu} = \left(\frac{\nu}{\mu^2}\right)\sum_{i=1}^{N} y_i - \left(\frac{\nu}{\mu}\right)N. \quad (6)$$

From calculus, we know that when the first derivative (with respect to μ) equals zero, the corresponding value for μ is either at its maximum or minimum. In this case, we do have the maximum—to determine this requires a working knowledge of second derivatives and is thus beyond the scope of this entry. Therefore, the last step involves setting the derivative in equation (6) to zero and solving for μ:

$$\left(\frac{v}{\mu^2}\right)\sum_{i=1}^{N} y_i - \left(\frac{v}{\mu}\right)N$$

$$= 0 \Rightarrow \hat{\mu} = \sum_{i=1}^{N} y_i/N. \qquad (7)$$

That is, the maximum likelihood estimator for μ, $\hat{\mu}$, for the gamma log-likelihood in equation (5) is the sample mean.

Importantly, these techniques are very general. Instead of μ, we could have been interested in the maximum likelihood solution of v in the gamma, a component of the variance of the random variable Y_i. In addition, in the social sciences, we are often interested not only in the distributional parameters for some variable (say, e.g., the parameters governing the distributions of wages, prestige, or power) but in the way some other variables (say, e.g., attributes of individuals, jobs, markets, and institutions) come together to affect those parameters. This requires our attention to shift to an additional layer of the problem—to model specification and functional forms linking variables to parameters of interest.

To take an overly simplistic example, we may posit that attributes X_i (e.g., gender, race, age, degree attained, social class, etc.) of individuals embedded in labor market institutions with attributes Z_j (e.g., degree of labor market regulation, closed vs. open systems of jobs, degree of market concentration, unionization rate, etc.) interact to affect the distribution of wages. Note that here i indexes individuals, whereas j indexes markets. Recall that Pearson's breakthrough in the late 1800s showed us that the distribution of any variable is entirely governed by the parameters in that distribution. So, if we link our factors in an informative way (as expected by our theory of how individual and market attributes combine to affect wages) to the distributional parameters, we can show how these factors come together to affect the distribution as a whole.

Staying with the gamma distribution, we would thus link these factors to the parameters μ, which governs the central tendency of the wage distribution, and v, which governs the shape of the wage distribution. Given that both μ and v must be positive in the gamma distribution, the function linking these distributional parameters to the factors in X_i and Z_j must reflect

this. So, the simplest model adhering to that condition would result in a log-linear link with additive effects. That is,

$$\mu_{ij} = \exp\{\beta_0 + \beta_1 X_i + \beta_2 Z_j\}, \qquad (8)$$

and

$$v_{ij} = \exp\{\gamma_0 + \gamma_1 X_i + \gamma_2 Z_j\}, \qquad (9)$$

where β_1, β_2, γ_1, and γ_2 are all vectors of model parameters with dimensions to accommodate the dimensions in X_i and Z_j. Maximum likelihood estimates for the βs and γs would then contain the information as to how the individual and market factors in X_i and Z_j affect the wage distribution, given the model specification in equations (8) and (9).

To be consistent with the simple example of embeddedness given above, however, we would at least require an interaction that in part governs the distribution of wages. Thus, we would still have a log-linear link function, but now with an interaction term included:

$$\mu_{ij} = \exp\{\beta_0 + \beta_1 X_i + \beta_2 Z_j + \beta_3 X_i Z_j\}, \qquad (10)$$

$$v_{ij} = \exp\{\gamma_0 + \gamma_1 X_i + \gamma_2 Z_j + \gamma_3 X_i Z_j\}. \qquad (11)$$

In linking these factors in this way to the distributional parameters, the researcher can answer important questions regarding how individual and market attributes come together to affect the distribution of wages.

Although the models in equations (8) through (11) provide an additional layer of complexity, the basic ideas are not much different from those in the previous example in which we had no model. That is, given the data, we would (a) choose an appropriate probability (density) function for the outcome variable of interest, (b) create the functions linking the independent variables of interest to the parameters governing the probability (density) function for the outcome variable, and (c) maximize that log-likelihood to obtain the maximum likelihood estimates for the model parameters. Any statistical software, such as SAS's NLP procedure, that allows the user to write and maximize an arbitrary function may be used to obtain maximum likelihood estimates in this fashion. Once obtained, for the above example, these maximum likelihood estimates would provide the foundation for interpreting the effects of the individual and market attributes, as well as their interactions, on the distribution of wages.

The above represents the core ideas underlying the method of maximum likelihood as developed initially by R. A. Fisher. In current-day computer packages, many distributional and model parameters are estimated with maximum likelihood routines and algorithms, oftentimes behind the scenes and not obvious to the user of point-and-click statistical packages such as SPSS. Maximum likelihood is in fact the workhorse behind the estimation of many statistical models used in social science research, including STRUCTURAL EQUATION MODELS, LOGISTIC REGRESSION models, PROBIT regression models, TOBIT models, censored regression models, EVENT HISTORY models, LOG-LINEAR MODELS, GENERALIZED LINEAR MODELS, and so on. Thus, understanding the logic behind maximum likelihood methods gives one a powerful tool for understanding these many disparate models used by social scientists.

Finally, there are many useful sources to learn more about maximum likelihood estimation. Eliason (1993) provides an accessible introductory treatment to the logic and practice of this method. King (1989) also provides a wonderfully useful text. Gill's (2001) monograph shows how maximum likelihood undergirds much of the estimation of generalized linear models. In addition, Cramer's (1986) text provides useful insights into this method. For a more in-depth discussion, Stuart, Ord, and Arnold (1999) provide a highly useful volume detailing maximum likelihood methods in comparison to other estimation methods, such as Bayesian estimation techniques.

—Scott R. Eliason

REFERENCES

Cramer, J. S. (1986). *Econometric applications of maximum likelihood methods*. Cambridge, UK: Cambridge University Press.

Eliason, S. R. (1993). *Maximum likelihood estimation: Logic and practice*. Newbury Park, CA: Sage.

Gill, J. (2001). *Generalized linear models: A unified approach*. Thousand Oaks, CA: Sage.

Hogg, R. V., & Tanis, E. A. (1988). *Probability and statistical inference*. New York: Macmillan.

King, G. (1989). *Unifying political methodology: The likelihood theory of statistical inference*. New York: Cambridge University Press.

Salsburg, D. (2001). *The lady tasting tea: How statistics revolutionized science in the twentieth century*. New York: Holt.

Stuart, A., & Ord, K. (1987). *Kendall's advanced theory of statistics: Vol. 1. Distributional theory* (5th ed.). New York: Oxford University Press.

Stuart, A., Ord, K., & Arnold, S. (1999). *Kendall's advanced theory of statistics: Vol. 2A. Classical inference & the linear model* (6th ed.). New York: Oxford University Press.

MCA. *See* MULTIPLE CLASSIFICATION ANALYSIS

McNEMAR CHANGE TEST. *See* McNEMAR'S CHI-SQUARE TEST

McNEMAR'S CHI-SQUARE TEST

Also known as the McNemar change test, this is the nonparametric analogue to the *T*-TEST for related samples, for data that do not meet the requirements of that PARAMETRIC test. In particular, this test covers situations in which the dependent variable is NOMINAL data (i.e., frequencies for categories). This test is literally looking for a significant change in the category of subjects.

To illustrate, let us consider the psychology and sociology departments at Freedonia University. They decided to recruit students into a common first-year social sciences program, letting the students select their degree subject at the end of the year. There was some suspicion that the sociology department would benefit more than the psychology department from this process in terms of students changing their minds. The sociology department suggested that it be left to a trial year and that a check be made at the end of the year based on the number of students changing, presenting the psychology department with a test of their "faith" in statistics. At the beginning of the year, the departments randomly selected two groups of 24 students claiming a strong commitment to pursuing one degree or the other from those in the class of 250. At the end of the year, they compared this to what they selected for a department for the next year. The results are shown in Figure 1. Was the psychology department always going to lose out because it ended up with 16 students

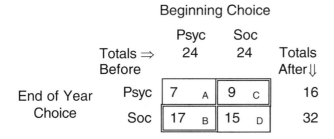

Figure 1   Before and After First-Year Course Choices for Degrees

and the sociology department with 32, or was this just a difference that was within the realm of random fluctuation?

This could be considered an example of a design that consists of pretest and posttest/observations on two groups using a dichotomous variable, in which each subject belongs to one of two alternative groups. The "treatment" here was seemingly the first-year course, although it could be said that it was the collective experience of learning what the two disciplines *and* teaching staff were really like.

The really important students to this test are the ones who changed their minds—the 9 in cell C who went from sociology to psychology and the 17 in cell B who went from psychology to sociology. Although one would expect some changes, if the first year exercised no differential effect on the students, one would expect as many going one way as the other. In other words, the expected change would have been

$$E = \frac{B + C}{2}.$$

Obviously, not every sample would produce exactly this number, so we resort to a statistical test to see what would be an acceptable variation from this. As this is a matter of categories, the chi-square test is appropriate. If we use B and C as the observed frequencies, these can be substituted into the following equation for the chi-square ratio:

$$\chi^2_{\text{ratio}} = \sum_{i=1}^{m} \frac{(O_i - E_i)^2}{E_i},$$

which would become

$$\chi^2_{\text{ratio}} = \frac{\left(B - \frac{B+C}{2}\right)^2}{\frac{B+C}{2}} + \frac{\left(C - \frac{B+C}{2}\right)^2}{\frac{B+C}{2}},$$

which reduces to

$$\chi^2_{\text{ratio}} = \frac{(B - C)^2}{B + C}, \quad df = 1 \text{ (McNemar change test)}.$$

Thus, for the example above,

$$\chi^2_{\text{ratio}} = \frac{(9 - 17)^2}{9 + 17} = \frac{64}{26} = 2.46.$$

Because $\chi^2(1, .05) = 3.84$, the result was considered nonsignificant; in other words, this was a chance occurrence. It was argued that this scheme would ultimately not influence the balance of the number of students changing their minds over a year.

—Thomas R. Black

REFERENCES

Black, T. R. (1999). *Doing quantitative research in the social sciences: An integrated approach to research design, measurement, and statistics.* London: Sage.

Howell, D. C. (2002). *Statistical methods for psychology* (5th ed.). Pacific Grove, CA: Duxbury.

Siegel, S., & Castellan, N. J. (1988). *Nonparametric statistics for the behavioral sciences.* New York: McGraw-Hill.

MEAN

The mean is one of the most commonly used ways of summarizing the values of a variable. The arithmetic mean is the sum of all the values of the variable divided by the number of observations—that is, $\sum x_i / n$, where x_i represents the ith value of the variable of interest, x, and n is the sample size. For example, Table 1 shows the incomes of a sample of 12 people. The sum of the incomes of the 12 people is $3,970 and, when divided by the n of 12, gives a mean of $331. The mean is commonly what is meant when people refer to the AVERAGE. The mean of x is often written as ξ and is used to represent the best estimate of x_i, to which improved estimates can be compared in, for example, ordinary least squares. The extent to which the mean effectively summarizes a distribution will depend on the levels of dispersion in the distribution and on the existence of a skewed distribution or of "outliers." For example, in the notional data in Table 1, Person F has an income ($944) that far exceeds the next highest income. If this outlying case is excluded, the mean falls to $275, which might be considered to be a value that is more typical of the incomes as a whole.

Table 1   Net Incomes of a Sample of 12 People

Person	Net Income ($ per week)
A	260
B	241
C	300
D	327
E	289
F	944
G	350
H	195
I	160
J	379
K	214
L	311
Total	3,970
Mean	331

Extreme values, over time, tend to move closer to the mean, as Galton first ascertained in his famous study of the relationship between fathers' and sons' heights (Galton, 1889). This is known as regression toward the mean and is the basis of regression analysis. The mean of a sample is, when combined with its CONFIDENCE INTERVALS, used to estimate the population mean for the given variable.

Less commonly used in the social sciences than the arithmetic mean are the geometric mean and the harmonic mean. The geometric mean is the nth root of the product of the data values, where n represents the number of cases. That is, it is given by

$$(x_1^* x_2^*, \ldots, x_n)^{1/n}.$$

Another way of thinking about this is that the log of the geometric mean is the arithmetic mean of the logs of the data values, or

$$\log G = 1/n \left(\sum \log x \right).$$

In the example in Table 1, therefore, $\log G$ is equal to 2.47, and the geometric mean is $296.5. The properties of the geometric mean make it more appropriate for measuring the mean in contexts in which the increase in values is itself geometrically related to the starting point. For example, geometric means are applied to price (or other sorts of) indexes, in which the prices are expressed as a ratio of the beginning of the series. Another example of an application can be found in estimating the size of a population between measurements at different time points by taking its mean. For example, the geometric mean of the populations from two consecutive decennial censuses would

provide an estimate of the population at the 5-year midpoint.

The harmonic mean, on the other hand, is used to summarize frequency data or data when results are grouped by outcome. The reciprocal of the harmonic mean is the arithmetic mean of the reciprocals of the data values. It is therefore given by

$$1/H = 1/n \sum 1/x \quad \text{or} \quad N \times 1 / \sum (1/x).$$

For example, if, in a study of 20 families, 7 had 1 child, 8 had 2 children, and 5 had 3 children, the harmonic mean of family size would be $1/(7 + 4 + 1.7)/20 = 1.6$ children. This is lower than the arithmetic mean, which would come to 1.9 children. In fact, the harmonic mean is always lower than the arithmetic mean. Because of the reciprocal nature of the calculation of the harmonic mean, it also represents the arithmetic mean when the relationship between the component frequencies is expressed in the reverse way. Thus, in this case, there is 1 family per child for 7 children, half a family per child for 8 children, and a third of a family per child for 5 children, which comes to .635 families per child or, standardizing per family, to 1.6 children per family. Thus, it can be used when one wishes to calculate the reciprocal arithmetic mean, for example, with means of prices when calculated via rates per dollar or via dollars for set quantities. How much lower it is than the arithmetic mean depends on the amount of dispersion and the size of the mean.

—Lucinda Platt

See also AVERAGE, CONFIDENCE INTERVALS, MEASURES OF CENTRAL TENDENCY

REFERENCES

Galton, F. (1889). *Natural inheritance.* London: Macmillan.

Stuart, A., & Ord, J. K. (1987). *Kendall's advanced theory of statistics: Vol. 1. Distribution theory* (5th ed.). London: Griffin.

Yule, G. U., & Kendall, M. G. (1950). *An introduction to the theory of statistics* (14th ed.). London: Griffin.

MEAN SQUARE ERROR

In REGRESSION, the mean square error is the total sum of squares minus the regression sum of squares, adjusted for the sample size (Norusis, 1990, p. B-75). The adjustment takes account of the DEGREES OF FREEDOM as well as sample size. The mean squared error is closely involved in the calculation of statistics measuring GOODNESS OF FIT, including the R^2 and the F statistic for regression.

The mean square error in regression relates to the mean squared variation for a single variable as follows. The mean squared variation is a unit-free measure of the dispersion of a continuous variable. The mean squared variation takes no account of skewness. The equation that defines the mean squared variation allows for sample size and for the deviations of each observation from the mean.

If we denote the mean by

$$\bar{X} = \frac{\sum_i X_i}{n}$$

and notice that $(n - 1)$ is the degrees of freedom for this statistic, then the mean squared variation can be written as follows (see SPSS, 2001):

$$\text{Mean squared variation} = \frac{\bar{X}}{n - 1} = \frac{\sum_i X_i}{n \cdot (n - 1)}.$$

By comparison, in multivariate regression, the mean squared variation is the total sum of squared variations (TSS) divided by n, the sample size. However, when an estimate of a regression line using p variables has been obtained, the mean squared variation can be broken up into two parts: the variation explained by the regression and the residual variation. The latter is commonly known as the mean squared error. Define terms as shown below.

$$\text{Total sum of squares} = \text{TSS} = \sum (Y_i - \bar{Y})^2.$$

The mean squared variation in total is $\frac{\text{TSS}}{n}$.

$$\text{Regression sum of squares} = \text{RSS} = \sum (\hat{Y} - \bar{Y})^2.$$

The residual error, denoted here as ESS, is the difference between TSS and RSS, as shown as follows:

$$\text{ESS} = \sum (Y_i - \hat{Y})^2.$$

Each sum of squares term is then divided by its degrees of freedom to get the corresponding mean squares term.

The mean square of regression, or mean sum of squares (MSS), is

$$\frac{\text{TSS}}{k}.$$

The mean squared error, MSE, is

$$\frac{\text{ESS}}{n - k - 1}.$$

The ratio of these two is the F statistic for regression (Hardy, 1993, p. 22).

$$F = \frac{\text{MSS}}{\text{MSE}} = \frac{\frac{\text{TSS}}{k}}{\frac{\text{ESS}}{n-k-1}} = \frac{\text{TSS}}{\text{ESS}} \cdot \frac{n - k - 1}{k}.$$

Thus, the mean square error is crucial for deciding on the significance of the R^2 in multiple regression. Mean squares generally, however, play a role in a range of statistical contexts.

In the ANALYSIS OF VARIANCE, or ANOVA, the total mean squares represent the variation in the dependent variable, whereas the mean squares explained by different combinations of the independent variables are compared relative to this starting point.

Thus, in general, mean squares give a unit-free measure of the dispersion of a dependent variable. By comparing the total squared deviation with the regression sum of squares and adjusting for sample size, we use mean squares to move toward summary indicators of goodness of fit. Inferences from these measures (i.e., from R^2, t-tests, and the F test) provide standard measures of the significance of inferences to the population.

It is important in regression analysis to adjust the resulting R^2 value; the ADJUSTED R^2 goes further in correcting the test statistic for the sample size. Its formula allows the estimator to be adjusted for the sample size, even beyond the corrections for degrees of freedom that give the mean squares of regression and the mean squared error.

Thus, although mean square error plays an important role in regression, further adjustments may be needed before inferences are drawn.

—Wendy K. Olsen

REFERENCES

Hardy, M. (1993). *Regression with dummy variables* (Quantitative Applications in the Social Sciences Series, No. 93). London: Sage.

Norusis, M. (1990). *SPSS/PC + Statistics 4.0*. Chicago: SPSS.

SPSS. (2001). *Reliability* (Technical section). Retrieved from www.spss.com/tech/stat/algorithms/11.0/reliability.pdf

MEAN SQUARES

In general, mean squares provide a statistic that estimates the average squared deviations across the cases in a group while adjusting for the degrees of freedom of the estimate. Mean squares rest on an assumption of RANDOM SAMPLING for inferences to be valid. The mean squares are used to calculate other test statistics.

In regression, the MEAN SQUARE ERROR is the total sum of squares minus the regression sum of squares, adjusted for n (cases) and k (independent variables).

The mean squared error, MSE, is

$$\frac{ESS}{n - k - 1},$$

with ESS the residual error.

MSE gives a unit-free estimate of the error relative to the mean, taking into account both sample size and the degrees of freedom.

Two examples illustrate two usages of mean squares: first in the ANALYSIS OF VARIANCE and second in the analysis of REGRESSION.

In the analysis of variance, a table such as Table 1 may be obtained.

The ratio of two mean square statistics follows an F distribution, whose significance (under the relevant set of assumptions) can be obtained from a table or from a statistical package.

Thus, for a set of 13 measures of citizens' confidence, with $n = 415$ cases, ANOVA gives the results shown in Table 1.

In this table, the F statistic is the ratio of 20.0803 and .3257 (SPSS, 1990, p. 868). When the ratio of mean squares explained to mean squares unexplained is high, one would reject the hypothesis that the between-measures variation is not substantial. In other words, citizens' confidence does not only vary between individuals but also varies considerably between measures. Formulas for the analysis of variance allow the calculation of degrees of freedom in such cases.

The second example illustrates results from regression estimation using ordinary least squares. In a study of logged wage rates with 31 independent variables in the equation, including years of education, years of

Table 1 ANOVA Mean Squares Results for Citizens' Data

Source of Variation	Sum of Squares	Degrees of Freedom	Mean Square	F Statistic
Between people	669	414	1.6177	
Within people	1,859	4,980	.3733	
Between measures	241	12	20.0803	61.66*
Residual	1,617	4,968	.3257	
Total	2,529	5,394	.4688	

SOURCE: SPSS (1990, p. 868).
*Significant at < 1% level.

full-time work experience, gender, and other variables, Table 2 results in the following:

Table 2 Mean Squares Table for Regression

	Sum of Squares	Degrees of Freedom	Mean Square	F Statistic	Significance
Regression	602	31	19.431	129	.000
Residual	549	3,643	0.151		
Total	1,152	3,674			

The table indicates that the regression mean square is huge relative to the mean squared error; R^2 adjusted is 52%. In the table, the first column is divided by the second to obtain the mean square. Then the regression mean square is divided by the residual mean square to give an F statistic with 31 and 3,643 degrees of freedom. The significance of this figure is near zero.

If a simpler regression were run, the degrees of freedom change, but the F statistic remains strong (see Table 3); R^2 is 38%. With smaller data sets, one may find that the larger regression has a low F statistic due to the loss of degrees of freedom.

Table 3 Revision of F Statistic Using Mean Squares for a Simpler Regression

	Sum of Squares	Degrees of Freedom	Mean Square	F Statistic	Significance
Regression	435	10	43	222	.000
Residual	717	3,664	0.196		
Total	1,152	3,674			

The predictor variables used here were age, years of unemployment, education in years, hours worked < 30, years of family care leave, number of years of part-time employment, degree of segregation (males as percentage of total in that occupation), number of years of full-time employment, and full-time years worked (squared). See Walby and Olsen (2002) for details of these variables. In this example, F is higher (222) for the simpler regression.

—Wendy K. Olsen

REFERENCES

SPSS. (1990). *SPSS reference guide*. Chicago: SPSS.

Walby, S., & Olsen, W. (2002). *The impact of women's position in the labour market on pay and implications for UK productivity*. Cabinet Office Women and Equality Unit, November. Retrieved from www.womenandequalityunit.gov.uk

---

MEASURE. *See* CONCEPTUALIZATION, OPERATIONALIZATION, AND MEASUREMENT

MEASURE OF ASSOCIATION

A measure of association is a statistic that indicates how closely two variables appear to move up and down together or to have a pattern of values that observably differs from a random distribution of the observations on each variable. Measures of association fall into two main classes: parametric and nonparametric.

Two cautions precede the measurement of bivariate relationships. First, the sampling used before data collection begins has spatial and temporal limits beyond which it is dangerous to draw inferences (Olsen, 1993; Skinner, Holt, & Smith, 1989). Second, evidence of a strong association is not necessarily evidence of a causal relation between the two things indicated by the variables.

Three main types of association can be measured: CROSS-TABULATION, ordinal relationships, and CORRELATION. For cross-tabulations with categorical data, the available tests include the Phi, Kappa, and Cramér's V coefficients; the McNemar change test; and the Fisher and CHI-SQUARE TESTS. When one variable is ordinal and the other categorical, one may use the MEDIAN TEST, the Wilcoxon-Mann-Whitney test, or KOLMOGOROV-SMIRNOV TEST, among others. When both variables are continuous and normally distributed, PEARSON'S CORRELATION COEFFICIENT offers an indicator of how strongly one can infer an association from the sample to the population. If both variables are ordinal, Spearman's rank-order correlation coefficient or Kendall's TAU b (τ_b) may be used. Kendall's τ_b has the advantage of being comparable across several bivariate tests, even when the variables are measured on different types of ordinal scale.

OPERATIONALIZATION decisions affect the outcomes of tests of association. Decisions about technique may influence the choice of level of measurement. In addition, the nature of reality may affect how things can be measured (e.g., categorical, ordinal, interval, continuous, and continuous normally distributed levels of measurement).

It is crucial to choose the right test(s) from among the available nonparametric and parametric tests. Choosing a test is done in three steps: operationalize both variables, decide on a LEVEL OF MEASUREMENT for each variable, and choose the appropriate test (see Siegel & Castellan, 1988).

An example illustrates the ordinal measurement of attitudes that lie on a continuous underlying distribution. The example illustrates the use of the paired t statistic; a nonparametric statistic such as the Kolgomorov-Smirnov test for nonnormal distributions would be an acceptable alternative (see Table 1).

Among individuals of various social backgrounds, 154 were randomly sampled and asked how well they

Table 1   The Paired t-Test in an Attitude Survey About Occupations in India

Job or Occupation	Mean of Attitudes About Young Men Doing Job	Mean of Attitudes About Young Women Doing Job	Paired t Statistic for the Paired Values
Buying and managing livestock	4.2	3.1	−13.8*
Garment stitching with a sewing machine	2.4	2.8	3.7*

SOURCE: Field survey, 1999, Andhra Pradesh, India.
NOTE: The preferences were recorded during one-to-one interviews as 1 = *strongly disapprove*, 2 = *disapprove*, 3 = *neutral*, 4 = *approve*, and 5 = *strongly approve*.
*Significant at the 1% level.

would hypothetically have liked a young woman (or a young man) to do a certain type of job or training. Their answers were coded on a 5-point Likert scale that was observed to have different shapes for different jobs. The *t*-test measures the association between each pair of Likert scales: preference for a young man doing that job versus preference for a young woman doing that job. The paired *t*-test is often used in repeated-measures situations.

The local norms were that young men should do livestock management, whereas young women were more suited to garment stitching. As usual with bivariate tests, the direction of causality has not been ascertained, and the strong observed association could even be spurious.

—Wendy K. Olsen

REFERENCES

Olsen, W. K. (1993). Random samples and repeat surveys in South India. In S. Devereux & J. Hoddinott (Eds.) *Fieldwork in Developing Countries* (pp. 57-72). Boulder, CO: Lynne Rienner.

Siegel, S., & Castellan, N. J. (1988). *Nonparametric statistics for the behavioral sciences* (2nd ed.). New York: McGraw-Hill.

Skinner, C. J., Holt, D., & Smith, T. M. F. (Eds.). (1989). *Analysis of complex surveys*. Chichester, UK: Wiley.

MEASURES OF CENTRAL TENDENCY

Measures of central tendency are ways of summarizing a distribution of values with reference to its central point. They consist, primarily, of the MEAN and the MEDIAN. The MODE, although not strictly a measure of central tendency, also provides information about the distribution by giving the most common value in the distribution. It therefore tells us something about what is typical, an idea that we usually associate with a central point. Table 1 shows the number of dependent children in seven notional families. We can summarize the midpoint of this distribution with reference to the arithmetic mean (the sum of the values divided by the number of the observations), the median (or midpoint of the distribution), or the mode (the most common value).

Table 2 identifies the values of each of these three measures of central tendency as applied to the family

Table 1   Number of Children in Seven Families

Family	Number of Children Younger Than Age 16
Jones	1
Brown	1
Singh	1
Roberts	2
O'Neill	2
Smith	3
Phillips	6

Table 2   Measures of Central Tendency Derived From Table 1

Measure	Result From Table 1
Mean	$16/7 = 2.3$
Median	2
Mode	1

sizes given in Table 1. It shows that each measure produces a different figure for summarizing the center of the distribution. In this case, the limited range of the variable and the observations means that the differences are not substantial, but when the range of values is much wider and the distribution is not symmetrical, there may be substantial differences between the values provided by the different measures.

Although the mean can only be used with interval data, the median may be used for ordinal data, and the mode can be applied to nominal or ordinal categorical data. On the other hand, when data are collected in continuous or near-continuous form, the mode may provide little valuable information: Knowing that, in a sample of 100 people, two people earn $173.56, whereas all the other sample members have unique earnings, tells us little about the distribution.

An additional, though rarely used, measure of central tendency is provided by the midrange, that is, the halfway point between the two ends of distribution. In the example in Table 1, the midrange would have the value 2.5. A modification of this is the midpoint between the 25th and 75th percentile of a distribution (i.e., the midpoint of the INTERQUARTILE RANGE).

Means can be related to any fixed point in the distribution, although they are usually assumed to be related to 0. For example, IQ tests set the standard for intelligence at 100. An average score for a class of students could be taken from the amount they differ from 100. The final average difference would then be added to (or subtracted from) 100. Such nonzero reference points are often taken as those in which the frequency of observations is greatest, as this can simplify the amount of calculation involved.

HISTORICAL DEVELOPMENT

Measures of central tendency were in use long before the development of statistics. That is because, by telling us about the middle of the distribution, they tell us something about what is "normal" and how to place ourselves in relation to them. People construct ideas of how tall, poor, thin, or clever they are by reference to a perceived midpoint. Arithmetic means were long used as a check on the reliability of repeat observations; however, it was not until the 19th century that the possibilities of measures of central tendency for statistical science began to be developed. Francis Galton first explored the utility of the midpoint of the interquartile range as a summary measure, and he also developed Adolphe Quetelet's work on the "average man" with investigations of deviation from both the mean and the median in his explorations of heredity (see AVERAGE). Francis Edgeworth explored the relevance of different means and the median to indexes, such as price indexes. Measures of central tendency remain critical to descriptive statistics and to understanding distributions, as well as to key statistical concepts such as regression.

APPLICATION OF MEASURES OF CENTRAL TENDENCY

Different measures of central tendency may be more relevant or informative in particular situations or with particular types of data. In addition, in combination, they may give us added information about a distribution. In a symmetrical distribution, the mean and the median will have the same value. However, if the distribution is skewed to the right (this is usually the case in income distributions, for example), then the median will have a lower value than the mean. If the distribution is skewed to the left (as, for example, with exam results), then the value of the mean will be lower than that of the median.

Table 3 illustrates a small data table of the characteristics across five variables of 15 British households in 1999, derived from an annual national household survey. The measures that are appropriate to summarize location, or central tendency, vary with these variables. For example, when looking at the number of rooms, we might be interested in the mean, the median, or the mode. It is worth noting, in this case, that the mean provides us with a number (5.1) that cannot, because it is fractional, represent the actual number of rooms of any household. It is the same apparent paradox that arises when we talk of the average number of children per family being 1.7, which conjures up notions of subdivided children. For housing tenure (1 = *owned outright,* 2 = *buying with a mortgage,* 3 = *renting*), only the mode is appropriate as this is a categorical variable without any ordering. By contrast, although the local tax bracket is also a categorical variable, it is ordered by the value of the property, and thus the median may also be of interest here. For the income values, the mean or the median may be pertinent (or both). It is left to the reader to calculate the relevant measures of central tendency for each of the variables.

Table 3   The Individual Characteristics of 15 Households, Britain 1999

Region	Number of Rooms	Housing Tenure	Household Income (£ per week)	Local Tax Bracket
West Midlands	6	2	202.45	1
West Midlands	4	1	301	3
West Midlands	6	3	192.05	2
West Midlands	6	1	359.02	4
West Midlands	3	3	209.84	1
West Midlands	4	3	491.8	1
West Midlands	5	2	422.7	2
East Midlands	9	1	434.43	5
East Midlands	4	3	353	1
East Midlands	6	2	192	1
East Midlands	6	2	490.86	3
East Midlands	5	2	550	4
East Midlands	3	2	372.88	3
East Midlands	3	3	303	2
East Midlands	7	2	693.87	5

Finally, we see that households come from one of two regions—East Midlands or West Midlands. We might be interested to consider whether there is systematic difference between the midpoints of the variables according to region. Applications often require the comparison for different groups within a sample or for different samples; the *T*-TEST provides a way of comparing means and ascertaining if there are significant differences between them, whereas the MEDIAN TEST is used to compare medians across samples.

—Lucinda Platt

See also AVERAGE, INTERQUARTILE RANGE, MEAN, MEDIAN, MEDIAN TEST, MODE, *T*-TEST

REFERENCES

Stuart, A., & Ord, J. K. (1987). *Kendall's advanced theory of statistics: Vol. 1. Distribution theory* (5th ed.). London: Griffin.

Yule, G. U., & Kendall, M. G. (1950). *An introduction to the theory of statistics* (14th ed.). London: Griffin.

MEDIAN

The median is the midpoint of the distribution of a variable such that half the distribution falls above the median and half falls below it. That is,

$$\text{Median} = (n + 1)/2.$$

If the distribution has an even number of cases, then the median is deemed to fall precisely between the two middle cases and is calculated as the arithmetic MEAN of those two cases. For example, in the set of cases

$$1, 2, 5, 6, 8, 11, 14, 17, 45,$$

the median value is 8. In the set of cases

$$1, 5, 6, 12, 18, 19,$$

however, the median is $(6 + 12)/2 = 9$.

When the data do not have discrete values but are grouped either in ranges or with a continuous variable (e.g., age is given whereby each year actually represents the continuous possible ages across that period), a different approach is used to calculate the median. For example, Table 1 shows the frequencies of children in a small specialist school who fall into particular age bands.

Table 1   Distribution of Children by Age Ranges in a Small Specialist School (constructed data)

Age Range (Years)	Frequency	Cumulative Frequency
3 to 5.9	16	16
6 to 8.9	35	51
9 to 11.9	62	113
12 to 14.9	63	176
15 to 17.9	21	197

There are 197 children, so the median value will be the age of the 99th child. The 99th child falls in the 9 to 11.9-year age bracket. In fact, it falls 48 observations into that bracket and so can be counted as the 48/62 share of that bracket of 3 years added on to the age of 8.9 that it has already passed. That is, the median can be calculated as

$$8.9 + ((48/62) \cdot 3) = 11.2.$$

The median is, therefore, one of several MEASURES OF CENTRAL TENDENCY, or location, that can be used to understand aspects of the distribution. It is also a form of the AVERAGE, even if that term is normally reserved in common parlance for the arithmetic mean. Although the median does not have as many applications as the mean, it has certain advantages in giving an understanding of a distribution. The principal advantage is that it is not as susceptible to OUTLIERS—that is, extreme, potentially erroneous and potentially distorting cases—that will influence the mean value but not the median (see MEAN). For example, in the first example above, the value of 45 would appear to be such an outlier. Similarly, the median may form a valuable average when the final value of a distribution is unknown, rendering the mean impossible to calculate. The median can also be used for ordinal data, that is, data for which there is a hierarchical order to categories but the distances between the categories are not equal. An example is measures of educational achievement, ranked 1 for no qualifications, 2 for midlevel qualifications, 3 for higher qualifications, and so on. In such cases, it is meaningless to calculate the mean as the values do not represent numeric quantities. However, the median may be of interest in such instances.

The median can also be considered the 50th percentile and, as such, is a special instance of percentiles as measures of distribution. Percentiles are the values at which the named proportion of cases falls below the value and the remainder fall above it. Thus, the

25th percentile (or lower quartile) represents the value at which 25% of cases are of smaller value and the remaining 75% are larger. The median is thus part of a general system of describing a distribution by the values that break it into specified divisions. There are 99 percentiles in a distribution that divide it into 100 parts, 9 deciles (of which the median is the 5th) that divide it into 10 parts, and 3 quartiles (of which the median is the central one) that divide it into 4 parts.

—Lucinda Platt

See also AVERAGE, MEASURES OF CENTRAL TENDENCY

REFERENCES

Agresti, A., & Finlay, B. (1997). *Statistical methods for the social sciences* (3rd ed.). Upper Saddle River, NJ: Prentice Hall.

Stuart, A., & Ord, J. K. (1987). *Kendall's advanced theory of statistics: Vol. 1. Distribution theory* (5th ed.). London: Griffin.

Yule, G. U., & Kendall, M. G. (1950). *An introduction to the theory of statistics* (14th ed.). London: Griffin.

MEDIAN TEST

The median test is a NONPARAMETRIC test to ascertain if different samples have the same location parameter, that is, the same *median.* That is, do the two samples come from the same population, with any differences between their medians being attributable to sampling variation? It can be generalized to other percentiles such as the 25th percentile (the first quartile) or the 75th percentile (the third quartile). Its origins have been dated to Alexander Mood's work on nonparametric methods from 1950 (see Mood & Graybill, 1963). It belongs to a group of simple linear rank statistics as they are concerned with the rank of an ordered distribution (see also WILCOXON TEST and KRUSKAL-WALLIS *H* TEST).

In the median test, a score is derived from the number of cases in the different samples that fall above the median (or other percentile) of the pooled sample. These are then compared with the score that would be expected under the null hypothesis (i.e., if the two samples belonged to the same population). The resulting test statistic has a CHI-SQUARE DISTRIBUTION, and its significance relative to the degrees of freedom can thus be calculated.

Table 1　　Scores for Men and Women on Duration of Unemployment Relative to the Median

		Male	Female	Total
Duration of	> Median	55	35	90
unemployment	≤ Median	44	70	114
Total		99	105	204

For example, let us consider an ordinal variable giving months' duration of unemployment in a British sample of 204 working-age adults who experienced unemployment at some time before the mid-1980s. The question is, then, whether the median duration of unemployment is the same for both men and women. For the pooled samples, the median value is 2, indicating between 6 months and a year of unemployment. Table 1 shows the numbers of men and women whose duration falls above this median and those falling below or equal to it.

The test gives us a CHI-SQUARE TEST statistic of 10.2 for 1 degree of freedom. This is significant at the .001 level, which indicates that the case for independence is weak and that we can reject the null hypothesis. That is, it is very unlikely that the median duration of unemployment for men and women is the same.

—Lucinda Platt

REFERENCES

Hajek, J., & Sidák, Z. (1967). *Theory of rank tests.* New York: Academic Press.

Hollander, M., & Wolfe, D. A. (1973). *Nonparametric statistical methods.* New York: John Wiley.

Mood, A. M., & Graybill, F. A. (1963). *Introduction to the theory of statistics* (2nd ed.). New York: McGraw-Hill.

MEDIATING VARIABLE

A mediating variable is one that lies intermediate between independent causal factors and a final outcome. Like MODERATING VARIABLES, mediating variables are seen as intervening factors that can change the impact of X on Y. Mediating variables aim to estimate the way a variable Z affects the impact of X on Y, and they can be estimated in one of four ways: through PATH ANALYSIS, STRUCTURAL EQUATION MODELING, proxies embedded in linear regression, and MULTILEVEL MODELING.

In PATH ANALYSIS, separate regressions are run for different causal processes. Recursive regressions are those that invoke variables used in another regression (and instrumental variables regression is a case in point). The X variables in one regression have standardized beta coefficients, defined as

$$\beta_i = \mathbf{B}_i \cdot \frac{\mathbf{S}_{X_i}}{\mathbf{S}_Y},$$

which lead toward the final outcome Y. However, in addition, a separate equation for the mediating variable Z measures the association of elements of the vector $\mathbf{X}$ with Z, and Z in turn is a factor associated with the final outcome Y.

Two examples illustrate the possible impact of Z.

1. In the analysis of breast cancer, social behavior patterns such as smoking and the decision to start or stop taking the contraceptive pill influence the odds of cancer developing, whereas genetic and biological factors form another path to the onset of cancer (Krieger, 1994). These two sets of factors then interact and can offset each other's influence when we examine the odds of the patient dying from cancer. A complex path diagram results (see Figure 1).

The biologist would consider the social factors "mediating variables."

2. In the analysis of how attitudes are associated with final outcomes, attitudes may play a role mediating the direct effect of a sociodemographic characteristic on an outcome. Gender, for instance, was not directly a factor influencing eating-out behaviors but was a strong mediating factor. Women were more likely to wish they could eat out more often compared with men. Gender

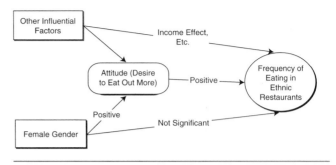

Figure 2 Causal Paths to Eating Out Frequently

thus mediated between the impact of income and other wealth indicators on the overall curiosity of a person regarding eating in ethnic restaurants (Olsen, 1999; Warde, Martens, & Olsen, 1999). See Figure 2.

Path analysis presents the error term as an unexplained causal process (Bryman & Cramer, 1997, chap. 10). In some economic analyses, the error term is presumed to represent a set of unrecorded causal factors, some of which are inherently unobservable, whereas in sociology, the error term might be thought to represent individual variation relative to a basic structuralist model.

Recent developments in the estimation of multilevel models using STATA software allow contextual effects to be represented through models in which the distribution to which a case is allocated is subject to conditional probabilities (allowing the contingent nature of contextual effects to be modeled) and is linked through a variety of functions (as in standard multilevel modeling) (Rabe-Hesketh, Pickles, & Skrondal, 2001). Thus, over time, new modeling structures for moderating factors become possible.

—Wendy K. Olsen

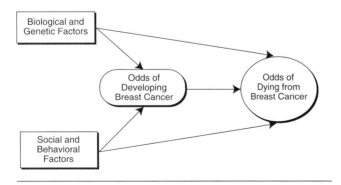

Figure 1 Causal Paths to Cancer Deaths

REFERENCES

Arbuckle, J. (1997). *Amos users' guide version 3.6.* Chicago: Smallwaters Corporation.

Bryman, A., & Cramer, D. (1997). *Quantitative data analysis with SPSS for Windows: A guide for social scientists.* New York: Routledge.

Krieger, N. (1994). Epidemiology and the web of causation: Has anyone seen the spider? *Social Science & Medicine, 39*(7), 887–903.

Olsen, W. K. (1999). *Path analysis for the study of farming and micro-enterprise* (Bradford Development Paper No. 3).

Bradford, UK: University of Bradford, Development and Project Planning Centre.

Rabe-Hesketh, S., Pickles, A., & Skrondal, A. (2001). *GLLAMM manual technical report 2001/01*. London: King's College, University of London, Department of Biostatistics and Computing, Institute of Psychiatry. Retrieved from www. iop. kcl. ac.uk/IoP/Departments/BioComp/programs/manual.pdf

Warde, A., Martens, L., & Olsen, W. K. (1999). Consumption and the problem of variety: Cultural omnivorousness, social distinction and dining out. *Sociology, 30*(1), 105–128.

MEMBER VALIDATION AND CHECK

Also called *member check* and *respondent validation,* member validation is a procedure largely associated with QUALITATIVE RESEARCH, whereby a researcher submits materials relevant to an investigation for checking by the people who were the source of those materials. The crucial issue for such an exercise is how far the researcher's understanding of what was going on in a social setting corresponds with that of members of that setting. Probably the most common form of member validation occurs when the researcher submits an account of his or her findings (such as a short report or interview transcript) for checking.

The chief problem when conducting a member validation exercise is deciding what is to be validated. In particular, there is the issue of how far the submitted materials should include the kinds of interpretation that a researcher engages in when writing up findings for a professional audience. Even if members are able to corroborate materials with which they are submitted, so that they can confirm the researcher's interpretations of their interpretations, it is unreasonable to expect them to do so in relation to the social-scientific rendering of those interpretations. Furthermore, there is a difficulty for the researcher in knowing how best to handle suggestions by members that there has been a failure to understand them. In many cases, if this occurs, all that is needed is for the researcher to modify an interpretation. Sometimes, however, the lack of corroboration may be the result of members disliking the researcher's gloss. Indeed, the presentation of interpreted research materials to members may be the starting point for defensive reactions and wrangles over interpretations.

On the basis of their experiences of using member validation, Emerson and Pollner (1988) have pointed to several other difficulties with its use: problems arising from a failure to read all of a report and/or from misunderstanding what was being said; difficulty establishing whether certain comments were indicative of assent or dissent; members, with whom the authors had been quite close, being unwilling to criticize or inadvertently asking member validation questions with which it would be difficult to disagree; and fears among members about the wider political implications of agreement or disagreement. Bloor (1997) has similarly argued that it is sometimes difficult to get members to give the submitted materials the attention the researcher would like, so that indifference can sound like corroboration.

Although member validation is clearly not an unproblematic procedure, as Lincoln and Guba (1985) observe, it can be crucial for establishing the credibility of one's findings and can also serve to alleviate researchers' anxieties about their capacity to comprehend the social worlds of others. It can be employed in connection with most forms of qualitative research. However, it is crucial to be sensitive to the limits of member validation when seeking such reassurance.

—Alan Bryman

See also RESPONDENT VALIDATION

REFERENCES

Bloor, M. (1997). Addressing social problems through qualitative research. In D. Silverman (Ed.), *Qualitative research: Theory, method and practice* (pp. 221–238). London: Sage.

Emerson, R. M., & Pollner, M. (1988). On the use of members' responses to researchers' accounts. *Human Organization, 47,* 189–198.

Lincoln, Y. S., & Guba, E. (1985). *Naturalistic inquiry.* Beverly Hills, CA: Sage.

MEMBERSHIP ROLES

ETHNOGRAPHERS must assume social roles that fit into the worlds they study. Their access to information, their relationships to subjects, and their sociological interpretations are greatly influenced by these roles' character. Early Chicago school proponents advocated various research postures, such as the complete observer, observer-as-participant, participant-as-observer, and complete participant (Gold, 1958), ranging from least to most involved in the group. These roles were popular when ethnographers were advised to be objective, detached, and distanced.

By the 1980s, ethnography partly relinquished its more OBJECTIVIST leanings, embracing its subjectivity. Ethnographers valued research roles that generated more depth in their settings. They sought positions offering regular, close contact with participants. Critical to these roles is their *insider* affiliation; when assuming *membership roles* in field research, individuals are not detached outsiders but instead take on participant status (Adler & Adler, 1987). This can vary between the *peripheral, active,* and *complete* membership roles.

Most marginal and least committed, the peripheral role still requires membership in the group's social world. Peripheral-member researchers seek an insider's perspective and direct, firsthand experience but do not assume functional roles or participate in core group activities. In our research on upper-level drug dealers and smugglers, we joined the social community and subculture, becoming accepted in the friendship network. We socialized with members, housed them, babysat their children, and formed long-term friendships. Yet, crucially, we refrained from participating in their drug trafficking (see Adler, 1985).

Less marginal and more central in the setting, active-member researchers take part in the group's core activities and assume functional and not merely social or research roles. Beyond sharing insider status, they interact with participants as colleagues. In our research on college athletics, Peter became an assistant coach on a basketball team, serving as the counselor and academic adviser. He regularly attended practices and functions, traveled with the team, and assisted in its routine functioning. However, his identity and job could detach from his coaching, and his professorial role remained primary (see Adler & Adler, 1991).

The complete membership role incorporates the greatest commitment. Researchers immerse themselves fully in their settings, are status equals with participants, and share common experiences and goals. Ethnographers may assume this role by selecting settings where they are already members or by converting. Although this position offers the deepest understanding and the least role pretense, it more frequently leads to conflicts between individuals' research and membership role demands. In gathering data on preadolescents' peer culture, we studied our children, their friends, and our neighbors, friends, schools, and community. Our parental membership role gave us naturally occurring access to children's social networks and "after-school" activities. We used our membership relationships to recruit interviews and to penetrate beyond surface knowledge. At times, though, we were torn between wanting to actively parent these youngsters and needing to remain accepting to keep open research lines of communication (see Adler & Adler, 1998).

Membership roles offer ethnographers, to varying degrees, the deepest levels of understanding in their research.

—Patricia A. Adler and Peter Adler

REFERENCES

Adler, P. A. (1985). *Wheeling and dealing.* New York: Columbia University Press.

Adler, P. A., & Adler, P. (1987). *Membership roles in field research.* Newbury Park, CA: Sage.

Adler, P. A., & Adler, P. (1991). *Backboards and blackboards.* New York: Columbia University Press.

Adler, P. A., & Adler, P. (1998). *Peer power.* New Brunswick, NJ: Rutgers University Press.

Gold, R. L. (1958). Roles in sociological field observations. *Social Forces, 36,* 217–223.

MEMOS, MEMOING

Memos are researchers' records of analysis. Although they take time to write, they are worth doing. Memos are a way of keeping the researcher aware and the research honest. All too often, researchers take shortcuts to the analytic process, writing notes in margins of transcripts, trusting their memories to fill in the details later when writing. Unfortunately, memories often fail, and the "golden nuggets" of insight that emerged during analysis are lost. Furthermore, memos are useful for trying out analytic ideas and working out the logic of the emergent findings. As memos grow in depth and breath, researchers can use them to note areas that need further investigation to round out the findings. When working in teams, memos can be used to keep everyone informed and to share ideas (Huberman & Miles, 1994). During the writing stage, researchers only have to turn to their memos to work out an outline.

There are no hard-and-fast rules for writing memos. However, here are a few suggestions for improving the quality of memos and enhancing their usefulness. Memos should be titled and dated. They should be analytic rather than descriptive, that is, focused on concepts that emerged during the analysis and not filled with raw data (Dey, 1993). With the computer programs that are available, one can mark the raw data from which concepts emerged and refer back to the items when necessary (Richards & Richards, 1994). Memos should ask questions of the data, such as, "Where do I go from here to get more data on this concept, or what should I be thinking about when doing my next observation or interview?" As more data about a concept emerge, memos should explore concepts in terms of their properties and dimensions, such as who, what, when, where, how, why, and so on. The researcher should keep a piece of paper and a pencil available at all times, even by the bedside. One never knows when that sudden insight will appear, when the pieces of the puzzle will fall into place. Analysts should not let a lot of time elapse between doing the analysis and writing the memos. Not only do thoughts get lost, so does momentum. Analysts should not be afraid to be creative and write down those insights, even if they seem far-fetched at the time. One can always toss them out if they are not verified by data. Finally, memos can be used to keep an account of one's own response to the research process, including the personal biases and assumptions that inevitably shape the tone and outcome of analysis. This record keeping will prove useful later when writing.

Writing memos stimulates thinking and allows one to interact with data in ways that foster creativity while staying grounded at the same time. At the beginning of a research project, memos will appear more exploratory and directive than analytic. Often, they seem foolish to the researcher when looking back. This is to be expected. Doing research is progressive and an act of discovery, a process one can only keep track of in memos.

—Juliet M. Corbin

REFERENCES

Dey, I. (1993). *Qualitative data analysis*. London: Routledge Kegan Paul.

Huberman, A. M., & Miles, M. B. (1994). Data management and analysis methods. In N. K. Denzin & Y. S. Lincoln (Eds.), *Handbook of qualitative research* (pp. 428–444). Thousand Oaks, CA: Sage.

Richards, T. J., & Richards, L. (1994). Using computers in qualitative research. In N. K. Denzin & Y. S. Lincoln (Eds.), *Handbook of qualitative research* (pp. 445–462). Thousand Oaks, CA: Sage.

META-ANALYSIS

The term *meta-analysis* refers to the statistical analysis of results from individual studies for purposes of integrating the findings. The person who coined the term in 1976, Gene Glass, felt that the accumulated findings of studies should be regarded as complex data points that were no more comprehensible without statistical analysis than the data points found in individual studies.

Procedures for performing meta-analysis had appeared in statistics texts and articles long before 1976, but instances of their application were rare. It took the expanding evidence in the social sciences and the growing need for research syntheses to provide impetus for the general use of meta-analysis. The explosion in social science research focused considerable attention on the lack of standardization in how scholars wishing to integrate literatures arrived at general conclusions from series of related studies. For many topic areas, a separate verbal description of each relevant study was no longer possible. One traditional strategy was to focus on one or two studies chosen from dozens or hundreds. This strategy failed to portray accurately the accumulated state of knowledge. First, this type of selective attention is open to confirmatory bias: A particular synthesist may highlight only studies that support his or her initial position. Second, selective attention to only a portion of all studies places little or imprecise weight on the volume of available tests. Finally, selectively attending to evidence cannot give a good estimate of the strength of a relationship. As evidence on a topic accumulates, researchers become more interested in "how much" rather than simply "yes or no."

Traditional synthesists also faced problems when they considered the variation between the results of different studies. Synthesists would find distributions of results for studies sharing a particular procedural characteristic but varying on many other characteristics. They found it difficult to conclude accurately whether a procedural variation affected study outcomes because the variability in results obtained by any single method meant that the distributions of results with different methods would overlap.

It seemed, then, that there were many situations in which synthesists had to turn to quantitative synthesizing techniques, or meta-analysis. The application of quantitative inference procedures to research synthesis was a necessary response to the expanding literature. If statistics are applied appropriately, they should enhance the validity of synthesis conclusions. Meta-analysis is an extension of the same rules of inference required for rigorous data analysis in primary research.

HISTORICAL DEVELOPMENT

At the beginning of the 20th century, Karl Pearson (1904) was asked to review the evidence on a vaccine against typhoid. He gathered data from 11 relevant studies, and for each study, he calculated a CORRELATION coefficient. He averaged these measures of the treatment's effect across two groups of studies distinguished by their outcome variable. On the basis of the average correlations, Pearson concluded that other vaccines were more effective. This is the earliest known quantitative research synthesis.

Three quarters of a century after Pearson's research synthesis, Robert Rosenthal and Donald Rubin (1978) undertook a synthesis of research studying the effects of interpersonal expectations on behavior in laboratories, classrooms, and the workplace. They found 345 studies that pertained to their hypothesis. Nearly simultaneously, Gene Glass and Mary Lee Smith (1978) conducted a review of the relation between class size and academic achievement. They found 725 estimates of the relation based on data from nearly 900,000 students. This literature revealed 833 tests of the treatment. John Hunter, Frank Schmidt, and Ronda Hunter (1979) uncovered 866 comparisons of the differential validity of employment tests for Black and White workers.

Largely independently, the three research teams rediscovered and reinvented Pearson's solution to their problem. They were joined quickly by others. In the 1980s, Larry Hedges and Ingram Olkin (1985) provided the rigorous statistical proofs that established meta-analysis as an independent specialty within the statistical sciences.

Meta-analysis was not without its critics, and some criticisms persist. The value of quantitative synthesizing was questioned along lines similar to criticisms of primary data analysis. That is, some wondered whether using numbers to summarize research literatures might lead to the impression of the greater precision of results than was truly warranted by the data. However, much of the criticism stemmed less from issues in meta-analysis than from more general inappropriate synthesizing procedures, such as a lack of operational detail, which were erroneously thought to be by-products of the use of quantitative procedures.

THE ELEMENTS OF META-ANALYSIS

Suppose a research synthesist is interested in whether fear-arousing advertisements can be used to persuade adolescents that smoking is bad. Suppose further that the (hypothetical) synthesist is able to locate eight studies, each of which examined the question of interest. Of these, six studies reported nonsignificant differences between attitudes of adolescents exposed and not exposed to fear-arousing ads, and two reported significant differences indicating less favorable attitudes held by adolescent viewers. One was significant at $p < .05$ and one at $p < .02$ (both two-tailed). Can the synthesist reject the NULL HYPOTHESIS that the ads had no effect?

The research synthesist could employ multiple methods to answer this question. First, the synthesist could cull through the eight reports, isolate those studies that present results counter to his or her position, discard these disconfirming studies due to methodological limitations, and present the remaining supportive studies as presenting the truth of the matter. Such a research synthesis would be viewed with extreme skepticism. It would contribute little to answering the question.

The Vote Count

As an alternative procedure, the synthesist could take each report and place it into one of three piles: statistically significant findings that indicate the ads were effective, statistically significant findings that indicate the ads created more positive attitudes toward smoking (in this case, this pile would have no studies), and nonsignificant findings that do not permit rejection of the hypothesis that the fear-arousing ads had no effect. The synthesist then would declare the largest pile the winner. In our example, the null hypothesis wins.

This vote count of significant findings has much intuitive appeal and has been used quite often. However, the strategy is unacceptably conservative. The problem is that chance alone should produce only about 5% of all reports falsely indicating that viewing the ads created more negative attitudes toward smoking. Therefore, depending on the number of studies, 10% or less of the positive and statistically significant findings might indicate a real difference due to the ads.

However, the vote-counting strategy requires that a minimum 34% of findings be positive and statistically significant before the hypothesis is ruled a winner. Thus, the vote counting of significant findings could and often does lead to the suggested abandonment of hypotheses (and effective treatment programs) when, in fact, no such conclusion is warranted.

A different way to perform vote counts in research synthesis involves (a) counting the number of positive and negative results, regardless of significance, and (b) applying the sign test to determine if one direction appears in the literature more often than would be expected by chance. This vote-counting method has the advantage of using all studies but suffers because it does not weight a study's contribution by its sample size. Thus, a study with 100 participants is given weight equal to a study with 1,000 participants. Furthermore, the revealed magnitude of the hypothesized relation (or impact of the treatment under evaluation) in each study is not considered—a study showing a small positive attitude change is given equal weight to a study showing a large negative attitude change. Still, the vote count of directional findings can be an informative complement to other meta-analytic procedures.

Combining Probabilities Across Studies

Taking these shortcomings into account, the research synthesist might next consider combining the precise probabilities associated with the results of each study. These methods require that the statistical tests (a) relate to the same hypothesis, (b) are independent, and (c) meet the initial statistical ASSUMPTIONS made by the primary researchers.

The most frequently applied method is called the method of adding Zs. In its simplest form, the adding Zs method involves summing Z-scores associated with p levels and dividing the sum by the square root of the number of inference tests. In the example of the eight studies of fear-arousing ads, the cumulative Z-score is 1.69, $p < .05$ (one-tailed). Thus, the null hypothesis is rejected.

Not all findings have an equal likelihood of being retrieved by the synthesist. Nonsignificant results are less likely to be retrieved than significant ones. This fact implies that the adding Zs method may produce a probability level that underestimates the chance of a Type I error. Rosenthal (1979) referred to this as the FILE DRAWER PROBLEM and wrote, "The extreme view of this problem . . . is that the journals are filled with

the 5% of studies that show Type I errors, while the file drawers back in the lab are filled with the 95% of studies that show insignificant (e.g., $p < .05$) results" (p. 638). The problem is probably not this dramatic, but it does exist.

The combining probabilities procedure overcomes the improper weighting problems of the vote count. However, it has severe limitations of its own. First, whereas the vote-counting procedure is overly conservative, the combining probabilities procedure is extremely powerful. In fact, it is so powerful that for hypotheses or treatments that have generated a large number of tests, rejecting the null hypothesis is so likely that it becomes a rather uninformative exercise. Furthermore, the combined probability addresses the question of whether an effect exists; it gives no information on whether that effect is large or small, important or trivial. Therefore, answering the question, "Do fear-arousing ads create more negative attitudes toward smoking in adolescents, yes or no?" is often not the question of greatest importance. Instead, the question should be, "How much of an effect do fear-arousing ads have?" The answer might be zero, or it might be either a positive or negative value. Furthermore, the research synthesist would want to ask, "What factors influence the effect of fear-arousing ads?" He or she realizes that the answer to this question could help make sound recommendations about how to both improve and target the smoking interventions. Given these new questions, the synthesists would turn to the calculation of average EFFECT SIZES, much like Pearson's correlation coefficient.

Estimating Effect Sizes

Cohen (1988) defined an effect size as "the degree to which the phenomenon is present in the population, or the degree to which the null hypothesis is false" (pp. 9–10). In meta-analysis, effect sizes are (a) calculated for the outcomes of studies (or sometimes comparisons within studies), (b) averaged across studies to estimate general magnitudes of effect, and (c) compared between studies to discover if variations in study outcomes exist and, if so, what features of studies might account for them.

Although numerous estimates of effect size are available, two dominate the social science literature. The first, called the d-index, is a scale-free measure of the separation between two group means. Calculating the d-index for any study involves dividing the difference between the two group means by either their average STANDARD DEVIATION or the standard deviation of the control group. The second effect size metric is the r-index or correlation coefficient. It measures the degree of linear relation between two variables. In the advertising example, the d-index would be the appropriate effect size metric.

Meta-analytic procedures call for the weighting of effect sizes when they are averaged across studies. The reason is that studies yielding more precise estimates— that is, those with larger sample sizes—should contribute more to the combined result. *The Handbook of Research Synthesis* (Cooper & Hedges, 1994) provides procedures for calculating the appropriate weights. Also, this book describes how CONFIDENCE INTERVALS for effect sizes can be estimated. The confidence intervals can be used instead of the adding Z-scores method to test the null hypothesis that the difference between two means, or the size of a correlation, is zero.

Examining Variance in Effect Sizes

Another advantage of performing a meta-analysis of research is that it allows the synthesist to test hypotheses about why the outcomes of studies differ. To continue with the fear-arousing ad example, the synthesist might calculate average d-indexes for subsets of studies, deciding that he or she wants different estimates based on certain characteristics of the data. For example, the reviewer might want to compare separate estimates for studies that use different outcomes, distinguishing between those that measured likelihood of smoking versus attitude toward smoking. The reviewer might wish to compare the average effect sizes for different media formats, distinguishing print from video advertisements. The reviewer might want to look at whether advertisements are differentially effective for different types of adolescents, say, males and females.

After calculating the average effect sizes for different subgroups of studies, the meta-analyst can statistically test whether these factors are reliably associated with different magnitudes of effect. This is sometimes called a homogeneity analysis. Without the aid of statistics, the reviewer simply examines the difference in outcomes across studies, groups them informally by study features, and decides (based on unspecified inference rules) whether the feature is a significant predictor of variation in outcomes. At best, this method is imprecise. At worst, it leads to incorrect inferences.

In contrast, meta-analysis provides a formal means for testing whether different features of studies explain variation in their outcomes. Because effect sizes are imprecise, they will vary somewhat even if they all estimate the same underlying population value. Homogeneity analysis allows the synthesist to test whether SAMPLING ERROR alone accounts for this variation or whether features of studies, samples, treatment designs, or outcome measures also play a role. If reliable differences do exist, the average effect sizes corresponding to these differences will take on added meaning.

Three statistical procedures for examining variation in effect sizes appear in the literature. The first approach applies standard inference tests, such as ANOVA or MULTIPLE REGRESSION. The effect size is used as the DEPENDENT VARIABLE, and study features are used as independent or predictor variables. This approach has been criticized based on the questionable tenability of the underlying assumptions.

The second approach compares the variation in obtained effect sizes with the variation expected due to sampling error. This approach involves calculating not only the observed variance in effects but also the expected variance, given that all observed effects are estimating the same population value. This approach also can include adjustments to effect sizes to account for methodological artifacts.

The third approach, called homogeneity analysis, was mentioned above. It provides the most complete guide to making inferences about a research literature. Analogous to ANOVA, studies are grouped by features, and the average effect sizes for groups can be tested for homogeneity. It is relatively simple to carry out a homogeneity analysis. The formulas for homogeneity analysis are described in Cooper (1998) and Cooper and Hedges (1994).

In sum, then, a meta-analysis might contain four separate sets of statistics: (a) a frequency analysis of positive and negative results, (b) combinations of the *p* levels of independent inference tests, (c) estimates of average effect sizes with confidence intervals, and (d) homogeneity analyses examining study features that might influence study outcomes. The need for combined probabilities diminishes as the body of literature grows or if the author provides confidence intervals around effect size estimates. In addition to these basic components, the techniques of meta-analysis have grown to include many descriptive and diagnostic techniques unique to the task of integrating the results of separate studies.

—Harris M. Cooper

REFERENCES

Cohen, J. (1988). *Statistical power analysis in the behavioral sciences.* Hillsdale, NJ: Lawrence Erlbaum.

Cooper, H. (1998). *Synthesizing research: A guide for literature reviews* (3rd ed.). Thousand Oaks, CA: Sage.

Cooper, H., & Hedges, L. V. (Eds.). (1994). *The handbook of research synthesis.* New York: Russell Sage Foundation.

Glass, G. V. (1976). Primary, secondary, and meta-analysis of research. *Educational Research, 5,* 3–8.

Glass, G. V., & Smith, M. L. (1978). Meta-analysis of research on the relationship of class size and achievement. *Educational Evaluation and Policy Analysis, 1,* 2–16.

Hedges, L. V., & Olkin, I. (1985). *Statistical methods for meta-analysis.* Orlando, FL: Academic Press.

Hunter, J. E., Schmidt, F. L., & Hunter, R. (1979). Differential validity of employment tests by race: A comprehensive review and analysis. *Psychological Bulletin, 86,* 721–735.

Pearson, K. (1904). Report on certain enteric fever inoculation statistics. *British Medical Journal, 3,* 1243–1246.

Rosenthal, R. (1979). The "file drawer problem" and tolerance for null results. *Psychological Bulletin, 86,* 638–641.

Rosenthal, R., & Rubin, D. (1978). Interpersonal expectancy effects: The first 345 studies. *Behavioral and Brain Sciences, 3,* 377–415.

META-ETHNOGRAPHY

Meta-ethnography is an approach to synthesizing qualitative studies, allowing interpretations to be made across a set of studies (Noblit & Hare, 1988). In contrast to quantitative META-ANALYSIS (Glass, 1977), meta-ethnography does not aggregate data across studies as this ignores the context-specific nature of qualitative research. Instead, meta-ethnography involves synthesizing the interpretations across qualitative studies in which context itself is also synthesized. The approach allows for the development of more interpretive literature reviews, critical examinations of multiple accounts of similar phenomena, systematic comparisons of case studies to allow interpretive cross-case conclusions, and more formal syntheses of ETHNO-GRAPHIC studies. In all these uses, meta-ethnography is both inductive and interpretive. It begins with the studies and inductively derives a synthesis by translating ethnographic and/or qualitative accounts into the terms of each other to inductively derive a new interpretation of the studies taken collectively.

A meta-ethnography is accomplished through seven phases. First, one starts by identifying an intellectual interest that can be addressed by synthesizing qualitative studies. Second, it is necessary to decide what is relevant to the intellectual interest by considering what might be learned and for which audiences. Third, after conducting an exhaustive search for relevant studies, one reads the studies in careful detail. Fourth, it is necessary to consider the relationships of the studies to one another by making lists of key metaphors, phrases, ideas, and concepts and their relations to one another. The relationships may be reciprocal (similarity between studies is evident), refutational (studies oppose each other), or line of argument (studies of parts infer a whole). Fifth, the studies are translated into one another in the form of an analogy that one account is like the other except in some ways. Sixth, the translations are synthesized into a new interpretation that accounts for the interpretations in the different studies. Seventh, the synthesis is expressed or represented in some form appropriate to the audience of the synthesis: text, play, video, art, and so on.

For example, Derek Freeman's refutation of Margaret Mead's ethnography of Samoa was covered in the popular media in the 1980s. Freeman's (1983) account was an attempt to discredit the work of Mead (1928), but the refutational synthesis in Noblit and Hare (1988) reveals that the studies come from different time periods, different paradigms of anthropology, different genders, and even different Samoas (American vs. Western). In short, the studies do not refute each other. They teach about different aspects of Samoan culture. Freeman's claim that he refutes Mead and Mead's claim to refute biological determinism both fail. Meta-ethnography, then, is a powerful tool used to reconsider what ethnographies are to mean to us taken together.

—George W. Noblit

REFERENCES

Freeman, D. (1983). *Margaret Mead and Samoa.* Cambridge, MA: Harvard University Press.

Glass, G. V. (1977). Integrating findings. *Review of Research in Education, 5,* 351–379.

Mead, M. (1928). *Coming of age in Samoa.* New York: William Morrow.

Noblit, G. W., & Hare, R. D. (1988). *Meta-ethnography.* Newbury Park, CA: Sage.

METAPHORS

Metaphor refers to a figure of speech in which one thing is understood or described in terms of another thing. The two things are not assumed to be literally the same. For instance, one might talk metaphorically about a thinker "shedding light on an issue." This does not mean that the thinker has actually lit a candle or turned on an electric light. In the social sciences, the use of metaphors has been studied as a topic, but also metaphors have contributed greatly to the development of theoretical thinking.

George Lakoff and Mark Johnson (1980), in their influential book *Metaphors We Live By,* argued that metaphors were socially and psychologically important. They suggested that culturally available metaphors influence how people think about issues. A metaphor that was once strikingly fresh becomes a shared cliché through constant repetition. The shared metaphor can provide a cognitive framework that directs our understanding of the social world. For instance, the competitiveness of politics, or of academic debate, is reinforced by the habitual use of warfare metaphors, which describe views as positions as being "attacked," "defended," or "shot down."

Within the social sciences, metaphors can constitute the core of theoretical insights. For example, the metaphor of social life as theater has been enormously influential in the history of sociology. This dramaturgical metaphor has given rise to terms such as *social actor, social role,* and *social scene.* One can see this metaphor being used in novel, creative ways in the work of Erving Goffman, particularly in his classic book *The Presentation of Self in Everyday Life* (Goffman, 1959).

Metaphors, like coins, lose their shine through circulation. The idea of a "social role" might have once been metaphorical, but now that it has become a standard sociological term, its meaning tends to be understood literally. Role theorists assume that social roles actually exist and that they can be directly observed, even measured. The more recent metaphor—that the social world is a text or discourse to be read—has also traveled along a similar route. What was once novel and metaphorical, as in the work of Roland Barthes (1977), becomes through repetition to be understood much more literally. The development of methodological practices, whether to identify social roles or to "read cultural practices," hastens this journey from the excitingly metaphorical to the routinely literal.

It is too simple to claim that metaphors in the social sciences invariably start by being nonliteral, for some have always been inherently ambiguous. Psychologists have often used the metaphor of "the mind as machine." Even early theorists seem to have been uncertain whether the mind should be understood to be "like a machine" or whether it was actually a machine (Soyland, 1994). What is clear, however, is that as later scientists take up the idea, transforming it into research programs with established methodologies, so progressively the metaphorical element gives way to the literal. When this happens, a field of inquiry may become successfully established, but it will be vulnerable to assault by a younger generation of thinkers, who are inspired by new metaphorical insights.

—Michael Billig

REFERENCES

Barthes, R. (1977). *Image music text.* London: Fontana.
Goffman, E. (1959). *The presentation of self in everyday life.* New York: Anchor.
Lakoff, G., & Johnson, M. (1980). *Metaphors we live by.* Chicago: University of Chicago Press.
Soyland, A. J. (1994). *Psychology as metaphor.* London: Sage.

METHOD VARIANCE

Method variance refers to the effects the method of measurement has on the things being measured. According to classical test theory, the observed VARIANCE among participants in a study on a variable can be attributable to the underlying TRUE SCORE or construct of interest plus RANDOM ERROR. Method variance is an additional source of variance attributable to the method of assessment. Campbell and Fiske (1959) gave examples of apparatus effects with Skinner boxes used to condition rats and format effects with psychological scales.

It has been widely assumed in the absence of solid evidence that when the same method is used to assess different variables, method effects (also called monomethod bias) will produce a certain level of SPURIOUS covariation among those variables. Many researchers, for example, are suspicious of survey studies in which all variables are contained in the same questionnaire, assuming that by being in the same questionnaire, there is a shared method that produces spurious correlation among items. Research on method variance has cast doubt on such assumptions. For example, Spector (1987) was unable to find evidence to support that method effects are widespread in organizational research. One of his arguments was that if method variance produced spurious correlations, why were so many variables in questionnaire studies unrelated? Williams and Brown (1994) conducted analyses showing that in most cases, the existence of variance due to method would serve to attenuate rather than inflate relations among variables.

Spector and Brannick (1995) noted that the traditional view that a method (e.g., questionnaire) would produce method effects across all variables was an oversimplification. They discussed how constructs and methods interacted, so that certain methods used to assess certain variables might produce common variance. Furthermore, they suggested that it was not methods themselves but rather features of methods that were important. For example, SOCIAL DESIRABILITY is a well-known potential BIAS of self-reports about issues that are personally sensitive or threatening (e.g., psychological adjustment), but it does not bias reports of nonsensitive issues. If the method is a self-report and the construct is sensitive, a certain amount of variance will be attributable to social desirability. With such constructs, it may be necessary to find a procedure that can control these effects.

—Paul E. Spector

REFERENCES

Campbell, D. T., & Fiske, D. W. (1959). Convergent and discriminant validation by the multitrait-multimethod matrix. *Psychological Bulletin, 56*, 81–105.

Spector, P. E. (1987). Method variance as an artifact in self-reported affect and perceptions at work: Myth or significant problem? *Journal of Applied Psychology, 72*, 438–443.

Spector, P. E., & Brannick, M. T. (1995). The nature and effects of method variance in organizational research. In C. L. Cooper & I. T. Robertson (Eds.), *International review of industrial and organizational psychology: 1995* (pp. 249–274). West Sussex, England: Wiley.

Williams, L. J., & Brown, B. K. (1994). Method variance in organizational behavior and human resources research: Effects on correlations, path coefficients, and hypothesis testing. *Organizational Behavior and Human Decision Processes, 57*, 185–209.

METHODOLOGICAL HOLISM

The opposite of METHODOLOGICAL INDIVIDUALISM, this doctrine holds that social wholes are more than the sum of individual attitudes, beliefs, and actions and that the whole can often determine the characteristics of individuals. Holism has been prominent in philosophy and social science since Hegel, and, arguably, it has its roots in the writings of Plato. Methodological holism (often abbreviated to *holism*) takes a number of forms across social science disciplines. Although very different in their views and emphases, Marx, Dewey, Durkheim, and Parsons can all be regarded as holists.

The quintessential holist thinker was the sociologist Emile Durkheim (1896/1952), who argued that social effects must be explained by social causes and that psychological explanations of the social were erroneous. His evidence for this came from his study of suicide statistics, over time, in several European countries. Although suicide rates rose and fell, the proportions attributed to individual causes by coroners remained constant, suggesting that even such an individual act as suicide was shaped by social forces.

Holism in anthropology and sociology was much encouraged by the biological "organicism" of Darwinism. Herbert Spencer (Dickens, 2000, pp. 20–24), for example, saw society evolving through the adaptation of structures, in much the same way as biological structures evolved. A more sophisticated version of organic thinking was advanced by Talcott Parsons (1968), in which, like the organs of the human body, the constituent parts of society function to maintain each other. Parsons's holism was explicitly functionalist, but critics of holism and functionalism have maintained that the latter is necessarily at least implicit in the former.

Notwithstanding Popper's and Hayek's political criticisms of holism (see METHODOLOGICAL INDIVIDUALISM), methodological critique has centered on the incompleteness of explanations that do not make ultimate reference to individual beliefs, desires, and actions. For example, although a reference to the Treaty of Versailles and the subsequent war reparations required of Germany might be offered as historical explanations of the origins of World War II, this cannot stand on its own without reference to the views and actions of agents responsible for its enactment and the response to it by other individuals, particularly Hitler.

Durkheim, as well as many after him, believed that sociology particularly depended, as a scientific discipline, on the existence of social facts with an ontological equivalence to that of objects in the physical world. In recent years, however, the language of (and the debate about) methodological holism and individualism has been superseded by that of "structure and agency." Only a few thinkers now refer to themselves as "holists" or "individualists," and although extreme forms of each position can be logically demonstrated, much recent debate concerns the extent to which the social can be explained by individual agency, or agents' beliefs, desires, and actions by the social.

In recent years, sociologists such as Anthony Giddens (1984) and philosophers such as Roy Bhaskar (1998) have attempted to bridge the gap between holism and individualism by advancing versions of "structuration theory," which, in Giddens's case, focuses on social practices, which he argues produce and are produced by structure (Giddens, 1984).

—Malcolm Williams

REFERENCES

Bhaskar, R. (1998). *The possibility of naturalism* (2nd ed.). London: Routledge Kegan Paul.

Dickens, P. (2000). *Social Darwinism.* Buckingham, UK: Open University Press.

Durkheim, E. (1952). *Suicide.* London: Routledge Kegan Paul. (Original work published 1896)

Giddens, A. (1984). *The constitution of society.* Cambridge, UK: Polity.

Parsons, T. (1968). *The structure of social action* (3rd ed.). New York: Free Press.

METHODOLOGICAL INDIVIDUALISM

There is a long tradition in the social sciences—going back to Hobbes and continued through J. S. Mill, Weber, and, more recently, George Homans and J. W. N. Watkins—that insists that explanations of social phenomena must derive from the characteristics and dispositions of individual agents. In recent decades, this *methodological* approach has become somewhat conflated with individualist political and economic doctrines (Lukes, 1994).

Most of the arguments for methodological individualism have been couched in response to the

opposite doctrine, METHODOLOGICAL HOLISM (and vice versa). Individualists reject the latter's claim that there can be social wholes existing beyond or separate to individuals—not by saying these social wholes do not exist, but rather claiming that the social world is brought into being by individuals acting according to the "logic of the situation." That is, individuals create social situations by directing their actions according to the expected behavior of other individuals in particular situations. Complex social situations (e.g., economic systems) are said to result from particular alignments of individual dispositions, beliefs, and physical resources or characteristics. In explaining a given economic system, reference to constituent parts (e.g., the role of merchant banks) can only be seen as partial explanation, although they may be constructed as heuristic models. A full explanation must, at rock bottom, refer to actual or possibly "ideal" (statistical) agents.

Since J. S. Mill, there has been an association between individualist political and economic philosophy in liberalism and an individualist methodological approach. This association became more explicit in the writings of Frederich von Hayek and Karl Popper. Popper maintained that "collective" (holist) explanation blinded us to the truth of the matter that the functioning of all social institutions results from the attitudes, decisions, and actions of individuals. Moreover, he claimed, collectivist views about what *is* lead to collectivist views about what *should* be and, ultimately, the totalitarianism of fascism and communism (Popper, 1986).

Whatever the merits or demerits of this political argument, it is widely acknowledged to be a non sequitur from the methodological argument, which has been associated with thinkers of both the right and left (Phillips, 1976). There are, however, a number of methodological objections to the doctrine, foremost among which is that it leads to the conclusion that social characteristics can only be described in terms of individual psychologies, yet most individual characteristics (such as being a banker, a teacher, or a police officer) can only be explained in terms of social institutions. A second REALIST objection concerns the ontological status of social practices or objects. Methodological individualists maintain that, unlike physical objects that have real properties, social phenomena are simply collective mental constructions. The response to this is that many things in the physical world can only be known by their observed effects (e.g., gravity), and much the same is true of social phenomena such as a foreign policy or a body of law, but they, nonetheless, are real for this.

—Malcolm Williams

REFERENCES

Lukes, S. (1994). Methodological individualism reconsidered. In M. Martin & L. McIntyre (Eds.), *Readings in the philosophy of social science* (pp. 451–459). Cambridge: MIT Press.

Phillips, D. (1976). *Holistic thought in social science.* Stanford, CA: Stanford University Press.

Popper, K. (1986). *The poverty of historicism.* London: ARK.

METRIC VARIABLE

A metric variable is a variable measured QUANTITATIVELY. The distance between the values is equal (e.g., the distance from scores 4 to 6 is the same as the distance from scores 6 to 8). INTERVAL, RATIO, and CONTINUOUS variables can have metric measurement and be treated as metric variables.

—Michael S. Lewis-Beck

See also INTERVAL

MICRO

Micro is the opposite of macro. Microanalysis is small scale, or at the individual level. Macroanalysis is large scale, or at the aggregate level.

—Michael S. Lewis-Beck

MICROSIMULATION

As with SIMULATION, the major purpose of microsimulation is to generate human, social behavior using computer ALGORITHMS. The distinctive feature of microsimulation, however, is that such a MODEL operates at the MICRO level, such as a person, family or household, or company. By simulating large representative MACRO-level POPULATIONS of these micro-level entities, conclusions are drawn to be applicable to an entire society or country. Microsimulation can

play a role not only in BASIC RESEARCH but also in assisting policymaking, such as helping U.S. states weigh different approaches to welfare reform.

—Tim Futing Liao

MIDDLE-RANGE THEORY

An idea that is associated with Robert Merton and his *Social Theory and Social Structure* (1949, 1957, 1968), middle-range theories fall between the working hypotheses of everyday research and unified, general theories of social systems. Merton was critical of the sociological quest for general theories, exemplified by Talcott Parsons's project, because he believed such theories to be too abstract to be empirically testable. However, he did not regard empirical generalizations about the relationship between variables as an adequate alternative. He believed, instead, that sociology should be committed to developing middle-range theories that are both close enough to observed data to be testable and abstract enough to inform systematic theory development. These theories are based on uniformities found in social life and take the form of causal laws (as opposed to empirical description). Merton meant for theories of the middle range to answer his own call for empirically informed sociological theorizing. His hope was that, over time, this program would generate an empirically verified body of social theory that could be consolidated into a scientific foundation for sociology.

Merton's commitments have roots in the philosophy of science and the empirically oriented sociology of his day. A sensitivity to the intellectual limits of extreme generality and particularity can be traced from Plato's *Theaetetus* to Francis Bacon and J. S. Mill. In *A System of Logic,* Mill (1865/1973) notably advocated limited causal theories based on classes of communities. Among sociologists, Merton cites Emile Durkheim's (1951) *Suicide,* with its limited causal theories based on national cases, as the classic example of middle-range theorizing. The ideal grew popular among American sociologists oriented toward research and concerned with the empirical applicability of theory during the first half of the past century. As it did so, space was created for theoretically informed research of a more scientific character than the grand theories of late 19th-century sociology.

Modeled on scientific inquiry, middle-range theories characteristically posit a central idea from which specific hypotheses can be derived and tested. Middle-range theorizing begins with a concept and its associated imagery and develops into a set of associated theoretical puzzles. For Merton, these puzzles centered on the operation of the social mechanisms that give rise to social behavior, organization, and change. Middle-range theorizing should produce causal models of social processes (such as theory of reference groups or social differentiation). The designation of the specific conditions under which a theory applies (scope conditions) fixes it in the middle range. Theorizing of this sort can be fruitfully conducted at both the micro-behavioral (such as the social psychology of small groups) and macro-structural levels (such as the interrelation among elements of social structure) as well as between the two (micro-macro or macro-micro relations).

Although structural functionalism is no longer *de mode,* sociological research in the spirit of middle-range theory continues to be produced, most notably by exchange and network theorists. The ideal of middle-range theory has again been the subject of attention and debate over the past few years. A collection of essays edited by Peter Hedstrom and Richard Swedberg (1998), featuring contributions by academicians from diverse backgrounds, is based on the premise that middle-range theorizing is the key to developing causal models of social processes, specifically focusing on the micro-macro linkage. In a similar spirit to Merton's program, these scholars call for empirically confirmed, rigorously delimited causal sociological theorizing.

—George Ritzer and Todd Stillman

REFERENCES

Durkheim, E. (1951). *Suicide.* New York: Free Press.

Hedstrom, P., & Swedberg, R. (1998). *Social mechanisms: An analytical approach to social theory.* Cambridge, UK: Cambridge University Press.

Merton, R. (1949). *Social theory and social structure.* New York: Free Press.

Merton, R. (1968). *Social theory and social structure* (3rd ed.). New York: Free Press.

Mill, J. S. (1973). *A system of logic.* Toronto: University of Toronto Press. (Original work published 1865)

Sztompka, P. (1990). *Robert Merton: An intellectual profile.* London: Macmillan.

MILGRAM EXPERIMENTS

In Milgram's (1963, 1974) obedience experiments, research participants, in the role of "teacher," were instructed to administer increasingly severe electric shocks to another participant, the "learner," for errors in a learning task. An unexpectedly high percentage of participants followed the experimenter's instructions to administer the maximum (apparently extremely painful) shock level. In fact, no shocks were administered, and all parties to the experiment, with the exception of the "teacher," were members of Milgram's research team. Despite their being, in many respects, so *unlike* any other research, these studies have been, for almost 40 years, the key reference point in discussions of ethical issues in social science research. Why have they been so prominent in the specific context of ethical issues?

1. The Milgram experiments have become the best-known and, for some, the most important research in psychology. Observing high rates of destructive obedience on the part of normal persons, they have been interpreted as revealing a major cause of the Nazi Holocaust (Miller, 1995). The unusual circumstance of a research program being both extraordinarily famous but also extremely controversial ethically has contributed to the unprecedented impact of these studies and created a highly instructive benchmark for discussing research ethics *in general.*

2. Milgram's first published account (1963) presented highly graphic portraits of stress and tension experienced by the research participants: "I observed a mature and initially poised businessman enter the laboratory smiling and confident. Within 20 minutes he was reduced to a twitching, stuttering wreck, who was rapidly approaching a point of nervous collapse" (Milgram, 1963, p. 377). It was in the context of these reports that the Milgram experiments came to be viewed as exposing participants to possibly dangerous levels of psychological risk.

3. A landmark citation was an early ethical critique of the Milgram experiments by Diana Baumrind (1964), published in the *American Psychologist.* Baumrind accused Milgram of (a) violating the experimenter's obligation to protect the emotional welfare of participants, (b) conducting an inadequate postexperimental DEBRIEFING, and (c) using a flawed methodology that produced highly questionable

results, thus arguing that the benefits of Milgram's research were not worth the ethical costs. She concluded that Milgram's participants would experience a loss of trust in authority figures and a permanent loss of self-esteem. Although Baumrind's criticisms were subsequently rebutted by Milgram and many others (Miller, 1986), her commentary had a powerful impact and became a model for ethical criticism.

4. A key feature of the Milgram experiments was the coercion built into the method. Participants who expressed a desire to withdraw from the study, were continuously prodded by the experimenter to continue in their role of shocking the other participant. By current ethical standards of the American Psychological Association (APA), this coercive aspect could make the obedience research unethical:

APA Ethics Codes Revision Draft 6,
October 21, 2001
8.02 INFORMED CONSENT to Research

When obtaining informed consent as required in Standard 3.10, Informed Consent, psychologists inform participants about (1) the purpose of the research, expected duration, and procedures; (2) their right to decline to participate and to withdraw from the research once participation has begun.

Although the use of DECEPTION and a lack of a truthful informed consent were also important features of the Milgram experiments, these factors, in themselves, are not a crucial feature of the legacy of the Milgram experiments. A significant proportion of contemporary psychological research (including the Ethical Guidelines of the APA) endorses a judicious use of deception (Epley & Huff, 1998).

In conclusion, the Milgram experiments have had a profound impact on considerations of ethical issues in research. The invaluable, often impassioned, debates surrounding these experiments have sensitized generations of students and researchers to the emotional and cognitive risk factors in research methods. The routine use of institutional review boards to assess, independent of primary investigators, ethical aspects of research prior to the conduct of such inquiry can also be viewed as a highly significant legacy of the Milgram experiments. Finally, the Milgram experiments have taught us that there may be inevitable ethical costs in the conduct of highly significant and potentially beneficial

psychological research. The rights of researchers to inquire must be honored while simultaneously gauging and protecting the vulnerabilities of their participants.

—Arthur G. Miller

REFERENCES

Baumrind, D. (1964). Some thoughts on ethics after reading Milgram's "Behavioral study of obedience." *American Psychologist, 19,* 421–423.

Epley, N., & Huff, C. (1998). Suspicion, affective response, and educational benefit of deception in psychology research. *Personality and Social Psychology Bulletin, 24,* 759–768.

Milgram, S. (1963). Behavioral study of obedience. *Journal of Abnormal and Social Psychology, 67,* 371–378.

Milgram, S. (1974). *Obedience to authority: An experimental view.* New York: Harper & Row.

Miller, A. G. (1986). *The obedience experiments: A case study of controversy in social science.* New York: Praeger.

Miller, A. G. (1995). Constructions of the obedience experiments: A focus upon domains of relevance. *Journal of Social Issues, 51,* 33–53.

MISSING DATA

In the social sciences, nearly all QUANTITATIVE DATA sets have missing data, which simply means that data are missing on some variables for some cases in the data set. For example, annual income may be available for 70% of the respondents in a sample but missing for the other 30%. There are many possible reasons why data are missing. Respondents may refuse to answer a question or may accidentally skip it. Interviewers may forget to ask a question or may not record the response. In longitudinal studies, persons may die or move away before the next follow-up interview. If data sets are created by merging different files, there may be matching failures or lost records.

Whatever the reasons, missing data typically create substantial problems for statistical analysis. Virtually all standard statistical methods presume that every case has complete information on all variables of interest. Until recently, there has been very little guidance for researchers on what to do about missing data. Instead, researchers have chosen from a collection of ad hoc methods that had little to recommend them except long and widespread usage. Fortunately, two principled methods for handling missing data are now available: maximum likelihood and multiple imputation. If appropriate assumptions are met, these methods have excellent statistical properties and are now within the reach of the average researcher. This entry first reviews conventional methods for handling missing data and then considers the two newer methods. To say meaningful things about the properties of any of these methods, one must first specify the assumptions under which they are valid.

ASSUMPTIONS

To keep things simple, let us suppose that a data set contains only two variables, X and Y. We observe X for all cases, but data are missing on Y for, say, 20% of the cases. We say that data on Y are *missing completely at random* (MCAR) if the probability that data are missing on Y depends on neither Y nor X. Formally, we have Pr(Y is missing$|X, Y$) = Pr(Y is missing). Many missing data techniques are valid only under this rather strong assumption.

A weaker assumption is that the data are *missing at random* (MAR). This assumption states that the probability that data are missing on Y may depend on the value of X but does *not* depend on the value of Y, holding X constant. Formally, we have Pr(Y is missing$|X, Y$) = Pr(Y is missing$|X$). Suppose, for example, that Y is a measure of income and X is years of schooling. The MAR assumption would be satisfied if the probability that income is missing depends on years of schooling, but within each level of schooling, the probability of missing income does not depend on income itself. Clearly, if the data are missing completely at random, they are also missing at random.

It is certainly possible to test whether the data are missing completely at random. For example, one could compare males and females to see whether they differ in the proportion of cases with missing data on particular variables. Any such difference would be a violation of MCAR. However, it is impossible to test whether the data are missing at random. For obvious reasons, you cannot tell whether persons with high income are less likely than those with moderate income to have missing data on income.

Missing data are said to be *ignorable* if the data are MAR and, in addition, the parameters governing the missing data mechanism are completely distinct from the parameters of the model to be estimated. This somewhat technical condition is unlikely to be violated in the real world. Even if it were, methods that assume ignorability would still perform very well if the data

are only MAR. It is just that one could do even better by modeling the missing data mechanism as part of the estimation process. So in practice, *missing at random* and *ignorability* are often used interchangeably.

CONVENTIONAL METHODS

The most common method for handling missing data—and the one that is the default in virtually all statistical packages—is known as LISTWISE DELETION or *complete case analysis*. The rule for this method is very simple: Delete any case that has missing data on any of the variables in the analysis of interest. Because the cases that are left all have complete data, statistical methods can then be applied with no difficulty.

Listwise deletion has several attractive features. Besides being easy to implement, it has the virtue that it works for *any* statistical method. Furthermore, if the data are missing completely at random, listwise deletion will not introduce any bias into the analysis. That is because under MCAR, the subset of the sample with complete data is effectively a SIMPLE RANDOM SAMPLE from the original data set. For the same reason, STANDARD ERRORS estimated by conventional methods will be valid estimates of the true standard errors.

The big problem with listwise deletion is that it often results in the elimination of a large fraction of the cases in the data set. Suppose, for example, that the goal is to estimate a multiple regression model with 10 variables. Suppose, furthermore, that each variable has 5% missing data and that the probability of missing on any variable is unrelated to whether or not data are missing on any other variables. Then, on average, half the cases would be lost under listwise deletion. The consequence would be greatly increased standard errors and reduced statistical power.

Other conventional methods are designed to salvage some of the data lost by listwise deletion, but these methods often do more harm than good. PAIRWISE DELETION, also known as *available case analysis,* is a method that can be easily implemented for a wide class of linear models, including MULTIPLE REGRESSION and FACTOR ANALYSIS. For each pair of variables in the analysis, the correlation (or covariance) is estimated using all the cases with no missing data for those two variables. These correlations are combined into a single correlation matrix, which is then used as input to linear modeling programs. Under MCAR, estimates produced by this method are consistent (and thus approximately unbiased), but standard errors and associated test statistics are typically biased. Furthermore, the method may break down entirely (if the correlation matrix is not positive definite).

Dummy variable adjustment is a popular method for handling missing data on independent variables in a regression analysis. When a variable X has missing data, a dummy (indicator) variable D is created with a value of 1 if data are present on that variable and 0 otherwise; for cases with missing data, X is set to some constant (e.g., the mean for nonmissing cases). Both X and D are then included as independent variables in the model. Although this approach would seem to incorporate all the available information into the model, it has been shown to produce biased estimates even if the data are MCAR.

A variety of missing data methods fall under the general heading of IMPUTATION, which means to substitute some plausible values for the missing data. After all the missing data have been imputed, the statistical analysis is conducted as if there were no missing data. One of the simplest methods is *unconditional mean imputation*: If a variable has any missing data, the mean for the cases without missing data is substituted for those cases with missing data. But this method is known to produce biased estimates of many parameters; in particular, variances are always underestimated. Somewhat better is *conditional mean imputation*: If a variable has missing data, one estimates a linear regression of that variable on other variables for those cases without missing data. Then, the estimated regression line is used to generate predicted values for the missing data. This method can produce approximately unbiased estimates of regression coefficients if the data are MCAR.

Even if one can avoid bias in parameter estimates, however, all conventional methods of imputation lead to underestimates of standard errors. The reason is quite simple. Standard methods of analysis presume that all the data are real. If some data are imputed, the imputation process introduces additional sampling variability that is not adequately accounted for.

MAXIMUM LIKELIHOOD

Much better than conventional methods is MAXIMUM LIKELIHOOD (ML). Under a correctly specified model, ML can produce estimates that are consistent (and, hence, approximately unbiased), ASYMPTOTICALLY efficient, and asymptotically normal, even when data are missing (Little & Rubin, 2002). If the

missing data mechanism is ignorable, constructing the likelihood function is relatively easy: One simply sums or integrates the conventional likelihood over the missing values. Maximization of that likelihood can then be accomplished by conventional numerical methods.

Although the general principles of ML for missing data have been known for many years, only recently have practical computational methods become widely available. One very general numerical method for getting ML estimates when data are missing is the EM algorithm. However, most EM software only produces estimates of means, variances, and covariances, under the assumption of multivariate normality. Furthermore, the method does not produce estimates of standard errors.

Much more useful is the incorporation of ML missing data methods into popular structural equations modeling programs, notably LISREL (www.ssicentral.com/lisrel), AMOS (www.smallwaters.com), and MPLUS (www.statmodel.com). Under the assumption of multivariate normality, these programs produce ML estimates for a wide class of linear models, including linear regression and factor analysis. Estimated standard errors make appropriate adjustments for the missing data.

For categorical data analysis, ML methods for missing data have been implemented in the program ℓEM (http://cwis.kub.nl/~fsw_1/mto/mto3.htm). This software estimates a large class of LOG-LINEAR and LATENT CLASS models with missing data. It will also estimate LOGISTIC REGRESSION models when all predictor variables are discrete.

MULTIPLE IMPUTATION

Although ML is a very good method for handling missing data, it still requires specialized software to do the statistical analysis. At present, such software is only available for a rather limited class of problems. A much more general method is *multiple imputation* (MI), which can be used for virtually any kind of data and for any kind of analysis. Furthermore, the analysis can be done with conventional software.

The basic idea of MI is simple. Instead of imputing a single value for each missing datum, multiple values are produced by introducing a random component into the imputation process. As few as three imputed values will suffice for many applications, although more are certainly preferable. These multiple imputations are used to construct multiple data sets. So if three imputed values are generated for each missing value, the result will be three "completed" data sets, all with the same values for the nonmissing data but with slightly different values for the imputed data.

Next, the analysis is performed on each completed data set using conventional software. Finally, the results of these replicated analyses are combined according to some very simple rules. For parameter estimates, one takes the mean of the estimates across the replications. Standard errors are calculated by averaging the squared standard errors across replications, adding the variance of the parameter estimates across replications (with a small correction factor), and then taking the square root. The formula is

$$SE(\bar{b})$$
$$= \sqrt{\frac{1}{M} \sum_k s_k^2 + \left(1 + \frac{1}{M}\right) \left(\frac{1}{M-1}\right) \sum_k (b_k - \bar{b})^2},$$

where b_k is the parameter estimate in replication k, s_k is the estimated standard error of b_k, and M is the number of replications.

This method accomplishes three things. First, appropriate introduction of random variation into the imputation process can eliminate the biases in parameter estimation that are endemic to deterministic imputation methods. Second, repeating the process several times and averaging the parameter estimates results in more stable estimates (with less sampling variability). Finally, the variability in the parameter estimates across replications makes it possible to get good estimates of the standard errors that fully reflect the uncertainty in the imputation process.

How do the statistical properties of MI compare with those of ML? If all the assumptions are met, MI produces estimates that are consistent and asymptotically normal, just like ML. However, they are not fully efficient unless there are an infinite number of imputations, something not likely to be seen in practice. In most cases, however, only a handful of imputations are necessary to achieve close to full efficiency.

Now that we have the basic structure of multiple imputation, the next and obvious question is how to generate the imputations. There are many different ways to do this. Like ML, the first step is to choose a model for the data. The most popular model, at present, is the multivariate normal model, which implies that (a) all variables are normally distributed and (b) each variable can be represented as a linear function of all

the other variables. The force of this assumption is that all imputations are based on linear regressions. The random variation in imputed values is accomplished by making random draws from NORMAL DISTRIBUTIONS that have the estimated residual variance from each linear regression. These random draws are added to the predicted values for each case with missing data.

The details of how to accomplish all this can get rather technical and are not worth pursuing here. (Schafer [1997] gives a very thorough treatment; Allison [2001] provides a less technical discussion.) Fortunately, there are now several readily available computer programs that produce multiple imputations with a minimum of effort on the part of the user. SAS has recently introduced procedures for producing multiple imputations and for combining results from multiple imputation analyses (www.sas.com). SOLAS is a commercial stand-alone program for doing MI (www.statsolusa.com). Freeware stand-alone programs include NORM (www.stat.psu.edu/~jls) and AMELIA (gking.harvard.edu/stats.shtml).

MI can seem very complicated and intimidating to the novice. Although it is certainly more work than most conventional methods for handling missing data, good software can make MI a relatively painless process. For example, to do MI for multiple regression in SAS, one needs only two lines of additional program code to do the imputation, one additional line in the regression procedure, and two lines of subsequent code to combine the results.

OTHER APPROACHES

Before closing, other methods currently under development deserve a brief mention. Although MI methods based on the multivariate normal model are the most widely and easily used, other parametric models may be less restrictive. For example, imputations can be generated under a log-linear model, a general location scale model (for both categorical and quantitative variables), or a sequential generalized regression model. There are also nonparametric and semiparametric methods available for multiple imputation.

Although the MI and ML methods discussed here are all based on the assumption that the missing data mechanism is ignorable, it is quite possible to apply both methods to nonignorable situations in which the probability of missing data on Y depends on the value of Y itself. Heckman's method for handling selectivity bias is a good example of how to accomplish this by ML. However, methods for nonignorable missing data tend to be extremely sensitive to the choice of models for the missing data mechanism.

—Paul D. Allison

REFERENCES

Allison, P. D. (2001). *Missing data.* Thousand Oaks, CA: Sage.

Little, R. J. A., & Rubin, D. B. (2002). *Statistical analysis with missing data* (2nd ed.). New York: John Wiley.

Schafer, J. L. (1997). *Analysis of incomplete multivariate data.* London: Chapman & Hall.

MISSPECIFICATION

Among the assumptions employed in classical linear REGRESSION, it is taken that the researcher has specified the "true" model for estimation. Misspecification refers to several and varied conditions under which this assumption is not met. The consequences of model misspecification for PARAMETER ESTIMATES and STANDARD ERRORS may be either minor or serious depending on the type of misspecification and other mitigating circumstances. Tests for various kinds of misspecification lead us to consider the bases for choice among competing MODELS.

TYPES OF MISSPECIFICATION

Models may be incorrectly specified in one or more of three basic ways: (a) with respect to the set of REGRESSORS selected, (b) in the measurement of model variables, and (c) in the specification of the stochastic term or ERROR, u_i. First, estimation problems created by incorrect selection of regressors will vary depending on whether the researcher has (a) omitted an important variable from the model (see OMITTED VARIABLE), (b) included an extraneous variable, or (c) misspecified the functional form of the relationship between X_i and Y. Under most circumstances, the first condition—omission of a relevant variable from the model—results in the most serious consequences for model estimates. Specifically, if some variable Z_i is responsible for a portion of the variation in Y, yet Z_i is omitted from the model, then parameter estimates will be both biased and inconsistent, unless Z is perfectly independent of the included variables. The extent and direction of BIAS depend on the CORRELATION between the omitted

Z_i and the included variables X_k. Inclusion of an extraneous variable (i.e., "overfitting" the model) is generally less damaging because all model parameters remain unbiased and consistent. However, a degree of inefficiency in those estimates is introduced in that the calculated standard errors for each parameter take account of the correlation between each "true" variable and the extraneous X_k. Because that correlation is likely to be nonzero in the sample, estimated standard errors are inflated unnecessarily. Misspecification of the functional form linking Y to X can be seen as a mixed case of overfitting as well as underfitting. Imagine a "true" model, $Y = \beta_0 + \beta_1 X_1 + \beta_2 X_2^2 + u_i$. If we now estimate a model in which Y is a simple linear function of X_1 and X_2 (rather than the square of X_2 found in the true model)—that is, $Y = \alpha_0 + \alpha_1 X_1 + \alpha_2 X_2 + e_i$—then parameter estimates and standard errors for α_0, α_1, and α_2 will be vitiated by the inclusion of the extraneous X_2 as well as by the omission of the squared term X_2^2.

Beyond the incorrect choice of regressors, measurement errors in the dependent and independent variables may be viewed as a form of model misspecification. This is true simply because such measurement error may result in the same variety of problems in parameter estimation as discussed above (i.e., estimated parameters that are biased, inconsistent, or inefficient). Finally, proper identification of the process creating the stochastic errors, u_i, can be seen as a model specification issue. To see this point, begin with the common assumption that the errors are distributed normally with mean zero and variance σ^2 (i.e., $u_i \sim N(0, \sigma^2)$). Now imagine that the true errors are generated by any other process (e.g., perhaps the errors may exhibit HETEROSKEDASTICITY or they are distributed log normal). In this instance, we will again face issues of bias, inconsistency, or inefficiency depending on the particular form of misspecification of the error term.

TESTS FOR MISSPECIFICATION

Good THEORY is by far the most important guide we have in avoiding misspecification. But given that social science theories are often weak or tentative, empirical tests of proper specification become more important. A variety of tests are associated with each of the specification problems described above. One should always begin with analysis of RESIDUALS from the initial estimation. Cases sharing common traits that cluster above or below the regression line often suggest an omitted variable. General patterns in those residuals may suggest a nonlinear relationship between X and Y (i.e., an issue of functional form) or perhaps other pathologies such as heteroskedasticity. In short, analysis of residuals is an important means whereby the researcher comes to know the cases and their relationship to the model specified. Specification, especially when theory is weak, is an iterative process between model and data.

If one suspects that some omitted variable, Z_i, may be part of the true model, the well-known DURBIN-WATSON d statistic may be employed to test this hypothesis. Simply arrange the original ordinary least squares (OLS) residuals according to values of Z_i and compute d by the usual means. Rejection of the null hypothesis indicates that Z_i has indeed been incorrectly omitted from the original specification. More general tests for omitted variables include Ramsey's RESET and the Lagrange multiplier (LM) test. Neither RESET nor the LM test, however, is capable of identifying the missing variable(s). That important step can only be informed by refinement of theory and deepened understanding of the cases, perhaps through techniques such as analysis of residuals. Gujarati (2003, pp. 518–524) describes specific steps to be taken with these tests in greater detail.

MODEL SPECIFICATION AND MODEL SELECTION

Given that we can never be certain that we have correctly identified the "true" model, modern practitioners argue that our efforts are better focused on assessing the adequacy of contending models of a given phenomenon Y. Imagine two contending models of Y. If all explanatory variables in one contender are a perfect subset of variables included in a second model, then we may say the first is "nested" within the second. Recalling that the regressand must be identical across equations, well-known statistics such as adjusted R-SQUARED, the F test and the likelihood ratio test (for nonlinear estimators) are entirely appropriate to assess the empirical adequacy of one model against another. Competing models are "nonnested" when the set of regressors in one contender overlaps partially or not at all with the regressors included in the second contending model of Y. Keynesian versus monetarist models of gross national product (GNP) growth, for example, would be nonnested competitors. Comparing the relative performance of nonnested models, the

researcher may turn again to adjusted R^2 and certain other GOODNESS-OF-FIT MEASURES such as the Akaike Information Criterion. Clarke (2001, pp. 732–735) also describes application of the Cox test and Vuong test for these purposes. Finally, the activity of model selection lends itself quite directly to BAYESIAN INFERENCE, especially when, practically speaking, our data are not subject to repeated sampling. The subject of model selection from a Bayesian perspective is introduced in Leamer (1978) and updated in an applied setting in Clarke (2001).

—Brian M. Pollins

REFERENCES

Clarke, K. A. (2001). Testing nonnested models of international relations: Reevaluating realism. *American Journal of Political Science, 45,* 724–744.

Gujarati, D. N. (2003). *Basic econometrics* (4th ed.). Boston: McGraw-Hill.

Leamer, E. E. (1978). *Specification searches.* New York: John Wiley.

MIXED DESIGNS

Mixed designs have long been a mainstay of experimentation, but in recent years, their importance has been made greater still by the development of a new statistical methodology. This methodology, called *mixed modeling,* enhances the VALIDITY of analyses of the data generated by a mixed design.

Mixed design is a term that sometimes has been loosely applied to any research plan involving both QUALITATIVE and QUANTITATIVE variables or, alternatively, involving both manipulated and unmanipulated variables. However, psychologists usually define it as a formal research plan that includes both *between*-subjects and *within*-subjects factors, and statisticians generally define it as a RESEARCH DESIGN that involves the estimation of both *fixed* factor effects and *random* factor effects.

With a between-subjects factor, each experimental unit is exposed to only a single level of that factor. The factor levels are mutually exclusive and (assuming a balanced design) involve an equal number of experimental units. In other words, each factor level will have the same number of exposed units. When the set of levels is exhaustive and not merely a sample, such a factor's effects are *fixed.*

With a within-subjects factor, each experimental unit is exposed to all factor levels. Such a factor's effect is *random* when it involves a random sampling of the set of levels that can be found for some larger population. Blocking effects may be treated as random when the experimental blocks are seen as a sample of the population of blocks about which inferences are to be drawn.

Consider this example: An EXPERIMENT tests, by gender, the effect of drug therapy on 100 severely depressed patients. The gender factor in the study has only two levels, male and female, both of which have equal numbers. Gender here is a between-subjects factor with fixed effects. The drug therapy factor, on the other hand, is based on a random selection of four drugs (levels) from the large set of antidepressant drugs now available for prescription. Such sampling permits estimation of the random (treatment) effect of the entire population of antidepressant drugs in dealing with depression. *Drug* here is a within-subjects factor. Note, however, that had the design involved not testing an overall (sampled) drug effect but rather the individual effect for each of the four drugs—and *only* these four—the drug factor effects would be considered fixed, not random. In either case, when the selection of subjects for the study can reasonably be assumed to be a random selection from a larger POPULATION of patients, *patient* also would be a factor with random effects.

There are numerous types of mixed designs. Although many are quite similar, each may require somewhat different data-analytic methods, depending on how treatments are applied to experimental units. Four common mixed designs are REPEATED MEASURES, SPLIT PLOT, NESTED or hierarchical, and RANDOMIZED BLOCKS. In *repeated-measures designs* (sometimes called within-subjects designs), experimental units are measured more than once. When a time series of effect data will be collected, measurement intervals are to be of equal length. These designs are fully randomized and may or may not include a between-subjects factor (other than the treatment). If such a factor is present, the design is said to have a split-plot/repeated-measures structure.

In basic *split-plot designs,* experimental units are of two different sizes, the larger being blocks of the smaller. Two treatments are involved. The first (the within-subjects factor) is assigned to the larger units, and the second (the between-subjects factor) is assigned to the smaller units separately within each larger block. There are similarities between repeated-measures designs and split-plot designs in that the treatment factor in the former is equivalent to the larger unit ("whole plot") treatment in the latter. In addition, the time factor in the repeated-measures design is equivalent to the smaller unit ("subplot") treatment in the split-plot design. However, the covariance structure of the data from a repeated-measures design usually requires methods of analysis different from those for data from a true split-plot design.

Nested or hierarchical designs involve the nesting of one experimental factor within another. (Nested designs are sometimes called between-subjects designs.) A simple version of this design is found when experimental units merely are nested within conditions. In a "purely hierarchical" design, every set of factors has an inside-outside relationship. When blocks are nested within a between-blocks factor, the nested design is equivalent to a split-plot design. With nesting of blocks, the inside factor groups are completely embedded within the larger factor grouping. Consequently, it is not possible to separate the insider factor's effects from an insider-outsider interaction.

In *randomized blocks designs,* treatments are randomly assigned to units within blocks. Treatment effects are usually considered fixed (no treatments other than those actually in the experiment are considered). Block effects are considered random, a sampling of the larger set of blocks about which conclusions are to be drawn. In cases when each treatment is applied in each block, the design is called a randomized complete blocks design.

The analysis of the data from mixed designs is made problematic by the random factor(s). The recently developed and now preferred approach uses MAXIMUM LIKELIHOOD ESTIMATION (rather that LEAST SQUARES), in which there is no assumption that variance components are independently and identically distributed. This is possible because the covariances are modeled within the analysis itself. Such mixed modeling can generate appropriate error terms even in the presence of MISSING DATA (and an unbalanced design). Nonetheless, valid SIGNIFICANCE TESTS for the random factors still must meet the SPHERICITY ASSUMPTION for F tests to be valid. Sphericity (or its equivalents: circularity, Huynh-Feldt structure, or Type H covariance structure) is found when all the variances of the differences (in the population sampled) are equal.

—Douglas Madsen

REFERENCES

Cobb, G. W. (1998). *Introduction to design and analysis of experiments*. New York: Springer-Verlag.

Littell, R. C., Milliken, G. A., Stroup, W. W., & Wolfinger. R. D. (1996). *SAS system for mixed models*. Cary, NC: SAS Institute, Inc.

Milliken, G. A., & Johnson, D. E. (1992). *Analysis of messy data: Vol. 1. Designed experiments*. London: Chapman & Hall.

MIXED-EFFECTS MODEL

ANALYSIS OF VARIANCE (ANOVA) models can be used to study how a dependent variable Y depends on one or several factors. A *factor* here is defined as a categorical independent variable—in other words, an explanatory variable with a nominal LEVEL OF MEASUREMENT. Factors can have fixed or random effects. For a factor with fixed effects, the parameters expressing the effect of the categories of each factor are fixed (i.e., nonrandom) numbers. For a factor with random effects, the effects of its categories are modeled as random variables. Fixed effects are appropriate when the statistical inference aims at finding conclusions that hold for precisely the categories of the factor that are present in the data set at hand. Random effects are appropriate when the categories of the factor are regarded as a random sample from some population, and the statistical inference aims at finding conclusions that hold for this population. If the model contains only fixed or only random effects, we speak of FIXED-EFFECTS MODELS or RANDOM-EFFECTS MODELS, respectively. A model containing fixed as well as random effects is called a mixed-effects model.

An example of a mixed-effects ANOVA model could be a study about work satisfaction of employees in several job categories in several organizations. If the researcher is interested in a limited number of specific job categories and in a population of organizations, as well as, inter alia, the amount of variability between the organizations in this population, then it is natural to use a mixed model, with fixed effects for the job categories and random effects for the organizations.

Random effects, as defined above and in the entry on random-effects models, can be regarded as random main effects of the levels of a given factor. Random interaction effects can be defined similarly. In the example from the previous paragraph, a random job category-by-organization interaction effect also could be included.

Mixed-effects models are also used for the analysis of data collected according to SPLIT-PLOT DESIGNS or REPEATED-MEASURES DESIGNS. In such designs, individual subjects (or other units) are investigated under several conditions. Suppose that the conditions form one factor, called B; the individual subjects are also regarded as a factor, called S. The mixed-effects model for this design has a fixed effect for B, a random effect for S, and a random $B \times S$ interaction effect.

THE LINEAR MIXED MODEL

A generalization is a random coefficient of a numerical explanatory variable. This leads to the generalization of the GENERAL LINEAR MODEL, which incorporates fixed as well as random coefficients, commonly called the linear mixed model or random coefficient regression model. In matrix form, this can be written as

$$Y = \mathbf{X}\boldsymbol{\beta} + \mathbf{Z}\mathbf{U} + \mathbf{E},$$

where Y is the dependent variable, $\mathbf{X}$ is the design matrix for the fixed effects, $\boldsymbol{\beta}$ is the vector of fixed regression coefficients, $\mathbf{Z}$ is the design matrix for the random coefficients, $\mathbf{U}$ is the vector of random coefficients, and $\mathbf{E}$ is the vector of random residuals. The standard assumption is that the vectors $\mathbf{U}$ and $\mathbf{E}$ are independent and have multivariate normal distributions with zero mean vectors and with covariance matrices $\mathbf{G}$ and $\mathbf{R}$, respectively. This assumption implies that Y has the multivariate normal distribution with mean $\mathbf{X}\boldsymbol{\beta}$ and covariance matrix $\mathbf{Z}\mathbf{G}\mathbf{Z}' + \mathbf{R}$. Depending on the study design, a further structure will usually be imposed on the matrices $\mathbf{G}$ and $\mathbf{R}$. For example, if there are K factors with random effects and the residuals are purely random, then the model can be specialized to

$$Y = \mathbf{X}\boldsymbol{\beta} + \mathbf{Z}_1\mathbf{U}_1 + \mathbf{Z}_2\mathbf{U}_2 + \cdots + \mathbf{Z}_K\mathbf{U}_K + \mathbf{E},$$

where now all vectors $\mathbf{U}_1, \ldots, \mathbf{U}_K$ and $\mathbf{E}$ are independent and have multivariate normal distributions with zero mean vectors and covariance matrices $\mathbf{G}_1, \ldots, \mathbf{G}_K$ and $\sigma^2\mathbf{I}$, respectively, and where no further restrictions are imposed on the matrices $\mathbf{G}_1$ to $\mathbf{G}_K$ and the scalar σ^2. This model is the matrix formulation of the HIERARCHICAL LINEAR MODEL but without the assumption that the factors with random effects are hierarchically nested, and it is a basic model for MULTI-LEVEL ANALYSIS. For $K = 1$, this is the two-level hierarchical linear model, often used for the analysis of longitudinal data (see Verbeke & Molenberghs, 2000, and the entry on MULTILEVEL ANALYSIS). For longitudinal data, the covariance matrix $\mathbf{R}$ can also be assumed to have specific nondiagonal forms, expressing autocorrelation or other kinds of time dependence.

Mixed-effects models can also be defined as extensions of the GENERALIZED LINEAR MODEL. In such models, the linear predictor $\eta = \mathbf{X}\boldsymbol{\beta}$, as defined in the entry on generalized linear models, is replaced by the term $\mathbf{X}\boldsymbol{\beta} + \mathbf{Z}\mathbf{U}$. This gives a general mathematical formulation of so-called generalized linear mixed models, which generalize HIERARCHICAL NONLINEAR MODELS to the case of random factors that are not necessarily nested.

—Tom A. B. Snijders

REFERENCES

Cobb, G. W. (1998). *Introduction to design and analysis of experiments.* New York: Springer-Verlag.

Longford, N. T. (1993). *Random coefficient models.* New York: Oxford University Press.

McCulloch, C. E., & Searle, S. R. (2001). *Generalized, linear and mixed models.* New York: John Wiley.

Neter, J., Kutner, M., Nachtsheim, C., & Wasserman, W. W. (1996). *Applied linear regression models.* New York: Irwin.

Verbeke, G., & Molenberghs, G. (2000). *Linear mixed models for longitudinal data.* New York: Springer.

MIXED-METHOD RESEARCH. *See* MULTIMETHOD RESEARCH

MIXTURE MODEL (FINITE MIXTURE MODEL)

Finite mixture model is another name for LATENT CLASS ANALYSIS. These models assume that parameters of a statistical model of interest differ across unobserved subgroups called *latent classes* or *mixture components*. The most important kinds of applications of finite mixture models are clustering, scaling, density estimation, and RANDOM-EFFECTS MODELING.

—Jeroen K. Vermunt

MLE. *See* MAXIMUM LIKELIHOOD ESTIMATION

MOBILITY TABLE

A mobility table is a two-way CONTINGENCY TABLE in which the individuals are classified according to the same variable on two occasions. It therefore distinguishes between the "immobile" (i.e., all the cases on the main diagonal of the table) and the "mobile," who are classified elsewhere. Mobility tables are very common in the social sciences (e.g., to study geographical mobility of households from one census to another or to examine electorate mobility between candidates during an election campaign). In sociology, intergenerational mobility tables cross-classify the respondents' own social class with their class of origin (usually father's class), whereas intragenerational mobility tables cross-classify their occupation or class at two points in time.

HISTORICAL DEVELOPMENT

Essentially developed in sociology from the 1950s, the statistical methodology of mobility tables was primarily based on the computation of indexes. The mobility ratio or Glass's index was proposed as the ratio of each observed frequency in the mobility table to the corresponding expected frequency under the hypothesis of statistical independence (also called "perfect mobility"). Yasuda's index and Boudon's index were based on the decomposition of total mobility as the sum of two components: structural or "forced" mobility (the dissimilarity between marginal distributions implies that all cases cannot be on the diagonal) and net mobility (conceived of as reflecting the intensity of association). However, with time, the shortcomings of mobility indexes became increasingly clear.

Since the 1980s, the new paradigm has been to analyze mobility tables from two perspectives. Total immobility rate $(\sum_i f_{ii}/f_{++})$, outflow percentages (f_{ij}/f_{i+}), and inflow percentages (f_{ij}/f_{+j}) are simple tools to describe absolute (or observed) mobility. But absolute mobility also results from the combination of the marginals of the table with an intrinsic pattern of ASSOCIATION between the variables. The study of relative mobility consists of analyzing the structure and strength of that association with LOG-LINEAR MODELS and ODDS RATIOS.

Among these models, "topological" or "levels" models are an important class based on the idea that different densities underlie the cells of the mobility table. In the two-way multiplicative (log-linear) model $F_{ij} = \alpha\beta_i\gamma_j\delta_{ij}$, positing $\delta_{ij} = 1$ for all i and all j leads to the independence model. It assumes that a single density applies for the entire table; that is, each of the mobility or immobility trajectories is equally plausible (net of marginal effects). Positing $\delta_{ij} = \delta$ if $i = j$ and $\delta_{ij} = 1$ otherwise corresponds to a two-density model (with one degree of freedom less than the independence model) called the *uniform inheritance model* because δ, which is usually more than 1, captures a propensity toward immobility common to all categories. Assuming that this propensity is specific to each category ($\delta_{ij} = \delta_i$ if $i = j$) leads to the *quasi-perfect mobility model*. With the insight that the same density can apply to cells on and off the diagonal, R. M. Hauser (1978), following previous work by Leo Goodman,

proposed the general levels model: $F_{ij} = \alpha\beta_i\gamma_j\delta_k$ if the cell (i, j) belongs to the kth density level.

EXAMPLE

Table 1 is a mobility table that cross-classifies the father's occupation by the son's first full-time civilian occupation for U.S. men between ages 20 and 64 in 1973. The total immobility rate is 39.9% $((1,414 + 524 + \cdots + 1,832)/19,912)$; that is, two out of five sons belong to the same category as their father. As regards the outflow perspective, 39.4% of farmers' sons are themselves farmers $(1,832/4,650)$; as regards the inflow perspective, 80.9% of farmers have farm origins $(1,832/2,265)$. These two figures and their contrast reflect (and confound) both the interaction effect (the propensity toward immobility into farming) and marginal effects (the importance of the farm category among fathers and among sons).

To isolate interaction effects, we need log-linear modeling. Although the perfect mobility model is very far from the data (the LIKELIHOOD RATIO STATISTIC L^2 is 6,170.13 with 16 degrees of freedom), the

Table 1   Mobility Table

Father's Occupation	Son's Occupation					
	Upper Nonmanual	Lower Nonmanual	Upper Manual	Lower Manual	Farm	Total
Upper nonmanual	1,414	521	302	643	40	2,920
Lower nonmanual	724	524	254	703	48	2,253
Upper manual	798	648	856	1,676	108	4,086
Lower manual	756	914	771	3,325	237	6,003
Farm	409	357	441	1,611	1,832	4,650
Total	4,101	2,964	2,624	7,958	2,265	19,912

Table 2   Five-Level Model of Mobility

Father's Occupation	Son's Occupation				
	Upper Nonmanual	Lower Nonmanual	Upper Manual	Lower Manual	Farm
Upper nonmanual	B	D	E	E	E
Lower nonmanual	C	D	E	E	E
Upper manual	E	E	E	E	E
Lower manual	E	E	E	D	D
Farm	E	E	E	D	A

uniform inheritance model yields a huge improvement ($L^2 = 2,567.66$, $df = 15$, $\delta = 2.62$). So, there is a marked inheritance effect. However, its strength varies from one category to another because the quasi-perfect mobility model is still much better ($L^2 = 683.34$, $df = 11$). Finally, Table 2 presents a levels model proposed by Featherman and Hauser (1978), which reproduces the observed data fairly well ($L^2 = 66.57$, $df = 12$). Given that $\delta_E = 1$, the estimated interaction parameters are $\delta_A = 30.04$, $\delta_B = 4.90$, $\delta_C = 2.47$, and $\delta_D = 1.82$. Thus, for instance, propensity toward immobility is the highest in the farm category, and the upward move from lower nonmanual to upper nonmanual is more probable than the corresponding downward move (net of marginal effects).

ADVANCED TOPICS

Although the levels model can be applied when the variables are nominal or ordinal, special models are also useful in the latter case: diagonals models, crossings parameters models, uniform association model, and row (and/or column) effect models. Log-multiplicative ASSOCIATION MODELS are relevant when the categories are assumed to be ordered, but their exact order is unknown and must be established from the data.

When several mobility tables are grouped together according to a third (layer) variable (e.g., country or time), log-linear modeling of the variation in the association over that dimension usually generates many supplementary parameters. Recent progress has been made in modeling such a variation very parsimoniously with log-multiplicative terms. These methods have, for instance, shown that the general strength of association between class of origin and destination has steadily decreased in France for men and women from the 1950s to the 1990s.

—Louis-André Vallet

REFERENCES

Featherman, D. L., & Hauser, R. M. (1978). *Opportunity and change.* New York: Academic Press.

Hauser, R. M. (1978). A structural model of the mobility table. *Social Forces, 56,* 919–953.

Hout, M. (1983). *Mobility tables.* Beverly Hills, CA: Sage.

Vallet, L.-A. (2001). Forty years of social mobility in France. *Revue Française de Sociologie: An Annual English Selection, 42*(Suppl.), 5–64.

Xie, Y. (1992). The log-multiplicative layer effect model for comparing mobility tables. *American Sociological Review, 57,* 380–395.

MODE

The mode is a MEASURE OF CENTRAL TENDENCY and refers to the value or values that appear most frequently in a distribution of values. Thus, in the series 9, 8, 2, 4, 9, 5, 2, 7, 10, there are two modes (2 and 9).

—Alan Bryman

MODEL

Social scientists use *model* to denote two distinct (although related) concepts: *empirical models* and *theoretical models.* An empirical model usually takes the form of an empirical test, often a statistical test, such as in a REGRESSION that is used to discern whether a set of independent variables influences a DEPENDENT VARIABLE. In such empirical models, the INDEPENDENT VARIABLES are identified from either a theory or observed empirical regularities.

A theoretical model, like an empirical model, represents an abstraction from reality. The goal, however, is different. In an empirical model, the analyst seeks to ascertain which independent variables actually exert a significant influence on the dependent variable of interest. The empirical test then indicates which of the potential influences are actual influences and which are not. In a theoretical model, on the other hand, the analyst seeks to provide an abstract account of how various forces interact to produce certain outcomes. The goal of such models is to capture what is sometimes referred to as the data-generating process, which is the source for data that exist in the real world (Morton, 2000). To capture this process, the analyst will create an argument, or "tell a story," about how real-world outcomes or events occur and, in so doing, will identify the key factors and mechanisms that will lead to these outcomes or events.

Some theoretical models are purely verbal and use words to construct their arguments. Others, however, use mathematics to construct their arguments. Generally, models that rely on mathematics to provide predictions about the world are known as *formal models.* These models consist of several components. First, there are constants, or undefined terms, which are those features of the model that are taken as given (e.g., members of a legislature). Second, there are defined terms (e.g., committees consist of members of the legislature). Third, there are assumptions about goals and preferences. For example, an analyst might assume that committees are driven by policy concerns. Finally, there is a sequence, which details the order in which events in the model take place (e.g., a bill is introduced in a legislature, a committee decides whether to send the bill to the chamber floor, etc.).

Once these various pieces are laid out, the analyst attempts to solve the model—that is, to identify the conditions under which different outcomes occur. Models can be solved in a variety of ways. GAME-THEORETIC models, for example, are usually solved analytically, in which the analyst identifies a solution, or equilibrium. Dynamic models, on the other hand, are usually solved computationally, in which the analyst sets initial values for the variables and then runs SIMULATIONS to provide insights about outcomes.

Formal models offer several benefits over verbal, or nonformal, models. First, the assumptions in formal models need to be stated more clearly. Second, the terms are defined more specifically. Third, the logic of the argument is spelled out more cleanly and transparently.

—Charles R. Shipan

REFERENCE

Morton, Rebecca B. (2000). *Methods and models: A guide to the empirical analysis of formal models in political science.* New York: Cambridge University Press.

MODEL I ANOVA

ANALYSIS OF VARIANCE (ANOVA) is a method that deals with differences in means of a variable across categories of observations. A classic example would be the comparison of a behavior of interest between an EXPERIMENTAL group and a control group. The question is whether the mean behavior (measured on an INTERVAL scale) of the subjects in the experimental group differs significantly from the mean behavior of the members of the control group. In other words, does the experimental treatment have an effect? ANOVA is a method that employs ratios of variances—hence

the name *analysis of variance*—to conduct a test of SIGNIFICANCE. So long as we have observations from all categories, as opposed to a subset of categories, ANOVA uses a FIXED-EFFECTS MODEL. In the example at hand, there are only two categories—namely, the experimental condition and the control condition. So, the fixed-effects model would apply. Note, however, that the fixed-effects model is not restricted to comparisons across just two categories.

ANOVA results typically appear in a table with the following layout (Table 1):

Table 1

Source	Sum of Squares	Degrees of Freedom	Mean Square	F Ratio	Significance
Between groups	10.0	1	10.0	1.21	.30
Within groups	66.0	8	8.3		
Total	76.0	9			

SOURCE: Iversen and Norpoth (1987, p. 21).

The "sum of squares" entries provide measures of variation between the groups and within each of the groups, with the assumption that the within-group variation is constant. To standardize those measures, we divide each sum of squares by the respective degrees of freedom. That gives us two estimates of VARIANCE (MEAN SQUARE). In the event that the between variance is no larger than the within variance, the ratio of those two quantities (F RATIO) should be 1.0. In that case, any difference between the two groups is entirely due to random chance and not to any group characteristic. In the case above, the F ratio only reaches 1.21, which is not significant at the .05 level. Hence, we have to conclude that the experimental treatment has no effect.

The fixed-effects model is not limited to testing for the effect of just one explanatory variable (ONE-WAY ANOVA). It can also accommodate two such variables (TWO-WAY ANOVA), in which one is designated as the row variable and the other as the column variable. It is advisable, however, to design the research in such a way that all the resulting combinations (cells) of rows and columns contain the same number of observations. That is possible, of course, only with experiments in which the investigators have that kind of control. With survey or other observational data, combinations of categories will have whatever observations occur. In that case, one cannot obtain unique estimates for the variance due to each of the explanatory factors. That limits the utility of two-way ANOVA to experimental designs.

Besides testing for the effect of each explanatory variable (MAIN EFFECTS), a two-way ANOVA also provides a test of the INTERACTION between those variables. Two variables (X_1 and X_2) are said to have an interaction effect on the dependent variable (Y) if the main effects are not additive. In other words, the addition of those effects does not predict the dependent variable of interest, even aside from random error. Being exposed to two experimental conditions has an effect on a behavior of interest that is systematically higher (or lower) than what the two separate effects add up to. With categorical data, such interaction effects are often difficult to interpret in the absence of good theory about their directions.

—Helmut Norpoth

See also FIXED-EFFECTS MODEL

REFERENCES

Hays, W. L. (1994). *Statistics* (5th ed.). New York: Harcourt Brace.

Iversen, G. R., & Norpoth, H. (1987). *Analysis of variance* (2nd ed., Sage University Paper Series on Quantitative Applications in the Social Sciences, 07–001). Newbury Park, CA: Sage.

Scheffe, H. (1959). *The analysis of variance.* New York: John Wiley.

MODEL II ANOVA. *See*
RANDOM-EFFECTS MODEL

MODEL III ANOVA. *See*
MIXED-EFFECTS MODEL

MODELING

Modeling is the process of creating "a simplified representation of a system or phenomenon . . . with any hypotheses required to describe the system or explain the phenomenon" (Random House, 1997). Through the modeling process, analysts seek to confirm or deny the HYPOTHESES they generate about the system or phenomenon of concern, usually accomplishing the task of confirmation or denial through the testing of the hypotheses using QUANTITATIVE DATA. The analyst hopes to arrive at conclusions from the exercise that are nontrivial, scientifically sound, and replicable using the same MODEL and data. The conclusions should also help both the analyst and the reader to explain what took place, predict future behavior, and present fresh conceptualizations that can better explain and predict societal behavior.

HISTORY

Model building became most prevalent in social science research during the behavioralist revolution that took place in social science beginning in the mid-20th century. At that time, social science scholars, inspired by the mathematical and logical sophistication of the physical sciences (biology, chemistry, physics), especially of economics, became particularly concerned with finding "universal" relationships between quantitatively measured variables that were similar to those found by physical scientists. The purpose behind seeking universal relationships was to build lawlike statements about human behavior. The variance in human behavior, particularly in the social science realm, was to be accounted for through the use of scientifically applied control variables that operated independently of the human behavior under study. Blalock (1969) considered inductive model building to be essential for more precise theorizing and, if necessary, for making adjustments to the original proposed theory based on the results of hypothesis testing. Over the years, studies using more deductive formal models that depend on the logical sequencing of arguments have become more popular and have taken their place alongside their inductive cousins in the social science literature.

As scientists in the physical sciences know the precise amount of acceleration to apply to a mass to produce a known quantity of force, expressed in the formula $f = m \times a$, behavioralist-minded social scientists could also know to a more refined extent the necessary amount of an INDEPENDENT VARIABLE to create an important impact on the DEPENDENT VARIABLE, which is the human behavior of interest. Thus, *voting behavior* became a term of choice in political science and political sociology because social scientists increasingly understood the power of models, within which several independent variables could be placed, to capture variation in individual voting choices at election time. Each independent variable in the model accounts for a different portion of the variance.

MODEL BUILDING

Social scientists build models to better understand the "real-world" environment. In particular, issues of cause and effect are addressed through modeling. What explains the number of votes cast for Candidate Brown for mayor? How can we account for changes in regime type in countries around the world? What factors are most important in explaining variation in spending on social welfare programs in the U.S. states?

Social science modeling creates an artificial and abstract societal environment that represents its most important features. For instance, social scientists attempt to account for the vote choice by ascertaining the most critical factors that voters consider in helping them to choose to vote for a particular candidate or against another candidate or candidates: party identification, ideology, and opinions about the condition of the economy. Then, through the measurement of these important (though hardly exhaustive list of) variables, the analyst can focus his or her attention on comprehending what is essential about the real-world environment. This should bring about a better understanding of the phenomenon under study (i.e., account for variation in vote choice).

TYPES OF MODELS

Models can be both conceptual and mathematical. The goal of the social scientist is to proceed from the conceptual model to the mathematical model. The difference between the two is that although conceptual models allow the analyst to play with competing theories in verbal form, mathematical models are made "OPERATIONAL" using variables that numerically measure a phenomenon of interest. The mathematical measures can be either direct or indirect. An example of a direct measure is votes cast for a particular candidate, which represents the support a candidate has garnered to win elective office. An example of an indirect measure is an index of democracy, in which different components of the measure are assembled to represent the concept of "democracy." Models further specify a path by which the variables influence one another to produce a behavior. Thus, mathematical models are "testable," in that one can estimate them using statistical techniques and come to conclusions about the hypotheses about the real world that inform them.

CONSTRUCTING AND EVALUATING MODELS

For instance, to better understand the occurrence of democratic regimes in different countries, a researcher could create a conceptual model in the following manner:

$$\text{Democracy} = f(\text{Economics, Culture}).$$

The researcher could further refine his or her effort by conceiving of variables that operationalize the above concepts as follows:

$$\text{Democracy} = f(\text{Economic Development,}$$
$$\text{Income Distribution, Religious}$$
$$\text{Practice, Ethnic Composition}).$$

In the model, economic development and income distribution (throughout the population of the country) represent "Economics," whereas religious practice (e.g., the percentage of the population that is Protestant) and ethnic composition of the country's population represent "Culture."

The modeler also hypothesizes, in this model, that the relationship between the independent variables and the dependent variable is linear and direct. Models can also be constructed that specify relationships that are linear and indirect (such as INTERACTION terms), nonlinear and direct (through a LOGARITHMIC TRANSFORMATION), and NONLINEAR and indirect.

How do we evaluate models? Do they accurately explain variance in the dependent variable of interest? If we estimate models using statistics, we generally use statistical standards to evaluate their performance. The multivariate nature of modeling lends itself to several standards. The R-SQUARED statistics is a common evaluation statistic for MULTIPLE REGRESSION models. The log-likelihood is another way to judge multivariate model performance—in this instance, MAXIMUM LIKELIHOOD ESTIMATION.

Models are created to answer specific research questions that are more comprehensive in scope than can be captured by a simple bivariate relationship. Models help social scientists to explain, predict, and understand societal phenomena. They can also be evaluated for their effectiveness in performing those three tasks.

—Ross E. Burkhart

REFERENCES

Asher, H. B. (1983). *Causal modeling* (2nd ed., Sage University Paper Series on Quantitative Applications in the Social Sciences, 07–003). Beverly Hills, CA: Sage.

Blalock, H. M., Jr. (1969). *Theory construction: From verbal to mathematical formulations.* Englewood Cliffs, NJ: Prentice Hall.

Lave, C., & March, J. G. (1978). *An introduction to models in the social sciences.* New York: Harper & Row.

Random House. (1997). *Random House Webster's college dictionary.* New York: Author.

Schrodt, P. A. (2002). Mathematical modeling. In J. B. Manheim, R. C. Rich, & L. Willnat (Eds.), *Empirical political analysis: Research methods in political science* (5th ed.). New York: Longman.

MODERATING. *See* MODERATING VARIABLE

MODERATING VARIABLE

A moderating variable represents a process or a factor that alters the impact of an independent variable X on a dependent variable Y. The moderating variable may take the form of an indicator variable (0/1 values), a categorical variable, or a continuous variable. Moderation of the effects of X on Y is usually of interest in the context of a well-theorized area of research, such as the provision of labor by individuals in which the human capital and labor market segmentation theories are both well established. Variables reflecting these two theories can be put together in a multiple regression equation, and a path analysis involving two stages (labor force participation in the first stage and wage determination in the second) can be developed. Paths through the model involve the multiplication of the coefficients from two regressions together, giving the moderated effect of X on Y through Z, and comparing that effect with the direct effect of X on Z (which is assumed to be additively separable) (Bryman & Cramer, 1997).

Furthermore, background factors can be tested for a moderating effect on the main impact of each X on the final outcome Y.

Moderating variables allow for testing the notion of contingent effects. Realists distinguish necessary effects from contingent effects (Sayer, 2000, p. 94). Researchers benefit from focusing on contingent effects that only occur in the absence of offsetting, blocking, or cross-cutting causal processes. The moderating variables may act as obstacles to the action of X in causing Y. Thus, divorce only results from "submitting divorce papers" *if* the case is well constructed, uncontested, or both; it is contingently caused by divorce papers.

Two main approaches are used for estimating the impact of moderating variables: PATH ANALYSIS and INTERACTION EFFECTS.

The path analysis approach allows for two or more equations to simultaneously represent the set of associations. These equations may involve independent variables X_{ij}, intermediate variables Z_{ij}, and final outcomes Y_{ij}. In each equation j, variables may be recursively affected by factors in other linked equations. Such models are structural equation models.

The alternative method of using interaction effects (Jaccard, Turrisi, & Wan, 1990) introduces an extra term that is the product of two existing variables into a single regression equation. The interaction terms may be numerous for categorical variables. The degrees of freedom of the new estimate are reduced.

For example, in researching the factors associated with eating out frequently, the interaction effect of marital status with having young children in the household was measured using dummy variables in a logistic regression context (Olsen, Warde, & Martens, 2000). The impact of [Divorced × Kids < 5 in Hhold] was a dramatic increase in the odds of eating out in a hotel or of eating an unusual ethnic meal. This interaction term offset one of the underlying associations: Divorced people in the United Kingdom were generally less likely than married/cohabiting people to eat in ethnic restaurants.

A simpler alternative is to use dummy variables to control for the impact of moderating factors. Another alternative is to use multilevel modeling to represent contextual moderating influences (Jones, 1997).

—Wendy K. Olsen

REFERENCES

Bollen, K. A. (1989). *Structural equations with latent variables.* New York: Wiley.

Bryman, A., & Cramer, D. (1997). *Quantitative data analysis with SPSS for Windows: A guide for social scientists.* New York: Routledge.

Jaccard, J., Turrisi, R., & Wan, C. K. (1990). *Interaction effects in multiple regression* (Quantitative Applications in the Social Sciences, No. 72). London: Sage.

Jones, K. (1997). Multilevel approaches to modelling contextuality: From nuisance to substance in the analysis of voting behaviour. In G. P. Westert & R. N. Verhoeff (Eds.), *Places and people: Multilevel modelling in geographical research* (Nederlandse Geografische Studies 227). Utrecht, The Netherlands: The Royal Dutch Geographical Society and Faculty of Geographical Sciences, Utrecht University.

Olsen, W. K., Warde, A., & Martens, L. (2000). Social differentiation and the market for eating out in the UK. *International Journal of Hospitality Management, 19*(2), 173–190.

Sayer, A. (2000). *Realism and social science.* London: Sage.

MOMENT

Moment is often used with an order value in statistical analysis. The kth moment of a variable is the average value of the observations of the variable raised to the kth power. Let N indicate sample size and the cases of the variable be indicated by $x_1, x_2, \ldots, x_N$, and then the kth moment of the variable is

$$\left(x_1^k + x_2^k + x_N^k\right)/N.$$

The kth moment of a random variable X is the expected value of X^k, or $E(X^k)$.

In qualitative research, the word *moment* often is used to refer to a specific combination of social and historical circumstances such as a sociohistorical moment.

—Tim Futing Liao

MOMENTS IN QUALITATIVE RESEARCH

The history of qualitative research in North America in the 20th century divides into seven phases, or moments. We define them as the *traditional* (1900–1950); the *modernist* or golden age (1950–1970); *blurred genres* (1970–1986); the *crisis of representation* (1986–1990); the *postmodern,* a period

of experimental and new ethnographies (1990–1995); *postexperimental* inquiry (1995–2000); and the *future,* which is now. The future, the seventh moment, is concerned with moral discourse; with the rejoining of art, literature, and science; and with the development of sacred textualities. The seventh moment asks that the social sciences and the humanities become sites for critical conversations about democracy, race, gender, class, nation, globalization, freedom, and community.

THE TRADITIONAL PERIOD

The first moment, the traditional period, begins in the early 1900s and continues until World War II. During this time, qualitative researchers wrote "objective," colonizing accounts of field experiences, reflective of the POSITIVIST scientist paradigm. They were concerned with offering VALID, RELIABLE, and OBJECTIVE interpretations in their writings. The other who was studied was often alien, foreign, and exotic.

MODERNIST PHASE

The modernist phase, or second moment, builds on the canonical works from the traditional period. Social REALISM, NATURALISM, and slice-of-life ETHNOGRAPHIES are still valued. It extended through the postwar years to the 1970s and is still present in the work of many. In this period, many texts sought to formalize and legitimize qualitative methods. The modernist ethnographer and sociological PARTICIPANT OBSERVER attempted rigorous, qualitative studies of important social processes, including deviance and social control in the classroom and society. This was a moment of creative ferment.

BLURRED GENRES

By the beginning of the third stage (1970–1986), "blurred genres," qualitative researchers had a full complement of paradigms, methods, and strategies to employ in their research. Theories ranged from SYMBOLIC INTERACTIONISM to CONSTRUCTIVISM, naturalistic inquiry, positivism and postpositivism, PHENOMENOLOGY, ETHNOMETHODOLOGY, critical Marxist theories, SEMIOTICS, STRUCTURALISM, FEMINISM, and various ethnic paradigms. APPLIED QUALITATIVE RESEARCH was gaining in stature, and the politics and ethics of qualitative research were topics of considerable concern. Research strategies and formats for reporting research ranged from GROUNDED

THEORY to CASE STUDY to methods of historical, biographical, ethnographic, action, and clinical research. Diverse ways of collecting and analyzing empirical materials became available, including qualitative interviewing (open-ended and semistructured), observational, visual, personal experience, and documentary methods. Computers were entering the situation, to be fully developed (to provide online methods) in the next decade, along with narrative, content, and semiotic methods of reading interviews and cultural texts. Geertz's two books, *The Interpretation of Cultures* (1973), and *Local Knowledge* (1983), defined the beginning and end of this moment.

CRISIS OF REPRESENTATION

A profound rupture occurred in the mid-1980s. What we call the fourth moment, or the crisis of representation, appeared with *Anthropology as Cultural Critique* (Marcus & Fischer, 1986), *The Anthropology of Experience* (Turner & Bruner, 1986), and *Writing Culture* (Clifford & Marcus, 1986). They articulated the consequences of Geertz's "blurred genres" interpretation of the field in the early 1980s as new models of truth, method, and representation were sought (Rosaldo, 1989).

THE POSTMODERN MOMENT

The fifth moment is the postmodern period of experimental ethnographic writing. Ethnographers struggle to make sense of the previous disruptions and crises. New ways of composing ethnography are explored. Writers struggle with new ways to represent the "other" in the text. Epistemologies from previously silenced groups have emerged to offer solutions to these problems. The concept of the aloof observer has been abandoned.

THE POSTEXPERIMENTAL AND BEYOND MOMENTS

The sixth (postexperimental) and seventh (future) moments are upon us. Fictional ethnographies, ethographic poetry, and multimedia texts are today taken for granted. Postexperimental writers seek to connect their writings to the needs of a free democratic society. The needs of a moral and sacred qualitative social science are actively being explored by a host of new writers (Clough, 1998).

We draw several conclusions from this brief history, noting that it is, like all histories, somewhat arbitrary. First, North Americans are not the only scholars struggling to create postcolonial, nonessentialist, feminist, dialogic, performance texts—texts informed by the rhetorical, narrative turn in the human disciplines. This international work troubles the traditional distinctions between science, the humanities, rhetoric, literature, facts, and fictions. As Atkinson and Hammersley (1994), observe, this discourse recognizes "the literary antecedents of the ethnographic text, and affirms the essential dialectic" (p. 255) underlying these aesthetic and humanistic moves.

Second, this literature is reflexively situated in multiple, historical, and national contexts. It is clear that America's history with qualitative inquiry cannot be generalized to the rest of the world (Atkinson, Coffey, & Delamont, 2001). Nor do all researchers embrace a politicized, cultural studies agenda that demands that interpretive texts advance issues surrounding social justice and racial equality.

Third, each of the earlier historical moments is still operating in the present, either as legacy or as a set of practices that researchers continue to follow or argue against. The multiple and fractured histories of qualitative research now make it possible for any given researcher to attach a project to a canonical text from any of the above-described historical moments. Multiple criteria of evaluation compete for attention in this field. Fourth, an embarrassment of choices now characterizes the field of qualitative research. There have never been so many paradigms, strategies of inquiry, or methods of analysis to draw on and use. Fifth, we are in a moment of discovery and rediscovery, as new ways of looking, interpreting, arguing, and writing are debated and discussed. Sixth, the qualitative research act can no longer be viewed from within a neutral or objective positivist perspective. Class, race, gender, and ethnicity inevitably shape the process of inquiry, making research a multicultural process.

—Norman K. Denzin and Yvonna S. Lincoln

REFERENCES

Atkinson, P., Coffey, A., & Delamont, S. (2001). Editorial: A debate about our canon. *Qualitative Research, 1,* 5–21.

Atkinson, P., & Hammersley, M. (1994). Ethnography and participant observation. In N. K. Denzin & Y. S. Lincoln (Eds.), *Handbook of qualitative research* (pp. 248–261). Thousand Oaks, CA: Sage.

Clifford, J., & Marcus, G. E. (Eds.). (1986). *Writing culture.* Berkeley: University of California Press.

Clough, P. T. (1998). *The end(s) of ethnography* (2nd ed.). New York: Peter Lang.

Geertz, C. (1973). *The interpretation of cultures.* New York: Basic Books.

Geertz, C. (1983). *Local knowledge.* New York: Basic Books.

Marcus, G., & Fischer, M. (1986). *Anthropology as cultural critique.* Chicago: University of Chicago Press.

Rosaldo, R. (1989). *Culture & truth.* Boston: Beacon.x

Turner, V., & Bruner, E. (Eds.). (1986). *The anthropology of experience.* Urbana: University of Illinois Press.

MONOTONIC

Monotonic refers to the properties of a function that links one set of scores to another set of scores. Stated formally, consider a set of scores Y that are some function of another set of scores, X, such that $Y = f(X)$. The function is said to be *monotonic increasing* if for any two scores, X_j and X_k, where $X_j < X_k$, the property holds that $f(X_j) \leq f(X_k)$. If $f(X_j) < f(X_k)$, then the function is said to be *monotonic strictly increasing*. If $f(X_j) \geq f(X_k)$, then the function is said to be *monotonic decreasing,* and if $f(X_j) > f(X_k)$, then the function is said to be *monotonic strictly decreasing.*

For example, consider five individuals on whom a measure of an X variable is taken as well as five additional variables, A, B, C, D, and E. The data are as follows in Table 1.

Table 1

Individual	X	A	B	C	D	E
1	12	44	44	47	47	47
2	13	45	44	46	46	46
3	14	46	45	45	45	45
4	15	47	46	44	44	46
5	16	48	47	43	44	47

A is a monotonic strictly increasing function of X because for any two individuals where X_j is less than X_k, it is the case that $A_j < A_k$. B is a monotonic increasing function of X because for any two individuals where X_j is less than X_k, it is the case that $B_j \leq B_k$. C is a monotonic strictly decreasing function of X because for any two individuals where X_j is less than X_k, it is the case that $C_j > C_k$. D is a monotonic decreasing function of X because for any two individuals where X_j is less than X_k, it is the case

that $B_j \geq B_k$. Finally, E is a nonmonotonic function of X because it satisfies none of the conditions described above.

—James J. Jaccard

MONTE CARLO SIMULATION

Monte Carlo simulation is the use of computer ALGORITHMS and pseudo-random numbers to conduct mathematical experiments on statistics. These experiments are used to understand the behavior of statistics under specified conditions and, ultimately, to make inferences to population characteristics. Monte Carlo simulation is most useful when strong analytic distributional theory does not exist for a statistic in a given situation.

EXPLANATION

The goal of INFERENTIAL STATISTICAL analysis is to make PROBABILITY statements about a POPULATION PARAMETER, θ, from a statistic, $\hat{\theta}$, calculated from a SAMPLE of data from a POPULATION. This is problematic because the calculated statistics from any two RANDOM SAMPLES from the same population will almost never be equal. For example, suppose you want to know the average IQ of the 20,000 students at your university (θ), but you do not have the time or resources to test them all. Instead, you draw a random sample of 200 and calculate the mean IQ score ($\hat{\theta}$) of these sampled students to be, say, 123. What does that tell you about the average IQ of the entire student body? This is not obvious, because if you drew another random sample of 200 from those same 20,000 students, their mean IQ might be 117. A third random sample might produce a mean of 132, and so on, through the very large number of potential random samples that could be drawn from this student body. So how can you move from having solid information about the sample statistic ($\hat{\theta}$) to being able to make at least a probability statement about the population parameter (θ)?

At the heart of making this inference from sample to population is the SAMPLING DISTRIBUTION. A statistic's sampling distribution is the range of values it could take on in a random sample from a given population and the probabilities associated with those values. So the mean IQ of a sample of 200 of our 20,000 students might be as low as, say, 89 or as high as 203, but there would probably be a much greater likelihood that the mean IQ of such a sample would be between 120 and 130. If we had some information about the structure of the sample mean's sampling distribution, we might be able to make a probability statement about the population mean, given a particular sample.

In the standard parametric inferential statistics that social scientists learn in graduate school (with the ubiquitous t-tests and p values), we get information about a statistic's sampling distribution from mathematical analysis. For example, the CENTRAL LIMIT THEOREM gives us good reason to believe that the sampling distribution of the mean IQ of our random sample of 200 students is distributed normally, with an expected value of the population mean and a STANDARD DEVIATION of approximately the standard deviation of the IQ in the population divided by the square root of 200. However, there are situations when either no such analytical distributional theory exists about a statistic or the assumptions needed to apply parametric statistical theory do not hold. In these cases, one can use Monte Carlo simulation to estimate the sampling distribution of a statistic empirically.

Monte Carlo simulation estimates a statistic's sampling distribution empirically by drawing a large number of random samples from a known "pseudo-population" of simulated data to track a statistic's behavior. The basic concept is straightforward: If a statistic's sampling distribution is the density function of the values it could take on in a given population, then the relative frequency distribution of the values of that statistic that are actually observed in many samples from a population is an estimate of that sampling distribution. Because it is impractical for social scientists to sample actual data multiple times, we use artificially generated data that resemble the real thing in relevant ways for these samples.

The basic steps of a Monte Carlo simulation are as follows:

1. Define in symbolic terms a pseudo-population that will be used to generate random samples. This usually takes the form of a computer algorithm that generates simulated data in a carefully specified manner.
2. Sample from the pseudo-population (yielding a pseudo-sample) in ways that simulate the statistical situation of interest, for example, with the same sampling scheme, sample size, and so on.

3. Calculate and save $\hat{\theta}$ from the pseudo-sample.
4. Repeat Steps 2 and 3 t times, where t is the number of trials. Usually, t is a large number, often 10,000 or more. This is done with a looping algorithm in a computer program.
5. Construct a relative frequency distribution of the resulting $\hat{\theta}_t$ values. This is the Monte Carlo estimate of the sampling distribution of $\hat{\theta}$ under the conditions specified by the pseudo-population and the sampling procedures.
6. Evaluate or use this estimated sampling distribution to understand the behavior of $\hat{\theta}$ given a population value, θ.

Thus, Monte Carlo simulation is conducted by writing and running a computer program that generates carefully structured, artificial, random data to conduct a mathematical experiment on the behavior of a statistic. Two crucial steps in the process are (a) specifying the pseudo-population in a computer algorithm and (b) using the estimated sampling distribution to understand social processes better.

Specifying the pseudo-population with a computer algorithm must begin with a clear understanding of the social process to be simulated. Such a computer algorithm will be as complex as the process being simulated is believed to be. Most theoretical models of social processes contain a deterministic and a probabilistic, or random, component. Writing the computer code for the deterministic component is often relatively straightforward. The random component of the simulation usually requires the most thought. This is appropriate because the random component of a social process largely determines the configuration of the statistics' sampling distributions and makes statistical inference an issue in the first place. It is the importance of the random component in this technique that led to it being named for the famous European casino.

The random component enters a Monte Carlo simulation of a social process in the distributions of the variables that go into it. In writing a simulation program, you specify these distributions based on theory and evidence about the phenomena you are modeling and the characteristics of the experiment you are undertaking. In theory, a social variable could take on any of an infinite range of distributions, but statisticians have identified and developed theory about relatively few. Most books on Monte Carlo simulation, including those listed below, discuss at length how to generate variables with various distributions and what observed variables might be best simulated by each of them.

APPLICATION

Monte Carlo simulation is based on a tradition of numerical experimentation that goes back at least to biblical times, but with renewed interest being sparked in it in the mid-20th century from such disparate fields as quantum physics and the development of telephone networks. However, it was not until very recently that the technique has become widely practical, due to the massive computer power available for the first time at the end of the 20th century. As a result, social scientists are only just beginning to develop general uses for Monte Carlo simulation (but the rise in its use has been rapid, with a key word search for *Monte Carlo* in the Social Sciences Citation Index yielding only 14 articles in 1987 compared to 270 articles in 2001). Some of the most important current applications of Monte Carlo simulation include the following:

- assessing the sampling distribution of a new statistic (or combination of statistics) for which mathematical analysis is intractable;
- assessing the sensitivity of an empirical analysis to variations in potential population conditions, including the violation of parametric inference assumptions; and
- being used in MARKOV CHAIN MONTE CARLO techniques, which have recently brought Bayesian statistical inference into the social science mainstream.

See Evans, Hastings, and Peacock (2000); Mooney (1997); Robert and Casella (2000); and Rubinstein (1981) for these and other uses of Monte Carlo simulation in the social sciences.

—Christopher Z. Mooney

REFERENCES

Evans, M., Hastings, N., & Peacock, B. (2000). *Statistical distributions* (3rd ed.). New York: John Wiley.

Mooney, C. Z. (1997). *Monte Carlo simulation.* Thousand Oaks, CA: Sage.

Robert, C. P., & Casella, G. (2000). *Monte Carlo statistical methods.* New York: Springer-Verlag.

Rubinstein, R. Y. (1981). *Simulation and the Monte Carlo method.* New York: John Wiley.

MOSAIC DISPLAY

Mosaic displays (or mosaic plots) are plots of cell frequencies in a cross-classified CONTINGENCY TABLE depicting the cell frequency $n_{ijk\ell...}$ as the area of a "tile" in a space-filling mosaic graphic. This is based on the idea that, for a two-way table, cell probabilities $p_{ij} = n_{ij}/n_{++}$ can always be expressed as $p_{ij} = p_{i+} \times p_{j|i}$, shown by the width and height of rectangles.

Thus, if a unit area is divided first in proportion to the marginal probabilities of one variable, p_{i+}, and those are each subdivided according to conditional probabilities, $p_{j|i}$, the tiles (a) will have area $\sim p_{ij}$ and (b) will align under independence (i.e., when $p_{ij} = p_{i+} \times p_{+j}$). This visual representation turns out to have a long and interesting history (Friendly, 2002).

Recently reintroduced to statistical graphics (Hartigan & Kleiner, 1981), the basic mosaic display generalizes this idea to n-way tables by recursive subdivision of areas according to the continued application of Bayes rule, so that $p_{ijk\ell...} = p_i \times p_{j|i} \times p_{k|ij} \times \cdots \times p_{n|ijk...}$.

This method for visualizing contingency tables was enhanced (Friendly, 1992, 1994, 1998) to (a) fit any log-linear model, (b) show the residuals (contributions to the overall Pearson or likelihood ratio chi-square) from the model by color and shading, and (c) permute the categories of variables so that the pattern of shading shows the nature of the associations among variables. As a consequence, mosaic displays have become a primary graphical tool for visualization and analysis of categorical data in the form of n-way contingency tables (Friendly, 1999, 2000; Valero, Young, & Friendly, 2003).

A two-way table and a three-way table example in Figure 1 show the relations among the categories of hair color, eye color, and sex. In these figures, the area of each tile is proportional to the observed cell frequency, but the tiles are shaded according to the residuals from a particular log-linear model, thus showing the pattern of associations that remain. (Color versions are far more effective and use shades of blue and red for positive and negative residuals, respectively.) In the left-hand two-way display, the model of independence has been fit to the table; the opposite-corner pattern of the shading shows that dark (light) hair is associated with dark (light) eyes.

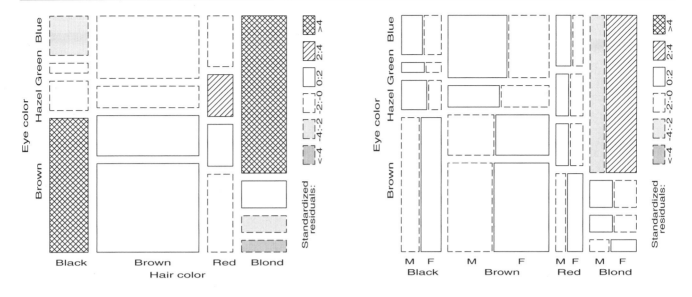

Figure 1   Mosaic Displays for Frequencies of Hair Color, Eye Color, and Sex

NOTE: Left: two-way table, hair color by eye color; right: three-way table, divided by sex.

In the right panel, the log-linear model [*Hair Eye*] [*Sex*] has been fit to the three-way table, which asserts that the combinations of hair color and eye color are independent of sex. Only one pair of cells has residuals large enough to be shaded—the blue-eyed blondes—in which there are more women and fewer men than would be the case under this model of independence.

Recent developments extend mosaic displays in several directions: (a) mosaic matrices and partial mosaics (Friendly, 1999, 2000) as discrete analogs of scatterplot matrices and coplots for continuous data; (b) several highly interactive, dynamic implementations (Hofmann, 2000; Theus, 1997; Valero et al., 2003) for exploration and "visual fitting"; and (c) application of same visual ideas to nested classifications or tree structures (Shneiderman, 1992).

—Michael Friendly

REFERENCES

Friendly, M. (1992). Mosaic displays for loglinear models. In American Statistical Association (Ed.), *Proceedings of the Statistical Graphics Section* (pp. 61–68). Alexandria, VA: American Statistical Association.

Friendly, M. (1994). Mosaic displays for multi-way contingency tables. *Journal of the American Statistical Association, 89,* 190–200.

Friendly, M. (1998). Mosaic displays. In S. Kotz, C. Reed, & D. L. Banks (Eds.), *Encyclopedia of statistical sciences* (Vol. 2, pp. 411–416). New York: John Wiley.

Friendly, M. (1999). Extending mosaic displays: Marginal, conditional, and partial views of categorical data. *Journal of Computational and Graphical Statistics, 8*(3), 373–395.

Friendly, M. (2000). *Visualizing categorical data.* Cary, NC: SAS Institute.

Friendly, M. (2002). A brief history of the mosaic display. *Journal of Computational and Graphical Statistics, 11*(1), 89–107.

Hartigan, J. A., & Kleiner, B. (1981). Mosaics for contingency tables. In W. F. Eddy (Ed.), *Computer science and statistics: Proceedings of the 13th Symposium on the Interface* (pp. 268–273). New York: Springer-Verlag.

Hofmann, H. (2000). Exploring categorical data: Interactive mosaic plots. *Metrika, 51*(1), 11–26.

Shneiderman, B. (1992). Tree visualization with treemaps: A 2-D space-filling approach. *ACM Transactions on Graphics, 11*(1), 92–99.

Theus, M. (1997). Visualization of categorical data. In W. Bandilla & F. Faulbaum (Eds.), *SoftStat'97: Advances in statistical software* (Vol. 6, pp. 47–55). Stuttgart, Germany: Lucius & Lucius.

Valero, P., Young, F., & Friendly, M. (2003). Visual categorical analysis in ViSta. *Computational Statistics and Data Analysis, 43*(4), 495–508.

MOVER-STAYER MODELS

The mover-stayer (MS) model is an extension of the MARKOV CHAIN MODEL for dealing with a very specific type of unobserved heterogeneity in the population.

The population is assumed to consist of two unobserved groups (latent classes): a stayer group containing persons with a zero probability of change and a mover group following an ordinary Markov process. Early references to the MS model are Blumen, Kogan, and McCarthy (1955) and Goodman (1961). Depending on the application field, the model might be known under a different name. In the biomedical field, one may encounter the term *long-term survivors,* which refers to a group that has a zero probability of dying or experiencing another type of event of interest within the study period. In marketing research, one uses the term *brand-loyal segments* as opposed to *brand-switching segments.* There is also a strong connection with zero-inflated models for binomial or Poisson counts.

Suppose the categorical variable Y_t is measured at T occasions, where t denotes a particular occasion, $1 \leq t \leq T$; D is the number of levels of Y_t; and y_t is a particular level of Y_t, $1 \leq y_t \leq D$. This could, for example, be a respondent's party preference measured at 6-month intervals. The vector notation $\mathbf{Y}$ and $\mathbf{y}$ is used to refer to a complete response pattern.

A good way to introduce the MS model is as a special case of the mixed Markov model. The latter is obtained by adding a discrete unobserved heterogeneity component to a standard Markov chain model. Let X denote a discrete latent variable with C levels. A particular latent class is enumerated by the index x, $x = 1, 2, \ldots, C$. The mixed Markov model has the form

$$P(\mathbf{Y} = \mathbf{y}) = \sum_{x=1}^{C} P(X = x) P(Y_1 = y_1 | X = x)$$
$$\times \prod_{t=2}^{T} P(Y_t = y_t | Y_{t-1} = y_{t-1}, X = x).$$

As can be seen, latent classes differ with respect to the initial state and the transition probabilities. A MS model is obtained if $C = 2$ and $P(Y_t = y_t | Y_{t-1} = y_t, X = 2) = 1$ for each y_t. In other words, the probability of staying in the same state equals 1 in latent class 2, the stayer class. Note that $P(X = x)$ is the proportion of persons in the mover and stayer classes, and $P(Y_1 = y_1 | X = x)$ is the initial distribution of these groups over the various states.

To identify the MS model, we need at least three occasions, but it is not necessary to assume the process to be stationary in the mover chain. With three time points ($T = 3$) and two states ($D = 2$), a nonstationary MS model is a saturated model.

A restricted variant of the MS model is the independence-stayer model, in which the movers are assumed to behave randomly; that is, $P(Y_t = y_t | Y_{t-1} = y_{t-1}, X = 1) = P(Y_t = y_t | X = 1)$. Another variant is obtained with absorbing states, such as first marriage and death. In such cases, everyone starts in the first state, $P(Y_1 = 1 | X = x) = 1$, and backward transitions are also impossible in the mover class, $P(Y_t = 2 | Y_{t-1} = 2, X = 1) = 1$.

The formulation as a mixed Markov model suggests several types of extensions, such as the inclusion of more than one class of movers or a LATENT MARKOV MODEL variant that corrects for measurement error. Another possible extension is the inclusion of covariates, yielding a model that is similar to a zero-inflated model for counts.

Two programs that can be used to estimate the MS model and several of its extensions are PANMARK and LEM.

—Jeroen K. Vermunt

REFERENCES

Blumen, I. M., Kogan, M., & McCarthy, P. J. (1955). *The industrial mobility of labor as a probability process.* Ithaca, NY: Cornell University Press.

Goodman, L. A. (1961). Statistical methods for the mover-stayer model. *Journal of the American Statistical Association, 56,* 841–868.

Langeheine, R., & Van de Pol, F. (1994). Discrete-time mixed Markov latent class models. In A. Dale & R. B. Davies (Eds.), *Analyzing social and political change: A casebook of methods* (pp. 171–197). London: Sage.

Vermunt, J. K. (1997). *Log-linear models for event histories.* Thousand Oaks, CA: Sage.

MOVING AVERAGE

A moving average process is the product of a RANDOM shock, or disturbance, to a TIME SERIES. When the pattern of disturbances in the dependent variable can best be described by a weighted average of current and lagged random disturbances, then it is a moving average process. There are both immediate effects and discounted effects of the random shock over time, occurring over a fixed number of periods before disappearing. In a sense, a moving average is a linear combination of WHITE-NOISE error terms. The number of periods that it takes for the effects of the random shock on the dependent variable to disappear is termed the ORDER of the moving average process, denoted q. The length of the effects of the random shock is not dependent on the time at which the shock occurs, making a moving average process independent of time.

The mathematical representation of a moving average process with mean $u = 0$ and of order q is as follows:

$$y_t = \varepsilon_t - \theta_1 \varepsilon_{t-1} - \theta_2 \varepsilon_{t-2} - \cdots - \theta_q \varepsilon_{t-q}.$$

Take, for instance, a moving average process of order $q = 1$: The effects of the random shock in period t would be evident in period t and period $t - 1$, then in no period after. Although observations one time period apart are correlated, observations more than one time period apart are uncorrelated. The memory of the process is just one period. The order of the process can be said to be the memory of the process. An example would be the effect of a news report about the price of hog feed in Iowa. The effect of this random shock would be felt for the first day and then discounted for 1 or more days (order q). After several days, the effects of the shock would disappear, resulting in the series returning to its mean.

Identifying a moving average process requires examining the AUTOCORRELATION (ACF) and partial autocorrelation (PACF) functions. For a first-order moving average process, the ACF will have one spike and then abruptly cut off, with the remaining lags of the function exhibiting the properties of white noise; the PACF of a first-order moving average process will dampen infinitely. Figure 1 shows the ACF for a first-order moving average process. Moving average processes of order q will have an ACF that spikes significantly for lags 1 through q and then abruptly cuts off after lag q. In contrast, the PACF will dampen infinitely. Statistical packages such as SAS and SPSS will generate correlograms for quick assessment of ACFs and PACFs, although higher-order moving average processes are rare in the social sciences.

A moving average process can occur simultaneously with serial correlation and a TREND. Autoregressive, integrated, moving average (ARIMA) modeling is useful to model time series that exhibit a combination of these processes because it combines an autoregressive process, an integrated or differenced process (which removes a trend), and a moving average process. Furthermore, a moving average process can be written as an infinite-order autoregressive process. Conversely, an infinite-order autoregressive process can be written as a first-order moving average process. This is

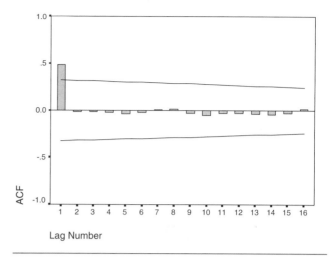

Figure 1   Theoretical Autocorrelation (ACF): MA(1) Process

important because it allows for parsimonious expressions of complex processes as small orders of the other process.

—Andrew J. Civettini

REFERENCES

Cromwell, J. B., Labys, W., & Terraza, M. (1994). *Univariate tests for time series models.* Thousand Oaks, CA: Sage.
Ostrom, C. W., Jr. (1990). *Time series analysis.* Thousand Oaks, CA: Sage.

MPLUS

Mplus is a statistical software package for estimating STRUCTURAL EQUATION MODELS and performing analyses that integrate RANDOM-EFFECTS FACTOR, and LATENT CLASS ANALYSIS in both cross-sectional and longitudinal settings and for both single-level and multilevel data. For further information, see the following Web site of the software: www.statmodel.com/index2.html.

—Tim Futing Liao

MULTICOLLINEARITY

Collinearity between two INDEPENDENT VARIABLES or multicollinearity between multiple independent variables in LINEAR REGRESSION analysis means that there are linear relations between these variables. In a vector model, in which variables are represented as vectors, exact collinearity would mean that two vectors lie on the same line or, more generally, for k variables, that the vectors lie in a subspace of a dimension less than k (i.e., that one of the vectors is a linear combination of the others). The result of such an exact linear relation between variables $\mathbf{X}$ would be that the cross-product matrix $\mathbf{X'X}$ is singular (i.e., its determinant would be equal to zero), so that it would have no inverse. In practice, an exact linear relationship rarely occurs, but the interdependence of social phenomena may result in "approximate" linear relationships. This phenomenon is known as multicollinearity.

In the analysis of interdependence, such as PRINCIPAL COMPONENTS and FACTOR ANALYSIS, multicollinearity is blissful because dimension reduction is the objective, whereas in the analysis of dependence structures, such as MULTIPLE REGRESSION ANALYSIS, multicollinearity among the independent variables is a problem. We will treat it here in the context of regression analysis.

CONSEQUENCES

Imagine an investigation into the causes of well-being of unemployed workers (measured as a scale from 0 to 100). A great number of EXPLANATORY VARIABLES will be taken into account, such as annual income (the lower the annual income, the lower the well-being), duration of unemployment (the higher the number of weeks of unemployment, the lower the well-being), and others. Now, some of these independent variables will be so highly correlated that conclusions from a multiple regression analysis will be affected. High multicollinearity is undesirable in a multicausal model because standard errors become much larger and CONFIDENCE INTERVALS much wider, thus affecting SIGNIFICANCE TESTING and STATISTICAL INFERENCE, even though the ORDINARY LEAST SQUARES (OLS) estimator still is unbiased. Like VARIANCES and COVARIANCES, multicollinearity is a sample property. This means analyses may be unreliable and sensitive to a few OUTLIERS or extreme cases.

The problem of correlated independent variables in a causal model is an old sore in social scientific research. In multiple regression analysis, it is referred to as multicollinearity (the predictors in a vector model almost overlap in a straight line), whereas in ANALYSIS OF VARIANCE and COVARIANCE, one tends to use the term *nonorthogonality* (the factors of the factor-response model are not perpendicular to each other). *Multicollinearity* and *nonorthogonality* are, in fact, synonyms.

Let us emphasize that strange things may happen in an analysis with high multicollinearity. Kendall and Stuart (1948) provided an extreme example of one dependent variable Y and two independent variables X_1 and X_2, in which the correlations $Y - X_1$ and $Y - X_2$ are weak (one of them even zero) and the correlation $X_1 - X_2$ is very strong (0.90, high multicollinearity), whereas the multiple correlation coefficient $R_{y \cdot 12}$ is approximately 1. This classic example shows a classic consequence of multicollinearity: insignificant results of testing individual parameters but high R-SQUARED values. The standardized coefficients (a direct function of sample variances), which normally cannot be greater than 1 because their squared values express a proportion of explained variance, exceed 2; consequently, both variables appear to explain each more than 400%, with only 100% to be explained!

DETECTIONS

How do we know whether the analysis is affected by high multicollinearity?

Most statistical software packages such as SPSS, SAS, and BMDP contain "collinearity diagnostics." Correlations with other independent variables, multiple correlations from the auxiliary regression of X_j on all other independent variables (R_j), TOLERANCE $(1 - R_j^2)$, variance-inflation factors $[1/(1 - R_j^2)]$, and eigenvalue analyses (cf. Belsley, Kuh, & Welsch, 1980) are part of the standard output and indicate which subset of variables is problematic. These diagnoses are more appropriate than the suggestion to draw the line at an arbitrary correlation value such as 0.60, as is stated in some textbooks. Besides, these diagnoses are to be used together with a SIGNIFICANCE TEST of the regression coefficients (or a calculation of the confidence intervals). Also, one should not take the correlation among X variables as proof enough for multicollinearity, for one should not forget that a correlation has to be evaluated in a multivariate context; that is, it might be affected by spurious relations, suppressor variables, and the like.

SOLUTIONS

A first option, ignoring the problem, can only be justified if multicollinearity only refers to subsets of variables, the individual effects of which the researcher is not interested in.

An obvious solution would be to delete one of these highly correlated variables. However, researchers often do not find this approach satisfactory from a theoretical point of view. To take the aforementioned example, both annual income and duration of unemployment offer a particular and fairly distinct explanation for well-being, even if they are statistically correlated.

A third possible solution, as suggested by econometricians, is to get more data. By obtaining more data, the current sample and its properties are modified. However, this solution is impractical most of the time because extra time and money are needed.

A fourth procedure removes the common variance of one collinear variable from another. In the current example, this would imply that the researcher keeps annual income but only keeps the residual of the duration of unemployment after regressing it on income. This procedure can be applied to all variables involved.

A fifth method is the creation of a summary index of the collinear variables if the researcher is not interested in seeing separate effects of the variables involved. But this method ignores measurement error and other possible factors.

A more sophisticated approach is the use of principal components analysis (PCA). All independent variables (often a great number) are to be used as the basis for a PCA and possibly combined with VARIMAX rotation, from which the component scores are taken and included in further regression analysis with, say, well-being as the dependent variable and the components as independent variables. The independent variables then will be at perpendicular angles to each other, thus avoiding multicollinearity. Interpretation of the new components can be a challenge, although the problem can be avoided by conducting the PCA on collinear variables only.

Finally, when the researcher intends to keep the highly correlated variables X_1 and X_2 in the regression model and yet produce a scientifically well-founded analysis, we can recommend *Ridge Regression* (e.g., Hoerl & Kennard, 1970) and *Bayes Regression* (e.g., Lindley & Smith, 1972), although they do not provide a 100% satisfactory solution either.

Ridge regression is an attempt to cope with multicollinearity by introducing some bias in the OLS estimation. Estimates from ridge regression have lower standard errors, but they are also slightly biased. In a $\mathbf{Y} = \mathbf{X}\boldsymbol{\beta} + \varepsilon$ regression, the coefficients $\hat{\beta}^* =$ $(\mathbf{X}'\mathbf{X} + k\mathbf{I})^{-1}\mathbf{X}'\mathbf{y}$ are used, in which small increments to the principal diagonal $(\mathbf{X}'\mathbf{X})$ are added. Now the entire system behaves more orthogonally. However, the choice of the small values k is arbitrary. Higher k values decrease standard errors but introduce greater bias in the estimates. Ridge regression is available in major statistical software programs today.

Similar to ridge regression, Bayes regression attempts to correct the problems of multicollinearity. However, while ridge regression relies on an arbitrary choice by the researcher of the small increments k, these are to be estimated from the data in Bayes regression. The disadvantage is that the Bayes strategy invariably presupposes the formulation of an a priori distribution.

—Jacques Tacq

REFERENCES

Belsley, D. A., Kuh, E., & Welsch, R. (1980). *Regression diagnostics*. New York: John Wiley.

Hoerl, A. E., & Kennard, R. W. (1970). Ridge regression. *Technometrics, 12*(1), 55–67, 69–82.

Kendall, M. G., & Stuart, A. (1948). *The advanced theory of statistics*. London: Griffin.

Lindley, D. V., & Smith, A. F. M. (1972). Bayes estimates for the linear model. *Journal of the Royal Statistical Society, 34*, 1–41.

MULTIDIMENSIONAL SCALING (MDS)

Multidimensional scaling (MDS) refers to a family of models in which the structure in a set of data is represented graphically by the relationships between a set of points in a space. MDS can be used on a wide variety of data, using different models and allowing different assumptions about the level of measurement.

In the simplest case, a data matrix giving information about the similarity (or DISSIMILARITY) between a set of objects is represented by the proximity (or distance) between corresponding points in a low-dimensional space. Given a set of data, interpreted as "distances," it finds the map locations that generated them.

For example, in a study of how people categorize drugs, a list of drugs was elicited from a sample of users and nonusers; 28 drugs were retained for a free-SORTING experiment, and the co-occurrence frequency was used as the measure of similarity. The

NewMDX FINAL CONFIGURATION: dimensions 1 and 2   Stress1 = 0.097

1. ALCOHOL
2. AMPHETAMINE
3. ASPIRIN
4. BARBITURATES
5. CAFFEINE
6. CANNABIS
7. CHOCOLATE
8. COCAINE
9. COUGH MIXTURE
10. CRACK
11. ECSTASY
12. GHP
13. GLUE
14. HEROIN
15. IMMODIUM
16. INSULIN
17. KETAMINE
18. LSD
19. MAGIC MUSHROOM
20. METHADONE
21. PCP
22. PENICILLIN
23. POPPERS
24. PROZAC
25. STEROIDS
26. TEMAZEPAM
27. TOBACCO
28. VIAGRA

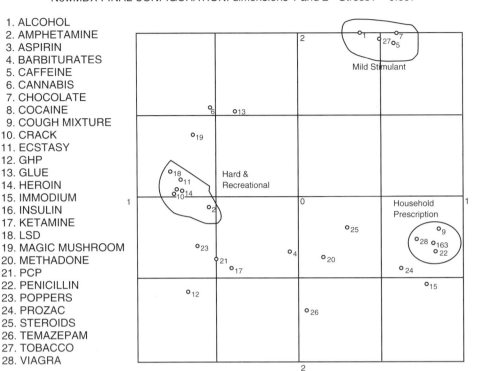

Figure 1

data were scaled in two dimensions, producing Figure 1.

In the case of perfect data, the correspondence between the dissimilarity data and the distances of the solution will be total, but with imperfect data, the degree of fit is given by the size of the normalized stress (residual sum of squares) value, which is a measure of badness of fit. In this case, the fit is excellent ($stress_1 = 0.097$), and it is three times smaller than random expectation. The solution configuration yields three highly distinct clusters (confirmed by independent hierarchical clustering) of *mild stimulant drugs* (core prototypes: tobacco, caffeine), *hard recreational* (core: cocaine, heroin), and *household prescription* (core: aspirin, penicillin).

MDS can be either exploratory (simply providing a useful and easily assimilable visualization of a data set) or explanatory (giving a geometric representation of the structure in a data set, in which the assumptions of the model are taken to represent the way in which the data were produced). Compared to other multivariate methods, MDS models are usually distribution free, make conservative demands on the structure of the data, are unaffected by nonsystematic missing data, and can

be used with a wide variety of measures; the solutions are also usually readily interpretable. The chief weaknesses are relative ignorance of the sampling properties of stress, proneness to local minima solutions, and inability to represent the asymmetry of causal models.

THE BASIC MDS MODEL

The basic type of MDS is the analysis of two-way, one-mode data (e.g., a matrix of correlations or other dissimilarity/similarity measures), using the Euclidean distance model. The original *metric* version, "classical" MDS converted the "distances" into scalar products and then factored or decomposed them into a set of locations in a low-dimensional space (hence "smallest space analysis"). The first *nonmetric* model was developed by Roger N. Shepard in 1962, who showed that the merely ordinal constraints of the data, if imposed in sufficient number, guarantee metric recovery, and he provided the first iterative computer program that implemented the claim. Kruskal (1964) gave ordinary least squares (OLS) statistical substance to it; Takane, Young, and DeLeeuw (1977) developed a frequently used Alternating Least Squares program (ALSCAL); and probabilistic MAXIMUM LIKELIHOOD versions of MDS have also subsequently been developed (e.g., MULTISCALE) (Ramsay, 1977).

VARIANTS OF MDS

The various types of MDS can be differentiated (Coxon, 1982) in terms of the following:

- **The data**, whose "shape" is described in terms of its *way* (rows, columns, "third-way" replications) and its *mode* (the number of sets of distinct objects, such as variables, subjects).
- **The transformation (rescaling) function**, or LEVEL OF MEASUREMENT, which specifies the extent to which the data properties are to be adequately represented in the solution). The primary distinction is *nonmetric* (ordinal or lower) versus *metric* (interval and ratio) scaling.
- **The model**, which is usually the Euclidean distance model but also covers simpler Minkowski metrics such as City-Block and the different composition functions such as the vector, scalar products, or FACTOR model.

TWO-WAY, ONE-MODE DATA

Any nonnegative, symmetric judgments or measures can provide input to the basic model: frequencies, counts, ratings/rankings of similarity, co-occurrence, colocation, confusion rates, measures of association, and so forth, and a two-dimensional solution should be stable with 12 or more points. Nonmetric analyses use distance models; metric models also may use vector/factor models. Stress values from simulation studies of random configurations provide an empirical yardstick for assessing obtained stress values.

TWO-WAY, TWO-MODE DATA

Rectangular data matrices (usually with subjects as rows and variables as columns) consist of profile data or preference ratings/rankings. Distance (unfolding) or vector models are employed to produce a joint BIPLOT of the row and column elements as points. The vector model (MDPREF) is formally identical to simple CORRESPONDENCE ANALYSIS and represents the row elements as unit vectors. Because such data are row conditional, caution is needed in interpreting interset relations in the solution. If the sorting data of the

example were entered directly as (Individual × Object matrix, with entries giving the category number), then a program such as MDSORT would represent both the objects and the categories.

THREE-WAY DATA

The "third way" consists of different individuals, time or spatial points, subgroups in the data, experimental conditions, different methods, and so forth. The most common variant is three-way, two-mode data (a stack of two-way, one-mode matrices)—which, when represented by the metric weighted distance model, is termed *individual differences scaling* (INDSCAL) (Carroll & Chang, 1970). In the INDSCAL solution, the objects are represented in a group space (whose dimensions are fixed and should be readily interpretable), and each element of the third way ("individual") has a set of nonnegative dimensional weights by which the individual differentially shrinks or expands each dimension of the group space to form a "private space." Individual differences are thus represented by a profile of salience weights applied to a common space. When plotted separately as the "subject space," the angular separation between the points represents the closeness of their profiles, and the distance from the origin approximately represents the variance explained. Returning to the example, if the individuals were divided into subgroups (such as Gender × Usage) and a co-occurrence matrix calculated within each group, then the set of matrices forms three-way, two-mode data, and their scaling by INDSCAL would yield information about how far the groups differed in terms of the importance (weights) attributed to the dimensions underlying the drugs configuration.

Other variants of MDS exist for other types of data (e.g., tables, triads), other transformations (parametric mapping, power functions), and other models (non-Euclidean metrics, simple conjoint models, discrete models such as additive trees), as well as for a wide range of three-way models and hybrid models such as CLASCAL (a development of INDSCAL that parameterizes latent *classes* of individuals). Utilities exist for comparing configuration (Procrustean rotation), and extensions for up to seven-way data are possible.

An extensive review of variants of MDS is contained in Carroll and Arabie (1980), and a wide-ranging bibliography of three-way applications is accessible at http://ruls01.fsw.leidenuniv.nl/~kroonenb/document/reflist.htm.

APPLICATIONS

For the basic model and for the input of aggregate measures, restrictions on the number of cases are normally irrelevant. But for two-way, two-mode data and three-way data, applications are rarely feasible (or interpretable) for more than 100 individual cases. In this case, "pseudo-subjects" (subgroups of individuals chosen either on analytic grounds or after CLUSTER ANALYSIS) are more appropriately used. Disciplines using MDS now extend well beyond the original focus in psychology and political science and include other social sciences, such as economics, as well as biological sciences and chemistry.

—Anthony P. M. Coxon

REFERENCES

Carroll, J. D., & Chang, J.-J. (1970). Analysis of individual differences in multidimensional scaling via a N-way generalisation of Eckart-Young decomposition. *Psychometrika, 35,* 283–299, 310–319.

Carroll, J. D., & Arabie, P. (1980). Multidimensional scaling. *Annual Review of Psychology, 31,* 607–649.

Coxon, A. P. M. (1982). *The user's guide to multidimensional scaling.* London: Heinemann Educational.

Kruskal, J. B. (1964). Multidimensional scaling by optimising goodness of fit to a nonmetric hypothesis. *Psychometrika, 29,* 1–27, 115–129.

Ramsay, J. O. (1977). Maximum likelihood estimation in MDS. *Psychometrika, 42,* 241–266.

Takane, Y., Young, F. W., & DeLeeuw, J. (1977). Nonmetric individual differences multidimensional scaling: An alternating least squares method with optimal scaling features. *Psychometrika, 42,* 7–67.

MULTIDIMENSIONALITY

A unidimensional structure exists in those situations in which a single, fundamental DIMENSION underlies a set of observations. Examples of this condition are measures used to evaluate the qualifications of political candidates, a SCALE of political activism, or a measure designed to describe a single personality trait. The presumption is that there is a single common dimension on which the candidates, citizens, or personality traits are arrayed.

Many theoretical CONSTRUCTS used in the social sciences are quite complex. A single, homogeneous, underlying dimension may not be adequate to express these complex concepts. This complexity may require us to turn to more elaborate explanations of the variables' behavior in which more than one latent dimension underlies a set of empirical observations. This is multidimensionality. For these concepts to be useful in further analysis, their multiple aspects must be reflected in their MEASUREMENT. In this regard, specifying multiple dimensions is a way of defining the complex concept by simplifying it into measurable and understandable aspects and may not represent substantive reality. Its utility is in OPERATIONALIZING the theoretical construct for ease of interpretation.

The substantive task of the researcher relative to dimensionality is to uncover these multiple dimensions and determine how many are scientifically important. We hypothesize their existence because THEORY suggests that they should exist or that we can predict these latent dimensions because of the variation in the empirical observations at hand. We hypothesize how they should relate to each other and then use some empirical technique to test our HYPOTHESES. Thus, there is a theoretical and an empirical basis to the concept.

For example, modeling the concept of political ideology by using a variable measuring only attitudes toward governmental intervention in the economy gives an entirely different picture of ideology than if we defined it by measuring only attitudes toward issues of race, such as busing or affirmative action. We could further model ideology by measuring attitudes on social-cultural issues such as abortion or homosexual rights. These are dimensions of the multidimensional concept of ideology.

An important consideration in the choice of dimensions is their importance for a particular purpose. Jacoby (1991) offers an example. Maps MODEL the physical world. The type of map, or its dimensionality, depends on its purpose and the audience at which it is directed. A person traveling by automobile may need a map depicting roadways. This usually involves only two dimensions—latitude and longitude. A topographical engineer, however, may require more detail in the form of another dimension, height above sea level. Thus, the number of dimensions deemed important is a contextual decision.

—Edward G. Carmines and James Woods

REFERENCES

Carmines, E. G., & McIver, J. P. (1981). *Unidimensional scaling* (Sage University Paper Series on Quantitative Applications in the Social Sciences, 07–024). Beverly Hills, CA: Sage.

Jacoby, W. G. (1991). *Data theory and dimensional analysis* (Sage University Paper Series on Quantitative Applications in the Social Sciences, 07–078). Newbury Park, CA: Sage.

Nunnally, J. C. (1978). *Psychometric theory.* New York: McGraw-Hill.

Weisberg, H. F. (1974). Dimensionland: An excursion into spaces. *American Journal of Political Science, 18,* 743–776.

MULTI-ITEM MEASURES

The item is the basic unit of a psychological scale. It is a statement or question in clear, unequivocal terms about the measured characteristics (Haladyna, 1994). In social science, SCALES are used to assess people's social characteristics, such as attitudes, personalities, opinions, emotional states, personal needs, and description of their living environment.

An item is a "mini" measure that has a molecular score (Thorndike, 1967). When used in social science, multi-item measures can be superior to a single, straightforward question. There are two reasons. First, the RELIABILITY of a multi-item measure is higher than a single question. With a single question, people are less likely to give consistent answers over time. Many things can influence people's response (e.g., mood, specific thing they encountered that day). They may choose yes to a question one day and say no the other day. It is also possible that people give a wrong answer or interpret the question differently over time. On the other hand, a multi-item measure has several questions targeting the same social issue, and the final composite score is based on all questions. People are less likely to make the above mistakes to multiple items, and the composite score is more consistent over time. Thus, the multi-item measure is more reliable than a single question. Second, the VALIDITY of a multi-item measure can be higher than a single question. Many measured social characteristics are broad in scope and simply cannot be assessed with a single question. Multi-item measures will be necessary to cover more content of the measured characteristic and to fully and completely reflect the construct domain.

These issues are best illustrated with an example. To assess people's job satisfaction, a single-item measure could be as follows:

I'm not satisfied with my work. (1 = *disagree,* 2 = *slightly disagree,* 3 = *uncertain,* 4 = *slightly agree,* 5 = *agree*)

To this single question, people's responses can be inconsistent over time. Depending on their mood or specific things they encountered at work that day, they might respond very differently to this single question. Also, people may make mistakes when reading or responding. For example, they might not notice the word *not* and agree when they really disagree. Thus, this single-item measure about job satisfaction can be notoriously unreliable. Another problem is that people's feelings toward their jobs may not be simple. Job satisfaction is a very broad issue, and it includes many aspects (e.g., satisfaction with the supervisor, satisfaction with coworkers, satisfaction with work content, satisfaction with pay, etc.). Subjects may like certain aspects of their jobs but not others. The single-item measure will oversimplify people's feelings toward their jobs.

A multi-item measure can reduce the above problems. The results from a multi-item measure should be more consistent over time. With multiple items, random errors could average out (Spector, 1992). That is, with 20 items, if a respondent makes an error on 1 item, the impact on the overall score is quite minimal. More important, a multi-item measure will allow subjects to describe their feelings about different aspects of their jobs. This will greatly improve the precision and validity of the measure. Therefore, multi-item measures are one of the most important and frequently used tools in social science.

—Cong Liu

See also SCALING

REFERENCES

Haladyna, T. M. (1994). *Developing and validating multiple-choice test items.* Hillsdale, NJ: Lawrence Erlbaum.

Spector, P. (1992). *Summated rating scale construction: An introduction.* Newbury Park, CA: Sage.

Thorndike, R. L. (1967). The analysis and selection of test items. In D. Jackson & S. Messick (Eds.), *Problems in human assessment* (pp. 201–216). New York: McGraw-Hill.

MULTILEVEL ANALYSIS

Most of statistical inference is based on replicated observations of UNITS OF ANALYSIS of one type (e.g., a sample of individuals, countries, or schools). The analysis of such observations usually is based on the assumption that either the sampled units themselves or the corresponding RESIDUALS in some statistical model are independent and identically distributed. However, the complexity of social reality and social science theories often calls for more COMPLEX DATA SETS, which include units of analysis of more than one type. Examples are studies on educational achievement, in which pupils, teachers, classrooms, and schools might all be important units of analysis; organizational studies, with employees, departments, and firms as units of analysis; cross-national comparative research, with individuals and countries (perhaps also regions) as units of analysis; studies in GENERALIZABILITY THEORY, in which each factor defines a type of unit of analysis; and META-ANALYSIS, in which the collected research studies, the research groups that produced them, and the subjects or respondents in these studies are units of analysis and sources of unexplained variation. Frequently, but by no means always, units of analysis of different types are hierarchically nested (e.g., pupils are nested in classrooms, which, in turn, are nested in schools). *Multilevel analysis* is a general term referring to statistical methods appropriate for the analysis of data sets comprising several types of unit of analysis. The *levels* in the multilevel analysis are another name for the different types of unit of analysis. Each level of analysis will correspond to a POPULATION, so that multilevel studies will refer to several populations—in the first example, there are four populations: of pupils, teachers, classrooms, and schools. In a strictly nested data structure, the most detailed level is called the first, or the lowest, level. For example, in a data set with pupils nested in classrooms nested in schools, the pupils constitute Level 1, the classrooms Level 2, and the schools Level 3.

HIERARCHICAL LINEAR MODEL

The most important methods of multilevel analysis are variants of REGRESSION analysis designed for hierarchically nested data sets. The main model is the HIERARCHICAL LINEAR MODEL (HLM), an extension of the GENERAL LINEAR MODEL in which the probability model for the errors, or residuals, has a structure reflecting the hierarchical structure of the data. For this reason, multilevel analysis often is called hierarchical linear modeling. As an example, suppose that a researcher is studying how annual earnings of college graduates well after graduation depend on academic achievement in college. Let us assume that

the researcher collected data for a reasonable number of colleges—say, more than 30 colleges that can be regarded as a sample from a specific population of colleges, with this population being further specified to one or a few college programs—and, for each of these colleges, a random sample of the students who graduated 15 years ago. For each student, information was collected on the current income (variable Y) and the grade point average in college (denoted by the variable X in a metric where $X = 0$ is the minimum passing grade). Graduates are denoted by the letter i and colleges by j. Because graduates are nested in colleges, the numbering of graduates i may start from 1 for each college separately, and the variables are denoted by Y_{ij} and X_{ij}. The analysis could be based for college j on the model

$$Y_{ij} = a_j + b_j X_{ij} + E_{ij}.$$

This is just a linear regression model, in which the INTERCEPTS a_j and the regression coefficients b_j depend on the college and therefore are indicated with the subscript j. The fact that colleges are regarded as a random sample from a population is reflected by the assumption of random variation for the intercepts a_j and regression coefficients b_j. Denote the population mean (in the population of all colleges) of the intercepts by a and the college-specific deviations by U_{0j}, so that $a_j = a + U_{0j}$. Similarly, split the regression coefficients into the population mean and the college-specific deviations $b_j = b + U_{1j}$. Substitution of these equations then yields

$$Y_{ij} = a + b X_{ij} + U_{0j} + U_{1j} X_{ij} + E_{ij}.$$

This model has three different types of residuals: the so-called Level-1 residual E_{ij} and the Level-2 residuals U_{0j} and U_{1j}. The Level-1 residual varies over the population of graduates; the Level-2 residuals vary over the population of colleges. The residuals can be interpreted as follows. For colleges with a high value of U_{0j}, their graduates with the minimum passing grade $X = 0$ have a relatively high expected income—namely, $a + U_{0j}$. For colleges with a high value of U_{1j}, the effect of one unit GPA extra on the expected income of their graduates is relatively high—namely, $b + U_{1j}$. Graduates with a high value of E_{ij} have an income that is relatively high, given their college j and their GPA X_{ij}.

This equation is an example of the HLM; in its general form, this model can have more than one independent variable. The first part of the equation, $a + bX_{ij}$, is called the fixed part of the model; this is a linear function of the independent variables, just like in linear regression analysis. The second part, $U_{0j} + U_{1j}X_{ij} + E_{ij}$, is called the random part and is more complicated than the random residual in linear regression analysis, as it reflects the unexplained variation E_{ij} between the graduates as well as the unexplained variation $U_{0j} + U_{1j}X_{ij}$ between the colleges. The random part of the model is what distinguishes the hierarchical linear model from the general linear model. The simplest nontrivial specification for the random part of a two-level model is a model in which only the intercept varies between Level-2 units, but the regression coefficients are the same across Level-2 units. This is called the random intercept model, and for our example, it reads

$$Y_{ij} = a + bX_{ij} + U_{0j} + E_{ij}.$$

Models in which also the regression coefficients vary randomly between Level –2 units are called random slope models (referring to graphs of the regression lines, in which the regression coefficients are the slopes of the regression lines).

The dependent variable Y in the HLM always is a variable defined at the lowest (i.e., most detailed) level of the hierarchy. An important feature of the HLM is that the independent, or explanatory, variables can be defined at any of the levels of analysis. In the example of the study of income of college graduates, suppose that the researcher is interested in the effect on earnings of alumni of college quality, as measured by college rankings, and that some meaningful college ranking score Z_j is available. In the earlier model, the college-level residuals U_{0j} and U_{1j} reflect unexplained variability between colleges. This variability could be explained partially by the college-level variable Z_j, according to the equations

$$a_j = a + c_0 Z_j + U_{0j}, \quad b_j = b + c_1 Z_j + U_{1j},$$

which can be regarded as linear regression equations at Level 2 for the quantities a_j and b_j, which are themselves not directly observable. Substitution of these equations into the Level-1 equation $Y_{ij} = a_j + b_j X_{ij} + E_{ij}$ yields the new model,

$$Y_{ij} = a + bX_{ij} + c_0 Z_j + c_1 X_{ij} Z_j + U_{0j}$$
$$+ U_{1j} X_{ij} + E_{ij},$$

where the parameters a and b and the residuals E_{ij}, U_{0j}, and U_{1j} now have different meanings than in the earlier model. The fixed part of this model is extended compared to the earlier model, but the random part has retained the same structure. The term $c_1 X_{ij} Z_j$ in the fixed part is the INTERACTION EFFECT between the Level-1 variable X and the Level-2 variable Z. The regression coefficient c_1 expresses how much the college context (Z) modifies the effect of the individual achievement (X) on later income (Y); such an effect is called a cross-level interaction effect. The possibility of expressing how context (the "macro level") affects relations between individual-level variables (the "micro level") is an important reason for the popularity of multilevel modeling (see DiPrete & Forristal, 1994).

A parameter that describes the relative importance of the two levels in such a data set is the INTRACLASS CORRELATION coefficient, described in the entry with this name and also in the entry on VARIANCE COMPONENT MODELS. The similar variance ratio, when applied to residual (i.e., unexplained) variances, is called the residual intraclass correlation coefficient.

ASSUMPTIONS, ESTIMATION, AND TESTING

The standard assumptions for the HLM are the linear model expressed by the model equation, normal distributions for all residuals, and independence of the residuals for different levels and for different units in the same level. However, different residuals for the same unit, such as the random intercept U_{0j} and the random slope U_{1j} in the model above, are allowed to be correlated; they are assumed to have a multivariate normal distribution. With these assumptions, the HLM for the example above implies that outcomes for graduates of the same college are correlated due to the influences from the college—technically, due to the fact that their equations for Y_{ij} contain the same college-level residuals U_{0j} and U_{1j}. This dependence between different cases is an important departure from the assumptions of the more traditional general linear model used in regression analysis.

The parameters of the HLM can be estimated by the MAXIMUM LIKELIHOOD method. Various ALGORITHMS have been developed mainly in the 1980s (cf. Goldstein, 2003; Longford, 1993); one important algorithm is an iterative reweighted least squares algorithm (see the entry on GENERALIZED LEAST SQUARES), which alternates between estimating the regression coefficients in the fixed part and the parameters of the random part. The regression coefficients can be tested by T-TESTS or Wald tests. The parameters defining the structure of the random part can be tested by LIKELIHOOD RATIO TESTS (also called deviance tests) or by chi-squared tests. These methods have been made available since the 1980s in dedicated multilevel software, such as HLM and MLwiN, and later also in packages that include multilevel analysis among a more general array of methods, such as M-Plus, and in some general statistical packages, such as SAS and SPSS. An overview of software capabilities is given in Goldstein (2003).

MULTIPLE LEVELS

As was illustrated already in the examples, it is not uncommon that a practical investigation involves more than two levels of analysis. In educational research, the largest contributions to achievement outcomes usually are determined by the pupil and the teacher, but the social context provided by the group of pupils in the classroom and the organizational context provided by the school, as well as the social context defined by the neighborhood, may also have important influences. In a study of academic achievement of pupils, variables defined at each of these levels of analysis could be included as explanatory variables. If there is an influence of some level of analysis, then it is to be expected that this influence will not be completely captured by the variables measured for this level of analysis, but there will be some amount of unexplained variation between the units of analysis for this level. This should then be reflected by including this unexplained variation as random residual variability in the model. The first type of residual variability is the random main effect of the units at this level, exemplified by the random intercepts U_{0j} in the two-level model above. In addition, it is possible that the effects of numerical variables (such as pupil-level variables) differ across the units of the level under consideration, which can again be modeled by random slopes such as the U_{1j} above. An important type of conclusion of analyses with multiple levels of analysis is the partitioning of unexplained variability over the various levels. This is discussed for models without random slopes in the entry on VARIANCE COMPONENT MODELS. How much unexplained variability is associated with each of the levels can provide the researcher with important directions about where to look for further explanation.

Levels of analysis can be nested or crossed. One level of analysis—the lower level—is said to be nested in another, higher level if the units of the higher level correspond to a partition into subsets of the units of the lower level (i.e., each unit of the lower level is contained in exactly one unit of the higher level). Otherwise, the levels are said to be crossed. Crossed levels of analysis often are more liable to lead to difficulties in the analysis than nested levels: Estimation algorithms may have more convergence problems, the empirical conclusions about partitioning variability over the various levels may be less clear-cut, and there may be more ambiguity in conceptual and theoretical modeling.

The use of models with multiple levels of analysis requires a sufficiently rich data set on which to base the statistical analysis. Note that for each level of analysis, the units in the data set constitute a sample from the corresponding population. Although any rule of thumb should be taken with a grain of sand, a sample size less than 20 (i.e., a level of analysis represented by less than 20 units) usually will give only quite restricted information about this population (i.e., this level of analysis), and sample sizes less than 10 should be regarded with suspicion.

LONGITUDINAL DATA

In LONGITUDINAL RESEARCH, the HLM also can be used fruitfully. In the most simple longitudinal data structure, with repeated measures on individuals, the repeated measures constitute the lower (first) and the individuals the higher (second) levels. Mostly, there will be a meaningful numerical time variable: For example, in an experimental study, this may be the time since onset of the experimental situation, and in a developmental study, this may be age. Especially for nonbalanced longitudinal data structures, in which the numbers and times of observations differ between individuals, multilevel modeling may be a natural and very convenient method. The dependence of the outcome variable on the time dimension is a crucial aspect of the model. Often, a linear dependence is a useful first approximation. This amounts to including the time of measurement as an explanatory variable; a random slope for this variable represents differential change (or growth) rates for different individuals. Often, however, dependence on time is nonlinear. In some cases, it will be possible to model this while remaining within the HLM by using several nonlinear transformations (e.g., polynomials or splines) of time and postulating a model that is linear in these transformed time variables (see Snijders & Bosker, 1999, chap. 12). In other cases, it is better to forgo the relative simplicity of linear modeling and construct models that are not linear in the original or transformed variables or for which the Level-1 residuals are autocorrelated (cf. Verbeke & Molenberghs, 2000).

NONLINEAR MODELS

The assumption of normal distributions for the residuals is not always appropriate, although sometimes this assumption can be made more realistic by transformations of the dependent variable. In particular, for dichotomous or discrete dependent variables, other models are required. Just as the GENERALIZED LINEAR MODEL is an extension of the general linear model of regression analysis, nonlinear versions of the HLM also provide the basis of, for example, multilevel versions of LOGISTIC REGRESSION and LOGIT MODELS. These are called hierarchical generalized linear models or generalized linear mixed models (see the entry on HIERARCHICAL NONLINEAR MODELS).

—Tom A. B. Snijders

REFERENCES

de Leeuw, J., & Kreft, I. G. G. (Eds.). (in press). *Handbook of quantitative multilevel analysis*. Dordrecht, The Netherlands: Kluwer Academic.

DiPrete, T. A., & Forristal, J. D. (1994). Multilevel models: Methods and substance. *Annual Review of Sociology, 20*, 331–357.

Goldstein, H. (2003). *Multilevel statistical models* (3rd ed.). London: Hodder Arnold.

Hox, J. J. (2002). *Multilevel analysis, techniques and applications*. Mahwah, NJ: Lawrence Erlbaum.

Longford, N. T. (1993). *Random coefficient models*. New York: Oxford University Press.

Raudenbush, S. W., & Bryk, A. S. (2001). *Hierarchical linear models: Applications and data analysis methods* (2nd ed.). Thousand Oaks, CA: Sage.

Snijders, T. A. B., & Bosker, R. J. (1999). *Multilevel analysis: An introduction to basic and advanced multilevel modeling*. London: Sage.

Verbeke, G., & Molenberghs, G. (2000). *Linear mixed models for longitudinal data*. New York: Springer.

MULTIMETHOD-MULTITRAIT RESEARCH. *See* MULTIMETHOD RESEARCH

MULTIMETHOD RESEARCH

Multimethod research entails the application of two or more sources of data or research methods to the investigation of a research question or to different but highly linked research questions. Such research is also frequently referred to as *mixed methodology*. The rationale for mixed-method research is that most social research is based on findings deriving from a single research method and, as such, is vulnerable to the accusation that any findings deriving from such a study may lead to incorrect inferences and conclusions if MEASUREMENT ERROR is affecting those findings. It is rarely possible to estimate how much measurement error is having an impact on a set of findings, so that monomethod research is always suspect in this regard.

MIXED-METHOD RESEARCH AND MEASUREMENT

The rationale of mixed-method research is underpinned by the principle of TRIANGULATION, which implies that researchers should seek to ensure that they are not overreliant on a single research method and should instead employ more than one measurement procedure when investigating a research problem. Thus, the argument for mixed-method research, which in large part accounts for its growth in popularity, is that it enhances confidence in findings.

In the context of measurement considerations, mixed-method research might be envisioned in relation to different kinds of situations. One form might be that when one or more constructs that are the focus of an investigation have attracted different measurement efforts (such as different ways of measuring levels of job satisfaction), two or more approaches to measurement might be employed in combination. A second form might entail employing two or more methods of data collection. For example, in developing an approach to the examination of the nature of jobs in a firm, we might employ structured observation and structured interviews concerning apparently identical job attributes with the same subjects. The level of agreement between the two sets of data can then be assessed.

THE MIXED-METHOD-MULTITRAIT MATRIX

One very specific context within which the term *mixed-method* is frequently encountered is in relation to the mixed-method-multitrait matrix developed by Campbell and Fiske (1959). Let us say that we have a construct that is conceptualized as comprising five dimensions or "traits" as they are referred to by Campbell and Fiske. We might develop subscales to measure each dimension and employ both structured interviewing and structured observation with respect to each trait. We can then generate a matrix that summarizes within- and between-method correlations between the different traits. The matrix allows two concerns to be addressed. First, it allows a test of the DISCRIMINANT VALIDITY of the measures because the within-method correlations should not be too large. Second, of particular importance to this entry is that the convergent validity of the between-method scores can be examined. The larger the resulting correlations, the greater the convergent validity and therefore the more confidence can be felt about the findings. Table 1 illustrates the resulting matrix.

In this matrix, a correlation of, say, $r_{i4,o2}$ indicates the correlation between trait T4, measured by a subscale administered by structured interview (i), and trait T2, measured by a subscale administered by structured observation (o). The five correlations in bold are the convergent validity correlations and indicate how well the two approaches to the measurement of each trait (e.g., $r_{i1,o1}$) are consistent.

Care is needed over the successful establishment of convergent validity within a mixed-method research context. It is easy to assume that measurement validity has been established when convergent validity is demonstrated. However, it may be that *both* approaches to the measurement of a construct or research problem are problematic. Convergent validity enhances our confidence but of course does not eliminate completely the possibility that error remains.

COMBINING QUANTITATIVE AND QUALITATIVE RESEARCH

The account of mixed-method research so far has been firmly rooted in the tradition of measurement and of the triangulation of measurements in particular. However, the discussion of mixed-method research has increasingly been stretched to include the collection of qualitative as well as quantitative data. In other words, increasingly mixed-method research includes the combination of quantitative research and qualitative research. In this way, the discussion of mixed-method research and, indeed, of triangulation is employed not just in relation to measurement issues but also to different approaches to collecting data.

QUANTITATIVE RESEARCH and QUALITATIVE RESEARCH are sometimes taken to refer to distinct PARADIGMS and, as such, as being incompatible. Several writers have argued that quantitative and qualitative research derive from completely different epistemological and ontological traditions. They suggest that

Table 1   Mixed-Method-Multitrait Matrix

	Interview					Observation				
Interview	*T1*	*T2*	*T3*	*T4*	*T5*	*T1*	*T2*	*T3*	*T4*	*T5*
T1	—									
T2	$r_{i2,i1}$	—								
T3	$r_{i3,i1}$	$r_{i3,i2}$	—							
T4	$r_{i4,i1}$	$r_{i4,i2}$	$r_{i4,i3}$	—						
T5	$r_{i5,i1}$	$r_{i5,i2}$	$r_{i5,i3}$	$r_{i5,i4}$	—					
Observation										
T1	$\boldsymbol{r_{i1,o1}}$					—				
T2	$r_{i2,o1}$	$\boldsymbol{r_{i2,o2}}$				$r_{o2,o1}$	—			
T3	$r_{i3,o1}$	$r_{i3,o2}$	$\boldsymbol{r_{i3,o3}}$			$r_{o3,o1}$	$r_{o3,o2}$	—		
T4	$r_{i4,o1}$	$r_{i4,o2}$	$r_{i4,o3}$	$\boldsymbol{r_{i4,o4}}$		$r_{o4,o1}$	$r_{o4,o2}$	$r_{o4,o3}$	—	
T5	$r_{i5,o1}$	$r_{i5,o2}$	$r_{i5,o3}$	$r_{i5,o4}$	$\boldsymbol{r_{i5,o5}}$	$r_{o5,o1}$	$r_{o5,o2}$	$r_{o5,o3}$	$r_{o5,o4}$	—

although it is possible to employ, for example, both a structured interview (as a quintessentially quantitative research method) and ETHNOGRAPHY (as a quintessentially qualitative research method) within a single investigation, this does not and indeed cannot represent a true integration because of the divergent principles on which the two approaches are founded. The combined use of such methods represents for such authors a superficial integration of incompatible approaches.

However, most researchers have adopted a more pragmatic stance and, although recognizing the fact that quantitative and qualitative research express different epistemological and ontological commitments (such as POSITIVISM VS. INTERPRETIVISM and OBJECTIVISM VS. CONSTRUCTIONISM), they accept that much can be gained by combining their respective strengths. The apparent incommensurability of quantitative and qualitative research is usually resolved either by ignoring the epistemological and ontological issues or by asserting that research methods and sources of data are in fact much less wedded to epistemological presuppositions than is commonly supposed. With the latter argument, a research method is no more than a technique for gathering data and is largely independent of wider considerations to do with the nature of valid knowledge.

When quantitative and qualitative research are combined, it is sometimes argued that what is happening is not so much mixed-method as MULTI-STRATEGY RESEARCH (Bryman, 2001). This preference reflects a view that quantitative and qualitative research are research strategies with contrasting approaches to social inquiry and that each is associated with a cluster of research methods and research designs. These distinctions suggest the fourfold classification presented in Table 2.

Mixed-method research associated with the mixed-method-multitrait matrix essentially belongs to cell 1 in Table 2 because such an investigation combines two data collection methods associated with quantitative research. Cell 4 includes investigations that combine two or more methods associated with qualitative research. In fact, much ethnography is almost inherently mixed-method research because ethnographers frequently do more than act as participant observers. They buttress their observations with such other sources as interviewing key informants, examining documents, and engaging in nonparticipant observation.

Table 2   Monostrategy and Multistrategy Approaches to Mixed-Method Research

	Quantitative Research Method	Qualitative Research Method
Quantitative research strategy	Monostrategy multimethod research 1	Multistrategy multimethod research 2
Qualitative research strategy	Multistrategy multimethod research 3	Monostrategy multimethod research 4

APPROACHES TO COMBINING QUANTITATIVE AND QUALITATIVE RESEARCH

Cells 2 and 3 are identical in that they comprise multistrategy mixed-method research, in which at least one research method or source of data associated with both quantitative and qualitative research is employed. They can be further refined by considering the different ways that the two research strategies can be combined, an issue that has been addressed by several writers. Morgan (1998) elucidates a mechanism for classifying multistrategy research in terms of two principles: whether the quantitative or the qualitative research method is the main approach to gathering data and which research method preceded the other. This pair of distinctions yields a fourfold classification of mixed-method studies (italics indicate the principal method):

1. qual → *quant.* Examples are when a researcher conducts semistructured interviewing to develop items for a multiple-item measurement scale or when an exploratory qualitative study is carried out to generate hypotheses that can be subsequently tested by a quantitative approach.

2. quant → *qual.* An example is when a social survey is conducted and certain individuals are selected on the basis of characteristics highlighted in the survey for further, more intensive study using a qualitative method.

3. *quant* → qual. An example would be when a researcher conducts some semistructured interviewing or participant observation to help illuminate some of the factors that may be responsible for relationships between variables that have been generated from a social survey investigation.

4. *qual* → quant. An illustration of such a study might be when an interesting relationship between variables is discerned in an ethnographic study and a survey is then conducted to establish how far that relationship has EXTERNAL VALIDITY.

These four types of multistrategy research constitute ways in which quantitative and qualitative research can be combined and, as such, are refinements of cells 2 and 3 in Table 2. Morgan's (1998) classification is not exhaustive in that it does not consider (a) multistrategy research in which quantitative and qualitative research are conducted more or less simultaneously and (b) multistrategy research in which there is no main approach to the collection of data (i.e., they are equally weighted). Creswell (1995) distinguishes two further types of multistrategy research that reflect these two points:

5. *Parallel/simultaneous studies.* Quantitative and qualitative research methods are administered more or less at the same time.

6. *Equivalent status studies.* Two research strategies have equal status within the overall research plan.

These two types frequently co-occur, as in mixed-method research in which different research methods are employed to examine different aspects of the phenomenon being investigated. One of the more frequently encountered arguments deployed in support of using multistrategy research is that using just quantitative or qualitative research is often not sufficient to get access to all dimensions of a research question. In such a context, the quantitative and qualitative research methods are likely to be employed more or less simultaneously and to have equivalent status.

Tashakkori and Teddlie (1998) further distinguish a seventh type of multistrategy research:

7. *Designs with multilevel use of approaches.* The researcher uses "different types of methods at different levels of data aggregation" (p. 18). An example of this type of study may occur when the researcher collects different types of data for different levels of an organization (a survey of organizational members, intensive interviews with section heads, observation of work practices).

In addition, Tashakkori and Teddlie (1998) observe that the kinds of multistrategy research covered thus far are what they call "mixed-method" studies. They observe that it is possible to distinguish these from mixed-model designs in which different phases of quantitative and qualitative research are combined. Mixed-model research occurs when, for example, a researcher collects qualitative data in an essentially exploratory manner but then submits the data to a quantitative, rather than a qualitative, data analysis.

One of the most frequently cited rationales for multistrategy research is that of seeking to establish the convergent validity of findings; in other words, this kind of rationale entails an appeal to the logic of triangulation. If quantitative findings can be confirmed with qualitative evidence (and vice versa), the credibility of the research is enhanced. Such a notion is not without problems, however. First, it is sometimes suggested that because quantitative and qualitative research derive from such contrasting epistemological and ontological positions, it is difficult to establish that one set of evidence can legitimately provide support or otherwise of the other. Second, as with all cases of triangulation, it is difficult to know how to deal with a disparity between the two sets of evidence. A common error is to assume that one is more likely to be valid than the other and to use the former as a yardstick of validity. Third, it is often suggested that the triangulation procedure is imbued with naive REALISM and that because many qualitative researchers subscribe to a constructionist position that denies the possibility of absolutely valid knowledge of the social world, it is inconsistent with much qualitative research practice. Fourth, it is easy to assume that multistrategy research is necessarily superior to monostrategy research, but this may not be so if the overall research design does not allow one research strategy to add substantially to what is known on the basis of the other research strategy. Fifth, although some social researchers are well rounded in terms of different methods and approaches, some may have strengths in one type of research rather than another, although this represents a good argument for teams with combinations of skills.

The idea of triangulation invariably presumes that the exercise is planned. However, when conducting any of the previously cited seven multistrategy research approaches, it is conceivable that the resulting quantitative and qualitative data may relate to a specific issue and therefore form an unplanned triangulation exercise. When the two sets of evidence provide convergent validity, the fact that this happens is likely to be unremarkable for the researcher, but when the two sets of data do not converge, the researcher will need to think further about the reasons that lie behind the clash of findings. Deacon, Bryman, and Fenton (1998) report that in the course of analyzing the results from a multistrategy investigation of the representation of social research in the mass media, they found a number of disparities between their quantitative and qualitative findings. These disparities did not derive from planned triangulation exercises. For example, they found that a survey of social scientists had found a general satisfaction with media representation, but when interviewed in depth about specific instances of media accounts of their research, they were much more critical. The disparity necessitated a consideration of the different kinds and contexts of questioning and their implications for understanding the role of the media in the social sciences.

Mixed-method research is undoubtedly being used increasingly in social research. Its appeal lies in the possibilities it offers in terms of increasing the validity of an investigation. It can be employed within and across research strategies and, as such, is a flexible way of approaching research questions, although it carries certain disadvantages in terms of time and cost. Mixed-method research and multistrategy research in particular can present problems of interpretation, especially when findings are inconsistent, but the preparedness of researchers to address such problems will enhance the credibility of their work.

—Alan Bryman

REFERENCES

Bryman, A. (2001). *Social research methods.* Oxford, UK: Oxford University Press.

Campbell, D. T., & Fiske, D. W. (1959). Convergent and discriminant validation by the multitrait-multimethod matrix. *Psychological Bulletin, 56,* 81–105.

Creswell, J. W. (1995). *Research design: Quantitative and qualitative approaches.* Thousand Oaks, CA: Sage.

Deacon, D., Bryman, A., & Fenton, N. (1998). Collision or collusion? A discussion of the unplanned triangulation of quantitative and qualitative research methods. *International Journal of Social Research Methodology, 1,* 47–63.

Morgan, D. L. (1998). Practical strategies for combining qualitative and quantitative methods: Applications for health research. *Qualitative Health Research, 8,* 362–376.

Tashakkori, A., & Teddlie, C. (1998). *Mixed methodology: Combining qualitative and quantitative approaches.* Thousand Oaks, CA: Sage.

MULTINOMIAL DISTRIBUTION

Suppose we have a RANDOM SAMPLE of N subjects, individuals, or items, and each subject is classified into exactly one of k possible categories that do not overlap in any way. That is, each subject can be classified into one and only one category. Define p_i as the probability that a subject is classified into category i for $i = 1, 2, \ldots, k$, where $0 \leq p_i \leq 1$ and $\sum p_i = 1$.

The categories are then said to be mutually exclusive and exhaustive.

Define the RANDOM VARIABLE X_i as the number of subjects in the sample (the count) that are classified into category i for $i = 1, 2, \ldots, k$. Obviously, we have $\sum X_i = N$. Then the joint PROBABILITY DISTRIBUTION of these k random variables is called the multinomial distribution, given by

$$f(X_1, X_2, \ldots, X_k)$$
$$= \binom{N}{X_1, X_2, \ldots, X_k} p_1^{X_1} p_2^{X_2} \cdots p_k^{X_k} \quad (1)$$
$$= \frac{N!}{X_1! X_2! \ldots X_k!} p_1^{X_1} p_2^{X_2} \cdots p_k^{X_k}. \quad (2)$$

The relevant PARAMETERS are $N, p_1, p_2, \ldots, p_k$. There are a total of only $k - 1$ random variables involved in this distribution because of the fixed sum $\sum X_i = N$. The mean and variance of each X_i are Np_i and $Np_i(1 - p_i)$, respectively, and the covariance of the pair X_i, X_j is $-Np_i p_j$. The marginal distribution of each X_i is the BINOMIAL DISTRIBUTION with parameters N and p_i.

As an example, suppose we roll a balanced die 10 times and want to find the probability that the faces 1 and 6 each occur once and each other face occurs twice, that is, $P(X_1 = X_6 = 1, X_2 = X_3 = X_4 = X_5 = 2)$. Each $p_i = 1/6$ for a balanced die, and the calculation is 0.003751.

The term in large parentheses in (1) or, equivalently, the term involving factorials in (2) is called the multinomial coefficient.

If $k = 2$, the multinomial distribution reduces to the familiar binomial distribution with parameters N and p_1, where the two categories are usually called success and failure, X_1 is the number of successes, and $X_2 = N - X_1$ is the number of failures.

—Jean D. Gibbons

MULTINOMIAL LOGIT

Multinomial logit (MNL) is a statistical model used to study problems with unordered categorical (nominal) dependent variables that have three or more categories. Multinomial logit estimates the PROBABILITY that each observation will be in each category of the dependent variable. MNL uses characteristics of the individual observations as independent variables, and the effects of the independent variables are allowed to vary across the categories of the dependent variable. This differs from the similar CONDITIONAL LOGIT model, which uses characteristics of the choice categories as independent variables and thus does not allow the effects of independent variables to vary across choice categories. Models that include both characteristics of the alternatives and characteristics of the individual observations are possible and are also usually referred to as conditional logits.

There are several different ways to derive the multinomial logit model. The most common approach in the social sciences is to derive the MNL as a DISCRETE choice model. Each observation is an actor selecting one alternative from a choice set of J alternatives, where J is the number of categories in the dependent variable. The utility an actor i would get from selecting alternative k from this choice set is given by

$$U_{ik} = X_i \beta_k + \varepsilon_{ik}.$$

Let y be the dependent variable with J unordered categories. Thus, the probability that an actor i would select alternative j over alternative k is

$$
\begin{aligned}
\Pr(y_i = k) &= \Pr(U_{ik} > U_{ij}) \\
&= \Pr(X_i \beta_k + \varepsilon_{ik} > X_i \beta_j + \varepsilon_{ij}) \\
&= \Pr(\varepsilon_{ik} - \varepsilon_{ij} > X_i \beta_j - X_i \beta_k).
\end{aligned}
$$

McFadden (1973) demonstrated that if the εs are independent and identical Gumbel distributions across all observations and alternatives, this discrete choice derivation leads to a multinomial logit. MNL estimates $\Pr(y_i = k | x_i)$, where k is one of the J categories in the dependent variable. The multinomial logit model is written as

$$\Pr(y_i = k | x_i) = \frac{e^{x_i \beta_k}}{\sum_{j=1}^{J} e^{x_i \beta_k}}.$$

Multinomial logits are estimated using MAXIMUM LIKELIHOOD techniques. To identify the model, one must place a constraint on the βs. Generally, the βs for one category are constrained to equal zero, although other constraints are possible (such as $\sum_{j=1}^{J} \beta_j = 0$). If the βs for one category are constrained to equal zero, this category becomes the baseline category, and all other β_js indicate the effect of the independent variables on the probability of being in category j as opposed to the baseline category. Multinomial logit coefficients cannot be interpreted as REGRESSION COEFFICIENTS, and other methods (such as examining changes in $\Pr(y_i = k)$ as independent variables change) must be used to determine what effect the independent variables have on the dependent variable.

Multinomial logit is logically equivalent to estimating a series of binary logits for every pairwise comparison of categories in the dependent variable, although it is more EFFICIENT because it uses all of the data at once. MNL also has the independence of irrelevant alternatives (IIA) property, which is undesirable in many choice situations.

As an example of an application of MNL, consider the problem of estimating the effects of age, gender, and education on occupation choice, where occupation is broken down into three categories: manual labor (M), skilled labor (S), and professional (P). The results of estimating a multinomial logit for this choice problem are presented in Table 1.

Notice the coefficients vary across alternatives, and the coefficients for one alternative have been normalized to zero. This MNL tells us that as education

Table 1   Multinomial Logit Estimates, Occupation Choice (Coefficients for Manual Labor Normalized to Zero)

Independent Variables	Coefficient Value	Standard Error
	S/M Coefficients	
Education	0.76*	0.18
Age	−0.09	0.10
Female	0.17	0.15
Constant	0.51	0.42
	P/M Coefficients	
Education	0.89*	0.16
Age	0.21	0.15
Female	0.27*	0.13
Constant	−0.03	0.67
Number of observations	1,000	

NOTE: M = manual labor; S = skilled; P = professional.
*Statistically significant at the 95% level.

increases, individuals are less likely to select a manual labor occupation in comparison to a skilled labor or professional occupation. Women are also more likely to select a professional occupation than a manual labor occupation.

—Garrett Glasgow

REFERENCES

Long, J. S. (1997). *Regression models for categorical and limited dependent variables.* Thousand Oaks, CA: Sage.

McFadden, D. (1973). Conditional logit analysis of qualitative choice behavior. In P. Zarembka (Ed.), *Frontiers of econometrics* (pp. 105–142). New York: Academic Press.

Train, K. (1986). *Qualitative choice analysis: Theory, econometrics, and an application to automobile demand.* Cambridge: MIT Press.

MULTINOMIAL PROBIT

REGRESSION analysis assumes a continuous (or at least interval-level) DEPENDENT VARIABLE. For many research questions in the social sciences, the CONTINUOUS VARIABLE may be unobserved and only manifested by a binomial or DICHOTOMOUS VARIABLE. For example, the unobserved variable may be the probability that a voter will choose Candidate A over Candidate B, and the observed variable is the actual choice between A and B. Analysts must choose alternative estimation procedures, such as PROBIT and LOGIT, when the continuity assumption is violated by a dichotomous dependent variable.

There are also instances when the unobserved continuous dependent variable manifests itself as three or more values or ordered categories. For example, survey respondents are often asked to indicate their reaction to a statement by responding on a 5-point scale ranging from *strongly disagree*, to *strongly agree*, or legislators may face the threefold choice of eliminating a program, funding it at the status quo, or increasing funding to a specified higher level. Variables measuring such data may be termed *multinomial, polychotomous*, or *n-chotomous*. Variations of standard probit and logit, called multinomial probit and MULTINOMIAL LOGIT, may be used to analyze polychotomous dependent variables.

The essence of binomial probit is to estimate the PROBABILITY of observing a 0 or 1 in the dependent variable given the values of the INDEPENDENT VARIABLES for a particular observation. Classifying the observations is simply a matter of determining which value has the higher probability estimate. In multinomial probit, threshold parameters, commonly denoted μ_j, are estimated along with the COEFFICIENTS of the independent variables. Keeping in mind that the number of threshold parameters necessary is one less than the number of categories in the dependent variable, in the case of three categories, only two threshold parameters need to be estimated and classification would proceed as follows:

$$
\begin{aligned}
y &= 1 \quad \text{if } y^* \le \mu_1, \\
y &= 2 \quad \text{if } \mu_1 \le y^* \le \mu_2, \\
y &= 3 \quad \text{if } \mu_2 \le y^*,
\end{aligned}
$$

where y is the observed dependent variable and y^* is the unobserved variable. As a practical matter, μ_1 is generally normalized to be zero. Thus, the number of estimated parameters is two less than the number of categories.

Every observation in the data set has an estimated ability that it falls into each of the categories of the dependent variable. In general, the probability that an observation falls into a category is calculated as

$$
\begin{aligned}
\text{Prob}(y = j) &= \Phi\left(\mu_j - \sum_{i=0}^{n} \beta_i x_i\right) \\
&\quad - \Phi\left(\mu_{j-1} - \sum_{i=0}^{n} \beta_i x_i\right),
\end{aligned}
$$

where j is the specific category, μ_j is the threshold parameter for that category, the $\beta_i x_i$ are the estimated coefficients multiplied by the values of the corresponding n independent variables (with $\beta_0 x_0$ the constant term), and Φ is the cumulative normal probability distribution. Note that for all the probabilities to be greater than or equal to zero, $\mu_1 < \mu_2 < \mu_3 < \cdots < \mu_j$ must hold (and recall that μ_1 is usually set to zero). Given the cumulative nature of the probability distribution, this can be restated more simply as $\text{Prob}(y = j) = \text{Prob}(y \le j) - \text{Prob}(y \le j - 1)$.

The significance of the μ_j may be tested using the familiar T-TEST. Significant and positive estimates of the μ_j confirm that the categories are ordered.

Table 1 presents sample multinomial probit results. The dependent variable, Y, is coded 1, 2, or 3. Each of the three independent variables, X_i, is coded 0 or 1. After normalizing one threshold parameter as

Table 1   Sample Results of Multinomial Probit Estimation

Dependent Variable: Y		
Independent Variables	Estimated Coefficient	Standard Error
X_1	0.90	0.29
X_2	0.55	0.26
X_3	−0.31	0.31
Constant	0.58	—
$\hat{\mu}$	0.97	0.15
N	107	
−2 Log-likelihood ratio, $df = 3$	96.23	

zero, the trichotomous dependent variable leaves only one threshold parameter to be estimated. In addition to being STATISTICALLY SIGNIFICANT, the estimated threshold parameter is positive and greater than the parameter normalized to zero.

To calculate the probabilities that a given observation falls into each of the response categories of the dependent variable, consider an observation whereby $X_1 = 1$, $X_2 = 1$, and $X_3 = 1$. From the formula above, we can use the cumulative normal probability distribution to calculate that

$$\text{Prob}(y = 1) = \Phi\left(-\sum_{i=0}^{3} \beta_i x_i\right) = .0418,$$

$$\text{Prob}(y = 2) = \Phi\left(\mu - \sum_{i=0}^{3} \beta_i x_i\right)$$
$$- \Phi\left(-\sum_{i=0}^{3} \beta_i x_i\right) = .1832,$$

$$\text{Prob}(y = 3) = 1 - \Phi\left(\mu - \sum_{i=0}^{3} \beta_i x_i\right) = .7750.$$

Notice that the calculated probabilities for the three possible categories correctly sum to 1.

As with their binary counterparts, the primary difference between the multinomial probit and multinomial logit models is the distributional function on which they are based: normal for probit, logistic for logit. The difference between the two distributions is often of little consequence unless the data set is very large or the number of observations in the tails of the

distribution is of particular importance. Interpretation of estimation results from the models is very similar, so the choice between them may lie in practical considerations such as availability of the procedure in computer programs or prior experience with one procedure or the other.

—Timothy M. Hagle

AUTHOR'S NOTE: As used here, *multinomial probit* refers to an ordered multinomial dependent variable. Some sources, however, use the term *multinomial* to refer to unordered or categorical dependent variables and simply use *ordered probit* to refer to the ordered case. Multinomial logit is the appropriate technique for estimating models with categorical dependent variables.

REFERENCES

Liao, T. F. (1994). *Interpreting probability models: Logit, probit, and other generalized linear models.* Thousand Oaks, CA: Sage.

Maddala, G. S. (1983). *Limited-dependent and qualitative variables in econometrics.* Cambridge, UK: Cambridge University Press.

McKelvey, R. D., & Zavoina, W. (1975). A statistical model for the analysis of ordinal level dependent variables. *Journal of Mathematical Sociology, 4,* 103–120.

MULTIPLE CASE STUDY

The CASE STUDY is a research method that focuses on understanding the dynamics of single settings. Although it can be used for description and deduction (Yin, 1994), our focus is on inductive theory development, an application for which the method is particularly well suited. In comparison with aggregated, statistical research, the primary advantage of case study research is its deeper understanding of specific instances of a phenomenon.

Multiple case study is a variant that includes two or more observations of the same phenomenon. This variant enables REPLICATION—that is, using multiple cases to independently confirm emerging CONSTRUCTS and propositions. It also enables extension—that is, using the cases to reveal complementary aspects of the phenomenon. The result is more robust, generalizable, and developed theory. In contrast to multiple case research, single cases may contain intriguing stories but are less likely to produce high-quality theory.

An example of the multiple case method is the inductive study by Galunic and Eisenhardt (2001) of 10 charter gains by divisions of a *Fortune* 100 high-technology firm. By studying different cases of divisions gaining new product/market responsibilities, the authors identified and described three distinct patterns for this phenomenon: new charter opportunities, charter wars, and foster homes. In addition, given the commonalities across the cases and the richness in the data, the authors were able to develop an elaborate theory of architectural innovation at the corporate level.

Multiple case research begins with data and ends with theory. Because deductive research simply reverses this order, it is not surprising that the two have similarities. These include a priori defined research questions, clearly designated POPULATION(s) from which observations are drawn, construct definition, and measurement of constructs with triangulated measures where possible. Yet, despite these similarities, there are crucial differences.

One is sampling logic. Instead of RANDOM SAMPLING of observations, THEORETICAL SAMPLING is used. That is, cases are selected to fill conceptual categories, replicate previous findings, or extend emergent theory. Furthermore, selection of cases can be adjusted during a study as it becomes clearer which cases and categories are needed to replicate or extend the emerging insights.

A second is data type. Instead of only quantitative data, both qualitative and quantitative data can be used. Indeed, the emphasis is typically on the former because qualitative data drawn from rich media such as observations, archival stories, and interviews are central to the in-depth understanding that cases provide. Qualitative data are also used because important constructs often cannot be predicted a priori. In addition, such data are invaluable for creating the underlying theoretical logic that connects constructs together into propositions.

A third difference is analysis. Instead of aggregating observations and examining them statistically, cases are treated as separate instances of the focal phenomenon, allowing replication. Because the goal is to create as close a match between data and theory, analysis involves iteratively developing tentative frameworks from one or several cases and then testing them in others (Glaser & Strauss, 1967). So, constructs are refined, patterns emerge, and relations between constructs are established. This close relationship between theory and data limits the researcher bias that

inexperienced scholars often believe is present. Once rough patterns emerge, existing literature is included in the iterations to further sharpen the emergent theory. The ultimate goal is high-quality theory.

—Filipe M. Santos and Kathleen M. Eisenhardt

REFERENCES

Eisenhardt, K. M. (1989). Building theories from case study research. *Academy of Management Review, 14,* 532–550.

Galunic, D. C., & Eisenhardt, K. M. (2001). Architectural innovation and modular corporate forms. *Academy of Management Journal, 44*(6), 1229–1249.

Glaser, B., & Strauss, A. L. (1967). *The discovery of grounded theory: Strategies for qualitative research.* Hawthorne, NY: Aldine de Gruyter.

Yin, R. K. (1994). *Case study research: Design and methods.* Thousand Oaks, CA: Sage.

MULTIPLE CLASSIFICATION ANALYSIS (MCA)

Also called factorial ANOVA, multiple classification analysis (MCA) is a QUANTITATIVE analysis procedure that allows the assessment of differences in subgroup means, which may have been adjusted for compositional differences in related factors and/or covariates and their effects. MCA produces the same overall results as MULTIPLE REGRESSION with DUMMY VARIABLES, although there are differences in the way the information is reported. For example, an MCA in SPSS produces an ANALYSIS OF VARIANCE with the appropriate F TESTS, decomposing the SUMS OF SQUARES explained by the model into the relative contributions of the factor of interest, the COVARIATE(s), and any INTERACTIONS that are specified. These F tests assess the ratio of the sums of squares explained by the factor(s) and covariates (if specified) adjusted by degrees of freedom ($k - 1$ categories on a k-category factor plus the number of covariates) to the unexplained sums of squares adjusted for its degrees of freedom ($N - df$ for explained sums of squares). F tests for each factor and for each covariate are also provided. Also reported is a table of predicted subgroup MEANS adjusted for factors and covariates as well as the DEVIATIONS (adjusted for factors and covariates) of subgroup means from the grand mean. A regression analysis in SPSS, which regresses a dependent variable on a series of DUMMY VARIABLES and covariate(s),

Table 1   Results from Multiple Classification Analysis

		Predicted Mean		Deviation	
Marital Status	n	Unadjusted	Adjusted for Covariate	Unadjusted	Adjusted for Covariate
Married	3,243	8814.4326	8737.7758	903.7891	827.1323
Widowed	124	3979.3468	4515.9674	−3931.2967	−3394.6761
Divorced	210	4696.4095	4818.3596	−3214.2340	−3092.2839
Separated	249	3257.3052	4069.9054	−4653.3383	−3840.7380
Never married	216	5087.3241	4878.8716	−2823.3194	−3035.7719

produces a comparable analysis of variance (although explained sums of squares are not decomposed) with an appropriate F test, as well as a set of regression COEFFICIENTS one can use to calculate a comparable set of subgroups means, adjusted for other factors and covariates specified in the model.

To illustrate, consider the effects of marital status and years of schooling (as the covariate) on total family income. Table 1 displays the MCA output from SPSS using the National Longitudinal Surveys cohort of mature women, who were ages 30 to 45 in 1967. The grand mean for total annual family income is $7,910.64 (in 1967 U.S.$). Column 1 reports marital status categories, and column 2 reports the number of cases in each subgroup. Columns 3 and 4 display the unadjusted and adjusted predicted means. The unadjusted means are the same as the subgroup means (i.e., mean family income for those in each category of marital status).

The adjusted predicted mean for each category of marital status is, for example, the predicted subgroup mean for married persons, controlling for years of schooling. The deviation column reports the comparison of the subgroup mean to the grand mean for all respondents. The unadjusted deviation indicates that the mean family income for married persons is about $903 higher than the grand mean of $7,911. About $76 of that difference is due to the fact that married persons have higher than average years of schooling, and years of schooling are positively associated with total family income. Subgroup differences in education have been held to the side.

Had we estimated a regression equation with total family income as the dependent variable, specifying years of schooling and a set of dummy variables representing differences in marital status as the independent variables, we would have generated the same F-test of model fit. Furthermore, we could have used the regression coefficients to reproduce the adjusted subgroup means by substituting mean years of schooling and the appropriate values of the dummy variables into the equation.

—Melissa A. Hardy and Chardie L. Baird

REFERENCES

Andrews, F. M., Morgan, J. N., & Sonquist, J. A. (1967). *Multiple classification analysis: A report on a computer program for multiple regression using categorical predictors.* Ann Arbor, MI: Survey Research Center, Institute for Social Research.

Retherford, R. D., & Choe, M. K. (1993). *Statistical models for causal analysis.* New York: John Wiley.

MULTIPLE COMPARISONS

Multiple comparisons compare $J \geq 3$ sample means from J levels of one classification variable. The ONE-WAY ANOVA, FIXED-EFFECTS MODEL simply detects the presence of significant differences in the means, not which means differ significantly.

A comparison ψ on J means is a linear combination of the following means:

$$\psi = c_1 \mu_1 + c_2 \mu_2 + \cdots + c_J \mu_J = \sum_{j=1}^{J} c_j \mu_j, \quad (1)$$

where the sum of the cs equals zero, but not all of the cs are zero. To estimate ψ, use

$$\hat{\psi} = c_1 \bar{Y}_1 + c_2 \bar{Y}_2 + \cdots + c_J \bar{Y}_J = \sum_{j=1}^{J} c_j \bar{Y}_j, \quad (2)$$

where the cs are as given for ψ. There can be many different comparisons—hence the name *multiple comparisons*. The history of tests for multiple comparisons (multiple comparison procedures [MCPs]) can be traced back to early work by Sir Ronald A. Fisher, who suggested using individual t-tests following a significant ANOVA F test: This idea is captured and modernized in the Fisher-Hayter MCP, which is presented below. Subsequent development by Henry Scheffé and John W. Tukey, among others, led not only to their MCPs (shown below) but also to the prominence of the topic of MCPs in applied literature. After a brief coverage of basic concepts used in the area of multiple comparisons, several different MCPs are given, followed by recent developments.

BASIC CONCEPTS

A pairwise comparison has weights of 1 and –1 for two of the J means and zero for all others and thus is a difference between two means. For example, with $J = 4$, the pairwise comparison of means one and two is

$$\hat{\psi}_1 = \bar{Y}_1 - \bar{Y}_2, \tag{3}$$

with $c_1 = 1$ and $c_2 = -1$, and the other cs are zero. A nonpairwise comparison is any comparison that is not pairwise, for example,

$$\hat{\psi}_2 = \bar{Y}_1 - \frac{\bar{Y}_2 + \bar{Y}_3}{2}, \tag{4}$$

with $c_1 = 1, c_2 = c_3 = -1/2$, and $c_4 = 0$.

Planned (or a priori) comparisons are planned by the researcher before the results are obtained. Often, planned comparisons are based on predictions from the theory that led to the research project. Post hoc (or a posteriori) comparisons are computed after the results are obtained. With post hoc comparisons, the researcher can choose comparisons based on the results. Post hoc comparisons may or may not have a theory base for their inclusion in the study.

Orthogonality of multiple comparisons is considered for each pair of comparisons. When all the samples have a common size n, comparisons one and two are orthogonal if

$$\sum_{j=1}^{J} c_{1j} c_{2j} = 0. \tag{5}$$

For J means, the maximum number of comparisons that are each orthogonal to each other is $J - 1$.

If the ANOVA ASSUMPTIONS are met, the SAMPLING DISTRIBUTION of a sample comparison has known mean, known variance and known estimate of the

variance, and known shape (normal). Given this information, it is possible to form a t statistic for any given comparison,

$$t_{\hat{\psi}} = \frac{\hat{\psi} - \psi}{\sqrt{MS_W \sum_{j=1}^{J} \frac{c_j^2}{n_j}}}. \tag{6}$$

For equal ns and pairwise comparisons, the t statistic simplifies to

$$t = \frac{\bar{Y}_j - \bar{Y}_k}{\sqrt{\frac{MS_{W}(2)}{n}}}, \tag{7}$$

which has $df_W = J(n - 1) = N - J$.

If there is only a single comparison of interest, and with the usual ANOVA assumptions met, the t statistic can be used to test the hypothesis of

$$H_0 : \psi = 0, \tag{8}$$

using a critical value from the t distribution with $df = df_W$. For multiple comparisons, there are multiple hypotheses as in (8), and the t statistics must be referred to appropriate critical values for the chosen MCP. Such tests are almost always TWO-TAILED TESTS.

All of the MCPs given below are able to provide the researcher with a test of this hypothesis. However, if the researcher desires to obtain an interval estimate of ψ, then some MCPs are not appropriate because they cannot give interval estimates of the population comparisons. For those methods that can give a CONFIDENCE INTERVAL, the interval is given as

$$\hat{\psi} - \text{crit} \sqrt{\frac{MS_W}{n} \sum_{j=1}^{J} c_j^2} \leq \psi \leq \hat{\psi}$$
$$+ \text{crit} \sqrt{\frac{MS_W}{n} \sum_{j=1}^{J} c_j^2}, \tag{9}$$

where crit is an appropriate two-tailed critical value at the α level, such as t. For those researchers desiring both to test hypotheses and to obtain interval estimates, the confidence interval can be used to test the hypothesis that the comparison is zero by rejecting H_0 if the interval does not contain zero.

A researcher's primary concern should be α-control and power (see ALPHA, POWER OF THE TEST, and TYPE I ERROR). There are two basic categories of α-control (error rates): α-control for each comparison versus α-control for some group of comparisons. The choice of category of α-control determines the value of α' to assign to each comparison and influences the power of the eventual statistic. Relative power of different MCPs can be assessed by comparing the critical values and choosing the MCP with the smallest critical value.

Setting $\alpha' = \alpha$ (typically .05) for each comparison and choosing an α-level t critical value is called error rate per comparison (ERPC). One problem with controlling α using ERPC is that p(at least one Type I error) increases as the number of comparisons (C) increases. For C orthogonal comparisons each at level α', this is shown as p(at least one Type I error) $= 1 - (1 - \alpha')C \le C\alpha'$. If the C comparisons are not orthogonal, then p(at least one Type I error) $\le 1 - (1 - \alpha'^{C} \le C\alpha'$, but empirical research shows that p(at least one Type I error) is fairly close to $1 - (1 - \alpha')^{C}$.

ERPC gives a large p(at least one Type I error), but the power also is large. Control of error rate using ERPC gives higher power than any other method of error rate control but at the expense of high p(at least one Type I error). As in basic hypothesis testing, in which there is a trade-off between control of α and power, allowing high p(at least one Type I error) gives high power.

The second of the two basic categories of α-control is to control α for some group (family) of comparisons. Error rate per family (ERPF) is the first of two types of α-control for a family of comparisons. ERPF is not a probability, as are the other definitions of error rate. ERPF is the average number of erroneous statements (false rejections, Type I errors) made in a family of comparisons. ERPF is accomplished by setting α' at some value smaller than α, and the simplest method for doing this is to set the α' such that they add up to α. For example, if α' is the same value for all comparisons, then for C orthogonal comparisons each at level α', ERPF is equal to $C\alpha'$. This method of controlling error rate appears in the logic of the Dunn method, as shown below.

The second type of α-control that functions for some family of comparisons is error rate familywise (ERFW). ERFW is a probability and is defined as p(at least one Type I error) $= 1 - (1 - \alpha')^{C}$. Even though ERFW and ERPF differ in definition and concept, in practice, if an MCP accomplishes one, it usually accomplishes the other. Thus, the basic decision a researcher faces with respect to α-control is whether

to control error rate for each comparison (ERPC) or some family of comparisons (ERPF or ERFW).

To see the relationships among these three different types of α-control, let α' be used for each of C comparisons: Using ERPC gives $\alpha = \alpha'$, using ERFW gives $\alpha < 1 - (1 - \alpha')^{C}$, and using ERPF gives $\alpha < C\alpha'$. Putting these together gives $\alpha' \le 1 - (1 - \alpha')^{C} \le C\alpha'$; thus, ERPC < ERFW < ERPF. If we set $\alpha' = .01$ for $C = 5$ orthogonal comparisons, then ERPC $= .01$, ERFW $= .049$, and ERPF $= .05$.

Types of hypotheses give configurations that exist in the population means where attention is paid to the equality, or equalities, in the means. An overall null hypothesis exists if all of the J means are equal. This is the null hypothesis tested by the overall F test—thus the name "overall null hypothesis" or "full" null hypothesis. Multiple null hypotheses exist if the overall null hypothesis is not true, but more than one subset of equal means does exist. The means must be equal within the subset, but there must be differences between the subsets. Then each of these subsets represents a null hypothesis. If there are M multiple subsets of means with equality within the subset, then there are M multiple null hypotheses. For example, if $J = 4$, and means one and two are equal but different from means three and four, which are equal, then there are $M = 2$ null hypotheses. A partial null hypothesis exists when the overall null hypothesis is not true, but some population means are equal. For $J = 4$, if the first three means are equal, but the fourth is larger than the first three, there would be a partial null hypothesis in the three equal means.

A stepwise MCP contains a test that depends in part on another test. A stepwise MCP may allow computation of comparisons only if the overall F is significant or may make testing one comparison allowable only if some other comparison is significant. MCPs that do not have such dependencies are called nonstepwise or simultaneous test procedures (STPs) because the tests may be done simultaneously.

MCPS

Many MCPs exist for the one-way ANOVA. If you are using a t statistic and have decided how to control error rate, then the choice of MCP is a choice of the critical value (theoretical distribution). Unless otherwise stated, confidence intervals can be computed from the critical value of each MCP.

Choosing α-control at ERPC gives the usual t MCP, which has the decision rule to reject H_0 if

$$|t_{\hat{\psi}}| \geq t_{df_W}^{\alpha} \qquad (10)$$

and otherwise retain H_0. Note that the usual t can be used for either pairwise or nonpairwise comparisons.

If the C comparisons are planned and α-control is chosen as ERPF (thus, ERFW), by dividing the total α into $\alpha' = \alpha/C$ for each comparison, the Dunn MCP (see BONFERRONI TECHNIQUE) is given by the decision rule to reject H_0 if

$$|t_{\hat{\psi}}| \geq t_{df_W}^{\alpha'} \qquad (11)$$

and otherwise retain H_0. The Dunn MCP can be used for either pairwise or nonpairwise comparisons.

The Tukey MCP accomplishes α-control by using an α-level critical value from the Studentized range distribution for J means and df_W, so control of α is built into the Studentized range critical value at the chosen ERFW α-level. The Tukey MCP is given by the decision rule to reject H_0 if

$$|t_{\hat{\psi}}| \geq \frac{q_{J,df_W}^{\alpha}}{\sqrt{2}} \qquad (12)$$

and otherwise retain H_0. The Tukey MCP can be used for pairwise comparisons.

The Scheffé MCP accomplishes α-control by using an α-level critical value from the F distribution for df_B and df_W, so control of α is built into the F critical value at the chosen ERFW α-level. The decision rule for Scheffé is to reject H_0 if

$$|t_{\hat{\psi}}| > \sqrt{(J-1) F_{J-1,df_W}^{\alpha}} \qquad (13)$$

and otherwise retain H_0. Literally infinitely many comparisons can be done with the Scheffé method while maintaining control of α using ERFW: pairwise comparisons, nonpairwise comparisons, orthogonal polynomials, and so on.

The Fisher-Hayter MCP allows testing of comparisons only after a significant overall ANOVA F. It has α-control at ERFW and uses a q critical value with $J-1$ as the number-of-means parameter. The decision rule is to perform the overall ANOVA F test and, if it is significant at level α, then reject H_0 if

$$|t_{\hat{\psi}}| \geq \frac{q_{J-1,df_W}^{\alpha}}{\sqrt{2}} \qquad (14)$$

and otherwise retain H_0. The Fisher-Hayter MCP is a stepwise procedure for pairwise comparisons; it does not allow computation of confidence intervals because its critical value does not take into account the first step of requiring the overall F test to be significant.

The Ryan MCP is a compilation of contributions of several statisticians. First, put the J means in order. Now consider the concept of stretch size of a comparison, the number of ordered means between and including the two means in the comparison. Stretch size is symbolized by p. The Ryan MCP has α-control at ERFW and uses a q critical value with p as the number-of-means parameter but an α that can be different depending on p. For the Ryan MCP, the decision rule is to reject H_0 if the means in the comparison are not contained in the stretch of a previously retained hypothesis and if

$$|t_{\hat{\psi}}| \geq \frac{q_{p,df_W}^{\alpha_p}}{\sqrt{2}},$$

where

$$\alpha_p = \alpha \quad \text{for } p = J, J-1$$
$$\alpha_p = 1 - (1-\alpha)^{p/J} \quad \text{for } p \leq J-2 \qquad (15)$$

and otherwise retain H_0. The Ryan MCP is a stepwise procedure for pairwise comparisons; it does not allow computation of confidence intervals because its critical value does not take into account prior steps.

The Games-Howell (GH) MCP takes into account both unequal ns and unequal variances. It has reasonably good α-control at ERFW and uses the statistic

$$t_{jk} = \frac{\bar{Y}_j - \bar{Y}_k}{\sqrt{\frac{s_j^2}{n_j} + \frac{s_k^2}{n_k}}} \qquad (16)$$

for each pair of means $j \neq k$. The decision is to reject H_0 if

$$|t_{jk}| \geq \frac{q_{J,df_{jk}}^{\alpha}}{\sqrt{2}} \qquad (17)$$

and otherwise retain H_0, where

$$df_{jk} = \frac{(s_j^2/n_j + s_k^2/n_k)^2}{\frac{(s_j^2/n_j)^2}{n_j-1} + \frac{(s_k^2/n_k)^2}{n_k-1}}. \qquad (18)$$

A practical suggestion is to round df_{jk} to the nearest whole number to use as the df for the q critical value.

The GH MCP is used for pairwise comparisons. For more on basic MCPs, see Toothaker (1993). A mathematical treatment of MCPs is given by Hochberg and Tamhane (1987) and Miller (1981).

RECENT DEVELOPMENTS

Following work by Tukey, several researchers have focused on the sensitivity to extreme scores (lack of robustness) of the following statistics: the sample mean, the sample variance, and tests of means. This work examines particularly the lack of robustness when the population is a heavy-tailed distribution. Heavy-tailed departure from normality leads to inflated variance of the mean (and variance) and lack of control of α and low power for tests using means. Recent research in the area of MCPs has concentrated on using 20% trimmed means and 20% Winsorized variances to form a t-statistic. First, compute the number of scores to be trimmed from each tail as $g = [.2n]$, where the $[.2n]$ notation means to take the whole number, or integer, part of $.2n$. For each of the J groups, the steps to compute the 20% trimmed mean, $\bar{Y}_t$ include TRIMMING the g most extreme scores from each tail of the sample, summing the remaining $h = n - 2g$ scores, and dividing by h. The variance of these 20% trimmed means is estimated by a function of Winsorized variances. A Winsorized variance is computed by again focusing on the g extreme scores in each tail of each of the J samples. Let $Y_{(1)} \le Y_{(2)} \le \cdots \le Y_{(n)}$ represent the n ordered scores in a group. The Winsorized mean is computed as

$$\bar{Y}_w = \frac{[(g + 1)Y_{(g+1)} + Y_{(g+2)} + \cdots + Y_{(n-g-1)} + (g + 1)_{(n-g)}]}{n}, \tag{19}$$

and the Winsorized variance is computed as

$$S_w^2 = \frac{(g + 1)(Y_{(g+1)} - \bar{Y}_w)^2 + (Y_{(g+2)} - \bar{Y}_w)^2 + \cdots + (Y_{(n-g-1)} - \bar{Y}_w)^2 + (g + 1)(Y_{(n-g)} - \bar{Y}_w)^2}{n - 1}. \tag{20}$$

Then we form estimates of variances of the trimmed means by using

$$d = \frac{(n - 1)S_w^2}{h(h - 1)} \tag{21}$$

for each of the J groups. The robust pairwise test statistic is

$$t_w = \frac{\bar{Y}_{tj} - \bar{Y}_{tk}}{\sqrt{d_j + d_k}}, \tag{22}$$

with estimated degrees of freedom of

$$df_w = \frac{(d_j + d_k)^2}{\frac{d_j^2}{h_j - 1} + \frac{d_k^2}{h_k - 1}}. \tag{23}$$

The robust statistic t_W with df_W can be used with a variety of MCPs, such as the Ryan MCP, above. For more on robust estimation, see Wilcox (2001). For robust estimation and subsequent MCPs, see Keselman, Lix, and Kowalchuk (1998).

—Larry E. Toothaker

REFERENCES

Hochberg, Y., & Tamhane, A. C. (1987). *Multiple comparison procedures.* New York: John Wiley.

Keselman, H. J., Lix, L. M., & Kowalchuk, R. K. (1998). Multiple comparison procedures for trimmed means. *Psychological Methods, 3,* 123–141.

Miller, R. G. (1981). *Simultaneous statistical inference* (2nd ed.). New York: Springer-Verlag.

Toothaker, L. E. (1993). *Multiple comparison procedures.* Newbury Park, CA: Sage.

Wilcox, R. (2001). *Fundamentals of modern statistical methods: Substantially improving power and accuracy.* New York: Springer.

MULTIPLE CORRELATION

The multiple correlation arises in the context of MULTIPLE REGRESSION ANALYSIS; it is a one-number summary measure of the accuracy of prediction from the regression model.

In multiple regression analysis, a single dependent variable Y (or criterion) is predicted from a set of independent variables (or predictors). In the most common form of multiple regression, multiple LINEAR REGRESSION (or ORDINARY LEAST SQUARES regression analysis), the independent variables are aggregated into a linear combination according to the following linear regression equation:

$$\hat{Y} = b_1 X_1 + b_2 X_2 + \cdots + b_p X_p + b_0.$$

The Xs are the predictors. Each predictor is multiplied by a weight, called the PARTIAL REGRESSION COEFFICIENT, $b_1, b_2, \ldots, b_p$. Then, according to the regression equation, the linear combination (or weighted sum) of the scores on the set of predictors is computed. This weighted sum, noted $\hat{Y}$, is termed the *predicted score*. The regression coefficients $b_1, b_2, \ldots, b_p$ are chosen in such a way that correlation between the actual dependent variable Y and the predicted score $\hat{Y}$ is as large as possible. This maximum correlation between a single criterion score Y and a linear combination of a set of Xs is the multiple correlation, $R_{Y\hat{Y}}$. In usual practice, the square of this correlation is reported, referred to as the squared multiple correlation $R^2_{Y\hat{Y}}$, or R-SQUARED.

The squared multiple correlation is a central measure in multiple regression analysis—it summarizes the overall adequacy of the set of predictors in accounting for the dependent variable. The squared multiple correlation is the proportion of variation in the criterion that is accounted for by the set of predictors.

As an example, consider an undergraduate statistics course in which three tests are given during the semester. Suppose in a class of 50 students, we predict scores on Test 3 from scores on Tests 1 and 2 using linear regression as the method of analysis. The resulting linear regression equation is as follows:

$$\hat{Y} = .15 \text{ Test } 1 + .54 \text{ Test } 2 + 28.91.$$

For each student, we substitute the scores on Test 1 and Test 2 into the regression equation and compute the predicted score $\hat{Y}$ on Test 3. We then correlate these predicted scores with actual scores on Test 3; the resulting correlation is the multiple correlation. Here the multiple correlation is $R_{Y\hat{Y}} = .65$, quite a substantial correlation. Students' performance on the third test is closely related to performance on the first two tests. The squared multiple correlation $R^2_{Y\hat{Y}} = .42$. We would describe this result by saying that 42% of the variation in the observed Test 3 scores is accounted for by scores on Test 1 and Test 2.

The multiple correlation ranges between 0 and 1. As predictors are added to the regression equation, the multiple correlation either remains the same or increases. The multiple correlation does not take into account the number of predictors. Moreover, the sample multiple correlation tends to overestimate the population multiple correlation. An adjusted squared multiple correlation that is less biased (though not

unbiased) is given as follows, where n is the number of cases and p is the number of predictors:

$$\text{Adjusted } R^2_{Y\hat{Y}} = 1 - \left(1 - R^2_{Y\hat{Y}}\right) \times [(n-1)/(n-p-1)].$$

For our analysis with $n = 50$ students and $p = 2$ predictors, the adjusted $R^2_{Y\hat{Y}} = .39$.

The multiple correlation as presented here pertains only to linear regression analysis. For other forms of regression analysis (e.g., LOGISTIC REGRESSION or POISSON REGRESSION), measures that are analogs of the multiple correlation (and squared multiple correlation) have been derived; they are not strictly multiple correlations as defined here.

—Leona S. Aiken

See also MULTIPLE REGRESSION ANALYSIS, REGRESSION ANALYSIS, R-SQUARED

REFERENCES

Cohen, J., Cohen, P., West, S. G., & Aiken, L. S. (2003). *Applied multiple regression/correlation analysis for the behavioral sciences* (3rd ed.). Mahwah, NJ: Lawrence Erlbaum.

Draper, N. R., & Smith, H. (1998). *Applied regression analysis* (3rd ed.). New York: John Wiley.

Neter, J., Kutner, M. H., Nachtsheim, C. J., & Wasserman, W. (1996). *Applied linear regression models* (3rd ed.). Chicago: Irwin.

MULTIPLE CORRESPONDENCE ANALYSIS. *See* CORRESPONDENCE ANALYSIS

MULTIPLE REGRESSION ANALYSIS

Multiple regression analysis subsumes a broad class of statistical procedures that relate a set of INDEPENDENT VARIABLES (the predictors) to a single DEPENDENT VARIABLE (the criterion). One product of multiple regression analysis (MR) is a multiple regression equation that quantifies how each predictor relates to the criterion when all the other predictors in the equation are simultaneously taken into account. Multiple regression analysis has broad applications. It may be used descriptively, simply to summarize the relationship of a set of predictors to a criterion. It may be used for

PREDICTION. It may be used for MODEL building and theory testing.

STRUCTURE OF MULTIPLE REGRESSION

The most common form of MR (i.e., multiple LINEAR REGRESSION analysis) has the following multiple regression equation:

$$\hat{Y} = b_1 X_1 + b_2 X_2 + \cdots + b_p X_p + b_0.$$

The Xs are the predictors. Each predictor is multiplied by a weight, called the PARTIAL REGRESSION COEFFICIENT, $b_1, b_2, \ldots, b_p$. The intercept of the equation b_0 is termed the *regression constant* or *regression* INTERCEPT. In the regression equation, scores on the set of predictors are combined into a single score $\hat{Y}$, the predicted score, which is a linear combination of all the predictors.

That the independent variables and dependent variable are termed *predictors* and *criterion,* respectively, reflects the use of MR to predict individuals' scores on the criterion based on their scores on the predictors. For example, a college admissions office might develop a multiple regression equation to predict college freshman grade point average (the criterion) from three predictors: high school grade point average plus verbal and quantitative performance scores on a college admissions examination. The predicted score for each college applicant would be an estimate of the freshman college grade point average the applicant would be expected to achieve, based on the set of high school measures.

In MR, the PARTIAL REGRESSION COEFFICIENT assigned to each predictor in the regression equation takes into account the relationship of that predictor to the criterion, the relationships of all the other predictors to the criterion, and the relationships among all the predictors. The partial regression coefficient gives the unique contribution of a predictor to overall prediction over and above all the other predictors included in the equation, that is, when all other predictors are held constant.

Multiple regression analysis provides a single summary number of how accurately the set of predictors reproduces or "accounts for" the criterion, termed the *squared* MULTIPLE CORRELATION, variously noted R^2 or $R^2_{Y\hat{Y}}$ or $R^2_{Y.12\ldots p}$. The second notation, $R^2_{Y\hat{Y}}$, indicates that the squared multiple correlation is the square of the correlation between the predicted and criterion scores. In fact, the multiple correlation is the highest possible correlation that can be achieved between a linear combination of the predictors and the criterion. The third notation, $R^2_{Y.12\ldots p}$, indicates that the correlation reflects the overall relationship of the set of predictors $1, 2, \ldots, p$ to the criterion. The squared multiple correlation measures the proportion of variation in the criterion that is accounted for by the set of predictors, a measure of EFFECT SIZE for the full regression analysis.

The values of the regression coefficients are chosen to minimize the errors of prediction. For each individual, we have a measure of prediction error, the discrepancy between the individual's observed criterion score and predicted score $(Y - \hat{Y})$, termed the *residual*. In ORDINARY LEAST SQUARES regression analysis (the most common approach to ESTIMATION of regression coefficients), the partial regression coefficients are chosen so as to minimize the sum of squared residuals, the ordinary least squares (OLS) criterion. The resulting OLS regression coefficients simultaneously yield the maximum achievable multiple correlation from the set of predictors.

BUILDING A REGRESSION MODEL

A fictitious example from health psychology illustrates aspects of regression analysis and its use in model building. We wish to build a model of factors that relate to the prevention of skin cancer. The target population is young Caucasian adults living either in the Southwest or the Northeast. As the criterion, we measure their intention to protect themselves against skin cancer (Intention) on a 10-point scale. There are four predictors: (a) objective risk for skin cancer based on skin tone (Risk); (b) region of the country, Southwest or Northeast, in which the participant resides (Region); (c) participant's rating of the advantages of being tanned (Advantage); and (d) participant's perception of the injunctive norms for sun protection, that is, what he or she "should" do about sun protection (Norm). We hypothesize that Risk will be a positive predictor of Intention to sun protect, whereas Advantage of tanning will be a negative predictor. We expect higher Intention to sun protect in the Southwest with its great sun intensity. We are uncertain about the impact of injunctive Norm because young people may well not adhere to recommendations for protecting their health.

The choice of predictors illustrates the flexibility of MR. Risk, Advantage, and Norm are CONTINUOUS VARIABLES, measured on 6-point scales. Region is

CATEGORICAL. Categorical predictors require special CODING schemes to capture the fact that they are categorical and not continuous. Three coding schemes in use are dummy coding (DUMMY VARIABLE CODING), EFFECT CODING, and CONTRAST CODING. For dummy coding in the DICHOTOMOUS (two-category) case, one category is assigned the number 1, and the other is assigned 0 on a single predictor. Dummy coding is employed here with Southwest = 1 and Northeast = 0.

CORRELATIONS among the predictors and criterion for $n = 100$ cases are given in Table 1a. The final column of the correlation matrix contains the correlations of each predictor with the criterion. The expected relationships obtain. We also note SIGNIFICANT correlations among pairs of predictors. Risk is negatively correlated with Advantage. Norm is positively correlated with Region. Because Southwest is coded 1 and Northeast is coded 0, the positive correlation signifies

that the injunctive norm that one should sun protect is stronger in the Southwest.

Table 1b provides a series of bivariate regression equations (i.e., a single predictor and the criterion). There is one equation for each predictor, along with the squared multiple correlations R^2. The regression coefficient in each single predictor equation measures the amount of change in Y for a one-unit change in the predictor. For example, Intention increases by .145 points on the 10-point scale for each 1-point increase in Risk. For the dummy-coded Region, the regression coefficient indicates that the arithmetic mean Intention is 1.049 points higher in the Southwest (coded 1) than in the Northeast (coded 0). In bivariate regression, the squared multiple correlation is simply the square of the correlation of the predictor with the criterion. We note that Risk is a statistically significant predictor of Intention. Risk alone accounts for 3.7% of the variation in

Table 1 Illustration of Multiple Regression Analysis

a. Correlations Among All Predictors and the Criterion

	Risk	*Region*	*Advantage*	*Norm*	*Intention*
Risk	1.000	−.075	−.203*	−.094	.193*
Region	−.075	1.000	.168+	.424*	.313*
Advantage	−.203*	.168+	1.000	.254*	−.374*
Norm	−.094	.424*	.254*	1.000	.028
Intention	.193*	.313*	−.374	.028	1.000

b. Bivariate Regression Analyses: Single-Predictor Regression Equation

1. Risk alone	$\hat{Y} = .145$ Risk* $+ 3.991$	$R^2 = .037$
2. Region alone	$\hat{Y} = 1.049$ Region* $+ 4.407$	$R^2 = .098$
3. Advantage alone	$\hat{Y} = -.474$ Advantage* $+ 6.673$	$R^2 = .140$
4. Norm alone	$\hat{Y} = .044$ Norm $+ 4.760$	$R^2 = .001$

c. Prediction From Risk Plus Advantage

$\hat{Y} = .180$ Risk $-.443$ Advantage* $+ 5.985$ $R^2 = .154$

d. Analysis of Regression: Test of the Squared Multiple Correlation, Risk Plus Advantage

Sources of Variance	Sums of Squares	Degrees of Freedom	Mean Square	F Ratio	p
Regression	43.208	2	21.606	8.858	.001
Residual	236.582	97	2.439		

e. Full Model: Prediction From All Four Predictors: Full Model

$\hat{Y} = .202$ Risk $-.516$ Advantage* $+ 1.349$ Region* $-.039$ Norm $+ 5.680$ $R^2 = .304$

f. Trimmed Model and Illustration of Suppression: Prediction From Risk Plus Region

Unstandardized equation	$\hat{Y} = .319$ Risk* $+ 1.104$ Region* $+ 3.368$	$R^2 = .145$
Standardized equation	$\hat{Y} = .218$ Risk* $+ .329$ Region*	$R^2 = .145$

*p < .05.

Y (i.e., $R^2 = .037$). Similarly, we note that Advantage is a statistically significant predictor that accounts for 14.0% of the variation in Y.

Now we use Risk and Advantage as the two predictors in a multiple regression equation, given in Table 1c. Two aspects are noteworthy. First, Risk is no longer a significant predictor of Intention as it was in the bivariate regression equation. This is so because (a) Advantage is more strongly correlated with Intention than is Risk, and (b) the two predictors are correlated ($r = -.203$). Second, together the predictors account for 15.4% of the variance (i.e., $R^2 = .154$), which is lower than the sum of the proportions of variance accounted for by each predictor taken separately, that is, $3.7\% + 14.0\% = 17.7\%$. This is due to the redundancy between Risk and Advantage in predicting Intention.

In MR, we partition (divide) the total variation in the criterion Y (typically noted SS_Y) into two nonoverlapping (orthogonal) parts. First is the predictable variation or REGRESSION SUMS OF SQUARES (typically noted $SS_{\text{regression}}$), which summarizes the extent to which the regression equation reproduces the differences among individuals on the criterion. It is literally the variation of the predicted scores around their mean. Second is the residual variation or RESIDUAL SUM OF SQUARES (noted SS_{residual}), that part of the criterion variation SS_Y that cannot be accounted for by the set of predictors. The squared multiple correlation is simply the ratio $SS_{\text{regression}}/SS_Y$, again the proportion of variation in the criterion accounted for by the set of predictors. These sources of variation are summarized into an analysis of regression summary table, illustrated in Table 1d. The two sources of variation are employed in testing the omnibus NULL HYPOTHESIS that the squared multiple correlation is zero in the population. For the numerical example, the F RATIO in the summary table leads us to reject this null hypothesis and conclude that we have accounted for a significant portion of variation in Intention from the predictors of Risk and Advantage.

Can we improve prediction by the addition of the other predictors? Hierarchical regression analysis answers this question. Hierarchical regression analysis consists of estimating a series of regression equations in which sets of predictors (one or more per set) are added sequentially to a regression equation, typically with tests of gain in the accuracy of prediction (i.e., increment in the squared multiple correlation) as each set is added. We add to our regression equation the predictors Region and Norm, yielding the four-predictor regression equation given in Table 1e, our final model including all predictors. We see that both Advantage and Region are significant predictors of Intention in the four-predictor equation. We are not surprised that Norm has a regression coefficient of approximately zero because it is uncorrelated with Intention. We note that there is substantial gain in the squared multiple correlation from $R^2 = .154$ with only Risk and Advantage as predictors to $R^2 = .304$ with all four predictors. The increase of .150 ($.304 - .154 = .150$) is the proportion of variation in the criterion predicted by Region and Norm over and above Risk and Advantage (i.e., with Risk and Advantage partialed out or held constant). In this instance, the gain is statistically significant. The final regression equation with all four predictors is our model of Intention to protect against skin cancer. We must take care in interpretation, particularly that Risk is not a statistically significant predictor of Intention because it does correlate with Intention. We must also explain the relationship of Risk to Advantage, another important predictor of Intention.

The interplay between predictors in multiple regression analysis can lead to surprising results. Consider Table 1f, the prediction of Intention from Risk and Region. We note from the bivariate regressions that from Risk alone, $R^2 = .037$, and from Region alone, $R^2 = .098$. Yet in the equation predicting Intention from Risk and Region, $R^2 = .145$, greater than the sum from the two individual predictors. This is a special (and rare) result referred to as suppression in multiple regression. The classic explanation of a SUPPRESSOR EFFECT is that one predictor is partialing from the other predictor some irrelevant variance, thus improving the quality of the latter predictor.

The regression coefficients that we have examined are unstandardized regression coefficients. Each such coefficient is dependent on the particular units of measure of the predictor. A second set of regression coefficients, STANDARDIZED REGRESSION COEFFICIENTS, is based on standardized scores (z scores with mean of 0, standard deviation of 1) for all predictors and the criterion. Standardized regression coefficients are all measured in the same units (i.e., standard deviation units). In Table 1f, the standardized regression equation is reported for Risk and Region. The coefficient of .218 for Risk signifies that for a 1 standard deviation increase in Risk, there is a .218 standard deviation increase in Intention.

Thus far, we have only considered linear relationships of each predictor to the criterion. NON-LINEAR relationships can also be handled in multiple linear regression using either of two approaches: POLYNOMIAL regression and TRANSFORMATIONS of the predictors and/or the criterion. Polynomial regression involves creating a regression equation that has higher order functions of the predictor in the linear regression equation, an equation of the form $\hat{Y} = b_1 X + b_2 X^2 + b_0$ for a quadratic (one-bend) relationship or $\hat{Y} = b_1 X + b_2 X^2 + b_3 X^3 + b_0$ for a cubic (two-bend) relationship and so forth. Suppose we expect that intention to sun protect will increase with level of habitual exposure to the sun, but only up to a point. If habitual exposure is very high, then individuals may simply ignore sun protection, so that intention to sun protect decreases at high levels of exposure. To test the hypothesis of an inverted U-shaped relationship (intention first rises and then falls as habitual sun exposure increases), we examine the b_2 coefficient for the X^2 term in a QUADRATIC EQUATION. For an inverted U-shaped relationship, this coefficient would be negative. If b_2 were essentially zero, this would indicate that the quadratic (inverted U-shaped) relationship did not hold. For a U-shaped relationship, the b_2 coefficient would be positive.

Multiple regression analysis can also treat INTER-ACTIONS between predictors. By *interaction,* we mean that the effect of one predictor on the criterion depends on the value of another predictor. Suppose, for example, that people in the Southwest (with relentless desert sun) were more aware of the risk of skin cancer than those in the Northeast, leading to a stronger relationship of Risk to Intention in the Southwest than in the Northeast (i.e., an interaction between Risk and Region). In multiple regression, we may specify an interaction by including an interaction term as a predictor, here between Risk and Region:

$$\hat{Y} = b_1 \text{ Risk} + b_2 \text{ Region} + b_3 \text{ Risk} \times \text{Region} + b_0.$$

A nonzero b_3 coefficient indicates the presence of an interaction between Risk and Region (when Risk and Region are also included in the regression equation).

ASSUMPTIONS AND DIFFICULTIES

The most common linear regression model assumes that predictors are measured without error (the FIXED-EFFECTS MODEL); error in the predictors introduces bias into the estimates of regression coefficients. For accurate statistical inference, the errors of prediction (the residuals) must follow a NORMAL DISTRIBUTION. MULTICOLLINEARITY (i.e., very high correlation among predictors) causes great instability of regression coefficients. Regression analysis is notoriously sensitive to the impact of individual errant cases (OUTLIERS); one case can markedly alter the size of a regression coefficient. REGRESSION DIAGNOSTICS assess the extent to which individual cases are INFLUENTIAL CASES that change the values of regression coefficients and, moreover, the overall fit of the regression equation.

HISTORY AND NEW EXTENSIONS

Regression analysis as a methodology made noteworthy entry into scientific literature around 1900 based on work by Galton and Pearson (see REGRESSION ANALYSIS for further exposition). The development of multiple regression as an easily implemented technique required the development of ALGORITHMS to handle numerical requirements of the analysis, particularly in the face of correlated predictors. In fact, R. A. Fisher developed the ANALYSIS OF VARIANCE with orthogonal factors due to computational difficulties in applying multiple regression analysis. With widespread availability of mainframe computers, the use of multiple regression analysis burgeoned in the 1960s and 1970s. New extensions have abounded. The GENERALIZED LINEAR MODEL subsumes methods of MR that treat a variety of dependent variables, among them LOGISTIC REGRESSION for binary and ordered category outcomes and POISSON REGRESSION for counts. Random coefficient regression and MULTILEVEL MODELING permit the analysis of clustered data with predictors measured at different levels of aggregation. Great flexibility is offered by NONPARAMETRIC REGRESSION, nonlinear regression, and ROBUST regression models.

—Leona S. Aiken

See also REGRESSION ANALYSIS

REFERENCES

Cohen, J., Cohen, P., West, S. G., & Aiken, L. S. (2003). *Applied multiple regression/correlation analysis for the behavioral sciences* (3rd ed.). Mahwah, NJ: Lawrence Erlbaum.

Draper, N. R., & Smith, H. (1998). *Applied regression analysis* (3rd ed.). New York: John Wiley.

Fox, J. (1997). *Applied regression analysis, linear models, and related methods.* Thousand Oaks, CA: Sage.

Neter, J., Kutner, M. H., Nachtsheim, C. J., & Wasserman, W. (1996). *Applied linear regression models* (3rd ed.). Chicago: Irwin.

MULTIPLE-INDICATOR MEASURES

MEASUREMENT of theoretical CONSTRUCTS is one of the most important steps in social research. Relating the abstract concepts described in a THEORY to empirical INDICATORS of those CONCEPTS is crucial to an unambiguous understanding of the phenomena under study. Indeed, the linkage of theoretical constructs to their empirical indicators is as important in social inquiry as the positing of the relationships between the theoretical constructs themselves.

Multiple-indicator measures refer to situations in which more than one indicator or item is used to represent a theoretical construct in contrast to a single indicator. There are several reasons why a multiple-item measure is preferable to a single item. First, many theoretical constructs are so broad and complex that they cannot be adequately represented in a single item. As a simple example, no one would argue that an individual true-false question on an American government examination is an adequate measure of the degree of knowledge of American government possessed by a student. However, if several questions concerning the subject are asked, we would get a more comprehensive assessment of the student's knowledge of the subject.

A second reason to use multiple-item measures is accuracy. Single items lack precision because they may not distinguish subtle distinctions of an attribute. In fact, if the item is dichotomous, it will only recognize two levels of the attribute.

A third reason for preferring multiple-item measures is their greater RELIABILITY. Reliability focuses on the consistency of a measure. Do repeated tests with the same instrument yield the same results? Do comparable but different tests yield the same results? Generally, multiple-indicator measures contain less RANDOM ERROR and are thus more reliable than single-item measures because random error cancels itself out across multiple measurements. For all of these reasons, multiple indicator measures usually represent theoretical constructs better than single indicators.

—Edward G. Carmines and James Woods

REFERENCES

Carmines, E. G., & McIver, J. P. (1981). *Unidimensional scaling* (Sage University Paper Series on Quantitative Applications in the Social Sciences, 07–024). Beverly Hills, CA: Sage.

Nunnally, J. C. (1978). *Psychometric theory.* New York: McGraw-Hill.

Spector, P. E. (1992). *Summated rating scale construction: An introduction* (Sage University Paper Series on Quantitative Applications in the Social Sciences, 07–082). Newbury Park, CA: Sage.

MULTIPLICATIVE

The term *multiplicative* refers to the case when one variable is multiplied by another variable. The term is frequently used in the context of regression models, in which an outcome variable, Y, is said to be some function of the product of two variables, X and Z. A common scenario is where Y is said to be a linear function of the XZ product, such that

$$Y = \alpha + \beta XZ,$$

where XZ is the product of variable X times variable Z. A REGRESSION model is said to be "multiplicative" if it includes a multiplicative term within it. The multiplicative term can be a PREDICTOR VARIABLE multiplied by another predictor variable or a predictor variable multiplied by itself, such as

$$Y = \alpha + \beta X^2.$$

MODELS with product terms between two different variables typically imply some form of statistical INTERACTION. Models with product terms that represent squared, cubic, or higher order terms typically imply a NONLINEAR relationship between Y and X.

The fit of multiplicative models such as those described above are affected by the METRIC of the predictor variables. One can obtain a different CORRELATION between Y and XZ depending on how X and Z are scored (e.g., from −5 to +5 vs. from 0 to 10). There are strategies one can employ to evaluate multiplicative models so that they are invariant to such metric assumptions. These are discussed in Anderson (1981) and Jaccard and Turrisi (2003).

—James J. Jaccard

REFERENCES

Anderson, N. H. (1981). *Methods of information integration theory.* New York: Academic Press.

Jaccard, J., & Turrisi, R. (2003). *Interaction effects in multiple regression.* Thousand Oaks, CA: Sage.

MULTISTAGE SAMPLING

Multistage sampling refers to SURVEY designs in which the POPULATION units are hierarchically arranged and the sample is selected in stages corresponding to the levels of the hierarchy. At each stage, only units within the higher level units selected at the previous stage are considered. (It should not be confused with *multiphase sampling.*)

The simplest type of multistage sampling is two-stage sampling. At the first stage, a sample of higher level units is selected. At the second stage, a sample of lower level units within the higher level units selected at the first stage is selected. For example, the first-stage units may be schools and the second-stage units pupils, or the first-stage units may be businesses and the second-stage units employees. In surveys of households or individuals covering a large geographical territory (e.g., national surveys), it is common for first-stage sampling units to be small geographical areas, with a modest number of addresses or households—perhaps 10 or 20—selected at the second stage within each selected first-stage unit.

Multistage designs result in samples that are "clustered" within a limited set of higher level units. If the design is to include *all* units at the latter stage—for example, all pupils in each selected school—then the sample is referred to as a CLUSTER SAMPLE because it consists of entire clusters. Otherwise, if the units are subsampled at the latter stage, the sample is said to be a *clustered sample.*

The main motivation for multistage sampling is usually cost reduction. In the case of field interview surveys, each cluster in the sample can form a workload for one interviewer. Thus, each interviewer has a number of interviews to carry out in the same location, reducing travel time relative to a single-stage (unclustered) sample. In consequence, the unit cost of an interview is reduced so a larger sample size can be achieved for a fixed budget. Often (not only for field interview surveys), there is a fixed cost associated with each first-stage unit included in the sample. For example, in a survey of school pupils, it may be necessary to liaise with each school. The cost of this liaison, which may include visits to the school, may be independent of the number of pupils to be sampled within the school. Again, then, the unit cost of data collection can be reduced by clustering the sample of pupils within a restricted number of schools.

However, sample clustering also has a disadvantage. Because units within higher stage units (e.g., pupils within schools, households within small areas) tend to be more homogeneous than units in the population as a whole, clustering tends to reduce the precision of survey estimates. In other words, clustering tends to have the opposite effect to proportionate sample stratification (see STRATIFIED SAMPLE). Whereas stratification ensures that *all* strata are represented in the sample, clustering causes only *some* clusters to be represented in the sample. The resultant reduction in precision can be measured by the DESIGN EFFECT due to clustering. In general, the reduction in precision will be greater the larger the mean sample size per cluster and the more homogeneous the clustering units. For example, a sample of 10 pupils from each of 100 classes will result in less precision than a sample of 10 pupils from each of 100 schools if pupils within classes are more homogeneous than pupils within schools.

In designing a survey sample, the choice of clustering units and the sample size to allocate to each is important. The choice should be guided by considerations of cost and precision. Ideally, with a fixed budget, the increase in precision due to being able to afford a larger sample size should be as large as possible relative to the loss in precision due to clustering per se. The overall aim should be to maximize the accuracy of survey estimates for a fixed budget or to minimize the cost of obtaining a particular level of accuracy.

One other important aspect of multistage sampling is the control of selection probabilities. If a sample is selected in a number of conditional stages, the overall probability of selection for a particular unit is the product of the (conditional) probabilities at each stage. For example, imagine a survey of school pupils in a particular school year, with a two-stage sample design: selection of schools, followed by selection of a sample of pupils in each school. Then, the probability of selecting pupil j at school i is $P_{ij} = P_i \times P_{j|i}$, where P_i is the probability of selecting school i, and $P_{j|i}$ is the probability of selecting pupil j conditional on having selected school i. (The idea extends in an obvious way to any number of stages.)

With multistage sampling, it is important to know and to capture on the data set the selection probabilities at each stage. Only then is it possible to construct UNBIASED estimates. Furthermore, it is important to control the overall probabilities as far as possible at the design stage. In particular, in many circumstances, the most efficient design will be one that gives all population units equal selection probabilities (see DESIGN EFFECT). But there are an infinite number of possible combinations of P_i and $P_{j|i}$ that would result in the same value of P_{ij}. One obvious solution is to make each of these probabilities a constant. This is sometimes done, but it has the disadvantage that the sample size will vary across clustering units in proportion to their size. This variation could be considerable, which could cause both practical and statistical problems. A more common design is to use "probability proportional to size" (PPS) selection at each but the last stage and then select the same number of final stage units within each selected previous stage unit. In other words, $P_i = K1 \times N_i$ and $P_{j|i} = K2/N_i$, where N_i is the number of second-stage units in the ith first-stage unit (e.g., the number of pupils in the relevant year in school i, in the example of the previous paragraph), and $K1$ and $K2$ are just constant numbers. It can easily be seen that this design gives all pupils in the relevant year, regardless of which school they attend, the same overall selection probability P_{ij} while also leading to the same sample size, $K2$, of pupils in each sampled school.

—Peter Lynn

REFERENCES

Cochran, W. G. (1977). *Sampling techniques* (3rd ed.). New York: John Wiley.

Scheaffer, R. L., Mendenhall, W., & Ott, L. (1990). *Elementary survey sampling*. Boston: PWS-Kent.

Stuart, A. (1984). *The ideas of sampling*. London: Griffin.

MULTISTRATEGY RESEARCH

Multistrategy research is a term employed by Layder (1993) and Bryman (2001) to refer to research that combines quantitative and qualitative research. The term has been coined to distinguish it from MULTIMETHOD RESEARCH. The latter entails the combined use of two or more methods, but these may or may not entail a combination of quantitative and qualitative research. Multimethod research may entail the use of two or more methods within quantitative research or within qualitative research. By contrast, multistrategy research reflects the notion that quantitative and qualitative research are contrasting research strategies, each with its own set of epistemological and ontological presuppositions and criteria. Therefore, multistrategy research entails a commitment to the view that the two contrasting research strategies do not represent incommensurable PARADIGMS but instead may fruitfully be combined for a variety of reasons and in different contexts.

Multistrategy research is sometimes controversial because some writers take the view that because of their contrasting epistemological commitments, quantitative and qualitative research cannot genuinely be combined (e.g., Smith & Heshusius, 1986). According to this view, what appears to be an example of the combined use of quantitative and qualitative research (e.g., the use of both a STRUCTURED INTERVIEW-based social SURVEY with SEMISTRUCTURED INTERVIEWING) does not represent a genuine integration of the two strategies because the underlying principles are not capable of reconciliation. Instead, there is a superficial complementarity at the purely technical level. In other words, although techniques of data collection or analysis may be combined, strategies cannot. Such a view subscribes to a particular position in relation to the debate about quantitative and qualitative research—namely, one that centers on the epistemological version of the debate.

Writers and researchers who subscribe to the view that quantitative and qualitative research can be combined essentially take the position that research methods are not ineluctably embedded in epistemological and ontological presuppositions. Several different contexts for multistrategy research have been identified (Bryman, 2001). These include the following:

- using TRIANGULATION, in which the results of quantitative and qualitative research are cross-checked;
- using qualitative research to facilitate quantitative research and vice versa (e.g., when a social survey is used to help identify suitable people to be interviewed using a qualitative instrument, such as a semistructured interview);
- using one strategy to fill in the gaps that are left by the other strategy;

- using the two strategies to answer different types of research question;
- conducting qualitative research to help explain findings deriving from quantitative research; and
- gleaning an appreciation of participants' perspectives as well as addressing the concerns of the researcher.

In practice, it is difficult to separate out these different contexts of multistrategy research. For example, in their research on the mass-media representation of social science in Britain, Deacon, Bryman, and Fenton (1998) used a variety of research methods to answer different kinds of research questions. However, they found that when some of their quantitative and qualitative findings clashed, they were in fact carrying out an unplanned triangulation exercise.

—Alan Bryman

REFERENCES

Bryman, A. (2001). *Social research methods.* Oxford, UK: Oxford University Press.

Deacon, D., Bryman, A., & Fenton, N. (1998). Collision or collusion? A discussion of the unplanned triangulation of quantitative and qualitative research methods. *International Journal of Social Research Methodology, 1,* 47–63.

Layder, D. (1993). *New strategies in social research.* Cambridge, UK: Polity.

Smith, J. K., & Heshusius, L. (1986). Closing down the conversation: The end of the quantitative-qualitative debate among educational enquirers. *Educational Researcher, 15,* 4–12.

MULTIVARIATE

Statistics that deal with three or more variables at once are multivariate. For example, a MULTIPLE CORRELATION COEFFICIENT correlates two or more independent variables with a dependent variable. In MULTIPLE REGRESSION, there is a dependent variable and at least two independent variables. Any time tabular controls on a third variable are imposed in CONTINGENCY TABLES, the results are multivariate. The term is commonly juxtaposed to BIVARIATE, which looks at only two variables at once. Although the multiple variables are usually independent, they can be dependent. For example, in CANONICAL CORRELATION ANALYSIS (CCA), multiple X variables can be related to multiple Y variables. Also, an analyst may try to explain more than one dependent variable, as in a system of SIMULTANEOUS EQUATIONS.

—Michael S. Lewis-Beck

MULTIVARIATE ANALYSIS

As the name indicates, multivariate analysis comprises a set of techniques dedicated to the analysis of data sets with more than two variables. Several of these techniques were developed recently in part because they require the computational capabilities of modern computers. Also, because most of them are recent, these techniques are not always unified in their presentation, and the choice of the proper technique for a given problem is often difficult.

This entry provides a (nonexhaustive) catalog to help researchers decide when to use a given statistical technique for a given type of data or statistical question and gives a brief description of each technique. This entry is organized according to the number of data sets to analyze: one or two (or more). With two data sets, we consider two cases: In the first case, one set of data plays the role of PREDICTORS (or INDEPENDENT) VARIABLES (IVs), and the second set of data corresponds to measurements or DEPENDENT VARIABLES (DVs). In the second case, the different sets of data correspond to different sets of DVs.

ONE DATA SET

Typically, the data tables to be analyzed are made of several measurements collected on a set of units (e.g., subjects). In general, the units are rows and the variables columns.

Interval or Ratio Level of Measurement: Principal Components Analysis (PCA)

This is the oldest and most versatile method. The goal of PCA is to decompose a data table with correlated measurements into a new set of uncorrelated (i.e., orthogonal) variables. These variables are called, depending on the context, PRINCIPAL COMPONENTS, FACTORS, EIGENVECTORS, singular vectors, or loadings. Each unit is also assigned a set of scores that correspond to its projection on the components.

The results of the analysis are often presented with graphs plotting the projections of the units onto the components and the loadings of the variables (the so-called "circle of correlations"). The importance of each component is expressed by the variance (i.e., eigenvalue) of its projections or by the proportion of the variance explained. In this context, PCA is interpreted as an orthogonal decomposition of the variance (also called *inertia*) of a data table.

Nominal or Ordinal Level of Measurement: Correspondence Analysis (CA), Multiple Correspondence Analysis (MCA)

CA is a generalization of PCA to CONTINGENCY TABLES. The factors of CA give an orthogonal decomposition of the CHI-SQUARE associated with the table. In CA, rows and columns of the table play a symmetric role and can be represented in the same plot. When several NOMINAL variables are analyzed, CA is generalized as MCA. CA is also known as dual or OPTIMAL SCALING or reciprocal averaging.

Similarity or Distance: Multidimensional Scaling (MDS), Additive Tree, Cluster Analysis

These techniques are applied when the rows and the columns of the data table represent the same units and when the measure is a distance or a similarity. The goal of the analysis is to represent graphically these distances or similarities. MDS is used to represent the units as points on a map such that their Euclidean distances on the map approximate the original similarities (classic MDS, which is equivalent to PCA, is used for distances, and nonmetric MDS is used for similarities). Additive tree analysis and CLUSTER ANALYSIS are used to represent the units as "leaves" of a tree with the distance "on the tree" approximating the original distance or similarity.

TWO DATA SETS, CASE 1: ONE INDEPENDENT VARIABLE SET AND ONE DEPENDENT VARIABLE SET

Multiple Linear Regression Analysis (MLR)

In MLR, several IVs (which are supposed to be fixed or, equivalently, are measured without error) are used to predict with a LEAST SQUARES approach one DV. If the IVs are orthogonal, the problem reduces to a set of bivariate regressions. When the IVs are correlated, their importance is estimated from the partial coefficient of correlation. An important problem arises

when one of the IVs can be predicted from the other variables because the computations required by MLR can no longer be performed: This is called perfect multicollinearity. Some possible solutions to this problem are described in the following section.

Regression With Too Many Predictors and/or Several Dependent Variables

Partial Least Squares (PLS) Regression (PLSR)

PLSR addresses the multicollinearity problem by computing latent vectors (akin to the components of PCA), which explain both the IVs and the DVs. This very versatile technique is used when the goal is to predict more than one DV. It combines features from PCA and MLR: The score of the units as well as the loadings of the variables can be plotted as in PCA, and the DVs can be estimated (with a confidence interval) as in MLR.

Principal Components Regression (PCR)

In PCR, the IVs are first submitted to a PCA, and the scores of the units are then used as predictors in a standard MLR.

Ridge Regression (RR)

RR accommodates the multicollinearity problem by adding a small constant (the ridge) to the diagonal of the correlation matrix. This makes the computation of the estimates for MLR possible.

Reduced Rank Regression (RRR) or Redundancy Analysis

In RRR, the DVs are first submitted to a PCA and the scores of the units are then used as DVs in a series of standard MLRs in which the original IVs are used as predictors (a procedure akin to an inverse PCR).

Multivariate Analysis of Variance (MANOVA)

In MANOVA, the IVs have the same structure as in a standard ANOVA and are used to predict a set of DVs. MANOVA computes a series of ordered orthogonal linear combinations of the DVs (i.e., factors) with the constraint that the first factor generates the largest F if used in an ANOVA. The sampling distribution of this F is adjusted to take into account its construction.

Predicting a Nominal Variable: Discriminant Analysis (DA)

DA, which is mathematically equivalent to MANOVA, is used when a set of IVs is used to predict the group to which a given unit belongs (which is a nominal DV). It combines the IVs to create the largest F when the groups are used as a fixed factor in an ANOVA.

Fitting a Model: Confirmatory Factor Analysis (CFA)

In CFA, the researcher first generates one (or a few) MODEL(S) of an underlying explanatory structure (i.e., a construct), which is often expressed as a graph. Then the correlations between the DVs are fitted to this structure. Models are evaluated by comparing how well they fit the data. Variations over CFA are called STRUCTURAL EQUATION MODELING (SEM), LISREL, or EQS.

TWO (OR MORE) DATA SETS, CASE 2: TWO (OR MORE) DEPENDENT VARIABLE SETS
Canonical Correlation Analysis (CC)

CC combines the DVs to find pairs of new variables (called canonical variables [CV], one for each data table) that have the highest correlation. However, the CVs, even when highly correlated, do not necessarily explain a large portion of the variance of the original tables. This makes the interpretation of the CV sometimes difficult, but CC is nonetheless an important theoretical tool because most multivariate techniques can be interpreted as a specific case of CC.

Multiple Factor Analysis (MFA)

MFA combines several data tables into one single analysis. The first step is to perform a PCA of each table. Then, each data table is normalized by dividing all the entries of the table by the first eigenvalue of its PCA. This transformation—akin to the univariate Z-score—equalizes the weight of each table in the final solution and therefore makes possible the simultaneous analysis of several heterogeneous data tables.

Multiple Correspondence Analysis (MCA)

MCA can be used to analyze several contingency tables; it generalizes CA.

Parafac and Tucker3

These techniques handle three-way data matrices by generalizing the PCA decomposition into scores and loadings to generate the three matrices of loading (one for each dimension of the data). They differ by the constraints they impose on the decomposition (Tucker3 generates orthogonal loadings, Parafac does not).

Indscal

Indscal is used when each of several subjects generates a data matrix with the same units and the same variables for all the subjects. Indscal generates a common Euclidean solution (with dimensions) and expresses the differences between subjects as differences in the importance given to the common dimensions.

Statis

Statis is used when at least one dimension of the three-way table is common to all tables (e.g., same units measured on several occasions with different variables). The first step of the method performs a PCA of each table and generates a similarity table (i.e., cross-product) between the units for each table. The similarity tables are then combined by computing a cross-product matrix and performing its PCA (without centering). The loadings on the first component of this analysis are then used as weights to compute the *compromise data table,* which is the weighted average of all the tables. The original table (and their units) is projected into the compromise space to explore their communalities and differences.

Procustean Analysis (PA)

PA is used to compare distance tables obtained on the same objects. The first step is to represent the tables by MDS maps. Then PA finds a set of transformations that will make the position of the objects in both maps as close as possible (in the least squares sense).

—Hervé Abdi

REFERENCES

Borg, I., & Groenen, P. (1997). *Modern multidimensional scaling.* New York: Springer-Verlag.

Escofier, B., & Pagès, J. (1988). *Analyses factorielles multiples* [Multiple factor analysis]. Paris: Dunod.

Johnson, R. A., & Wichern, D. W. (2002). *Applied multivariate statistical analysis.* Upper Saddle River, NJ: Prentice Hall.

Naes, T., & Risvik, E. (Eds.). (1996). *Multivariate analysis of data in sensory science.* New York: Elsevier.

Weller, S. C., & Romney, A. K. (1990). *Metric scaling: Correspondence analysis.* Newbury Park, CA: Sage.

MULTIVARIATE ANALYSIS OF VARIANCE AND COVARIANCE (MANOVA AND MANCOVA)

The word *multi* here refers to the use of several DEPENDENT VARIABLES in a single analysis. This is in spite of the often-used term for several EXPLANATORY variables, as in MULTIPLE REGRESSION. These multiple analyses can successfully be used in fields as separate as psychology and biology—in psychological testing, each test item becomes a separate dependent variable, and in biology, there are several observations on a particular organism.

MANOVA and MANCOVA are models for the joint statistical analysis of several QUANTITATIVE dependent variables in one analysis, using the same explanatory variables for all the dependent variables. In MANOVA, all the explanatory variables are NOMINAL variables, whereas in MANCOVA, some of the explanatory variables are quantitative and some are QUALITATIVE (nominal). These models can also be extended to the regression case in which all the explanatory variables are quantitative. These three approaches are special cases of the so-called multivariate GENERAL LINEAR MODEL.

With several dependent variables and a set of explanatory variables, it is possible to separately analyze the relationship of each dependent variable to the explanatory variables, using ANALYSIS OF VARI-ANCE or ANALYSIS OF COVARIANCE. The difference in MANOVA and MANCOVA is that here all the dependent variables are used in the same, one analysis. This can be desirable when the several dependent variables have something in common, such as scores on different items in a psychological test. This multivariate approach also eliminates the problem of what to do for an overall significance level when many statistical tests are run on the same data.

EXPLANATION

As a simple example, suppose there are data on both the mathematics and verbal Scholastic Aptitude Test (SAT) scores for a group of students. Are there gender and race differences in the two sets of SAT scores? It is possible to do a separate ANALYSIS OF VARIANCE for each SAT score, as expressed in the following two equations:

$$\text{Math SAT} = \text{Gender} + \text{Race} + \text{Gender} \cdot \text{Race} + \text{Residual},$$

$$\text{Verbal SAT} = \text{Gender} + \text{Race} + \text{Gender} \cdot \text{Race} + \text{Residual}.$$

Each analysis would provide the proper SUMS OF SQUARES and *P* VALUES, and it would be possible to conclude what the impacts are on the SAT scores of the two explanatory variables and their STATISTICAL INTERACTIONS.

However, two such separate analyses do not use the fact that the two explanatory variables themselves are related. If there were some way of taking this information into account, it would be possible to perform a stronger analysis and perhaps even find significant results that were not apparent in the two separate analyses. This can now be done using *one* MANOVA analysis instead of *two* separate ANOVAs.

HISTORICAL ACCOUNT

The computational complexity increases dramatically by going from analysis of variance and analysis of covariance to the corresponding multivariate analyses. Thus, the methods were not well developed and used until the necessary statistical software became available in the latter parts of the past century. Now, all major statistical software packages have the capacity to perform MANOVA and MANCOVA. Also, many of the software manuals have good explanations of the methods and how to interpret the outputs.

APPLICATIONS

Let us consider the two SAT scores and one explanatory variable, say, gender. With two separate analyses of variance, we study the distributions of the math and verbal scores separately, and we may or may not find gender differences. However, with two dependent variables, we can now create a scatterplot for the two test scores, showing their relationship. To identify the gender of each respondent, we can color the points in two different colors. It will then be clear whether the points for the two groups overlap, or the groups may show up as two very different sets of points in a variety of possible ways. We can now see differences between the two groups that were not obvious when each variable was only considered separately. In the extreme, it is even possible to have the same mean value for both females and males on one of the two test scores. However, in the scatterplot, we may see the way in which the two groups of scores differ in major ways. Such differences would be found using one multivariate analysis of variance instead of two separate analyses.

The first step in both MANOVA and MANCOVA is to test the overall NULL HYPOTHESIS that all groups have the same means on the various dependent variables. In the example above, that implies testing that females and males have the same math scores and verbal scores and that all races have the same math scores and verbal scores. If these null hypotheses are rejected, the next step is to find *which* group means are different, just as we do in the univariate case.

Typically, there are four different ways to test the overall null hypothesis. They are known as Wilks's lambda, the Pillai-Bartlett trace, Roy's greatest characteristic root, and the Hotelling-Lawley trace. The four methods may not agree in their test of the same null hypotheses, and the choice is usually governed by issues having to do with robustness of the tests and their statistical power. Wilks's test is the most commonly used, and his test statistic has a distribution that can be approximated by an F DISTRIBUTION when the proper assumptions are met.

Assumptions

As with other statistical procedures, the data have to satisfy certain assumptions for the procedure to work, especially to produce meaningful p values. The data need to form a proper statistical random sample from an underlying population. The observations need to be obtained independently of one another. The dependent variables need to have a multivariate NORMAL DISTRIBUTION, which may be the case when each dependent variable has a normal distribution. Finally, homogeneity of variance must be the case for each dependent variable, and the correlation between any two dependent variables must be the same in all groups of observations.

—Gudmund R. Iversen

AUTHOR'S NOTE: A search on the World Wide Web of MANOVA will bring up several good explanations and examples of uses of these methods.

REFERENCES

Bray, J. H., & Maxwell, S. E. (1985). *Multivariate analysis of variance* (Sage University Paper Series on Quantitative Applications in the Social Sciences, 07–054). Beverly Hills, CA: Sage.

Velleman, P. F. (1988). *DataDesk version 6.0 statistics guide.* Ithaca, NY: Data Description, Inc.

N

N (n)

The symbol(s) for SAMPLE size. Most social science research is carried out on samples from a POPULATION, rather than on the population itself. Whenever the DATA are from a sample, it is standard practice to report the sample size, such as $N = 256$, or $n = 256$. (There is no difference in practice between N and n, and each seems used about equally in the literature.) Furthermore, the reported N normally excludes cases with missing data on variables in the analysis. Thus, for example, a survey may have interviewed 1,000 respondents, but for the analysis of the six variables of interest, only 873 had no missing data, for an effective $N = 873$, not the original 1,000.

—Michael S. Lewis-Beck

N6

N6 (formerly NUD*IST), like NVivo, is a specialized computer program package for qualitative data analysis. For further information, see the website: www.scolari.co.uk/frame.html or www.scolari.co.uk/qsr/qsr.htm

—Tim Futing Liao

NARRATIVE ANALYSIS

Narrative analysis in the human sciences refers to a family of approaches to diverse kinds of texts that have in common a storied form. As nations and governments construct preferred narratives about history, so do social movements, organizations, scientists, other professionals, ethnic/racial groups, and individuals in stories of experience. What makes such diverse texts "narrative" is sequence and consequence: Events are selected, organized, connected, and evaluated as meaningful for a particular audience. Storytellers interpret the world and experience in it; they sometimes create moral tales—how the world should be. Narratives represent storied ways of knowing and communicating (Hinchman & Hinchman, 1997). I focus here on oral narratives of personal experience.

Research interest in narrative emerged from several contemporary movements: the "narrative turn" in the human sciences away from POSITIVIST modes of inquiry and the master narratives of theory (e.g., Marxism); the "memoir boom" in literature and popular culture; identity politics in U.S., European, and transnational movements—emancipation efforts of people of color, women, gays and lesbians, and other marginalized groups; and the burgeoning therapeutic culture—exploration of personal life in therapies of various kinds. "Embedded in the lives of the ordinary, the marginalized, and the muted, personal narrative responds to the disintegration of master narratives as people make sense of experience, claim identities, and 'get a life' by telling and writing their stories" (Langellier, 2001, p. 700).

Among investigators, there is considerable variation in definitions of personal narrative, often linked to discipline. In social history and anthropology, narrative can refer to an entire life story, woven from the threads of interviews, observation, and documents (e.g., Barbara Myerhoff's ethnography of elderly Jews in Venice, California). In sociolinguistics and other fields, the concept of narrative is restricted, referring to brief, topically specific stories organized around characters, setting, and plot (e.g., Labovian narratives in answer to a single interview question). In another tradition (common in psychology and sociology), personal narrative encompasses long sections of talk—extended accounts of lives in context that develop over the course of single or multiple interviews. Investigators' definitions of narrative lead to different methods of analysis, but all require them to construct texts for further analysis, that is, select and organize documents, compose FIELDNOTES, and/or choose sections of interview TRANSCRIPTS for close inspection. Narratives do not speak for themselves or have unanalyzed merit; they require interpretation when used as data in social research.

MODELS OF NARRATIVE ANALYSIS

Several typologies exist (cf. Cortazzi, 2001; Mishler, 1995). The one I sketch is an heuristic effort to describe a range of contemporary approaches particularly suited to oral narratives of personal experience (on organizational narratives, see Boje, 2001). The typology is not intended to be either hierarchical or evaluative, although I do raise questions about each. In practice, different approaches can be combined; they are not mutually exclusive, and, as with all typologies, boundaries are fuzzy. I offer several examples of each, admittedly my favorites, drawn from the field of health and illness.

Thematic Analysis

Emphasis is on the content of a text, "what" is said more than "how" it is said, the "told" rather than the "telling." A (unacknowledged) philosophy of language underpins the approach: Language is a direct and unambiguous route to meaning. As GROUNDED THEORISTS do, investigators collect many stories and inductively create conceptual groupings from the data. A typology of narratives organized by theme is the typical representational strategy, with case studies or vignettes providing illustration.

Gareth Williams (1984), in an early paper in the illness narrative genre, shows how individuals manage the assault on identity that accompanies rheumatoid arthritis by narratively reconstructing putative causes—an interpretive process that connects the body,

illness, self, and society. From analysis of how 30 individuals account for the genesis of their illness, he constructs a typology, using three cases as exemplars; they illustrate thematic variation and extend existing theory on chronic illness as biographical disruption. His interview excerpts often take the classic, temporally ordered narrative form, but analysis of formal properties is not attempted.

Carole Cain (1991) goes a bit further in her study of identity acquisition among members of an Alcoholics Anonymous group, in which she uses observation and interviews. There are common propositions about drinking in the classic AA story, which new members acquire as they participate in the organization; over time, they learn to place the events and experiences in their lives into a patterned life story that is recognizable to AA audiences. She identifies a general cultural story and analyzes how it shapes the "personal" stories of group members—key moments in the drinking career, often told as episodes. By examining narrative structure in a beginning way, her work segues into the text type.

The thematic approach is useful for theorizing across a number of cases—finding common thematic elements across research participants and the events they report. A typology can be constructed to elaborate a developing theory. Because interest lies in the content of speech, analysts interpret what is said by focusing on the meaning that any competent user of the language would find in a story. Language is viewed as a resource, not a topic of investigation. But does the approach mimic OBJECTIVIST modes of inquiry, suggesting themes are unmediated by the investigator's theoretical perspective, interests, and mode of questioning? The contexts of an utterance—in the interview, in wider institutional and cultural discourses—are not usually studied. Readers must assume that when many narratives are grouped into a similar thematic category, everyone in the group means the same thing by what he or she says. What happens to ambiguities, "deviant" responses that don't fit into a typology, the unspoken?

Structural Analysis

Emphasis shifts to the telling, the *way* a story is told. Although thematic content does not slip away, focus is equally on form—how a teller, by selecting particular narrative devices, makes a story persuasive. Unlike the thematic approach, language is treated seriously—an object for close investigation—over and beyond its referential content.

Arguably the first method of narrative analysis developed by William Labov and colleagues more than 30 years ago, this structural approach analyzes the *function* of a clause in the overall narrative—the communicative work it accomplishes. Labov (1982) later modified the approach to examine first-person accounts of violence—brief, topically centered, and temporally ordered stories—but he retained the basic components of a narrative's structure: the abstract (summary and/or point of the story); orientation (to time, place, characters, and situation); complicating action (the event sequence, or plot, usually with a crisis and turning point); evaluation (where the narrator steps back from the action to comment on meaning and communicate emotion—the "soul" of the narrative); resolution (the outcome of the plot); and a coda (ending the story and bringing action back to the present). Not all stories contain all elements, and they can occur in varying sequences. Labov's microanalysis convincingly shows how violent actions (in bars, on the street, etc.) are the outcome of speech acts gone awry. From a small corpus of narratives and the prior work of Goffman, he develops a theory of the rules of requests that explains violent eruptions in various settings experienced by a diverse group of narrators.

An ethnopoetic structural approach is suitable for lengthy narratives that do not take the classic temporal story form. Building on the work of Dell Hymes and others, James Gee (1991) analyzes the speech of a woman hospitalized with schizophrenia and finds it artful and meaningful. Episodically (rather than temporally) organized, the narrative is parsed into idea units, stanzas, strophes, and parts based on how the narrative is *spoken*. Meaning and interpretation are constrained by features of the spoken narrative. Gee develops a theory of units of discourse that goes beyond the sentential.

Because structural approaches require examination of syntactic and prosodic features of talk, they are not suitable for large numbers, but they can be very useful for detailed case studies and comparison of several narrative accounts. Microanalysis of a few cases can build theories that relate language and meaning in ways that are missed when transparency is assumed, as in thematic analysis. Investigators must decide, depending on the focus of a project, how much transcription detail is necessary. There is the danger that interview excerpts can become unreadable for those unfamiliar with sociolinguistics, compromising communication across disciplinary boundaries.

Like the thematic approach, strict application of the structural approach can decontextualize narratives by ignoring historical, interactional, and institutional factors. Research settings and relationships constrain what can be narrated and shape the way a particular story develops.

Interactional Analysis

Here, the emphasis is on the dialogic process between teller and listener. Narratives of experience are occasioned in particular settings, such as medical, social service, and court situations, where storyteller and questioner jointly participate in conversation. Attention to thematic content and narrative structure are not abandoned in the interactional approach, but interest shifts to storytelling as a process of coconstruction, where teller and listener create meaning collaboratively. Stories of personal experience, organized around the life-world of the teller, may be inserted into question-and-answer exchanges. The approach requires transcripts that include all participants in the conversation, and it is strengthened when paralinguistic features of interaction are included as well.

Some research questions require interactional analysis. Jack Clark and Elliot Mishler (1992) sought to distinguish the features that differentiated "attentive" medical interviews from others. By analyzing pauses, interruptions, topic chaining, and other aspects of conversation, they show how medical interviews can (and cannot) result in patient narratives that provide knowledge for accurate diagnosis and treatment.

Susan Bell (1999) compares the illness narratives of two women, separated in time by the women's health movement and activism. Interrogating her participation in the research interviews, she shows how the emergent narratives are situated historically and politically. Contexts shape possibilities in the women's lives, their experiences of illness, and the specific illness narratives the women produce collaboratively with the author. Microanalysis of language and interaction, in addition to narrative organization and structure, are essential to her method.

An interactional approach is useful for studies of relationships between speakers in diverse field settings (courts of law, classrooms, social service organizations, psychotherapy offices, and the research interview itself). Like structural approaches, studies of interaction typically represent speech in all its complexity, not simply as a vehicle for content. As in CONVERSATION ANALYSIS, transcripts may be difficult for the uninitiated. Pauses, disfluencies, and other aspects of talk are typically included, but what cannot be represented in a transcript (unlike a videotape) is the unspoken. What happens to gesture, gaze, and other displays that are enacted and embodied?

Performative Analysis

Extending the interactional approach, interest goes beyond the spoken word, and, as the stage metaphor implies, storytelling is seen as performance by a "self" with a past who involves, persuades, and (perhaps) moves an audience through language and gesture, "doing" rather than telling alone. Variation exists in the performative approach, ranging from dramaturgic to narrative as praxis—a form of social action. Consequently, narrative researchers may analyze different features: actors allowed on stage in an oral narrative (e.g., characters and their positionings in a story, including narrator/protagonist); settings (the conditions of performance and setting of the story performed); the enactment of dialogue between characters (reported speech); and audience response (the listener[s] who interprets the drama as it unfolds, and the interpreter in later reading[s]). Performative analysis is emergent in narrative studies, although the dramaturgic view originated with Goffman, and researchers are experimenting with it in studies of identities— vested presentations of "self" (Riessman, 2003).

Kristin Langellier and Eric Peterson (2003) provide a compelling theory and many empirical examples, ranging from detailed analysis of family (group) storytelling to an illness narrative told by a breast cancer survivor. They analyze the positioning of storyteller, audience, and characters in each performance; storytelling is a communicative practice that is embodied, situated, material, discursive, and open to legitimation and critique.

The performative view is appropriate for studies of communication practices and for detailed studies of identity construction—how narrators want to be known and precisely how they involve the audience in "doing" their identities. The approach invites study of how audiences are implicated in the art of narrative performance. As Wolfgang Iser and reader-response theorists suggest, readers are the ultimate interpreters, perhaps reading a narrative differently from either teller or investigator. Integrating the visual (through filming and photography) with the spoken narrative represents an innovative contemporary turn (Radley & Taylor, 2003).

CONCLUSION

Analysis of narrative is no longer the province of literary study alone; it has penetrated all of the human sciences and practicing professions. The various methods reviewed are suited to different kinds of projects and texts, but each provides a way to systematically study personal narratives of experience. Critics argue (legitimately, in some cases) that narrative research can reify the interior "self," pretend to offer an "authentic" voice—unalloyed subjective truth—and idealize individual agency (Atkinson & Silverman, 1997; Bury, 2001). There is a real danger of overpersonalizing the personal narrative.

Narrative approaches are not appropriate for studies of large numbers of nameless and faceless subjects. Some modes of analysis are slow and painstaking, requiring attention to subtlety: nuances of speech, the organization of a response, relations between researcher and subject, social and historical contexts— cultural narratives that make "personal" stories possible. In a recent reflexive turn, scholars in AUTOETHNO-GRAPHY and other traditions are producing their own narratives, relating their biographies to their research materials (Riessman, 2002).

Narratives do not mirror the past, they refract it. Imagination and strategic interests influence how storytellers choose to connect events and make them meaningful for others. Narratives are useful in research precisely because storytellers interpret the past rather than reproduce it as it was. The "truths" of narrative accounts are not in their faithful representations of a past world but in the shifting connections they forge among past, present, and future. They offer storytellers a way to reimagine lives (as narratives do for nations, organizations, and ethnic/racial and other groups forming collective identities). Building on C. Wright Mills, narrative analysis can forge connections between personal biography and social structure—the personal and the political.

—Catherine Kohler Riessman

REFERENCES

Atkinson, P., & Silverman, D. (1997). Kundera's "immortality": The interview society and the invention of self. *Qualitative Inquiry, 3*(3), 304–325.

Bell, S. E. (1999). Narratives and lives: Women's health politics and the diagnosis of cancer for DES daughters. *Narrative Inquiry, 9*(2), 1–43.

Boje, D. M. (2001). *Narrative methods for organizational and communication research.* Thousand Oaks, CA: Sage.

Bury, M. (2001). Illness narratives: Fact or fiction? *Sociology of Health and Illness, 23*(3), 263–285.

Cain, C. (1991). Personal stories: Identity acquisition and self-understanding in Alcoholics Anonymous. *Ethos, 19,* 210–253.

Clark, J. A., & Mishler, E. G. (1992). Attending to patients' stories: Reframing the clinical task. *Sociology of Health and Illness, 14,* 344–370.

Cortazzi, M. (2001). Narrative analysis in ethnography. In P. Atkinson, A. Coffey, S. Delamont, J. Lofland, & L. Lofland (Eds.), *Handbook of ethnography.* Thousand Oaks, CA: Sage.

Gee, J. P. (1991). A linguistic approach to narrative. *Journal of Narrative and Life History, 1,* 15–39.

Hinchman, L. P., & Hinchman, S. K. (Eds.). (1997). *Memory, identity, community: The idea of narrative in the human sciences.* Albany: State University of New York Press.

Labov, W. (1982). Speech actions and reactions in personal narrative. In D. Tannen (Ed.), *Analyzing discourse: Text and talk.* Washington, DC: Georgetown University Press.

Langellier, K. M. (2001). Personal narrative. In M. Jolly (Ed.), *Encyclopedia of life writing: Autobiographical and biographical forms* (Vol. 2). London: Fitzroy Dearborn.

Langellier, K. M., & Peterson, E. E. (2003). *Performing marrative: The communicative practice of storytelling.* Philadelphia: Temple University Press.

Mishler, E. G. (1995). Models of narrative analysis: A typology. *Journal of Narrative and Life History, 5*(2), 87–123.

Radley, A., & Taylor, D. (2003). Remembering one's stay in hospital: A study in recovery, photography and forgetting. *Health: An Interdisciplinary Journal for the Social Study of Health, Illness and Medicine, 7*(2), 129–159.

Riessman, C. K. (2002). Doing justice: Positioning the interpreter in narrative work. In W. Patterson (Ed.), *Strategic narrative: New perspectives on the power of personal and cultural storytelling* (pp. 195–216). Lanham, MA: Lexington Books.

Riessman, C. K. (2003). Performing identities in illness narrative: Masculinity and multiple sclerosis. *Qualitative Research, 3*(1), 5–33.

Williams, G. (1984). The genesis of chronic illness: Narrative re-construction. *Sociology of Health & Illness, 6*(2), 175–200.

NARRATIVE INTERVIEWING

How does narrative interviewing differ from the classic in-depth interview? The first term suggests the generation of detailed "stories" of experience, not generalized descriptions. But narratives come in many forms, ranging from tightly bounded ones that recount specific past events (with clear beginnings, middles, and ends) to narratives that traverse temporal and geographical space—biographical accounts that refer to entire lives or careers.

The idea of narrative interviewing represents a major shift in perspective in the human sciences about the research interview itself. The question-and-answer (stimulus/response) model gives way to viewing the interview as a discursive accomplishment. Participants engage in an evolving conversation; narrator and listener/questioner, collaboratively, produce and make meaning of events and experiences that the narrator reports (Mishler, 1986). The "facilitating" interviewer and the vessel-like "respondent" are replaced by two active participants who jointly produce meaning (Gubrium & Holstein, 2002). Narrative interviewing has more in common with contemporary ETHNOGRAPHY than with mainstream social science interviewing practice that relies on discrete OPEN-ENDED QUESTIONS and/or CLOSED-ENDED QUESTIONS.

ENCOURAGING NARRATION

When the interview is viewed as a conversation—a discourse between speakers—rules of everyday conversation apply: turn taking; relevancy; and entrance and exit talk to transition into, and return from, a story world. One story can lead to another; as narrator and questioner/listener negotiate spaces for these extended turns, it helps to explore associations and meanings that might connect several stories. If we want to learn about experience in all its complexity, details count: specific incidents, not general evaluations of experience. Narrative accounts require longer turns at talk than are typical in "natural" conversation, certainly in mainstream research practice.

Opening up the research interview to extended narration by a research participant requires investigators to give up some control. Although we have particular experiential paths we want to cover, narrative interviewing means following participants down their trails. Genuine discoveries about a phenomenon can come from power sharing in interviews.

Narratives can emerge at the most unexpected times, even in answer to fixed-response (yes/no) questions (Riessman, 2002). But certain kinds of open-ended questions are more likely than others to provide narrative opportunities. Compare "When did X happen?" which requests a discrete piece of information, with "Tell me what happened . . . and then what happened?" which asks for an extended account of some past time. Some investigators, after introductions, invite a participant to tell their story—how an illness began, for example. But experience always exceeds its description and narrativization; events may be fleetingly summarized and given little significance. Only with further questioning can participants recall the details, turning points, and other shifts in cognition, emotion, and action. In my own research on disruptions in the expected life course, such as divorce, I have posed the question: "Can you remember a particular time when . . .?" I might probe further: "What happened that makes you remember that particular moment in your marriage?" Cortazzi and colleagues (Cortazzi, Jin, Wall, & Cavendish, 2001), studying the education of health professionals, asked: "Have you had a breakthrough in your learning recently?" "Oh yes" typically followed, and then a long narrative with an outpouring of emotion and metaphor about a breakthrough—"a clap of thunder," as one student said.

In general, less structure in interview schedules gives greater control to research participants—interviewee and interviewer alike—to jointly construct narratives using available cultural forms. Not all parents tell stories to children on a routine basis, and not all cultures are orally based (in some groups, of course, stories are the primary way to communicate about the past). Storytelling as a way of knowing and telling is differentially invoked by participants in research interviews. Not all narratives are "stories" in the strict (sociolinguistic) sense of the term.

Collecting and comparing different forms of telling about the past can be fruitful. A graduate student in my class, Janice Goodman, studied a group of Sudanese boys that had traversed many countries before the boys were finally accepted into the United States as "legitimate" refugees. Their narrative accounts differed from one another in significant ways, but all contained particular events in the narrative sequence—for example, crossing a river filled with crocodiles in which many boys perished. The absence of emotion and evaluation in the narratives contrasts with accounts of other refugee groups, reflecting perhaps the young age of my student's participants, their relationship to her, and cultural and psychological factors.

Sometimes, it is next to impossible for a participant to narrate experience in spoken language alone. Wendy Luttrell (2003), working as an ethnographer in a classroom for pregnant teens, most of whom were African American, expected "stories" from each girl about key events: learning of her pregnancy, telling her mother and boyfriend, making the decision to keep the baby, and other moments. She confronted silence instead, only to discover a world of narrative as she encouraged the girls' artistic productions and role-plays. When she asked them to discuss their artwork, they performed narratives about the key moments for each other—group storytelling. It is a limitation for investigators to rely only on the texts we have constructed from individual interviews, our "holy transcripts." Innovations among contemporary scholars include combining observation, sustained relationships and conversations over time with participants, even visual data with narrative interviewing (e.g., videotaping of participants' environments, photographs they take, and their responses to photographs of others).

In sum, narrative interviewing is not a set of techniques, nor is it necessarily natural. If used creatively in some research situations, it offers a way for us to forge dialogic relationships and greater communicative equality in social research.

—Catherine Kohler Riessman

REFERENCES

Cortazzi, M., Jin, L., Wall, D., & Cavendish, S. (2001). Sharing learning through narrative communication. *International Journal of Language and Communication Disorders, 36,* 252–257.

Gubrium, J. F., & Holstein, J. A. (2002). From the individual interview to the interview society. In J. F. Gubrium & J. A. Holdstein (Eds.), *Handbook of interview research: Context and method.* Thousand Oaks, CA: Sage.

Luttrell, W. (2003). *Pregnant bodies, fertile minds: Gender, race, and the schooling of pregnant teens.* New York: Routledge.

Mishler, E. G. (1986). *Research interviewing: Context and narrative.* Cambridge, MA: Harvard University Press.

Riessman, C. K. (2002). Positioning gender identity in narratives of infertility: South Indian women's lives in context. In M. C. Inhorn & F. van Balen (Eds.), *Infertility around the globe: New thinking on childlessness, gender, and reproductive technologies.* Berkeley: University of California Press.

NATIVE RESEARCH

The predominance of POSITIVISM in EPISTE-MOLOGY and science has long emphasized the necessity for researchers to conduct their work with OBJECTIVITY and methodologies through which concerns about VALIDITY, RELIABILITY, and generalizability are obviated. The phrase "GOING NATIVE" is often attributed to Bronislaw Malinowski based upon his extensive experience studying the Trobriand Islanders of New Guinea (Malinowski, 1922). In his reflections upon the relationship between the anthropologist and "subjects" in the field, Malinowski suggested that, contrary to the tradition of distancing oneself from objects of study research, one should instead "grasp the native's point of view, his relations to life, to realize *his* vision of *his* world" (p. 290). That is, scientists in a foreign milieu should go native, engaging in the research endeavor in a more interactive and reflexive manner with those peoples and cultures they study.

Over the seven decades since Malinowski first suggested the notion of going native, researchers across disciplines have focused upon the ways they might gain access to or study those populations and/or topics that are dissimilar to the researcher by gender, race, class, nationality, or other characteristics. Over the past 10 years, however, the field of anthropology has been primarily responsible for coining the nomenclature of the "native," "indigenous," or "insider" researcher (Hayano, 1979; Kanuha, 2000; Malinowski, 1922; Narayan, 1993; Ohnuki-Tierney, 1984; Reed-Danahay, 1997) in which ethnographers study social or identity groups of which they are members and/or social problem areas about which they have direct and often personal experience. Examples of native research would be female researchers studying breast cancer, ethnographers with HIV/AIDS conducting focus groups with HIV-positive clients, or Hiroshima-born scientists surveying Japanese survivors of the atomic bomb.

The benefits of researchers conducting studies by/about themselves include access to previously unstudied or hard-to-reach populations, the nature and depth of "insider" knowledge that accentuates the possibilities and levels of analytical interpretation, and a complex understanding of methods and data that can be born only of LIVED EXPERIENCE in a specific cultural context. However, native research also includes challenges. Balancing the multiple identities of being at once a PARTICIPANT OBSERVER *and* researcher requires unique skills and understandings to distance emotionally and intellectually from data in order to enhance analyses without predisposition. This is particularly difficult when the native researcher's primary social

identities often mirror those he or she is studying. In addition, an essential criterion for the native researcher is to have not only some prior knowledge of the population, but also the ability to be accepted as a member of one's own group (an insider) even while conducting oneself as a researcher (an outsider).

The conundrums of native research require sensitivity to those native researchers who bring both "insider" perspectives and "outsider" methods for studying them.

—Valli Kalei Kanuha

REFERENCES

Hayano, D. (1979). Auto-ethnography: Paradigms, problems and prospects. *Human Organization, 38*(1), 99–104.

Kanuha, V. (2000). "Being" native vs. "going native": The challenge of doing research as an insider. *Social Work, 45*(5), 439–447.

Malinowski, B. (1922). *Argonauts of the Western Pacific.* New York: Holt, Rinehart and Winston.

Narayan, K. (1993). How native is the "native" anthropologist? *American Anthropologist, 95,* 671–686.

Ohnuki-Tierney, E. (1984). "Native" anthropologists. *American Ethnologist, 11,* 584–586.

Reed-Danahay, D. E. (Ed.). (1997). *Auto/ethnography: Rewriting the self and the social.* Oxford, UK: Berg.

NATURAL EXPERIMENT

The natural or naturalistic experiment is "natural" in the sense that it makes investigative use of real-life, naturally occurring happenings as they unfold, without the imposition of any CONTROL or manipulation on the part of the researcher(s), and usually without any preconceived notions on what the research outcomes will be. In the social sciences, empirical inquiries of this kind make use of natural settings such as playgrounds, schools, workplaces, neighborhoods, communities, and people's homes. With their naturally occurring events, these contexts provide scope for social scientists to unobtrusively gather and then analyze experimental data making use of QUANTITATIVE RESEARCH and/or QUALITATIVE RESEARCH methods (e.g., IN-DEPTH INTERVIEWS, CASE STUDIES, OBSERVATIONS, QUESTIONNAIRES, ATTITUDE SCALES, ratings, test scores). Experiments of this kind study the effect of natural phenomena on the response/DEPENDENT VARIABLE.

The naturalistic experiment is often contrasted with LABORATORY EXPERIMENTS or FIELD EXPERIMENTS, where events under investigation are intentionally and systematically manipulated by the researcher. For example, the researcher introduces, withdraws, or manipulates some variables while holding others constant. But despite these differences, the two methodologies can complement each other, with the natural experiment helping to determine whether or not the outcomes of carefully controlled laboratory studies occur in real life (i.e., establishing EXTERNAL VALIDITY). On the other hand, indicative results may prompt more rigorous experimental work. Another merit of the natural experiment is that certain research may be undertaken only by using this approach, because experimental research would be unethical, too costly, or too difficult.

Potential weaknesses include problems to do with SAMPLING, limitations in generalizing results to wider populations, and problems in extrapolating causal inferences from data. Although sampling can be randomized in experimental research, it may be outside the researchers' control in the naturalistic experiment. Thus, researchers may be obliged to depend upon self-selection. In the St. Helena study (see Charlton, Gunter, & Hannan, 2002), for example, comparisons were made between viewers and nonviewers. Problems about whether findings can be generalized to other places, times, and people are also linked to sampling. Findings can be generalized only when there is evidence to suggest that the sample under scrutiny is a REPRESENTATIVE SAMPLE of the general population. Finally, causal inferences can be difficult to make unless controls are in place to show that other factors have not influenced results. For example, Cook, Campbell, and Peracchio (1990) talk of four general kinds of natural experimental research design, only one of which allows—but does not guarantee—causal inferences.

The study by Charlton et al. (2002) is an example of the naturalistic experiment. Researchers monitored children's behavior before and then for 5 years after the availability of broadcast television using a MULTIMETHOD research approach (observations, ratings, self-reports, questionnaires, FOCUS GROUP discussions, DIARIES, and CONTENT ANALYSIS) to take advantage of a naturally occurring event in order to assess television's impact upon viewers.

—Tony Charlton

REFERENCES

Charlton, T., Gunter, B., & Hannan, A. (2002). *Broadcast television effects in a remote community.* Hillsdale, NJ: Lawrence Erlbaum.

Cook, T. D., Campbell, D. T., & Peracchio, L. (1990). Quasi-experimentation. In M. D. Dunnette & L. M. Hough (Eds.), *Handbook of industrial and organisational psychology* (2nd ed., Vol. 1, pp. 491–576). Chicago: Rand McNally.

NATURALISM

The term is used in three different ways. *Philosophical naturalism* is the assertion that there is an objective, natural order in the world to which all things belong (see Papineau, 1993). It is, then, a denial of Cartesian dualism, which assumes a separation of physical things and mind. Philosophical naturalism usually implies materialism, that what we experience as mind can be accounted for materially (although it would be just as consistent with a naturalistic position to say all was reducible to mind). Philosophical naturalism is no more than metaphysical reasoning or speculation, but it underlies the most important version of naturalism, *scientific naturalism.*

SCIENTIFIC NATURALISM

Scientific naturalism spans a wide range of views. Some maintain that a unity of nature implies a unity of approach to investigating nature, and this is likely to entail the best methods of science currently available to us. At the other extreme is a much harder version of naturalism that embraces an extreme form of physicalism and reductionism. In this view, all phenomena are reducible to physical properties, and things such as the senses and moral values are simply epiphenomena.

Although natural scientists will place themselves at different points on such a continuum, almost by definition they are naturalists of some kind, but this is not always the case with those who study the social world and even call themselves social "scientists." If the ontological assumptions of naturalism are applied to the social world, then it must follow that the latter is continuous with, or arises from, the physical world (Williams, 2000, p. 49). Furthermore, if we are to explain the relation of humans to the world in terms of that order, with appropriate adaptations, scientific methods can be used to study the social world. This view underlies two of the most prominent approaches in social science, POSITIVISM and REALISM.

What kind of assumptions we can make about the world and the methods that follow from these assumptions divide realists in both the natural and the social sciences, but they are united in the belief that those things considered the proper outcomes of natural science—explanations and generalizations—are appropriate for social science. Naturalists do not deny that there are important differences in the way the social world (as compared to the physical world) manifests itself to other human beings, and it is accepted that this will produce methodological differences. However, it is argued, such differences already exist in natural science. Physicists, for example, use experimental methods, whereas astronomers use passive observational methods.

OBJECTIONS TO NATURALISM

There are a number of objections to naturalism from within both philosophy and social studies.

Antirationalists, such as postmodernists and those in the social studies of science, direct their attack not at the ontological claims of naturalism, but at science itself, claiming that it is "just one kind of conversation or one form of social organisation" (Kincaid, 1996, p. 8) and can claim no special epistemological privilege. This renders naturalism redundant, because it has no means by which it can demonstrate the existence of a natural order. However, the counterargument must come not from a defense of naturalism, but from scientific method itself (Williams, 2000, chap. 4).

A second argument against scientific naturalism is that it is tautological. Science is the only way we can know the natural order, and what counts as natural are those things discovered by science. Again, this can be answered only obliquely by maintaining that naturalism does not depend on any particular historical form science might take, only that form of science that provides the best approximation to the truth about puzzles of nature or society.

The most important objections to naturalism as a basis for study of the *social* world are methodological. Most of these are agnostic as to whether there is a "unity of nature," but instead focus on the way the social world manifests itself as a product of consciousness. It is said that the resulting feedback mechanisms produce an indeterminacy that renders impossible the identification of the regularities necessary for explanation and generalization. Therefore, studies of the social world cannot be scientific in the way that, say, physics or biology are. This claim leads to two broad methodological positions, although the first is something of an antimethodology: (a) science is the most reliable way to discover truths about the world, but unfortunately, social science is unable to be scientific, and it follows, therefore, that there can be no reliable route to knowledge of the social world; (b) the social world can be investigated, but it must be studied from a humanistic perspective that places emphasis on understanding rather than explanation.

There are a number of responses to the above methodological objections. The first is that naturalism and methodology are relatively independent of each other, because the natural sciences and different social sciences, or even research problems, will require different methods. For the most part, anthropology would not be well served by an explanatory survey, and, conversely, political polling would be impossible with ethnographic methods. Second, explanations and generalizations are just as possible in many areas of the social world as they are in any other complex system. They are likely to be probabilistic, but this is the case in many studies of the physical world (e.g., turbulence, genetic mutation, etc.). Third, some aspects of the social world will defy our efforts to know about them, but this is equally true in the physical world.

The debate about naturalism in social science is made difficult by its conflation with positivism. Critics of the latter position in social science have seen its particular conception of science as standing in for all scientific study of the social world. This conflation is problematic partly because it is misleading, but also because it ignores that although natural scientists are naturalists, they are often antipositivists.

NATURALISM IN ETHNOGRAPHY

The third use of the term *naturalism* is found in ethnography. This usage has nothing to do with the previous, older employment of the term and is indeed commonly used by humanists opposed to scientific naturalism. What might be termed *ethnographic naturalism* is the view that people create their own social realities from meanings, and to know those social realities, the researcher should minimize the amount of interference he or she makes in that reality while conducting research. This position is principally associated with SYMBOLIC INTERACTIONISM.

—Malcolm Williams

REFERENCES

Kincaid, H. (1996). *Philosophical foundations of the social sciences: Analyzing controversies in social research.* Cambridge, UK: Cambridge University Press.

Papineau, D. (1993). *Philosophical naturalism.* Oxford, UK: Basil Blackwell.

Williams, M. (2000). *Science and social science: An introduction.* London: Routledge.

NATURALISTIC INQUIRY

Research designs are naturalistic to the extent that the research takes place in real-world settings and the researcher does not attempt to manipulate the phenomenon of interest (e.g., a group, event, program, community, relationship, or interaction). The phenomenon of interest unfolds "naturally" in that it has no predetermined course established by and for the researcher such as would occur in a laboratory or other controlled setting. Observations take place in real-world settings, and people are interviewed with open-ended questions in places and under conditions that are comfortable for and familiar to them.

Egon Guba's (1978) classic treatise on naturalistic inquiry identified two dimensions along which types of scientific inquiry can be described: (a) the extent to which the scientist manipulates some phenomenon in advance in order to study it; and (b) the extent to which constraints are placed on outputs, that is, the extent to which *predetermined* categories or variables are used to describe the phenomenon under study. He then defined naturalistic inquiry as a discovery-oriented approach that minimizes investigator manipulation of the study setting and places no prior constraints on what the outcomes of the research will be. Naturalistic inquiry contrasts with controlled EXPERIMENTAL DESIGNS, where, ideally, the investigator controls study conditions by manipulating, changing, or holding constant external influences and where a limited set of outcome variables is measured. Open-ended, conversation-like interviews as a form of naturalistic inquiry contrast with questionnaires that have predetermined response categories.

In the simplest form of controlled experimental inquiry, the researcher gathers data at two points in time, pretest and posttest, and compares the treatment group to some control group on a limited set of standardized measures. Such designs assume a single, identifiable, isolated, and measurable treatment. Moreover, such designs assume that, once introduced, the treatment remains relatively constant and unchanging.

In program evaluation, for example, controlled experimental evaluation designs work best when it is possible to limit program adaptation and improvement so as not to interfere with the rigor of the research design. In contrast, under real-world conditions where programs are subject to change and redirection, naturalistic inquiry replaces the fixed treatment/outcome emphasis of the controlled experiment with a dynamic process orientation that documents actual operations and impacts of a process, program, or intervention over a period of time. The evaluator sets out to understand and document the day-to-day reality of participants in the program, making no attempt to manipulate, control, or eliminate situational variables or program developments, but accepts the complexity of a changing program reality. The data of the evaluation include whatever emerges as important to understanding what participants experience.

Natural experiments occur when the observer is present during a real-world change to document a phenomenon before and after the change. Natural experiments can involve comparing two groups, one of which experiences some change while the other does not. What makes such studies naturalistic is that real-world participants direct the changes, not the researcher, as in the laboratory.

However, the distinction is not as simple as being in the field versus being in the laboratory; rather, the degree to which a design is naturalistic falls along a continuum with completely open fieldwork on one end and completely controlled laboratory conditions on the other end, but with varying degrees of researcher control and manipulation between these endpoints. For example, the very presence of a researcher asking questions can be an intervention that reduces the natural unfolding of events. Or, in the case of a program evaluation, providing feedback to staff can be an intervention that reduces the natural unfolding of events. *Unobtrusive observations* are used as an inquiry strategy when the inquirer wants to minimize data collection as an intervention.

Alternative approaches to agricultural research illuminate the differences between controlled and naturalistic inquiries. In agricultural testing stations, field experiments are conducted in which researchers carefully vary an intervention with predetermined measures and rigorous controls, as in crop fertilizer studies. In contrast, naturalistic inquiry in agricultural research involves observing, documenting, and studying farmers' own "experiments" on their own farms, undertaken without researcher direction or interference.

Anthropologists engage in naturalistic inquiry when they do ethnographic fieldwork. Sociologists use naturalistic inquiry to do PARTICIPANT OBSERVATION studies in neighborhoods and organizations. Program evaluators employ naturalistic inquiry to observe how a program is being implemented by staff. Naturalistic inquiry is used by social scientists generally to study how social phenomena and human interactions unfold in real-world settings.

EMERGENT DESIGN FLEXIBILITY

Naturalistic inquiry designs cannot be completely specified in advance of fieldwork. Although the design will specify an initial focus, plans for observations, and initial guiding interview questions, the naturalistic and inductive nature of the inquiry makes it both impossible and inappropriate to specify operational variables, state testable hypotheses, finalize either instrumentation, or completely predetermine sampling approaches. A naturalistic design unfolds or emerges as fieldwork unfolds (Patton, 2002). Design flexibility stems from the open-ended nature of naturalistic inquiry.

—Michael Quinn Patton

REFERENCES

Guba, E. G. (1978). *Toward a methodology of naturalistic inquiry in educational evaluation.* CSE Monograph Series in Evaluation, No. 8. Los Angeles: Center for the Study of Evaluation, University of California, Los Angeles.

Patton, M. Q. (2002). *Qualitative research and evaluation methods.* Thousand Oaks, CA: Sage.

NEGATIVE BINOMIAL DISTRIBUTION

A PROBABILITY distribution is the full range of conceivable values that a RANDOM VARIABLE could take on, as well as the probabilities associated with those values. A random variable, Y, has a negative binomial probability distribution if its probability mass function (pmf) follows the form:

$$p(y) = \binom{y-1}{r-1} p^r q^{y-r},$$

$$y = r, r+1, r+2, \ldots, 0 \le p \le 1,$$

where p is the probability of success (occurrence of an event), q is the probability of failure (no occurrence of event), and r is the first success (occurrence). The data follow from a process that can have only two outcomes: success or failure (occurrence or non-occurrence). A random variable following a negative binomial distribution has the following mean and variance:

$$\mu = E(Y) = \left(\frac{r}{p}\right) \quad \text{and} \quad \sigma^2 = V(Y) = \frac{r(1-p)}{p^2}.$$

The type of REGRESSION model and underlying probability distribution on which you decide to base your estimates depends on the characteristics of the data. The principles that are used to derive the distribution parallel the principles (characteristics) of the data. When your data are of the event count form, certain characteristics are implicit, namely, that there is a lower bound of zero and that there is a finite number your observations may take. Such data cannot follow a NORMAL DISTRIBUTION. The POISSON REGRESSION model is often appropriate for such data.

However, in some situations, two fundamental assumptions of the Poisson do not hold, namely, that the data are independent and identically distributed. The negative binomial distribution generalizes the Poisson by relaxing these assumptions, which makes it a better distribution on which to base your estimates if you have reason to believe your observations are not independent or occurring constantly. To test whether the Poisson or the negative binomial is appropriate, it is necessary to check for under- and overdispersion of the Poisson regression. Overdispersion is present if the sample mean is larger than the variance of the dependent event count variable. The effect of overdispersion on standard errors and significance statistics is similar to HETEROSKEDASTICITY in OLS estimation.

The negative binomial regression model is useful if, for example, you are studying participation in protests. It is likely that one person's decision to participate is not entirely independent from another's; some members of a student political organization may be more prone to take part than those who are not affiliated with any political organizations. This is a situation of violating the Poisson assumption of independence. The second assumption is violated if you, say, studied the establishment of left-wing social movements over time. If the government of a country shifted from authoritarian to democratic, it is plausible that you would find an inconstant rate of occurrence—social movement development would be more restricted under the repressive regime than under the new government. This is obviously not restricted to the TIME SERIES case; the rate of occurrence may not, for example, be constant across states in cross-sectional analysis.

If you decide that the negative binomial regression model is appropriate for your data, keep in mind that you will have to identify the distribution of the rate of change (if you suspect inconsistency). This has the potential to be very difficult, and MISSPECIFICATION will lead to inaccurate PARAMETER ESTIMATES. If you do not have a theoretical basis on which to project a λ, you may consider using a generalized event count model.

—Christine Mahoney

REFERENCES

Cameron, A. C., & Trivedi, P. K. (1998). *Regression analysis of count data.* Cambridge, UK: Cambridge University Press.

King, G. (1998). *Unifying political methodology: The likelihood theory of statistical inference.* Ann Arbor: University of Michigan Press.

Long, J. S. (1997). *Regression models for categorical and limited dependent variables.* Thousand Oaks, CA: Sage.

NEGATIVE CASE

In qualitative analysis, data are usually grouped to form patterns (identified as constructs) with the expectation that there will be some degree of VARIATION within those patterns. However, either through the process of purposeful searching or by happenstance, it is possible to come across a case that does not fit within the pattern, however broadly the construct is defined. This case is usually referred to as a "negative case" because it seems contrary to the general pattern. For example, suppose one was studying caregivers of people with Alzheimer's disease, and one of

the constructs identified from the study is "emotional distress" (Khurana, 1995). All of the caregivers who are interviewed express some degree of emotional distress. However, as data gathering continues, the researcher happens upon a participant who expresses little, if any, distress. Coming across this one participant does not necessarily negate the general pattern, but the case does provide additional insight into the construct of "emotional distress."

Negative cases can serve as comparative cases enabling analysts to explain more clearly what a CONCEPT is and what it is not in terms of its properties (i.e., identify the boundaries of a concept). Negative cases can help delineate important conditions pertaining to a concept, for instance, enabling the researcher to explain why some people who are caregivers are more or less likely to develop emotional distress. They also enable analysts to extend or modify the original construct, possibly adding to its explanatory power. Negative cases can also lend a degree of VALIDITY to a study by demonstrating that the analyst is willing to consider alternatives and has indeed searched for other possible explanations (Miles & Huberman, 1994). Because social science research deals with human beings, one can expect that there will always be exceptions to every identified pattern (Patton, 1990).

Does one always discover negative cases when conducting research? The answer is that whether or not one discovers the negative case depends on how hard and how long one looks. At the same time, there are no set rules for how long one should continue the search for the "negative case" (Glaser & Strauss, 1967). There are always constraints on a research project in terms of time, money, and access to a population. However, a researcher should make a concerted effort to find the exceptions to the pattern and include reference to the search process when writing up the research; then, when and if such a case is discovered, he or she should bring the additional insights and alternative explanations into the discussion of findings. This will not only add to the credibility to the research but also enhance understanding of the phenomenon under investigation, benefiting participants and users of the research.

—Juliet M. Corbin

REFERENCES

Glaser, B., & Strauss, A. (1967). *The discovery of grounded theory.* Chicago: Aldine.

Khurana, B. (1995). *The older spouse caregiver: Paradox and pain of Alzheimer's disease.* Unpublished doctoral dissertation, Center for Psychological Studies, Albany, CA.

Miles, M. B., & Huberman, A. M. (1994). *Qualitative data analysis* (2nd ed.). Thousand Oaks, CA: Sage.

Patton, M. Q. (1990). *Qualitative evaluation and research methods* (2nd ed.). Newbury Park, CA: Sage.

NESTED DESIGN

Nested design is a research design in which levels of one factor (say, Factor *B*) are hierarchically subsumed under (or nested within) levels of another factor (say, Factor *A*). As a result, assessing the complete combination of *A* and *B* levels is not possible in a nested design. For example, one might wish to study the effect of Internet search strategies (Factor *A*) on college students' information-seeking efficiency (the dependent variable). Six classes of freshmen English at a state college are randomly selected; three classes are assigned to the "linear search" condition and the other three to the "nonlinear search" condition. Table 1 illustrates the research design.

Because freshmen enrolled in these classes form "intact groups," they cannot be randomly assigned to the two treatment conditions on an individual basis. Furthermore, their learning processes and behaviors are likely to be mutually dependent; differences in students' information-seeking behavior among classes are embedded within each treatment condition. This restriction makes this design a nested design rather than a fully crossed design, and the nested design is denoted as $B(A)$.

The statistical model assumed for the above nested design is

$$Y_{ijk} = \mu + \alpha_j + \beta_{k(j)} + \varepsilon_{i(jk)},$$
$$(i = 1, \ldots, n; j = 1, \ldots, p,$$
$$\text{and } k = 1, \ldots, q),$$

where

Y_{ijk} is the score of the ith observation in the jth level of Factor *A* and kth level of Factor *B*.

μ is the grand mean, therefore, a constant, of the population of observations.

α_j is the effect of the jth treatment condition of Factor *A*; algebraically, it equals the deviation of the population mean ($\mu_{.j}$) from the grand mean (μ). It is a constant for all observations' dependent score in the jth condition, subject to the restriction that all α_j sum to zero across all treatment conditions.

$\beta_{k(j)}$ is the effect for the kth treatment condition of Factor *B*, nested within the jth level of Factor *A*; algebraically, it equals the deviation of the population mean ($\mu_{jk.}$) in the kth and jth combined level from the grand mean (μ). It is a constant for all observations' dependent score in the kth condition, nested within Factor *A*'s jth condition. The effect is assumed to be normally distributed in its underlying population.

$\varepsilon_{i(jk)}$ is the random error effect associated with the ith observation in the jth condition of Factor A and kth condition of Factor *B*. It is a random variable that is normally distributed in the underlying population and is independent of $\beta_{k(j)}$.

Table 1

| | | Factor A Internet Search Strategy | | |
		Treatment 1 Linear Search Strategy	Treatment 2 Nonlinear Search Strategy	Row Mean
Factor B	*Class 1*	$\bar{Y}_{1(1)}$		$\bar{Y}_{.1}$
Freshman English Class	*Class 2*	$\bar{Y}_{2(1)}$		$\bar{Y}_{.2}$
	Class 3	$\bar{Y}_{3(1)}$		$\bar{Y}_{.3}$
	Class 4		$\bar{Y}_{4(2)}$	$\bar{Y}_{.4}$
	Class 5		$\bar{Y}_{5(2)}$	$\bar{Y}_{.5}$
	Class 6		$\bar{Y}_{6(2)}$	$\bar{Y}_{.6}$
	Column mean	$\bar{Y}_{1.}$	$\bar{Y}_{2.}$	Grand mean $= \bar{Y}_{...}$

Table 2

		Factor C Prior Experience With Internet	Factor A Internet Search Strategy — Treatment 1 Linear Search Strategy	Factor A Internet Search Strategy — Treatment 2 Nonlinear Search Strategy	Row Mean
Factor B Freshman English Class	Class 1	High	$\bar{Y}_{1(1)1}$		$\bar{Y}_{.1.}$
		Low	$\bar{Y}_{1(1)2}$		
	Class 2	High	$\bar{Y}_{2(1)1}$		$\bar{Y}_{.2.}$
		Low	$\bar{Y}_{2(1)2}$		
	Class 3	High	$\bar{Y}_{3(1)1}$		$\bar{Y}_{.3.}$
		Low	$\bar{Y}_{3(1)2}$		
	Class 4	High		$\bar{Y}_{4(2)1}$	$\bar{Y}_{.4.}$
		Low		$\bar{Y}_{4(2)2}$	
	Class 5	High		$\bar{Y}_{5(2)1}$	$\bar{Y}_{.5.}$
		Low		$\bar{Y}_{5(2)2}$	
	Class 6	High		$\bar{Y}_{6(2)1}$	$\bar{Y}_{.6.}$
		Low		$\bar{Y}_{6(2)2}$	
	Column mean		$\bar{Y}_{1..}$	$\bar{Y}_{2..}$	Grand mean = $\bar{Y}_{..}$

The example represents a balanced, completely randomized nested design. Each cell (i.e., the combination of A and B levels) has $n = 4$ observations; thus, the design is balanced. It is also completely randomized because observations are assigned randomly to levels (or conditions) of A, and no blocking variable is involved in this example. Additionally, if the researcher wishes to control for individual differences on a blocking variable such as "prior experience with Internet search," the design suitable for his or her research is the completely randomized block nested design. Table 2 explains the layout of this design and its difference from the completely randomized nested design.

Variations of the balanced, completely randomized nested design include the following: unbalanced nested design, balanced or unbalanced randomized block nested design, balanced or unbalanced randomized factorial nested design, and balanced or unbalanced randomized block factorial nested design. For details on these designs, readers should consult Kirk (1995) and Maxwell and Delaney (1990).

Nested design is alternatively called hierarchical design; it is used most often in QUASI-EXPERIMENTAL studies in which researchers have little or no control over random assignment of observations into treatment conditions. The design is popular, and sometimes necessary, among curriculum studies and clinical, sociological, and ethological research in which observations (units of analysis) belong to intact groups (such as classes, therapeutic groups, gangs, cages); these intact groups cannot be dismantled to allow for a random assignment of observations into different treatment conditions. Because of the nonindependence among units of observations in nested designs, methodologists have recommended using group means (i.e., class means in the example above) to perform statistical analyses. This recommendation proves to be restrictive, unnecessary, and less powerful than alternatives derived directly from individual data and proper statistical models (Hopkins, 1982). A better treatment of the interdependence among units of observation is to employ an efficient statistical modeling technique known as hierarchical linear modeling (HLM). In a typical educational setting in which students are taught in classrooms, classrooms are embedded within schools, and schools are embedded within school districts. HLM can model data at three levels: students at Level 1, classrooms at Level 2, and schools at Level 3. Each higher-level (say, Level 2) model takes into account the nested nature of data collected at a lower level (say, Level 1). Thus, the hierarchical nature of the data is completely and efficiently captured in HLM (Raudenbush & Bryk, 1988).

—Chao-Ying Joanne Peng

See also CROSS-SECTIONAL DESIGN

REFERENCES

Hopkins, K. D. (1982). The unit of analysis: Group means versus individual observations. *American Educational Research Journal, 19*(1), 5–18.

Huck, S. (2000). *Reading statistics and research* (3rd ed.). New York: Addison-Wesley Longman.

Kirk, R. E. (1995). *Experimental design: Procedures for the behavioral sciences* (3rd ed.). Belmont, CA: Brooks/Cole.

Kirk, R. E. (1999). *Statistics: An introduction* (4th ed.). Orlando, FL: Harcourt Brace.

Maxwell, S. E., & Delaney, H. D. (1990). *Designing experiments and analyzing data: A model comparison perspective.* Belmont, CA: Wadsworth.

Raudenbush, S. W., & Bryk, A. S. (1988). Methodological advances in analyzing the effects of schools and classrooms on student learning. *Review of Research in Education, 15,* 423–476.

NETWORK ANALYSIS

Network analysis is the interdisciplinary study of social relations and has roots in anthropology, sociology, psychology, and applied mathematics. It conceives of social structure in relational terms, and its most fundamental construct is that of a *social network,* comprising at the most basic level a set of *social actors* and a set of *relational ties* connecting pairs of these actors. A primary assumption is that social actors are interdependent and that the relational ties among them have important consequences for each social actor as well as for the larger social groupings that they comprise.

The *nodes* or *members* of the network can be groups or organizations as well as people. Network analysis involves a combination of theorizing, model building, and empirical research, including (possibly) sophisticated data analysis. The goal is to study network structure, often analyzed using such concepts as density, centrality, prestige, mutuality, and role. Social network data sets are occasionally multidimensional and/or longitudinal, and they often include information about *actor attributes*, such as actor age, gender, ethnicity, attitudes, and beliefs.

A basic premise of the social network paradigm is that knowledge about the structure of social relationships enriches explanations based on knowledge about the attributes of the actors alone. Whenever the social context of individual actors under study is relevant, relational information can be gathered and studied. Network analysis goes beyond measurements taken on individuals to analyze data on patterns of relational ties and to examine how the existence and functioning of such ties are constrained by the social networks in which individual actors are embedded. For example, one might measure the relations "communicate with," "live near," "feel hostility toward," and "go to for social support" on a group of workers. Some network analyses are longitudinal, viewing changing social structure as an outcome of underlying processes. Others link individuals to events (affiliation networks), such as a set of individuals participating in a set of community activities.

Network structure can be studied at many different levels: the dyad, triad, subgroup, or even the entire network. Furthermore, network theories can be postulated at a variety of different levels. Although this multilevel aspect of network analysis allows different structural questions to be posed and studied simultaneously, it usually requires the use of methods that go beyond the standard approach of treating each individual as an independent unit of analysis. This is especially true for studying a *complete* or whole network: a census of a well-defined population of social actors in which all ties, of various types, among all the actors are measured. Such analyses might study structural balance in small groups, transitive flows of information through indirect ties, structural equivalence in organizations, or patterns of relations in a set of organizations.

For example, network analysis allows a researcher to model the interdependencies of organization members. The paradigm provides concepts, theories, and methods to investigate how informal organizational structures intersect with formal bureaucratic structures in the unfolding flow of work-related actions of organizational members and in their evolving sets of knowledge and beliefs. Hence, it has informed many of the topics of organizational behavior, such as leadership, attitudes, work roles, turnover, and computer-supported cooperative work.

HISTORICAL BACKGROUND

Network analysis has developed out of several research traditions, including (a) the birth of sociometry in the 1930s spawned by the work of the psychiatrist Jacob L. Moreno; (b) ethnographic efforts in the 1950s and 1960s to understand migrations from tribal villages to polyglot cities, especially the research of A. R. Radcliffe-Brown; (c) survey research since the 1950s to describe the nature of personal communities, social support, and social mobilization; and (d) archival analysis to understand the structure of interorganizational and international ties. Also noteworthy is the work of Claude Lévi-Strauss, who was the first to introduce formal notions of kinship, thereby leading to a mathematical algebraic theory of relations, and the work of Anatol Rapoport, perhaps the first to propose an elaborate statistical model of relational ties and flow through various nodes.

Highlights of the field include the adoption of sophisticated mathematical models, especially discrete mathematics and graph theory, in the 1940s and 1950s. Concepts such as transitivity, structural equivalence, the strength of weak ties, and centrality arose from network research by James A. Davis, Samuel Leinhardt, Paul Holland, Harrison White, Mark Granovetter, and Linton Freeman in the 1960s and 1970s. Despite the separateness of these many research beginnings, the field grew and was drawn together in the 1970s by formulations in graph theory and advances in computing. Network analysis, as a distinct research endeavor, was born in the early 1970s. Noteworthy in its birth are the pioneering text by Harary, Norman, and Cartwright (1965); the appearance in the late 1970s of network analysis software, much of it arising at the University of California, Irvine; and annual conferences of network analysts, now sponsored by the International Network for Social Network Analysis. These well-known "Sunbelt" Social Network Conferences now draw as many as 400 international participants. A number of fields, such as organizational science, have experienced rapid growth through the adoption of a network perspective.

Over the years, the social network analytic perspective has been used to gain increased understanding of many diverse phenomena in the social and behavioral sciences, including (taken from Wasserman & Faust, 1994)

- Occupational mobility
- Urbanization
- World political and economic systems
- Community elite decision making
- Social support
- Community psychology
- Group problem solving
- Diffusion and adoption of information
- Corporate interlocking
- Belief systems
- Social cognition
- Markets
- Sociology of science
- Exchange and power
- Consensus and social influence
- Coalition formation

In addition, it offers the potential to understand many contemporary issues, including

- The Internet
- Knowledge and distributed intelligence
- Computer-mediated communication
- Terrorism
- Metabolic systems
- Health, illness, and epidemiology, especially of HIV

Before a discussion of the details of various network research methods, we mention in passing a number of important measurement approaches.

MEASUREMENT

Complete Networks

In complete network studies, a census of network ties is taken for all members of a prespecified population of network members. A variety of methods may be used to observe the network ties (e.g., survey, archival, participant observation), and observations may be made on a number of different types of network tie. Studies of complete networks are often appropriate when it is desirable to understand the action of network members in terms of their location in a broader social system (e.g., their centrality in the network, or more generally in terms of their patterns of connections to other network members). Likewise, it may be necessary to observe a complete network when properties of the network as a whole are of interest (e.g., its degree of centralization, fragmentation, or connectedness).

Ego-Centered Networks

The size and scope of complete networks generally preclude the study of all the ties and possibly all the nodes in a large, possibly unbounded population. To study such phenomena, researchers often use survey research to study a sample of personal networks (often called *ego-centered* or *local* networks). These smaller networks consist of the set of specified ties that links *focal persons* (or *egos*) at the centers of these networks to a set of close "associates" or *alters*. Such studies focus on an ego's ties and on ties among ego's alters. Ego-centered networks can include relations such as kinship, weak ties, frequent contact, and provision of emotional or instrumental aid. These relations can be characterized by their variety, content, strength, and structure. Thus, analysts might study network member *composition* (such as the percentage of women providing social or emotional support, for example, or basic actor attributes more generally); network characteristics (e.g., percentage of dyads that are mutual); measures of *relational association* (do strong ties with immediate kin also imply supportive relationships?); and network structure (how densely knit are various relations? do actors cluster in any meaningful way?).

SNOWBALL SAMPLING AND LINK TRACING STUDIES

Another possibility, to study large networks, is simply to sample nodes or ties. Sampling theory for networks contains a small number of important results (e.g., estimation of subgraphs or subcomponents; many originated with Ove Frank) as well as a number of unique techniques or strategies such as snowball sampling, in which a number of nodes are sampled, then those linked to this original sample are sampled, and so forth, in a multistage process. In a link-tracing sampling design, emphasis is on the links rather than the actors—a set of social links is followed from one respondent to another. For hard-to-access or hidden populations, such designs are considered the most practical way to obtain a sample of nodes.

COGNITIVE SOCIAL STRUCTURES

Social network studies of *social cognition* investigate how individual network actors perceive the ties of others and the social structures in which they are contained. Such studies often involve the measurement of multiple perspectives on a network, for instance, by observing each network member's view of who is tied to whom in the network. David Krackhardt referred to the resulting data arrays as *cognitive social structures*. Research has focused on clarifying the various ways in which social cognition may be related to network locations: (a) People's positions in social structures may determine the specific information to which they are exposed, and hence, their perception; (b) structural position may be related to characteristic patterns of social interactions; (c) structural position may frame social cognitions by affecting people's perceptions of their social locales.

METHODS

Social network analysts have developed methods and tools for the study of relational data. The techniques include graph theoretic methods developed by mathematicians (many of which involve counting various types of subgraphs); algebraic models popularized by mathematical sociologists and psychologists; and statistical models, which include the social relations model from social psychology and the recent family of random graphs first introduced into the network literature by Ove Frank and David Strauss. Software packages to fit these models are widely available.

Exciting recent developments in network methods have occurred in the statistical arena and reflect the increasing theoretical focus in the social and behavioral sciences on the interdependence of social actors in dynamic, network-based social settings. Therefore, a growing importance has been accorded the problem of constructing theoretically and empirically plausible parametric models for structural network phenomena and their changes over time. Substantial advances in statistical computing are now allowing researchers to more easily fit these more complex models to data.

SOME NOTATION

In the simplest case, network studies involve a single type of directed or nondirected tie measured for all pairs of a node set $N = \{1, 2, \ldots, n\}$ of individual actors. The observed tie linking node i to node j $(i, j \in N)$ can be denoted by x_{ij} and is often defined to take the value 1 if the tie is observed to be present and 0 otherwise. The network may be either *directed* (in which case x_{ij} and x_{ji} are distinguished and may take different values) or *nondirected* (in which case x_{ij} and x_{ji} are not distinguished and are necessarily equal in value). Other cases of interest include the following:

1. *Valued* networks, where x_{ij} takes values in the set $\{0, 1, \ldots, C - 1\}$.
2. *Time-dependent* networks, where x_{ijt} represents the tie from node i to node j at time t.
3. *Multiple relational* or *multivariate* networks, where x_{ijk} represents the tie of type k from node i to node j (with $k \in R = \{1, 2, \ldots, r\}$, a fixed set of *types* of tie).

In most of the statistical literature on network methods, the set N is regarded as fixed and the network ties are assumed to be random. In this case, the tie linking node i to node j may be denoted by the random variable X_{ij} and the $n \times n$ array $X = [X_{ij}]$ of random variables can be regarded as the adjacency matrix of a *random (directed) graph* on N. The state space of all possible realizations of these arrays is Ω_n. The array $x = [x_{ij}]$ denotes a realization of X.

GRAPH THEORETIC TECHNIQUES

Graph theory has played a critical role in the development of network analysis. Graph theoretical techniques underlie approaches to understanding cohesiveness, connectedness, and fragmentation in networks. Fundamental measures of a network include its *density* (the proportion of possible ties in the network that are actually observed) and the degree sequence of its nodes. In a nondirected network, the *degree* d_i of node i is the number of distinct nodes to which node i is connected ($d_i = \Sigma_{j \in N} x_{ij}$). In a directed network, sequences of *indegrees* ($\Sigma_{j \in N} x_{ji}$) and *outdegrees* ($\Sigma_{j \in N} x_{ij}$) are of interest. Methods for characterizing and identifying cohesive subsets in a network have depended on the notion of a *clique* (a subgraph of network nodes, every pair of which is connected) as well as on a variety of generalizations (including k-clique, k-plex, k-core, LS-set, and k-connected subgraph).

Our understanding of connectedness, connectivity, and centralization is also informed by the distribution of path lengths in a network. A *path* of length k from one node i to another node j is defined by a sequence $i = i_1, i_2, \ldots, i_{k+1} = j$ of distinct nodes such that i_h and i_{h+1} are connected by a network tie. If there is no path from i to j of length $n - 1$ or less, then j is not reachable from i and the distance from i to j is said to be infinite; otherwise, the distance from i to j is the length of the shortest path from i to j. A directed network is *strongly connected* if each node is reachable from each other node; it is *weakly connected* if, for every pair of nodes, at least one of the pair is reachable from the other. For nondirected networks, a network is connected if each node is reachable from each other node, and the *connectivity,* κ, is the least number of nodes whose removal results in a disconnected (or trivial) subgraph.

Graphs that contain many cohesive subsets as well as short paths, on average, are often termed *small world* networks, following early work by Stanley Milgram, and more recent work by Duncan Watts. Characterizations of the centrality of each actor in the network are typically based on the actor's degree (*degree* centrality), on the lengths of paths from the actor to all other actors (*closeness* centrality), or on the extent to which the shortest paths between other actors pass through the given actor (*betweenness* centrality). Measures of network *centralization* signify the extent of heterogeneity among actors in these different forms of centrality.

ALGEBRAIC TECHNIQUES

Closely related to graph theoretic approaches is a collection of algebraic techniques that has been developed to understand social roles and structural regularities in networks. Characterizations of role have developed in terms of mappings on networks, and descriptions of structural regularities have been facilitated by the construction of algebras among labeled network walks. An important proposition about what it means for two actors to have the same social role is embedded in the notion of *structural equivalence:* Two actors are said to be *structurally equivalent* if they relate to and are related by every other network actor in exactly the same way (thus, nodes i and j are structurally equivalent if, for all $k \in N$, $x_{ik} = x_{jk}$ and $x_{ki} = x_{kj}$). Generalizations to automorphic and regular equivalence are based on more general mappings on N and capture the notion that similarly positioned network nodes are related to *similar* others in the same way.

Approaches to describing structural regularities in multiple networks have grown out of earlier characterizations of structure in kinship systems, and can be defined in terms of labeled walks in multiple networks. Two nodes i and j are connected by a labeled *walk* of type $k_1 k_2 \cdots k_h$ if there is a sequence of nodes $i = i_1, i_2, \ldots, i_{h+1} = j$ such that i_q is connected to i_{q+1} by a tie of type k_q (note that the nodes in the sequence need not all be distinct, so that a walk is a more general construction than a path). Each sequence $k_1 k_2 \cdots k_h$ of tie labels defines a derived network whose ties signify the presence of labeled walks of that specified type among pairs of network nodes. Equality and ordering relations among these derived networks lead to various algebraic structures (including *semigroups* and partially ordered semigroups) and describe observed regularities in the structure of walks and paths in the multiple network. For example, *transitivity* in a directed network with ties of type k is a form of structural regularity associated with the observation that walks of type kk link two nodes only if the nodes are also linked by a walk of type k.

STATISTICAL TECHNIQUES

A simple statistical model for a (directed) graph assumes a BERNOULLI distribution, in which each edge, or tie, is statistically independent of all others and governed by a theoretical probability P_{ij}. In addition to edge independence, simplified versions also assume equal probabilities across ties; other versions allow the probabilities to depend on structural parameters. These distributions often have been used as models for at least 40 years, but are of questionable utility because of the independence assumption.

Dyadic Structure in Networks

Statistical models for social network phenomena have been developed from their edge-independent beginnings in a number of major ways. The p_1 model recognized the theoretical and empirical importance

of dyadic structure in social networks, that is, of the interdependence of the variables x_{ij} and x_{ji}. This class of Bernoulli dyad distributions and their generalization to valued, multivariate, and time-dependent forms gave parametric expression to ideas of reciprocity and exchange in dyads and their development over time. The model assumes that each dyad (x_{ij}, x_{ji}) is independent of every other and, in a commonly constrained form, specifies

$$
\begin{aligned}
P(X = x) \\
= \pi_{i<j} \exp \Bigg[\lambda_{ij} + \theta \left(\sum_{i<j} x_{ij} \right) + \rho \left(\sum_{i<j} x_{ij} x_{ji} \right) \\
+ \alpha_i \left(\sum_j x_{ij} \right) + \beta_j \left(\sum_i x_{ij} x_{ji} \right) \Bigg],
\end{aligned}
$$

(1)

where θ is a density parameter, ρ is a reciprocity parameter, the parameters α_i and β_j reflect individual differences in expansiveness and popularity, and λ_{ij} ensures that probabilities for each dyad sum to 1. This is a LOG-LINEAR MODEL and easily fit. Generalizations of this model are numerous, and include *stochastic block models,* representing hypotheses about the interdependence of social positions and the patterning of network ties; mixed models, such as p_2; and *latent space models* for networks.

Null Models for Networks

The assumption of dyadic independence is questionable. Thus, another series of developments has been motivated by the problem of assessing the degree and nature of departures from simple structural assumptions like dyadic independence. A number of *conditional uniform* random graph distributions were introduced as null models for exploring the structural features of social networks. These distributions, denoted by $U|Q$, are defined over subsets Q of the state space Ω_n of directed graphs and assign equal probability to each member of Q. The subset Q is usually chosen to have some specified set of properties (e.g., a fixed number of mutual, asymmetric, and null dyads). When Q is equal to Ω_n, the distribution is referred to as the *uniform* (di)graph distribution, and is equivalent to a Bernoulli distribution with homogeneous tie probabilities. Enumeration of the members of Q and simulation of $U|Q$ are often straightforward, although certain cases, such as the distribution that is conditional on the indegree and outdegree of each node i in the network, require more complicated approaches.

A typical application of these distributions is to assess whether the occurrence of certain higher-order (e.g., triadic) features in an observed network is unusual, given the assumption that the data arose from a uniform distribution that is conditional on plausible lower-order (e.g., dyadic) features. This general approach has also been developed for the analysis of multiple networks. The best known example is probably Frank Baker and Larry Hubert's Quadratic Assignment Procedure (QAP) for networks. In this case, the association between two graphs defined on the same set of nodes is assessed using a uniform multigraph distribution that is conditional on the unlabeled graph structure of each constituent graph.

Extradyadic Local Structure in Networks

A significant step in the development of parametric statistical models for social networks was taken by Frank and Strauss (1986) with the introduction of the class of *Markov random graphs*. This class of models permitted the parameterization of extradyadic local structural forms and so allowed a more explicit link between some important theoretical propositions and statistical network models. These models are based on the fact that the Hammersley-Clifford theorem provides a general probability distribution for X from a specification of which pairs (X_{ij}, X_{k1}) of tie random variables are conditionally dependent, given the values of all other random variables.

Specifically, define a *dependence graph* $\mathbf{D}$ with node set $N(\mathbf{D}) = \{(X_{ij}: i, j \in N, i \neq j)\}$ and edge set $E(\mathbf{D}) = \{(X_{ij}, X_{k1}): X_{ij} \text{ and } X_{k1} \text{ are assumed to be}$ conditionally dependent, given the rest of $X\}$. Frank and Strauss used $\mathbf{D}$ to obtain a model for $\Pr(X = x)$, denoted p^* by later researchers, in terms of parameters and substructures corresponding to cliques of $\mathbf{D}$. The model has the form

$$\Pr(X = x) = p^*(x)$$

$$= (1/c) \exp \left[\sum_{P \supseteq N(D)} \alpha_P z_P(x) \right], \quad (2)$$

where

1. The summation is over all cliques P of $\mathbf{D}$ [with a *clique* of $\mathbf{D}$ defined as a nonempty subset P of $N(\mathbf{D})$ such that $|P| = 1$ or $(X_{ij}, X_{k1}) \in E(\mathbf{D})$ for all $X_{ij}, X_{k1} \in P$].
2. $z_P(x) = \Pi_{X_{ij} \in P} x_{ij}$ is the (observed) *network statistic* corresponding to the clique P of $\mathbf{D}$
3. $c = \sum_{\mathbf{x}} \exp \left\{ \sum_P \alpha_P z_P(x) \right\}$ is a *normalizing* quantity.

One possible dependence assumption is Markov, in which $(X_{ij}, X_{k1}) \in E(\mathbf{D})$ whenever $\{i, j\} \cap \{k, l\} \neq \varnothing$. This assumption implies that the occurrence of a network tie from one node to another is conditionally dependent on the presence or absence of other ties in a *local neighborhood* of the tie. A Markovian local neighborhood for X_{ij} comprises all possible ties involving i and/or j. Many other dependence assumptions are also possible, and the task of identifying appropriate dependence assumptions in any modeling venture poses a significant theoretical challenge.

These random graph models permit the parameterization of many important ideas about local structure in univariate social networks, including transitivity, local clustering, degree variability, and centralization. Valued, multiple, and temporal generalizations also lead to parameterizations of substantively interesting multirelational concepts, such as those associated with balance and clusterability, generalized transitivity and exchange, and the strength of weak ties. Pseudo-maximum likelihood estimation is easy; maximum likelihood estimation is difficult, but not impossible.

Dynamic Models

A significant challenge is to develop models for the emergence of network phenomena, including the evolution of networks and the unfolding of individual actions (e.g., voting, attitude change, decision making) and interpersonal transactions (e.g., patterns of communication or interpersonal exchange) in the context of long-standing relational ties. Early attempts to model the evolution of networks in either discrete or continuous time assumed dyad independence and Markov processes in time. A step toward continuous time MARKOV CHAIN models for network evolution that relaxes the assumption of dyad independence has been taken by Tom Snijders and colleagues. This approach also illustrates the potentially valuable role of simulation techniques for models that make empirically plausible assumptions; clearly, such methods provide a promising focus for future development. Computational models based on simulations are becoming increasingly popular in network analysis; however, the development of associated model evaluation approaches poses a significant challenge.

Current research (as of 2003), including future challenges, such as statistical estimation of complex model parameters, model evaluation, and dynamic statistical models for longitudinal data, can be found in Carrington, Scott, and Wasserman (2003). Applications of the techniques and definitions mentioned here can be found in Scott (1992) and Wasserman and Faust (1994).

—Stanley Wasserman and Philippa Pattison

AUTHOR'S NOTE: Research supported by the U.S. Office of Naval Research and the Australian Research Council.

REFERENCES

Boyd, J. P. (1990). *Social semigroups: A unified theory of scaling and blockmodeling as applied to social networks.* Fairfax, VA: George Mason University Press.

Carrington, P. J., Scott, J., & Wasserman, S. (Eds.). (2003). *Models and methods in social network analysis.* New York: Cambridge University Press.

Frank, O., & Strauss, D. (1986). Markov graphs. *Journal of the American Statistical Association, 81,* 832–842.

Friedkin, N. (1998). *A structural theory of social influence.* New York: Cambridge University Press.

Harary, F., Norman, D., & Cartwright, D. (1965). *Structural models for directed graphs.* New York: Free Press.

Monge, P., & Contractor, N. (2003). *Theories of communication networks.* New York: Oxford University Press.

Pattison, P. E. (1993). *Algebraic models for social networks.* New York: Cambridge University Press.

Scott, J. (1992). *Social network analysis.* London: Sage.

Wasserman, S., & Faust, K. (1994). *Social network analysis: Methods and applications.* New York: Cambridge University Press.

Wasserman, S., & Galaskiewicz, J. (Eds.). (1994). *Advances in social network analysis.* Thousand Oaks, CA: Sage.

Watts, D. (1999). *Small worlds: The dynamics of networks between order and randomness.* Princeton, NJ: Princeton University Press.

Wellman, B., & Berkowitz, S. D. (Eds.). (1997). *Social structures: A network approach* (updated ed.). Greenwich, CT: JAI.

NEURAL NETWORK

Neural networks are adaptive statistical models based on an analogy with the structure of the brain. They are *adaptive* because they can learn to estimate the PARAMETERS of some population using a small number of exemplars (one or a few) at a time. They do not differ *essentially* from standard statistical MODELS. For example, one can find neural network architectures akin to DISCRIMINANT ANALYSIS, PRINCIPAL COMPONENTS ANALYSIS, LOGISTIC REGRESSION, and other techniques. In fact, the same mathematical tools can be used to analyze standard statistical models and neural networks. Neural networks are used as *statistical tools* in a variety of fields, including psychology, statistics, engineering, econometrics, and even physics. They are used also as *models* of cognitive processes by neuro- and cognitive scientists.

Basically, neural networks are built from simple units, sometimes called *neurons* or cells by analogy with the real thing. These units are linked by a set of weighted connections. Learning is usually accomplished by modification of the connection weights. Each unit CODES or corresponds to a feature or a characteristic of a pattern that we want to analyze or that we want to use as a PREDICTOR VARIABLE.

These networks usually organize their units into several layers. The first layer is called the *input* layer, and the last one is the *output* layer. The intermediate layers (if any) are called the *hidden* layers. The information to be analyzed is fed to the neurons of the first layer and then propagated to the neurons of the second layer for further processing. The result of this processing is then propagated to the next layer and so on until the last layer. Each unit receives some information from other units (or from the external world through some devices) and processes this information, which will be converted into the output of the unit.

The goal of the network is to learn or to discover some association between input and output patterns, or to analyze, or to find the structure of the input patterns. The learning process is achieved through the modification of the connection weights between units. In statistical terms, this is equivalent to interpreting the value of the connections between units as parameters (e.g., like the values of a and b in the REGRESSION equation $y = a + bx$) to be estimated. The learning process specifies the "ALGORITHM" used to estimate the parameters.

THE BUILDING BLOCKS OF NEURAL NETWORKS

Neural networks are made of basic units (see Figure 1) arranged in layers. A unit collects information provided by other units (or by the external world) to which it is connected with *weighted* connections called *synapses.* These weights, called *synaptic weights,* multiply (i.e., amplify or attenuate) the input information: A positive weight is considered excitatory, a negative weight inhibitory.

Each of these units is a simplified model of a neuron and transforms its input information into an output response. This transformation involves two steps: First, the activation of the neuron is computed as the weighted sum of its inputs, and second, this activation is transformed into a response by using a *transfer* function. Formally, if each input is denoted x_i, and each weight w_i, then the activation is equal to $a = \Sigma x_i w_i$, and the output, denoted o, is obtained as $o = f(a)$. Any function whose domain is real numbers can be used as a transfer function. The most popular ones are the linear function ($o \propto a$); the step function (activation values less than a given threshold are set to 0 or to -1 and the other values are set to $+1$); the logistic function $\left[f(x) = \frac{1}{1+\exp\{-x\}} \right]$, which maps the real numbers into the interval $[-1 +1]$ and whose derivative, needed for learning, is easily computed $\{f'(x) = f(x)[1 - f(x)]\}$; and the normal or Gaussian function $[o = (\sigma\sqrt{2\pi})^{-1} \times \exp\{-\frac{1}{2}(a/\sigma)^2\}]$. Some of these functions can include

probabilistic variations; for example, a neuron can transform its activation into the response $+1$ with a probability of $\frac{1}{2}$ when the activation is larger than a given threshold.

The architecture (i.e., the pattern of connectivity) of the network, along with the transfer functions used by the neurons and the synaptic weights, completely specify the behavior of the network.

LEARNING RULES

Neural networks are adaptive statistical devices. This means that they can change iteratively the values of their parameters (i.e., the synaptic weights) as a function of their performance. These changes are made according to *learning rules,* which can be characterized as *supervised* (when a desired output is known and used to compute an error signal) or *unsupervised* (when no such error signal is used).

The Widrow-Hoff (also called the gradient descent or delta rule) is the most widely known supervised learning rule. It uses the difference between the actual input of the cell and the desired output as an error signal for units in the output layer. Units in the hidden layers cannot compute directly their error signal, but they estimate it as a function (e.g., a weighted average) of the error of the units in the following layer. This adaptation of the Widrow-Hoff learning rule is known as *error backpropagation.* With Widrow-Hoff learning, the correction to the synaptic weights is proportional to the error signal multiplied by the value of the activation given by the derivative of the transfer function. Using the derivative has the effect of making finely tuned corrections when the activation is near its extreme values (minimum or maximum) and larger corrections when the activation is in its middle range. Each correction has the immediate effect of making the error signal *smaller* if a similar input is applied to the unit. In general, supervised learning rules implement optimization algorithms akin to *descent* techniques because they search for a set of values for the free parameters (i.e., the synaptic weights) of the system such that some error function computed for the whole network is minimized.

The Hebbian rule is the most widely known unsupervised learning rule. It is based on work by the Canadian neuropsychologist Donald Hebb, who theorized that neuronal learning (i.e., synaptic change) is a local phenomenon expressible in terms of the temporal correlation between the activation values of neurons. The

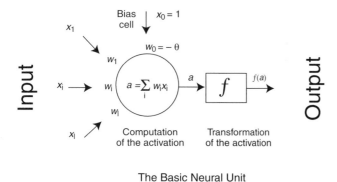

The Basic Neural Unit

Figure 1   The Basic Neural Unit Processes the Input Information Into the Output Information

synaptic change depends on both the presynaptic and activities and states that the change in a synaptic weight is a function of the temporal correlation between the presynaptic and postsynaptic activities. Specifically, the value of the synaptic weight between two neurons increases whenever they are in the same state and decreases when they are in different states.

SOME IMPORTANT NEURAL NETWORK ARCHITECTURE

One the most popular architectures in neural networks is the *multilayer perceptron* (see Figure 2). Most of the networks with this architecture use the Widrow-Hoff rule as their learning algorithm and the logistic function as the transfer function of the units of the hidden layer (the transfer function is, in general, nonlinear for these neurons). These networks are very popular because they can approximate any multivariate function relating the input to the output. In a statistical framework, these networks are akin to MULTIVARIATE NONLINEAR REGRESSION. When the input patterns are the same as the output patterns, these networks are called *auto-associators.* They are closely related to linear (if the hidden units are linear) or nonlinear (if not) PRINCIPAL COMPONENT ANALYSIS and other statistical techniques linked to the GENERAL LINEAR MODEL (see Abdi, Valentin, Edelman, & O'Toole, 1996), such as DISCRIMINANT ANALYSIS or CORRESPONDENCE ANALYSIS.

A recent development generalizes the *radial basis function* (RBF) networks (see Abdi, Valentin, & Edelman, 1999) and integrates them with *statistical learning theory* (see Vapnik, 1999) under the name of *support vector machine* or SVM (see Schölkopf & Smola, 2003). In these networks, the hidden units (called the support vectors) represent possible (or even real) input patterns, and their response is a function of their similarity to the input pattern under consideration. The similarity is evaluated by a *kernel* function (e.g.,

dot product; in the radial basis function, the kernel is the Gaussian transformation of the Euclidean distance between the support vector and the input). In the specific case of RBF networks—which we will use as an example of SVM—the output of the units of the hidden layers are connected to an output layer composed of linear units. In fact, these networks work by breaking the difficult problem of a nonlinear approximation into two more simple ones. The first step is a simple nonlinear mapping (the Gaussian transformation of the distance from the kernel to the input pattern), and the second step corresponds to a linear transformation from the hidden layer to the output layer. Learning occurs at the level of the output layer. The main difficulty with these architectures resides in the choice of the support vectors and the specific kernels to use. These networks are used for pattern recognition, classification, and clustering data.

VALIDATION

From a statistical point of view, neural networks represent a class of nonparametric adaptive models. In this framework, an important issue is to evaluate the performance of the model. This is done by separating the data into two sets: the training set and the testing set. The parameters (i.e., the value of the synaptic weights) of the network are computed using the training set. Then, learning is stopped and the network is evaluated with the data from the testing set. This cross-validation approach is akin to BOOTSTRAPPING or the JACKKNIFE METHOD.

USEFUL REFERENCES

Neural network theory connects several domains from the neurosciences to engineering, including statistical theory. This diversity of sources also creates a real heterogeneity in the presentation of the material, because textbooks often try to address only one portion of the interested readership. The following references should be helpful to the reader interested in the statistical properties of neural networks: Abdi et al. (1999), Bishop (1995), Cherkassky and Mulier (1998), Duda, Hart, and Stork (2001), Hastie, Tibshirani, and Friedman (2001), Looney (1997), Ripley (1996), and Vapnik (1999).

—Hervé Abdi

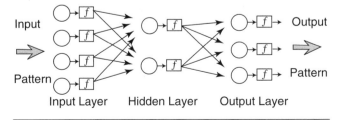

Figure 2 A Multilayer Perceptron

REFERENCES

Abdi, H., Valentin, D., & Edelman, B. (1999). *Neural networks.* Thousand Oaks, CA: Sage.

Abdi, H., Valentin, D., Edelman, B., & O'Toole, A. J. (1996). A Widrow-Hoff learning rule for a generalization of the linear auto-associator. *Journal of Mathematical Psychology, 40,* 175–182.

Bishop, C. M. (1995). *Neural networks for pattern recognition.* Oxford, UK: Oxford University Press.

Cherkassky, V., & Mulier, F. (1998). *Learning from data.* New York: Wiley.

Duda, R., Hart, P. E., & Stork, D. G. (2001). *Pattern classification.* New York: Wiley.

Hastie, T., Tibshirani, R., & Friedman, J. (2001). *The elements of statistical learning.* New York: Springer-Verlag

Looney, C. G. (1997). *Pattern recognition using neural networks.* Oxford, UK: Oxford University Press.

Ripley, B. D. (1996). *Pattern recognition and neural networks.* Cambridge, UK: Cambridge University Press.

Schölkopf, B., & Smola, A. J. (2003). *Learning with kernel.* Cambridge: MIT Press.

Vapnik, V. N. (1999). *Statistical learning theory.* New York: Wiley.

NOMINAL VARIABLE

This variable is simply a categorization of cases. It allows us to show that the cases are different in terms of the categories, and no more than that. For example, unlike an ordinal variable, we are not able to rank order the categories in any way. An example of a nominal variable is the voting behavior of a sample. We can classify members of the sample in terms of the political party for which they voted at the most recent election, but we cannot infer any more about the differences between people in terms of that classification.

—Alan Bryman

See also ATTRIBUTE, CATEGORICAL, DISCRETE

NOMOTHETIC. *See*
NOMOTHETIC/IDIOGRAPHIC

NOMOTHETIC/IDEOGRAPHIC

The distinction between nomothetic, which pertains to the construction of general models and laws in science, and ideographic, which is concerned with the detailed understanding of particular circumstances, was proposed by Wilhelm Windleband in 1894 (Smith, 1998, pp. 141–142). Although intended to demarcate the natural (nomothetic) from the cultural (ideographic) sciences, the positioning of the demarcation, and even whether one can talk of such, has been controversial ever since.

Windleband held that although all science and knowledge referred to the same reality, different disciplines will have distinct concerns and view reality accordingly. Although this was not an assertion of a divide between "mind" and "matter" (see NATURALISM), he nevertheless thought that, in practice, there is a divide between the cultural world—produced by autonomous, self-reflecting human agents—and the physical world. The latter may be known objectively by human observers, but the social world must be studied subjectively through a strategy of interpretation.

The debates of the mid to late 20th century between INTERPRETIVISTS and POSITIVISTS have their origins in Windleband's distinction, although ironically, one of the best arguments for a fluidity of any divide between the nomothetic and ideographic comes from one of the key figures in interpretivist social science, Max Weber (1975). He saw the distinction not as a scientific versus nonscientific mode of inquiry; rather, he saw both as forms of scientific inquiry. The former Weber equates with abstract generalizations, as in law-like statements. The second he regarded as a science of concrete reality, of specific instances.

If one takes Weber's view, then virtually all of the sciences, natural and social, have both nomothetic and ideographic characteristics, and their forms of inquiry reflect this. Astronomers, for example, will provide detailed individual descriptions of particular bodies, but explain them in the context of abstract generalizations about wider phenomena. Likewise, an interpretation of a specific human interaction will require a contextualization within a wider social setting. The latter requires at least some form of taxonomy and idealization that can be grounded in ideographic interpretation and description. A statistical claim such as "20% of pensioners lived in poverty" can tell us nothing about any given individual pensioner, only pensioners in the abstract, yet the description "poverty" is likely to have been derived from an examination of specific, individual cases of poverty.

The maintenance of a clear divide has been challenged from another direction, that of the philosophy and sociology of natural science. Windleband's original distinction, and, to an extent, Weber's redefinition, left untouched the positivistic view of natural science as value free and phenomenalist. However, since the Popper-Kuhn "revolution" of the early 1960s (see Lakatos & Musgrave, 1965), most accept that, at least to some degree, subjectivity must enter natural science through moral positioning, theory choice, and observation. Finally, in recent years, complex approaches to understanding physical and social systems (see Byrne, 1998) have emphasized the ontological continuities and similarities between such systems and consequently have raised objections to the epistemological and methodological divide of the kind proposed by Windleband.

—Malcolm Williams

REFERENCES

Byrne, D. (1998). *Complexity theory and the social sciences: An introduction.* London: Routledge.

Lakatos, I., & Musgrave, A. (Eds.). (1970). *Criticism and the growth of knowledge.* Cambridge, UK: Cambridge University Press.

Smith, M. (1998). *Social science in question.* London: Sage.

Weber, M. (1975). *Roscher and Knies.* New York: Free Press.

NONADDITIVE

Nonadditive is a term used to describe a function that relates one set of scores (e.g., scores on a variable, Y) to two or more other sets of scores (e.g., scores on variables X_1 and X_2). The relationship between Y and the other variables is said to be additive if Y can be expressed as a sum of those other variables. The sum can be a weighted sum and has the general expression

$$Y = a + w_1X_1 + w_2X_2 + \cdots + w_kX_k,$$

where a and the various ws are constants.

In some applications, restrictions are placed on the constants. For example, if $a = 0$ and each weight is set to 1.0, then Y is literally the sum of the X variables. Another type of restriction that a researcher might apply is that the weights must sum to 1.0 in accordance with the formulation

$$w_j = c_j \Big/ \sum c_j,$$

where c_j is an absolute weight for variable X_j. The summation is across the k weights. As an example,

suppose that Y is an additive function of X_1 and X_2, and that $a = 0$, $c_1 = 1$, and $c_2 = 1$. Then, $w_1 = 1/(1 + 1) = 0.50$, and $w_2 = 1/(1 + 1) = 0.50$, yielding

$$Y = 0 + 0.50X_1 + 0.50X_2.$$

Note that this expression is equivalent to

$$Y = (X_1 + X_2)/2,$$

so that Y is the average of X_1 and X_2. This example shows that expressing Y as an average of a set of variables is a type of additive function.

A nonadditive function is one where Y cannot be expressed as a (weighted) sum of the other variables. Nonadditive functions can take many forms—indeed, there is an infinite number of such functions. An example of a nonadditive function is a MULTIPLICATIVE function, where Y is said to equal the product of two variables, X_1 and X_2.

Traditional MULTIPLE REGRESSION ANALYSIS is based on an additive model,

$$Y = \alpha + \beta_1X_1 + \beta_2X_2 + \cdots + \beta_kX_k,$$

where α is the intercept and the various βs are the REGRESSION COEFFICIENTS.

—James J. Jaccard

REFERENCE

Anderson, N. H. (1981). *Methods of information integration theory.* New York: Academic Press.

NONLINEAR DYNAMICS

Nonlinear dynamics refers to a broad range of behavior that can occur with many varieties of mathematical models that are structured with respect to time. Nonlinear dynamics can occur with both linear and nonlinear algebraic specifications, as with $dy/dt = ay$ or $dy/dt = ay^2$, respectively, where the parameter "a" is a constant. Minimally, the basic idea is that change occurs over time with respect to one or more variables such that this change cannot be represented as a straight line on a graph that places time on the horizontal axis. More specifically, nonlinear variation is change that does not follow an incremental pattern in which the same increment of change recurs with every sequential and equally spaced change in time. The most frequent uses of the term *nonlinear dynamics* refer to more complex situations in which phenomena with longitudinal change are modeled using nonlinear algebraic formulations (often involving systems of interdependent equations with more than one variable) that either implicitly or explicitly reference time. A thorough mathematical introduction to nonlinear dynamics as it appears in both linear and nonlinear mathematical specifications can be found in Hirsch and Smale (1974). Treatments and examples of this same subject matter from a social science perspective can be found in Brown (1995a, 1995b, 1991).

In the physical and natural sciences, nonlinear dynamics is normally encountered using continuous-time differential equation model specifications, which is a consequence of the continuous-time processes of change that are naturally encountered in these fields. Exceptions are not rare, however, especially in the biological sciences, in which generational or seasonal changes are the focus of study. In those cases, difference equation approaches are sometimes employed. In the social sciences, nonlinear dynamics is often modeled using discrete-time difference equation structures, almost always due to the manner in which social scientific data are collected (e.g., periodic elections, decade-spaced census reports, periodically spaced survey data, etc.). Exceptions do occur here as well, and the technical difficulties involved in using continuous-time models with discretely measured data sets as are commonly encountered in the social sciences now have clear solutions (e.g., see Brown, 1995b). The choice of using a continuous- or discrete-time approach to modeling social phenomena has substantive consequences that can be important in certain settings, and a discussion of these substantive consequences can be found in Brown (1995b, pp. 13–30).

Nonlinear dynamics is normally described in terms of the following processes of change: regular, periodic, chaotic, and catastrophe. A regular process begins with a bifurcation, or a point in which a new process of change begins that differs structurally from a previous process of change. This bifurcation is followed by growth that normally experiences positive feedback and that later changes to negative feedback as the growth process slows. The classic example of a regular process involving nonlinear dynamics is the logistic equation $dy/dt = ay(k - y)$, where growth in the variable y continues smoothly as its values asymptotically approach the equilibrium value k. In the

neighborhood of an equilibrium, the growth process eventually approaches zero net change. Because of other processes of change that are temporarily external to this regular process, the regular process eventually becomes "ripe" for experiencing another bifurcation, which can lead to the initiation of a new process of change that can be any of the four listed above (including a new regular process).

A periodic process is one in which the values of the relevant variables recur at specified intervals. Periodic processes normally have periodic limit cycles, as compared with fixed-point equilibria that are typically associated with regular processes. A chaotic process (see CHAOS THEORY) differs from a periodic process in that changes in the values of the relevant variables never recur exactly, and this lack of repetition is not a consequence of a stochastic element. Chaotic processes often exhibit dramatically diverse variations in variable values. Thus, chaotic processes lack periodic limit cycles, although variable variations typically "hover" within an identifiable neighborhood of an unstable equilibrium (a "strange attractor").

Catastrophe processes (see CATASTROPHE THEORY) experience sudden and dramatic changes that depart from previously existing dynamic processes. An earthquake is an obvious candidate for a phenomenon that can be modeled as a catastrophe process because incremental (i.e., regular process) changes in the positions of tectonic plates eventually lead to a sudden departure from a previously established, pressure-defined equilibrium. In essence, a catastrophe process is such that the previously dominant equilibrium and its basin disappears, and a new equilibrium and its basin becomes dominant for the dynamical system. Examples of catastrophe models using social scientific data can be found in Brown (1995a, 1995b).

—Courtney Brown

REFERENCES

Brown, C. (1995a). *Chaos and catastrophe theories.* Thousand Oaks, CA: Sage.

Brown, C. (1995b). *Serpents in the sand: Essays on the nonlinear nature of politics and human destiny.* Ann Arbor: University of Michigan Press.

Brown, C. (1991). *Ballots of tumult: A portrait of volatility in American voting.* Ann Arbor: University of Michigan Press.

Hirsch, M. W., & Smale, S. (1974). *Differential equations, dynamical systems, and linear algebra.* New York: Academic Press.

NONLINEARITY

Nonlinearity refers to a RELATIONSHIP between two or more variables that is not linear. A nonlinear relationship *cannot* be represented by a line in two dimensions or by a plane in three dimensions. A linear relationship, for two variables Y and X, is defined by the equation for a line, $Y = a + bX$, where a and b are the intercept and slope coefficients, respectively. However, in the social sciences, relationships are rarely deterministic and usually are specified in a REGRESSION model that includes an error term to account for unexplained variation in Y. The equation for a two-variable LINEAR REGRESSION model, specifying a linear relationship between Y and X_1 with the error term ε, and the intercept and slope PARAMETERS β_0 and β_1, is $Y = \beta_0 + \beta_1 X_1 + \varepsilon$. The general form of a MULTIVARIATE linear regression model is $Y = \beta_0 + \beta_1 X_1 + \beta_2 X_2 + \cdots + \beta_k X_k + \varepsilon$, which specifies a linear relationship between each X and Y if other Xs are held constant.

Nonlinearity in regression models is any other pattern of relationship *not* defined by these linear MODELS. Therefore, nonlinearity can take many forms. It may be curvilinear, represented by a quadratic polynomial, $Y = \beta_0 + \beta_1 X_1 + \beta_2 X_2^2 + \varepsilon$, or a cubic polynomial, $Y = \beta_0 + \beta_1 X_1 + \beta_2 X_2^2 + \beta_3 X_3^3 + \varepsilon$. It may involve transcendental FUNCTIONS such as natural LOGARITHMS (ln) (e.g., $Y = \beta_0 + \beta_1 X_1 + \beta_2 \ln X_2 + \varepsilon$), or exponentials ($e$) (e.g., $Y = \beta_0 e^{\beta_1 X_1} + \varepsilon$). It may be MULTIPLICATIVE, such as this LOG-LINEAR MODEL, $Y = \beta_0 X_1^{\beta_1} X_2^{\beta_2}, \ldots, X_k^{\beta_k} e^{\varepsilon}$.

It is important to differentiate between nonlinear models that are "intrinsically linear" and those that are "intrinsically nonlinear." Intrinsically linear models are nonlinear models that can be reduced to linear models by means of TRANSFORMATIONS on Y and/or the Xs. This amounts to simply substituting the transformed variables for the original variables into a linear regression model. Common intrinsically linear models and their linearizing transformations are reported in Table 1.

A nonlinear model that is intrinsically linear is nonlinear with respect to the variables but linear with respect to the PARAMETERs to be estimated. In contrast, intrinsically nonlinear models are nonlinear with respect to the variables and the parameters. Once transformed, the parameters of intrinsically linear models can be estimated using ORDINARY LEAST SQUARES (OLS). Intrinsically nonlinear models, on the other hand, require more elaborate techniques for estimating the parameters. Often, they do not have unique parameter estimates that minimize the SUM OF SQUARED ERRORS (SSE), as in OLS. Instead, the parameters are estimated iteratively through a series of improved guesses.

As demonstrated in Table 1, the nonlinear model, $Y = \beta_0 e^{\beta_1 X_1} \varepsilon$, can be linearized by taking natural logarithms of both sides, $\ln Y' = \ln \beta_0 + \beta_1 X_1 + \ln \varepsilon$. However, if the nonlinear model assumes an additive error term instead of a multiplicative error term, $Y = \beta_0 e^{\beta_1 X_1} + \varepsilon$, the model cannot be linearized and must be estimated with nonlinear techniques instead of OLS. Another common example of an intrinsically nonlinear model is the LOGISTIC REGRESSION model with a BINARY outcome variable,

$$Y = \frac{1}{1 + e^{-(\beta_0 + \beta_1 X_1 + \cdots + \beta_k X_k)}} + \varepsilon.$$

—Jani S. Little

Table 1 Linearizing Transformations for Nonlinear Models

Nonlinear Form	Transformation(s) to Linearize	Linear Form
$Y = \beta_0 + \beta_1 X_1^2 + \varepsilon$	$X_1' = X_1^2$	$Y = \beta_0 + \beta_1 X_1' + \varepsilon$
$Y = \beta_0 + \beta_1 \ln X_1 + \varepsilon$	$X_1' = \ln X_1$	$Y = \beta_0 + \beta_1 X_1' + \varepsilon$
$Y = \beta_0 e^{\beta_1 X_1} \varepsilon$	$Y' = \ln Y$	$Y' = \beta_0' + \beta_1 X_1 + \varepsilon'$
	$\beta_0' = \ln \beta_0$	
	$\varepsilon' = \ln \varepsilon$	
$Y = \beta_0 X_1^{\beta_1} X_2^{\beta_2} e^{\varepsilon}$	$Y' = \ln Y$	$Y' = \beta_0' + \beta_1 X_1' + \beta_2 X_2' + \varepsilon$
	$\beta_0' = \ln \beta_0$	
	$X_1' = \ln X_1$	
	$X_2' = \ln X_2$	

REFERENCES

Devore, J. L. (1991). *Probability and statistics for engineering and the sciences* (3rd ed.). Pacific Grove, CA: Brooks/Cole.

Greene, W. H. (2000). *Econometric analysis* (4th ed.). Upper Saddle River, NJ: Prentice Hall.

Hamilton, L. C. (1992). *Regression with graphics: A second course in applied statistics.* Pacific Grove, CA: Brooks/Cole.

Kmenta, J. (1986). *Elements of econometrics* (2nd ed.). New York: Macmillan.

NONPARAMETRIC RANDOM-EFFECTS MODEL

Random-effects modeling is one of the several alternative approaches to deal with dependent observations such as those that occur in repeated measures or multilevel data structures. Nonparametric random effects models differ from standard (parametric) random effects models in that no assumptions are made about the distribution of the random effects. Actually, this is a form of LATENT CLASS ANALYSIS: The mixing distribution is modeled by means of a finite mixture structure. Early references to the nonparametric approach are Laird (1978) and Heckman and Singer (1982).

Let y_{ij} denote the response variable of interest, where the index j refers to a group and i to a replication within a group. Note that with repeated measures, groups and replications refer to individuals and time points. It is easiest to explain the random effects models within a GENERALIZED LINEAR MODELING framework; that is, to assume that the response variable comes from a distribution belonging to the exponential family and that the expectation of y_{ij}, $E(y_{ij})$, is modeled via a linear function after an appropriate transformation $g[\cdot]$.

A simple random intercept model without predictors has the following form:

$$g[E(y_{ij})] = \alpha_j.$$

To utilize a parametric approach, a distributional form is specified for α_j, typically normal: $\alpha_j \sim N(\mu, \tau^2)$. The unknown parameters to be estimated are the mean, μ, and the variance, τ^2. An equivalent parameterization is $g[E(y_{ij})] = \mu + \tau u_j$, with $u_j \sim N(0, 1)$.

A nonparametric approach characterizes the distribution of α_j by an unspecified discrete mixing distribution with C nodes (latent classes), where a particular latent class (LC) is enumerated by x, $x = 1, 2, \ldots, C$. The intercept associated with class x is denoted by α_x and the size of class x by $P(x)$. The α_x and $P(x)$ are sometimes referred to as the location and weight of node x. The nonparametric model can be specified as follows:

$$g[E(y_{ij}|x)] = \alpha_x.$$

The nonparametric maximum likelihood estimator is obtained by increasing the number of latent classes until a saturation point is reached. In practice, however, researchers prefer solutions with less than the maximum number of classes.

The similarity between the parametric and nonparametric approaches becomes clear when one realizes that the α_x and $P(x)$ parameters can be used to compute the mean (μ) and the variance (τ^2) of the random effects, which are the unknown parameters in the parametric approach. Using elementary statistics, we get $\mu = \sum_{x=1}^{C} \alpha_x P(x)$ and $\tau^2 = \sum_{x=1}^{C} (\alpha_x - \mu)^2 P(x)$.

A more general model is obtained by including predictors z_{ijk}, yielding a two-level regression model with a random intercept:

$$g[E(y_{ij}|\mathbf{z}_{ij}, x)] = \alpha_x + \sum_{k=1}^{K} \beta_k z_{ijk}.$$

A special case is the (semiparametric) Rasch model, which is obtained by adding a dummy predictor for each replication i.

Also, the regression coefficient can be allowed to differ across latent classes, which is analogous to having random slopes in a MULTILEVEL ANALYSIS. This yields

$$g[E(y_{ij}|\mathbf{z}_{ij}, x)] = \alpha_x + \sum_{k=1}^{K} \beta_{kx} z_{ijk},$$

a model that is often referred to as a latent class (LC) or mixture regression model. In fact, this is one of the most important applications of latent class analysis: Unobserved subgroups are identified that differ with respect to the parameters of the regression model of interest.

Two computer programs for estimating LC regression models are GLIMMIX and Latent GOLD.

—Jeroen K. Vermunt and Jay Magidson

REFERENCES

Heckman, J. J., & Singer, B. (1982). Population heterogeneity in demographic models. In K. Land & A. Rogers (Eds.), *Multidimensional mathematical demography.* New York: Academic Press.

Laird, N. (1978). Nonparametric maximum likelihood estimation of a mixture distribution. *Journal of the American Statistical Association, 73,* 805–811.

Lindsay, B., Clogg, C. C., & Grego, J. (1991). Semiparametric estimation in the Rasch model and related models, including a simple latent class model for item analysis. *Journal of the American Statistical Association, 86,* 96–107.

Wedel, M., & DeSarbo, W. S. (1994). A review of recent developments in latent class regression models. In R. P. Bagozzi (Ed.), *Advanced methods of marketing research* (pp. 352–388). Cambridge, UK: Basil Blackwell.

NONPARAMETRIC REGRESSION.

See LOCAL REGRESSION

NONPARAMETRIC STATISTICS

Experimental, QUASI-EXPERIMENTAL, ex post facto, and correlation designs often generate results that are not continuous data (INTERVAL or ratio), but nominal or ordinal data instead. Thus, parametric statistics are not the appropriate tools to resolve the hypotheses or describe associations between variables. There is a need for tests and measures that basically do not have all the constraints of parametric ones, some for which there are no demands for continuous data, or NORMAL DISTRIBUTIONS for this data (thus, they are sometimes described as "distribution-free"). Also, there is a need for tests where group characteristics are nominal, the data consisting of the frequency of subjects having specified traits. Not surprisingly, these are referred to as nonparametric tests, and they are appropriate for analyzing nominal and rank/ordinal data in order to make inferences about POPULATIONS based upon REPRESENTATIVE SAMPLES.

NATURE OF DATA AND SOURCES

Nonparametric tests do have some requirements of their own, and their disadvantage is that their use is more likely to incur a TYPE II ERROR than a

Table 1 Criteria for Choosing Between Parametric and Nonparametric Tests

Parametric	Nonparametric
Continuous data (scores), and	Nominal data (frequencies in categories), or
Normal distributions for all groups	Ordinal data (ranks), or Non-normal distributions of continuous data

parallel parametric test. They are often rated against comparable parametric tests in terms of *power efficiency.* Siegel and Castellan (1988) describe a test that has a power efficiency of 90%: "When all the conditions of the parametric statistical test are satisfied the appropriate parametric test would be just as effective with a sample which is 10% smaller than that used in the non-parametric analysis" (p. 36). Thus, one could conceivably replace parametric tests with nonparametric counterparts by degrading the data from continuous to ranks, but at a cost to the power of the test. Table 1 summarizes the requirements for the two types of statistics.

Having noted some of the differences between parametric and nonparametric tests and the limitations of the latter, it is worth noting the advantages of using them. To summarize Siegel and Castellan (1988), the advantages are that such tests

1. Are applicable to small samples where the underlying distribution is not known.
2. May be more appropriate for the research question.
3. Contend with ranked data.
4. Contend with categorical (nominal) data.

TESTS OF SIGNIFICANT DIFFERENCE

Research designs often wish to determine whether the differences between two groups (or three or more groups) is greater than what could be attributed to natural variation. In other words, no matter how random a set of samples is from a population, the samples will not all be the same. When they are too different, they are not considered part of the same population. Although this is reasonably easy to understand when comparing means for scores for groups of subjects using parametric tests, it can be more difficult to comprehend with nonparametric counterparts, and they do not follow a

Table 2   Comparing Some Typical Parametric and Nonparametric Tests of Significance

| | | *Independent Variables or Groups* | | | |
| | | *Two Groups* | | *Three Groups* | |
Measure of Dependent Variable	*One-Sample*	*Independent*	*Related/ Matched*	*Independent*	*Related/ Matched*
Interval/Ratio	z-test	t-tests	$t_{related}$-test	One-way ANOVA	Randomized block ANOVA
Ordinal	t-test ($n < 30$) Kolmogorov-Smirnov test	Mann-Whitney U-test	Wilcoxon signed ranks test	Factorial ANOVA Kruskal-Wallis one-way analysis of variance	ANCOVA Friedman two-way analysis of variance by ranks
Nominal	χ^2-test, goodness-of-fit	χ^2-test, $k \times 2$ tables	McNemar change test	χ^2-test for $m \times k$ tables	Cochran Q-test

Table 3   Contrasting Some Typical Parametric and Nonparametric Measures of Correlation and Association

| | | | *Nominal* | |
	Interval/Ratio	*Ordinal*	$m \geq 2$	$m = 2$
Interval/Ratio	Pearson product moment, r_{xy} (linear relationship). If nonlinear, monotonic: both reduced to ordinal	(Interval/ratio variable reduced to ordinal) ↓		Point biserial, r_{pb}
Ordinal		Spearman's rho, r_s (linear relationship)	(Ordinal variable reduced to nomial) ↓	
Nominal $k \geq 2$			Cramer's C (V, ϕ_c)	
$k = 2$				Phi, ϕ (dichotomies)

common theme. The differences of interest for these tests typically can be differences in

- *Proportions* or frequencies in categories of samples as compared to what would be expected (e.g., is the proportion of male to female nurses consistent with the national pattern?)
- *Distribution* of values as compared to what would be expected (e.g., salaries of different groups of employees compared to medians)
- *Order* or sequence of discrete events (e.g., are they really random?)

The number and variety of tests are considerable (see Siegel & Castellan, 1988, and Gibbons & Chakraborti, 1992, which have comprehensive coverage of tests), and Table 2 illustrates the roles of a variety in contrast with their parametric counterparts. If there is a need

to test whether a sample is typical of all samples that could be drawn from a population, the analogue to the z-test for ordinal data (ranks) is the KOLMOGOROV-SMIRNOV TEST, and for nominal data (frequencies for categories), it is the chi-square goodness-of-fit test. In both cases, population data are needed with which to compare the sample data. Similarly, there are analogues to the t-tests for two groups to test whether they belong to the same population. For ordinal data, the MANN-WHITNEY U-TEST will compare two unrelated groups, and for nominal data, the chi-square test for two groups will resolve the hypotheses. For related or matched groups, the corresponding test to the t-test for related groups is the Wilcoxon signed ranks test, and for nominal data, it is MCNEMAR'S CHI-SQUARE TEST (sometimes referred to as the McNemar change test). As can be seen from Table 3, there are similar analogues for three and more groups as well.

DESCRIPTORS OF CORRELATION AND ASSOCIATION

The results of surveys of single groups often endeavor to describe correlations (continuous and ordinal data) or associations (nominal) between pairs of variables. The statistic that is most appropriate depends on the nature of the data and, in this case, how each of the variables is measured, as shown in Table 3. If they are both the same (e.g., both are continuous), then it is a straightforward decision: the Pearson product moment correlation. But if they are not the same, then the choice is determined by the *lowest*. For example, if one variable was age (continuous) and the second was social class (ordinal), then the age data would have to be considered ordinal (ages changed to ranks) and the Spearman's rho would be most appropriate (see Table 3).

AN EXAMPLE OF A COMPARISON BETWEEN PARAMETRIC AND NONPARAMETRIC TESTS

Although the type of data is the ultimate determining factor in the choice between parametric and nonparametric tests, it is worth considering the types of research questions nonparametric tests can resolve and what the differences are between these and the ones answered by parametric tests. Sometimes, the questions may have to be changed because of the nature of the data that can be collected. To illustrate the issue, an example will be presented contrasting the use of parametric and nonparametric tests.

Two common tests will be used in an example to illustrate the basic differences: the *t*-test and chi-square or χ^2. The latter is used primarily with nominal data, but is sometimes used with ordinal data where frequencies of ranked categories are used, due to its simplicity, although it may increase slightly the probability of making a Type II error.

Imagine the situation in which the research question asked whether there was a difference between two groups in the conservativeness of their political views. If the study were to use, say, an instrument on strength of conservative political views and generate a score for each person, then the means scores of the two groups could be compared to see if there were a difference using the *t*-test. On the other hand, if one were to record which party each group said they voted for in a recent election, assuming one party were identifiably conservative, then the frequency of voters for each party for each group constitutes the data. To resolve the difference in voting patterns for the two groups, the χ^2-test would be appropriate. But note that two different questions are being answered:

- Is there a difference in voting patterns between the two groups?
- Is there a difference in level of conservatism between the two groups?

Thus, one must be aware that the type of data collected may influence what question is being answered. In both cases, one might wish to infer whether there is a difference in conservatism between the two groups, but only the first really answers that question. We will come back to a numerical example of this question, but let us first look at some examples of nonparametric tests that are parallel to the *z*-test and *t*-test.

WHICH TO USE: *T*-TEST OR CHI-SQUARE?

This question was raised at the beginning of the entry. As was noted, the most obvious criteria for deciding the answer to this question are based upon the type of data collected to answer a research question. For example, if the question were

Is there a difference in how conservative patrons of two English pubs are?

then we would have to look at what data were used to answer the question. Simply put, if the data were scores from a random sample of patrons that would meet the criteria in the left column of Table 1, then the parametric *t*-test would be appropriate. But if the sample of patrons was classified into categories from more to less conservative, and frequencies belonging to each category tallied, then the data would require the nonparametric chi-square test.

To be more specific, let us map out two answers to the question by elaborating on two ways the variable could be operationally defined. We could define "how conservative" by designing a purpose-made test that would give a score relative to the level of conservatism and then administer it to patrons. Alternatively, we could take the view that action speaks louder than words and simply ask them which party they voted for (or would vote for) in an election, where the three main British political parties (at least in the past) have espoused political philosophies from conservative to socialist. Following the two lines of logic results in

Table 4   An Example of Two Ways to Ostensibly Answer the Same Question: "Is There a Difference in How Conservative Patrons of Two Pubs Are?"

Parametric	Nonparametric
Are patrons of one pub more conservative than another?	Do the patrons of two pubs vote along different party lines?
Questionnaire (20 questions, 5 point scale) as a measure of "conservatism." The higher the score, the more conservative a person is. Individual score range: 20–100.	How many voted for (or would vote for) each of the political parties represented in local elections (frequencies for each party).
Compare mean scores for each pub with a t-test.	Compare voting frequencies for the two pubs using chi-square.

two different tests, as outlined in Table 4, and, logically following, the two statistical tests.

We can even illustrate the results with hypothetical data to show what could be the kind of outcomes in each case (we could use a more sensitive test for ordinal data, but the results would be much the same). This is shown in Table 5, with sample data for each of the two approaches. This raises a question about the measurements of the variable "conservatism": Are they really measuring the same thing with two different instruments? Or, could there be other components or factors that might influence the outcomes of either instrument that may distort their responses? Who is asking the question? This is where the arguments begin.

The researcher using the questionnaire on conservatism could maintain that the instrument is independent of *who* is running for office, the argument being that personality may encourage or discourage voters regardless of their political affiliation, and the choice of parties may not validly reflect how conservative a voter is. Although it might be argued that Conservatives are most conservative, Liberal Democrats are in between, and Labour voters are least conservative, for some specific issues and candidates, such a distinction is not valid and these are not strictly in order. Yet the researcher asking patrons to indicate which party they will vote for claims that this avoids abstractions and gets them to commit their beliefs to action, focusing on party and ideological commitment. What becomes apparent is that the tests are definitely appropriate for the data collected, but there is an issue as to which is most appropriate to answer the research question. In other words, the greatest potential for disagreement lies with the choice of OPERATIONAL DEFINITION (i.e., instrument) as a logical extension of the research question, and *not* with the choice of statistical test!

HISTORY

The brief history of nonparametric tests is highlighted by the developers and publication dates of selected tests (drawn from references in Howell, 2002; Kerlinger & Lee, 2000; Siegel & Castellan, 1988). This starts with Karl Pearson, who developed the chi-square test around 1900; the chi-square test is sometimes referred to as Pearson's chi-square. Milton Friedman, later best known as an economist, devised his two-way analysis of variance for ranked data for related samples in 1937. A. Kolmogorov developed tests of ordinal data for goodness of fit for single samples and for comparing two independent samples about 1941,

Table 5   Data and Results for the Example of Two Ways to Ostensibly Answer the Same Question: "Is There a Difference in Political Persuasion for Patrons of Two Pubs?"

	Parametric			Nonparametric		
	Green Toad	Red Herring			Green Toad	Red Herring
Mean	78	68	Conservative		35	20
Standard Deviation	22	24	Liberal Democrats		33	36
Number	87	76	Labour		19	20
			Total		87	76

$t = 2.76$ ($p < .05$)

∴ Reject H_0: There probably is a difference in level of conservatism.

$\chi^2 = 3.52$ (n.s.)

∴ Accept H_0: There is probably no difference in voting patterns.

and N. V. Smirnov published a table for the test in 1948. Wilcoxon (in 1945) and Mann and Whitney (in 1947) proposed other tests of two independent samples for ordinal data that are equivalent. W. H. Kruskal and W. A. Wallis proposed their one-way analysis of variance test for ordinal data in 1952. Quinn McNemar outlined his sign test for two related nominal groups in 1969.

—Thomas R. Black

REFERENCES

Black, T. R. (1999). *Doing quantitative research in the social sciences: An integrated approach to research design, measurement, and statistics.* London: Sage.

Bradley, J. V. (1985). *Distribution-free statistical tests.* Englewood Cliffs, NJ: Prentice Hall.

Gibbons, J. D., & Chakraborti, S. (1992). *Nonparametric statistical inference* (3rd ed.). New York: Marcel Dekker.

Howell, D. C. (2002). *Statistical methods for psychology* (5th ed.). Pacific Grove, CA: Duxbury.

Kerlinger, F. N., & Lee, H. B. (2000). *Foundations of behavioral research.* Ft. Worth, TX: Harcourt.

Siegel, S., & Castellan, N. J. (1988). *Nonparametric statistics for the behavioral sciences.* New York: McGraw-Hill.

NONPARTICIPANT OBSERVATION

Observation-based research that is conducted without subjects' awareness of being studied is often known as nonparticipant, unobtrusive, or nonreactive research. Two forms of nonparticipant observation, disguised observation and NATURAL EXPERIMENTS, in which permission is not sought, were once acceptable but are no longer ethically viable because they violate the principles of INFORMED CONSENT. Other styles of unobtrusive methodology, however, remain in the repertoire of sociologists, cultural anthropologists, and social psychologists.

Behavior trace studies, ARCHIVAL RESEARCH, and CONTENT ANALYSIS are three commonly used unobtrusive methods, although they do not consistently require the researcher to be involved in on-site observation of actual behavior. Researchers who use UNOBTRUSIVE METHODS with a strong component of on-site observation tend to rely on the systematic recording of data, often with the use of precoded checklists. Because they cannot verify their interpretations by asking informants questions about their behaviors, they must be especially careful to record their data in the most objective way possible. They must also be sure to

report their findings in aggregated ways so as not to compromise inadvertently the privacy of individuals whose identity might be revealed. When such observations are carried out by multiple researchers at multiple sites, care must be taken to ensure that data are recorded in a consistent fashion.

Nonparticipant observation is especially important when the subject is one about which participants might not be forthcoming when asked direct questions (e.g., covert behavior, such as the ways adolescents flirt with one another, or behavior in which the researcher cannot legally or ethically participate, such as drug use). Nonparticipant observation has been used in a variety of ETHNOGRAPHIC studies, for example, to characterize nonverbal communications (i.e., to understand how people use spatial arrangements or body gestures) or to describe the ways in which people make purchasing choices (but not to analyze the reasons behind their decisions). For example, Price (1989) studied the behaviors of customers in two urban pharmacies in Ecuador. She wanted to find out if any prescription drugs were being bought without prescriptions, and she was able to determine, after observing more than 600 sales transactions, that 51% of purchases were for prescription drugs for which the buyer had no prescriptions. She also learned that in such cases, pharmacy customers bought capsules in very small quantities (two or three pills at a time). In addition, Price unexpectedly learned that pharmacists (and even untrained drugstore clerks) were major purveyors of medical advice, especially for lower-class customers, who typically had limited access to physicians.

Richard Lee's (1993) widely cited study of the !Kung San people of southern Africa focused on food sources and the composition of diet. He set out to measure the distance people walked from camp to the gathering or hunting sites. He also calculated the weight of nuts collected or animals killed per hour of labor, the average caloric intake from both plant and animal resources, the number of different foods consumed, and the social relationships of those who shared foods of different types. On the basis of these observations, Lee was able to formulate more intelligent questions about food, diet, and social networks for a later phase of research than would have been the case had he entered the field armed only with his outsider's preconceptions about the people's behaviors.

Despite the reluctance of nonparticipant observers to interact directly with those being observed, it is sometimes necessary to ask questions to elicit contextual information; such background material can be collected before the actual observation begins. By the same token, some observational researchers have found that it is sometimes necessary to ask questions designed to clarify the observed action; such questions can be asked after the observation has ended. But in nonparticipant observation, the main part of the research process should flow without the researcher's intervention.

—Michael V. Angrosino

REFERENCES

Lee, R. B. (1993). *The Dobe !Kung.* New York: Holt, Rinehart and Winston.

Price, L. J. (1989). In the shadow of biomedicine: Self-medication in two Ecuadorian pharmacies. *Social Science and Medicine, 28,* 905–915.

Sechrest, L. (Ed.). (1979). *Unobtrusive measures today.* San Francisco: Jossey-Bass.

Webb, E. J., Campbell, D. T., Schwartz, R. D., & Sechrest, L. (1966). *Unobtrusive measures: Nonreactive research in the social sciences.* Chicago: Rand McNally.

NONPROBABILITY SAMPLING

A nonprobability sample is one not based on random selection methods.

The purpose of sampling is to obtain an accurate representation of the population from which the SAMPLE is drawn, so that accurate inferences about the population can be made on the basis of it. The samples most likely to be representative are large and randomly drawn (see RANDOM SAMPLING)—every member of the population has a known, nonzero probability of being part of the sample. (In *simple* random samples, every member would have an equal probability of being chosen, but there are also other variants.)

Often, random sampling is not possible or too expensive. It requires a complete list of the population or some other way of guaranteeing that every member is considered, and selected units cannot be replaced if they prove to be unavailable or refuse to take part. Under these circumstances, survey organizations often resort to the QUOTA SAMPLE, which is a *non*probability method. Here, the representation of the population is not left to chance but built into the sampling pattern. Knowing that gender is a variable of interest, for example, and that the relevant population is equally divided between men and women, the survey design will require interviewers to select equal numbers of men

and women—they will be given a quota of men and women to find. Properly conducted, this kind of sample is necessarily representative of the population in terms of the quota variables; this is built into the design.

It may not be representative in other terms, however, because the interviewers are left free to exercise choice about how they fill the quota. In a survey that British Open University students carried out as part of their coursework, for example, every student was responsible for collecting four cases according to a quota system that took account of gender, age, and social class. (This yielded a sample of about 2,000 people nationally.) When we came to analyze the data, we found that this sample appeared representative of most of the known facts about the population. However, despite the national tendency for middle-class people of both genders to vote Conservative, in our sample the middle-class women were more likely to vote for the Labour Party. The explanation was almost certainly that when the students were looking for middle-class women, they tended to go to their children's schools and approach teachers—and research had shown that middle-class people in the public sector of the economy were, in fact, more likely than others to vote for the Labour Party.

Quota samples at least represent the population in certain respects, but other forms of nonprobability sample are less likely to do so (see CONVENIENCE SAMPLE). Much research is conducted on what may best be described as a *haphazard* sample—stopping people "at random" in the street, for example. Other studies are carried out on "samples of opportunity"—education research carried out on the class you happen to be teaching, for example. Other studies use *volunteer* samples—they advertise for participants. In all of these cases, it is very likely indeed that the representation of the population will be imperfect. We shall fail to contact the kind of people who would not be on the street at that time. Our class may be untypical of the school, which in turn may not be representative of the total population of the town (which in turn may not be typical of the country as a whole). Volunteer samples cannot reach those who do not volunteer, and volunteers are most likely to include people with strong views on the advertised subject and less likely to include those who are indifferent to it.

Information based on nonprobability samples is therefore to be treated with caution. Alternatively, the researcher needs to think carefully about what population *is* represented. A survey on loneliness with a volunteer sample drawn by advertising in coffee bars, for example, will not represent true social isolates—who do not go out to coffee bars—and it will not represent people too shy to respond to the advertisement. Within those limitations, however, it may provide useful information.

One point of view is that the *achieved* sample is nonrandom in *all* surveys, however rigorous the design. The sampling pattern may have been random, but the people whom we fail to reach or who refuse to participate are very unlikely to be a random subset of the planned sample; they will differ from those who do respond in systematic ways.

—Roger Sapsford

NONRECURSIVE

Many social scientific theories specify MODELS of more than one equation. A nonrecursive system of equations is a type of SIMULTANEOUS EQUATION system where the equations are linked through RECIPROCAL RELATIONSHIPS between dependent variables, or correlations between errors in the equations. In nonrecursive models, either (a) there is reciprocal causation or feedback loops, and/or (b) the errors in the equations are correlated. The presence of either reciprocal causation or correlated errors (or both) indicates that a model is nonrecursive. In contrast, if there is neither reciprocal causation nor correlated errors, a simultaneous equation system is called RECURSIVE. SEEMINGLY UNRELATED REGRESSION models are a special case of nonrecursive models where the equations are related only through correlations between the errors.

A simple nonrecursive model with reciprocal causation can be represented by the following PATH DIAGRAM:

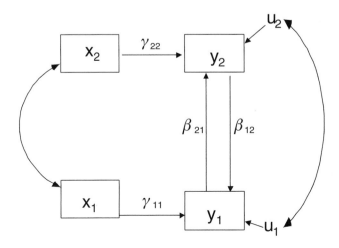

Here, y_1 affects y_2 while y_2 in turn affects y_1. Therefore, a change in y_1 feeds back upon itself. Notice also that the errors in the equations are correlated.

A nonrecursive model with a feedback loop could appear as follows:

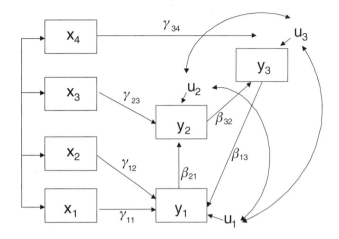

Here, y_1 affects y_2, y_2 affects y_3, and y_3 returns to affect y_1. Again, a change in y_1 will feed back upon itself.

Consider the two-equation nonrecursive system of equations corresponding to the first diagram:

$$y_1 = \beta_{12}y_2 + \gamma_{11}x_1 + u_1$$
$$y_2 = \beta_{21}y_1 + \gamma_{22}x_2 + u_2$$

where $\text{Cov}(u_1, u_2) \neq 0$.

In the system of equations, ENDOGENOUS VARIABLES are denoted with ys, while EXOGENOUS VARIABLES are denoted with xs. βs indicate the effect of an endogenous variable on another endogenous variable, whereas γs indicate the effect of an exogenous variable on an endogenous variable. The us indicate errors in the equations. In order for the system to be in equilibrium, $|\beta_{12}\beta_{21}| < 1$.

Nonrecursive systems of equations must avoid the IDENTIFICATION PROBLEM. That is, whether the parameters of the model are estimable must be established. Many methods to identify nonrecursive models are possible, including the order condition and the rank condition (see Bollen, 1989, pp. 98–103). Rigdon (1995) provides a straightforward way to identify many types of nonrecursive models.

Estimation of nonrecursive systems of equations requires that estimation take account of the information from other equations in the system. Therefore, if ORDINARY LEAST SQUARES (OLS) regression is applied to a nonrecursive simultaneous equation system, the estimates are likely to be biased and inconsistent. Instead, nonrecursive models can be estimated by two-stage least squares, three-stage least squares, and MAXIMUM LIKELIHOOD ESTIMATION. It is possible to view all of these estimators as INSTRUMENTAL VARIABLE estimators.

—Pamela Paxton

REFERENCES

Bollen, K. A. (1989). *Structural equations with latent variables.* New York: Wiley.

Greene, W. H. (1997). *Econometric analysis* (3rd ed.). Upper Saddle River, NJ: Prentice Hall.

Rigdon, E. E. (1995). A necessary and sufficient identification rule for structural models estimated in practice. *Multivariate Behavioral Research, 30,* 359–383.

Heise, D. R. (1975). *Causal analysis.* New York: Wiley.

NONRESPONSE

There are two broad categories of nonresponse in survey research: unit nonresponse, when a subject does not complete the survey instrument, and item nonresponse, when a respondent fails to answer one or more of the questions posed.

UNIT NONRESPONSE

Generally speaking, response rates have been declining in surveys of households and establishments over the past few decades. This nonresponse contributes to increased costs of data collection and may introduce nonresponse BIAS.

Groves and Couper (1998) have created a typology of exogenous and endogenous factors influencing survey cooperation. Exogenous factors, which are largely out of the control of the survey researcher, include the social environment (e.g., level of urbanicity in the area to be surveyed or the amount of advance publicity about the survey) and sample members' social psychological attributes and levels of knowledge about the topic of interest. Endogenous factors include the data collection protocols (mode of administration, incentives, length of the instrument, etc.) and, in interviewer-administered surveys, interviewer selection and training.

It can be challenging to enlist cooperation in surveys of establishments. In many cases, one individual does not have all the information necessary to respond. In telephone studies, it can be difficult for interviewers to get past gatekeepers to speak directly with respondents. Some companies have "blanket" policies that prohibit survey participation by their employees. Even in establishments without such a policy, the person receiving the invitation to participate may have to get authorization to participate from someone else in the organization.

There are research design features that have demonstrated positive effects on response rates. The numbers and types of contacts with sample members are important factors in enlisting cooperation. Mail surveys often include postcard reminders, replacement mailings of questionnaire packets, and telephone reminder calls to nonresponders. In TELEPHONE SURVEYS, the timing of calls is important to increasing the odds of finding the potential participant at home. COMPUTER-ASSISTED DATA COLLECTION systems can incorporate rules to make sure that calls are attempted during daytime and evening hours, on weekdays and weekends, and that calls are placed in different weeks. Other design features that have been shown to influence response include the length of the field period (generally the longer, the better); the survey sponsor; advance letters that provide information about the study and let participants know that an interviewer will be calling; and monetary and nonmonetary incentives. Prepaid cash incentives have proven to be the most productive type of incentive. Refusal conversions and increasing the numbers of call attempts also tend to increase response rates.

Information on nonrespondents is often limited. In nonresponse studies, a random sample of nonrespondents is selected, and intensive recruitment efforts are undertaken (e.g., offering or increasing incentives, offering different modes of administration, and/or increasing the numbers of contacts). Usually, these surveys include a few key questions from the survey and demographic questions. The data collected can be used to characterize nonrespondents and make postsurvey adjustments to the data.

When respondents are systematically different from nonrespondents in ways that are relevant to the research questions being addressed by the survey, NONRESPONSE BIAS occurs. Nonresponse is widely acknowledged as a major source of ERROR in survey research. Raising response rates is desirable in itself because it increases the credibility of data. However, the most important result is that improving response rates also tends to reduce nonresponse bias. The effects of additional efforts to reduce nonresponse bias depend on the size of the difference between respondents and nonrespondents. The substantive significance of nonresponse reduction will inevitably vary by topic, population, and methods of data collection.

ITEM NONRESPONSE

Respondents can fail to follow skip patterns accurately, intentionally omit an answer to a question they are uncomfortable answering, or stop answering survey items before the questionnaire is completed. This item nonresponse is more of an issue when surveys are self-administered than when an interviewer is present. Interviewers develop rapport with respondents and help them negotiate the instrument, and they can repeat questions or provide standardized definitions for unfamiliar terms when necessary.

Missing answers are more likely in questions about sensitive issues than in less threatening items. Questions concerning income levels and socially undesirable behaviors, such as recreational drug use or criminal behavior, often have MISSING DATA. Items that ask for the respondent's income often have the highest level of item nonresponse in a given survey. Asking about income in a series of nested questions and/or providing income ranges as response options can help to improve the quality of these data.

Poorly designed questions (e.g., ambiguous or double-barreled items) often yield missing data, either unit or item. Items that increase respondent burden by requiring extra effort on the part of the respondent also increase the likelihood of nonresponse. Examples are questions that ask respondents to answer in percentages that sum to 100%, items with long recall periods, and open-ended items in self-administered questionnaires. During instrument development, the testing of candidate items in cognitive interviews with people who mirror key characteristics of the population to be surveyed and in field PRETESTS will help identify problematic questions. These items can then be reworked before the survey is fielded.

Skip instructions embedded in an instrument indicate what question the respondent should answer next based on the answer to the trigger item. Faulty skip patterns can occur when respondents fail to answer a question they should, and when they answer items that should have been skipped. Well-designed instruments will minimize skip errors. Survey researchers need to carefully consider the content of both visual and textual information about skip instructions presented to respondents.

The issue of the differences between "purely" missing answers—items about which respondents have not formulated an opinion and items that are not applicable to a respondent—also should be considered when thinking about item nonresponse. The use of screening questions is recommended. These "trigger" questions are used to identify the appropriate denominator for substantive questions by allowing respondents who do not have relevant experience to inform their answers to factual items or those who do not have a position on opinion items to skip the "target" item. There is, however, concern that offering a no-opinion option may give respondents an easy way out of responding to questions where it is reasonably certain they have an opinion.

Item nonresponse in establishment surveys can result when respondents are asked to provide information the company either does not collect or collects in units that do not fit the response choices offered. Firms also consider some information proprietary—employees may be prohibited from releasing certain requested information.

Research design that maximizes response rates and instrument development that optimizes question design are pivotal to reducing nonresponse in surveys.

—Patricia M. Gallagher

REFERENCES

Fowler, F. J., Jr. (1995). *Improving survey questions: Design and evaluation.* Thousand Oaks, CA: Sage.

Groves, R. M., & Couper, M. P. (1998). *Nonresponse in household interview surveys.* New York: Wiley.

Groves, R. M., Dillman, D. A., Eltinge, J. L., & Little, R. J. A. (Eds.). (2002). *Survey nonresponse.* New York: Wiley.

Schwarz, N., & Sudman, S. (Eds.). (1996). *Answering questions: Methodology for determining cognitive and communicative processes in survey research.* San Francisco: Jossey-Bass.

NONRESPONSE BIAS

NONRESPONSE occurs when a study fails to gather data from all the elements that have been sampled from the frame. This can occur in any form of research, not just in sample surveys. Measurement of the size of the nonresponse is the response rate, and it can be computed in several informative ways (cf. AAPOR, 2000). Although response rates provide useful information about the study's efficiency in measuring all sampled elements, they do not directly provide any information about whether the data have any nonresponse bias. That is, "low" response rates do not automatically mean that nonresponse bias is present (cf. Curtin, Presser, & Singer, 2000; Merkle & Edelman, 2002). However, whenever nonresponding elements differ from the responding elements on the measures of interest, then nonresponse error occurs, most typically in the form of bias. Nonresponse bias is a function of *both* the size of the nonresponse and the size of the differences between responders and nonresponders (e.g., Groves, 1989).

If responders and nonresponders are not different on measures of interest, then there will be no nonresponse bias, regardless of the study's response rate. Nonresponse bias can occur at the unit level (e.g., person) or at the item level (e.g., a survey question). Many methodological techniques have been devised to try to reduce the likelihood of nonresponse, which in surveys occurs most often because of noncontacts, refusals, and language barriers. Many statistical WEIGHTING and IMPUTATION techniques have been devised to adjust for possible nonresponse bias at both the unit and item levels. However, typically no information is available from the nonresponding elements; thus, there is no guarantee that these statistical adjustments will, in fact, reduce any nonresponse bias that may be present. Special follow-up studies of nonresponders can gather information that can be used to determine how the nonresponders in the original study differed from responders.

—Paul J. Lavrakas

REFERENCES

American Association for Public Opinion Research (AAPOR). (2000). *Standard definitions: Final dispositions for case codes and outcome rates for surveys.* Ann Arbor, MI: Author.

Curtin, R., Presser, S., & Singer, E. (2000). The effects of response rate changes on the index of consumer sentiment. *Public Opinion Quarterly, 64,* 413–428.

Groves, R. M. (1989). *Survey errors and survey costs.* New York: Wiley.

Merkle, D. M., & Edelman, M. (2002). Nonresponse in exit polls: A comprehensive analysis. In R. M. Groves, D. A. Dillman, J. L. Eltinge, & R. J. A. Little (Eds.), *Survey nonresponse* (pp. 243–258). New York: Wiley.

NONSAMPLING ERROR

There are many forms of potential error in social research that a prudent researcher will (a) try to minimize and/or (b) measure (cf. Groves, 1989). Error is due to the various causes of BIAS (i.e., constant error) and VARIANCE (i.e., variable error) that can occur whenever data are gathered, regardless of whether the research is QUANTITATIVE RESEARCH or QUALITATIVE RESEARCH. SAMPLING ERROR is the variance associated with any research sample that is not a census of the population of interest. *Nonsampling error* is the term that traditionally has been used to refer to all other sources of bias and variance, and it includes coverage error, nonresponse error, and measurement error.

Coverage error refers to the bias that may result when the frame (the list) used to represent the population of interest fails to adequately cover (include) the entire population. NONRESPONSE *error* refers to the bias and variance that may result when data are not gathered from all of the elements sampled from the frame. *Measurement error* refers to potential bias and variance that can be caused by any of the following: (a) the person who gathers the data (e.g., an interviewer, observer, or coder); (b) the instrument that is used to gather the data (e.g., a questionnaire, observational or coding form); (c) the subject/respondent being measured; (d) the mode of data collection (e.g., in-person vs. self-administered). The literature abounds with methodological and statistical studies that address various techniques that can be used to try to reduce the possibility that nonsampling errors will occur and/or ways to measure and adjust for such errors when they do result. Of note, many think that these forms of errors apply only to sample surveys, when, in fact, each type of error has its counterpart in any form of social research, including OBSERVATIONAL RESEARCH, CONTENT ANALYSIS, and all forms of qualitative research.

—Paul J. Lavrakas

REFERENCE

Groves, R. M. (1989). *Survey errors and survey costs.* New York: Wiley.

NORMAL DISTRIBUTION

The normal distribution (sometimes referred to as the Gaussian distribution) has been applied to problems in the social sciences many times. Many continuous random variables can be modeled as a normal PROB-ABILITY distribution whose density function produces a symmetric, bell-shaped curve. The normal density function for a continuous random variable Y is

$$f(y) = \frac{1}{\sigma\sqrt{2\pi}}e^{-\frac{(y-\mu)^2}{2\sigma^2}},$$

where $-\infty < y < \infty$, $-\infty < \mu < \infty$, and $\sigma > 0$, and μ and σ are the POPULATION mean and STAN-DARD DEVIATION, respectively, such that $E(Y) = \mu$, and $V(Y) = \sigma^2$. Notice that these are the only two PARAMETERS that define the density of the normal distribution.

The normal distribution has a special property that holds across parameter values: 68% of the distribution lies within 1 standard deviation above and below the mean, 95% of the distribution lies within 2 standard deviations above and below the mean, and 99.7% of the distribution lies within 3 standard deviations of the mean. However, because the distribution lies between $-\infty$ and ∞, a normally distributed random variable

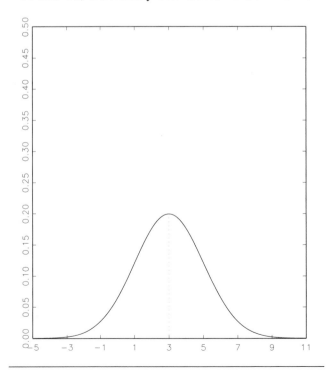

Figure 1 $Y_i \sim$ Normal, $\mu = 3$, $\sigma = 2$

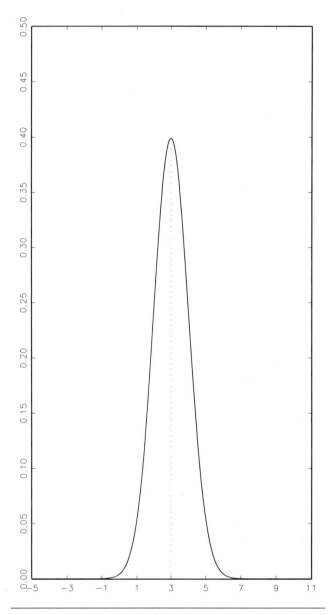

Figure 2 $Y_i \sim$ Normal, $\mu = 3$, $\sigma = 1$

has events with nonzero probability occurring any-where on the real-number line. In addition, because the distribution is symmetric and has a unique maximum, its MEAN, MEDIAN, and MODE are the same. Furthermore, the two inflection points are located 1 standard deviation away from the mean. Figures 1 and 2 demonstrate these points. Note that the two distributions are both centered around 3, but the spread of the first is greater than that of the second. However, a very high or very low number is a possible event (even with very low probability) in both distributions.

A major reason for the centrality of the normal distribution in the social sciences is the CENTRAL LIMIT THEOREM. The theorem links any probability function (as long as its μ and σ are finite) to the normal distribution by proving that regardless of the distribution of the original variable, the mean and the sum of the variable are normally distributed for large enough SAMPLES (or, more strictly, as n approaches infinity). A particular application of the theorem is the normal approximation to the BINOMIAL distribution. The application establishes that a fraction of successes in a series of n BERNOULLI trials with a probability of success in each one, p, is approximately normally distributed with a mean p and variance $\frac{p(1-p)}{n}$.

In addition, following the ASSUMPTION that the ERROR terms in the frequently used LEAST SQUARES REGRESSION are distributed normally, the least squares estimators are distributed normally, a property that helps with many questions of STATISTICAL INFERENCE.

THE STANDARD NORMAL DISTRIBUTION

To compare values of two normally distributed variables, each drawn from a different normal distribution, a standardization is required. The standardization shifts the means of the distributions and adjusts their variances to comparable grounds, such that a comparison of, say, a grade in Advanced Akkadian and a grade in Introduction to Astrophysics is made possible.

The standardization procedure is $Z_i = \frac{Y_i - \mu}{\sigma}$, such that each value Z_i represents the difference from Y_i to its mean in units of its standard deviation (σ) of the original variable Y_i. Therefore, the mean value of Z_i must be zero, and the standard deviation is equal to 1.

Thus, the density function for the standard normal distribution is

$$f(z) = \frac{1}{\sqrt{2\pi}} e^{-\frac{z^2}{2}}.$$

Evaluating the probability of a normal variable being between points a and b [$P(a \leq Y_i \leq b)$] requires evaluation of the area under the normal density function between points a and b, or, in other words, evaluation of the integral

$$\int_a^b \frac{1}{\sigma\sqrt{2\pi}} e^{-\frac{(y-\mu)^2}{2\sigma^2}}\,dy.$$

Unfortunately, a closed-form expression for the integral does not exist, hence, numerical techniques are used, and in practice, statistical tables that summarize the density are often put to use. Because the distribution

is symmetric around μ, symmetric areas need to be calculated only on one side of the mean. Otherwise, for convenience, areas to the left of the mean are calculated as if they were to the right of the mean. Figure 3 demonstrates this point with respect to the standard normal distribution.

$$\begin{aligned}
P(a < Y_i < b) &= P(Y_i < b) - P(Y_i < a) \\
&= P(Y_i < b) - P(Y_i > -a) \\
&= P(Y_i < b) - [1 - P(Y_i < -a)] \\
&= P(Y_i < b) + P(Y_i < -a) - 1.
\end{aligned}$$

Suppose $a = -1.5$ and $b = 0.8$. Then

$$\begin{aligned}
P(-1.5 < Y_i < 0.8) &= P(Y_i < 0.8) \\
&\quad + P(Y_i < 1.5) - 1 = 0.7881 \\
&\quad + 0.9332 - 1 = 0.7213.
\end{aligned}$$

LINEAR TRANSFORMATION

Often, social scientists would work with a variable that is a LINEAR TRANSFORMATION of an original variable of interest. For example, a researcher might measure income in dollars or thousands of dollars, or distance in kilometers or miles. When the original variable is distributed normally, the linear transformation of it is also distributed normally. Furthermore, if we know the mean and standard deviation of the original variable, it is easy to extract the parameter values of the transformed variable when they are linearly related. If $Y_i \sim N$ such that $E(Y) = \mu$ and $V(Y) = \sigma^2$, and X is a linear transformation of Y such that $X_i = aY_i + b$, then $E(X_i) = E(aY_i + b) = aE(Y_i) + b = a\mu + b$, and $V(X_i) = V(aY_i + b) = a^2 V(Y_i) = a^2\sigma^2$.

MULTIVARIATE NORMAL DISTRIBUTION

If, rather than a single variable, Y_i is a vector of N random variables normally distributed, we need a multivariate distribution to model this vector. The multivariate normal distribution with N random variables can be written as a function of an $N \times 1$ vector μ and an $N \times N$ variance-covariance matrix Σ, such that

$$f(y) = \frac{1}{\sqrt{|\Sigma|}(2\pi)^{-\frac{N}{2}}} e^{-\frac{1}{2}[(y_i - \mu)\Sigma^{-1}(y_i - \mu)]}.$$

When Y_i includes only one random variable, this expression reduces to the univariate normal density, and its variance-covariance matrix is simply σ^2.

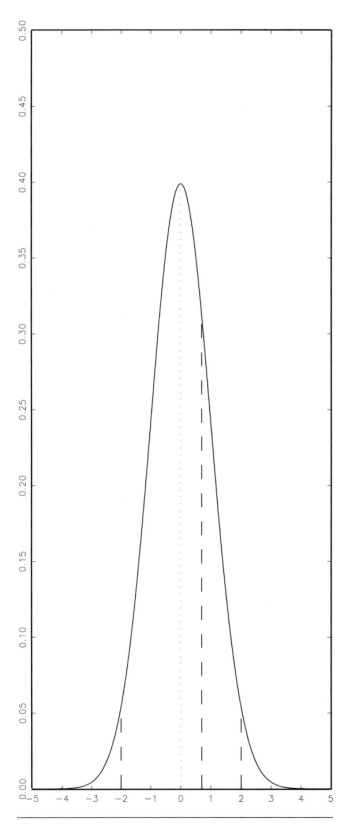

Figure 3 $Y_i \sim$ Standard Normal ($\mu = 0, \sigma = 1$)

When the variables are independent, $\sum$ is diagonal (i.e., the off-diagonal entries are equal to zero). In this special case, the product of the univariate normal distributions will equal the multivariate normal distribution.

LOG-NORMAL DISTRIBUTION

A distribution that might be helpful to describe variables that can take only a non-negative value (such as income or weight) is the log-normal distribution. If Z_i is distributed standard normal such that $Z_i = \frac{\ln Y_i - \mu}{\sigma}$, then Y_i is distributed log-normal with mean μ and variance σ^2, such that $Y_i = e^{\sigma Z_i + \mu}$.

HISTORICAL DEVELOPMENT

The normal distribution is often associated with Carl Friedrich Gauss (1777–1855). In a book published in 1809, Gauss associated the normal density with the method of least squares. Yet Gauss cites work by Laplace from 1774, where he touches on the distribution, and indeed, some works refer to the distribution as Gauss-Laplace. However, historical scholarship traces the distribution's origin back even further to a publication by De Moivre from 1733 (Stigler, 1999, pp. 284–285).

Indeed, the idea that a normal distribution can describe statistical processes was developed in the 18th century. For much of the 19th century, they were called "error curves" because they were first used to describe the distribution of measurement errors. It was not until the 1870s that the phrase "normal distribution" was introduced.

—Orit Kedar

REFERENCES

Greene, W. H. (1993). *Econometric analysis.* Englewood Cliffs, NJ: Prentice Hall.

King, G. (1989). *Unifying political methodology.* New York: Cambridge University Press.

Stigler, S. M. (1986). *The history of statistics.* Cambridge, MA: Harvard University Press.

Stigler, S. M. (1999). *Statistics on the table.* Cambridge, MA: Harvard University Press.

Wackerly, D. D., Mendelhall, W., III, & Scheaffer, R. L. (1996). *Mathematical statistics with applications* (5th ed.). Belmont, CA: Duxbury.

NORMALIZATION

In many popular statistical models, we assume that some component of a variable Y has a NORMAL DISTRIBUTION. For example, in the LINEAR REGRESSION model $Y = \alpha + \beta X + \varepsilon$, we typically assume that the error term ε is normal. Although minor departures from normality may be acceptable, distributions with heavier-than-normal tails can compromise statistical estimates. In such cases, it may be preferable to transform Y so that the pertinent component is closer to normality. Transforming a variable in this way is called *normalization.*

If the pertinent component of Y has one heavy tail (SKEWED), then we often apply a *power transformation.* True to their name, power transformations raise Y to some power p (i.e., they transform Y into Y^p). Powers greater than 1 reduce *negative* skew: An example is the quadratic transformation $Y^2 (p = 2)$. Powers between 0 and 1 reduce *positive* skew: An example is the square-root transformation or $\sqrt{Y}$ or $\sqrt{Y + 1/2}$ $(p = 0.5)$, which is common when Y represents counts or frequencies. For a power of 0, the power transformation is defined to be log(Y), which reduces positive skew in much the same way as a very small power. Negative powers have the same effect as positive powers applied to the reciprocal $\frac{1}{Y}$ and are used when the reciprocal has a natural interpretation—as when Y is a rate (events per unit time), so that $\frac{1}{Y}$ is the time between events.

In sum, the family of power transformations can be written as follows:

$$t(Y; p) = \begin{cases} Y^p & \text{if } p \neq 0, \\ \ln(Y) & \text{if } p = 0. \end{cases}$$

Power transformations assume that Y is positive; if Y can be zero or negative, we commonly make Y positive by adding a constant. There are formal procedures for estimating the best constant to add, as well as the power p that yields the best approximation to normality (Box & Cox, 1964). However, the optimal power and additive constant are usually treated only as rough guidelines.

If the pertinent component of Y has *two* heavy tails (excess KURTOSIS), we may use a *modulus transformation* (John & Draper, 1980),

$$t(Y; p) = \begin{cases} \text{sign}(Y)][\frac{(|Y|+1)^p - 1}{p}] & \text{if } p \neq 0, \\ \text{sign}(Y)][\ln(Y) + 1] & \text{if } p = 0, \end{cases}$$

which is a modified power transformation applied to each tail separately. Non-negative powers p less than 1 reduce kurtosis, while powers greater than 1 increase kurtosis. Again, there are formal procedures for estimating the optimal power p (John & Draper, 1980). If Y is symmetric around 0, then the modulus transformation will change the kurtosis without introducing skew. If Y is not centered at 0, it may be advisable to add a constant before applying the modulus transformation.

Other normalizations are typically used if Y represents proportions between 0 and 1: the arcsine or angular transformation $\sin^{-1}(\sqrt{Y})$, the logit or logistic transformation $\ln(\frac{Y}{1-Y})$, and the probit transformation $\Phi^{-1}(Y)$, where Φ^{-1} is the inverse of the cumulative standard normal density. The logit and probit are better normalizations than the arcsine, which is gradually disappearing from practice.

Even the best transformation may not provide an adequate approximation to normality. Moreover, a transformed variable may be hard to interpret, and conclusions drawn from it may not apply to the original, untransformed variable (Levin, Liukkonen, & Levine, 1996). Fortunately, modern researchers often have good alternatives to normalization. When working with non-normal data, we can use a GENERALIZED LINEAR MODEL that assumes a different type of distribution. Or we can make weaker assumptions by using statistics that are "distribution-free" or nonparametric.

In addition to the definition given here, the word *normalization* is sometimes used when a variable is STANDARDIZED. It is also used when constraints are imposed to ensure that a system of SIMULTANEOUS EQUATIONS is identified (e.g., Greene, 1997).

—Paul T. von Hippel

REFERENCES

Box, G. E. P., & Cox, D. R. (1964). An analysis of transformations. *Journal of the Royal Statistical Society (B), 26*(2), 211–252.

Cook, R. D., & Weisberg, S. (1996). *Applied regression including computing and graphics.* New York: Wiley.

Greene, W. H. (1997). *Econometric analysis* (3rd ed.). Upper Saddle River, NJ: Prentice Hall.

John, N. R., & Draper, J.A. (1980). An alternative family of transformations. *Applied Statistics, 29*(2), 190–197.

Levin, A., Liukkonen, J., & Levine, D. W. (1996). Equivalent inference using transformations. *Communications in Statistics, Theory and Methods, 25*(5), 1059–1072.

Yeo, I.-K., & Johnson, R. (2000). A new family of power transformations to improve normality or symmetry. *Biometrika, 87,* 954–959.

NUD*IST

A software program designed for computer-assisted qualitative data analysis. As such, it allows qualitative data to be coded and retrieved. It also supports GROUNDED THEORY practices, such as the generation of MEMOS. The name is an abbreviation of Non-numerical Unstructured Data Indexing, Searching, and Theorizing.

—Alan Bryman

NUISANCE PARAMETERS

A nuisance parameter is a type of parameter that is of no or only secondary interest in parametric ESTIMATION. For example, in a certain statistical model that involves a normally distributed random variable, the researcher's interest often focuses on the estimation of the expectation of the variable μ, whereas the variance of the random variable σ^2 is of no interest and is then considered a nuisance parameter.

—Tim Futing Liao

NULL HYPOTHESIS

The null hypothesis is an essential component of HYPOTHESIS TESTING in social research. It is relevant when quantitative measures of social activities have been made and when hypotheses derived from theories are to be tested. The theoretical (or research) hypothesis defines a certain pattern to be found in the data, and the statistical analysis is designed to evaluate the extent to which the evidence from the collected measurements supports the existence of that pattern. The null hypothesis is the hypothesis that the pattern of data found has occurred simply by chance.

Take an example of a RANDOM SAMPLING of participants drawn from the human POPULATION, which is randomly divided into two groups. One group may receive a treatment, such as a small dose of alcohol, whereas the other receives a placebo (to conceal from the participants which group they are in). Their performance on a driving task (or other related skill) may then be measured. The research hypothesis will be that the two groups will have different levels of performance. The null hypothesis is that the alcohol has no effect and any resulting difference between the two groups is due to random chance. If the null hypothesis is true, we expect the mean performance of the two groups to be the same. However, any RANDOM ASSIGNMENT of participants into two groups almost always will produce two groups whose measured performance differs by some amount, even when both groups are treated exactly the same. However, the larger the difference in the means, the less probable is such an outcome. Hypothesis testing relies on estimating the probability (or chance) of obtaining the results we measure.

If it is assumed that the null hypothesis is true (in this example, that the alcohol has no effect), it is possible to calculate the chance of getting any pattern of data that may result from the measurement of two randomly allocated groups of participants. Usually, this is done by using this assumption (that the null hypothesis is true) to calculate (or otherwise estimate) the SAMPLING DISTRIBUTION of a statistic (such as T RATIO or CHI-SQUARE). This distribution is then used to compare with the sample statistic calculated from the measurements taken.

In principle, even if there is no effect of the treatment (so the null hypothesis is true), any mathematically possible pattern in the data may be found by chance alone, however unlikely. The smaller the probability of finding a given pattern of results by chance, the more we consider that we have evidence that supports the research hypothesis. Some statistical methods set a conventional probability level, below which the procedure allows the decision to be made that the null hypothesis may be rejected and the research hypothesis accepted. Other methods consider that there is no hard-and-fast decision rule that can be universally applied, and that the evidence obtained with one set of measurements can be fully evaluated only in the context of other research that has investigated similar problems in similar ways (see, e.g., MacDonald, 2002).

—Martin Le Voi

See also SIGNIFICANCE TESTING, *P* VALUES, HYPOTHESIS.

REFERENCE

MacDonald, R. R. (2002). The incompleteness of probability models and the resultant implications for theories of statistical inference. *Understanding Statistics, 1*(3), 167–189.

NUMERIC VARIABLE. *See* METRIC VARIABLE

NVIVO

NVivo or NUD*IST Vivo is a software program designed for computer-assisted qualitative data analysis. As such, it allows qualitative data to be coded and retrieved. It also supports GROUNDED THEORY practices, such as the generation of MEMOS. It is a variant (but not a new release) of NUD*IST but is often regarded as more suited to the fine-grained analysis that is particularly popular among practitioners of QUALITATIVE RESEARCH.

—Alan Bryman

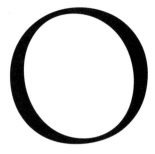

OBJECTIVISM

Objectivism is the view that there can be a "permanent, ahistorical matrix or framework to which we can ultimately appeal in determining the nature of rationality, knowledge, truth, reality, goodness or rightness" (Bernstein, 1983, p. 8). Although long challenged by the phenomenological and hermeneutic traditions in social science, it was nevertheless the default position in both the natural and social sciences until the 1960s. Thomas Kuhn's *The Structure of Scientific Revolutions*, first published in 1962 (Kuhn, 1970), challenged this orthodoxy in natural science (and by extension in social science) by claiming that there is no linear progress in science; rather, there are "paradigms" of thought and practice that are taken to represent scientific truth at particular times. These are subject to occasional and dramatic revolution that can be accounted for more readily by social and psychological factors than by objective facts about the world. Indeed, so opposed are competing paradigms that they are epistemologically incommensurate.

Kuhn's work influenced a number of antiobjectivist positions in social science (or perhaps more correctly social studies, for in these positions there was often a denial the social world could be studied scientifically): RELATIVISM, social CONSTRUCTIONISM, and subjectivism. Though sometimes an antiobjectivist view will incorporate all these oppositions, they are not necessarily synonymous. Relativists will deny that knowledge and/or morality can be judged from a perspective that is not embedded in subjective epistemological or moral positions, and thus they claim there can be no privileging of any one truth or morality. Subjectivists will deny the existence of an objective reality existing outside of agents' perceptions or constructions of it. Social constructionism, though similar, places stress on the social construction of what we call "reality."

Objectivism, like so many other "isms," is often something of a straw person, and there are few now who would wholeheartedly embrace either it or its complete denial. There are, however, more moderate successor positions in respect of objectivity as an achievable goal or REALISM as an ontological stance in social theory and methodology. In the first case, the question addressed is to what extent can objectivity, as a pursuit of truth in the social world, be retained when the social world is actively constructed by its participants? Realists have attempted to find a middle ground by accepting that the social world is socially constructed, but once it comes into being it exists as an objective reality independent of any individual conception of it.

One influential attempt to transcend objectivism and its oppositions came from Pierre Bourdieu (1977), who associated it with the STRUCTURALISM of Durkheim, Althusser, and Lévi-Strauss and the consequent "disappearance" of the agent from social theory. Conversely, he saw the ETHNOMETHODOLOGISTS and SYMBOLIC INTERACTIONISTS as overly concentrating on agents' subjectivity and ignoring the objective structures acting upon them. Instead, he proposed that there existed a dialectic relationship between subjective and objective factors in the practice of the construction of social reality. Objective structures bear upon day-to-day interactions, and although agents will reproduce and transform them, the ways in which they are presented will make a difference in how they will be reproduced and transformed.

—Malcolm Williams

REFERENCES

Bernstein, R. (1983). *Beyond objectivism and relativism: Science, hermeneutics and praxis*. Oxford, UK: Basil Blackwell.

Bourdieu, P. (1977). *Outline of a theory of practice*. Cambridge, UK: Cambridge University Press.

Kuhn, T. (1970). *The structure of scientific revolutions* (2nd ed.). Chicago: University of Chicago Press. (Original work published 1962.)

OBJECTIVITY

The central meaning of the term "objectivity" concerns whether inquiry is pursued in a way that maximizes the chances that the conclusions reached will be true. As will become clear, however, the word has a number of other related meanings.

The fortunes of this concept underwent a dramatic change in the second half of the 20th century. It had been treated by most researchers as identifying an essential requirement of research, but it came to be regarded by some as little more than an ideological disguise for the interests of scientists, especially those who are male, white, and from Western countries.

The various meanings of "objectivity" can be clarified by distinguishing its adjectival and adverbial forms. Confusion often arises from conflating these. First, "objective" can be applied as an adjective to phenomena in the world. In this sense, it is sometimes taken to imply that a thing exists, rather than being a mere appearance or figment of imagination. Alternatively, "objectivity" can mean that a thing belongs to the "external" world, not to the "internal," psychological world of a subject. In this sense, whereas tables and chairs are objective, thoughts and feelings are not, even though they both may be real rather than mere appearances.

"Objective" also can be applied as an adjective to research findings, and here it is equivalent in meaning to "true." This is what is sometimes referred to as "ontological objectivity" (Newell, 1986). However, given the equivalence, this usage seems superfluous and in most cases is best avoided.

By contrast, the central meaning identified in the first paragraph is adverbial, and here the term "objective" is applied to a process of inquiry and/or to an inquirer. This is sometimes referred to as "procedural objectivity," though this is misleading because it implies mere following of a method. What this adverbial sense of "objectivity" refers to is whether or not inquiry has been BIASED through the effects of factors extrinsic to it, notably the researcher's own motives and interests, social background, political and religious commitments, and so on. It is important to notice that objectivity does not require that these factors have no influence on the research process, only that they do not deflect it from its rational course.

As this makes clear, the adverbial sense of "objective" is evaluative rather than factual in character: It involves judging a course of inquiry, or an inquirer, against some rational standard of how an inquiry *ought to have been pursued in order to maximize the chances of producing true findings*. It is concerned not with all deviations from this path but with systematic error caused by factors associated with the researcher. It is perhaps worth underlining that these factors are not necessarily subjective in the psychological sense.

Objectivity as a regulative ideal, in its adverbial form, has been challenged on a number of grounds. Some commentators have claimed that it can never be achieved, because this would imply a researcher with no background characteristics. On this basis, it has been argued that the notion of objectivity is simply a rhetorical device by which researchers privilege their own views. As already noted, however, objectivity does not require an absence of background characteristics, only that any systematic negative effects of these be avoided. Furthermore, even if it is true that objectivity can never be fully achieved—in that we cannot entirely avoid such negative effects, or at least know that we have avoided them—it does not follow that striving to achieve objectivity is undesirable. It might be argued that the more closely inquiry approximates this ideal, the more likely it is that the knowledge produced will be sound.

It has been proposed that particular categories of actors are more able to gain objectivity than others. One version of this is put forward by Harding (1992). She argues in favor of what she calls "strong objectivity," which amounts to privileging the perspectives of those who are socially marginalized, on the grounds that they are more capable of gaining genuine knowledge about society because they are not blinded by any commitment to sustaining the status quo. This approach builds on Hegelian and Marxist ideas to the effect that objectivity is a sociohistorical product, rather than a matter of individual orientation.

Another criticism of objectivity as an ideal stems from rejection of the concepts of rationality and/or truth on which it depends, these being treated as themselves mythological or merely rhetorical. This criticism arises from various forms of skepticism and RELATIVISM, most recently inspired by POSTSTRUCTURALISM.

A rather different criticism of objectivity as a regulative ideal argues that it encourages ethical irresponsibility on the part of researchers. This is because it requires research to be carried out in ways that do not treat important values other than truth as part of its goal. Here, the concepts of truth and rationality are not rejected; the claim is simply that inquiry should involve rational pursuit of other goals besides knowledge, with these other goals—such as social justice—being assumed to have an elective affinity to truth, or as properly overriding it.

Defenders of the older concept of objectivity reject these criticisms, arguing that "objectivity" simply means avoiding bias arising from irrelevant factors, that no one is uniquely privileged or debarred from gaining knowledge of the social world, that any denial of the possibility of knowledge is self-refuting, and that there is good reason to believe that different goals imply divergent lines of rational action and therefore cannot be pursued simultaneously. Defenders of objectivity claim that the success of scientific inquiry has arisen from its institutionalization in research communities, and that seeking to avoid deflection by irrelevant considerations is just as important in research as it is in rational pursuit of any other activity (see Rescher, 1997).

—Martyn Hammersley

REFERENCES

Harding, S. (1992). After the neutrality ideal: Science, politics, and "strong objectivity." *Social Research, 59*, 568–587.
Newell, R. W. (1986). *Objectivity, empiricism and truth.* London: Routledge and Kegan Paul.
Rescher, N. (1997). *Objectivity: The obligations of impersonal reason.* Notre Dame, IN: University of Notre Dame Press.

OBLIQUE ROTATION. *See* ROTATIONS

OBSERVATION SCHEDULE

Observation schedules are used in research employing observational methods to study behavior and interaction in a structured and systematic fashion (see STRUCTURED OBSERVATION). They consist of pre-defined systems for classifying and recording behavior and interactions as they occur, together with sets of rules and criteria for conducting observation and for allocating events to categories. An observation schedule normally will include a time dimension for locating observations in time and will contain variables relating to different aspects of behavior and interaction, each consisting of a set of categories describing particular behaviors and interactions. The observation schedule is the means by which a researcher operationalizes the aspects of the social world that are the focus of the study; it is used to collect systematic and reliable data that can be used in analysis. The categories and definitions used in observation schedules should be explicit and should be capable of being used identically by different observers.

TYPES OF OBSERVATION SCHEDULE

There are a variety of types of schedule, in particular with regard to how they locate observations in time and whether they provide data on the duration, frequency, time of occurrence, and sequence of the behaviors studied. *Continuous* and *quasi-continuous* observation systems provide a continual, ongoing record of behavior. These systems are the most complete but practical only for limited sets of categories. For example, Hilsum and Cane (1971) studied the work of schoolteachers through continuous observation throughout the day, classifying activities into categories such as "instruction," "marking," and "administration." *Event recording* is essentially a checklist system that notes whenever a particular type of event takes place. It is a good measure of frequency of occurrence. Wheldall and Merrett (1989) used such an approach to compare different ways of managing classroom behavior based on simple counts of every time a teacher praised or reprimanded a pupil. Many systems use various types of time sampling to structure the observations, such as *instantaneous time sampling* and *partial interval* and *whole interval* time sampling. Galton, Simon, and Croll (1980) studied school classrooms using instantaneous time sampling; the interactions and behavior of selected pupils and their teacher were coded at precisely timed 25-second intervals. Further details of approaches to time sampling are given by Croll (1986) and Suen and Ary (1989).

DESIGNING OBSERVATION SCHEDULES

Before designing a new observation schedule, researchers should consider whether one of the many systems already in use would serve their purpose. If existing schedules are not suitable, it is still worth considering modifying something already in use or at least incorporating variables from another schedule as benchmark measures for comparative purposes. Guidelines for the development of observation systems are given by Robson (1993, chap. 8). These include criteria such as ease of use in the research situation, low levels of inference or judgment needed by the observer, and explicit definition of categories. The categories used should be *exhaustive*, in that all behaviors encountered can be coded, and *exclusive*, in that each behavior observed fits into only one category of a variable (although there may, of course, be several variables). Researchers intending to use observation schedules may find it helpful to start observing in an unstructured fashion and then to progressively introduce structure into the observation procedure. This can help both to focus their conceptualization of the field of study and to identify ways of more precisely operationalizing the relevant variables.

—Paul Croll

REFERENCES

Croll, P. (1986). *Systematic classroom interaction*. Lewes, UK: Falmer.

Galton, M., Simon, B., & Croll, P. (1980). *Inside the primary classroom*. London: Routledge and Kegan Paul.

Hilsum, S., & Cane, B. (1971). *The teacher's day*. Windsor, UK: National Foundation for Educational Research.

Robson, C. (1993). *Real world research*. Oxford, UK: Blackwell.

Suen, H. K., & Ary, D. (1989). *Analyzing quantitative behavioural observation data*. London: Lawrence Erlbaum.

Wheldall, K., & Merrett, F. (1989). *Positive teaching: The behavioural approach*. Birmingham, UK: Positive Products.

OBSERVATION, TYPES OF

Observation is a data collection strategy involving the systematic collection and examination of verbal and nonverbal behaviors as they occur in a variety of contexts. This method of data collection is particularly important when there are difficulties in obtaining relevant information through self-report because subjects are unable to communicate (e.g., with infants or confused adults) or provide sufficiently detailed information (e.g., about complex interaction patterns). Observations also are used to validate or extend data obtained using other data collection methods. Both unstructured and structured observations are used by researchers. Unstructured observations are most useful in exploratory, descriptive research. STRUCTURED OBSERVATIONS are used when behaviors of interest are known, and this type of observation often involves the use of an OBSERVATION SCHEDULE (e.g., a checklist). Efforts usually are made to observe participants in as natural a setting as possible. Data collection involving observation involves INFORMED CONSENT of the participants.

There are two main types of observation: observation in person (PARTICIPANT OBSERVATION or NONPARTICIPANT OBSERVATION) and video recordings. Observation in person involves sustained direct observations by the researcher and focuses on the context as well as the behaviors of individuals to understand the meaning of certain behaviors or beliefs. This type of observation typically is linked with ETHNOGRAPHY. For example, participant observation is a useful method to study privacy in nursing home settings. The participant role or degree of involvement that the researcher has with others in the setting may vary. In nonparticipant observation, researchers focus primarily on the task of observation, while minimizing their participation in interactions in the setting. In other situations, a researcher may be more a participant than observer by taking on some of the roles and responsibilities of insiders in a research setting while observations are carried out. The advantages of in-person observation are that (a) over time, participants accommodate to the presence of the researcher, increasing the likelihood of the possibility of observing the phenomena of interest as it really occurs; (b) the researcher has the opportunity to interact with participants to clarify and extend observations; (c) events can be understood as they unfold in everyday life; and (d) differences between what participants say and do can be made apparent (Bogdewic, 1999). Observations conducted in this context encompass all the researcher's senses and are recorded as "jottings" in the field, then later are expanded into detailed FIELDNOTES with the researcher's interpretations (Emerson, Fretz, & Shaw, 1995). Usually, it is recognized that participants may limit disclosing some information and define the boundaries of observation.

In the second type of observation, video cameras are used to capture behaviors of interest. The advantage of video recordings is that a permanent record of observations is available for detailed microanalysis or for multiple kinds of analysis (Bottorff, 1994). Video recording typically is used in qualitative ethology and some forms of CONVERSATION ANALYSIS. For example, video recordings provide a rich data source for studying interaction patterns between health care providers and patients. This observational approach is particularly useful when researchers are interested in examining the sequence of behaviors, concurrent behaviors, and nonverbal behaviors that are difficult to observe in real time. In-depth descriptions of behavior can result from the microanalysis of video recorded behaviors.

—Joan L. Bottorff

REFERENCES

Angrosino, M. V., & Mays de Perez, K. (2000). Rethinking observation: From method to context. In N. K. Denzin & Y. S. Lincoln (Eds.), *Handbook of qualitative research* (2nd ed., pp. 673–702). Thousand Oaks, CA: Sage.

Bogdewic, S. P. (1999). Participant observation. In B. J. Crabtree & W. L. Miller (Eds.), *Doing qualitative research* (pp. 47–69). Thousand Oaks, CA: Sage.

Bottorff, J. L. (1994). Using videotaped recordings in qualitative research. In J. M. Morse (Ed.), *Critical issues in qualitative research* (pp. 224–261). Newbury Park, CA: Sage.

Emerson, R. M., Fretz, R. I., & Shaw, L. L. (1995). *Writing ethnographic fieldnotes.* Chicago: University of Chicago Press.

OBSERVATIONAL RESEARCH

Observation is one of the fundamental techniques of research conducted by sociologists, cultural anthropologists, and social psychologists. It can either stand on its own as a data collection method or be paired with one or more other means of data collection. The purpose of observational research is to record group activities, conversations, and interactions as they happen and to ascertain the meanings of such events to participants. Observations may take place either in laboratory settings designed by the researcher or in field settings that are the natural loci of selected activities. Data derived from observation may be either encoded quantitatively, often through the use of standardized checklists or research guides, or rendered as open-ended narrative descriptions. Data are recorded in either written or taped (audio and/or video) form and may consist of either numerical or narrative depictions of physical settings, actions, interaction patterns, meanings (expressed or implicit), and expressions of emotion.

Researchers may strive to attempt to accomplish one or more of the following, depending on the type of observation they employ: (a) to see events through the eyes of the people being studied, (b) to attend to seemingly mundane details (i.e., to take nothing for granted), (c) to contextualize observed data in the widest possible social and historical frame (without overgeneralizing from limited data), (d) to attain maximum flexibility of research design (i.e., to use as many means as feasible to collect data to supplement basic observational data), and (e) to construct theories or explanatory frameworks only after careful analysis of objectively recorded data.

TYPES OF OBSERVATIONAL RESEARCH

There are three main ways in which social scientists have conducted observational research. There is considerable overlap in these approaches, but it is useful to distinguish them for purposes of definition: (a) PARTICIPANT OBSERVATION, a style of research favored by field-workers, requires the establishment of rapport in study communities and the long-term immersion of researchers in the everyday life of those communities; (b) reactive observation, associated with controlled settings, assumes that the people being studied are aware of being studied but interact with the researcher only in response to elements in the research design; and (c) unobtrusive (nonreactive) observation is the study of people who are unaware of being observed.

Each of the three types of observational research involves three procedures of increasing levels of specificity:

(a) Descriptive observation involves the annotation and description of all details by an observer who assumes a nearly childlike stance, eliminating all preconceptions and taking nothing for granted. This procedure yields a huge amount of data, some of which will prove irrelevant. It takes a certain amount of experience in the setting to be able to determine what is truly irrelevant to the participants.

(b) Focused observation entails the researcher looking only at that material pertinent to the issue at hand, often concentrating on well-defined categories of group activity (e.g., religious rituals, political elections).

(c) Selective observation requires honing in on a specific form of a more general category (e.g., initiation rituals; city council elections).

QUESTIONS OF OBJECTIVITY IN OBSERVATIONAL RESEARCH

Social scientists have long realized that their very presence can affect the activities and settings under observation, and they also have endeavored to adhere to careful standards of objective data collection and analysis so as to minimize the effects of observer bias. Objectivity is the result of agreement between participants in and observers of activities and settings as to what is happening; in other words, the researcher has not imposed theoretical or other preconceptions on the events being analyzed.

Social researchers of the first half of the 20th century adopted one of four observational roles of increasing degrees of presumed scientific objectivity: (a) the complete participant, or insider; (b) the participant-as-observer (an insider with scientific training); (c) the observer-as-participant (an outsider who becomes a member of the community, a stance actually preferred by cultural anthropologists); and (d) the complete observer (a researcher without ties to the people or setting being observed who conducts his or her observations unobtrusively, with a minimal amount of interaction with those being observed).

The ideal of complete objectivity, however, has been compromised by modern ethical concerns about INFORMED CONSENT. Researchers who take pains to inform subjects about the nature and purposes of the research, as required by most institutional review boards, would almost certainly be involved in more interaction than the old ideal would accommodate. Modern researchers therefore prefer to characterize their roles in terms of degrees of membership in the setting under observation, on the assumption that no one can function as an ethical researcher without being a member in some fashion. Membership roles may include (a) peripheral member researchers (those who develop an insider's perspective without participating in activities constituting the core of group membership), (b) active member researchers (those who become involved with the central activities of the group, sometimes even assuming leadership responsibilities, but without necessarily giving a full endorsement of the group's values and goals), and (c) complete member researchers (those who study settings in which they already are members or with which they become fully affiliated as they conduct their research). Researchers in the latter group still, however, strive to make sure that their insider status does not alter the flow of interaction in an unnatural manner—their status as insiders presumably making it possible for them to detect the natural from the unnatural flow of events.

Contemporary observational researchers demonstrate an increased willingness to affirm an existing membership (or to develop a new one) in the group they are studying. They recognize that it might be neither feasible nor desirable to filter out their own perceptions in a quest for the "truth" of a given social situation. In other words, the classic goal of systematic rigor leading to results as nearly objectively rendered as possible has been replaced by an attitude in which multiple versions of "truth" are possible and in which observations are, among other things, records of encounters between specific researchers and specific subjects at specific points in time, rather than reflections of some sort of timeless, abstract social reality. (This attitude shift is more prominent among observational field researchers; experimental researchers, who still have the option of controlling for extraneous variables, continue to strive for rigorous objectivity.)

Field researchers, unlike laboratory researchers, are also redefining the people they study. They prefer to avoid the traditional term for those people, "subjects," and refer to them instead as "partners," "collaborators," or participants in research. The term "subjects" can seem paternalistic, perpetuating an undesirable image of the all-knowing scientist putting human beings under the microscope in a detached, controlled, abstract (and, by implication, unrealistic) manner. Because ethical rules mandate informing "subjects" about their rights and about the nature and scope of a research project, those people are no longer passive actors being observed by a distant authority figure; their values, beliefs, and ideas must necessarily inform the research.

QUESTIONS OF VALIDITY AND RELIABILITY IN OBSERVATIONAL RESEARCH

Social researchers are becoming increasingly skeptical of using observations of specific people in specific settings to generate large-scale descriptions of cultures supposedly represented by those who are observed. Observational researchers commonly use several techniques to enhance the validity of their data. Cautious about making inferences beyond the study population, yet interested in large-scale patterns, observational researchers may rely on composite portraits generated by standardized observational checklists (see STRUC-TURED OBSERVATION) used by a team of researchers in many different settings rather than on inferences from a single observed site. It is sometimes suggested that the members of the team should represent a diversity of age, gender, and other demographic characteristics, to make sure that such factors do not inadvertently color any one researcher's perceptions. The "Six Cultures Study," created by John Whiting and his associates in the 1950s to generate cross-culturally valid information about child-rearing practices, is the classic example of this approach. A more recent example is the study of needle hygiene among injection drug users in 20 sites in the United States, led by Stephen Koester, Michael Clatts, and Laurie Price for the National Institute on Drug Abuse.

Data reliability is enhanced by TRIANGULATION—the inclusion of observation in a package of data collection methods so as to achieve a reasonably comprehensive conclusion. The fact that one can reach the same conclusion by means of different data collection techniques makes it more likely that the data are reliable.

OBSERVATIONAL RESEARCH IN SELECTED SCHOOLS OF SOCIAL RESEARCH THEORY AND PRACTICE

Observational research has been favored by followers of several major theoretical or conceptual traditions in the social sciences. For example, the school of formal sociology (of which Georg Simmel was an early representative) focuses on the forms or structures that pattern social interactions and relations, rather than on the specific content of those relations. More modern

formal sociologists, such as Manfred Kuhn and Carl Couch, see social reality as constructed by an interaction of the self and the other through more or less institutionalized forms of interconnectedness. Proponents of this school have advocated the use of video technology to record observational data; those with a cultural anthropological orientation favor videotaping in the field, whereas others favor bringing subjects into a specially designed setting in which they can be taped. Such studies tend to focus on the ways in which people develop and sustain relationships, although modifications of the technique also have been used to study the operation of large bureaucracies.

Dramaturgical sociology, associated with the work of Erving Goffman, has focused on how people present themselves in social settings and, in effect, act out their self-conceptions in front of an "audience"—the social group. Goffman's approach, sometimes criticized as unsystematic and hence overly subjective, nonetheless enables the researcher to capture a range of acts of people at all levels of society. Followers of Goffman such as Spencer Cahill have attempted to introduce a degree of systematization in the method; Cahill in particular has made use of teams of researchers, although he has used Goffman's approach of unstructured recording (making notes on the spot and categorizing them afterward, rather than immediately sorting observed behavior into precoded categories) in public and semipublic places. By contrast, Laud Humphreys has attempted to develop a systematic method for capturing dramaturgical detail. In his study of homosexual encounters in a public restroom, he made sure to record his observations on a checklist, although the fact that this method made it possible to identify participants (who, being engaged in a covert activity, probably would not have given permission to be observed so closely) has led critics to express concern about the ethics of such research.

Auto-observation (or AUTOETHNOGRAPHY) is a technique that moves the unit of observation from groups in public or semipublic places to the individual and his or her intimate relationships. More often than not, the individual in question is the researcher himself or herself. This approach, sometimes referred to as existential sociology, traces its philosophical roots to sociologist Wilhelm Dilthey, who advocated a stance of *verstehen* (understanding through empathy). An important modern practitioner is Carolyn Ellis, recognized for her powerfully personal account of the death of her partner and the ways in which she dealt with grief. Although the case example is the sociologist herself, the theme of the study is universal, and the reactions she exhibits are meant to be representative of the culture and society of which she is a part. This approach is linked conceptually to the school of reflexive anthropology, in which participant observers shed their pose of strict objectivity and insert themselves into the narratives of the cultures they are describing. Vincent Crapanzano and Peter Wilson, who structured their ethnographies (of a community in Morocco and of a Caribbean island, respectively) through the lens of their personal relationships with their principal informants, are two prominent practitioners of this approach.

Perhaps no school of social research has placed more emphasis on observational techniques than that of ETHNOMETHODOLOGY. Advocates of this approach believe that social life is constructed in terms of subconscious processes—minute gestures that everyone takes for granted and that cannot, therefore, be captured by asking people questions about what they are doing. Ethnomethodologists favor the analysis of minutely detailed data, usually by means of an intricate notational system, an approach they share with the cognitive anthropologists who have turned their attention to the analysis of discourse with an emphasis on conversational overlaps, pauses, and intonations. Sociologist Douglas Maynard used this technique to study the language of courtroom negotiation, and anthropologist Michael Agar used it to study the behavior of drug addicts in a rehabilitation program. Nonverbal discourse also may be recorded by means of this approach, as in the methodology of proxemics (the study of the ways in which people in a given culture use space and how the arrangement of people in space—e.g., the positioning of furniture in a house; the patterns by which people fill in seats in an airport lounge—conveys cultural meanings about relationships), which was pioneered by Edward Hall, and the methodology of kinesics (the academic version of the study that has entered pop psychology as "body language") developed by R. L. Birdwhistle.

THE ETHICAL DIMENSION OF OBSERVATIONAL RESEARCH

Observational researchers resist the notion that they are engaged in harmfully intrusive work, although, as noted above, they certainly are aware of the necessity of increasing their interactions with members of study populations. Observational research that is defined as "public" (e.g., studies of patterns in the ways people orient themselves in elevators) may be exempt from institutional review, although examples of purely observational research with minimal interaction are becoming increasingly rare. The more interaction there is, the more opportunities there will be for doing harm in ways that cannot always be adequately anticipated at the outset of a project. It is therefore considered important for observational researchers, regardless of degree of interaction, to be as open as possible with the people they study, and to disclose as much about the project's methods and aims as they can.

—Michael V. Angrosino

REFERENCES

Adler, P. A., & Adler, P. (1994). Observational techniques. In N. K. Denzin & Y. S. Lincoln (Eds.), *Handbook of qualitative research* (pp. 377–392). Thousand Oaks, CA: Sage.

Agar, M. (1973). *Ripping and running.* New York: Academic Press.

Angrosino, M. V., & Pérez, K. (2000). Rethinking observation: From method to context. In N. K. Denzin & Y. S. Lincoln (Eds.), *Handbook of qualitative research* (2nd ed., pp. 73–702). Thousand Oaks, CA: Sage.

Cahill, S. (1987). Children and civility: Ceremonial deviance and the acquisition of ritual competence. *Social Psychology Quarterly, 50,* 312–321.

Crapanzano, V. (1980). *Tuhami: Portrait of a Moroccan.* Chicago: University of Chicago Press.

Ellis, C. (1995). *Final negotiations: A story of love, loss, and chronic illness.* Philadelphia: Temple University Press.

Gold, R. L. (1958). Roles in sociological field observation. *Social Forces, 36,* 217–223.

Humphreys, L. (1975). *Tearoom trade: Impersonal sex in public places.* Chicago: Aldine.

Maynard, D. W. (1984). *Inside plea bargaining: The language of negotiation.* New York: Plenum.

Price, L. J. (2002). Carrying out a structured observation. In M. V. Angrosino (Ed.), *Doing cultural anthropology* (pp. 107–114). Prospect Heights, IL: Waveland.

Schensul, J. J., & LeCompte, M. D. (Eds.). (1999). *Ethnographer's toolkit.* Walnut Creek, CA: AltaMira.

Whiting, J. W., Child, I. L., & Lambert, W. W. (1966). *Field guide for the study of socialization.* New York: Wiley.

Wilson, P. J. (1974). *Oscar: An inquiry into the nature of sanity.* New York: Vintage.

OBSERVED FREQUENCIES

A frequency can be defined simply as the number of times an event, which we are measuring, happens.

Table 1 Number of Cars Parked During the Week

Day of the Week	Total Number of Cars Parked
Monday	10
Tuesday	9
Wednesday	10
Thursday	8
Friday	1
Saturday	3
Sunday	2

The event is the VARIABLE on which we are interested in gaining information. Consider the data in Table 1.

The event/variable we are measuring is that of parking lot occupancy. Thus, on Monday, the frequency (i.e., the number of cars parked) is 10, on Tuesday the frequency is 9, on Wednesday it is 10, and so on.

An observed frequency is defined as the *actual* number of times we see the event, which we are measuring, happening. Does this mean we have to stand in the car park and record every car that is parked? In some cases, yes, we would, and could, measure an event by physically being there and counting its frequency. In reality, we tend to gain details about the event/variable we are measuring by using a research instrument (e.g., QUESTIONNAIRE). For example, we could ask the parking lot attendant to fill in a questionnaire about the occupancy of the lot on the days of the week and, using that information, construct Table 1.

We can elaborate on this analysis by looking at the RELATIVE FREQUENCY, which is derived from the observed frequency. The relative frequency is the proportion of cases that include the phenomena we are examining, in relation to the total number of cases in the study.

For example, the total number of cars parked in the parking lot example during the week was 43. We can calculate the relative frequency for each day of the week by using the following formula:

$$\text{relative frequency} = \frac{\text{number of cars parked in the lot on a particular day}}{\text{total number of cars parked during the week}}.$$

Thus, on Monday there were 10 cars parked, and the total during the week was 43; therefore, the relative frequency for Monday is as follows:

$$\text{relative frequency (Monday)} = 10/43 = 0.23.$$

From this calculation, we would state that the relative frequency of occupancy on Monday was 0.23.

We could repeat these calculations and compute the relative frequency for the remaining days of the week.

Observed frequency should not be confused with *expected* frequency. Although the two are joined by the fact that they are looking at the same event/variable, they are quite different in their calculation and interpretation.

An expected frequency is *not* an observed frequency, although it may be based upon one. Expected frequencies are what we *expect* to happen, as opposed to what *actually* happens. Expected frequencies usually are based upon some previous information that a researcher has acquired, calculated, or noted, and from which he or she attempts to predict what will happen. For example, we could observe how many cars were parked on four consecutive Mondays and from this attempt to predict what we expect to happen on the fifth Monday.

—Paul E. Pye

REFERENCES

Kerr, A. W., Hall, H. K., & Kozub, A. (2002). Descriptive statistics. Chapter 2 in *Doing statistics with SPSS*. London: Sage.

Hinton, P. R. (1996). *Statistics explained: A guide for social science students*. London: Routledge.

OBSERVER BIAS

Although they may strive for OBJECTIVITY in the recording and analysis of data, social researchers who use observational methods are aware of the possibility that bias arising out of the nature of observation itself may compromise their work. It is therefore desirable for researchers to become consciously aware of such possibilities and then to take steps to avoid them.

Observer bias may arise out of unconscious assumptions or preconceptions harbored by the researcher. In some cases, these preconceptions take the form of ethnocentrism—the unreflective acceptance of the values, attitudes, and practices of one's own culture as somehow normative, leading to the inability to see, let alone to understand, behaviors that do not conform to that norm. Feminist scholars have increased researchers' awareness of the unspoken assumptions based in gender and in the power relationships implied by gender roles. Other critics have pointed out ethnocentrism rooted in the social class, religious background, and even age (the "generation gap"), all of which may contribute to researchers missing important points about the lives of people who are in any way different from themselves.

The effects of ethnocentric observer bias usually can be mitigated by a rigorous and sustained effort at making conscious all the unconscious assumptions that might lead to misperception. Somewhat more subtle—and hence more difficult to overcome—is the bias resulting from the tendency of people to change their behavior when they know they are being observed, even if the researcher doing the observation is doing all the right things to minimize his or her ethnocentrism. Traditional cultural anthropology was based on the establishment of long-term relationships in a study community so that, in effect, the members of the community would forget that they were in fact being observed by someone who had ceased to be a stranger. It is no longer always possible, even for anthropologists, to arrange for long-term field studies. It is therefore necessary to devise other ways to mitigate observer effects in short-term research; for example, the researcher can enhance the level of comfort and trust in the study population by being introduced to the community by someone who already is respected by that group. It is also desirable to practice TRIANGULATION—the collection of impressions gleaned from observation with other sources of data, the better to ensure that unintended cues emanating from any one researcher have not skewed the results.

Most contemporary social researchers recognize that they cannot predict every potential effect that they may have on a study community, and they admit that it is unreasonable to strive to be strictly neutral presences. Some aspects of a researcher's self-presentation can be easily modified to minimize his or her obtrusiveness in a study community (e.g., style of dress, tone of voice). Other factors (e.g., race, gender, age) cannot be changed; it is therefore ethically desirable for researchers, when reporting results, to be candid about such factors, so that readers can judge for themselves whether or not they seriously compromised the study population's response to the conditions of research.

—Michael V. Angrosino

REFERENCES

Gouldner, A. W. (1962). Anti-minotaur: The myth of a value-free sociology. *Social Problems, 9*, 199–213.

Schensul, S. L., Schensul, J. J., & LeCompte, M. D. (1999). *Essential ethnographic methods: Observations, interviews, and questionnaires*. Walnut Creek, CA: AltaMira.

ODDS

The odds that a state exists (for example, that someone is a computer user) or that an event occurs (for example, that someone commits a crime) is the ratio of the probability that the state or event occurs to the probability that the state or event does not occur. If we symbolize the probability of the state or event by $P(Y)$, then the odds of Y, $\text{odds}(Y) = P(Y)/[1 - P(Y)]$. If the event or state is impossible, the probability is zero and the odds are zero. If the probability is less than 0.5, the odds will be between zero and 1; if the probability is exactly 0.5, the odds will be 1; if the probability is greater than 0.5, the odds will be greater than 1; and if the state or event is certain, $P(Y) = 1$ and $\text{odds}(Y) = 1/0$, which is positive and infinitely large in magnitude. The idea of the odds of an outcome, or the comparison of the odds of two alternative outcomes, is common in gambling, which provided some of the impetus for the early development of probability theory and statistics (Stigler, 1986, pp. 62–63).

The odds is the ratio of two "opposite" probabilities, the first equal to one minus the second. Another related ratio of two probabilities is the *relative risk* or *risk ratio*, the ratio of two different but not necessarily opposite probabilities. For example, if the probability of computer use is .60 for males, then the odds of computer use for males, $\text{odds}(Y)$, is $(0.60)/(1 - 0.60) = 1.5$; if the probability of computer use is .45 for females, then the odds of computer use for females is $(0.45)/(1 - 0.45) = 0.82$, and the ratio of the probabilities (or risks) of computer use for males compared to females is the relative risk $= 0.60/0.45 = 1.33$. In other words, males are 1.33 times as likely to use computers as females. A second related ratio, the ODDS RATIO, is the ratio of two different but not opposite odds. In the above example, the odds ratio of males as opposed to females being computer users is odds ratio = (odds of male using computer)/(odds of female using computer) = $1.5/0.82 = 1.83$. In other words, the odds of computer use is 1.83 times as high, or 83% higher, for males as for females. Notice that the relative risk and the odds ratio are not the same. A common mistake is to calculate an odds ratio, then interpret it as though it were a relative risk, for instance, in the above example, saying that males are 1.83 times as likely to use computers as females (when, as shown above, males are only 1.33 times as likely as females to be computer users). It is important to keep clear the distinction between (a) probabilities or ratios of probabilities and (b) odds or ratios of odds.

—Scott Menard

REFERENCES

Stigler, S. M. (1986). *The history of statistics: The measurement of uncertainty before 1900.* Cambridge, MA: Belknap Press and Harvard University Press.

ODDS RATIO

An odds ratio is the division of two ODDS. An odds is formed by two numbers representing two different events (most often event vs. nonevent), such as the odds of winning versus losing, or the odds of voting for the Democratic candidate versus voting for the Republican candidate (or a non-Democratic candidate). As such, it is different from a rate, which gives the number of events occurring in a population standardized to a base, such as per hundred or per thousand. Odds ratios are useful statistical tools in CATEGORICAL DATA ANALYSIS for studying association or concordance in the data.

G. Udny Yule was notably the first statistician to apply odds ratios to measure the association in CONTINGENCY TABLES. Odds ratios and log-odds ratios are common tools for LOG-LINEAR MODELING. To demonstrate the application of odds ratios, let us examine in Table 1 some classic data presented by M. Greenwood and G. U. Yule in their classic 1915 study of the effect of antityphoid inoculations.

This is a typical 2×2 table with the columns recording the two outcomes and the rows representing the two categories in the exposure variable. More generally, the columns may contain any response or dependent variable and the rows, any explanatory or

Table 1   Data on Antityphoid Inoculations

	Typhoid: No	Typhoid: Yes	Total
Inoculation: Yes	6,759	56	6,815
Inoculation: No	11,396	272	11,668
Total	18,155	328	18,483

SOURCE: Data are from Greenwood and Yule (1915).

Table 2   A Two-by-Two Table Layout

	Variable 1, Category 1	Variable 1, Category 2	Total
Variable 2, Category 1	A	B	A + B
Variable 2, Category 2	C	D	C + D
Total	A + C	B + D	A + B + C + D

independent variable; indeed, the rows and columns can simply contain two variables whose association is under investigation. The cells can be indicated by A, B, C, and D (see Table 2).

There are three nonredundant ways of forming odds ratios (OR) in a 2×2 table:

$$OR_1 = \frac{A/C}{D/B}, \quad OR_2 = \frac{A/B}{D/C}, \quad \text{and} \quad OR_3 = \frac{A/B}{C/D}.$$

For studying association between two categorical variables, OR_3 typically is used. This odds ratio is also known as the cross-product ratio because

$$OR = \frac{A/B}{C/D} = \frac{AD}{BC},$$

where hereafter we ignore the subscript because it is the only odds ratio we examine. Returning to the data on antityphoid inoculations, we find the odds ratio or cross-product ratio to be

$$OR = \frac{(6,759)(272)}{(56)(11,396)} = 2.881.$$

The ratio suggests that there is an association between inoculations and typhoid occurrences. The odds of having typhoid prevented are close to three times greater for those who had received inoculations than for those who had not. Statistics like these may give some evidence to government agencies for policy making such as implementing vaccination programs.

Note that YULE'S Q is simply a function of the odds ratio that has been normed to fall between -1 and $+1$:

$$Q = \frac{OR - 1}{OR + 1} = \frac{2.881 - 1}{2.881 + 1} = 0.485.$$

Because the Q statistic is close to 0.5 (with zero indicating no relationship), it suggests some moderate positive association between inoculations and typhoid prevention.

Often, it is convenient to work with (natural-) log-odds ratios, which have two useful properties. Log-odds ratios have zero as the value for indicating no relation between the two variables, whereas the value for odds ratios is one. Zero for no relationship may be intuitively appealing for some researchers. One also can compute asymptotic standard errors for log-odds ratios,

$$\sigma_{\log(OR)} = \sqrt{\frac{1}{A} + \frac{1}{B} + \frac{1}{C} + \frac{1}{D}}$$
$$= \sqrt{\frac{1}{6,759} + \frac{1}{56} + \frac{1}{11,396} + \frac{1}{272}} = 0.148,$$

and calculate related Z ratios that follow the standard normal distribution:

$$Z = \frac{\log(OR)}{\sigma_{\log(OR)}} = \frac{0.460}{0.148} = 3.108.$$

The Z statistic indicates a highly significant result (i.e., it is very unlikely that the odds is observed by chance). One can go one step further by constructing confidence intervals for log-odds ratios using the Z obtained (or for odds ratios by going through the anti-log function).

—Tim Futing Liao

REFERENCE

Greenwood, M. & Yule, G. U. (1915). The statistics of antityphoid and anticholera inoculations, and the interpretation of such statistics in general. *Proceedings of the Royal Society of Medicine 8* (part 2), 113–194.

Rudas, T. (1997). *Odds ratios in the analysis of contingency tables*. Thousand Oaks, CA: Sage.

OFFICIAL STATISTICS

Counts made by administrators on behalf of their rulers for the purposes of gathering taxes or conscripting soldiers were a feature of many ancient civilizations, but the organized compilation of facts and figures for the use of states in much broader ways became systematized only following the age of Enlightenment, the scientific revolution, and the growth of European nationalism. Nowadays, modern states collect and publish a whole a range of DATA about their populations, trade, finances, housing, health, consumption, leisure activities, and many other aspects of their societies, both to reflect performance and as a guide for future policy formation. In addition, supranational bodies

such as the European Commission, the United Nations and its subsidiary organizations, the World Health Organization, and the World Bank all monitor their areas of competence, to produce a broader picture of regional and global developments.

MAIN TYPES OF OFFICIAL STATISTICS

Some official statistics are generated routinely as a result of administrative procedures, and there often is a legal requirement for information to be provided to the state. Tax details, births, marriages,s divorces, deaths, and certain notifiable diseases are recorded in this way, as are data about employment and unemployment, crime, and education. STATISTICS about these collections of data are reported at regular intervals in many countries.

Although apparently comprising a full record, such statistics have often been questioned on the grounds that they provide an incomplete picture of the areas they claim to cover. Most vulnerable to this type of criticism have been official figures about crime, employment, and unemployment. Alternative means of gathering information about crime, such as victim SURVEYS, have revealed the gulf between levels of crime experienced by the population and published statistics of recorded crime. This discrepancy, known as the "dark figure," stems partly from the fact that many offenses are not reported, for a wide variety of reasons including disbelief by victims or witnesses that effective action will be taken, fear of retaliation by perpetrators, or simply apathy (Coleman & Moynihan, 1996).

Similarly, official employment statistics fail to take account of those working in the informal or illegal economy, and unemployment statistics omit those who have become discouraged about finding work and have dropped out of the labor market, as in depressed market situations when jobs are scarce. Because unemployment rates are politically sensitive, governments may take administrative measures to reduce still further the reported numbers out of work, such as by excluding the long-term unemployed and others not eligible for compensatory benefits.

The most widely known and longest established form of official statistics are the results of the CENSUS of population, a compendium of information about all inhabitants of a state. The U.S. Bureau of the Census conducts the national census at 10-year intervals. Although a census is regarded as the most comprehensive source of information about the entire population of a country, the broad scope of its focus usually renders it inadequate for more detailed investigation.

Recent decades have seen a growth of government surveys, usually targeted at specific topic areas to investigate inevitable gaps left by censuses. For reasons of cost, if no other, many kinds of official statistics generated in this way are not based on all of those from whom data might be gathered. Instead a subset, consisting of a large-scale REPRESENTATIVE SAMPLE, is approached, and consequent findings are then generalized to provide estimates about the whole POPULATION. Using either INTERVIEWING or mail QUESTIONNAIRES to gather data, these surveys often achieve high response rates, inspiring confidence in their inferences.

Typical examples of such surveys in the United Kingdom are the Family Expenditure Survey, established as early as the 1950s, and the 1970s General Household Survey. As its name implies, the latter is a general purpose data-gathering tool for use by a wide range of researchers and is flexible enough to be modified by the introduction of new questions to take account of changing social trends or policy priorities. Other major surveys include cohort studies such as the Longitudinal Survey, which tracks a 1% sample of the U.K. population, the Labour Force Survey, and the British Household Panel Survey.

These last two studies are examples of state-sponsored surveys designed to be compatible with those of other countries so that results contribute to international statistical reports. Such cross-national statistics are increasingly the norm, and the adoption of standard measures provides not only comparability but also safeguards against manipulation by individual governments. Nevertheless, problems remain, and where statistics relate to politically sensitive issues, such as asylum seekers, this can affect their dissemination (Singleton, 1999).

CHANGING ACCESS TO OFFICIAL STATISTICS

During the last decades of the 20th century, the significance of the long-standing practice of gathering and compiling official statistics was completely transformed. Although the census of population had long been automated by the use of punched card processing (1880 in the United States and 1911 in the United Kingdom), in the later years of the 20th century the expansion in computing capacity available to the ordinary citizen through the rapid spread and quantum leap in processing power of personal computers was matched by the explosive growth of the World Wide Web and the proliferation of databases holding vast amounts of statistical information. These parallel processes meant that it was no longer necessary to rely entirely on the published accounts of governmental or other official agencies: Individuals now had the potential to interrogate data sets for themselves and make their own interpretations.

These technological developments did not take place in a political vacuum. Governments, particularly in OECD countries, embraced a democratizing agenda to make more information available to their citizens so that they could gain a fuller understanding of the changing nature of their society and participate more actively in debates about the governance of their states. Many governments and organizations now provide free access to databases held on their Web sites. Meanwhile, international statistics are coordinated and made available by supranational agencies such as Eurostat. At the same time, it should be recognized that ways in which data are produced and released place subtle constraints on this new paradise where a wealth of apparently reliable and objective information is freely available.

THE POLITICAL CONTEXT OF OFFICIAL STATISTICS

Attempts by the U.K. government in the 1980s to suppress the publication of research findings that revealed a growing mortality gap between rich and poor, as well as problems such as those about unemployment statistics discussed above, serve as reminders of the highly sensitive political context of some statistics (Townsend, Davidson, & Whitehead, 1988). It should never be forgotten that although certain published figures are termed "official," this offers no guarantee of their accuracy or impartiality or that hidden censorship or pressure has not occurred. The issue of impartiality remains a concern for all users of official statistics worldwide, and in the United Kingdom the debate continues despite government pledges to freedom of information and an independent national statistical service.

—Will Guy

REFERENCES

Coleman, C., & Moynihan, J. (1996). *Understanding crime data: Haunted by the dark figure.* Buckingham, UK: Open University Press.

Singleton, A. (1999). Measuring international migration: A case study of European cross-national comparisons. In D. Dorling & S. Simpson (Eds.), *Statistics in society: The arithmetic of politics* (pp. 148–158). London: Arnold.

Townsend, P., Davidson, N., & Whitehead, M. (1988). *Inequalities in health: The Black report and the health divide.* Harmondsworth: Penguin.

OGIVE. *See* CUMULATIVE FREQUENCY POLYGON

OLS. *See* ORDINARY LEAST SQUARES

OMEGA SQUARED

Omega squared (ω^2) is a measure of the strength (or magnitude) of an effect. There are various measures of the strength of an effect relevant to different data measurements (e.g., the CORRELATION COEFFICIENT is one kind of effect strength measure). Omega squared is relevant to experimental studies that have been analyzed using one-way or factorial ANALYSIS OF VARIANCE. It is one of a group of measures of the strength of effect for analysis of variance that are related to R-SQUARED (R^2) (the measure of the strength of effect in regression and correlation). The strength of an effect is scientifically important because it gives a comparative measurement of how much a treatment (in an experimental study) has affected the behavioral measure. An effect size of zero means the treatment had no effect, and measures of strength of effect related to R-squared have a maximum of 1 (as does the correlation coefficient).

In a one-way (unrelated measures) analysis of variance, the results table looks like Table 1.

Table 1   A One-Way Analysis of Variance

Source	Degrees of Freedom	Sum of Squares	Mean Square	F Ratio
Treatment	k	a	x	$\frac{x}{y}$
Error	$n - k - 1$	b	y	
Total	$n - 1$	c		

NOTE: k is the number of treatment groups and n is the total number of measurements (in social science research, usually participants).

Table 2   Example Results From a One-Way Analysis of Variance

Source	Degrees of Freedom	Sum of Squares	Mean Square	F Ratio
Treatment	3	600	200	2
Error	20	2,000	100	
Total	23	2,600		

For fixed treatment effects, the mathematical definition of ω^2 is

$$\omega^2 = \frac{a - (k - 1)y}{c + y}.$$

Suppose a one-way ANOVA produced results like Table 2.
Then

$$\omega^2 = \frac{600 - (3 - 1)100}{2,600 + 100}.$$

The definition for random effects differs because the variance component calculation is different from that for fixed effects.

A more general formula is

$$\omega^2_{\text{effect}} = \frac{\hat{\sigma}^2_{\text{effect}}}{\hat{\sigma}^2_{\text{total}}}.$$

where $\hat{\sigma}^2_{\text{effect}}$ is the VARIANCE COMPONENT for an effect. This formula can be used for fixed and random effects, assuming the variance components are calculated appropriately (e.g., see Howell, 2002).

There are other potential measures of effect strength for analysis of variance. These include ETA squared (η^2), which is also related to R^2, and phi prime (ϕ'), which is a measure of standardized effect size, related to Cohen's d.

Omega squared is a less biased measure of magnitude of effect than is eta squared (see Fowler, 1985). This means it is a better estimate of the treatment effect in the population, as opposed to the magnitude of the effect found in the current sample. Insofar as there are differences between ω^2 and η^2, ω^2, is always smaller and more useful when we are interested in generalizing results to a population.

—Martin Le Voi

See also BIAS, ETA, FIXED-EFFECTS MODEL, R-SQUARED, VARIANCE

REFERENCES

Fowler, R. L. (1985). Point estimates and confidence intervals in measures of association. *Psychological Bulletin, 98*, 160–165.

Howell, D. C. (2002). *Statistical methods for psychology* (5th ed.). Duxbury, UK: Thomson Learning.

OMITTED VARIABLE

In any research situation, the estimated effect of one variable on another may change when a third variable is introduced. The direction of a relationship between two variables may change or the relationship may disappear altogether when controlling for a third variable. Social scientists must beware the danger of excluding relevant variables from a research design. Failure to account for relevant variables may result in omitted variable bias.

Suppose we want to estimate the effect of INDEPENDENT VARIABLE X_1 on DEPENDENT VARIABLE Y. The effect of X_1 on Y is denoted as β_1. If we use REGRESSION analysis, our estimate of β_1 is b_1. If omitted variable bias is present in our research, our estimate b_1 is incorrect because we have failed to account for another independent variable, X_2.

How do we know if omitting X_2 biases our estimate of β_1? If X_2 has no effect on the dependent variable Y, then omitting X_2 will not induce bias. In other words, if an independent variable is irrelevant to the phenomenon under study, then excluding that independent variable will not cause bias.

An omitted variable will bias our estimate of β_1 only if the omitted variable is correlated with our explanatory variable X_1. Introducing X_2 into the regression equation will change our estimate of β_1 only if X_2 is correlated with X_1. If X_2 is uncorrelated with X_1, we can safely omit it from our analysis, even if X_2 is strongly related to Y. Thus, we can omit variables that are not correlated with our explanatory variables, even if the omitted variables have a strong relationship with the dependent variable. We will induce omitted variable bias only if we exclude variables that are correlated with the included explanatory variables.

However, if our goal is predicting values of Y, then we should include in our regression every explanatory variable that is strongly related to the dependent variable. Explaining as much variation in the dependent variable as possible will increase the accuracy of our predictions, and we will explain more variation if we include all relevant explanatory variables. When FORECASTING is our goal, we should include all independent variables strongly related to Y. If we do not want to forecast values of Y but simply want to know the effect of X_1 on Y, we can safely exclude any variables not correlated with X_1.

—Megan L. Shannon

REFERENCE

King, G., Keohane, R. O., & Verba, S. (1994). *Designing social inquiry: Scientific inference in qualitative research.* Princeton, NJ: Princeton University Press.

ONE-SIDED TEST. *See* ONE-TAILED TEST

ONE-TAILED TEST

A NULL HYPOTHESIS most often specifies one particular value of a population PARAMETER. We do not necessarily believe this to be the true value of the parameter, but if we can reject the null hypothesis and thereby eliminate this particular value of the parameter, then it follows that the parameter must be equal to something else. In the study of the relationship between two variables, using REGRESSION as an example, the null hypothesis is most often stated in such a way that there is no relationship between the variables. In symbols, H_0: $\beta = 0$, where β is the SLOPE of the population regression line.

If we can reject this null hypothesis, then we have shown that β is not equal to 0, meaning that a relationship exits between the variables. Next, if the population slope is not equal to 0, then what can we conclude about the value of this slope? One possibility is that we do not know anything about the slope, meaning that it can be either greater than or less than zero. Another possibility is that we have additional knowledge about the slope. Say that we know, from previous research, that the slope cannot be negative. The ALTERNATIVE HYPOTHESIS can then be stated as H_1: $\beta > 0$. Because the null hypothesis has been rejected, the conclusion follows from the alternative hypothesis that the value of β must be larger than 0.

This is an example of a *one-tailed* (also called one-sided) test. It is called one-tailed, or one-sided, because of the one-sided form of the alternative hypothesis. The alternative hypothesis includes values only in one direction away from the value of the parameter of the null hypothesis.

When there is a one-tailed alternative hypothesis, the null hypothesis gets rejected for only one range of the test statistic. When we have a normal test statistic and a 5% SIGNIFICANCE LEVEL, a null hypothesis with a two-tailed alternative hypothesis gets rejected for $z < -1.96$ or $z > 1.96$. Half of the significance level is located at each tail of the test statistic, and we reject for large, negative values or large, positive values. For a one-tailed test with a 5% significance level, however, the null hypothesis is rejected for $z > 1.64$. That means the rejection region is located here only in one (the positive) tail of the distribution of the test statistic. This is because we make use of the additional knowledge we have about the parameter—that it is greater than zero.

The distinction between a two-tailed and a one-tailed alternative hypothesis could matter for a normal test statistic, say if $z = 1.85$. With a two-tailed alternative here, the null would not be rejected, but it would be rejected for a one-tailed alternative. This situation, however, does not occur very often.

Also, with the change from a prechosen significance level to a P VALUE computed from the data, the distinction is not as important. If we report a one-tailed p value, then the reader can easily change it to a two-tailed p value by multiplying by 2. Statistical software must be clear on whether it computes one-tailed or two-tailed p values.

—Gudmund R. Iversen

REFERENCES

Mohr, L. B. (1990). *Understanding significance testing* (Sage University Papers series on Quantitative Applications in the Social Sciences, series 07–073). Newbury Park, CA: Sage.

Morrison, D. E., & Henkel, R. (Eds.). (1970). *The significance test controversy*. Chicago: Aldine.

ONE-WAY ANOVA

Analysis of variance, which is abbreviated as ANOVA, was developed by Sir Ronald Fisher (1925) to determine whether the means of one or more factors and their interactions differed significantly from that expected by chance. "One-way" refers to an analysis that involves only one factor. "Two-way" (or more ways) refers to an analysis with two or more factors and the interactions between those factors. A factor comprises two or more groups or levels. Analysis of variance is based on the assumption that each group is drawn from a population of scores that is normally distributed. In addition, the variance of scores in the different groups should be equal, or homogeneous.

The scores in the different groups may be related or unrelated. *Related* scores may come from the same cases or cases that have been matched to be similar in certain respects. An example of related scores is where the same variable (such as job satisfaction) is measured at two or more points in time. *Unrelated* or *independent* scores come from different cases. An example of unrelated scores is where the same variable is measured in different groups of people (such as people in different occupations). An analysis of variance consisting of only two groups is equivalent to a *t*-test where the variances are assumed to be equal.

A one-way analysis of variance for unrelated scores compares the population estimate of the variance between the groups with the population estimate of the variance within the groups. This ratio is known as the *F*-test, *F*-statistic, or *F*-value in honor of Fisher and is calculated as

$$F = \frac{\text{between-groups variance estimate}}{\text{within-groups variance estimate}}.$$

The bigger the between-groups variance is in relation to the within-groups variance estimate, the larger F will be and the more likely it is to be statistically significant. The statistical significance of F is determined by two sets of degrees of freedom: those for the between-groups variance estimate (the numerator or upper part of the F ratio) and those for the within-groups variance estimate (the denominator or lower part of the F ratio). The between-groups DEGREES OF FREEDOM are the number of groups minus 1. The within-groups degrees of freedom are the number of cases minus the number of groups.

In a one-way analysis of variance for related scores, the denominator of the F ratio is the population estimate of the within-groups variance minus the population estimate of the variance due to the cases. The degrees of freedom for this denominator are the number of cases minus 1 multiplied by the number of groups minus 1.

Where the factor consists of more than two groups and F is statistically significant, which of the means differ significantly from each other needs to be determined by comparing them two at a time. Where there are good grounds for predicting the direction of these differences, these comparisons should be carried out with the appropriate t-test. Otherwise, these comparisons should be made with a post hoc test. There are a number of such tests, such as the SCHEFFÉ TEST.

—Duncan Cramer

REFERENCE

Fisher, R. A. (1925). *Statistical methods for research workers.* London: Oliver and Boyd.

ONLINE RESEARCH METHODS

The development of computer technology and the Internet has greatly enhanced the ability of social scientists to find information, collaborate with colleagues, and collect data through computer-assisted experiments and surveys. A number of different tools and techniques fall within the rubric of online research methods, including Internet search engines, online databases and data archiving, and online experiments. Although the Internet itself, as a collection of networked computer systems, has existed in some form for at least 25 years, the development of the World Wide Web in the early 1990s significantly improved its usability and began the explosion of interconnected information. At the same time, the development of powerful personal computers has brought to the desktop the ability to develop sophisticated data analyses. Combined, these technological advances have provided social scientists with an important array of new tools.

INTERNET SEARCH ENGINES

The Internet is essentially a collection of interconnected computer networks, which themselves are made up of any number of individual computer systems. Information on these systems is made available to Internet users by placing it on a server, of which there are several types, including Web, news, and file transfer protocol (FTP) servers. As of 2002, there were approximately 200,000,000 servers (or hosts) accessible through the Internet. In order to find material within this overwhelming collection, a wide range of search engines have been developed. A search engine takes the keywords or a sentence entered and returns a list of Web pages that contain the requested words. Some search engines, such as Google (www.google.com) and AltaVista (www.altavista.com) are primarily that; they incorporate a very simple user interface and attempt to return matches that are best using some type of best-fit algorithm. Other engines, such as the one associated with Yahoo! (www.yahoo.com) are more comprehensive, combining an attempt to organize Web sites according to categories, as well as keyword and category searching. Other well-known search engines include Lycos (www.lycos.com) and AskJeeves (www.askjeeves.com). Like Yahoo!, Lycos aims to be more than a search engine, providing a portal service, where users can not only search the Web but also gain access to news and a range of online services. Recent enhancements in search engine technology include options to search for graphical materials such as pictures, as well as for text in word processing documents embedded within Web sites.

Using Internet search engines is as much an art as a science, because for many searches, hundreds and even thousands of potential matches may be returned. In general, the more specific the phrase or keywords used, the better, but the state of search engine technology is such that users often have to wade through many matches to find exactly what they need. In fact, an entire Internet site, www.searchenginewatch.com, is dedicated to helping researchers get the most out of the many different search engines.

ONLINE DATABASES/DATA ARCHIVING

The development of the Internet has greatly improved the ability of scientists to share data. Many data sets now reside on the World Wide Web and are accessible through generalized or specialized search engines. The National Election Studies, for example, provide free access to the full set of data collected since 1948 (www.umich.edu/~nes). Researchers need only register with the site to gain access. The General Printing Office (GPO) of the U.S. federal government has created a single access point to search a range of online databases, including the *Congressional Record* and the *Federal*

Register (www.access.gpo.gov/su_docs/multidb.html). This site also points up a typical problem with online databases—their lack of completeness. The GPO *Federal Register* database, for example, does not begin until 1994, and some of the other constituent data sets are even more recent. Thus, researchers wishing to access significant historical material often cannot find it online. Even so, data sets as broad based as the U.S. Census (www.census.gov) and as specific as the Victorian Database Online (www.victoriandatabase.com) have radically changed the way researchers find information.

For academic researchers, many journals have begun online full-text databases of their articles, maintained either specifically by the journal or as part of a collection of journals. JSTOR (www.jstor.org) is one large full-text database, incorporating page images of 275 journals incorporating more than 73,000 issues, dating back to the first issue for many journals. An even more comprehensive service is provided by EBSCO (www.ebscohost.com), providing access to full text for some 1,800 periodicals and the indices for 1,200 more. Whereas JSTOR provides access back to Volume 1 for many journals, EBSCO full text dates only to 1985 but makes up for this by providing access to current issues, whereas JSTOR limits availability to issues at least 3 years old. Most academic libraries provide users with the ability to use these services, as well as a wide range of other services, including Lexis-Nexus (legal research, news periodicals, and reference information) and ERIC (education).

ONLINE EXPERIMENTS

Although experimentation has been a standard tool in some social science fields for many years, the ability to mount experiments online increases the number and variety of subjects who can participate as well as the sophistication that can be used in the design of the experiment. Computers can be used to manipulate textual and nontextual materials presented to subjects while tracking the way in which the subjects respond. Using computers to mount an experiment simplifies data collection because the experiment can be designed to directly generate the data set as the experiment proceeds, thus avoiding data entry errors. Researchers in decision making and in experimental economics have pioneered much of the use of online experiments, perhaps because their fields lend themselves to simpler experimental designs and experiments that

can be completed quickly. Even so, it is likely that the number of INTERNET SURVEYS is far greater than the number of true experiments running on the Internet. A Hanover College psychology department site (http://psych.hanover.edu/research/exponnet.html) maintains a listing of known Internet-based psychology projects, many of which are surveys rather than experiments.

Even so, the use of the Internet for experimentation is growing rapidly. Software such as MediaLab (www.empirisoft.com/medialab/) and Web-based guides (Kevin O'Neil, *A Guide to Running Surveys and Experiments on the World-Wide Web*, http://psych.unl.edu/psychlaw/guide/guide.asp) can simplify the process of generating online experiments. Researchers who wish to use this technique must consider several points, however. Will the experiment lend itself to being run without direct personal guidance from the experimenter? Participants will have to negotiate their own way through the experiment using only whatever information can be provided on the Web site. Can the experiment be completed reasonably quickly? Most existing online experiments are relatively short; Web users often will not devote significant time to participation in such experiments. Can the experiment be designed to ensure random assignment to experimental conditions? Although RANDOM ASSIGNMENT is important in any EXPERIMENT, the recruitment of subjects in Internet experiments cannot be controlled as easily as in traditional research, so random assignment is potentially critical. An especially interesting challenge comes in acquiring INFORMED CONSENT from potential subjects. For experiments carried out with students for instructional purposes, this is not an issue, but for data collection to be used in research projects aimed at publication and using the general public as subjects, informed consent must be obtained. The standard approach has become a front end to the experiment that provides the consent document and requires subjects to click on a button on the screen to indicate assent to the document. PsychExperiments at the University of Mississippi (http://psychexps.olemiss.edu/About PE/IRB%20procedures1.htm) uses this technique, along with the requirement that subjects affirmatively click on a Send Data button to have their results included in the data set.

—David P. Redlawsk

See also COMPUTER-ASSISTED PERSONAL INTERVIEWING, INTERNET SURVEYS

REFERENCES

Birnbaum, M. H. (2001). *Introduction to behavioral research on the Internet.* Upper Saddle River, NJ: Prentice Hall.

Krantz, J. H., & Dalal, R. (2000). Validity of Web-based psychological research. In M. H. Birnbaum (Ed.), *Psychological experiments on the Internet* (pp. 35–60). New York: Academic Press.

Musch, J., & Reips, U. (2000). A brief history of Web experimenting. In M. H. Birnbaum (Ed.), *Psychological experiments on the Internet* (pp. 61–88). San Diego, CA: Academic Press.

Nesbary, D. K. (2000). *Survey research and the World Wide Web.* Boston, MA: Allyn and Bacon.

University of Mississippi. (n.d.). PsychExperiments. Retrieved from http://psychexps.olemiss.edu

ONTOLOGY, ONTOLOGICAL

Ontology is a branch of philosophy that is concerned with the nature of what exists. It is the study of theories of being, theories about what makes up reality. In the context of social science: All theories and methodological positions make assumptions (either implicit or explicit) about what kinds of things do or can exist, the conditions of their existence, and the way they are related.

Theories about the nature of social reality fall into two categories: What exists is viewed either as a set of material phenomena or as a set of ideas that human beings have about their world. The materialist position assumes that, from a human viewpoint, both natural and social phenomena have an independent existence, and both types of phenomena have the potential to constrain human actions (see REALISM). Natural constraints may be in the form of gravity, climate, and our physical bodies, whereas social constraints include culture, social organization, and the productive system. Materialism is associated with the doctrine of naturalism, which claims that because there is little difference between the behavior of inanimate objects and that of human beings, the logics of enquiry appropriate in the natural sciences can also be used in the social sciences. The idealist position, on the other hand, claims that there are fundamental differences between natural and social phenomena, that humans have culture and live in a world of their shared interpretations (see IDEALISM). Social action is not mere behavior but instead involves a process of meaning giving. It is these meanings that constitute social reality (Johnson, Dandeker, & Ashworth, 1984, pp. 13–15).

Ontological assumptions underpin all social theories and methodological positions; they make different claims about what exists in their domain of interest. For example, POSITIVISM and FALSIFICATIONISM entail ontological assumptions of an ordered universe made up of discrete and observable events. Human activity is regarded as observable behavior taking place in observable, material circumstances. Social reality is regarded as a complex of causal relations between events that are depicted as a patchwork of relations between variables. INTERPRETIVISM, on the other hand, assumes that social reality is the product of processes by which human beings together negotiate the meanings of actions and situations. Human experience is characterized as a process of interpretation rather than direct perception of an external physical world. Hence, social reality is not some "thing" that may be interpreted in different ways; it is those interpretations (Blaikie, 1993, pp. 94, 96).

Because ontological claims are inevitably linked with epistemological claims (see EPISTEMOLOGY), it is difficult to discuss them separately (Crotty, 1998, p. 10). Assertions about what constitutes social phenomena have implications for the way in which it is possible to gain knowledge of such phenomena. Differences in the types of ontological and epistemological claims cannot be settled by empirical enquiry. Although they are open to philosophical debate, the proponents of the various positions ultimately make their claims as an act of faith.

—Norman Blaikie

REFERENCES

Blaikie, N. (1993). *Approaches to social enquiry.* Cambridge, UK: Polity Press.

Crotty, M. (1998). *The foundations of social research.* London: Sage.

Johnson, T., Dandeker, C., & Ashworth, C. (1984). *The structure of social theory.* London: Macmillan.

OPEN QUESTION. *See* OPEN-ENDED QUESTION

OPEN-ENDED QUESTION

Open-ended questions, also called open, unstructured, or qualitative questions, refer to those questions for which the response patterns or answer categories are provided by the respondent, not the interviewer. This is in contrast to closed-ended or structured questions, for which the interviewer provides a limited number of response categories from which the respondent makes a selection. Thus, respondents can provide answers to open questions in their own terms or in a manner that reflects the respondents' own perceptions rather than those of the researcher.

This type of question works well in face-to-face interviews but less well in mail, electronic, or telephone interviews. The open-ended question is effective particularly when phenomenological purposes guide the research. People usually like to give an opinion, making the open-ended question potentially therapeutic for the respondent. In addition, open-ended questions often will generate unanticipated accounts or response categories. The open-ended question also is appropriate when the range of possible responses exceeds what a researcher would provide on response list (e.g., recreation preference); when the question requires a detailed, expanded response; when the researcher wants to find out what a respondent knows about a topic; and when it is necessary to flesh out details of a complicated issue (Fowler, 1995). Open-ended questions also are useful in generating answer categories for closed or structured questions.

The open-ended question is, however, more demanding on respondents, particularly those with less education (Frey, 1989). The detail and depth of a response are also affected by the extent to which a respondent is familiar with or has an investment in the research topic. An open-ended question can prompt a lengthy, detailed response, much of which might be irrelevant to the topic, and which may be difficult to code. Open-ended questions in interviews also typically take longer to ask and to record responses, thereby increasing survey costs. Cost is perhaps the primary reason that the open-ended question is utilized in a limited way in survey research today; survey researchers will use this type of question when it is the only way certain responses can be obtained.

Finally, the open-ended question becomes a "linguistic event" where the interviewer is not simply a neutral or passive conduit of the research questions. Rather, the interview becomes a negotiated text reflecting the interaction of respondent and interviewer (Fontana & Frey, 2000). The interview is a social encounter amplified by the open-ended questions, and the process has the potential to provide an outcome that is not representative of a respondent's perception of events; it is, in a sense, distorted by the interaction of interviewer and respondent.

Open-ended questions are valuable means of obtaining information despite problems associated with burden, cost, and context effects. Some of the difficulties can be overcome by adding some structure or limits to responses (Fowler, 1995) and through proper interviewer training on the administration of open-ended questions.

—James H. Frey

REFERENCES

Fontana, A., & Frey, J. H. (2000). The interview: From structured questions to negotiated text. In N. K. Denzin & Y. S. Lincoln (Eds.), *Handbook of qualitative research* (2nd ed., pp. 645–672). Thousand Oaks, CA: Sage.

Fowler, F. J. (1995). *Improving survey questions*. Thousand Oaks, CA: Sage.

Frey, J. F. (1989). *Survey research by telephone*. Newbury Park, CA: Sage.

OPERATIONAL DEFINITION. *See*
CONCEPTUALIZATION, OPERATIONALIZATION, AND MEASUREMENT

OPERATIONISM/OPERATIONALISM

Operationalism began life in the natural sciences in the work of Percy Bridgman and is a variant of positivism. It specifies that scientific concepts must be linked to instrumental procedures in order to determine their values. "Although a concept such as 'mass' may be conceived theoretically or metaphysically as a property, it is only pious opinion.... 'Mass' as a property is equivalent to 'mass' as inferred from pointer readings" (Blalock, 1961, p. 6).

In the social sciences, operationalism enjoyed a brief spell of acclaim through the work of sociologist George Lundberg (1939). He maintained that sociologists are wrong in believing that measurement can be carried out only after things have been appropriately defined—for example, the idea that we must have a workable definition of alienation before we can measure it. For Lundberg, the definition comes about through measurement. He maintained that social values can be measured (and therefore defined) by an examination of the extent to which particular things are valued. Do people value X? If so, how much do they value X?

Operationalism remained fairly uncontroversial while the natural and social sciences were dominated by POSITIVISM but was an apparent casualty of the latter's fall from grace. In the social sciences, three main difficulties have been identified. First—and this is a problem shared with natural science—is that of underdetermination. How can the researcher know if testable propositions fully operationalize a theory? Concepts such as homelessness, poverty, and alienation take on a range of distinctive dimensions and appearances in different social environments. Homelessness, for instance, will depend for its definition on the historically and socially variable relationship between concepts of "shelter" and "home." Second, the objective external definition of a phenomenon may not (or even cannot) accord with the subjective definition of those who experience it. What for one person seems to be poverty may be riches for another. The third problem is that of definitional disagreement between social scientists. Although individual researchers may find local practical solutions to the second problem, their solutions are likely to be different from and/or contradictory to those of other researchers.

These difficulties would appear to provide an undeniable refutation of the methodological approach, yet despite its apparent demise, operationalism remains an unresolved issue. All survey researchers are familiar with the process of *operationalization*, where one "descends the ladder of abstraction" from theory to measurement. This process is logically equivalent to that of operationalism. It is, for example, possible to state a broad, nonoperationalizable theory of homelessness, but if one wants to measure or describe homelessness using a social survey, then homelessness must be defined operationally (Williams, 1998). The difference between operationalization and operationalism perhaps lies in the relationship between theory and research. Operationalism leads to a division of labor between theory construction and measurement, but most survey researchers these days instead emphasize the importance of a dynamic relationship between theory building and the specification of variables that can test a theory.

—Malcolm Williams

REFERENCES

Blalock, H. (1961). *Causal inference in nonexperimental research.* Chapel Hill: University of North Carolina Press.

Lundberg, G. (1939). *Foundations of sociology.* New York: Macmillan.

Williams, M. (1998). The social world as knowable. In T. May & M. (Eds.), *Knowing the social world* (pp. 5–21). Buckingham, UK: Open University Press.

OPTIMAL MATCHING

Optimal matching (sometimes referred to as optimal alignment) is a metric technique for analyzing the overall resemblance between two strings or sequences of data. This approach makes it possible to compare sequences of uneven length or sequences composed of repeating elements. Combined with scaling or clustering ALGORITHMS, optimal matching can be used to detect empirically common sequential patterns across many cases.

The optimal matching approach was first developed by Vladimir Levenshtein in 1965 and since then has been widely used in the natural sciences for identifying similarity in DNA strings and in computer science as the basis of word- and speech-recognition algorithms. Andrew Abbott (1986) introduced the method to the social sciences.

Optimal matching rests on the premise that resemblance in sequential data can be quantified by calculating how easily one string can be turned into another. The transformation of one sequence into the other is accomplished via a set of elementary operators, usually including insertion of elements (I_i), deletion of elements (D_i), and substitution of one element for another (S_{ij}). Use of each of these operators is associated with a fixed penalty (which may vary for each element i or element pair ij). Using the costs associated with the operators, optimal matching algorithms identify the minimal total cost of transforming one sequence into another; this value is typically called the *distance* between the pair of sequences. Pairs of sequences with small distances resemble each other more than do pairs of sequences with larger distances.

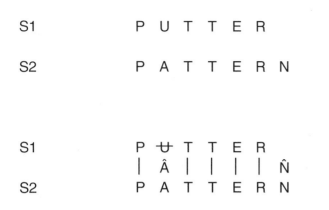

Figure 1   Optimal Matching

If we consider words as sequences of letters, we can use optimal matching to calculate the resemblance between PUTTER and PATTERN (see Figure 1). If each operation exacts the same cost ($S_{ij} = I_i = D_i$ for all elements i and j), it is easy to see that in this example the simplest alignment involves two transformations: replacing the U in position 2 of PUTTER with an A, and inserting an N in position 8.

Although in some situations it may be reasonable to assign each transformation the same cost, most social sciences applications require a more complex cost scheme. For instance, optimal matching frequently is used to reveal patterns in career structures, where careers are built from jobs. Because some jobs are empirically more prevalent—and therefore more easily "substituted"—than are others, a common solution is to order the universe of elements (jobs) into a linear scale and then generate a MATRIX of substitution costs for each pair of elements by calculating the difference in their scores on the scale. Thus $S_{ij} = |i - j|$. In other substantive settings—such as sequences of collective action events or the history of policy changes—nonlinear substitution schemes with increasing or decreasing marginal costs may be more appropriate. Typically, insertion and deletion costs are equal and are set at a value close to the maximum substitution cost.

Although optimal matching is fundamentally a dyadic technique, it can be applied to large data sets with many cases of sequential data. In this situation, optimal matching algorithms produce a matrix in which each cell contains the distance between a pair of sequences. As with any distance matrix, scaling or clustering algorithms can be used to detect groups of cases that are close to one another; the interpretation here is that small distances between cases reflect strong resemblance in the underlying sequential strings of data. Cases also can be classified in terms of their resemblance to theoretically derived or empirically typical sequences; such classifications can be used as VARIABLES in standard regression models.

—Katherine Stovel

REFERENCES

Abbott, A., & Forrest, J. (1986). Optimal matching methods for historical sequences. *Journal of Interdisciplinary History, 16*, 471–494.

Abbott, A., & Hrycak, A. (1990). Measuring resemblance in sequence data. *American Journal of Sociology, 96*, 144–185.

Levenshtein, V. I. (1966). Binary codes capable of correcting deletions, insertions, and reversals. *Cybernetics and Control Theory, 10*, 707–710. (Original work published 1965.)

Sankoff, D., & Kruskal, J. B. (1983). *Time warps, string edits, and macromolecules*. Reading, MA: Addison-Wesley.

OPTIMAL SCALING

Optimal scaling, a term coined by R. Darrell Bock in 1960 for scaling of multivariate categorical data, is mathematically equivalent to DUAL SCALING, CORRESPONDENCE ANALYSIS, and homogeneity analysis of incidence data.

—Shizuhiko Nishisato

ORAL HISTORY

Oral history—research into the past that records the memories of witnesses to the past in order to draw on direct and personal experience of events and conditions—occupies an area of overlap between history, sociology, cultural studies, and psychology. Arguments in support of oral history turn on the challenge that it presents to official and dominant accounts of the past that are based in documentary sources. It is argued that oral history contributes to the broadening of the explanatory base and provides a "voice" to those whose experiences might otherwise go unrecorded. This emancipatory and critical thrust is, for many researchers, the attraction of the method (Perks & Thomson, 1998; Thompson, 2000). Critics question the validity of DATA that depend on the reliability of lifetime survivors' memories.

THE INTERVIEW AND ITS ANALYSIS

At the heart of oral history is INTERVIEWING, a method of data collection that is central to social science practice but equally familiar to historians researching contemporary and 20th century history. For oral historians, the spoken immediacy of the interview, its social relations, and its inevitably interrogative nature are its defining characteristics, yet oral history remains a broad church. Depending on the disciplinary base of the oral historian and on the chosen topic, approaches to finding interviewees and interviewing may vary.

In an early and formative study, Paul Thompson (2000, pp. 145ff) used a QUOTA SAMPLE, taking a sociological approach to find subjects from populations that could not be subjected to randomized selection. When oral historians draw on late-life memories, they are working with survivors. In the Thompson case, a quota sample was used to fill predetermined categories with interview subjects, matching occupational groups identified in the 1911 U.K. census. Such an approach is favored when the focus is general social trends over time, for example, explorations of family relationships, gender, migration, employment, or political generations.

In such studies, interviews tend to be based on standardized areas for questioning, with topic areas identified, most frequently within a LIFE HISTORY perspective. Because the aim is to draw out comparable sources of evidence, to find regularities and patterns in what is presented, interviews tend to follow a closely prescribed form. Studies of this type are likely to be based on sample sizes nearer 100.

In contrast, studies that seek to explore particular events, or that draw on the experiences of a highly select group of survivors, or that focus on one individual's story tend to take a rather different approach to finding and interviewing subjects. In such cases, the most usual approaches to finding interviewees are SNOWBALL SAMPLING, appealing through the media, and using membership lists, representative bodies, or networks among older people's organizations to advertise for witness accounts.

Where studies draw on only a few accounts, the approach to interviewing may be rather different. For one thing, there may be a return to interview the same person more than once, the aim being to secure a full account and one that will enable free expression of subjective experience on the part of the interviewee. Approaches vary again. For some oral historians, a more psychoanalytic, free-associative interaction has proved to be attractive. Explorations of memories of such events as childhood separation, experiences of segregation on the basis of race and disability, and strikes or conflicts can release powerful evocations, particularly when linked to other sources of evidence, documentary or visual, and when situated and explored in the interview as part of a whole life experience.

The identification of silences and suppression of experience has engaged the interest of oral historians whether or not they are influenced by psychoanalytic theories. Generally, among oral historians there has been a shift toward acceptance of more subjective, sometimes mythic accounts (Perks & Thomson, 1998). Recognizing that data such as these may have both cultural and psychological significance represents a move away from more empirically and positivistically situated approaches, with consequent implications for the interpretation of data and criticisms that focus on validity.

Analysis of interview data typically has followed the thematic approach used by both historians and sociologists with themes determined either in advance, according to the research design or the chosen theoretical framework, or deriving from the data itself with GROUNDED THEORY (Thompson, 2000, p. 151). Use of electronic methods has become more common, particularly with larger samples of interviews, though here again with an emphasis on the significance of language and expression. Researchers draw on the interpretive powers afforded by their particular disciplinary base— for example, history, psychology, sociology, or social policy—cross-referencing to other sources, both documentary and oral, seeking to locate and validate their analysis historically and structurally.

DEVELOPMENTS AND ISSUES

Oral history researchers, in common with developments in BIOGRAPHICAL METHODS and NARRATIVE ANALYSIS, anthropology, and ETHNOGRAPHY, have developed discussion relating to methods, significantly in the areas of FEMINIST RESEARCH, ethics, and ownership.

The position of women as subjects of research and as researchers has posed questions of power in the process of interviewing. The essentialist position argues that women share understandings and experience with their interviewees, giving particular resonance to their position as researchers. A contrasting position, equally feminist though more critical and reflective, acknowledges the salience of other aspects of difference in the interview relationship, notably class, color, and generation. A key contribution to these debates has been the edited volume by Sherna Berger Gluck and Daphne Patai (1991), which includes some searchingly self-critical accounts by feminists engaged in oral history research.

Ethical issues deriving from questions of consent and ownership now play a central role in oral history research. Under European Union law, copyright in the interview rests with the interviewee, which means that no part of the interview can be published unless copyright has been assigned to the interviewer or to his or her employing organization (Ward, 2002). Such a requirement is a legal expression of what some oral historians regard as central ethical issues, namely consent to participation in the process and ownership of what is recorded. Providing interviewees with control over the destination of the interview tape and transcript is regarded as a necessary stage in the interview process, with standard documentation now available on oral history Web sites and in key texts relating to ARCHIVE deposit and access.

—Joanna Bornat

REFERENCES

Gluck, S. B., & Patai, D. (Eds.). (1991). *Women's words: The feminist practice of oral history*. London: Routledge.

Perks, R., & Thomson, A. (Eds.). (1998). *The oral history reader*. London: Routledge.

Thompson, P. (2000). *The voice of the past* (3rd ed.). Oxford, UK: Oxford University Press.

Ward, A. (2002). *Oral history and copyright*. Retrieved June 7, 2002 from http://www.oralhistory.org.uk

ORDER

Order refers to the number of additional variables controlled or held constant in statistical analyses of a relationship between two variables. A zero-order relationship measures the magnitude or strength of an association between two variables, without controlling for any other factors (Knoke, Bohrnstedt, & Mee, 2002, p. 213). Familiar examples include CONTINGENCY TABLES for two categorical variables, CORRELATION between two continuous variables, and simple REGRESSION of a dependent variable on one independent variable.

A first-order relationship involves controlling for the effects of a third variable to determine whether a bivariate relationship changes. In cross-tabulation analysis, this procedure is called ELABORATION (Kendall & Lazarsfeld, 1950). A relationship between variables X and Y is elaborated by splitting their zero-order cross-tabulation into first-order subtables, also called partial tables. Each subtable exhibits the $X - Y$ association within one category of control variable Z. If the $X - Y$ association is not affected by Z, then measures of association such as PHI COEFFICIENT or GAMMA will have identical values in each first-order table. If the association is spurious because Z causes both variables, then the association disappears in each subtable; hence, Z "explains" the $X - Y$ relationship. The same outcome occurs if Z intervenes in a causal sequence linking X to Y; hence, Z "interprets" the $X - Y$ relationship. Elaboration often uncovers a "specification" or INTERACTION EFFECT, where the strength or direction of association differs across subtables, indicating that the $X - Y$ relationship is contingent or conditional on the specific categoric of Z.

A first-order relationship for three continuous variables can be estimated using the PARTIAL CORRELATION coefficient, which shows the "magnitude and direction of covariation between two variables that remain after the effects of a control variable have been held constant" (Knoke et al., 2002, p. 223). Its formula is a function of three zero-order correlations:

$$r_{XY \times Z} = \frac{r_{XY} - r_{XZ}\, r_{XZ}}{\sqrt{1 - r_{XZ}^2}\sqrt{1 - r_{YZ}^2}}.$$

If X and Y are uncorrelated with variable Z, their partial correlation equals their zero-order correlation, $r_{XY \times Z} = r_{XY}$; that is, their linear relationship is unaffected by the control variable. However, if Z correlates strongly in the same direction with both variables, their reduced (or zero) partial correlation reveals that some of or all the $X - Y$ relationship is spurious.

Second- and higher-order relationships generalize these methods for analyzing zero-order relations using multiple control variables. LOG-LINEAR MODELING estimates complex interaction effects in multivariate cross-tabulations. In MULTIPLE REGRESSION ANALYSIS equations, each partial regression coefficient shows the effect on a dependent variable of one-unit differences in an independent variable after controlling for ("partialing out") additive effects of other predictor variables. Detecting INTERACTION EFFECTS involves forming product terms or other independent variable combinations (Jaccard, Turrisi, & Wan, 1990).

Order also refers to a MOMENT of the distribution of a random variable X. Moments about the origin are defined for the kth positive integer as the expected value of X^k, or $E(X^k)$; thus, the first moment about the origin, $E(X)$, is the MEAN. If the mean is subtracted from X before exponentiation, the moments about the mean are defined as $E[X - E(X)]^k$. The first moment of X about its mean equals zero, while its second moment is the VARIANCE. The third and fourth moments about the mean are called, respectively, skewness and KURTOSIS.

—David H. Knoke

REFERENCES

Jaccard, J., Turrisi, R., & Wan, C. K. (1990). *Interaction effects in multiple regression.* Newbury Park, CA: Sage.

Kendall, P. L., & Lazarsfeld, P. F. (1950). Problems of survey analysis. In R. K. Merton & P. Lazarsfeld (Eds.), *Continuities in social research* (pp. 133–196). New York: Free Press.

Knoke, D., Bohrnstedt, G. W., & Mee, A. P. (2002). *Statistics for social data analysis* (4th ed.). Itasca, IL: Peacock.

ORDER EFFECTS

Question and response-order effects in SURVEY interviews and QUESTIONNAIRES have become the focus of numerous methodological experiments by sociologists, political scientists, public opinion researchers, and cognitive social psychologists. Just as the meaning of a word or phrase in spoken and written communication cannot be separated from the context in which it occurs, so too have researchers discovered that the meaning of a survey question can be influenced significantly by the respondent's reactions to previous questions in an INTERVIEW or SELF-ADMINISTERED QUESTIONNAIRE. They also have learned that order effects can occur within, as well as between, survey questions because of the serial presentation of response alternatives. Respondents evidently use the order of the questions and the response categories to make inferences about the meaning of the questions asked of them.

Question order and context effects often arise when respondents are asked two or more questions about the same subject or about closely related topics. They can show up even if multiple items in the interview or questionnaire separate closely related questions. Initial attempts to understand such effects have included the development of conceptual classifications of the types of relations among questions: (a) part-whole relationships involving two or more questions, in which one of them is more general than the other and therefore implies or subsumes the other question, but not necessarily the reverse (e.g., how happy one is with life in general vs. one's marital happiness); and (b) part-part relationships involving questions asked at the same level of specificity (e.g., permitting an abortion in the case of rape vs. a case of a potential birth defect). Two types of effects have likewise been identified: (a) consistency effects, in which respondents bring answers to subsequent questions more in line with their answers to earlier questions (e.g., voting preferences and their political party identification); and (b) contrast effects, in which they differentiate their responses to later questions from those given to previous questions (e.g., their approval of the way George W. Bush has handled the economy vs. how he has handled foreign relations). The net result is a fourfold typology of question order effects: part-part consistency effects, part-whole contrast effects, part-part contrast effects, and part-whole consistency effects (Schuman & Presser, 1981, chap. 2). Smith (1992) later demonstrated that order effects depend not only on the holistic context of previous questions, as identified in Schuman and Presser's typology, but also on how respondents actually answered the prior questions. Conceptually, this interaction between question order and responses to antecedent questions has become known as "conditional order effects." More recent psychological research has used the heuristic of cognitive accessibility, models of belief sampling, the logic of conversation, and cognitive models of assimilation and contrast effects to make theoretical sense of various types of question order and context effects (see, e.g., Sudman, Bradburn, and Schwarz, 1996).

Response-order effects within survey questions can appear in several ways. When the response categories for a question are read aloud, as in a telephone interview or in a face-to-face interview without a visible response card, respondents will tend to select the last-mentioned response alternative: a *recency effect*. If the response categories are presented in a visual format, as in a self-administered mail survey, Web-based poll, or exit poll, respondents will tend to choose one of the first listed alternatives: a *primacy effect*. Judgmental *contrast effects* among response categories can arise as well when a questionnaire item is preceded by another item that generates more extreme ratings on some response scale dimension, as for example when an extremely well-liked or disliked political figure is presented in the middle of a list of other figures to be rated. Explanations of response-order effects have ranged from the conventional opinion crystallization hypothesis, which predicts that such effects will be less likely to occur among respondents with intensely held prior opinions on the topic; to the memory limitations hypothesis, which postulates that such effects occur because of the inability of respondents to remember all the response alternatives; to more current cognitive elaboration and satisficing models (see, e.g., the review by Bishop and Smith, 2001). Derived from the literature on attitude persuasion in cognitive social psychology, the cognitive elaboration model assumes that the mediating process underlying response-order effects is the opportunity respondents have to think about (elaborate on) the response alternatives presented to them. When a list of response alternatives is read aloud to respondents, as for example in a TELEPHONE SURVEY, respondents have more opportunity to think about (elaborate on) choices presented to them later in the list, which often generates a recency effect. In contrast, the satisficing model rooted in Herbert Simon's theory of economic decision making, assumes that most survey respondents answer survey questions by selecting the first satisfactory or acceptable response alternative offered to them rather than taking the time to select an optimal answer. Selecting the last-mentioned category in a telephone survey question, for example, demonstrates the tendency of respondents to satisfice rather than optimize. Despite these promising cognitive theoretical developments, both question and response-order effects have continued to resist ready explanation and prediction.

—George F. Bishop

REFERENCES

Bishop, G., & Smith, A. (2001). Response-order effects and the early Gallup split-ballots. *Public Opinion Quarterly, 65,* 479–505.

Schuman, H., & Presser, S. (1981). *Questions and answers in attitude surveys*. New York: Academic Press.

Smith, T. W. (1992). Thoughts on the nature of context effects. In N. Schwarz & S. Sudman (Eds.), *Context effects in social and psychological research* (pp. 163–184). New York: Springer-Verlag.

Sudman, S., Bradburn, N. M., & Schwarz, N. (1996). *Thinking about answers: The application of cognitive processes to survey methodology*. San Francisco: Jossey-Bass.

ORDINAL INTERACTION

Distinctions often are made between *ordinal* interactions and *disordinal* interactions. The distinction usually is made in the context of REGRESSION analyses, where one is comparing the slope of Y on X for one group with the slope of Y on X for another group. An INTERACTION is implied if the slopes for the two groups are not equal. For each group, one can specify a regression line that characterizes the relationship between Y and X across the range of X values observed in the groups. Nonparallel regression lines for the two groups imply the presence of interaction. A disordinal interaction is one in which the regression line that regresses Y onto X for one group intersects the corresponding regression line for the other group. This also is referred to as a *crossover* interaction. An ordinal interaction is one in which the regression lines are nonparallel, but they do not intersect within the range of data being studied.

For any given pair of nonparallel regression lines, there is always a point where the lines will intersect. In this sense, all interactions are disordinal in theory. Interactions are classified as being ordinal if, *within the range of scores being studied* (e.g., for IQ scores between 90 and 110), the regression lines do not intersect.

If one knows the values of the INTERCEPT and SLOPE for the two regression lines, the value of X where the two regression lines intersect can be calculated algebraically. Let $\beta_{0,A}$ be the intercept for group A, $\beta_{1,A}$ be the slope for group A, $\beta_{0,B}$ be the intercept for group B, and $\beta_{1,B}$ be the intercept for group B. The point of intersection is

$$PI = (\beta_{0,A} - \beta_{0,B})/(\beta_{1,B} - \beta_{1,A}).$$

Applied researchers express some wariness about ordinal interactions. Such interactions, they contend, may be an artifact of the nature of the metric of the outcome variable. Nonparallel regression lines frequently can be made parallel by simple MONOTONIC transformations of scores on the outcome variable. If the metric of the outcome variable is arbitrary, then some scientists argue that one should consider removing the interaction through transformation in the interest of MODEL parsimony. Ordinal interactions, however, should not be dismissed if the underlying metric of the variables is meaningful.

—James J. Jaccard

ORDINAL MEASURE

A measure is a data point. In many research applications, a measure is a number assigned to an individual, organism, or research participant that reflects his or her or its standing on some construct. A measure is taken at a given time, on a given individual, in a given setting, using a given type of recording device. A set of measures refers to multiple data points. For example, a measure of height on each of 10 individuals represents a set of 10 measures.

Ordinal measures can be described from different vantage points. Ordinality as applied to a set of measures describes a property of the function that relates observed measures of a CONSTRUCT to the true values of that construct. A set of measures of a construct has the property of ordinality if the values of the measure are a strictly MONOTONIC function of the true values of the construct, that is, if the relative ordering of individuals on the true construct is preserved when one uses the observed measure to order individuals. For example, 10 individuals may differ in their height, and they can be ordered from shortest to tallest. A researcher may develop a strategy for measuring height such that higher scores on the index imply greater height. The set of measures taken on the 10 individuals is said to have ordinal properties if the ordering of individuals on the index is the same as the ordering of individuals on the underlying dimension of height.

Strictly speaking, ordinal measures do not convey information about the magnitude of differences between individuals or organisms on the underlying dimension. They only permit us to state that one individual has more or less of the dimension than another individual.

—James J. Jaccard

REFERENCE

Anderson, N. H. (1981). *Methods of information integration theory.* New York: Academic Press.

ORDINARY LEAST SQUARES (OLS)

Consider a linear relationship in which there is a stochastic dependent variable with values y_i that are a function of the values of one or more nonstochastic independent variables, $x_{1i}, x_{2i} \ldots x_{ki}$. We could write such a relationship as $y_i = \beta_0 + \beta_1 x_{1i} + \cdots + \beta_k x_{ki} + \varepsilon_i$. For any such relationship, there is a *prediction equation* that produces predicted values of the dependent variable. For example, $\hat{y}_i = \hat{\beta}_0 + \hat{\beta}_1 x_{1i} + \cdots + \hat{\beta}_k x_{ki}$. Predicted values usually are designated by the symbol $\hat{y}_i$. If we subtract the predicted values from the actual values ($y_i - \hat{y}_i$), then we produce a set of RESIDUALS (ε_i), each of which measures the distance between a prediction and the corresponding actual observation on y_i. Ordinary Least Squares (OLS) is a method of point estimation of parameters that minimizes the function defined by the sum of squares of these residuals (or distances) with respect to the parameters.

OLS ESTIMATION

For example, consider the simple bivariate regression given by $y_i = \beta_0 + \beta_1 x_i + \varepsilon_i$. The prediction equation is $\hat{y}_i = \hat{\beta}_0 + \hat{\beta}_1 x_i$. The residuals can be calculated as $\varepsilon_i = y_i - \hat{\beta}_0 - \hat{\beta}_1 x_i = y_i - \hat{y}_i$. Then the OLS estimator is defined by finding the minimum of the function $S = \sum_{i=1}^{n} (y_i - \hat{\beta}_0 - \hat{\beta}_1 x_i)^2$ with respect to the parameters β_0 and β_1. This is a concave quadratic function that always has a single minimum. This simple minimization problem can be solved analytically. The standard approach to minimizing such a function is to take first partial derivatives with respect to the two parameters β_0 and β_1, then solve the resulting set of two simultaneous equations in two unknowns. Performing these operations, we have the following:

$$\frac{\partial \left[\sum_{i=1}^{n} (y_i - \hat{\beta}_0 - \hat{\beta}_1 x_i)^2 \right]}{\partial \beta_0}$$

$$= \sum_{i=1}^{n} 2(y_i - \hat{\beta}_0 - \hat{\beta}_1 x_i)(-1) = 0$$

$$\frac{\partial\left[\sum_{i=1}^{n}(y_i - \hat{\beta}_0 - \hat{\beta}_1 x_i)^2\right]}{\partial\beta_1}$$

$$= \sum_{i=1}^{n} 2(y_i - \hat{\beta}_0 - \hat{\beta}_1 x_i)(-x_i) = 0.$$

Simplifying this result and rearranging produces what are called the normal equations:

$$\sum_{i=1}^{n} y_i = n\hat{\beta}_0 + \left(\sum_{i=1}^{n} x_i\right)\hat{\beta}_1,$$

$$\sum_{i=1}^{n} x_i y_i = \left(\sum_{i=1}^{n} x_i\right)\hat{\beta}_0 + \left(\sum_{i=1}^{n} x_i^2\right)\hat{\beta}_1.$$

Because we can easily calculate the sums in the preceding equations, we have only to solve the resulting set of two simultaneous equations in two unknowns to have OLS estimates of the regression parameters. These analytical procedures are easily extended to the multivariate case, resulting in a set of normal equations specific to the dimension of the problem. For example, see Greene (2003, p. 21).

CLASSICAL ASSUMPTIONS FOR OLS ESTIMATION

The OLS estimator is incorporated into virtually every statistical software package and is extremely popular. The reason for this popularity is its ease of use and very convenient statistical properties. Recall that *parameter estimation* is concerned with finding the value of a population parameter from sample statistics. We can never know with certainty that a sample statistic is representative of a population parameter. However, using well-understood statistical theorems, we can know the properties of the estimators used to produce the sample statistics.

According to the GAUSS-MARKOV THEOREM, an OLS regression estimator is a BEST LINEAR UNBIASED ESTIMATOR (BLUE) under the following assumptions.

1. The expected value of the population disturbances is zero ($E[\varepsilon_i] = 0$). This assumption implies that any variables omitted from the population regression function do not result in a systematic effect on the mean of the disturbances.
2. The expected value of the covariance between the population independent variables and disturbances is zero ($E[X_i, \varepsilon_i] = 0$).

This assumption implies that the independent variables are nonstochastic, or, if they are stochastic, they do not covary systematically with the disturbances.

3. The expected value of the population correlation between disturbances is zero ($E[\varepsilon_i, \varepsilon_j] = 0$). This is the so-called nonautocorrelation assumption.
4. The expected value of the population variance of the disturbances is constant, ($E[\varepsilon_i^2] = 0$). This is the so-called nonheteroskedasticity assumption.

These four assumptions about the population disturbances are commonly called the Gauss-Markov assumptions. Other conditions, however, are relevant to the statistical properties of OLS. If disturbances are normal, then the OLS estimator is the best unbiased estimator (BUE), but if disturbances are non-normal, then the OLS estimator is only the best linear unbiased estimator (BLUE). That is, another estimator that is either nonlinear or robust may be more efficient depending on the nature of the non-normality.

Additionally, the population regression function must be correctly specified by the sample regression function. All relevant independent variables should be included, and no nonrelevant independent variables should be included. The functional form of the population regression function should be linear.

Another requirement of the OLS estimator is the absence of perfect MULTICOLLINEARITY. Perfect multicollinearity exists when one of the independent variables is a perfect linear combination of one or more other independent variables. If perfect multicollinearity exists, then the OLS estimator is undefined and the standard error of the sampling distribution is infinite. High multicollinearity may be problematic for enabling the researcher to disentangle the independent effects of the regressors. However, even in the presence of high multicollinearity, the OLS estimator is BLUE.

STATISTICAL INFERENCE USING OLS ESTIMATORS

Knowing that the OLS estimator is BLUE provides absolute certainty that *on average*, under repeated sampling, the estimated sample statistic will equal the population parameter. Additionally, the variance of sample statistics under repeated sampling when using OLS will be the smallest possible among all possible estimators of this variance.

Although we can never be certain that the sample statistic for any particular sample is representative of the population, knowledge of the estimator that produced the sample statistic enables assessing the degree of confidence we can have about estimates. For example, the standard deviation of the OLS sampling distribution of regression slope coefficients is given as

$$SE(\hat{\beta}_k) = \sqrt{\frac{\hat{\sigma}_e^2}{\sum_{i=1}^{n}(X_i - \bar{X})^2(1 - R_j^2)}},$$

where R_j^2 is the explained variance from the regression of variable j on all other independent variables. This is also referred to as the standard error. Using the standard error, we can make probability statements about the likelihood that a sample statistic is representative of a population parameter. Relying on knowledge that the distribution of the sample statistic under repeated sampling is normal, the probability of an estimate being more than s standard deviations away from the true parameter can be calculated easily. More often, however, the t-distribution is used to take into account the fact that the disturbance variance in the numerator of the preceding equation is an estimate, rather than the true population variance.

Although not technically a requirement for OLS estimation, the assumption of normally distributed population disturbances usually is made. The consequence of non-normal disturbances, however, is quite serious. Non-normality of the "fat-tailed" kind means that hypothesis tests cannot be done meaningfully. In this situation, there are two options. First, the data often can be transformed to produce normally distributed disturbances. Second, one can employ one of the available robust estimators that takes into account the non-normally distributed disturbances.

—B. Dan Wood and Sung Ho Park

REFERENCES

Greene, W. H. (2003). *Econometric analysis* (5th ed.). Englewood Cliffs, NJ: Prentice-Hall.

Gujarati, D. N. (1995). *Basic econometrics* (3rd ed.). New York: McGraw-Hill.

Judge, G. G., Hill, R. C., Griffiths, W. E., Lutkepohl, H., & Lee, T. (1988). *Introduction to the theory and practice of econometrics* (2nd ed.). New York: John Wiley & Sons.

Schroeder, L. D., Sjoquist, D. L., & Stephan, P. E. (1986). *Understanding regression analysis: An introductory guide.* Beverly Hills, CA: Sage.

ORGANIZATIONAL ETHNOGRAPHY

Dating from the 19th century, ETHNOGRAPHY ("nation-description") has meant the portrayal of a people: their customs, manners, and beliefs. Organizational ethnography emerged in the 1980s with the growing interest in culture, symbolism, and folklore. Through the use of FIELD RESEARCH, ethnographers document traditions and symbolic behaviors that reveal people's feelings, opinions, and customary ways of doing things as well as the ethos of an organization. Goals include understanding organizational behavior and contributing to organization development.

The early 1980s witnessed a search for new paradigms with which to think about organizations: perspectives that would direct attention toward the human dimension in ways that mechanistic and super-organic models did not. In 1980, the *Academy of Management Review* published an article by Dandridge, Mitroff, and Joyce on "organizational symbolism." A special issue of *Administrative Science Quarterly* appeared in 1983 devoted to the subject of "organizational culture." A conference directed by Michael Owen Jones that same year titled "Myth, Symbols & Folklore: Expanding the Analysis of Organizations" introduced the notion of "organizational folklore." Although John Van Maanen (1979) employed the term *organizational ethnography* earlier, probably Evergreen State College in Olympia, Washington, should receive credit as the first institution to publicly seek one. In May, 1990, it advertised for an ethnographer to uncover its culture, selecting Peter Tommerup (1993), a PhD candidate in folklore and mythology. Through interviews and observations focusing on stories, rituals, and other expressive forms (Georges & Jones, 1995), he gathered data to describe the nature and assess the impact of the teaching and learning cultures at the college.

Organizational ethnography relies on in-depth interviewing, observation, and PARTICIPANT OBSERVATION in order to capture the "feel" of the organization from the inside, the perceptions of individual members, and the community of shared symbols (Jones, 1996). Researchers elicit participants' accounts of events in their own words and expressive media, whether story, celebration, ritual, proverb, or objects. They note the personal decoration of workspace, graffiti, poster and flyer art, photographs, bulletin boards, images and sayings posted on people's doors, photocopy lore, and other material manifestations of behavior and culture. They record verbal expressions such as traditional sayings, metaphors, slogans, oratory, rumors, beliefs, personal experience stories, and oft-told tales. They observe (and sometimes participate in) customs, rituals, rites of passage, festive events, play, gestures, social routines, and ceremonies.

By documenting and analyzing examples of organizational symbolism, ethnographers gain insights into leadership style, climate, ambiguity and contradictions, tensions and stress, conflicts, and coping in organizations. Ethnography also brings to light values and ways of doing things long taken for granted that guide people's actions, inform decision making, and aid or hinder organizational effectiveness.

—Michael Owen Jones

REFERENCES

Dandridge, T. C., Mitroff, I., & Joyce, W. F. (1980). Organizational symbolism: A topic to expand organizational analysis. *Academy of Management Review, 5,* 77–82.

Georges, R. A., & Jones, M. O. (1995). *Folkloristics: An introduction.* Bloomington: Indiana University Press.

Jones, M. O. (1996). *Studying organizational symbolism: What, how, why?* Thousand Oaks, CA: Sage.

Tommerup, P. (1993). *Adhocratic traditions, experience narratives and personal transformation: An ethnographic study of the organizational culture and folklore of the Evergreen State College, an innovative liberal arts college.* Unpublished doctoral dissertation, University of California, Los Angeles.

Van Maanen, J. (1979). The fact and fiction in organizational ethnography. *Administrative Science Quarterly, 24,* 539–550.

ORTHOGONAL ROTATION.

See ROTATIONS

OTHER, THE

The *other* is a term used in human science discourses that are concerned with themes such as identity, difference, selfhood, recognition, and ethics. *Other* can mean the other person but also the self as other. Philosophy has a long-standing interest in addressing the notion of the other but often has done so by reducing the "other" to the "same" or the "self." Self-discovery or self-recognition can be seen as a process of becoming, whereby the self recognizes itself in the alterity (otherness) of objects. For example, Hegel showed how self-consciousness and freedom can be achieved only through the overcoming of what is other.

Much of contemporary human science literature dealing with the notion of other finds its impetus in the early phenomenological writings of Emmanuel Levinas. Here, the other transcends the self and cannot be reduced to the self. For Levinas, the otherness of the other is first of all an ethical event and appears to us in the nakedness and vulnerability of the face. When we have a Levinassian encounter with a person who is weak or vulnerable, then this other makes an appeal on us that we have already experienced as an ethical response before we are reflectively aware of it. "From the start, the encounter with *other* is my responsibility for him," said Levinas (1998, p. 103).

In her classic book *The Second Sex* (1949/1970), Simone de Beauvoir examined by means of historical, literary, and mythical sources how the oppression of women is associated with patriarchal processes of systematic objectification. The result is that the male is seen as "normal" and the female as "other," leading to the loss of women's social and personal identity. In Kate Millett's *Sexual Politics* (first published in 1970, with revisions afterward) and in the work of contemporary feminists, women consistently appear as "other" against male constructions of social norms.

French poststructuralists in particular have developed a range of interpretations of the notions of other, otherness, and othering. Othering is what people do when they consider themselves normal but notice differences in other peoples. In the works of Michel Foucault (1995), others are those who have been victimized and marginalized—the mentally ill, prisoners, women, gays, lesbians, and people of color among them. Genealogical analysis consists of recovering the social, cultural, and historical roots of the practices of institutionalization and marginalization of the ones who are our others.

Paul Ricoeur has explored the dialectical ties between selfhood and otherness in his study of personal and narrative identity. He is especially interested in the experience of otherness that resides in the body of the self. There are several levels of otherness, said Ricoeur. There is the otherness of "myself as flesh," the otherness of the other person (the foreigner), and the otherness experienced in "the call" of conscience. These distinctions may help us to understand the programs of inquiry of early and contemporary scholars.

In Julia Kristeva's *Strangers to Ourselves* (1991), the notion of the other refers to the foreigners, outsiders, or aliens around us. She asks how we can live in peace with these foreigners if we cannot come to terms with the other inside ourselves. In her analysis she aims to show how alterity of the other is the hidden face of our own identity. Poststructuralist studies of the other in intersubjective relations is further exemplified in the influential work of Jacques Derrida where the other is a theme for raising the question of responsibility, duty, and moral choice. He said, "I cannot respond to the call, the request, the obligation, or even the love of another without sacrificing the other other, the other others" (Derrida, 1995, p. 68).

The question of the meaning of other and otherness figures prominently in qualitative inquiries in fields such as multiculturalism, gender studies, queer theory, ethnicity, and postcolonial studies. In writings on the politics of multiculturalism by Charles Taylor, the "significant other" is addressed in terms of the searches for self-identity and complex needs for social recognition that are sometimes incommensurable. In philosophy too, the notion of other has become a common concern. Especially worth mentioning are the phenomenological studies of the other by Alphonso Lingis, who translated some of the main works of Levinas. In his book *The Community of Those Who Have Nothing in Common* (1994b), Lingis started an inquiry into the question how we can experience moral responsibility and community with respect to cultural others with whom we have no racial kinship, no language, no religion, and no economic interests in common. He continued this line of research in studies such as *Abuses* (1994a) and *The Imperative* (1998) that constitute an entirely new approach to philosophy. In his work, Lingis has blended evocative methods of travelogue, letter writing, ethics, and meditations on themes such as torture, war, identity, lust, passions, and the rational in his "face to face" encounters with marginalized others in India, Bali, Bangladesh, and Latin America.

—Max van Manen

REFERENCES

de Beauvoir, S. (1970). *The second sex.* New York: Alfred A. Knopf. (Original work published 1949.)

Derrida, J. (1995). *The gift of death.* Chicago: The University of Chicago Press.

Foucault, M. (1995). *Discipline and punish: The birth of the prison.* New York: Vintage Books.

Kristeva, J. (1991). *Strangers to ourselves.* New York: Columbia University Press.

Levinas, E. (1998). *On thinking-of-the-Other: Entre nous.* New York: Columbia University Press.

Lingis, A. (1994a). *Abuses.* Berkeley: The University of California Press.

Lingis, A. (1994b). *The community of those who have nothing in common.* Bloomington: Indiana University Press.

Lingis, A. (1998). *The imperative.* Bloomington: Indiana University Press.

Millett, K. (1970). *Sexual politics.* Garden City, NY: Doubleday.

Ricoeur, P. (1992). *Oneself as another.* Chicago: The University of Chicago Press.

Taylor, C. (1994). The politics of recognition. In C. Taylor & A. Gutmann (Eds.), *Multiculturalism and the politics of recognition* (pp. 25–73). Princeton, NJ: Princeton University Press.

OUTLIER

An outlier is an OBSERVATION whose value falls very far from the other values. For example, in a community income study, suppose there is a millionaire with an income of $2,000,000, well beyond the next highest income of $150,000. That millionaire is a outlier on the income variable. Outliers can pose problems of inference, especially if they are extremely far out, or if there are very many of them. For example, in an income study of community leaders, $N = 100$, where a handful of them are multimillionaires, the estimated mean income would give a distorted view of the income of the typical community leader. A better measure of central tendency, in this instance, would be the MEDIAN. Outliers also can distort other statistics, such as the REGRESSION COEFFICIENT. A common remedy is to exclude them from analysis, but that approach is flawed in that it loses information. TRANSFORMATION of the outliers may be the ideal solution, for it can pull these extreme values in, at the same time maintaining the full sample.

—Michael S. Lewis-Beck

See also INFLUENTIAL STATISTICS

P

P VALUE

The *p* value for a statistical test of a hypothesis is defined as the PROBABILITY, calculated under the assumption that the NULL HYPOTHESIS is true, of obtaining a sample result as extreme as, or more extreme than, that observed in a particular direction. This direction is determined by the direction of the ONE-TAILED (or ONE-SIDED) alternative. As an example, consider the SIGN TEST for the null hypothesis that a coin is balanced. The coin is tossed 10 times, and we observe heads 9 times. The sample size is $n = 10$, and the test statistic is S, defined as the number of heads in this sample. The observed sample result is $S = 9$. This sample result is a fact. The question is whether this sample result is consistent with the claim (in the null hypothesis) that the coin is balanced. If it is not, then the claim must be in error, and hence the null hypothesis should be rejected. To determine whether the sample result is consistent with this claim, we calculate the probability of obtaining 9 or more heads in a sample of 10 tosses when the coin is balanced. This probability is found from the binomial distribution with $n = 10$ and $p = 0.50$ for the probability of a head when the coin is balanced, or

$$p \text{ value} = p(S \geq 9) = \sum_{t=9}^{10} \binom{10}{t}(0.50)^t(0.50)^{10-t}$$

$$= 0.0020.$$

This represents a 2 in 1,000 chance, which is quite a rare occurrence. Therefore, our decision is to reject the null hypothesis and conclude that the coin is not balanced. The coin seems to be weighted in favor of the occurrence of a head over a tail; that is, $p > 0.50$.

The traditional or classical approach to this hypothesis-testing problem is to preselect a numerical value for α, the probability of a TYPE I ERROR, and use that α to determine a critical region or rejection region for the value of S; for example, reject if $S \geq c$ for some constant c. This preselected α value is almost always completely arbitrary (0.05 may be traditional, but it is totally arbitrary), but it can have a tremendous effect on the decision that is reached.

Reporting the *p* value is an alternative method of carrying out a test of a null hypothesis against a one-sided alternative. Instead of reaching a definitive decision to reject or not to reject the null hypothesis at a chosen level α, the researcher lets the readers or users make their own decision based on the magnitude of this *p* value. The readers can choose their own α. Then the decision made by the readers is to reject if $p \leq \alpha$ and not to reject if $p > \alpha$.

If the ALTERNATIVE HYPOTHESIS does not predict a particular direction—that is, if the alternative is TWO-TAILED (or TWO-SIDED)—then the *p* value is not uniquely defined. There are essentially two different *p* values, one in each possible direction. The smaller of these two possible *p* values is the only relevant one. Then the researcher can either report this smaller *p* value, indicating that it is a one-sided *p* value, or double this one-sided *p* value.

—Jean D. Gibbons

PAIRWISE CORRELATION. *See*

CORRELATION

PAIRWISE DELETION

Pairwise deletion is a term used in relation to computer software programs such as SPSS in connection with the handling of MISSING DATA. Pairwise deletion of missing data means that only cases relating to each pair of variables with missing data involved in an analysis are deleted. Consider the following scenario: We have a sample of 200 cases and want to produce a set of PEARSON CORRELATIONS for 10 variables. Let us take the first 3 variables. Variable 1 has 4 missing cases, Variable 2 has 8 missing cases, and Variable 3 has 2 missing cases. Let us also assume that the missing cases are different for each of the variables; that is, Variable 1's 4 missing cases are not among Variable 2's 8 missing cases. (In practice, this will not always be the case because if a person does not answer questions relating to both Variable 1 and Variable 2, he or she will be a case with missing data on both variables.) When we analyze the 10 variables, the correlation between Variables 1 and 2 will be based on 188 cases (because between them, Variable 1 and Variable 2 have 12 missing cases). The correlation between Variable 1 and Variable 3 will be based on 194 cases (because between them, they have 6 missing cases), and between Variable 2 and Variable 3, it will be based on 190 cases (because between them, they have 10 missing cases).

—Alan Bryman

See also DELETION, LISTWISE DELETION

PANEL

The term *panel* refers to a RESEARCH DESIGN in which the DATA are gathered on at least two occasions on the same units of analysis. Most commonly, that unit of analysis is an individual in a SURVEY. In a two-wave panel survey, respondents at time t are reinterviewed at time $t + 1$; in a three-wave panel, they would be reinterviewed yet again at time $t + 2$.

Sometimes, the units of analysis of the panel are aggregates, such as nations. For example, a sample of European countries might be measured at time t and again at $t + 1$. A special value of a panel design is that it incorporates the temporality required for strong CAUSAL inference because the potential causal variables, the Xs, can actually be measured before Y occurs. In addition, panel studies allow social change to be gauged. For example, with repeated INTERVIEWING over a long time, panel surveys (unlike COHORT designs) have the potential to distinguish age effects, PERIOD EFFECTS, and cohort effects.

A chief disadvantage of the panel approach is the data ATTRITION from time point to time point, especially with panel surveys in which individuals drop out of the sample. A related problem is the issue of addition to the panel, in that demographic change may, over time, suggest that the original panel is no longer representative of the POPULATION initially SAMPLED. For example, as a result of an influx of immigrants, it may be that the panel should have respondents added to it to better reflect the changed population.

—Michael S. Lewis-Beck

PANEL DATA ANALYSIS

Panel data refer to data sets consisting of multiple observations on each sampling unit. This could be generated by pooling time-series observations across a variety of cross-sectional units, including countries, states, regions, firms, or randomly sampled individuals or households. This encompasses longitudinal data analysis in which the primary focus is on individual histories. Two well-known examples of U.S. panel data are the Panel Study of Income Dynamics (PSID), collected by the Institute for Social Research at the University of Michigan, and the National Longitudinal Surveys of Labor Market Experience (NLS) from the Center for Human Resource Research at Ohio State University. An inventory of national studies using panel data is given at http://www.ceps.lu/Cher/Cherpres.htm. These include the Belgian Household Panels, the German Socioeconomic Panel, the French Household Panel, the British Household Panel Survey, the Dutch Socioeconomic Panel, the Luxembourg Household Panel, and, more recently, the European Community household panel. The PSID began in 1968 with 4,802 families and includes an oversampling of poor households. Annual interviews were conducted and socioeconomic characteristics of each family and roughly 31,000 individuals who had been in these or derivative families were recorded. The list of variables collected is more than 5,000. The NLS followed five distinct segments of the labor force. The original samples include 5,020 men ages 45 to 59 years in 1966, 5,225 men ages 14 to 24 years in 1966, 5,083 women ages 30 to 44 years in 1967, 5,159 women ages 14 to 24 years in 1968, and 12,686 youths ages 14 to 21 years in 1979. There was an oversampling of Blacks, Hispanics, poor Whites, and military in the youths survey. The variables collected run into the thousands. Panel data sets have also been constructed from the U.S. Current Population Survey (CPS), which is a monthly national household survey conducted by the Census Bureau. The CPS generates the unemployment rate and other labor force statistics. Compared with the NLS and PSID data sets, the CPS contains fewer variables, spans a shorter period, and does not follow movers. However, it covers a much larger sample and is representative of all demographic groups.

Some of the benefits and limitations of using panel data are given in Hsiao (1986). Obvious benefits include a much larger data set because panel data are multiple observations on the same individual. This means that there will be more variability and less COLLINEARITY among the variables than is typical of cross-section or time-series data. For example, in a demand equation for a given good (say, gasoline) price and income may be highly correlated for annual time-series observations for a given country or state. By stacking or pooling these observations across different countries or states, the variation in the data is increased and collinearity is reduced. With additional, more informative data, one can get more reliable estimates and test more sophisticated behavioral models with less restrictive assumptions. Another advantage of panel data is their ability to control for individual heterogeneity. Not controlling for these unobserved individual specific effects leads to BIAS in the resulting estimates. For example, in an earnings equation, the wage of an individual is regressed on various individual attributes, such as education, experience, gender, race, and so on. But the error term may still include unobserved individual characteristics, such as ability, which is correlated with some of the regressors, such as education. Cross-sectional studies attempt to control for this unobserved ability by collecting hard-to-get data on twins. However, using individual panel data, one can, for example, difference the data over time and wipe out the unobserved individual invariant ability. Panel data sets are also better able to identify and estimate effects that are not detectable in pure cross-section or pure time-series data. In particular, panel data sets are better able to study complex issues of dynamic behavior. For example, with cross-section data, one can estimate the rate of unemployment at a particular point in time. Repeated cross-sections can show how this proportion changes over time. Only panel data sets can estimate what proportion of those who are unemployed in one period remains unemployed in another period.

Limitations of panel data sets include the following: problems in the design, data collection, and data management of panel surveys (see Kasprzyk, Duncan, Kalton, & Singh, 1989). These include the problems of coverage (incomplete account of the population of interest), nonresponse (due to lack of cooperation of the respondent or because of interviewer error), recall (respondent not remembering correctly), frequency of interviewing, interview spacing, reference period, the use of bounding to prevent the shifting of events from outside the recall period into the recall period, and time-in-sample bias. Another limitation of panel data sets is the distortion due to measurement errors. Measurement errors may arise because of faulty response due to unclear questions, memory errors, deliberate distortion of responses (e.g., prestige bias), inappropriate informants, misrecording of responses, and interviewer effects. Although these problems can occur in cross-section studies, they are aggravated in panel data studies. Panel data sets may also exhibit bias due to sample selection problems. For the initial wave of the panel, respondents may refuse to participate, or the interviewer may not find anybody at home. This may cause some bias in the inference drawn from this sample. Although this nonresponse can also occur in cross-section data sets, it is more serious with panels because subsequent waves of the panel are still subject to nonresponse. Respondents may die, move, or find that the cost of responding is high. The rate of attrition differs across panels and usually increases from one wave to the next, but the rate of increase declines over time. Typical panels involve annual data covering a short span of time for each individual. This means that asymptotic arguments rely crucially on the number of individuals in the panel tending to infinity. Increasing the time span of the panel is not without cost either. In fact, this increases the chances of attrition with every new wave, as well as the degree of computational difficulty in estimating qualitative limited dependent variable panel data models (see Baltagi, 2001).

Although RANDOM-COEFFICIENT MODELS can be used in the estimation and specification of panel data models (Hsiao, 1986), most panel data applications have been limited to a simple regression with error components disturbances, such as the following:

$$y_{it} = \mathbf{x}'_{it}\boldsymbol{\beta} + \mu_i + v_{it}, \quad i = 1, \ldots, N; t = 1, \ldots, T$$

where y_{it} may denote log(wage) for the ith individual at time t, and $\mathbf{x}_{it}$ is a vector of observations on k explanatory variables such as education, experience, race, sex, marital status, union membership, hours worked, and so on. In addition, $\boldsymbol{\beta}$ is a k vector of unknown coefficients, μ_i is an unobserved individual specific effect, and v_{it} is a zero mean random disturbance with variance σ_v^2. The error components disturbances follow a one-way analysis of variance (ANOVA). If μ_i denote fixed parameters to be estimated, this model is known as the FIXED-EFFECTS (FE) MODEL. The $\mathbf{x}_{it}$s are assumed independent of the v_{it}s for all i and t. Inference in this case is conditional on the particular N individuals observed. Estimation in this case amounts to including $(N-1)$ individual dummies to estimate these individual invariant effects. This leads to an enormous loss in degrees of freedom and attenuates the problem of MULTICOLLINEARITY among the regressors. Furthermore, this may not be computationally feasible for large N panels. In this case, one can eliminate the μ_is and estimate $\boldsymbol{\beta}$ by running least squares of $\tilde{y}_{it} = y_{it} - \bar{y}_{i\cdot}$ on the $\tilde{\mathbf{x}}_{it}$s similarly defined, where the dot indicates summation over that index and the bar denotes averaging. This transformation is known as the within transformation, and the corresponding estimator of $\boldsymbol{\beta}$ is called the within estimator or the FE estimator. Note that the FE estimator cannot estimate the effect of any time-invariant variable such as gender, race, religion, or union participation. These variables are wiped out by the within transformation. This is a major disadvantage if the effect of these variables on earnings is of interest. Ignoring the individual unobserved effects (i.e., running ordinary least squares [OLS] without individual dummies) leads to biased and inconsistent estimates of the regression coefficients.

If μ_i denotes independent random variables with zero mean and constant variance σ_μ^2, this model is known as the random-effects model. The preceding moments are conditional on the $\mathbf{x}_{it}$s. In addition, μ_i and v_{it} are assumed to be conditionally independent. The random-effects (RE) model can be estimated by generalized least squares (GLS), which can be obtained using a least squares regression of $y_{it}^* = y_{it} - \theta\bar{y}_{i\cdot}$ on $\mathbf{x}_{it}^*$ similarly defined, where θ is a simple function of the variance components σ_μ^2 and σ_v^2 (Baltagi, 2001). The corresponding GLS estimator of $\boldsymbol{\beta}$ is known as the RE estimator. Note that for this RE model, one can estimate the effects of individual-invariant variables. The best quadratic unbiased (BQU) estimators of the variance components are ANOVA-type estimators based on the true disturbances, and these are minimum variance unbiased (MVU) under normality of the disturbances. One can obtain feasible estimates of the variance components by replacing the true disturbances by OLS or fixed-effects residuals. For the random-effects model, OLS is still unbiased and consistent but not efficient.

Fixed versus random effects has generated a lively debate in the biometrics and econometrics literature. In some applications, the random- and fixed-effects models yield different estimation results, especially if T is small and N is large. A specification test based on the difference between these estimates is given by Hausman (1978). The null hypothesis is that the individual effects are not correlated with the $\mathbf{x}_{it}$s. The basic idea behind this test is that the fixed-effects estimator $\tilde{\boldsymbol{\beta}}_{FE}$ is consistent, whether or not the effects are correlated with the $\mathbf{x}_{it}$s. This is true because the fixed-effects transformation described by $\tilde{y}_{it}$ wipes out the μ_i effects from the model. In fact, this is the modern econometric interpretation of the FE model—namely, that the μ_is are random but hopelessly correlated with all the $\mathbf{x}_{it}$s. However, if the null hypothesis is true, the fixed-effects estimator is not efficient under the random-effects specification because it relies only on the within variation in the data. On the other hand, the random-effects estimator $\hat{\boldsymbol{\beta}}_{RE}$ is efficient under the null hypothesis but is biased and inconsistent when the effects are correlated with the $\mathbf{x}_{it}$s. The difference between these estimators $\hat{q} = \tilde{\boldsymbol{\beta}}_{FE} - \hat{\boldsymbol{\beta}}_{RE}$ tends to zero in probability limits under the null hypothesis and is nonzero under the alternative. The variance of this difference is equal to the difference in variances, $\text{var}(\hat{q}) = \text{var}(\tilde{\boldsymbol{\beta}}_{FE}) - \text{var}(\hat{\boldsymbol{\beta}}_{RE})$ because $\text{cov}(\hat{q}, \hat{\boldsymbol{\beta}}_{RE}) = 0$ under the null hypothesis. Hausman's test statistic is based on $m = \hat{q}'[\text{var}(\hat{q})]^{-1}\hat{q}$ and is asymptotically distributed as a chi-square with k degrees of freedom under the null hypothesis.

For maximum likelihood as well as generalized method of moments estimation of panel models, the reader is referred to Baltagi (2001). Space limitations do not allow discussion of panel data models that include treatment of missing observations, dynamics, measurement error, qualitative limited dependent variables, endogeneity, and nonstationarity of the regressors. Instead, we focus on some frequently encountered special panel data sets—namely, pseudo-panels and rotating panels. Pseudo-panels refer to the construction of a panel from repeated cross sections, especially in countries where panels do not exist but where independent surveys are available over time. The United Kingdom Family Expenditure Survey, for example, surveys about 7,000 households annually. These are independent surveys because it may be impossible to track the same household across surveys, as required in a genuine panel. Instead, one can track cohorts and estimate economic relationships based on cohort means. Pseudo-panels do not suffer the attrition problem that plagues genuine panels and may be available over longer time periods. One important question is the optimal size of the cohort. A large number of cohorts will reduce the size of a specific cohort and the samples drawn from it. Alternatively, selecting few cohorts increases the accuracy of the sample cohort means, but it also reduces the effective sample size of the panel.

Rotating panels attempt to keep the same number of households in the survey by replacing the fraction of households that drop from the sample in each period with an equal number of freshly surveyed households. This is a necessity in surveys in which a high rate of attrition is expected from one period to the next. Rotating panels allow the researcher to test for the existence of time-in-sample bias effects. These correspond to a significant change in response between the initial interview and a subsequent interview when one would expect the same response.

With the growing use of cross-country data over time to study purchasing power parity, growth convergence, and international research and development spillovers, the focus of panel data econometrics has shifted toward studying the asymptotics of macro panels with large N (number of countries) and large T (length of the time series) rather than the usual asymptotics of micro panels with large N and small T. Researchers argue that the time-series components of variables such as per capita gross domestic product growth have strong nonstationarity. Some of the distinctive results that are obtained with nonstationary panels are that many test statistics and estimators of interest have Normal limiting distributions. This is in contrast to the nonstationary time-series literature in which the limiting distributions are complicated functionals of Weiner processes. Several unit root tests applied in the time-series literature have been extended to panel data (see Baltagi, 2001). However, the use of such panel data methods is not without their critics, who argue that panel data unit root tests do not rescue purchasing power parity (PPP). In fact, the results on PPP with panels are mixed depending on the group of countries studied, the period of study, and the type of unit root test used. More damaging is the argument that for PPP, panel data tests are the wrong answer to the low power of unit root tests in single time series. After all, the null hypothesis of a single unit root is different from the null hypothesis of a panel unit root for the PPP hypothesis. Similarly, panel unit root tests did not help settle the question of growth convergence among countries. However, it was useful in spurring much-needed research into dynamic panel data models.

Over the past 20 years, the panel data methodological literature has exhibited phenomenal growth. One cannot do justice to the many theoretical and empirical contributions to date. Space limitations prevented discussion of many worthy contributions. Some topics are still in their infancy but growing fast, such as nonstationary panels and semiparametric and nonparametric methods using panel data. It is hoped that this introduction will whet the reader's appetite and encourage more readings on the subject.

—Badi H. Baltagi

REFERENCES

Baltagi, B. H. (2001). *Econometric analysis of panel data.* Chichester, UK: Wiley.

Hausman, J. A. (1978). Specification tests in econometrics. *Econometrica, 46,* 1251–1271.

Hsiao, C. (1986). *Analysis of panel data.* Cambridge, UK: Cambridge University Press.

Kasprzyk, D., Duncan, G. J., Kalton, G., & Singh, M. P. (1989). *Panel surveys.* New York: John Wiley.

PARADIGM

In everyday usage, *paradigm* refers either to a model or an example to be followed or to an established system or way of doing things. The concept was introduced into the philosophy of science by Thomas

Kuhn (1970) in his discussion of the nature of scientific progress.

As a reaction against philosophies of science that prescribed *the* appropriate scientific method, such as Popper's FALSIFICATIONISM, Kuhn (1970) focused on the practices of communities of scientists. He saw such communities as sharing a paradigm or "discipline matrix" consisting of their views of the nature of the reality they study (their ONTOLOGY), including the components that make it up and how they are related; the techniques that are appropriate for investigating this reality (their EPISTEMOLOGY); and accepted examples of past scientific achievements (exemplars) that provide both the foundation for further practice and models for students who wish to become members of the community. He suggested that a mature science is dominated by a single paradigm.

According to Kuhn (1970), most of the time, scientists engage in *normal science,* research that is dominated by "puzzle-solving" activities and is firmly based on the assumptions and rules of the paradigm. Normal science extends the knowledge that the paradigm provides by testing its predictions and further articulating and filling out its implications; it does not aim for unexpected novelty of fact or theory. In the course of normal science, the paradigm is not challenged or tested; failure to solve a puzzle will be seen as the failure of the scientist, not the paradigm.

Occasions arise when some puzzles cannot be solved, or gaps appear between what the paradigm would have anticipated and what is observed. These anomalies may be ignored initially, as commitment to a paradigm produces inherent resistance to their recognition. Kuhn (1970) argued that a paradigm is a prerequisite to perception itself, that what we see depends both on what we look at and also on what our previous visual-conceptual experience has taught us to see. Adherence to a paradigm is analogous to an act of faith, and to suggest that there is something wrong with it is likely to be interpreted as heresy.

Anomalies may lead to a crisis of confidence in the paradigm. There emerges a period of *extraordinary science,* accompanied by a proliferation of competing articulations, the willingness to try anything, the expression of discontent, the recourse to philosophy, and debates over fundamentals. The situation is ripe for the emergence of a new paradigm and novel theories.

Kuhn (1970) has described the process of replacing the old paradigm with a new one as a *scientific revolution.* A new paradigm may be proposed to replace an existing one—a paradigm that can solve the new puzzles raised by the anomalies and can handle the puzzles that the previous paradigm had solved. However, such revolutions occur only slowly, usually taking a generation or longer. According to Kuhn, the process by which a scientist moves from working with the old paradigm to the new is analogous to a religious conversion; it involves not just adopting a fundamentally different way of viewing the world but also living in a different world. Once a new paradigm is established, a new phase of normal science will commence. In time, new anomalies will emerge and further revolutions will occur.

Kuhn (1970) argued that rival paradigms are incommensurable. This is because the concepts and propositions of theories produced by a community of scientists depend on the assumptions and beliefs in their paradigm for their particular meaning. As paradigms embody different and incompatible worldviews, it will be difficult for members of different scientific communities to communicate effectively, and it will be impossible to adjudicate between competing theories. There is no neutral language of observation, no common vocabulary, and no neutral ground from which to settle claims.

For Kuhn, scientific progress is not achieved by the accumulation of generalizations derived from observation (INDUCTION) or by the critical testing of new hypotheses (deduction/FALSIFICATIONISM)—it is achieved by scientific revolutions that change the way a scientific community views the world and defines and goes about solving puzzles (for reviews, see Blaikie, 1993, pp. 105–110; Riggs, 1992, pp. 22–59).

Kuhn's work has spawned a vast literature and has received detailed criticism by philosophers and historians of science, such as Lakatos and Laudan (for a review, see Riggs, 1992). It was used as a framework for understanding the crisis in sociology in the 1960s and 1970s (see, e.g., Friedricks, 1970), when there were vigorous disputes between competing paradigms (see, e.g., Ritzer, 1980).

—Norman Blaikie

REFERENCES

Blaikie, N. (1993). *Approaches to social enquiry.* Cambridge, UK: Polity.

Friedricks, R. (1970). *A sociology of sociology.* New York: Free Press.

Kuhn, T. S. (1970). *The structure of scientific revolutions* (2nd ed.). Chicago: University of Chicago Press.

Riggs, P. J. (1992). *Whys and ways of science.* Melbourne, Australia: Melbourne University Press.

Ritzer, G. (1980). *Sociology: A multiple paradigm science.* Boston: Allyn & Bacon.

PARAMETER

A parameter is any quantity that reveals a certain characteristic of a POPULATION. One conceptualization of a population is the set containing all outcomes of interest to the researcher. However, in statistics, a population is defined more technically as the set of all possible outcomes from a random EXPERIMENT. For example, the random experiment might consist of observations on the taxes paid by individual U.S. citizens. The population would then consist of the tax bill for each and every U.S. citizen. A population can be fully characterized by a RANDOM VARIABLE X (e.g., tax paid) and its associated PROBABILITY distribution $f(x)$ (e.g., a probability function or density function on tax paid). A population is considered known when we know the probability distribution $f(x)$ of the associated random variable X. If the population is known, parameters can be calculated easily from the population data. Parameters are therefore fixed quantities representing features of a population.

Two commonly used parameters in descriptive analysis are the MEAN and VARIANCE of a population. The population mean shows the numerical average of the population, whereas the population variance shows the average squared deviations of the observed values about the mean. For example, in the taxation experiment above, there is an average tax paid, as well as a variance in tax paid by all U.S. citizens. Other examples of parameters would be the population SKEWNESS, KURTOSIS, CORRELATION, and REGRESSION partial SLOPE parameter.

Parameters have no variability because they can be calculated from a known population. However, it is often inconvenient or impossible to work with a population. The population may be quite large, as in the taxpayer example above, and the researcher may not want to obtain or enter the data. It is also often difficult to obtain a population in the social sciences. The data may not be readily available to the researcher or may be nonexistent.

Most of the time in social science research, the population is not available, so the parameter is a theoretical construct that is unknown. The parameter exists somewhere in the real world, but researchers must estimate its value from a sample. In estimating a parameter from sample data, we regard all the entries of the sample as observations on *random variables* that are drawn from the population by random experiment. They are assumed to have the same probability distribution and to be drawn independently. *Sample statistics* that reveal certain characteristics of the sample are obtained from these random variables to estimate the population parameters. For example, in the tax experiment above, the sample mean is obtained by summing across all sample observations the products of sample entries and their respective probabilities. This is then considered as an estimator for population mean.

—B. Dan Wood and Sung Ho Park

REFERENCES

Blalock, H. M., Jr. (1979). *Social statistics.* New York: McGraw-Hill.

Casella, G., & Berger, R. L. (2001). *Statistical inference* (2nd ed.). New York: Wadsworth.

Spiegel, M. R., Schiller, J., & Srinivasan, R. A. (2000). *Schaum's outline of probability and statistics* (2nd ed.). New York: McGraw-Hill.

PARAMETER ESTIMATION

Parameter estimation is concerned with finding the value of a population parameter from sample statistics. Population parameters are fixed and generally unknown quantities. If we know all possible entries of a population and their respective PROBABILITIES, we can calculate the value of a population parameter. However, we usually have only a sample from a population, so we have to estimate population parameters based on sample statistics. *Sample statistics* are constructed to reveal characteristics of the sample that may be considered ESTIMATORS of corresponding population parameters. Notice that sample statistics are themselves RANDOM VARIABLES because they are based on draws from a population.

Sample statistics are used as estimators of fixed population parameters. For example, the sample mean can be used as an estimator of the population mean. However, there is no guarantee that any particular estimate, based on the estimator, will be an accurate reflection of the population parameter. There will always be uncertainty about the estimate due to SAMPLING ERROR. We can, however, minimize uncertainty about parameter estimates by using good estimators. A good estimator should satisfy certain statistical properties, such as UNBIASEDNESS, EFFICIENCY, asymptotic efficiency, or consistency. The first two are finite-sample properties, and the last two are asymptotic properties.

Unbiasedness requires that the expected value of an estimator should be equal to the true population parameter. That is, unbiasedness requires $E(\hat{\theta}) = \theta$, where θ is a population parameter and $\hat{\theta}$ is an estimator of the parameter. Notice again that this does not mean that a specific estimate will be equal to the true parameter. Instead, it is a property of repeated sampling. We expect only that the mean of the estimates that are calculated from repeated samples will be equal to the true parameter. *Efficiency* requires that the variance of an estimator be less than or equal to that of other unbiased estimators of the same parameter. That is, $\text{Var}(\hat{\theta}_1) \le \text{Var}(\hat{\theta}_2)$, where $\hat{\theta}_2$ comes from any estimator other than $\hat{\theta}_1$. It is sometimes the case that an estimator is biased but has smaller variance than other estimators that are unbiased. In this case, the minimum MEAN SQUARED ERROR (MSE) criterion can be useful. This is calculated as $\text{MSE}(\hat{\theta}|\theta) = \text{Var}(\hat{\theta}) + \text{Bias}(\hat{\theta}|\theta)^2$. The estimator with the smallest MSE, regardless of bias, is generally considered the better estimator.

If an estimator satisfies both the unbiasedness and efficiency requirements, it is always a good estimator. However, it often happens that an estimator fails these requirements in small samples but, as the sample size increases, attains desirable statistical properties. Such estimators may be called asymptotically efficient or consistent. *Asymptotic efficiency* means that the variance of the asymptotic distribution of an estimator is smaller than the variance of any other asymptotically unbiased estimator. *Consistency* means that an estimator converges with unit probability to the value of the population parameter as we increase the sample size to infinity. These two properties are asymptotic equivalents of efficiency and unbiasedness in finite samples.

—B. Dan Wood and Sung Ho Park

REFERENCES

Blalock, H. M., Jr. (1979). *Social statistics.* New York: McGraw-Hill.

Casella, G., & Berger, R. L. (2001). *Statistical inference* (2nd ed.). New York: Wadsworth.

Judge, G. G., Hill, R. C., Griffiths, W. E., Lutkepohl, H., & Lee, T. (1988). *Introduction to the theory and practice of econometrics.* New York: John Wiley.

Spiegel, M. R., Schiller, J., & Srinivasan, R. A. (2000). *Schaum's outline of probability and statistics* (2nd ed.). New York: McGraw-Hill.

PART CORRELATION

The part correlation coefficient $r_{y(1\cdot2)}$, which is also called the semipartial correlation coefficient by Hays (1972), differs from the partial correlation coefficient $r_{y1\cdot2}$ in the following respect: The influence of the control variable X_2 is removed from X_1 but not from Y.

The three steps in PARTIAL CORRELATION analysis are now reduced to two. In the first step, the RESIDUAL scores $X_1 - \hat{X}_1$ from a bivariate REGRESSION analysis of X_1 on X_2 are calculated. In a second and last step, we calculate the ZERO-ORDER correlation coefficient between these residual scores $X_1 - \hat{X}_1$ and the original Y scores. This, then, is the part correlation coefficient $r_{y(1\cdot2)}$. For HIGHER-ORDER coefficients, such as $r_{y(1\cdot23)}$, it holds in the same way that the influence of the control variables X_2 and X_3 is removed from X_1 but not from Y. An example of $r_{y(1\cdot2)}$ can be the correlation between the extracurricular activity of students (variable X_1) and their popularity (variable Y), controlling for their scholastic achievement (X_2). To clarify the mechanism of PART CORRELATION, we give a simple (fictitious) sample of five students with the following scores on the three variables: 1, 3, 2, 6, 4 for Y; 0, 1, 3, 6, 8 for X_1; and 4, 4, 1, 2, 0 for X_2. The part correlation coefficient $r_{y(1\cdot2)}$ is now calculated as the ZERO-ORDER correlation between the $X_1 - \hat{X}_1$ scores –0.70, 0.30, –2.53, 2.08, 0.86 and the original Y scores 1, 3, 2, 6, 4, which yields $r_{y(1\cdot2)} = 0.83$. This is then the correlation between popularity and extracurricular activity, in which the latter is cleared of the influence of scholastic achievement.

When dealing with considerations of content, part correlation finds little application. One reason why part correlation could be preferred to partial correlation in concrete empirical research is that the variance of Y would almost disappear when removing the influence of the control variable X_2 from it, so that there would be little left to explain. In such a case, the control variable would, of course, be a very special one because it would share its variance almost entirely with one of the considered variables.

An example of a more appropriate use of the part correlation coefficient can be found in Colson's (1977, p. 216) research of the influence of the mean age (A) on the crude birth rate (B) in a sample of countries. But as the latter is not independent of the age structure and vice versa, because the mean age A contains a fertility component, a problem of contamination arose. This problem can be solved in two ways if we include the total (period) fertility rate as a variable, which is measured as the total of the age-specific fertility rates (F) and is independent of the age structure. A first procedure is the calculation of the correlation coefficient between A and F (i.e., the association between the mean age and age-free fertility). A second procedure, which was chosen by the author, is the calculation of the part correlation coefficient $r_{B(A \cdot F)}$ between crude birth rates (measured as B) and the fertility-free age structure (residual scores of A after removing the influence of F).

This is an example of an appropriate use of part correlation analysis, provided that one is aware that one does not always know which concepts remain after the removal of contamination effects. It is therefore advisable, if possible, to preserve a conceptual distance between the original concepts (age structure and birth rate) to avoid contamination.

COMPUTATION OF THE PARTIAL AND PART CORRELATION

In the foregoing, we attempted to demonstrate the relevance of the part correlation in terms of contents. However, its power is predominantly formal in nature. Many formulas can be developed for the part correlation coefficient, and for each of these formulas, an equivalent for the partial correlation coefficient can be derived. We will now make some derivations for coefficient $r_{y(1 \cdot 23)}$, in which original Y scores are correlated with scores of X_1 controlled for X_2 and X_3.

The part correlation is, in its squared form, the increase in the proportion of the explained variance of Y that emerges when adding X_1 to the $\{X_2, X_3\}$ set:

$$r^2_{y(1 \cdot 23)} = R^2_{y \cdot 123} - R^2_{y \cdot 23}.$$

We get a bit more insight into this formula when we rewrite it as follows:

$$R^2_{y \cdot 123} = R^2_{y \cdot 23} + r^2_{y(1 \cdot 23)}.$$

The multiple determination coefficient $R^2_{y \cdot 123}$ is the proportion of the variance of Y that is explained by X_1, X_2, and X_3 together. This proportion can be split additively in two parts. The first part, $R^2_{y \cdot 23}$, is the proportion of the variance of Y that is explained by X_2 and X_3 together. The second part is the proportion that is also due to X_1, after the latter is freed from the influence of X_2 and X_3. This is the squared part correlation coefficient $r^2_{y(1 \cdot 23)}$.

If X_1 is uncorrelated with X_2 and X_3, then this increase in R^2 is simply equal to r^2_{y1}. On the other hand, if X_1 is strongly associated with X_2 and X_3, then the squared part correlation will be very different from the original squared correlation r^2_{y1}.

Now, if the other variables X_2 and X_3 together explain a substantial proportion of the variance of Y, then there is not much left for X_1 to explain. In such a case, the part correlation $r_{y(1 \cdot 23)}$ is unfairly small and will be hardly comparable with the situation in which the control variables do not explain a great amount. It is therefore wiser to divide the "absolute" increase in R^2 by the proportion of the variance of Y that is not explained by X_2 and X_3. In doing so, we obtain the squared partial correlation coefficient, which is thus equal to the "relative" increase in the proportion of the explained variance of Y that emerges when adding X_1 to the $\{X_2, X_3\}$ set:

$$r^2_{y1 \cdot 23} = \frac{R^2_{y \cdot 123} - R^2_{y \cdot 23}}{1 - R^2_{y \cdot 23}}.$$

Consequently, the squared partial correlation is obtained by dividing the squared part correlation by the part that is not explained by the control variables:

$$r^2_{y1 \cdot 23} = \frac{r^2_{y(1 \cdot 23)}}{1 - R^2_{y \cdot 23}}$$

where

$$r_{y1 \cdot 23} = \frac{r_{y(1 \cdot 23)}}{(1 - R^2_{y \cdot 23})^{\frac{1}{2}}}.$$

SIGNIFICANCE TEST

The significance tests of the part correlation coefficient and of the partial correlation coefficient are identical to the significance test of partial regression coefficients in regression analysis.

—Jacques Tacq

REFERENCES

Blalock, H. M. (1972). *Social statistics.* Tokyo: McGraw-Hill Kogakusha.

Brownlee, K. (1965). *Statistical theory and methodology in science and engineering.* New York: John Wiley.

Colson, F. (1977). *Sociale indicatoren van enkele aspecten van bevolkingsgroei.* Doctoral dissertation, Katholieke Universiteit Leuven, Department of Sociology, Leuven.

Hays, W. L. (1972). *Statistics for the social sciences.* New York: Holt.

Tacq, J. J. A. (1997). *Multivariate analysis techniques in social science research: From problem to analysis.* London: Sage.

PARTIAL CORRELATION

Partial correlation is the correlation between two variables with the effect of (an)other variable(s) held constant. An often-quoted example is the correlation between the number of storks and the number of babies in a sample of regions, where the correlation disappears when the degree of rurality is held constant. This means that regions showing differences in the numbers of storks will also differ in birth rates, but this covariation is entirely due to differences in rurality. For regions with equal scores on rurality, this relationship between storks and babies should disappear. The correlation is said to be "spurious."

As the correlation does not have to become zero but can change in whatever direction, we give here the example of the partial correlation between the extracurricular activity of students (variable X_1) and their popularity (variable Y), controlling for their scholastic achievement (X_2). To clarify the mechanism of partial correlation, we give a simple (fictitious) sample of five students with the following scores on the three variables:

Table 1

Y	X_1	X_2
1	0	4
3	1	4
2	3	1
6	6	2
4	8	0

To calculate the partial correlation, we remove the influence of X_2 from X_1 as well as from Y, so that the partial correlation becomes the simple ZERO-ORDER correlation between the residual terms $X_1 - \hat{X}_1$ and $Y - \hat{Y}$. This mechanism involves three steps.

First, a bivariate regression analysis is performed from X_1 on X_2. The estimated $\hat{X}_1$ values are calculated, and the difference of $X_1 - \hat{X}_1$ yields the residual scores that are freed from control variable X_2.

Second, a bivariate regression analysis of Y on X_2 is performed. The estimated $\hat{Y}$ values are calculated, and the difference of $Y - \hat{Y}$ yields the residual scores.

Third, $X_1 - \hat{X}_1$ and $Y - \hat{Y}$ are correlated. This zero-order correlation between the residuals is the partial correlation coefficient $r_{y1 \cdot 2}$ (i.e., the zero-order product-moment correlation coefficient between Y and X_1 after the common variance with X_2 is removed from both variables).

This partial correlation coefficient is a FIRST-ORDER coefficient because one controls for only one variable. The model can be extended for HIGHER-ORDER partial correlations with several control variables. In the third-order coefficient $r_{y1 \cdot 234}$, the partial correlation between Y and X_1 is calculated, controlling for X_2, X_3, and X_4. In that case, the first step is not a bivariate but a multiple regression analysis of X_1 on X_2, X_3, and X_4, resulting in the residual term $X_1 - \hat{X}_1$. The second step is a multiple regression analysis of Y on X_2, X_3, and X_4, yielding the residual term $Y - \hat{Y}$. The zero-order correlation between $X_1 - \hat{X}_1$ and $Y - \hat{Y}$ is, then, the coefficient $r_{y1 \cdot 234}$.

For the population, Greek instead of Latin letters are used. The sample coefficients $r_{y1 \cdot 2}$ and $r_{y1 \cdot 234}$, which are indicated above, are then written as $\rho_{y1 \cdot 2}$ and $\rho_{y1 \cdot 234}$.

CALCULATION OF THE PARTIAL CORRELATION

All the aforementioned operations are brought together in Table 2.

We can see here that the mechanism of partial correlation analysis should not be naively understood as the disappearance of a relationship when controlling for a third factor. In this case, the original correlation between Y and X_1 is $r_{y1} = 0.75$, and the partial correlation is $r_{y1 \cdot 2} = 0.89$. So, the relationship between extracurricular activity and popularity appeared to be strong at first sight and now proves to be even stronger when controlling for scholastic achievement.

When calculating the partial correlation between Y and X_2, controlling for X_1 (exercise for the reader), we clearly see how drastic the mechanism can be. The original correlation is $r_{y2} = -0.38$, and the partial correlation is $r_{y2 \cdot 1} = 0.77$, which means that the sign has changed. The relationship between scholastic

Table 2

X_1	X_2	$\hat{X}_1$	$X_1 - \hat{X}_1$		Y	X_2	$\hat{Y}$	$Y - \hat{Y}$
0	4	0.70	-0.70		1	4	2.45	-1.45
1	4	0.70	0.30		3	4	2.45	0.55
3	1	5.53	-2.53		2	1	3.68	-1.68
6	2	3.92	2.08		6	2	3.27	2.73
8	0	7.14	0.86		4	0	4.09	-0.09

Step 1: $\hat{X}_1 = 7.14 - 1.61X_2$ _Step_ 2: $\hat{Y} = 4.09 - 0.41X_2$

Step 3: $r_{(x_1 - \hat{x}_1)(y - \hat{y})} = r_{y1\cdot2} = 0.89$

achievement and popularity originally appeared to be moderate and negative (the better school results, the less popular), but for students with the same level of extracurricular activity, it proves to be strong and positive (the better school results, the more popular). The reason for this drastic difference between the correlation and the partial correlation is that there is a strong association between the control variable X_1 and each of the variables X_2 and Y ($r_{12} = -0.86$ and $r_{1y} = 0.75$).

Computation of the Partial Correlation Coefficient

It can be easily shown that the partial correlation coefficient ($r_{y1\cdot2}$) is equal to a fraction, of which the numerator is the difference between the original correlation (r_{y1}) and the product of the marginal relationships ($r_{y2} r_{12}$), and the denominator is the geometric mean (the $\sqrt{}$ of the product) of the proportions of variance of the original variables Y and X_1 that cannot be explained by the control variable X_2 (i.e., of the residual variances: $1 - r_{y2}^2$ and $1 - r_{12}^2$):

$$r_{y1\cdot2} = \frac{r_{y1} - r_{y2}r_{12}}{\sqrt{[(1 - r_{y2}^2)(1 - r_{12}^2)]}}.$$

We can obtain this formula in many ways. The derivation can be found in matrix notation in Kendall and Stuart (1969, pp. 317–318) and in more elaborate algebraic notation in Brownlee (1965, pp. 429–430). Kendall and Stuart (1969, pp. 328–329) also succeed in deriving the formula geometrically in the vector

model, a derivation that is warmly recommended to the reader who enjoys intellectual pieces of art.

Still another way to find the formula for $r_{y1\cdot2}$ is the one used in PATH ANALYSIS. Path coefficients are standardized partial regression coefficients, and these can be expressed as functions of zero-order correlation coefficients as follows:

$$b_{y1\cdot2}^* = (r_{y1} - r_{y2}r_{12})/(1 - r_{12}^2).$$

With X_1 as the dependent variable and Y as the independent variable, this is

$$b_{1y\cdot2}^* = (r_{y1} - r_{y2}r_{12})/(1 - r_{y2}^2).$$

Just as the zero-order correlation coefficient r_{y1} is the geometric mean of the two regression coefficients b_{y1} and b_{1y}, the first-order partial correlation coefficient $r_{y1\cdot2}$ is the geometric mean of the two partial regression coefficients $b_{y1\cdot2}$ and $b_{1y\cdot2}$ or of their standardized versions $b_{y1\cdot2}^*$ and $b_{1y\cdot2}^*$. Indeed, we see that

$$b_{y1\cdot2}^* b_{1y\cdot2}^* = \left[\frac{(r_{y1} - r_{y2}r_{12})}{(1 - r_{12}^2)}\frac{(r_{y1} - r_{y2}r_{12})}{(1 - r_{y2}^2)}\right]^{\frac{1}{2}}$$
$$= \frac{(r_{y1} - r_{y2}r_{12})}{[(1 - r_{12}^2)(1 - r_{y2}^2)]^{\frac{1}{2}}} = r_{y1\cdot2}.$$

This formula can be easily extended for higher-order coefficients. For example, if we, in addition to X_2, introduce X_3 as a control variable in the investigation of the relationship between X_1 and Y, then we simply write down the formula of $r_{y1\cdot2}$ and add the control for X_3 to each zero-order correlation in the formula. Or, reversing the order, we write the formula for $r_{y1\cdot3}$ and add the control for X_2 everywhere:

$$r_{y1\cdot23} = \frac{r_{y1\cdot3} - r_{y2\cdot3}r_{12\cdot3}}{[(1 - r_{12\cdot3}^2)(1 - r_{y2\cdot3}^2)]^{\frac{1}{2}}}$$
$$= \frac{r_{y1\cdot2} - r_{y3\cdot2}r_{13\cdot2}}{[(1 - r_{13\cdot2}^2)(1 - r_{y3\cdot2}^2)]^{\frac{1}{2}}}.$$

We see that the second-order partial correlation coefficient is a function of first-order coefficients. Each higher-order coefficient can be written in this way (i.e., in terms of coefficients of which the order is one lower).

SIGNIFICANCE TEST

The significance tests of the partial correlation coefficient and of the corresponding partial regression coefficient are identical. See REGRESSION ANALYSIS for further details.

–Jacques Tacq

REFERENCES

Blalock, H. M. (1972). *Social statistics*. Tokyo: McGraw-Hill Kogakusha.

Brownlee, K. (1965). *Statistical theory and methodology in science and engineering*. New York: John Wiley.

Hays, W. L. (1972). *Statistics for the social sciences*. New York: Holt.

Kendall, M., & Stuart, A. (1969). *The advanced theory of statistics: Vol. 2. Inference and relationship*. London: Griffin.

Tacq, J. J. A. (1997). *Multivariate analysis techniques in social science research: From problem to analysis*. London: Sage.

PARTIAL LEAST SQUARES REGRESSION

Partial least squares (PLS) regression is a recent technique that generalizes and combines features from PRINCIPAL COMPONENTS ANALYSIS and MULTIPLE REGRESSION. It is particularly useful when we need to predict a set of dependent variables from a (very) large set of independent variables (i.e., predictors). It originated in the social sciences (specifically, economics; Wold, 1966) but became popular first in chemometrics, due in part to Wold's son Svante (see, e.g., Geladi & Kowalski, 1986), and in sensory evaluation (Martens & Naes, 1989). But PLS regression is also becoming a tool of choice in the social sciences as a multivariate technique for nonexperimental and experimental data alike (e.g., neuroimaging; see McIntosh, Bookstein, Haxby, & Grady, 1996). It was first presented as an algorithm akin to the power method (used for computing eigenvectors) but was rapidly interpreted in a statistical framework (Frank & Friedman, 1993; Helland, 1990; Höskuldsson, 1988; Tenenhaus, 1998).

PREREQUISITE NOTIONS AND NOTATIONS

The I observations described by K dependent variables are stored in an $I \times K$ matrix denoted $\mathbf{Y}$, and the values of the J predictors collected on these I observations are collected in the $I \times J$ matrix $\mathbf{X}$.

GOAL

The goal of PLS regression is to predict $\mathbf{Y}$ from $\mathbf{X}$ and to describe their common structure. When $\mathbf{Y}$ is a vector and $\mathbf{X}$ is full rank, this goal could be accomplished using ORDINARY LEAST SQUARES (OLS). When the number of predictors is large compared to the number of observations, $\mathbf{X}$ is likely to be singular, and the regression approach is no longer feasible (i.e., because of MULTICOLLINEARITY). Several approaches have been developed to cope with this problem. One approach is to eliminate some predictors (e.g., using STEPWISE methods); another one, called principal component regression, is to perform a PRINCIPAL COMPONENTS ANALYSIS (PCA) of the $\mathbf{X}$ matrix and then use the principal components of $\mathbf{X}$ as regressors on $\mathbf{Y}$.

The orthogonality of the principal components eliminates the multicollinearity problem. But the problem of choosing an *optimum* subset of predictors remains. A possible strategy is to keep only a few of the first components. But they are chosen to explain $\mathbf{X}$ rather than $\mathbf{Y}$, and so nothing guarantees that the principal components, which "explain" $\mathbf{X}$, are relevant for $\mathbf{Y}$.

By contrast, PLS regression finds components from $\mathbf{X}$ that are also relevant for $\mathbf{Y}$. Specifically, PLS regression searches for a set of components (called *latent vectors*) that perform a simultaneous decomposition of $\mathbf{X}$ and $\mathbf{Y}$ with the constraint that these components explain as much as possible of the *covariance* between $\mathbf{X}$ and $\mathbf{Y}$. This step generalizes PCA. It is followed by a regression step in which the decomposition of $\mathbf{X}$ is used to predict $\mathbf{Y}$.

SIMULTANEOUS DECOMPOSITION OF PREDICTORS AND DEPENDENT VARIABLES

PLS regression decomposes both $\mathbf{X}$ and $\mathbf{Y}$ as a product of a common set of orthogonal factors and a set of specific loadings. So, the independent variables are *decomposed* as $\mathbf{X} = \mathbf{TP}^T$ with $\mathbf{T}^T\mathbf{T} = \mathbf{I}$, with $\mathbf{I}$ being the identity matrix (some variations of the technique do not require $\mathbf{T}$ to have unit norms). By analogy, with PCA, $\mathbf{T}$ is called the *score* matrix and $\mathbf{P}$ the *loading* matrix (in PLS regression, the loadings are not orthogonal). Likewise, $\mathbf{Y}$ is *estimated* as $\hat{\mathbf{Y}} = \mathbf{TBC}^T$, where $\mathbf{B}$ is a diagonal matrix with the "regression weights" as diagonal elements (see below for more details on these weights). The columns of $\mathbf{T}$ are the *latent vectors*. When their number is equal to the rank of $\mathbf{X}$, they perform an exact decomposition of $\mathbf{X}$. Note, however, that they only *estimate* $\mathbf{Y}$ (i.e., in general, $\hat{\mathbf{Y}}$ is not equal to $\mathbf{Y}$).

PLS REGRESSION AND COVARIANCE

The latent vectors could be chosen in a lot of different ways. In fact, in the previous formulation, any set of orthogonal vectors spanning the column space of $\mathbf{X}$ could be used to play the role of $\mathbf{Y}$. To specify $\mathbf{T}$, additional conditions are required. For PLS regression, this amounts to finding two sets of weights $\mathbf{w}$ and $\mathbf{c}$ to create (respectively) a linear combination of the columns of $\mathbf{X}$ and $\mathbf{Y}$ such that their covariance is maximum. Specifically, the goal is to obtain a first pair of vectors $\mathbf{t} = \mathbf{Xw}$ and $\mathbf{u} = \mathbf{Yc}$ with the constraints that $\mathbf{w}^T\mathbf{w} = 1$, $\mathbf{t}^T\mathbf{t} = 1$, and $\mathbf{t}^T\mathbf{u}$ be maximal. When the first latent vector is found, it is *subtracted* from both $\mathbf{X}$ and $\mathbf{Y}$ (this guarantees the orthogonality of the latent vectors), and the procedure is reiterated until $\mathbf{X}$ becomes a null matrix (see the algorithm section for more).

A PLS REGRESSION ALGORITHM

The properties of PLS regression can be analyzed from a sketch of the original algorithm. The first step is to create two matrices: $\mathbf{E} = \mathbf{X}$ and $\mathbf{F} = \mathbf{Y}$. These matrices are then column centered and normalized (i.e., transformed into Z-scores). The sums of squares of these matrices are denoted SS_X and SS_Y. Before starting the iteration process, the vector $\mathbf{u}$ is initialized with random values (in what follows, the symbol $\propto$ means "to normalize the result of the operation").

Step 1. $\mathbf{w} \propto \mathbf{E}^T\mathbf{u}$ (estimate $\mathbf{X}$ weights).
Step 2. $\mathbf{t} \propto \mathbf{Ew}$ (estimate $\mathbf{X}$ factor scores).
Step 3. $\mathbf{c} \propto \mathbf{F}^T\mathbf{t}$ (estimate $\mathbf{Y}$ weights).
Step 4. $\mathbf{u} = \mathbf{Fc}$ (estimate $\mathbf{Y}$ scores).

If $\mathbf{t}$ has not converged, then go to Step 1; if $\mathbf{t}$ has converged, then compute the value of b, which is used to predict $\mathbf{Y}$ from $\mathbf{t}$ as $b = \mathbf{t}^T\mathbf{u}$, and compute the factor loadings for $\mathbf{X}$ as $\mathbf{p} = \mathbf{E}^T\mathbf{t}$. Now subtract (i.e., partial out) the effect of $\mathbf{t}$ from both $\mathbf{E}$ and $\mathbf{F}$ as follows $\mathbf{E} = \mathbf{E} - \mathbf{tp}^T$ and $\mathbf{F} = \mathbf{F} - b\mathbf{tc}^T$. The vectors $\mathbf{t}$, $\mathbf{u}$, $\mathbf{w}$, $\mathbf{c}$, and $\mathbf{p}$ are then stored in the corresponding matrices, and the scalar b is stored as a diagonal element of $\mathbf{B}$. The sum of squares of $\mathbf{X}$ (or, respectively, $\mathbf{Y}$) explained by the latent vector is computed as $\mathbf{p}^T\mathbf{p}$ (or, respectively, b^2), and the proportion of variance explained is obtained by dividing the explained sum of squares by the corresponding total sum of squares (i.e., SS_X and SS_Y).

If $\mathbf{E}$ is a null matrix, then the whole set of latent vectors has been found; otherwise, the procedure can be reiterated from Step 1 on.

PLS REGRESSION AND THE SINGULAR VALUE DECOMPOSITION

The iterative algorithm presented above is similar to the power method, which finds eigenvectors. So PLS regression is likely to be closely related to the eigenvalue and singular value decompositions, and this is indeed the case. For example, if we start from Step 1, which computes $\mathbf{w} \propto \mathbf{E}^T\mathbf{u}$, and substitute the rightmost term iteratively, we find the following series of equations: $\mathbf{w} \propto \mathbf{E}^T\mathbf{u} \propto \mathbf{E}^T\mathbf{Fc} \propto \mathbf{E}^T\mathbf{FF}^T\mathbf{t} \propto \mathbf{E}^T\mathbf{FF}^T\mathbf{Ew}$. This shows that the first weight vector $\mathbf{w}$ is the first right singular vector of the matrix $\mathbf{X}^T\mathbf{Y}$. Similarly, the first weight vector $\mathbf{c}$ is the left singular vector of $\mathbf{X}^T\mathbf{Y}$. The same argument shows that the first vectors $\mathbf{t}$ and $\mathbf{u}$ are the first eigenvectors of $\mathbf{XX}^T\mathbf{YY}^T$ and $\mathbf{YY}^T\mathbf{XX}^T$.

PREDICTION OF THE DEPENDENT VARIABLES

The dependent variables are predicted using the multivariate regression formula as $\hat{\mathbf{Y}} = \mathbf{TBC}^T = \mathbf{XB}_{\text{PLS}}$ with $\mathbf{B}_{\text{PLS}} = (\mathbf{P}^{T+})\mathbf{BC}^T$ (where $\mathbf{P}^{T+}$ is the Moore-Penrose pseudo-inverse of $\mathbf{P}^T$). If all the latent variables of $\mathbf{X}$ are used, this regression is equivalent to principal components regression. When only a subset of the latent variables is used, the prediction of $\mathbf{Y}$ is optimal for this number of predictors.

An obvious question is to find the number of latent variables needed to obtain the best generalization for the prediction of *new* observations. This is, in general, achieved by cross-validation techniques such as BOOTSTRAPPING.

The interpretation of the latent variables is often helped by examining graphs akin to PCA graphs (e.g., by plotting observations in a $t_1 \times t_2$ space).

A SMALL EXAMPLE

We want to predict the subjective evaluation of a set of five wines. The dependent variables that we want to predict for each wine are its likeability and how well it goes with meat or dessert (as rated by a panel of experts) (see Table 1). The predictors are the price and the sugar, alcohol, and acidity content of each wine (see Table 2).

Table 2   The **Y** Matrix of Dependent Variables

Wine	Hedonic	Goes With Meat	Goes With Dessert
1	14	7	8
2	10	7	6
3	8	5	5
4	2	4	7
5	6	2	4

Table 3   The **X** Matrix of Predictors

Wine	Price	Sugar	Alcohol	Acidity
1	7	7	13	7
2	4	3	14	7
3	10	5	12	5
4	16	7	11	3
5	13	3	10	3

The different matrices created by PLS regression are given in Tables 3 to 11. From Table 11, one can find that two latent vectors explain 98% of the variance of **X** and 85% of **Y**. This suggests keeping these two dimensions for the final solution. The examination of the two-dimensional regression coefficients (i.e., B_{PLS}; see Table 8) shows that sugar content is mainly responsible for choosing a dessert wine and that price is negatively correlated with the perceived quality of the wine, whereas alcohol content is positively correlated with it (at least in this example). The latent vectors show that t_1 expresses price and t_2 reflects sugar content.

Table 4   The Matrix **T**

Wine	t_1	t_2	t_3
1	0.4538	−0.4662	0.5716
2	0.5399	0.4940	−0.4631
3	0	0	0
4	−0.4304	−0.5327	−0.5301
5	−0.5633	0.5049	0.4217

Table 5   The Matrix **U**

	u_1	u_2	u_3
1	1.9451	−0.7611	0.6191
2	0.9347	0.5305	−0.5388
3	−0.2327	0.6084	0.0823
4	−0.9158	−1.1575	−0.6139
5	−1.7313	0.7797	0.4513

Table 6   The Matrix **P**

	p_1	p_2	p_3
Price	−1.8706	−0.6845	−0.1796
Sugar	0.0468	−1.9977	0.0829
Alcohol	1.9547	0.0283	−0.4224
Acidity	1.9874	0.0556	0.2170

Table 7   The Matrix **W**

	w_1	w_2	w_3
Price	−0.5137	−0.3379	−0.3492
Sugar	0.2010	−0.9400	0.1612
Alcohol	0.5705	−0.0188	−0.8211
Acidity	0.6085	0.0429	0.4218

Table 7   The Matrix B_{PLS} When Three Latent Vectors Are Used

	Hedonic	Goes With Meat	Goes With Dessert
Price	−1.0607	−0.0745	0.1250
Sugar	0.3354	0.2593	0.7510
Alcohol	−1.4142	0.7454	0.5000
Acidity	1.2298	0.1650	0.1186

RELATIONSHIP WITH OTHER TECHNIQUES

PLS regression is obviously related to CANONICAL CORRELATION and to multiple FACTOR ANALYSIS (Escofier & Pagès, 1988). These relationships are explored in detail by Tenenhaus (1998) and Pagès and Tenenhaus (2001). The main originality of PLS regression is preserving the asymmetry of the relationship

Table 8   The Matrix $\mathbf{B}_{PLS}$ When Two Latent Vectors Are Used

	Hedonic	Goes With Meat	Goes With Dessert
Price	−0.2662	−0.2498	0.0121
Sugar	0.0616	0.3197	0.7900
Alcohol	0.2969	0.3679	0.2568
Acidity	0.3011	0.3699	0.2506

Table 9   The Matrix $\mathbf{C}$

	$\mathbf{c}_1$	$\mathbf{c}_2$	$\mathbf{c}_3$
Hedonic	0.6093	0.0518	0.9672
Goes with meat	0.7024	−0.2684	−0.2181
Goes with dessert	0.3680	−0.9619	−0.1301

Table 10   The $\mathbf{b}$ Vector

b_1	b_2	b_3
2.7568	1.6272	1.1191

Table 11   Variance of $\mathbf{X}$ and $\mathbf{Y}$ Explained by the Latent Vectors

Latent Vector	% of Explained Variance for $\mathbf{X}$	Cumulative % of Explained Variance for $\mathbf{X}$	% of Explained Variance for $\mathbf{Y}$	Cumulative % of Explained Variance for $\mathbf{Y}$
1	70	70	63	63
2	28	98	22	85
3	2	100	10	95

between predictors and dependent variables, whereas these other techniques treat them symmetrically.

SOFTWARE

PLS regression necessitates sophisticated computations, and its application depends on the availability of software. For chemistry, two main programs are used: the first one, called SIMCA-P, was originally developed by Wold; the second one, called the UNSCRAMBLER, was first developed by Martens, who was another pioneer in the field. For brain imaging, SPM, which is one of the most widely used programs in the field, has recently (2002) integrated a PLS regression module. Outside these fields, SAS PROC PLS is probably the most easily available program. In addition, interested readers can download a set of MATLAB programs from the author's home page (www.utdallas.edu/~ herve). A public domain set of MATLAB programs

is available from the home page of the *N*-Way project (www.models.kvl.dk/source/nwaytoolbox/), along with tutorials and examples. Finally, a commercial MATLAB toolbox has also been developed by EIGENRESEARCH.

—Hervé Abdi

REFERENCES

Escofier, B., & Pagès, J. (1988). *Analyses factorielles multiples* [Multiple factor analyses]. Paris: Dunod.

Frank, I. E., & Friedman, J. H. (1993). A statistical view of chemometrics regression tools. *Technometrics, 35,* 109–148.

Geladi, P., & Kowalski, B. (1986). Partial least square regression: A tutorial. *Analytica Chemica Acta, 35,* 1–17.

Helland, I. S. (1990). PLS regression and statistical models. *Scandinavian Journal of Statistics, 17,* 97–114.

Höskuldsson, A. (1988). PLS regression methods. *Journal of Chemometrics, 2,* 211–228.

Martens, H., & Naes, T. (1989). *Multivariate calibration.* London: Wiley.

McIntosh, A. R., Bookstein, F. L., Haxby, J. V., & Grady, C. L. (1996). Spatial pattern analysis of functional brain images using partial least squares. *Neuroimage, 3,* 143–157.

Pagès, J., & Tenenhaus, M. (2001). Multiple factor analysis combined with PLS path modeling: Application to the analysis of relationships between physicochemical variables, sensory profiles and hedonic judgments. *Chemometrics and Intelligent Laboratory Systems, 58,* 261–273.

Tenenhaus, M. (1998). *La régression PLS* [PLS regression]. Paris: Technip.

Wold, H. (1966). Estimation of principal components and related models by iterative least squares. In P. R. Krishnaiaah (Ed.), *Multivariate analysis* (pp. 391–420). New York: Academic Press.

PARTIAL REGRESSION COEFFICIENT

The partial regression coefficient is also called the REGRESSION COEFFICIENT, regression weight, partial regression weight, SLOPE coefficient, or partial slope coefficient. It is used in the context of multiple linear regression (MLR) analysis and gives the amount by which the DEPENDENT VARIABLE (DV) increases when one INDEPENDENT VARIABLE (IV) is increased by one unit and all the other independent variables are held constant. This coefficient is called partial because its value depends, in general, on the other independent variables. Specifically, the value of the partial coefficient for one independent variable will vary, in general, depending on the other independent variables included in the regression equation.

MULTIPLE REGRESSION FRAMEWORK

In MLR, the goal is to PREDICT, knowing, from the measurements collected on N subjects, the value of the dependent variable Y from a set of K independent variables $\{X_1, \ldots, X_k, \ldots, X_K\}$. We denote by $\mathbf{X}$ the $N \times (K + 1)$ augmented MATRIX collecting the data for the independent variables (this matrix is called *augmented* because the first column is composed only of 1s), and we denote by $\mathbf{y}$ the $N \times 1$ vector of observations for the dependent variable (see Figure 1).

$$\mathbf{X} = \begin{pmatrix} 1 & x_{11} & \cdots & x_{1k} & \cdots & x_{1K} \\ \vdots & \vdots & \ddots & \vdots & \ddots & \vdots \\ 1 & x_{n1} & \cdots & x_{nk} & \cdots & x_{nK} \\ \vdots & \vdots & \ddots & \vdots & \ddots & \vdots \\ 1 & x_{N1} & \cdots & x_{Nk} & \cdots & x_{NK} \end{pmatrix}$$

$$\mathbf{y} = \begin{pmatrix} y_1 \\ \vdots \\ y_n \\ \vdots \\ y_N \end{pmatrix}.$$

Figure 1   The Structure of the X and y Matrices

Multiple regression finds a set of partial regression coefficients b_k such that the dependent variable could be approximated as well as possible by a linear combination of the independent variables (with the b_ks being the weights of the combination). Therefore, a predicted value, denoted $\hat{Y}$, of the dependent variable is obtained as

$$\hat{Y} = b_0 + b_1 X_1 + b_2 X_2 + \cdots + b_k X_k + \cdots + b_K X_K. \tag{1}$$

The value of the partial coefficients is found using ORDINARY LEAST SQUARES (OLS). It is often convenient to express the MLR equation using matrix notation. In this framework, the predicted values of the dependent variable are collected in a vector denoted $\hat{\mathbf{y}}$ and are obtained using MLR as

$$\hat{\mathbf{y}} = \mathbf{X}\mathbf{b} \quad \text{with} \quad \mathbf{b} = (\mathbf{X}^T\mathbf{X})^{-1}\mathbf{X}^T\mathbf{y}. \tag{2}$$

The quality of the prediction is evaluated by computing the multiple coefficient of correlation squared $R^2_{Y,1,\ldots k,\ldots,K}$, which is the squared coefficient of correlation between the dependent variable (Y) and the predicted dependent variable ($\hat{Y}$). The *specific* contribution of each IV to the regression equation is assessed by the partial coefficient of correlation associated with each variable. This coefficient, closely associated with the partial regression coefficient, corresponds to the increment in explained variance obtained by adding this variable to the regression equation after all the other IVs have been already included.

PARTIAL REGRESSION COEFFICIENT AND REGRESSION COEFFICIENT

When the independent variables are pairwise orthogonal, the effect of each of them in the regression is assessed by computing the slope of the regression between this independent variable and the dependent variable. In this case (i.e., orthogonality of the IVs), the partial regression coefficients are equal to the regression coefficients. In all other cases, the regression coefficient will differ from the partial regression coefficients.

Table 1   A Set of Data: Y Is Predicted From X_1 and X_2

Y (Memory Span)	14	23	30	50	39	67
X_1 (Age)	4	4	7	7	10	10
X_2 (Speech Rate)	1	2	2	4	3	6

SOURCE: Abdi, Dowling, Valentin, Edelman, and Posamentier (2002).
NOTE: Y is the number of digits a child can remember for a short time (the "memory span"), X_1 is the age of the child, and X_2 is the speech rate of the child (how many words the child can pronounce in a given time). Six children were tested.

For example, consider the data given in Table 1, in which the dependent variable Y is to be predicted from the independent variables X_1 and X_2. In this example, Y is a child's memory span (i.e., number of words a child can remember in a set of short-term memory tasks) that we want to predict from the child's age (X_1) and the child's speech rate (X_2). The prediction equation (using equation (2)) is $\hat{Y} = 1.67 + X_1 + 9.50X_2$, where b_1 is equal to 1 and b_2 is equal to 9.50. This means that children increase their memory span by one word every year and by 9.50 words for every additional word they can pronounce (i.e., the faster they speak, the more they can remember).

A multiple linear regression analysis of this data set gives a multiple coefficient of correlation squared of $R^2_{Y \cdot 1,2} = .9866$. The coefficient of correlation between X_1 and X_2 is equal to $r_{1,2} = .7500$, between X_1 and Y is equal to $r_{Y,1} = .8028$, and between X_2 and Y is equal to $r_{Y,2} = .9890$. The squared partial regression coefficient between X_1 and Y is computed as $r^2_{Y \cdot 1 | 2} = R^2_{Y \cdot 12} - r^2_{Y,2} = .9866 - .9890^2 = .0085$; likewise, $r^2_{Y \cdot 2 | 1} = R^2_{Y \cdot 12} - r^2_{Y,1} = .9866 - .8028^2 = .3421$.

F AND *T*-TESTS FOR THE PARTIAL REGRESSION COEFFICIENT

The NULL HYPOTHESIS stating that a partial regression coefficient is equal to zero can be tested by using a standard F TEST, which tests the equivalent null hypothesis stating that the associated partial coefficient of correlation is zero. This F test has $\nu_1 = 1$ and $\nu_2 = N - K - 1$ degrees of freedom (with N being the number of observations and K being the number of predictors). Because ν_1 is equal to 1, the square root of F gives a Student t-test. The computation of F is best described with an example: The F for the variable X_1 in our example is obtained as follows:

$$
\begin{aligned}
F_{Y \cdot 1,2} &= \frac{r^2_{Y \cdot 1 | 2}}{1 - R^2_{Y \cdot 1,2}} \times df_{\text{regression}} \\
&= \frac{r^2_{Y \cdot 1 | 2}}{1 - R^2_{Y \cdot 1,2}} \times (N - K - 1) \\
&= \frac{.0085}{1 - .9866} \times 3 = 1.91.
\end{aligned}
$$

This value of F is smaller than the critical value for $\nu_1 = 1$ and $\nu_2 = N - K - 1 = 3$, which is equal to 10.13 for an alpha level of .05. Therefore, b_1 (and $r^2_{Y \cdot 1 | 2}$) cannot be considered different from zero.

STANDARD ERROR AND CONFIDENCE INTERVAL

The STANDARD ERROR of the partial regression coefficient is useful to compute CONFIDENCE INTERVALS and perform additional statistical tests. The standard error of coefficient b_k is denoted S_{b_k}. It can be computed directly from F as $S_{b_k} = b_k \times \sqrt{1/F_k}$, where F_k is the value of the F test for b_k. For example, we find for the first variable that: $S_{b_k} = 1 \times \sqrt{1/1.91} = .72$.

The confidence interval of b_j is computed as $b_k \pm S_{b_k} \sqrt{F_{\text{critical}}}$, with F_{critical} being the critical value for the F test. For example, the confidence interval of b_1 is equal to $1 \pm .72 \times \sqrt{10.13} = 1 \pm 2.29$, and therefore the 95% confidence interval b_1 goes from -1.29 to $+3.29$. This interval encompasses the zero value, and this corresponds to the failure to reject the null hypothesis.

β WEIGHTS AND PARTIAL REGRESSION COEFFICIENTS

There is some confusion here because, depending on the context, β is the parameter estimated by b, whereas in some other contexts, β is the regression weight obtained when the regression is performed with all variables being expressed in Z-scores. In the latter case, β is called the *standardized partial regression coefficient* or the *β-weight*. These weights have the advantage of being comparable from one independent variable to the other because the unit of measurement has been eliminated. The β-weights can easily be computed from the bs as $\beta_k = \frac{S_k}{S_y} b_k$ (with S_k being the standard deviation of the kth independent variable and S_y being the standard deviation of the dependent variable).

—Hervé Abdi

REFERENCES

Abdi, H., Dowling, W. J., Valentin, D., Edelman, B., & Posamentier, M. (2002). *Experimental design and research methods*. Unpublished manuscript, University of Texas at Dallas, Program in Cognition and Neuroscience.

Cohen, J., & Cohen, P. (1984). *Applied multiple regression/correlation analysis for the behavioral sciences* (2nd ed.). Hillsdale, NJ: Lawrence Erlbaum.

Darlington, R. B. (1990). *Regression and linear models*. New York: McGraw-Hill.

Draper, N. R., & Smith, H. (1998). *Applied regression analysis*. New York: John Wiley.

Pedhazur, E. J. (1997). *Multiple regression in behavioral research* (3rd ed.). New York: Wadsworth.

PARTICIPANT OBSERVATION

Participant observation is a method of data collection in which the investigator uses participation in an area of ongoing social life to observe it. The investigator may or may not already be a natural member of the social setting studied. The classic form that such participation takes has been relatively long-term membership in a small face-to-face group, but it can also extend to the anonymous joining of a crowd; the boundary between participant and nonparticipant observation is thus not a clear one. Raymond L. Gold's (1969) distinctions among possible field roles—from complete participant to participant as observer/observer as participant/complete observer—have been widely used to indicate the range of possibilities. What participant observers actually do can vary considerably and may include elements sometimes counted as separate methods in their own right such as UNSTRUCTURED INTERVIEWS, observation of physical features of settings, or the collection of printed materials.

It has become conventional to classify participant observation as a qualitative method, but its data can sometimes be quantified, even if the circumstances may often make the collection of standardized material difficult. Equally, it is conventionally assumed that the observer does not set out to test hypotheses but enters the field with an open mind to see what life is like. The mode of data collection as such does not prevent the testing of hypotheses, but the assumption is that adequate hypotheses cannot be formed without close familiarity with a situation and the meanings of members in it. Participant observation has mainly been used for studies of groups in work settings or of informal groupings in small communities or the social life of groups of friends; these are situations in which patterns of face-to-face interaction develop, and a single researcher or a small group of workers can gain access and establish a role. However, there also, for example, have been studies of football crowds, right-wing political groups, and schools. The method is not well suited to the study of large populations or to the collection of representative data about causal relations among predefined variables; the logic of the CASE STUDY rather than of the RANDOM SAMPLE applies.

HISTORY

The history of the *practice* of "participant observation" needs to be distinguished from the history of the use of the *term* and of its application in the modern sense. Observers reported on their findings from personal participation before the term emerged, some well before the development of social science as an academic field. The term was first used in the literature of sociology, in 1924, for the role of informants

who reported to the investigator on meetings they had attended. (Bronislaw Malinowski was inventing the form that it came to take in social-anthropological fieldwork in the Trobriand islands during World War I, although the anthropological and sociological traditions were largely independent.) The body of work produced at the University of Chicago in the 1920s and 1930s, under the leadership of Robert Park, is generally regarded as providing the first examples in sociology of participant observation in the modern sense, although they did not then call it that. Some of these studies were ones in which Park encouraged his students to write up prior experiences, or ones that arose naturally in their daily lives, rather than undertaking them for research purposes. These studies drew on many sources of data, without privileging participation as giving special access to meanings. It was only after World War II that the methodological literature developed, again led by Chicago and authors there such as Howard S. Becker, which focused on participant observation as one of the major alternative modes of data collection. The direct empathetic access it provided to real social behavior and its meanings was contrasted with the newly dominant questionnaire survey, and its data were seen as superior to the answers to standardized questions that merely reported on behavior.

PRACTICAL AND ETHICAL PROBLEMS

Some special research problems, practical and ethical, follow from the use of participant observation. ACCESS to the research situation needs to be gained. Negotiation with gatekeepers, when identified, may solve that for overt research. But what particular researchers can do depends, more than with any other method of data collection, on their personal characteristics; a man and a woman, or a Black and a White researcher, do not have the same ranges of opportunities, although such conventional boundaries have sometimes been transcended. Conducting research covertly may solve some problems of access but, in addition to raising acute ethical issues, makes the possibility of exposure a continual anxiety; important work, however, has been done covertly that could not have been done overtly. Even when participant observation is overt, research subjects can forget, once the researcher has become a friend, that their interaction may become data; the researcher's dilemma is then that continual renewal of consent would jeopardize the naturalness of the relationship and so damage the data. This is part of two broader problems: how to live psychologically with using the self for research purposes, perhaps for many hours a day, without GOING NATIVE, and how to deal with the fact that the researcher's presence must, to some extent, change the situation that is being studied. The issue of sampling as such is seldom addressed for participant observation but arises in the form of the need to avoid relying on unrepresentative informants and to observe interaction at different times and places in the life of the group studied. The physical task of recording the data has to be fitted in around making the observations; solutions have ranged from writing up notes every night from memory to frequent trips to the toilet or the use of pocket counting devices. How satisfactory such arrangements are will depend on the social situation and the nature of the data sought.

EXAMPLES

Three well-known examples of the method are William F. Whyte's (1943/1955) *Street Corner Society*; Howard S. Becker, Everett C. Hughes, and Anselm L. Strauss's (1961) *Boys in White*; and Laud Humphreys's (1970) *Tearoom Trade*. Whyte's study of a gang in Boston is not only of substantive interest but also important for the detailed methodological appendix added to later editions, which did much to create discussion of the practical issues involved in such work. *Boys in White* was a study of medical students that adopted exceptionally systematic and clearly documented methods of observation and analysis. *Tearoom Trade* has become notorious for its observation of homosexual activity in public toilets, as well as the ethical issues raised by Humphreys's indirect methods of identifying the participants.

—Jennifer Platt

REFERENCES

Becker, H. S., Hughes, E. C., & Strauss, A. L. (1961). *Boys in white*. Chicago: University of Chicago Press.

Gold, R. L. (1969). Roles in sociological field observations. In G. J. McCall & J. L. Simmons (Eds.), *Issues in participant observation* (pp. 30–38). Reading, MA: Addison-Wesley.

Humphreys, L. (1970). *Tearoom trade*. Chicago: Aldine.

Whyte, W. F. (1955). *Street corner society*. Chicago: University of Chicago Press. (Original work published in 1943.)

PARTICIPATORY ACTION RESEARCH

Participatory action research (PAR) is research involving the collaboration between local communities, organizations, or coalitions with a legitimate personal interest in solving a problem that affects them directly and expert outside facilitators. Together they define the problem, learn how to study it, design the research, analyze the outcomes, and design and execute the needed actions. PAR rests on a belief in the importance of local knowledge and the ability of people of all social conditions to take action on their own behalf to democratize the situations they live in.

Key elements in participatory action research include the belief that the purpose of research is to promote democratic social change by enhancing the capacity of people to chart the course of their own future, that insider-outsider collaboration is both possible and desirable, that local knowledge is essential to the success of any social change project, and that nothing of importance happens if power imbalances are not ameliorated to some degree. PAR also aims to enhance local stakeholders' ability to take on further change projects on their own rather than relying on outside experts.

A wide variety of ideological positions and methodological practices are associated with PAR. Some practitioners believe in a strong model of external leadership or even provocation. Others believe that people can organize themselves effectively if given a favorable protected space to work in. Some see radical social change as the defining characteristic of PAR, whereas others believe that any changes that enhance well-being, sustainability, or fairness are sufficient.

The terminological field surrounding PAR is dense and complex. Many varieties of activist research bear some relationship to each other (see the entry on ACTION RESEARCH for additional information). Among these are action research, action science, action learning, collaborative inquiry, and the methodological traditions of GROUNDED THEORY and general systems theory. These approaches differ in the disciplinary backgrounds they draw on (education, sociology, social movement analysis, applied anthropology, psychology, social work). They differ in what they define as a good outcome, and they differ in how strong a role expert outsiders are expected to play in the change process.

PAR has long had a controversial relationship to the academic disciplines and to the academy in general. A purposely engaged form of research, PAR rejects the separation of thought and action on which the academic social sciences and humanities generally rest and fundamentally questions the notions of objectivity, control, distance, and quality control by disciplinary standards.

PAR is practiced in many different contexts—communities, organizations, a business unit, a voluntary coalition, and so on—and so no single example can do justice to the variety of approaches. There are diverse ways of beginning a project: being invited as an outside consultant to a group or coalition, being a member of a thematic organization known for expertise with certain issues, being invited to work with community partners, and so forth. How one begins matters, but what matters most is not how one begins but the democratic quality of the process as it develops—its openness, its flexibility, its consistency with democratic purposes. Despite all the differences, a single brief example, drawn from my own work, will help clarify how such projects begin and develop.

In a small town in south central Spain, the agrarian economy has become increasingly vulnerable. More than 300 men leave daily to work in construction in Madrid, and hundreds of women do piecework sewing. A highly stratified community with a history of class conflict, the town faces the loss of most of its young people to other cities, something affecting all classes equally in a society that strongly values family ties. To address this, we convened a planning group of municipal officials and public and private school teachers who planned an action research search conference for 40 people selected from all ages, classes, genders, and ideologies. This 2-day event involved developing a shared view of the history, the ideal future, and the probable future of the community; the development of plans to improve future prospects for the young; and the creation of voluntary action teams to work on the different problems identified. The teams met for months after this, elaborating plans, acquiring resources, and taking actions with the outside facilitator in contact by e-mail and reconvening groups at 3-month intervals in person.

The concrete experience of the ability of people with very different social positions, wealth, and ideologies to collaborate and discover that each held a "piece of the puzzle" was a lasting contribution of the project. A number of the small action projects prospered, but some also failed. Now, elements and processes drawn from those initial activities are coalescing in a public initiative to create an ethnographic museum, civic center, and in tourism promotion efforts.

—Davydd J. Greenwood

REFERENCES

Fals-Borda, O., & Anisur Rahman, M. (Eds.). (1991). *Action and knowledge: Breaking the monopoly with participatory action-research.* New York: Apex.

Greenwood, D., & Levin, M. (1998). *Introduction to action research: Social research for social change.* Thousand Oaks, CA: Sage.

Horton, M., & Freire, P. (2000). *We make the road by walking* (Bell, B., Gaventa, J., & Peters, J., Eds.). Philadelphia: Temple University Press.

Reason, R., & Bradbury, H. (Eds.). (2001). *The handbook of action research.* London: Sage.

Whyte, W. F. (Ed.). (1991). *Participatory action research.* Newbury Park, CA: Sage.

PARTICIPATORY EVALUATION

Participatory evaluation is an umbrella term for approaches to program evaluation that actively involve program staff and participants in the planning and implementation of evaluation studies. This involvement ranges on a continuum from shared responsibility for evaluation questions and activities, including data collection and analysis, to complete control of the evaluation process and its outcomes, where the evaluator serves as a coach to ensure the quality of the effort. *Collaborative evaluation,* a related term, is a form of participatory evaluation near the center of this continuum; program participants take an active role, for example, in designing questions and data collection instruments, but the program evaluator remains a partner in the process, rather than a coach.

What all forms of participatory evaluation share is the purposeful and explicit involvement of program participants in the evaluation process to effect change, either in a program or organization locally or in society more generally. Many also seek to build the capacity of an organization or group to conduct additional evaluation without the assistance of a professional evaluator. Weaver and Cousins (2001) provide five dimensions for analyzing participatory evaluation studies: the extent to which stakeholders control decisions about the evaluation, the diversity of individuals selected to participate in the discussions, the power relations of participants, the ease with which the study can be implemented, and the depth of people's participation.

The origins of participatory evaluation reflect the general nature of the term, with roots in disparate traditions from around the world. Building on the work of Cousins and Whitmore (1998), theorists distinguish between two categories of approaches: practical participatory evaluation (P-PE) and transformative participatory evaluation (T-PE). Practical participatory evaluation evolved from approaches that seek to increase the ownership and use of evaluation results by involving program staff and participants in the evaluation process. Michael Quinn Patton's (1997) utilization-focused evaluation highlights the importance of the "personal factor" (i.e., connecting with individuals who are interested in the evaluation and providing information of use to them). Organization development and organizational learning point to the value of cyclic processes over time for asking questions, collecting and analyzing data, reflecting on them, and making changes as appropriate. In P-PE, evaluators can provide leadership of the evaluation process as they teach it to others by having them engage in it.

In T-PE, by contrast, program participants (at least theoretically) become the leaders of evaluation efforts to support social change and social justice through the development of empowered citizens. Whereas P-PE can improve the status quo by making programs more effective or efficient (e.g., improving service delivery in mental health programs), T-PE is a process that seeks to better the world for disenfranchised and oppressed people (e.g., reducing poverty among rural communities in a developing country). This category now encompasses a number of citizen-based evaluation/research approaches of the past 50 years, including, for example, participatory action research, participatory rural appraisal (renamed *participatory learning and action*), participatory monitoring and evaluation, and, more recently, empowerment evaluation.

—Jean A. King

REFERENCES

Cousins, J. B. (2003). Utilization effects of participatory evaluation. In T. Kellaghan, D. L. Stufflebeam, & L. A. Wingate (Eds.), *International handbook of educational evaluation* (pp. 245–266). Dordrecht, The Netherlands: Kluwer Academic.

Cousins, J. B., & Whitmore, E. (1998). Framing participatory evaluation. *New Directions in Evaluation, 80,* 5–23.

King, J. A. (1998). Making sense of participatory evaluation practice. *New Directions for Evaluation, 80,* 57–67.

Patton, M. Q. (1997). *Utilization-focused evaluation* (3rd ed.). Thousand Oaks, CA: Sage.

Weaver, L., & Cousins, B. (2001, November). *Unpacking the participatory process.* Paper presented at the annual meeting of the American Evaluation Association, St. Louis, MO.

PASCAL DISTRIBUTION

The Pascal distribution is used to model the number of independent BERNOULLI trials (x) needed to obtain a specific number of successes (r). The discrete RANDOM VARIABLE X can take on any integer value from r to infinity. If one is lucky and every trial results in a success, then $X = r$. To have $X = x$, it is necessary for there to be a success in trial x following exactly $r - 1$ successes during the preceding $x - 1$ trials. The definition here is opposite to that of the BINOMIAL distribution. That is, the random variable in the Pascal distribution is the number of trials before a certain number of successes, whereas in the binomial distribution, the random variable is the number of successes within a certain number of trials. For this reason, the Pascal distribution is also referred to as the NEGATIVE BINOMIAL DISTRIBUTION. Although these two distributions are often used synonymously, the Pascal distribution is actually a special case of the negative binomial in which the random variable X must be an integer. A special case of the Pascal distribution, the geometric distribution, occurs when $r = 1$, that is, how many trials are necessary to obtain the first success.

The probability mass function (pmf) for the Pascal distribution is given by

$$P(X = x | r, p) = \binom{x - 1}{r - 1} p^r (1 - p)^{x - r}$$

for $x = r, r + 1, r + 2, \ldots,$

$0 \leq p \leq 1, 0 < r \leq \infty.$

The mean of a Pascal distributed random variable is

$$\mu = \frac{r}{p}$$

and the variance is

$$\sigma^2 = \frac{r(1-p)}{p^2}.$$

The Pascal distribution is an extension of the POISSON DISTRIBUTION in which the restrictions on the parameter λ are relaxed. Rather than requiring a constant rate of events over an observation period, the Pascal distribution assumes this rate to vary according to the gamma distribution. For this reason, the Pascal distribution is more flexible than the Poisson distribution and is often used to model overdispersed EVENT COUNT data, or data in which the variance exceeds the mean.

For example, the Pascal distribution could be used to model the number of bills that must be proposed to a legislature before 10 bills are passed. Alternatively, the results of such an experiment can be used to determine the number of failures before the rth success.

—Ryan Bakker

REFERENCES

Johnson, N. L., & Kotz, S. (1969). *Discrete distributions.* Boston: Houghton-Mifflin.

King, G. (1998). *Unifying political methodology: The likelihood theory of statistical inference.* Ann Arbor: University of Michigan Press.

PATH ANALYSIS

Although the dictum "Correlation does not imply causation" is well rehearsed in research methods courses throughout the social sciences, its converse actually serves as the basis for *path analysis* and the larger STRUCTURAL EQUATION MODELING (SEM) family of quantitative data analysis methods (which also includes, for example, MULTIPLE REGRESSION ANALYSIS and CONFIRMATORY FACTOR ANALYSIS). Specifically, under the right circumstances, "Causation does imply correlation." That is to say, if one variable has a causal bearing on another, then a CORRELATION (or COVARIANCE) should be observed in the data when all other relevant variables are controlled statistically and/or experimentally. Thus, path analysis may be described, in part, as the process of hypothesizing a model of causal (structural) relations among measured variables—as often represented in a *path diagram*—and then formally examining observed data relations for degree of fit with the initial hypotheses' expected relations.

Most modern treatments of path analysis trace the technique's beginnings to the work of the biometrician Sewell Wright (e.g., Wright, 1918), who first applied path analysis to correlations among bone measurements. The method was barely noticed in the social sciences until Otis Duncan (1966) and others introduced the technique in sociology. Spurred by methodological, computational, and applied developments mainly during the 1970s and 1980s by such scholars as K. G. Jöreskog, J. Ward Keesling, David Wiley, Dag Sörbom, Peter Bentler, and Bengt Muthén, countless applications have appeared throughout the social and behavioral sciences. For example, shifting focus from correlations to covariances allowed for the development of a formal statistical test of the fit between observed data and the hypothesized model. Furthermore, the possibility of including latent (i.e., unobserved) factors into path models and the development of more general estimation techniques (e.g., MAXIMUM LIKELIHOOD, asymptotically DISTRIBUTION FREE) addressed major initial limitations of traditional correlational path analysis. Continuous refinements in specialized computer software throughout the 1980s, 1990s, and today (e.g., LISREL, EQS, AMOS, Mplus) have led to a simultaneous increase in technical sophistication and ease of use and thus have contributed to the proliferation of path analysis and more general SEM applications over the past three decades.

In this entry, typical steps in the path analysis process are introduced theoretically and via example. These steps include model conceptualization, parameter identification and estimation, effect decomposition, data-model fit assessment, and potential model modification and cross-validation. More detail about path analysis and SEM in general may be found in, for example, Bollen (1989), Kaplan (2000), Kline (1998), and Mueller (1996).

FOUNDATIONAL PRINCIPLES

As an example, an education researcher might have a theory about the relations among four constructs: Mathematics Self-Concept (MSC), Reading Self-Concept (RSC), Task Goal Orientation (TGO),

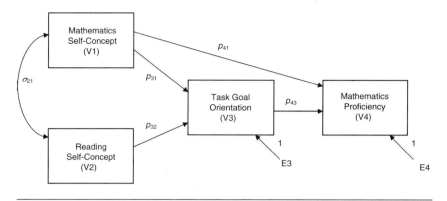

Figure 1 Hypothetical Path Model

and Mathematics Proficiency (MP). The first three constructs are operationalized as scores from rating scale instruments, whereas the latter is operationalized as a standardized test score. Using the measured variables as proxies for their respective constructs, the theory may be expressed as shown in Figure 1. Each box represents a measured variable, labeled as V. A single-headed arrow represents a formal theoretical statement that the variable at the tail of the arrow might have a direct causal bearing on the variable at the head of the arrow (but not vice versa). As seen in the figure, RSC is hypothesized to affect TGO directly, MSC to affect TGO and MP, and TGO to affect MP. Variables that have no causal inputs within a model are said to be *independent* or *exogenous* variables (MSC and RSC), whereas those with causal inputs are *dependent* or *endogenous* variables (TGO and MP). Two other single-headed arrows appear in the figure, one into TGO and the other into MP. These signify all unrelated residual factors ("Errors," labeled E) affecting each endogenous variable. Finally, a two-headed arrow indicates that the variables could be related but for reasons other than one causing the other (e.g., both influenced by some other variable(s) external to this model). MSC and RSC are hypothesized to have such a relation. Note that the two-headed arrow does *not* symbolize reciprocal causation (when variables are hypothesized to have a direct or indirect causal bearing on each other). Such would be an example of a larger class of *nonrecursive models* that is beyond the scope of this entry (see Berry, 1984; Kline, 1998).

On each single-headed arrow is an unstandardized *path coefficient* for the population, p, indicating the direction and magnitude of the causal relation between the relevant variables. These are akin to, but not necessarily identical to, unstandardized partial regression

weights. With regard to the two-headed arrow, as it represents a covariance between two variables, the symbol appearing atop the arrow is the familiar σ. Using these symbols, we may express the relations from the figure in two ways: as *structural equations* and as *model-implied relations*. Structural equations are regression-type equations expressing each endogenous variable as a function of its direct causal inputs. Assuming variables are mean centered (thereby eliminating the need for intercept terms), the structural equations for the current model are as follows:

$$V3 = p_{31}V1 + p_{32}V2 + 1E3,$$
$$V4 = p_{41}V1 + p_{43}V3 + 1E4.$$

These equations, along with any noncausal relations contained in the model (i.e., two-headed arrows), have implications for the variances and covariances one should observe in the data. Specifically, if the hypothesized model is true in the population, then the algebra of EXPECTED VALUES applied to the structural equations yields the following model-implied variances (Var) and covariances (Cov) for the population:

$$\mathrm{Var}(V1) = \sigma_1^2$$
$$\mathrm{Var}(V2) = \sigma_2^2$$
$$\mathrm{Var}(V3) = p_{31}^2\sigma_1^2 + p_{32}^2\sigma_2^2 + 2p_{31}\sigma_{21}p_{32} + \sigma_{E3}^2$$
$$\mathrm{Var}(V4) = p_{41}^2\sigma_1^2 + 2p_{43}p_{31}p_{41}\sigma_1^2$$
$$+ 2p_{43}p_{32}\sigma_{21}p_{41}$$
$$+ p_{43}^2\big(p_{31}^2\sigma_1^2 + p_{32}^2\sigma_2^2$$
$$+ 2p_{31}\sigma_{21}p_{32} + \sigma_{E3}^2\big) + \sigma_{E4}^2$$
$$\mathrm{Cov}(V1, V2) = \sigma_{21}$$
$$\mathrm{Cov}(V1, V3) = p_{31}\sigma_1^2 + p_{32}\sigma_{21}$$
$$\mathrm{Cov}(V1, V4) = p_{41}\sigma_1^2 + p_{31}p_{43}\sigma_1^2 + p_{32}p_{43}\sigma_{21}$$
$$\mathrm{Cov}(V2, V3) = p_{32}\sigma_2^2 + p_{31}\sigma_{21}$$
$$\mathrm{Cov}(V2, V4) = p_{32}p_{43}\sigma_2^2 + p_{41}\sigma_{21}$$
$$\mathrm{Cov}(V3, V4) = p_{43}\big(p_{31}^2\sigma_1^2 + p_{32}^2\sigma_2^2 + 2p_{31}\sigma_{21}p_{32}$$
$$+ \sigma_{E3}^2\big) + p_{31}p_{41}\sigma_1^2 + p_{32}p_{41}\sigma_{21}$$

These 10 equations constitute the covariance structure of the model, with 9 unknown population parameters appearing on the right side (p_{31}, p_{32}, p_{41}, p_{43}, σ_{21}, σ_1^2, σ_2^2, σ_{E3}^2, σ_{E4}^2). If one had the population variances and covariances among the four variables, those numerical values could be placed on the left, and the unknowns on the right could be solved for (precisely, if the hypothesized model is correct). Given only sample (co)variances, such as those shown in Table 1 for a hypothetical sample of $n = 1,000$ ninth graders, they may similarly be placed on the left, and estimates of the parameters on the right may be derived. To this end, each parameter in a model must be expressible as a function of the (co)variances of the observed variables. When a system of such relations can be uniquely solved for the unknown parameters, the model is said to be *just-identified*. When multiple such expressions exist for one or more parameters, the model is *overidentified*; in this case, a best-fit (although not unique) estimate for each parameter is derived. If, however, at least one parameter cannot be expressed as a function of the observed variables' (co)variances, the model is *underidentified*, and some or all parameters cannot be estimated on the basis of the data alone. This underidentification might be the result of the researcher attempting to impose a model that is too complex (i.e., too many parameters to be estimated) relative to the number of (co)variances of the observed variables. Fortunately, underidentification is rare in most path analysis applications, occurring only with less common model features (e.g., nonrecursive relations).

Table 1   Sample Matrix of Variances and Covariances

	$V1$	$V2$	$V3$	$V4$
V1 (mathematics self-concept)	1.951			
V2 (reading self-concept)	−.308	1.623		
V3 (task goal orientation)	.262	.242	1.781	
V4 (mathematics proficiency)	28.795	−4.317	17.091	1375.460

The model in Figure 1 is overidentified with 10 observed (co)variances and 9 parameters to be estimated: 1 covariance, 4 direct paths, 2 variable variances, and 2 error variances. The model thus has $10 - 9 = 1$ degree of freedom (*df*). Given that a model is just- or (preferably) overidentified, parameter estimates can be obtained through a variety of estimation methods. These include maximum likelihood and generalized least squares, both of which assume multivariate normality and are asymptotically equivalent as well as asymptotically distribution-free estimation methods that generally require a substantially larger sample size. These methods iteratively minimize a function of the discrepancy between the observed (co)variances and those reproduced by substitution of iteratively changing parameter estimates into the model-implied relations. Using any SEM software package, the maximum likelihood estimates for the key paths in the current model are found to be (in the variables' original units) as follows: $\hat{p}_{31} = .163$, $\hat{p}_{32} = .180$, $\hat{p}_{41} = 13.742$, $\hat{p}_{43} = 7.575$, and $\hat{\sigma}_{21} = -.308$ (all of which are statistically significant at a .05 level). Standardized path coefficients, similar to beta weights in multiple regression, would be .170, .172, .518, .273, and −.173, respectively. Before focusing on these main parameter estimates, however, we should consider whether there is any evidence suggesting data-model misfit and any statistical—and theoretically justifiable—rationale for modifying the hypothesized model.

DATA–MODEL FIT ASSESSMENT AND MODEL MODIFICATION

One of the advantages of modern path analysis is its ability to assess the quality of the fit between the data and the model. A multitude of measures exists that assist the researcher in deciding whether to reject or tentatively retain an a priori specified overidentified model. In general, measures to assess the fit between the (co)variances observed in the data and those reproduced by the model and its parameter estimates can be classified into three categories: absolute, parsimonious, and incremental. Absolute fit indices are those that improve as the discrepancy between observed and reproduced (co)variances decreases, that is, as the number of parameters approaches the number of nonredundant observed (co)variances. Examples of such measures include the model chi-square statistic that tests the stringent null hypothesis that there is no data-model misfit in the population, the standardized root mean square residual (SRMR) that roughly assesses the average standardized discrepancy between observed and reproduced (co)variances, and the goodness-of-fit index (GFI) designed to evaluate the amount of observed (co)variance information that can be accounted for by the model.

Parsimonious fit indices take into account not just the overall absolute fit but also the degree of model complexity (i.e., number of parameters) required to achieve that fit. Indices such as the adjusted goodness-of-fit index (AGFI), the parsimonious goodness-of-fit index (PGFI), and the root mean square error of approximation (RMSEA) indicate greatest data-model fit when data have reasonable absolute fit and models are relatively simple (i.e., few parameters). Finally, incremental fit indices such as the normed fit index (NFI) and the comparative fit index (CFI) gauge the data-model fit of a hypothesized model relative to that of a baseline model with fewer parameters.

The three types of fit indices together help the researcher to converge on a decision regarding a path model's acceptability. Hu and Bentler (1999) suggested joint criteria for accepting a model, such as CFI values of 0.96 or greater together with SRMR values less than 0.09 (or with RMSEA values less than 0.06). In the current example, the nonsignificant model chi-square of 2.831 (with 1 df) indicates that the observed (co)variances could reasonably occur if our model correctly depicted the true population relations. Although bearing good news for the current model, this statistic is typically ignored as it is notoriously sensitive to very small and theoretically trivial model misspecifications under large sample conditions. As such, other fit indices are generally preferred for model evaluation. For the current model, no appreciable data-model inconsistency is suggested when applying the standards presented above: CFI = 0.997, SRMR = 0.013, and RMSEA = 0.043.

After the data-model fit has been assessed, a decision about that model's worth must be reached. Acceptable fit indices usually lead to the conclusion that no present evidence exists warranting a rejection of the model or the theory underlying it. This is not to say that the model and theory have been confirmed, much less proven as correct; rather, the current path model remains as one of possibly many that satisfactorily explain the relations among the observed variables. On the other hand, when fit indices suggest a potential data-model misfit, one might be reluctant to dismiss the model entirely. Instead, attempts are often made to modify the model post hoc, through the addition of paths, so that acceptable fit indices can be obtained. Most path analysis software packages will facilitate such model "improvement" by providing modification indices (Lagrange multiplier tests) indicating what changes in the model could reap the greatest increase in absolute fit, that is, decrease in the model chi-square statistic. Although such indices constitute a potentially useful tool for remedying incorrectly specified models, it seems imperative to warn against an atheoretical hunt for the model with the best fit. Many alternative models exist that can explain the observed data equally well; hence, attempted modifications must be based on a sound understanding of the specific theory underlying the model. Furthermore, when modifications and reanalyses of the data are based solely on data-model misfit information, subsequent fit results might be due largely to chance rather than true improvements to the model. Modified structures therefore should be cross-validated with an independent sample whenever possible. From the current analysis, none of the modification indices suggested changes to the model that would result in a statistically significant improvement in data-model fit (i.e., a significant decrease in the model chi-square statistic); indeed, as the overall model chi-square value is 2.831 (significance level > 0.05), there is no room for statistically significant improvement. Thus, no model modification information is reported here.

At last, given satisfactory data-model fit, one may draw conclusions regarding the specific model relations. Interpretation of path coefficients is similar to that of regression coefficients but generally with a causal bent. For example, $\hat{p}_{31} = 0.163$ implies that, under the hypothesized model, a 1-unit increase in scores on the MSC scale directly causes a 0.163-unit increase in scores on the TGO scale, on average, holding all else constant. Recall that this was a statistically significant impact. Alternatively, one may interpret the standardized path coefficients, such as the corresponding value of 0.170. This implies that, under the hypothesized model, a 1 standard deviation increase in scores on the MSC scale directly causes a 0.170 standard deviation increase in scores on the TGO scale, on average, holding all else constant. Other direct paths, unstandardized and standardized, are interpreted similarly as the *direct effect* of one variable on another under the hypothesized model.

In addition to the direct effects, other *effect coefficients* may be derived as well. Consider the modeled relation between RSC and MP. RSC does not have a direct effect on MP, but it does have a direct effect on TGO, which, in turn, has a direct effect on MP. Thus, RSC is said to have an *indirect effect* on MP because, operationally speaking, one may follow a series of two or more single-headed arrows flowing in the same direction to get from one variable to the other. The magnitude of the indirect effect is the product of its constituent direct effects, $(0.180)(7.575) \approx 1.364$ for the unstandardized solution. This unstandardized indirect effect value implies that a 1-unit increase in scores on the RSC scale indirectly causes a 1.364-unit increase in scores on the MP test, on average, holding all else constant. Similarly, for the standardized solution, the standardized indirect effect is $(0.172)(0.273) \approx 0.047$, which implies that a 1 standard deviation increase in scores on the RSC scale indirectly causes a .047 standard deviation increase in scores on the MP test, on average, holding all else constant.

Finally, notice that MSC actually has both a direct effect and an indirect effect on MP. In addition to the unstandardized and standardized direct effects of 13.742 and 0.518, respectively, the indirect effect may be computed as $(0.163)(7.575) \approx 1.235$ in the unstandardized metric and $(0.170)(0.273) = 0.046$ in the standardized metric. This implies that the total causal impact of MSC on MP, the *total effect,* is the sum of the direct and indirect effects. For the unstandardized solution, this is $13.742 + 1.235 \approx 14.977$, implying that a 1-unit increase in scores on the MSC scale causes in total a 14.977-unit increase in scores on the MP test, on average, holding all else constant. Similarly, for the standardized solution, this is $0.518 + 0.046 = 0.564$, implying that a 1 standard deviation increase in scores on the MSC scale causes in total a 0.564 standard deviation increase in scores on the MP test, on average, holding all else constant. Thus, through this type of *effect decomposition,* which uses the full context of the hypothesized model, one can learn much more about the relations among the variables than would be provided by the typically atheoretical correlations or covariances alone.

SUMMARY

Path analysis has become established as an important analysis tool for many areas of the social and behavioral sciences. It belongs to the family of structural equation modeling techniques that allow for the investigation of causal relations among observed and latent variables in a priori specified, theory-derived models. The main advantage of path analysis lies in its ability to aid researchers in bridging the often-observed gap between theory and observation. As has been highlighted in this entry, path analysis is best understood as a process starting with the theoretical and proceeding to the statistical. If the theoretical underpinnings are ill-conceived, then interpretability of all that follows statistically can become compromised. Researchers interested in more detail regarding path analysis, as well as its extension to the larger family of SEM methods, are referred to such resources as Bollen (1989), Kaplan (2000), Kline (1998), and Mueller (1996). Parallel methods involving categorical variables, which have foundations in LOG-LINEAR MODELING, may also be of interest (see Goodman, 1973; Hagenaars, 1993).

—Gregory R. Hancock and Ralph O. Mueller

REFERENCES

Berry, W. D. (1984). *Nonrecursive causal models.* Beverly Hills, CA: Sage.

Bollen, K. A. (1989). *Structural equations with latent variables.* New York: John Wiley.

Duncan, O. D. (1966). Path analysis: Sociological examples. *American Journal of Sociology, 72,* 1–16.

Goodman, L. A. (1973). The analysis of multidimensional contingency tables when some variables are posterior to others: A modified path analysis approach. *Biometrika, 60,* 179–192.

Hagenaars, J. A. (1993). *Loglinear models with latent variables.* Newbury Park, CA: Sage.

Hu, L., & Bentler, P. M. (1999). Cutoff criteria for fit indexes in covariance structure analysis: Conventional criteria versus new alternatives. *Structural Equation Modeling: A Multidisciplinary Journal, 6,* 1–55.

Kaplan, D. (2000). *Structural equation modeling: Foundations and extensions.* Thousand Oaks, CA: Sage.

Kline, R. B. (1998). *Principles and practice of structural equation modeling.* New York: Guilford.

Mueller, R. O. (1996). *Basic principles of structural equation modeling: An introduction to LISREL and EQS.* New York: Springer.

Wright, S. (1918). On the nature of size factors. *Genetics, 3,* 367–374.

PATH COEFFICIENT. *See* PATH ANALYSIS

PATH DEPENDENCE

Originally formulated for use in economics, the concept of path dependence now appears with increasing frequency in other social sciences, notably historical sociology and political science. It is used to explain how certain outcomes are the result of a particular sequence of events and how that unique sequence constrains future options.

When an outcome is the result of path dependency, some general factors about the outcome's history can be observed. First, there is an aspect of unpredictability. This means that despite all prior knowledge of a certain hoped-for outcome, some events will take place that could not have been foreseen—they will be historically contingent. Second, path dependence emphasizes the importance of small events. Economist W. Brian Arthur (1994) notes that "many outcomes are possible, and heterogeneities, small indivisibilities, or chance meetings become magnified by positive feedbacks to 'tip' the system into the actual outcome" (p. 27). Most important, however, is the third factor, which is "lock-in." As small, seemingly inconsequential decisions are made along an outcome's path, these decisions are constantly being reinvented and reinforced. This is the logic of increasing returns. Once a decision is made (about a new technology or an institution, for example), that initial decision becomes very difficult to change. It is "locked in"—because it is constantly used and revised. In this way, path-dependent processes are unforgiving: After a decision is made, it is very costly to change and becomes even more costly as time passes. This persistence often leads to suboptimal outcomes, another hallmark of a path-dependent trajectory.

Illustrations of path dependence are useful to fully understand the concept. Economist Paul David (1985) first described path dependence in a study of the "QWERTY" keyboard arrangement. David argued that the now familiar arrangement of keys on a typewriter was the result of a random decision, and once typewriters were manufactured with that particular arrangement and people began to learn to use it, the arrangement became too costly to reverse. Although there were likely many alternatives (some of them perhaps more efficient) to the QWERTY keyboard, the initial decision to use that arrangement became "locked in" over time, and more and more people used it. As a result, changing the arrangement of keys now is virtually unthinkable.

A frequent criticism of explanations that employ path dependence is that they simply assert the importance of history. Paul Pierson (2000) emphatically notes, however, that "it is not the past *per se* but the unfolding of events over time that is theoretically central" (p. 264). This sentiment is echoed by other proponents of path dependence, notably James Mahoney. Mahoney (2000) offers a framework for path-dependent analysis, suggesting that all path-dependent arguments must demonstrate (a) that the outcome under investigation was particularly sensitive to events occurring early in the historical sequence, (b) that these early events were historically contingent (unpredictable), and (c) that the historical events must render the "path" to the outcome relatively inertial or DETERMINISTIC (Mahoney, 2000, pp. 510–511). Such an analysis allows for a clear explanation of how, for example, certain institutions emerge, persist, and become resistant to change.

—Tracy Hoffmann Slagter

REFERENCES

Arthur, W. B. (1994). *Increasing returns and path dependence in the economy.* Ann Arbor: University of Michigan Press.

David, P. (1985). Clio and the economics of QWERTY. *American Economic Review, 75,* 332–337.

Mahoney, J. (2000). Path dependence in historical sociology. *Theory and Society, 29,* 507–548.

Pierson, P. (2000). Increasing returns, path dependence, and the study of politics. *American Political Science Review, 94,* 251–267.

PATH DIAGRAM. *See* PATH ANALYSIS

PEARSON'S CORRELATION COEFFICIENT

The Pearson's correlation coefficient (denoted as r_{xy}) best represents the contemporary use of the SIMPLE CORRELATION that assesses the LINEAR relationship between two variables. The coefficient indicates the strength of the relationship, with values ranging from 0 to 1 in absolute value. The larger the magnitude of the coefficient, the stronger the relationship between the variables. The sign of the coefficient indicates the direction of the relationship as null, positive, or negative. A null relationship between variables X and Y suggests that an increase in variable X is accompanied with both an increase and a decrease in variable Y and vice versa. A positive relationship indicates that an increase (or decrease) in variable X is associated with an increase (or decrease) in variable Y. In contrast, a negative relationship suggests that an increase (or decrease) in variable X is associated with a decrease (or increase) in variable Y.

ORIGIN OF PEARSON'S CORRELATION COEFFICIENT

In the 19th century, Darwin's theory of evolution stimulated interest in making various measurements of living organisms. One of the best-known contributors of that time, Sir Francis Galton, offered the statistical concept of correlation in addition to the law of heredity. In his 1888 article (cited in Stigler, 1986), "Co-Relations and Their Measurement, Chiefly from Anthropometric Data," Galton demonstrated that the REGRESSION lines for the lengths of the forearm and head had the same slope (denoted as r) when both variables used the same scale for the measurement. He labeled the r as an index of *co-relation* and characterized its identity as a REGRESSION COEFFICIENT. The spelling of *co-relation* was deliberately chosen to distinguish it from the word *correlation,* which was already being used in other disciplines, although the spelling was changed to *correlation* within a year. However, it was not until Karl Pearson (1857–1936) that Pearson's correlation coefficient was introduced.

COMPUTATIONAL FORMULAS

The Pearson's correlation coefficient is also called the Pearson product-moment correlation, defined by

$$\frac{\sum z_{X_i} z_{Y_i}}{n},$$

because it is obtained by multiplying the z-SCORES of two variables (i.e., the products), followed by taking the average (i.e., the moment) of these products. Various computational formulas for Pearson's correlation coefficient can be derived from the above formula (Chen & Popovich, 2002), as demonstrated as follows:

$$\frac{\sum z_{X_i} z_{Y_i}}{n} = \frac{\sum \left(\frac{(X_i - \bar{X})}{s_X}\right)\left(\frac{(Y_i - \bar{Y})}{s_Y}\right)}{n}$$

$$= \frac{\frac{1}{s_X s_Y} \sum (X_i - \bar{X})(Y_i - \bar{Y})}{n}$$

$$= \frac{\sum \frac{(X_i - \bar{X})(Y_i - \bar{Y})}{n}}{s_X s_Y}$$

$$= \frac{\sum X_i Y_i - \frac{\sum X_i \sum Y_i}{n}}{\sqrt{\left(\sum X_i^2 - \frac{(\sum X_i^2)}{n}\right)\left(\sum Y_i^2 - \frac{(\sum Y_i)^2}{n}\right)}}.$$

INTERPRETATION OF PEARSON'S CORRELATION COEFFICIENT

Pearson's correlation coefficient does not suggest a cause-and-effect relationship between two variables. It cannot be interpreted as a proportion, nor does it represent the proportionate strength of a relationship. For example, a correlation of .40 is not twice as strong a relationship compared to a correlation of .20. In contrast to Pearson's correlation coefficient, r_{xy}^2 (also labeled as the COEFFICIENT OF DETERMINATION) should be interpreted as a proportion. Say the Pearson's correlation coefficient for class grade and intelligence is .7. The r_{xy}^2 value of .49 suggests that 49% of the variance is shared by intelligence and class grade. It can also be interpreted that 49% of the variance in intelligence is explained or predicted by class grade and vice versa.

SPECIAL CASES OF PEARSON'S CORRELATION COEFFICIENT

There are several well-known simple correlations such as the point-biserial correlation coefficient, the phi coefficient, the SPEARMAN CORRELATION COEFFICIENT, and the ETA COEFFICIENT. All of them are special cases of Pearson's correlation coefficient. Suppose we use Pearson's correlation coefficient to assess the relationship between a dichotomous variable (e.g., gender) and a continuous variable (e.g., income). This correlation is often referred to as the point-biserial correlation coefficient. We can also use it to gauge the relationship between two dichotomous variables (e.g., gender and infection), and we refer to this coefficient as the Phi coefficient. If both variables are measured at the ORDINAL level and ranks of their characteristics are assigned, Pearson's correlation coefficient can also be applied to gauge the relationship. This coefficient is often labeled as the *Spearman correlation coefficient.* Finally, Pearson's correlation coefficient, when applied to measure the relationship between a multichotomous variable (e.g., races, schools, colors) and a continuous variable, is referred to as the Eta coefficient (Wherry, 1984).

USES OF PEARSON'S CORRELATION COEFFICIENT

The Pearson's correlation coefficient can be used in various forms for many purposes. It can be used for, although is not limited to, any of the following functions: (a) describing a relationship between two

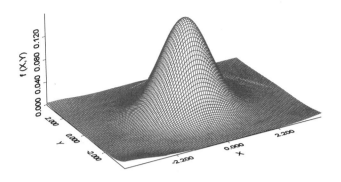

Figure 1   Bivariate Normal Distribution, Given $\rho = 0$ and $N = 1,000$

variables as a descriptive statistic; (b) examining a relationship between two variables in a POPULATION as an INFERENTIAL STATISTIC; (c) providing various RELIABILITY estimates such as CRONBACH'S ALPHA, TEST-RETEST RELIABILITY, and SPLIT-HALF RELIABILITY; (d) evaluating VALIDITY evidence; and (e) gauging the strength of effect for an intervention program. When Pearson's correlation coefficient is used to infer population RHO, the assumption of a bivariate NORMAL DISTRIBUTION is required. Both variables X and Y follow a bivariate normal distribution if and only if, for every possible linear combination W, where

$W = c_1 X + c_2 Y$, the distribution of W is normal, with neither c values being zero (Hays, 1994). An example of a bivariate normal distribution when $\rho = 0$ is depicted in Figure 1.

SAMPLING DISTRIBUTION OF PEARSON'S CORRELATION COEFFICIENT

The shape of the SAMPLING DISTRIBUTION for Pearson's correlation coefficient varies as a function of population rho (ρ) and sample size, although the impact of sample size is minimal when it is large. When population ρ equals zero, the sampling distribution is symmetrical and distributed as a T-DISTRIBUTION, as depicted in Figure 2. As seen below, the sampling distribution—based on 1,000 randomly generated samples, given $\rho = 0$ and $n = 20$—is overall symmetrical. Therefore, to test the NULL HYPOTHESIS of $\rho = 0$, a T-TEST can be conducted, $t = \frac{r\sqrt{n-2}}{\sqrt{1-r^2}}$ with DEGREES OF FREEDOM of $n - 2$.

However, the sampling distribution becomes negatively SKEWED when $|\rho|$ increases, given small sample sizes, as seen in Figure 3. The distribution can be made normal if each Pearson's correlation coefficient in the distribution is TRANSFORMED into a new

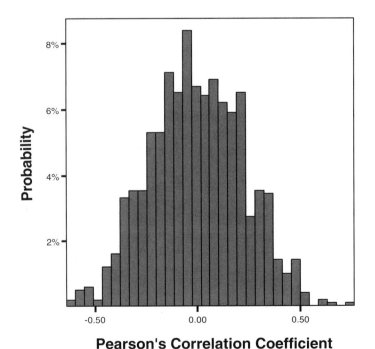

Range	1.41
Minimum	-.64
Maximum	.77
Mean	-.0003
Std. Deviation	.22692
Skewness	.020

Figure 2   Sampling Distributions of 1,000 Pearson's Correlation Coefficients, Given $n = 20$ and $\rho = 0$

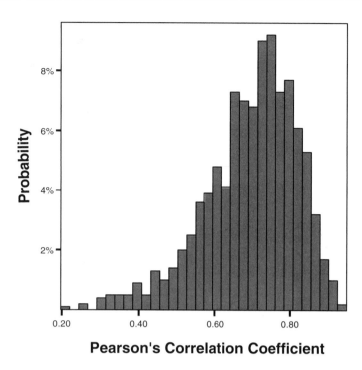

Range	.75
Minimum	.20
Maximum	.95
Mean	.6961
Std. Deviation	.12236
Skewness	-.827

Figure 3   Sampling Distributions of 1,000 Pearson's Correlation Coefficients, Given $n = 20$ and $\rho = 0.7$

variable, labeled Fisher's z (denoted as z_r), based on $0.5 \times \log_e(\frac{1+r}{1-r})$, where $\log_e$ is the natural LOGARITHM function. Consequently, to examine the null hypothesis that ρ equals any nonzero value (denoted as $\rho_\emptyset$), we can conduct a z-test, $z = (z_r - z_\emptyset)\sqrt{(n-3)}$, where z_r is the transformed value of the Pearson's correlation coefficient for a sample, and $z_\emptyset$ is the transformed value of $\rho_\emptyset$.

FACTORS THAT AFFECT PEARSON'S CORRELATION COEFFICIENT

The size of Pearson's correlation coefficient can be affected by many factors. First, the size of the coefficient can be either 1 or −1 only if the distributions of both variables are symmetrical and have the same form or shape. It can also be affected by the degree of linearity and small sample sizes, particularly when OUTLIERS exist. In addition, the size of the coefficient can either increase or decrease as a result of RANGE restriction. When the range of either variable is restricted on either end of the distribution, Pearson's correlation coefficient tends to decrease. In contrast, it tends to increase when the middle range of the distribution is restricted. Furthermore, the size of the coefficient may be misleading when it is calculated based on heterogeneous samples. Finally, it

can be influenced by measurement errors associated with the variables. The more ERRORS the measured variables contain, the smaller the correlation between the variables.

—Peter Y. Chen and Autumn D. Krauss

REFERENCES

Chen, P. Y., & Popovich, P. M. (2002). *Correlation: Parametric and nonparametric measures.* Thousand Oaks, CA: Sage.

Hays, W. L. (1994). *Statistics* (5th ed.). New York: Harcourt Brace College.

Stigler, S. M. (1986). *The history of statistics.* Cambridge, MA: Belknap Press of Harvard University Press.

Wherry, R. J., Sr. (1984). *Contributions to correlational analysis.* New York: Academic Press.

PEARSON'S *R. See* PEARSON'S CORRELATION COEFFICIENT

PERCENTAGE FREQUENCY DISTRIBUTION

Percentage frequency distribution is a form of RELATIVE FREQUENCY DISTRIBUTION when the y-axis is a percentage (instead of an absolute frequency) scale of cases subsumed by each category of a VARIABLE. For example, of the 22,000 undergraduate students registered at a certain American university during a certain spring semester, 30% were freshmen, 27% were sophomores, 20% were juniors, and 23% were seniors.

—Tim Futing Liao

See also RELATIVE FREQUENCY DISTRIBUTION

PERCENTILE

Percentiles may be defined as a system of measurement based on percentages as opposed to the absolute values of a variable. Percentages are based on a SCALE of 100 (i.e., there are 100 divisions), with each division being one percentage or percentile.

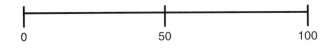

Figure 1   Division of a Line

The line in Figure 1 may be divided into 100 equal pieces. Halfway would be 50 equal divisions of the line. This position is 50% of the total length of the line and would also be known as the 50th percentile. If we stopped at the 75th division, this would be 75% of the total length of the line and would be the 75th percentile. If we stopped at the 62nd division, this would be 62% of the total length of the line and would be the 62nd percentile.

Clearly, there is no problem when the variable we are measuring is measured out of 100—the absolute measuring system and the percentage measuring system are one and the same thing. That is, the absolute measuring system has 100 equal divisions, as does the percentage measuring system. An exam score of 42 would represent a percentage score of 42% and be considered to be the 42nd percentile.

What happens when the two measuring systems are not the same? How would we work out percentiles if the maximum score on an examination paper were 30? The answer is to convert the absolute score into a percentage.

Example: Candidate 1 scores 25 marks out of 30 in a statistics examination.

We need to translate the actual 25 marks out of 30 into a percentage, and this is done using the following formulas:

Percentage mark = (actual mark/maximum mark) × 100/1.

From our example is the following (remember the rule of mathematics—perform the calculations inside the brackets first):

Percentage mark = (25/30) × 100/1
= 83.33% or the 83.33 percentile.

The score of 25 would be considered to be the 83rd percentile (rounded down to the nearest whole number). Both the candidate and the examiner are now in a better position regarding interpretation and what conclusions to draw.

We can take percentile analysis slightly further by RANKING the percentiles. To do this, we need to know the frequency attributable to the scores of the variable we are interested in. A percentile rank is the percentage of scores in a DISTRIBUTION that is equal to, or greater than, a specified absolute score.

If the examiner of the statistics paper knows that there were 40 students out of 46 who achieved a mark of 25 or more, then we can calculate the percentile RANK by changing the absolutes into percentages:

(40/46) × 100/1 = 86.95%.

That is, 86.95% of all students achieved a mark of 25 or more, and the student is in the 87th percentile (rounded up to nearest whole number). The percentile RANK would be 87.

By dividing the DISTRIBUTION of a VARIABLE into percentiles, it is now possible to analyze each percentile as a group, examining the similarities and differences between these groups. More often than not, we group the variables into DECILES and QUARTILES to produce such an analysis. Alternatively, by calculating the RANK percentile, we can indicate the RANK of a person RELATIVE to others in the study.

Let us assume we have collected data on salary, sex, expenditure on goods and services, and so forth. By dividing the salary range into percentiles, we could analyze each percentile group to look for differences and similarities regarding the sex of a respondent and his or her salary. In addition, we could also examine the relationship between salary and the patterns of expenditure on goods and services. By using DECILES and

QUARTILES, we can reduce the number of groups and widen the salary range and are more likely to identify similarities and differences.

Ranking percentiles allows us to see the position we occupy out of 100, with the 100th percentile being the highest. In the example of the student who scored 25 on the statistics examination (which equated to the 83rd percentile), this informs us that this student could be ranked 83rd in this examination. We could produce percentiles ranks for all students, thereby allowing us to see how one student compares with another. Alternatively, we could take an individual student and calculate rank percentiles for all of their examinations, allowing us to see the range of the individual student's performance. This would allow us to identify individual strengths and weaknesses.

—Paul E. Pye

REFERENCES

Collican, H. (1999). *Research methods and statistics in psychology.* London: Hodder & Staughton.

Saunders, M. N. K., & Cooper, S. A. (1993). *Understanding business statistics: An active learning approach.* London: DP Publications.

PERIOD EFFECTS

Individual human subjects and sometimes other entities, such as cities or nations, can be regarded as existing in two time dimensions, subjective and objective. The subjective time dimension for an individual begins at birth, and parallels to birth can be found for other entities. The objective time dimension is measured with respect to events external to the individual or entity, dating from the beginning of the universe or, at a more modest level, the beginning of a research study. We call the subjective time dimension *age* and the objective time dimension *history.* Entities whose subjective time begins at the same objective time are said to belong to the same *cohort.*

In LONGITUDINAL RESEARCH, patterns of change in variables and patterns of relationships among variables are studied with respect to both age and history. The impact of age on variables or relationships among variables, ignoring historical time, is called a *developmental effect* or *age effect.* Examples of age effects include language acquisition and development of other cognitive skills. The impact of living at a certain historical time on variables or relationships among variables, ignoring age, is called a *period effect* or *historical effect.* Examples of period effects include the use of computers, cell phones, and other devices, which depend on the level of technology in the historical period rather than on the age of the individual in that period, and attitudes and behaviors shaped by political and military events, such as expressing more patriotic attitudes or displaying the American flag more frequently in the United States after the bombing of Pearl Harbor or the destruction of the World Trade Center. The impact of being a certain age at a certain period (in other words, of being born in a certain year) is called a *cohort effect.* One of the principal problems in longitudinal research is separating the impacts of age, period, and cohort (Menard, 2002). The problem arises because if we use age, period, and cohort as predictors and assume a linear relationship of each with the dependent variable, the predictors are perfectly collinear, related by the equation, period = age + cohort, when cohort is measured as year of birth.

Different approaches to the separation of period effects from age and cohort effects are reviewed in Menard (2002). As noted by Hobcraft, Menken, and Preston (1982), period effects provide a proxy—often a weak proxy—for an explanation that is not really a matter of "what year is it" but rather a matter of what events occurred in that year, or before that year, at some significant period in the past. As Menard (2002) suggests, to the extent that it is possible, period effects should be replaced in longitudinal analysis by the historical events or trends for which they are proxies. At the aggregate level, it may also be possible to separate period effects from age or cohort effects by examining age-specific indicators of the variables of interest. This is commonly done in social indicators research, for example, by using trends in infant mortality or rates of labor force participation for individuals 16 to 64 years old as indicators of trends in national health and employment conditions.

—Scott Menard

REFERENCES

Hobcraft, J., Menken, J., & Preston, S. (1982). Age, period, and cohort effects in demography: A review. *Population Index, 42,* 4–43.

Menard, S. (2002). *Longitudinal research* (2nd ed.). Thousand Oaks, CA: Sage.

PERIODICITY

Periodic variation is a trademark of time that has long mystified ordinary people, inspired philosophers, and frustrated mathematicians. Through thousands of years, famines have alternated with prosperity, war with peace, ice ages with warming trends, among others, in a way that hinted at the existence of cycles. A cycle is a pattern that is "continually repeated with little variation in a periodic and fairly regular fashion" (Granger, 1989, p. 93). With the help of trigonometric functions, the cyclical component of a time series z_t may be expressed as follows:

$$z_t = A \sin(2\pi f t + \varphi) + u_t,$$

where A represents the amplitude, f the frequency, and φ the initial phase of the periodic variation, with u_t denoting WHITE-NOISE error. The amplitude indicates how widely the series swings during a cycle (the distance from peak to valley), whereas the frequency f measures the speed of the cyclical movement:

$$f = 1/P,$$

where P refers to the period of a cycle, the number of time units it takes for a cycle to be completed. Hence a 4-year cycle would operate at a frequency of 0.25 (cycles per unit time). The shortest cycle that can be detected with any given data would have a period of two time units. It would correspond to a frequency of 0.5, which is the fastest possible one. Any cycle that is done in fewer than two time units is not detectable. The longer the cycle—that is, the more time units it takes—the lower the frequency. A time series without a cycle would register a frequency of zero, which corresponds to an infinite period.

SPECTRAL ANALYSIS provides the major tool for identifying cyclical components in time series (Gottman, 1981; Jenkins & Watts, 1968). The typical plot of a spectral density function features spectral density along the vertical axis and frequency (ranging from 0 to 0.5) along the horizontal axis. A time series with a 4-year cycle (a year being the time unit of the series) would show a density peak at a frequency of $1/4$ or 0.25. The problem is that few time series of interest are generated in such perfectly cyclical fashion that their spectral density functions would be able to tell us so.

Aside from strictly seasonal phenomena, many apparent cycles do not repeat themselves with constant regularity. Economic recessions, for example, do not occur every 7 years. Nor do they hurt the same each time. Although boom and bust still alternate, the period of this "cycle" is not fixed. Nor is its "amplitude." That lack of constancy undermines the utility of DETERMINISTIC MODELS such as sine waves. As an alternative, Yule (1927/1971) proposed the use of PROBABILISTIC models for time series with cycles whose period and amplitude are irregular. His pioneering idea was to fashion a second-order autoregressive model to mimic the periodic, albeit irregular, fluctuations of sunspot observations over a span of 175 years. Yule's AR(2) model had the following form:

$$z_t = b_1 z_{t-1} - b_2 z_{t-2} + u_t.$$

With only two PARAMETERS and LAGS going no further than two, this model succeeded in estimating the periodicity of the sunspot fluctuations (10.6 years). The model also provided estimates of the RANDOM disturbances that continually affected the amplitude and phase of those fluctuations. BOX-JENKINS MODELING has extended the use of probability models for identifying and estimating periodic components in time series, with a special set of models for seasonal fluctuations.

—Helmut Norpoth

REFERENCES

Gottman, J. M. (1981). *Time-series analysis: A comprehensive introduction for social scientists.* Cambridge, UK: Cambridge University Press.

Granger, C. W. J. (1989). *Forecasting in business and economics.* Boston: Academic Press.

Jenkins, G. M., & Watts, D. G. (1968). *Spectral analysis and its applications.* San Francisco: Holden-Day.

Yule, G. U. (1971). On a method of investigating periodicities in disturbed series with special reference to Wolfer's sunspot numbers. In A. Stuart & M. Kendall (Eds.), *Statistical papers of George Udny Yule* (pp. 389–420). New York: Hafner. (Original work published 1927)

PERMUTATION TEST

The permutation test is a NONPARAMETRIC test using the resampling method. The basic procedure of a permutation test is as follows:

1. Set the hypothesis.
2. Choose a test statistic and compute the test statistic T for the original samples (T_0).

3. Rearrange or permute the samples and recompute the test statistic for the rearranged samples $(T_1, T_2, \ldots, T_x)$. Repeat this process until you obtain the distribution of the test static for all the possible permutations or sufficiently many permutations by random rearrangement.

4. Compare T_0 with the permutation distribution of T_1 to T_x and calculate the p value. Then, judge whether to accept or reject the hypothesis.

The permutation test is similar to the BOOTSTRAP: Both are computer intensive and limited to the data at hand. However, the methods of resampling are different: In the permutation test, you will permute the samples to construct the distribution, but in the bootstrap, you take a series of samples with replacement from the whole samples.

When you need to compare samples from two populations, the only requirement of the permutation test is that under the null hypothesis, the distribution from which the data in the treatment group are taken is the same as the distribution from which the untreated sample is taken.

The permutation test provides an exact statistic, not an approximation. The permutation test is as powerful as the parametric test if the sample size is large, and it is more powerful if the sample size is small. Thus, it is useful if it is difficult to obtain large samples such as sociometric data in a small group.

Let us look at hypothetical data on a new medicine to control blood pressure. The effect of the medicine is compared with a placebo. The data are collected by using 20 people whose usual blood pressures are around 165. These 20 people are evenly divided into two groups (each group consists of 10 people). The first 10 people get the placebo, and the last 10 people get the new medicine. The data for the placebo group are {132, 173, 162, 168, 140, 165, 190, 199, 173, 165}, and the data for the treatment group are {150, 124, 133, 162, 190, 132, 158, 144, 165, 152}. Is there any evidence that the new medicine is really effective in reducing blood pressure? Let us take the mean of both groups. For the placebo group, the mean is 166.7, and for the treatment group, it is 151.0. The difference of the means is 15.7. Now, we permute the data of 20 people. However, there are

$$\binom{20}{10} = 184,756$$

different combinations. We do not have to be concerned with all of those because dealing with this would be too time-consuming. So, we randomly permute the 20 data sufficiently many times—say, 100 times—and calculate the difference of the means of the first 10 and the last 10 permuted data. Then, we count the number of the cases such that the difference of the means of the original data, 15.7, is greater than the difference of the means of the permuted data. If we get 4 such cases out of 100 cases ($p = .04$), we conclude that the new medicine is effective in reducing blood pressure at $\alpha < .05$.

The permutation test can be applied in many social science research situations involving a variety of data; one such example is valued sociometric (network) data. Let us define the degree of symmetry between i and j as $s_{ij} = |A_{ij} - A_{ji}|$, where A is an adjacency matrix of a relation, and A_{ij} is a degree of the relation from i to j. The larger s implies that the relation deviates from symmetry or is less symmetric. Let us also define the symmetry in a whole group as

$$S = \frac{1}{\binom{N}{2}} \sum_{i=1}^{N-1} \sum_{j>i}^{N} s_{ij}.$$

We can calculate S, but we may wonder how large or small it is compared with symmetry in other groups because the distribution of S is unknown yet. So, we conduct a permutation test for symmetry with the test statistic S.

There are some practical guidelines for permutation tests dealing with sociometric data. First, we do not permute diagonal values because they usually hold a theoretically defined value such as 0 or 1. Second, we need to decide how to permute the matrix. For example, we may choose to permute the whole matrix, within each row, and so on, depending on your interest. In general, we can conduct a better test with a more restricted permutation. In the case of symmetry S, permutation within each row may make more sense because we calculate s (thus S), keeping each individual's properties such as the means and the variances.

For symmetry and transitivity tests, a computer program PermNet is available at the following Web site: www.meijigakuin.ac.jp/~rtsuji/en/software.html.

You can execute permutation tests with common statistics software packages. A macro is available for SAS (www2.sas.com/proceedings/sugi27/p251–27.

pdf). The Exact Test package of SPSS, StatXact, and LogXact will also do the test.

—Ryuhei Tsuji

REFERENCES

Boyd, J. P., & Jonas, K. J. (2001). Are social equivalences ever regular? Permutation and exact tests. *Social Networks, 23,* 87–123.

Good, P. (1994). *Permutation tests: A practical guide to resampling methods for testing hypotheses.* New York: Springer.

Tsuji, R. (1999). Trusting behavior in prisoner's dilemma: The effects of social networks. *Dissertation Abstracts International Section A: Humanities & Social Sciences, 60*(5-A), 1774. (UMI No. 9929113)

PERSONAL DOCUMENTS. *See*

DOCUMENTS, TYPES OF

PHENOMENOLOGY

In its most influential philosophical sense, the term *phenomenology* refers to descriptive study of how things appear to consciousness, often with the purpose of identifying the essential structures that characterize experience of the world. In the context of social science methodology, the term usually means an approach that pays close attention to how the people being studied experience the world. What is rejected here is any immediate move to evaluate that experience (e.g., as true or false by comparison with scientific knowledge) or even causally to explain why people experience the world the way that they do. From a phenomenological viewpoint, both these tendencies risk failing to grasp the complexity and inner logic of people's understanding of themselves and their world. Phenomenological sociology shares something in common with anthropological relativism, which insists on studying other cultures "in their own terms"; and with SYMBOLIC INTERACTIONIST approaches, which emphasize that people are constantly *making* sense of what happens, and that this process generates diverse perspectives or "worlds."

The phenomenological movement in philosophy was founded by Edmund Husserl at the end of the 19th century and was later developed in diverse directions by, among others, Heidegger, Merleau-Ponty, Sartre, and (most influentially of all for social science) Schutz. The fundamental thesis of phenomenology is the intentionality of consciousness: that we are always conscious *of* something. The implication is that the experiencing subject and the experienced object are intrinsically related; they cannot exist apart from one another. The influence of phenomenology has been especially appealing to those social scientists who oppose both POSITIVISM's treatment of natural science as the only model for rational inquiry *and* all forms of speculative social theorizing. It serves as an argument against these, as well as an alternative model for rigorous investigation.

One of the phenomenological concepts that has been most influential in social science is what is referred to as the "natural attitude." Husserl argued that rather than people experiencing the world in the way that traditional EMPIRICISTS claimed, as isolated sense data, most of the time they experience a familiar world containing all manner of recognizable objects, including other people, whose characteristics and behavior are taken as known (until further notice). Although there are areas of uncertainty in our experience of the world, and although sometimes our expectations are not met, it is argued that these problems always emerge out of a taken-for-granted background. The task of phenomenological inquiry, particularly as conceived by later phenomenologists such as Schutz (1973), is to describe the constitutive features of the natural attitude: how it is that we come to experience the world as a taken-for-granted and shared reality. They argue that this must be explicated if we are to provide a solid foundation for science of any kind.

Phenomenology has probably had its most direct influence on social research through the work of Berger and Luckmann (1967)—which stimulated some kinds of social CONSTRUCTIONISM—and through ETHNOMETHODOLOGY.

—Martyn Hammersley

REFERENCES

Berger, P., & Luckmann, T. (1967). *The social construction of reality.* Harmondsworth, UK: Penguin.

Embree, L., Behnke, E. A., Carr, D., Evans, J. C., Huertas-Jourda, J., Kockelmans, J. J., et al. (Eds.). (1996). *The encyclopedia of phenomenology.* Dordrecht, The Netherlands: Kluwer.

Hammond, M., Howarth, J., & Keat, R. (1991). *Understanding phenomenology.* Oxford, UK: Blackwell.

Schutz, A. (1973). *Collected papers* (4 vols.). Dordrecht, The Netherlands: Kluwer.

PHI COEFFICIENT. *See*
Symmetric Measures

PHILOSOPHY OF SOCIAL RESEARCH

The philosophy of social research is a branch of the PHILOSOPHY OF SOCIAL SCIENCE. It involves a critical examination of social research practice, as well as the various components of social research and their relationships.

The social researcher is confronted with a plethora of choices in the design and conduct of social research. These include the research problem; the RESEARCH QUESTION(S) to investigate this problem; the research strategies to answer these questions; the approaches to social enquiry that accompany these strategies; the concepts and theories that direct the investigation; the sources, forms, and types of data; the methods for making selections from these data sources; and the methods for collecting and analyzing the data to answer the research questions (Blaikie, 2000). At each point in the research process, philosophical issues are encountered in the evaluation of the options available and in the justification of the choices made. It is becoming increasingly difficult for social researchers to avoid these issues by simply following uncritically the practices associated with a particular PARADIGM.

PHILOSOPHICAL ISSUES

The philosophical issues that enter into these choices include types of ontological and epistemological assumptions, the nature of EXPLANATION, the types of THEORY and methods of construction, the role of language, the role of the researcher, OBJECTIVITY and truth, and generalizing results across time and space (Blaikie, 2000). As these issues are interrelated, the choice made on some issues has implications for the choice on other issues. This brief discussion of some of these issues is dependent on the more detailed discussion of related key concepts in this encyclopedia.

Ontological and Epistemological Assumptions

A key concern of philosophers of science and social science is the examination of claims that are made by theorists and researchers about the kinds of things that exist in the world and how we can gain knowledge of them. Social researchers, whether they realize it or not, have to make assumptions about both of these to proceed with their work. A range of positions can be adopted. To defend the position taken, social researchers need to have an understanding of the arguments for and against each position and be able to justify the stance taken. (See ONTOLOGY and EPISTEMOLOGY for a discussion of the range of positions.)

Theory Types and Their Construction

Philosophers have given considerable attention to the forms that theory takes and the processes by which theory is generated. In the social sciences, it is useful to distinguish between two types of theory: theoreticians' theory and researchers' theory. The former uses abstract concepts and ideas to understand social life at both the macro and micro levels. The latter is more limited in scope and is developed and/or tested in the context of social research. Although these two types of theory are related, their form and level of abstraction are different (Blaikie, 2000, pp. 142–143, 159–163). It is researchers' theory that is of concern here.

Some researchers' theories consist of general laws that are related in networks and are generated by INDUCTION from DATA. Others take the form of a set of propositions, of differing levels of generality, which form a deductive argument. Their origin is regarded as being unimportant, but their empirical testing is seen to be vital (see FALSIFICATIONISM). Some theories consist of descriptions of generative structures or mechanisms that are hypothesized to account for some phenomenon and are arrived at by the application of an informed imagination to a problem (see RETRODUCTION). Other theories consist of either rich descriptions or abstractions, perhaps in the form of ideal types of actors, courses of action, and situations. They are derived from social actors' concepts and interpretations (see ABDUCTION and INTERPRETIVISM). Philosophers of social science have put forward arguments for and criticisms of all four types of theory construction (see Blaikie, 1993).

The Nature of Explanation

One of the most vexed questions in the social sciences is how to explain social life. One controversy centers on the source of the explanation, whether it lies in social structures or in individual motives, that is, holism versus individualism. The issue is whether the source is to be found external to social actors or within them.

A related controversy is concerned with types of explanations, with the distinction between causal explanations and reason explanation. The former, which can take various forms, follows the logics of explanation used in the natural sciences, whereas the latter rejects these as being appropriate in the social sciences and replaces them with the reasons or motives social actors can give for their actions. Whether the use of reasons or motives can be regarded as explanations or just provide understanding is a matter of some debate.

Causal explanations, whether in the natural or social sciences, are of three major forms: pattern, deductive, and retroductive. In pattern explanations (see INDUCTION and POSITIVISM), a well-established generalization about regularities in social life can provide low-level explanations. For example, if it has been established that "juvenile delinquents come from broken homes," it is possible to use this to explain why some young people commit crimes—it is their family background. Deductive explanations (see FALSIFICATIONISM) start with one or more abstract theoretical premises and, by the use of deductive logic and other propositions, arrive at a conclusion that can either be treated as a hypothesis or as the answer to a "why" research question. Retroductive explanations (see RETRODUCTION and CRITICAL REALISM) rely on underlying causal structures or mechanisms to explain patterns in observed phenomena.

The Role of Language

The philosophical issue here is what relationship there should be, if any, between scientific language and objects in the world. The positions adopted on this issue are dependent on the ontological assumptions adopted. For example, in POSITIVISM, the use of a theory-neutral observation language is considered to be unproblematic, whereas in FALSIFICATIONISM, this is rejected on the grounds that all observations are theory dependent.

In positivism, language is regarded as a medium for describing the world, and it is assumed that there is an isomorphy between the structural form of language and the object-worlds to which language gives access. However, in some branches of INTERPRETIVISM, language is regarded as the medium of everyday, practical social activity. The issue here is the relationship between this lay language and social scientific language, with a number of writers advocating that the latter should be derived from the former by a process of ABDUCTION. The choice is between the imposition of technical language on the social world and the derivation of technical language from the everyday language.

The Role of the Researcher

Social researchers have adopted a range of stances toward the research process and the participants. These positions range from complete detachment to committed involvement. Philosophers of social science have critically examined these stances in terms of their achievability and their consequences for research outcomes.

Each stance is associated with the use of particular approaches to social enquiry and research strategies. The role of *detached observer* is concerned with OBJECTIVITY and is associated with positivism and the logics of induction and deduction. The role of *faithful reporter* is concerned with social actors' points of view and is associated with some branches of interpretivism. The role of *mediator of languages* is concerned with generating understanding and is associated with some branches of HERMENEUTICS and with the logic of abduction. The role of *reflective partner* is concerned with emancipation and is associated with both critical theory and feminism. Finally, the role of *dialogic facilitator* is associated with POSTMODERNISM and is concerned with reducing the researcher's authorial influence by allowing a variety of "voices" to be expressed (see Blaikie, 2000, pp. 52–56).

Objectivity

No concept associated with social research evokes both more emotion and confusion than objectivity. Researchers frequently aim to produce objective results and are often criticized when they are seen to fail. Some research methods are praised because they are seen to be objective, and others are criticized because they are assumed not to be objective. The philosophical issues are as follows: What does it mean to be "objective," and what do methods and results have to be like to be objective?

In positivism, being objective means keeping facts and values separate, that is, not allowing the researcher's values and prejudices to contaminate the data. This is a deceptively simple idea but one that turns out to be impossible to achieve. For a start, the notion of a "fact" is a complex one, and the difference between facts and values is not clear-cut. For some philosophers, keeping facts and values separate can mean not taking sides on issues involved in the research. However, some researchers favor a particular point of view (in feminism, women's points of view). Values themselves can also be a topic for investigation.

For some philosophers, objectivity is achieved by using methods that are regarded as being appropriate by a community of scientists. This, of course, means adopting a particular set of values. Objectivity is also considered by some to entail the use of replicability. Procedures are used that other researchers can repeat, thus making possible the validation of results. Again, acceptability of particular methods is the criterion.

Some interpretive social scientists eschew concerns with objectivity and argue that researchers should be as subjective as possible. What this means is that researchers should immerse themselves completely in the life of the people they study, as this is seen to be the only way another form of life can be understood. What they aim for is an authentic account of that form of life, an account that is faithful to social actors' points of view.

Truth

Philosophers have developed a number of theories to defend their views of the nature of "truth." The *correspondence* theory of truth appeals to evidence gained from "objective" observation. It is assumed that an unprejudiced observer will be able to see the world as it really is and will be able to report these observations in a theory-neutral language. It is assumed that a theory is true because it agrees with the facts (see POSITIVISM). Of course, to achieve this, there has to be agreement about what are the facts. The *tentative* theory of truth argues that the theory-dependence of observations and the nature of the logic of falsification mean that the testing of deductively derived theory can never arrive at the truth. Although finding the truth is the aim, the results of deductive theory testing are always subject to future revision. In contrast, the *consensus* theory

of truth is based on the idea of rational discussion free from all constraints and distorting influences. Although evidence may be important, it is rational argument that will determine the truth. Then there is the *pragmatic* theory of truth, which argues that something is true if it is useful, if it can be assimilated into and verified by the experiences of a community of people. In the correspondence theory, truth is seen to be established for all time. In the consensus theory, disinterested logical argument by anyone should arrive at the same truth. However, in the tentative theory, truth is seen to change as testing proceeds and, in the pragmatic theory, as experience changes. Finally, in the *relativist* theory of truth, there are many truths because it is assumed that there are multiple social realities. As no one has a privileged or neutral position from which to judge the various truths, it is impossible to determine which is the "truest." This range of positions makes the concept of truth rather less secure than common sense would suggest.

Generalizing

There seems to be a desire among practitioners of all sciences to be able to generalize their findings beyond the context in which they were produced, that their theories will apply across space and time (see GENERALIZATION). This is particularly true of positivism, in which inductive logic is used. Despite the fact that generalizations are based on finite observations, the aim is to produce universal laws, such as, "juvenile delinquents come from broken homes." Many philosophers have argued that this aim is impossible and have suggested less ambitious aspirations. Falsificationists, for example, accept the tentative nature of their theories, as well as the possibility that they may be replaced by better theories in the future. In addition, they may state some propositions in their theories in a general form but also include conditions that limit their applicability. In fact, it is the search for such conditions to which much scientific activity is devoted. For example, although the general proposition that "juvenile delinquents come from broken homes" may be included at the head of a deductive theory, limiting conditions—such as, "in some broken homes, children are inadequately socialized into the norms of society"—limit the theory to certain kinds of broken homes. The search for underlying mechanisms in CRITICAL REALISM is based on an assumption that they are real and not just the creation of scientists. However, such researchers see their task as not only finding the appropriate mechanisms but also establishing the conditions and contexts under which they operate. Mechanisms may be general, but their ability to operate is always dependent on the circumstances. Hence, these theories are always limited in time and space. Within interpretivism, it is generally accepted that any social scientific account of social life must be restricted in terms of time and space. Any understanding must be limited to the context from which it was abductively derived. Whether the same type of understanding is relevant in other social contexts will be dependent on further investigation. In any case, all understanding is time bound.

One aspect of generalizing that causes considerable confusion is the difference between the form of theoretical propositions and what happens in sample surveys (see SURVEY). If a PROBABILITY SAMPLE is drawn from a defined POPULATION, and if response rates are satisfactory, the results obtained from the sample can be statistically generalized back to the population from which the sample was drawn. Beyond that population, all generalizations have to be based on other evidence and argument, not on statistical procedures. In this regard, generalizing beyond sampled populations is essentially the same as generalizing from NONPROBABILITY SAMPLES and CASE STUDIES (Blaikie, 2000).

ASPECTS OF SOCIAL RESEARCH

A number of aspects of social research practice are associated with the issues discussed in the previous section. The ones reviewed here involve choices from among alternatives.

Approaches to Social Enquiry

At an abstract level, social research is conducted within theoretical and methodological perspectives, that is, within different approaches to social enquiry. These approaches have been characterized in various ways and usually include positivism, falsificationism (or critical rationalism), hermeneutics, interpretivism, critical theory, critical realism, structuration theory, and feminism (Blaikie, 1993). Each approach works with its own combination of ontological and epistemological assumptions (see Blaikie, 1993, pp. 94–101). The choice of approach and its associated research strategy has a major bearing on other RESEARCH DESIGN

decisions and the conduct of a particular research project.

Research Strategies

Four basic strategies can be adopted in social research, based on the logics of induction, deduction, retroduction, and abduction (Blaikie, 1993, 2000). Each research strategy has a different starting point and arrives at a different outcome. The inductive strategy starts out with the collection of data, from which generalizations are made, and these can be used as elementary explanations. The deductive strategy starts out with a theory that provides a possible answer to a "why" research question. The conclusion that is logically deduced from the theory is the answer that is required. The theory is tested in the context of a research problem by the collection of relevant data. The retroductive strategy starts out with a hypothetical model of a mechanism that could explain the occurrence of the phenomenon under investigation. It is then necessary to conduct research to demonstrate the existence of such a mechanism. The abductive strategy starts out with lay concepts and meanings that are contained in social actors' ACCOUNTS of activities related to the research problem. These accounts are then redescribed in technical language, in social scientific accounts. The latter provide an understanding of the phenomenon and can be used as the basis for more elaborate theorizing.

The four research strategies work with different ontological assumptions. The inductive and deductive strategies share the same ontological assumptions (see POSITIVISM, INDUCTION, FALSIFICATIONISM, and DEDUCTION); the retroductive strategy works with a tiered notion of reality, which particularly distinguishes between the domains of the actual (what we can observe) and the real (underlying structures and mechanisms) (see CRITICAL REALISM and RETRODUCTION). The abductive strategy adopts a social constructionist view of social reality (see INTERPRETIVISM and ABDUCTION). It is important for researchers to be aware of these differences as they have implications for other choices and for the interpretation of results.

The inductive strategy is only really useful for answering "what" research questions as generalizations from data have been shown to be an inadequate basis for answering "why" questions. The deductive and retroductive strategies are exclusively used for answering "why" questions, although both require that descriptions of observed patterns first be established. The abductive strategy can be used to answer both "what" and "why" questions.

There are extensive philosophical criticisms of each strategy and debates about their relative merits. None of them is without some controversial features. In the end, the social researcher has to evaluate the arguments and then make a judgment about their suitability for the problem at hand while, at the same time, recognizing their limitations.

CONCLUSION

All this suggests that an understanding of the issues dealt with in the philosophy of social research is essential for any social scientist. The choices that have to be made in doing social research require social scientists to take sides on philosophical issues. A lack of understanding of what is involved in making these choices can lead to naive and inconsistent research practices.

—Norman Blaikie

REFERENCES

Blaikie, N. (1993). *Approaches to social enquiry.* Cambridge, UK: Polity.

Blaikie, N. (2000). *Designing social research: The logic of anticipation.* Cambridge, UK: Polity.

Hughes, J. A. (1990). *The philosophy of social research* (2nd ed.). Harlow, UK: Longman.

Williams, M., & May, T. (1996). *Introduction to the philosophy of social research.* London: UCL Press.

PHILOSOPHY OF SOCIAL SCIENCE

The philosophy of social science is a branch of the philosophy of science, an important field of philosophy. The discipline of philosophy is difficult to define precisely. The original Greek meaning is the love of wisdom, but today it is associated with techniques of critical analysis. Although philosophy has no subject matter of its own and cannot produce new facts about the world, philosophers may be able to provide new understanding of known facts. They make the first principles of our knowledge clearer by exposing what is implicit in concepts and theories and exploring their implications. By analyzing the kind of language we use to talk about the world, philosophers can

help us to understand it. In particular, philosophers provide a critical reflection on our taken-for-granted interpretations of reality.

In the philosophy of science, critical analysis focuses on such topics as "what is reality" and "what constitutes knowledge of that reality," on issues of ONTOLOGY and EPISTEMOLOGY. More specifically, this field of philosophy examines the nature of science, the logics of enquiry used to advance knowledge that is regarded as scientific, and the justifications offered for the views adopted.

The philosophy of social science is primarily concerned with three issues: the variety of ontological and epistemological assumptions that social researchers adopt in their theories and approaches to social enquiry, as well as the justifications given for these; the logics of enquiry that can be used to produce answers to RESEARCH QUESTIONS; and the appropriateness of the methods of data collection and analysis that are used within a particular logic of enquiry.

Many of the issues dealt with in the philosophy of science are also relevant in the philosophy of social science. However, the issue that particularly distinguishes the latter and that has divided philosophers and methodologists for about a hundred years is whether the methods or, more correctly, the logics of enquiry that have been developed and successfully used in the natural sciences should also be used in the social sciences. A problem with this debate is that there has also been a parallel debate about which logic of enquiry is the most appropriate in the natural sciences— INDUCTION, DEDUCTION, or some other procedure?

A fundamental choice for all social scientists is whether to use one of these logics of enquiry or one that is regarded by some philosophers as being more appropriate for the particular subject matter of the social sciences. The ontological assumptions adopted will determine whether social reality is seen to be essentially the same as natural reality or fundamentally different. In the latter case, a different logic (ABDUCTION) will have to be adopted, and this can restrict the choice of methods of data collection and analysis.

A central issue in this controversy is how to explain human action. Adopting the logics used in the natural sciences entails a concern with establishing causal explanations, with identifying the factors or mechanisms that produce those actions under particular conditions (see CAUSALITY). However, those social scientists who argue for a different kind of logic content themselves with achieving some kind of understanding based on the reasons social actors give for their actions.

Hence, the choices that social scientists make about the kinds of research questions to investigate, as well as the logics of enquiry used to answer these questions, commit them to taking sides on profound and complex philosophical issues.

—Norman Blaikie

REFERENCES

Blaikie, N. (1993). *Approaches to social enquiry.* Cambridge, UK: Polity.

Chalmers, A. (1982). *What is this thing called science?* St. Lucia, Australia: University of Queensland Press.

O'Hear, A. (1989). *Introduction to the philosophy of science.* Oxford, UK: Clarendon.

Rosenberg, A. (1988). *Philosophy of social science.* Oxford, UK: Clarendon.

PHOTOGRAPHS IN RESEARCH

Photographs have had a limited but important role in social science research. In recent years, this role has increased. Photography has had to overcome the fact that social science reasoning generally relies on the analysis of aggregate data, and photography, by definition, fixes attention on the particular. Second, the most vigorous focus on the visual aspects of society has been mustered by cultural studies and semiotics theorists, who have studied domination, resistance, and other cultural themes as in media, architecture, and other visual forms of society. This is not the use of photographs to gather data but rather analysis of the visually constructed world.

Photographs were first used in social science to catalogue aspects of material culture or social interaction. In the first 20 volumes of the *American Journal of Sociology,* between 1896 and 1916, sociologists used photographs to study such topics as the working conditions in offices and factories and living conditions in industrializing cities. As sociology sought a more scientific posture, the photographs were, for a half century, largely abandoned.

Anthropologists also used photography extensively in its formative decades to document and classify human groups. As anthropology abandoned paradigms based on the taxonomic organization of racial classifications, photography declined in importance.

The full development of photography in ethnography is attributed to Gregory Bateson and Margaret Mead's (1942) study of Balinese culture. The authors studied social rituals, routine behavior, and material culture through extensive photographic documentation. Subsequently, photography has flourished in anthropological ETHNOGRAPHY.

Howard Becker was the first modern sociologist to link photography and sociology (Becker, 1974). Becker noted that photography and sociology, since their inception, had both been concerned with the critical examination of society. Early 20th-century photographers, such as Lewis Hine and Jacob Riis, documented urbanization and industrialization, the exploitation of labor, and the conditions of immigrants, all topics of concern to sociologists. Becker suggested that visual sociology should emerge from documentary practice engaged with sociological theory, and the sociological use of photographs developed in the context of concerns about VALIDITY, RELIABILITY, and SAMPLING.

In the meantime, sociologists demonstrated the utility of photographs to study social change (Rieger, 1996) and several other conventional sociological topics. Photographs, however, remain the exception rather than the rule in empirical studies. The challenge of using photographs to explore society at a macro or structural level is also beginning to be met in research such as Deborah Barndt's (1997) photo collage/field study of globalization and tomato production and consumption.

Researchers may employ photographs to elicit cultural information. This process, referred to as *photo elicitation,* uses photographs to stimulate culturally relevant reflections in interviews (Harper, 2002). The photographs may be made by the researcher during field observations, or they may come from historical or personal archives. In a recent study, for example (Harper, 2001), photos from an archive made 50 years ago that depicted the routines of work, community life, and family interaction were used to encourage elderly farmers to critically reflect on the meaning of change in an agricultural community.

Photo elicitation explores the taken-for-granted assumptions of both researcher and subject. Furthermore, because photo elicitation stimulates reflection based on the analysis of visual material, the quality of memory and reflection is different than in words-alone interviews. Finally, photo elicitation challenges the authority of the researcher and redefines the research project to a collaborative search for meaning, rather than a mining of information. This places photo elicitation squarely in the emerging practices of "new ethnography" or "postmodern research methods."

There are at least three ethical challenges in photographic social science. The first concerns the matter of anonymity, the second concerns the matter of INFORMED CONSENT, and the third represents the burden of "telling the visual truth."

In conventional research, individuals are represented by words or, more commonly, as unidentified data in tables and graphs. Thus, the identity of research subjects is easily hidden. In the case of photographic research, however, it is often impossible to protect the PRIVACY of subjects. Thus, photographic research challenges a fundamental principle of social science research. The full resolution of this issue remains.

VISUAL RESEARCHERS face this problem partly through informed consent. When possible, subjects must be made aware of implications of publishing their likeness in social science research, and agreement to participate should be made clearly and in writing. Informed consent, however, is not possible when social scientific photographers make images in spaces such as public gatherings in parks, urban landscapes, and other sites of informal interaction. The full resolution of this problem also remains.

Visual researchers must maintain a firm commitment to "tell the visual truth" by not altering images to change their meaning and by presenting a visual portrait of reality that is consistent with the scientifically understood reality of the situation. This guiding principle is maintained as an overriding ethical consideration that overshadows the technical considerations listed above.

New methodologies, such as computer-based multimedia, the World Wide Web, CD publication, and virtual reality all offer possibilities for the innovative use of photography as a social science method. The future of photographs in social research will depend in part on how well these new technologies are integrated into social science methods and thinking. However, new journals devoted to visual studies and a growing list of books that use photographs as a primary form of data and communication

suggest that the day of the image is dawning in social science.

—Douglas Harper

REFERENCES

Barndt, D. (1997). Zooming out/zooming in: Visualizing globalization. *Visual Sociology, 12*(2), 5–32.

Bateson, G., & Mead, M. (1942). *Balinese character: A photographic analysis.* New York: New York Graphic Society.

Becker, H. S. (1974). Photography and sociology. *Studies in the Anthropology of Visual Communication, 1*(1), 3–26.

Harper, D. (2001). *Changing works: Visions of a lost agriculture.* Chicago: University of Chicago Press.

Harper, D. (2002). Talking about pictures: A case for photo elicitation. *Visual Studies, 17*(1), 13–26.

Rieger, J. (1996). Photographing social change. *Visual Sociology, 11*(1), 5–49.

PIE CHART

A pie chart is a circle segmented to illustrate shares or percentages of the total; each category appears as a "slice" of the "pie." Bar charts can be used for the same purpose, but a pie chart gives a more readily comprehensible picture of how cases are "shared out" between categories, provided there are relatively few categories. (A HISTOGRAM or bar chart would be used in preference to a pie chart for showing trends across a variable—e.g., over time or by geographical locality.)

Figure 1, for example, illustrates what people living in a town center had to say about their area and what was good about it.

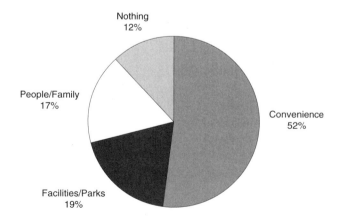

Figure 1   What Is Good About Living in Your Area?

SOURCE: Data from Hobson-West and Sapsford (2001).

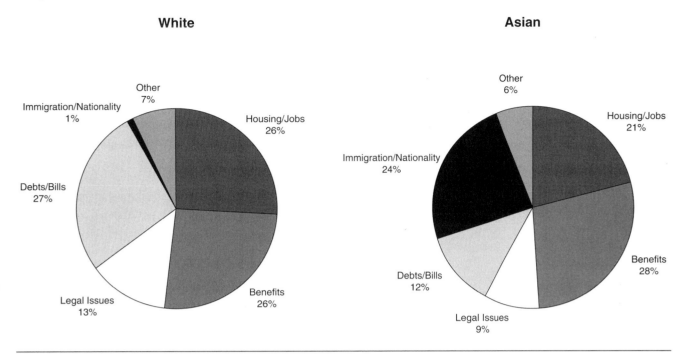

White

Asian

Figure 2   Purpose of Visit to the Citizens' Advice Bureau in Middlesbrough

SOURCE: McGuinness and Sapsford (2002).

Pie charts can also be used to make simple comparisons between categories. Again, bar charts can be used for the same purpose and may, indeed, be preferable when there are several different groups to be compared, but pie charts give a graphic contrast between, say, two groups that can be seen easily and immediately. The "pies" in Figure 2, for instance, illustrate the difference in reasons for using a Citizens' Advice Bureau by ethnic group. The Citizens' Advice Bureaus are a network of volunteer offices across Britain that offer advice and guidance on dealing with the bureaucracy in the face of which the poor are otherwise powerless—with central and local government, taxation, landlords, shops, and other financial and legal matters—and they also offer counseling on debt and financial management. Figure 2 shows, unsurprisingly, that immigration and nationality are issues that are often brought up by the Asian population of Middlesbrough and very seldom by the White population. The White population is a little more likely than the Asian population to raise issues about housing and benefits (government support payments) and substantially more likely to have debt problems that they want to discuss.

—Roger Sapsford

REFERENCES

Hobson-West, P., & Sapsford, R. (2001). *The Middlesbrough Town Centre Study: Final report.* Middlesbrough, UK: University of Teesside, School of Social Sciences.

McGuinness, M., & Sapsford, R. (2002). *Middlesbrough Citizens' Advice Bureau: Report for 2001.* Middlesbrough, UK: University of Teesside, School of Social Sciences.

PIECEWISE REGRESSION.

See SPLINE REGRESSION

PILOT STUDY

Pilot study refers to

1. feasibility or small-scale versions of studies conducted in preparation for the main study and
2. the pretesting of a particular research instrument.

Good pilot studies increase the likelihood of success in the main study. Pilot studies should warn of possible project failures, deviations from PROTOCOLS, or problems with proposed methods or instruments and, it is hoped, uncover local politics or problems that may affect the research (see Table 1).

Table 1   Reasons for Conducting Pilot Studies

- Developing and testing adequacy of research instruments
- Assessing feasibility of (full-scale) study
- Designing research protocol
- Assessing whether research protocol is realistic and workable
- Establishing whether sampling frame and technique are effective
- Assessing likely success of proposed recruitment approaches
- Identifying possible logistical problems in using proposed methods
- Estimating variability in outcomes to determine sample size
- Collecting preliminary data
- Determining resources needed for study
- Assessing proposed data analysis techniques to uncover potential problems
- Developing research question and/or research plan
- Training researcher(s) in elements of the research process
- Convincing funding bodies that research team is competent and knowledgeable
- Convincing funding bodies that the study is feasible and worth funding
- Convincing stakeholders that the study is worth supporting

Pilot studies can be based on quantitative (QUANTITATIVE RESEARCH) and/or qualitative methods (QUALITATIVE RESEARCH), whereas large-scale studies may employ several pilots. The pilot of a QUESTIONNAIRE survey could begin with interviews or focus groups to establish the issues to be addressed in the questionnaire. Next, the wording, order of the questions, and the range of possible answers may be piloted. Finally, the research process could be tested, such as different ways of distributing and collecting the questionnaires, and precautionary procedures or safety nets devised to overcome problems such as poor recording and response rates (RESPONSE BIAS).

Difficulties can arise from conducting a pilot:

- Contamination of sample: Participants (RESPONDENTS) who have already been exposed to the pilot may respond differently from those who have not previously experienced it.
- Investment in the pilot may lead researchers to make considerable changes to the main study, rather than decide that it is not possible.
- Funding bodies may be reluctant to fund the main study if the pilot has been substantial as the research may be seen as no longer original.

Full reports of pilot studies are relatively rare and often only justify the research methods and/or research tool used. However, the processes and outcomes from pilot studies might be very useful to others embarking on projects using similar methods or instruments. Researchers have an ethical obligation to make the best use of their research experience by reporting issues arising from all parts of a study, including the pilot phase.

—Edwin R. van Teijlingen and Vanora Hundley

REFERENCES

De Vaus, D. A. (1995). *Surveys in social research* (4th ed.). Sydney, Australia: Allen & Unwin.

Peat, J., Mellis, C., Williams, K., & Xuan, W. (2002). *Health science research: A handbook of quantitative methods.* London: Sage.

van Teijlingen, E., & Hundley, V. (2002). The importance of pilot studies. *Nursing Standard, 16*(40), 33–36.

PLACEBO

This term *placebo* is used in connection with EXPERIMENTS. Its main use is in connection with medical investigations in which a CONTROL GROUP is led to believe that it is being given a treatment, such as a medicine, but the treatment is in fact a dummy one. The term is also sometimes used to refer to a treatment given to a control group that is not designed to have an effect. As such, its main role is to act as a point of comparison to the treatment or experimental group. A placebo effect occurs when people's behavior or state of health changes as a result of believing the placebo was meant to have a certain kind of effect, such as making them feel calmer.

—Alan Bryman

PLANNED COMPARISONS. *See*
MULTIPLE COMPARISONS

POETICS

Poetics takes language both as its substance and as a conspicuous vehicle for wider ends of communication. It is a universal aspect of language-centered behavior that can be emphasized or de-emphasized according to the purposes at hand. The focus on composition and the conspicuous display of the language used in poetics are the keys to understanding it, not simply its forms of production (e.g., poetic prose, rich with metaphor and allegory; poetry as prose or verse; chanting, singing) or the kinds of messages sent (e.g., aesthetic, didactic, mythic, ritualized). It appears with increasing frequency today as a matter of special interest in the social sciences, especially in their concerns with texts as cultural artifacts. Rooted in part in the conflicts of POSTMODERNISM and in part in increasing awareness of the common denominators of cultural diversity, this "literary turn" has led to expanded research on semiotic behavior and the production of meaning in discourse, text construction and authority in performance, and, more generally, the place of poetics in the philosophical and critical problems associated with the representation and communication of experience in any form. It includes among its broad topics of inquiry the mutually constructed viewpoints of critical dialogics, the histories and forms of poetries in the world (from tribal societies to modern theater), studies of ritual and worldview and their relationships to language and culture, and the self-conscious filings of autoethnography and ethnographic fieldwork. It is rich with implications for social science.

ANTHROPOLOGICAL POETICS

The specific challenge of anthropological poetics includes developing sensitive and realistic cross-cultural translation skills and a genre of reporting that systematically incorporates edifying poetic qualities without sacrificing the essence of ethnographic accountability. We need to know something of the substance and what it means to be situated differently in language and culture from the actor's point of view while, at the same time, finding ways to combine and communicate those differences. On the assumption that all human beings are sufficiently alike to be open to discovery and mutually empathetic communications, anthropological poetics attempts to evoke a comparable set of experiences through the reader's (or hearer's) exposure to the text. Ethnographers have been attracted to these kinds of arguments precisely because they help to define the constraints on self-conscious research and writing. This increasing "literariness" has also led some social scientists to a classic obsession with lines, punctuation, and white spaces—in a word, to poetry as an alternative form of representation.

Poetry is by far the most celebrated category of poetic communication. Denying mind-body separations in concept and argument, it is cut very close to experiential ground. It takes place simultaneously in the deepest level of minding and in that part of consciousness where ideas and opinions are formed, constructing the poet as a cultural and sentient being even as the experience is unfolding. It is a self-revealing, self-constructing form of discovery, like writing in general and that fundamental human activity, "storying." It takes its motivations and saturations from the exotic and the quotidian and from our dreams, creating and occupying sensuous and meaningful space in the process. Everything we do has meaning, from the simple act of digging up a sweet potato to the launching of rockets to the moon, and every meaning is ultimately anchored in the senses. Nevertheless, it is mostly only the poets who write about experience consistently from a sensual perspective—centering, decoding, reframing, and discoursing literally as "embodied" participant observers, full of touch, smell, taste, hearing, and vision, open to the buzz and joy, the sweat and tears, the erotics and anxieties of daily life. Poets offer their take on the world sometimes with a view closer than a bug's eye on a plant, sometimes deep into the sublime, the universal. At work in ethnography, poets hope to reveal that world for what it is to themselves and to Others through mutual authorships, getting especially at the work that cannot take place within a single language or culture, as it is experienced in distinctive patterns and puzzles and can be shared with coparticipants, and yet doing so ultimately in a manner that makes the Otherness of obvious strangers collapse on close inspection. Poetry insists on being about all of us. But adding it to the repertoire of social science methods is problematic. Among other things, it opens those disciplines up to the whole complicated realm of aesthetics and to what appears to the received wisdom to be a truckload of counterintuitive arguments about ethnographic representation, including the place of language (and writer consciousness) in scientific writing.

SCIENCE AND POETICS

Scientific inquiry can give us a more or less dispassionate glimpse of causal relationships among things and behaviors, in both small- and large-scale patterns. It does not give us ordinary reality, the world we live in *as* we live it. Instead of writing or talking exclusively *about* their experiences through abstract concepts, as one might do in applying productive scientific theory, trying to make language as invisible as possible while focusing on the objects of scientific expressions, poets report more concretely, *in and with* the facts and frameworks of what they see in themselves *in relation to* Others, in particular landscapes and emotional and social situations. They aim for representation from one self-conscious interiority to another in a manner that flags their language, stirs something up in us, finds the strange in the everyday, and takes us out of ourselves for a moment to show us something about ourselves in principle if not in precisely reported fact. Keeping people from jumping to culturally standardized conclusions about what is reported and evoking a larger sense of shared humanity in the process make the poetic effort both didactic and comparative.

The use of metaphor as a tool of and for discovery sets a similar instructional table. The idea that grandfather is an oak or that subatomic particles are best conceptualized as billiard balls in motion might prove to be the source for unraveling the very things that puzzle us most and the kinds of insights not available to us any other way. Knowing that, and consciously exploiting the "as if" world of analogies and creative equivalencies that is metaphor and that binds *all* interpretations of experience (for scientist and poet alike, albeit at different levels of disciplinary recognition), poets argue that the most productive form of inquiry depends on the nature of the problem to be addressed. Just as *Finnegan's Wake* refuses reduction to the subject of free masonry or river journeys and resurrection or to critical summaries of its formal properties and

inspirations, so the statistical expression of cross-cultural trait distribution in aboriginal California cannot yield its exactness and rhetorical integrity to interpretive statements high in poeticity or uncommon metaphor. The implications of that are important, not only for helping us unravel the cultural constructions of a shared world that both differentiates and consolidates through various levels and circumstances, but also because changing the language of our descriptions, as Wittgenstein (1974) says, changes the analytic game itself, including changing the premises for research entry points. So poetics is not well conceived as a simple supplement to existing quantitative methods. It is a radically different form of interpreting, and therefore of knowing and reporting, whose domain is decidedly qualitative but no less complementary to other kinds of studies as a result.

Poetic inquiry can give us provocative and enlightening information about the nature of the world and our place in it, some of which is not available to the same extent, in the same form, or at all through other means. Ensuring interpretations grounded in self-awareness, it is also designed to keep premature closure on thinking in check while encouraging creativity in research and reporting. It is a way of reminding us that, despite numerous common denominators, science and poetics do different work; that no single genre or method can capture it all; that nothing we say can be nested in the entirely new; and that the field of experience and representation is by definition both culturally cluttered and incomplete for all of us at some level. Softening or solving such problems (e.g., by reaching beyond analytic categories whose only reality lies in the minds and agreements of the researchers themselves) matters if we are ever going to get a handle on the ordinary realities of the people we study—the universe *they* know, interpret, and act in as sentient beings. Such realities escape only at great cost to understanding ourselves, how we are articulated socially and semiotically, how we construct our Selves as meaningful entities in our own minds and in relation to each other, and what that contributes to acting responsibly in the shrinking space of a shared planet. For these and other reasons, privileging one form over the other as the source of Truth for all purposes is to confuse apples and hammers—to be satisfied with one tool for all jobs and with the politics of the moment. Inclusive is better. The combination of ethnological science and anthropological poetics can yield a more robust and complete accounting for and representation of our existence as meaning-making and meaning-craving Beings-in-the-World.

—Ivan Brady

REFERENCES

Brady, I. (2000). Anthropological poetics. In N. K. Denzin & Y. S. Lincoln (Eds.), *Handbook of qualitative research* (2nd ed., pp. 949–979). Thousand Oaks, CA: Sage.

Brady, I. (2003). *The time at Darwin's Reef: Poetic explorations in anthropology and history.* Walnut Creek, CA: AltaMira.

Rothenberg, J., & Rothenberg, D. (Eds.). (1983). *Symposium of the whole: A range of discourse toward an ethnopoetics.* Berkeley: University of California Press.

Tedlock, D. (1999). Poetry and ethnography: A dialogical approach. *Anthropology and Humanism, 24*(2), 155–167.

Wittgenstein, L. (1974). *On certainty* (G. E. M. Anscombe & G. H. Von Wright, Eds.). Oxford, UK: Blackwell.

POINT ESTIMATE

A point estimate is the estimated value of a population PARAMETER from a SAMPLE. Point estimates are useful summary statistics and are ubiquitously reported in QUANTITATIVE analyses. Examples of point estimates include the values of such coefficients as the SLOPE and the INTERCEPT obtained from REGRESSION analysis. A point estimate can be contrasted with an *interval estimate,* also known as a CONFIDENCE INTERVAL. A confidence interval reflects the uncertainty, or ERROR, of the point estimate. A point estimate provides a single value for the population parameter, whereas a confidence interval provides a range of possible values for the population parameter. Although the true parameter cannot be known, the point estimate is the best approximation.

A point estimate facilitates description of the relationship between VARIABLES. The relationship may be STATISTICALLY SIGNIFICANT, but the magnitude of the relationship is also of interest. A point estimate provides more information about the relationship under examination. A hypothetical simple REGRESSION analysis is provided here to illustrate the concept of a point estimate. Given an INDEPENDENT VARIABLE X and a DEPENDENT VARIABLE Y in the regression equation $Y = a + bX + e$, let X = number of hours of sleep the night before a test, Y = exam grade (in the form of a percentage) in a sample of students in an American politics seminar, b = slope, a = y-intercept, and e = error. An analysis of our hypothetical data produces the following regression equation: $\hat{Y} = -2 + 9.4X$. A point estimate is the value obtained for any sample statistic; here we are interested in the values of the intercept and the slope. The slope suggests that, on average, 1 additional hour of sleep is associated with an increase of 9.4 percentage points on the exam. If the slope estimate is also significant, the point estimate indicates that students who sleep more the night before a test perform substantially better. If, on the other hand, the slope estimate were very small—say, .5—the relationship would not appear to be substantively meaningful despite statistical significance. The example illustrates that point estimates provide valuable information about the relationship under examination.

The value of the intercept is also of interest. For this example, the value of the intercept is –2. The intercept indicates that, on average, students with zero hours of sleep received a score of –2 percentage points; however, this value does not make sense because the grading scale ranges from 0 to 100. Also, if we were to plot these data along an x-axis and a y-axis, we would see that none or perhaps just a couple of students slept very little—say, 0 to 2 hours—the night before the test. With so few data points, PREDICTION of test scores for such little sleep should be avoided (in this case, we obtain a nonsensical result). Point estimates are useful for illustrating the relationship in more concrete terms and for making predictions but contain more error when based on relatively little data. In this case, the y-intercept underscores the caution that must be taken with point estimates.

The hypothetical example given here to illustrate the concept of a point estimate employed ORDINARY LEAST SQUARES as the ESTIMATOR; however, point estimates of parameters may be obtained using other estimators, such as MAXIMUM LIKELIHOOD. In fact, the point estimate, or the value obtained for the sample statistic, depends in part on the estimator chosen by the researcher. Thus, it is important for the researcher to select an appropriate or *preferred* estimator given the particular properties of the research question (Kennedy, 1998, pp. 5–6). Point estimates are also sensitive to the SPECIFICATION of the model, the presence of measurement error, the sample size, and the SAMPLE draw.

—Jacque L. Amoureux

REFERENCES

Kennedy, P. (1998). *A guide to econometrics.* Cambridge: MIT Press.

Lewis-Beck, M. S. (1980). *Applied regression: An introduction* (Sage University Paper Series on Quantitative Applications in the Social Sciences, 07–022). Newbury Park, CA: Sage.

Lewis-Beck, M. S. (1995). *Data analysis: An introduction* (Sage University Paper Series on Quantitative Applications in the Social Sciences, 07–103). Thousand Oaks, CA: Sage.

POISSON DISTRIBUTION

The Poisson distribution measures the PROBABILITY that a DISCRETE positive variable takes on a given value for an observation period. For a given period, we observe the sum of "successes" among a possibly infinite number of trials. This sum has no upper bound. Trials or events are INDEPENDENT of one another and cannot occur simultaneously. In a given hour, for example, we might receive 10 phone calls from telemarketers; in this case, our Poisson variable takes on a value of 10. We define the EXPECTED VALUE ($E[Y]$) of a Poisson RANDOM variable as λ, or the anticipated rate of occurrence for the next period. Once having calculated a value for λ (drawing on results from previous periods), we can determine the probability with which Y takes on the value k using the Poisson PROBABILITY DENSITY FUNCTION:

$$\Pr(Y = k) = \frac{e^{-\lambda}\lambda^k}{k!}.$$

Although Siméon-Denis Poisson (1791–1840) originally developed the Poisson as an approximation for the binomial probability distribution function, scholars have since derived the Poisson from a simple set of propositions.

The Poisson bears a striking resemblance to the BINOMIAL DISTRIBUTION, which summarizes the outcome of n Bernoulli trials. Poisson derived the function as a way of approximating the probability that a binomial random variable takes on a particular value when the number of trials (n) is large, the chance of success (p) is small, and $\lambda = np$ is moderate in size—that is, in the case of rare events. (For a derivation, see Ross, 2002.) The variance formula for the Poisson follows from that for the binomial as well: $\text{Var}(Y) = np(1 - p) \approx \lambda$ when n is large and p is small. The key difference between the binomial and the Poisson is that we know the number of trials (n) in a binomial distribution, whereas the number of trials in the Poisson is unknown and approaches infinity.

Social scientists have since begun to use the Poisson as a probability distribution in its own right to describe phenomena as diverse as the number of wars per year and the incidence of certain rare behaviors within a given population. Consider the case of the number of presidential vetoes during a given year. This example satisfies assumptions underlying the more general Poisson derivation (see King, 1998). Vetoes on particular bills are independent of one another. No two vetoes can occur at exactly the same time. Given a λ of 3.5 (the average of presidential veto rates during previous years), we can calculate the probability that the president would veto at least three bills in the next year (see Figure 1):

$$\Pr(k \geq 3) = 1 - P(k = 0) - P(k = 1) - P(k = 2)$$
$$= 1 - e^{-3.5} - 3.5e^{-3.5} - \frac{(3.5)^2}{2}e^{-3.5}$$
$$= 1 - 10.625e^{-3.5} = 0.8641.$$

Were we to vary the length of the interval, we would need an adjusted version of the equation that takes t (the length of the interval) as an additional PARAMETER. In this case, we would calculate instead the probability that the president will veto at least three bills during the next 2 years (see Figure 1):

$$\Pr(Y = k) = \frac{e^{-\lambda t}(\lambda t)^k}{k!}.$$

$$\Pr(k \geq 3) = 1 - P(k = 0) - P(k = 1) - P(k = 2)$$
$$= 1 - e^{-7} - 7e^{-7} - \frac{(7)^2}{2}e^{-7}$$
$$= 1 - 32.5e^{-7} = 0.9704.$$

Although the Poisson distribution as described above applies to single observations, social scientists have developed the POISSON REGRESSION technique to estimate λ for a set of observations.

—Alison E. Post

REFERENCES

King, G. (1998). *Unifying political methodology.* Ann Arbor: University of Michigan Press.

Poisson Distribution for λ = 3.5

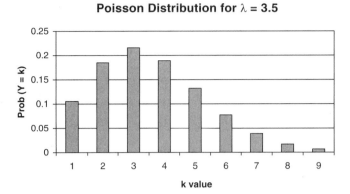

Figure 1   Poisson Distribution

Larsen, R. J., & Marx, M. L. (1990). *Statistics.* Englewood Cliffs, NJ: Prentice Hall.

Ross, S. (2002). *A first course in probability.* Upper Saddle River, NJ: Prentice Hall.

POISSON REGRESSION

A Poisson regression is a REGRESSION MODEL in which a dependent variable that consists of counts is modeled with a POISSON DISTRIBUTION. Count-dependent variables, which can take on only nonnegative integer values, appear in many social science contexts. For example, a sociologist might be interested in studying the factors that affect the number of times that an individual commits criminal behaviors. In this case, each individual in a data set would be associated with a number that specifies how many criminal behaviors he or she committed in a given time frame. Individuals who committed no such behaviors would receive a count value of 0, individuals who committed one crime would receive a count value of 1, and so forth. The sociologist in question could use a Poisson regression to determine which of a set of specified independent variables (e.g., an individual's level of educational attainment) has a significant relationship with an individual's criminal activity as measured by counts of criminal acts.

Poisson regressions are, as noted above, based on the Poisson distribution. This one-parameter univariate DISTRIBUTION has positive support over the nonnegative integers, and hence it is appropriate to use such a distribution when studying a dependent variable that consists of counts.

MODEL SPECIFICATION

The MODEL SPECIFICATION for a Poisson regression is based on assuming that a count-dependent variable y_i has, conditional on a vector of independent variables $\mathbf{x}_i$, a Poisson distribution independent across other observations i with mean μ_i and the following probability DISTRIBUTION function:

$$f(y_i|\mathbf{x}_i) = \frac{e^{-\mu_i}\mu_i^{y_i}}{y_i!}. \qquad (1)$$

The link between μ_i and x_i is assumed to be

$$\mu_i = \exp(\mathbf{x}_i'\boldsymbol{\beta}), \qquad (2)$$

where $\boldsymbol{\beta}$ is a parameter vector (with the same dimension as $\mathbf{x}_i$) to be estimated. Note that the exponential link function between μ_i and $\mathbf{x}_i$ ensures that μ_i is strictly positive; this is essential because the mean of the Poisson distribution cannot be nonpositive. Based on a set of n observations $(y_i, \mathbf{x}_i)$, equations (1) and (2) together generate a log-likelihood function of

$$\log L = \sum_{i=1}^{n}[y_i\mathbf{x}_i'\boldsymbol{\beta} - \exp(\mathbf{x}_i'\boldsymbol{\beta}) - \log(y_i!)], \qquad (3)$$

where $\log(\cdot)$ denotes natural LOGARITHM. The first-order conditions from this log-likelihood function—there is one such condition per each element of $\boldsymbol{\beta}$—are NONLINEAR in $\boldsymbol{\beta}$ and cannot be solved in closed form. Therefore, numerical methods must be used to solve for the value of $\hat{\boldsymbol{\beta}}$ that maximizes equation (3).

Interpretation of Poisson regression output is similar to interpretation of other nonlinear regression models. If a given element of $\hat{\boldsymbol{\beta}}$ is positive, then it follows that increases in the corresponding element of $\mathbf{x}_i$ are associated with relatively large count values in y_i. However, comparative statics in a Poisson regression model are complicated by the fact that the derivative of μ_i with respect to an element of $\mathbf{x}_i$ in equation (2) depends on all the elements of $\mathbf{x}_i$ (cross-partial derivatives of μ_i with respect to different elements of $\mathbf{x}_i$ are not zero, as they are in an ORDINARY LEAST SQUARES regression). Hence, with a vector estimate $\hat{\boldsymbol{\beta}}$, one can vary an element of $\mathbf{x}_i$ and, substituting $\hat{\boldsymbol{\beta}}$ for $\boldsymbol{\beta}$ in equation (2), generate a sequence of estimated μ_i values based on a modified $\mathbf{x}_i$ vector. It is then straightforward to generate a probability distribution over the nonnegative integers—an estimated distribution for y_i—using the link function in equation (2). This distribution, it is important to point out, will be conditional on the elements of $\mathbf{x}_i$ that are not varied.

The log likelihood in equation (3) satisfies standard regularity conditions, and from this it follows that inference on $\hat{\beta}$ can be carried out using standard asymptotic theory. Accordingly, significance tests, likelihood ratio tests, and so forth can easily be calculated based on $\hat{\beta}$ and an estimated covariance matrix for this parameter vector. The Poisson regression model is a special case of a GENERALIZED LINEAR MODEL (McCullagh & Nelder, 1989); hence, generalized linear model theory can be applied to Poisson regressions.

EXTENSIONS

The standard Poisson regression model—encapsulated in equations (1) and (2)—can be extended in a number of ways, many of which are described in Cameron and Trivedi (1998), a detailed and very broad reference on count regressions. One very common extension of the Poisson model is intended to reflect the fact that a count-dependent variable y_i can, in practice, have greater variance than it should based on the nominal Poisson variance conditional on a vector $\mathbf{x}_i$. Note that a Poisson random variable with mean λ has variance λ as well. This means that modeling the mean of y_i as in equation (2) imposes a strong constraint on the variance of y_i as well.

When, given observations $(y_i, \mathbf{x}_i)$, the variance of y_i exceeds μ_i because of unmodeled HETEROGENEITY, then y_i is said to suffer from overdispersion (i.e., it has greater variance than one would expect given observed y_i and $\mathbf{x}_i$). An overdispersed count-dependent variable can be studied using a negative binomial regression model; the standard Poisson model should not be applied to overdispersed data as results based on this model can be misleading.

Moreover, the Poisson regression model is a special case of the negative binomial model. Thus, when applying a negative binomial regression model to a given count data set, it is straightforward to test whether the data set, conditional on independent variables in the associated $\mathbf{x}_i$ vector, is overdispersed, implying that a standard Poisson model should not be used to analyze it.

Another extension of the standard Poisson model, due to Lambert (1992), is intended to model a count-dependent variable with an excessive number of zero observations (i.e., an excessive number of values of y_i such that $y_i = 0$). Such a set of dependent variable values can be labeled zero inflated, and Lambert's zero-inflated Poisson regression model assumes that some observations y_i are drawn from a standard Poisson regression model (or a negative binomial model) and that some values of y_i are from an "always zero" model. Consequently, associated with each y_i that is observed zero is a latent probability of being drawn from the always zero model and, correspondingly, a latent probability of being drawn from a regular Poisson model that puts positive weight on zero and also on all positive integers. A standard Poisson regression is not a special case of Lambert's zero-inflated Poisson model, and as pointed out in Greene's (2000) discussion and survey of count regressions, testing for excess zeros requires nonnested hypothesis testing.

Additional extensions of the Poisson regression model can be found in Cameron and Trivedi (1998) and in Greene (2000). Cameron and Trivedi, for example, discuss TIME-SERIES extensions of the Poisson model as well as generalizations that allow the modeling of vectors of counts.

—Michael C. Herron

REFERENCES

Cameron, A. C., & Trivedi, P. K. (1998). *Regression analysis of count data.* New York: Cambridge University Press.

Greene, W. H. (2000). *Econometric analysis* (4th ed.). Upper Saddle River, NJ: Prentice Hall.

Lambert, D. (1992). Zero-inflated Poisson regression with an application to defects in manufacturing. *Technometrics, 34,* 1–14.

McCullagh, P., & Nelder, J. A. (1989). *Generalized linear models* (2nd ed.). London: Chapman & Hall.

POLICY-ORIENTED RESEARCH

Policy-oriented research is designed to *inform* or *understand* one or more aspects of the public and social policy process, including decision making and policy formulation, implementation, and evaluation. A distinction may be made between research *for* policy and research *of* policy. Research *for* policy is research that informs the various stages of the policy process (before the formation of policy through to the implementation of policy). Research *of* policy is concerned with how problems are defined, agendas are set, policy is formulated, decisions are made, and how policy is implemented, evaluated, and changed (Nutley & Webb, 2000, p. 15). Policy-oriented research (POR) can simultaneously be of both types.

How POR actually informs policy (if at all) is a debated issue. Young, Ashby, Boaz, and Grayson (2002) identify various models that help us understand this process. A *knowledge-driven model* assumes that research (conducted by experts) *leads* policy. A *problem-solving model* assumes that research *follows* policy and that policy issues shape research priorities. An *interactive model* portrays research and policy as mutually influential. A *political/tactical model* sees policy as the outcome of a political process, where the research agenda is politically driven. An *enlightenment model* sees research as serving policy in indirect ways, addressing the context within which decisions are made and providing a broader frame for understanding and explaining policy. Each model can help us understand the links between POR and specific policy developments. Young and colleagues (2002, p. 218) suggest that the role of policy research "is less one of problem solving than of clarifying issues and informing the wider public debate."

Thus, POR may serve several functions and can have a diverse range of audiences. It provides a *specialist* function of informing and influencing the policy process and understanding how policy works and what works for target audiences of policy makers, policy networks and communities, research-aware practitioners, and academics; it also provides a *democratic* function, in which research findings contribute to the development of an informed and knowledge-based society as well as to the broader democratic process. Here the users of research will include organized groups with vested interests, service users, and the public as a whole.

Policymakers and those who implement policy (e.g., social workers, health care workers) are increasingly looking to base their policy and practice on "evidence," particularly on evidence of effectiveness and "what works." What counts as evidence (and who says so) are highly contested areas. Although POR can be a key source of "evidence," what actually counts as evidence—especially in informing policy and practice—will be far broader than research findings alone.

POR can draw from the full range of possible research designs and methods (Becker & Bryman, 2004). Depending on the specific research question(s) to be addressed, in some cases, just one method will be used. In other cases, there may be an integration of different methods either within a single piece of research or as part of a wider program of research being conducted across multiple sites or cross-nationally. Although each method and design has its own strengths and limitations, RANDOMIZED CONTROLLED TRIALS, followed by SYSTEMATIC REVIEWS and statistical META-ANALYSIS, are seen by many as the "gold standards." This is particularly the case in medical and health policy research, and there is an ongoing debate concerning which research designs and methods are the most appropriate for POR in social care, education, criminal justice, and other fields of public and social policy.

—Saul Becker

REFERENCES

Becker, S., & Bryman, A. (Eds.). (2004). *Understanding research for social policy and practice: Themes, methods and approaches.* Bristol, UK: Policy Press.

Nutley, S., & Webb, J. (2000). Evidence and the policy process. In H. Davies, S. Nutley, & P. Smith (Eds.), *What works? Evidence-based policy and practice in public services* (pp. 13–41). Bristol, UK: Policy Press.

Young, K., Ashby, D., Boaz, A., & Grayson, L. (2002). Social science and the evidence-based policy movement. *Social Policy and Society, 1*(3), 215–224.

POLITICS OF RESEARCH

With politics in relation to research, the issue is how far it can be or should seek to be value free. The early and traditional argument was that social research should strive to be scientific and OBJECTIVE by emulating the practices and assumptions of the natural sciences, a philosophical position known as POSITIVISM. The key characteristics focused on using a value-free method, making logical arguments, and testing ideas against that which is observable to produce social facts. Such principles have always been subject to dispute. Nevertheless, they dominated mainstream thought during the 19th century and a considerable part of the 20th century.

More recently, alternative positions have prevailed. Positivism has been challenged as inappropriate to the social sciences, which is concerned with social actors' meanings, beliefs, and values. The reliance on quantitative methods, such as SURVEYS, has been modified as greater legitimacy is afforded to in-depth qualitative studies. There has been a blurring of the boundaries between social research and policy and practice (Hammersley, 2000). As a result, the assumption that social science can produce objective knowledge has been challenged.

Hammersley (1995) has argued that it is necessary to ask three different questions as to whether social research is political. *Can* research be nonpolitical? Does research as *practiced* tend to be political? *Should* research be political? Some social scientists argue that it is impossible for research not to involve a political dimension. All research is, necessarily, influenced by social factors, such as how the topic is framed, what access to participants is possible, and the role of the researcher in the research process. Funding bodies also have a major impact in terms of which projects they finance and the conditions relating to this.

Others also claim that it is neither possible nor desirable for social scientists to adopt a disinterested attitude to the social world. Sociology, for instance, has always been driven by a concern for the "underdog" and by its willingness to challenge the status quo. Currently, feminist and antiracist research is explicitly aimed at bringing about change. However, there are still those who argue that research should not be directly concerned with any goal other than the production of knowledge. From this view, research has a limited capacity to deliver major political transformations, and such pursuits limit the value of research itself (Hammersley, 1995).

A possible way out of this conundrum is to distinguish between politics, on one hand, and objectivity in producing knowledge, on the other. Asking questions that are guided by a political or ethical point of view need not prevent a researcher from striving toward objectivity in the actual research. This involves using rigorous and systematic procedures throughout the research process, including during the analysis and when producing an account. Researchers are arguing that, even if there is no utopia of absolute objectivity for social scientists, this must still be an aspiration in the interest of generating robust knowledge and understandings (Christians, 2000).

—Mary Maynard

REFERENCES

Christians, C. (2000). Ethics and politics in qualitative research. In N. K. Denzin & Y. S. Lincoln (Eds.), *The handbook of qualitative research* (pp. 133–155). Thousand Oaks, CA: Sage.

Hammersley, M. (1995). *The politics of social research.* London: Sage.

Hammersley, M. (2000). *Taking sides in social research.* London: Routledge.

POLYGON

Polygon is a type of chart that displays a variable of ordinal, interval, or grouped ratio scale on the x-axis and another variable of interest, most often frequencies of observations, on the y-axis.

—Tim Futing Liao

See also FREQUENCY POLYGON

POLYNOMIAL EQUATION

When an equation contains right-side variables that are exponentiated to some power greater than 1, we call it a *polynomial equation.* Polynomial equations are observed in research in economics more frequently than in other social sciences. For example, the theory of marginal cost suggests a U-shaped relation between output and marginal cost. As we increase output of a commodity, the marginal cost for producing one unit of the commodity decreases due to the economy of scale. As we keep production beyond a certain amount of output, however, the cost tends to increase due to saturation of the production facility. Mathematically, this relationship can be captured with a quadratic equation of the form $\hat{Y} = \beta_0 + \beta_1 X + \beta_2 X^2$.

STOCHASTIC FORM OF POLYNOMIAL EQUATIONS

Statistical specifications sometimes represent the theory associated with polynomial equations in a STOCHASTIC form. For example, the stochastic version of the preceding equation is $Y = \beta_0 + \beta_1 X + \beta_2 X^2 + \varepsilon$. If we expand our discussion to a more general case in which there are more than two powers for several variables, we have the following general expression of the stochastic polynomial equation:

$$Y = \beta_0 + \sum_{i=1}^{m} \beta_i X^i + \cdots + \sum_{j=1}^{n} \zeta_j Z^j + \varepsilon.$$

In the remainder of this entry, we shall consider polynomial equations in a stochastic context.

For example, polynomial specification of a REGRESSION model is a special case of a NONLINEAR model, which can be represented more generally as

$$Y = \alpha g_1(\mathbf{z}) + \beta g_2(\mathbf{z}) + \cdots + \zeta g_k(\mathbf{z}) + \varepsilon$$
$$= \alpha X_1 + \beta X_2 + \cdots + \zeta X_k + \varepsilon.$$

Here a vector $\mathbf{z}$ consists of several independent variables. A series of TRANSFORMATION functions, such as $g_1(\mathbf{z})$, $g_2(\mathbf{z})$, $g_k(\mathbf{z})$, specify various nonlinear relations among the variables in $\mathbf{z}$. Notice that we begin with a nonlinear specification of independent variables but end up with a familiar expression of the right side of the classic linear regression equation, $\alpha X_1 + \beta X_2 + \cdots + \zeta X_k + \varepsilon$, through the transformation of the independent variables. This shows the intrinsic linearity of the model. If we find the nature of the nonlinear relationship, we can often transform our complex model into a simple linear form. A polynomial equation is one of the possible specifications of the transformation function. LOGARITHMIC, exponential, and reciprocal equations can also be alternatives, depending on the nature of the nonlinearity.

ESTIMATION OF POLYNOMIAL REGRESSIONS

We can estimate a polynomial regression by classic ORDINARY LEAST SQUARES. This is because nonlinearity in independent variables does not violate the assumption of linearity in parameters. We can just put the transformed values of independent variables into the equation. Then, we get a simplified form of LINEAR REGRESSION. Polynomial terms are often associated with MULTICOLLINEARITY because variables in quadratic and cubic forms will be correlated. However, estimates from polynomial regression equations are best linear unbiased estimates (BLUE) if all of the regression assumptions are met.

DETECTION OF POLYNOMIAL RELATIONSHIPS

Given this basic definition and characteristics of the polynomial regression equation, a natural question is how we can specify and detect polynomial relationships. There are two approaches to answering this question. The first is grounded in theory, and the second is grounded in statistical testing. Based on a well-developed theory of the phenomenon we are studying, such as the marginal cost theory mentioned above, we could specify a priori predicted relations among variables and then just check the STATISTICAL SIGNIFICANCE of the coefficients. Obviously, this test of significance is a natural test of the theory. However, in many cases, theory will be too weak to specify particular polynomial or nonlinear forms.

Thus, we can also address the problem of specifying and detecting polynomial relationships statistically. Three approaches are commonly used. First, we can analyze the residuals from a simple linear regression graphically. Let's think of a simple polynomial equation with one variable. Suppose the true model is $Y = \beta_0 + \beta_1 X + \beta_2 X^2 + \varepsilon$, but we estimated it with a sample regression of $Y = \hat{\beta}_0 + \hat{\beta}_1 X + \varepsilon$. Then, the residuals will reflect $\beta_2 X^2$ as well as ε. In other words, the residuals will contain systematic variations of the true model in addition to the pure disturbances. If we rearrange the observations in ascending order of the x values, then we will easily find a pattern in the residuals.

Second, we can run piecewise linear regressions. Taking the same example of the residual analysis, we can rearrange the observations again in ascending order and divide the sample into several subgroups. If we run separate regressions on the subgroups, we will have coefficient estimates that are consistently increasing or decreasing depending on whether the sign of β_2 is positive or negative.

Third, if we deal with the problem of specification and detection in the more general context of nonlinearity, then we can use a Box-Cox specification. According to the Box-Cox transformation, we specify a nonlinear functional form of the independent variables as

$$X = \frac{Z^\lambda - 1}{\lambda}$$

Here λ is an unknown parameter, so we have a variety of possible functional forms depending on the value of λ. Critical to our current interest is the case of $\lambda = 1$, where we have X as a linear function of Z. A LIKELIHOOD RATIO test is often used to see whether the likelihood ratio statistics that are estimated with and without the restriction of $\lambda = 1$ suggest a difference between the two specifications. If we find a statistically significant difference between the two, we reject the null hypothesis of linearity in variables. Given the results of these statistical procedures, we can make a judgment on the existence of nonlinearity. However, the existence of nonlinearity itself does not tell us about the true nature and form of nonlinearity. In a general specification of nonlinearity, we can use the Box-Cox transformation equation for estimating the value of λ. The value of λ is indicative of the nature of the nonlinearity. However, the Box-Cox approach does not cover all possible forms of nonlinear relations. Moreover, the Box-Cox approach does not pertain specifically to polynomial-based nonlinearity.

CONCLUSION

In summary, specification and detection of nonlinearity, including polynomial forms, should be grounded in theory and confirmed through statistical testing. A purely theoretical specification may miss the exact form of nonlinearity. A purely statistical basis for specifying nonlinearity is likely to provide a weak basis for using nonlinear forms. Thus, considerable judgment is required in specifying polynomial and other forms of nonlinearity.

—B. Dan Wood and Sung Ho Park

REFERENCES

Greene, W. H. (2003). *Econometric analysis* (5th ed.). Mahwah, NJ: Prentice Hall.
Gujarati, D. N. (1995). *Basic econometrics* (3rd ed.). New York: McGraw-Hill.

POLYTOMOUS VARIABLE

A polytomous variable is a variable with more than two distinct categories, in contrast to a DICHOTOMOUS variable. In principle, any CONTINUOUS variable or any INTERVAL or RATIO variable with more than two observed values is a polytomous variable, but the term is usually reserved for NOMINAL and ORDINAL variables, called unordered and ordered polytomous variables. Usually, when applied to ordinal variables, the term is used to refer to ordinal variables with relatively few (e.g., less than 10) distinct categories; ordinal variables with large numbers of categories (e.g., more than 20) are sometimes described as, and often treated the same as, continuous interval or ratio variables. Also, although in principle the term is applicable to either INDEPENDENT or DEPENDENT VARIABLES in any analysis, the term is usually reserved for dependent variables in LOGIT and LOGISTIC

REGRESSION models. Other terms sometimes used for polytomous variables are *polychotomous* (just an extra syllable, also in contrast to dichotomous variables) and *multinomial* (in contrast to binomial). Because the terms *binomial* and *multinomial* refer to specific probability distributions and to variables having those distributions, the term *polytomous* may be preferred when no implication about the distribution of the variable is intended.

—Scott Menard

POOLED SURVEYS

Pooled surveys represent the combining of different SURVEYS into one data set. Usually, the surveys are essentially the same measuring instruments, applied repeatedly over time. For example, the analyst might combine, or pool, the presidential election year surveys of the American National Election Study from, say, 1952 to 2000. That would mean a pool of 13 cross-sectional surveys conduced across a time period of 48 years. Advantages of the pooled survey are a great increase in SAMPLE size and VARIANCE. Analysis complications can arise from the mix of TIME-SERIES and CROSS-SECTIONAL DESIGNS. Also, the study may be forced to restrict itself to the narrower range of items that were posed in all the surveys.

—Michael S. Lewis-Beck

POPULATION

A population is the universe of units of analysis, such as individuals, social groups, organizations, or social artifacts about which a researcher makes conclusions. In the course of the study, the researcher collects measurable DATA about a specific population in which he or she is interested. In a study, the units of analysis that comprise the population are referred to as subjects. Although the goal of all studies is to make inferences about population, in most cases, it is virtually impossible to gather data about all members of the population in which the researcher is interested. Because some populations, such as college students or Native Americans, are very large, attempts at complete enumeration of all cases are extremely time-consuming, prohibitively expensive, and prone to data collection error. Selecting a representative subset of the population, called a SAMPLE, is often preferable to enumeration. By using inferential statistical methods, the researcher is able to make conclusions about characteristics of a population, based on a RANDOM SAMPLE of that population.

Some social studies focus on populations that actually exist, such as freshman students of the New York University. Alternatively, a study can be focused on a conceptual population that does not exist in reality but can be hypothetically conceptualized, such as divorced middle-class males age 45 and older.

Characteristics of the population are generally referred to as PARAMETERS. By convention, parameters are denoted by Greek letters, such as μ for population mean and σ for population standard deviation. Population parameters are fixed values and are, in most cases, unknown. For example, the percentage of people in favor of abortions in Utah may be unknown, but theoretically, if several researchers measured this parameter at a specific time, they would come up with the same number. In contrast, sample statistics vary from one sample to another. It would be extremely unlikely for several random samples measuring the percentage of pro-choice Utah residents to arrive at the same number. In contrast to population parameters, the values of statistics for a particular sample are either known or can be calculated. What is often unknown is how representative the sample actually is of the population from which it was drawn or how accurately the statistics of this sample represent population parameters.

Prior to conducting the actual study, the researcher usually makes ASSUMPTIONS about the population to which he or she is generalizing and the SAMPLING procedures he or she uses for the study. These assumptions usually fall into one of two categories: (a) assumptions of which the researcher is virtually certain or is willing to accept and (b) assumptions that are subject to debate and empirical proof and in which the researcher is therefore most interested. Assumptions in the first category are called the MODEL. The assumptions in the second category are called the HYPOTHESIS. In the course of the study, after the assumptions about the unknown population parameters are made, the researcher tests the hypothesis and tries to determine how likely his or her sample statistics would be if these assumptions were actually true.

—Alexei Pavlichev

REFERENCES

Agresti, A., & Finlay, B. (1997). *Statistical methods for social sciences* (3rd ed.). Upper Saddle River, NJ: Prentice Hall.
Babbie, E. R. (1995). *The practice of social research* (7th ed.). Belmont, CA: Wadsworth.
Blalock, H. M., Jr. (1979). *Social statistics* (Rev. 2nd ed.). New York: McGraw-Hill.

POPULATION PYRAMID

The age-sex composition of a POPULATION is often portrayed in a stylized graph called a *population pyramid,* which shows the numbers of people, expressed in absolute numbers, percentages, or proportions, in each age (or year of birth) interval arrayed by sex. The name derives from the typical triangular or pyramidal shape of the image for populations that are growing because of high levels of fertility sustained over a substantial period of time. Pyramids for populations that are growing very slowly or are stable in size tend to be shaped like beehives, whereas pyramids for populations that are decreasing in size because of low rates of fertility show marked constrictions at the base.

The merits of population pyramids lie in their clear presentation of the relative sizes of age (or year of birth) cohorts and thus the relative sizes of important age-bounded groups such as the potential labor force or dependent populations such as children and the elderly. Population pyramids can also show the impact of trends and fluctuations in historic and recent levels of vital rates, especially fertility rates, on the population's age structure. Because population pyramids show both sexes, they also show the impact of the sex ratio at birth, which approximates 105 males to 100 females in most national populations, and the impact of sex-specific differentials in mortality and migration. Population pyramids also sometimes indicate patterns of error in age-specific counts. It is becoming very common for national statistical agencies to publish the age-sex tabulations necessary for constructing population pyramids on the Web.

The population pyramid displayed in Figure 1 shows the age-sex structure of the population of the Republic of Ecuador in 1990, with age reported in single years. The graph shows the typical features of a population pyramid for a developing country. Its overall shape is triangular, the result of historically high levels of fertility. It is asymmetric with respect to sex: The base

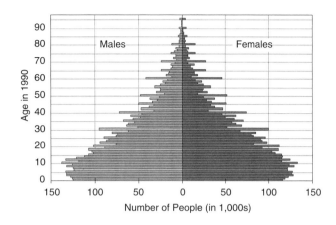

Figure 1   Population Pyramid for Ecuador, 1990

SOURCE: Instituto Nacional de Estadistica y Censos, 1990, wws4.inec.gov.ed/poblac/pobla03.txt.

of the pyramid has a slight preponderance of males because of the male-biased sex ratio among births, and the top has a slight preponderance of females because mortality rates slightly favor females. There is also clear evidence of error in the age-specific counts due to "age heaping," a common pattern of age misreporting in which people are more likely to report ages ending in selected digits (often 0 and 5, as observed here) than ages ending in other digits. (This type of error is often masked by the common practice of aggregating age or year of birth categories into 5-year intervals.) The inward cut at the bottom of the pyramid could reflect either the underenumeration of children in the census or a decline in fertility rates in Ecuador during the 1980s. Comparing the sizes of the cohorts ages 0 to 9 enumerated in the 1990 census with the sizes of the cohorts ages 10 to 19 enumerated in the 2000 census suggest that the constriction at the base of the pyramid is mostly attributable to underenumeration of children in the 1990 census.

—Gillian Stevens

POSITIVISM

Positivism is a philosophy of science that rejects metaphysical speculation in favor of systematic observation using the human senses. "Positive" knowledge of the world is based on GENERALIZATIONS from such observations that, given sufficient number and consistency, are regarded as producing laws of how phenomena coexist or occur in sequences. In the 19th century, positivism was not merely a philosophy of science; it expressed a more general worldview that lauded the achievements of science.

CENTRAL TENETS

Although numerous attempts have since been made to identify the central tenets of positivism, the following are generally accepted as its main characteristics.

1. *Phenomenalism.* Knowledge must be based on experience, on what observers can perceive with their senses. This perception must be achieved without the subjective activity of cognitive processes; it must be "pure experience" with an empty consciousness.

2. *Nominalism.* Any abstract concepts used in scientific explanation must also be derived from experience; metaphysical notions about which it is not possible to make any observations have no legitimate existence except as names or words. Hence, the language used to describe observations must be uncontaminated by any theoretical notions.

3. *Atomism.* The objects of experience, of observation, are regarded as discrete, independent atomic impressions of events, which constitute the ultimate and fundamental elements of the world. Insofar as these atomic impressions are formed into generalizations, they do not refer to abstract objects in the world, only regularities among discrete events.

4. *General laws.* Scientific theories are regarded as a set of highly general lawlike statements; establishing such general laws is the aim of science. These laws summarize observations by specifying simple relations or constant conjunctions between phenomena. EXPLANATION is achieved by subsuming individual cases under appropriate laws. These laws are general in scope, in that they cover a broad range of observations, and are universal in form, in that they apply, without exception, across time and space.

5. *Value judgments and normative statements.* "Facts" and "values" must be separated as values do not have the status of knowledge. Value statements have no empirical content that would make them susceptible to any tests of their validity based on observations.

6. *Verification.* The truth or falsity of any scientific statement can be settled with reference to an observable

state of affairs. Scientific laws are verified by the accumulation of confirming evidence.

7. *Causation.* There is no CAUSALITY in nature, only regularities or constant conjunctions between events, such that events of one kind are followed by events of another kind. Therefore, if all we have are regularities between types of events, then explanation is nothing more than locating an event within a wider ranging regularity.

VARIETIES OF POSITIVISM

According to Halfpenny (1982), it is possible to identify 12 varieties of positivism. However, following Outhwaite (1987), these can be reduced to 3. The first was formulated by August Comte (1798–1857) as an alternative to theological and metaphysical ways of understanding the world. He regarded all sciences as forming a unified hierarchy of related levels, building on mathematics at the lowest level, followed by astronomy, physics, chemistry, biology, and, finally, sociology.

The second version, known as *logical positivism,* was founded in Vienna in the 1920s. The catch-cry of these philosophers was that any concept or proposition that does not correspond to some state of affairs (i.e., cannot be verified by experience) is regarded as being meaningless (*phenomenalism*). At the same time, it is argued that the concepts and propositions of the higher level sciences *can* be reduced to those of the lower ones. In other words, they adopted the reductionist position that the propositions of the social sciences could ultimately be analyzed down to those of physics.

The third version, which was derived from the second and is sometimes referred to as the "standard view" in the philosophy of science, dominated the English-speaking world in the post–World War II period. Its fundamental tenet is that all sciences, including the social sciences, are concerned with developing explanations in the form of universal laws or generalizations. Any phenomenon is explained by demonstrating that it is a specific case of some such law. These laws refer to "constant conjunctions" between events or, in the case of the social sciences, statistical correlations or regularities ("general law").

This third version is based on the belief that there can be a *natural* scientific study of people and society, the doctrine known as the *unity of scientific method.* It is argued that despite the differences in subject matter of the various scientific disciplines, both natural and social, the same method or logic of explanation can be used, although each science must elaborate these in a way appropriate to its objects of enquiry.

At its most general, positivism is a theory of the nature, omnicompetence and unity of science. In its most radical shape it stipulates that the only valid kind of (non-analytic) knowledge is scientific, that such knowledge consists in the description of the invariant patterns, the co-existence in space and succession over time, of observable phenomena. . . . Its naturalistic insistence on the unity of science and scientistic disavowal of any knowledge apart from science induce its aversion to metaphysics, insistence upon a strict value/fact dichotomy and tendency to historicist confidence in the inevitability of scientifically mediated progress. (Bhaskar, 1986, p. 226)

POSITIVISM IN THE SOCIAL SCIENCES

It was through the work of August Comte and Emile Durkheim that positivism was introduced into the social sciences. Forms of positivism have dominated sociology, particularly in the decades immediately following World War II, and continue to do so today in disciplines such as psychology and economics. However, in recent years, positivism has been subjected to devastating criticism (for reviews, see Blaikie, 1993, pp. 101–104; Bryant, 1985).

CRITICISM

Some of the main points of dispute are the claim that experience can be a sound basis for scientific knowledge, that science should deal only with observable phenomena and not with abstract or hypothetical entities, that it is possible to distinguish between an atheoretical observation language and a theoretical language, that theoretical concepts have a 1:1 correspondence with "reality" as it is observed, that scientific laws are based on constant conjunctions between events in the world, and that "facts" and "values" can be separated.

Positivism has been attacked from many perspectives, including INTERPRETIVISM, FALSIFICATIONISM, and CRITICAL REALISM. The interpretive critique has focused on positivism's inadequate view of the nature of social reality—its ONTOLOGY. Positivism takes for granted the socially constructed world that interpretivism regards as social reality. Positivists construct fictitious social worlds out of the meaning it has for *them* and neglect what it means to the social actors.

The central feature of the falsificationist critique is positivism's process for "discovering" knowledge and the basis for justifying this knowledge. First, because they regard experience as an inadequate source of knowledge, and as all observation involves interpretation, falsificationists have argued that it is not possible to distinguish between observational statements and theoretical statements; all statements about the world are theoretical, at least to some degree. Second, it is argued that experience is an inadequate basis for justifying knowledge because it leads to a circular argument. On what basis can experience be established as a justification for knowledge except by reference to experience?

Positivism's claim that reality can be perceived directly by the use of the human senses has been thoroughly discredited. Even if it is assumed that a single, unique physical world exists independently of observers—and this assumption is not universally accepted—the process of observing it involves both conscious and unconscious interpretation. Observations are "theory laden." The processes that human beings use to observe the world around them, be it in everyday life or for scientific purposes, are not analogous to taking photographs. In "reading" what impinges on our senses, we have to engage in a complex process that entails both the use of concepts peculiar to the language of a particular culture and expectations about what is "there." Furthermore, we do not observe as isolated individuals but as members of cultural or subcultural groups that provide us with ontological assumptions. Therefore, observers are active agents, not passive receptacles.

The realist solution to the theory-laden nature of observation and description is to draw the distinction between the transitive and intransitive objects of science. Although our descriptions of the *empirical* domain may be theory dependent, the structures and mechanisms of the *real* domain exist independently of our descriptions of them. Reality is not there to be observed as in positivism, nor is it just a social construction; it is just there. Therefore, according to the realists, the relative success of competing theories to represent this reality can be settled as a matter of rational judgment (see REALISM and CRITICAL REALISM).

As well as accusing positivism of having an inadequate ontology, critical realism also attacked the positivist method of explanation in terms of constant conjunctions between events. Even if two kinds of phenomena can be shown to occur regularly together, there is still the question of why this is the case. According to critical realism, establishing regularities between observed events is only the starting point in the process of scientific discovery. Constant conjunctions of events occur only in closed systems, those produced by experimental conditions. However, positivism treats the world of nature as a closed system. In open systems characteristic of both nature and society, a large number of generative mechanisms will be exercising their powers to cause effects at the same time. What is observed as an "empirical" conjunction may, therefore, not reflect the complexity of the mechanisms that are operating.

—Norman Blaikie

REFERENCES

Bhaskar, R. (1986). *Scientific realism and human emancipation.* London: Verso.

Blaikie, N. (1993). *Approaches to social enquiry.* Cambridge, UK: Polity.

Bryant, C. G. A. (1985). *Positivism in social theory and research.* London: Macmillan.

Halfpenny, P. (1982). *Positivism and sociology: Explaining social life.* London: Allen & Unwin.

Outhwaite, W. (1987). *New philosophies of social science: Realism, hermeneutics and critical theory.* London: Macmillan.

POST HOC COMPARISON. *See* MULTIPLE COMPARISONS

POSTEMPIRICISM

EMPIRICISM has long appeared synonymous with science. After all, if science could not gain an insight into reality, what could? In the history of empiricism, it was John Locke who argued that our understanding of the world arises from our experiences. Nevertheless, he also emphasized that classification must be based on a view of the essential qualities of objects. Therefore, there is no privileged access to things in themselves but to their properties (color, shape, feel, etc.). The empiricist philosopher David Hume was even more of a skeptic and held that only appearances can be known and nothing beyond them.

In what is a complicated history, EMPIRICISM provided the basis for a unity of method in the sciences. It also provided for a strict demarcation between the social and natural sciences centered on, for example, such issues as the neutrality of the process of observation, the unproblematic nature of experience, a strict separation of DATA from THEORY, and a universal approach to the basis of knowledge. In their different ways, Thomas Kuhn, Paul Feyerabend, and Mary Hesse added to postempiricist insights that take aim at these idealist assumptions and, in so doing, open up science to a more social and historical understanding that is rooted in EXPLANATIONS and understandings of the conditions that inform knowledge production, development, and application.

To simplify his argument, Kuhn (1970), in *The Structure of Scientific Revolutions,* characterized science as consisting of periods of "normal science" in which "puzzle solving" took place against the background of particular PARADIGMS. These comprise the intellectual standards and practices of a scientific community and are based on shared sets of assumptions. From time to time, however, anomalies are bound to occur, and key theories will seem to be falsified. When this happens and key scientists begin to challenge the orthodoxy, crises will occur. This will then spread, with a resulting revolution that leads to a new paradigm being established and so on.

A number of implications followed from Kuhn's (1970) groundbreaking work and the work of the postempiricists. First, the LOGICAL POSITIVISTS had held that there must be a strict separation between the language of theory and the language of OBSERVATION. Although Karl Popper (1959) has submitted this to critique, Kuhn took it a step further. The simple demarcation between the social and natural sciences could no longer hold as one between facts and values. The anti-essentialism of the postempiricists met with their commitment to detailed analysis based on the social context of production as a practical activity rooted within particular circumstances. Therefore, the social was not a separate activity to scientific endeavor but was fundamentally a part of it. Paul Feyerabend (1978) took this even further than the conservative orientation of Kuhn and held not only that local factors determined

how science progressed but, because of this, that there could be no grounds on which any rule might inform the practice of science.

The postempiricist critiques opened up a rich tradition of social studies of science. It has also left a legacy around a central problem neatly expressed by James Bohman (1991): "how to derive standards for the comparison and evaluation of competing explanations and research programs without falling back into ahistorical and essentialist epistemology" (p. 4).

—Tim May

REFERENCES

Bohman, J. (1991). *New philosophy of social science: Problems of indeterminacy.* Cambridge, UK: Polity.

Feyerabend, P. (1978). *Against method.* London: Verso.

Kuhn, T. (1970). *The structure of scientific revolutions.* Chicago: University of Chicago Press.

Popper, K. R. (1959). *The logic of scientific discovery.* London: Hutchinson.

Williams, M., & May, T. (1996). *Introduction to the philosophy of social research.* London: Routledge Kegan Paul.

POSTERIOR DISTRIBUTION

A posterior distribution $p(\theta|\mathbf{x})$ is a probability distribution describing one's subjective belief about an unknown quantity θ after observing a data set $\mathbf{x}$. Posterior distributions are constructed using Bayes' rule and occupy a central position in BAYESIAN INFERENCE. Denote the PRIOR DISTRIBUTION by $p(\theta)$ and the likelihood function by $p(\mathbf{x}|\theta)$. Bayes' rule is often written as

$$p(\theta|\mathbf{x}) \propto p(\mathbf{x}|\theta)p(\theta).$$

Bayes' rule describes the process of learning from data. It explains how two people with different prior beliefs can be drawn toward similar conclusions after observing $\mathbf{x}$. The proportionality in Bayes' rule is resolved by the fact that $p(\theta|\mathbf{x})$ is a probability distribution, so its integral over all possible values of θ must equal 1. The proportionality constant is usually difficult or impossible to compute except in special cases. Monte Carlo simulation methods are often employed to compute marginal distributions or other low-dimensional summaries of $p(\theta|\mathbf{x})$ when analytic computation is difficult. Exact analytic results are easily obtained when $p(\mathbf{x}|\theta)$ and $p(\theta)$ are conjugate. A likelihood function and prior distribution are conjugate if

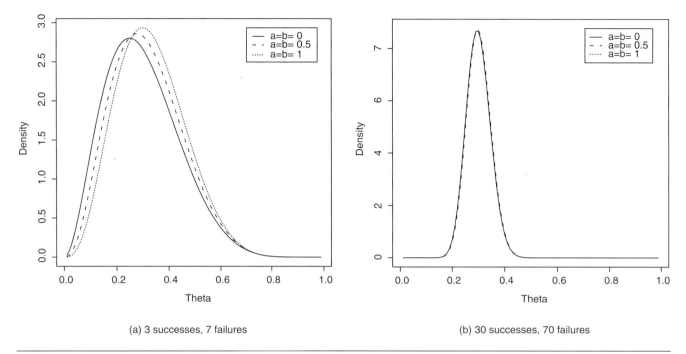

(a) 3 successes, 7 failures

(b) 30 successes, 70 failures

Figure 1　Posterior Distribution of θ Given Different Numbers of Successes and Failures and Different Beta Prior Distributions

they combine to form a posterior distribution from the same distributional family as the prior. The entry on PRIOR DISTRIBUTION lists several conjugate prior-likelihood pairs.

For an example, suppose one flips a coin n times, observes Y heads, and wishes to infer θ, the probability that the coin shows heads with each flip. The likelihood function is the binomial likelihood

$$p(Y|\theta) = \binom{n}{Y} \theta^Y (1-\theta)^{n-Y}.$$

If one assumes the beta (a, b) prior distribution,

$$p(\theta) = \frac{\theta^{a-1}(1-\theta)^{b-1}}{\beta(a,b)}, \qquad \theta \in (0, 1),$$

which is conjugate to the binomial likelihood, then the posterior distribution

$$
\begin{aligned}
p(\theta|Y) &\propto \binom{n}{Y} \theta^Y (1-\theta)^{n-Y} \frac{\theta^{a-1}(1-\theta)^{b-1}}{\beta(a,b)} \\
&\propto \theta^{Y+a-1}(1-\theta)^{n-Y+b-1}
\end{aligned}
$$

is proportional to the beta $(a + Y, b + n - Y)$ distribution. Conjugate priors eliminate the need to perform complicated integrations because the family of the

posterior distribution is known. One merely needs to examine the unnormalized distribution to determine its parameters.

The parameters of the beta distribution are interpretable as counts of successes and failures. Bayesian updating simply adds the number of successes to a and the number of failures to b. Interpreting parameters as prior observations provides a means of understanding the sensitivity of the posterior distribution to the prior. The beta (a, b) prior adds $a + b$ observations worth of information to the data. A Bayesian analysis requires that one specify a and b, but if there are a large number of successes and failures in the data set relative to a and b, then the choice of prior parameters will have little impact on the posterior distribution. In small samples, the choice of prior parameters can noticeably affect the posterior distribution.

Figure 1 plots the posterior distributions of θ given different numbers of successes and failures and different prior distributions. These distributions can be used to construct point estimates of θ using the posterior mean, median, or mode. Interval estimates of θ (known as credible intervals) may be obtained by locating the $\alpha/2$ and $1 - \alpha/2$ quantiles of the relevant beta distribution or by the method of highest posterior density (HPD). The posterior distribution for θ in Figure 1(a) exhibits desirable qualities, despite its sensitivity to the prior. It is unimodal, constrained to lie within the interval (0, 1), and is skewed to reflect the asymmetry in the number of successes and failures. Prior sensitivity is usually a signal that the data provide only limited information and that frequentist methods will also encounter difficulty. For example, the standard frequentist method for Figure 1(a) centers on the point estimate $\hat{\theta} = .3$ with a standard error of roughly .15. If $\alpha < .05$, then the frequentist approximation produces confidence intervals that include negative values.

For more on the use of posterior distributions in Bayesian inference, consult Gelman, Carlin, Stern, and Rubin (1995) or Carlin and Louis (1998).

—Steven L. Scott

REFERENCES

Carlin, B. P., & Louis, T. A. (1998). *Bayes and empirical Bayes methods for data analysis.* London: Chapman & Hall/CRC.
Gelman, A., Carlin, J. B., Stern, H. S., & Rubin, D. B. (1995). *Bayesian data analysis.* London: Chapman & Hall.

POSTMODERN ETHNOGRAPHY

Postmodern ethnography is an ETHNOGRAPHY that goes beyond its traditional counterpart by expanding its REFLEXIVITY and its commitment to the groups it studies; it questions its truth claims and experiments with new modes of reporting. Postmodern ethnography derives its new goals from POSTMODERNISM. Postmodernism comprises a set of beliefs that span many disciplines, from architecture to literary criticism, from anthropology to sociology. It rejects grand narratives and meta-theories of modernism, with their preconceived and sweeping statements. Postmodernism proposes to "fragment" these narratives and study each fragment on its own. It does so, in sociology, by studying the interactions and details of everyday life and by analyzing each one separately, based on its situation and context.

Reflexivity is a paramount concern of postmodern ethnography, based on the belief that for too long, the role and power of the researcher have been ignored by ethnographers. The researcher chooses what to observe, when to observe it, what is relevant, and what is worth reporting. Whenever quotes from the members of society are used, they are snippets tailored to support the argument put forth by the researcher. Yet, the study ignores these problems and tends to claim neutrality and objectivity, under the guise of letting the "natives" (subjects being studied) speak for themselves. Postmodern ethnography attempts to remedy these problems by reporting about the role and decision making of the researcher. Thus, although the ethnographer still controls the selectivity process, at least the readers are informed on how it is carried out. Furthermore, postmodern ethnography attempts to allow the voices of the "natives" to be heard to a greater degree. Various reporting modes, discussed below, are employed toward this end.

Commitment is another important element of postmodern ethnography. Traditional ethnographers tend to study the weak and the oppressed, yet the information obtained is rarely used to ameliorate the plight of the group studied. Postmodern ethnographers openly pledge political commitment to those studied and promise to share their findings to somehow help those being studied. Thus, the researcher, rather than control the study and exploit the subject for his or her own purpose, becomes a partner with those being studied, in a quest for their betterment.

A third concern of postmodern ethnography focuses on truth claims. Traditional ethnographies tend to be written in the "I was there" style (Geertz, 1988; Van Maanen, 1988). That is, the legitimacy and credibility of the study are achieved through the "eyewitnessing" of the researcher. He (or, seldom, she) narrates the ethnography by summarizing and categorizing the concerns of the subjects. The ethnographer inserts appropriate illustrative quotations from field notes here and there to underscore his or her thesis and create the illusion that the "natives" are speaking for themselves. Postmodern ethnography questions the fact that closer proximity to the respondents makes one closer to the "truth." In fact, it questions the very notion of an absolute truth, holding, instead, that all we can achieve is a relative, temporal perspective that is contextually and historically bound. All we can hope to reach in ethnography is the understanding of a slice of life as we see it and as told to us by the respondents.

The belief in the relativity and bias of ethnography influences postmodern modes of reporting. Rather than relying of the researcher's (*qua* writer) authority, the postmodern ethnographers try to minimize it as much as possible. Some postmodern ethnographies allow many of the subjects to voice their own concerns and keep the author's comments to a minimum

(Krieger, 1983). Others expand the ethnographic data to include movies, television, ballads, folk tales, painting, dreams, and more. Some write AUTOETHNOGRAPHIES, looking at the past through the eyes of the present, by concentrating on the feelings and reactions of the researcher to the interaction. A few are trying out poetry as a form of ethnographic reporting. Plays and performances have become popular modes of reporting postmodern ethnography. In addition, short story format has become popular among postmodern ethnographers. All of these modes are ways to experiment in the attempt to capture a larger audience and to depict the events in a more immediate and compelling way.

A type of postmodern ethnography relies on the teaching of Michael Foucault. According to Foucault (1985), society uses its powers to control its members by creating for them formal sets of knowledge through which they apprehend reality; for example, an atlas is a way to understand and describe the sky, a dental chart provides names and organization for small enamel objects in our mouth, and so on. These ethnographers focus on the ways in which various groups create and control reality for its members.

Some feminists are pursuing postmodern ethnography. They reject traditional ethnographies as male dominated and criticize the work of traditional ethnographers by showing their male-centered concerns and biases (Clough, 1998). They advocate the use of females studying females to eliminate male dominance and allow women to express themselves freely. Also, they reject what they consider the exploitation of male researchers and promote support and cooperation for the women studied.

A final type of postmodern ethnography is VIRTUAL ETHNOGRAPHY. Some researchers are using the Internet to study various subcultures by becoming members of various chat rooms or joining Internet groups. This type of ethnography no longer relies on face-to-face communication but studies subjects whose existence can only be apprehended through the electronic media.

Finally, postmodern researchers address concerns of RELIABILITY and VALIDITY for their alternative ethnographies. Although there is no clear consensus, a very flexible set of principles based on a combination of aesthetic and political beliefs seems to emerge. Postmodern ethnographers pursue a self-admittedly utopian paradigm, based on the understanding that writing is not neutral but political and that it does not merely describe the world but changes it. Postmodern ethnography wishes to describe the world in an engaging way; it desires to ameliorate the plight of the underprivileged groups studied, and all along it wants to remain as faithful as possible to the views of the social reality of the individuals studied.

—Andrea Fontana

REFERENCES

Clough, T. P. (1998). *The end(s) of ethnography: From realism to social criticism.* New York: Peter Lang.

Foucault, M. (1985). *Power/knowledge: Selected interviews and other writings: 1972–1977* (C. Gordon, Ed.). New York: Pantheon.

Geertz, C. (1988). *Works and lives: The anthropologist as author.* Stanford, CA: Stanford University Press.

Krieger, S. (1983). *The mirror's dance: Identity in a women's community.* Philadelphia: Temple University Press.

Markham, A. N. (1998). *Life online: Researching real experience in virtual space.* Walnut Creek, CA: AltaMira.

Van Maanen, J. (1988). *Tales of the field: On writing ethnography.* Chicago: University of Chicago Press.

POSTMODERNISM

Postmodernism is a term used in a variety of intellectual and cultural areas in rather different ways. The use of the same word creates a confusing and misleading impression of unity and coherence in developments across societal, academic, and cultural fields. There are three broad ways of talking about postmodernism: as an orientation in architecture and art, as a way of describing contemporary (Western or possibly global) society, and as a philosophy. This article mainly focuses on postmodernism in the third sense (i.e., as a philosophy or intellectual style within the social sciences), but a brief overview of other ways of using the term is also called for, especially because they are often viewed as linked. Postmodernism is impossible to define; it even runs against its spirit to try to do so. Many people do, however, use the term to refer to a style of thinking/cultural orientation emphasizing fragmentation and instability of meaning: an unpacking of knowledge, rationality, social institutions, and language.

Postmodernism began to be used in the 1970s as a term for a traditionally and locally inspired approach in architecture, in contrast to the ahistoric and superrational functionalism. Postmodernism also involves the mixing of architectural styles. In the arts, postmodernism represents a partial continuation but also a partial break with modernism. Characterized by a rejection of the idea of representation and an emphasis on the challenge and the unfamiliar (e.g., Picasso), modernism in the arts actually has some affinity with postmodern philosophy. Nevertheless, the postmodern idea of "de-differentiation" between different spheres—such as high culture and low (mass) culture—and the break with elite ideas of a specific space and function of art make it possible to point at some overall features of postmodernism as an overall label that seems to work broadly in a diversity of fields:

> the effacement of the boundary between art and everyday life; the collapse of the hierarchical distinction between high and mass/popular culture; a stylistic promiscuity favouring eclecticism and the mixing of codes; parody, pastiche, irony, playfulness and the celebration of the surface "depthlessness" of culture; the decline of the originality/genius of the artistic producer and the assumption that art can only be repetitive. (Featherstone, 1988, p. 203)

To the extent that there is such a trend in the arts—and some skeptics say that postmodernism is a favored idea among certain art critics rather than among larger groups of artists—that is indicative of wider societal developments, it fits into the idea of postmodernism representing a new society or a period in societal development.

Postmodernism started to be used in the social sciences in the late 1970s, drawing on French and, to some extent, Anglo-Saxon philosophers and social scientists (e.g., Derrida, Foucault, Baudrillard, Lyotard, Jameson, Harvey, and Bauman). Some of these rejected the term *postmodernism*; Foucault also resisted the idea of a "postmodern society or a period." In particular, Jameson and Harvey, but also to some extent Lyotard, have been influential in forming ideas about a new period in societal development.

With references to a distinct societal period, we move postmodernism from culture to social science. Many authors then talk about *postmodernity* instead of postmodernism, and we will follow this custom here. There are various opinions about the meaning of this epoch. Some say that postmodernity signals postindustrialism as well as postcapitalism, but others suggest that postmodernity refers to cultural changes *within* capitalism. The periodization

idea typically indicates some notion of sequentiality—postmodernism (postmodernity) comes after modernism (modernity), but what this means is debated: Opinions vary from postmodernism emerging from the 1920s to the time after the Second World War and to the more recent time. An influential author is Jameson (1983), who refers to

> a general feeling that at some point following World War II a new kind of society begun to emerge (variously described as postindustrial society, multinational capitalism, consumer society, media society and so forth). New types of consumption, planned obsolescence; an ever more rapid rhythm of fashion and styling changes; the penetration of advertising, television and the media generally to a hitherto unparalleled degree throughout society; the replacement of the old tension between city and country, center and province, by the suburb and by universal standardization; the growth of the great networks of superhighways and the arrival of automobile culture—these are some of the features which would seem to mark a radical break with that older prewar society. (pp. 124–125)

Postmodernity presupposes modernity, an orientation associated with the Enlightenment project. The most common point of departure in describing modernity—and thus postmodernity—is to focus on rationality seen as guiding principle as well as an attainable objective for the modern project. Rationality is embodied especially in the certainty and precision of science and knowledge, as well as the far-reaching control and manipulation of nature that this knowledge makes possible. Postmodernity then often refers to the idea of a society characterized by widely dispersed cultural orientations that doubt the possibilities and blessings of this rationalizing project, manifested in science, formal organizations (bureaucracies), and social engineering. "Postmodern society" thus goes against the claimed certainty, objectivity, and progress orientation of modernity.

There are different opinions of the relationship between modernity/postmodernity in terms of sequentiality/overlap. Whether the emergence of postmodernity means replacement of modernity or the emergence of a stream existing parallel with and in opposition to it is debated. For many commentators, postmodernity is better seen as a kind of reaction or comment on modernism than a developmental phase coming after and replacing modernism. Arguably, principles and practices of modernity still seem to dominate a great deal of contemporary Western society.

Postmodernity is sometimes linked to postmodernism as a basic way of thinking about the world. It is then argued that societal developments call for sensitizing vocabularies and ideas that can say something interesting about recent developments and contemporary society. Conventional (modernist) social science and its language are viewed as outdated, incapable of representing subtle but pervasive societal developments. But opponents argue that discussions around postmodernity and postmodernism should be kept separated and confusions avoided: Matters of periodization and identification of social trends are empirical issues, whereas postmodernism is based on philosophical ideas and preferences for intellectual style uncoupled from how to describe contemporary society and social changes. One should be clear when addressing postmodernity and when being postmodernist, it is said.

Leaving postmodernity and the relationship between the period and the intellectual style and moving over to the latter, we enter frameworks and ideas in strong opposition to conventional ideas of social theory and methodology. *Postmodernism,* in this sense, strongly overlaps what is referred to as *poststructuralism,* and the two terms are frequently, when it comes to intellectual agenda and commitments, used as synonyms. There is still a tendency that postmodernism—also when separated from the postmodernity/period issues—refers to a societal/cultural context (e.g., Lyotard, 1984), whereas poststructuralism has a more strict interest in philosophy, particularly around language issues. The points of departures of the two "isms" also differ; postmodernism, in the case of Lyotard (1984), departs from changes in the conditions of knowledge production, whereas poststructuralists move away from the ideas of French structuralism (e.g., de Saussure). But increasingly in social science, postmodernism and poststructuralism are viewed as referring to the same agenda, but with *postmodernism* being the more popular term.

Very briefly, postmodernism can be described as "an assault on unity" (Power, 1990). For postmodernists, social science is a humble and subjective enterprise, characterized by tentativeness, fragmentation, and indeterminacy. Actually, many postmodernists would hesitate in labeling their work as social science. The social and the science part becomes downplayed, if not rejected, by those taking postmodernism into its more extreme positions. For postmodernists, the social, as conventionally understood—systems, structures, agents, shared meanings, a dominant social order, and so forth—is replaced by discourse (language with strong constructing effects), images, and simulations in circulation.

The label of *postmodernism* in social science often summarizes the following five assumptions and foci (Alvesson & Deetz, 2000; Smart, 2000):

- *The centrality of discourse—textuality—where the constitutive power of language is emphasized and "natural" objects are viewed as discursively produced.* This means that there are no objects or phenomena outside or independent of language. Instead, language is an active force shaping our worlds. Different discourses thus mean different social realities.

- *Fragmented identities—emphasizing subjectivity as a process and the death of the individual, autonomous, meaning-creating subject.* The discursive production of the individual replaces the conventional "essentialistic" understanding of people. Against the conventional, "modernist" view of the human being as an integrated whole—the origin of intentions, motives, and meaning—postmodernists suggest a decentered, fragmented, and discourse-driven subject. There is, for example, no true meaning or experience associated with being a "woman"—instead, dominating discourses produce different versions of "woman" (e.g., mother, worker, voter, sexual being) with different effects on temporal subjectivities.

- *The critique of the idea of representation, where the indecidabilities of language take precedence over language as a mirror of reality and a means for the transport of meaning.* It is not possible to represent an objective reality out there. Pure descriptions or a separation of documentation and analysis become impossible. We cannot control language, but must struggle with—or simply accept—the locally context-dependent, metaphorical, and constitutive nature of language. Issues around texts and authorship then become crucial in social science (as well as in other fields of cultural work).

- *The loss of foundations and the power of grand narratives, where an emphasis on multiple voices and local politics is favored over theoretical frameworks and large-scale political projects.* Against the ambition to produce valid general truths guiding long-term, broad-scaled social and scientific projects, knowledge and politics are seen as local and governed by short-term, performance-oriented criteria. Sometimes multiple voices and diversity are privileged.

● *The power-knowledge connection, where the impossibilities in separating power from knowledge are assumed and knowledge loses a sense of innocence and neutrality.* Power and knowledge are not the same, but they are intertwined and dependent on each other. Knowledge always has power effects; it produces a particular version of reality and—through being picked up and affecting how people relate to their worlds—shapes it.

Taking these five ideas seriously leads to a drastic reconceptualization of the meaning of social studies. Some people expect and hope that "the postmodern turn," leading to a stress on "the social construction of social reality, fluid as opposite to fixed identities of the self, and the partiality of truth will simply overtake the modernist assumptions of an objective reality" (Lincoln & Guba, 2000, p. 178).

Postmodernist ideas are pushed more or less far and in somewhat different directions. A possible distinction is between skeptical and affirmative postmodernism (Rosenau, 1992). The skeptical version promotes a "negative" agenda, based on the idea of the impossibility of establishing any truth. Representation becomes a matter of imposing an arbitrary meaning on something. Research becomes a matter of deconstruction, the tearing apart of texts by showing the contradictions, repressed meanings, and thus the fragility behind a superficial level of robustness and validity. This approach strongly discourages empirical work, at least as conventionally and positively understood.

Affirmative postmodernism also questions the idea of truth and validity but has a more positive view of social research. Playfulness, irony, humor, eclecticism, and methodological pluralism are celebrated. So is local knowledge (including a preference for situated knowledge and a rejection of the search for abstract, universal truths). This version is not antithetical to empirical work and empirical claims, but issues around description, interpretation, and researcher authority become problematic. This has triggered profound methodological debates in many fields of social and behavioral science, especially in anthropology (Clifford & Marcus, 1986) and feminism (Nicholson, 1990).

Postmodernism can be seen as a key part in a broader trend in philosophy and social science, summarized as the "linguistic turn." This means a radical reconceptualization of language: It is seen *not* as a passive medium for the transport of meaning, a fairly unproblematic part of social life and institutions and carefully mastered by the competent social scientist. Instead, language (discourse) becomes a crucial constituting social force to be targeted by social researchers, who are themselves forced to struggle with basic problems around representation and authorship.

The implications for social research are substantial but, as said, may be taken more or less far and may inspire and rejuvenate rather than finish empirical social science (Alvesson, 2002). Interviews can, for example, be seen not as simple reports of reality or sites for the expression of the meanings and experiences of the interviewees but as local settings in which dominant discourses constitute subjects and their responses. Ethnographies are less viewed as the authoritative reports of other cultures based on carefully carried out fieldwork and more as fictional texts in which the authorship and the constructions of those being studied matter as much or more than the phenomena "out there" claimed to be studied. Rather than capturing meanings, finding patterns, and arriving at firm conclusions, postmodernistically inspired social research shows the indecisiveness of meaning, gives space for multiple voices, and opens up for alternative readings.

—Mats Alvesson

REFERENCES

Alvesson, M. (2002). *Postmodernism and social research.* Buckingham, UK: Open University Press.

Alvesson, M., & Deetz, S. (2000). *Doing critical management research.* London: Sage.

Clifford, J., & Marcus, G. E. (Eds.). (1986). *Writing culture.* Berkeley: University of California Press.

Featherstone, M. (1988). In pursuit of the postmodernism: An introduction. *Theory, Culture & Society, 5,* 195–215.

Jameson, F. (1983). Postmodernism and consumer society. In H. Foster (Ed.), *Postmodern culture.* London: Pluto.

Lincoln, Y., & Guba, E. (2000). Paradigmatic controversies, contradictions, and emerging confluences. In N. Denzin & Y. Lincoln (Eds.), *Handbook of qualitative research* (2nd ed., pp. 163–188). Thousand Oaks, CA: Sage.

Lyotard, J.-F. (1984). *The postmodern condition: A report on knowledge.* Minneapolis: University of Minnesota Press.

Nicholson, L. (Ed.). (1990). *Feminism/postmodernism.* New York: Routledge Kegan Paul.

Power, M. (1990). Modernism, postmodernism and organisation. In J. Hassard & D. Pym (Eds.), *The theory and philosophy of organisations.* London: Routledge Kegan Paul.

Rosenau, P. M. (1992). *Post-modernism and the social sciences: Insights, inroads and intrusions.* Princeton, NJ: Princeton University Press.

Smart, B. (2000). Postmodern social theory. In B. Turner (Ed.), *The Blackwell companion to social theory* (pp. 447–480). Oxford, UK: Blackwell.

POSTSTRUCTURALISM

The post–World War II French intellectual climate was characterized not only by existentialism and PHENOMENOLOGY, Marxism and psychoanalysis, but also by the structuralist writings of de Saussure. STRUCTURALISM may be distinguished from other traditions through its contention that knowledge cannot be grounded in individuals or their historically given situations. Structuralism also rejects empiricism for its failure to distinguish between the appearance of a phenomenon and its underlying "reality." It is a "science of relationships," with the emphasis of holistic structuralism being on the interconnections or interdependencies between different social relations within society.

What has become known as poststructuralism rejects the universalist aspirations of structuralism in, for example, the work of Lévi-Strauss. However, as with many such terms, poststructuralism can work to alleviate researchers of the need for engagement, as much as to define a distinct tradition of social thought.

Under this school of thought, a diversity of thinkers has been included, with the German philosopher Friedrich Nietzsche providing one clear influence. Nietzsche espoused the doctrine of perspectivism: That is, there is no transcendental vantage point from which one may view truth, and the external world is interpreted according to different beliefs and ideas whose VALIDITY is equal to one another.

The poststructuralist movement—among whom have been included Michel Foucault, Jacques Derrida, Jacques Lacan, Jean-François Lyotard, Gilles Deleuze, Hélèle Cixious, Luce Irigaray, and Julia Kristeva—was to subject received wisdom to critical scrutiny under the banners of anti-humanism and anti-essentialism, together with an absence of a belief in reason unfolding in history. A resulting critique of the unity of the subject has provoked a strong critical reaction. To understand this and its implications for social research, take the

works of two thinkers who have themselves engaged in debate: Jacques Derrida and Michel Foucault.

Derrida's DECONSTRUCTIONIST project is driven by the desire to expose the "dream" of Western philosophy to find the transparent subject. For de Saussure, signs were divided into two parts: the signifier (the sound) and the signified (the idea or concepts to which the sound refers). The meaning of terms was then argued to be fixed through language as a self-referential system. In contrast, Derrida argues that when we read a sign, its meaning is not immediately clear to us. Not only do signs refer to what is absent, so too is meaning. Meaning is then left to flow along a chain of signifiers, with the result that it can never be fixed or readily apparent. An inability to find a fixed point is based on the idea of *différance*: That is, meaning will always elude us because of the necessity of continual clarification and definition. More language is thus required for this purpose, but language can never be the final arbiter. As a result, signs can only be studied in terms of other signs whose meanings continually evade us. This leaves Derrida constantly on the lookout for those who desire an unmediated truth by smuggling into their formulations a "transcendental signified."

With this critique in mind, methodology can be opened up to alternative readings. Science may, for example, be read as a series of attempts at obfuscation, as opposed to liberation through illumination. Values and interests can be exposed where they are assumed not to exist to demonstrate that perspectivism, not universality, lies deep within its assumptions. RHETORIC buries its presuppositions away from the gaze of those who have not served its lengthy apprenticeships, and we cannot allude to language to solve this problem for the principle of "undecidability" will always obtain. The idea of questioning the metaphysics of presence affects social research practice in terms of, for example, its use of "consciousness" and "intentionality" as explanatory frameworks in the study of human relations. Instead, the study rests on how the social world is fabricated through what is known as "intertextuality." TEXTS are seen as social practices, and observations become acts of writing, not the reportings of an independent reality.

To take research beyond ideas of intentionality without lapsing into structuralism takes us into the realms of what has been characterized as Foucault's "interpretive analytics." The basis on which representations are formed and the potential for a transparent relationship between language and reality are abandoned for the study of discourses in which a politics of truth combines to constitute subject and object. To analyze discourses in this manner means insisting on the idea that the social world cannot be divided into two realms: the material and the mental. Discourses provide the limits to what may be experienced as well as the attribution of meanings to those experiences. Expressed in these terms, a social researcher would examine not only the forms of appropriation of discourses but also their limits of appropriation (the latter being a neglected feature of research influenced by Foucault).

As part of this overall strategy that saw Foucault's work move from archaeology to genealogy, the notion of "eventalization" sees the singularity of an event not in terms of some historical constant or anthropological invariant. Instead, the use of Foucault's methods provides for what is argued to be a subversive strategy that breaches the self-evident to demonstrate how "things" might have been otherwise. A series of possibilities, without any allusion to a unified subject or reason waiting to be discovered in history, may then emerge. The social researcher is thereby required to "rediscover" possibility rather than engage in transcendent critique: "the connections, encounters, supports, blockages, plays of forces, strategies and so on which at a given moment establish what subsequently counts as being self-evident, universal and necessary. In this sense one is indeed effecting a sort of multiplication or pluralization of causes" (Foucault, 1991, p. 76).

There is no doubt that poststructuralism provides a rich vein of thought that provides new insights into social life. At the same time, some of this work is not always amenable to assisting social researchers in their endeavors. That is not to say it is not of importance beyond such a relationship, simply that one must always seek in thought the possibilities for illumination, clarification, and engagement.

—Tim May

REFERENCES

Foucault, M. (1991). Questions of method. In G. Burchell, C. Gordon, & P. Miller (Eds.), *The Foucault effect: Studies in governmentality* (pp. 73–86). London: Harvester Wheatsheaf.

Game, A. (1991). *Undoing the social: Towards a deconstructive sociology.* Buckingham, UK: Open University Press.

Kendall, G., & Wickham, G. (1999). *Using Foucault's methods.* London: Sage.

POWER OF A TEST

In the SIGNIFICANCE TESTING of a HYPOTHESIS, there are two kinds of mistakes an analyst may make: TYPE I ERROR and TYPE II ERROR. One minus the Type II error of a statistical test defines the power of the same test. The power of a test is related to the true POPULATION PARAMETER, the population VARIANCE of the distribution related to the test, the SAMPLE size, and the LEVEL OF SIGNIFICANCE for the test.

—Tim Futing Liao

POWER TRANSFORMATIONS. *See* POLYNOMIAL EQUATION

PRAGMATISM

Pragmatism, in the technical rather than everyday sense of the word, refers to a philosophical movement that emerged in the United States in the second half of the 19th century and continued to have an influence throughout the 20th century. The core idea of pragmatism is that the meaning of any concept is determined by its practical implications; and that the truth of any judgment is determined in and through practical activity, whether in the context of science or in life more generally.

These central ideas are usually connected with a few others. One is rejection of the assumption, shared by many RATIONALISTS and EMPIRICISTS, that we can find some indubitable foundation on which knowledge can be built. Thus, for Charles S. Peirce, generally recognized to be the founder of pragmatism, inquiry always starts from a problem that emerges out of previous experience, and always involves taking much of that experience for granted: Only what is open to *reasonable* doubt is questioned, not all that is open to *possible* doubt. Similarly, the knowledge produced by inquiry is always fallible; it cannot be known to be valid with absolute certainty. However, in the long run, inquiry is self-corrective: It is geared toward the discovery and rectification of errors.

Another central pragmatist idea is that all cognition must be viewed as part of the ongoing transaction between individual organisms and their environments. This is at odds with the influential ancient Greek view that true knowledge is produced by spectators detached from everyday human life. Thus, for William James, another influential pragmatist philosopher, the function of cognition is not to copy reality but to satisfy the individual organism's needs and interests, enabling it to achieve a flourishing relationship with its environment. For him, truth consists of what it proves generally expedient to believe. Indeed, for pragmatists, even philosophy and the sciences have a pragmatic origin and function. Thus, John Dewey viewed the procedures of scientific inquiry as central to the democratic ideal and as the proper basis for societal development.

There is diversity as well as commonality within the pragmatist tradition. Where some have taken science as the model for rational thinking, others have adopted a more catholic approach. Where some have assumed a form of REALISM, others have insisted that we only ever have access to how things appear in experience, not to some reality beyond it.

During the 20th century, pragmatist ideas were developed by a number of influential philosophers, notably C. I. Lewis, W. van O. Quine, H. Putnam, R. Rorty, and S. Haack. Rorty's work, in particular, has generated much controversy, not least about whether it represents a genuine form of pragmatism or a break with the older tradition.

Pragmatism has had considerable influence on thinking about social research methodology, notably but not exclusively through the Chicago school of sociology. A valuable, early text that draws heavily on pragmatism is Kaplan's (1964) *The Conduct of Inquiry.*

—Martyn Hammersley

REFERENCES

Haack, S. (1993). *Evidence and inquiry: Toward a reconstruction of epistemology.* Oxford, UK: Blackwell.
Kaplan, A. (1964). *The conduct of inquiry.* New York: Chandler.
Mounce, H. O. (1997). *The two pragmatisms: From Peirce to Rorty.* London: Routledge and Kegan Paul.

PRECODING

A *code* is a number (or letter or word) that will be recorded on a data file as the answer to a particular

---

> Which of the following best describes your employment situation? (Please circle *one* answer):
>
> 1. Employed
> 2. Self-employed
> 3. In full-time education/training
> 4. Unemployed
> 5. Retired

Figure 1   A Precoded Variable on Employment Status

CLOSED-ENDED QUESTION from a particular respondent or informant in a quantitative study. An efficient study will code most of its information at the point of collection—precoding. The interviewer (or the informant, in a self-completion questionnaire) will circle a number corresponding to his or her response, and this number will be typed into the data file without further thought or coding. For example, Figure 1 shows a precoded "employment status" variable.

For precoding to be an effective procedure, two things are necessary:

• The categories must be unambiguous, with no overlap between them. The coding scheme in Figure 1 fails in this respect: It is possible to be both employed and in full-time education (on an army scholarship to university, for example) or full-time training (as an apprentice, for example).

• The categories must be exhaustive, covering the whole field. Again, Figure 1 fails in this respect: There is no category covering full-time homemakers. Some may put themselves down as "unemployed"; others may consider themselves "retired." Those who consider homemaking and the care of children a job in its own right are constrained to these two answers, however, or to a misleading use of one of the "employed" categories. In other words, the survey question structures the social world in a way that may not be acceptable to some of the respondents—a not uncommon fault in precoded survey questions.

One way around this problem is to provide an "Other" category in which respondents write in their status if it is not reflected in any of the precoded

Please circle the number that best describes your *highest* educational qualification.

GCE or equivalent	1
"O" level or equivalent	2
AS level or equivalent	3
A + level or equivalent	4
Higher education qualification lower than an honors degree	5
Honors degree or equivalent	6
Qualification higher than an honors degree	7

Figure 2   A Question on Educational Level

categories. The responses will then have to be "office coded" after the event—assigned to one of the existing categories, a new category, or a catchall "other" category. This takes additional time and effort, however, and its use is to be avoided whenever possible.

Mostly, we go for single-coded variables—sets of codes from which the respondent is required to select one and only one (see Figure 2). It is possible to handle multicoded variables—variables that carry more than one code (e.g., "Circle all the choices that apply to you from the following list"), but these need special thought at the data entry stage if they are to be interpretable in the analysis.

—Roger Sapsford

See also INTERVIEW SCHEDULE, QUESTIONNAIRE

PREDETERMINED VARIABLE

The exogenous variables and lagged ENDOGENOUS VARIABLES included in a SIMULTANEOUS EQUATION MODEL are typically called *predetermined variables*. The classification of variables is crucial for model IDENTIFICATION because there are endogenous variables among the independent (or explanatory) variables in a system of SIMULTANEOUS EQUATIONS.

To introduce the idea of predetermined variables, one must distinguish between endogenous variables and exogenous variables. *Endogenous variables* (or jointly determined variables) have outcomes values determined within the model. In other words, endogenous variables have values that are determined

through joint interaction with other variables within the model. One is interested in the behavior of endogenous variables because they are explained by the rest of the model. The term *endogeneity* (or *simultaneity*) reflects the simultaneous character and feedback mechanism of the model that determines these variables.

Exogenous variables differ from endogenous variables in that they contribute to provide explanations for the behavior of endogenous variables. These variables affect the outcome values of endogenous variables, but their own values are determined completely outside the model. In this sense, exogenous variables are CAUSAL, characterizing the model in which endogenous variables are determined, but values of exogenous variables are not RECIPROCALLY affected. In other words, no feedback interaction or simultaneity between exogenous variables is assumed.

Consider a very simple macroeconomic model that is specified as a simultaneous equation model with three equations:

$$C_t = \alpha_0 + \alpha_1 Y_t + \alpha_2 Y_{t-1} + \alpha_3 R_t + \varepsilon_{Ct}, \quad (1a)$$

$$I_t = \beta_0 + \beta_1 R_t + \varepsilon_{It}, \quad (1b)$$

$$Y_t = C_t + I_t + G_t. \quad (1c)$$

In this system of equations, contemporaneous consumption (C_t), investment (I_t), and income (Y_t) are endogenous because their values are explained by other variables and determined within the system. There is a feedback mechanism between the endogenous variables because C_t is conditional on Y_t in the behavioral equation (1a), and Y_t depends on C_t through the identity equation (1c) at the same time. Interest rates (R_t) and government spending (G_t) are exogenous variables because they explain the behavior of endogenous variables, but their values are determined by factors outside the system. We visualize no feedback mechanism between these two exogenous variables.

There is one LAGGED endogenous variable, Y_{t-1}, included in this simple macroeconomic model. The value of this lagged endogenous variable is determined by its past value. For the current value of income (Y_t), its past value (Y_{t-1}) is observed and predetermined. Thus, past endogenous variables may be placed in the same category as the exogenous variables. In other words, lagged endogenous variables and exogenous variables are two subsets of predetermined variables. More information on the classification of variables with respect to identifying and estimating a system of equations may be found in Kmenta (1986); Judge,

Griffiths, Hill, Lütkepohl, and Lee (1985); and Wooldridge (2003).

—Cheng-Lung Wang

REFERENCES

Judge, G. G., Griffiths, W. E., Hill, R. C., Lütkepohl, H., & Lee, T.-C. (1985). *The theory and practice of econometrics* (2nd ed.). New York: John Wiley.

Kmenta, J. (1986). *Elements of econometrics* (2nd ed.). New York: Macmillan.

Wooldridge, J. M. (2003). *Introductory econometrics: A modern approach* (2nd ed.). Cincinnati, OH: South-Western College Publishing.

PREDICTION

Prediction involves inference from known to unknown events, whether in the past, present, or future. In the natural sciences, theories often predict the existence of entities that are subsequently discovered. In the social sciences, prediction usually refers to statements about future outcomes. To be more than a lucky guess, a scientific prediction requires supporting empirical evidence and must be grounded in a body of theory. Thus, Randall Collins (1995) justifies his successful prediction of the collapse of communism by its grounding in geopolitical theory.

FORECASTING, generally used by economists in preference to *prediction,* is sometimes synonymous with it. Forecasting is also used in a more restricted sense to refer to predictions that hold true only for a concrete instance, in a given place and time frame: forecasting automobile sales in the United States over the next 5 years, for example. A forecast in this narrower sense is not generalizable beyond the specific case.

One form of prediction is EXTRAPOLATION, whereby past trends are projected into the future. To yield successful predictions, extrapolation assumes that the causes and social processes underlying the trends remain constant. Extrapolation is typically accurate only in the short run. Not all extrapolations, however, are intended to be predictive. They may be offered as possible scenarios, warning us to change our behavior lest the undesired outcome occur. Thus, extrapolations about the effects of global warming may be given not as predictions but as exhortations to reduce consumption of fossil fuels.

Retrodiction involves predicting backwards from outcomes to their causes, showing why an already known outcome was to be expected. Although retrodiction can be no more than the spurious wisdom of hindsight, there are good reasons why retrodiction can be valid even though prediction was difficult or impossible. Timur Kuran (1995) argues that a problem in predicting revolutions is *preference falsification,* that is, people misrepresenting their preferences because of perceived social pressures. The citizens of an oppressive regime may be reluctant to express any dissatisfaction to a social researcher. After the revolution has occurred, evidence of preexisting discontent becomes abundant. To improve our prediction of revolutions, we might therefore need to analyze sources of information other than standard social surveys (e.g., diaries and memoirs, confidential letters, and secret archives).

A key problem for social prediction is that predictions frequently interact with the phenomena they predict. In a *self-fulfilling prophecy,* the prediction comes true because it has been enunciated; conversely, a *self-negating prophecy*'s enunciation ensures that it will be false. A practical solution is to insulate the prediction from the audiences that might react to it. In some cases, proclaiming self-fulfilling or self-negating prophecies may be a deliberate attempt to influence events so as to avert or mitigate adverse outcomes or increase the probability of desired outcomes.

Predicting future states of a system from its initial state requires that minor variations in initial states have a limited impact on future states. This does not hold true in *chaotic* systems (CHAOS THEORY), as in meteorology, in which undetectable differences in initial conditions produce widely divergent outcomes.

A major difficulty is the necessary unpredictability of future knowledge (Popper, 1957). We cannot rationally claim to have full predictive knowledge of that which has not yet been conceptualized or discovered.

—Alan Aldridge

REFERENCES

Collins, R. (1995). Prediction in macrosociology: The case of the Soviet collapse. *American Journal of Sociology, 100*(6), 1552–1593.

Kuran, T. (1995). The inevitability of future revolutionary surprises. *American Journal of Sociology, 100*(6), 1528–1551.

Popper, K. R. (1957). *The poverty of historicism.* Boston: Beacon.

PREDICTION EQUATION

Any REGRESSION-like analysis provides two kinds of information. First, it tells us the estimated effect of one or more INDEPENDENT VARIABLES on a DEPENDENT VARIABLE. Estimates of COEFFICIENTS and STANDARD ERRORS suggest the relative strengths of effects and their estimation precision. Second, a regression-like analysis can provide an ability to predict values of a dependent variable. The *prediction equation* relates to this second kind of information. More specifically, the prediction equation is an equation that links the independent variables to predicted values of the dependent variable. In a LINEAR REGRESSION analysis, the prediction equation is formed by taking only the systematic components of the model, $\hat{Y} = \hat{\beta}_0 + \hat{\beta}_1 X_1 + \cdots + \hat{\beta}_k X_k$, and using these for calculating predictions of the dependent variable. In other forms of analysis, such as LOGIT, PROBIT, and other latent index models, the prediction equation is linked in NONLINEAR fashion to a PROBABILITY function that enables prediction.

Generally, the average prediction error within a sample is a useful criterion for assessing model fit in a population. An effective prediction equation should produce predictions that, on average, lie close to the actual values of the sampled dependent variable. We can then test the significance of average prediction error in attempting to relate the model fit in the sample to a population.

A prediction equation can also be used as a FORECASTING tool for predicting *individual values* of a dependent variable that lie either within or outside of the sample. For example, suppose we have a linear regression for which we want to predict the value of $\hat{y}_i^0$, a single observation that lies either within or outside of the sample. Then we would use the prediction equation $\hat{y}_i^0 = \hat{\beta}_0 + \hat{\beta}_1 x_{1i}^0 + \cdots + \hat{\beta}_k x_{ki}^0$. An effective prediction equation should be able to forecast accurately single observations that lie either inside or outside the sample. So forecasting individual observations is an alternative approach to assessing the quality of a model.

AVERAGE PREDICTION ERROR

In using a prediction equation for assessing *average* prediction error for a linear regression, there are two accepted standards: R^2 and the STANDARD ERROR of

estimate (*SEE*, sometimes written as $\hat{\sigma}_e$). The R^2 statistic is calculated as

$$R^2 = 1 - \frac{\sum_{i=1}^{n} (Y_i - \hat{Y}_i)^2}{\sum_{i=1}^{n} (Y_i - \bar{Y})^2}.$$

Note that this calculation takes the sum of the squared prediction errors (calculated using the prediction equation) and then standardizes these prediction errors relative to a naive or worst-case prediction. Subtracting this quantity from 1 yields a measure of fit ranging from 0 to 1. At the 0 end of the scale, we can conclude that the model has no predictive ability. At the 1 end of the scale, we can conclude that the model predicts every observation without error. Values between 0 and 1 provide a scaled assessment of average predictive ability.

A disadvantage of R^2 for assessing average model prediction error is that it provides no indication of how much prediction error can be expected in the metric of the analysis. The R^2 statistic is scaled from 0 to 1, but for intermediate values, it is unclear how much actual prediction error will occur. For this reason, some analysts prefer using the STANDARD ERROR OF ESTIMATE (*SEE*). This is calculated as

$$SEE = \sqrt{\frac{\sum_{i=1}^{n} (Y_i - \hat{Y}_i)^2}{N - k}}.$$

Note that the *SEE* calculation takes the square root of the variance in prediction error, again calculated using the prediction equation. The result is an average prediction error scaled in the metric of the dependent variable. The value contained in the *SEE* statistic tells the analyst how much error can be expected, on average, in units of the dependent variable when using the prediction equation. This provides a more intuitive description of a model's predictive ability.

In relating average prediction error from the sample to the population using either R^2 or *SEE*, the analyst usually calculates an F statistic for the null hypothesis that the model has no predictive ability. In terms of R^2, the null hypothesis is that the R^2 statistic equals zero. In terms of *SEE*, the null hypothesis is that the average prediction error is just the average deviation of observations about the mean. The two hypotheses are equivalent and enable the analyst to infer how much prediction error could be expected, on average, in repeated sampling from the same population.

INDIVIDUAL PREDICTION

Average prediction error, as gauged by R^2 and *SEE*, provide a measure of overall model fit. However, if the analyst is interested in using the prediction equation to forecast particular values of the dependent variable, then these statistics provide a poor assessment of how much prediction error can be expected. One reason is that observations nearer the ends of the distribution of the independent variables become increasingly atypical. Toward the ends of the distribution of X, we have less data and therefore more uncertainty about individual predictions. Individual prediction error gets larger the further an observation on X gets from the typical value of X. For example, suppose we are interested in predicting an individual observation of the dependent variable using the prediction equation $\hat{y}_i^0 = \hat{\beta}_0 + \hat{\beta}_1 x_i^0$. The prediction error for a single observation using this equation would be

$$SE[y_i^0 - \hat{y}_i^0] = SEE\sqrt{1 + \frac{1}{n} + \frac{(x_i^0 - \bar{X})^2}{\sum_{i=1}^{n}(X_i - \bar{X})^2}}.$$

Note that this statistic weights the average prediction error (*SEE* discussed above) by a function capturing the distance of the predicted value from the center of the distribution. A multivariate version of this statistic requires the use of linear algebra and is given in Greene (2003).

If we are interested in individual predictions for multiple observations, then the average error in individual predictions is used as a measure of forecasting accuracy. This is called the ROOT MEAN SQUARED error (RMSE) or sometimes Theil's U statistic. This statistic is given as

$$RMSE = \sqrt{\frac{1}{m}\sum_{i=1}^{m}\left(y_i^0 - \hat{y}_i^0\right)^2},$$

where m is the number of individual predictions. Note that this is just the square root of the average sum of squared prediction errors. Smaller values of RMSE imply stronger forecasting capability when using a prediction equation.

—B. Dan Wood and Sung Ho Park

REFERENCES

Greene, W. H. (2003). *Econometric analysis* (5th ed.). Mahwah, NJ: Prentice Hall.

King, G. (1990). Stochastic variation: A comment on Lewis-Beck and Skalaban's "The *R*-squared." *Political Analysis, 2,* 185–200.

Lewis-Beck, M. S., & Skalaban, A. (1990). The *R*-squared: Some straight talk. *Political Analysis, 2,* 153–171.

PREDICTOR VARIABLE

In every RESEARCH DESIGN, there is a set of INDEPENDENT VARIABLES that can be thought of as antecedent conditions that affect a DEPENDENT VARIABLE. These variables are either manipulated by the researcher (as in the case of EXPERIMENTS) or simply observed by the researcher (as in the case of SECONDARY ANALYSIS OF SURVEY DATA). If an antecedent condition is simply observed by the researcher (i.e., is not manipulated by them), it is often referred to as a predictor variable.

The distinction between predictor and independent variables is a function of the research design. In experimental studies, there can be a meaningful distinction between the two because the independent variable is presumed to be under the control of the researcher (i.e., it is the manipulation or treatment in the experiment), whereas the predictor variable is seen simply as an antecedent condition (e.g., the gender of a subject) that predicts values on the dependent variable. In nonexperimental studies (e.g., CORRELATIONAL studies), however, the distinction is moot because the researcher manipulates none of the variables in the MODEL.

Consider the following two research designs in which the researcher is interested in assessing the effects of campaign advertisements on vote choice. In the first case, the researcher gathers data for a RANDOM SAMPLE of voters on each of the following variables: (a) whether the respondent was likely to vote for Candidate Smith, (b) gender, (c) age, (d) party identification, and (e) exposure to campaign advertisements for Candidate Smith. Using these data, the researcher then estimates the following REGRESSION equation:

$$\text{Vote for Smith} = \beta_0 + \beta_1\,\text{Gender} + \beta_2\,\text{Age} + \beta_3\,\text{PID} + \beta_4\,\text{Ads} + \varepsilon. \quad (1)$$

In the second case, the researcher gathers data for a random sample of voters on only (a) gender, (b) age, and (c) party identification. Voters are then randomly assigned to either a control or an experimental group. Voters in the experimental group are shown Candidate Smith's campaign advertisements, and those in the control group view only product advertisements. After the treatment (viewing campaign advertisements or not) is administered, respondents in both groups are asked whether they would likely vote for Candidate Smith. On the basis of the results, the researcher estimates the regression equation given in (1).

Conventionally, *all* of the variables on the right-hand side of the regression equation in the first design are referred to as independent variables (or REGRESSORS). In the second design, however, we can distinguish between independent variables and predictor variables. The independent variable in this case is whether the respondent saw the candidate's advertisements. It is the key EXPLANATORY VARIABLE of interest and the one that is manipulated by the researcher. The predictor variables in the model, then, are (a) age, (b) gender, and (c) party identification. Each subject in the study has some value on these variables prior to the researcher applying the treatment (thus they are correctly seen as antecedent conditions), and the values are thought to predict a respondent's score on the dependent variable (thus the nomenclature "predictor" variable).

Because the distinction between predictor variables and independent variables is of no consequence in the statistical analysis of the data (note that in the above example, the statistical technique employed did not vary from the first design to the second), it is often ignored in practice. However, the distinction is important for the design of a study (i.e., what variable is the treatment in experimental designs) and in the interpretation and explanation of the results.

—Charles H. Ellis

REFERENCES

Frankfort-Nachmias, C., & Nachmias, D. (1996). *Research methods in the social sciences* (5th ed.). New York: St. Martin's.

Howell, D. C. (1999). *Fundamental statistics for the behavioral sciences* (4th ed.). Belmont, CA: Duxbury.

Jaeger, R. M. (1993). *Statistics: A spectator sport* (2nd ed.). Newbury Park, CA: Sage.

PRETEST

A field pretest is a dress rehearsal for a SURVEY. These PILOT tests are extremely useful tools, allowing researchers to identify potential problems with survey items and/or data collection PROTOCOLS prior to fielding a study. Although all surveys should undergo a trial run before they are launched, pretests are particularly valuable in preparation for large and/or complex surveys. They are imperative in any study that involves COMPUTER-ASSISTED DATA COLLECTION. Potentially costly mistakes can be identified and remedied during this phase of survey development.

Basically, a pretest involves collecting data from a relatively small number of RESPONDENTS using the data collection procedures specified for the study. Ideally, the pretest sample is selected from the study's SAMPLING FRAME. When this is not practical or feasible, respondents are often selected on the basis of convenience and availability. However, the more closely the pretest SAMPLE mirrors the survey sample in terms of the characteristics being studied, the better. For studies calling for INTERVIEWER administration, it is advisable to have at least three interviewers involved in pretesting the questionnaire.

Pretest responses are tabulated and the MARGINAL distribution of responses is examined for indications of potential problems—for example, little VARIATION in response (either for the VARIABLE as a whole or for subgroups of interest) or incorrect skip patterns. Items for which a large percentage of respondents either report that they do not know the answer to the question or refuse to respond should probably be revised and retested.

Although it is possible to pretest an instrument in all modes of administration—interviewer administered (by telephone and in person) and self-administered (by mail or electronically)—interviewer-mediated studies offer researchers opportunities to study the interaction between interviewer and respondent and identify questions that are not performing well. Once interviewers are briefed about the research goals of both the project in general and specific questions, they contact members of a small practice sample under conditions that mimic those of the larger study to follow.

The interviews are tape-recorded with the respondents' express permission. Later, specially trained CODING personnel listen to the tapes and "behavior CODE" the interaction between interviewer and respondent. For each question asked, both sides of the interaction are coded. On the interviewer side, it is noted whether the question was read exactly as worded, whether items that were not applicable to a particular respondent were navigated correctly, and whether PROBES or clarifications were offered. On the respondent side, tallies are kept of how often respondents interrupted interviewers before the entire question was read or requested clarifications and definitions and whether the answers provided fit the response alternatives offered. BEHAVIOR CODING allows the identification of items that interviewers find difficult to administer in a standardized way, as well as questions or terminology that are not consistently understood by respondents. If any problems are found, the instrument or protocols can be revised prior to fielding the survey.

—Patricia M. Gallagher

REFERENCES

Fowler, F. J., Jr. (1995). *Improving survey questions.* Thousand Oaks, CA: Sage.

Oksenberg, L., Cannell, C., & Kalton, G. (1991). New strategies for pretesting survey questions. *Journal of Official Statistics,* 7(3), 349–365.

PRETEST SENSITIZATION

When participants in an EXPERIMENT are pretested, there is a risk that they will be alerted or sensitive to the variable that the pretest is measuring and that, as a result, their posttest scores will be affected. In other words, experimental subjects who are affected by pretest sensitization become sensitized to what the experiment is about, and this affects their behavior. The SOLOMON FOUR-GROUP DESIGN is sometimes used to deal with this problem.

—Alan Bryman

PRIMING

An individual's experiences in the environment temporarily activate concepts that are mentally represented. The activation of these concepts, which can include traits, schemata, attitudes, stereotypes, goals, moods, emotions, and behaviors, heightens their accessibility. These concepts are said to be *primed*; that is, they become more likely to influence one's subsequent thoughts, feelings, judgments, and behaviors. Priming also refers to an experimental technique that is used to simulate the activation of concepts that usually occurs through real-world experiences.

The term *priming* was first used by Karl Lashley (1951) to refer to the temporary internal activation of response tendencies. The process of priming begins when a mentally represented concept becomes activated through one's experiences in the environment. The level of activation does not immediately return to its baseline level; rather, it dissipates over time. This lingering activation can then affect subsequent responses. Thus, recently used concepts can be activated more quickly and easily than other concepts due to their heightened accessibility. Through this mechanism, priming creates a temporary state of internal readiness. Importantly, priming is a passive, cognitive process that does not require motivation or intent on the part of the perceiver.

Several types of priming techniques are commonly used in psychology research (see Bargh & Chartrand, 2000). Perhaps the simplest is *conceptual priming.* In this technique, the researcher activates one concept unobtrusively in a first task. The activated concept then automatically affects individuals' responses in a second, later task outside of their awareness or intent. A seminal experiment in social psychology using conceptual priming showed that activated concepts could affect future social judgments (Higgins, Rholes, & Jones, 1977). Participants were primed in a first task with positive or negative traits (e.g., reckless, adventurous). Those primed with positive traits formed more favorable impressions of a target person engaging in ambiguous behaviors than those primed with negative traits. There are two types of conceptual priming. In *supraliminal priming,* the individual is consciously aware of the priming stimuli but not aware of the priming stimuli's influence on his or her later responses. In *subliminal priming,* the individual is aware of neither the priming stimuli nor the influence those stimuli have on subsequent responses.

A second priming technique is *carryover priming.* In this type of priming, the researcher first has participants deliberately and consciously make use of the concept to be primed. This can include having participants think or write about a goal, mind-set, memory, person, or other topic that activates the to-be-primed construct. The individual then engages in a second, unrelated task. The construct that was primed in the first task influences the person's responses in the second task. Critically, he or she is not aware of this influence. Oftentimes, carryover priming is used when the key concept is too abstract or detailed to be conceptually primed.

A third priming technique is *sequential priming*. This method tests the associations between various mental representations. The researcher presents a prime stimulus, followed by a target stimulus. The participant must respond in some way to the target (e.g., pronouncing it, determining whether it is a word, evaluating it). To the extent that the prime facilitates the response to the target, there is an associative link in memory between the two constructs.

All priming research should end with a check for suspicion and awareness of the influence of the prime.

—Tanya L. Chartrand and Valerie E. Jefferis

REFERENCES

Bargh, J. A., & Chartrand, T. L. (2000). Mind in the middle: A practical guide to priming and automaticity research. In H. T. Reis & C. M. Judd (Eds.), *Handbook of research methods in social and personality psychology* (pp. 253–285). New York: Cambridge University Press.

Higgins, E. T., Rholes, W. S., & Jones, C. R. (1977). Category accessibility and impression formation. *Journal of Experimental Social Psychology, 13,* 141–154.

Lashley, K. S. (1951). The problem of serial order in behavior. In L. A. Jeffress (Ed.), *Cerebral mechanisms in behavior: The Hixon symposium* (pp. 112–136). New York: John Wiley.

PRINCIPAL COMPONENTS ANALYSIS

Principal components analysis (PCA) is the workhorse of exploratory multivariate data analysis, especially in those cases when a researcher wants to gain an insight into and an overview of the relationships between a set of variables and evaluate individuals with respect to those variables. The basic technique is designed for continuous variables, but variants have been developed that cater for variables of categorical and ordinal MEASUREMENT LEVELS, as well as for sets of variables with mixtures of different types of measurement levels. In addition, the technique is used in conjunction with other techniques, such as REGRESSION ANALYSIS. In this entry, we will concentrate on standard PCA, but overviews of PCA at work in different contexts can, for instance, be found in the books by Joliffe (1986) and Jackson (1991), and an exposé of PCA for variables with different measurement levels is contained in Meulman and Heiser (2000).

THEORY

Suppose that we have the scores of I individuals on J variables and that the relationships between the variables are such that no variable can be perfectly predicted by all the remaining variables. Then these variables form the axes of a J-dimensional space, and the scores of the individuals on these J variables can be portrayed in this J-dimensional space. However, looking at a high-dimensional space is not easy; moreover, most of the variability of the high-dimensional arrangement of the individuals can often be displayed in a low-dimensional space without much loss in variability. As an example, we see in Figure 1 that the two-dimensional ellipse A of scores of Sample A can be reasonably well represented in one dimension by the first principal component, and one only needs to interpret the variability along this single dimension. However, for the scores of Sample B, the one-dimensional representation is much worse (i.e., the variance accounted for by the first principal component is much lower in Case B than in Case A, and interpreting a single dimension might not suffice in Case B).

The coordinate axes of the low-dimensional dimensional space are commonly called *components*. If the components are such that they successively account for most of the variability in the data, they are called *principal* components. The coordinates of the individuals on the components are called *component scores*. To interpret components, the coordinates for the variables

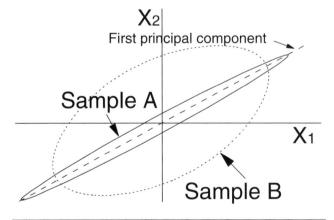

Figure 1   Two Samples, A and B, With Scores on Variables X_1 and X_2

NOTE: The ellipses indicate the approximate contour of the sample points. The first principal component is a good one-dimensional approximation to the scores of Sample A but much less so to the scores of Sample B.

on these components need to be derived as well, and the common approach to do this is via EIGENVALUE-EIGENVECTOR techniques. If both the variables and the components are standardized, the variable coordinates are the correlations between variables and components. By inspecting these correlations, commonly known as *component loadings,* one may assess the extent to which the components measure the same quantities as (groups of) variables. In particular, when a group of variables has high correlations with a component, the component has something in common with all of them, and on the basis of the substantive content of the variables, one may try to ascertain what the common element between the variables may be and hypothesize that the component is measuring this common element.

Unfortunately, the principal components do not always have high correlations with one specific group of variables because they are derived to account successively for the maximum variance of all the variables, not to generate optimal interpretability. This can also be seen in plots of the variables in the space determined by the components (see Figure 2). Such plots may show that there are other directions in this space for which components align with groups of variables and allow for a relatively simpler interpretation. Therefore, principal components are often rotated or transformed in such a way that the rotated components align with groups of variables if they exist. Such transformations do not affect the joint fit of the components to the data because they are restricted to the space of the principal components. When the rotation leads to correlated axes (oblique rotation; see the example), the coefficients reported for the variables are no longer correlations and are often called *pattern coefficients.* When the (rotated) components are uncorrelated, the square of each variable-component correlation is the size of the explained variance of a variable by a component, and the sum over all derived components of such squared correlations for a variable is the squared multiple correlation (often called COMMUNALITY) for predicting that variable by the derived components.

An essential part of any component analysis is the joint graphical portrayal of the relationships between the variables and the scores of the subjects through a BIPLOT. For visual inspection, such plots should be at most three-dimensional, but when more dimensions are present, several plots need to be constructed (e.g., one plot for the first two dimensions and another for the third and fourth dimensions).

EXAMPLE

Suppose, as an extremely simplified example, that we have scores of nine children on an intelligence test consisting of four subtests and that a principal component analysis showed that two components are sufficient for an adequate description of the variability. Figure 2 (a biplot) gives the results of the two-dimensional solution, portraying the subtests A, B, C, and D as vectors and children 1 through 9 as points. Clearly, the subtests form two groups, and inspection of the contents of the subtests shows that A and D tap verbal intelligence and B and C numerical intelligence. The subtests do not align with the principal components, but an oblique transformation puts two axes right through the middle of the groups, and thus they may be hypothesized to represent numerical and verbal intelligence, respectively. The angle between the rotated axes indicates that they are correlated, which is not surprising considering all subtests measure intelligence. Due to their position near the positive side of the numerical intelligence axis, Children 6 and 8 did particularly well on the numeric subtests, whereas Children 3 and 5 scored considerably below average on the verbal subtests. Child 7 scores about average on all subtests, as she is close to the origin (see also the entry on BIPLOTS for rules of interpretation).

—Pieter M. Kroonenberg

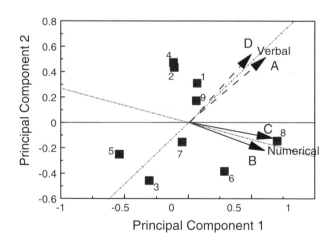

Figure 2   Example of a Biplot of the Four Subtests and Nine Children for the First Two Principal Components

NOTE: Subtests A and D measure numerical ability, and Subtests B and D measure verbal ability. The obliquely rotated components pass through each of the groups of subtests.

REFERENCES

Jackson, J. E. (1991). *A user's guide to principal components.* New York: John Wiley.

Joliffe, I. T. (1986). *Principal component analysis.* New York: Springer.

Meulman, J. J., & Heiser, W. J. (2000). *Categories.* Chicago: SPSS.

PRIOR DISTRIBUTION

A prior distribution $p(\theta)$ is a probability distribution describing one's subjective belief about an unknown quantity θ before observing a data set $\mathbf{x}$. BAYESIAN INFERENCE combines the prior distribution with the likelihood of the data to form the POSTERIOR DISTRIBUTION used to make inferences for θ. This entry describes the prior distribution's role in Bayesian inference from four points of view: subjective probability, objective Bayes, penalized likelihood, and hierarchical models.

At its foundation, Bayesian inference is a theory for updating one's subjective belief about θ upon observing $\mathbf{x}$. Subjectivists use probability distributions to formalize an individual's beliefs. Each individual's prior distribution is to be elicited by considering his or her willingness to engage in a series of hypothetical bets about the true value of θ. Models are required to make prior elicitation practical for continuous parameter spaces. Because of their computational convenience, *conjugate* priors are often used when they are available. A model has a conjugate prior if the prior and posterior distributions belong to the same family. Table 1 lists conjugate likelihood-prior relationships for several members of the exponential family. The prior parameters in many conjugate prior-likelihood families may be thought of as prior data, which provides a straightforward way to measure the strength of the prior (e.g., "one observation's worth of prior information"). See the entry on POSTERIOR DISTRIBUTION for an example calculation using conjugate priors.

One often finds that any reasonably weak prior has a negligible effect on the posterior distribution. Yet counterexamples exist, and critics of the Bayesian approach find great difficulty in prior elicitation (Efron, 1986). *Objective Bayesians* answer this criticism by deriving "reference priors," which attempt to model prior ignorance in standard situations. Kass and Wasserman (1996) review the extensive literature on

Table 1 Conjugate Prior Distributions for Several Common Likelihoods

Likelihood	Conjugate Prior
Univariate normal	Normal (mean parameter) gamma (inverse variance parameter)
Multivariate normal	Multivariate normal (mean vector) Wishart (inverse variance matrix)
Binomial	Beta
Poisson/exponential	Gamma
Multinomial	Dirichlet

reference priors. Many reference priors are improper (i.e., they integrate to ∞). For example, a common "noninformative" prior for mean parameters is the uniform prior $p(\theta) \propto 1$, which is obviously improper if the parameter space of θ is unbounded. Improper priors pose no difficulty so long as the likelihood is sufficiently well behaved for the posterior distribution to be proper, which usually happens in simple problems in which frequentist procedures perform adequately. However, when improper priors are used in complicated models, the propriety of the posterior distribution can be difficult to check (Hobert & Casella, 1996).

One difficulty with reference priors is that noninformative priors on one scale become informative after a change of variables. For example, a uniform prior on $\log \sigma^2$ becomes $p(\sigma^2) \propto 1/\sigma^2$ because of the Jacobian introduced by the log transformation. *Jeffreys' priors* are an important family of reference prior that are invariant to changes of variables. The general Jeffreys' prior for a model $p(\mathbf{x}|\theta)$ is $p(\theta) \propto \det(J(\theta))^{1/2}$, where $J(\theta)$ is the Fisher information from a single observation.

Although objective Bayesians strive to minimize the influence of the prior, practitioners of *penalized likelihood* actively seek out priors that will tame the highly variable parameter estimates that occur in high-dimensional models (Hastie, Tibshirani, & Friedman, 2001). For example, consider the regression model $\mathbf{y} \sim N(\mathbf{X}\beta, \sigma^2 I_n)$, where $\mathbf{X}$ is the $n \times p$ design matrix and $\mathbf{y}$ is the $n \times 1$ vector of responses. If $\mathbf{X}$ is ill-conditioned, then the least squares estimate of β is unreliable. An ill-conditioned design matrix can occur either because of an explicit collinearity in the data set or because $\mathbf{X}$ has been expanded by adding multiple interaction terms, polynomials, or other nonlinear basis functions such as splines.

A prior distribution $\beta \sim N(0, \tau^2 I_p)$ leads to a posterior distribution for β equivalent to ridge regression:

$$p(\beta \mid \mathbf{X}, \mathbf{y}, \tau, \sigma^2) = N(B, \Omega^{-1}).$$

The posterior precision (inverse variance) $\Omega = (\mathbf{X}^T\mathbf{X}/\sigma^2 + I_p/\tau^2)$ is the sum of the prior precision $\Omega_0 = I_p/\tau^2$ and the data precision $\Omega_1 = \mathbf{X}^T\mathbf{X}/\sigma^2$. If $\hat{\beta}$ is the least squares estimate of β, then the posterior mean B can be written as

$$B = \Omega^{-1}\Omega_1\hat{\beta}.$$

Thus, B is a precision-weighted average of β and the prior mean of zero. It is a compromise between information in the prior and the likelihood. The prior distribution ensures that Ω is positive definite. When $\mathbf{X}$ is ill-conditioned, the prior stabilizes the matrix inversion of Ω, which dramatically reduces the posterior variance of β.

Finally, a prior distribution can be used as a mechanism to model relationships between complicated data structures. HIERARCHICAL (NON)LINEAR MODELS, which are often used to model nested data, provide a good example. A hierarchical model considers observations in a subgroup of the data (e.g., exam scores for students in the same school) to be conditionally independent given parameters for that subgroup. The parameters for the various subgroups are linked by a prior distribution whose parameters are known as hyperparameters. The prior allows subgroup parameters to "borrow strength" from other subgroups so that parameters of sparse subgroups can be accurately estimated.

To make the example concrete, let y_{ij} denote the score for student j in school i. Suppose exam scores for students in the same school are conditionally independent, given school parameters, with $y_{ij} \sim N(\theta_i, \sigma^2)$. A prior distribution that assumes each $\theta_i \sim N(\alpha, \tau^2)$ induces a posterior correlation on students in the same school. If one conditions on $(\alpha, \tau^2, \sigma^2)$ but averages over θ_i, then the correlation between any two individual scores in the same school is $\tau^2/(\sigma^2 + \tau^2)$. Figure 1 provides a graphical description (known as the directed acyclic graph [DAG]) for the model.

To see how the prior allows one to "borrow strength" across population subsets, visualize information about (α, τ^2) flowing up from the data level. Then, given data and all other parameters, the posterior mean for θ_i is

$$E\left(\theta_i \mid y, \alpha, \sigma^2, \tau^2\right) = \frac{\frac{n_i}{\sigma^2}\bar{y}_i + \frac{1}{\tau^2}\alpha}{\frac{n_i}{\sigma^2} + \frac{1}{\tau^2}}.$$

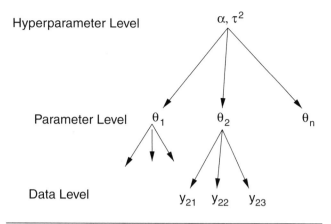

Figure 1 Graphical Depiction of a Hierarchical Model
NOTE: Each variable in the graph, given its parents, is conditionally independent of its nondescendents.

This expression is known as a *shrinkage estimate* because the data-based estimate is shrunk toward the prior. It combines information obtained from the entire sample, summarized by (α, τ^2) with data specific to subset i. The variation between subsets, measured by τ^2, determines the amount of shrinkage. If $\tau^2 \to \infty$, then θ_i is estimated with the sample mean from subset i, but if $\tau^2 \to 0$, then all subsets share a common mean α. The posterior variance for θ_i is

$$\text{Var}\left(\theta_i \mid \mathbf{y}, \alpha, \tau^2, \sigma^2\right) = \left(\frac{n_i}{\sigma^2} + \frac{1}{\tau^2}\right)^{-1}.$$

In words, the posterior precision is the sum of the data precision and prior precision. When n_i is small, shrinkage estimation can greatly reduce the posterior variance of θ_i, compared to estimating each θ_i independently. For a complete discussion of hierarchical models, consult Carlin and Louis (1998).

—Steven L. Scott

REFERENCES

Carlin, B. P., & Louis, T. A. (1998). *Bayes and empirical Bayes methods for data analysis.* London: Chapman & Hall/CRC.

Efron, B. (1986). Why isn't everyone a Bayesian? *The American Statistician, 40,* 1–5.

Hastie, T., Tibshirani, R., & Friedman, J. (2001). *The elements of statistical learning.* New York: Springer.

Hobert, J. P., & Casella, G. (1996). The effect of improper priors on Gibbs sampling in hierarchical linear mixed models. *Journal of the American Statistical Association, 91,* 1461–1473.

Kass, R. E., & Wasserman, L. (1996). The selection of prior distributions by formal rules. *Journal of the American Statistical Association, 91,* 1343–1370.

PRIOR PROBABILITY

A certain kind of PROBABILISTIC reasoning uses the observed data to update PROBABILITIES that existed before the data were collected, the so-called prior probabilities. This approach is called BAYESIAN INFERENCE and is in sharp contrast to the other existing approach, which is called *frequentist.* In the frequentist approach, the probabilities themselves are considered fixed but unknown quantities that can be observed through the RELATIVE FREQUENCIES. If the Bayesian approach is applied to a certain event, the researcher is assumed to have some knowledge regarding the probability of the event—the *prior probability*—and this is converted, using the BAYES THEOREM, into a posterior probability. The prior probability expresses the knowledge available before the actual observations become known, and the posterior probability is a combination of the prior probability with the information in the data. This updating procedure uses the BAYES FACTOR.

The prior probabilities are similar to ordinary probabilities, and they are called prior only if the goal is to update them using new data. One situation when this approach seems appropriate is when the prior probability comes from a census or an earlier large SURVEY and updating is based on a recent, smaller survey. Although census data, in most cases, are considered more reliable than survey data, they may become outdated, and a newer survey may reflect changes in the society that have taken place since the census was conducted. In such cases, a combination of the old and new pieces of information is achieved by considering the probability of a certain fact, computed from the census, as a prior probability and updating it using the recent survey information. A similar situation occurs when the prior information is taken from a large survey.

For example, suppose that the efficiency of a retraining program for unemployed people is investigated, in terms of the chance (probability) that someone who finishes the program will find employment within a certain period of time. When the program is launched, its efficiency is monitored in great detail, and the data are used to determine employment probabilities for different groups of unemployed people. After the first year of operation, to cut costs, complete monitoring is stopped, and only small-scale surveys are conducted to provide figures for the efficiency of the program. In this case, the probabilities from the complete monitoring are more reliable than those computed from the later surveys. On the other hand, the efficiency of the program may have changed in the meantime for a number of reasons, and the survey results may reflect this change. Therefore, it is appropriate to consider the original probabilities as prior probabilities and to update them using the new data.

The simplest updating procedure uses the so-called BAYES THEOREM and may be applied to update the prior probabilities of certain events that cannot occur at the same time (e.g., different religious affiliations) and may all be compatible with a further event (e.g., agreeing with a certain statement about the separation of state and church). If the former events have known (prior) probabilities (e.g., taken from census data) and it is known what the conditional probability is for someone belonging to one of the religions to agree with the statement, then if agreement with the statement is observed for a respondent, the probabilities of the different religious affiliations may be updated to produce new probabilities for the respondent.

—Tamás Rudas

REFERENCE

Iversen, G. R. (1984). *Bayesian statistical inference* (Quantitative Applications in the Social Sciences, 07–043). Beverly Hills, CA: Sage.

PRISONER'S DILEMMA

A prisoner's dilemma (PD) is a game used to study motives and behavior when people interact seeking personal gain. In a typical PD game, two players each choose between two behavioral options: cooperation and defection. The payoff each player receives depends on not only what that player chooses but also what the other chooses. Neither knows the other's choice until both have chosen. Payoffs are structured so that whatever the other player does, choosing to defect always produces the highest payoff to the chooser; yet, if both players defect, each gets less than if both cooperate—hence the dilemma.

Table 1   Typical Payoffs in a Prisoner's Dilemma

		Choices of Player 2	
		C_2	D_2
Choices of Player 1	C_1	3,3	0,5
	D_1	5,0	1,1

SOURCE: Adapted from Rapoport and Chammah (1965).

NOTE: The first number in each cell is the payoff for Player 1; the second is for Player 2. C_1 and C_2 represent the cooperating choices by Players 1 and 2, respectively; D_1 and D_2 represent the defecting choices.

The name *prisoner's dilemma* comes from an imaginary situation in which two prisoners committed a serious crime together, but the authorities only have proof that they committed a minor crime. The authorities offer each prisoner a deal: inform on the other and get a lighter sentence. If only one prisoner informs, he will get a very light sentence and the other a very heavy sentence. If both inform, each will get a moderately heavy sentence. If neither informs, each will get a moderately light sentence.

In research, PD payoffs are usually positive rather than negative. Standard payoffs are presented in Table 1.

Iterated PD games have repeated trials, and both players learn at the end of each trial what the other did. In an iterated PD, players can use their own behavior strategically to influence the other's behavior. It has been suggested that social competition for nature's resources is an iterated PD, and the strategy producing the highest payoff over trials should be favored by natural selection. Accordingly, Axelrod and Hamilton (1981) invited game theorists in economics, sociology, political science, and mathematics to propose strategies, which were then pitted against one another in iterated PD games. The strategy that proved best of the 14 often quite elaborate strategies proposed was *tit for tat*. This strategy is quite simple; it involves cooperating on the first trial, then doing whatever the other player did on the preceding trial. The success of tit for tat has led some to argue that a tendency to reciprocate is part of our evolutionary heritage.

One-trial PD games are used to study social motives, not strategies. Game theory, which assumes that each person is motivated solely to maximize personal gain, predicts universal defection in a one-trial PD. Yet, when people are placed in a one-trial PD, about one third to one half cooperate (Poundstone,

1992). This finding has cast doubt on the assumption that maximization of personal gain is the sole motive underlying interpersonal behavior.

—C. Daniel Batson

REFERENCES

Axelrod, R., & Hamilton, W. D. (1981). The evolution of cooperation. *Science, 211,* 1390–1396.

Poundstone, W. (1992). *Prisoner's dilemma.* New York: Doubleday.

Rapoport, A., & Chammah, A. M. (1965). *Prisoner's dilemma.* Ann Arbor: University of Michigan Press.

PRIVACY. *See* ETHICAL CODES; ETHICAL PRINCIPLES

PRIVACY AND CONFIDENTIALITY

Jing was alone, elderly, lonely, and in failing health. She was delighted to be visited by a courteous Mandarin-speaking researcher who asked about Jing's health and housing. Jing served tea and cookies and poured out her health problems, until it occurred to her that the city's financial problems might be solved by reducing benefits of indigent elderly in failing health. To prevent this from happening to her, she explained that her (nonexistent) children take care of her health care needs and that she is free to live with them as required. However, the researcher was simply a doctoral student seeking to understand the needs of Jing's community.

What devices did Jing use to regulate the interviewer's access to her? What may have accounted for Jing's initial granting of access and later curtailment of access? What did Jing assume about confidentiality? What are the implications for informed consent?

Privacy and *confidentiality* have been variously defined. Here, *privacy* refers to persons and to having control over the access by others to oneself. *Confidentiality* refers to *data* about oneself and to agreements regarding who may have access to such information.

These definitions take into account the subjective nature of privacy. Behavior that one person gladly discloses to others, another person wants hidden from others, similarly for data *about* such behavior.

Valid and ethical research requires sensitivity to factors that affect what research participants consider as private. Failure to recognize and respect these factors may result in refusal to participate in research or to respond honestly, yet many sensitive or personal issues need to be researched. How do researchers learn to respectfully investigate such issues? Regulations of human research may appear to suggest that one size fits all and provide little definitional or procedural guidance. However, regulations direct researchers to find solutions to privacy issues. Depending on the research context, privacy-related dilemmas may be idiosyncratic and require special insights into the privacy interests of the specific research population and ways to respect those interests. The following is intended to guide the pursuit of such insight.

PRIVACY

The meaning of privacy inheres in the culture and personal circumstances of the individual, the nature of the research, and the social and political environment in which the research occurs. Laufer and Wolfe (1977) present a theory of personal privacy that recognizes the manifold cultural, developmental, and situational elements through which individuals orchestrate their privacy. It recognizes people's desire to control the time, place, and nature of the information they give to others and to control the kinds of information or experiences that are proffered to them. This theory embodies four dimensions of privacy, as follows.

1. The *self-ego dimension* refers to development of autonomy and personal dignity. Young children dislike being alone or separated from their parents. In research settings, they regard parents as a welcome presence, not an invasion of their privacy. By middle childhood, children seek time alone to establish a sense of self and nurture new ideas that become the basis of self-esteem, personal strength, and dignity; they seek privacy, sometimes manifested as secret hideouts and "Keep Out" signs on bedroom doors. Teenagers are intensely private, self-conscious, and self-absorbed as they forge an identity separate from their parents. They are embarrassed to be interviewed about personal matters in the presence of others, especially their parents. Adults continue to need time alone and may become adroit at subtly protecting their privacy. (In the anecdote above, Jing shifted to polite lies when she decided that was in her best interests.)

2. The *environmental dimension* includes socio-physical, cultural, and life cycle dimensions. *Sociophysical* elements are physical or technological elements that offer privacy (e.g., private rooms, telephones). *Cultural* elements include norms for achieving privacy (e.g., cultural acceptability of white lies). *Life cycle* elements vary with age, occupation, available technology, and changing economic and sociocultural patterns.

3. The *interpersonal dimension* refers to how interaction and information are managed. Social settings and their physical characteristics provide options for managing social interaction; physical and social boundaries can be used to control people's access to one another.

4. The *control-choice dimension* grows out of the other three dimensions. Gradually, persons learn to use personal, cultural, and physical resources to control their privacy. Events that would threaten one's privacy early in the development of control/choice are later easy to control and pose no threat to privacy.

Using the dimensions described above to guide one's inquiry, discussion with networks of persons who are acquainted with the research population can provide useful information. Such networks might include, for example, relevant local researchers, educators, and outreach workers (e.g., social workers, farm agents, public health nurses, and other professionals). Focus groups and other forms of community consultation are useful ways to learn how a given community might perceive the research, what might be objectionable to them, how it can be made more acceptable, and how to recruit and inform prospective subjects (see, e.g., Melton, Levine, Koocher, Rosenthal, & Thompson, 1988). Talking with formal or informal gatekeepers and stakeholders, volunteering to work for relevant community outreach services, or using ethnographic methods can also provide useful insight into a population's privacy concerns. As the anecdote about Jing illustrates, it is in the best interests of the research program to understand and respect the privacy interests of subjects, as people have a host of techniques for covertly protecting their privacy and thereby confounding the goals of the researcher.

CONFIDENTIALITY

Confidentiality is an extension of the concept of privacy. It refers to identifiable data (e.g., videotape of subjects, nonanonymous survey data, data containing enough description to permit deductive identification of subjects) and to agreements about how access to those data is controlled. Research planning should consider needs for confidentiality and how access will be controlled. It should incorporate those plans into the methodology, institutional review board (IRB) protocol, informed consent, data management, training of research assistants, and any contractual agreements with subsequent users of the data. If feasible, problems of confidentiality should be avoided by gathering data in anonymous form, that is, so that the identity of the subject is never recorded. Identifiers include any information such as address, license number, or Social Security number, which can connect data with a specific person. When personal data are gathered, subjects may be particularly interested in knowing what steps will be taken to prevent possible disclosure of information about them.

However, promises of confidentiality do not necessarily contribute much to some subjects' willingness to participate in research, and extensive assurances of confidentiality accompanying nonsensitive research actually raise suspicion and diminish willingness to participate (Singer, von Thurn, & Miller, 1995). Many respondents, especially minorities, do not trust promises of confidentiality (Turner, 1982). Creative solutions to problems of subject distrust include consultation and collaboration with trusted community leaders in useful service connected with the research.

To whom or what does *confidentiality* pertain? Regulations of human research define *human subjects* as individually identifiable (not anonymous) living individuals. For many purposes, however, the researcher may also consider the privacy interests of entire *communities,* organizations, or even the deceased and their relatives (see Andrews & Nelkin, 1998). Issues of professional courtesy and maintaining the goodwill of gatekeepers to research sites may be as important to science and to individual investigators as protecting individual human subjects.

Issues of confidentiality have many ramifications as the following vignette illustrates:

In response to funding agency requirements, Professor Freeshare stated in his proposal that he would make his data available to other scientists as soon as his results are published. Thus, others could build on his data, perhaps linking them to related data from the same sample or reanalyzing his original data by different methods.

"Not so fast, Dr. Freeshare!" said his IRB. "There is a troubling disconnect in your description of your project. In your informed consent statement you promise confidentiality, but you must attach unique identifiers if other scientists are to link to your data. True, data sharing increases benefit and decreases cost of research, but that doesn't justify breach of confidentiality."

Dr. Freeshare revised his protocol to read as follows: Rigorous standards for protecting confidentiality will be employed to de-identify data that are to be shared, employing sophisticated methods developed by the U.S. Bureau of Census and other federal agencies that release data to academic scientists and the general public for further analysis. There are two kinds of data that might be shared, tabular data (tables of grouped data) and micro-data (data files on individual subjects, showing values for each of selected variables). There are also various methods of ensuring confidentiality: (a) de-identify the data before they are released to the public or to an archive (restricted data); (b) restrict who, when, or where the data may be used subsequently (restricted access); or (c) a combination of the two methods. It is anticipated that micro-data files will be prepared for release to other qualified scientists after the data have been carefully scrutinized, employing the Checklist on Disclosure Potential of Proposed Data Releases developed by the Confidentiality and Data Access Committee (CDAC). Restriction of data will be carried out using appropriate techniques described in the Federal Committee on Statistical Methodology (FCSM) "primer" (Chapter 2, FCSM, 1994). If qualified scientists present proposals for important research requiring use of unique identifiers, "restricted access" arrangements will be made to conduct the needed analyses at this university by statisticians who are familiar with the data and who are paid the marginal costs of organizing and conducting those analyses for the secondary user.

PROBLEMS

Preventing careless disclosure of information about subjects requires training of research personnel and planning of how raw data will be kept secure. As soon as possible, unique identifiers should be removed from the data and, if necessary, code numbers substituted; any key linking names to code numbers should be kept off-site in a secure place.

There are various possible threats to confidentiality apart from the researcher's own careless disclosure of subjects' identity. These include the following:

- Deductive identification based on demographic information contained in the data
- Recognition of unique characteristics of individual subjects (e.g., from videotapes, qualitative descriptions, case studies)
- Hacker break-in to computer data files containing unique identifiers
- Subpoena of data
- Legally mandated reporting by investigator (e.g., of child or elder abuse)
- Linkage of related data sets (from different sources or from longitudinal sequences)
- Audit of data by the research sponsor

Researchers are responsible for identifying possible threats to the confidentiality of data they plan to gather, employing appropriate means of ensuring confidentiality, and communicating to potential subjects how confidentiality has been ensured or whether there remain risks to confidentiality. Researchers must not promise confidentiality they cannot ensure.

SOLUTIONS

A major literature describes ways of ensuring confidentiality. The following summarizes main approaches to ensuring confidentiality. Each approach is accompanied by two sources of information: (a) a key bibliographic reference and (b) key words to employ with an online search engine such as Google. The Internet has become a rapidly evolving resource as new confidentiality problems and solutions emerge.

Broadened Categories and Error Inoculation. Deductive identification is possible when someone who knows distinctive identifying demographic facts about an individual (e.g., age, income, medical status, ZIP code) wishes to pry into other information on that individual. This can be prevented by broadening

data categories to obscure data from unique individuals (e.g., a billionaire can be included in a category containing many subjects labeled "annual income of over $100,000"), or data can be "error inoculated" so that no individual case is necessarily correct. (Boruch & Cecil, 1979; confidentiality raw data)

Unique Characteristics of Individual Subjects or Settings in Case Descriptions and Videotapes. These can be disguised by various means, but elimination of all possible identifying characteristics may destroy the scientific value of the data. A second precaution is to assume that identities can be guessed and to avoid use of pejorative or unnecessarily personal language. (Johnson, 1982; confidentiality qualitative data)

Subpoena of Data. This is a possibility whenever data might be considered material to legal proceedings. In the United States, a subpoena can be blocked with a Certificate of Confidentiality obtained by the researcher from the National Institutes of Health prior to gathering data that might be subpoenaed. Obviously, data on criminal activities of subjects would call for a Certificate of Confidentiality. Less obvious are data that might be useful in future class-action suits, child custody disputes, or other civil legal actions; such threats to confidentiality are next to impossible to anticipate. A safer way to protect data from subpoena is to remove all unique identifiers as soon as possible. (National Institutes of Health, 2003; confidentiality, subpoena of data)

Linkage of Data to Unique Identifiers. Anonymity is the best practice when feasible. However, linkage with identifiers may be needed to permit, for example, follow-up testing for sampling validity or longitudinal research. Temporarily identified responses, use of brokers, aliases, or file-linkage systems can permit linkages without disclosure of subject identity. (Campbell, Boruch, Schwartz, & Steinberg, 1977; confidentiality file linkage)

Audits of Data. Audits of data by research sponsors require that the funder be able to recontact subjects to ensure that the data were actually gathered from the ostensible subject. To satisfy this requirement while protecting the privacy interests of subjects, the researcher (or the researcher's institution) may develop contractual agreements with such secondary users about how they will ensure confidentiality. Researchers should disclose these arrangements in the informed consent so that potential subjects understand what researchers may do with the data subsequent to the project. (Boruch & Cecil, 1979; confidentiality data sharing)

Legally Mandated Reporting Requirements. Legally mandated reporting requirements (e.g., of child abuse) vary in the United States by state and county with respect to what constitutes abuse and who are mandated reporters. These requirements pertain mostly to helping professionals (therapists, physicians, teachers); many researchers happen to also be helping professionals. Moreover, in nine states—Florida, Indiana, Kentucky, Minnesota, Nebraska, New Hampshire, New Jersey, New Mexico, and North Carolina—anyone who has reason to suspect child maltreatment must report. Child abuse may include a wide range of activities—for example, neglect, physical abuse, psychological abuse, sexual abuse, and child pornography. Informed consent for research that may reveal reportable incidents should state that confidentiality could be promised except if the researcher believes that there is reasonable suspicion that a child has been abused. Researchers who have reasonable suspicion of child abuse should consult professionals who have a better understanding of reporting requirements (e.g., nurses, social workers, physicians) before proceeding to report the incident to local authorities. (Kalichman, 1999; reporting child abuse)

Laws concerning prevention and reporting of elder abuse are rapidly evolving. Most elder abuse is perpetrated by family members. It may include slapping, bruising, sexually molesting, or restraining; financial exploitation without their consent for someone else's benefit; and failure to provide goods or services necessary to avoid physical harm, mental anguish, or mental illness. (Bonnie & Wallace, 2002; reporting elder abuse)

Protection of Computer Files. Researchers routinely store electronic data on their institution's server. Such data are vulnerable to hackers, masqueraders, users of the local-area network (LAN), and Trojan horses. It is unwise to store data with unique identifiers where unauthorized users can possibly gain access. Understanding of these risks and relevant safeguards is evolving rapidly; the best current sources are found online (Skoudis, 2002; computer files hackers; confidentiality)

Online Research. Surveys, focus groups, personality studies, experiments, ethnography, and other kinds of social and behavioral research are increasingly being conducted online, enabling researchers to reach far-flung subjects quickly, inexpensively, around the clock, and without a research staff. Accompanying problems and solutions to issues of confidentiality change rapidly as new technologies evolve. There are emerging technologies for protecting communication and personal identity and emerging cohorts of technology-sophisticated privacy activists. However, policies and methods of data protection cannot evolve fast enough to anticipate emerging problems. There are already digital communication networks on a global scale; hackers with a laptop computer and Internet technology could download any electronic data stored on any server anywhere in the world. (Nosek, Banaji, & Greenwald, 2002; Internet-based research)

IMPLICATIONS

There is an implicit understanding within social science that subjects' privacy will be respected and access to identified data appropriately limited. But what are subjects' privacy interests, and what limitations are appropriate? If there are special privacy interests, then special precautions (e.g., a Certificate of Confidentiality, error inoculation) may be needed and should be discussed with subjects and gatekeepers. When subjects are situated differently from the researcher, the problem is compounded by the difficulty of gaining insight into the subject's situation and privacy interests. For example, does the subject trust researcher promises of confidentiality? Are there "snoopers" who would engage in deductive identification of subjects or who would subpoena data? Clarity about such issues is elusive and cannot be settled definitively in regulatory language or in articles such as this. Such issues require that researchers know the culture and circumstances of those they study.

—Joan E. Sieber

REFERENCES

Andrews, L., & Nelkin, D. (1998). Do the dead have interests? Policy issues of research after life. *American Journal of Law & Medicine, 24,* 261.

Bonnie, R. J., & Wallace, R. B. (2002). *Elder mistreatment: Abuse, neglect, and exploitation in an aging America.* Washington, DC: Joseph Henry Press.

Boruch, R. F., & Cecil, J. S. (1979). *Assuring the confidentiality of social research data.* Philadelphia: University of Pennsylvania Press.

Campbell, D. T., Boruch, R. F., Schwartz, R. D., & Steinberg, J. (1977). Confidentiality-preserving modes of access to files and to interfile exchange for useful statistical analysis. *Evaluation Quarterly, 1,* 269–300.

Confidentiality and Data Access Committee. (1999). *Checklist on disclosure potential of proposed data releases.* Washington, DC: Office of Management and Budget, Office of Information and Regulatory Affairs, Statistical Policy Office. Retrieved from www.fcsm.gov/committees/cdac/checklist_799.doc

Federal Committee on Statistical Methodology. (1994). *Report on statistical disclosure limitation methodology* (Statistical Policy Working Paper #22). Prepared by the Subcommittee on Disclosure Limitation Methodology. Washington, DC: Office of Management and Budget, Office of Information and Regulatory Affairs, Statistical Policy Office. Retrieved from www.fcsm.gov/working-papers/wp22.html

Johnson, C. (1982). Risks in the publication of fieldwork. In J. E. Sieber (Ed.), *The ethics of social research: Fieldwork, regulation and publication* (pp. 71–92). New York: Springer-Verlag.

Kalichman, S. C. (1999). *Mandated reporting of suspected child abuse: Ethics, law and policy.* Washington, DC: American Psychological Association.

Laufer, R. S., & Wolfe, M. (1977). Privacy as a concept and a social issue: A multidimensional developmental theory. *Journal of Social Issues, 33,* 44–87.

Melton, G. B., Levine, R. J., Koocher, G. P., Rosenthal, R., & Thompson, W. (1988). Community consultation in socially sensitive research. *American Psychologist, 43,* 573–581.

National Institutes of Health. (2003, July 22). *Certificates of confidentiality.* Retrieved from http://grants1.nih.gov/grants/policy/coc/index.htm

Nosek, B. A., Banaji, M. R., & Greenwald, A. G. (2002). E-research: Ethics, security, design, and control in psychological research on the Internet. *Journal of Social Issues, 58,* 161–176.

Singer, E., von Thurn, D., & Miller, E. (1995). Confidentiality assurances and response. *Public Opinion Quarterly, 59,* 66–77.

Skoudis, E. (2002). *Counter Hack: A step-by-step guide to computer attacks and effective defenses.* Upper Saddle, NJ: Prentice Hall.

Turner, A. C. (1982). What subjects of survey research believe about confidentiality. In J. E. Sieber (Ed.), *The ethics of social research: Surveys and experiments* (pp. 151–165). New York: Springer-Verlag.

PROBABILISTIC

A model or an argument is probabilistic if it is STOCHASTIC (i.e., incorporates uncertainty) and uses the concept of PROBABILITY. Probabilistic models and arguments are often used in scientific inquiry when the researcher does not have sufficient information to apply a DETERMINISTIC approach and the available information is best formulated in terms of probabilities. A probabilistic model for a social phenomenon is a set of assumptions that describe the likely behavior of the entities involved, in terms of relationships, associations, causation, or other concepts that each have their specific probabilities. A probabilistic argument is often based on a probabilistic model and is not aimed at proving that a certain fact is true or will be the result of the discussed actions or developments. Rather, it assesses the probabilities of certain implications and outcomes.

The probabilities applied in a probabilistic model or argument may be results of subjective considerations, previous knowledge, or experience, and the results of the analysis of the model or of the argument are often used to assess whether the probabilities assumed seem realistic. In such cases, the probabilistic argument is applied iteratively.

In the social sciences, there are two major situations when probabilistic models and arguments are used. In one of these, the exact laws governing the relationships between certain variables are not precisely known. For example, in most societies, sons of fathers with higher levels of education have better chances of achieving a high level of education than sons of fathers with lower levels of education do. Based on educational mobility data, the conditional probabilities that a son whose father has a given level of education achieves a basic, medium, or high level of education may be estimated. These probabilities may be further modified depending on other factors that potentially influence educational attainment, such as the mother's educational level, ethnic or religious background of the family, the type of the settlement where the family lives, and so forth. By taking the effects of several factors into account, the probabilities are refined and may yield a good approximation of reality. This is a probabilistic model because not all factors are taken into account and the effects are not precisely known; rather, they are described using probabilities. The predictions from the model may be compared to reality to get better estimates of the probabilities used in the model and to find out if further factors need to be taken into account.

The other important situation when probabilistic arguments and models are used is when the precise factors and their effects are of secondary interest only and the researcher is more interested in PREDICTING, based on data from a SAMPLE, the behavior of the entire POPULATION. A typical example of this situation is when data from opinion polls are used to predict election results. If, for example, 25% of the population would vote for a candidate, then with a sample size of 2,500, the pollster has 0.95 probability of finding a result between 23% and 27%. Based on this fact, if the poll results in, say, 26% popularity of the candidate, the pollster has (24%, 28%) as a 95% CONFIDENCE INTERVAL for the true value.

—Tamás Rudas

REFERENCE

Bennett, D. J. (1998). *Randomness*. Cambridge, MA: Harvard University Press.

PROBABILISTIC GUTTMAN SCALING

Probabilistic Guttman scaling is an extension to the classical GUTTMAN SCALING method, which is deterministic. In contrast, a probabilistic treatment is stochastic, and there exist numerous variations, the most prominent and earliest of which is a method proposed by Proctor (1970).

—Alan Bryman

See also GUTTMAN SCALING

REFERENCE

Proctor, C. H. (1970). A probabilistic formulation and statistical analysis of Guttman scaling. *Psychometrika, 35,* 73–78.

PROBABILITY

The modern theory of probability is one of the most widely applied areas of mathematics. Whenever an empirical investigation involves uncertainty, due to SAMPLING, insufficient understanding of the actual procedure or of the laws governing the observed phenomena, or for other reasons, the concept of probability may be applied. In general, probability is considered a numerical representation of how likely is the occurrence of certain observations.

HISTORY

The concept of probability developed from the investigation of the properties of various games, such as rolling dice, but in addition to the very practical desire of understanding how to win, it also incorporates deep philosophical thought. First, questions concerning the chance of certain results in gambling were computed, and these led to working out the rules associated with probability, but the concept of probability itself was not defined. It took quite some time to realize that the existence of a PROBABILISTIC background or framework cannot be automatically assumed, and the question, "What is probability?" became a central one. In the late 19th century, it became widely accepted among philosophers and mathematicians that the correct approach to define the fundamentals of a precise theory (not only for probability but also for many other concepts underlying our present scientific thinking) is the axiomatic approach. The axiomatic approach does not aim at precisely defining what is probability; rather, it postulates its properties and derives the entire theory from these. It was Kolmogorov, who, in the early 20th century, developed an axiomatic theory of probability. Although the philosophical thinking about the nature of probability continues to this date, Kolmogorov's theory has been able to incorporate the newer developments, and this theory led to widespread applications in statistics.

EXAMPLES AND AXIOMS

Usually, several constructions possess the properties postulated in a system of axioms and can serve as models for the concept, but the concept itself is not derived from, rather is only illustrated by, these CONSTRUCTS. For probability, a simple illustration is rolling a die with all outcomes being equally likely. Then, each outcome has probability equal to 1/6, the probability of having a value less than 4 (i.e., 1, 2, or 3) is equal to 1/2, and the probability of having an even outcome (i.e., 2, 4, or 6) is also 1/2. The probability of having an outcome less than 4 and even is 1/6, as this only happens for 2. There are, however, events that are possible but that cannot occur at the same time. For example, having a value less than 4 and greater than 5 is not possible. The event that cannot occur is called the impossible event and is denoted by 0.

Another example is the so-called geometric probability, for which a model is obtained by shooting at a target in such a way that hitting any point of the target has the same probability. Here, hitting the right-hand half has 1/2 probability, just like hitting the left-hand half or hitting the upper half. The probability that one hits the right-hand side and the upper side, at the same time, is 1/4.

In a precise theory, the events associated with the observation of an EXPERIMENT possess probabilities. To define the properties of probability, one has to define certain operations on these events. The product of two events A and B occurs if both A and B occur and is denoted by AB. For example, one event may be, when rolling a die, having a value less than 4; another event may be having an even value. The product of these is having a value that is less than 4 and is even, that is, 2. Or, an event may be hitting the right-hand side of the target, another may be hitting its upper half, and the product is hitting the upper right-hand side quarter of the table. If two events cannot occur at the same time, their product is the impossible event. Another operation is the sum of two events, denoted as $A + B$. The sum occurs if at least one of the two original events occurs. The sum of having a value less than 4 and of having an even value is having anything from among 1, 2, 3, 4, 6. The sum of the right-hand side of the target and of its upper half is three quarters of the target, obtained by omitting the lower left-hand side quarter.

One can even think of more complex operations on the events. For example, consider the upper right-hand corner of the target and denote it by $A1$, then the one eighth of the target immediately below it (let this be $A2$), then the one sixteenth of the target next to it ($A3$), then the one thirty-second of the target ($A4$), and so forth. One has here infinitely many events, and it is intuitively clear that they also have a sum— namely, the left-hand side half of the target. This is illustrated in Figure 1. The sum of these infinitely many events is denoted as $A1 + A2 + A3 + A4\ldots$. Probability theory also applies to these more general operations.

Now we are ready to formulate the axioms of probability. The probability is a system of numbers (the probabilities) assigned to events associated with an experiment. The probabilities are assigned to the events in such a way that

1. The probability of an event is a value between 0 and 1:

$$0 \leq P(A) \leq 1.$$

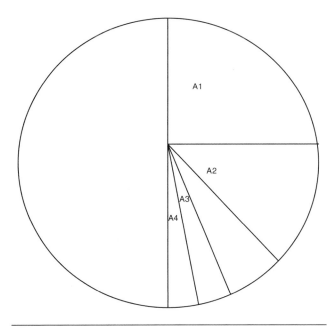

Figure 1   The Sum of Infinitely Many Events Illustrated on a Target

2. If an event occurs all the time (surely), its probability is 1:

$$P(S) = 1.$$

3. If two events are such that they cannot occur at the same time, then the probability of their sum is the sum of their probabilities:

$$P(A + B) = P(A) + P(B), \quad \text{if } AB = \emptyset.$$

The last property may be extended to cover the sum of infinitely many events, as in the case of hitting certain fractions of the target. A more general form of Axiom 3 postulates the following:

4. If a sequence of events $A1, A2, A3, \ldots$ is such that no two events can occur at the same time, then the probability of their sum is the sum of their probabilities:

$$P(A1 + A2 + A3 + \cdots)$$
$$= P(A1) + P(A2) + P(A3) + \cdots$$
$$\text{if } AiAj = \emptyset \quad \text{for } i \neq j.$$

INDEPENDENCE

All properties of probability can be derived from Axioms 1 to 3 (or $1 - 3'$) and the further concepts in probability theory that are precisely defined in this framework. One of the frequently used notions in probability theory is independence. The events A and B are independent if

$$P(AB) = P(A)P(B).$$

Notice that this formula is not the rule of computing the joint probability if independence is true; rather, it is the definition of independence. In the die-rolling example, the events of having an even number and of having a value less than 5 are independent because the former (2, 4, 6) has probability $1/2$ and the latter (1, 2, 3, 4) probability $2/3$, whereas the intersection (2, 4) has probability $1/3$, that is, their product. On the other hand, the events of having an even number and having something less than 4 are not independent because the former has probability $1/2$, the latter has probability $1/2$, and their product has probability $1/6$. The interpretation of this fact may be that within the first three numbers, even numbers are less likely than among the first six numbers. Indeed, among the first six numbers, three are even, but among the first three, only one is even.

CONDITIONAL PROBABILITY

The latter interpretation, in fact, points to another useful concept related to probability, called conditional probability. The conditional probability shows how the probability of an event changes if one knows that another event occurred. For example, when rolling the die, the probability of having an even number is $1/2$, because one half of all possible outcomes is even. If, however, one knows that the event of having a value less than 4 has occurred, then, knowing this, the probability of having an even number is different, and this new probability is called the conditional probability of having an even number, given that the number is less than 4. To see this, consider the list of possible outcomes of the experiment:

Possible outcomes: 1, 2, 3, 4, 5, 6
Even numbers from among these: 2, 4, 6
Probability of having an even number: $1/2$

Possible outcomes if the number is less than 4: 1, 2, 3
Even numbers from among these: 2
Conditional probability of having an even number if the number is less than 4: $1/3$

The conditional probability of A given B is denoted by $P(A|B)$ and is precisely defined as

$$P(A|B) = P(AB)/P(B),$$

that is, the probability of the product of the events, divided by the probability of the condition. In the example above, we have seen that the probability of having a value that is even and also less than 4 is $1/6$, and the probability of having a value less than 4 is $1/2$, and their ratio is $1/3$.

It follows from the definition directly that if A and B are independent, then $P(A|B) = P(A)$; that is, conditioning on the occurrence of B does not change the probability of A if these are independent. Indeed, if A and B are independent,

$$P(A|B) = P(AB)/P(B)$$
$$= P(A)P(B)/P(B) = P(A),$$

where the first equality is the definition of conditional probability, and the second one is based on the definition of independence. Therefore, independence of events means no relevance for each other. The probability of A is the same, whether or not B occurred, if A and B are independent.

In the target-shooting example, hitting the right-hand side half and hitting the lower half are easily seen to be independent of each other, by an argument similar to the one presented for the die-rolling example. This relies heavily on the fact that the two examples are similar in the sense that all outcomes are equally likely. In the case of rolling a die, the outcomes are the numbers 1, 2, 3, 4, 5, 6; in the target-shooting example, the outcomes are the points of the target. Although one is inclined to accept that the outcomes are equally likely in both cases, this assumption is straightforward for the six outcomes of die rolling but much less apparent for the infinitely many outcomes that are possible with the target shooting. It shows the strength of the underlying mathematical theory that such assumptions may be precisely incorporated into a probabilistic model. In the social sciences, models for experiments with infinitely many outcomes are used routinely; for example, approximations based on the NORMAL DISTRIBUTION assume that a variable may take on any number as its value, and there are infinitely many different numbers, just like infinitely many points on the target. In such cases, one uses a so-called density function to specify the probabilistic behavior.

APPLICATIONS

The foregoing simple examples are not meant to suggest that formulating and applying probabilistic models is always straightforward. Sometimes, even relatively simple models lead to technically complex analyses, but, more important, it is relatively easy to be mistaken on a basic conceptual level. The following example illustrates some of the dangers. The CEO of a corporation interviews three applicants for the position of secretary. The applicants—say, A, B, and C—know that three of them were interviewed and, as they have no information with respect to each other's qualifications, may assume that they all have equal chances of getting the job. Therefore, all of them think that the probability of being hired is 1/3 for each of them. After the interviews were conducted, the CEO reached a decision, but this decision was not yet communicated to the applicants. Applicant A calls the CEO and says the following: As there are three interviewees and only one of them will be given the position, it is certain that from among B and C, there will be at least one who will not get the job. The CEO gives no information with respect to the chances of A by naming one from among B and C, who will not be given the position. The CEO tells A that C will certainly not get the position. After finishing the call, A thinks that now that C is out of the race, out of the remaining two candidates, A and B, each has 1/2 probability of getting the job, that is, the probability changed from 1/3 to 1/2. Did or did not the CEO give information, with respect to the chances of A, by naming a person who would not get the job, if such a person exists, whether named or not? And what is the correct probability of A getting the job: 1/3 or 1/2? The situation is somewhat paradoxical, as one could argue for and also against both possible responses for both questions. The important point here is that assuming three candidates (and thinking that the probability is 1/3) or assuming two candidates (and thinking that the probability is 1/2) are two different probabilistic models and therefore cannot be directly compared. More precisely, asking whether 1/3 or 1/2 is the correct probability makes sense only if they are computed within the same model (and in that case, there is a clear answer). In the first model (three applicants), it is true that naming one who will not be given the job is not informative. But when the CEO named one candidate who would not be given the job, A defined, based on this information, a new probabilistic model, and in the new model (two applicants),

1/2 is the correct probability. The inference based on a probabilistic model (and this also applies to any kind of STATISTICAL INFERENCE) is only relevant if, in addition to the correct analysis of the model itself, it is also based on a model that appropriately describes the relevant aspects of reality. The results will largely depend on the choice of the model.

Probability theory has many applications in the social sciences. It is the basis of RANDOM SAMPLING, in which the units of the population of interest, usually people, are selected into the sample with probabilities specified in advance. The simplest case is SIMPLE RANDOM SAMPLING, in which every person has the same chance of being selected into the sample, and the steps of the selection process are independent from each other. In such cases, probability models with all outcomes having equal probability may be relevant, but the more complex sampling schemes used in practice require other models. Probabilistic methods are also used to model the effects of errors of MEASUREMENT and, more generally, to model the effects of not measured or unknown factors.

—Tamás Rudas

REFERENCES

Bennett, D. J. (1998). *Randomness.* Cambridge, MA: Harvard University Press.

Feller, W. (1968). *An introduction to probability theory and its applications* (3rd ed.). New York: John Wiley.

Wonnacott, T. H., & Wonnacott, R. J. (1990). *Introductory statistics for business and economics* (4th ed.). San Francisco: Jossey-Bass.

PROBABILITY DENSITY FUNCTION

The probabilistic behavior of a CONTINUOUS VARIABLE is best described by its probability density function. Although in the case of a DISCRETE VARIABLE, the probabilities belonging to its different values can be specified separately, such a description of the behavior of a continuous variable is not possible. A continuous variable takes on all its values with zero PROBABILITY, and therefore specification of the individual probabilities would not be informative either. What is informative and, in fact, characterizes entirely the behavior of a continuous variable is the probability of having a value on an arbitrary interval. The

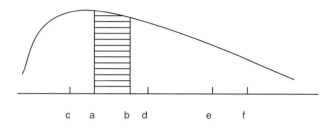

Figure 1   A Probability Density Function

probability of having an observation on an interval can be read off from the density function by determining the integral of the density function over this interval, that is, by taking the area under the function over this interval. This procedure is illustrated in Figure 1. The shaded area is the probability of observing a value on the interval (a, b). The probability of other intervals is determined similarly. This probability depends on the length of the interval (the longer interval (c, d) has a higher probability) and on the location of the interval. For example, the interval (e, f) has the same length as (a, b), but it is less likely to have an observation on it than on (a, b). Interval probabilities determined by this method are easily seen to possess the properties of probability. For example, if an interval is the union of two other nonoverlapping intervals, then the area associated with it is the sum of the areas associated with the two intervals.

Density functions may also be used to determine the probability that a variable is smaller or greater than a certain value by calculating the relevant areas. To be a density function, the function, in addition to other properties, has to be nonnegative, and the total area under the function has to be equal to 1.

Density functions can be considered as being the theoretical counterparts of HISTOGRAMS, obtained by using shorter and shorter intervals. Parallel to this, the number of intervals increases and the boundary of the histogram becomes finer and finer.

The name of the density function comes from the fact that the probability of an interval determines how densely one can expect the observations on the interval. When the variable is observed, one can expect the number of observations on the interval to be proportional to the probability of the interval: On an interval with higher probability, the observations occur more densely than on an interval with lower probability.

The value of the density function for a possible value of the variable is called the *likelihood of the value*. For example, the likelihood of the value a is larger than the likelihood of the value e. In everyday language, the words *probability* and *likelihood* are used interchangeably, but in probability and statistics, they have different meanings. Both the values a and e have probability zero, but they have different likelihoods. A precise interpretation of the difference is that values in the vicinity of a are more likely to occur than values in the vicinity of e. It is also true that a short interval centered on a has a larger probability than an interval of the same length centered on e.

—Tamás Rudas

REFERENCE

Chatfield, C. (1983). *Statistics for technology* (3rd ed.). London: Chapman & Hall.

PROBABILITY SAMPLING. *See*
RANDOM SAMPLING

PROBABILITY VALUE

The probability value (or p value) or the achieved probability level is a measure of the amount of evidence the data provide against a statistical HYPOTHESIS. It shows how extreme the data would be if the hypothesis were true. The p value is essentially the probability of observing data that are not more likely than the actually observed data set. Hypothesis tests are usually based on the p values. If the achieved probability level is smaller than a specified value—usually .05 but sometimes .01 or .10—the hypothesis is rejected. Most software packages routinely print the p values, and SIGNIFICANCE TESTING can be performed by comparing these values to the desired SIGNIFICANCE LEVELS.

As a simple example, consider the BINOMIAL TEST with $n = 10$ observations and the assumption that the success probability is $p = .5$. Out of the several properties of the observations, only the number of successes is relevant to test the hypothesis. Table 1 lists all possible results with their respective probabilities. If the data contain 7 successes (and 3 failures), the outcomes that

Table 1   Possible Results of the Binomial Test With $n = 10$ and $p = .5$

Number of Successes	Probability
0	0.000977
1	0.009766
2	0.04395
3	0.117188
4	0.205078
5	0.246094
6	0.205078
7	0.117188
8	0.04395
9	0.009766
10	0.000977

are more likely than the present outcome are those with 6, 5, or 4 successes. The outcomes that are as likely as or less likely than the actual data contain 0, 1, 2, 3, 7, 8, 9, or 10 successes; their combined probability is 0.3475, and this is the p value associated with the data and the test. Therefore, the actual data (with 7 successes) do not belong to the least likely 5% of the observations and do not suggest rejecting the hypothesis. If, on the other hand, the observations contain 1 success only, the outcomes that are as likely or less likely than this contain 0, 1, 9, or 10 successes, and their combined probability is 0.021484. This achieved probability level is less than .05, and the hypothesis is rejected because observing these data would be very unlikely if the hypothesis were true.

As another example, consider a 2×2 CONTINGENCY TABLE, and let the hypothesis be INDEPENDENCE. The data are given in Table 2. In this case, there are many possible independent tables, and the probability of a sample depends on which one of these is the true distribution. In such cases, MAXIMUM LIKELIHOOD ESTIMATION is used to select the distribution that would give the highest probability to the actual observations, and the p value is determined based on this distribution. To determine the probability value, we first compute

Table 2   Hypothetical Observations in a 2×2 Table

10	20
30	40

the value of a CHI-SQUARE statistic. The samples that have smaller likelihoods than the actual data are characterized by having a larger value of this STATISTIC. The combined probability of these samples (i.e., the p value) is equal to the probability that the statistic takes on a value greater than its actual value. The value of the Pearson CHI-SQUARE statistic is 0.793651 for the present data; the probability that the statistic exceeds this value is .37, and this is the p value of the data.

—Tamás Rudas

REFERENCE

Schervish, M. J. (1996). *P*-values: What they are and what are they not. *American Statistician, 50,* 203–206.

PROBING

Probing, a technique used during an in-person INTERVIEW to acquire additional information, is used to gather more explanation or clarification following an OPEN-ENDED QUESTION. It supplements the specific questions of the interview protocol. The technique allows the investigator to attain the precise information on which the research project is centered.

Research designs may employ different types of interview forms, varying in the degree of structure. At one end of the spectrum, there is a highly STRUCTURED INTERVIEW schedule, with the interviewer asking all respondents the same direct questions; protocols for these types of interviews may be very similar in design to a MAIL survey. A well-known example is the National Election Survey. At the other end, there is a much more loosely focused interview form, with the interviewer asking some general questions and allowing the interview to develop from there; such interviews have the feel of natural dialogue. More probing is required in less structured interviews. The interviewer will ask general questions and probe the respondent throughout the discussion to get at the information of interest.

Probes, as well as the primary interview questions, must not lead or suggest the interviewee's response. Probes should be simple prods for the interviewee to elaborate on his or her initial response. In interviewing, keep in mind that sometimes the most appropriate probe is a moment of silence; a pause alone is often enough to provoke the interviewee to develop the point.

Interviewees are different; some are much more loquacious than others, requiring little probing. Others may be quite reticent. For example, if a respondent is asked if his or her organization used more than one institutional route to communicate its message and the interviewee responds with a simple "Oh we used every route in the book, you name it we tried it," a probe could simply be, "Such as?" or "Could you describe that process a bit more?" prompting further explanation on the part of the interviewee.

—Christine Mahoney

REFERENCES

Berry, J. (2002). Validity and reliability issues in elite interviewing. *PS—Political Science and Politics, 35*, 679–682.

Dexter, L. A. (1970). *Elite and specialized interviewing.* Evanston, IL: Northwest University Press.

PROBIT ANALYSIS

Probit analysis originated as a method of analyzing quantal (dichotomous) responses. Quantal responses involve situations in which there is only one possible response to a stimulus, sometimes referred to as "all-or-nothing." Early applications of probit analysis involved biological assays. A classic example involves the determination of death when an insect is exposed to an insecticide. Although theoretically the health of the insect deteriorates as exposure to the insecticide is increased, measurement limitations or focus on a specific result necessitate the use of a DICHOTOMOUS VARIABLE to represent the quantal response. Current applications in the social sciences often involve individual-level behavior such as whether a member of Congress votes for or against a bill or when a judge affirms or reverses a lower court decision.

Analytical work in the social sciences often uses a form of linear REGRESSION analysis (e.g., ORDINARY LEAST SQUARES [OLS]). A fundamental assumption of regression analysis is that the DEPENDENT VARIABLE is CONTINUOUS, which allows for a linear model. Many research questions, however, involve situations with a dichotomous dependent variable (such as the decision making of human actors, with a prime example being individual voting behavior). Because certain regression assumptions are violated when the dependent variable is dichotomous, which in turn may lead to serious errors of INFERENCE, analysis of dichotomous variables generally requires a nonlinear estimation procedure, and probit is a common choice.

The conceptual approach of regression is to estimate the coefficients for a linear model that minimizes the sum of the squared errors between the observed and predicted values of the dependent variable given the values of the independent variables. In contrast, the approach of probit is to estimate the coefficients of a nonlinear model that maximizes the likelihood of observing the value of the dependent variable given the values of the independent variables. As such, probit estimates are obtained by the method known as MAXIMUM LIKELIHOOD ESTIMATION.

The probit model makes four basic assumptions. First, the error term is normally distributed. With this assumption, the probit estimates have a set of properties similar to those of OLS estimates (e.g., unbiasedness, normal sampling distributions, minimum variance). Second, the probability that the dependent variable takes on the value 1 (given the choices 0 and 1) is a function of the independent variables. Third, the observations of the dependent variable are statistically independent. This rules out SERIAL CORRELATION. Fourth, there are no perfect linear dependencies among the independent variables. As with OLS, near but not exact linear dependencies may result in MULTICOLLINEARITY.

Although probit estimates appear similar to those of OLS regression, their interpretation is less straightforward. Probit estimates are probabilities of observing a 0 or 1 in the dependent variable given the values of the independent variables for a particular observation. The coefficient estimate for each independent variable is the amount the probability of the dependent variable taking on the value 1 increases (or decreases if the estimate is negative), and it is given in standard deviations, a Z-SCORE, based on the cumulative normal probability distribution. Thus, the estimated probability that $y = 1$ for a given observation is

$$P(y = 1) = \Phi \left(\sum_{i=1}^{n} \hat{\beta}_0 + \hat{\beta}_i x_i \right),$$

where $\hat{\beta}_0$ is the estimated coefficient for the constant term, $\hat{\beta}_i$ are the estimated coefficients for the n independent variables (x_i), and Φ is the cumulative normal probability distribution.

Table 1 presents sample probit results for a model containing three independent variables, all of which are measured dichotomously (0/1). The probability that $y = 1$ for a particular observation is

$P(y = 1)$

$= \Phi((2.31) * \text{constant}$

$+ (-2.16) * x_1 + (-1.06) * x_2 + (-2.27) * x_3).$

Table 1   Sample Results of Probit Estimation

Dependent Variable: y		
Independent Variables	Estimated Coefficient	Standard Error
Constant	2.31	.56
x_1	−2.16	.42
x_2	−1.06	.45
x_3	−2.27	.80
N	107	
−2LLR 3 df	65.28	

If all three of the x_i take on the value 1, the Z-score is −3.18. Computer programs may automatically calculate the probability, or one can look it up in a table to determine that the probability that $y = 1$ for this observation is only .0007. If all three of the x_i take on the value 0, the Z-score is 2.31, for a probability of .9896 that $y = 1$.

The marginal effect of a change in value for one of the x_i is often demonstrated by holding the other x_i at some value and calculating the change in probability based on the variable of interest. The values selected for the other x_i may be their means, although this can be theoretically troubling when the variables cannot actually take on such values, or some representative combination of values. For example, if we wish to know the effect of x_1, then we might set $x_2 = 0$ and $x_3 = 1$ and calculate that if $x_1 = 1$, the probability that $y = 1$ is .0170, and the probability increases to .5160 when $x_1 = 0$. Note that the apparent effect of a particular variable will appear larger when the Z-score is closer to 0. For example, if the Z-score of the other variables equals 0, then a one standard deviation change will increase the probability from .5 to .8413. In contrast, if the starting Z-score is 2.0, then the same one standard deviation change will increase the probability from .9772 to .9987.

Significance tests of the estimated coefficients are achieved by dividing the estimate by its standard error to obtain a t-statistic. In the sample results for the first variable, $-2.16/.56 = -5.14$, which is significant at $p < .001$. The log-likelihood ratio is used to test the overall significance of the model. Specifically, $-2(\ln L_0 - \ln L_1)$, where $\ln L_1$ is the natural log of the likelihood value for the full model, and $\ln L_0$ is the value when all the variables except the constant are 0. The log-likelihood ratio, often denoted $-2LLR$, is a chi-square value that tests the hypothesis that all the coefficients except that of the constant are 0. The degrees of freedom are the number of independent variables.

There are two basic types of GOODNESS-OF-FIT MEASURES for probit results. The first are the pseudo-R^2 measures that attempt to evaluate how much variance is explained by the model. One problem with such measures is that they do not consider the success of the model in correctly classifying the observations into the two categories of the dependent variable. This is particularly troublesome when there is a substantial imbalance in the percentage of observations in each category. Even a highly significant model will have difficulty correctly classifying observations into the nonmodal category when a large imbalance exists. An alternative measure considers how much the model reduces the error that would occur if one simply guessed the modal category for each observation. For example, if there were 70 observations in the modal category in a sample of 100, and the model correctly classified 80 observations, there would be a reduction of error of 33% (i.e., the model correctly classified 10 of the 30 errors one would make in simply guessing the modal category).

—Timothy M. Hagle

REFERENCES

Aldrich, J. H., & Cnudde, C. F. (1975). Probing the bounds of conventional wisdom: A comparison of regression, probit, and discriminant analysis. *American Journal of Political Science, 19,* 571–608.

Aldrich, J. H., & Nelson, F. D. (1984). *Linear probability, logit and probit models.* Beverly Hills, CA: Sage.

Hagle, T. M., & Mitchell, G. E., II. (1992). Goodness-of-fit measures for probit and logit. *American Journal of Political Science, 36,* 762–784.

Liao, T. F. (1994). *Interpreting probability models: Logit, probit, and other generalized linear models.* Thousand Oaks, CA: Sage.

Maddala, G. S. (1983). *Limited-dependent and qualitative variables in econometrics.* Cambridge, UK: Cambridge University Press.

McKelvey, R. D., & Zavoina, W. (1975). A statistical model for the analysis of ordinal level dependent variables. *Journal of Mathematical Sociology, 4,* 103–120.

PROJECTIVE TECHNIQUES

A projective technique is defined as an instrument that requires a subject to look at an ambiguous stimulus and to give it structure—for example, by saying what he or she sees on an inkblot. It is assumed that the subject "projects" his or her personality into the response.

It is useful to contrast projective techniques with objective tests. The former have ambiguous stimuli, and the subject can, for example, see anything on an inkblot from an aadvark to a zebra. This great freedom of response enhances the projective nature of the response but can produce quantification problems. On an objective test, subjects might have to choose only between the answers "yes" and "no" in reference to self statements. Such limited responses enhance possibilities for statistical analysis. We might thus say that projective and objective tests are opposites in terms of their strengths and weaknesses. This has led some psychologists to suggest that they provide different kinds of information, with the projective test providing more about what is unique in the individual (IDIOGRAPHIC data) and the objective test telling us more about how the individual compares with a group in terms of personality traits (NOMOTHETIC data).

An example of the type of information provided by a projective technique might be the associations of the patient to having seen "four pink geese" on an inkblot. "When I was little I worked on my uncle's farm—he would slaughter geese and the feathers would turn pink with blood. I recently remembered that he molested me. Funny—he had four daughters." An example of the information provided by an objective test is finding that the score obtained on items measuring depression is very high when contrasted with the normative sample, suggesting that clinical depression is present.

Projective techniques have received much criticism from academic psychologists, usually pertaining to weak psychometric qualities. Nonetheless, they continue to be highly popular among clinically oriented psychologists.

Some of the better known projective techniques include the Rorschach technique, consisting of 10 inkblots in which the subject has to say what he or she sees. A second popular projective technique is the Thematic Apperception Test (TAT), in which the subject has to construct stories for ambiguous pictures of interpersonal scenes. Although there are scoring systems for the TAT and similar techniques, analysis is typically done impressionistically without using scores. A third common projective techinique is the DAP (Draw-A-Person) test, in which the subject draws people and also possibly such things as a house, a tree, a family in action, and so forth. A fourth genre of projective techniques is an incomplete sentences test,

in which subjects have to complete a sentence stem, such as "most women. . . ." Answers to such items are usually analyzed impressionistically. (See SENTENCE COMPLETION TEST.)

Some recent trends in projective technique research include a standardization of different approaches to scoring and accompanying efforts to make the techniques more psychometrically sound (Exner, 2002), the development of alternate techniques designed for minority populations (Constantino, Malgady, & Vazquez, 1981), and use of the techniques as an actual part of the psychotherapy process (Aronow, Reznikoff, & Moreland, 1994).

—Edward Aronow

REFERENCES

Aronow, E., Reznikoff, M., & Moreland, K. (1994). *The Rorschach technique.* Needham Heights, MA: Allyn & Bacon.

Costantino, G., Malgady, R. G., & Vazquez, C. (1981). A comparison of the Murray–TAT and a new Thematic Apperception Test for urban Hispanic children. *Hispanic Journal of Behavior Sciences, 3,* 291–300.

Exner, J. E. (2002). *The Rorschach: A comprehensive system* (Vol. 1). New York: John Wiley.

PROOF PROCEDURE

The proof procedure is a central feature of CONVERSATION ANALYSIS (CA), in which the analysis of what a turn at talk is doing is based on, or referred to, how it is responded to in the next speaker's turn. Thus, a "request" may be identifiable as such, not simply on the basis of its content and grammar or on what an analyst may intuitively interpret it to be, but on the basis that it is treated as such in next turn. It may be constituted interactionally as a request, for example, by being complied with, or by noncompliance being accounted for, or by questioning its propriety, or by some other relevant orientation.

The proof procedure is not merely a method for checking the validity of an analysis that has already been produced. Rather, it is a basic principle of how CA proceeds in the first place. It is available as part of CA's methodology because it is, in the first instance, a participants' procedure, integral to how conversational participants themselves accomplish and check their own understandings of what they are saying and doing. Insofar as participants produce next turns on the basis of what *they* take prior turns to be doing, analysts are able to use next turns for analysis (Sacks, Schegloff, & Jefferson, 1974). The proof procedure is therefore linked to the basic phenomena of conversational turn taking, including "conditional relevance" and "repair" (Schegloff, 1992); see entry on conversation analysis.

An important point to note here is that the proof procedure is *not* a way of establishing or proving what speakers may have "actually intended" to say. Next turns can be understood as displaying or implying participants' hearings of prior turns, but such hearings may transform or subvert any such intentions rather than stand merely as hearers' best efforts to understand them (cf. Schegloff, 1989, p. 200, on how "a next action can recast what has preceded"). But this is not a failure of the next-turn proof procedure because CA's analytic goal is not speakers' intentions, understood psychologically, but rather the methods (in the sense of ETHNOMETHODOLOGY) by which conversational interaction is made to work. Again, it is a participants' option, having heard how a first turn has been responded to, to "repair" that displayed understanding in a subsequent "third turn." What we then have is CA's object of study—not speakers' intentional meanings, but their interactional procedures for achieving orderly talk. Meaning is taken to be an interactional accomplishment, and the proof procedure takes us directly to the interactionally contingent character of meaning for participants, as well as the basis on which it can be studied in the empirically available details of recorded talk.

—Derek Edwards

REFERENCES

Sacks, H., Schegloff, E. A., & Jefferson, G. (1974). A simplest systematics for the organization of turn-taking for conversation. *Language, 50*(4), 696–735.

Schegloff, E. A. (1989). Harvey Sacks—lectures 1964–1965: An introduction/memoir. *Human Studies, 12,* 185–209.

Schegloff, E. A. (1992). Repair after next turn: The last structurally provided defence of intersubjectivity in conversation. *American Journal of Sociology, 97*(5), 1295–1345.

PROPENSITY SCORES

The propensity score is defined as the PROBABILITY of an individual being exposed to a new treatment, rather than the control treatment, conditional on a set of covariates. Propensity scores are typically used in the context of CAUSAL inference, in which the objective is to estimate the effect of some intervention (the new treatment) by comparing the outcomes in two groups of subjects: one group that has been exposed to the intervention (the treated group) and an unexposed group (the control group).

Rosenbaum and Rubin (1983), who coined the term *propensity score,* show that subclassification, pair MATCHING, and model-based adjustment for the propensity score all lead to UNBIASED estimates of the treatment effect when treatment assignment is based on the set of COVARIATES that are in the propensity score. Subclassification involves classifying the observations (treated and control) into blocks based on the propensity score. Within each such block, the distribution of all covariates will be the same in the treated and control groups, at least in large SAMPLES. This outcome can be checked through statistical tests such as T-TESTS. Methods for causal inference in RANDOMIZED studies can then be used within each block. Pair matching chooses for each treated member the control member with the closest value of the propensity score. Analysis is done on the matched samples. The assumptions inherent in modeling (such as linearity) will be better satisfied in the matched groups than in the full treated and control samples because there is less EXTRAPOLATION. Other matching methods can also be used.

Conditional on the propensity score, treatment assignment is independent of the covariates, which implies that at the same value of the propensity score, the distribution of observed covariates is the same in the treated and control groups. This result justifies the use of the one-dimensional propensity score for matching or subclassification, in place of the multidimensional full set of covariates.

In randomized EXPERIMENTS, the propensity scores are known. In observational studies, however, they must be estimated from the data. Propensity scores are often estimated with LOGISTIC REGRESSION. Other classification methods such as CART or DISCRIMINANT ANALYSIS can also be used. Dehejia and Wahba (1999) provide an example of an observational study that uses propensity scores, including details on estimation.

OBSERVATIONAL studies designed by using subclassification and/or blocking on propensity scores resemble randomized experiments in two important ways. The first is that the analysis is done on treated and control groups with similar distributions of the observed covariates. In randomized experiments, however, the distributions of all covariates are the same in the treated and control groups as a direct consequence of the randomization. Propensity scores can be used to replicate this as much as possible in observational studies.

The second way that an observational study designed using propensity scores resembles a randomized experiment is that the outcome data are not used in the design stage. The propensity score is estimated and assessed, and matched samples and/or subclasses are formed, without involving the outcome. Rubin (2001) discusses in more detail the use of propensity scores in the design of observational studies.

—Elizabeth A. Stuart

REFERENCES

Dehejia, R. H., & Wahba, S. (1999). Causal effects in nonexperimental studies: Reevaluating the evaluation of training programs. *Journal of the American Statistical Association, 94*, 1053–1062.

Rosenbaum, P. R. (2002). *Observational studies.* New York: Springer-Verlag.

Rosenbaum, P. R., & Rubin, D. B. (1983). The central role of the propensity score in observational studies for causal effects. *Biometrika, 70*, 41–55.

Rubin, D. B. (2001). Using propensity scores to help design observational studies: Application to the tobacco litigation. *Health Services and Outcomes Research Methodology, 2*, 169–188.

Winship, C., & Morgan, S. L. (1999). The estimation of causal effects from observational data. *Annual Review of Sociology, 25*, 659–706.

PROPORTIONAL REDUCTION OF ERROR (PRE)

Assume we have two models for predicting a variable Y and that for each MODEL, we have some measure of the inaccuracy of our PREDICTIONS. Also assume that Model 1 is the more "naive" or less informed model, for instance, predicting the value of Y without knowing anything about any of the predictors of Y; Model 2 is a more informed model, using information about one or more predictors of Y to predict the value of Y. The measure of inaccuracy for Model 1, E_1, may be a measure of the VARIATION of the observed values of Y about the predicted value of Y, an *actual count* of the number of ERRORS, or, when different

predictions under the same (naive) rule (e.g., given the number of cases in each category, randomly guessing which cases belonged in which category) would produce different numbers for E_1, the *expected number* of errors based on the rule for prediction in Model 1. The measure of inaccuracy for Model 2, E_2, would be the variation of the estimated value of Y in the second model or the *actual* number (not expected, because the more informed Model 2 should produce a unique prediction for each case) of errors of prediction made with the second model.

The *proportional change in error* is the ratio $(E_1 - E_2)/E_1$. As described in Menard (2002) and Wilson (1969), it is possible that the naive prediction of Model 1 may be better, by some measures of error, than the more informed prediction of Model 2, in which case we have a *proportional increase in error.* If the value of $(E_1 - E_2)/(E_1)$ is positive, however, it indicates that we are better able to predict the value of Y from Model 2 than from Model 1, and using Model 2 results in a *proportional reduction in error* (PRE) $= (E_1 - E_2)/(E_1)$. Multiplying the PRE by 100 gives us a *percentage reduction in error,* the percentage by which we reduce our error of prediction by using Model 2 instead of Model 1. The clear interpretation of PRE measures has led Costner (1965) and others to argue that PRE measures should be used in preference to other measures of association in social science research.

Examples of PRE measures include Goodman and Kruskal's τ_{YX} and λ_{YX} for bivariate association between nominal variables, in which Y is the variable being predicted and X is the predictor (Reynolds, 1984); the square of Kendall's τ_b, $(\tau_b)^2$, for bivariate ASSOCIATION between ORDINAL variables (Wilson, 1969); and the square of PEARSON'S r, r^2, for ratio variables. For prediction tables, such as those generated by LOGISTIC REGRESSION or DISCRIMINANT ANALYSIS, PRE measures include λ_p, τ_p, and φ_p, similar but not identical to the corresponding measures for CONTINGENCY TABLES (Menard, 2002). For the special case of 2×2 contingency tables (but *not* more generally), several of these PRE measures produce the same numerical value: $r^2 = \tau_b^2 = \tau_{YX}^2$. In models with more than one predictor for a dependent variable, the familiar R^2 for ORDINARY LEAST SQUARES regression analysis and the LIKELIHOOD RATIO R^2, R_L^2 for logistic regression analysis are also PRE measures (Menard, 2002).

—Scott Menard

REFERENCES

Costner, H. L. (1965). Criteria for measures of association. *American Sociological Review, 30,* 341–353.

Menard, S. (2002). *Applied logistic regression analysis* (2nd ed.). Thousand Oaks, CA: Sage.

Reynolds, H. T. (1984). *Analysis of nominal data* (2nd ed.). Beverly Hills, CA: Sage.

Wilson, T. P. (1969). A proportional reduction in error interpretation for Kendall's tau-b. *Social Forces, 47,* 340–342.

PROTOCOL

Protocol has several usages in the literatures of social science methodology, but with all of them, the core meaning, generally construed, is "a detailed statement of procedures for all or part of a research or analytic undertaking." This core meaning is found across fields ranging from psychiatry to sociology and from political science to epidemiology. (Note, however, that *protocol* also is a very common term in the literatures of computer and information science, and there its meaning is rather different—that is, "a set of rules for transferring information among diverse processing units." The processing units in question will often be computers, but they may be sentient beings.)

One early social science use of the term was in research employing questionnaires (whether in broad sample surveys or in more focused interviewing), in which *interview protocol* was used synonymously with QUESTIONNAIRE or INTERVIEW SCHEDULE. Of course, here the detailed statement of procedures is limited entirely to matters of sequence and wording for the questions being asked.

Another early use was in ARTIFICIAL INTELLIGENCE models of problem solving, where "thinking-aloud protocols" or VERBAL PROTOCOLS were used first to provide human points of comparison with model behaviors and later to provide direct insight into how people reason (Ericsson & Simon, 1984; Newell & Simon, 1961, 1971). Thinking-aloud protocols represented participants' step-by-step recounting of their analytic thoughts while in the process of solving puzzles or problems. These recountings became the raw data of an investigation. Perhaps because sophisticated (as opposed to, say, keyword) analysis of verbal protocols is such a daunting task, we now find little use of such protocols in most of the social sciences. However, they remain important in some areas of psychology (Carroll, 1997).

At the present time, an increasingly popular social science use of *protocol* is borrowed from medicine, where it has long been paired with TREATMENT or research. The meaning is akin to RESEARCH DESIGN, although a *treatment protocol* in medicine has infinitely more detail to it than is found in the typical non-experimental research design in the social sciences. Especially in clinical trials, a "protocol" covers every facet and every particular of all procedures in an effort to totally standardize data collection across times and sites. In contrast, the areas of standardization in research designs for the nonexperimental social sciences are for the most part focused loosely on measurement procedures. In many field studies, for example, there will be an effort to standardize questioning and the coding of answers. Fully standardized CODING will also be sought in the treatments of texts of one kind or another.

By their very nature, EXPERIMENTS require detailed research designs/protocols so that investigators can run multiple sessions under conditions that are as close as possible to true constancy. Hence, the growing use of experimental methods in many of the social sciences will be accompanied by increased use of explicit research protocols. Also, in an important contribution to the research enterprise, the publication of those protocols will make exact REPLICATIONS more common than they have been to date.

—Douglas Madsen

REFERENCES

Carroll, J. M. (1997). Human-computer interaction: Psychology as a science of design. *Annual Review of Psychology, 48,* 61–83.

Ericsson, K. A., & Simon, H. A. (1984). *Protocol analysis: Verbal reports as data.* Cambridge: MIT Press.

Newell, A., & Simon, H. A. (1961). Computer simulation of human thinking. *Science, 134,* 2011–2017.

Newell, A., & Simon, H. A. (1971). *Human problem solving.* Englewood Cliffs, NJ: Prentice Hall.

PROXY REPORTING

Proxy reporting refers to two related situations in conducting social surveys. If, by certain preset criteria, survey researchers consider a sample person as being unable to answer the survey, then the proxy or substitute respondent is used. More generally, the situation in which a person who reports information on other persons can be defined as proxy reporting.

—Tim Futing Liao

PROXY VARIABLE

A proxy variable is a variable that is used to measure an unobservable quantity of interest. Although a proxy variable is not a direct measure of the desired quantity, a good proxy variable is strongly related to the unobserved variable of interest. Proxy variables are extremely important to and frequently used in the social sciences because of the difficulty or impossibility of obtaining measures of the quantities of interest.

An example clarifies both the importance and the problems resulting from the use of proxy variables. Suppose a researcher is interested in the effect of intelligence on income, controlling for age. If it were possible to know the intelligence of an individual and assuming (for purposes of illustration) that the relationship is linear, then the relationship could be estimated using MULTIPLE REGRESSION by

$$\text{Income}_i = \alpha + \beta_1 \cdot \text{Intelligence}_i + \beta_2 \cdot \text{age}_i + \varepsilon_i.$$

Unlike age, intelligence is not a quantity that can be directly measured. Instead, the researcher interested in the above relationship must rely on measures arguably related to intelligence such as years of education and standardized test results. Using years of education as a proxy variable for intelligence assumes: $\text{Intelligence}_i = \text{Years of Education}_i + \delta_i$. Consequently, the researcher estimates the following:

$$\text{Income}_i = \alpha + \beta_1 \cdot \text{Years of Education}_i + \beta_2 \cdot \text{age}_i + \varepsilon_i.$$

Strictly speaking, β_1 does not measure the covariation between intelligence and income unless $\delta_i = 0$ for all individuals i. However, because it is impossible to assess how well a proxy variable measures the unobservable quantity of interest (i.e., what the value of δ_i is), and because the relationship between income and years of education is of interest only insofar as it permits an understanding of the relationship between income and intelligence, β_1 is frequently interpreted in terms of the latter. Some suggest that when several measures are available (as is arguably the case in the above example), specification searches may be used to try to select the best proxy variable (Leamer, 1978).

Statistically, the decision of whether to use a proxy variable entails weighing two possible consequences. If a proxy variable is used, then the researcher necessarily encounters the traditional problems associated with "errors-in-variables" (i.e., all PARAMETER ESTIMATES are inconsistent) (Fuller, 1987). However, if no proxy variable is used and the unmeasured quantity is related to the specification of interest, then failure to use a proxy variable will result in omitted variable bias (see OMITTED VARIABLE and BIAS). Econometric investigation of the trade-off reveals that it is generally advisable to include a proxy variable, even one that is relatively poor (Kinal & Lahiri, 1983).

—Joshua D. Clinton

REFERENCES

Fuller, W. A. (1987). *Measurement error models*. New York: John Wiley.

Kinal, T., & Lahiri, K. (1983). Specification error analysis with stochastic regressors. *Econometrica, 54,* 1209–1220.

Leamer, E. (1978). *Specification searches: Ad hoc inferences with nonexperimental data*. New York: John Wiley.

Maddala, G. S. (1992). *Introduction to econometrics*. Englewood Cliffs, NJ: Prentice Hall.

PSEUDO-*R*-SQUARED

A commonly used GOODNESS-OF-FIT MEASURE in REGRESSION analysis is the COEFFICIENT OF (MULTIPLE) DETERMINATION, also known as *R*-SQUARED or R^2. R^2 essentially measures the proportion of the variance in the DEPENDENT VARIABLE that is explained by the MULTIPLE REGRESSION model. Although some disagreement exists as to the overall utility of R^2, it does provide a widely used measure of model performance.

Regression analysts have available a wide array of diagnostic tools and goodness-of-fit measures. Such tools and measures are less well developed for models using PROBIT and LOGIT. In particular, there is no direct analog to R^2 as a goodness-of-fit measure. Several substitutes, pseudo-R^2s, are available and are often present in the results of various computer programs. A difficulty facing probit and logit analysts is in choosing among the pseudo-R^2s. An initial question to be addressed when choosing a pseudo-R^2 will be the use to which the measure will be put (e.g., explanation of VARIANCE, HYPOTHESIS testing, classifying the dependent variable).

The most common use is as a measure of how much variation in the dependent variable is explained or accounted for by the model. One frequently used method, developed by McKelvey and Zavoina (1975), is to use the estimated probit or logit coefficients to compute the variance of the forecasted values for the LATENT DEPENDENT VARIABLE, denoted $\text{var}(\hat{y}_i)$. The disturbances have unit variance, and the total variance then reduces to explained variance plus 1. This pseudo-R^2 is then calculated as

$$R^2 = \frac{\text{var}(\hat{y}_i)}{1 + \text{var}(\hat{y}_i)}.$$

Another popular alternative pseudo-R^2, developed by Aldrich and Nelson (1984), uses the chi-square statistic, $-2LLR$, defined as $-2\ln(L_0/L_1)$ with k, the number of independent variables estimated, DEGREES OF FREEDOM. This measure requires two passes through the data—the first with only the constant to determine L_0 and the second with the full model to determine L_1. The pseudo-R^2 is then calculated as

$$R^2 = \frac{-2LLR}{N - 2LLR},$$

where N is the number of observations.

Both measures proved to be good estimates of the ORDINARY LEAST SQUARES R^2 in a test conducted by Hagle and Mitchell (1992) using SIMULATION data. The Aldrich and Nelson (1984) measure produced slightly smaller errors and was more ROBUST when the assumption of a NORMAL DISTRIBUTION in the dependent variable was violated. A theoretical limitation in the calculation of the Aldrich and Nelson measure is easily corrected based on the percentage of observations in the modal category.

The utility of pseudo-R^2s for probit and logit is based on the assumption of an unobserved continuous variable that manifests itself only as an observed dichotomous variable. For example, the unobserved variable may be the probability that a voter will choose Candidate A over Candidate B, and the observed variable is the actual choice between A and B. Because variations in the unobserved variable will produce the same observed variable, analysts may place greater emphasis on the model's ability to correctly classify the observations. One issue in using the correct classification rate as a goodness-of-fit measure is that it often becomes difficult for probit and logit to correctly classify observations into the nonmodal category when the percentage of observations in the modal category is quite high. On the whole, a combination of different measures may provide the best understanding of model performance.

—Timothy M. Hagle

REFERENCES

Aldrich, J. H., & Nelson, F. D. (1984). *Linear probability, logit and probit models.* Thousand Oaks, CA: Sage.

Hagle, T. M., & Mitchell, G. E., II. (1992). Goodness-of-fit measures for probit and logit. *American Journal of Political Science, 36,* 762–784.

McKelvey, R. D., & Zavoina, W. (1975). A statistical model for the analysis of ordinal level dependent variables. *Journal of Mathematical Sociology, 4,* 103–120.

PSYCHOANALYTIC METHODS

Psychoanalysis is both a clinical psychotherapeutic practice and a body of theory concerning people's mental life, including its development and expression in activities and relationships. Empirical findings are basic to psychoanalysis, but rather than being based on a claim to objectivity, these findings are recognized to be the product of both the patient's and analyst's subjectivities. Objections to the scientific status of psychoanalytic data have been on the grounds that the psychoanalytic method was based in the consulting room, not the laboratory, and produced single case studies, not generalizable findings. However, following the challenge to positivist methods in social science research, the resulting linguistic, qualitative, and hermeneutic turns have opened a space for psychoanalysis in qualitative methods.

Psychoanalytic theory has proved influential in questioning the Enlightenment subject—the rational, unitary, consciously intentional subject that usually underpins social scientists' assumptions about research participants. The premise of unconscious conflict and defenses casts doubt on the idea of a self-knowledgeable, transparent respondent, an idea underpinning interview-based, survey, and attitude scale research (Hollway & Jefferson, 2000). Such unconscious contents necessarily require interpretation, and these are warranted by psychoanalytic concepts (e.g., the idea of denying an action when its recall would be painful). Such concepts have been built up and refined through clinical psychoanalytic practice (Dreher, 2000).

Psychoanalytic methods require modification if extended beyond the consulting room, where research findings are subordinate to therapeutic purpose. Clinical and research applications both use psychoanalytic interpretation. In the consulting room, analysts' interpretations are a small part of their therapeutic method, offered directly to patients whose emotional responses provide a test of the interpretation's correctness. In generating and interpreting research data psychoanalytically, other methods of validation are sought (e.g., looking for supporting and countervailing examples in the whole text or detecting a recognizable pattern of defenses).

The method of free association, on which psychoanalysis is based, encourages patients to report their thoughts without reservation on the assumption that uncensored thoughts lead to what is significant. The use of free association can inform the production and analysis of interview data (see FREE ASSOCIATION NARRATIVE INTERVIEW METHOD), tapping aspects of human social life of which methods relying on the self-knowledgeable transparent research subject remain unaware (e.g., the desires and anxieties that affect family and work relationships). The concept of transference refers to the displacement of unconscious wishes from an earlier figure, such as a parent, on to the analyst, where they are experienced with the immediacy of feelings for the current person. Albeit diluted in a nonclinical setting, researchers sensitive to their own and participants' transferences and countertransferences can use these as data (e.g., Walkerdine, Lucey, & Melody, 2001). Epistemologically, these concepts enhance the critique of objectivity and supplement the understanding of researcher reflexivity, an important but undertheorized concept in qualitative social science.

Interviewing and observation both include psychoanalytic influences. Kvale (1999) argues that knowledge produced in the psychoanalytic interview is relevant for research. Two currents of observation work use psychoanalytic methods—namely, ethnographic field studies (Hunt, 1989) and baby observation (Miller, Rustin, Rustin, & Shuttleworth, 1989). In Germany, ethnopsychoanalysis applies psychoanalysis to the study of culture. Psychoanalytic observation—dating from the 1940s in England, when detailed once-weekly observation of babies in their families became a part of training at the Tavistock Institute—now extends to research on wider topics.

—Wendy Hollway

REFERENCES

Dreher, A. U. (2000). *Foundations for conceptual research in psychoanalysis* (Psychoanalytic Monograph 4). London: Karnac.

Hollway, W., & Jefferson, T. (2000). *Doing qualitative research differently: Free association, narrative and the interview method.* London: Sage.

Hunt, J. C. (1989). *Psychoanalytic aspects of fieldwork* (University Paper Series on Qualitative Research Methods 18). Newbury Park, CA: Sage.

Kvale, S. (1999). The psychoanalytic interview as qualitative research. *Qualitative Inquiry, 5*(1), 87–113.

Miller, L., Rustin, M., Rustin, M., & Shuttleworth, J. (1989). *Closely observed infants.* London: Duckworth.

Walkerdine, V., Lucey, H., & Melody, J. (2001). *Growing up girl: Psychosocial explorations of gender and class.* Basingstoke, UK: Palgrave.

PSYCHOMETRICS

Psychometrics deals with the measurement of individual differences between people. The instruments used for measurement can be psychological tests, questionnaires, personality inventories, and observational checklists. The measurement values quantify either the levels of a psychological property or the ordering of these levels. These properties can be abilities (e.g., verbal intelligence, analytical reasoning, spatial orientation), skills (e.g., in manipulating control panels for traffic regulation, in chairing a meeting in a work situation), personality traits (e.g., introversion, friendliness, neuroticism), preferences (e.g., for consumer goods, politicians, authors), and attitudes (e.g., toward abortion, the political right wing, NATO intervention in other countries). "John is more introvert than Mary" is an example of an ordering with respect to a personality trait, and "Carol's general intelligence is high enough to admit her to the course" compares Carol's general cognitive ability level to the absolute level required to pass the course entrance.

The measurement values obtained through tests, questionnaires, or other instruments must be reliable and valid. A measurement is reliable to the degree it can be generalized across independent replications of the same measurement procedure. A broader definition says that generalization can also be across the measurement units (the items from a test), different measurement occasions (time points), or different psychologists who assessed a pupil or a client.

A measurement has CONSTRUCT VALIDITY to the degree it is based on an adequate operationalization of the underlying property. This means that the measurement instrument measures introversion and not, say, the respondent's idealized self-image. Predictive validity holds to the degree the measurement permits making correct predictions about individuals' future behavior (e.g., the degree to which analytical reasoning predicts people's suitability for computer programmer).

Psychometrics studies and develops mathematical and statistical measurement methods. Older psychometric methods are classical test theory, mostly due to Charles Spearman; LIKERT SCALING for rating scale data; FACTOR ANALYSIS as developed in the 1920s and 1930s by Spearman, Thurstone, and Thompson; Thurstone's method for paired comparison data; Guttman's scalogram analysis for dominance data; and Coombs's unfolding method for preference data. GENERALIZABILITY THEORY, mostly due to Cronbach, broadens classical test theory by using an analysis of variance layout of sources that explain test performance. ITEM RESPONSE THEORY models are a large family of modern psychometric models, initially developed in the 1950s and 1960s by Lord, Birnbaum, Rasch, and Mokken. Since then, this development has been taken up by many researchers and has dominated psychometrics over the past few decades.

Traditionally, MULTIVARIATE ANALYSIS methods have been part of psychometrics. In particular, factor analysis and CLUSTER ANALYSIS have been used for the investigation of construct validity and regression methods for establishing test batteries to be used for prediction. Methods for psychophysical measurement, such as the determination of visual or aural thresholds, are mainly aimed at establishing general laws of behavior and less at measuring individual differences.

Psychometrics also includes the technology of constructing measurement instruments of all sorts, including standard paper-and-pencil tests and item banks for computerized adaptive testing procedures that enable a more efficient measurement procedure. Other applications identify items that put certain minority groups at a disadvantage (differential item functioning) and respondents who produced aberrant patterns of item scores (person-fit analysis). Also included are applications that study the cognitive processes and solution strategies respondents use to solve the items in the test (cognitive modeling).

—Klaas Sijtsma

See also ITEM RESPONSE THEORY

PSYCHOPHYSIOLOGICAL MEASURES

Psychophysiological measures are physiological measures used to index psychological constructs (e.g., psychological states or processes). Researchers began to explore mind-body relationships scientifically early in the 20th century. However, psychophysiology did not emerge as a subdiscipline separate from physiological psychology until mid-century. Until that time (and beyond), physiological psychologists explored the effects of physiological changes, particularly neurophysiological ones, on behavioral and mental outcome measures, typically conducting animal experiments. In contrast, psychophysiologists explored effects of psychological changes on physiological outcome measures, typically conducting human experiments. Now, the distinctions between psychophysiology and physiological psychology have blurred, with both subsumed within neuroscience more generally.

Nevertheless, psychophysiologists have made enduring general contributions to psychology and behavioral science as well as contributing many important and useful physiological measures of indexes of psychological states. The utility of physiological indexes of psychological states rests on the assumption that the observation and recording of biological or physiological processes, particularly less consciously controllable ones, are methodologically advantageous.

Physiological and, hence, psychophysiological measures are typically online, covert, and continuous. Online physiological measures provide pinpoint temporal accuracy. They can be linked in time to the expected occurrence of the psychological state or process being indexed, thereby providing simultaneous evidence of the strength or operation of the state or process, while avoiding some pitfalls of post hoc, measures such variations in memory. For example, an online physiological measure of happiness would avoid any measurement error due to participant recall.

Covert physiological measures provide data not readily observable either to the participant being assessed or to outside observers, thereby increasing their veridicality. Given their covert nature, physiological measures provide no conscious feedback to

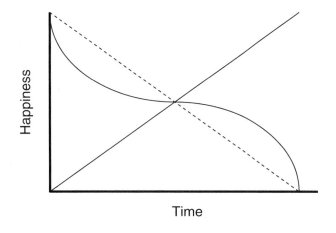

Figure 1   Psychophysiological Measures

participants, thereby providing little if any basis for participant control of their responses. Hence, by their covert nature, physiological measures void participant impression management strategies in experimental contexts. For example, a covert measure of happiness would void attempts of participants to appear more or less happy than they actually were.

Continuous physiological measures provide topographical accuracy. Experimenters can sample physiological measures repeatedly at high rates. Indeed, given computer technology, physiological measures can be recorded with near-perfect fidelity over time. Hence, researchers can produce topographical physiological records that increase available information without increasing cost. For example, a topographical record of happiness would allow investigators to examine trends and variability in happiness within an epoch. Even if measurements share CENTRAL TENDENCY values (i.e., means, medians, modes), topographical differences can provide important psychological information. Figure 1 illustrates a few of the many possible topographical differences among participant responses sharing the same central tendencies.

However, the fact that physiological measures typically provide online, covert, and continuous data, with corresponding temporal, veridical, and topographical accuracy, does not mean they have CONSTRUCT VALIDITY. Here, the legacy of psychophysiology for methodologists is less obvious. Indeed, the happiness examples above mention no specific physiological index or metric. Even though a literature search of happiness studies would probably turn up quite a few

physiological measures that have been used, such as electrodermal activity, heart rate, blood flow to the cerebral cortex, and so forth, explicit theory linking any of these or other physiological measures to the happiness construct might be quite fuzzy.

Physiological measures, like other measures used in psychological research, must have construct validity. As stated elsewhere (Blascovich, 2000; Cacioppo, Tassinary, & Berntson, 2000), *invariance* is the ideal association between a psychological construct and its index, whether physiological or not. This means that the construct and its index should co-occur, with the presence of one ensuring the presence of the other and vice versa. However, invariance proves a difficult ideal to achieve between psychological constructs and physiological indexes because the constructs (e.g., happiness, love, risk taking, prejudice, learning) are difficult to define explicitly, the body operates more as a general-purpose system than a specific purpose one, or both.

Here, as for nonphysiological measures, one needs a specific measurement theory on which to base any invariance assumption. For physiological measures, the measurement theory must be based on psychophysiological theory connecting the construct with its purported index. This is no mean feat. Nevertheless, several strong theories have been applied or developed to provide the necessary justification for many psychological constructs, including ones within many psychological domains such as affect, motivation, and cognition (for reviews, see Blascovich, 2000; Cacioppo, Tassinary, & Berntson, 2000).

For example, Cacioppo, Petty, Losch, and Kim (1986) suggested using patterns of zygomaticus major and corrugator supercilii (facial) muscle responses assessed via electromyographic (EMG) techniques to index and distinguish positive and negative affect. The psychophysiological basis for their assertion involved Darwinian work on the evolutionary significance of facial expressions for social interactions. They reasoned that positive affect should be accompanied by increases in zygomaticus major (the "smile muscle") EMG and decreases in corrugator supercilii (the "frown muscle") EMG but that negative affect should be accompanied by the reverse pattern. Subsequently, they validated these patterns experimentally.

Blascovich and his colleagues (e.g., Blascovich & Tomaka, 1996) suggested using patterns of cardiovascular responses assessed using electrocardiographic (ECG), impedance cardiographic (ZKG), and hemodynamic blood pressure monitoring techniques to index challenge and threat motivational states. The psychophysiological basis for their assertion involved Dienstbier's (1989) neuroendocrine theory of physiological toughness. Blascovich and colleagues demonstrated that challenge, which they identified as a benign motivational state (i.e., when resources are sufficient to meet situational demands), is accompanied by sympathetic adrenal medullary (SAM)-driven increases in cardiac contractility and cardiac output accompanied by vasodilation, whereas threat, which they identified as a malignant motivational state (i.e., when resources are insufficient to meet situational demands), is accompanied by pituitary adrenal cortical (PAC) inhibition of the SAM axis, resulting in increases in cardiac contractility but little change in cardiac output and vasomotor tone.

Many other theoretically based physiological indexes of psychological constructs have appeared and continue to add to the store of such measures. With new technology, such as brain imaging techniques, constantly emerging and increased appreciation of the utility of physiological measures for psychological research, we can look forward to even more and better ones being developed.

—Jim Blascovich

REFERENCES

Blascovich, J. (2000). Psychophysiological indexes of psychological processes. In H. T. Reis & C. M. Judd (Eds.), *Handbook of research methods in social and personality psychology* (pp. 117–137). Cambridge, UK: Cambridge University Press.

Blascovich, J., & Tomaka, J. (1996). The biopsychosocial model of arousal regulation. In M. Zanna (Ed.), *Advances in experimental social psychology* (pp. 1–51). New York: Academic Press.

Cacioppo, J. T., Petty, R. E., Losch, M. E., & Kim, H. S. (1986). Electromyographic specificity during simple physical and attitudinal tasks: Location and topographical features of integrated EMG responses. *Biological Psychology, 18,* 85–121.

Cacioppo, J. T., Tassinary, L. G., & Berntson, G. G. (2000). *Handbook of psychophysiology* (2nd ed.). Cambridge, UK: Cambridge University Press.

Dienstbier, R. A. (1989). Arousal and physiological toughness: Implications for mental and physical health. *Psychological Review, 96,* 84–100.

PUBLIC OPINION RESEARCH

Public opinion research involves the CONCEPTUALIZATION and MEASUREMENT of what people think or how they behave. Since the development of the field in conjunction with rise of survey research, practitioners have disagreed about the meaning and measurement of each of these aspects, and research on "public opinion research" remains an active and contested area today. Although an argument can be made that "public opinion" can be represented as well by various forms of collective action, such as strikes and protest marches, as it can by survey responses, SURVEYS and polls remain the predominant basis for measuring and reporting it.

One of the key conceptual points is whether public opinion is an individual or an AGGREGATED concept. Although an individual may have or express attitudes and opinions, does a public exist only as the aggregated combination of the views of individuals? If individuals hold views but they are not measured, aggregated, and communicated to others, is there in fact any prospect of collective action based on such opinions? Another important point is whether public opinion exists if it is not expressed. This argument has been used to distinguish between "measured" opinion and "considered" opinion. This raises the prospect that anything that can be measured with a survey can be considered "opinion" no matter what the quality of the questions asked, the definition of the groups that were queried, or how much thought an individual has given to an issue. *Measured opinion* is reflected in the responses that individuals give to questions they are asked, whether or not they have devoted any attention to the topic, whereas *considered opinion* is the end result of a process of deliberation that takes place over time.

Generally, public opinion is associated with the results from a survey, typically involving measurements taken from a REPRESENTATIVE SAMPLE of a relevant POPULATION. Typically, this would be designed to reflect the attitudes of all adults in a society or political constituency. Some researchers would argue that there are other behavioral measures of public opinion, such as voting, demonstrations, or letters that are written to a newspaper.

The study of public opinion has focused on two key areas: the conceptual dimensions of the opinions themselves and the effects of survey methodology on the views expressed. Most populations are stratified in opinion terms, with a very small proportion comprising political elites who hold complex, well-structured views on issues and who can provide survey responses that seem to be ideologically consistent and constrained (Converse, 1964). Research shows that elites, in addition to their discourse through the media, provide significant cues to the mass public about the salience or importance of specific issues, as well as the specific domains along which they should be considered. Information about the party affiliation or political ideology of elites can be very useful to citizens when evaluating such reports, helping them to make judgments without a significant investment in learning or assimilating new information (Lupia, McCubbins, & Popkin, 1998; Popkin, 1991). But information is not the only basis for holding opinions; other social psychological concepts such as stereotypes may support their formation. This is especially true for attitudes about race and gender, for example, or about individuals on welfare or in poverty.

Another aspect of opinions is the intensity with which the attitudes are held. In the political arena, strength of feelings among a minority may be more powerful in explaining policy or legislative changes than the distribution of opinions in the entire population. This can be especially important if such intensity is related to forms of political behavior such as protest, letter writing, or voting.

From a methodological perspective, public opinion researchers are concerned that survey respondents often answer questions posed to them as a matter of courtesy or an implied social contract with an interviewer. As a result, they express opinions that may be lightly held or come off the top of their heads in response to a specific question or its wording. The use of CLOSED-ENDED QUESTIONS, especially those that do not provide an explicit alternative such as "Don't know" or "Have not thought about that," can produce measured opinions that are weakly held at best.

Increasingly, other methodological issues may relate to potential BIASES in the selection of those whose opinions are measured. They include problems of self-selected respondents who answer questions on the growing number of Web sites that simulate polls, problems of the increased use of cell phones that are generally unavailable in the standard RANDOM DIGIT DIALING (RDD) sample, and declining response rates.

Because of concerns about the meaning of public opinion and the ways that survey methodology can affect how it is measured, public opinion research will remain an active area of substantive and methodological attention.

—Michael W. Traugott

REFERENCES

Converse, P. E. (1964). The nature of belief systems in mass publics. In D. Apter (Ed.), *Ideology and discontent* (pp. 206–261). New York: Free Press.

Lupia, A., McCubbins, M. D., & Popkin, S. L. (Eds.). (1998). *Elements of reason.* Cambridge, UK: Cambridge University Press.

Popkin, S. L. (1991). *The reasoning voter.* Chicago: University of Chicago Press.

Price, V. (1992). *Public opinion.* Newbury Park, CA: Sage.

Zaller, J. R. (1992). *The nature and origins of mass opinion.* Cambridge, UK: Cambridge University Press.

PURPOSIVE SAMPLING

Purposive sampling in qualitative inquiry is the deliberate seeking out of participants with particular characteristics, according to the needs of the developing analysis and emerging theory. Because, at the beginning of the study, the researcher does not know enough about a particular phenomenon, the nature of the sample is not always predetermined. Often, midway through data analysis, the researcher will realize that he or she will need to interview participants who were not envisioned as pertinent for the study at the beginning of the project. For example, Martin (1998), in her study of sudden infant death syndrome (SIDS), discovered issues of control over the responsibility for these infants between the groups of first responders (emergency medical technicians and the firefighters) and realized that she would have to interview these professionals, extending her study beyond the interviews with parents, as originally perceived.

Types of purposive sampling are nominated or SNOWBALL SAMPLING (in which participants are referred by members of the same group who have already been enrolled in the study) and THEORETICAL SAMPLING (in which participants are deliberately sought according to information required by the analysis as the study progresses).

In nominated or snowball sampling, the researcher locates a "good" participant and, at the end of the interview, asks the participant to help with the study by referring the researcher to another person who may like to participate in the study. Thus, sampling follows a social network. Nominated or snowball sampling is particularly useful when groups are hard to identify or may not volunteer or respond to a notice advertising for participants. It is a useful strategy when locating participants who would otherwise be hard to locate, perhaps because of shame of fear of reprisal for illegal activities, such as drug use; a closed group, such as a motorcycle gang; or those who have private behaviors or a stigma associated with a disease. Gaining trust with the first participant and allowing that person to assure the group that the research is "OK" provides access to participants who would otherwise be unobtainable.

The final use of a nominated sample is by researchers who are using theoretical sampling. They may use a form of nominated sample by requesting recommendations from the group for participants who have certain kind of experiences or knowledge needed to move the analysis forward.

—Janice M. Morse

REFERENCE

Martin, K. (1998). *When a baby dies of SIDS: The parents' grief and searching for a reason.* Edmonton, Canada: Qual Institute Press.

PYGMALION EFFECT

The term *Pygmalion effect* has both a general and a specific meaning. Its general meaning is that of an *interpersonal expectancy effect* or an *interpersonal self-fulfilling prophecy.* These terms refer to the research finding that the behavior that one person expects from another person is often the behavior that is, in fact, obtained from that other person. The more specific meaning of the *Pygmalion effect* is the effect of teachers' expectations on the performance of their students.

The earliest EXPERIMENTAL studies of Pygmalion effects were conducted with human research participants. Experimenters obtained ratings of photographs of stimulus persons from their research participants, but half the experimenters were led to expect high photo ratings and half were led to expect low photo ratings. In a series of such studies, experimenters expecting higher photo ratings obtained substantially higher photo ratings than did experimenters expecting lower photo ratings (Rosenthal, 1976).

To investigate the generality of these interpersonal expectancy effects in the laboratory, researchers conducted two studies employing animal subjects (Rosenthal, 1976). Half the experimenters were told their rats had been specially bred for maze (or Skinner box) brightness, and half were told their rats had been specially bred for maze (or Skinner box) dullness. In both experiments, when experimenters had been led to expect better learning from their rat subjects, they obtained better learning from their rat subjects.

The "Pygmalion experiment," as it came to be known, was a fairly direct outgrowth of the studies just described. If rats became brighter when expected to by their experimenters, then it did not seem far-fetched to think that children could become brighter when expected to by their teacher. Accordingly, all of the children in the study (Rosenthal & Jacobson, 1968, 1992) were administered a nonverbal test of intelligence, which was disguised as a test that would predict intellectual "blooming." There were 18 classrooms in the school, 3 at each of the six grade levels. Within each grade level, the 3 classrooms were composed of children with above-average ability, average ability, and below-average ability, respectively. Within each of the 18 classrooms, approximately 20% of the children were chosen at random to form the experimental group. Each teacher was given the names of the children from his or her class who were in the experimental condition. The teacher was told that these children had scored on the predictive test of intellectual blooming such that they would show surprising gains in intellectual competence during the next 8 months of school. The only difference between the experimental group and the control group children, then, was in the mind of the teacher.

At the end of the school year, 8 months later, all the children were retested with the same test of intelligence. Considering the school as a whole, the children from whom the teachers had been led to expect greater intellectual gain showed a significantly greater gain than did the children of the control group.

There are now nearly 500 experiments investigating the phenomenon of interpersonal expectancy effects or the Pygmalion effect broadly defined. The typical obtained magnitude of the effect is very substantial; when we have been led to expect a certain behavior from others, we are likely to obtain it about 65% of the time, compared to about 35% of the time, when we have not been led to expect that behavior.

—Robert Rosenthal

See also EXPERIMENTER EXPECTANCY EFFECT, INVESTIGATOR EFFECTS

REFERENCES

Blanck, P. D. (Ed.). (1993). *Interpersonal expectations: Theory, research, and applications.* New York: Cambridge University Press.

Eden, D. (1990). *Pygmalion in management: Productivity as a self-fulfilling prophecy.* Lexington, MA: D. C. Heath.

Rosenthal, R. (1976). *Experimenter effects in behavioral research: Enlarged edition.* New York: Irvington.

Rosenthal, R., & Jacobson, L. (1968). *Pygmalion in the classroom.* New York: Holt, Rinehart & Winston.

Rosenthal, R., & Jacobson, L. (1992). *Pygmalion in the classroom: Expanded edition.* New York: Irvington.

Appendix
Bibliography

Abbott, A., & Forrest, J. (1986). Optimal matching methods for historical sequences. *Journal of Interdisciplinary History, 16,* 471–494.

Abbott, A., & Hrycak, A. (1990). Measuring resemblance in sequence data. *American Journal of Sociology, 96,* 144–185.

Abdi, H., Dowling, W. J., Valentin, D., Edelman, B., & Posamentier, M. (2002). *Experimental design and research methods.* Unpublished manuscript, University of Texas at Dallas, Program in Cognition and Neuroscience.

Abdi, H., Valentin, D., & Edelman, B. (1999). *Neural networks.* Thousand Oaks, CA: Sage.

Abdi, H., Valentin, D., Edelman, B., & O'Toole, A. J. (1996). A Widrow-Hoff learning rule for a generalization of the linear auto-associator. *Journal of Mathematical Psychology, 40,* 175–182.

Abell, P. (1987). *The syntax of social life: The theory and method of comparative narratives.* Oxford, UK: Clarendon.

Abraham, B., & Ledolter, J. (1983). *Statistical methods for forecasting.* New York: Wiley.

Abraham, B., & Ledolter, J. (1986). Forecast functions implied by ARIMA models and other related forecast procedures. *International Statistical Review, 54,* 51–66.

Achen, C. H. (1975). Mass political attitudes and the survey response. *American Political Science Review, 69,* 1218–1231.

Achen, C. H. (1977). Measuring representation: Perils of the correlation coefficient. *American Journal of Political Science, 21,* 805–815.

Achen, C. H. (1982). *Interpreting and using regression.* Beverly Hills, CA: Sage.

Achen, C., & Shively, W. P. (1995). *Cross-level inference.* Chicago: University of Chicago Press.

Achinstein, P. (1983). *The nature of explanation.* New York: Oxford University Press.

Achinstein, P., & Barker, S. F. (1969). *The legacy of logical positivism.* Baltimore: Johns Hopkins University Press.

Adair, J. G., Sharpe, D., & Huynh, C. L. (1989). Hawthorne control procedures in educational experiments: A reconsideration of their use and effectiveness. *Review of Educational Research, 59,* 215–228.

Aday, L. A. (1996). *Designing and conducting health surveys: A comprehensive guide* (2nd ed.). San Francisco: Jossey-Bass.

Adler, P. A. (1985). *Wheeling and dealing.* New York: Columbia University Press.

Adler, P. A., & Adler, P. (1991). *Backboards and blackboards.* New York: Columbia University Press.

Adler, P. A., & Adler, P. (1994). Observational techniques. In N. K. Denzin & Y. S. Lincoln (Eds.), *Handbook of qualitative research* (pp. 377–392). Thousand Oaks, CA: Sage.

Adler, P. A., & Adler, P. (1998). *Peer power.* New Brunswick, NJ: Rutgers University Press.

Adler, P., & Adler, P. A. (1987). *Membership roles in field research* (Qualitative Research Methods Series vol. 6). Newbury Park, CA: Sage.

Adorno, T., & Horkheimer, M. (1979). *Dialectic of enlightenment* (J. Cumming, Trans.). London: Verso. (Original work published 1944).

Afifi, A. A., & Clark, V. A. (1996). *Computer-aided multivariate analysis* (3rd ed.). Boca Raton, FL: Chapman & Hall.

Agar, M. (1973). *Ripping and running.* New York: Academic Press.

Aggresti, A., & Finlay, B. (1997). *Statistical methods for the social sciences* (3rd ed.). Upper Saddle River, NJ: Prentice Hall.

Agresti, A. (1984). *An introduction to categorical data analysis.* New York: John Wiley.

Agresti, A. (1984). *Analysis of ordinal categorical data.* New York: John Wiley.

Agresti, A. (1990). *Categorical data analysis.* New York: John Wiley.

Agresti, A. (1996). *An introduction to categorical data analysis* (2nd ed.). New York: John Wiley.

Agresti, A. (2002). *Categorical data analysis* (2nd ed.). New York: Wiley Interscience.

Agresti, A., & Cato, B. (2000). Simple and effective confidence intervals for proportions and differences of proportions result from adding two successes and two failures. *American Statistician, 54*(4), 280–288.

Agresti, A., & Finlay, B. (1997). *Statistical methods for social sciences* (3rd ed.). Upper Saddle River, NJ: Prentice Hall.

Aiken, L. S., & West, S. G. (1991). *Multiple regression: Testing and interpreting interactions.* Newbury Park, CA: Sage.

Albrow, M. (1990). *Max Weber's construction of social theory.* London: Macmillan.

Aldrich, J. H., & Cnudde, C. F. (1975). Probing the bounds of conventional wisdom: A comparison of regression, probit, and discriminant analysis. *American Journal of Political Science, 19,* 571–608.

Aldrich, J. H., & Nelson, F. D. (1984). *Linear probability, logit and probit models.* Beverly Hills, CA: Sage.

Algina, J., Oshina, T. C., & Lin, W.-Y. (1994). Type I error rates for Welch's test and James's second order test under non-normality and inequality of variance when there are two groups. *Journal of Educational and Behavorial Statistics, 19,* 275–291.

Alkin, M. (1990). *Debates on evaluation.* Newbury Park, CA: Sage.

Allison, P. D. (2003). Event history analysis. In M. A. Hardy & A. Bryman (Eds.), *Handbook of data analysis.* London: Sage.

Allison, P. D. (1978). Measures of inequality. *American Sociological Review, 43,* 865–880.

Allison, P. D. (1987). Estimation of linear models with incomplete data. In C. C. Clogg (Ed.), *Sociological methodology 1987.* San Francisco: Jossey-Bass.

Allison, P. D. (1999). *Multiple regression: A primer.* Thousand Oaks, CA: Pine Forge.

Allison, P. D. (2001). *Missing data.* Thousand Oaks, CA: Sage.

Allport, G. (1942). *The use of personal documents in psychological science.* New York: Social Science Research Council.

Alonso, E. (2002). AI and agents: State of the art. *AI Magazine, 23*(3), 25–29.

Altheide, D. L. (1987). Ethnographic content analysis. *Qualitative Sociology, 10,* 65–77.

Altheide, D. L. (1996). *Qualitative media analysis.* Newbury Park, CA: Sage.

Altheide, D. L. (2002). *Creating fear: News and the construction of crisis.* Hawthorne, NY: Aldine de Gruyter.

Altheide, D., & Johnson, J. (1994). Criteria for assessing interpretive validity in qualitative research. In N. K. Denzin & Y. S. Lincoln (Eds.), *Handbook of qualitative research* (pp. 485–499). Thousand Oaks, CA: Sage.

Altman, D. G., Machin, D., Bryant, T. N., & Gardner, M. J. (2000). *Statistics with confidence: Confidence intervals and statistical guidelines* (2nd ed.). London: British Medical Journal Books.

Altman, M., Gill, J., & McDonald, M. P. (2003). *Numerical methods in statistical computing for the social sciences.* New York: Wiley.

Alvarez, R. M., & Glasgow, G. (2000). Two-stage estimation of nonrecursive choice models. *Political Analysis, 8,* 147–165.

Alveson, M., & Sköldberg, K. (2000). *Reflexive methodology.* London: Sage.

Alvesson, M. (2002). *Postmodernism and social research.* Buckingham, UK: Open University Press.

Alvesson, M., & Deetz, S. (2000). *Doing critical management research.* London: Sage.

Amemiya, T. (1985). *Advanced econometrics.* Cambridge, MA: Harvard University Press.

Amemiya, T. (1994). *Introduction to statistics and econometrics.* Cambridge, MA: Harvard University Press.

American Association for Public Opinion Research (AAPOR). (2000). *Standard definitions: Final dispositions for case codes and outcome rates for surveys.* Ann Arbor, MI: Author.

American Educational Research Association, American Psychological Association, & National Council on Educational Measurement. (1999). *Standards for educational and psychological testing.* Washington, DC: American Psychological Association.

American Educational Research Association, American Psychological Association, & National Council on Measurement in Education. (1985). *Standards for educational and psychological testing.* Washington, DC: American Psychological Association.

American Psychological Association. (1992). Ethical principles of psychologists and code of conduct. *American Psychologist, 47,* 1597–1611.

American Psychological Association. (2002, October 28). *PsycINFO database records* [electronic database]. Washington, DC: Author.

Anastasi, A. (1988). *Psychological testing* (6th ed.). New York: Macmillan.

Anastasi, A., & Urbina, S. (1996). *Psychological testing* (7th ed.). New York: Prentice Hall.

Anderberg, M. R. (1973). *Cluster analysis for applications.* New York: Academic Press.

Anderson, N. H. (1981). *Methods of information integration theory.* New York: Academic Press.

Anderson, S., Auquier, A., Hauck, W. W., Oakes, D., Vandaele, W., & Weisberg, H. I. (1980). On the use of matrices in certain population mathematics. In *Statistical methods for comparative studies: Techniques for bias reduction.* New York: Wiley.

Andersson, B. E., & Nilsson, S. G. (1964). Studies in the reliability and validity of the critical incident technique. *Journal of Applied Psychology, 48*(1), 398–403.

Andrews, F. M., Morgan, J. N., & Sonquist, J. A. (1967). *Multiple classification analysis: A report on a computer program for multiple regression using categorical predictors.* Ann Arbor, MI: Survey Research Center, Institute for Social Research.

Andrews, L., & Nelkin, D. (1998). Do the dead have interests? Policy issues of research after life. *American Journal of Law & Medicine, 24,* 261.

Angle, J. (1986). The Surplus Theory of Social Stratification and the size distribution of personal wealth. *Social Forces, 65,* 293–326.

Angle, J. (2002). The statistical signature of pervasive competition on wage and salary incomes. *Journal of Mathematical Sociology, 26,* 217–270.

Angrasino, M. V., & Mays de Perez, K. (2000). Rethinking observation: From method to context. In N. K. Denzin & Y. S. Lincoln (Eds.), *Handbook of qualitative research* (2nd ed., pp. 673–702). Thousand Oaks, CA: Sage.

Angrist, J. D., Imbens, G. W., & Rubin, D. B. (1996). Identification of causal effects using instrumental variables. *Journal of the American Statistical Association, 91,* 444–455.

Angst, D. B., & Deatrick, J. A. (1996). Involvement in health care decisions: Parents and children with chronic illness. *Journal of Family Nursing, 2*(2), 174–194.

Anselin, L. (1988). *Spatial econometrics.* Boston: Kluwer Academic.

Anselin, L., & Bera, A. (1998). Spatial dependence in linear regression models, with an introduction to spatial econometrics. In A. Ullah & D. Giles (Eds.), *Handbook of applied economic statistics* (pp. 237–289). New York: Marcel Dekker.

Antoni, M. H., Baggett, L., Ironson, G., LaPerriere, A., August, S., Kilmas, N., et al. (1991). Cognitive-behavioral stress management intervention buffers distress responses and immunologic changes following notification of HIV-1 seropositivity. *Journal of Consulting and Clinical Psychology, 59*(6), 906–915.

Arabie, P., & Boorman, S. A. (1973). Multidimensional scaling of measures of distance between partitions. *Journal of Mathematical Psychology, 10,* 148–203.

Arbuckle, J. (1997). *Amos users' guide version 3.6.* Chicago: Smallwaters Corporation.

Arch, D. C., Bettman, J. R., & Kakkar, P. (1978). Subjects' information processing in information display board studies. In K. Hunt (Ed.), *Advances in consumer research, Vol. 5* (pp. 555–559). Ann Arbor, MI: Association for Consumer Research.

Archer, M. (1995). *Realist social theory: The morphogenetic approach.* Cambridge, UK: Cambridge University Press.

Archer, M., Bhaskar, R., Collier, A., Lawson, T., & Norrie, A. (Eds.). (1998). *Critical realism: Essential readings.* London: Routledge Kegan Paul.

Aristotle. (1977). *Metaphysica.* Baarn: Het Wereldvenster.

Armacost, R. L., Hosseini, J. C., Morris, S. A., & Rehbein, K. A. (1991). An empirical comparison of direct questioning, scenario, and randomized response methods for obtaining sensitive business information. *Decision Sciences, 22,* 1073–1090.

Armitage, P., & Colton, T. (Eds.). (1998). *Encyclopedia of biostatistics.* New York: John Wiley.

Armstrong, J. S. (Ed.). (2001). *Principles of forecasting.* Boston: Kluwer.

Aronow, E., Reznikoff, M., & Moreland, K. (1994). *The Rorschach technique.* Needham Heights, MA: Allyn & Bacon.

Aronson, E., Carlsmith, M., & Ellsworth, P. C. (1990). *Methods of research in social psychology.* New York: McGraw-Hill.

Arrow, K. J. (1963). *Social choice and individual values* (2nd ed.). New Haven, CT: Yale University Press.

Arthur, W. B. (1994). *Increasing returns and path dependence in the economy.* Ann Arbor: University of Michigan Press.

Asch, S. E. (1946). Forming impressions of personality. *Journal of Abnormal and Social Psychology, 41,* 258–290.

Asch, S. E. (1951). Effects of group pressure upon the modification and distortion of judgments. In H. Guetzkow (Ed.), *Groups, leadership, and men* (pp. 177–190). Pittsburgh, PA: Carnegie Press.

Asher, H. B. (1983). *Causal modeling* (2nd ed., Sage University Paper Series on Quantitative Applications in the Social Sciences, 07–003). Beverly Hills, CA: Sage.

Ashmore, M. (1989). *The reflexive thesis: Wrighting sociology of scientific knowledge.* Chicago: University of Chicago Press.

Ashmore, M. (1995). Fraud by numbers: Quantitative rhetoric in the Piltdown forgery discovery. *South Atlantic Quarterly, 94*(2), 591–618.

Atkinson, J. M., & Heritage, J. (Eds.). (1984). *Structures of social action: Studies in conversation analysis.* Cambridge, UK: Cambridge University Press.

Atkinson, P. (1990). *The ethnographic imagination: Textual constructions of reality.* London: Routledge.

Atkinson, P., & Hammersley, M. (1994). Ethnography and participant observation. In N. K. Denzin & Y. S. Lincoln (Eds.), *Handbook of qualitative research* (pp. 248–261). Thousand Oaks, CA: Sage.

Atkinson, P., & Silverman, D. (1997). Kundera's "immortality": The interview society and the invention of self. *Qualitative Inquiry, 3*(3), 304–325.

Atkinson, P., Coffey, A., & Delamont, S. (2001). Editorial: A debate about our canon. *Qualitative Research, 1,* 5–21.

Atkinson, R. (1998). *The life story interview* (Qualitative Research Methods Series, Vol. 44). Thousand Oaks, CA: Sage.

Axelrod, R. (1984). *The evolution of cooperation.* New York: Basic Books.

Axelrod, R. (1995). A model of the emergence of new political actors. In N. Gilbert & R. Conte (Eds.), *Artificial societies.* London: UCL.

Axelrod, R. (1997). *The complexity of cooperation: Agent-based models of competition and collaboration.* Princeton, NJ: Princeton University Press.

Axelrod, R., & Hamilton, W. D. (1981). The evolution of cooperation. *Science, 211,* 1390–1396.

Ayer, A. J. (1936). *Language, truth and logic.* London: Victor Gollancz.

Babbie, E. (1979). *The practice of social research.* Belmont, CA: Wadsworth.

Babbie, E. R. (1995). *The practice of social research* (7th ed.). Belmont, CA: Wadsworth.

Baillie, R. T. (1996). Long memory processes and fractional integration in econometrics. *Journal of Econometrics, 73,* 5–59.

Bainbridge, E. E., Carley, K. M., Heise, D. R., Macy, M. W., Markovsky, B., & Skvoretz, J. (1994). Artificial social intelligence. *Annual Review of Sociology, 20,* 407–436.

Bakeman, R., & Gottman, J. M. (1997). *Observing interaction: An introduction to sequential analysis* (2nd ed.). New York: Cambridge University Press.

Bakeman, R., & Quera, V. (1995). *Analyzing interaction: Sequential analysis with SDIS and GSEQ.* New York: Cambridge University Press.

Baker, B. O., Hardyck, C. D., & Petrinovich, L. F. (1966). Weak measurement vs. strong statistics: An empirical critique of

S.S. Stevens' proscriptions on statistics. *Educational and Psychological Measurement, 26,* 291–309.

Baltagi B. H. (2001). *Econometric analysis of panel data.* Chichester, UK: Wiley.

Banerjee, A., Dolado, J. J., Galbraith, J., & Hendry, D. F. (1993). *Cointegration, error correction and the econometric analysis of nonstationary series.* New York: Oxford University Press.

Banks, M. (2001). *Visual methods in social research.* London: Sage.

Bargh, J. A., & Chartrand, T. L. (2000). Mind in the middle: A practical guide to priming and automaticity research. In H. T. Reis & C. M. Judd (Eds.), *Handbook of research methods in social and personality psychology* (pp. 253–285). New York: Cambridge University Press.

Barnard, J., & Rubin, D. B. (1999). Small-sample degrees of freedom with multiple imputation. *Biometrika, 86,* 948–955.

Barndt, D. (1997). Zooming out/zooming in: Visualizing globalization. *Visual Sociology, 12*(2), 5–32.

Barnes, D. B., Taylor-Brown, S., & Weiner, L. (1997). "I didn't leave y'all on purpose": HIV-infected mothers' videotaped legacies for their children. *Qualitative Sociology, 20*(1), 7–32.

Barnett, V. (1974). *Elements of sampling theory.* Sevenoaks, UK: Hodder & Stoughton.

Barr, R. (1996). A comparison of aspects of the US and UK censuses of population. *Transactions in GIS, 1,* 49–60.

Barthes, R. (1967). *Elements of semiology.* London: Jonathan Cape.

Barthes, R. (1977). *Image music text.* London: Fontana.

Barthes, R. (1977). Rhetoric of the image. In *Image, music, text* (S. Heath, Trans.). London: Fontana.

Bartholomew, D. J., & Knott, M. (1999). *Latent variable models and factor analysis.* London: Arnold.

Bartlett, M. S. (1947). Multivariate analysis. *Journal of the Royal Statistical Society, Series B, 9,* 176–197.

Bartunek, J. M., & Louis, M. R. (1996). *Insider-outsider team research.* Thousand Oaks, CA: Sage.

Bates, D. M., & Watts, D. G. (1988). *Nonlinear regression analysis and its applications.* New York: John Wiley.

Bateson, G., & Mead, M. (1942). *Balinese character: A photographic analysis.* New York: New York Graphic Society.

Baudrillard, J. (1998). *The consumer society.* London: Sage. (Originally published in 1970)

Bauman, Z. (1978). *Hermeneutics and social science.* London: Hutchinson.

Baumrind, D. (1964). Some thoughts on ethics after reading Milgram's "Behavioral study of obedience." *American Psychologist, 19,* 421–423.

Bayer, A. E., & Smart, J. C. (1991). Career publication patterns and collaborative "styles" in American academic science. *Journal of Higher Education, 62,* 613–636.

Bayes, T. (1763). An essay towards solving a problem in the doctrine of chances. *Philosophical Transactions of the Royal Society, 53,* 370–418.

Bayes, T. (1958). An essay towards solving a problem in the doctrine of chances. *Biometrika, 45,* 293–315.

Baym, N. (2000). *Tune in, log on: Soaps, fandom and online community.* Thousand Oaks, CA: Sage.

Beck, N. (1991). Comparing dynamic specifications: The case of presidential approval. *Political Analysis, 3,* 51–87.

Beck, N., & Jackman, S. (1998). Beyond linearity by default: Generalized additive models. *American Journal of Political Science, 42,* 596–627.

Beck, N., & Katz, J. N. (1995). What to do (and not to do) with time-series cross-section data. *American Political Science Review, 89,* 634–647.

Becker, H. S. (1967). Whose side are we on? *Social Problems, 14,* 239–247.

Becker, H. S. (1974). Photography and sociology. *Studies in the Anthropology of Visual Communication, 1*(1), 3–26.

Becker, H. S. (1986). *Doing things together.* Evanston, IL: Northwestern University Press.

Becker, H. S. (1998). *Tricks of the trade.* Chicago: University of Chicago Press.

Becker, H. S., Hughes, E. C., & Strauss, A. L. (1961). *Boys in white.* Chicago: University of Chicago Press.

Becker, S., & Bryman, A. (Eds.). (2004). *Understanding research for social policy and practice: Themes, methods and approaches.* Bristol, UK: Policy Press.

Bell, C. (1969). A note on participant observation. *Sociology, 3,* 417–418.

Bell, S. E. (1999). Narratives and lives: Women's health politics and the diagnosis of cancer for DES daughters. *Narrative Inquiry, 9*(2), 1–43.

Bellman, B. L., & Jules-Rosette, B. (1977). *A paradigm for looking: Cross-cultural research with visual media.* Norwood, NJ: Ablex.

Belsley, D. A., Kuh, E., & Welsch, R. E. (1980). *Regression diagnostics: Identifying influential data and sources of collinearity.* New York: John Wiley.

Beltrami, E. J. (1999). *What is random? Chance and order in mathematics and life.* New York: Copernicus.

Benfer, R. A., Brent, E. E., Jr., & Furbee, L. (1991). *Expert systems.* Newbury Park, CA: Sage.

Bennet, D. J. (1998). *Randomness.* Cambridge, MA: Harvard University Press.

Bennett, A. (1999). *Condemned to repetition? The rise, fall, and reprise of Soviet-Russian military interventionism, 1973–1996.* Cambridge: MIT Press.

Benton, T. (1977). *Philosophical foundations of the three sociologies.* London: Routledge Kegan Paul.

Benton, T. (1998). Realism and social science. In M. Archer, R. Bhaskar, A. Collier, T. Lawson, & A. Norrie (Eds.), *Critical realism: Essential readings.* London: Routledge Kegan Paul.

Benzécri, J.-P. (1973). *Analyse des Données. Tome 2: Analyse des Correspondances* [Data analysis: Vol. 2. Correspondence analysis]. Paris: Dunod.

Berelson, B. (1954). Content analysis. In G. Lindzey (Ed.), *Handbook of social psychology* (Vol. 1, pp. 488–522). Reading, MA: Addison-Wesley.

Berg, B. L. (2001). *Qualitative research methods for the social sciences.* Boston: Allyn and Bacon.

Berger, J. O., & Wolpert, R. L. (1984). *The likelihood principle: A review, generalizations, and statistical implications.* Hayward, CA: Institute of Mathematical Statistics.

Berger, J., Fisek, H., Norman, R., & Zelditch, M. (1977). *Status characteristics and social interaction: An expectation states approach.* New York: Elsevier.

Berger, P., & Luckmann, T. (1967). *The social construction of reality.* Harmondsworth, UK: Penguin.

Bergner, R. M. (1974). The development and evaluation of a training videotape for the resolution of marital conflict. *Dissertation Abstracts International, 34,* 3485B. (UMI No. 73–32510)

Bergsma, W. (1997). *Marginal models for categorical data.* Tilburg, The Netherlands: Tilburg University Press.

Berk, R. A., & Freedman, D. A. (1995). Statistical assumptions as empirical commitments. In T. G. Blomberg & S. Cohen (Eds.), *Law, punishment, and social control: Essays in honor of Sheldon Messinger* (pp. 245–258). New York: Aldine de Gruyter.

Bernardo, J. M., & Smith, A. F. M. (1994). *Bayesian theory.* New York: Wiley.

Bernstein, R. (1983). *Beyond objectivism and relativism: Science, hermeneutics and praxis.* Oxford, UK: Basil Blackwell.

Berry, J. (2002). Validity and reliability issues in elite interviewing. *PS—Political Science and Politics, 35,* 679–682.

Berry, W. D. (1984). *Nonrecursive causal models.* Beverly Hills, CA: Sage.

Berry, W. D. (1993). *Understanding regression assumptions.* Newbury Park, CA: Sage.

Beverley, J. (1989). The margin at the center: On testimonio. *Modern Fiction Studies, 35*(1), 11–28.

Beverley, J., & Zimmerman, M. (1990). *Literature and politics in the Central American revolutions.* Austin: University of Texas Press.

Bhaskar, R. (1978). *A realist theory of science.* Hassocks, UK: Harvester Press.

Bhaskar, R. (1979). *The possibilities of naturalism: A philosophical critique of the contemporary human sciences.* Brighton, UK: Harvester.

Bhaskar, R. (1986). *Scientific realism and human emancipation.* London: Verso.

Bhaskar, R. (1997). *A realist theory of science.* London: Verso. (Original work published 1978)

Bhaskar, R. (1998). *The possibility of naturalism* (2nd ed.). Hemel Hempstead, UK: Harvester Wheatsheaf. (Original work published 1979)

Bickman, L., & Rog, D. J. (Eds.). (1998). *Handbook of applied social research methods.* Thousand Oaks, CA: Sage.

Biemer, P. P., Groves, R. M., Lyberg, L. E., Mathiowetz, N. A., & Sudman, S. (Eds.). (1991). *Measurement errors in surveys.* New York: Wiley.

Biggs, D., De Ville, B., & Suen, E. (1991). A method of choosing multiway partitions for classification and decision trees. *Journal of Applied Statistics, 18,* 49–62.

Bijleveld, C. C. J. H., & van der Kamp, L. J. Th. (with Mooijaart, A., van der Kloot, W. A., van der Leeden, R., & van der Burg, E.). (1998). *Longitudinal data analysis: Designs, models, and methods.* London: Sage.

Billig, M. (1996). *Arguing and thinking.* Cambridge, UK: Cambridge University Press.

Bimler, D., & Kirkland, J. (1999). Capturing images in a net: Perceptual modeling of product descriptors using sorting data. *Marketing Bulletin, 10,* 11–23.

Birdwhistell, R. L. (1970). *Kinesics and context: Essays on body motion communication.* Philadelphia: University of Pennsylvania Press.

Birnbaum, A. L. (1968). Some latent trait models and their use in inferring an examinee's ability. In F. M. Lord & M. R. Novick (Eds.), *Statistical theories of mental test scores.* Reading, MA: Addison-Wesley.

Birnbaum, M. H. (2001). *Introduction to behavioral research on the Internet.* Upper Saddle River, NJ: Prentice Hall.

Bishop, C. M. (1995). *Neural networks for pattern recognition.* Oxford, UK: Oxford University Press.

Bishop, G., & Smith, A. (2001). Response-order effects and the early Gallup split-ballots. *Public Opinion Quarterly, 65,* 479–505.

Black, D. (1958). *The theory of committees and elections.* Cambridge, UK: Cambridge University Press.

Black, T. R. (1999). *Doing quantitative research in the social sciences: An integrated approach to research design, measurement, and statistics.* London: Sage.

Blaikie, N. (1993). *Approaches to social enquiry.* Cambridge, UK: Polity.

Blaikie, N. (2000). *Designing social research: The logic of anticipation.* Cambridge, UK: Polity.

Blalock, H. (1961). *Causal inference in nonexperimental research.* Chapel Hill: University of North Carolina Press.

Blalock, H. M. (1960). *Social statistics.* New York: McGraw-Hill.

Blalock, H. M. (1961). Theory, measurement and replication in the social sciences. *American Journal of Sociology, 66*(1), 342–347.

Blalock, H. M. (1972). *Social statistics* (2nd ed.). Tokyo: McGraw-Hill Kogakusha.

Blalock, H. M. (1979). *Social statistics* (rev. 2nd ed.). New York: McGraw-Hill.

Blalock, H. M., Jr. (1969). *Theory construction: From verbal to mathematical formulations.* Englewood Cliffs, NJ: Prentice Hall.

Blanck, P. D. (Ed.). (1993). *Interpersonal expectations: Theory, research, and applications.* New York: Cambridge University Press.

Blascovich, J. (2000). Psychophysiological indexes of psychological processes. In H. T. Reis & C. M. Judd (Eds.), *Handbook of research methods in social and personality psychology* (pp. 117–137). Cambridge, UK: Cambridge University Press.

Blascovich, J., & Tomaka, J. (1996). The biopsychosocial model of arousal regulation. In M. Zanna (Ed.), *Advances in experimental social psychology* (pp. 1–51). New York: Academic Press.

Blau, P. M. (1974). Parameters of social structure. *American Sociological Review. 39*, 615–635.

Bloor, M. (1997). Addressing social problems through qualitative research. In D. Silverman (Ed.), *Qualitative research: Theory, method and practice* (pp. 221–238). London: Sage.

Blossfeld, H.-P., & Rohwer, G. (2002). *Techniques of event history modeling: New approaches to causal analysis*. Mahwah, NJ: Lawrence Erlbaum Associates.

Blumen, I. M., Kogan, M., & McCarthy, P. J. (1955). *The industrial mobility of labor as a probability process*. Ithaca, NY: Cornell University Press.

Blumen, I., Kogan, M., & McCarthy, P. J. (1968). Probability models for mobility. In P. F. Lazarsfeld & N. W. Henry (Eds.), *Readings in mathematical social science* (pp. 318–334). Cambridge: MIT Press.

Blumer, H. (1956). Sociological analysis and the "variable." *American Sociological Review, 21*, 683–690.

Blumer, H. (1969). *An empirical appraisal of Thomas and Znaniecki (1918–20) The Polish Peasant in Europe and America*. New Brunswick, NJ: Transaction Books. (Original work published 1939)

Blumer, H. (1969). *Symbolic interactionism: Perspective and method*. Englewood Cliffs, NJ: Prentice Hall.

Blundell, R. W., & Smith, R. J. (1989). Estimation in a class of simultaneous equation limited dependent variable models. *Review of Economic Studies, 56*, 37–58.

Blurton Jones, N. (Ed.). (1972). *Ethological studies of child behaviour*. London: Cambridge University Press.

Bobko, P. (1995). *Correlation and regression : Principles and applications for industrial organizational psychology and management*. New York: McGraw-Hill.

Bogartz, R. S. (1994). *An introduction to the analysis of variance*. Westport, CT: Praeger.

Bogdewic, S. P. (1999). Participant observation. In B. J. Crabtree & W. L. Miller (Eds.), *Doing qualitative research* (pp. 47–69). Thousand Oaks, CA: Sage.

Bohman, J. (1991). *New philosophy of social science: Problems of indeterminacy*. Cambridge, UK: Polity.

Boje, D. M. (2001). *Narrative methods for organizational and communication research*. Thousand Oaks, CA: Sage.

Bolger, N., Davis, A., & Rafaeli, E. (in press). Diary methods: Capturing life as it is lived. *Annual Review of Psychology*.

Bollen, K. (1989). *Structural equations with latent variables*. New York: John Wiley.

Bollen, K. A., & Curran, P. J. (in press). *Latent curve models: A structural equation approach*. New York: John Wiley.

Bollen, K. A., & Jackman, R. W. (1990). Regression diagnostics: An expository treatment of outliers and influential cases. In J. Fox & J. S. Long (Ed.), *Modern methods of data analysis* (pp. 257–291). Newbury Park, CA: Sage.

Bonnie, R. J., & Wallace, R. B. (2002). *Elder mistreatment: Abuse, neglect, and exploitation in an aging America*. Washington, DC: Joseph Henry Press.

Boomsma, A., Van Duijn, M. A. J., & Snijders, T. A. B. (Eds.). (2001). *Essays on item response theory*. New York: Springer.

Borg, I., & Groenen, P. (1997). *Modern multidimensional scaling*. New York: Springer-Verlag.

Borgatta, E. F., & Bohrnstedt, G. W. (1980). Level of measurement: Once over again. *Sociological Methods and Research, 9*, 147–160.

Borgatta, E. F., & Jackson, D. J. (Eds.). (1980). *Aggregate data: Analysis and interpretation*. Beverly Hills, CA: Sage.

Bornstein, R. F. (2002). A process dissociation approach to objective-projective test score interrelationships. *Journal of Personality Assessment, 78*, 47–68.

Bornstein, R. F., Rossner, S. C., Hill, E. L., & Stepanian, M. L. (1994). Face validity and fakability of objective and projective measures of dependency. *Journal of Personality Assessment, 63*, 363–386.

Boruch, R. F. (1997). *Randomized experiments for planning and evaluation: A practical guide*. Thousand Oaks, CA: Sage.

Boruch, R. F., & Cecil, J. S. (1979). *Assuring the confidentiality of social research data*. Philadelphia: University of Pennsylvania Press.

Boster, J. S. (1994). The successive pile sort. *Cultural Anthropology Methods, 6*(2), 7–8.

Bosworth, M. (1999). *Engendering resistance: Agency and power in women's prisons*. Aldershot, UK: Ashgate/Dartmouth.

Bottorff, J. L. (1994). Using videotaped recordings in qualitative research. In J. M. Morse (Ed.), *Critical issues in qualitative research* (pp. 224–261). Newbury Park, CA: Sage.

Boucke, O. F. (1923). The limits of social science: II. *American Journal of Sociology, 28*(4), 443–460.

Bourdieu, P. (1977). *Outline of a theory of practice*. Cambridge, UK: Cambridge University Press.

Bourdieu, P. (2000). *Pascalian meditations* (R. Nice, Trans.). Cambridge, UK: Polity.

Bourdieu, P., & Waquant, L. J. D. (1992). *An invitation to reflexive sociology*. Chicago: University of Chicago Press.

Bourque, L. B., & Clark, V. A. (1992). *Processing data: The survey example* (Sage University Paper Series on Quantitative Applications in the Social Sciences, 07–085). Newbury Park, CA: Sage.

Bourque, L. B., & Fielder, E. P. (2003). *How to conduct self-administered and mail surveys* (2nd ed.). Thousand Oaks, CA: Sage.

Bourque, L. B., & Russell, L. A. (with Krauss, G. L., Riopelle, D., Goltz, J. D., Greene, M., McAffee, S., & Nathe, S.) (1994, July). *Experiences during and responses to the Loma Prieta earthquake.* Oakland: Governor's Office of Emergency Services, State of California.

Bourque, L. B., Shoaf, K. I., & Nguyen, L. H. (1997). Survey research. *International Journal of Mass Emergencies and Disasters, 15,* 71–101.

Box, G. E. P., & Cox, D. R. (1964). An analysis of transformations. *Journal of the Royal Statistical Society (B), 26*(2), 211–252.

Box, G. E. P., & Jenkins, G. M. (1976). *Time series analysis: Forecasting and control* (rev. ed.). San Francisco: Holden-Day.

Box, G. E. P., & Tiao, G. C. (1965). A change in level of nonstationary time series. *Biometrika, 52,* 181–192.

Box, G. E. P., & Tiao, G. C. (1973). *Bayesian inference in statistical analysis.* New York: Wiley.

Box, G. E. P., & Tiao, G. C. (1975). Intervention analysis with applications to economic and environmental problems. *Journal of the American Statistical Association, 70,* 70–92.

Box, G. E. P., Hunter, W. G., & Hunter, J. S. (1978). *Statistics for experimenters.* New York: Wiley.

Box, G. E. P., Jenkins, G. M., & Reinsel, G. C. (1994). *Time series analysis: Forecasting and control* (3rd ed.). New York: Prentice Hall.

Box-Steffensmeier, J. M., & Jones, B. S. (1997). Time is of the essence: Event history models in political science. *American Journal of Political Science, 41,* 336–383.

Box-Steffensmeier, J. M., & Zorn, C. J. W. (2001). Duration models and proportional hazards in political science. *American Journal of Political Science, 45,* 951–967.

Box-Steffensmeier, J. M., & Zorn, C. J. W. (2002). Duration models for repeated events. *The Journal of Politics, 64*(4), 1069–1094.

Boyd, J. P. (1990). *Social semigroups: A unified theory of scaling and bockmodeling as applied to social networks.* Fairfax, VA: George Mason University Press.

Boyd, J. P., & Jonas, K. J. (2001). Are social equivalences ever regular? Permutation and exact tests. *Social Networks, 23,* 87–123.

Bracken, B. (Ed.). (1995). *Handbook of self concept: Developmental, social and clinical consequences.* New York: Wiley.

Bradley, J. V. (1985). *Distribution-free statistical tests.* Englewood Cliffs, NJ: Prentice Hall.

Brady, I. (2000). Anthropological poetics. In N. K. Denzin & Y. S. Lincoln (Eds.), *Handbook of qualitative research* (2nd ed., pp. 949–979). Thousand Oaks, CA: Sage.

Brady, I. (2003). *The time at Darwin's Reef: Poetic explorations in anthropology and history.* Walnut Creek, CA: AltaMira.

Bray, J. H., & Maxwell, S. E. (1985). *Multivariate analysis of variance* (Sage University Paper Series on Quantitative Applications in the Social Sciences, 07–054) Beverly Hills, CA: Sage.

Breen, R. (1996). *Regression models: Censored, sample selected, or truncated data* (Sage University Paper Series on Quantitative Applications in the Social Sciences, 07–111). Thousand Oaks, CA: Sage.

Breiman, L., Friedman, J., Olshen, R., & Stone, C. (1984). *Classification and regression trees.* Monterey, CA: Wadsworth.

Brennan, R. L. (1983). *Elements of generalizability.* Iowa City, IA: American College Testing Program.

Brennan, R. L. (2001). *Generalizability theory.* New York: Springer-Verlag.

Brewer, K. (2002). *Combined survey sampling inference: Weighing Basu's elephants.* London: Arnold.

Briggs, C. (1986). *Learning how to ask.* Cambridge, UK: Cambridge University Press.

Broad, W., & Wade, N. (1982). *Betrayers of the truth: Fraud and deceit in the halls of science.* New York: Simon & Schuster.

Brockmeyer, E., Halstrom, H. L., & Jensen, A. (1960). *The life and works of A. K. Erlang.* Kobenhavn: Akademiet for de Tekniske Videnskaber.

Bronfenbrenner, U. (1979). *The ecology of human development.* Cambridge, MA: Harvard University Press.

Bronner, S. E., & Kellner, D. M. (1989). *Critical theory and society: A reader.* New York: Routledge.

Bronshtein, I. N., & Semendyaev, K. A. (1985). *Handbook of mathematics* (K. A. Hirsch, Trans. & Ed.). New York: Van Nostrand Reinhold. (Originally published in 1979)

Brown, C. (1991). *Ballots of tumult: A portrait of volatility in American voting.* Ann Arbor: University of Michigan Press.

Brown, C. (1995). *Chaos and catastrophe theories.* Thousand Oaks, CA: Sage.

Brown, C. (1995). *Serpents in the sand: Essays on the nonlinear nature of politics and human destiny.* Ann Arbor: University of Michigan Press.

Brown, H. I. (1987). *Observation and objectivity.* New York: Oxford University Press.

Brown, S. R., & Melamed, L. E. (1998). *Experimental design and analysis* (Sage University Paper Series on Quantitative Applications in the Social Sciences, 07–074). Thousand Oaks, CA: Sage.

Brown, S. R., Durning, D. W., & Selden, S. C. (1999). Q methodology. In G. J. Miller & M. L. Whicker (Eds.), *Handbook of research methods in public administration* (pp. 599–637). New York: Dekker.

Brown, W. (1910). Some experimental results in the correlation of mental abilities. *British Journal of Psychology, 12,* 296–322.

Browne, M. W. (1982). Covariance structures. In D. M. Hawkins (Ed.), *Topics in applied multivariate analysis* (pp. 72–141). Cambridge, UK: Cambridge University Press.

Browne, M. W. (1984). Asymptotic distribution free methods in the analysis of covariance structures. *British Journal of Mathematical and Statistical Psychology, 37,* 62–83.

Brownlee, K. (1965). *Statistical theory and methodology in science and engineering.* New York: John Wiley.

Bruner, J. (1960). *The process of education.* Cambridge, MA: Harvard University Press.

Bruner, J. (1966). *Toward a theory of instruction.* Cambridge, MA: Harvard University Press.

Brunk, G. G., Caldeira, G. A., & Lewis-Beck, M. S. (1987). Capitalism, socialism, and democracy: An empirical inquiry. *European Journal of Political Research, 15,* 459–470.

Brunswik, E. (1943). Organismic achievement and environmental probability. *The Psychological Review, 50,* 255–272.

Bryant, C. G. A. (1985). *Positivism in social theory and research.* London: Macmillan.

Bryk, A. S., & Raudenbush, S. W. (1992). *Hierarchical linear models.* Newbury Park, CA: Sage.

Bryman, A. (2001). *Social research methods.* Oxford, UK: Oxford University Press.

Bryman, A., & Cramer, D. (1997). *Quantitative data analysis with SPSS for Windows: A guide for social scientists.* New York: Routledge Kegan Paul.

Bryun, T. S. (1966) *The human perspective in sociology: The methodology of participant observation.* Englewoood Cliffs, NJ: Prentice Hall.

Bulmer, M. (Ed.). (1982). *Social research ethics.* London: Macmillan.

Bulmer, M., & Solomos, J. (Eds.). (2003). *Researching race and racism.* London: Routledge Kegan Paul.

Bunge, M. (1959). *Causality: The place of the causal principle in modern science.* Cambridge, MA: Harvard University Press.

Burawoy, M. (1998). The extended case method. *Sociological Theory, 16*(1), 4–33.

Burgess, R. (1984). *In the field.* London: Allen & Unwin.

Burgess, R. G. (Ed.). (1982). *Field research: A sourcebook and field manual.* London: Allen & Unwin.

Burkhart, R. E. (2000). Economic freedom and democracy: Post-cold war tests. *European Journal of Political Research, 37,* 237–253.

Burkhart, R. E., and Lewis-Beck, M. S. (1994). Comparative democracy: The economic development thesis. *American Political Science Review, 88,* 903–910.

Burr, V. (1995). *An introduction to social constructionism.* London: Routledge.

Burton, M. L. (1975). Dissimilarity measures for unconstrained sorting data. *Multivariate Behavioral Research, 10,* 409–424.

Bury, M. (2001). Illness narratives: Fact or fiction? *Sociology of Health and Illness, 23*(3), 263–285.

Buttny, R., & Morris, G. H. (2001). Accounting. In W. P. Robinson & H. Giles (Eds.), *The new handbook of language and social psychology* (pp. 285–301). Chichester, England: Wiley.

Byrne, D. (1998). *Complexity theory and the social sciences: An introduction.* London: Routledge.

Byrne, D. (2002). *Interpreting quantitative data.* London: Sage.

Byrne, D. S., McCarthy, P., Harrison, S., & Keithley, J. (1986). *Housing and health.* Aldershot, UK: Gower.

Cacioppo, J. T., Petty, R. E., Losch, M. E., & Kim, H. S. (1986). Electromyographic specificity during simple physical and attitudinal tasks: Location and topographical features of integrated EMG responses. *Biological Psychology, 18,* 85–121.

Cacioppo, J. T., Tassinary, L. G., & Berntson, G. G. (2000). *Handbook of psychophysiology* (2nd ed.). Cambridge, UK: Cambridge University Press.

Cahill, S. (1987). Children and civility: Ceremonial deviance and the acquisition of ritual competence. *Social Psychology Quarterly, 50,* 312–321.

Cain, C. (1991). Personal stories: Identity acquisition and self-understanding in Alcoholics Anonymous. *Ethos, 19,* 210–253.

Cale, G. (2001). *When resistance becomes reproduction: A critical action research study.* Proceedings of the 42nd Adult Education Research Conference. East Lansing: Michigan State University.

Callendar, J. C., & Osburn, H. G. (1977). A method for maximizing split-half reliability coefficients. *Educational and Psychological Measurement, 37,* 819–825.

Cameron, A. C., & Trivedi, P. K. (1998). *Regression analysis of count data.* New York: Cambridge University Press.

Campbell, D. T. (1969). Reforms as experiments. *American Psychologist, 24,* 409–429.

Campbell, D. T. (1988). *Methodology and epistemology for social science: Selected papers* (E. S. Overman, Ed.). Chicago: University of Chicago Press.

Campbell, D. T. (1991). Methods for the experimenting society. *Evaluation Practice, 12,* 223–260.

Campbell, D. T., & Fiske, D. W. (1959). Convergent and discriminant validation by the multitrait-multimethod matrix. *Psychological Bulletin, 56,* 81–105.

Campbell, D. T., & Kenny, D. A. (1999). *A primer on regression artifacts.* New York: Guilford.

Campbell, D. T., & Stanley, J. C. (1963). Experimental and quasi-experimental designs for research on teaching. In N. L. Gage (Ed.), *Handbook of research on teaching* (pp. 171–246). Chicago: Rand McNally.

Campbell, D. T., Boruch, R. F., Schwartz, R. D., & Steinberg, J. (1977). Confidentiality-preserving modes of access to files and to interfile exchange for useful statistical analysis. *Evaluation Quarterly, 1,* 269–300.

Cannell, C., Fowler, J., & Marquis, K. (1968). *The influence of interviewer and respondent psychological and behavioral variables on the reporting of household interviews* (Vital and Health Statistics Series 2, No. 6). Washington, DC: National Center for Health Statistics.

Capdevila, R., & Stainton Rogers, R. (2000). If you go down to the woods today . . . : Narratives of Newbury. In H. Addams & J. Proops (Eds.), *Social discourse and environmental policy: An application of Q methodology* (pp. 152–173). Cheltenham, UK: Elgar.

Carless, S. A. (1998). Assessing the discriminant validity of the transformational leadership behaviour as measured by the MLQ. *Journal of Occupational and Organizational Psychology, 71,* 353–358.

Carley, K., & Prietula, M. (Eds.). (1994). *Computational organization theory.* Hillsdale, NJ: Lawrence Erlbaum.

Carlin, B. P., & Louis, T. A. (1998). *Bayes and empirical Bayes methods for data analysis.* London: Chapman & Hall/CRC.

Carlson, M., & Mulaik, S. A. (1993). Trait ratings from descriptions of behavior as mediated by components of meaning. *Multivariate Behavioral Research, 28,* 111–159.

Carmines, E. G., & McIver, J. P. (1981). *Unidimensional scaling* (Sage University Paper Series on Quantitative Applications in the Social Sciences, 07–024). Beverly Hills, CA: Sage.

Carmines, E. G., & Zeller, R. A. (1979). *Reliability and validity assessment.* Beverly Hills, CA: Sage.

Carrington, P. J., Scott, J., & Wasserman, S. (Eds.). (2003). *Models and methods in social network analysis.* New York: Cambridge University Press.

Carroll, J. B. (2002). The five-factor personality model: How complete and satisfactory is it? In H. I. Braun, D. N. Jackson, & D. E. Wiley (Eds.), *The role of constructs in psychological and educational measurement* (pp. 97–126). Mahwah, NJ: Lawrence Erlbaum.

Carroll, J. D., & Arabie, P. (1980). Multidimensional scaling. *Annual Review of Psychology, 31,* 607–649.

Carroll, J. D., & Chang, J.-J. (1970). Analysis of individual differences in multidimensional scaling via a N-way generalisation of Eckart-Young decomposition. *Psychometrika, 35,* 283–299, 310–319.

Carroll, J. M. (1997). Human-computer interaction: Psychology as a science of design. *Annual Review of Psychology, 48,* 61–83.

Cartwright, N. (1989). *Nature's capacities and their measurement.* Oxford, UK: Oxford University Press.

Casella, G., & Berger, R. L. (1990). *Statistical inference.* Belmont, CT: Duxbury.

Casella, G., & Berger, R. L. (2001). *Statistical inference* (2nd ed.). New York: Wadsworth.

Cattell, R. B. (1966). The scree test for the number of factors. *Multivariate Behavioral Research, 1,* 245–276.

Chadhuri, A., & Mukerjee, R. (1987). *Randomized response: Theory and techniques.* New York: Marcel Dekker.

Chalmers, A. (1982). *What is this thing called science?* St. Lucia, Australia: University of Queensland Press.

Chalmers, A. (1999). *What is this thing called science?* (3rd ed.). Buckingham, UK: Open University Press.

Chamberlayne, P., Bornat, J., & Wengraf, T. (2000). *The turn to biographical methods in social science.* London: Routledge Kegan Paul.

Chamberlayne, P., Rustin, M., & Wengraf, T. (Eds.). (2002). *Biography and social exclusion in Europe: Experiences and life journeys.* Bristol, UK: Policy Press.

Charemza, W. W., & Deadman, D. F. (1997). *New directions in econometric practice* (2nd ed.). Cheltenham, UK: Edward Elgar.

Charlton, J., Patrick, D. L., Matthews, G., & West, P. A. (1981). Spending priorities in Kent: A Delphi study. *Journal of Epidemiology and Community Health, 35,* 288–292.

Charlton, T., Gunter, B., & Hannan, A. (2002). *Broadcast television effects in a remote community.* Hillsdale, NJ: Lawrence Erlbaum.

Charmaz, K. (2000). Grounded theory: Constructivist and objectivist methods. In N. K. Denzin & Y. S. Lincoln (Eds.), *Handbook of qualitative research* (2nd ed., pp. 509–535). Thousand Oaks, CA: Sage.

Chatfield, C. (1983). *Statistics for technology* (3rd ed.). London: Chapman & Hall.

Chatfield, C. (1996). *The analysis of time series: An introduction.* New York: Chapman & Hall.

Chavez, L., Hubbell, F. A., McMullin, J. M., Marinez, R. G., & Mishra, S. I. (1995). Structure and meaning in models of breast and cervical cancer risk factors: A comparison of perceptions among Latinas, Anglo women and physicians. *Medical Anthropology Quarterly, 9,* 40–74.

Checkland, P. B. (1981). *Systems thinking, systems practice.* Chichester, UK: Wiley.

Chell, E. (1998). Critical incident technique. In G. Symon & C. Cassell (Eds.), *Qualitative methods and analysis in organizational research: A practical guide* (pp. 51–72). London: Sage.

Chell, E., & Baines, S. (1998). Does gender affect business performance? A study of micro-businesses in business services in the U.K. *International Journal of Entrepreneurship and Regional Development, 10*(4), 117–135.

Chen, P. Y., & Popovich, P. M. (2002). *Correlation: Parametric and nonparametric measures.* Thousand Oaks, CA: Sage.

Cheng, P. W. (1997). From covariation to causation: A causal power theory. *Psychological Review, 104*(2), 367–405.

Cherkassky, V., & Mulier, F. (1998). *Learning from data.* New York: Wiley.

Chernick, M. R. (1999). *Bootstrap methods: A practioner's guide.* New York: Wiley-Interscience.

Cherryholmes, C. H. (1999). *Reading pragmatism.* New York: Teachers College Press.

Chiang, A. C. (1984). *Fundamental methods of mathematical economics* (3rd ed.). New York: McGraw-Hill.

Chiari, G., & Nuzzo, M. L. (1996). Psychological constructivisms: A metatheoretical differentiation. *Journal of Constructivist Psychology, 9,* 163–184.

Chipman, J. S. (1979). Efficiency of least squares estimation of linear trend when residuals are autocorrelated. *Econometrica, 47,* 115–128.

Chouliaraki, L., & Fairclough, N. (1999). *Discourse in late modernity.* Edinburgh, UK: Edinburgh University Press.

Chow, G. (1961). Tests of equality between sets of regression coefficients in linear regression models. *Econometrica, 28*(3), 591–605.

Chrisman, N. (1997). *Exploring geographic information systems.* New York: Wiley.

Christians, C. (2000). Ethics and politics in qualitative research. In N. K. Denzin & Y. S. Lincoln (Eds.), *The handbook of qualitative research* (2nd ed., pp. 133–155). Thousand Oaks, CA: Sage.

Cicerelli, V. G., & Associates. (1969). *The impact of Head Start: An evaluation of the effects of Head Start on children's cognitive and affective development* (2 vols.). Athens: Ohio University and Westinghouse Learning Corp.

Cicourel, A. V. (1974). *Theory and method in a critique of Argentine fertility.* New York: John Wiley.

Clark, J. A., & Mishler, E. G. (1992). Attending to patients' stories: Reframing the clinical task. *Sociology of Health and Illness, 14,* 344–370.

Clarke, H. D., Norpoth, H., & Whiteley, P. F. (1998). It's about time: Modeling political and social dynamics. In E. Scarborough & E. Tanenbaum (Ed.), *Research strategies in the social sciences* (pp. 127–155). Oxford, UK: Oxford University Press.

Clarke, K. A. (2001). Testing nonnested models of international relations: Reevaluating realism. *American Journal of Political Science, 45,* 724–744.

Clayman, S. E., & Maynard, D. (1995). Ethnomethodology and conversation analysis. In P. ten Have & G. Psathas (Eds.), *Situated order: Studies in the social organization of talk and embodied activities* (pp. 1–30). Washington, DC: University Press of America.

Clayman, S., & Heritage, J. (2002). *The news interview: Journalists and public figures on the air.* Cambridge, UK: Cambridge University Press.

Cleary, T. A., & Linn, R. L. (1969). Error of measurement and the power of a statistical test. *The British Journal of Mathematical and Statistical Psychology, 22*(1), 49–55.

Clegg, C. W., & Walsh, S. (1998). Soft systems analysis. In G. Symon & C. M. Cassell (Eds.), *Qualitative methods and analysis in organisational research: A practical guide.* London: Sage.

Cleveland, W. S. (1979). Robust locally-weighted regression and smoothing scatterplots. *Journal of the American Statistical Association, 74,* 829–836.

Cleveland, W. S. (1993). *Visualizing data.* Summit, NJ: Hobart.

Cleveland, W. S., & Devlin, S. J. (1988). Locally weighted regression: An approach to regression analysis by local fitting. *Journal of the American Statistical Association, 83,* 596–610.

Clifford, J., & Marcus, G. E. (Eds.). (1986). *Writing culture: The poetics and politics of ethnography.* Berkeley: University of California Press.

Clogg, C. C. (1978). Adjustment of rates using multiplicative models. *Demography, 15,* 523–539.

Clogg, C. C. (1982). Some models for the analysis of association in multiway cross-classifications having ordered categories. *Journal of the American Statistical Association, 77,* 803–815.

Clogg, C. C. (1982). Using association models in sociological research: Some examples. *American Journal of Sociology, 88,* 114–134.

Clogg, C. C., & Eliason, S. R. (1988). A flexible procedure for adjusting rates and proportions, including statistical methods for group comparisons. *American Sociological Review, 53,* 267–283.

Clogg, C. C., & Shihadeh, E. S. (1994). *Statistical models for ordinal variables.* Thousand Oaks, CA: Sage.

Clogg, C. C., Shockey, J. W., & Eliason, S. R. (1990). A general statistical framework for adjustment of rates. *Sociological Methods & Research, 19,* 156–195.

Clough, T. P. (1998). *The end(s) of ethnography: From realism to social criticism* (2nd ed.). New York: Peter Lang.

Cobb, G. W. (1998). *Introduction to design and analysis of experiments.* New York: Springer-Verlag.

Cochran, W. G. (1950). The comparison of percentages in matched samples. *Biometrika, 37,* 256–266.

Cochran, W. G. (1957). Analysis of covariance: Its nature and uses. *Biometrics, 13*(3), 261–281.

Cochran, W. G. (1965). The planning of observational studies in human populations. *Journal of the Royal Statistical Society, Series A, 128,* 134–155.

Cochran, W. G. (1953). *Sampling techniques.* New York: Wiley.

Cochran, W. G. (1977). *Sampling techniques* (3rd ed.). New York: John Wiley.

Cochrane, D., & Orcutt, G. H. (1949). Application of least squares relationships containing autocorrelated error terms. *Journal of the American Statistical Association, 44,* 32–61.

Coffey, A., & Atkinson, P. (1996). *Making sense of qualitative data: Complementary research strategies.* Thousand Oaks, CA: Sage.

Cohen, A., Doveh, E., & Eick, U. (2001). Statistical properties of the $r_{WG(J)}$ index of agreement. *Psychological Methods, 6,* 297–310.

Cohen, J. (1960). A coefficient of agreement for nominal scales. *Educational and Psychological Measurement, 20,* 37–46.

Cohen, J. (1978). Partialed products are interactions; partialed powers are curve components. *Psychological Bulletin, 85,* 858–866.

Cohen, J. (1988). *Statistical power analysis in the behavioral sciences* (2nd ed.). Hillsdale, NJ: Lawrence Erlbaum.

Cohen, J. (2001). Smallpox vaccinations: How much protection remains? *Science, 294,* p. 985.

Cohen, J., & Cohen, P. (1983). *Applied multiple regression/ correlation analysis for the behavioral sciences* (2nd ed.). Hillsdale, NJ: Lawrence Erlbaum.

Cohen, J., Cohen, P., West, S. G., & Aiken, L. S. (2003). *Applied multiple regression/correlation analysis for the behavioral sciences* (3rd ed.). Mahwah, NJ: Lawrence Erlbaum.

Cole, M. (1996). *Cultural psychology: A once and future discipline.* Cambridge, MA: Belknap Press of Harvard University Press.

Coleman, C., & Moynihan, J. (1996). *Understanding crime data: Haunted by the dark figure.* Buckingham, UK: Open University Press.

Collett, D. (1991). *Modelling binary data.* New York: Chapman and Hall.

Collican, H. (1999). *Research methods and statistics in psychology.* London: Hodder & Staughton.

Collier, A. (1994). *Critical realism.* London: Verso.

Collins, H. M. (1985). *Changing order: Replication and induction in scientific practice.* London: Sage.

Collins, P. H. (1997). Comment on Heckman's "Truth and method: Feminist standpoint theory revisited": Where's the power? *Signs, 22*(21), 375–381.

Collins, R. (1995). Prediction in macrosociology: The case of the Soviet collapse. *American Journal of Sociology, 100*(6), 1552–1593.

Colson, F. (1977). *Sociale indicatoren van enkele aspecten van bevolkingsgroei.* Doctoral dissertation, Katholieke Universiteit Leuven, Department of Sociology, Leuven.

Comstock, D. E. (1994). A method for critical research. In M. Martin & L. C. McIntyre (Eds.), *Readings in the philosophy of social science* (pp. 625–639). Cambridge: MIT Press.

Confidentiality and Data Access Committee. (1999). *Checklist on disclosure potential of proposed data releases.* Washington, DC: Office of Management and Budget, Office of Information and Regulatory Affairs, Statistical Policy Office. Retrieved from www.fcsm.gov/committees/cdac/checklist _799.doc

Conger, A. J. (1974). Revised definition for suppressor variables: A guide to their identification and interpretation. *Educational and Psychological Measurement, 34,* 35–46.

Connell, R. W. (2002). *Gender.* Cambridge, UK: Polity.

Conover, W. J. (1980). *Practical nonparametric statistics.* New York: Wiley.

Conover, W. J. (1998). *Practical nonparametric statistics* (3rd ed.). New York: Wiley.

Conte, R., & Dellarocas, C. (2001). Social order in info societies: An old challenge for innovation. In R. Conte & C. Dellarocas (Eds.), *Social order in multi-agent systems* (pp. 1–16). Boston: Kluwer Academic.

Converse, J. (1987). *Survey research in the United States.* Berkeley: University of California Press.

Converse, J., & Presser, S. (1986). *Survey questions.* Beverly Hills, CA: Sage.

Converse, P. E. (1964). The nature of belief systems in mass publics. In D. Apter (Ed.), *Ideology and discontent* (pp. 206–261). New York: Free Press.

Converse, P. E., & Markus, G. B. (1979). Plus ca change . . . : The new CPS Election Study Panel. *American Political Science Review, 73,* 32–49.

Cook, D. (1996). On the interpretation of regression plots. *Journal of the American Statistical Association, 91,* 983–992.

Cook, D. R., & Weisberg, S. (1999). *Applied regression including computing and graphics.* New York: Wiley.

Cook, R. D., & Weisberg, S. (1982). *Residuals and influence in regression.* New York: Chapman and Hall.

Cook, T. D., & Campbell, D. T. (1979). *Quasi-experimentation: Design and analysis issues for field settings.* Chicago: Rand McNally College Publishing.

Cook, T. D., & Payne, M. R. (2002). Objecting to the objections to using random assignment in educational research. In F. Mosteller & R. Boruch (Eds.), *Evidence matters: Randomized trials in education research.* Washington, DC: Brookings Institution.

Cook, T. D., Campbell, D. T., & Peracchio, L. (1990). Quasi-experimentation. In M. D. Dunnette & L. M. Hough (Eds.), *Handbook of industrial and organisational psychology* (2nd ed., Vol. 1, pp. 491–576). Chicago: Rand McNally.

Cooke, B., & Kothari, U. (Eds.). (2001). *Participation: The new tyranny?* London: Zed.

Cooksy, L. J., Gill, P., & Kelly, P. A. (2001). The program logic model as an integrative framework for a multimethod evaluation. *Evaluation and Program Planning, 24,* 119–128.

Cooley, W., & Lohnes, P. (1971). *Multivariate data analysis.* New York: Wiley.

Coombs, C. H. (1964). *A theory of data.* New York: Wiley.

Cooper, H. (1998). *Synthesizing research: A guide for literature reviews* (3rd ed.). Thousand Oaks, CA: Sage.

Cooper, H., & Hedges, L. V. (Eds.). (1994). *The handbook of research synthesis.* New York: Russell Sage Foundation.

Copi, I. M., & Cohen, C. (1990). *Introduction to logic* (8th ed.). New York: Macmillan.

Cordova, D. I., & Lepper, M. R. (1996). Intrinsic motivation and the process of learning: Beneficial effects of contextualization, personalization, and choice. *Journal of Educational Psychology, 88*(4), 715–730.

Cormack, R. (2001). Population size estimation and capture-recapture methods. In N. J. Smelser & P. B. Baltes (Eds.), *International encyclopedia of the social and behavioral sciences* (Vol. 17). Amsterdam: Elsevier.

Cormen, T. H., Leiserson, C. E., Rivest, R. L., & Stein, C. (2001). *Introduction to algorithms* (2nd ed.). Cambridge: MIT Press.

Correll, S. (1995). The ethnography of an electronic bar: The lesbian cafe. *Journal of Contemporary Ethnography, 24*(3), 270–298.

Cortazzi, M. (2001). Narrative analysis in ethnography. In P. Atkinson, A. Coffey, S. Delamont, J. Lofland, & L. Lofland (Eds.), *Handbook of ethnography.* London: Sage.

Cortazzi, M., Jin, L., Wall, D., & Cavendish, S. (2001). Sharing learning through narrative communication. *International Journal of Language and Communication Disorders, 36,* 252–257.

Corter, J. E. (1996). *Tree models of similarity and association* (Sage University Paper Series on Quantitative Applications in the Social Sciences, 07–112). Thousand Oaks, CA: Sage.

Corti, L. (1993). Using diaries in social research (*Social Research Update,* Iss. 2). Guildford, UK: University of Surrey, Department of Sociology.

Corti, L., Foster, J., & Thompson, P. (1995). *Archiving qualitative research data* (Social Research Update No. 10). Surrey, UK: Department of Sociology, University of Surrey.

Cortina, J. M. (1993). What is coefficient alpha? An examination of theory and applications. *Journal of Applied Psychology, 78,* 98–104.

Costantino, G., Malgady, R. G., & Vazquez, C. (1981). A comparison of the Murray–TAT and a new Thematic

Apperception Test for urban Hispanic children. *Hispanic Journal of Behavior Sciences, 3,* 291–300.

Costigan, P., & Thomson, K. (1992). Issues in the design of CAPI questionnaires for complex surveys. In A. Westlake, R. Banks, C. Payne, & T. Orchard (Eds.), *Survey and statistical computing* (pp. 47–156). London: North Holland.

Costner, H. L. (1965). Criteria for measures of association. *American Sociological Review, 30,* 341–353.

Couper, M. P. (2000). WEB surveys: A review of issues and approaches. *Public Opinion Quarterly, 64,* 464–494.

Couper, M. P., Baker, R. P., Bethlehem, J., Clark, C. Z. F., Martin, J., Nichols, W. L., et al. (Eds.). (1998). *Computer assisted survey information collection.* New York: John Wiley.

Courant, Richard. (1988). *Differential and integral calculus* (2 vols.) (E. J. McShane, Trans.). New York: Wiley. (Originally published in 1934)

Courville, T., & Thompson, B. (2001). Use of structure coefficients in published multiple regression articles: β is not enough. *Educational and Psychological Measurement, 61,* 229–248.

Cousins, J. B. (2003). Utilization effects of participatory evaluation. In T. Kellaghan, D. L. Stufflebeam, & L. A. Wingate (Eds.), *International handbook of educational evaluation* (pp. 245–266). Dordrecht, The Netherlands: Kluwer Academic.

Cousins, J. B., & Whitmore, E. (1998). Framing participatory evaluation. *New Directions in Evaluation, 80,* 5–23.

Cox, D. R. (1972). Regression models and life-tables (with discussion). *Journal of the Royal Statistical Society, B, 34,* 187–220.

Cox, D. R., & Oakes, D. (1984). *Analysis of survival data.* New York: Chapman and Hall.

Cox, R. T. (1990). Probability, frequency, and reasonable expectation. In G. Shafer & J. Pearl (Eds.), *Readings in uncertain reasoning* (pp. 353–365). New York: Morgan Kaufmann. (Original work published 1946)

Coxon, A. P. M. (1982). *The user's guide to multidimensional scaling.* London: Heinemann Educational.

Coxon, A. P. M. (1999). *Between the sheets: Sexual diaries and gay men's sex in the era of AIDS.* London: Cassell.

Coxon, A. P. M. (1999). *Sorting data: Collection and analysis* (Sage University Paper Series on Quantitative Applications in the Social Sciences, 07–127). Thousand Oaks, CA: Sage.

Cramer, J. S. (1986). *Econometric applications of maximum likelihood methods.* Cambridge, UK: Cambridge University Press.

Crano, W. D., & Brewer, M. B. (2002). *Principles and methods of social research* (2nd ed.). Mahwah, NJ: Lawrence Erlbaum.

Crapanzano, V. (1980). *Tuhami: Portrait of a Moroccan.* Chicago: University of Chicago Press.

Crenshaw, K., Gotanda, N., Peller, G., & Thomas, K. (Eds.). (1995). *Critical race theory.* New York: The New York Press.

Cressey, D. (1950). The criminal violation of financial trust. *American Sociological Review, 15,* 738–743.

Cressey, D. (1953). *Other people's money.* Glencoe, IL: Free Press.

Cressie, N. (1993). *Statistics for spatial data.* New York: Wiley.

Cressie, N., & Read, T. (1984). Multinomial goodness of tests. *Journal of Royal Statistical Society Series B, 46,* 440–464.

Creswell, J. W. (1995). *Research design: Quantitative and qualitative approaches.* Thousand Oaks, CA: Sage.

Crocker, L., & Algina, J. (1986). *Introduction to classical & modern test theory.* New York: Harcourt Brace Jovanovich.

Croll, P. (1986). *Systematic classroom observation.* Lewes, UK: Falmer.

Cromwell, J. B., Labys, W., & Terraza, M. (1994). *Univariate tests for time series models.* Thousand Oaks, CA: Sage.

Cronbach, L. J. (1943). On estimates of test reliability. *Journal of Educational Psychology, 34,* 485–494.

Cronbach, L. J. (1946). A case study of the split-half reliability coefficient. *Journal of Educational Psychology, 37,* 473–480.

Cronbach, L. J. (1951). Coefficient alpha and the internal structure of tests. *Psychometrika, 16,* 297–334.

Cronbach, L. J. (1955). Processes affecting scores on "understanding of others" and "assumed similarity." *Psychological Bulletin, 52,* 177–193.

Cronbach, L. J. (1990). *Essentials of psychological testing* (5th ed.). New York: HarperCollins.

Cronbach, L. J., & Meehl, P. E. (1955). Construct validity in psychological tests. *Psychological Bulletin, 52,* 281–302.

Cronbach, L. J., Gleser, G. C., Nanda, H., & Rajaratnam, N. (1972). *The dependability of behavioral measurements: Theory of generalizability of scores and profiles.* New York: Wiley.

Croon, M. A., Bergsma, W., & Hagenaars, J. A. (2000). Analyzing change in categorical variables by generalized log-linear models. *Sociological Methods & Research, 29,* 195–229.

Crotty, M. (1998). *The foundations of social research: Meaning and perspective in the research process.* London: Sage.

Crowne, D., & Marlowe, D. (1964). *The approval motive: Studies in evaluative dependence.* New York: Wiley.

Cruse, D. A. (1986). *Lexical semantics.* Cambridge, UK: Cambridge University Press.

Cullen, C. G. (1990). *Matrices and linear transformations* (2nd ed.). New York: Dover.

Curtin, R., Presser, S., & Singer, E. (2000). The effects of response rate changes on the index of consumer sentiment. *Public Opinion Quarterly, 64,* 413–428.

Czaja, R., Blair, J., & Sebestile, J. P. (1982). Respondent selection in a telephone survey: Comparison of three techniques. *Journal of Marketing Research, 21,* 381–385.

Czyzewski, M. (1994). Reflexivity of actors versus reflexivity of accounts. *Theory, Culture and Society, 11,* 161–168.

D'Andrade, R. (1995). *The development of cognitive anthropology.* Cambridge, UK: Cambridge University Press.

Dale, A., & Marsh, C. (Eds.). (1993). *The 1991 census user's guide.* London: HMSO.

Dale, A., Arber, S., & Procter, P. (1988). *Doing secondary analysis*. London: Unwin Hyman.

Dale, A., Fieldhouse, E., & Holdsworth, C. (2000). *Analyzing census microdata*. London: Arnold.

Dandridge, T. C., Mitroff, I., & Joyce, W. F. (1980). Organizational symbolism: A topic to expand organizational analysis. *Academy of Management Review, 5*, 77–82.

Daniel, W. W. (1993). *Collecting sensitive data by randomized response: An annotated bibliography* (2nd ed.). Atlanta: Georgia State University Business Press.

Daniels, H. E. (1944). The relation between measures of correlation in the universe of sample permutations. *Biometrika, 35*, 129–135.

Darlington, R. B. (1990). *Regression and linear models*. New York: McGraw-Hill.

Darnell, A. C. (1995). *A dictionary of econometrics*. Cheltenham, UK: Edward Elgar.

Darroch, J. N., Lauritzen, S. L., & Speed, T. P. (1980). Markov fields and log-linear models. *Annals of Mathematical Statistics, 43*, 1470–1480.

David, H. A., & Moeschberg, M. L. (1978). *The theory of competing risks* (Griffin's Statistical Monograph #39). New York: Macmillan.

David, P. (1985). Clio and the economics of QWERTY. *American Economic Review, 75*, 332–337.

Davidson, J., Hendry, D. F., Srba, F., & Yeo, S. (1978). Econometric modelling of the aggregate time-series relationship between consumers' expenditure and income in the United Kingdom. *Economic Journal, 88*, 661–692.

Davidson, R., & MacKinnon J. G. (1993). *Estimation and inference in econometrics*. New York: Oxford University Press.

Davis, J. A. (1985). *The logic of causal order* (Sage University Paper Series on Quantitative Applications in the Social Sciences, 07–055). Beverly Hills, CA: Sage.

Davis, J. A., & Smith, T. W. (1992). *The NORC General Social Survey: A user's guide*. Newbury Park, CA: Sage.

Davison, A. C., & Hinkley, D. V. (1997). *Bootstrap methods and their application*. Cambridge, UK: Cambridge University Press.

Day, N. E. (1969). Estimating the components of a mixture of two normal distributions. *Biometrika, 56*, 463–474.

De Beauvoir, S. (1970). *The second sex*. New York: Alfred A. Knopf. (Original work published 1949)

de Leeuw, J., & Kreft, I. G. G. (Eds.). (in press). *Handbook of quantitative multilevel analysis*. Dordrecht, The Netherlands: Kluwer Academic.

de Leeuw, J., & van der Heijden, P. G. M. (1988). The analysis of time-budgets with a latent time-budget model. In E. Diday (Ed.), *Data analysis and informatics* (Vol. 5, pp. 159–166). Amsterdam: North-Holland.

de Saussure, F. (1979). *Cours de linguistique générale* (T. de Mauro, Ed.). Paris: Payot.

de Vaus, D. (Ed.). (2002). *Social surveys* (4 vols.). London: Sage.

de Vaus, D. A. (1995). *Surveys in social research* (4th ed.). Sydney, Australia: Allen & Unwin.

de Vaus, D. A. (2001). *Research design in social research*. London: Sage.

Deacon, D., Bryman, A., & Fenton, N. (1998). Collision or collusion? A discussion of the unplanned triangulation of quantitative and qualitative research methods. *International Journal of Social Research Methodology, 1*, 47–63.

Deacon, D., Pickering, M., Golding, P., & Murdock, G. (1999). *Researching communications*. London: Arnold.

DeBoef, S., & Granato, J. (2000). Testing for cointegrating relationships with near-integrated data. *Political Analysis, 8*, 99–117.

Deckner, D. F., Adamson, L. B., & Bakeman, R. (2003). Rhythm in mother-infant interactions. *Infancy, 4*, 201–217.

DeGroot M. H., & Schervish, M. J. (2002). *Probability and statistics* (3rd ed.). Reading, MA: Addison-Wesley.

Dehejia, R. H., & Wahba, S. (1999). Causal effects in non-experimental studies: Reevaluating the evaluation of training programs. *Journal of the American Statistical Association, 94*, 1053–1062.

Del Monte, K. (2000). Partners in inquiry: Ethical challenges in team research. *International Social Science Review, 75*, 3–14.

Delanty, G. (1997). *Social science: Beyond constructivism and realism*. Buckingham, UK: Open University Press.

DeMaris, A. (1992). *Logit modeling*. Newbury Park, CA: Sage.

Deming, W. E. (1997). *Statistical adjustment of data*. New York. Dover.

DeNavas-Walt, C., & Cleveland, R. W. (2002). *Money income in the United States* (United States Census Bureau, Current Population Reports, P60–218). Washington, DC: Government Printing Office. Available: www.census.gov/prod/2002pubs/p60-218.pdf

Denzin, N. (1983). Interpretive interactionism. In G. Morgan (Ed.), *Beyond method: Strategies for social research* (pp. 128–142). Beverly Hills, CA: Sage.

Denzin, N. (1992). *Symbolic interactionism: The politics of interpretation*. Oxford, UK: Blackwell.

Denzin, N. K. (1970). *The research act in sociology*. Chicago: Aldine.

Denzin, N. K. (1989). *Interpretive biography*. Newbury Park, CA: Sage.

Dezin, N. K., (1989). *Interpretive interactionism*. Newbury Park, CA: Sage.

Denzin, N. K., (1997). *Interpretive enthnography*. Thousand Oaks, CA: Sage.

Denzin, N. K., & Lincoln, Y. S. (2000). The discipline and practice of qualitative research. In N. K. Denzin & Y. S. Lincoln (Eds.), *Handbook of qualitative research* (2nd ed., pp. 1–28). Thousand Oaks, CA: Sage.

Denzin, N. K., & Lincoln, Y. S. (Eds.). (2000). *Handbook of qualitative research* (2nd ed.). Thousand Oaks, CA: Sage.

Denzin, N. K. & Lincoln, Y. S. (2000). Introduction: The discipline and practice of qualitative research. In N. K. Denzin & Y. S. Lincoln (Eds.), *Handbook of qualitative research* (2nd ed., pp. 1–28). Thousand Oaks, CA: Sage.

Derrida, J. (1976). *Of grammatology* (G. Spivak, Trans.). Baltimore, MD: Johns Hopkins University Press.

Derrida, J. (1995). *The gift of death.* Chicago: The University of Chicago Press.

Derrida, J., & Ferraris, F. (2001). *A taste for the secret.* Cambridge, UK: Polity.

DeVellis, R. F. (1991). *Scale development: Theory and applications.* Newbury Park, CA: Sage.

Devore, J. L. (1991). *Probability and statistics for engineering and the sciences* (3rd ed.). Pacific Grove, CA: Brooks/Cole.

Dexter, L. A. (1970). *Elite and specialized interviewing.* Evanston, IL: Northwest University Press.

Dey, I. (1993). *Qualitative data analysis.* London: Routledge Kegan Paul.

Diamond, S. S. (2000). Reference guide on survey research, in *Reference manual on scientific evidence.* (2nd ed., pp. 229–276). Washington, D. C.: Federal Judicial Center.

Dickens, P. (2000). *Social Darwinism.* Buckingham, UK: Open University Press.

Diebold, F. X. (2001). *Elements of forecasting* (2nd ed.). Cincinnati, OH: South-Western.

Dienstbier, R. A. (1989). Arousal and physiological toughness: Implications for mental and physical health. *Psychological Review, 96,* 84–100.

Diesing, P. (1991). *How does social science work?* Pittsburgh, PA: University of Pittsburgh Press.

Digman, J. M. (1990). Personality structure: Emergence of the five-factor model. *Annual Review of Psychology, 41,* 417–440.

Dillman, D. A. (1978). *Mail and telephone surveys: The total design method.* New York: Wiley.

Dillman, D. A. (2000). *Mail and Internet surveys: The tailored design method.* New York: Wiley.

Dilthey, W. (1985). *Poetry and experience: Selected works* (Vol. 5). Princeton, NJ: Princeton University Press.

Dion, K. K., Berscheid, E., & Walster, E. (1972). What is beautiful is good. *Journal of Personality and Social Psychology, 24,* 285–290.

DiPrete, T. A., & Forristal, J. D. (1994). Multilevel models: Methods and substance. *Annual Review of Sociology, 20,* 331–357.

Dixon-Woods, M., Fitzpatrick, R., & Roberts, K. (2001). Including qualitative research in systematic reviews: Problems and opportunities. *Journal of Evaluation in Clinical Practice, 7,* 125–133.

Doksum, K. A., & Sievers, G. L. (1976). Plotting with confidence: Graphical comparisons of two populations. *Biometrika, 63,* 421–434.

Doreian, P., Batagelj, V., & Ferligoj, A. (1994). Partitioning networks based on generalized concepts of equivalence. *Journal of Mathematical Sociology, 19,* 1–27.

Douglas, J. D. (1985). *Creative interviewing.* Beverly Hills, CA: Sage.

Douglass, B., & Moustakas, C. (1985). Heuristic inquiry: The internal search to know. *Journal of Humanistic Psychology, 25,* 39–55.

Dovidio, J. F., Kawakami, K., & Beach, K. R. (2001). Implicit and explicit attitudes: Examination of the relationship between measures of intergroup bias. In R. Brown & S. L. Gaertner (Eds.), *Blackwell handbook of social psychology: Intergroup processes* (pp. 175–197). Malden, MA: Blackwell.

Downs, A. (1957). *An economic theory of democracy.* New York: HarperCollins.

Doyle, P., Martin, B., & Moore, J. (2000). *Improving income measurement.* The Survey of Income Program Participation (SIPP) Methods Panel. Washington, DC: U.S. Bureau of the Census.

Draper, N. R., & Smith, H. (1998). *Applied regression analysis* (3rd ed.). New York: Wiley.

Dreher, A. U. (2000). *Foundations for conceptual research in psychoanalysis* (Psychoanalytic Monograph 4). London: Karnac.

Drew, P., & Heritage, J. (Eds.). (1992). *Talk at work: Interaction in institutional settings.* Cambridge, UK: Cambridge University Press.

Dryzek, J. S., & Holmes, L. T. (2002). *Post-communist democratization.* Cambridge, UK: Cambridge University Press.

Dubin, J. A., & Rivers, D. (1989). Selection bias in linear regression, logit and probit models. *Sociological Methods & Research, 18,* 360–390.

Duda, R., Hart, P. E., & Stork, D. G. (2001). *Pattern classification.* New York: Wiley.

Dukes, R. L., Ullman, J. B., & Stein, J. A. (1995). An evaluation of D.A.R.E. (Drug Abuse Resistance Education), using a Solomon four-group design with latent variables. *Evaluation Review, 19*(4), 409–435.

Duncan, O. D. (1966). Path analysis: Sociological examples. *American Journal of Sociology, 72,* 1–16.

Duncan, O. D. (1975). *Introduction to structural equation models.* New York: Academic Press.

Duncan, O. D., Haller, A., & Portes, A. (1968). Peer influence on aspiration: A reinterpretation. *American Journal of Sociology, 75,* 119–137.

Dupré, J. (2001). *Human nature and the limits of science.* Oxford, UK: Oxford University Press.

Dupré, J., & Cartwright, N. (1988). Probability and causality: Why Hume and indeterminism don't mix. *Nous, 22,* 521–536.

Durbin, J., & Watson, G. S. (1950). Testing for serial correlation in least squares regressions I. *Biometrika, 37,* 409–428.

Durkheim, E. (1951). *Suicide.* Glencoe, IL: Free Press.

Durkheim, E. (1952). *Suicide.* London: Routledge Kegan Paul. (Original work published 1896)

Durkheim, E. (1964). *The rules of scientific method.* Glencoe, IL: Free Press.

Duval, S., & Tweedie, R. (2000). Trim and fill: A simple funnel plot based method of testing and adjusting for publication bias in meta-analysis. *Biometrics, 56,* 276–284.

Eagly, A. H., Ashmore, R. D., Makhijani, M. G., & Longo, L. C. (1991). What is beautiful is good but . . . A meta-analytic review of research on the physical attractiveness stereotype. *Psychological Bulletin, 110,* 109–128.

Easterby-Smith, M., Thorpe, R., & Holman, D. (1996). Using repertory grids in management. *Journal of European Industrial Training, 20,* 1–30.

Easterby-Smith, M., Thorpe, R., & Lowe, A. (2002). *Management research: An introduction* (2nd ed.). London: Sage.

Eatwell, J., Milgate, M., & Newman, P. (1987). *The new Palgrave: A dictionary of economics.* London: Macmillan.

Eckstein, H. (1975). Case study and theory in political science. In F. I. Greenstein & N. W. Polsby (Eds.), *Handbook of political science: Vol. 7, Strategies of inquiry* (pp. 79–137). Reading, MA: Addison-Wesley.

Eco, U. (1972). Towards a semiotic inquiry into the television message. In *Working papers in cultural studies* (Vol. 3, pp. 103–121). Birmingham: Centre for Contemporary Cultural Studies. (Original work published 1965)

Eco, U. (1976). *A theory of semiotics.* Bloomington: Indiana University Press.

Eco, U. (1981). *The role of the reader: Explorations in the semiotics of texts.* London: Hutchinson.

Economic and Social Research Council Research Centre on Micro-Social Change. (2001, February 28). *British Household Panel Survey* [computer file] (Study Number 4340). Colchester, UK: The Data Archive [distributor].

Eden, D. (1990). *Pygmalion in management: Productivity as a self-fulfilling prophecy.* Lexington, MA: D. C. Heath.

Edwards, A. (1948). On Guttman's scale analysis. *Educational and Psychological Measurement, 8,* 313–318.

Edwards, A. L. (1957). *Techniques of attitude construction.* New York: Appleton- Century-Crofts.

Edwards, A. W. F. (1972). *Likelihood: An account of the statistical concept of likelihood and its application to scientific inference.* Cambridge, UK: Cambridge University Press.

Edwards, D. (1997). *Discourse and cognition.* London: Sage.

Edwards, D. (2000). *Introduction to graphical modelling* (2nd ed.). New York: Springer-Verlag.

Edwards, D., & Potter, J. (1992). *Discursive psychology.* London: Sage.

Edwards, D., Ashmore, M., & Potter, J. (1995). Death and furniture: The rhetoric, politics, and theology of bottom line arguments against relativism. *History of the Human Sciences, 8,* 25–49.

Edwards, W. S., Winn, D. M., Kurlantzick, V. et al. (1994). *Evaluation of National Health Interview Survey diagnostic reporting.* National Center for Health Statistics. Vital Health Stat 2(120).

Efron, B. (1979). Bootstrap methods: Another look at the jackknife. *Annals of Statistics, 7,* 1–26.

Efron, B. (1982). *The jackknife, the bootstrap, and other resampling plans.* Philadelphia: Society for Industrial and Applied Mathematics.

Efron, B. (1986). Why isn't everyone a Bayesian? *The American Statistician, 40,* 1–5.

Efron, B., & Tibshirani, R. J. (1993). *An introduction to the bootstrap.* New York: Chapman & Hall.

Egger, M., Davey Smith, G., & Altman, D. G. (2001). *Systematic reviews in health care: Meta-analysis in context* (2nd ed.). London: BMJ Books.

Egger, M., Smith, G., Schneider, M., & Minder, C. (1997). Bias in meta-analysis detected by a simple, graphical test. *British Medical Journal, 315,* 629–634.

Eibl-Eibesfeldt, I. (1989). *Human ethology.* Hawthorne, NY: Aldine de Gruyter.

Eisenhardt, K. M. (1989). Building theories from case study research. *Academy of Management Review, 14,* 532–550.

Eisenhart, M. (1998). On the subject of interpretive reviews. *Review of Educational Research, 68*(4), 391–399.

Eisner, E. W. (1997). The new frontier in qualitative research methodology. *Qualitative Inquiry, 3,* 259–273.

Elder, G., Pavalko, E. K., & Clipp, E. C. (1993). *Working with archival lives: Studying lives* (Sage University Papers on Quantitative Applications on the Social Sciences, 07–088). Newbury Park, CA: Sage.

Eliason, S. R. (1993). *Maximum likelihood estimation: Logic and practice.* Newbury Park, CA: Sage.

Ellis, B. D., & Lierse, C. (1994). Dispositional essentialism. *Australasian Journal of Philosophy, 72*(1), 27–45.

Ellis, C. (1995). *Final negotiations: A story of love, loss, and chronic illness.* Philadelphia: Temple University Press.

Ellis, C. (2003). *The ethnographic "I": A methodological novel on doing autoethnography.* Walnut Creek, CA: AltaMira.

Ellis, C. S. (1991). Sociological introspection and emotional experience. *Symbolic Interaction, 14,* 23–50.

Ellis, C., & Bochner, A. P. (2000). Autoethnography, personal narrative, reflexivity: Researcher as subject. In N. K. Denzin & Y. S. Lincoln (Eds.), *Handbook of qualitative research* (2nd ed., pp. 733–768). Thousand Oaks, CA: Sage.

Ellis, C., & Bochner, A. P. (Eds.). (1996). *Composing ethnography: Alternative forms of qualitative writing.* Walnut Creek, CA: AltaMira.

Elmasri, R. A., & Navathe, S. B. (2001). *Fundamentals of database systems.* New York: Addison-Wesley.

Elster, J. (1989). *Nuts and bolts for the social sciences.* Cambridge, UK: Cambridge University Press.

Elster, J. (1989). *The cement of society: A study of social order.* Cambridge, UK: Cambridge University Press.

Elster, J. (Ed.). (1986). *Rational choice.* Oxford, UK: Basil Blackwell.

Ember, C. R., & Ember, M. (2001). *Cross-cultural research methods.* Walnut Creek, CA: AltaMira.

Embree, L., Behnke, E. A., Carr, D., Evans, J. C., Huertas-Jourda, J., Kockelmans, J. J., et al. (Eds.). (1996). *The encyclopedia of phenomenology.* Dordrecht, The Netherlands: Kluwer.

Embretson, S. E., & Reise, S. P. (2000). *Item response theory for psychologists.* Mahwah, NJ: Lawrence Erlbaum.

Emerson, R. M., & Pollner, M. (1988). On the use of members' responses to researchers' accounts. *Human Organization, 47,* 189–198.

Emerson, R. M., Fretz, R. I., & Shaw, L. L. (1995). *Writing ethnographic fieldnotes.* Chicago: University of Chicago Press.

Emirbayer, M., & Mische, A. (1998). What is agency? *American Journal of Sociology, 103*(4), 962–1023.

Emmison, M., & Smith, P. (2000). *Researching the visual.* London: Sage.

Engle, R. F., & Granger, C. W. J. (1987). Co-integration and error correction: Representation, estimation and testing. *Econometrica, 55,* 251–276.

Engle, R. F., Granger, C. W. J. (1991). *Long run relationships: Readings in cointegration.* New York: Oxford University Press.

Engle, R. F., Hendry, D. F., & Richard, J. F. (1983). Exogeneity. *Econometrica, 51,* 277–304.

Epley, N., & Huff, C. (1998). Suspicion, affective response, and educational benefit of deception in psychology research. *Personality and Social Psychology Bulletin, 24,* 759–768.

Epstein, J. M., & Axtell, R. (1996). *Growing artificial societies: Social science from the bottom up.* Cambridge: MIT Press.

Ericsson, K. A., & Simon, H. A. (1984). *Protocol analysis: Verbal reports as data.* Cambridge: MIT Press.

Erikson, E. H. (1975). *Life history and the historical moment.* New York: Norton.

Erikson, R., Goldthorpe, J. H., & Portocarero, L. (1979). Intergenerational mobility in three Western European societies. *British Journal of Sociology, 30.*

Erlang, A. K. (1935). *Fircifrede logaritmetavler og andre regnetavler til brug ved undervisning og i praksis.* Kobenhavn: G.E.C. Gads.

Ermarth, M. (1978). *Wilhelm Dilthey: The critique of historical reason.* Chicago: University of Chicago Press.

Escofier, B., & Pagès, J. (1988). *Analyses factorielles multiples* [Multiple factor analyses]. Paris: Dunod.

Essed, Ph., & Goldberg, T. D. (Eds.). (2002). *Race critical theories: Text and context.* Malden, MA: Blackwell.

Eubank, R. L. (1988). Quantiles. In S. Kotz, N. L. Johnson, & C. B. Read (Eds.), *Encyclopedia of statistical sciences* (Vol. 7, pp. 424–432). New York: Wiley.

European Social Survey Central Co-ordinating Team. (2001). *European Social Survey (ESS): Specification for participating countries.* London: Author.

Eurostat. (1998). *Labour force survey: Methods and definitions* (1998 ed.). Luxembourg: Author.

Evans, J. L. (2000). *Early childhood counts.* Washington, DC: World Bank.

Evans, M., Hastings, N., & Peacock, B. (2000). *Statistical distributions* (3rd ed.). New York: Wiley.

Everitt, B. S. (1992). *The analysis of contingency tables.* London: Chapman & Hall.

Everitt, B., Landau, S., & Leese, M. (2001). *Cluster analysis* (4th ed.). Oxford, UK: Oxford University Press.

Exner, J. E. (2002). *The Rorschach: A comprehensive system* (Vol. 1). New York: John Wiley.

Fairclough, N. (2000). *New labour, new language?* London: Routledge Kegan Paul.

Fairclough, N., & Wodak, R. (1997). Critical discourse analysis. In T. van Dijk (Ed.), *Discourse as social interaction.* Thousand Oaks, CA: Sage.

Fals-Borda, O., & Anisur Rahman, M. (Eds.). (1991). *Action and knowledge: Breaking the monopoly with participatory action-research.* New York: Apex.

Fan, J., & Gijbels, I. (1996). *Local polynomial modelling and its applications.* London: Chapman & Hall.

Faugier, J., & Sargeant, M. (1997). Sampling hard to reach populations. *Journal of Advanced Nursing, 26,* 790–797.

Fazio, R. H., & Olson, M. A. (2003). Implicit measures in social cognition research: Their meaning and use. *Annual Review of Psychology, 54,* 297–327.

Featherman, D. L., & Hauser, R. M. (1978). *Opportunity and change.* New York: Academic Press.

Featherstone, M. (1988). In pursuit of the postmodernism: An introduction. *Theory, Culture & Society, 5,* 195–215.

Fechner, G. T. (1860). *Elemente der Psychophysik.* Leipzig: Breitkopf & Härtel.

Fechner, G. T. (1877). *In sachen der Psychophysik.* Leipzig: Breitkopf & Härtel.

Federal Committee on Statistical Methodology. (1994). *Report on statistical disclosure limitation methodology* (Statistical Policy Working Paper #22). Prepared by the Subcommittee on Disclosure Limitation Methodology. Washington, DC: Office of Management and Budget, Office of Information and Regulatory Affairs, Statistical Policy Office. Retrieved from www.fcsm.gov/working-papers/wp22.html

Feldt, L. S., & Brennan, R. L. (1989). Reliability. In R. L. Linn (Ed.), *Educational measurement* (3rd ed., pp. 105–146). New York: Macmillan.

Feller, W. (1968). *An introduction to probability theory and its applications* (3rd ed.). New York: John Wiley.

Ferrell, J., & Hamm, M. S. (1998). True confessions: Crime, deviance, and field research. In J. Ferrell & M. Hamm (Eds.), *Ethnography at the edge: Crime, deviance and field research* (pp. 2–19). Boston: Northeastern University Press.

Fetterman, D. M. (1998). *Ethnography: Step by step* (2nd ed.). Thousand Oaks, CA: Sage.

Fetterman, D. M. (2002). Web surveys to digital movies: Technological tools of the trade. *Educational Researcher, 31*(6), 29–37.

Feyerabend, P. (1978). *Against method.* London: Verso.

Feynman, R. P., & Weinberg, S. (1987). *Elementary particles and the laws of physics: The 1986 Dirac Memorial Lectures.* Cambridge, UK: Cambridge University Press.

Field, A. (1998). A bluffer's guide to . . . sphericity. *British Psychological Society: Mathematical, Statistical & Computing Newsletter, 6,* 13–22.

Fielding, J. (1993). Coding and managing data. In N. Gilbert (Ed.), *Researching social life* (pp. 218–238). Thousand Oaks, CA: Sage.

Fielding, N. G., & Lee, R. M. (1998). *Computer analysis and qualitative research.* London: Sage.

Fienberg, S. E. (1977). *The analysis of cross-classified categorical data.* Cambridge: MIT Press.

Fienberg, S. E. (1980). *The analysis of cross-classified categorical data* (2nd ed.). Cambridge: MIT Press.

Fillmore, C. (1975). An alternative to checklist theories of meaning. In C. Cogen, H. Thompson, G. Thurgood, K. Whistler, & J. Wright (Eds.), *Proceedings of the First Annual Meeting of the Berkeley Linguistics Society* (pp. 123–131). Berkeley, CA: Berkeley Linguistics Society.

Filmer, P. (1998). Analysing literary texts. In C. Seale (Ed.), *Researching society and culture.* London: Sage.

Fink, A., & Kosecoff, J. (1988). *How to conduct surveys: A step-by-step guide.* Newbury Park, CA: Sage.

Firebaugh, G. (2001). Ecological fallacy. *International encyclopedia for the social and behavioral sciences* (Vol. 6, pp. 4023–4026). Oxford, UK: Pergamon.

Fisher, C. B., & Wallace, S. A. (2000). Through the community looking glass: Reevaluating the ethical and policy implications of research on adolescent risk and psychopathology. *Ethics & Behavior, 10*(2), 99–118.

Fisher, R. A. (1925). *Statistical methods for research workers* (1st ed.). Edinburgh, UK: Oliver & Boyd.

Fisher, R. A. (1925). Theory of statistical estimation. *Proceedings of the Cambridge Philosophical Society, 22,* 700–725.

Fisher, R. A. (1934). Two new properties of mathematical likelihood. *Proceedings of the Royal Society of London, Series A, 144,* 285–307.

Fisher, R. A. (1935). *The design of experiments* (1st ed.). Edinburgh, UK: Oliver and Boyd.

Fisher, R. A. (1971). *Design of experiments.* New York: Hafner Press. (Original work published 1935).

Fisher, R. A., & Yates, F. (1934). The six by six Latin squares. *Proceedings of the Cambridge Philosophical Society, 30,* 492–507.

Flanagan, J. C. (1954). The critical incident technique. *Psychological Bulletin, 51*(4), 327–358.

Flick, U. (2002). *An introduction to qualitative research* (2nd ed.). London: Sage.

Foley, D. E. (1990). *Learning capitalist culture: Deep in the heart of Texas.* Philadelphia: University of Pennsylvania Press.

Fontana, A., & Frey, J. H. (1994). Interviewing: The art of science. In N. K. Denzin & Y. S. Lincoln (Eds.), *Handbook of qualitative research* (pp. 361–376). Thousand Oaks, CA: Sage.

Fontana, A., & Frey, J. H. (2000). The interview: From structured questions to negotiated text. In N. K. Denzin & Y. S. Lincoln (Eds.), *Handbook of qualitative research* (2nd ed., pp. 645–672). Thousand Oaks, CA: Sage.

Forrester, J. W. (1961). *Industrial dynamics.* Cambridge: MIT Press.

Forster, E., & McCleery, A. (1999). Computer assisted personal interviewing: A method of capturing sensitive information. *IASSIST Quarterly, 23*(2), 26–38.

Foster, J., & Sheppard, J. (1995). *British archives: A guide to archival resources in the United Kingdom* (3rd ed.). London: Macmillan.

Foucault, M. (1985). *Power/knowledge: Selected interviews and other writings: 1972–1977* (C. Gordon, Ed.). New York: Pantheon.

Foucault, M. (1991). Questions of method. In G. Burchell, C. Gordon, & P. Miller (Eds.), *The Foucault effect: Studies in governmentality* (pp. 73–86). London: Harvester Wheatsheaf.

Foucault, M. (1991). *Remarks on Marx: Conversations with Duccio Trombadori* (R. J. Goldstein & J. Cascaito, Trans.). New York: Semiotext(e).

Foucault, M. (1995). *Discipline and punish: The birth of the prison.* New York: Vintage Books.

Foucault, M. (1998). *The will to knowledge: The history of sexuality* (Vol. 1). London: Penguin.

Foucault, M. (2002). *Archeology of knowledge.* London: Routledge.

Fowler, F. J., Jr. (1988). *Survey research methods* (Rev. ed.). Newbury Park, CA: Sage.

Fowler, F. J., Jr. (1995). *Improving survey questions: Design and evaluation.* Thousand Oaks, CA: Sage.

Fowler, F. J., Jr. (2002). *Survey research methods* (3rd ed.). Thousand Oaks, CA: Sage.

Fowler, F. J., Jr., & Mangione, T. W. (1990). *Standardized survey interviewing.* Newbury Park, CA: Sage.

Fowler, R. L. (1985). Point estimates and confidence intervals in measures of association. *Psychological Bulletin, 98,* 160–165.

Fowler, R. L. (1985). Testing for substantive significance in applied research by specifying non-zero effect null-hypotheses. *Journal of Applied Psychology, 70,* 215–218.

Fox, J. (1991). *Regression diagnostics* (Sage University Paper Series on Quantitative Applications in the Social Sciences, 07–079). Newbury Park, CA: Sage.

Fox, J. (1997). *Applied regression analysis, linear models, and related methods.* Thousand Oaks, CA: Sage.

Fox, J. (2000). *Nonparametric simple regression: Smoothing scatterplots.* Thousand Oaks, CA: Sage.

Fox, J. (2000). *Multiple and generalized nonparametric regression.* Thousand Oaks, CA: Sage.

Fox, J. (2002). *An R and S-PLUS companion to applied regression.* Thousand Oaks, CA: Sage.

Fox, J. A., & Tracy, P. E. (1986). *Randomized response: A method for sensitive surveys.* Beverly Hills, CA: Sage.

Fox, J., & Monette, G. (1992). Generalized collinearity diagnostics. *Journal of the American Statistical Association, 87,* 178–183.

Fox, W. (1998). *Social statistics* (3rd ed.). Bellevue, WA: MicroCase.

Frank, I. E., & Friedman, J. H. (1993). A statistical view of chemometrics regression tools. *Technometrics, 35,* 109–148.

Frank, O., & Strauss, D. (1986). Markov graphs. *Journal of the American Statistical Association, 81,* 832–842.

Frankfort-Nachmias, C., & Nachmias, D. (1996). *Research methods in the social sciences* (5th ed.). New York: St. Martin's.

Frankfort-Nachmias, C., & Nachmias, D. (2000). *Research methods in the social sciences* (6th ed.). New York: Worth.

Fransella, F., & Bannister, D. (1977). *A manual for repertory grid technique.* London: Academic Press.

Franses, P. H. (1998). *Time series models for business and economic forecasting.* Cambridge, UK: Cambridge University Press.

Franzese, R. (2002). *Macroeconomic policy of developed democracies.* Cambridge, UK: Cambridge University Press.

Franzosi, R. (2003). *From words to numbers.* Cambridge, UK: Cambridge University Press.

Fraser, N. (1997). *Justice interruptus: Critical reflections on the 'postsocialist' condition.* London: Routledge Kegan Paul.

Frederick, B. N. (1999). Partitioning variance in the multivariate case: A step-by-step guide to canonical commonality analysis. In B. Thompson (Ed.), *Advances in social science methodology* (Vol. 5, pp. 305–318). Stamford, CT: JAI.

Frederick, R. I., & Crosby, R. D. (2000). Development and validation of the Validity Indicator Profile. *Law and Human Behavior, 24,* 59–82.

Freedman, D. A. (2001). Ecological inference and the ecological fallacy. *International encyclopedia for the social and behavioral sciences* (Vol. 6, pp. 4027–4030). Oxford, UK: Pergamon.

Freedman, D. A., & Wachter, K. W. (2001). *On the likelihood of improving the accuracy of the census through statistical adjustment* (Tech. Rep. 612). Berkeley: University of California, Department of Statistics.

Freedman, D. A., Klein, S. P., Ostland, M., & Roberts, M. R. (1998). Review of "A solution to the ecological inference problem." *Journal of the American Statistical Association, 93,* 1518–1522. (Discussion appears in Vol. 94, pp. 352–357)

Freedman, D. A., Pisani, R., & Purves, R. A. (1998). *Statistics.* 3rd ed. New York: W. W. Norton, Inc.

Freeman, D. (1983). *Margaret Mead and Samoa.* Cambridge, MA: Harvard University Press.

Freeman, J. F. (1983). Granger causality and the time series analysis of political relationships. *American Journal of Political Science, 27,* 325–355.

Frey, J. H. (1989). *Survey research by telephone* (2nd ed.). Newbury Park, CA: Sage.

Frey, J. H., & Fontana, A. (1991). The group interview in social research. *The Social Science Journal, 28,* 175–187.

Frey, J. H., & Oishi, S. M. (1995). *How to conduct interviews by telephone and in person.* Thousand Oaks, CA: Sage.

Fricker, R. D., & Schonlau, M. (2002). Advantages and disadvantages of Internet research surveys: Evidence from the literature. *Field Methods, 14*(4), 347–365.

Friedkin, N. (1998). *A structural theory of social influence.* New York: Cambridge University Press.

Friedman, M. (1937). The use of ranks to avoid the assumption of normality implicit in the analysis of variance. *Journal of the American Statistical Association, 32,* 675–701.

Friedman, M. (1962). The interpolation of time series by related series. *Journal of the American Statistical Association, 57,* 729–757.

Friedman, M. (1991). The re-evaluation of logical positivism. *Journal of Philosophy, 88*(10), 505–519.

Friedricks, R. (1970). *A sociology of sociology.* New York: Free Press.

Friendly, M. (1992). Mosaic displays for loglinear models. In American Statistical Association (Ed.), *Proceedings of the Statistical Graphics Section* (pp. 61–68). Alexandria, VA: American Statistical Association.

Friendly, M. (1994). Mosaic displays for multi-way contingency tables. *Journal of the American Statistical Association, 89,* 190–200.

Friendly, M. (1998). Mosaic displays. In S. Kotz, C. Reed, & D. L. Banks (Eds.), *Encyclopedia of statistical sciences* (Vol. 2, pp. 411–416). New York: John Wiley.

Friendly, M. (1999). Extending mosaic displays: Marginal, conditional, and partial views of categorical data. *Journal of Computational and Graphical Statistics, 8*(3), 373–395.

Friendly, M. (2000). *Visualizing categorical data.* Cary, NC: SAS Institute.

Friendly, M. (2002). A brief history of the mosaic display. *Journal of Computational and Graphical Statistics, 11*(1), 89–107.

Fu, V., Mare, R., & Winship, C. (2003). Sample selection bias models. In M. A. Hardy & A. Bryman (Eds.), *Handbook of data analysis.* London: Sage.

Fuller, D. (1999). Part of the action, or "going native"? Learning to cope with the politics of integration. *Area, 31*(3), 221–227.

Fuller, W. A. (1987). *Measurement error models.* New York: John Wiley.

Fuss, D. (1989). *Essentially speaking.* New York: Routledge.

Gabriel, K. R. (1971). The biplot graphic display of matrices with application to principal component analysis. *Biometrika, 58,* 453–467.

Gadamer, H.-G. (1975). *Truth and method.* New York: Seabury.

Gadamer, H-G. (1989). *Truth and method* (rev. 2nd ed.). New York: Crossroad.

Gaito, J. (1980). Measurement scales and statistics: Resurgence of an old misconception. *Psychological Bulletin, 87,* 564–567.

Gallmeier, C. P. (1991). Leaving, revisiting, and staying in touch: Neglected issues in field research. In W. B. Shaffir & R. A. Stebbins (Eds.), *Fieldwork experience: Qualitative approaches to social research* (pp. 224–231). London: Sage.

Galton, F. (1886). Regression toward mediocrity in hereditary stature. *Journal of the Anthropological Institute, 15,* 246–263.

Galton, F. (1889) *Natural inheritance.* London: Macmillan.

Galton, M., Simon, B., & Croll, P. (1980). *Inside the primary classroom*. London: Routledge and Kegan Paul.

Galunic, D. C., & Eisenhardt, K. M. (2001). Architectural innovation and modular corporate forms. *Academy of Management Journal, 44*(6), 1229–1249.

Game, A. (1991). *Undoing the social: Towards a deconstructive sociology*. Buckingham, UK: Open University Press.

Garfinkel, H. (1967). *Studies in ethnomethodology*. Englewood Cliffs, NJ: Prentice Hall.

Garfinkel, H. (1974). On the origins of the term "ethnomethodology." In R. Turner (Ed.), *Ethnomethodology* (pp. 15–18). Harmondsworth, UK: Penguin.

Garfinkel, H. (2002). *Ethnomethodology's program: Working out Durkheim's aphorism*. Blue Ridge Summit, PA: Rowman and Littlefield.

Garman, M. (1990). *Psycholinguistics*. Cambridge, UK: Cambridge University Press.

Garson, G. D. (2002, June). *Statnotes: An online textbook* [Online]. Retrieved from http://www2.chass.ncsu.edu/garson/pa765/statnote.htm.

Gaventa, J. (1980). *Power and powerlessness: Quiescence and rebellion in an Appalachian valley*. Chicago: University of Chicago Press.

Gee, J. P. (1991). A linguistic approach to narrative. *Journal of Narrative and Life History, 1,* 15–39.

Geertz, C. (1973). *The interpretation of cultures*. New York: Basic Books.

Geertz, C. (1983). *Local knowledge*. New York: Basic Books.

Geertz, C. (1988). *Works and lives: The anthropologist as author*. Stanford, CA: Stanford University Press.

Geertz, C. (2000). *The interpretation of cultures: Selected essays*. New York: Basic Books.

Geladi, P., & Kowlaski, B. (1986). Partial least square regression: A tutorial. *Analytica Chemica Acta, 35,* 1–17.

Gelfand, A. E., & Smith, A. F. M. (1990). Sampling based approaches to calculating marginal densities. *Journal of the American Statistical Association, 85,* 398–409.

Gelman, A., Carlin, J. B., Stern, H. S., & Rubin, D. B. (1995). *Bayesian data analysis*. London: Chapman & Hall.

Geman, S., & Geman, D. (1984). Stochastic relaxation, Gibbs distributions, and the Bayesian restoration of images. *IEEE Transactions on Pattern Analysis and Machine Intelligence, 6,* 721–741.

Gensler, H. J. (2002). *Introduction to logic*. London: Routledge Kegan Paul.

Gentle, J. (2003). *Computational statistics*. New York: Springer-Verlag.

George, A. L. (1979). Case studies and theory development: The method of structured, focused comparison. In P. G. Lauren (Ed.), *Diplomacy: New approaches in history, theory, and policy* (pp. 43–68). New York: Free Press.

George, A. L., & McKeown, T. J. (1985). Case studies and theories of organizational decision making. *Advances in Information Processing in Organizations, 2,* 21–58.

George, A. L., & Smoke, R. (1974). *Deterrence in American foreign policy: Theory and practice*. New York: Columbia University Press.

Georges, R. A., & Jones, M. O. (1995). *Folkloristics: An introduction*. Bloomington: Indiana University Press.

Gephart, R. P. (1986). Deconstructing the defence for quantification in social science: A content analysis of journal articles on the parametric strategy. *Qualitative Sociology, 9,* 126–144.

Gephart, R. P. (1988). *Ethnostatistics: Qualitative foundations for quantitative research*. Newbury Park, CA: Sage.

Gephart, R. P. (1997). Hazardous measures: An interpretive textual analysis of quantitative sensemaking during crises. *Journal of Organizational Behavior, 18,* 583–622.

Gerber, A. S., & Green, D. P. (2000). The effects of personal canvassing, telephone calls, and direct mail on voter turnout: A field experiment. *The American Political Science Review, 94,* 653–664.

Gergen, K. J. (1994) *Realities and relationships*. Cambridge, MA: Harvard University Press.

Gergen, K. J. (1999). *An invitation to social construction*. London: Sage.

Gerhardt, U. (1985). Erzähldaten und Hypothesenkonstruktion. *Kölner Zeitschrift für Soziologie und Sozialpsychologie, 37,* 230–256.

Gerhardt, U. (1986). *Patientenkarrieren: Eine idealtypenanalytische Studie*. Frankfurt: Suhrkamp.

Gerhardt, U. (1994). The use of Weberian ideal-type methodology in qualitative data interpretation: An outline for ideal-type analysis. *BMS Bulletin de Methodologie Sociologique* (International Sociological Association, Research Committee 33), *45,* 76–126.

Gerhardt, U. (1999). *Herz und Handlungsrationalität: Eine idealtypen-analytische Studie*. Frankfurt: Suhrkamp.

Gershuny, J. (2000). *Changing times: Work and leisure in postindustrial societies*. Oxford, UK: Oxford University Press.

Ghiselli, E. E., Campbell, J. P., & Zedeck, S. (1981). *Measurement theory for the behavioral sciences*. San Francisco: W. H. Freeman.

Gibbons, J. D. (1988). Truncated data. In S. Kotz, N. L. Johnson, & C. B. Read (Eds.), *Encyclopedia of statistical sciences* (Vol. 9, p. 355). New York: Wiley.

Gibbons, J. D. (1993). *Nonparametric statistics: An introduction*. Newbury Park, CA: Sage.

Gibbons, J. D. (1997). *Nonparametric methods for quantitative analysis* (3rd ed.). Columbus, OH: American Sciences Press.

Gibbons, J. D., & Chakraborti, S. (1992). *Nonparametric statistical inference* (3rd ed.). New York: Marcel Dekker.

Gibson, N., Gibson, G., & Macaulay, A. C. (2001). Community-based research: Negotiating agendas and evaluating outcomes. In J. Morse, J. Swanson, & A. J. Kuzel (Eds.), *The nature of qualitative evidence* (pp. 160–182). Thousand Oaks, CA: Sage.

Giddens, A. (1976). *New rules of sociological method*. London: Hutchinson.

Giddens, A. (1979). *Central problems in social theory.* Berkeley: University of California Press.

Giddens, A. (1984). *The constitution of society: Outline of the theory of structuration.* Cambridge, UK: Polity.

Giele, J. Z., & Elder, G. H. (1998). *Methods of life course research: Qualitative and quantitative approaches.* Thousand Oaks, CA: Sage.

Gifi, A. (1990). *Nonlinear multivariate analysis.* New York: Wiley.

Gigerenzer, G., & Goldstein, D. G. (1996). Reasoning the fast and frugal way: Models of bounded rationality. *Psychological Review, 103,* 650–669.

Gilbert, G. N., & Mulkay, M. (1984). *Opening Pandora's box: A sociological analysis of scientists' discourse.* Cambridge, UK: Cambridge University Press.

Gilbert, N., & Troitzsch, K. G. (1999). *Simulation for the social scientist.* Milton Keynes, UK: Open University Press.

Gill, J. (2000). *Generalized linear models: A unified approach.* Thousand Oaks, CA: Sage.

Gill, J. (2002). *Bayesian methods: A social and behavioral sciences approach.* London: Chapman & Hall.

Gintis, H. (2000). *Game theory evolving.* Princeton, NJ: Princeton University Press.

Girden, E. R. (1992). *ANOVA: Repeated measures* (Sage University Paper Series on Quantitative Applications in the Social Sciences, 07–084). Newbury Park, CA: Sage.

Glaser, B. (1992). *Emergence vs. forcing: Basics of grounded theory analysis.* Mill Valley, CA: Sociology Press.

Glaser, B. G. (1978). *Theoretical sensitivity.* Mill Valley, CA: Sociology Press.

Glaser, B. G. (2002). Grounded theory and gender relevance. *Health Care for Women International, 23,* 786–793.

Glaser, B. G., & Strauss, A. L. (1967). *Discovery of grounded theory: Strategies for qualitative research.* Chicago: Aldine.

Glass, G. V., & Hopkins, K. D. (1984). *Statistical methods in education and psychology* (2nd ed.). Englewood Cliffs, NJ: Prentice Hall.

Glass, G. V., & Hopkins, K. D. (1996). *Statistical methods in education and psychology* (3rd ed.). Boston: Allyn & Bacon.

Glass, G. V., Peckham, P. D., & Sanders, J. R. (1972). Consequences of failure to meet assumptions underlying the analysis of variance and convariance. *Review of Educational Research, 42,* 237–288.

Glass, G. V. (1976). Primary, secondary, and meta-analysis of research. *Educational Research, 5,* 3–8.

Glass, G. V. (1977). Integrating findings. *Review of Research in Education, 5,* 351–379.

Glass, G. V., & Smith, M. L. (1978). Meta-analysis of research on the relationship of class size and achievement. *Educational Evaluation and Policy Analysis, 1,* 2–16.

Glenn, N. D. (2003). Distinguishing age, period, and cohort effects. In J. Mortimer & M. Shanahan (Eds.), *Handbook of the life course* (pp. 465–476). New York: Kluwer Academic/Plenum.

Gluck, S. B., & Patai, D. (Eds.). (1991). *Women's words: The feminist practice of oral history.* London: Routledge.

Glymour, C. N. (1980). *Theory and evidence.* Princeton, NJ: Princeton University Press.

Goffman, E. (1959). *The presentation of self in everyday life.* Garden City, NY: Doubleday.

Goffman, E. (1983). The interaction order. *American Sociological Review, 48,* 1–17.

Gold, R. L. (1958). Roles in sociological field observation. *Social Forces, 36,* 217–223.

Gold, R. L. (1969). Roles in sociological field observations. In G. J. McCall & J. L. Simmons (Eds.), *Issues in participant observation* (pp. 30–38). Reading, MA: Addison-Wesley.

Goldberger, A. S. (1964). *Econometric theory.* New York: John Wiley & Sons.

Goldmann, L. (1981). *Method in the sociology of literature* (W. Boelhower, Trans. & Ed.). Oxford, UK: Basil Blackwell.

Goldstein, H. (1987). *Multilevel models in educational and social research.* London: Griffin.

Goldstein, H. (1995). *Multilevel statistical models.* London: Edward Arnold.

Goldstein, H. (2003). *Multilevel statistical models* (3rd ed.). London: Hodder Arnold.

Golub, G. H., & Van Loan, G. F. (1996). *Matrix computations* (3rd ed.). Baltimore: Johns Hopkins University Press.

Gomm, R., Hammersley, M., & Foster, P. (2000). Case study and generalisation. In R. Gomm, M. Hammersley, & P. Foster (Eds.), *Case study method: Key issues, key texts.* London: Sage.

Gomm, R., Hammersley, M., & Foster, P. (Eds.). (2000). *Case study method.* London: Sage.

Good, I. J. (1988). The interface between statistics and philosophy of science. *Statistical Science, 3,* 386–397.

Good, P. (1994). *Permutation tests: A practical guide to resampling methods for testing hypotheses.* New York: Springer.

Goode, W. J. (1978). *The celebration of heroes: Prestige as a control system.* Berkeley: University of California Press.

Goodenough, W. (1957). Cultural anthropology and linguistics. In P. L. Garvin (Ed.), *Report of the 7th Annual Roundtable on Linguistics and Language Study* (pp. 167–173). Washington, DC: Georgetown University Press.

Goodman, A., Johnson, P., & Webb, S. (1997). *Inequality in the UK.* Oxford, UK: Oxford University Press.

Goodman, L. (1953). Ecological regression and the behavior of individuals. *American Sociological Review, 18,* 663–664.

Goodman, L. A. (1961). Statistical methods for the mover-stayer model. *Journal of the American Statistical Association, 56,* 841–868.

Goodman, L. A. (1973). Causal analysis of data from panel studies and other kinds of surveys. *American Journal of Sociology, 78,* 1135–1191.

Goodman, L. A. (1973). The analysis of multidimensional contingency tables when some variables are posterior to others: A modified path analysis approach. *Biometrika, 60,* 179–192.

Goodman, L. A. (1974). The analysis of systems of qualitative variables when some of the variables are unobservable: I. A modified latent structure approach. *American Journal of Sociology, 79,* 1179–1259.

Goodman, L. A. (1978). *Analyzing qualitative/categorical data.* Cambridge, MA: Abt.

Goodman, L. A. (1979). Simple models for the analysis of association in cross-classifications having ordered categories. *Journal of the American Statistical Association, 74,* 537–552.

Goodman, L. A. (1984). *The analysis of cross-classified data having ordered categories.* Cambridge, MA: Harvard University Press.

Goodman, L. A. (1986). Some useful extensions of the usual correspondence analysis approach and the usual log-linear models approach in the analysis of contingency tables. *International Statistical Review, 54,* 243–309.

Goodman, L. A., & Hout, M. (1998). Understanding the Goodman-Hout approach to the analysis of differences in association and some related comments. In A. E. Raftery (Ed.), *Sociological methodology* (pp. 249–261). Washington, DC: American Sociological Association.

Goodman, L. A., & Kruskal, W. H. (1954). Measures of association for cross classification. *Journal of the American Statistical Association, 49,* 732–764.

Goodman, S. N. (1999). Toward evidence-based medical statistics: 1. The *p* value fallacy. *Annals of Internal Medicine, 130,* 995–1004.

Goodwin, C. (1981). *Conversational organization: Interaction between speakers and hearers.* New York: Academic Press.

Gopaul-McNicol, S.-A., & Armour-Thomas, E. (2002). *Assessment and culture: Psychological tests with minority populations.* San Diego: Academic Press.

Gottman, J. M. (1981). *Time-series analysis: A comprehensive introduction for social scientists.* Cambridge, UK: Cambridge University Press.

Gottschalk, L., Kluckhohn, C., & Angell, R. (1945). *The use of personal documents in history, anthropology, and sociology.* New York: Social Science Research Council.

Gouldner, A. V. (1973). *For sociology.* Harmondsworth, UK: Penguin.

Gouldner, A. W. (1962). Anti-minotaur: The myth of a value-free sociology. *Social Problems, 9,* 199–213.

Gower, J. C., & Hand, D. J. (1996). *Biplots.* London: Chapman & Hall.

Gower, J. C., & Legendre, P. (1986). Metric and Euclidean properties of dissimilarity coefficients. *Journal of Classification, 5,* 5–48.

Graham, J. M., Guthrie, A. C., & Thompson, B. (2003). Consequences of not interpreting structure coefficients in published CFA research: A reminder. *Structural Equation Modeling, 10,* 142–153.

Grammer, K., Fink, B., & Renninger, L. (2002). Dynamic systems and inferential information processing in human communication. *Neuroendocrinology Letters, 23*(Suppl. 4), 15–22.

Gramsci, A. (1971). *Selections from the prison notebooks.* London: Lawrence and Wishart.

Granger, C. W. J. (1964). *Spectral analysis of economic time series.* Princeton, NJ: Princeton University Press.

Granger, C. W. J. (1969). Investigating causal relations by econometric models and cross-spectral methods. *Econometrica, 37,* 24–36.

Granger, C. W. J. (1981). Some properties of time series data and their use in econometric models specification. *Journal of Econometrics, 16,* 121–130.

Granger, C. W. J. (1983). *Co-integrated variables and error-correcting models.* Discussion Paper No. 1983–13, University of California, San Diego.

Granger, C. W. J. (1989). *Forecasting in business and economics.* Boston: Academic Press.

Granger, C. W. J., & Newbold, P. (1986). *Forecasting economic time series* (2nd ed.). New York: Academic Press.

Gravetter, F. J., & Wallnau, L. B. (2000). *Statistics for the behavioral sciences* (5th ed.). Belmont, CA: Wadsworth.

Gray, J., & Reuter, A. (1992). *Transaction processing: Concepts and techniques.* San Francisco: Morgan Kaufmann.

Green, D. P., & Gerber, A. S. (2002). Reclaiming the experimental tradition in political science. In I. Katznelson & H. V. Milner (Eds.), *Political science: State of the discipline* (3rd ed., pp. 805–832). New York: W.W. Norton.

Green, D. P., Gerber, A. S., & De Boef, S. L. (1999). Tracking opinion over time: A method for reducing sampling error. *Public Opinion Quarterly, 63,* 178–192.

Green, P. (1978). *Analyzing multivariate data.* Hinsdale, IL: Dryden.

Green, W. H. (2000). *Econometric analysis* (4th ed.). Upper Saddle River: Prentice Hall.

Greenacre, M. J. (1984). *Theory and method of correspondence analysis.* London: Academic Press.

Greenacre, M. J. (1993). *Correspondence analysis in practice.* London: Academic Press.

Greenacre, M. J., & Blasius, J. (1994). *Correspondence analysis in the social sciences.* London: Academic Press.

Greenbaum, T. L. (1998). *The handbook for focus group research.* London: Sage.

Greene, R. L. (2000). *The MMPI-2: An interpretive manual.* Boston: Allyn & Bacon.

Greene, W. H. (1993). *Econometric analysis* (2nd ed.). New York: Macmillan.

Greene, W. H. (1997). *Econometric analysis* (3rd ed.). Englewood Cliffs, NJ: Prentice-Hall.

Greene, W. H. (2000). *Econometric analysis* (4th ed.). Englewood Cliffs, NJ: Prentice Hall.

Greene, W. H. (2003). *Econometric analysis* (5th ed.). Englewood Cliffs, NJ: Prentice-Hall.

Greenfield, P. (1997). You can't take it with you: Why ability assessments don't cross cultures. *American Psychologist, 52*(10), 1115–1124.

Greenhouse, G. W., & Geisser, S. (1959). On methods in the analysis of profile data. *Psychometrika, 55,* 431–433.

Greenland, S. (2003). Quantifying biases in causal models. *Epidemiology, 14,* 300–306.

Greenland, S., & Brumback, B. A. (2002). An overview of relations among causal modelling methods. *International Journal of Epidemiology, 31,* 1030–1037.

Greenland, S., & Robins, J. M. (1986). Identifiability, exchangeability, and epidemiological confounding. *International Journal of Epidemiology, 15,* 413–419.

Greenland, S., Robins, J. M., & Pearl, J. (1999). Confounding and collapsibility in causal inference. *Statistical Science, 14,* 29–46.

Greenwald, A. G., Banaji, M. R., Rudman, L. A., Farnham, S. D., Nosek, B. A., & Mellott, D. S. (2002). A unified theory of implicit attitudes, stereotypes, self-esteem, and self-concept. *Psychological Review, 109,* 3–25.

Greenwood, D., & Levin, M. (1998). *Introduction to action research: Social research for social change.* Thousand Oaks, CA: Sage.

Greimas, A. J., & Courtés, J. (1982). *Semiotics and language: An analytical dictionary.* Bloomington: Indiana University Press.

Griffin, L., Caplinger, C., Lively, K., Malcom, N. L., McDaniel, D., & Nelsen, C. (1997). Comparative-historical analysis and scientific inference: Disfranchisement in the U.S. South as a test case. *Historical Methods, 30,* 13–27.

Griliches, Z. (1957). Hybrid corn: An exploration in the economics of technological change. *Econometrica, 25,* 501–522.

Grinyer, A. (2002). The anonymity of research participants: Assumptions, ethics, and practicalities. *Social Research Update, 36,* 1–4.

Grofman, B., & Davidson, C. (1992). *Controversies in minority voting: The voting rights act in perspective.* Washington, DC: Brookings Institution.

Gross, D., & Harris, C. M. (1998). *Fundamentals of queueing theory* (3rd ed.). New York: Wiley.

Groves, E. R., & Ogburn, W. F. (1928). *American marriage and family relationships.* New York: Holt.

Groves, R. M. (1989). *Survey errors and survey costs.* New York: Wiley.

Groves, R. M., & Couper, M. P. (1998). *Nonresponse in household interview surveys.* New York: Wiley.

Groves, R. M., Dillman, D. A., Eltinge, J. L., & Little, R. J. A. (Eds.). (2001). *Survey nonresponse.* New York: Wiley.

Guba, E. G. (1978). *Toward a methodology of naturalistic inquiry in educational evaluation.* CSE Monograph Series in Evaluation, No. 8. Los Angeles: Center for the Study of Evaluation, University of California, Los Angeles.

Guba, E. G. (1981). Criteria for assessing the trustworthiness of naturalistic inquiries. *Educational Communications and Technology Journal, 29,* 75–92.

Guba, E. G., & Lincoln, Y. S. (1985). *Naturalistic inquiry.* Beverly Hills, CA: Sage.

Guba, E. G., & Lincoln, Y. S. (1989). *Fourth generation evaluation.* Newbury Park, CA: Sage.

Guba, E., & Lincoln, Y. (1994). Competing paradigms in qualitative research. In N. K. Denzin & Y. S. Lincoln (Eds.), *Handbook of qualitative research* (pp. 105–117). Thousand Oaks, CA: Sage.

Gubrium, J. F., & Buckholdt, D. R. (1979). Production of hard data in human service organizations. *Pacific Sociological Review, 22,* 115–136.

Gubrium, J. F., & Holstein, J. A. (1997). *The new language of qualitative method.* New York: Oxford University Press.

Gubrium, J. F., & Holstein, J. A. (2002). From the individual interview to the interview society. In J. F. Gubrium & J. A. Holstein (Eds.), *Handbook of interview research: Context and method* (pp. 3–32). Thousand Oaks, CA: Sage.

Gujarati, D. (1995). *Basic econometrics* (3rd ed.). New York: McGraw-Hill.

Gujarati, D. (2002). *Basic econometrics* (4th ed.). New York: McGraw-Hill.

Gulliksen, H. (1950). *The theory of mental tests.* New York: Wiley.

Guttman, L. (1941). An outline for the statistical theory of prediction. In P. Horst (with collaboration of P. Wallin & L. Guttman) (Ed.), *The prediction of personal adjustment* (Bulletin 48, Supplementary Study B-1, pp. 253–318). New York: Social Science Research Council.

Guttman, L. (1944). A basis for scaling quantitative data. *American Sociological Review, 9,* 139–150.

Guttman, L. (1953). Image theory for the structure of quantitative variates. *Psychometrika, 18,* 277–296.

Guttman, L. (1954). Some necessary conditions for common-factor analysis. *Psychometrika, 19,* 149–161.

Guttman, L. (1956). "Best possible" systematic estimates of communalities. *Psychometrika, 21,* 273–285.

Haack, S. (1993). *Evidence and inquiry: Toward a reconstruction of epistemology.* Oxford, UK: Blackwell.

Haavelmo, T. (1944). The probability approach in econometrics. *Econometrica, 12*(Suppl.), preface, p. iii.

Haberman, S. J. (1979). *Analysis of qualitative data: Vol. 2. New developments.* New York: Academic Press.

Hacking, I. (1965). *The logic of statistical inference.* Cambridge, UK: Cambridge University Press.

Hacking, I. (2001). *An introduction to probability and inductive logic.* Cambridge, UK: Cambridge University Press.

Hagenaars, J. A. (1990). *Categorical longitudinal data: Log-linear analysis of panel, trend and cohort data.* Newbury Park, CA: Sage.

Hagenaars, J. A. (1993). *Loglinear models with latent variables.* Newbury Park, CA: Sage.

Hagenaars, J. A. (1998). Categorical causal modeling: Latent class analysis and directed log-linear models with latent variables. *Sociological Methods and Research, 26,* 436–486.

Hagenaars, J. A., & McCutcheon, A. L. (2002). *Applied latent class analysis.* Cambridge, UK: Cambridge University Press.

Hagle, T. M., & Mitchell, G. E., II. (1992). Goodness-of-fit measures for probit and logit. *American Journal of Political Science, 36,* 762–784.

Haight, B. K., Michel, Y., & Hendrix, S. (1998). Life review: Preventing despair in newly relocated nursing home residents: Short- and long-term effects. *International Journal of Aging and Human Development, 47*(2), 119–142.

Hajek, J., & Sidák, Z. (1967). *Theory of rank tests.* New York: Academic Press.

Hakim, C. (1982). *Secondary analysis of social research.* London: George Allen and Unwin.

Haladyna, T. M. (1994). *Developing and validating multiple-choice test items.* Hillsdale, NJ: Lawrence Erlbaum.

Hald, A. (1952). *Statistical theory with engineering applications.* New York: John Wiley.

Hald, A. (1990). *A history of probability and statistics and their applications before 1750.* New York: John Wiley and Sons.

Halfpenny, P. (1982). *Positivism and sociology: Explaining social life.* London: Allen & Unwin.

Hall, E. T. (1974). *Handbook for proxemic research.* Washington, DC: Society for the Anthropology of Visual Communication.

Hall, S. (1974). The television discourse—Encoding and decoding. In *Education and culture* (Vol. 35, pp. 8–14). Paris: United Nations Educational, Social, and Cultural Organization.

Hambleton, R. K., Swaminathan, H., & Rogers, H. J. (1991). *Fundamentals of item response theory.* Newbury Park, CA: Sage.

Hamilton, D. (1980). Some contrasting assumptions about case study research and survey analysis. In H. Simons (Ed.), *Towards a science of the singular: Essays about case study in educational research and evaluation* (pp. 78–92). Norwich, UK: Centre for Applied Research in Education University of East Anglia.

Hamilton, J. D. (1994). *Time series analysis.* Princeton, NJ: Princeton University Press.

Hamilton, L. C. (1990). *Modern data analysis: A first course in applied statistics.* Pacific Grove, CA: Brooks/Cole.

Hamilton, L. C. (1992). *Regression with graphics: A second course in applied statistics.* Pacific Grove, CA: Brooks/Cole.

Hamlyn, D. W. (1967). Empiricism. In P. Edwards (Ed.), *The encyclopedia of philosophy* (pp. 499–505). New York: Macmillan.

Hammersley, M. (1989). *The dilemma of qualitative method: Herbert Blumer and the Chicago school of sociology.* London: Routledge and Kegan Paul.

Hammersley, M. (1989). The problem of the concept: Herbert Blumer on the relationship between concepts and data. *Journal of Contemporary Ethnography, 18,* 133–160.

Hammersley, M. (1990). *Reading ethnographic research.* London: Longman.

Hammersley, M. (1992). *What's wrong with ethnography.* London: Routledge Kegan Paul.

Hammersley, M. (1995). *The politics of social research.* London: Sage.

Hammersley, M. (1995). Theory and evidence in qualitative research. *Quality and Quantity, 29,* 55–66.

Hammersley, M. (1997). Qualitative data archiving: Some reflections on its prospects and problems. *Sociology, 31*(1), 131–142.

Hammersley, M. (1999). Sociology, what's it for? A critique of the grand conception. *Sociological Research Online, 4*(3). Retrieved from http://www.socresonline.org.uk/socresonline/4/3/hammersley.html

Hammersley, M. (2000). *Taking sides in social research.* London: Routledge.

Hammersley, M. (2001). On "systematic" reviews of research literatures: A "narrative" reply to Evans and Benefield. *British Educational Research Journal, 27*(5), 543–554.

Hammersley, M., & Atkinson, P. (1995). *Ethnography: Principles in practice.* London: Routledge.

Hammond, M., Howarth, J., & Keat, R. (1991). *Understanding phenomenology.* Oxford, UK: Blackwell.

Handcock, M. S., & Morris, M. (1999). *Relative distribution methods in the social sciences.* New York: Springer-Verlag.

Haney, C., Banks, C., & Zimbardo, P. (1973). Interpersonal dynamics in a simulated prison. *International Journal of Criminology and Penology, 1,* 69–97.

Hansen, M. H., Hurwitz, W. N., & Madow, W. G. (1953). *Sample survey methods and theory.* New York: John Wiley & Sons.

Hansen, P. R., & Johansen, S. (1998). *Workbook on cointegration.* Oxford, UK: Oxford University Press.

Hantrais, L., & Mangen, S. (Eds.). (1996). *Cross-national research methods in the social sciences.* London: Pinter.

Harary, F., Norman, D., & Cartwright, D. (1965). *Structural models for directed graphs.* New York: Free Press.

Hardin, J. W., & Hilbe, J. M. (2003). *Generalized estimating equations.* London: Chapman & Hall.

Harding, S. (1991). *Whose science? Whose knowledge?* Milton Keynes, UK: Open University Press.

Harding, S. (1992). After the neutrality ideal: Science, politics, and "strong objectivity." *Social Research, 59,* 568–587.

Harding, S. (Ed.). (1987). *Feminism and methodology.* Milton Keynes, UK: Open University Press.

Hardy, M. A. (1993). *Regression with dummy variables* (Sage University Paper Series on Quantitative Applications in the Social Sciences, 07–093). Newbury Park, CA: Sage.

Hardy, M. A., & Reynolds, J. (2003). Incorporating categorical information into regression models: the utility of dummy variables. In M. A. Hardy & A. Bryman (Eds.), *Handbook of data analysis.* London: Sage.

Hare, R. D. (1966). Temporal gradient of fear arousal in psychopaths. *Journal of Abnormal and Social Psychology, 70,* 442–445.

Harper, D. (2001). *Changing works: Visions of a lost agriculture.* Chicago: University of Chicago Press.

Harper, D. (2002). Talking about pictures: A case for photo elicitation. *Visual Studies, 17*(1), 13–26.

Harré, R. (1961). *Theories and things.* London: Sheed & Ward.

Harré, R. (1986). *Varieties of realism.* Oxford, UK: Blackwell.

Harré, R., & Secord, P. F. (1972). *The explanation of social behaviour.* Oxford, UK: Basil Blackwell.

Harris, C. W. (1962). Some Rao-Guttman relationships. *Psychometrika, 27,* 247–263.

Harris, J. A. (1913). On the calculation of intraclass and interclass coefficients of correlation from class moments when the number of possible combinations is large. *Biometrika, 9,* 446–472.

Harris, M. (1976). History and significance of the emic/etic distinction. *Annual Review of Anthropology, 5,* 329–350.

Hart, C. (1998). *Doing a literature review: Releasing the social science research imagination.* London: Sage.

Hartigan, J. A., & Kleiner, B. (1981). Mosaics for contingency tables. In W. F. Eddy (Ed.), *Computer science and statistics: Proceedings of the 13th Symposium on the Interface* (pp. 268–273). New York: Springer-Verlag.

Hartsock, N. C. M. (1998). *The feminist standpoint revisited and other essays.* Boulder, CO: Westview.

Hartwig, F., & Dearing, B. E. (1979). *Exploratory data analysis* (Sage University Papers on Quantitative Applications in the Social Sciences). Beverly Hills, CA: Sage.

Harvey, A. (1990). *The econometric analysis of time series* (2nd ed.). Cambridge: MIT Press.

Harvey, A. C. (1990). *Forecasting, structural time series models, and the Kalman filter.* New York: Cambridge University Press.

Harvey, A. S. (1999). Guidelines. In W. E. Pentland, A. S. Harvey, M. P. Lawton, & M. A. McColl (Eds.), *Time use research in the social sciences* (pp. 19–45). New York: Kluwer.

Harvey, D. (1973). *Social justice and the city.* Baltimore: Johns Hopkins University Press.

Harvey, D. (1989). *The condition of postmodernity.* Oxford, UK: Basil Blackwell.

Harvey, L. (1987). *Myths of the Chicago school of sociology.* Aldershot, England: Avebury.

Hastie, T. J. (1992). Generalized additive models. In J. M. Chambers & T. J. Hastie (Eds.), *Statistical models in S* (pp. 249–307). Pacific Grove, CA: Wadsworth and Brooks/Cole.

Hastie, T. J., & Tibshirani, R. J. (1990). *Generalized additive models.* New York: Chapman & Hall.

Hastie, T., Tibshirani, R., & Friedman, J. (2001). *The elements of statistical learning.* New York: Springer-Verlag

Hastings, W. K. (1970). Monte Carlo sampling methods using Markov chains. *Biometrika, 57,* 97–109.

Hauser, R. M. (1978). A structural model of the mobility table. *Social Forces, 56,* 919–953.

Hausman, J. A. (1978). Specification tests in econometrics. *Econometrica, 46,* 1251–1271.

Hausman, J., & McFadden, D. (1984). Specification tests for the multinomial logit model. *Econometrica, 52,* 1219–1240.

Hayano, D. (1979). Auto-ethnography: Paradigms, problems and prospects. *Human Organization, 38*(1), 99–104.

Hayes, S. C., White, D., & Bissett, R. T. (1998). Protocol analysis and the "silent dog" method of analyzing the impact of self-generated rules. *Analysis of Verbal Behavior, 15,* 57–63.

Hays, W. L. (1972). *Statistics for the social sciences.* New York: Holt.

Hays, W. L. (1988). *Statistics.* New York: Holt, Rinehart and Winston.

Hays, W. L. (1994). *Statistics* (5th ed.). Fort Worth, TX: Harcourt Brace.

Headland, T. N., Pike, K. L., & Harris, M. (1990). *Emics and etics: The insider/outsider debate.* Newbury Park, CA: Sage.

Healey, J. F. (1995). *Statistics: A tool for social research* (3rd ed.). Belmont, CA.: Wadsworth.

Heaton, J. (1998). Secondary analysis of qualitative data [Online]. *Social Research Update, 22.* Retrieved April 28, 2002, from http://www.soc.surrey.ac.uk/sru/SRU22.html.

Heckman, J. J. (1979). Sample selection bias as a specification error. *Econometrica, 47,* 153–161.

Heckman, J. J., & Singer, B. (1982). Population heterogeneity in demographic models. In K. Land & A. Rogers (Eds.), *Multidimensional mathematical demography* (pp. 567–599). New York: Academic Press.

Heckman, J. J., & Singer, B. (1984). A method for minimizing the impact of distributional assumptions in econometric models for duration data. *Econometrica, 52*(2), 271–320.

Heckman, J. J., & Smith, J. A. (1995). Assessing the case for social experiments. *Journal of Economic Perspectives, 9,* 85–110.

Hedges, L. V., & Olkin, I. (1985). *Statistical methods for meta-analysis.* Orlando, FL: Academic Press.

Hedstrom, P., & Swedberg, R. (1998). *Social mechanisms: An analytical approach to social theory.* Cambridge, UK: Cambridge University Press.

Heider, K. G. (1976). *Ethnographic film.* Austin: University of Texas Press.

Heinen, T. (1996). *Latent class and discrete latent trait models: Similarities and differences.* Thousand Oaks, CA: Sage.

Heise, D. (1971). The semantic differential and attitude research. In G. F. Summers (Ed.), *Attitude measurement* (pp. 235–253). Chicago: Rand McNally.

Heise, D. R. (1975). *Causal analysis.* New York: Wiley.

Heise, D. R. (1987). Affect Control Theory: Concepts and model. *Journal of Mathematical Sociology, 13,* 1–33.

Hektner, J. M., & Csikszentmihalyi, M. (2002). The experience sampling method: Measuring the context and the content of lives. In R. B. Bechtel & A. Churchman (Eds.), *Handbook of environmental psychology* (pp. 233–243). New York: John Wiley & Sons.

Helland, I. S. (1990). PLS regression and statistical models. *Scandinavian Journal of Statistics, 17,* 97–114.

Hempel, C. (1965). *Aspects of scientific explanation, and other essays in the philosophy of science.* New York: Free Press.

Hempel, C. (1965). Confirmation, induction, and rational belief. In C. Hempel (Ed.), *Aspects of scientific explanation.* New York: Free Press.

Hempel, C. G. (1966). *Philosophy of natural science.* Englewood Cliffs, NJ: Prentice Hall.

Hendrick, T., Bickman, L., & Rog, D. J. (1993). *Applied research design: A practical guide.* Newbury Park, CA: Sage.

Hendry, D. F. (1995). *Dynamic econometrics.* New York: Oxford University Press.

Henkel, R. E. (1976). *Tests of significance* (Sage University Paper Series on Quantitative Applications in the Social Sciences, 07-004). Beverly Hills, CA: Sage.

Henle, M., & Hubble, M. B. (1938). Egocentricity in adult conversation. *Journal of Social Psychology, 9,* 227–234.

Henry, G. T. (1990). *Practical sampling.* Newbury Park, CA: Sage.

Henry, G. T., & Gordon, C. S. (2001). Tracking issue attention: Specifying the dynamics of the public agenda. *Public Opinion Quarterly, 65*(2), 157–177.

Hepburn, A. (2000). On the alleged incompatibility between feminism and relativism. *Feminism and Psychology, 10,* 91–106.

Heritage, J. (1984). *Garfinkel and ethnomethodology.* Cambridge, UK: Polity.

Herrnstein, R., & Murray, C. (1994). *The bell curve: Intelligence and class structure in American life.* New York: Free Press.

Hess, I. (1985). *Sampling for social research surveys 1947–1980.* Ann Arbor, MI: Institute for Social Research.

Hewitt, J. (1989). *Dilemmas of the American self.* Philadelphia: Temple University Press.

Heyde, C. C., & Seneta, E. (Eds.). (2001). *Statisticians of the centuries.* New York: Springer.

Hibbs, D. A. (1982). The dynamics of political support for American presidents among occupational and partisan groups. *American Journal of Political Science, 26,* 312–332.

Higgins, E. T., Rholes, W. S., & Jones, C. R. (1977). Category accessibility and impression formation. *Journal of Experimental Social Psychology, 13,* 141–154.

Hill, A. B. (1953). Observation and experiment. *New England Journal of Medicine, 248,* 995–1001.

Hill, M. M. (1993). *Archival strategies and techniques* (Qualitative Research Methods Series No. 31). Newbury Park, CA: Sage.

Hill, M. S. (1992). *The panel study of income dynamics: A user's guide.* Newbury Park, CA: Sage.

Hilsum, S., & Cane, B. (1971). *The teacher's day.* Windsor, UK: National Foundation for Educational Research.

Himmelfarb, G. (1987). *The new history and the old.* Cambridge, MA: Harvard University Press.

Hinchman, L. P., & Hinchman, S. K. (Eds.). (1997). *Memory, identity, community: The idea of narrative in the human sciences.* Albany: State University of New York Press.

Hinds, P. S., Vogel, R. J. . & Clarke-Steffen, L. (1997). The possibilities and pitfalls of doing a secondary analysis of a qualitative data set. *Qualitative Health Research, 7,* 408–424.

Hine, C. (2000). *Virtual ethnography.* London: Sage.

Hinton, P. R. (1996). *Statistics explained: A guide for social science students.* London: Routledge.

Hirsch, M. W., & Smale, S. (1974). *Differential equations, dynamical systems, and linear algebra.* New York: Academic Press.

Hoaglin, D. C., Mosteller, F., & Tukey, J. W. (Eds.). (1983). *Understanding robust and exploratory data analysis.* New York: Wiley.

Hobcraft, J., Menken, J., & Preston, S. (1982). Age, period, and cohort effects in demography: A review. *Population Index, 42,* 4–43.

Hobert, J. P., & Casella, G. (1996). The effect of improper priors on Gibbs sampling in hierarchical linear mixed models. *Journal of the American Statistical Association, 91,* 1461–1473.

Hobson-West, P., & Sapsford, R. (2001). *The Middlesbrough Town Centre Study: Final report.* Middlesbrough, UK: University of Teesside, School of Social Sciences.

Hochberg, Y., & Tamhane, A. C. (1987). *Multiple comparison procedures.* New York: John Wiley.

Hoerl, A. E., & Kennard, R. W. (1970). Ridge regression. *Technometrics, 12*(1), 55–67, 69–82.

Hoey, M. (2001). *Textual interaction.* London: Routledge.

Hofmann, H. (2000). Exploring categorical data: Interactive mosaic plots. *Metrika, 51*(1), 11–26.

Hogg, R. V., & Craig, A. T. (1978). *Introduction to mathematical statistics* (4th ed.). New York: Macmillan.

Hogg, R. V., & Tanis, E. A. (1988). *Probability and statistical inference.* New York: Macmillan.

Hollander, M., & Wolfe, D. A. (1973). *Nonparametric statistical inference.* New York: Wiley.

Hollander, M., & Wolfe, D. A. (1999). *Nonparametric statistical methods* (2nd ed.). New York: Wiley.

Hollis, M. (1977). *Models of man.* Cambridge, UK: Cambridge University Press.

Hollis, M., & Smith, S. (1990). *Explaining and understanding international relations.* New York: Oxford University Press.

Hollway, W., & Jefferson, T. (2000). *Doing qualitative research differently: Free association, narrative and the interview method.* London: Sage.

Holmes, D. (1976). Debriefing after psychological experiments: Effectiveness of post-experimental desensitizing. *American Psychologist, 32,* 868–875.

Holmwood, J. (2001). Gender and critical realism: A critique of Sayer. *Sociology, 35,* 947–965.

Holstein, J. A., & Gubrium, J. F. (1995). *The active interview.* Thousand Oaks, CA: Sage.

Holstein, J. A., & Gubrium, J. F. (2000). *The self we live by: Narrative identity in a postmodern world.* New York: Oxford University Press.

Holsti, O. R. (1969). *Content analysis for the social sciences and humanities.* Reading, MA: Addison-Wesley.

Homan, R. (1992). *The ethics of social research.* London: Longman.

Homans, G. C. (1964). Contemporary theory in sociology. In R. E. L. Faris (Ed.), *Handbook of modern sociology* (pp. 951–977). Chicago: Rand McNally.

Homans, G. C. (1967). *The nature of social science.* New York: Harcourt, Brace, & World.

Honneth, A. (1996). *The struggle for recognition: The moral grammar of social conflicts* (J. Anderson, Trans.). Cambridge: MIT Press.

Hopkins, K. D. (1982). The unit of analysis: Group means versus individual observations. *American Educational Research Journal, 19*(1), 5–18.

Horn, R. (1996). Negotiating research access to organizations. *Psychologist, 9*(12), 551–554.

Horst, P. (1941). The role of the predictor variables which are independent of the criterion. *Social Science Research Council, 48,* 431–436.

Horton, M., & Freire, P. (2000). *We make the road by walking* (Bell, B., Gaventa, J., & Peters, J., Eds.). Philadelphia: Temple University Press.

Horton, N. J., & Lipsitz, S. R. (2001). Multiple imputation in practice: Comparison of software packages for regression models with missing variables. *American Statistician, 55,* 244–254.

Horvitz, D. G., Shah, B. U., & Simmons, W. R. (1967). The unrelated question randomized response model. In E. D. Goldfield (Ed.), *Proceedings of the Social Statistics Section* (pp. 65–72). Washington, DC: American Statistical Association.

Hoskins, J. (1998). *Biographical objects: How things tell the stories of people's lives.* London: Routledge.

Höskuldsson, A. (1988). PLS regression methods. *Journal of Chemometrics, 2,* 211–228.

Hotelling, H. (1933). Analysis of a complex of statistical variables into principal components. *Journal of Educational Psychology, 24,* 417–441, 498–520.

Hougaard, P. (2000). *Analysis of multivariate survival data.* New York: Springer-Verlag.

House, E. R., & Howe, K. R. (1999). *Values in evaluation and social research.* Thousand Oaks, CA: Sage.

Hout, M. (1983). *Mobility tables.* Beverly Hills, CA: Sage.

Howell, D. C. (1999). *Fundamental statistics for the behavioral sciences* (4th ed.). Belmont, CA: Duxbury.

Howell, D. C. (2002). *Statistical methods for psychology* (5th ed.). Duxbury, UK: Thomson Learning.

Hox, J. J. (2002). *Multilevel analysis, techniques and applications.* Mahwah, NJ: Lawrence Erlbaum.

Hoyle, R. H. (2000). Confirmatory factor analysis. In H. E. A. Tinsely & S. D. Brown (Eds.), *Handbook of applied multivariate statistics and mathematical modeling* (pp. 465–497). New York: Academic Press.

Hsiao, C. (1986). *Analysis of panel data.* Cambridge, UK: Cambridge University Press.

Hu, L., & Bentler, P. M. (1999). Cutoff criteria for fit indexes in covariance structure analysis: Conventional criteria versus new alternatives. *Structural Equation Modeling: A Multidisciplinary Journal, 6,* 1–55.

Huber, P. (1981). *Robust statistics.* New York: Wiley.

Huberman, A. M., & Miles, M. B. (1994). Data management and analysis methods. In N. K. Denzin & Y. S. Lincoln (Eds.), *Handbook of qualitative research* (pp. 428–444). Thousand Oaks, CA: Sage.

Huck, S. (2000). *Reading statistics and research* (3rd ed.). New York: Addison Wesley Longman.

Huff, A. S. (2000). Changes in organizational knowledge production. *Academy of Management Review, 25*(2), 288–293.

Hughes, J. A. (1990). *The philosophy of social research* (2nd ed.). Harlow, UK: Longman.

Hughes, K., MacKintosh, A. M., Hastings, G., Wheeler, C., Watson, J., & Inglis, J. (1997). Young people, alcohol, and designer drinks: A quantitative and qualitative study. *British Medical Journal, 314,* 414–418.

Hughes, R. (1998). Considering the vignette technique and its application to a study of drug injecting and HIV risk and safer behaviour. *Sociology of Health and Illness, 20,* 381–400.

Hujala, E. (1998). Problems and challenges in cross-cultural research. *Acta Universitatis Ouluensis, 35,* 19–31.

Hume, D. (1786). *Treatise on human nature.* Oxford, UK: Claridon.

Humphreys, L. (1975). *Tearoom trade: Impersonal sex in public places.* Chicago: Aldine.

Hunt, J. C. (1989). *Psychoanalytic aspects of fieldwork* (University Paper Series on Qualitative Research Methods 18). Newbury Park, CA: Sage.

Hunter, J. E., Schmidt, F. L., & Hunter, R. (1979). Differential validity of employment tests by race: A comprehensive review and analysis. *Psychological Bulletin, 86,* 721–735.

Husserl, E. (1970). *Logical investigations* (Vols. 1–2). London: Routledge Kegan Paul.

Hutcheson, G., & Sofroniou, N. (1999). *The multivariate social scientist: Introductory statistics using generalized linear models.* London: Sage.

Huynh, H., & Feldt, L. S. (1970). Conditions under which mean square ratios in repeated measurements designs have exact F-distributions. *Journal of the American Statistical Association, 65,* 1582–1589.

Hyde, R. (2003). *The art of assembly language.* San Francisco: No Starch Press.

Hyman, H. (1955). *Survey design and analysis.* New York: Free Press.

Hyman, H. H. (1972). *Secondary analysis of sample surveys.* Glencoe, IL: Free Press.

Hyvärinen, A., Karhunen, J., & Oja, E. (2001). *Independent component analysis.* New York: Wiley.

ICPSR. (2002). *Guide to social science data preparation and archiving* [Online]. Available: http://www.ifdo.org/archiving _distribution/datprep_archiving_bfr.htm.

IFDO. (n.d.). [Online]. Available: http://www.ifdo.org/.

Imber, J. B. (Ed.). (2001). Symposium: Population politics. *Society, 39,* 3–53.

Inkeles, A., & Sasaki, M. (Eds.). (1996). *Comparing nations and cultures.* Englewood Cliffs, NJ: Prentice Hall.

International Centre for Diarrhoeal Disease Research, Bangladesh (ICDDRB). (1992). *Demographic surveillance system—Matlab: Registration of demographic events—1985* (Scientific Report 68). Dhaka, Bangladesh: Author.

Inter-University Consortium for Political and Social Research. (2002). *Guide to social science data preparation and archiving* [Online]. Supported by the Robert Wood Johnson Foundation. Available: www.ICPSR.umich.edu

Iversen, G. R. (1973). Recovering individual data in the presence of group and individual effects. *American Journal of Sociology, 79,* 420–434.

Iversen, G. R. (1984). *Bayesian statistical inference* (Sage University Paper Series on Quantitative Applications in the Social Sciences, 07–043). Beverly Hills, CA: Sage.

Iversen, G. R. (1991). *Contextual analysis* (Sage University Paper Series on Quantitative Applications in the Social Sciences, 07–081). Newbury Park, CA: Sage.

Iversen, G. R., & Norpoth, H. (1987). *Analysis of variance* (2nd ed., Sage University Paper Series on Quantitative Applications in the Social Sciences, 07–001). Newbury Park, CA: Sage.

Iversen, G., & Gergen, M. (1997). *Statistics: The conceptual approach.* New York: Springer-Verlag.

Iyengar, S., Peters, M. E., & Kinder, D. R. (1982). Experimental demonstrations of the "not-so-minimal" consequences of television news programs. *The American Journal of Political Science, 4,* 848–858.

Jaccard, J. (1998). *Interaction effects in factorial analysis of variance* (Sage University Paper Series on Quantitative Applications in the Social Sciences, 07–118). Thousand Oaks, CA: Sage.

Jaccard, J., & Turrisi, R. (2003). *Interaction effects in multiple regression* (2nd ed., Sage University Paper Series on Quantitative Applications in the Social Sciences, 07–72). Thousand Oaks, CA: Sage.

Jaccard, J., Turrisi, R, & Wan, C. K. . (1990). *Interaction effects in multiple regression.* Newbury Park, CA: Sage.

Jackman, R. W. (1973). On the relationship of economic development to political performance. *American Journal of Political Science, 17,* 611–621.

Jackson, D. N. (2002). The constructs in people's heads. In H. I. Braun, D. N. Jackson, & D. E. Wiley (Eds.), *The role of constructs in psychological and educational measurement* (pp. 3–18). Mahwah, NJ: Lawrence Erlbaum.

Jackson, J. E. (1991). *A user's guide to principal component analysis.* New York: John Wiley.

Jackson, S., & Brashers, D. E. (1994). *Random Factors in ANOVA* (Sage University Paper Series on Quantitative Applications in the Social Sciences, 07–098). Thousand Oaks, CA: Sage.

Jacobs, H. A. (1861). *Incidents in the life of a slave girl: Written by herself.* Boston.

Jacoby, L. L., Debner, J. A., & Hay, J. F. (2001). Proactive interference, accessibility bias, and process dissociations: Valid subject reports of memory. *Journal of Experimental Psychology: Memory, Learning, and Cognition, 27,* 686–700.

Jacoby, W. G. (1991). *Data theory and dimensional analysis* (Sage University Paper Series on Quantitative Applications in the Social Sciences, 07–078). Newbury Park, CA: Sage.

Jacoby, W. G. (1997). *Statistical graphics for univariate and bivariate data.* Thousand Oaks, CA: Sage.

Jaeger, R. M. (1993). *Statistics: A spectator sport* (2nd ed.). Newbury Park, CA: Sage.

Jahoda, G. (1977). In pursuit of the emic-etic distinction: Can we ever capture it? In Y. H. Poortinga (Ed.), *Basic problems in cross-cultural research* (pp. 55–63). Amsterdam: Swets & Zeitlinger.

James, J. B., & Sørensen, A. (2000, December). Archiving longitudinal data for future research: Why qualitative data add to a study's usefulness. *Forum Qualitative Sozialforschung* [Forum: Qualitative Social Research] [Online journal], *1*(3). Available: http://qualitative-research.net/fqs/fqs-eng.htm

James, L. R., Demaree, R. G., & Wolf, G. (1984). Estimating within-group interrater reliability with and without response bias. *Journal of Applied Psychology, 69,* 85–98.

James, W. (1952). *The varieties of religious experience: A study in human nature.* London: Longmans, Green & Co. (Original work published 1902)

Jameson, F. (1983). Postmodernism and consumer society. In H. Foster (Ed.), *Postmodern culture.* London: Pluto.

Jasso, G. (1988). Principles of theoretical analysis. *Sociological Theory, 6,* 1–20.

Jasso, G. (1990). Methods for the theoretical and empirical analysis of comparison processes. *Sociological Methodology, 20,* 369–419.

Jasso, G. (2001). Formal theory. In J. H. Turner (Ed.), *Handbook of sociological theory* (pp. 37–68). New York: Kluwer Academic/Plenum.

Jasso, G. (2001). Rule-finding about rule-making: Comparison processes and the making of norms. In M. Hechter & K.-D. Opp (Eds.), *Social norms* (pp. 348–393). New York: Russell Sage.

Jasso, G. (2001). Comparison theory. In J. H. Turner (Ed.), *Handbook of sociological theory* (pp. 669–698). New York: Kluwer Academic/Plenum.

Jasso, G. (2001). Studying status: An integrated framework. *American Sociological Review, 66,* 96–124.

Jasso, G. (2002). Seven secrets for doing theory. In J. Berger & M. Zelditch (Eds.), *New directions in contemporary sociological theory* (pp. 317–342). Boulder, CO: Rowan & Littlefield.

Jasso, G. (in press). The tripartite structure of social science analysis. *Sociological Theory.*

Jasso, G., & Rossi, P. H. (1977). Distributive justice and earned income. *American Sociological Review, 42,* 639–651.

Jeffreys, H. (1961). *Theory of probability* (3rd ed.). Oxford, UK: Clarendon.

Jenkins, G. M., & Watts, D. G. (1968). *Spectral analysis and its applications.* San Francisco: Holden-Day.

Jenkins, R. (1984). Bringing it all back home: An anthropologist in Belfast. In C. Bell & H. Roberts (Eds.), *Social researching: Politics, problems, practice* (pp. 147–164). London: Routledge and Kegan Paul.

JMP Introductory Guide. (2000). Cary, NC: SAS Institute.

Johansen, S. (1988). Statistical analysis of cointegration vectors. *Journal of Economic Dynamics and Control, 12,* 231–254.

Johansen, S. (1991). Estimation and hypotheses testing of cointegrating vectors in Gaussian vector autoregressive models. *Econometrica, 59,* 1551–1580.

Johansen, S. (1995). *Likelihood-based inference in cointegrated vector autoregressive models.* Oxford, UK: Oxford University Press.

John, K. E. (1989). The polls—A report. *Public Opinion Quarterly, 53,* 590–605.

John, N. R., & Draper, J.A. (1980). An alternative family of transformations. *Applied Statistics, 29*(2), 190–197.

Johnson, C. (1982). Risks in the publication of fieldwork. In J. E. Sieber (Ed.), *The ethics of social research: Fieldwork, regulation and publication* (pp. 71–92). New York: Springer-Verlag.

Johnson, C. (1994). Gender, legitimate authority, and leader-subordinate conversations. *American Sociological Review, 59,* 122–135.

Johnson, J. C. (1990). *Selecting ethnographic informants.* Newbury Park, CA: Sage.

Johnson, J. C., & Weller, S. C. (2002). Elicitation techniques for interviewing. In J. F. Gubrium & J. A. Holstein (Eds.), *The handbook of interview research.* Thousand Oaks, CA: Sage.

Johnson, N. L., & Kotz, S. (1969). *Discrete distributions.* Boston: Houghton-Mifflin.

Johnson, N. L., Kotz, S., & Balakrishnan, N. (1994). *Continuous univariate distributions, Vol. 1.* New York: Wiley.

Johnson, R. A., & Bhattacharyya, G. K. (2001). *Statistics: Principles and methods* (4th ed.). New York: Wiley.

Johnson, R. A., & Wichern, D. W. (2002). *Applied multivariate statistical analysis.* Upper Saddle River, NJ: Prentice Hall.

Johnson, T., Dandeker, C., & Ashworth, C. (1984). *The structure of social theory.* London: Macmillan.

Johnston, J., & Dinardo, J. (1997). *Econometric methods* (4th ed.). New York: McGraw-Hill.

Joint Committee on Standards for Educational Evaluation. (1994). *The program evaluation standards.* Thousand Oaks, CA: Sage.

Joliffe, I. T. (1986). *Principal component analysis.* New York: Springer-Verlag.

Jones, J. M. G., & Hunter, D. (1995). Consensus methods for medical and health services research. *British Medical Journal, 311,* 376–380.

Jones, K. (1997). Multilevel approaches to modelling contextuality: From nuisance to substance in the analysis of voting behaviour. In G. P. Westert & R. N. Verhoeff (Eds.), *Places and people: Multilevel modelling in geographical research* (Nederlandse Geografische Studies 227). Utrecht, The Netherlands: The Royal Dutch Geographical Society and Faculty of Geographical Sciences, Utrecht University.

Jones, M. B. (1959). *Simplex theory* (U.S. Naval School of Aviation Medicine Monograph Series No. 3). Pensacola, FL: U.S. Naval School of Aviation Medicine.

Jones, M. O. (1996). *Studying organizational symbolism: What, how, why?* Thousand Oaks, CA: Sage.

Jones, S. R. (1992). Was there a Hawthorne effect? *American Journal of Sociology, 98,* 451–468.

Jöreskog, K. G. (1967). Some contributions to maximum likelihood factor analysis. *Psychometrika, 32,* 443–482.

Jöreskog, K. G. (1969). A general approach to confirmatory maximum likelihood factor analysis. *Psychometrika, 34,* 183–202.

Jöreskog, K. G. (1973). A general method for estimating a linear structural equation system. In A. S. Goldberger & O. D. Duncan (Eds.), *Structural equation models in the social sciences* (pp. 85–112). New York: Academic Press.

Jöreskog, K. G. (1979). Statistical models and methods for analysis of longitudinal data. In K. G. Jöreskog & D. Sörbom (Eds.), *Advances in factor analysis and structural equation models.* Cambridge, MA: Abt.

Josselson, R., & Lieblich, A. (Eds.). (1993–1999). *The narrative study of lives* (Vols. 1–6). Newbury Park, CA: Sage.

Josselsyn, R. (Ed.). (1996). *Ethics and process in the narrative study of lives.* Thousand Oaks, CA: Sage.

Joynson, R. B. (1989). *The Burt affair.* London: Routledge.

Judd, C. M., & McClelland, G. H. (1998). Measurement. In D. T. Gilbert, S. T. Fiske, & G. Lindzey (Eds.), *The handbook of social psychology* (4th ed., Vol. 1). Boston: McGraw-Hill.

Judd, C. M., Smith, E. R., & Kidder, L. H. (1991). *Research methods in social relations* (6th ed.). Fort Worth, TX: Harcourt Brace Jovanovich.

Judge, G. G., Griffiths, W. E., Hill, R. C., & Lee, T.-C. (1980). *The theory and practice of econometrics* (Wiley Series in Probability and Mathematical Statistics). New York: John Wiley.

Judge, G. G., Griffiths, W. E., Hill, R. C., Lütkepohl, H., & Lee, T.-C. (1985). *The theory and practice of econometrics* (2nd ed.). New York: John Wiley.

Judge, G. G., Hill, R. C., Griffiths, W. E., Lütkepohl, H., & Lee, T. (1988). *Introduction to the theory and practice of econometrics* (2nd ed.). New York: John Wiley.

Julian, D. A. (1997). The utilization of the logic model as a system level planning and evaluation device. *Evaluation and Program Planning, 20*(3), 251–257.

Juster, F. T., & Stafford, F. P. (1985). *Time, goods and well-being.* Ann Arbor, MI: Institute for Social Research

Kalichman, S. C. (1999). *Mandated reporting of suspected child abuse: Ethics, law and policy.* Washington, DC: American Psychological Association.

Kalton, G. (1983). *Introduction to survey sampling* (Sage University Paper Series on Quantitative Applications in the Social Sciences, 07–035). Beverly Hills, CA: Sage.

Kan, M. (2002). Reinterpreting the Multifactor Leadership Questionnaire. In K. W. Parry & J. R. Meindl (Eds.), *Grounding leadership theory and research: Issues, perspectives and methods* (pp. 159–173). Greenwich, CT: Information Age Publishing.

Kane, M. (2002). Validating high-stakes testing programs. *Educational Measurement: Issues and Practice, 21*(1), 31–41.

Kant, I. (1781). *Kritik der reinen Vernunft* [Critique of pure reason]. Hamburg: Felix Meiner.

Kanuha, V. K. (2000). "Being" native versus "going native": Conducting social work research as an insider. *Social Work, 45*(5), 439–447.

Kaplan, A. (1943). Content analysis and the theory of signs. *Philosophy of Science, 10,* 230–247.

Kaplan, A. (1964). *The conduct of inquiry.* New York: Chandler.

Kaplan, D. (1990). Evaluation and modification of covariance structure models: A review and recommendation. *Multivariate Behavioral Research, 25,* 137–155.

Kaplan, D. (2000). *Structural equation modeling: Foundations and extensions.* Thousand Oaks, CA: Sage.

Kaplan, E. L., & Meier, P. (1958). Nonparametric estimation from incomplete observations. *Journal of the American Statistical Association, 53,* 457–481.

Kashy, D. A., & Kenny, D. A. (2000). The analysis of data from dyads and groups. In H. T. Reis & C. M. Judd (Eds.), *Handbook of research methods in social and personality psychology* (pp. 451–477). New York: Cambridge University Press.

Kasprzyk, D., Duncan, G. J., Kalton, G., & Singh, M. P. (1989). *Panel surveys.* New York: John Wiley.

Kass, G. (1980). An exploratory technique for investigating large quantities of categorical data. *Applied Statistics, 29*(2), 119–127.

Kass, R. E., & Wasserman, L. (1996). The selection of prior distributions by formal rules. *Journal of the American Statistical Association, 91,* 1343–1370.

Kazdin, A. E. (2003). *Research design in clinical psychology, 4th Edition.* Boston: Allyn & Bacon.

Keat, R., & Urry, J. (1975). *Social theory as science.* London: Routledge Kegan Paul.

Keeter, S., Miller, C., Kohut, A., Groves, R. M., & Presser, S. (2000). Consequences of reducing nonresponse in a national telephone survey. *Public Opinion Quarterly, 64,* 125–148.

Keleman, M., & Bansal, P. (2002). The conventions of management research and their relevance to management practice. *British Journal of Management, 13,* 97–108.

Kelle, U. (Ed.). (1995). *Computer-aided qualitative data analysis: Theory, methods and practice.* London: Sage.

Kelly, G. (1955). *The psychology of personal constructs.* New York: Norton.

Kendall, G., & Wickham, G. (1999). *Using Foucault's methods.* London: Sage.

Kendall, M. G. (1962). *Rank correlation methods* (3rd ed.). London: Griffin.

Kendall, M. G., & Buckland, W. R. (1971). *A dictionary of statistical terms* (3rd ed.). Edinburgh: Oliver & Boyd.

Kendall, M., & Gibbons, J. D. (1990). *Rank correlation methods* (5th ed.). New York: Oxford University Press.

Kendall, M., & Stuart, A. (1969). *The advanced theory of statistics: Vol. 2. Inference and relationship.* London: Griffin.

Kendall, P. L., & Lazarsfeld, P. F. (1950). Problems of survey analysis. In R. K. Merton & P. F. Lazarsfeld (Eds.), *Continuities in social research: Studies in the scope and method of "the American soldier"* (pp. 160–176). Glencoe, IL: Free Press.

Kennedy, P. (1992). *A guide to econometrics* (3rd ed.). Cambridge: MIT Press.

Kennedy, P. (1998). *A guide to econometrics* (4th ed.). Cambridge: MIT Press.

Kennedy, P. E. (2002). More on Venn diagrams for regression. *Journal of Statistics Education, 10*(1) [Online]. Retrieved from http://www.amstat.org/publications/jse/v10n1/kennedy.html

Kenny, D. A. (1979). *Correlation and causality.* New York: John Wiley.

Kenny, D. A. (1994). *Interpersonal perception: A social relations analysis.* New York: Guilford.

Kenny, D. A., & La Voie, L. (1984). The social relations model. In L. Berkowitz (Ed.), *Advances in experimental social psychology* (Vol. 18, pp. 142–182). Orlando, FL: Academic Press.

Keppel, G. (1991). *Design and analysis: A researcher's handbook* (3rd ed.). Englewood Cliffs, NJ: Prentice Hall.

Keren, G., & Lewis, C. (Eds.). (1993). *A handbook for data analysis in the behavioral sciences: Methodological issues.* Hillsdale, NJ: Lawrence Erlbaum.

Kerlinger, F. N., & Lee, H. B. (2000). *Foundations of behavioral research.* Ft. Worth, TX: Harcourt.

Kerr, A. W., Hall, H. K., & Kozub, A. (2002). Descriptive statistics. Chapter 2 in *Doing statistics with SPSS.* London: Sage.

Keselman, H. J., Lix, L. M., & Kowalchuk, R. K. (1998). Multiple comparison procedures for trimmed means. *Psychological Methods, 3,* 123–141.

Kessler, R., & Greenberg, D. (1981). *Linear panel analysis.* New York: Academic Press.

Keyfitz, N. (1985). *Applied mathematical demography* (2nd ed.). New York: Wiley.

Keynes, J. M. (1936). *The general theory of employment, interest, and money.* New York: Harcourt Brace Jovanovich.

Khurana, B. (1995). *The older spouse caregiver: Paradox and pain of Alzheimer's disease.* Unpublished doctoral dissertation, Center for Psychological Studies, Albany, CA.

Kiel, L. D., & Elliott, E. (1996). *Chaos theory in the social sciences.* Ann Arbor: University of Michigan Press.

Kim, J. O., & Mueller, C. W. (1978). *Factor analysis: Statistical methods and practical issues.* Beverly Hills, CA: Sage.

Kinal, T., & Lahiri, K. (1983). Specification error analysis with stochastic regressors. *Econometrica, 54,* 1209–1220.

Kincaid, H. (1994). Defending laws in the social sciences. In M. Martin & L. McIntyre (Eds.), *Readings in the philosophy of social science* (pp. 111–130). Cambridge: MIT Press.

Kincaid, H. (1996). *Philosophical foundations of the social sciences: Analyzing controversies in social research.* Cambridge, UK: Cambridge University Press.

King, G. (1988). Statistical models for political science event counts: Bias in conventional procedures and evidence for the exponential Poisson regression model. *American Journal of Political Science, 32,* 838–863.

King, G. (1989). *Unifying political methodology: The likelihood theory of statistical inference.* New York: Cambridge University Press.

King, G. (1990). Stochastic variation: A comment on Lewis-Beck and Skalaban's "The R-Squared." *Political Analysis, 2,* 185–200.

King, G. (1997). *A solution to the ecological inference problem.* Princeton, NJ: Princeton University Press

King, G. (1998). *Unifying political methodology: The likelihood theory of statistical inference.* Ann Arbor: University of Michigan Press.

King, G., & Zeng, L. (2001). Logistic regression in rare events data. *Political Analysis, 9,* 137–163.

King, G., Keohane, R. O., & Verba, S. (1994). *Designing social inquiry: Scientific inference in qualitative research.* Princeton, NJ: Princeton University Press.

King, J. A. (1998). Making sense of participatory evaluation practice. *New Directions for Evaluation, 80,* 57–67.

Kirk, J., & Miller, M. L. (1986). *Reliability and validity in qualitative research.* Beverly Hills, CA: Sage.

Kirk, R. E. (1995). *Experimental design: Procedures for the behavioral sciences* (3rd ed.). Pacific Grove, CA: Brooks/Cole.

Kirk, R. E. (1999). *Statistics: An introduction* (4th ed.). Orlando, FL: Harcourt Brace. .

Kirkman, B. L., Rosen, B., Gibson, C. B., Tesluk, P. E., & McPherson, S. O. (2003). Five challenges to virtual team success: Lessons from Sabre, Inc. *Academy of Management Executive, 16*(3), 67–79.

Kish, L. (1949). A procedure for objective respondent selection within a household. *Journal of the American Sociological Association, 44,* 380–387.

Kish, L. (1962). Studies of interviewer variance for attitudinal variables. *Journal of the American Statistical Association, 57,* 92–115.

Kish, L. (1965). *Survey sampling.* New York: Wiley.

Kish, L. (1987). *Statistical design for research.* New York: Wiley.

Kish, L. (1995). Methods for design effects. *Journal of Official Statistics, 11*(1), 55–77.

Kitagawa, E. (1955). Components of a difference between two rates. *Journal of the American Statistical Association, 50,* 1168–1194.

Kitcher, P., & Salmon, W. C. (Eds.). (1989). *Scientific explanation* (Minnesota Studies in the Philosophy of Science, Vol. 13). Minneapolis: University of Minnesota Press.

Kivlahan, D. R., Marlatt, G. A., Fromme, K., Coppel, D. B., & Williams, E. (1990). Secondary prevention with college drinkers: Evaluation of an alcohol skills training program. *Journal of Consulting and Clinical Psychology, 58*(6), 805–810.

Kleiber, C., & Kotz, S. (2003). *Statistical size distributions in economics and actuarial sciences.* Hoboken, NJ: Wiley.

Kleinbaum, D. G., Kupper, L. L., & Morgensten, H. (1982). *Epidemiologic research: Principles and quantitative methods.* New York: Van Nostrand Reinhold.

Kleinman, A. L., Eisenberg, L., & Good, B. J. (1978). Culture, illness and care: Clinical lessons from anthropologic and cross-cultural research. *Annals of Internal Medicine, 88,* 251–258.

Kleinman, S., & Copp, M. A. (1993). *Emotions and fieldwork.* Thousand Oaks, CA: Sage.

Kline, P. (1994). *An easy guide to factor analysis.* Thousand Oaks, CA: Sage.

Kline, R. B. (1998). *Principles and practice of structural equation modeling.* New York: Guilford.

Klir, G. J., & Folger, T. A. (1988). *Fuzzy sets, uncertainty, and information.* Englewood Cliffs, NJ: Prentice Hall.

Kmenta, J. (1997). *Elements of econometrics* (2nd ed.). Ann Arbor: University of Michigan Press.

Knoke, D., & Burke, P. J. (1980). *Log-linear models.* Beverly Hills, CA: Sage.

Knoke, D., Bohrnstedt, G. W., & Mee, A. P. . (2002). *Statistics for social data analysis* (4th ed.). Itasca, IL: Peacock.

Knuth, D. E. (1997). *Fundamental algorithms: The art of computer programming* (Vol. 1, 3rd ed.). Reading, MA: Addison-Wesley.

Knuth, D. E. (1997). *The art of computer programming, volume 2: Seminumerical algorithms.* Reading, MA: Addison-Wesley.

Koch, W., Schulz, E. M., Wright, R., Smith, R. M., Lang, S. et al. (1996). What is a ratio scale? *Rasch Measurement Transactions, 9,* 457.

Kohn, L. T., Corrigan, J. M., & Donaldson, M. S. (Eds.). (2000). *To err is human: Building a safer health system.* Washington, DC: National Academy Press.

Kondo, D. K. (1990). *Crafting selves: Power, gender and discourses of identity in a Japanese workplace.* Chicago: University of Chicago Press.

Korczynski, M. (2000). The political economy of trust. *Journal of Management Studies, 37*(1), 1–22.

Kornberg, A. (1997). *Basic research, the lifeline of medicine.* Retrieved from http://www.nobel.se/medicine/articles/research/

Körner, S. (1955). *Kant.* Harmondsworth, UK: Penguin.

Kotz, S., & Johnson, N. (Eds.). (1983). *Encyclopedia of statistical sciences.* New York: Wiley.

Kotz, S., Johnson, N. L., & Read, C. B. (1982). Censoring. In S. Kotz, N. L. Johnson, & C. B. Read (Eds.), *Encyclopedia of statistical sciences* (Vol. 1, p. 396). New York: Wiley.

Koutsoyiannis, A. (1978). *Theory of econometrics: An introductory exposition of econometric methods* (2nd ed.). London: Macmillan.

Kozlowski, S. W., & Hattrup, K. (1992). A disagreement about within-group agreement: Disentangling issues of consistency versus consensus. *Journal of Applied Psychology, 77,* 161–167.

Kracauer, S. (1952–1953). The challenge of qualitative content analysis. *Public Opinion Quarterly, 16,* 631–642.

Krantz, J. H., & Dalal, R. (2000). Validity of Web-based psychological research. In M. H. Birnbaum (Ed.), *Psychological experiments on the Internet* (pp. 35–60). New York: Academic Press.

Krieger, N. (1994). Epidemiology and the web of causation: Has anyone seen the spider? *Social Science & Medicine, 39*(7), 887–903.

Krieger, S. (1983). *The mirror's dance: Identity in a women's community.* Philadelphia: Temple University Press.

Krippendorf, K. (1980). *Content analysis: An introduction to its methodology.* Beverly Hills, CA: Sage.

Kristeva, J. (1991). *Strangers to ourselves.* New York: Columbia University Press.

Kroenke, D. M. (2001). *Database processing: Fundamentals, design and implementation.* Upper Saddle River, NJ: Prentice Hall.

Krosnick, J. A. (1999). Survey methodology. *Annual Review of Psychology, 50,* 537–567.

Krueger, R. A. (1994). *Focus groups: A practical guide for applied research* (2nd ed.). Thousand Oaks, CA: Sage.

Krueger, R. A., & Casey, M. A. (2000). *Focus groups: A practical guide for applied research* (3rd ed.). Thousand Oaks, CA: Sage.

Kruskal, J. B. (1964). Multidimensional scaling by optimising goodness of fit to a nonmetric hypothesis. *Psychometrika, 29,* 1–27, 115–129.

Kruskal, J. B. (1968). Transformation of data. In D. L. Sills (Ed.), *International encyclopedia of the social sciences* (Vol. 15, pp. 182–192). New York: Macmillan.

Kruskal, W. H. (1958). Ordinal measures of association. *Journal of the American Statistical Association, 53,* 814–861.

Kuhn, M., & McPartland, T. S. (1954). An empirical investigation of self attitudes. *American Sociological Review, 19,* 68–76.

Kuhn, T. (1970). *The structure of scientific revolutions* (2nd ed.). Chicago: University of Chicago Press. (Original work published 1962)

Kuran, T. (1995). The inevitability of future revolutionary surprises. *American Journal of Sociology, 100*(6), 1528–1551.

Kuusela, H., Spence, M. T., & Kanto, A. J. (1998). Expertise effects on prechoice decision processes and final outcomes: A protocol analysis. *European Journal of Marketing, 32,* 5–6, 559.

Kvale, S. (1996). *InterViews: An introduction to qualitative research interviewing.* Thousand Oaks, CA: Sage.

Kvale, S. (1999). The psychoanalytic interview as qualitative research. *Qualitative Inquiry, 5*(1), 87–113.

Labov, W. (1982). Speech actions and reactions in personal narrative. In D. Tannen (Ed.), *Analyzing discourse: Text and talk.* Washington, DC: Georgetown University Press.

Lachenbruch, P.A. (1975). *Discriminant analysis.* New York: Hafner.

LaFreniere, P., & Charlesworth, W. R. (1983). Dominance, attention, and affiliation in a preschool group: A nine-month longitudinal study. *Ethology and Sociobiology, 4*(2), 55–67.

Lagopoulos, A. Ph., & Boklund-Lagopoulou, K. (1992). *Meaning and geography: The social conception of the region in northern Greece.* Berlin: Mouton de Gruyter.

Laird, N. (1978). Nonparametric maximum likelihood estimation of a mixture distribution. *Journal of the American Statistical Association, 73,* 805–811.

Lakatos, I. (1978). *The methodology of scientific research programmes: Philosophical papers. Vol. 1.* Cambridge, UK: Cambridge University Press.

Lakatos, I., & Musgrave, A. (Eds.). (1970). *Criticism and the growth of knowledge.* Cambridge, UK: Cambridge University Press.

Lakoff, G., & Johnson, M. (1980). *Metaphors we live by.* Chicago: University of Chicago Press.

Lambert, D. (1992). Zero-inflated Poisson regression with an application to defects in manufacturing. *Technometrics, 34,* 1–14.

Langeheine, R., & van de Pol, F. (1990). A unifying framework for Markov modeling in discrete space and discrete time. *Sociological Methods & Research, 18,* 416–441.

Langeheine, R., & Van de Pol, F. (1994). Discrete-time mixed Markov latent class models. In A. Dale & R. B. Davies (Eds.), *Analyzing social and political change: A casebook of methods* (pp. 171–197). London: Sage.

Langellier, K. M. (2001). Personal narrative. In M. Jolly (Ed.), *Encyclopedia of life writing: Autobiographical and biographical forms* (Vol. 2). London: Fitzroy Dearborn.

Langellier, K. M., & Peterson, E. E. (2003). *Performing narrative: The communicative practice of storytelling.* Philadelphia: Temple University Press.

Lapadat, J. C., & Lindsay, A. C. (1999). Transcription in research and practice: From standardization of technique to interpretive positionings. *Qualitative Inquiry, 5*(1), 64–86.

Larsen, R. J., & Marx, M. L. (1990). *Statistics.* Englewood Cliffs, NJ: Prentice Hall.

Lashley, K. S. (1951). The problem of serial order in behavior. In L. A. Jeffress (Ed.), *Cerebral mechanisms in behavior: The Hixon symposium* (pp. 112–136). New York: John Wiley.

Latham, G. P., Skarlicki, D., Irvine, D., & Siegel, J. P. (1993). The increasing importance of performance appraisals to employee effectiveness in organizational settings in North America. In C. L. Cooper & I. T. Robertson (Eds.), *International review of industrial and organizational psychology 1993* (Vol. 8, pp. 87–132). Chichester, UK: Wiley.

Lather, P. (1993). Fertile obsession: Validity after post-structuralism. *Sociological Quarterly, 35,* 673–694.

Lather, P. (1999). To be of use: The work of reviewing. *Review of Educational Research, 69*(1), 2–7.

Laudan, L. (1977). *Progress and its problems: Toward a theory of scientific growth.* Berkeley: University of California Press.

Lauder, M. (2003). Covert participant observation of a deviant community: Justifying the use of deception. *Journal of Contemporary Religion, 18*(2), 185–196.

Laufer, R. S., & Wolfe, M. (1977). Privacy as a concept and a social issue: A multidimensional developmental theory. *Journal of Social Issues, 33,* 44–87.

Laurie, H., Smith, R., & Scott, L. (1999). Strategies for reducing nonresponse in a longitudinal panel survey. *Journal of Official Statistics, 15*(2), 269–282.

Lave, C., & March, J. G. (1978). *An introduction to models in the social sciences.* New York: Harper & Row.

Lavrakas, P. J. (1987). *Telephone survey methods.* Newbury Park, CA: Sage.

Lavrakas, P. J. (1993). *Telephone survey methods: Sampling, selection, and supervision* (2nd ed.). Newbury Park, CA: Sage.

Lavrakas, P. J. (1998). Methods for sampling and interviewing in telephone surveys. In L. Bickman & D. J. Rog (Eds.), *Handbook of applied social research methods* (pp. 429–472). Thousand Oaks, CA: Sage.

Lawlis, G. F., & Lu, E. (1972). Judgment of counseling process: Reliability, agreement, and error. *Psychological Bulletin, 78,* 17–20.

Lawshe, C. H. (1975). A quantitative approach to content validity. *Personnel Psychology, 28,* 563–575.

Lax, D. A. (1985). Robust estimators of scale: Finite-sample performance in long-tailed symmetric distributions. *Journal of the American Statistical Association, 80,* 736–741.

Layder, D. (1993). *New strategies in social research.* Cambridge, UK: Polity.

Lazarsfeld, P. F. (1950). The logical and mathematical foundation of latent structure analysis & the interpretation and mathematical foundation of latent structure analysis. In S. A. Stoufffer.(Ed.), *Measurement and prediction* (pp. 362–472). Princeton, NJ: Princeton University Press.

Lazarsfeld, P. F. (1955). Interpretation of statistical relations as a research operation. In P. F. Lazarsfeld & M. Rosenberg (Eds.), *The language of social research* (pp. 111–125). Glencoe, IL: Free Press.

Lazarsfeld, P. F. (1958). Evidence and inference in social research. *Daedalus, 87,* 120–121.

Lazarsfeld, P. F., & Henry, N. W. (1968). *Latent structure analysis.* Boston: Houghton Mifflin.

Leach, C., Freshwater, K., Aldridge, J., & Sunderland, J. (2001). Analysis of repertory grids in clinical practice. *British Journal of Clinical Psychology, 40,* 225–248.

Leamer, E. (1978). *Specification searches: Ad hoc inference with nonexperimental data.* New York: Wiley.

Leamer, E. E. (1978). *Specification searches: Ad hoc inference with nonexperimental data.* New York: John Wiley.

Leamer, E. E. (1983). Let's take the con out of econometrics. *American Economic Review, 73*(1), 31–43.

Lebart, L., Morineau, A., & Warwick, K. M. (1984). *Multivariate descriptive statistical analysis.* New York: Wiley.

Lebreton, J.-D., Burnham, K. P., Clobert, J., & Anderson, D. R. (1992). Modeling survival and testing biological hypotheses using marked animals: A unified approach with case studies. *Ecological Monographs, 62,* 67–118.

Lee, A. M. (1978). *Sociology for whom.* New York: Oxford University Press.

Lee, P. M. (1997). *Bayesian statistics: An introduction* (2nd ed.). London: Arnold.

Lee, R. (2000). *Unobtrusive methods in social research.* Buckingham, UK: Open University Press.

Lee, R. B. (1993). *The Dobe !Kung.* New York: Holt, Rinehart and Winston.

Lee, R. M. (1993). *Doing research on sensitive topics.* London: Sage.

Lee, R. M. (1995). *Dangerous fieldwork.* London: Sage.

Lehtonen, M. (2000). *The cultural analysis of texts.* London: Sage.

Leisering, L., & Leibfried, S. (1999). *Time and poverty in Western welfare states.* New York: Cambridge University Press.

Lemaitre, G. (1992). *Dealing with the seam problem* (Survey of Labour and Income Dynamics Research Papers 92–05). Ottawa: Statistics Canada.

Lenski, G. (1966). *Power and privilege.* New York: McGraw-Hill.

Lepkowski, J. M., & Couper, M. P. (2002). Nonresponse in the second wave of longitudinal household surveys. In R. M. Groves, D. A. Dillman, J. L. Eltinge, & R. J. A. Little (Eds.), *Survey nonresponse* (pp. 259–272). New York: John Wiley.

Leslie, P. H. (1945). On the use of matrices in certain population mathematics. *Biometrika, 33,* 183–212.

Lett, J. (1987). The importance of the emic/etic distinction. In *The human enterprise: A critical introduction to anthropological theory.* Boulder, CO: Westview.

Levene, H. (1960). Robust tests for equality of variances. In I. Olkin (Ed.), *Contributions to probability and statistics* (pp. 278–292). Stanford, CA: Stanford University Press.

Levenshtein, V. I. (1966). Binary codes capable of correcting deletions, insertions, and reversals. *Cybernetics and Control Theory, 10,:* 707–710. (Original work published 1965)

Levin, A., Liukkonen, J., & Levine, D. W. (1996). Equivalent inference using transformations. *Communications in Statistics, Theory and Methods, 25*(5), 1059–1072.

Levin, I. P. (1999). *Relating statistics and experimental design: An introduction* (Sage University Paper Series on

Quantitative Applications in the Social Sciences, 07–125). Thousand Oaks, CA: Sage.

Levin, J. R., & Subkoviak, M. J. (1977). Planning an experiment in the company of measurement error. *Applied Psychological Measurement, 1*(3), 331–338.

Levinas, E. (1998). *On thinking-of-the-Other: Entre nous.* New York: Columbia University Press.

Levine, E. K. (1982). Old people are not all alike: Social class, ethnicity/race, and sex are bases for important differences. In J. E. Sieber (Ed.), *The ethics of social research: Surveys and experiments* (pp. 127–144). New York: Springer-Verlag.

Lévi-Strauss, C. (1963). *Structural anthropology.* New York: Basic Books.

Lévi-Strauss, C. (1969). *The elementary structures of kinship.* London: Eyre and Spottiswoode.

Levy, P. S., & Lemeshow, S. (1999). *Sampling of populations: Methods and applications.* New York: Wiley.

Lewin, K. (1943). Defining the "field at a given time." *Psychological Review, 50,* 292–310.

Lewin, K. (1959). *A dynamic theory of personality: Selected papers* (D. K. Adams & K. E. Zener, Trans.). New York: McGraw-Hill. (Original work published 1935)

Lewin, K. (1997). Experiments in social space. In G. W. Lewin (Ed.), *Resolving social conflicts: Field theory in social science* (pp. 59–67). Washington, DC: American Psychological Association. (Originally published in 1939)

Lewis, D. K. (1973). *Counterfactuals.* Cambridge, MA: Harvard University Press.

Lewis-Beck, M. S. (1980). *Applied regression: An introduction* (Sage University Paper Series on Quantitative Applications in the Social Sciences, series 07–022). Beverly Hills, CA: Sage.

Lewis-Beck, M. S. (1995). *Data analysis: An introduction* (Sage University Paper Series on Quantitative Applications in the Social Sciences, 07–103). Thousand Oaks, CA: Sage.

Lewis-Beck, M. S. (Ed.). (1993). *Regression analysis.* London: Sage/Toppan.

Lewis-Beck, M. S., & Skalaban, A. (1990). The *R*-squared: Some straight talk. *Political Analysis, 2,* 153–171.

Li, H., Rosenthal, R., & Rubin, D. (1996). Reliability of measurement in psychology: From Spearman-Brown to maximal reliability. *Psychological Methods, 1*(1), 98–107.

Liang, K.-Y., & Zeger, S. L. (1986). Longitudinal data analysis using generalized linear models. *Biometrika, 73,* 13–22.

Liao, T. F. (1989). A flexible approach for the decomposition of rate differences. *Demography, 26,* 717–726.

Liao, T. F. (1994). *Interpreting probability models: Logit, probit, and other generalized linear models.* Thousand Oaks, CA: Sage.

Liao, T. F. (2001). How responsive is U.S. population growth to immigration? A situational sensitivity analysis. *Mathematical Population Studies, 9,* 217–229.

Liao, T. F. (2002). *Statistical group comparison.* New York: Wiley.

Lichfield, N. (1996). *Community impact evaluation.* London: University College Press.

Lieberson, S. (1987). *Making it count: The improvement of social research and theory.* Berkeley: University of California Press.

Light, R. J., & Pillemer, D. B. (1984). *Summing up: The science of reviewing research.* Cambridge, MA: Harvard University Press.

Likert, R. (1932). A technique for the measurement of attitudes. *Archives of Psychology, 140,* 44–53.

Lincoln, Y. S., & Guba, E. (1985). *Naturalistic inquiry.* Beverly Hills, CA: Sage.

Lincoln, Y. S. & Guba, E. (2000). Paradigmatic controversies, contradictions, and emerging confluences. In N. K. Denzin & Y. S. Lincoln (Eds.), *Handbook of qualitative research* (2nd ed., pp. 163–188). Thousand Oaks, CA: Sage.

Lind, J. (1753). *A treatise of the scurvy: Of three parts containing an inquiry into the nature, causes and cure of that disease.* Edinburgh, UK: Sands, Murray and Cochran.

Lindahl, L. (2002). *Do birth order and family size matter for intergenerational income mobility? Evidence from Sweden* (Working Paper No. 5). Stockholm: Swedish Institute for Social Research.

Lindell, M. K., & Brandt, C. J. (1999). Assessing interrater agreement on the job relevance of a test: A comparison of the CVI, T, $r_{WG(J)}$, and $r^*_{WG(J)}$ indexes. *Journal of Applied Psychology, 84,* 640–647.

Lindell, M. K., Brandt, C. J., & Whitney, D. J. (1999). A revised index of interrater agreement for multi-item ratings of a single target. *Applied Psychological Measurement, 23,* 127–135.

Lindesmith, A. (1968). *Addiction and opiates.* Chicago: Aldine.

Lindley, D. V. (2001). Thomas Bayes. In C. C. Heyde & E. Seneta (Eds.), *Statisticians of the centuries* (pp. 68–71). New York: Springer-Verlag.

Lindley, D. V., & Smith, A. F. M. (1972). Bayes estimates for the linear model. *Journal of the Royal Statistical Society, 34,* 1–41.

Lindquist, E. F. (1953). *Design and analysis of experiments in psychology and education.* Boston: Houghton Mifflin.

Lindsay, B., Clogg, C. C., & Grego, J. (1991). Semiparametric estimation in the Rasch model and related models, including a simple latent class model for item analysis. *Journal of the American Statistical Association, 86,* 96–107.

Lingis, A. (1994). *Abuses.* Berkeley: The University of California Press.

Lingis, A. (1994). *The community of those who have nothing in common.* Bloomington: Indiana University Press.

Lingis, A. (1998). *The imperative.* Bloomington: Indiana University Press.

Linn, R. L. (Ed.). (1989). *Educational measurement* (3rd ed.). New York: Macmillan.

Linstone, H. A. (1978). The Delphi technique In R. B. Fowles (Ed.), *Handbook of futures research.* Westport, CT: Greenwood.

Littell, R. C., Milliken, G. A., Stroup, W. W., & Wolfinger. R. D. (1996). *SAS system for mixed models.* Cary, NC: SAS Institute, Inc.

Little, D. (1991). *Varieties of social explanation: An introduction to the philosophy of social science.* Boulder, CO: Westview.

Little, D. (1998). *Microfoundations, method and causation: On the philosophy of the social sciences.* New Brunswick, NJ: Transaction Publishers.

Little, R. J. A. (1988). Missing data adjustments in large surveys. *Journal of Business and Economic Statistics, 6,* 287–301.

Little, R. J. A., & Rubin, D. B. (1987). *Statistical analysis with missing data.* New York: John Wiley.

Little, R. J. A., & Rubin, D. B. (2002). *Statistical analysis with missing data* (2nd ed.). New York: John Wiley.

Litwin, M. S. (1995). *How to measure survey reliability and validity.* Thousand Oaks, CA: Sage.

Livingston, G. (1999). Beyond watching over established ways: A review as recasting the literature, recasting the lived. *Review of Educational Research, 69*(1), 9–19.

Loader, C. (1999). *Local regression and likelihood.* New York: Springer.

Locke, K. D. (2000). *Using grounded theory in management research.* London: Sage.

Loehlin, J. C. (1998). *Latent variable models: An introduction to factor, path, and structural analysis* (3rd ed.). Mahwah, NJ: Lawrence Erlbaum.

Loevinger, J. (1957). Objective tests as instruments of psychological theory. *Psychological Reports, 3*(Suppl. 9), 635–694.

Loewenthal, L. (1989). Sociology of literature in retrospect. In P. Desan et al. (Eds.), *Literature and social practice.* Chicago and London: University of Chicago Press.

Lofland, J., & Lofland, L. H. (1995). *Analyzing social settings: A guide to qualitative observation and analysis.* Belmont, CA: Wadsworth.

Loman, L. A., & Larkin, W. E. (1976). Rejection of the mentally ill: An experiment in labeling. *Sociological Quarterly, 17,* 555–560.

Long, J. S. (1997). *Regression models for categorical and limited dependent variables.* Thousand Oaks, CA: Sage.

Long, J. S., & Cheng, S. (2003). Regression models for categorical outcomes. In M. A. Hardy & A. Bryman (Eds.), *Handbook of data analysis.* London: Sage.

Long, J. S., & Ervin, L. H. (2000) Using heteroskedasticity consistent standard errors in the linear regression model. *American Statistician, 54,* 217–224.

Longford, N. T. (1993). *Random coefficient models.* New York: Oxford University Press.

Looney, C. G. (1997). *Pattern recognition using neural networks.* Oxford, UK: Oxford University Press.

Lord, F. M. (1956). Sampling error due to choice of split in split-half reliability coefficients. *Journal of Experimental Education, 24,* 245–249.

Lord, F. M., & Novick, M. R. (1968). *Statistical theories of mental test scores.* Reading, MA: Addison-Wesley.

Lorencz, B. (1991). Becoming ordinary: Leaving the psychiatric hospital. In J. M. Morse & J. Johnson (Eds.), *The illness experience: Dimensions of suffering* (pp. 140–200). Newbury Park, CA: Sage.

Lorenz, E. N. (1963). Deterministic non-periodic flow. *Journal of Atmospheric Science, 20,* 130–141.

Lorenz, K. (1981). *The foundations of ethology.* New York: Simon and Schuster.

Lotka, A. J. (1998). *Analytical theory of biological populations: Part II: Demographic analysis with particular application to human populations* (D. P. Smith & H. Rossert, Trans.). New York: Plenum. (Original work published 1939)

Luger, G. F. (2002). *Artificial intelligence: Structures and strategies for complex problem solving* (4th ed.). Reading, MA: Addison-Wesley.

Lukes, S. (1994). Methodological individualism reconsidered. In M. Martin & L. McIntyre (Eds.), *Readings in the philosophy of social science* (pp. 451–459). Cambridge: MIT Press.

Lundberg, G. (1939). *Foundations of sociology.* New York: Macmillan.

Lupia, A., McCubbins, M. D., & Popkin, S. L. (Eds.). (1998). *Elements of reason.* Cambridge, UK: Cambridge University Press.

Luttrell, W. (2003). *Pregnant bodies, fertile minds: Gender, race, and the schooling of pregnant teens.* New York: Routledge.

Lykken, D. T. (1957). A study of anxiety in the sociopathic personality. *Journal of Abnormal and Social Psychology, 55,* 6–10.

Lykken, D. T. (1995). *The antisocial personalities.* Mahwah, NJ: Lawrence Erlbaum.

Lynch, M. (2000). Against reflexivity as an academic virtue and source of privileged knowledge. *Theory, Culture and Society, 17*(3), 26–54.

Lyotard, J.-F. (1984). *The postmodern condition: A report on knowledge.* Minneapolis: University of Minnesota Press.

Macaulay, A. C., Paradis, G., Potvin, L., Cross, E. J., Saad-Haddad, C., McComber, A., et al. (1997). The Kahnawake Schools Diabetes Prevention Project: Intervention, evaluation, and baseline results of a diabetes primary prevention program with a native community in Canada. *Preventive Medicine, 26*(6), 79–90.

MacDonald, I. L., & Zucchini, W. (1997). *Hidden Markov models and other types of models for discrete-valued time series.* London: Chapman & Hall.

MacDonald, R. R. (2002). The incompleteness of probability models and the resultant implications for theories of statistical inference. *Understanding Statistics, 1*(3), 167–189.

MacDougall, D. (2001). Renewing ethnographic film: Is digital video changing the genre? *Anthropology Today, 17*(3), 15–21.

Machlin, S. R., & Taylor, A. K. (2000). *Design, methods, and field results of the 1996 Medical Expenditure Panel Survey Medical Provider Component* (MEPS Methodology Report No. 9, AHRQ Pub. No. 00–0028). Rockville, MD: Agency for Healthcare Research and Quality.

Mackay, A. L. (1977). *Scientific quotations*. New York: Crane, Russak.

Mackie, J. L. (1974). *The cement of the universe: A study of causation*. Oxford, UK: Oxford University Press.

Mackintosh, N. J. (1995). *Cyril Burt: Fraud or framed?* Oxford, UK: Oxford University Press.

Macy, M. W., & Willer, R. (2002). From factors to actors: Computational sociology and agent-based modeling. *Annual Review of Sociology, 28*, 143–166.

Maddala, G. S. (1983). *Limited-dependent and qualitative variables in econometrics*. Cambridge, UK: Cambridge University Press.

Maddala, G. S. (1992). *Introduction to econometrics*. Englewood Cliffs, NJ: Prentice Hall.

Madden, D. (2000). Towards a broader explanation of male-female wage differences. *Applied Economics Letters, 7*, 765–770.

Madjar, I. (2001). The lived experience of pain in the context of clinical practice. In S. K. Toombs (Ed.), *Handbook of phenomenology and medicine* (pp. 263–277). Boston: Kluwer Academic.

Magidson, J. (1993). The CHAID approach to segmentation modeling: CHi-squared Automatic Interaction Detection. In R. Bagozzi (Ed.), *Handbook of marketing research* (pp. 118–159). London: Blackwell.

Magidson, J., & Vermunt, J. K. (2001). Latent class factor and cluster models, bi-plots and related graphical displays. *Sociological Methodology, 31*, 223–264.

Magnusson, D. (1967). *Test theory*. Reading, MA: Addison-Wesley.

Mahoney, J. (2000). Path dependence in historical sociology. *Theory and Society, 29*, 507–548.

Maines, D. R. (1992). Theorizing movement in an urban transportation system by use of the constant comparative method in field research. *Social Science Journal, 29*, 283–292.

Maines, D. R. (2001). *The faultline of consciousness: A view of interactionism in sociology*. New York: Aldine De Gruyter.

Makridakis, S., & Hibbon, M. (2000). The M3-competition: Results, conclusions, and implications. *International Journal of Forecasting, 16*, 451–476.

Malinoswki, B. (1989). *A diary in the strict sense of the term*. Stanford, CA: Stanford University Press.

Malinowski, B. (1922). *Argonauts of the Western Pacific*. London: Routledge & Kegan Paul.

Manski, C. F. (1995). *Identification problems in the social sciences*. Cambridge, MA: Harvard University Press.

Manton, K. G., & XiLiang, G. (2003). *Variation in disability decline and Medicare expenditures*. Working Monograph, Center for Demographic Studies.

Manton, K. G., & Stallard, E. (1988). *Chronic disease modelling: Vol. 2. Mathematics in medicine*. New York: Oxford University Press.

Manton, K. G., Singer, B., & Woodbury, M. A. (1992). Some issues in the quantitative characterization of heterogeneous populations. In J. Trussell, R. Hankinson, & J. Tilton (Eds.), *Demographic application of event history analysis* (pp. 9–37). Oxford, UK: Clarendon.

Manton, K. G., Woodbury, M. A., & Tolley, H. D. (1994). *Statistical applications using fuzzy sets*. Wiley Series in Probability and Mathematical Statistics. New York: John Wiley.

Marcus, G., & Fischer, M. (1986). *Anthropology as cultural critique*. Chicago: University of Chicago Press.

Marcuse, H. (1964). *One dimensional man*. Boston: Beacon.

Marcuse, H. (1968). *One dimensional man: The ideology of industrial society*. London: Sphere.

Mare, R. D. (1994). Discrete-time bivariate hazards with unobserved heterogeneity: A partially observed contingency table approach. In P. V. Marsden (Ed.), *Sociological methodology 1984* (pp. 341–383). Cambridge, MA: Blackwell.

Markham, A. N. (1998). *Life online: Researching real experience in virtual space*. Walnut Creek, CA: AltaMira.

Marquardt, D. W. (1970). Generalized inverses, ridge regression, biased linear estimation, and nonlinear estimation. *Technometrics, 12*, 591–612.

Marquis, K. (1984). Record checks for sample surveys. In T. Jabine, E. Loftus, M. Straf et al. (Eds.), *Cognitive aspects of survey methodology: Building a bridge between disciplines*. Washington, DC: National Academy Press.

Marsh, C. (1982). *The survey method: The contribution of surveys to sociological explanation*. London: Allen & Unwin.

Marsh, C. (1988). *Exploring data: An introduction to data analysis for social scientists*. Cambridge, UK: Polity.

Marsh, L. C., & Cormier, D. R. (2001). *Spline regression models*. Thousand Oaks, CA: Sage.

Marshall, P. A. (1992). Research ethics in applied anthropology. *IRB: A Review of Human Subjects Research, 14*(6), 1–5.

Martens, H., & Naes, T. (1989). *Multivariate calibration*. London: Wiley.

Martin, J. A., Hamilton, B. E., Ventura, S. J., Menacker, F., & Park, M. M. (2002, February 12). *Births: Final data for 2000* (National Vital Statistics Report, Vol. 50, No. 5). Hyattsville, MD: National Center for Health Statistics.

Martin, K. (1998). *When a baby dies of SIDS: The parents' grief and searching for a reason*. Edmonton, Canada: Qual Institute Press.

Mason, J. (1996). *Qualitative researching*. London: Sage.

Mason, J. (2002). *Qualitative researching* (2nd ed.). London: Sage.

Mason, K. O., Mason, W. M., Winsborough, H. H., & Poole, W. K. (1973). Some methodological issues in the cohort analysis of archival data. *American Sociological Review, 38*, 242–258.

Mathiowetz, N., & McGonagle, K. (2000). An assessment of the current state of dependent interviewing in household surveys. *Journal of Official Statistics, 16*(4), 401–418.

Matza, D. (1969). *Becoming deviant*. Englewood Cliffs, NJ: Prentice-Hall.

Maxim, P. S. (1999). *Quantitative research methods in the social sciences*. New York: Oxford University Press.

Maxwell, J. A. (1996). *Qualitative research design.* Thousand Oaks, CA: Sage.

Maxwell, S. E., & Delaney, H. D. (1990). *Design experiments and analyzing data: A model comparison perspective.* Belmont, CA: Wadsworth.

May, R. M. (1976). Simple mathematical models with very complicated dynamics. *Nature, 26,* 459–467.

Maynard, D. W. (1984). *Inside plea bargaining: The language of negotiation.* New York: Plenum.

McAdams, D. P., & Constantian, C. A. (1983). Intimacy and affiliation motives in daily living: An experience sampling analysis. *Journal of Personality and Social Psychology, 45,* 851–861.

McCleary, R., & Hay, R. A., Jr. (1980). *Applied time series analysis for the social sciences.* London: Sage.

McCloskey, D. N. (1986). *The rhetoric of economics.* Madison: University of Wisconsin Press.

McCullagh, P. (1980). Regression models for ordinal data. *Journal of the Royal Statistical Society, Series B, 42,* 109–142.

McCullagh, P., & Nelder, J. A. (1989). *Generalized linear models* (2nd ed.). London: Chapman & Hall.

McCulloch, C. E., & Searle, S. R. (2001). *Generalized, linear and mixed models.* New York: John Wiley.

McCullough, B. D., & Vinod, H. D. (1997). The numerical reliability of econometric software. *Journal of Economic Literature, 37*(2), 633–665.

McDonald, J. F., & Moffitt, R. A. (1980). The uses of Tobit analysis. *Review of Economics and Statistics, 62,* 318–321.

McDowall, D., McCleary, R., Meidinger, E. E., & Hay, R. A., Jr. (1980). *Interrupted time series analysis.* Beverly Hills, CA: Sage.

McFadden, D. (1973). Conditional logit analysis of qualitative choice behavior. In P. Zarembka (Ed.), *Frontiers of econometrics* (pp. 105–142). New York: Academic Press.

McGraw, K. O., & Wong, S. P. (1996). Forming inferences about some intraclass correlation coefficients. *Psychological Methods, 1,* 30–46.

McGrew, W. (1972). *An ethological study of children's behavior.* New York: Academic Press.

McGuigan, J. (1992). *Cultural populism.* London: Routledge.

McGuinness, M., & Sapsford, R. (2002). *Middlesbrough Citizens' Advice Bureau: Report for 2001.* Middlesbrough, UK: University of Teesside, School of Social Sciences.

McIntosh, A. R., Bookstein, F. L., Haxby, J. V., & Grady, C. L. (1996). Spatial pattern analysis of functional brain images using partial least squares. *Neuroimage, 3,* 143–157.

McIver, J. P., & Carmines, E. G. (1980). *Unidimensional scaling.* Beverly Hills, CA: Sage.

McKean, K. (1987, January). The orderly pursuit of pure disorder. *Discover,* pp. 72–81.

McKelvey, R. D., & Zavoina, W. (1975). A statistical model for the analysis of ordinal level dependent variables. *Journal of Mathematical Sociology, 4,* 103–120.

McLachlan, G. J., & Basford, K. E. (1988). *Mixture models: Inference and application to clustering.* New York: Marcel Dekker.

McSweeny, A. J. (1978). Effects of response cost on the behavior of a million persons: Charging for directory assistance in Cincinnati. *Journal of Applied Behavior Analysis, 11,* 47–51.

Meacham, S. J. (1998). Threads of a new language: A response to Eisenhart's "On the subject of interpretive reviews." *Review of Educational Research, 68*(4), 401–407.

Mead, M. (1928). *Coming of age in Samoa.* New York: William Morrow.

Meadows, L. M., & Dodendorf, D. M. (1999). Data management and interpretation: Using computers to assist. In B. F. Crabtree & W. L. Miller (Eds.), *Doing qualitative research* (pp. 195–218). Thousand Oaks, CA: Sage.

Melton, G. B., Levine, R. J., Koocher, G. P., Rosenthal, R., & Thompson, W. C. (1988). Community consultation in socially sensitive research: Lessons from clinical trials on treatments for AIDS. *American Psychologist, 43,* 573–581.

Menard, S. (1995). *Applied logistic regression analysis* (Sage University Paper Series on Quantitative Applications in the Social Sciences, 07–106). Thousand Oaks, CA: Sage.

Menard, S. (2002). *Applied logistic regression analysis* (2nd ed., Sage University Paper Series on Quantitative Applications in the Social Sciences, 07–106). Thousand Oaks, CA: Sage.

Menard, S. (2002). *Longitudinal research* (2nd ed.). Thousand Oaks, CA: Sage.

Menard, S. (in press). *Logistic regression.* Thousand Oaks, CA: Sage.

Menard, S., & Elliott, D. S. (1990). Longitudinal and cross-sectional data collection and analysis in the study of crime and delinquency. *Justice Quarterly, 7,* 11–55.

Menchú, R. (1984). *I, Rigoberta Menchú: An Indian woman in Guatemala.* (Ed. and intro. Elisabeth Burgos-Debray, Trans. Ann Wright.) London: Verso.

Mendel, G. (1866). Versuche über Pflanzen-Hybriden [Experiments in plant hybridization]. In *Verhandlungen des natur-forschenden Vereins* [Proceedings of the Natural History Society]. Available in both the original German and the English translation at www.mendelweb.org

Merkle, D. M., & Edelman, M. (2002). Nonresponse in exit polls: A comprehensive analysis. In R. M. Groves, D. A. Dillman, J. L. Eltinge, & R. J. A. Little (Eds.), *Survey nonresponse* (pp. 243–258). New York: Wiley.

Merleau-Ponty, M. (1962). *Phenomenology of perception.* London: Routledge Kegan Paul.

Merton, R. K. (1949). *Social theory and social structure.* New York: Free Press.

Merton, R. K. (1968). *Social theory and social structure* (3rd ed.). New York: Free Press.

Merton, R. K. (1987). The focused interview and focus groups: Continuities and discontinuities. *Public Opinion Quarterly, 51,* 550–566.

Merton, R. K., & Kendall, P. L. (1946). The focused interview. *American Journal of Sociology, 51*(6), 514–557.

Merton, R. K., Fiske, M., & Kendall, P. L. (1990). *The focused interview: A manual of problems and procedures* (2nd ed.). New York: Free Press.

Messick, S. (1989). Meaning and values in test validation: The science and ethics of assessment. *Educational Researcher, 18*(2), 5–11.

Messick, S. (1989). Validity. In R. L. Linn (Ed.), *Educational measurement* (3rd ed., pp. 13–103). New York: American Council on Education.

Messick, S. (1992). Validity of test interpretation and use. In M. C. Alkin (Ed.), *Encyclopedia of educational research* (6th ed., p. 1487–1495). New York: Macmillan.

Messick, S. (1995). Validity of psychological assessment: Validation of inferences from persons' responses and performances as scientific inquiry into score meaning. *American Psychologist, 50*(9), 741–749.

Metropolis, N., Rosenbluth, A. W., Rosenbluth, M. N., Teller, A. H., & Teller, E. (1953). Equation of state calculation by fast computing machines. *Journal of Chemical Physics, 21,* 1087–1092.

Meulman, J. J. (1998). Book review of W. J. Krzanowski, & F. H. C. Marriott, *Multivariate Analysis. Part I. Distributions, Ordinations, and Inference,* London: Edward Arnold, 1994. *Journal of Classification, 15,* 287–293

Meulman, J. J., & Heiser, W. J. (2000). *Categories.* Chicago: SPSS.

Michel, Y., & Haight, B. K. (1996). Using the Solomon four design. *Nursing Research, 45*(6), 367–369.

Miles, M. B., & Huberman, A. M. (1994). *Qualitative data analysis* (2nd ed.). Thousand Oaks, CA: Sage.

Milgram, S. (1963). Behavioral study of obedience. *Journal of Abnormal and Social Psychology, 67,* 371–378.

Milgram, S. (1974). *Obedience to authority.* London: Tavistock.

Milgram, S. (1974). *Obedience to authority: An experimental view.* New York: Harper & Row.

Mill, J. S. (1947). *A system of logic.* London: Longman, Green. (Originally published in 1879)

Mill, J. S. (1956). *A system of logic, ratiocinative and inductive.* London: Longmans, Green & Company. (Original work published 1843)

Mill, J. S. (1973). *A system of logic.* Toronto: University of Toronto Press. (Original work published 1865)

Mill, J. S. (1974). *Collected works of John Stuart Mill: Vol. 8. A system of logic* (Books 4–6). Toronto: University of Toronto Press.

Millar, A., Simeone, R. S., & Carnevale, J. T. (2001). Logic models: A system tool for performance management. *Evaluation and Program Planning, 24,* 73–81.

Miller, A. G. (1986). *The obedience experiments: A case study of controversy in social science.* New York: Praeger.

Miller, A. G. (1995). Constructions of the obedience experiments: A focus upon domains of relevance. *Journal of Social Issues, 51,* 33–53.

Miller, A. J. (1990). *Subset selection in regression.* New York: Chapman Hall.

Miller, D. (1998). Writing and retelling multiple ethnographic tales of a soup kitchen for the homeless. *Qualitative Inquiry, 4,* 469–492.

Miller, L., Rustin, M., Rustin, M., & Shuttleworth, J. (1989). *Closely observed infants.* London: Duckworth.

Miller, R. G. (1981). *Simultaneous statistical inference* (2nd ed.). New York: Springer-Verlag.

Miller, R. W. (1987). *Fact and method: Explanation, confirmation and reality in the natural and the social sciences.* Princeton, NJ: Princeton University Press.

Miller, W. L., & Crabtree, B. F. (1999). Clinical research: A multimethod typology and qualitative roadmap. In B. F. Crabtree & W. L. Miller (Eds.), *Doing qualitative research* (2nd ed., pp. 3–32). Thousand Oaks, CA: Sage.

Millett, K. (1970). *Sexual politics.* Garden City, NY: Doubleday.

Milligan, G. W. (1979). Ultrametric hierarchical clustering algorithms. *Psychometrika, 44*(3), 343–346.

Milliken, G. A., & Johnson, D. A. (1984). *Analysis of messy data: Vol. 1. Designed experiments.* New York: Van Nostrand Reinhold.

Milliken, G. A., & Johnson, D. E. (1992). *Analysis of messy data: Vol. 1. Designed experiments.* London: Chapman & Hall.

Mills, C. W. (1959). *The sociological imagination.* New York: Oxford University Press.

Mills, T. C. (1990). *Time series techniques for economists.* Cambridge, UK: Cambridge University Press.

Millward, L. J. (2000). Focus groups. In G. M. Breakwell, C. Fife-Schaw, & S. Hammond (Eds.), *Research methods in psychology* (2nd ed., pp. 303–324). London: Sage.

Milner, A. (1996). *Literature, culture and society.* London: UCL Press.

Mincer, J. (1958). Investment in human capital and personal income distribution. *Journal of Political Economy, 66,* 281–302.

Mincer, J. (1974). *Schooling, experience and earnings.* New York: Columbia University Press.

Mishler, E. G. (1986). *Research interviewing: Context and narrative.* Cambridge, MA: Harvard University Press.

Mishler, E. G. (1991). Representing discourse: The rhetoric of transcription. *Journal of Narrative and Life History, 1*(4), 255–280.

Mishler, E. G. (1995). Models of narrative analysis: A typology. *Journal of Narrative and Life History, 5*(2), 87–123.

Mitchell, J. (1983). Case and situation analysis. *Sociological Review, 31*(2), 186–211.

Mitchell, J. (1986). Measurement scales and statistics: A clash of paradigms. *Psychological Bulletin, 100,* 398–407.

Mittelhammer, R. C., Judge, G. G, & Miller, D. J. (2000). *Econometric foundations.* New York: Cambridge University Press.

Mohr, D. C., Likosky, W., Bertagnolli, A., Goodkin, D. E., Van der Wende, J., Dwyer, P., et al. (2000). Telephone administered cognitive-behavioral therapy for the treatment of depressive symptoms in multiple sclerosis. *Journal of Consulting and Clinical Psychology, 68*(2), 356–361.

Mohr, L. B. (1990). *Understanding significance testing* (Sage University Paper Series on Quantitative Applications in the Social Sciences, 07–073). Newbury Park, CA: Sage.

Monge, P., & Contractor, N. (2003). *Theories of communication networks.* New York: Oxford University Press.

Monk-Turner, E., & Turner, C. G. (2001). Sex differentials in the South Korean labour market. *Feminist Economics, 7*(1), 63–78.

Mood, A. M., & Graybill, F. A. (1963). *Introduction to the theory of statistics* (2nd ed.). New York: McGraw-Hill.

Mooney, C. Z. (1997). *Monte Carlo simulation.* Thousand Oaks, CA: Sage.

Mooney, C. Z., & Duval, R. D. (1993). *Bootstrapping: A nonparametric approach to statistical inference.* Thousand Oaks, CA: Sage.

Moore, D. S. (1997). *Statistics: Concepts and controversies* (4th ed.). New York: W. H. Freeman.

Moore, D. S., & McCabe, G. P. (1998). *Introduction to the practice of statistics.* New York: W. H. Freeman.

Moore, D. W. (1999, June/July). Daily tracking polls: Too much "noise" or revealed insights? *Public Perspective,* pp. 27–31.

Moorman, R. H., & Podsakoff, P. M. (1992). A meta-analytic review and empirical test of the potential confounding effects of social desirability response sets in organizational behaviour research. *Journal of Occupational and Organizational Psychology, 65,* 131–149.

Moreno, L. (1994). Frailty selection in bivariate survival models: A cautionary note. *Mathematical Population Studies, 4,* 225–233.

Morgan, D. L. (1988). *Focus groups as qualitative research.* Newbury Park, CA: Sage.

Morgan, D. L. (1993). *Successful focus groups: Advancing the state of the art.* London: Sage.

Morgan, D. L. (1998). Practical strategies for combining qualitative and quantitative methods: Applications for health research. *Qualitative Health Research, 8,* 362–376.

Morgan, D. L., & Krueger R. A. (Eds.). (1998). *Focus group kit.* Thousand Oaks, CA: Sage.

Morley, D. (1980). *The "Nationwide" audience.* London: British Film Institute.

Morley, D. (1986). *Family television—Cultural power and domestic leisure.* London: British Film Institute.

Morris, M., & Western, B. (1999). Inequality in earnings at the close of the 20th century. *Annual Review of Sociology, 25,* 623–657.

Morrison, D. E., & Henkel, R. (Eds.). (1970). *The significance test controversy.* Chicago: Aldine.

Morrow, R. A. (with Brown, D. D.). (1994). *Critical theory and methodology.* London: Sage.

Morse, J. M. (1989). Strategies for sampling. In J. Morse (Ed.), *Qualitative nursing research: A contemporary dialogue* (pp. 117–131). Rockville, MD: Aspen.

Morse, J. M. (1997). Considering theory derived from qualitative research. In J. Morse (Ed.), *Completing a qualitative project: Details and dialogue* (pp. 2163–2188). Thousand Oaks, CA: Sage.

Morse, J. M., & Richards, L. (2002). *Read me first for a user's guide to qualitative methods.* Thousand Oaks, CA: Sage.

Morse, J. M., Swanson, J. M., & Kuzel, A. J. (Eds.). (2001). *The nature of qualitative evidence.* Thousand Oaks, CA: Sage.

Morton, Rebecca B. (2000). *Methods and models: A guide to the empirical analysis of formal models in political science.* New York: Cambridge University Press.

Moser, C. A., & Kalton, G. (1971). *Survey methods in social investigation* (2nd ed.). Aldershot, UK: Gower.

Mosteller, F., & Tukey, J. W. (1977). *Data analysis and regression: A second course in statistics.* Reading, MA: Addison-Wesley.

Mounce, H. O. (1997). *The two pragmatisms: From Peirce to Rorty.* London: Routledge and Kegan Paul.

Moustakas, C. (1990). *Heuristic research: Design, methodology, and applications.* Newbury Park, CA: Sage.

Moustakas, C. (1994). *Phenomenological research methods.* Thousand Oaks, CA: Sage.

Moyé, L. A. (2000). *Statistical reasoning in medicine.* New York Springer-Verlag.

Mruck, K., Corti, L., Kluge, S. & Opitz, D. (Eds.). (2000, December). Text archive: Re-analysis. *Forum Qualitative Sozialforschung* [Forum: Qualitative Social Research] [Online Journal], *1*(3). Available: http://qualitative-research.net/fqs/fqs-eng.htm

Muchinsky, P. M. (1996). The correction for attenuation. *Educational and Psychological Measurement, 56,* 63–75.

Mueller, D. J. (1986). *Measuring social attitudes: A handbook for researchers and practitioners.* New York: Teachers College, Columbia University.

Mueller, R. O. (1996). *Basic principles of structural equation modeling: An introduction to LISREL and EQS.* New York: Springer.

Mulaik, S. A. (1972). *The foundations of factor analysis.* New York: McGraw-Hill.

Mulaik, S. A. (1987). A brief history of the philosophical foundations of exploratory factor analysis. *Multivariate Behavioral Research, 22,* 267–305.

Murphy, M. (1990). Minimising attrition in longitudinal studies: Means or end? In D. Magnusson & L. R. Bergman (Eds.), *Data quality in longitudinal research* (pp. 148–156). Cambridge, UK: Cambridge University Press.

Murphy, M. K., Black, N. A., Lamping, D. L., McKee, C. M., Sanderson, C. F. B., Ashkam, J., & Marteau, T. (1998). Consensus development methods, and their use in clinical guideline development [Entire issue]. *Health Technology Assessment, 2*(3).

Musch, J., & Reips, U. (2000). A brief history of Web experimenting. In M. H. Birnbaum (Ed.), *Psychological experiments on the Internet* (pp. 61–88). San Diego, CA: Academic Press.

Muthén, B. (1984). A general structural equation model with dichotomous, ordered categorical, and continuous latent variable indicators. *Psychometrika, 49,* 115–132.

Muthén, B. O. (2002). Beyond SEM: General latent variable modeling. *Behaviormetrika, 29*(1), 81–117.

Muthén, B., Kaplan, D., & Hollis, M. (1987). On structural equation modeling with data that are not missing completely at random. *Psychometrika, 51,* 431–462.

Myers, J. L., & Well, A. D. (1995). *Research design and statistical analysis.* Hillsdale, NJ: Lawrence Erlbaum.

Naes, T., & Risvik, E. (Eds.). (1996). *Multivariate analysis of data in sensory science.* New York: Elsevier.

Nagel, E. (1979). *The structure of science: Problems in the logic of scientific explanation.* Indianapolis, IN: Hackett.

Nagler, J. (1995). Coding style and good computing practices. *Political Methodologist, 6,* 2–8.

Namboodiri, K. (1984). *Matrix algebra: An introduction.* Beverly Hills, CA: Sage.

Narayan, K. (1993). How native is the "native" anthropologist? *American Anthropologist, 95,* 671–686.

National Center for Health Statistics. (2003). *United States life tables, 2000.* Retrieved from www.cdc.gov/nchs/data/lt2000.pdf.

National Commission for the Protection of Human Subjects of Biomedical and Behavioral Research. (1979). *The Belmont Report: Ethical principles and guidelines for the protection of human subjects of research* (DHEW Publication No. (OS) 78–0012). Washington, DC: Government Printing Office.

National Institutes of Health. (2003, July 22). *Certificates of confidentiality.* Retrieved from http://grants1.nih.gov/grants/policy/coc/index.htm

National Research Council. (2001). *The 2000 census: Interim assessment.* Washington, DC: National Academy Press.

Naughton, J. (1984). *Soft systems analysis: An introductory guide.* Milton Keynes, UK: Open University Press.

Neisser, U. (1976). *Cognition and reality: Principles and implications of cognitive psychology.* San Francisco: W. H. Freeman.

Nelder, J. A., & Lane, P. W. (1995). The computer analysis of factorial experiments: In memoriam—Frank Yates. *The American Statistician, 49,* 382–385.

Nelder, J. A., & Wedderburn, R. W. M. (1972). Generalized linear models. *Journal of the Royal Statistical Society, Series A, 135,* 370–384.

Nelson, J. S., Megill, A., & McCloskey, D. N. (Eds.). (1987). *The rhetoric of the human sciences.* Madison: University of Wisconsin Press.

Nesbary, D. K. (2000). *Survey research and the World Wide Web.* Boston, MA: Allyn and Bacon.

Neter, J., Kutner, M. H., Nachtsheim, C. J., & Wasserman, W. (1996). *Applied linear regression models* (3rd ed.). Chicago: Irwin.

Neter, J., Wasseman, W., & Kutner, M. H. (1989). *Applied linear regression models* (2nd ed.). Boston: Irwin.

Neter, J., Wasserman, W., & Kutner, M. (1990). *Applied linear statistical models* (3rd ed.). Homewood, IL: Irwin.

Nevo, B. (1985). Face validity revisited. *Journal of Educational Measurement, 22,* 287–293.

New, C. (1996). *Agency, health and social survival.* London: Taylor & Francis.

Newbold, P., & Bos, T. (1985). *Stochastic parameter regression models* (Sage University Paper Series on Quantitative Applications in the Social Sciences, 07–051). Beverly Hills, CA: Sage.

Newbold, P., & Bos, T. (1994). *Introductory business forecasting* (2nd ed.). Cincinnati, OH: South-Western.

Newby, H. (1977). In the field: Reflections on a study of Suffolk farm workers. In C. Bell & H. Newby (Eds.), *Doing sociological research* (pp. 108–129). London: Allen and Unwin.

Newell, A., & Simon, H. A. (1961). Computer simulation of human thinking. *Science, 134,* 2011–2017.

Newell, A., & Simon, H. A. (1971). *Human problem solving.* Englewood Cliffs, NJ: Prentice Hall.

Newell, R. W. (1986). *Objectivity, empiricism and truth.* London: Routledge and Kegan Paul.

Newey, W. K., & West, K. D. (1987). A simple, positive semi-definite, heteroskedasticity and autocorrelation consistent covariance matrix. *Econometrica, 55,* 703–708.

Newton, I. (1952). *Mathematical principles of natural philosophy.* Chicago: Britannica. (Originally published in 1686)

Newton, R. R., & Rudestam, K. E. (1999). *Your statistical consultant: Answers to your data analysis questions.* Thousand Oaks, CA: Sage.

NHS Centre for Reviews and Dissemination. (2001). *Undertaking systematic reviews of research on effectiveness: CRD's guidance for those carrying out or commissioning reviews* (Report number 4, 2nd ed.). York, UK: CRD.

Nicholson, L. (Ed.). (1990). *Feminism/postmodernism.* New York: Routledge Kegan Paul.

Nida, E. A. (1975). *Componential analysis of meaning: An introduction to semantic structures.* The Hague, The Netherlands: Mouton.

Nishisato, S. (1980). *Analysis of categorical data: Dual scaling and its applications.* Toronto: University of Toronto Press.

Nishisato, S. (1994). *Elements of dual scaling: An introduction to practical data analysis.* Hillsdale, N.J.: Lawrence Erlbaum.

Nishisato, S. (1996). Gleaning in the field of dual scaling. *Psychometrika, 61,* 559–599.

Nishisato, S., & Clavel, J. G. (2003). A note on between-set distances in dual scaling and correspondence analysis. *Behaviormetrika, 30,* 87–98.

NIST/SEMATECH. (2003). *E-handbook of statistical methods.* Retrieved from http://www.itl.nist.gov/div898/handbook/eda

Noblit, G. W., & Hare, R. D. (1988). *Meta-ethnography: Synthesizing qualitative studies.* Newbury Park, CA: Sage.

Nocedal, J., & Wright, S. (1999). *Numerical optimization.* New York: Springer-Verlag.

Noldus, L. P. J. J., Trienes, R. J. H., Hendriksen, A. H. M., Jansen, H., & Jansen, R. G. (2000). The Observer

Video-Pro: New software for the collection, management, and presentation of time-structured data from videotapes and digital media files. *Behavior Research Methods, Instruments & Computers, 32,* 197–206.

Norpoth, H. (1995). Is Clinton doomed? An early forecast for 1996. *Political Science & Politics, 27,* 201–206.

Norton, H. W. (1939). The 7 × 7 squares. *Annals of Eugenics, 9,* 269–307.

Norusis, M. (1990). *SPSS/PC+ Statistics 4.0.* Chicago: SPSS.

Norusis, M. J. (1990). *SPSS base system user's guide.* Chicago: SPSS.

Nosek, B. A., Banaji, M. R., & Greenwald, A. G. (2002). E-research: Ethics, security, design, and control in psychological research on the Internet. *Journal of Social Issues, 58,* 161–176.

Nowak, A., & Latané, B. (1994). Simulating the emergence of social order from individual behaviour. In N. Gilbert & J. Doran (Eds.), *Simulating societies: The computer simulation of social phenomena* (pp. 63–84). London: UCL.

Noymer, A. (2001). The transmission and persistence of "urban legends": Sociological application of age-structured epidemic models. *Journal of Mathematical Sociology, 25,* 299–323.

Nunnally, J. C. (1978). *Psychometric theory* (2nd ed.). New York: McGraw-Hill.

Nunnally, J. C., & Bernstein, I. H. (1994). *Psychometric theory* (3rd ed.). New York: McGraw-Hill.

Nutley, S., & Webb, J. (2000). Evidence and the policy process. In H. Davies, S. Nutley, & P. Smith (Eds.), *What works? Evidence-based policy and practice in public services* (pp. 13–41). Bristol, UK: Policy Press.

O'Brien, R. M. (2000). Age-period-cohort-characteristic models. *Social Science Research, 29,* 123–139.

O'Hear, A. (1989). *An introduction to the philosophy of science.* Oxford, UK: Clarendon.

O'Hear, A. (Ed.). (1996). *Verstehen and humane understanding.* Supplement to *Philosophy,* Royal Institute of Philosophy Supplement 41. Cambridge, UK: Cambridge University Press.

O'Rourke, D., & Blair, J. (1983). Improving random respondent selection in telephone surveys. *Journal of Marketing Research, 20,* 428–432.

Oakley, A. (2000). *Experiments in knowing: Gender and method in the social sciences.* Cambridge, UK: Polity.

Ohnuki-Tierney, E. (1984). "Native" anthropologists. *American Ethnologist, 11,* 584–586.

Oksenberg, L., Cannell, C., & Kalton, G. (1991). New strategies for pretesting survey questions. *Journal of Official Statistics, 7*(3), 349–365.

Olmsted, P., & Weikart, D. P. (Eds.). (1994). *Families speak: Early childhood care and education in 11 countries.* Ypsilanti, MI: High/Scope Press.

Olsen W. K. (1993) Random samples and repeat surveys in South India. In S. Devereux & J. Hoddinott (Eds.) *Fieldwork in Developing Countries,* (pp. 57–72). Boulder, CO: Lynne Rienner.

Olsen, W. K. (1999). *Path analysis for the study of farming and micro-enterprise* (Bradford Development Paper No. 3). Bradford, UK:University of Bradford, Development and Project Planning Centre.

Olsen, W. K., Warde, A., & Martens, L. (2000). Social differentiation and the market for eating out in the UK. *International Journal of Hospitality Management, 19*(2), 173–190.

Oneal, J. R., & Russett, B. (1997). The classical liberals were right: Democracy, interdependence, and conflict, 1950–1985. *International Studies Quarterly, 41,* 267–294.

Orne, M. T. (1962). On the social psychology of the psychological experiment: With particular reference to demand characteristics and their implications. *American Psychologist, 17,* 776–783.

Orne, M. T. (1969). Demand characteristics and the concept of quasi-controls. In R. Rosenthal & R. L. Rosnow (Eds.), *Artifact in behavioral research* (pp. 143–179). New York: Academic Press.

Orr, L. L. (1999). *Social experiments: Evaluating public programs with experimental methods.* Thousand Oaks, CA: Sage.

Orwin, R. (1983). A fail-safe N for effect size in meta-analysis. *Journal of Educational Statistics, 8,* 157–159.

Osburn, H. G. (2000). Coefficient alpha and related internal consistency reliability coefficients. *Psychological Methods, 5,* 343–355.

Osgood, C. E. (1952). The nature of and measurement of meaning. *Psychological Bulletin, 49,* 197–237.

Osgood, C. E., & Tzeng, O. C. S. (Eds.). (1990). *Language, meaning, and culture: The selected papers of C. E. Osgood.* New York: Praeger.

Osgood, C. E., Suci, C. J., & Tannenbaum, P. H. (1957). *The measurement of meaning.* Urbana: University of Illinois Press.

Ostrom, C. W., Jr. (1990). *Time series analysis.* Thousand Oaks, CA: Sage.

Otis, D. L., Burnham, K. P., White, G. C., & Anderson, D. R. (1978). Statistical inference from capture data on closed animal populations. *Wildlife Monographs, 62,* 1–135.

Outhwaite, W. (1975). *Understanding social life: The method called verstehen.* London: Allen & Unwin.

Outhwaite, W. (1987). *New philosophies of social science: Realism, hermeneutics and critical theory.* London: Macmillan.

Paccagnella, L. (1997). Getting the seats of your pants dirty: Strategies for ethnographic research on virtual communities. *Journal of Computer Mediated Communication, 3*(1). Retrieved from http://www.ascusc.org/jcmc/vol3/issue1/paccagnella.html

Paechter, C. (1996). Power, knowledge and the confessional in qualitative research. *Discourse: Studies in the Politics of Education, 17*(1), 75–84.

Page, B. I., & Shapiro, R. Y. (1992). *The rational public.* Chicago: University of Chicago Press.

Page, S. (2000). The lost art of unobtrusive measures. *Journal of Applied Social Psychology, 30*(10), 2126–2128.

Pagès, J., & Tenenhaus, M. (2001). Multiple factor analysis combined with PLS path modeling: Application to the analysis of relationships between physicochemical variables, sensory profiles and hedonic judgments. *Chemometrics and Intelligent Laboratory Systems, 58,* 261–273.

Palmer, R. E. (1969). *Hermeneutics: Interpretation theory of Schleiermacher, Dilthey, Heidegger, and Gadamer.* Evanston, IL: Northwestern University Press.

Pampel, F. C. (2000). *Logistic regression: A primer.* Thousand Oaks, CA: Sage.

Pankratz, L. (1979). Symptom validity testing and symptom retraining: Procedures for the assessment and treatment of functional sensory deficits. *Journal of Consulting and Clinical Psychology, 47,* 409–410.

Papineau, D. (1993). *Philosophical naturalism.* Oxford, UK: Basil Blackwell.

Park, A., & Jowell, R. (1997). *Consistencies and differences in a cross-national survey.* London: SCPR.

Parker, I. (1988). Deconstructing accounts. In C. Antaki (Ed.), *Analysing everyday explanation: A casebook of methods* (pp. 184–198). London: Sage.

Parkin, F. (1973). *Class inequality and political order.* London: Paladin.

Parkinson, B., & Manstead, A. S. R. (1993). Making sense of emotion in stories and social life. *Cognition and Emotion, 7,* 295–323.

Parsons, T. (1968). Émile Durkheim. In D. L. Sills (Ed.), *International encyclopedia of the social sciences, Vol. 4.* New York: Macmillan.

Parsons, T. (1968). *The structure of social action* (3rd ed.). New York: Free Press.

Passmore, J. (1967). Logical positivism. In P. Edwards (Ed.), *The encyclopedia of philosophy* (Vol. 5, pp. 52–57). New York: Macmillan.

Paterson, B. L., Thorne, S. E., Canam, C., & Jillings, C. (2001). *Meta-study of qualitative health research: A practical guide to meta-analysis and meta-synthesis.* Thousand Oaks, CA: Sage.

Patrick, C. J. (1994). Emotion and psychopathy: Startling new insights. *Psychophysiology, 31,* 415–428.

Pattison, P. E. (1993). *Algebraic models for social networks.* New York: Cambridge University Press.

Patton, M. Q. (1990). *Qualitative evaluation and research methods* (2nd ed.). Newbury Park, CA: Sage.

Patton, M. Q. (1997). *Utilization-focused evaluation: The new century text* (3rd ed.). Thousand Oaks, CA: Sage.

Patton, M. Q. (1999). *Grand Canyon celebration: A father-son journey of discovery.* Amherst, NY: Prometheus.

Patton, M. Q. (2002). *Qualitative research and evaluation methods* (3rd ed.). Thousand Oaks, CA: Sage.

Paulhus, D. L. (1984). Two-component models of socially desirable responding. *Journal of Personality and Social Psychology, 46,* 598–609.

Pawson, R., & Tilley, N. (1997). *Realistic evaluation.* London: Sage.

Pearl, J. (2000). *Causality: Models, reasoning, and inference.* Cambridge, UK: Cambridge University Press.

Pearson, K. (1901). On lines and planes of closest fit to systems of points in space. *Philosophical Magazine, 6*(2), 559–572.

Pearson, K. (1904). Report on certain enteric fever inoculation statistics. *British Medical Journal, 3,* 1243–1246.

Peat, J., Mellis, C., Williams, K., & Xuan W. (2002). *Health science research: A handbook of quantitative methods.* London: Sage.

Pedhazer, E. J., & Schmelkin, L. P. (1991). *Measurement, design, and analysis: An integrated approach.* Hillsdale, NJ: Lawrence Erlbaum.

Pedhazur, E. J. (1982). *Multiple regression in behavioral research* (2nd ed.). New York: Holt, Rinehart and Winston.

Pedhazur, E. J. (1997). *Multiple regression in behavioral research* (3rd ed.). New York: Wadsworth.

Peirce, C. S. (1931–1958). *Collected papers of Charles Sanders Peirce.* Cambridge, MA: Harvard University Press.

Pelusi, J. (1997). The lived experience of surviving breast cancer. *Oncology Nursing Forum, 24*(8), 1343–1353.

Perks, R., & Thomson, A. (Eds.). (1998). *The oral history reader.* London: Routledge.

Peterson, R. A. (1994). A meta-analysis of Cronbach's coefficient alpha. *Journal of Consumer Research, 21,* 381–391.

Pettofrezzo, A. J. (1978). *Matrices and transformations.* New York: Dover.

Pfungst, O. (1965). *Clever Hans: The horse of Mr. von Osten.* New York: Holt, Rinehart, & Winston. (Original work published 1911)

Phillips, D. (1976). *Holistic thought in social science.* Stanford, CA: Stanford University Press.

Phillips, N., & Brown, J. (1993). Analyzing communication in and around organizations: A critical hermeneutic approach. *Academy of Management Journal, 36*(6), 1547–1576.

Phillips, P. C. B. (1991). Optimal inference in cointegrated systems. *Econometrica, 59,* 283–306.

Piaget, J. (1929). *The child's conception of the world.* New York: Harcourt, Brace Jovanovich.

Piaget, J. (1955). *The construction of reality in the child.* New York: Routledge Kegan Paul. (Original work published 1937)

Pickering, M. (2001). *Stereotyping: The politics of representation.* Basingstoke, UK: Palgrave.

Pierce, J. L., Gardner, D. G., Cummings, L. L., & Dunham, R. B. (1989). Organization-based self-esteem: Construct definition, measurement, and validation. *Academy of Management Journal, 32,* 622–648.

Pierson, P. (2000). Increasing returns, path dependence, and the study of politics. *American Political Science Review, 94,* 251–267.

Pike, K. L. (1967). *Language in relation to a unified theory of the structure of human behavior* (2nd ed.). The Hague: Mouton. (Original work published 1954)

Pindyck, R. S., & Rubinfeld, D. L. (1991). *Econometric models and economic forecasts* (3rd ed.). New York: McGraw-Hill.

Pindyck, R. S., & Rubinfeld, D. L. (1998). *Econometric models and economic forecasts* (4th ed.). New York: McGraw-Hill.

Pink, S. (2001). *Doing visual ethnography: Images, media and representation in research.* London: Sage.

Plackett, R. L. (1972). The discovery of the method of least squares. *Biometrika, 59,* 239–251.

Plake, B. S., & Impara, J. C. (Eds.). (2001). *The fourteenth mental measurements yearbook.* Lincoln, NE: Buros Institute of Mental Measurements.

Platt, J. (2002). The history of the interview. In J. F. Gubrium & J. A. Holstein (Eds.), *Handbook of interview research: Context and method* (pp. 33–54). Thousand Oaks, CA: Sage.

Plessy v. Ferguson, 163 U.S. 537 (1896).

Plewis, I. (1985). *Analysing change: Measurement and exploration using longitudinal data.* Chichester, UK: Wiley.

Plummer, K. (2001). *Documents of life 2: An invitation to a critical humanism.* London: Sage.

Poland, B. (2001). Transcription quality. In J. Gubrium & J. Holstein (Eds.), *Handbook of interview research.* Thousand Oaks, CA: Sage.

Poland, B. D. (1995). Transcript quality as an aspect of rigor in qualitative research. *Qualitative Inquiry, 1*(3), 290–310.

Pollock, K. H., Nichols, J. D., Brownie, C., & Hines, J. E. (1990). Statistical inference for capture-recapture experiments. *Wildlife Monographs, 107,* 1–97.

Pope, C., & Mayes, N. (1995). Qualitative research: Reaching the parts other methods cannot reach: An introduction to qualitative methods in health and health services research. *British Medical Journal, 311,* 42–45.

Popkin, S. L. (1991). *The reasoning voter.* Chicago: University of Chicago Press.

Popper, K. (1959). *The logic of scientific discovery.* London: Hutchinson.

Popper, K. (1965). *Conjectures and refutations: The growth of scientific knowledge* (2nd ed.). New York: Basic Books.

Popper, K. (1966). *The open society and its enemies* (5th ed., Vol. 1). London: Routledge. (Original work published 1945)

Popper, K. (1972). *Objective knowledge: An evolutionary approach.* Oxford, UK: Clarendon.

Popper, K. R. (1957). *The poverty of historicism.* Boston: Beacon.

Popper, K. R. (1959). *The logic of scientific discovery.* London: Hutchinson.

Popper, K. R. (1961). *The poverty of historicism.* London: Routledge & Kegan Paul.

Popper, K. R. (1963). *Conjectures and refutations: The growth of scientific knowledge.* New York: Basic Books.

Popper, K. R. (1965). *The logic of scientific discovery.* New York: Harper & Row.

Popper, K. R. (1972). *Conjectures and refutation.* London: Routledge & Kegan Paul.

Popper, K. E. (1986). *The poverty of historicism.* London: ARK.

Porter, S. (1993). Critical realist ethnography: The case of racism and professionalism in a medical setting. *Sociology, 27,* 591–609.

Potter, J. (1996). *Representing reality: Discourse, rhetoric and social construction.* London: Sage.

Potter, J., & Wetherell, M. (1987). *Discourse and social psychology: Beyond attitudes and behaviour.* London: Sage.

Poundstone, W. (1988). *Labyrinths of reason: Paradoxes, puzzles and the frailty of knowledge.* New York: Anchor/Doubleday.

Poundstone, W. (1992). *Prisoner's dilemma.* New York: Doubleday.

Power, M. (1990). Modernism, postmodernism and organisation. In J. Hassard & D. Pym (Eds.), *The theory and philosophy of organisations.* London: Routledge Kegan Paul.

Powers, D. A., & Xie, Y. (2000). *Statistical methods for categorical data analysis.* San Diego: Academic Press.

Prais, S. J., & Winsten, C. B. (1954). *Trend estimators and serial correlation.* Chicago: Cowles Commission.

Prendergast, C. (1995). *Cultural materialism: On Raymond Williams.* Minneapolis: University of Minnesota Press.

Prentice, R. L., & Zhao, L. P. (1991). Estimating equations for parameters in mean and covariances of multivariate discrete and continuous responses. *Biometrics, 47,* 825–839.

Preston, S. H., & Coale, A. J. (1982). Age structure, growth, attrition and accession: A new synthesis. *Population Index, 48*(2), 217–259.

Preston, S. H., Heuveline, P., & Guillot, M. (2001). *Demography: Measuring and modeling population processes.* Oxford, UK: Basil Blackwell.

Price, L. J. (1989). In the shadow of biomedicine: Self-medication in two Ecuadorian pharmacies. *Social Science and Medicine, 28,* 905–915.

Price, L. J. (2002). Carrying out a structured observation. In M. V. Angrosino (Ed.), *Doing cultural anthropology* (pp. 107–114). Prospect Heights, IL: Waveland.

Price, V. (1992). *Public opinion.* Newbury Park, CA: Sage.

Proctor, C. H. (1970). A probabilistic formulation and statistical analysis of Guttman scaling. *Psychometrika, 35,* 73–78.

Przeworski, A., & Teune, H. (1970). *The logic of comparative social inquiry.* New York: John Wiley.

Quenouille, M. (1949). Approximate tests of correlation in time series. *Journal of the Royal Statistical Society, Series B, 11,* 18–84.

Rabe-Hesketh, S., Pickles, A., & Skrondal, A. (2001). *GLLAMM manual technical report 2001/01.* London: King's College, University of London, Department of Biostatistics and Computing, Institute of Psychiatry. Retrieved from www.iop.kcl.ac.uk/IoP/Departments/BioComp/programs/manual.pdf

Rachlin, H. (2000). *The science of self-control.* Cambridge, MA: Harvard University Press.

Radest, H. B. (1996). *Humanism with a human face: Intimacy and the enlightenment.* London: Praeger.

Radley, A., & Taylor, D. (2003). Remembering one's stay in hospital: A study in recovery, photography and forgetting.

Health: An Interdisciplinary Journal for the Social Study of Health, Illness and Medicine, 7(2), 129–159.

Rae, D. W., & Yates, D. (1981). *Equalities.* Cambridge, MA: Harvard University Press.

Raftery, A. E. (1996). Bayesian model selection in social research. In P. V. Marsden (Ed.), *Sociological methodology* (Vol. 25, pp. 111–163). Oxford, UK: Basil Blackwell.

Raftery, A. E. (1996). Hypothesis testing and model selection. In W. R. Gilks, S. Richardson, & D. J. Spiegelhalter (Eds.), *Markov chain Monte Carlo in practice* (pp. 163–187). London: Chapman and Hall.

Raghunathan, T. E., & Grizzle, J. E. (1995). A split questionnaire survey design. *Journal of the American Statistical Association, 90,* 54–63.

Ragin, C. C. (1987). *The comparative method: Moving beyond qualitative and quantitative strategies.* Berkeley: University of California Press.

Ragin, C. C. (1994). *Constructing social research.* Thousand Oaks, CA: Pine Forge Press.

Ragin, C. C. (2000). *Fuzzy-set social science.* Chicago: University of Chicago Press.

Ragin, C. C., & Becker, H. S. (1992). *What is a case? Exploring the foundations of social inquiry.* New York: Cambridge University Press.

Ramazanoglu, C., with Holland, J. (2002). *Feminist methodology.* London: Sage.

Ramsay, J. O. (1977). Maximum likelihood estimation in MDS. *Psychometrika, 42,* 241–266.

Ramsey, F. P. (1960). Truth and probability. In R. B. Braithwaite (Ed.), *The foundations of mathematics and other logical essays.* New York: Harcourt Brace.

Random House. (1997). *Random House Webster's college dictionary.* New York: Author.

Rao, P., & Griliches, Z. (1969). Small-sample properties of several two-stage regression methods in the context of auto-correlated errors. *Journal of the American Statistical Association, 64,* 253–272.

Rapoport, A., & Chammah, A. M. (1965). *Prisoner's dilemma.* Ann Arbor: University of Michigan Press.

Rässler, S. (2002). Statistical matching: A frequentist theory, practical applications, and alternative Bayesian approaches. *Lecture Notes in Statistics, 168.* New York: Springer.

Raudenbush, S. W., & Bryk, A. S. (1988). Methodological advances in analyzing the effects of schools and classrooms on student learning. *Review of Research in Education, 15,* 423–476.

Raudenbush, S. W., & Bryk, A. S. (2002). *Hierarchical linear models: Applications and data analysis methods* (2nd ed.). Thousand Oaks, CA: Sage.

Rawlings, J. O., Pantula, S. G., & Dickey, D. A. (1999) *Applied regression analysis: A research tool.* New York: Springer.

Reason, R., & Brabury, H. (Eds.). (2001). *Handbook of action research: Participative inquiry and practice.* London: Sage.

Redington, M., & Chater, N. (1997). Probabilistic and distributional approaches to language acquisition. *Trends in the Cognitive Sciences, 1*(7), 273–281.

Reed-Danahay, D. (2001). Autobiography, intimacy and ethnography. In P. Atkinson, A. Coffey, S. Delamont, J. Lofland, & L. Lofland (Eds.), *Handbook of ethnography* (pp. 405–425). London: Sage.

Reed-Danahay, D. E. (Ed.). (1997). *Auto/ethnography: Rewriting the self and the social.* Oxford, UK: Berg.

Rees, P., Martin, D., & Williamson, P. (Eds.). (2002). *The census data system.* Chichester, UK: Wiley.

Reichenbach, H. (1951). *The rise of scientific philosophy.* Berkeley: University of California Press.

Reis, H. T., & Gable, S. L. (2000). Event-sampling and other methods for studying everyday experience. In H. T. Reis & C. M. Judd (Eds.), *Handbook of research methods in social and personality psychology* (pp. 190–222). New York: Cambridge University Press.

Rengger, J. (1996). *Retreat from the modern: Humanism, postmodernism and the flight from modernist culture.* Exeter, UK: Bowerdean.

Rescher, N. (1997). *Objectivity: The obligations of impersonal reason.* Notre Dame, IN: University of Notre Dame Press.

Retherford, R. D., & Choe, M. K. (1993). *Statistical models for causal analysis.* New York: John Wiley.

Rex, J. (1974). *Sociology and the demystification of the modern world.* London: Routledge & Kegan Paul.

Reyment, R. A., & Jöreskog, K. G. (1993). *Applied factor analysis in the natural sciences.* Cambridge, UK: Cambridge University Press.

Reynolds, H. T. (1984). *Analysis of nominal data* (2nd ed.). Beverly Hills, CA: Sage.

Rhee, J. W. (1996). How polls drive campaign coverage. *Political Communication, 13,* 213–229.

Rice, J. A. (1995). *Mathematical statistics and data analysis* (2nd ed.). Belmont, CA: Duxbury.

Richards, T. J., & Richards, L. (1994). Using computers in qualitative research. In N. K. Denzin & Y. S. Lincoln (Eds.), *Handbook of qualitative research* (pp. 445–462). Thousand Oaks, CA: Sage.

Richardson, L. (1985). *The new other woman: Contemporary single women in affairs with married men.* London: Collier-Macmillan.

Richardson, L. (1997). *Fields of play: Constructing an academic life.* New Brunswick, NJ: Rutgers University Press.

Richardson, L. (2000). Writing: A method of inquiry. In N. K. Denzin & Y. S. Lincoln (Eds.), *Handbook of qualitative research* (2nd ed., pp. 923–948). Thousand Oaks, CA: Sage.

Richardson, L., & Lockridge, E. (in press). *Travels with Ernest: Crossing the Literary-Ethnographic Divide.* Walnut Creek, CA: AltaMira.

Ricoeur, P. (1981). *Hermeneutics and the human sciences: Essays on language, action and interpretation.* New York: Cambridge University Press.

Ricoeur, P. (1992). *Oneself as another.* Chicago: The University of Chicago Press.

Ridgeway, C. L. (2001). Inequality, status, and the construction of status beliefs. In J. H. Turner (Ed.), *Handbook of sociological theory* (pp. 323–340). New York: Kluwer Academic/Plenum.

Rieger, J. (1996). Photographing social change. *Visual Sociology, 11*(1), 5–49.

Riessman, C. K. (2002). Doing justice: Positioning the interpreter in narrative work. In W. Patterson (Ed.), *Strategic narrative: New perspectives on the power of personal and cultural storytelling* (pp. 195?216). Lanham, MA: Lexington Books.

Riessman, C. K. (2002). Positioning gender identity in narratives of infertility: South Indian women's lives in context. In M. C. Inhorn & F. van Balen (Eds.), *Infertility around the globe: New thinking on childlessness, gender, and reproductive technologies.* Berkeley: University of California Press.

Riessman, C. K. (2003). Performing identities in illness narrative: Masculinity and multiple sclerosis. *Qualitative Research, 3*(1), 5–33.

Rigdon, E. E. (1995). A necessary and sufficient identification rule for structural models estimated in practice. *Multivariate Behavioral Research, 30,* 359–383.

Riggs, P. J. (1992). *Whys and ways of science.* Melbourne, Australia: Melbourne University Press.

Riker, W. H. (1980). Implications from the disequilibrium of majority rule for the study of institutions. *American Political Science Review, 74,* 432–446.

Ripley, B. D. (1996). *Pattern recognition and neural networks.* Cambridge, UK: Cambridge University Press.

Ritchie, J., & Lewis, J. (2003). *Qualitative research practice.* London: Sage.

Ritzer, G. (1980). *Sociology: A multiple paradigm science.* Boston: Allyn & Bacon.

Rivers, D., & Vuong, Q. H. (1988). Limited information estimators and exogeneity tests for simultaneous probit models. *Journal of Econometrics, 39,* 347–366.

Robert, C. P. (2001). *The Bayesian choice: A decision theoretic motivation* (2nd ed.). New York: Springer-Verlag.

Robert, C. P., & Casella, G. (1999). *Monte Carlo statistical methods.* New York: Springer-Verlag.

Roberts, B. (2002). *Biographical research.* Buckingham, UK: Open University Press.

Roberts, N., Andersen, D. F., Deal, R. M., Grant, M. S., & Shaffer, W. A. (1983). *Introduction to computer simulation: A system dynamics modeling approach.* Reading, MA: Addison-Wesley.

Robey, B., Rutstein, S. O., & Morris, L. (1992). The reproductive revolution: New survey findings (Technical Report M-11). *Population Reports.* Baltimore, MD: Johns Hopkins University Center for Communication Programs.

Robins, J. M. (1998). Correction for non-compliance in equivalence trials. *Statistics in Medicine, 17,* 269–302.

Robinson, J. (1994). White women researching/representing "others": From anti-apartheid to postcolonialism. In A. Blunt & G. Rose (Eds.), *Writing, women and space* (pp. 97–226). New York: Guilford.

Robinson, J. P., & Godbey, G. (1997). *Time for life.* University Park: Pennsylvania State University Press.

Robinson, W. S. (1950). Ecological correlations and the behavior of individuals. *American Sociological Review, 15,* 351–357.

Robinson, W. S. (1951). The logical structure of analytic induction. *American Sociological Review, 16,* 812–818.

Robson, C. (1993). *Real world research.* Oxford, UK: Blackwell.

Rochford, E. B., Jr. (1992). On the politics of member validation: Taking findings back to Hare Krishna. In G. Miller & J. A. Holstein (Eds.), *Perspectives on social problems* (Vol. 3, pp. 99–116). Greenwich, CT: JAI.

Rodgers, J. L. (1999). The bootstrap, the jackknife, and the randomization test: A sampling taxonomy. *Multivariate Behavioral Research, 34,* 441–456.

Rodríguez, G. (1994). Statistical issues in the analysis of reproductive histories using hazard models. In K. L. Campbell & J. W. Wood (Eds.), *Human reproductive ecology: Interaction of environment, fertility and behavior* (pp. 266–279). New York: New York Academy of Sciences.

Roethlisberger, F. J., & Dickson, W. J. (1939). *Management and the worker.* Cambridge, MA: Harvard University Press.

Rogers, A. (1995). *Multiregional demography.* Chichester, UK: Wiley.

Rohrer, L. G. (1965). The great response-style myth. *Psychological Bulletin, 63,* 129–156.

Romney, A. K., Weller, S. C., & Batchelder, W. (1986). Culture as consensus: A theory of culture and informant accuracy. *American Anthropologist, 88,* 313–338.

Ronan, W. W., & Latham, G. P. (1974). The reliability and validity of the critical incident technique: A closer look. *Studies in Personnel Psychology, 6*(1), 33–64.

Roncek, D. W. (1992). Learning more from Tobit coefficients. *American Sociological Review, 57,* 503–507.

Rorty, R. (1991). *Objectivity, relativism, and truth: Philosophical papers volume 1.* Cambridge, UK: Cambridge University Press.

Rosaldo, R. (1989). *Culture & truth.* Boston: Beacon.

Rose, G. (2001). *Visual methodologies.* London: Sage.

Rosenau, P. M. (1992). *Post-modernism and the social sciences: Insights, inroads and intrusions.* Princeton, NJ: Princeton University Press.

Rosenbaum, P. R. (1995). *Observational studies.* New York: Springer-Verlag.

Rosenbaum, P. R. (1998). Multivariate matching methods. *Encyclopedia of Statistical Sciences, 2,* 435–438.

Rosenbaum, P. R., & Rubin, D. B. (1983). The central role of the propensity score in observational studies for causal effects. *Biometrika, 70,* 41–55.

Rosenberg, A. (1988). *Philosophy of social science.* Oxford, UK: Clarendon.

Rosenberg, M. (1968). *The logic of survey analysis.* New York: Basic Books.

Rosenberg, M. J. (1969). The conditions and consequences of evaluation apprehension. In R. Rosenthal &

R. L. Rosnow (Eds.), *Artifact in behavioral research* (pp. 279–349). New York: Academic Press.

Rosenberg, S., & Kim, M. P. (1975). The method of sorting as a data-gathering method in multivariate research. *Multivariate Behavioral Research, 10,* 489–502.

Rosenberger, J. L., & Gasko, M. (1983). Comparing location estimators: Trimmed means, medians, and trimean. In D. C. Hoaglin, F. Mosteller, & J. W. Tukey (Eds.), *Understanding robust and exploratory data analysis.* New York: Wiley.

Rosenhan, D. (1973). On being sane in insane places. *Science, 179,* 250–258.

Rosenthal, G. (Ed.). (1998). *The Holocaust in three generations: Families of victims and persecutors of the Nazi regime.* London: Cassell.

Rosenthal, R. (1966). *Experimenter effects in behavioral research.* New York: Appleton-Century-Crofts.

Rosenthal, R. (1976). *Experimenter effects in behavioral research* (rev. ed.). New York: Irvington.

Rosenthal, R. (1979). The "file drawer problem" and tolerance for null results. *Psychological Bulletin, 86,* 638–641.

Rosenthal, R., & Jacobson, L. (1968). *Pygmalion in the classroom.* New York: Holt, Rinehart & Winston.

Rosenthal, R., & Jacobson, L. (1992). *Pygmalion in the classroom: Expanded edition.* New York: Irvington.

Rosenthal, R., & Rosnow, R. L. (1975). *The volunteer subject.* New York: Wiley.

Rosenthal, R., & Rosnow, R. L. (1991). *Essentials of behavioral research: Methods and data analysis* (2nd ed.). New York: McGraw-Hill.

Rosenthal, R., & Rosnow, R. L. (Eds.). (1969). *Artifact in behavioral research.* New York: Academic Press.

Rosenthal, R., & Rubin, D. (1978). Interpersonal expectancy effects: The first 345 studies. *Behavioral and Brain Sciences, 3,* 377–415.

Rosenzweig, M. R., & Wolpin, K. I. (2000). Natural "natural experiments" in economics. *Journal of Economic Literature, 38,* 827–874.

Rosenzweig, S. (1933). The experimental situation as a psychological problem. *Psychological Review, 40,* 337–354.

Rosnow, R. L., & Rosenthal, R. (1970). Volunteer effects in behavioral research. In K. H. Craik, B. Kleinmuntz, R. L. Rosnow, R. Rosenthal, J. A. Cheyne, & R. H. Walters (Eds.), *New directions in psychology* (pp. 213–277). New York: Holt, Rinehart and Winston.

Rosnow, R. L., & Rosenthal, R. (1997). *People studying people: Artifacts and ethics in behavioral research.* New York: W. H. Freeman.

Ross, S. (1999). *A first course in probability.* Upper Saddle River, NJ: Prentice Hall.

Rossi, P. H. (1951). *The application of latent structure analysis to the study of social stratification.* Unpublished doctoral dissertation, Columbia University.

Rossi, P. H. (1979). Vignette analysis: Uncovering the normative structure of complex judgments. In R. K. Merton, J. S. Coleman, & P. H. Rossi (Eds.), *Qualitative and quantitative social research: Papers in honor of Paul F. Lazarsfeld* (pp. 176–186). New York: Free Press.

Rossi, P. H., & Anderson, A. B. (1982). The factorial survey approach: An introduction. In P. H. Rossi & S. L. Nock (Eds.), *Measuring social judgments: The factorial survey approach* (pp. 15–67). Beverly Hills, CA: Sage.

Rossi, P. H., & Berk, R. A. (1985). Varieties of normative consensus. *American Sociological Review, 50,* 333–347.

Rossi, P. H., Freeman, H. E., & Lipsey, M. (1998). *Evaluation: A systematic approach* (6th ed.). Thousand Oaks, CA: Sage.

Rossi, P. H., Sampson, W. A., Bose, C. E., Jasso, G., & Passel, J. (1974). Measuring household social standing. *Social Science Research, 3,* 169–190.

Rothenberg, J., & Rothenberg, D. (Eds.). (1983). *Symposium of the whole: A range of discourse toward an ethnopoetics.* Berkeley: University of California Press.

Rothman, K. J. (1977). Epidemiologic methods in clinical trials. *Cancer, 39,* 1771–1775.

Rothman, K. J. (1986). *Modern epidemiology.* Boston: Little, Brown.

Rothman, K. J., & Greenland, S. (1998). *Modern epidemiology* (2nd ed.). Philadelphia: Lippincott.

Rousseau, J.-J. (1953) *The confessions.* Harmondsworth, UK: Penguin. (Original work published 1781)

Rousseeuw, P. J., & Leroy, A. M. (1987). *Robust regression & outlier detection.* New York: Wiley.

Routledge, P. (1996). The third space as critical engagement. *Antipode, 28*(4), 399–419.

Rowell, R. K. (1996). Partitioning predicted variance into constituent parts: How to conduct commonality analysis. In B. Thompson (Ed.), *Advances in social science methodology* (Vol. 4, pp. 33–44). Greenwich, CT: JAI.

Royston, J. P. (1993). A toolkit for testing for non-normality in complete and censored samples. *The Statistician, 42,* 37–43.

Rubenstein, A. (1998). *Modeling bounded rationality.* Cambridge: MIT Press.

Rubin, D. B. (1986). Statistical matching using file concatenation with adjusted weights and multiple imputations. *Journal of Business and Economic Statistics, 4,* 87–95.

Rubin, D. B. (1987). *Multiple imputation for nonresponse in surveys.* New York: Wiley.

Rubin, D. B. (2001). Using propensity scores to help design observational studies: Application to the tobacco litigation. *Health Services and Outcomes Research Methodology, 2,* 169–188.

Rubin, D. B., & Schenker, N. (1986). Multiple imputation for interval estimation from simple random samples with ignorable nonresponse. *Journal of the American Statistical Association, 81,* 366–374.

Rubinstein, R. Y. (1981). *Simulation and the Monte Carlo method.* New York: John Wiley.

Rudas, T. (1997). *Odds ratios in the analysis of contingency tables.* Thousand Oaks, CA: Sage.

Rummel, R. J. (1970). *Applied factor analysis.* Evanston, IL: Northwestern University Press.

Ruskey, F. (2001). A survey of Venn diagrams. *The Electronic Journal of Combinatorics,* Dynamic Survey #5 [Online]. Retrieved from http://www.combinatorics.org/Surveys/ds5/VennEJC.html

Russell, B. (1912). *Mysticism and logic.* London: Allen & Unwin.

Russett, B. (1969). Inequality and instability: The relation of land tenure to politics. In D. Rowney & J. Graham (Eds.), *Quantitative history: Selected readings in the quantitative analysis of historical data* (pp. 356–367). Homewood, IL: Dorsey.

Ryle, G. (1971). Thinking and reflecting. In G. Ryle, *Collected papers, Volume 2.* London: Hutchinson.

Ryssevik, J., & Musgrave, S. (2001). The social science dream machine: Resource discovery, analysis, and delivery on the Web. *Social Science Computing Review, 19*(2), 163–174.

Sackett, G. P. (1979). The lag sequential analysis of contingency and cyclicity in behavioral interaction research. In J. D. Osofsky (Ed.), *Handbook of infant development* (1st ed., pp. 623–649). New York: Wiley.

Sacks, H. (1992). *Lectures on conversation* (2 vols.). Oxford, UK: Blackwell.

Sacks, H., Schegloff, E. A., & Jefferson, G. (1974). A simplest systematics for the organization of turn-taking for conversation. *Language, 50*(4), 696–735.

Sade, A. (1951). An omission in Norton's list of 7 × 7 squares. *Annals of Mathematical Statistics, 22,* 306–307.

Sale, J. E. M., Lohfeld, L. H., & Brazil, K. (2002). Revisiting the quantitative-qualitative debate: Implications for mixed-methods research. *Quality and Quantity, 36,* 43–53.

Salem, A., & Mount, T. (1974). A convenient descriptive model of income distribution: The gamma density. *Econometrica, 42,* 1115–1127.

Salmon, W. C. (1984). *Scientific explanation and the causal structure of the world.* Princeton, NJ: Princeton University Press.

Salsburg, D. (2001). *The lady tasting tea: How statistics revolutionized science in the twentieth century.* New York: Holt.

Sandelowski, M., Docherty, S., & Emden, C. (1997). Qualitative metasynthesis: Issues and techniques. *Research in Nursing & Health, 20,* 365–371.

Sankoff, D., & Kruskal, J. B. (1983). *Time warps, string edits, and macromolecules.* Reading, MA: Addison-Wesley.

Sapir, E. (1951). Culture, genuine and spurious. In D. G. Mandelbaum (Ed.), *Selected writings of Edward Sapir in language, culture and personality* (pp. 308–331). Berkeley: University of California Press.

Saris, W. E. (1991). *Computer-assisted interviewing.* Newbury Park, CA: Sage.

Saris, W. E., Satorra, A., & Sörbom, D. (1987). The detection and correction of specification errors in structural equation models. In C. C. Clogg (Ed.), *Sociological methodology 1987* (pp. 105–129). San Francisco: Jossey-Bass.

Särndal, C. E., Swensson, B., & Wretman, J. (1992). *Model assisted survey sampling.* New York: Springer-Verlag.

Saunders, M. N. K., & Cooper, S. A. (1993). *Understanding business statistics: An active learning approach.* London: DP Publications.

Saunders, P. (1979). *Urban politics: A sociological interpretation.* London: Hutchinson.

Saunders, P. T. (1980). *An introduction to catastrophe theory.* New York: Cambridge University Press.

Saussure, F. (1966). *Course in general linguistics.* New York: McGraw-Hill. (Originally published in 1915)

Saussure, F. de (1974). *Course in general linguistics.* London: Fontana/Collins.

Sayer, A. (1992). *Method in social science: A realist approach* (2nd ed.). London: Routledge.

Sayer, A. (1997). Essentialism, social constructionism and beyond. *Sociological Review, 45,* 453–487.

Sayer, A. (2000). *Realism and social science.* London: Sage.

Sayer, A. (2000). System, lifeworld and gender: Associational versus counterfactual thinking. *Sociology, 34,* 707–725.

Sayer, A. (2001). Reply to Holmwood. *Sociology, 35,* 967–984.

Schafer, J. L. (1997). *Analysis of incomplete multivariate data.* London: Chapman & Hall.

Scheaffer, R. L., Mendenhall, W., & Ott, L. (1990) *Elementary survey sampling.* Boston: PWS-Kent.

Scheffé, H. (1953). A method for judging all contrasts in the analysis of variance. *Biometrika, 40,* 87–104.

Scheffé, H. (1959). *The analysis of variance.* New York: Wiley.

Schegloff, E. A. (1968). Sequencing in conversational openings. *American Anthropologist, 70,* 1075–1095.

Schegloff, E. A. (1989). Harvey Sacks—lectures 1964–1965: An introduction/memoir. *Human Studies, 12,* 185–209.

Schegloff, E. A. (1992). Repair after next turn: The last structurally provided defence of intersubjectivity in conversation. *American Journal of Sociology, 97*(5), 1295–1345.

Schegloff, E.A. (1996). Confirming allusions: Toward an empirical account of action. *American Journal of Sociology, 2,* 161–216.

Schelling, T. C. (1971). Dynamic models of segregation. *Journal of Mathematical Sociology, 1,* 143–186.

Schelling, T. C. (1978). *Micromotives and macrobehavior.* New York: Norton.

Schensul, J. J., & LeCompte, M. D. (Eds.). (1999). *Ethnographer's toolkit.* Walnut Creek, CA: AltaMira.

Schensul, S. L., Schensul, J. J., & LeCompte, M. D. (1999). *Essential ethnographic methods: Observations, interviews, and questionnaires.* Walnut Creek, CA: AltaMira.

Schervish, M. J. (1996). *P*-values: What they are and what are they not. *American Statistician, 50,* 203–206.

Schlesselman, J. J. (1982). *Case-control studies: Design, conduct, analysis.* New York: Oxford University Press.

Schmidt, P. (1976). *Econometrics.* New York: Marcel Dekker.

Schmidt, P., & Witte, A. D. (1988). *Predicting recidivism using survival models.* New York: Springer-Verlag.

Schneider, H. (1986). *Truncated and censored samples from normal populations.* New York: Marcel Dekker.

Schober, M., & Conrad, F. (1997). Does conversational interviewing reduce survey measurement error? *Public Opinion Quarterly, 61,* 576–602.

Schoenberg, R. (1977). Dynamic models and cross-sectional data: The consequences of dynamic misspecification. *Social Science Research, 6,* 133–144.

Schölkopf, B., & Smola, A. J. (2003). *Learning with kernel.* Cambridge: MIT Press.

Schrodt, P. A. (2002). Mathematical modeling. In J. B. Manheim, R. C. Rich, & L. Willnat (Eds.), *Empirical political analysis: Research methods in political science* (5th ed.). New York: Longman.

Schroeder, L. D., Sjoquist, D. L., & Stephan, P. E. . (1986). *Understanding regression analysis: An introductory guide.* Beverly Hills, CA: Sage.

Schuman, H., & Presser, S. (1981). *Questions and answers in attitude surveys.* New York: Academic Press.

Schuman, H., & Presser, S. (1996). *Questions & answers in attitude surveys.* Thousand Oaks, CA: Sage.

Schütz, A. (1963). Concept and theory formation in the social sciences. In M. A. Natanson (Ed.), *Philosophy of the social sciences* (pp. 231–249). New York: Random House.

Schutz, A. (1964). Don Quixote and the problem of reality. In *Collected papers, Vol. 2.* The Hague: Martinus Nijhoff.

Schütz, A. (1967). *Der sinnhafte Aufbau der sozialen Welt* [Phenomenology of the social world]. Evanston, IL: Northwestern University Press. (Originally published in 1932)

Schutz, A. (1973). *Collected papers* (4 vols.). Dordrecht, The Netherlands: Kluwer.

Schütz, A. (1976). Equality and the meaning structure of the social world. In *Collected Papers II* (pp. 226–273). The Hague: Martinus Nijhoff. (Originally published in 1955)

Schütz, A. (1976). *The phenomenology of the social world* (G. Walsh & F. Lehnert, Trans.). London: Heinemann.

Schwandt, T. (1996). Farewell to criteriology. *Qualitative Inquiry, 2,* 58–72.

Schwandt, T. A. (1998). The interpretive review of educational matters: Is there any other kind? *Review of Educational Research, 68*(4), 409–412.

Schwarz, N., & Sudman, S. (Eds.). (1996). *Answering questions: Methodology for determining cognitive and communicative processes in survey research.* San Francisco: Jossey-Bass.

Schwarz, N., Hippler, H.-J., Deutsch, B., & Strack, F. (1985). Response scales: Effects of category range on reported behavior and comparative judgments. *Public Opinion Quarterly, 49*(3), 388–395.

Scott, J. (1990). *A matter of record: Documentary sources in social research.* Cambridge, UK: Polity.

Scott, J. (1992). *Social network analysis.* London: Sage.

Scott, J. W. (1988). *Gender and the politics of history.* New York: Columbia University Press.

Scott, M. B., & Lyman, S. (1968). Accounts. *American Sociological Review, 33,* 46–62.

Scott, W. A. (1955). Reliability of content analysis: The case of nominal scale coding. *Public Opinion Quarterly, 19,* 321–325.

Scott, W. A. (1968). Attitude measurement. In G. Lindzey & E. Aronson (Eds.), *The handbook of social psychology.* Reading, MA: Addison-Wesley.

Scriven, M. (1959). Explanation and prediction in evolutionary theory. *Science, 130,* 477–482.

Scriven, M. (1991). *Evaluation thesaurus* (4th ed.). Newbury Park, CA: Sage.

Scriven, M. (2001). Evaluation: Future tense. *The American Journal of Evaluation, 22,* 301–307.

Seal, H. L. (1967). The historical development of the Gauss linear model. *Biometrika, 54,* 1–23.

Seale, C. F. (1999). *The quality of qualitative research.* London: Sage.

Searle, S. R., Casella, G., & McCulloch, C. E. (1992). *Variance components.* New York: Wiley.

Sechrest, L. (Ed.). (1979). *Unobtrusive measures today.* San Francisco: Jossey-Bass.

Segrè, E. (1970). *Enrico Fermi: Physicist.* Chicago: University of Chicago Press.

Sen, A. (1973). *On economic inequality.* New York: Norton.

Sewell, W. H. (1942). The development of a sociometric scale. *Soociometry, 5*(3), 279–297.

Shadish, W. R. (2000). The empirical program of quasi-experimentation. In L. Bickman (Ed.), *Validity and social experimentation: Donald Campbell's legacy* (pp. 13–35). Thousand Oaks, CA: Sage.

Shadish, W. R., Cook, T. D., & Campbell, D. T. (2002). *Experimental and quasi-experimental designs for generalized causal inference.* Boston: Houghton-Mifflin.

Shadish, W. R., Jr., Cook, T. D., & Leviton, L. C. (1991). *Foundations of program evaluation: Theories of practice.* Newbury Park, CA: Sage.

Shadish, W. R., Jr., Newman, D. L., Scheirer, M. A., & Wye, C. (1995). *Guiding principles for evaluators* (New Directions for Program Evaluation, No. 66). San Francisco: Jossey-Bass.

Shapiro, G., & Markoff, J. (1998). *Revolutionary demands: A content analysis of the Cahier de Doléances of 1789.* Stanford, CA: Stanford University Press.

Shapiro, S. S., & Wilk, M. B. (1965). An analysis of variance test for normality (complete samples). *Biometrika, 52,* 591–611.

Shavelson, R. J., & Webb, N. M. (1991). *Generalizability theory: A primer.* Newbury Park, CA: Sage.

Shaw, C. (1966). *The jack roller.* Chicago: University of Chicago Press.

Shaw, I., Bloor, M., Cormack, R., & Williamson, H. (1996). Estimating the prevalence of hard-to-reach populations: The illustration of mark-recapture methods in the study of homelessness. *Social Policy and Administration, 30*(1), 69–85.

Sheskin, D. J. (1997). *Handbook of parametric and nonparametric statistical procedures.* Boca Raton, FL: CRC Press.

Shneiderman, B. (1992). Tree visualization with treemaps: A 2-D space-filling approach. *ACM Transactions on Graphics, 11*(1), 92–99.

Shrout, P. E., & Fleiss, J. L. (1979). Intraclass correlation: Uses in assessing rater reliability. *Psychological Bulletin, 86,* 420–428.

Shryock, H. S., Siegel, J. S., & Associates. (1973). *The methods and materials of demography.* New York: Academic Press. (Condensed edition by Edward G. Stockwell.)

Si, M., Neufeld, R. R., & Dunbar, J. (1999). Removal of bedrails on a short-term nursing home rehabilitation unit. *The Gerontologist, 39,* 611–614.

Sieber, J. E. (1992). *Planning ethically responsible research.* Newbury Park, CA: Sage.

Sieber, J. E. (1996). Typically unexamined communication processes in research. In B. H. Stanley, J. E. Sieber, & G. B. Melton (Eds.), *Research ethics: A psychological approach.* Lincoln: University of Nebraska Press.

Sieber, J. E. (Ed.). (1991). *Sharing social science data: Advantages and challenges.* Newbury Park, CA: Sage.

Siegel, J. S. (2002). *Applied demography.* San Diego, CA: Academic Press.

Siegel, S. (1956). *Nonparametric statistics for the behavioral sciences.* New York: McGraw-Hill.

Siegel, S., & Castellan, N. J. (1988). *Nonparametric statistics for the behavioral sciences* (2nd ed.). New York: McGraw-Hill.

Sijtsma, K., & Molenaar, I. W. (2002). *Introduction to nonparametric item response theory.* Thousand Oaks, CA: Sage.

Silverman, D. (1993). *Interpreting qualitative data: Methods for analysing talk, text, and interaction.* London: Sage.

Simon, H. A. (1954). Spurious correlation: A causal interpretation. *Journal of the American Statistical Association, 49,* 467–479.

Simon, H. A. (1957). *Models of man.* New York: Wiley.

Simon, H. A. (1976). Discussion: Cognition and social behavior. In J. S. Carroll & J. W. Payne (Eds.), *Cognition and social behavior.* Hillsdale, NJ: Erlbaum.

Simons, H. (1996). The paradox of case study. *Cambridge Journal of Education, 26*(2), 225–240.

Sims, C. A. (1972). Money income and causality. *American Economic Review, 62,* 540–552.

Singer, E. (1978). Informed consent: Consequences for response rate and response quality in social surveys. *American Sociological Review, 43,* 144–162.

Singer, E., & Frankel, M. R. (1982). Informed consent procedures in telephone interviews. *American Sociological Review, 47,* 416–427.

Singer, E., vonThurn, D., & Miller, E. (1995). Confidentiality assurances and response. *Public Opinion Quarterly, 59,* 66–77.

Singleton, A. (1999). Measuring international migration: A case study of European cross-national comparisons. In D. Dorling & S. Simpson (Eds.), *Statistics in society: The arithmetic of politics* (pp. 148–158). London: Arnold.

Skinner, C. J., Holt, D., & Smith, T. M. F. (Eds.). (1989). *Analysis of complex surveys.* Chichester, UK: Wiley.

Sklodowska, E. (1992). *Testimonio hispanoamericano: Historia, teoría, poética.* New York: Peter Lang.

Skoudis, E. (2002). *Counter Hack: A step-by-step guide to computer attacks and effective defenses.* Upper Saddle, NJ: Prentice Hall.

Skvoretz, J., & Faust, K. (1999). Logit models for affiliation networks. *Sociological Methodology, 29,* 253–280.

Slavin, R. E. (1986). Best-evidence synthesis: An alternative to meta-analytic and traditional reviews. *Educational Researcher, 15*(9), 5–11.

Smart, B. (2000). Postmodern social theory. In B. Turner (Ed.), *The Blackwell companion to social theory* (pp. 447–480). Oxford, UK: Blackwell.

Smelser, N. (1997). *Problems of sociology.* Berkeley: University of California Press.

Smith, B. H. (1997). *Belief and resistance: Dynamics of contemporary intellectual controversy.* Cambridge, MA: Harvard University Press.

Smith, D. (1997). Comment on Heckman's "Truth and method: Feminist standpoint theory revisited." *Signs, 22*(21): 392–397.

Smith, D. P. (1992). *Formal demography.* New York: Plenum.

Smith, G. (1997, Winter). Do statistics test scores regress toward the mean? *Chance,* pp. 42–45.

Smith, J. (1993). *After the demise of empiricism: The problem of judging social and educational inquiry.* Norwood, NJ: Ablex.

Smith, J. K. (1989). *The nature of social and educational inquiry: Empiricism versus interpretation.* Norwood, NJ: Ablex.

Smith, J. K., & Heshusius, L. (1986). Closing down the conversation: The end of the quantitative-qualitative debate among educational enquirers. *Educational Researcher, 15,* 4–12.

Smith, J., & Deemer, D. (2000). The problem of criteria in the age of relativism. In N. K. Denzin & Y. S. Lincoln (Eds.), *Handbook of qualitative research* (2nd ed., pp. 877–922). Thousand Oaks, CA: Sage.

Smith, L. M. (1978). An evolving logic of participant observation, educational ethnography and other case studies. *Review of Research in Education, 6,* 316–377.

Smith, M. (1998). *Social science in question.* London: Sage.

Smith, N. W. (2001). *Current systems in psychology.* Belmont, CA: Wadsworth.

Smith, S. K., Tayman, J., & Swanson, D. A. (2001). *State and local population projections: Methodology and analysis.* New York: Kluwer Academic/Plenum Publishers.

Smith, S., & Watson, J. (2001). *Reading autobiography: A guide for interpreting life narratives.* Minneapolis: University of Minnesota Press.

Smith, T. W. (1992). Thoughts on the nature of context effects. In N. Schwarz & S. Sudman (Eds.), *Context effects in social and psychological research* (pp. 163–184). New York: Springer-Verlag.

Smithson, M. (1987). *Fuzzy set analysis for behavioral and social sciences.* New York: Springer-Verlag.

Smithson, M. (2003). *Confidence intervals* (Sage University Papers on Quantitative Applications in the Social Sciences, 07–140). Thousand Oaks, CA: Sage.

Sneath, P. H. A., & Sokal, R. R. (1973). *Numerical taxonomy: The principles and practice of numerical classification.* San Francisco: Freeman.

Snedecor, G. W. (1937). *Statistical methods.* Ames: Iowa State University Press.

Snedecor, G. W. (1956). *Statistical methods* (5th ed.). Ames: Iowa State College Press.

Snider, J. G., & Osgood, C. E. (Eds.). (1969). *Semantic differential technique: A sourcebook.* Chicago: Aldine.

Snijders, T. (2001). The statistical evaluation of social network dynamics. *Sociological Methodology, 31,* 361–395.

Snijders, T. A. B., & Bosker, R. J. (1999). *Multilevel analysis: An introduction to basic and advanced multilevel modeling.* London: Sage.

Snow, D. (1980). The disengagement process: A neglected problem in participant observation research. *Qualitative Sociology, 3,* 100–122.

Sobel, M. E. (1995). Causal inference in the social and behavioral sciences. In G. Arminger, C. C. Clogg, & M. E. Sobel (Eds.), *Handbook of statistical modeling for the social and behavioral sciences* (pp. 1–38). New York: Plenum.

Sobel, M., & Bohrnstedt, G. W. (1985). Use of null models in evaluating the fit of covariance structure models. In N. B. Tuma (Ed.), *Sociological methodology 1985* (pp. 152–178). San Francisco: Jossey-Bass.

Sokal, R. R., & Michener, C. D. (1958). A statistical method for evaluating systematic relationships. *University of Kansas Science Bulletin, 38,* 1409–1438.

Sokal, R. R., & Rohlf, F. J. (1981). *Biometry* (2nd ed.). San Francisco: W.H. Freeman.

Sokal, R., & Sneath, P. (1963). *Principles of taxonomy.* San Francisco: Freeman.

Solomon, R. L. (1949). An extension of control group design. *Psychological Bulletin, 46,* 137–150.

Solomon, W. D. (1978). Ethics: Rules and principles. In W. T. Reich (Ed.), *Encyclopedia of bioethics.* New York: Free Press.

Sørensen, A. B. (1979). A model and a metric for the analysis of the intragenerational status attainment process. *American Journal of Sociology, 85,* 361–384.

Sørensen, J. B. (2002). The use and misuse of the coefficient of variation in organizational demography research. *Sociological Methods & Research, 30,* 475–491.

Soulliere, D., Britt, D. W., & Maines, D. R. (2001). Conceptual modeling as a toolbox for grounded theorists. *Sociological Quarterly, 42,* 233–251.

Soyland, A. J. (1994). *Psychology as metaphor.* London: Sage.

Spanos, A. (1999). *Probability and statistical inference: Econometric modeling with observational data.* Cambridge, UK: Cambridge University Press.

Spearman, C. (1904). General intelligence, objectively determined and measured. *American Journal of Psychology, 15,* 366–374.

Spearman, C. (1904). The proof and measurement of association between two things. *American Journal of Psychology, 15,* 72–101.

Spearman, C. (1910). Correlation calculated from faulty data. *British Journal of Psychology, 12,* 271–295.

Special section: Speaking in the name of the real: Freeman and Mead on Samoa. (1983). *American Anthropologist, 85,* 908–947.

Spector, P. E. (1987). Method variance as an artifact in self-reported affect and perceptions at work: Myth or significant problem? *Journal of Applied Psychology, 72,* 438–443.

Spector, P. E. (1992). *Summated rating scale construction: An introduction* (Sage University Paper Series on Quantitative Applications in the Social Sciences, 07–082). Newbury Park, CA: Sage.

Spector, P. E. (1994). Using self-report questionnaires in OB research: A comment on the use of a controversial method. *Journal of Organizational Behavior, 15,* 385–392.

Spector, P. E., & Brannick, M. T. 91995). The nature and effects of method variance in organizational research. In C. L. Cooper & I. T. Robertson (Eds.), *International review of industrial and organizational psychology: 1995* (pp. 249–274). West Sussex, England: Wiley.

Spector, P. E., Van Katwyk, P. T., Brannick, M. T., & Chen, P. Y. (1997). When two factors don't reflect two constructs: How item characteristics can produce artifactual factors. *Journal of Management, 23,* 659–677.

Spiegel, M. R., Schiller, J., & Srinivasan, R. A. (2000). *Schaum's outline of probability and statistics* (2nd ed.). New York: McGraw-Hill.

Spradley, J. P. (1979). *The ethnographic interview.* New York: Holt, Rinehart and Winston.

SPSS base 10.0 user's guide. (1999). Chicago: SPSS.

SPSS. (1990). *SPSS reference guide.* Chicago: SPSS.

SPSS. (2001). *Reliability* (Technical section). Retrieved from www.spss.com/tech/stat/algorithms/11.0/reliability.pdf

SPSS. (2002, August). Crosstabs. In *SPSS 11.0 statistical algorithms* [Online]. Available: http://www.spss.com/tech/stat/algorithms/11.0/crosstabs.pdf

Stanley, L. (1992). *The auto/biographical I: Theory and practice of feminist auto/biography.* Manchester, UK: Manchester University Press.

Stanley, L., & Wise, S. (1993). *Breaking out again: Feminist ontology and epistemology.* London: Routledge Kegan Paul.

Stanton, A. L., Burker, E. J., & Kershaw, D. (1991). Effects of researcher follow-up of distressed subjects: Tradeoff between validity and ethical responsibility? *Ethics & Behavior, 1*(2), 105–112.

Staudte, R. G., & Sheather, S. J. (1990). *Robust estimation and testing.* New York: Wiley.

Stem, D. E., Jr., & Lamb, C. W., Jr. (1981). The marble-drop technique: A procedure for gathering sensitive information. *Decision Sciences, 12,* 702–707.

Stern, J., Stackowiack, R., & Greenwald, R. (2001). *Oracle essentials: Oracle9i, Oracle8i and Oracle 8.* Sebastopol, CA: O'Reilly.

Stevens, J. (2001). *Applied multivariate statistics for the social sciences* (4th ed.). Mahwah, NJ: Lawrence Erlbaum.

Stevens, S. S. (1946). On the theory of scales of measurement. *Science, 103,* 677–680.

Stevens, S. S. (1951). *Handbook of experimental psychology.* New York: Wiley.

Stevens, S. S. (1968). Measurement, statistics, and the schemapiric view. *Science, 161,* 849–861.

Stewart, D. K., & Love, W. A. (1968). A general canonical correlation index. *Psychological Bulletin, 70,* 160–163.

Stewart, D. W., & Shamdasani, P. N. (1990). *Focus groups: Theory and practice* (Applied Social Research Methods Series, Vol. 20). Newbury Park, CA: Sage.

Stigler, S. M. (1986). *The history of statistics: The measurement of uncertainty before 1900.* Cambridge, MA: Belknap Press of Harvard University Press.

Stigler, S. (1986). Laplace's 1774 memoir on inverse probability. *Statistical Science, 1,* 359–378.

Stigler, S. M. (1999). *Statistics on the table: The history of statistical concepts and methods.* Cambridge, MA: Harvard University Press.

Stoll, D. (1999). *Rigoberta Menchú and the story of all poor Guatemalans.* Boulder, CO: Westview.

Stone, A. A., Shiffman, S., & DeVries, M. (1999). Ecological momentary assessment. In D. Kahneman, E. Diener, & N. Schwarz (Eds.), *Well-being: The foundations of hedonic psychology* (pp. 27–38). New York: Russell Sage.

Stone, A. A., Turkkan, J. S., Bachrach, C. A., Jobe, J. B., Kurtzman, H. S., & Cain, V. S. (Eds.). (2000). *The science of self-report: Implications for research and practice.* Mahwah, NJ: Lawrence Erlbaum.

Stouffer, S. A. (1950). Some observations on study design. *American Journal of Sociology, 55,* 355–361.

Strauss, A. (1987). *Qualitative analysis for social scientists.* New York: Cambridge University Press

Strauss, A. L., Corbin, J., Fagerhaugh, S., Glaser, B., Maines, D., Suczek, B., & Weiner, C. (1984). *Chronic illness and the quality of life.* St. Louis, MO: Mosby.

Strauss, A., & Corbin, J. (1990). *Basics of qualitative research: Grounded theory procedures and techniques.* Newbury Park, CA: Sage.

Strauss, A., & Corbin, J. (1998). *Basics of qualitative research: Grounded theory procedures and techniques* (2nd ed.). Thousand Oaks, CA: Sage.

Stringer, E. T. (1996). *Action Research: A handbook for practitioners.* Thousand Oaks, CA: Sage.

Strohmetz, D. B., & Rosnow, R. L. (1994). A mediational model of research artifacts. In J. Brzezinski (Ed.), *Probability in theory-building: Experimental and nonexperimental approaches to scientific research in psychology* (pp. 177–196). Amsterdam: Editions Rodopi.

Stuart, A. (1984). *The ideas of sampling.* London: Griffin.

Stuart, A., & Ord, J. K. (1987). *Kendall's advanced theory of statistics* (Vol. 1). London: Edward Arnold.

Stuart, A., Ord, J. K., & Arnold, S. (1999). *Kendall's advanced theory of statistics: Vol. 2A. Classical inference & the linear model* (6th ed.). New York: Oxford University Press.

Studenmund, A. H. (1992). *Using econometrics: A practical guide* (2nd ed.). New York: HarperCollins.

Student. (1908). The probable error of a mean. In E. S. Pearson & J. Wishart (Eds.), *Student's collected papers.* London: University College.

Suchman, E. A. (1967). *Evaluative research: Principles and practice in public service and social action programs.* New York: Russell Sage.

Sudman, S. (1976). *Applied sampling.* New York: Academic Press.

Sudman, S., & Bradburn, N. (1982). *Asking questions.* San Francisco: Jossey-Bass.

Sudman, S., Bradburn, N. M., & Schwarz, N. (1996). *Thinking about answers: The application of cognitive processes to survey methodology.* San Francisco: Jossey-Bass.

Sudnow, D. (1978). *Ways of the hand.* Cambridge, MA: Harvard University Press.

Sudnow, D. (2001). *Ways of the hand* (Rev. ed.). Cambridge, MA: MIT Press.

Suen, H. K., & Ary, D. (1989). *Analyzing quantitative behavioural observation data.* London: Lawrence Erlbaum.

Suppes, P. (1970). *A probabilistic theory of causality.* Amsterdam: North Holland.

Swokowski, E. W. (1979). *Calculus with analytic geometry* (2nd ed.). Boston: Prindle, Weber & Schmidt.

Symon, G. J., & Clegg, C. W. (1991). Technology-led change: A study of the implementation of CADCAM. *Journal of Occupational Psychology, 64,* 273–290.

Szalai, A. (Ed.). (1972). *The use of time.* The Hague: Mouton.

Sztompka, P. (1990). *Robert Merton: An intellectual profile.* London: Macmillan.

Tabachnick, B. G., & Fidell, L. S. (2001). *Computer-assisted research design and analysis.* Boston: Allyn and Bacon.

Tacq, J. J. A. (1984). *Causaliteit in Sociologisch Onderzoek. Een Beoordeling van Causale Analysetechnieken in het Licht van Wijsgerige Opvattingen over Causaliteit* [Causality in sociological research: An evaluation of causal techniques of analysis in the light of philosophical theories of causality]. Deventer, The Netherlands: Van Loghum Slaterus.

Tacq, J. J. A. (1997). *Multivariate analysis techniques in social science research: From problem to analysis.* London: Sage.

Takane, Y. (1981). Multidimensional scaling of sorting data. In Y. P. Chaubey & T. D. Dwivedi (Eds.), *Topics in applied statistics.* Montreal: Concordia University Press.

Takane, Y., Young, F. W., & DeLeeuw, J. (1977). Non-metric individual differences multidimensional scaling: An alternating least squares method with optimal scaling features. *Psychometrika, 42,* 7–67.

Tanner, M. A., & Wong, W. H. (1987). The calculation of posterior distributions by data augmentation (with discussion). *Journal of the American Statistical Association, 82,* 528–550.

Taris, T. W. (2000). *A primer in longitudinal data analysis.* London: Sage.

Tashakkori, A., & Teddlie, C. (1998). *Mixed methodology: Combining qualitative and quantitative approaches.* Thousand Oaks, CA: Sage.

Taylor, C. (1994). The politics of recognition. In C. Taylor & A. Gutmann (Eds.), *Multiculturalism and the politics of recognition* (pp. 25–73). Princeton, NJ: Princeton University Press.

Taylor, M. F., with Brice, J., Buck, N., & Prentice-Lane, E. (Eds.). (2000). *British Household Panel Survey user manual volume B9: Codebook.* Colchester, UK: University of Essex.

Taylor, S. J., & Bogdan, R. (1998). *Introduction to qualitative research methods: A guide & resource.* New York: Wiley.

Tedlock, D. (1999). Poetry and ethnography: A dialogical approach. *Anthropology and Humanism, 24*(2), 155–167.

ten Have, P. (1999). *Doing conversation analysis.* Thousand Oaks, CA: Sage.

Tenenhaus, M. (1998). *La régression PLS* [PLS regression]. Paris: Technip.

The 1980 U.S. census [Special issue]. (1992). *Survey Methodology, 18.*

The 1990 U.S. census [Special issue]. (1993). *Journal of the American Statistical Association, 88.*

The 1990 U.S. census [Special issue]. (1994). *Statistical Science, 9.*

The 2000 U.S. census. (2001). *Society, 39,* 2–53.

Therneau, T. M., & Grambsch, P. M. (2000). *Modeling survival data: Extending the Cox model.* New York: Springer-Verlag.

Theus, M. (1997). Visualization of categorical data. In W. Bandilla & F. Faulbaum (Eds.), *SoftStat '97: Advances in statistical software* (Vol. 6, pp. 47–55). Stuttgart, Germany: Lucius & Lucius.

Thom, R. (1975). *Structural stability and morphogenesis.* Reading, MA: Benjamin.

Thomas, H. (1997). Dancing: Representation and difference. In J. McGuigan (Ed.), *Cultural methodologies.* London: Sage.

Thomas, J. (1992). *Doing critical ethnography.* Newbury Park, CA: Sage.

Thomas, W. I., & Znaniecki, F. (1918–1920). *The Polish peasant in Europe and America* (5 vols.). New York: Dover.

Thomas, W. I., & Znaniecki, F. (1958). *The Polish peasant in Europe and America* (2 vols.). New York: Dover. (Original five-volume work published in 1918–1920).

Thompson, B. (1985). Alternate methods for analyzing data from experiments. *Journal of Experimental Education, 54,* 50–55.

Thompson, B. (1997). The importance of structure coefficients in structural equation modeling confirmatory factor analysis. *Educational and Psychological Measurement, 57,* 5–19.

Thompson, B. (2000). Canonical correlation analysis. In L. Grimm & P. Yarnold (Eds.), *Reading and understanding more multivariate statistics* (pp. 285–316). Washington, DC: American Psychological Association.

Thompson, J. (1981). *Critical hermeneutics: A study in the thought of Paul Ricoeur and Jürgen Habermas.* Cambridge, UK: Cambridge University Press.

Thompson, J. (1990). *Ideology and modern culture.* Stanford, CA: Stanford University Press.

Thompson, P. (2000). *The voice of the past* (3rd ed.). Oxford, UK: Oxford University Press.

Thorndike, R. L. (1967). The analysis and selection of test items. In D. Jackson & S. Messick (Eds.), *Problems in human assessment* (pp. 201–216). New York: McGraw-Hill.

Thorne, S. (1994). Secondary analysis in qualitative research: Issues and implications. In J. Morse (Ed.), *Critical issues in qualitative research methods* (pp. 263–279). Thousand Oaks, CA: Sage.

Thurstone, L. L. (1925). A method of scaling psychological and educational tests. *Journal of Educational Psychology, 16,* 433–451.

Thurstone, L. L. (1926). The scoring of individual performance. *Journal of Educational Psychology, 17,* 446–457.

Thurstone, L. L. (1927). A law of comparative judgment. *Psychological Review, 34,* 273–286.

Thurstone, L. L. (1928). Attitudes can be measured. *American Journal of Sociology, 23,* 529–554.

Thurstone, L. L. (1929). Fechner's law and the method of equal-appearing intervals. *Journal of Experimental Psychology, 12,* 214–224.

Thurstone, L. L. (1931). Measurement of social attitudes. *Journal of Abnormal and Social Psychology, 26,* 249–269.

Thurstone, L. L. (1947). *Multiple factor analysis.* Chicago: University of Chicago Press.

Thurstone, L. L., & Chave, E. J. (1929). *The measurement of attitudes.* Chicago: University of Chicago Press.

Timm, N. H. (1975). *Multivariate analysis with applications in education and psychology.* Monterey, CA: Brooks/Cole.

Tinbergen, N. (1963). On aims and methods of ethology. *Zeitschrift für Tierpsychologie, 20,* 410–433.

Tinsley, H. E., & Weiss, D. J. (1975). Interrater reliability and agreement of subjective judgments. *Journal of Counseling Psychology, 22,* 358–376.

Tintner, G. (1968). *Methodology and mathematical economics and econometrics.* Chicago: University of Chicago Press.

Titon, J. (1980). The life story. *Journal of American Folklore, 93*(369), 276–292.

Titscher, S., Meyer, M., Wodak, R., & Vetter, R. (2000). *Methods of text and discourse analysis.* London: Sage.

Tobin, J. (1958). Estimation of relationships for limited dependent variables. *Econometrica, 26,* 24–36.

Tolley, H. D., & Manton, K. G. (1992). Large sample properties of estimates of discrete grade of membership model. *Annals of the Institute of Statistical Mathematics, 41,* 85–95.

Tolley, H. D., Kovtun, M., Manton, K. G., & Akushevich, I. (2003). Statistical properties of grade of membership models for categorical data. Manuscript to be submitted to *Proceedings of National Academy of Sciences,* 2003.

Tommerup, P. (1993). *Adhocratic traditions, experience narratives and personal transformation: An ethnographic study of the organizational culture and folklore of the Evergreen State College, an innovative liberal arts college.* Unpublished doctoral dissertation, University of California, Los Angeles.

Toombs, S. K. (2001). Reflections on bodily change: The lived experience of disability. In S. K. Toombs (Ed.), *Handbook of phenomenology and medicine* (pp. 247–261). Boston: Kluwer Academic.

Toothaker, L. E. (1991). *Multiple comparisons for researchers.* Newbury Park, CA: Sage.

Toothaker, L. E. (1993). *Multiple comparison procedures.* Newbury Park, CA: Sage.

Torgerson, W. S. (1958). *Theory and methods of scaling.* New York: Wiley.

Toulmin, S. E. (1978). Science, philosophy of. In *Encyclopaedia Britannica* (15th ed., Vol. 16, pp. 375–393). Chicago: Britannica.

Tourangeau, R., Rips, L. J., & Rasinski, K. (2000). *The psychology of survey response.* Cambridge, UK: Cambridge University Press.

Townsend, J. T., & Ashby, F. G. (1984). Measurement scales and statistics: The misconception misconceived. *Psychological Bulletin, 96,* 394–401.

Townsend, P., Davidson, N., & Whitehead, M. (1988). *Inequalities in health: The Black report and the health divide.* Harmondsworth: Penguin.

Tracy, K. (2002). *Everyday talk: Building and reflecting identities.* New York: Guilford.

Tracy, P. E., & Fox, J. A. (1981). The validity of sensitive measurements: A comparison of two measurement strategies. *American Sociological Review, 46,* 187–200.

Train, K. (1986). *Qualitative choice analysis: Theory, econometrics, and an application to automobile demand.* Cambridge: MIT Press.

Tranfield, D., & Starkey, K. (1998). The nature, organization and promotion of management research: Towards policy. *British Journal of Management, 9,* 341–353.

Traugott, M. W., & Katosh, J. P. (1979). Response validity in surveys of voting behavior. *Public Opinion Quarterly, 43*(3), 359–377.

Trice, A. D. (1987). Informed consent: VII: Biasing of sensitive self-report data by both consent and information. *Journal of Social Behavior and Personality, 2,* 369–374.

Triplett, N. (1898). The dynamogenic factors in pacemaking and competition. *American Journal of Psychology, 9,* 507–533.

Troyna, B. (1994). Reforms, research and being reflexive about being reflective. In D. Halpin & B. Troyna (Eds.), *Researching education policy.* London: Falmer.

Trussell, J., & Rodríguez, G. (1990). Heterogeneity in demographic research. In J. Adams, D. A. Lam, A. I. Hermalin, &

P. E. Smouse (Eds.), *Convergent issues in genetics and demography* (pp. 111–132). Oxford, UK: Oxford University Press.

Truzzi, M. (1974). *Verstehen: Subjective understanding in the social sciences.* Reading, MA: Addison-Wesley.

Tsay, R. S. (2002). *Analysis of financial time series.* New York: Wiley.

Tsiatis, A. (1975). A nonidentifiability aspect of the problem of competing risks. *Proceedings of the National Academy of Sciences, 72,* 20–22.

Tsuji, R. (1999). Trusting behavior in prisoner's dilemma: The effects of social networks. *Dissertation Abstracts International Section A: Humanities & Social Sciences, 60*(5-A), 1774. (UMI No. 9929113)

Tuchman, G. (1994). Historical social science: Methodologies, methods, and meanings. In N. K. Denzin & Y. S. Lincoln (Eds.), *Handbook of qualitative research* (pp. 306–323). Thousand Oaks, CA: Sage.

Tucker, L. R. (1960). Intra-individual and inter-individual multidimensionality. In H. Gulliksen & S. Messick (Eds.), *Psychometric scaling: Theory and applications* (pp. 155–167). New York: Wiley.

Tufte, E. R. (1983). *The visual display of quantitative information.* Cheshire, CT: Graphics Press.

Tukey, J. W. (1958). Bias and confidence in not quite large samples [abstract]. *Annals of Mathematical Statistics, 29,* 614.

Tukey, J. W. (1960). A survey of sampling from contaminated normal distributions. In I. Olkin et al. (Eds.), *Contributions to probability and statistics.* Stanford, CA: Stanford University Press.

Tukey, J. W. (1977). *Exploratory data analysis.* Reading, MA: Addison-Wesley.

Tuma, N. B., & Hannan, M. T. (1984). *Social dynamics: Models and methods.* Orlando, FL: Academic Press.

Turner, A. C. (1982). What subjects of survey research believe about confidentiality. In J. E. Sieber (Ed.), *The ethics of social research: Surveys and experiments* (pp. 151–165). New York: Springer-Verlag.

Turner, R. H. (1951). The quest for universals. *American Sociological Review, 18*(6), 604–611.

Turner, S. P., & Factor, R. A. (1981). Objective possibility and adequate causality in Weber's methodological writings. *Sociological Review, 29*(1), 5–28.

Turner, V., & Bruner, E. (Eds.). (1986). *The anthropology of experience.* Urbana: University of Illinois Press.

Tversky, A., & Kahneman, D. (1974). Judgement under uncertainty: Heuristics and biases. *Science, 185,* 1124–1131.

Tversky, A., & Kahneman, D. (1986). Rational choice and the framing of decisions. *Journal of Business, 59,* 251–278.

Tzelgov, J., & Henik, A. (1991). Suppression situations in psychological research: Definitions, implications, and applications. *Psychological Bulletin, 109,* 524–536.

U.S. Census Bureau. (2001). *Report of the Executive Steering Committee for Accuracy and Coverage Evaluation Policy on Adjustment for Non-Redistricting Uses* (With supporting documentation, Reps. 1–24). Washington, DC: Government Printing Office.

U.S. Federal Regulations of Human Research 45 CFR 46. Retrieved from http://ohrp.osophy.dhhs.gov.

UK Data Archive (n.d.). [Online]. Available: http://www.data-archive.ac.uk/.

United Nations Statistics Division. (2001). *Handbook on census management for population and housing censuses–Series F* (No. 83, Revision 1). New York: United Nations.

United Nations. (1995). *World population prospects: The 1994 revision.* New York: Author.

United Nations. (1996). *Demographic yearbook 1994.* New York: Author.

University of Mississippi. (n.d.). PsychExperiments. Retrieved from http://psychexps.olemiss.edu

Utts, J. M. (1996). *Seeing through statistics.* Belmont, CA: Duxbury.

Valero, P., Young, F., & Friendly, M. (2003). Visual categorical analysis in ViSta. *Computational Statistics and Data Analysis, 43*(4), 495–508.

Vallet, L.-A. (2001). Forty years of social mobility in France. *Revue Française de Sociologie: An Annual English Selection, 42*(Suppl.), 5–64.

Valsiner, J., & Benigni, L. (1986). Naturalistic research and ecological thinking in the study of child development. *Developmental Review, 6*(3), 203–223.

Van de Geer, J. (1971). *Introduction to multivariate analysis for the social sciences.* San Francisco: Freeman.

Van den Ende, H. W. (1971). *Beschrijvende Statistiek voor Gedragswetenschappen.* Amsterdam/Brussel: Agon Elsevier.

van der Ark, L. A., & van der Heijden, P. G. M. (1998). Graphical display of latent budget analysis and latent class analysis, with special reference to correspondence analysis. In M. Greenacre & J. Blasius (Eds.), *Visualization of categorical data* (pp. 489–508). San Diego: Academic Press.

van der Ark, L. A., van der Heijden, P. G. M., & Sikkel, D. (1999). On the identifiability of the latent model. *Journal of Classification, 16,* 117–137.

van der Heijden, P. G. M., Mooijaart, A., & de Leeuw, J. (1992). Constrained latent budget analysis. In P. Marsden (Ed.), *Sociological methodology* (pp. 279–320). Cambridge, UK: Basil Blackwell.

van der Heijden, P. G. M., van der Ark, L. A., & Mooijaart, A. (2002). Some examples of latent budget analysis and its extensions. In J. A. Hagenaars & A. McCutcheon (Eds.), *Applied latent class analysis* (pp. 107–136). Cambridge, UK: Cambridge University Press.

Van der Heijden, P. G. M., van Gils, G., Bouts, J., & Hox, J. J. (2000). A comparison of randomized response, computer-assisted self-interview, and face-to-face direct questioning: Eliciting sensitive information in the context of welfare and unemployment benefit. *Sociological Methods & Research, 28,* 505–537.

Van der Linden, W. J., & Hambleton, R. K. (Eds.). (1997). *Handbook of modern item response theory.* New York: Springer.

Van Dijk, T. A. (Ed.). (1985). *Handbook of discourse analysis: Vols. 1–4.* London: Academic Press.

Van Maanen, J. (1979). The fact and fiction in organizational ethnography. *Administrative Science Quarterly, 24,* 539–550.

Van Maanen, J. (1988). *Tales of the field: On writing ethnography.* Chicago: University of Chicago Press.

van Manen, M. (1997). *Researching lived experience: Human science for an action sensitive pedagogy.* London, Ontario: Althouse.

van Teijlingen, E., & Hundley, V. (2002). The importance of pilot studies. *Nursing Standard, 16*(40), 33–36.

Vapnik, V. N. (1999). *Statistical learning theory.* New York: Wiley.

Vaupel, J. W. (1990). Relatives' risks: Frailty models of life history data. *Theoretical Population Biology, 37,* 220–234.

Vaupel, J. W., & Yashin, A. I. (1985). The deviant dynamics of death in heterogenous populations. In N. B. Tuma (Ed.), *Sociological methodology* (pp. 179–211). San Francisco: Jossey-Bass.

Vaupel, J. W., & Yashin, A. I. (1985). Heterogeneity's ruses: Some surprising effects of selection on population dynamics. *American Statistician, 39,* 176–185.

Vaupel, J. W., Manton, K. G., & Stallard, E. (1979). The impact of heterogeneity in individual frailty on the dynamics of mortality. *Demography, 16,* 439–454.

Velleman, P. F. (1988). *DataDesk version 6.0 statistics guide.* Ithaca, NY: Data Description, Inc.

Velleman, P. F., & Wilkinson, L. (1993). Nominal, ordinal, interval and ratio typologies are misleading. *American Statistician, 47,* 65–72.

Venables, W. N., & Ripley, B. D. (2002). *Modern applied statistics with S* (4th ed.). New York: Springer-Verlag.

Verbeke, G., & Molenberghs, G. (2000). *Linear mixed models for longitudinal data.* New York: Springer.

Verbrugge, L. (1980). Health diaries. *Medical Care, 18,* 73–95.

Vermunt, J. K. (1997). *Log-linear models for event histories.* Thousand Oaks, CA: Sage.

Vermunt, J. K., & Magidson, J. (2002). Latent class cluster analysis. In J. A. Hagenaars & A. L. McCutcheon (Eds.), *Applied latent class analysis* (pp. 89–106). Cambridge, UK: Cambridge University Press.

Vermunt, J. K., Rodrigo, M. F., & Ato-Garcia, M. (2001). Modeling joint and marginal distributions in the analysis of categorical panel data. *Sociological Methods & Research, 30,* 170–196.

Vogt, P. W. (1993). *Dictionary of statistics and methodology: A nontechnical guide for the social sciences.* Newbury Park, CA: Sage.

Vogt, W. P. (1999). *Dictionary of statistics and methodology: A nontechnical guide for the social sciences* (2nd ed.). Thousand Oaks, CA: Sage.

Von Collani, E., & Drager, K. (2001). *Binomial distribution handbook.* Basel, Switzerland: Birkhauser.

von Glasersfeld, E. (1984). An introduction to radical constructivism. In P. Watzlawick (Ed.), *The invented reality.* New York: Norton.

von Neumann, J., & Morgenstern, O. (1944). *Theory of games and economic behaviour.* Princeton, NJ: Princeton University Press.

von Wright, G. H. (1971). *Explanation and understanding.* Ithaca, NY: Cornell University Press.

Wachter, K. W., & Trussell, J. (1982). Estimating historical heights. *Journal of the American Statistical Association,* 77(378), 279–293.

Wackerly, D. D., Mendelhall, W., III, & Scheaffer, R. L. (1996). *Mathematical statistics with applications* (5th ed.). Belmont, CA: Duxbury.

Wahba, G. (1990). *Spline models for observational data.* Philadelphia: SIAM.

Walby, S., & Olsen, W. (2002, November). *The impact of women's position in the labour market on pay and implications for UK productivity.* Cabinet Office Women and Equality Unit. Retrieved from www.womenandequalityunit.gov.uk.

Wald, A., & Wolfowitz, J. (1940). On a test whether two samples are from the same population. *Annals of Mathematical Statistics, 11,* 147–162.

Walker, E., & Lev, J. (1953). *Statistical inference.* New York: Henry Holt.

Walker, R. (Ed.). (1985). *Applied qualitative research.* Aldershot, UK: Gower.

Walkerdine, V., Lucey, H., & Melody, J. (2001). *Growing up girl: Psycho-social explorations of gender and class.* Basingstoke, UK: Palgrave.

Wallgren, A. et al. (1996). *Graphing statistics and data: Creating better data.* Thousand Oaks, CA: Sage.

Walsh, A., & Ollenburger, J. C. (2001). *Essential statistics for the social and behavioral sciences: A conceptual approach.* Upper Saddle River, NJ: Prentice Hall.

Walt, S. M. (1987). *The origins of alliances.* Ithaca, NY: Cornell University Press.

Walton Braver, M., & Braver, S. L. (1996). Statistical treatment of the Solomon four-group design: A meta-analytic approach. *Psychological Bulletin, 104*(1), 150–154.

Walton, J. (1992). Making the theoretical case. In C. C. Ragin & H. S. Becker (Eds.), *What is a case? Exploring the foundations of social inquiry* (pp. 121–137). New York: Cambridge University Press.

Ward, A. (2002). *Oral history and copyright.* Retrieved June 7, 2002 from http://www.oralhistory.org.uk

Warde, A., Martens, L., & Olsen, W. K. (1999). Consumption and the problem of variety: Cultural omnivorousness, social distinction and dining out. *Sociology, 30*(1), 105–128.

Warner, R. M. (1998). *Spectral analysis of time-series data.* New York: Guilford.

Warner, S. L. (1965). Randomized response: A survey technique for eliminating evasive answer bias. *Journal of the American Statistical Association, 60,* 63–69.

Warren, C. A. B. (1987). *Madwives: Schizophrenic women in the 1950s.* New Brunswick, NJ: Rutgers University Press.

Warren, C. A. B. (2002). Qualitative interviewing. In J. F. Gubrium & J. A. Holstein (Eds.), *Handbook of interview research: Context and method* (pp. 83–101). Thousand Oaks, CA: Sage.

Warren, C. A. B., & Hackney, J. K. (2000). *Gender issues in ethnography* (Qualitative Research Methods Series vol. 9, 2nd ed.). Thousand Oaks, CA: Sage.

Wasserman, S., & Faust, K. (1994). *Social network analysis: Methods and applications.* New York: Cambridge University Press.

Wasserman, S., & Galaskiewicz, J. (Eds.). (1994). *Advances in social network analysis.* Thousand Oaks, CA: Sage.

Watson, J. B. (1959). *Behaviorism.* Chicago: University of Chicago Press.

Watson, M. W. (1994). Vector autoregression and cointegration. In R. F. Engle & D. L. McFadden (Eds.), *Handbook of econometrics* (Vol. 4, pp. 2843–2915). Amsterdam: Elsevier.

Watts, D. (1999). *Small worlds: The dynamics of networks between order and randomness.* Princeton, NJ: Princeton University Press.

Weaver, L., & Cousins, B. (2001, November). *Unpacking the participatory process.* Paper presented at the annual meeting of the American Evaluation Association, St. Louis, MO.

Webb, E. J., Campbell, D. T., Schwartz, R. D., & Sechrest, L. (1966). *Unobtrusive measures: Nonreactive measures in the social sciences.* Chicago: Rand McNally.

Webb, E. J., Campbell, D. T., Schwartz, R. D., Sechrest, L., & Grove, J. B. (1981). *Nonreactive measures in the social sciences* (2nd ed.). Boston: Houghton Mifflin.

Webb, J. F., Khazen, R. S., Hanley, W. B., Partington, M. S., Percy, W. J. L., & Rathborn, J. C. (1973). PKU screening—is it worth it? *Canadian Medical Association Journal, 108,* 328–329.

Weber, M. (1949). Die "Objektivität" sozialwissenschaftlicher und sozialpolitischer Erkenntnis ["Objectivity" in social science and social policy]. In *The methodology of the social sciences: Max Weber* (pp. 50–112). New York: Free Press. (Originally published in 1904)

Weber, M. (1964). *The theory of social and economic organization* (A. M. Henderson & T. Parsons, Trans.). New York: Free Press.

Weber, M. (1975). *Roscher and Knies.* New York: Free Press.

Weber, R. P. (1990). *Basic content analysis.* Newbury Park, CA: Sage.

Wedel, M., & DeSarbo, W. S. (1994). A review of recent developments in latent class regression models. In R. P. Bagozzi (Ed.), *Advanced methods of marketing research* (pp. 352–388). Cambridge, UK: Basil Blackwell.

Weisberg, H. F. (1974). Dimensionland: An excursion into spaces. *American Journal of Political Science, 18,* 743–776.

Weisberg, H. F. (1974). Models of statistical relationship. *American Political Science Review, 68,* 1638–1655.

Weisberg, H. F. (1992). *Central tendency and variability* (Sage University Paper Series on Quantitative Applications in the Social Sciences, 07–083). Newbury Park, CA: Sage.

Weisberg, S. (1985). *Applied linear regression.* New York: Wiley.

Weiss, C. (1977). *Use of social research in public policy.* Lexington, MA: D. C. Heath.

Weiss, C. H. (1972). A treeful of owls. In C. H. Weiss (Ed.), *Evaluating action programs* (pp. 3–27). Boston: Allyn & Bacon.

Weiss, C. H., & Bucuvalas, M. (1980). Truth test and utility test: Decision makers' frame of reference for social science research. *American Sociological Review, 45,* 302–313.

Weiss, H. M. (2002). Deconstructing job satisfaction: Separating evaluations, beliefs and affective experiences. *Human Resources Management Review, 12,* 173–194.

Weiss, R. (1995). *Learning from strangers.* New York: Free Press.

Weitzman, E. A., & Miles, M. B. (1995). *Computer programs for qualitative data analysis: A software source book.* Thousand Oaks, CA: Sage.

Welch, B. L. (1947). The generalization of student's problem when several different population variances are involved. *Biometrika, 34,* 28–35.

Weller, S. C., & Romney, A. K. (1988). *Systematic data collection* (Qualitative Research Methods, Vol. 10). Newbury Park, CA: Sage.

Weller, S. C., & Romney, A. K. (1990). *Metric scaling: Correspondence analysis.* Newbury Park, CA: Sage.

Wellman, B., & Berkowitz, S. D. (Eds.). (1997). *Social structures: A network approach* (updated ed.). Greenwich, CT: JAI.

Wengraf, T. (2001). *Qualitative research interviewing: Biographic-narrative and semi-structured method.* London: Sage.

Werner, O., & Schoepfle, G. M. (1987). *Systematic fieldwork* (2 vols.). Newbury Park, CA: Sage.

West, S. G., Hepworth, J. T., McCall, M. A., & Reich, J. W. (1989). An evaluation of Arizona's July 1982 drunk driving law: Effects on the City of Phoenix. *Journal of Applied Social Psychology, 19,* 1212–1237.

Wetherell, M., & Potter, J. (1992). *Mapping the language of racism: Discourse and the legitimation of exploitation.* Brighton, UK: Harvester Wheatsheaf.

Wetherell, M., Taylor, S., & Yates, S. J. (Eds.). (2001). *Discourse theory and practice.* London: Sage.

Wheldall, K., & Merrett, F. (1989). *Positive teaching: The behavioural approach.* Birmingham, UK: Positive Products.

Wherry, R. J., Sr. (1984). *Contributions to correlational analysis.* New York: Academic Press.

Whewell, W. (1847). *The philosophy of the inductive sciences* (Vols. 1 & 2). London: Parker.

White, H. (1980). A heteroskedasticity-consistent covariance matrix estimator and a direct test for heteroskedasticity. *Econometrica, 48,* 817–838.

White, H. (1984). *Asymptotic theory for econometricians.* Orlando, FL: Academic Press.

White, L. (1999). *Political analysis: Technique and practice* (4th ed.). Orlando, FL: Harcourt Brace.

Whiting, J. W., Child, I. L., & Lambert, W. W. (1966). *Field guide for the study of socialization.* New York: Wiley.

Whittaker, J. (1990). *Graphical models in applied multivariate statistics.* Chichester, UK: Wiley.

Whyte, W. F. (1955). *Street corner society: The social structure of an Italian slum* (2nd ed.). Chicago: University of Chicago Press. (Original work published 1943)

Whyte, W. F. (1984). *Learning from the field: A guide from experience.* Beverly Hills, CA: Sage.

Whyte, W. F. (Ed.). (1991). *Participatory action research.* Newbury Park, CA: Sage.

Wiggershaus, R. (1995). *The Frankfurt School: Its history, theories and political significance* (M. Robertson, Trans.). Cambridge, UK: Polity.

Wiggins, L. M. (1973). *Panel analysis.* Amsterdam: Elsevier.

Wilcox, R. (2001). *Fundamentals of modern statistical methods: Substantially improving power and accuracy.* New York: Springer.

Wilcox, R. R. (1996). *Statistics for the social sciences.* San Diego, CA: Academic Press.

Wilcox, R. R. (2001). *Fundamentals of modern statistical methods.* New York: Springer.

Wilcox, R. R. (2003). *Applying contemporary statistical techniques.* San Diego, CA: Academic Press.

Wilcoxon, F. (1945). Individual comparisons by ranking methods. *Biometrics, 1,* 80–83.

Wildt, A. R., & Ahtola, O. T. (1978). *Analysis of covariance* (Sage University Paper Series on Quantitative Applications in the Social Sciences, 07–012). Beverly Hills, CA: Sage.

Willer, D. (1967). *Scientific sociology: Theory and method.* Englewood Cliffs, NJ: Prentice Hall.

Williams, G. (1984). The genesis of chronic illness: Narrative re-construction. *Sociology of Health & Illness, 6*(2), 175–200.

Williams, L. J., & Brown, B. K. (1994). Method variance in organizational behavior and human resources research: Effects on correlations, path coefficients, and hypothesis testing. *Organizational Behavior and Human Decision Processes, 57,* 185–209.

Williams, M. (1998). The social world as knowable. In T. May & M. (Eds.), *Knowing the social world* (pp. 5–21). Buckingham, UK: Open University Press.

Williams, M. (2000). Interpretivism and generalisation. *Sociology, 34*(2), 209–224.

Williams, M. (2000). *Science and social science: An introduction.* London: Routledge.

Williams, M., & May, T. (1996). *Introduction to the philosophy of social research.* London: UCL Press.

Williams, R. (1977). *Marxism and literature.* Oxford, UK: Oxford University Press.

Willson, V. L., & Putnam, R. R. (1982). A meta-analysis of pretest sensitization effects in experimental design. *American Educational Research Journal, 19,* 249–258.

Wilson, P. J. (1974). *Oscar: An inquiry into the nature of sanity.* New York: Vintage.

Wilson, T. P. (1969). A proportional reduction in error interpretation for Kendall's tau-b. *Social Forces, 47,* 340–342.

Winch, P. (1990). *The idea of a social science and its relation to philosophy.* London: Routledge. (Originally published in 1958)

Winer, B. J. (1962). *Statistical principles in experimental designs.* New York: McGraw-Hill.

Winer, B. J., Brown, D. R., & Michels, K. M. (1991). *Statistical principles in experimental design* (3rd ed.). New York: McGraw-Hill.

Winship, C., & Mare, R. D. (1992). Models for sample selection bias. *Annual Review of Sociology, 18,* 327–350.

Winship, C., & Morgan, S. L. (1999). The estimation of causal effects from observational data. *Annual Review of Sociology, 25,* 659–706.

Winship, C., & Radbill, L. (1994). Sampling weights and regression analysis. *Sociological Methods & Research, 23*(2), 230–257.

Wiseman, F., Moriarty, M., & Schafer, M. (1975–1976). Estimating public opinion with the randomized response model. *Public Opinion Quarterly, 39*(4), 507–513.

Wishart, J. (1938). Growth-rate determinations in nutritional studies with the Bacon pig, and their analysis. *Biometrika, 30,* 16–28.

Wittgenstein, L. (1974). *On certainty* (G. E. M. Anscombe & G. H. Von Wright, Eds.). Oxford, UK: Blackwell.

Wodak, R., & Meyer, M. (2001). *Methods in critical discourse analysis.* Thousand Oaks, CA: Sage.

Wold, H. (1966). Estimation of principal components and related models by iterative least squares. In P. R. Krishnaiaah (Ed.), *Multivariate analysis* (pp. 391–420). New York: Academic Press.

Wolf, M. (1992). *A thrice told tale: Feminism, postmodernism and ethnographic responsibility.* Stanford, CA: Stanford University Press.

Wolfe, J. H. (1970). Pattern clustering by multivariate mixtures. *Multivariate Behavioral Research, 5,* 329–350.

Wonnacott, T. H., & Wonnacott, R. J. (1990). *Introductory statistics for business and economics* (4th ed.). San Francisco: Jossey-Bass.

Wood, B. D. (1992). Modeling federal implementation as a system: The clean air case. *American Journal of Political Science, 1,* 40–67.

Wood, J. W., & Weinstein, M. (1990). Heterogeneity in fecundability: The effect of fetal loss. In J. Adams, D. A. Lam, A. I. Hermalin, & P. E. Smouse (Eds.), *Convergent issues in genetics and demography* (pp. 171–188). Oxford, UK: Oxford University Press.

Wood, J. W., Holman, D. J., Yasin, A., Peterson, R. J., Weinstein, M., & Chang, M.-C. (1994). A multistate model of fecundability and sterility. *Demography, 31,* 403–426.

Wood, S. (2001). mgcv: GAMs and generalized ridge regression for R. *R News, 1,* 20–25.

Woodbury, M. A., & Clive, J. (1974). Clinical pure types as a fuzzy partition. *Journal of Cybernetics, 4*(3), 111–121.

Woodward, J. (1995). Causation and explanation in econometrics. In D. Little (Ed.), *On the reliability of economic models: Essays in the philosophy of economics* (pp. 9–61). Boston: Kluwer Academic.

Wooldridge, J. M. (2000). *Introductory econometrics: A modern approach.* Cincinnati, OH: South-Western.

Wooldridge, J. M. (2002). *Econometric analysis of cross section and panel data.* Cambridge: MIT Press.

Wooldridge, J. M. (2003). *Introductory econometrics: A modern approach* (2nd ed.). Cincinnati, OH: South-Western College Publishing.

Woolgar, S. (Ed.). (1988). *Knowledge and reflexivity.* London: Sage.

World Bank, International Economics Department. (1997). *World tables of economic and social indicators, 1950–1992* [Computer file]. Ann Arbor, MI: Interuniversity Consortium for Political and Social Science Research.

Wright, B. D. (1997). S. S. Stevens revisited. *Rasch Measurement Transactions, 11,* 552–553.

Wright, S. (1918). On the nature of size factors. *Genetics, 3,* 367–374.

Wright, S. (1934). The method of path coefficients. *Annals of Mathematical Statistics, 5,* 161–215.

Wright, W. (1975). *Six guns and society.* Berkeley: University of California Press.

Wu, L. L., & Martinson, B. C. (1993). Family structure and the risk of a premarital birth. *American Sociological Review, 58*(2), 210–232.

Wu, L. L., & Tuma, N. B. (1990). Local hazard models. In C. C. Clogg (Ed.), *Sociological methodology 1990* (pp. 141–180). Oxford, UK: Basil Blackwell.

Wylie, R. (1974). *The self concept: A review of methodological considerations and measuring instruments.* Lincoln: University of Nebraska Press.

Xie, Y. (1989). An alternative purging method: Controlling the composition-dependent interaction in an analysis of rates. *Demography, 26,* 711–716.

Xie, Y. (1992). The log-multiplicative layer effect model for comparing mobility tables. *American Sociological Review, 57,* 380–395.

Xie, Y., & Pimentel, E. E. (1992). Age patterns of marital fertility: Revising the Coale-Trussell method. *Journal of the American Statistical Association, 87,* 977–984.

Yates, F. (1934). The analysis of multiple classifications with unequal numbers in the different classes. *Journal of the American Statistical Association, 29,* 51–66.

Yeo, I.-K., & Johnson, R. (2000). A new family of power transformations to improve normality or symmetry. *Biometrika, 87,* 954–959.

Yin, R. K. (1989). *Case study research: Design and methods.* Newbury Park, CA: Sage.

Yin, R. K. (1994). *Case study research: Design and methods* (2nd ed.). Thousand Oaks, CA: Sage.

Yin, R. K. (1998). The abridged version of case study research. In L. Bickman & D. J. Rog (Eds.), *Handbook of applied social research methods* (pp. 229–259). Thousand Oaks, CA: Sage.

Young, F. W., & Hamer, R. M. (1987). *Multidimensional scaling: History, theory, and applications.* Hillsdale, NJ: Lawrence Erlbaum.

Young, K., Ashby, D., Boaz, A., & Grayson, L. (2002). Social science and the evidence-based policy movement. *Social Policy and Society, 1*(3), 215–224.

Yuen, K. K. (1974). The two-sample trimmed *t* for unequal populations variances. *Biometrika, 61,* 165–170.

Yule, G. U. (1903). Notes on the theory of association of attributes in statistics. *Biometrika, 2,* 121–134.

Yule, G. U. (1971). On a method of investigating periodicities in disturbed series with special reference to Wolfer's sunspot numbers. In A. Stuart & M. Kendall (Eds.), *Statistical papers of George Udny Yule* (pp. 389–420). New York: Hafner. (Original work published 1927)

Yule, G. U., & Kendall, M. G. (1950). *An introduction to the theory of statistics* (14th ed.). London: Griffin.

Yule, G. U., & Kendall, M. G. (1968). *An introduction to the theory of statistics.* New York: Hafner.

Zadeh, L. (1965). Fuzzy sets. *Information and Control, 8,* 338–353.

Zaller, J. R. (1992). *The nature and origins of mass opinion.* Cambridge, UK: Cambridge University Press.

Zaman, A. (1996). *Statistical foundations for econometric techniques.* New York: Academic Press.

Zanna, M. P., & Cooper, J. (1974). Dissonance and the pill: An attribution approach to studying the arousal properties of dissonance. *Journal of Personality and Social Psychology, 29,* 703–709.

Zeeman, E. C. (1972). Differential equations for the heartbeat and nerve impulse. In C. H. Waddington (Ed.), *Towards a theoretical biology* (Vol. 4, pp. 8–67). Edinburgh, UK: Edinburgh University Press.

Zeisel, H., & Kaye, D. H. (1997). *Prove it with figures.* New York: Springer.

Zellner, A. (1962). An efficient method of estimating seemingly unrelated regressions and tests for aggregation bias. *Journal of the American Statistical Association, 57,* 348–368.

Zellner, A., & Theil, H. (1962). Three-stage least squares: Simultaneous estimation of simultaneous equations. *Econometrica, 30,* 54–78.

Zetenyi, T. (Ed.). (1988). *Fuzzy sets in psychology.* Amsterdam: North-Holland.

Zimmerman, D. H., & Wieder, D. (1977). The diary-interview method. *Urban Life, 5,* 479–498.

Zimmerman, M. (2001–2002). Rigoberta Menchú, David Stoll, subaltern narrative and testimonial truth: A personal testimony. *Antípodas: Journal of Hispanic and Galician Studies, 13/14,* 103–124.

Znaniecki, F. (1934). *The method of sociology.* New York: Farrar and Rhienhart.

Znaniecki, F. (1969). *On humanistic sociology: Selected papers* (R. Bierstadt, Ed.). Chicago: University of Chicago Press.

Zorn, C. J. W. (2001). Generalized estimating equation models for correlated data: A review with applications. *American Journal of Political Science, 45,* 470–490.

Zwick, W. R., & Velicer, W. F. (1986). Comparison of five rules for determining the number of components to retain. *Psychological Bulletin, 99,* 432–442.

Zwillinger, D. (1995). *CRC standard mathematical tables and formulae* (30th ed.). Boca Raton, FL: CRC Press.